Educational Psychology
Windows on Classrooms

Global Edition
Tenth Edition

Paul Eggen
University of North Florida

Don Kauchak
University of Utah

PEARSON

Boston   Columbus   Indianapolis   New York   San Francisco   Amsterdam
Cape Town   Dubai   London   Madrid   Milan   Munich   Paris   Montreal   Toronto   Delhi
Mexico City   Sao Paulo   Sydney   Hong Kong   Seoul   Singapore   Taipei   Tokyo

Vice President and Editorial Director: Jeffery W. Johnston

Vice President and Publisher: Kevin M. Davis

Development Editor: Gail Gottfried

Editorial Assistant: Caitlin Griscom

Executive Field Marketing Manager: Krista Clark

Senior Product Marketing Manager: Christopher Barry

Project Manager: Lauren Carlson

Senior Acquisitions Editor, Global Edition: Sandhya Ghosal

Associate Project Editor, Global Edition: Amrita Kar

Project Manager, Global Edition: Ruchi Sachdev

Manager, Media Production, Global Edition: Vikram Kumar

Senior Manufacturing Controller, Production, Global Edition: Trudy Kimber

Procurement Specialist: Carol Melville

Senior Art Director: Diane Lorenzo

Text Designer: Studio Montage

Cover Designer: Studio Montage

Cover Art: FWstudio/Shutterstock

Media Project Manager: Caroline Fenton

Full-Service Project Management: Cenveo® Publisher Services

Composition: Cenveo® Publisher Services

Printer/Binder: Vivar, Malaysia

Cover Printer: Vivar, Malaysia

Credits and acknowledgments for material borrowed from other sources and reproduced, with permission, in this textbook appear on the appropriate page within the text.

Every effort has been made to provide accurate and current Internet information in this book. However, the Internet and information posted on it are constantly changing, so it is inevitable that some of the Internet addresses listed in this textbook will change.

Pearson Education Limited
Edinburgh Gate
Harlow
Essex CM20 2JE
England

and Associated Companies throughout the world

Visit us on the World Wide Web at:
www.pearsonglobaleditions.com

© Pearson Education Limited 2016

ISBN-10: 1-292-10756-1
ISBN-13: 978-1-292-10756-1

British Library Cataloguing-in-Publication Data
A catalogue record for this book is available from the British Library

10 9 8 7 6 5 4 3 2 1

Typeset by Cenveo® Publisher Services
Printed in Malaysia (CTP-VVP)

To Judy and Kathy,
teachers who have changed many lives.

About the Authors

Paul Eggen

Paul has worked in higher education for nearly 40 years. He is a consultant for public schools and colleges in his university service area and has provided support to teachers in 12 states. Paul has also worked with teachers in international schools in 23 countries in Africa, South Asia, the Middle East, Central America, South America, and Europe. He has published several articles in national journals, is the co-author or co-editor of six other books, and presents regularly at national and international conferences.

Paul is strongly committed to public education. His wife is a middle school teacher in a public school, and his two children are graduates of public schools and state universities.

Don Kauchak

Don has taught and worked in schools and in higher education in nine states for over 40 years. He has published in a number of scholarly journals, including the *Journal of Educational Research, Journal of Experimental Education, Journal of Research in Science Teaching, Teaching and Teacher Education, Phi Delta Kappan,* and *Educational Leadership.* In addition to this text, he has co-authored or co-edited six other books on education. He has also been a principal investigator on federal and state grants examining teacher development and evaluation practices, and presents regularly at the American Educational Research Association. He currently volunteer-tutors first, second, and third graders in a local elementary school. These students have taught him a lot about educational psychology.

Preface

Welcome to the tenth edition of *Educational Psychology: Windows on Classrooms*. We have redoubled our efforts to make this edition the clearest, most comprehensive, and up-to-date presentation of theory and research, combined with the most specific and usable applications, of any text in the field. Our text is generally recognized as the most applied in educational psychology, and in this edition we've tried to achieve the optimal balance of theory, research, and application.

To meet this goal we have much that is new to this edition. We outline these changes in the sections that follow.

Content New to This Edition

To provide students with the most complete and up-to-date information on recent developments in educational psychology, we have included the following new content in our tenth edition.

- *Major reorganization of the learning section of the book—Chapters 6–9:* Learning is at the heart of educational psychology, and we've reorganized these chapters to reflect recent developments in our understanding of how students in classrooms, and people of all ages, learn.
- *Analyzing Theories:* Research in every field is grounded in theory, but all theories have both strengths and weaknesses. "Analyzing Theories," a new feature in this edition, analyzes all the major theories discussed in the text. For instance, Piaget's and Vygotsky's theories of cognitive development are analyzed in Chapter 2, behaviorism and social cognitive theory are analyzed in Chapter 6, and constructivism is analyzed in Chapter 9. This analysis includes a summary of the major concepts within each theory, together with the contributions the theories make to our understanding of teaching and learning and common criticisms directed at each. We believe the addition of this feature will provide students with a more complete and accurate view of the theoretical foundation of educational psychology.
- *New chapter—Knowledge Construction in Social Contexts:* Educational psychology generally accepts the idea that learners construct their own knowledge and that learning is substantively a social process. This new chapter reflects and integrates these ideas in a comprehensive presentation that explains how these powerful ideas influence teaching and learning.
- *Extensive coverage of the learning sciences:* The learning sciences focus on learning as it exists in real-world settings and how teachers can facilitate that learning. This is the essential message of our text, and this new content explains how to apply these ideas to increase learning for all students.
- *Expanded coverage of technology's impact on learning:* To say that technology is an integral part of our lives is a vast understatement. Expanded coverage of technology throughout the text examines how it influences learning, development, and motivation, in addition to the general impact it is having on the way we live.
- *Greatly expanded coverage of neuroscience:* Neuroscience is providing researchers, educational leaders, teachers, and students with new insights into the teaching–learning process. As one powerful example, the concept of *neuroplasticity* helps us understand that our learning potential is much greater than we once believed possible, and with the right kinds of experiences, we can literally get smarter. This

expanded coverage helps teachers capitalize on this information to increase learning for all students regardless of their backgrounds.

- *Extensive coverage of the role of personality and emotion on learning and development:* Learning and development consist of much more than cognitive processes alone; personality and emotion play an important role in our motivation and how effectively we learn and develop. Further, both home and school environments have an important impact on the healthy development of learners' personalities and emotions. This coverage helps teachers create the kinds of environments that capitalize on these insights.
- *Updated descriptions of standards, accountability, and value-added teacher assessment and how they impact teaching and learning:* Standards—including the Common Core State Standards—combined with accountability, are facts of teaching life, and our discussion of these topics in this edition, including the controversies involved with each, is designed to prepare teachers to adapt to this new reality.

This new content adds to our expanded and detailed descriptions of traditional theories combined with the latest research. Our goal is to make the content presented in this text the most comprehensive and up-to-date discussion of learning, development, motivation, instruction and classroom management, classroom and standardized assessment, and learner diversity of any text in the field.

Applications New to This Edition

The content of educational psychology isn't useful if teachers don't know how to apply it to increase their students' learning and shape their development. To prepare teachers for the real world, and to help all students understand how educational psychology applies to their lives today, we have again redoubled our efforts to improve what is already the most applied educational psychology text in the field.

The following applications are new to this edition:

- *Explicit suggestions for applying educational psychology in teaching:* Instructors often tell us that their students can describe the theories and research that make up educational psychology, but these same students "don't know what to do with the content" when they go out into the real world of teaching. We attempt to solve this problem in this edition. Each chapter now includes specific sections titled "Educational Psychology and Teaching," which provide teachers with specific and concrete suggestions for applying the content of each chapter in their teaching. For instance, in Chapter 2, "Educational Psychology and Teaching: Applying Piaget's Theory with Your Students" provides teachers with specific suggestions for using Piaget's theory to advance their students' development, and a similar section does the same with Vygotsky's theory. As another example, in Chapter 4, "Educational Psychology and Teaching: Teaching Students in Your Classes Who Are Culturally and Linguistically Diverse" provides specific suggestions for accommodating and capitalizing on the diversity that our students are increasingly bringing to our classes. These suggestions are combined with concrete illustrations of teachers in the real world demonstrating these applications. "Educational Psychology and Teaching" sections are included in every chapter in the text.
- *Case studies linked to standards:* Standards have become a part of teachers' lives in today's classrooms. Case studies that introduce each chapter in the book are now linked to standards so prospective teachers can now see how their colleagues in the real world have adjusted to this new reality and have incorporated standards into their instruction.

- *Case studies in both written and video formats:* In the etext version of this edition, students can read case studies embedded in the text and can now see in video form the very lesson on which the case study is based. So they can read the case studies, and then with a simple click of their mouse see the actual lesson and how the teacher in the lesson applies the content of educational psychology to the real world of classrooms. No other text in the field applies the content of educational psychology to classrooms in this way.
- *Ed Psych and You:* This feature, which first appeared in our ninth edition, has been expanded to help students see that educational psychology applies not only to teaching but also to our lives as we live them every day. This feature is also designed to make the content of educational psychology more meaningful to students who may not plan to be teachers.

These new applications, combined with other features such as "Classroom Connections" and "Developmentally Appropriate Practice," make this edition even more usable in the real world of teaching. Further, we would like to believe that the text can be a resource for both new and veteran teachers as they move through their careers.

The Most Applied Educational Psychology Book in the Field

This is the most applied text in the field. The following illustrate these applications.

Educational Psychology and Teaching: Applying Information Processing and the Model of Human Memory with Your Students

Applying your understanding of information processing and the model of human memory in your teaching can increase learning for all your students. Guidelines for applying this information in your teaching are outlined below and discussed in the sections that follow.

- Conduct reviews to activate schemas and check perceptions
- Begin learning activities with attention-getting experiences
- Develop learners' background knowledge with high-quality representations of content
- Interact with students to promote cognitive activity and reduce cognitive load
- Capitalize on meaningful encoding strategies
- Model and encourage metacognition

The guidelines overlap and interact with each other. We will see how as we discuss each.

CONDUCT REVIEWS TO ACTIVATE SCHEMAS AND CHECK PERCEPTIONS

To begin this section let's return to Mike's Thursday lesson before he had his students work in their groups.

He begins, "What were we talking about yesterday? . . . Alexandria?"
". . . Figurative language . . . and figures of speech," Alexandria responds hesitantly.

Explicit Suggestions for Applying Educational Psychology in Teaching. "Educational Psychology and Teaching," which appears in every chapter, provides teachers with specific suggestions for applying the content of educational psychology to increase learning for all their students. The excerpt you see here appears on page 320 of Chapter 7 in the text.

Ed Psych and You. This feature helps students see how educational psychology applies to our lives and the people around us. The example you see here appears on page 66 in Chapter 2 of the text.

Ed Psych and You

Are you bothered when something doesn't make sense? Do you want, and even expect, the world to be predictable? Are you more comfortable in classes where the instructor specifies the requirements, outlines the grading practices, and consistently follows through? For most people, the answer to these questions is "Yes." Why do you think this is the case?

Case Studies Linked to Standards. The case studies that appear in this edition are now linked to standards. The excerpt you see here appears on page 379–380 in Chapter 9 of the text.

The students in this case are third graders, and their teacher, Alicia Evans, is working with them on *Common Core State Standard* ***CCSS.ELA-Literacy.L.3.1f "Ensure subject-verb and pronoun-antecedent agreement"*** (Common Core State Standards Initiative, 2014f).

After completing her routines for the beginning of language arts, Alicia explains and demonstrates the rules with some examples on the board. She then displays the following short paragraph on her document camera.

Bill takes his lunch to the cafeteria when it's time to eat. His friend Leroy and his other friend Antonio (takes, take) (his, theirs) to the cafeteria, too. Each of the boys has (his, their) own lunch box with pictures of cars on (it, them). Bill doesn't like apples, so he will give his to anyone else if (he, they) (wants, want) it.

"Now," she directs, "Read the paragraph carefully, . . . think about it, and then decide which one of the words in the parentheses in each case is correct. Remember, our reasons and thinking are as important as the actual answers."

After giving the students a couple minutes to study the paragraph, she begins, "How about the first one?" pointing to the first set of parentheses (takes, take) in the paragraph.

The students conclude that "take" is correct in the sentence because "Leroy and Antonio" is a plural subject, so it requires the plural verb "take." They also conclude that "theirs" is correct in the sentence because "theirs" agrees with its antecedent (Leroy and Antonio).

"Now, how about this one?" she asks, pointing to the next set of parentheses (his, their) in the third sentence—Each of the boys has (his, their) own lunch box with pictures of cars on (it, them). "What do you think, and why do you think so . . . Brittany?"

Classroom Connections at Elementary, Middle School, and High School Levels. These features in each chapter offer suggestions and illustrations for applying topics discussed in the chapter at different grade levels. Each strategy is illustrated with a classroom example, derived from teachers' experiences in elementary, middle, and high schools. The example you see here appears on page 427 of Chapter 10 of the text.

Developmentally Appropriate Practice. These features in each chapter describe developmental differences in our students and help teachers ensure that their instruction will best meet the needs of learners at all developmental levels. The example you see here appears on page 146 of Chapter 3 in the text.

Supplementary Materials

This edition of *Educational Psychology: Windows on Classrooms* provides a comprehensive and integrated collection of supplements to assist students and professors in maximizing learning and instruction. The following resources are available for instructors to download from **www. pearsonhighered.com/educator.** Enter the author, title of the text, or the ISBN number, then select this text, and click on the "Resources" tab. Download the supplement you need. If you require assistance in downloading any resources, contact your Pearson representative.

Instructor's Resource Manual

The Instructor's Resource Manual includes chapter overviews and outcomes, lists of available PowerPoint® slides, presentation outlines, teaching suggestions for each chapter, and questions for discussion and analysis along with feedback.

Powerpoint® Slides

The PowerPoint® slides highlight key concepts and summarize text content. The slides also include questions and problems designed to stimulate discussion, encourage students to elaborate and deepen their understanding of the topics in each chapter, and apply the content of the chapter to both the real world of teaching and their daily lives. The slides are further designed to help instructors structure the content of each chapter to make it as meaningful as possible for students.

Test Bank

The Test Bank provides a comprehensive and flexible assessment package. The Test Bank for this edition has been revised and expanded to make it more applicable to students. To provide complete coverage of the content in each chapter, all multiple-choice and essay items are grouped under the chapters' main headings and are balanced between knowledge/ recall items and those that require analysis and application.

TestGen®

TestGen is a powerful test generator available exclusively from Pearson Education publishers. You install TestGen on your personal computer (Windows or Macintosh) and create your own tests for classroom testing and for other specialized delivery options, such as over a local area network or on the web. A test bank, which is also called a Test Item File (TIF), typically contains a large set of test items, organized by chapter and ready for your use in creating a test, based on the associated textbook material. Assessments may be created for both print and testing online. The tests can be downloaded in the following formats:

TestGen Testbank file—PC
TestGen Testbank file—MAC
TestGen Testbank—Blackboard 9 TIF
TestGen Testbank—Blackboard CE/Vista (WebCT) TIF
Angel Test Bank (zip)
D2L Test Bank (zip)
Moodle Test Bank
Sakai Test Bank (zip)

Acknowledgments

Every book reflects the work of a team that includes the authors, the staff of editors, and the reviewers. We appreciate the input we've received from professors and students who have used previous editions of the book, and we gratefully acknowledge the contributions of the reviewers who offered us constructive feedback to guide us in this new edition:

Elizabeth Levine Brown, George Mason University; Jeffrey Liew, Texas A&M University; Serena Shim, Ball State University; Douglas W. Smith, Coastal Carolina University; and Rayne A. Sperling, Penn State University.

In addition, we acknowledge, with our thanks, the reviewers of our previous editions:

Patricia Barbetta, Florida International University; David Bergin, University of Toledo; Scott W. Brown, University of Connecticut; Kay S. Bull, Oklahoma State University; Barbara Collamer, Western Washington University; Jerome D'Agostino, University of Arizona; Betty M. Davenport, Campbell University; Brenda M. Davis, Randolph-Macon College; Ronna F. Dillon, Southern Illinois University; Oliver W. Edwards, University of Central Florida; Thomas G. Fetsco, Northern Arizona University; Leena Furtado, California State University, Dominguez Hills; Newell T. Gill, Florida Atlantic University; Claire Gonzalez, University of North Florida; Charles W. Good, West Chester University; Amy Hogan, Ottawa University; Robert L. Hohn, University of Kansas; Joel B. Judd, Adams State College; Pamela K. Kidder, Fort Valley State University; Dov Liberman, University of Houston; Hermine H. Marshall, San Francisco State University; Tes Mehring, Emporia State University; Luanna H. Meyer, Massey University–New Zealand; Michelle Morris, Northwestern State University; Nancy Perry, University of British Columbia; Evan Powell, University of Georgia; Anne N. Rinn, Western Kentucky University; Jay Samuels, University of Minnesota; Gregory Schraw, University of Nebraska, Lincoln; Dale H. Schunk, Purdue University; James A. Shuff, Henderson State University; Rozanne Sparks, Pittsburgh State University; Robert J. Stevens, Pennsylvania State University; Julianne C. Turner, Notre Dame University; Nancy Vye, University of Washington; Steven Whitney, University of Missouri; Glenda Wilkes, University of Arizona; Dylinda Wilson-Younger, Alcorn State University; and Karen M. Zabrucky, Georgia State University.

In addition to the reviewers who guided our revisions, our team of editors gave us support in many ways. Kevin Davis, our publisher, guided us with his intelligence, insight, and understanding of the field. Gail Gottfried, our development editor, was available whenever we had questions or needed help and provided us with invaluable support. Kathy Pruno, our copy editor, has been thoroughly professional in her efforts to make the content of the book clear and understandable.

Our appreciation goes to all of these fine people who have taken our words and given them shape. We hope that all of our efforts will result in increased learning for students and more rewarding teaching for instructors.

Finally, we would sincerely appreciate any comments or questions about anything that appears in the book or any of its supplements. Please feel free to contact either of us at any time. Our e-mail addresses are: peggen@unf.edu and don.kauchak@gmail.com.

Good luck and best wishes.

Paul Eggen
Don Kauchak

Acknowledgments

Pearson would like to acknowledge and thank Adilia Suzette Feio Silva (Clinical Psychologist) for her contribution to the Global Edition, and Manchong Limlunthang Zou (Zakir Hussain Delhi College), Alizeh Batra (New York University Abu Dhabi) and Elena-Maria N. Andrioti (Licensed Counselor) for reviewing the Global Edition.

Brief Contents

Contents

chapter 9

chapter 10

c h a p t e r 14

c h a p t e r 15

a p p e n d i x

g l o s s a r y

r e f e r e n c e s

n a m e i n d e x

s u b j e c t i n d e x

Educational Psychology: Understanding Learning and Teaching

OUTLINE	LEARNING OUTCOMES
	After you've completed your study of this chapter, you should be able to:
The Preeminence of Teachers	1. Describe expert teaching and explain how expert teaching influences student learning.
Educational Psychology, Professional Knowledge, and Expert Teaching Professional Knowledge Professional Knowledge and Reflective Practice ▶ Developmentally Appropriate Practice: Using Knowledge of Learners and Learning to Promote Achievement in Students at Different Ages	2. Describe the different kinds of professional knowledge that expert teachers possess.
The Role of Research in Acquiring Professional Knowledge Quantitative Research Qualitative Research Action Research Design-Based Research Research and the Development of Theory	3. Describe different types of research, and explain how research and theory contribute to teachers' professional knowledge.
Teaching in Today's Classrooms Standards and Accountability Teacher Licensure and Evaluation Learner Diversity Technology The Influence of Neuroscience Educational Psychology and Teaching: Applying Your Professional Knowledge in Today's Classrooms	4. Identify factors that influence teaching in today's classrooms.

You've just opened your textbook, and you're probably wondering what this class will be like and how it will make you a better teacher. So, let's start right off with a couple questions. First, why do children go to school? To learn and develop is the obvious answer. Easy question, right?

Second, which of the following factors contributes the most to students learning and development?

- *Curriculum and materials available to them*—the content students study and the quality of their textbooks.
- *Facilities and extracurricular activities*—access to a good library, the Internet, and athletics, clubs, and after-school music and drama.
- *Class size*—the number of students in a class.
- *Leadership*—such as the school principal and district superintendent.
- *You*—their teacher.

The unequivocal answer is *you, their teacher*! Unlike our first question, however, this answer hasn't always been obvious to educational leaders. We'll explore the importance of excellent teachers in more detail as the chapter unfolds, but before we do, let's turn to a conversation between Keith Jackson, a struggling, first-year, middle school math teacher, and Jan Davis, a four-year "veteran" who has become his confidant. As you read this case study, think about Jan's teaching and how it might influence her students' learning.

As Keith walks into the work room at Lakeside Middle School, Jan looks up and asks, "Hi, Keith. How's it going?"

"My last period class is getting to me," Keith replies. "The students are okay when we just stick to mechanics, but they simply can't do word problems. . . . And they hate them. . . . They just try to memorize formulas and enough to get by.

"I have a good math background, and I was going to be so great when I got here. . . . I'm not so sure any more. . . . I explain the stuff so carefully, but some of the kids just sit with blank looks on their faces. Then, I explain it even more carefully, and . . . nothing.

"And, there's Kelly. She disrupts everything I do. I gave her a referral, and I even called her mother. . . . The only thing that seemed to work was taking her aside and asking her straight out why she was giving me such a hard time."

"Sounds like you're becoming a *teacher*," Jan smiles. "There are few easy answers for what we do. . . . But then, that's what makes it both the toughest and the most rewarding work in the world.

"Like working with Kelly. She might not have another adult she can talk to, and she may simply need someone to care about her.

"As for the blank looks, I'm taking a class at the university. The instructor emphasizes involving the kids, and he keeps talking about research that says how important it is to call on all the kids as equally as possible.

"So, here's an example of how I'm approaching word problems now. We're working on decimals and percents, ultimately to help the kids reach this standard," she says as she shows Keith a lesson plan:

CCSS.Math.Content.6.RP.A.3c **Find a percent of a quantity as a rate per 100 (e.g., 30% of a quantity means 30/100 times the quantity); solve problems involving finding the whole, given a part and the percent. (Common Core State Standards Initiative, 2014v).**

"So, here's what I'm doing. I brought in a 12-ounce soft drink can from a machine, a 20-ounce bottle, and a 6-pack with price tags on them.

"I put the kids into pairs and told them to figure out a way to determine which one was the best buy. To figure it out, they needed to apply their understanding of decimals and percents, which helps us reach the standard. I helped them along, and we created a table, so we could compare the groups' answers. They're beginning to see how math relates to their lives. . . . Some of them even said they think it's important. And, now that they're used to being called on, they really like it. It's one of the most important things I do.

"When I think about it, I realize that I sometimes jump in too soon when they can figure it out themselves, and at other times I let them stumble around too long, and they waste time. So, then I adapt for the next lesson."

"I hate to admit this," Keith says, "but some of my university courses suggested just what you did. It was fun, but I didn't think it was real teaching."

"You couldn't relate to it at the time. You didn't have a class with live students who 'didn't get it.'

"Hang in there," Jan smiles. "You're becoming what teaching needs—a real pro."

Now, as you study this chapter, keep the following questions in mind:

1. How was Jan's approach to teaching word problems different from Keith's?
2. Why were their approaches so different, and how will these differences affect their students' learning?

We answer these and other questions about teaching and learning as the chapter unfolds. We begin by revisiting the idea we introduced at the beginning of the chapter.

The Preeminence of Teachers

In our introduction we asked, "Which of the following factors contributes the most to student's learning and development?" and we said that the answer hasn't always been obvious to educational leaders. In an effort to improve schooling, a great deal has been written about this question, and reformers have offered a variety of answers, including different organizational structures, such as open classrooms, and a variety of curricular and instructional approaches, such as Whole Language, or what was commonly described as "New Math." However, none of them were as successful as hoped (Thomas & Wingert, 2010).

The solution, however, is simple (but admittedly not easy). No organization, system, institution, or enterprise is any better than the people in it, and the same applies to schools. The quality of a school is determined by the quality of its teachers. *You* are the most important factor influencing your students' learning! Surprisingly, in spite of many years of research documenting the importance of teachers, only within approximately the last two decades have educational leaders begun to understand and appreciate this fact (Thomas & Wingert, 2010).

Let's look at some of this research. One widely publicized study conducted 20 years ago found that students who had expert teachers in third, fourth, and fifth grades scored more than 50 percentile points higher on standardized math tests than those in the same three grades who were taught by teachers less skilled (Sanders & Rivers, 1996). Another study revealed that five years in a row of expert teaching was nearly enough to close the achievement gap between disadvantaged and advantaged students (Hanushek, Rivkin, & Kain, 2005). Additional research has found that expert teaching in later grades could substantially, though not completely, make up for poor teaching in earlier grades (Rivkin, Hanushek, & Kain, 2001). More recent research corroborates the assertion that the expertise of teachers is the key to increased student achievement (Konstantopoulos, 2011; Kraus et al., 2008; Kunter et al., 2013).

The importance of teachers even caught the attention of the popular press. "The Key to Saving American Education" appeared on the cover of the March 15, 2010, issue of *Newsweek*, identifying teachers as the "key," and the *New York Times* included a lengthy article, "Building a Better Teacher," in its March 7, 2010, issue (Green, 2010). "Teacher quality is now a national priority" (Margolis, 2010, Introduction, para. 1). The American people agree. According to an annual poll of the public's attitudes toward public education, "Americans singled out improving the quality of teachers as the most important action for improving education" (Bushaw & Lopez, 2010, p. 15). Also, the quality of teachers is linked to the widely publicized success of students in other countries (Friedman, 2013). And, some good news: public opinion polls indicate that "More than 70% of Americans have trust and confidence in the men and women who teach in public schools" (Bushaw & Lopez, 2013, p. 12).

Some, including many educational leaders, once believed that expert teaching is essentially instinctive, a kind of magic performed by born superstars. And, just as is the case with other domains, such as athletics, music, or art, some teachers do indeed have more natural ability than others. However, research dating back to the 1960s and 1970s indicates that expert teachers possess knowledge and skills that are not purely instinctive. They are acquired through study and practice (Fisher et al., 1980), and more recent work corroborates these earlier findings (Kunter et al., 2013; Lemov, 2010). This is true in all domains. For example, many athletes, through awareness and hard work, perform better than their counterparts with more natural ability.

We referred to "expert" teachers in the preceding paragraphs. **Experts** are people who are highly knowledgeable and skilled in a particular domain, such as music, architecture, medicine, or teaching. Expert teachers' professional knowledge and skills are what set them apart from their less effective colleagues. This knowledge and these skills make them capable of producing learning in students that less able teachers cannot produce.

This leads us to the reason we wrote this book and the reason you're taking this course. Your goal is to begin acquiring the knowledge and skills that will ultimately lead to expertise, and our goal is to help you in this process. We turn to this topic next.

Educational Psychology, Professional Knowledge, and Expert Teaching

If expertise is so important to effective teaching, how do teachers gain the knowledge and skills needed to become experts? This leads us to the study of **educational psychology (ed psych)**, the academic discipline that examines human teaching and learning (Berliner, 2006). The content of educational psychology contributes to the professional knowledge base you will need to become an expert teacher. We discuss this professional knowledge in the following sections.

Ed Psych and You

How much do you know about teaching and learning? To test your knowledge, complete the following Learning and Teaching Inventory. It will introduce you to the kinds of knowledge you'll need to become an expert teacher.

Professional Knowledge

Professional knowledge refers to the body of information and skills that are unique to an area of study, such as law, medicine, architecture, or engineering. The same applies to teaching. In this section we focus on how educational psychology can increase your professional knowledge, and with it, your expertise.

To introduce you to the idea of professional knowledge in teaching, respond to each of the items in the *Learning and Teaching Inventory* below.

Learning and Teaching Inventory

Look at each of the 12 items, and decide if the statement is true or false.

1. The thinking of children in elementary schools tends to be limited to the concrete and tangible, whereas the thinking of middle and high school students tends to be abstract.
2. Students generally understand how much they know about a topic.

3. Experts in the area of intelligence view knowledge of facts, such as "On what continent is Brazil?," as one indicator of intelligence.
4. Expert teaching is essentially a process of presenting information to students in succinct and organized ways.
5. Preservice teachers who major in a content area, such as math, are much more successful than nonmajors in providing clear examples of the ideas they teach.
6. To increase students' motivation to learn, teachers should praise as much as possible.
7. The key to successful classroom management is to stop disruptions quickly.
8. Preservice teachers generally believe they will be more effective than teachers who are already in the field.
9. Teachers learn by teaching; in general, experience is the primary factor involved in learning to teach.
10. Testing detracts from learning, because students who are tested frequently develop negative attitudes and consequently learn less than those who are tested less often.
11. Criticizing students damages their self-esteem and should be avoided.
12. Because some students are left-brained thinkers and others are right-brained thinkers, teachers should make an effort to accommodate these differences in their students.

Let's see how you did. The correct answers for each item are outlined in the following paragraphs. As you read the answers, remember that they describe students or other people in general, and exceptions will exist.

1. *The thinking of children in elementary schools tends to be limited to the concrete and tangible, whereas the thinking of middle and high school students tends to be abstract.*
   False: Research indicates that middle school, high school, and even university students can effectively think in the abstract only when they have considerable prior knowledge and experience related to the topic they're studying (Berk, 2013; Cole, Cole, & Lightfoot, 2009). When you study the development of students' thinking in Chapter 2, you'll see how understanding this research can improve your teaching.
2. *Students generally understand how much they know about a topic.*
   False: Learners, in general, and young children in particular, often cannot accurately assess their own understanding (Hacker, Bol, Horgan, & Rakow, 2000). Students' awareness of what they know and how they learn strongly influences understanding, and cognitive learning theory helps us understand why. (You will study cognitive learning theory in Chapters 7, 8, and 9.)
3. *Experts in the area of intelligence view knowledge of facts, such as "On what continent is Brazil?," as one indicator of intelligence.*
   True: The Wechsler Intelligence Scale for Children—Fourth Edition (Wechsler, 2003), the most popular intelligence test in use today, includes several items similar to this example. We examine theories of intelligence, including controversies involved in these theories, in Chapter 5.
4. *Expert teaching is essentially a process of presenting information to students in succinct and organized ways.*
   False: The better we understand learning, the more we realize that simply explaining information to students is often ineffective for promoting learning (Kunter et al., 2013; Mayer, 2008). Learners construct their own knowledge based on what they already know, and their emotions, beliefs, and expectations all influence the process (Bruning, Schraw, & Norby, 2011; Schunk, Meece, & Pintrich, 2014). You will study the process of knowledge construction in Chapter 9.
5. *Preservice teachers who major in a content area, such as math, are much more successful than nonmajors in providing clear examples of the ideas they teach.*
   False: One of the most pervasive misconceptions about teaching is the idea that knowledge of subject matter is all that is necessary to teach effectively. In a study of

teacher candidates, researchers found that math majors were no more capable than nonmajors of effectively illustrating math concepts in ways that learners could understand (U.S. Department of Education, 2008). Knowledge of content is essential for expert teaching, but understanding how to make that content meaningful to students requires additional knowledge (Darling-Hammond & Baratz-Snowden, 2005; Kunter et al., 2013). You will study ways of making knowledge accessible to learners in Chapters 2, 6–9, and 13.

6. *To increase students' motivation to learn, teachers should praise as much as possible.*
   False: Although appropriate use of praise is effective, overuse detracts from its credibility. This is particularly true for older students, who discount praise if they believe it is invalid or insincere. Older students may also interpret praise given for easy tasks as indicating that the teacher thinks they have low ability (Schunk et al., 2014). Your study of motivation in Chapters 10 and 11 will help you understand this and other factors influencing students' motivation to learn.

7. *The key to successful classroom management is to stop disruptions quickly.*
   False: Research indicates that classroom management, a primary concern of beginning teachers, is most effective when teachers prevent management problems from occurring in the first place, instead of responding to problems after they occur (Brophy, 2006; Emmer & Evertson, 2013; Evertson & Emmer, 2013). You will study classroom management in Chapter 12.

8. *Preservice teachers generally believe they will be more effective than teachers who are already in the field.*
   True: Preservice teachers (like you) are often optimistic and idealistic. They believe they'll be effective with young people, and they generally believe they'll be better than teachers now in the field (Feiman-Nemser, 2001; Ingersoll & Smith, 2004). They are also sometimes "shocked" when they begin work and face the challenge of teaching on their own for the first time (Grant, 2006; Johnson & Birkeland, 2003). Keith's comments in the opening case study are typical of many beginning teachers: "I was going to be so great when I got here. . . . I'm not so sure anymore." Teaching is complex and challenging, and the more knowledge you have about learners, learning, and the teaching process, the better prepared you'll be to cope with the realities of your first job.

9. *Teachers learn by teaching; in general, experience is the primary factor involved in learning to teach.*
   False: Experience is essential in learning to teach, but it isn't sufficient by itself (Darling-Hammond & Bransford, 2005; Song & Felch, 2009; Kunter et al., 2013). In some cases, experience results in repeating the same actions year after year, regardless of their effectiveness. Knowledge of learners and learning, combined with experience, however, can lead to high levels of teaching expertise.

10. *Testing detracts from learning, because students who are tested frequently develop negative attitudes and consequently learn less than those who are tested less often.*
    False: In comprehensive reviews of the literature on assessment, experts have found that frequent, thorough assessment is one of the most powerful and positive influences on learning that exist (Rohrer & Pashler, 2010; Stiggins & Chappuis, 2012). This emphasis focuses on assessment *for* learning, however, and not the emphasis—and many argue *overemphasis*—on high-stakes standardized testing (Stiggins & Chappuis, 2012).

11. *Criticizing students damages their self-esteem and should be avoided.*
    False. Under certain circumstances, criticism can increase motivation and learning. For instance, criticism, such as a teacher saying, "Come on, you can do better work than this," communicates high expectations to students and the belief that they are capable learners. We're not suggesting that you make criticizing students

a habit, but periodic and well-timed criticism can enhance motivation (Deci & Ryan, 2008).

12. *Because some students are left-brained thinkers and others are right-brained thinkers, teachers should make an effort to accommodate these differences in their students.* **False.** The idea that we tend to be right-brained or left-brained is a myth (Boehm, 2012; Jarrett, 2012; Nielsen, Zielinski, Ferguson, Lainhart, & Anderson, 2013). "This popular myth, which conjures up an image of one side of our brains crackling with activity while the other lies dormant, has its roots in outdated findings from the 1970s . . ." (Boehm, 2012, para. 1).

The items you've just examined briefly introduce you to the professional knowledge base that will help you acquire teaching expertise. In the next section we examine this knowledge in more detail. Research indicates that four related types of knowledge are essential for expert teaching (Darling-Hammond & Baratz-Snowden, 2005; Kunter et al., 2013; Shulman, 1987). They are outlined in Figure 1.1 and discussed in the sections that follow.

KNOWLEDGE OF CONTENT

We obviously can't teach what we don't understand. To effectively teach about the American Revolutionary War, for example, a social studies teacher needs to know not only basic facts about the war but also how the war relates to other aspects of history, such as the French and Indian War, the colonies' relationship with England before the Revolution, and the unique characteristics of the colonies. The same is true for any topic in any other content area, and research confirms the relationship between what teachers know and how they teach (Bransford, Brown, & Cocking, 2000).

PEDAGOGICAL CONTENT KNOWLEDGE

Knowledge of content is essential, but, alone, not sufficient for expert teaching. We must also possess **pedagogical content knowledge**, an understanding of how to represent topics in ways that make the content understandable to learners, as well as an understanding of what makes specific topics easy or difficult to learn (Darling-Hammond & Bransford, 2005; Kunter et al., 2013; Shulman, 1986). It also includes teachers' abilities to identify students' most common misconceptions and to help students resolve their misunderstandings (Sadler, Sonnert, Coyle, Smith, & Miller, 2013).

The following quote supports the idea that pedagogical content knowledge (PCK) is essential for teaching expertise. "Yet as a new insight, our study also showed that teachers' PCK affects not only students' achievement but also their motivation, specifically their enjoyment of the subject . . ." (Kunter et al., 2013, p. 815). Expert teachers understand the

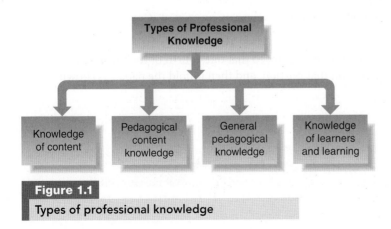

Figure 1.1
Types of professional knowledge

content they teach, and they also know how to make it understandable and interesting to students.

Knowledge of content and pedagogical content knowledge are related but not identical. For example, understanding the factors that led to the American Revolution reflects knowledge of content; knowing how to illustrate this content so students can understand it reflects pedagogical content knowledge. Expert teachers possess both (Kunter et al., 2013; Loughran, Mulhall, & Berry, 2004; Segall, 2004). So, as you study specific topics in your content area, such as math, social studies, science, or any other, ask yourself, "How can I illustrate this topic so students can understand it?" The ability to do so will reflect your pedagogical content knowledge, and it is one of the most important aspects of teaching expertise.

Demonstrating Pedagogical Content Knowledge. To further illustrate what we mean by pedagogical content knowledge in expert teaching, let's look at several examples. First, think about how you might help students understand the process of multiplying fractions, such as $1/4 \times 1/3 = 1/12$. This is neither easy to understand nor easy to teach. Our experience tells us that the product of two numbers is larger than either (e.g., $6 \times 5 = 30$), but with fractions the product is smaller, so the results are counterintuitive. As a result, students often simply memorize the process with little understanding.

Now, try the following activity. Fold a sheet of plain paper into thirds, and shade the center one-third of the paper, as shown:

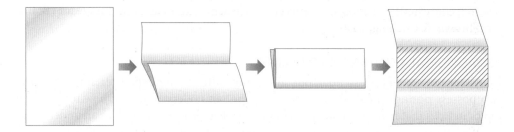

Now, refold your paper so that the shaded third is exposed:

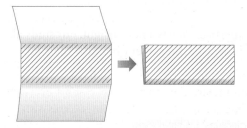

Now fold the paper in half, and in half again, so that one-fourth of the shaded one-third is visible. Put additional shading on that portion, and then unfold the paper, as shown:

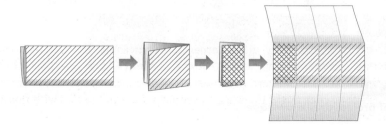

You've just prepared a concrete example demonstrating that $1/4 \times 1/3 = 1/12$ (the cross-hatched portion of the paper). This example helps students see that the product of multiplying two fractions results in a smaller number and also helps them apply their understanding in real-world settings (Mayer, 2008). This also demonstrates why pedagogical content knowledge is so important. Without examples, such as this one, students grasp what they can, memorize as much as possible, and little understanding develops (Donovan & Bransford, 2005; Kunter et al., 2013).

Now, let's look at an example in science. Consider the concept *density,* which represents the amount of mass (material) in a certain volume—and a concept with which many students, including those who are older, struggle. You can simply illustrate this concept for your students with cotton balls in a transparent drink cup as you see here.

Then, when you compress the cotton in the cup, your students can see that the same amount of cotton (mass) takes up less space (occupies less volume), so the cotton is more dense.

Illustrating the concept this way is much more meaningful for students than using the formula $D = m/v$, which is the way *density* is usually represented, and which students memorize with little understanding.

As a third example, suppose you are a language arts teacher and you want to teach your students about *gerunds,* verb forms that behave as nouns, and *participles,* verb forms that behave as adjectives. To illustrate these concepts you might display the following short paragraph for your students.

> Running is a very good form of exercise, and athletes, such as running backs in football, have to be in very good physical shape. I'm running a three miler this afternoon.

Here students can see that "running" is first used as a noun (*Running* is a very good form of exercise); then as an adjective (. . . such as *running* backs in football); and finally as a verb (I'm *running* a three miler this afternoon). An important point here is that students *can see* how the verb forms are used. They don't have to understand the concepts based on your explanation. The ability to represent topics in this way again illustrates pedagogical content knowledge.

Finally, suppose you're a geography teacher and you want to illustrate the concepts *longitude* and *latitude* for your students. You might draw lines on a beach ball as you see here.

As with the language arts example, your students *can see* that the latitude lines are parallel to each other, and the longitude lines meet at the poles. Then, during your discussion, you can guide your students to recognize that lines of longitude are farthest apart at the equator, but lines of latitude are the same distance apart everywhere, and that longitude measures distance east and west, whereas latitude measures distance north and south.

These are merely examples, and you will find many others when you teach. Depending on the content area, you can represent the topics you teach in several ways:

- *Examples.* Examples are useful when you're teaching a well-defined topic (Renkl, 2011). The illustrations we outlined above to help students understand multiplication of fractions and the concepts *density, gerund, participle, longitude,* and *latitude* are all examples Demonstrations, such as using the cotton balls in the drink cup, are also forms of examples.
- *Case studies.* We use case studies throughout this text to illustrate the topics you're studying. Together with vignettes (short case studies), they effectively illustrate complex topics that are hard to represent with simple examples. For instance, an English teacher might illustrate the concept *internal conflict* with this brief vignette:

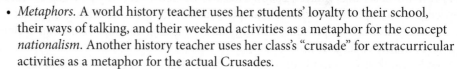

Andrea didn't know what to do. She was looking forward to the class trip, but if she went, she wouldn't be able to take the scholarship-qualifying test.

- *Metaphors.* A world history teacher uses her students' loyalty to their school, their ways of talking, and their weekend activities as a metaphor for the concept *nationalism.* Another history teacher uses her class's "crusade" for extracurricular activities as a metaphor for the actual Crusades.
- *Simulations.* Simulations can be effective because they provide concrete models that illustrate complex systems and processes (de Jong, 2011). For instance, an American government teacher creates a mock trial to simulate the workings of our country's judicial system, and a history teacher has students role-play delegates in a simulated Continental Congress to help students understand forces that shaped our country.
- *Models.* Models allow students to visualize what they can't observe directly. For instance, a science teacher uses a model of an atom to help students visualize the organization of the nucleus and electrons, as you see here.

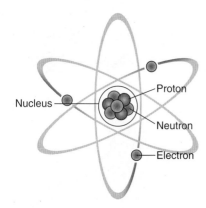

This list further illustrates why knowledge of content and pedagogical content knowledge are related but not identical, and it also helps us understand why item 5 in our Learning and Teaching Inventory ("Preservice teachers who major in a content area, such as math, are much more successful than nonmajors in providing clear examples of the ideas they teach") is false. Earning a degree in a content area, such as math, doesn't ensure that someone will be able to create examples like the one involving the multiplication of fractions, nor does majoring in history ensure that we would be able to think of using a campaign to save a school's extracurricular activities as a metaphor for the Crusades. The ability to represent topics in ways that are understandable to learners requires a special form of knowledge—pedagogical content knowledge—in addition to understanding content (Kunter et al., 2013). If we lack either, we commonly paraphrase information in learners' textbooks or provide abstract explanations that aren't meaningful to our students. We need both to become expert teachers.

GENERAL PEDAGOGICAL KNOWLEDGE

Knowledge of content and pedagogical content knowledge are domain specific, that is, they're related to knowledge of a particular content area, such as the Crusades, multiplying fractions, or the concepts *density, gerund, participle, internal conflict,* and many others. In comparison, general pedagogical knowledge involves an understanding of instructional strategies and classroom management that apply to all subject matter areas and topics (Borko & Putnam, 1996; Darling-Hammond & Bransford, 2005).

Instructional Strategies. Instructional strategies, such as knowing how to structure effective lessons that involve students in learning and check for understanding, are important regardless of the grade level, content area, or topic. For example, involving all students in a lesson by calling on them as equally as possible is important whether you're teaching first graders, middle school learners, or advanced high school students (Good & Brophy, 2008; Lemov, 2010). These strategies are essential aspects of general pedagogical knowledge, and you will study them in detail in Chapter 13.

Classroom Management. Classroom management is a second major component of general pedagogical knowledge. To be effective we need to create classroom environments that are safe, orderly, and focused on learning (Emmer & Evertson, 2013; Evertson & Emmer, 2013). Meeting this goal requires that we know how to plan, implement, and monitor rules and procedures; organize groups; and intervene when misbehavior occurs. The complexities of these processes help us see why item 7 in the Learning and Teaching Inventory ("The key to successful classroom management is to stop disruptions quickly") is false. It's impossible to maintain an orderly classroom if we wait for misbehavior to occur. Ideally, classroom environments are designed to prevent, rather than stop, disruptions. Chapter 12 describes how to do this in your classroom.

KNOWLEDGE OF LEARNERS AND LEARNING

Knowledge of learners and learning, the fourth type of professional knowledge, is also essential, "arguably the most important knowledge a teacher can have" (Borko & Putnam, 1996, p. 675). Let's see how this knowledge can influence the way we teach.

Knowledge of Learners. The following items from the Learning and Teaching Inventory all involve knowledge of learners.

> Item 1: The thinking of children in elementary schools tends to be limited to the concrete and tangible, whereas the thinking of middle and high school students tends to be abstract.
>
> Item 2: Students generally understand how much they know about a topic.
>
> Item 6: To increase students' motivation to learn, teachers should praise as much as possible.

For instance, with respect to item 1, we know that students need to have abstract ideas illustrated with concrete examples, and this is true for older as well as younger students. Chapter 2 helps us understand how students' thinking develops, and helps us understand how to represent topics in developmentally appropriate ways.

Item 2 suggests that learners often aren't good judges of either how much they know or the way they learn. Chapters 7 and 8 help us understand how to make our students more aware of the way they think and how to become more strategic in their approaches to learning (Bruning et al., 2011; Veenman, 2011).

Item 6 has implications for the ways we interact with our students. Intuitively, it seems that providing as much praise as possible is desirable and effective. However, motivation research, which you will study in Chapters 10 and 11, helps us understand why this isn't always the case.

Knowledge of Learning. As we better understand the different ways people learn, we can understand why item 4 ("Expert teaching is essentially a process of presenting information to students in succinct and organized ways") on the Learning and Teaching Inventory is false. For example, evidence consistently indicates that we don't behave like video recorders; we don't simply remember what we hear or read. Rather, in our attempts to make sense of the information, we interpret it in personal and sometimes idiosyncratic ways (Dubinsky, Roehrig, & Varma, 2013; Edwards, Esmonde, & Wagner, 2011; Hattie & Gan, 2011). In the process, meaning can be distorted, sometimes profoundly. For instance, the following statements were actually made by students:

> "The phases of the moon are caused by clouds blocking out the unseen parts."
> "Coats keep us warm by generating heat, like a stove or radiator."
> "A triangle which has an angle of 135 degrees is called an obscene triangle."

Obviously, students didn't acquire these ideas from their teachers' explanations. Rather, they interpreted what they heard, experienced, or read; related it to what they already knew; and attempted to make sense of it.

These examples help us understand Keith's comments in the case study at the beginning of the chapter: "I explain the stuff so carefully, but some of the kids just sit with blank looks on their faces. Then, I explain it even more carefully, and ... nothing." Expert teaching is much more than simply explaining, and expert teachers have a thorough understanding of how learning occurs and what they can do to promote it. (We examine learning in detail in Chapters 6 through 9.)

Developmentally Appropriate **Practice**

Using Knowledge of Learners and Learning to Promote Achievement in Students at Different Ages

While much of what we know about learners and learning applies to students of all ages, developmental differences, age-related changes in students' thinking, personalities, and social skills, exist.

Because the developmental level of your students affects their learning and your teaching, a feature titled "Developmentally Appropriate Practice" appears in each chapter. Developmentally appropriate practice refers to instruction that matches teacher actions to the capabilities and needs of learners at different developmental levels. The feature describes ways to adapt each chapter's content to the different learning needs of early childhood and elementary, middle school, and high school students.

Here's how the feature will appear in subsequent chapters:

FAMILY CIRCUS

"How do they fit so much water in that little spigot?"

Working with Students in Early Childhood Programs and Elementary Schools

Young children's thinking differs from the thinking of older students. As an example, look at the accompanying cartoon. Wondering how all the water could fit in the spigot is characteristic of the thinking of young children. Older students would of course realize that a vast reservoir of water exists that we can't see. Young children's personal and social characteristics also differ from those of older students and influence how they interact and learn in classrooms. We examine these differences in each of the chapters in the book.

Working with Students in Middle Schools

As a result of maturation and experience, the thinking and social skills of middle school students differ from those of young children. For example, older students are more likely to realize that they don't understand an idea being discussed in class and raise their hands to ask for an explanation. In addition, middle schoolers are increasingly social and find the opposite sex more interesting. These developmental differences have important implications for how we teach and interact with these students.

Working with Students in High Schools

As with differences between elementary and middle school students, additional differences exist between high school learners and their younger counterparts. For example, many high school students are quite mature, and discussing personal and social issues with them on an adult-to-adult level can be effective. They are capable of more abstract thinking than their younger counterparts, although they still need concrete examples to understand new or difficult topics.

We now understand why item 9 ("Teachers learn by teaching; in general, experience is the primary factor involved in learning to teach") on the Learning and Teaching Inventory is false. Experience is important, but we can't acquire all the knowledge we need to be effective from experience alone. Acquiring this knowledge is the primary reason you're studying educational psychology.

Professional Knowledge and Reflective Practice

You will make a staggering number of decisions in your teaching; some historical research suggests as many as 800 per day (Jackson, 1968). For example, the following are only a few of the aspects of her teaching about which Jan made decisions in her lesson earlier in the chapter:

- The learning objectives for her lesson
- The examples she would use to help students reach the objectives
- Which students she would call on and the order in which she would call on them
- The specific questions she would ask and how she would respond to students if they answered incorrectly

No one is there to help you make these decisions; you're essentially on your own. Learning how to make them leads us to the idea of **reflective practice**, the process of conducting a critical self-examination of one's teaching (Clarke, 2006; McGregor, 2011). Every professional decision we make is designed to promote student learning, and research suggests that reflective practice can help us become more sensitive to student differences (Berrill & Whalen, 2007). And it can make us more aware of the impact of our instruction on learning (Gimbel, 2008). For example, Jan's comment, "When I think about it, I realize that I sometimes jump in too soon . . . and at other times I let them stumble around too long. . . . So, then I adapt for the next lesson," illustrates the process of reflective practice and its influence on her instruction.

The Role of Research in Acquiring Professional Knowledge

To this point in the chapter, we've found that professional knowledge is essential for expert teaching, and we've examined the different types of professional knowledge we need to become experts. But, where does this knowledge originate, how does it accumulate, and how can we acquire it?

One answer is experience, sometimes called "the wisdom of practice" (Berliner, 2000). Well-designed teacher education programs help people like you acquire the beginnings of "the wisdom of practice" by integrating clinical experiences in schools with the topics you study in your classes.

Research, the process of systematically gathering information in an attempt to answer professional questions, is a second important source of the knowledge needed for expert teaching. All professions use research to guide their practice (Gall, Gall, & Borg, 2010; Van Horn, 2008). For example, in an effort to answer the question "How does teacher questioning influence student learning?" researchers have conducted large numbers of studies examining the numbers and types of questions teachers ask and the ways they are asked and distributed among students (Good & Brophy, 2008). The influence of teacher questioning on student learning is part of the professional literature of educational psychology. Jan drew from it when she talked about the changes she made in her teaching based on the class she is taking and her instructor who "keeps talking about research that says how important it is to call on all the kids as equally as possible." Jan is a veteran teacher but continues to grow professionally by staying up to date on current research.

Research in education exists in several forms, each of which answers different kinds of questions. The different types include:

- Quantitative research, which includes descriptive research, correlational research, and experimental research
- Qualitative research
- Action research
- Design-based research

Quantitative Research

Quantitative research refers to the systematic, empirical investigation of phenomena using numerical data and often involving statistical and mathematical techniques. Quantitative research can exist in descriptive, correlational, or experimental forms. We discuss them next.

DESCRIPTIVE RESEARCH

Descriptive research uses tools such as tests, surveys, and observations to describe the status or characteristics of a situation or phenomenon (Gall et al., 2010). For example, "How much are our students learning?" is an important question facing all educators. To answer this question, the National Assessment of Educational Progress (NAEP), often called "The Nation's Report Card," assesses our country's students in a variety of areas, including math, science, reading and writing, the arts, economics, geography and U.S. history, and beginning in 2014, in technology and engineering literacy (TEL) (National Center for Education Statistics, 2012). This is a form of descriptive research, and educators use it to measure the effectiveness of different programs and to make comparisons with other countries.

Surveys, such as the annual Phi Delta Kappan/Gallup Poll of the Public's Attitude Toward the Public Schools (Bushaw & Lopez, 2013), are also forms of descriptive research, as are firsthand observations. Jean Piaget (1959), a pioneer in the study of cognitive development, used systematic observations of children as his primary research technique. (You will study Piaget's work in Chapter 2.)

Descriptive research provides valuable information about a variety of topics related to education, but it doesn't allow us to predict future events, and it doesn't identify relationships. Finding relationships between variables leads us to correlational research.

CORRELATIONAL RESEARCH

Consider the following questions: Does a relationship exist between

- Students' grade-point averages (GPAs) and their scores on the SAT?
- Students' absences and their grades in school?
- Students' heights and high school GPAs?

Correlational research is the process of looking for relationships between variables that enables researchers to predict changes in one variable on the basis of changes in another. A **correlation** is a relationship, either positive or negative, between two or more variables. In our first example, the variables are *grade-point averages* and *SAT scores*; in the second, *absences* and *grades*; and in the third, *height* and *high school GPAs*. The variables are positively correlated in the first example; in general, the higher students' GPAs, the higher their SAT scores. In the second example, the variables are negatively correlated; the more school students miss, the lower their grades. No correlation exists in the third; height and high school GPAs are not related.

It's important to remember that a correlation doesn't imply that one variable *causes* the other. For example, a high GPA—by itself—obviously doesn't cause a high SAT score. Rather, time spent studying, effective study strategies, and general intelligence are likely to be causes of both. Similarly, being absent, per se, doesn't cause low grades. Instead, missing opportunities to learn, not completing homework assignments, and losing chances to interact with peers are likely causes.

Much of what we know about the relationships between teaching and learning is based on correlational research (Springer, 2010).

EXPERIMENTAL RESEARCH

Whereas correlational research looks for relationships in existing situations, such as the relationship between teacher questioning and student achievement, **experimental research** systematically manipulates variables in attempts to determine cause and effect (Springer, 2010). To illustrate this process, imagine that researchers randomly assign teachers to two groups (random assignment is important to ensure, as much as possible, that the groups are comparable). The researchers then train teachers in one group to call on their students equally, as Jan did with hers, but the other group receives no training. If the students taught by the trained teachers exhibit higher levels of achievement than the students taught by teachers who receive no training, researchers can then conclude that training in equitable distribution of questions causes an increase in achievement (Springer, 2010).

Qualitative Research

Quantitative research, and particularly experimental studies, can be costly, and conducting this research can be a challenge. For example, training interventions are often time consuming, and access to classrooms and teachers may be difficult. **Qualitative research**, which attempts to describe a complex educational phenomenon in a holistic fashion using nonnumerical data, such as words and pictures, is an alternative (Johnson & Christensen, 2011). It relies on interviews, field notes, and other descriptive techniques, and then looks for patterns, as does quantitative research. The results of qualitative studies, however, are published in narrative reports with detailed descriptions of settings and participants, whereas quantitative studies typically result in reports with correlations and other statistical techniques (Gay, Mills, & Airasian, 2012).

A classic qualitative study of teaching, *First-Year Teacher* (Bullough, 1989), illustrates these characteristics. The researcher's goal was to describe, from the teacher's perspective, what it's like to be a first-year teacher. He spent a year observing a first-year, middle school language arts teacher, interviewing her, and collecting artifacts such as lesson plans and assignments. A realistic account of the triumphs and difficulties encountered by one teacher emerged from the study. As in other qualitative studies, the researcher did not claim that this teacher's experience generalized to the experiences of all first-year teachers. Instead, he simply attempted to describe one teacher's experience in as much detail as possible and then allow readers to draw their own conclusions about that teacher's experiences.

Each of these forms of research contributes to professional knowledge, the knowledge expert teachers understand and apply in their work with students.

Action Research

When you teach, and as you gain experience, you'll have questions about the effects your actions have on your students' learning. Some might include:

- How much homework should I give?
- Should I systematically grade homework, or merely check to see if students have completed it?
- How often should I give quizzes?
- Should I ever give my students free time to socialize with their classmates?

Many other examples exist, and to answer these questions, you might conduct your own studies, which are forms of **action research**, applied research designed to answer a specific school- or classroom-related question. It can use either quantitative or qualitative methods (Gay et al., 2012). For example, you might want to compare your students' achievement when you give a quiz every week during one grading period to a previous grading period when you gave only three quizzes for the 9 weeks. In doing so, you are conducting action research.

If carefully organized and systematically conducted, action research can be published in professional journals or presented at conferences just as is done by professional researchers (Bransford et al., 2000). If you do so, you will also be contributing to the body of professional knowledge that expert teachers possess.

Design-Based Research

Research in education has received a considerable amount of criticism over the years, with its lack of impact on classroom practice being one of the most important. "It is both surprising and depressing that many educators cannot think of a single research output or can think of only trivial outputs that meet this most practical and important outcome of research" (Anderson & Shattuck, 2012, p. 18).

In response to these criticisms, design-based research has evolved. In addition to the goal of impacting classroom practice, it has the following characteristics (Anderson & Shattuck, 2012; McKenney & Reeves, 2013):

- It is conducted in a real-world context, such as a classroom.
- It focuses on the design and testing of educational interventions, which could be a specific learning activity, type of assessment, administrative innovation (such as starting school later in the morning), or application of some form of technology, among many others.
- It uses mixed methods, such as combining experimental and qualitative methods.
- It involves multiple iterations, that is, it repeats the process with the aim of approaching a desired goal. The result of one iteration is used as a starting point for the next one.
- It involves a partnership between researchers and practitioners.
- It is intended to contribute to theory.

Design-based research is not the same as action research. When action research is conducted, the educator, such as a teacher or administrator, is both researcher and teacher, whereas a design-based study involves a partnership between researchers and practitioners. "The partnership in a design-based study recognizes that teachers are usually too busy and often ill trained to conduct rigorous research" (Anderson & Shattuck, 2012, p. 17). It also recognizes that teachers working in the real world of classrooms are essential for a study's validity. Further, design-based research doesn't focus exclusively on a local need, as would be the case with action research; as we saw above, it also attempts to contribute to theories that are applicable to a variety of settings.

From your perspective as someone involved in a teacher preparation program, design-based research's attempt to have a practical impact on classroom practice is probably its most important characteristic. When successful, design-based research provides us with concrete and practical suggestions for improving our teaching.

Research and the Development of Theory

As we saw in the discussion of design-based research, contributing to theory is one of its goals. Arguably, this is the goal of all research. As research results accumulate, patterns emerge. For instance, after many studies researchers have concluded that the thinking of young children tends to be dominated by their perceptions (Piaget, 1970, 1977; Wadsworth, 2004). For example, when first graders see an inverted cup of water with a card beneath it, as we see in the accompanying picture, they commonly explain that the card doesn't fall because the water somehow holds it against the cup. They focus on the most perceptually obvious aspect of the object—the water—and ignore atmospheric pressure, the actual reason the card stays on the cup.

The statement "The thinking of young children tends to be dominated by their perceptions" is a pattern found in large numbers of research studies. Some additional examples of research-based patterns include:

- Behaviors rewarded some of the time, but not all of the time, persist longer than behaviors rewarded every time they occur.
- People tend to imitate behaviors they observe in others.
- People strive for a state of order, balance, and predictability in the world.

As additional research is conducted, related patterns are found, which in turn generate further studies. As knowledge accumulates, **theories**, sets of related patterns that researchers use to explain and predict events in the world, are gradually constructed (Cooper, 2006). In our everyday world, the term is used more loosely. For instance, one person makes a point in a conversation, and a second responds, "I have a theory about that." In this case, the person is merely offering an explanation for the point. In educational psychology, theory is reserved for the more systematic collection of data and the forming of patterns over time.

Theories help organize research findings and can provide valuable guidance for our teaching. Let's look at a brief example. One research-based pattern states, "Reinforced behaviors increase in frequency," and a related pattern we mentioned earlier indicates that intermittently reinforced behaviors persist longer than those that are continuously reinforced (Baldwin & Baldwin, 2001; Schunk, 2012; Skinner, 1957). Further, too much reinforcement can actually decrease its effectiveness. So, for example, if you reinforce your students for their attempts to answer questions by praising them, they are likely to increase their efforts, but they will persist longer if they are praised for some, but not all, of their attempts (intermittently reinforced). If you praise them too much, they may actually reduce their efforts (Deci & Ryan, 2008).

These related patterns are part of behaviorism, a theory that studies the effects of external influences on behavior. Our illustration, of course, is only a minor portion of the complete theory. (We examine behaviorism in depth in Chapter 6.) The key feature of any theory is the large number of research-based patterns that are integrated into a coherent body of knowledge.

Theories are useful in two important ways. First, they allow us to *explain* events in our classrooms and the world at large. For instance, look again at the cartoon on page 35. Piaget's theory of cognitive development (1970, 1977), which includes the pattern we mentioned earlier ("The thinking of young children tends to be dominated by their perceptions"), helps us explain why the child in the cartoon thinks the way he does. We can explain this behavior by saying that the child can see only the water and the faucet, and because his thinking is dominated by his perception—what he can see—he concludes that all the water is in the faucet. Similarly, using behaviorist theory, we can explain why casino patrons persist in playing slot machines, though coins infrequently fall into the trays, by observing that they are being intermittently reinforced.

Theories also allow us to *predict* behavior and events. For instance, based on behaviorism, we would predict that students who periodically receive positive comments on essays will try harder than either students who receive no comments at all, or students who receive effusive positive comments.

In both instances, theories—cognitive development theory and behaviorist theory—help us understand learning and teaching by allowing us to explain and predict our students' behavior and how our actions will influence their learning. Throughout this book, you will study a number of theories, and we will discuss and illustrate ways that you can apply them in your teaching. These theories, together with a large body of research, make up the professional knowledge you need to become an expert teacher.

Teaching in Today's Classrooms

The world of teaching is rapidly changing, and in many ways it's more challenging than it was only a few years ago. But at the same time more potential rewards also exist. To start you on the path toward meeting these challenges and reaping these rewards, we want to provide you with an overview of what you will encounter when you begin your teaching career. In it we'll discuss the following:

- Standards and accountability
- Teacher licensure and evaluation
- Learner diversity
- Technology
- The influence of neuroscience

Standards and Accountability

In 1983 a very influential report, called *A Nation at Risk: The Imperative for Educational Reform,* was published (National Commission on Excellence in Education, 1983). This widely read document, considered to be a landmark in American educational history, argued that our country's schools were failing to meet the national need for a competitive workforce, and since its publication, a great deal has been written about American students' lack of knowledge and skills. For instance, one survey found more than half of high school students identified Germany, Japan, or Italy, instead of the Soviet Union, as America's World War II ally (Bauerlein, 2008). And in 2010 the National Assessment of Educational Progress (NAEP) found that only 12% of American 12th graders scored well enough to be considered "proficient" in American history (National Center for Education Statistics, 2010). Further, NAEP results for 2013 showed that student performance in math and reading remains well below where government and education leaders want it to be (National Center for Education Statistics, 2013a).

American adults also fare poorly. For example, a report from the Organization for Economic Cooperation and Development (OECD), which focused on people aged 16–64 in 24 countries, found that, compared with their international counterparts, American adults are weak in both literacy and math (OECD, 2013).

In response to these concerns, educational leaders have established academic **standards**, statements that describe what students should know or be able to do at the end of a prescribed period of study. All states and the District of Columbia have established standards. The following are two examples, the first in world history from the state of California and the second in third-grade math from Texas.

> Students analyze the effects of the Industrial Revolution in England, France, Germany, Japan and the United States.
> 1. Analyze why England was the first country to industrialize (California State Board of Education, 2008).

> (3) Number and operations. The student applies mathematical process standards to represent and explain fractional units. The student is expected to:
>> (A) represent fractions greater than zero and less than or equal to one with denominators of 2, 3, 4, 6, and 8 using concrete objects and pictorial models, including strip diagrams and number lines (Texas Education Agency, 2012)

Analysis of standards from different states has identified significant variations in expectations, rigor, and even content. Also, charges have been made suggesting that many states lowered their standards to meet federal mandates (Ginsburg, Leinwand, & Decker, 2009).

Further, American students still remain behind other nations in academic achievement, readiness for college, and the world of work. For instance, according to some measures,

American students rank 25th in math, 17th in science, and 14th in reading compared with students in 27 industrialized countries around the world (Broad Foundation, 2013).

Because of these issues, the Common Core State Standards Initiative (CCSSI) was developed. Let's look at it.

THE COMMON CORE STATE STANDARDS INITIATIVE

The **Common Core State Standards Initiative (CCSSI)** is a state-led effort to establish a single set of clear educational standards for all states (Common Core State Standards Initiative, 2014a). The standards exist in mathematics and English-language arts together with literacy in history/social studies, science, and technical subjects. States can voluntarily adopt and share the standards. The CCSSI is coordinated by the National Governors Association Center for Best Practices (NGA Center) and the Council of Chief State School Officers (CCSSO). By 2012, 45 states, the District of Columbia, four territories, and the Department of Defense Education Activities had adopted the Common Core standards (Common Core State Standards Initiative, 2014a).

The CCSSI standards are designed to ensure that students graduating from high school are prepared to go to college or enter the workforce and that parents, teachers, and students have a clear understanding of what is expected of them. The standards are also linked to international benchmarks to hopefully ensure that American students are competitive in the emerging global marketplace (Ginsburg et al., 2009; Lee & Spratley, 2010).

The following is an example from first-grade math:

> CCSS.Math.Content.1.OA.B.3 Apply properties of operations as strategies to add and subtract. Examples: If $8 + 3 = 11$ is known, then $3 + 8 = 11$ is also known. (Commutative property of addition.) To add $2 + 6 + 4$, the second two numbers can be added to make a ten, so $2 + 6 + 4 = 2 + 10 = 12$. (Associative property of addition.) (Common Core State Standards Initiative, 2014p).

As another example, a literacy standard in History/Social Studies for Grade 9–10 appears as follows.

> CCSS.ELA-Literacy.RH.9-10.8 Assess the extent to which the reasoning and evidence in a text support the author's claims. (Common Core State Standards Initiative, 2014d).

The Common Core State Standards are similar to many of the standards that already exist in the states. The consistency that the standards provide—both among states in our country and internationally—is a primary advantage of the CCSSI.

Controversies with the Common Core. The Common Core enjoyed widespread acceptance until the fall of 2012, but then criticisms began to surface (Bushaw & Lopez, 2013). For example, some critics argued that the uniformity of standards across states represented federal overreach and an attempt to establish a national curriculum (Strauss, 2013).

Public understanding of the CCSSI was also a problem. For instance, one poll found that "almost two of three Americans have never heard of the Common Core State Standards, . . . and most of those who say they know about the Common Core neither understand it nor embrace it" (Bushaw & Lopez, 2013, p. 9).

On the other hand, supporters point out that the CCSSI is not a federal program; it originated in the states, where the standards were developed by governors and state school officials. Also, initial impetus for the standards began at the annual meeting of the Council of Chief State School Officers in 2007 during the George W. Bush presidential administration (Schoof, 2013). And the Common Core isn't a mandate, and it doesn't prescribe curriculum. Individual teachers interpret the standards, set their own objectives, design their own learning activities, and create their own assessments.

Further, the Common Core has variously been described as "The most important educational reform in the country's history" (New York Times Editorial Board, 2013, para. 2),

"[A]rguably one of the most important education initiatives in decades" (Bushaw & Lopez, 2013, p. 9), and "[A]rguably the most serious educational reform of our lifetime" (Keller, 2013, para. 3). The standards have been endorsed by most professional groups, and business leaders have come out in formal support of the Common Core (Molnar, 2014). Also, more than 8 of 10 Americans strongly agree that schools should teach critical thinking skills, which are integral to the Common Core (Bushaw & Lopez, 2013).

Despite controversies, the Common Core appears to be moving forward and will likely be a part of your professional life when you begin teaching. This is the reason we link most of our case studies in this book to Common Core standards—so you will be ready when you begin your career.

ACCOUNTABILITY

Accountability is the process of requiring students to demonstrate that they have met standards as measured by standardized tests. States that have adopted the Common Core standards have collaborated to develop common assessments that are aligned with the standards and replace existing end-of-year state assessments. These assessments linked to the Common Core were intended to be made available for the 2014–2015 school year (Common Core State Standards Initiative, 2014a). So, if your state is one that has adopted the Common Core standards, your students will be held accountable for meeting them.

Prior to the development of tests aligned with the Common Core State Standards, states developed their own end-of-year tests designed to assess the extent to which students have met state standards. If your state has not adopted the Common Core, your students will be held accountable for meeting the standards established by your state.

Either way, standards and accountability will be a part of your teaching life when you begin your career, and the sooner you become comfortable with them, the easier your job will be. Our goal in introducing them in this chapter is to help you hit the ground running.

Teacher Licensure and Evaluation

In addition to standards and accountability, teacher licensure and evaluation are part of the reality of teacher preparation programs and teaching in today's classroom. For you, this process will exist at two levels. The first will occur before you begin teaching and will require you to pass a licensure exam; the second is ongoing evaluation that will be conducted throughout your career. Let's first look at licensure exams.

LICENSURE EXAMS

As you saw earlier in the chapter, teacher quality is now a national priority, and, for many, "teacher quality" is synonymous with teacher knowledge. In an attempt to ensure that teachers possess adequate professional knowledge, all states now require prospective teachers to pass one or more tests before they receive a teaching license. These tests commonly measure general knowledge, as well as the types of professional knowledge that we described earlier in the chapter. It is a virtual certainty that you will be required to pass an exam that measures your professional knowledge before you receive your teaching license.

The Praxis Series™, published by the Educational Testing Service, is the test most widely used for teacher licensure (*praxis* means putting theory into practice). A majority of the states in our country use this series (Educational Testing Service, 2014a). States that don't use the Praxis Series™ have created their own licensure exams, and these exams are quite similar to the Praxis in design and content.

The Praxis Series™ tests include (Educational Testing Service, 2014a):

- Praxis™ Core Academic Skills for Educators (Core). These tests measure academic skills in reading, writing, and mathematics. They're designed to assess the knowledge and skills of candidates entering teacher preparation programs.

- Praxis I® Pre-Professional Skills Tests (PPST®). These tests measure basic skills in reading, writing, and mathematics. In addition to licensure, these tests are often used to qualify candidates for entry into a teacher education program.
- Praxis II® Subject Assessments. These tests measure subject-specific content knowledge, together with general and subject-specific teaching skills that are needed to succeed as a teacher.

The *Principles of Learning and Teaching (PLT)* tests are important parts of the Praxis II® series. The PLT tests are designed for teachers seeking licensure in early childhood or grades K–6, 5–9, and 7–12. Each of the four tests is 2 hours long and consists of 70 questions that are multiple-choice combined with four constructed-response questions that are based on two "case histories" similar to the case study that you read at the beginning of this chapter (Educational Testing Service, 2014b, 2014c, 2014d, 2014e). The content of educational psychology makes up much of what is measured on the tests, and in our "Preparing for Your Licensure Exam" feature, which appears at the end of each chapter, you can practice responding to multiple-choice and short-answer questions similar to those you'll encounter on the PLT tests. In addition, Appendix C provides a matrix that correlates the content covered in this text with the content measured on the Praxis PLT exams.

TEACHER EVALUATION

Teacher evaluation, the process of assessing teachers' classroom performance and providing feedback they can use to increase their expertise, is another aspect of reality that you will encounter when you begin your career. Teacher evaluation has become an increasingly important issue in education, because evidence suggests that, historically, evaluation procedures have done little to reward good teachers and eliminate those that are incompetent. Criticisms of these procedures vary from calling them inefficient and ineffective (Weisberg, Sexton, Mulhern, & Keeling, 2009) to calling them perfunctory and haphazard (Pallas, 2010/2011). Current reforms are attempting to remedy this problem by creating more valid and reliable teacher evaluation systems (Hull, 2013; MET, 2013).

The use of student achievement data is one aspect of these systems. This leads us to the concept of value-added modeling in teacher evaluation.

Value-Added Modeling in Teacher Evaluation. **Value-added modeling** is a method of teacher evaluation that measures a teacher's contribution to student learning in a given year by comparing the current test scores of their students to the scores of those same students in previous school years, and to the scores of other students in the same grade. For example, if a second grader scores at the 50th percentile on a reading test at the beginning of the year and on the 60th percentile at the end of the year, researchers conclude that the gain is a result of the teacher's expertise, and *value* had been added. This approach seeks to isolate the contribution that each teacher provides (the value added) during the year, which can then be compared with the performance of other teachers (Corcoran, 2010; Darling-Hammond, Amrein-Beardsley, Haertel, & Rothstein, 2011).

Value-added models are controversial (Fuhrman, 2013). Students are rarely randomly assigned to teachers, which can impact the validity of test results (Paufler & Amrein-Beardsley, 2014). Critics also question whether tests can accurately capture what teachers are actually accomplishing, such as learning gains that might not show up immediately, and other outcomes, such as social skills, motivation, and self-regulation, that can't be measured on tests (Baker et al., 2010; Corcoran, 2010; Darling-Hammond et al., 2011). "[T]here is broad agreement among statisticians, psychometricians, and economists that student test scores alone are not sufficiently reliable and valid indicators of teacher effectiveness . . . even when the most sophisticated statistical applications such as value-added modeling are employed" (Baker et al., 2010, p. 2). As a result of these criticisms, no state in our country evaluates teachers on the basis of student test scores alone (Hull, 2013).

Trends in Teacher Evaluation. So, how will you be evaluated when you begin your teaching career? A report issued in 2013 by National School Boards Association Center for Public Education outlines the patterns among the states in our country with respect to teacher evaluation (Hull, 2013). The following is a summary of them:

- Forty-seven states require or recommend that stakeholders, including teachers, provide input into the design of evaluation systems. This means that you and/or your colleagues will have input into the way your teaching will be evaluated.
- Forty-one states require or recommend that teachers be evaluated on multiple measures. In addition to student test scores and classroom observations, these evaluations may include measures such as student and parent surveys, examinations of lesson plans, teacher self-assessments, student artifacts, and teacher portfolios.
- Forty-six states require or recommend that evaluations include measures on how teachers impact their students' achievement, and 23 states have mandated that achievement measures comprise half of teachers' evaluations. And some research suggests that high-quality measures of student achievement correlate strongly with other measures of teacher effectiveness (MET, 2013). So, it's highly likely that your students' test scores will make up part of your evaluation.
- Classroom observations are a component of every state's evaluation system, and several evaluations during a school year are recommended. The goal is to use well-trained observers to ensure that teachers being evaluated receive similar scores regardless of who conducts the observations, and observation instruments are supposed to be based on practices most likely to increase student learning.
- Most states are focusing on using evaluation for the purpose of raising teacher performance, but some are also using the results to inform personnel decisions, such as teacher retention and salary increases.

To identify your state's specific practices, go to the website that includes the report conducted by the National School Boards Association Center for Public Education (Hull, 2013).

What are the implications of these changes for you when you begin teaching? First, evaluation will be an important part of your teaching life, so become thoroughly familiar with the criteria that will be used to evaluate you. Study the observation instruments that will be used, so that demonstrating the teaching skills identified in them become essentially automatic. For instance, if the instrument has a category saying, "Learning objectives are displayed for students," make writing your learning objectives on the board one of your routines. If the amount of student involvement is a category, make high levels of student involvement part of your teaching repertoire. (This is a win-win for you. Student involvement promotes learning, and you will earn positive evaluations.)

Since it's likely that your students' performance on standardized tests will make up part of your evaluation, become as familiar as possible with the content measured on the tests, as well as test formats, and do everything you can to ensure that your students have mastered the content and are familiar with test formats and procedures. (This suggestion is different from "teaching to the test," which focuses on specific test items and provides practice with those items.)

The same is true for other measures, such as lesson plans or student artifacts, if they're used as part of your evaluation. You will undoubtedly feel some pressure to perform well when you're evaluated, but teacher evaluation should not be onerous or punitive. Rather, it should be an opportunity for you to demonstrate your expertise and receive feedback that will help you improve in areas where needed. None of us teach perfect lessons, and we can all improve. If this is the spirit in which your district and school conducts evaluations, they can become a positive professional growth experience.

Learner Diversity

The demographic trends in our country are changing rapidly, and increasing diversity is one of the most significant. For example, you probably have friends whose ethnic backgrounds are different from your own, and they may speak a native language other than English. In fact, English may not be your first language.

The following projections illustrate some of these demographic changes, comparing the status in 2010 to predictions for 2021 (National Center for Education Statistics, 2013b):

- The total population in our country is projected to increase slightly more than 7%.
- The Hispanic population is projected to increase from approximately 23% to 26% of the total.
- The Black population, approximately 16% of the total, is projected to remain stable.
- The percentage of other ethnic groups, such as Asian/Pacific Islander, Native Americans, and multi-ethnic groups, is projected to increase.
- In 2010 the non-Hispanic white population in our country made up 52% of the total, but by 2021 that figure is projected to drop to 47%. This means that by that year, no ethnic group will be a majority in our country.

Prior to 2010, more than 40% of Californians spoke a language at home other than English. In Texas it was more than 33%; in New York nearly 30%; and it was more than 25% in Florida (Center for Public Education, 2012). Those figures are almost certainly higher today. In an event that symbolizes some of the potential issues related to this diversity, 20,000 students sued California educators in the spring of 2013 for failing to teach English to non-native English speakers (Mohajer, 2013).

The diversity in our country is more complex than culture and language. For example, children coming from low-income families are now a major factor in today's schools. Consider the following statistics (Southern Education Foundation, 2013):

- All states in our country experienced rising rates of low-income students between the years 2000 and 2011.
- Forty-eight percent of all students in our country were eligible for free or reduced-price lunch in 2011.
- Urban areas in every part of our country now have majorities of students who come from low-income families, and nationwide, two out of five students in the suburbs also are poor.

In addition, over a million homeless students attended our schools in 2011–2012, with substantial subgroups of learners with disabilities and non-native English speakers among this number. Forty states reported an increase in the number of homeless students, with 10 reporting an increase of 20% or more (National Center for Homeless Education, 2013).

Finally, statistics indicate that approximately 12% of the students who attend our nation's schools have exceptionalities that may require extra services in order for them to reach their full potential (Center for Public Education, 2013; Heward, 2013).

This all means that your students will have very diverse backgrounds, and this diversity will be both enriching and challenging. Different cultural habits, attitudes, and values can make learning experiences more enriching for all your students, while at the same time, for example, working with children from low-income families will be a challenge. Because learner diversity is such an important influence on teaching and learning in today's world, we include one or more sections examining diversity topics in each of the chapters of this book.

Technology

Think about the following questions.

1. When was the last time you went to a print encyclopedia to find some information, or to a print dictionary to find the definition of a word?
2. When was the last time you took a picture with a camera that uses film?

3. How often do you "Google" something?
4. Are you a Facebook user?
5. Do you own a smartphone or tablet computer?
6. Do you prefer to "text" rather than talk on the phone?

The answer to the first two questions might be "Never" or "Can't remember when." "Daily" or even more often might be the answer to the third, and "Yes" is probably the most common answer to the last three. We could ask many more similar questions, but you get the idea. Technology is now so much a part of our world that, until we stop to think about it, we almost don't realize it.

As with the other topics we've discussed in this section, technology will be an integral part of your teaching life, and it will have benefits and present challenges. As a simple example, instead of sending a letter in print form home to parents you will likely email it. You may teach some classes online. You will store lesson plans and a myriad of examples and other resources in your computer, which you will access and display for your students at the touch of your keyboard. Your classroom will likely be equipped with an **interactive whiteboard**, a device that includes a display screen connected to a computer and projector that allows information displayed on the screen to be manipulated with hands or special pens, stored in the computer, and recovered later for further use (Roblyer & Doering, 2013). Technology such as this is being used in classrooms across the country ranging from early elementary (Linder, 2013) to university levels (Greene & Kirpalani, 2013). Also, an increasing number of teachers are using social media, such as blogs, wikis, Twitter, and others, to promote classroom learning (Seo, 2013). And students are becoming increasingly "tech savvy." For example, many kindergarten students are now experienced tablet users—for both entertainment and learning. This technology is merely the tip of an iceberg. The list of potential technological influences is virtually endless, and we can only imagine what the future world has in store (Kaku, 2011).

Challenges will also exist. For instance, one survey found that nearly half of university students text at least once per class session (Johnson, 2013), and another determined that more than 9 of 10 bring their cell phones to class every day and use their phones to send texts during class time (Tindell & Bohlander, 2013). These issues also exist at the P–12 level.

The point here is that technology has permeated students' very existence, and it will also be an integral part of your teaching life. So, the sooner you begin preparing to capitalize on its benefits and meet its challenges the better off you'll be. Because technology is such an integral part of teaching and learning in our nation's schools, we include discussions of it in special features throughout this book.

The Influence of Neuroscience

Ed Psych and You

Is it possible for us to literally "get smarter" if the conditions are right? To what extent do emotions, such as joy and anger, influence our learning? We've all heard the old adage, "Let's sleep on it?" Can this make a difference?

Neuroscience is the study of how the nervous system develops, how it's structured, and what it does. Traditionally seen as a branch of biology, neuroscience is now viewed as an interdisciplinary science that collaborates with other fields such as chemistry, computer science, and medicine, and it's also linked to such disciplines as law, psychology, and education. Neuroscience began its march to prominence in the 1980s, and in the 1990s it gathered momentum that continues today (van Ommen, 2013).

Neuroscience research contributes to our understanding of learning and teaching in two ways. First, it provides evidence that confirms teaching practices that we have long believed are important, such as the need for active learning. "Many research studies suggest that active engagement is a prerequisite for changes in the brain. Not surprisingly, just listening to a presentation or lecture will not lead to learning" (Van Dam, 2013, p. 32). This quote implies that we won't learn from lectures, and while this is probably overstated, we have long known that students learn much more when they are cognitively active—consciously *thinking about* the content they're studying—than they do when they sit passively listening (Edwards et al., 2011; Veenman, 2011).

As a second example, intuitively it makes sense that stress and fatigue will have a negative impact on cognitive functioning, and neuroscience research confirms this sensible idea (Palmer, 2013). This research was done on university students, and it has implications for you as you move through your university experience; simply, understand that stress and fatigue affect learning and make every effort to manage your stress levels and get enough rest.

Second, neuroscience provides us with insights into the brain and the way it works. Neuroplasticity (sometimes called *brain plasticity,* or simply *plasticity*), the brain's ability to physically remodel itself in response to experience, is one of the most important of these insights (Dubinsky et al., 2013; Pascual-Leone, Amedi, Fregni, & Merabet, 2005). In other words, as we acquire experiences, the brain can literally rewire itself (Schachter, 2012). "People have different genetic predispositions, but experience continuously shapes our brain structure and modifies behavior" (Van Dam, 2013, p. 32). This is a very different view of the brain; until recently scientists thought the structure of the brain developed during childhood and that once developed there was little room for change (Pascual-Leone et al., 2005).

The concept of neuroplasticity helps answer the first question we asked in *Ed Psych and You*. It suggests that yes, if we have the right kinds of experiences, we can indeed literally get smarter. This is very good news, and it also has enormous implications for teaching and learning. It suggests that providing meaningful experiences—in areas varying from academic to personal, social, and emotional—is arguably our most important task as teachers. When we succeed, we don't just help our students acquire knowledge and skills; we literally change their brains. It has implications for learners as well. "Students who understand that their brains are plastic are more willing to struggle to learn difficult content" (Dubinsky et al., 2013, p. 319).

Neuroscience also helps us answer the second and third questions we asked in *Ed Psych and You*. Emotions do indeed influence both motivation and learning. Positive emotions, such as joy, are generally linked to increased motivation and achievement, whereas the opposite is true for negative emotions (Legault & Inzlicht, 2013; Lövheim, 2012). There's something to the old adage, "Let's sleep on it"; neuroscience research indicates that memories are often consolidated and linked during sleep, resulting in more coherent and usable patterns (Nieuwenhuis, Folia, Forkstam, Jensen, & Petersson, 2013).

Because neuroscience contributes to our understanding of learning and its implications for teaching, we include sections on the topic in several of the chapters of this text.

Educational Psychology and Teaching: Applying Your Professional Knowledge in Today's Classrooms

Much of educational psychology is interesting for its own sake, because it provides insights into how we all learn and develop. It can also make an important contribution to your teaching, but only if you know how to apply its content to your work. As you see in the title of this section, *applying* the content of educational psychology to your teaching is the focus here, and one or more sections devoted to application will appear in each chapter of this book. This is why you're taking this course and studying this text—so you can use your knowledge of learning and teaching, the content of educational psychology, to increase your students' achievement.

To understand how applications of educational psychology can influence your teaching, let's return to the questions we asked at the beginning of the chapter.

> "How was Jan's approach to teaching word problems different from Keith's?"

and

> "Why were their approaches so different, and how will these differences affect their students' learning?"

We now want to examine these questions again, using professional knowledge as the lens through which we look. Let's begin by considering the first. Keith's approach to teaching word problems was to ". . . explain the stuff so carefully," and when the kids sat with blank looks on their faces, to ". . . explain it even more carefully." He was conscientious and sincere in his attempts to help his students learn to solve problems, and his approach—to explain—is the one most commonly used in classrooms. The problem he encountered is also common; explaining—alone—is often ineffective in helping students understand difficult ideas, such as problem solving. In contrast, Jan built her lesson around concrete and real-world examples—the costs of the 12-ounce soft drink can, the 20-ounce bottle, and the 6 pack.

To promote student involvement, she had them work in pairs to determine which one was the best buy, and she provided them with enough guidance to ensure that they were making progress toward a solution. In contrast with Keith, she didn't use explaining as her primary approach to helping them learn to solve problems.

Now, let's answer the second question. Their approaches were different because Jan possessed more professional knowledge than did Keith, and, as a result, Jan's students are likely to learn more. They both had ample knowledge of content; they both understood decimals and percents and the processes involved in problem solving. However, the fact that Keith used verbal explanations—an often ineffective teaching strategy—as his only approach indicated that he lacked pedagogical content knowledge, general pedagogical knowledge, and knowledge of learners and learning—the other forms of professional knowledge needed for expert teaching. He explained, and when that didn't work, he was only able to explain some more. In contrast, Jan was able to provide concrete and real-world examples of decimals, percents, and problem solving, which demonstrated her pedagogical content knowledge. The fact that she knew her students needed the concrete examples and needed to be actively involved in the learning activity indicated her knowledge of learners and learning.

The differences between Jan's and Keith's professional knowledge are not surprising. Keith is a first-year teacher, whereas Jan has four years of experience, and she continues to grow professionally by taking classes that focus on this knowledge. Because Keith is a rookie, he is less knowledgeable than Jan, but he is no less committed. With study and practice he will learn and grow, and the same applies to you. You won't be an expert immediately, but with effort you can be, and in doing so, you *will* become more effective and more satisfied with your teaching.

chapter

1 Summary

1. Describe expert teaching and explain how expert teaching influences student learning.
   - Experts are people who are highly knowledgeable and skilled in a particular domain, such as teaching. Students taught by expert teachers learn more than students taught by teachers with less expertise.
   - Expert teachers can produce learning in their students and do so despite challenging circumstances.

2. Describe the different kinds of professional knowledge that expert teachers possess.
   - Expert teachers thoroughly understand the topics they teach, and their knowledge is reflected in their actions when they use their pedagogical content knowledge to illustrate those topics in ways that make sense to learners.
   - Expert teachers apply general pedagogical knowledge to organize learning environments and use basic instructional skills in ways that promote learning for their students.
   - Expert teachers' knowledge of learners and learning allows them to design learning activities that involve students, promote motivation to learn, and use developmentally appropriate practice.

3. Describe different types of research, and explain how research and theory contribute to teachers' professional knowledge.
   - Research is the process of systematically gathering information in an attempt to answer professional questions, and it is an important source of the knowledge needed for expert teaching.
   - Quantitative research is the systematic examination of events using numerical data and statistical and mathematical techniques. Quantitative research exists in descriptive, correlational, and experimental forms.
   - Descriptive research uses tests, surveys, and observations to describe the characteristics of some phenomena; correlational research looks for relationships among variables that allows the prediction of changes in one variable based on changes in another variable; experimental research systematically manipulates variables in attempts to determine cause and effect.
   - Qualitative research attempts to describe complex educational phenomen in a holistic fashion using nonnumerical data.
   - Action research is applied research designed to answer a specific school- or classroom-related question. It can use both quantitative and qualitative methods.
   - Influencing classroom practice is the goal of design-based research, and its characteristics include collaboration between researchers and teachers, a focus on educational interventions, the use of multiple iterations, and mixed methods. Unlike action research, it includes both the solution of local problems and efforts to contribute to theory.
   - Theories are sets of related patterns that help explain and predict events in the world. Theories can provide valuable guidance for teaching.

4. Identify factors that influence teaching in today's classrooms.
   - Standards, statements describing what students should know or be able to do after a given period of study, and accountability, the process of requiring students to demonstrate that they have met standards as measured by standardized tests, are parts of professional reality in today's classrooms.
   - Teachers are required to pass a licensure exam before they're allowed to work full time in today's classrooms, and they will also be regularly evaluated during their teaching careers.
   - Teacher evaluation systems commonly include a combination of measures. Virtually all include classroom observations, but they may also include other items, such as student and parent surveys, lesson plans, and student artifacts. A number of states are now including student scores on standardized tests as well.
   - Today's schools are now attended by students whose backgrounds are the most diverse in our country's history. In addition to differences in cultural and language backgrounds, large numbers of students from low-income backgrounds are now attending our nation's schools.
   - Technology is now an integral part of our lives, and it is becoming an increasingly significant factor in today's classrooms.
   - Neuroscience, the study of how the nervous system develops, how it's structured, and what it does, is contributing to our understanding of teaching and learning, with neuroplasticity, the ability of the brain to physically remodel itself in response to experience, a being one of the most important. It suggests that providing high-quality experiences for students might arguably be teachers' most important role.

Preparing for Your Licensure Exam

Understanding Professional Knowledge

You will be required to take a licensure exam before you go into your own classroom. This exam will include information related to the different types of professional knowledge teachers need to become experts, and the following exercises are similar to those that appear on licensure exams. They are designed to help you prepare for the exam in your state. This book and these exercises will be a resource for you later in your program as you prepare for the exam.

The following episodes illustrate four teachers at different classroom levels working with their students. As you read the episodes, think about the different types of professional knowledge that the teachers demonstrate in their lessons.

The segments you study here are based on the video episode you saw in "Practice Using What You Have Learned" Exercise 1.1. To make the written segments more meaningful, you may want to review the video episode again.

Rebecca Atkins, a kindergarten teacher, is talking with her children about planting a garden. She sits on a small chair at the front of the room and has the children seated on the floor in a semicircle in front of her.

She begins, "We had a story about gardening the other day. Who remembers the name of the story? . . . Shereta?"

"'Together,'" Shereta softly responds.

"Yes, 'Together,'" Rebecca repeats. "What happened in 'Together'? . . . Andrea?"

"They had a garden."

"They planted a garden together, didn't they?" Rebecca smiles. "The boy's father helped them plant the garden."

She continues by referring the children to previous science lessons during which they had talked about plants and soil. She then asks them about their own experiences helping their parents plant a garden.

"I helped put the seeds in the ground and put the dirt on top of it," Robert offers.

"What kinds of vegetables did you plant? . . . Kim?"

"I planted lots of vegetables . . . tomatoes, carrots."

"Travis?"

"I planted okra."

"Raphael?"

"I planted beans."

She continues, "Tell about the story 'Together.' What did they have to do to take care of the garden? . . . Carlita?"

"Water it."

"Bengemar?"

"Pull the weeds from it."

"Pull the weeds from it," Rebecca smiles. "What would happen if we left those weeds in there? . . . Latangela?"

"It would hurt the soil."

"What's another word for soil?"

"Dirt," several of the children say in unison.

"How many of you like to play in the dirt?"

Most of the children raise their hands.

"So, planting a garden would be fun because you get to play in the dirt," Rebecca says enthusiastically.

"I like to play in the mud," Travis adds.

"You like to play in the mud," Rebecca repeats, attempting to stifle a laugh.

We turn now to Richard Nelms, a middle school science teacher, as he illustrates the concept of symmetry for his seventh graders.

Richard begins his discussion of symmetry by holding up a sponge as an example of an asymmetrical animal; he demonstrates radial symmetry using a starfish; and he then turns to bilateral symmetry.

"We have one more type of symmetry," he says. "Jason, come up here. . . . Stand up here."

Jason comes to the front of the room and stands on a stool.

"Would you say," Richard begins, "that Jason is asymmetrical—that there is not uniformity in his shape?"

The students shake their heads.

He has Jason extend his arms out from his sides as you see here and then asks, "Would you consider this radial, because he has extensions that go out in all directions? . . . Jarrett?"

"No."

"Why not? Explain that for us."

"There's nothing there," Jarrett says, pointing to Jason's sides.

"There's nothing coming from here, is there, and the arms, legs and head are all different?" Richard adds.

"So, we move to the third type of symmetry," he continues, as Jason continues to stand with his arms extended. "It's called *bilateral*. . . . Bilateral means that the form or

shape of the organism is divided into two halves, and the two halves are consistent. . . . If I took a tree saw and started at the top," he says, pointing at Jason's head as the class laughs, "the two halves would be essentially the same."

"Now, tomorrow," he continues, "we're going to see how symmetry influences the ways organisms function in their environments."

Let's look in now at Didi Johnson, a 10th-grade chemistry teacher, as she attempts to help her students understand Charles's law of gases, the law stating that an increase in the temperature of a gas causes an increase in its volume if the pressure on the gas doesn't change.

To illustrate that heat causes gases to expand, Didi prepares a demonstration in which she places three identical balloons filled with the same amount of air into three beakers of water. She puts the first into a beaker of hot water, the second into a beaker of water at room temperature, and the third into a beaker of ice water, as you see here.

"This water is near boiling," Didi explains as she places the first balloon in the beaker. "This is room temperature, and this has had ice in it, so it is near the freezing point," she continues as she puts the other two balloons into the beakers.

"Today," she continues as she begins writing on the board, "we're going to discuss Charles's law, but before we put it on the board and discuss it, we're going to see what happened to the balloons. . . . Look up here. . . . How is the size of the balloon related to the temperature of the water we placed it in?"

"The balloon in the hot water looks bigger," Chris responds.

"Can you see any difference in these two?" Didi continues, pointing to the other two balloons.

"The one in the cold water looks smaller than the one in the room-temperature water," Shannon adds.

"So, from what we see, if you increase temperature, what happens to the volume of the gas?"

"It increases," several students volunteer.

Didi writes, "Increase in temperature increases volume" on the board, emphasizes that the amount of air and the pressure in the balloons were kept essentially constant, and then asks, "Who can state Charles's law based on what we've seen here?"

"Increased temperature will increase volume if you have constant pressure and mass," Jeremy offers.

Didi briefly reviews Charles's law, writes an equation for it on the board, and has the students solve a series of problems using the law.

Finally, let's look at Bob Duchaine's work with his students. An American history teacher, he is discussing the Vietnam War with his 11th graders.

Bob begins by saying, "To understand the Vietnam War, we need to go back to the beginning. Vietnam had been set up as a French colony in the 1880s, but by the mid-1900s, the military situation had gotten so bad for the French that they only controlled certain enclaves like the little city of Dien Bien Phu."

He explains that the French surrendered this city in the summer of 1954, and peace talks followed. The talks resulted in Vietnam being split, and provisions for free elections were set up.

"These elections were never held," Bob continues. "Ngo Dinh Diem, in 1956, said there will be no free elections: 'I am in charge of the South. You can have elections in the North if you want, but there will be no elections in the South.'"

He continues by introducing the "domino theory," which suggested that countries such as South Vietnam, Cambodia, Laos, Thailand, Burma, and even India would fall into communist hands much as dominos tip over and knock each other down. The way to prevent the loss of the countries, he explains, was to confront North Vietnam.

"And that's what we're going to be talking about throughout this unit," he says. "The war that we took over from the French to stop the fall of the dominos soon was eating up American lives at the rate of 12 to 15 thousand a year. . . . This situation went from a little simple plan—to stop the dominos from falling—to a loss of over 53,000 American lives that we know of.

"We'll pick up with this topic day after tomorrow. . . . Tomorrow, you have a fun day in the library."

Questions for **Case Analysis**

In answering these questions, use information from the chapter, and link your responses to specific information in the case.

Multiple-Choice Questions

1. The two teachers who most nearly demonstrated pedagogical content knowledge were:

   a. Rebecca and Richard.

   b. Richard and Didi.

   c. Richard and Bob.

   d. Didi and Bob.

2. The teacher who *least* demonstrated general pedagogical knowledge was:

   a. Rebecca.

   b. Richard.

   c. Didi.

   d. Bob.

Constructed-Response Question

3. What type or types of professional knowledge did Bob most nearly demonstrate?

Important **Concepts**

accountability
action research
Common Core State
   Standards Initiative
   (CCSSI)
correlation
correlational research
descriptive research

design-based research
developmental differences
developmentally appropriate
   practice
educational psychology
   (ed psych)
experimental research
experts

general pedagogical
   knowledge
interactive whiteboard
neuroplasticity
neuroscience
pedagogical content
   knowledge
professional knowledge

qualitative research
quantitative research
reflective practice
research
standards
teacher evaluation
theories
value-added modeling

chapter

2 Cognitive and Language Development

OUTLINE	LEARNING OUTCOMES
	After you've completed your study of this chapter, you should be able to:
What Is Development? Principles of Development Bronfenbrenner's Bioecological Model of Development ▶ Analyzing Theories: Assessing Bronfenbrenner's Bioecological Model of Development The Neuroscience of Development	**1.** Describe development, and explain how Bronfenbrenner's theory and neuroscience research contribute to our understanding of development.
Piaget's Theory of Cognitive Development The Drive for Equilibrium The Development of Schemes Responding to Experiences: Assimilation and Accommodation Stages of Development Neo-Piagetian Views of Cognitive Development Educational Psychology and Teaching: Applying Piaget's Theory with Your Students	**2.** Use concepts from Piaget's theory of intellectual development to explain both classroom and everyday events.
Vygotsky's Sociocultural Theory of Cognitive Development Learning and Development in a Cultural Context Zone of Proximal Development Scaffolding: Interactive Instructional Support Diversity: Culture and Development Educational Psychology and Teaching: Applying Vygotsky's Theory with Your Students ▶ Analyzing Theories: Piaget's and Vygotsky's Views of Cognitive Development ▶ Developmentally Appropriate Practice: Promoting Cognitive Development with Learners at Different Ages	**3.** Use Vygotsky's sociocultural theory to explain how language, culture, and instructional support influence development.
Language Development Theories of Language Development Early Language Development Language Development in the School Years Using Language to Learn ▶ Technology, Learning, and Development: Is Technology Interfering with Cognitive and Language Development? Educational Psychology and Teaching: Helping Your Students Develop Language Abilities" ▶ Developmentally Appropriate Practice: Promoting Language Development with Learners at Different Ages	**4.** Use theories of language development to explain language patterns in children.

The way we conduct our lives depends, to a large extent, on the experiences we have. Rich experiences can lead to healthy personalities, advanced social skills, and sophisticated thinking, whereas lack of quality experiences can leave people disadvantaged.

Our focus in this chapter is on cognitive development—the development of thinking. As you read the following case study, think about the influence of experience on students' thinking as you witness a teacher's frustration with her students' seeming inability to understand basic science concepts.

On Friday morning Karen Johnson, an eighth-grade science teacher, walks into the teachers' workroom with a discouraged look on her face.

"What's happening?" Ken, one of her colleagues, asks.

"I just had the most frustrating class. . . . I was working on the Common Core Standard that addresses key concepts and terms in science:

CCSS.ELA-Literacy.RST.6-8.4: Determine the meaning of symbols, key terms, and other domain-specific words and phrases as they are used in a specific scientific or technical context relevant to grades 6–8 texts and topics. (Common Core State Standards Initiative, 2014k).

"The standard says that all students should understand basic science terms, and this is basic information everyone should know. Concepts like *mass, weight, volume,* and *density* certainly are key terms in science, and they're commonly used in our everyday world. We hear about dense fog, "massive" changes, high-volume business, and on and on. But my third-period students are really struggling. For example, today we were working on the concept *density*. They memorize the formula for finding the density of some material and try to solve problems, but they don't actually understand it. And they're confused about related concepts, such as *mass, weight, volume*—everything. To them, *mass, weight,* and *density* are all the same. If it's bigger, it's more dense. The class was a disaster."

"You know how these kids are; they're not used to thinking on their own," Ken responds.

"I guess so, but there's more," Karen nods. "They've never really done anything other than memorize definitions and formulas. So, I guess, what do we expect?

We'll return to the conversation between Karen and Ken later in the chapter, but for now, think about these questions:

1. Why did Karen's students struggle with a concept as basic as *density?*
2. What, specifically, can she do in response to her students' struggles?
3. How will an understanding of the way students think increase your expertise as a teacher?

Theories of cognitive development help answer these questions, and in this chapter you'll see how these theories can be applied to your teaching.

Ed Psych and You

Think back to when you were in elementary and middle school. What kinds of abilities do you have now that you didn't have then? How about your high school years? How has your thinking changed since you graduated from high school?

What Is Development?

The questions in *Ed Psych and You* relate to the concept of **development**, the changes that occur in all of us as we go through our lives. We recognize these changes in ourselves, and we observe them in our sisters, brothers, and friends. Development exists in several forms.

Physical development describes changes in the size, shape, and functioning of our bodies and explains why we could, for example, run faster as a high school student than as a fifth grader. **Personal, social, and emotional development** refer to changes in our personalities, the ways we interact with others, and the ability to manage our feelings.

As we said in our introduction, in this chapter we focus on **cognitive development**, changes in our thinking that occur as a result of maturation and experience. The question, "How has your thinking changed?" in *Ed Psych and You* relates to cognitive development, and it was an important factor in Karen's students' inability to understand the concept *density*.

Understanding development is valuable for two important reasons. First, because we've all gone through the process, and will continue to go through it our entire lives, it gives us insights into ourselves and the people around us. Second, understanding development can make us better teachers because it helps us understand why our students think and act the way they do. This understanding can help reduce frustrations, such as those Karen is experiencing, and amplify the rewards we feel when we observe advances in our students' thinking and know we've contributed to these advances.

Principles of Development

Three general principles apply to all forms of development (Berk, 2013; Boyd & Bee, 2012; Feldman, 2014).

- *Development depends on both heredity and the environment.* **Maturation**, genetically driven, age-related changes in individuals, plays an important role in development. For instance, high school students are more cognitively mature than elementary or middle school students, which helps us understand why we don't teach calculus or physics to younger learners. Heredity interacts with the environment, through the experiences we provide, to maximize development.
- *Development proceeds in orderly and predictable patterns.* Development is relatively systematic and predictable. For example, we babble before we talk, crawl before we walk, and learn concrete concepts like *mammal* and *car* before abstract ones like *density* and *democracy*. These patterns exist in virtually all human beings.
- *People develop at different rates.* While development is generally systematic and orderly, the rate at which individuals progress varies. We've all heard phrases such as "He's a late bloomer" or "She never quite grew up," which describe individual differences in people's rates of development. These differences influence the effectiveness of our instruction and our interactions with our students.

With these principles in mind, we turn now to Bronfenbrenner's theory of development, which helps explain how the environment interacts with our genes to produce the unique individuals we each become.

Bronfenbrenner's Bioecological Model of Development

Bronfenbrenner's bioecological model offers a comprehensive description of the environmental factors influencing all forms of development (Bronfenbrenner, 1979, 2005; Bronfenbrenner & Morris, 2006). Figure 2.1 outlines this comprehensive view.

Ed Psych and You

Do you have brothers or sisters? In what ways are you and they similar or different? Why do you think these similarities and differences exist?

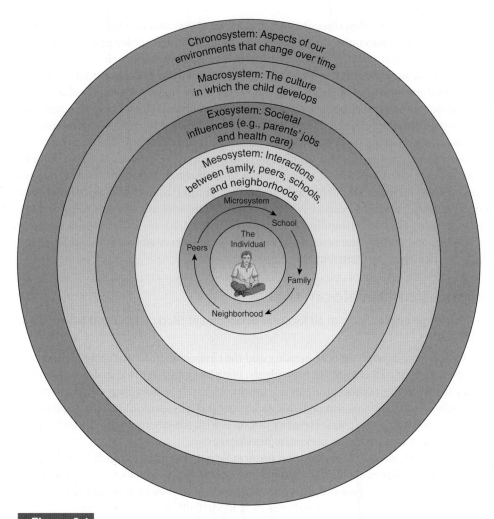

Figure 2.1

Bronfenbrenner's bioecological model of human development

As you see in Figure 2.1, individuals are at the center of his model, and the *bio* in the title reflects the influence of genetics on development. For instance, height and some aspects of body build, health, and intelligence are determined by genetics.

The *ecological* component in Bronfenbrenner's model suggests that our development is influenced by a complex set of systems in the environment, including family, peers, social institutions, such as churches and schools, and individuals' communities and cultures (Bronfenbrenner & Morris, 2006). As you see in the figure, each system is nested in a larger system, and each layer is viewed as impacting development (Dodge, 2011; Lee, 2010). Let's look at these systems.

The microsystem, the innermost level, is composed of the people and activities in our immediate surroundings, such as family, peers, neighborhood, and school. For instance, your parents probably expected you to do your homework, accept responsibility, and follow through on your commitments. These expectations were all part of the environmental influence on your development. Similarly, some neighborhoods are safe and nurturant, whereas others are dangerous and toxic (Dunn, Schaefer-McDaniel, & Ramsey, 2010; Bornstein, Hahn, & Haynes, 2011; Gauvain & Parke, 2010). Also, schools can be caring and supportive or sterile and impersonal (Fauth, Roth, & Brooks-Gunn, 2007; Kozol, 2005). These elements of Bronfenbrenner's microsystem provide different levels of support for healthy development.

The **mesosystem** consists of interactions among the elements of the microsystem, and healthy development depends on how effectively the elements work together (Lee, 2010; Lerner, Lewin-Bizan, & Warren, 2011). For instance, schools that promote high levels of parental involvement provide a more effective environment for development than those that don't (Lezotte & Snyder, 2011; O'Connor, Dearing, & Collins, 2011).

The **exosystem** includes societal influences, such as parents' jobs, school systems, and workplace conditions, such as health care, that influence both the microsystem and meso-system. For example, parents' jobs affect the amount of time they have to spend with their children, and wealthier school systems are more likely to provide nurses, counselors, psychologists, and smaller class sizes.

The **macrosystem** is the culture in which a child develops, and it influences all the other systems (Cole & Packer, 2011; Goodnow, 2010). For example, some cultures, such as ours, focus on the individual and emphasize autonomy, whereas others, such as those in parts of Asia, focus more strongly on social influences and conformity (Goodnow, 2010).

Finally, environments change over time. For example, your home environment was similar, but not identical, to that of your siblings. If you're the oldest child in your family, your parents were younger and less experienced in the process of parenting, and they might have been less secure economically. As a result, they probably treated you differently than your younger brothers and sisters. Also, other changes in our broader environments occur over time. For instance, the "Great Recession" that began in the first decade of the 21st century had a major impact on our country and particularly our country's middle class. As an example, more than one of five American public school students are in families living in poverty, and all states in our country experienced rising rates of poverty among public schoolchildren between the years 2000 and 2011 (Southern Education Foundation, 2013). When people live in poverty, they can't provide the kind of environments that promote healthy development.

Many other examples exist, including the influence of technology, changes in domestic and world politics, and societal changes. Bronfenbrenner calls this time-dependent element of our environments the **chronosystem**.

So now we can understand why similarities and differences exist between us and our siblings, and they help answer the questions we asked earlier in *Ed Psych and You*. We have a common genetic background, although we're all genetically unique. And the environments we grew up in were different enough to produce different, and sometimes *very different*, individuals.

Analyzing **Theories**

Bronfenbrenner's Bioecological Theory of Development

Bronfenbrenner's theory helps us better understand differences in our students and why children the same age and even from the same families often think and act very differently. It also helps us understand why home–school partnerships are so important and why involving the larger community in our children's education is valuable. For example, research tells us that the children of involved parents are more likely to do their homework, attend school more regularly, achieve more, and graduate from high school (Kersey & Masterson, 2009; Weinstein, Romano, & Mignano, 2011). You and your classroom will be embed-ded within larger contexts, all of which influence the development of the children you teach.

The model has weaknesses, however, and its tendency to ignore the role that cognition plays in development is an important one. The ways children think about themselves, their abilities, and their relationships with others also influence development. Further, Bronfenbrenner's assertions are difficult to examine with research, so his theory is difficult to assess empirically. Bronfenbrenner's theory, including its contributions and criticisms, is summarized in Table 2.1.

Table 2.1	Analyzing theories: Bronfenbrenner's bioecological theory of development
Key question	How do genetics and different levels of environmental influence interact to impact all forms of development?
Key concepts	Microsystem—family, peers, neighborhood, schools Mesosystem—interactions among the elements of the microsystem Exosystem—societal influences, such as parents' jobs and access to health care Macrosystem—culture in which the child develops Chronosystem—changes in a child's environment that occur over time
Description of development	Development occurs as different levels of environmental influence interact in dynamic systems with each other and with a child's genetic makeup to produce growth.
Catalyst for development	• Genetics • Multiple levels of environmental factors
Contributions	• Provides a detailed description of how genetics and different levels of environmental factors interact to influence children's development • Reminds educators that many factors outside of classrooms have important influences on children's learning and development
Criticisms	• Descriptions of how different levels of the environment interact with each other and with a child's genetics to influence development are somewhat vague. • Theory is difficult to empirically test with research and refine because the components of the theory lack specificity.

Sources: Berk, 2013; Bronfenbrenner, 1979, 2005; Bronfenbrenner & Morris, 2006; Feldman, 2014.

Ed Psych and You

Imagine you have a new experience, which might be as simple as learning a new word. Then, sometime later you use the word in your speech and writing. Expanding your vocabulary is a form of cognitive development. What, if anything, happens in your brain when this occurs? Neuroscience provides some answers.

The Neuroscience of Development

A great deal of research on the brain has occurred in the last 20 years, and it has contributed to the growing interest in healthy brain functioning in both children and adults (Gogtay & Thompson, 2010; Marx, 2013). Also, the fact that we now live in an information age has contributed to this interest. In recognition of the increasing importance of intellectual skills as central to our country's economic success, President Obama, during his second term, announced a broad, interdisciplinary research initiative to examine the human brain (Markoff & Gorman, 2013). This initiative, which was intended to receive 100 million dollars in 2014, involves scientists from a range of fields in an effort to better understand the brain and what can be done to promote its healthy development.

Before we examine the physiology of the brain and cognitive development, let's look briefly at what research has uncovered about our brains (Anguera et al., 2013; Dubinsky, Roehrig, & Varma, 2013; Kurzweil, 2012; Quiroga, Fried, & Koch, 2013):

- The brain is our body's most complex organ. The complexity of an organism's nervous system determines the range of behaviors it's able to produce. Humans have the most complex nervous systems of any animal.

- Genetically determined electrical circuits are the foundation of the nervous system. The basic wiring of the brain is similar for individuals within a species; variations at the brain-cell level account for differences.
- Intelligence grows as the brain reasons and solves problems. The brain is the foundation of the mind and thinking.
- The brain makes it possible to communicate through language. Language allows information exchange and creative thought.
- The brain instinctively looks for patterns in the way the world works. The brain tries to make sense of incoming sensory information, recognizes conflicts, and creates predictions and expectations that guide behavior.
- The brain is plastic. The concept of **neuroplasticity** describes the brain's ability to physically remodel itself in response to experience. In other words, experience can literally rewire our brains. "People have different genetic predispositions, but experience continuously shapes our brain structure and modifies behavior" (Van Dam, 2013, p. 32). This is a very different view of the brain; until around the 1980s scientists thought that the structure of the brain developed during childhood and that once developed, there was little room for change (Pascual-Leone et al., 2005).

Now, with these basic characteristics of our brains in mind, let's look at the physiology of the brain and how it relates to cognitive development.

THE PHYSIOLOGY OF THE BRAIN AND COGNITIVE DEVELOPMENT

The human brain is incredibly complex. Estimates suggest that it is composed of between 100 and 200 billion nerve cells, called **neurons** (Carlson, 2011; Seung, 2012). The neuron is the learning unit of the brain and is central to cognitive development. As you see in Figure 2.2, a neuron is composed of a cell body; **dendrites**, relatively short, branchlike structures that extend from the cell body and receive messages from other neurons; and **axons**, longer branches that also extend from the cell body and transmit messages.

Neurons communicate with each other, but don't actually touch; instead, signals are sent across **synapses**, tiny spaces between neurons that allow messages to be transmitted from one neuron to another. When an electrical impulse is sent down an axon, it produces a chemical that crosses the synapse and stimulates the dendrites of neighboring neurons. Frequent transmission of information between neurons can establish a permanent physical relationship between them, and evidence from animal studies indicates that learning experiences increase the number of synaptic connections per neuron (Johnson, 2011). For example, laboratory rats provided with mazes, and objects to manipulate, develop and retain 25% more synaptic connections than rats developed in sterile environments (Nelson, Thomas, & de Haan, 2006).

In other words, "What gets fired, gets wired," and this is why experiences are so important for development; they influence the connections between neurons that can remain throughout our lives. So, as a simple example, once a child learns to ride a bicycle, for all intents and purposes, that child will always be able to ride. Similarly, as young athletes practice shooting jump shots in basketball over and over, the experience gradually produces neurological connections that result in the development of a smooth and accurate shot. Without these experiences, the aspiring athlete will never develop into a skilled jump shooter, and the same is true for all forms of development.

These examples involve motor skills, but the same applies to cognitive tasks. And as we saw earlier in our discussion, the brain instinctively looks for patterns in experiences and tries to make sense of those experiences (Dubinsky et al., 2013; Quiroga, Fried, & Koch, 2013). So, for example, when young children correctly answer $2 + 4 = ?$, they not only know that the answer is 6 but identify a number of other patterns, such as 2 and 4 can each represent a variety of objects, both are even numbers, and many others. Identifying patterns is important for learning. Knowledge organized in this way is retained longer and is more

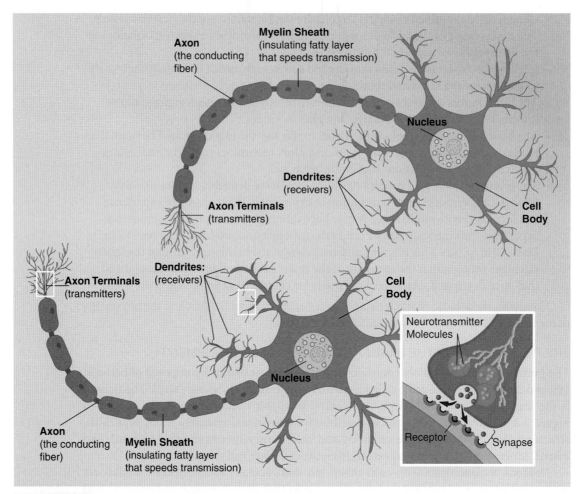

Figure 2.2

The structure of neurons

likely to connect to other information (Bruning, Schraw, & Norby, 2011; Schunk, 2012). This has important implications for instruction, which we'll discuss later in this section.

During the first 3 years of our lives, so many new synapses are created that they far exceed adult levels. Psychologists believe that generating more synapses than they will ever need allows children to adapt to the wide variety of circumstances they'll encounter throughout their lives (Davidson, 2011; Johnson, 2011).

Two important processes occur in the brain during development. The first is **myelination**, which occurs when cells grow around neurons to give them structural support, and a fatty coating of myelin, called the *myelin sheath*, develops to insulate axons and enable them to conduct electrical charges quickly and efficiently (see Figure 2.2). The second, **synaptic pruning**, eliminates synapses that are infrequently used. As the brain recognizes patterns in our environments, it physically reorganizes, keeping the synaptic connections that are used and useful, and discarding those that aren't. Cognitive development involves both creating and eliminating these synaptic connections (Siegel, 2012), and it is somewhat analogous to what we do when we clean and update our computer files; it makes the brain more efficient and effective.

This process is related to the concept of *neuroplasticity,* which we described earlier (Dubinsky et al., 2013; Pascual-Leone, Amedi, Fregni, & Merabet, 2005). This is a very powerful developmental idea. It suggests that, as we acquire experiences, we can change our brains' "wiring," that is, we can literally change the physiology of our brains (Schachter,

2012). It also debunks the old maxim, "You can't teach an old dog new tricks." Our brains retain the capacity to change and grow throughout our lives (Anguera et al., 2013).

Neuroplasticity is arguably the brain's most important characteristic and one that has enormous implications for teaching. It suggests that with the right kinds of experiences, we can literally "get smarter," which is indeed very good news. It is also cause for optimism as we work with students who have learning problems related to causes ranging from genetic issues to the lack of a stimulating home environment to environmental toxins such as lead, drugs, or alcohol. With effective experiences, these problems can, at least to a certain extent, be overcome (Auyeung & Baron-Cohen, 2012).

THE CEREBRAL CORTEX

The cerebral cortex is the part of the brain that rests on its top and sides, and much of human thinking occurs in this area (Anderson, 2010; Carlson, 2011). Not surprisingly, it is proportionately much larger in humans than in other animals, comprising 85% of the brain's total weight and containing the greatest number of neurons and synaptic connections (Berk, 2013).

The left and right hemispheres of the cortex specialize in different functions (Carlson, 2011). The right controls the left side of our bodies and vice versa. Also, in most people the left hemisphere controls language and logical thinking, and the right deals with synthesizing information—especially visual images—into meaningful patterns. This hemispheric specialization is sometimes misinterpreted, resulting in the misconception that some people are "right brained" and others "left brained." People are neither, and efforts to teach to the left or right brain are both overly simplistic and misguided (Siegel, 2012; Sprenger, 2010). The two hemispheres function as an integrated whole, especially with respect to the cognitive tasks found in schools (Carlson, 2011).

The Prefrontal Cortex. The prefrontal cortex (see Figure 2.3), a portion of the cortex located near the forehead, is the area of the brain largely responsible for a range of complex human activities. As development occurs, the prefrontal cortex monitors and guides other parts of the brain's activities including planning, maintaining attention, reasoning, decision making, emotional control, and the inhibition of unhealthy thoughts and behaviors (Cartwright, 2012; Casey, Jones, & Somerville, 2011; Kurzweil, 2012; Yang & Raine, 2009). Some authors also suggest that an integral link exists between a person's personality and the functions of the prefrontal cortex (DeYoung et al., 2010).

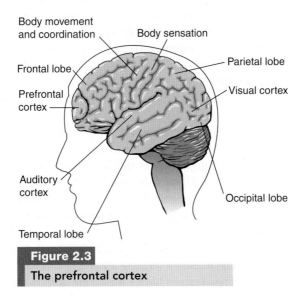

Figure 2.3
The prefrontal cortex

When we identified principles of development at the beginning of the chapter, we said that people develop at different rates, and this is true for brain development as well (Berk, 2013). The part controlling physical movement develops first, followed by vision and hearing, and ending with the prefrontal cortex. This area may not be fully developed until we are in our twenties.

The lag in development of the prefrontal cortex helps us understand a variety of behaviors, such as the temper tantrums of 2-year-olds and the sometimes undisciplined and dangerous behaviors of teenagers, such as drinking and driving, drug use, and unprotected sex. While equipped with the bodies of adults, teenagers' abilities to assess risk and make sound decisions are still developing. This helps explain why it's against the law to sell liquor and cigarettes to minors, and it also helps us understand why firm and consistent home and school environments that support learning and development are so important, particularly for adolescents. Rules and limits that simplify decisions help teenagers through this often confusing period.

CONTROVERSIES IN NEUROSCIENCE

As with most areas, some controversies with neuroscience exist. Critics argue, for instance, that people get caught up in the breakthroughs that neuroscience researchers have made, overreact, and try to use neuroscience to explain everything (Brooks, 2013).

Other authors go farther. Sally Satel and Scott Lilienfeld (2013) in their book *Brainwashed: The Seductive Appeal of Mindless Neuroscience* offer a biting criticism of attempts to use neuroscience to explain certain behaviors, such as how people will vote in elections or what products they will buy, attempts they argue are dramatic overreach and well beyond what neuroscience is capable of predicting. Their criticism is reinforced by other authors, such as Shulman (2013), who criticizes conclusions based on brain imaging studies that he believes are too broad.

These criticisms suggest that we need to view claims based on neuroscience research with caution, and we should be particularly cautious about prescriptions for teaching based on this field of study.

For example, a number of "brain-based learning" prescriptions exist. They're controversial, with proponents (e.g., Murphy & Benton, 2010; Wolfe, 2010) lining up on one side and critics (e.g., Miller, 2010; Varma, McCandliss, & Schwartz, 2008; Satel & Lilienfeld, 2013; Steinberg, 2009) on the other.

One of the controversies centers on the role of early stimulation for cognitive development. Research on synaptic connections and evidence supporting early stimulation in animals have resulted in some brain-based advocates recommending specialized instruction during children's early years. Other experts disagree. Early stimulus deprivation can indeed impede cognitive development, but evidence doesn't support the application of added stimulation, such as expensive toys or computers. In fact, one widely publicized study found that extensive media viewing in young children is associated with reduced language development (Zimmerman, Christakis, & Meltzoff, 2007), and others have criticized the sale of videos and other products designed to promote early stimulation as blatant commercialization (Linn, 2009).

The existence of critical periods for maximum development is a second controversy. For instance, young children who grow up in bilingual homes learn to speak both languages flawlessly, but adults who learn a language later in life struggle to produce certain sounds that are effortless for native speakers (Gluszek & Dovidio, 2010; Kuhn, 2009). Extrapolating from these findings, some educators suggest designing schools around these critical periods, such as introducing foreign languages to preschoolers to take advantage of a critical period in language development.

Critics counter that our brains retain the capacity to benefit from stimulation throughout our lives, and they caution against intensive training for young children. "No evidence exists for a sensitive period in the first few years of life for mastering skills that depend on extensive training, such as reading, musical performance, or gymnastics" (Berk, 2013, p. 192). Further, Berk (2013) argues that rushing early learning may harm the brain by overwhelming its neural circuits, making it less sensitive to the routine experiences it needs for a healthy start in life.

Instruction is a third area of controversy. Brain-based-instruction advocates emphasize the importance of deliberate practice and active learning strategies such as guided discovery, problem solving, and hands-on learning. Critics counter that these are strategies that have been widely accepted for years, and describing them as "brain based" adds nothing new (Byrnes, 2007). To this point, brain research is unable to provide specific guidance to teachers facing the myriad of decisions they make every day (Murphy & Benton, 2010).

Research and theory consistently indicate, however, that the stimulation that occurs in a healthy environment is essential for normal cognitive development, and, as teachers, we play major roles in the process. Understanding this research and theory is part of your professional knowledge. Piaget's and Vygotsky's theories of cognitive development are two of the most important contributions to this knowledge base. We begin with Piaget's work.

Piaget's Theory of Cognitive Development

Jean Piaget (1896–1980) was a Swiss developmental psychologist whose career took a major turn when he became fascinated by the changes in thinking that he observed in his own children. This shift led him to a life of research examining the thinking of children as they matured, acquired experiences, and attempted to make sense of the world around them. He is one of the most famous and influential psychologists in history.

As an introduction to Piaget's theory, consider the following problem.

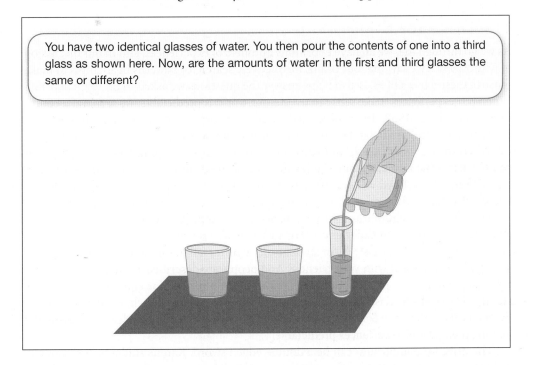

You have two identical glasses of water. You then pour the contents of one into a third glass as shown here. Now, are the amounts of water in the first and third glasses the same or different?

The question may seem silly; the amounts are obviously the same. However, when Piaget posed this problem to young children (such as 4- and 5-year-olds), he found that they believed more water was in the taller glass. These intriguing differences in children's thinking proved fascinating to Piaget and resulted in one of the most widely studied theories of cognitive development (Inhelder & Piaget, 1958; Piaget, 1952, 1959, 1980). We examine his theory in this section.

> **Overview of Piaget's Theory**
>
> Piaget believed that—consistent with what we know about the way our brains work—people in general, and children in particular, construct mental structures and ideas in attempts to make sense of their experiences. This helps them achieve a state of cognitive balance and predictability and the view that the world is an orderly place. When they have new experiences that don't make sense to them, this cognitive order is disrupted, and they make an effort to reestablish it. In doing so, their thinking becomes more sophisticated and development advances. These developmental advances occur in general patterns that fit within approximate age ranges.

Ed Psych and You

Are you bothered when something doesn't make sense? Do you want, and even expect, the world to be predictable? Are you more comfortable in classes where the instructor specifies the requirements, outlines the grading practices, and consistently follows through? For most people, the answer to these questions is "Yes." Why do you think this is the case?

The Drive for Equilibrium

As we go through life, we all have enormous numbers of experiences, and in our discussion of neuroscience we saw that our brains instinctively search for patterns in attempts to make sense of these experiences. It also helps answer the questions we asked in *Ed Psych and You*. When our experiences make sense to us and our world is predictable, we arrive at a condition Piaget (1952, 1959, 1980) described as **equilibrium**, which is the state of cognitive order, balance, and predictability that we described in our overview.

When we're able to explain our experiences using our existing understanding, we're at equilibrium. When we can't, our equilibrium is disrupted, and we're motivated to reestablish it (Berk, 2013; Boyd & Bee, 2012; Feldman, 2014). Development advances when our knowledge and skills increase as a result of equilibrium being disrupted and restored.

The concept of equilibrium helps explain many events common in our lives. Think about some of your own experiences. For instance, do you sit in essentially the same seat every time you come to class? Most students do. Do you fall into familiar patterns of interaction when you're out with your friends? And people are described as "creatures of habit." Following familiar habits and patterns is the result of our need for equilibrium. Teachers are urged to establish classroom routines as early as possible in the school year (Emmer & Evertson, 2013; Evertson & Emmer, 2013). Doing so helps students establish equilibrium by making their school experiences predictable.

The drive for equilibrium can be a double-edged sword. Karen's students, for example, were at equilibrium when they thought that *mass* and *density* were the same. This helps us understand why people retain misconceptions (Vosniadou, 2009) and why critical thinking is so difficult for many (Willingham, 2009).

The drive for equilibrium is the cornerstone of Piaget's theory. It provides the foundation for the rest of his ideas. Let's look at them now.

The Development of Schemes

To make sense of our experiences and reach equilibrium, people construct **schemes**, mental operations that represent our understanding of the world (the mental structures we described in our overview). Piaget believed that schemes are the building blocks of thinking. For instance, when you learned to drive a car, you had a series of experiences with attempting to start the engine, maneuver in traffic, and make routine driving decisions. As you (cognitively) organized these experiences, they became your "driving" scheme.

As suggested by our example with the containers of water, the schemes we construct vary with age, and they also vary with respect to accuracy and comprehensiveness. Infants develop psychomotor schemes, such as grasping objects and looking for them when they disappear; school-age children develop more abstract schemes like classification and proportional reasoning. Piaget used the idea of schemes to refer to a narrow range of operations, such as children's conservation-of-volume scheme (the idea that the amount of liquid doesn't change when poured into a different-shaped container, as you saw in our example) (Piaget, 1952). However, teachers and some researchers (e.g., Wadsworth, 2004) find it useful to extend Piaget's idea to include content-related schemes, such as *adding-fractions-with-unlike-denominators, creating-a-persuasive-essay,* or *reptile* schemes. As with our driving scheme, each represents our developing understanding based on our experiences, and they are commonly described as *schemas* rather than schemes. We use this expanded view in our description of Piaget's work.

Responding to Experiences: Assimilation and Accommodation

As we go through life and have new experiences, we either interpret them with our existing schemes, if doing so makes sense to us, or we modify our schemes (change our thinking) if we're not able to make sense of our new experiences with our existing schemes. For instance, suppose you first learned to drive your parents' car with an automatic transmission, and later you bought a Toyota Camry, also with an automatic. You were easily able to drive the Camry, because your thinking about driving didn't change. You *assimilated* the experience with the Camry into your original driving scheme. **Assimilation** is the process of using existing schemes to interpret new experiences.

Then you buy a Honda hybrid, but it has a stick shift. You must change your thinking about driving, or, in other words, you must *accommodate* your driving scheme. **Accommodation** is the process of changing our thinking to create new schemes or adjust old ones when they can no longer explain new experiences.

HOW EXPERIENCES ADVANCE DEVELOPMENT

Now, let's see how experiences advance development. Because you had the experience with your Honda hybrid, you are now able to drive cars with either automatic transmissions or stick shifts. This capability marks an advance in development with respect to your driving. If you hadn't had the experience with your Honda, you would only have been able to drive cars with automatics and your driving would not have developed. This developmental process is potentially never ending. For instance, if you acquired experiences with driving 18-wheelers or heavy equipment, such as bulldozers, your driving expertise would be even more fully developed.

The same processes apply in schools. For instance, if young children are given the problem

$$
\begin{array}{r}
47 \\
-\ 23 \\
\hline
\end{array}
$$

and they get 24 as an answer, their *subtracting-whole-numbers* scheme suggests that they subtract smaller numbers from larger ones. However, if they are then given this problem,

$$
\begin{array}{r}
43 \\
-\ 27 \\
\hline
\end{array}
$$

and they also get 24 as an answer, they have—mistakenly—assimilated the new experience into their existing scheme. Their thinking didn't change, and they still subtracted the smaller numbers from the larger ones, ignoring the positioning of the numbers. Now, suppose their teacher models and explains the process for subtracting numbers where regrouping is required, such as with the problem

$$
\begin{array}{r}
43 \\
-\ 27 \\
\hline
\end{array}
$$

so they get a correct answer of 16. Then, with guidance and practice they learn to solve a variety of problems. The problems, and their teacher's modeling, explaining, guidance, and practice, are experiences that lead to this capability. Because they've had this experience, they can now subtract numbers both when regrouping is and is not required. This increased capability represents an advance in development with respect to subtraction.

The essential role experience plays in cognitive development helps us answer our first question at the beginning of the chapter: "Why did Karen's students struggle with a concept as basic as *density*?" Lack of the direct, concrete experiences they needed to understand the concept is the answer. For example, many of us have used the formula Density = Mass/Volume ($d = m/v$), inserted numbers, and got answers that meant little to us. We lacked meaningful experiences with these concepts. We will see how Karen responds to this issue with her students in the section "Educational Psychology and Teaching: Applying Piaget's Theory with Your Students" later in our discussion.

SOCIAL EXPERIENCE

To this point we've emphasized the role of direct experiences with the physical world as a major factor influencing development. However, social experience, the process of interacting with other people, also contributes (Piaget, 1952, 1959, 1970, 1980). Social experiences allow us to test our schemes against those of others. When our schemes match, we remain at equilibrium; when they don't, our equilibrium is disrupted, we are motivated to reestablish it, we adjust our thinking, and our development advances (Howe, 2009, 2010; Siegler & Lin, 2010). As an example, let's look at a conversation between two students.

Devon: (Holding a beetle between his fingers and pointing at a spider) Look at the bugs.

Gino: Yech. . . . Put that thing down. (gesturing to the spider) Besides, that's not a bug. It's a spider.

Devon: What do you mean? A bug is a bug.

Gino: Nope. Bugs . . . actually, insects . . . have six legs. See (touching the legs of the beetle). This one has eight. . . . Look (pointing to the spider).

Devon: So, . . . bugs . . . insects . . . have six legs, and spiders have eight . . . I didn't know that.

Gino: Yeah . . . so, what do you think this is (holding up a grasshopper)?

Piaget would interpret this episode in the following way: As a result of the social interaction, Devon's equilibrium was disrupted. And, because it was disrupted, he was motivated to reestablish it, which he did by changing his thinking—the process of accommodation—about "bugs" and "spiders." The accommodation led to an advance in his development.

EXPERIENCE AND PIAGET'S INFLUENCE ON EDUCATION

Piaget's emphasis on experience has strongly influenced education in general, and preschool and kindergarten programs in particular (Berk, 2013; Trawick-Smith, 2014). For instance, in many early childhood classrooms, you'll see water and sand tables, building blocks, and other concrete materials that provide young children with the concrete experiences they need to form new schemes.

Maria Montessori, an Italian educator who stressed the importance of exploration and discovery, developed what is probably the best-known early childhood program (Feldman, 2014). In her work with children of poverty, Montessori concluded that learning environments, in which children simultaneously "worked" on both academic and social activities, were needed for development. It wasn't really *work*, however, because children could freely explore learning centers that provided hands-on activities and opportunities for social interaction with other students. Make-believe was encouraged with dress-up costumes and other accessories like play telephones.

Today, however, many early childhood programs, influenced by standards and accountability, emphasize early reading skills, such as knowing the letters of the alphabet, understanding basic concepts such as *left* and *right*, and math skills—counting, number recognition, and even adding to and taking away, for instance. As a result, child-centered programs have decreased in favor of those more academically oriented. "Yet despite grave concerns about its appropriateness, even preschool and kindergarten teachers have felt increased pressure to stress teacher-directed, academic training" (Berk, 2013, p. 639). Despite the influence and popularity of Piaget's emphasis on experience with the physical and social worlds, academically oriented early childhood programs are likely to grow.

Stages of Development

Stages of development—general patterns of thinking for children at different ages or with different amounts of experience—are among the most widely known elements of Piaget's theory. As you examine these stages, keep the following ideas in mind (Green & Piel, 2010; Meece & Daniels, 2011; Miller, 2011):

- Movement from one stage to another represents a qualitative change in thinking—a difference in the *way* children think, not the *amount* they know. As an analogy, a qualitative change occurs when a caterpillar metamorphoses into a butterfly, and a quantitative change occurs as the butterfly grows larger.
- Children's development is steady and gradual, and experiences in one stage form the foundation for movement to the next.
- All people pass through each stage in the same order but at different rates. Students at the same age may be at different stages, and the thinking of older children and even adults may be similar to that of younger children if they lack experience in that area (Kuhn, Pease, & Wirkala, 2009; Siegler, 2012).

Piaget's stages are summarized in Table 2.2 and described in the sections that follow.

THE SENSORIMOTOR STAGE (0 TO 2 YEARS)

In the sensorimotor stage, children use their motor capacities, such as grasping objects, to understand the world, and they don't initially represent the objects in memory; the

Table 2.2	Piaget's stages and characteristics	
Stage	**Characteristics**	**Example**
Sensorimotor (0–2)	Goal-directed behavior	Makes jack-in-the-box pop up
	Object permanence (represents objects in memory)	Searches for object behind parent's back
Preoperational (2–7)	Rapid increase in language ability with overgeneralized language	"We goed to the store."
	Symbolic thought	Points out car window and says, "Truck!"
	Dominated by perception	Concludes that all the water in a sink came out of the faucet (the cartoon in Chapter 1)
Concrete Operational (7–11)	Operates logically with concrete materials	Concludes that two objects on a "balanced" balance have the same mass even though one is larger than the other
	Classifies and serial orders	Orders containers according to decreasing volume
Formal Operational (11–Adult)	Solves abstract and hypothetical problems	Considers outcome of WWII if the Battle of Britain had been lost
	Thinks combinatorially	Systematically determines how many different sandwiches can be made from three different kinds of meat, cheese, and bread

objects are literally "out of sight, out of mind" early in this stage. Later, they acquire **object permanence**, the understanding that objects exist even when out of sight. As any parent will attest, young children at this stage of development learn many concrete concepts (e.g., Mom, Dad, doggie) and they form a conceptual foundation for later learning (Rakison, 2010). Children at this stage also develop the ability to imitate, which allows them to learn by observing others.

THE PREOPERATIONAL STAGE (2 TO 7 YEARS)

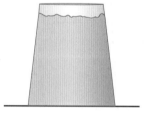

The term *preoperational* derives from the idea of "operation," or mental activity. A child who identifies different animals as dogs, cats, and bears, for example, is performing a mental operation.

Perception dominates children's thinking in this stage. For instance, look at the drawing here, which represents an inverted glass filled with water, and a card on the bottom. (Go ahead and try this.) Since they can see the glass, water, and card, preoperational thinkers conclude that the water is holding the card on the glass (atmospheric pressure is what actually holds the card next to the glass).

Many cognitive changes occur in children as they pass through this stage. For example, they make enormous progress in language development, reflecting their growth in the ability to use symbols, and they also learn huge numbers of concepts. For example, a child on a car trip will point excitedly and say, "truck," "horse," and "tree," delighting in exercising these newly formed schemes. These concepts are concrete, however, and children in this stage have limited notions of abstract ideas such as *fairness, democracy,* and *energy.*

The influence of perceptual dominance is also seen in another prominent idea from Piaget's theory: preoperational thinkers' inability to conserve.

Conservation. Conservation refers to the idea that the "amount" of some substance stays the same regardless of its shape or the number of pieces into which it is divided. A number of conservation tasks exist. The example with the glasses of water that we used to introduce our discussion of Piaget's work is one, and two others are outlined in Figure 2.4.

Conservation Task	Initial Presentation by Observer	Change in Presentation by Observer	Typical Answer from Preoperational Thinker
Number	The observer shows the child two identical rows of objects. The child agrees that the number in each row is the same.	The observer spreads the bottom row apart while the child watches. The observer then asks the child if the two rows have the same number of objects or if there are more in one row.	The preoperational child typically responds that the row that has been spread apart has more objects. The child centers on the length, ignoring the number.
Mass	The observer shows the child two balls of clay. The child agrees that the amount of clay is the same in each. (If the child doesn't agree that they have the same amount, the observer then asks the child to move some clay from one to the other until the amount is the same.)	The observer flattens and lengthens one of the balls while the child watches. The observer then asks the child if the two have the same amount of clay or if one has more.	The preoperational child typically responds that the longer, flattened piece has more clay. The child centers on the length.

Figure 2.4

Conservation tasks for number and mass

In Figure 2.4 we see that preoperational children don't "conserve," that is, it makes sense to them that the amount of water, the number of coins, or the amount of clay can somehow change without adding or subtracting anything from them. Let's see how this occurs using the example with the water.

First, they tend to *center* on the height of the water in the glass. Centration (or centering) is the tendency to focus on the most perceptually obvious aspect of an object or event and ignore other features. The height is most perceptually obvious, so preoperational children conclude that the tall, narrow glass has more water. Second, young children lack transformation, the ability to mentally record the process of moving from one state to another, such as pouring the water from the first to the third glass. To them it's a new and different container of liquid. Third, they also lack reversibility, the ability to mentally trace the process of moving from an existing state back to a previous state, such as being able to mentally reverse the process of pouring the water from one glass to another. When lack of transformation and reversibility are combined with their tendency to center, we can see why they conclude that the tall, narrow glass has more water in it, even though no water was added or removed.

Egocentrism. Preoperational thinkers also demonstrate egocentrism, the inability to see objects and events from others' perspectives. In a famous experiment, Piaget and Inhelder (1956) showed young children a three-dimensional model of several mountains and asked them to describe how the mountains would look to a doll seated on the opposite side. Preoperational children described the doll's view as identical to their own. Preoperational thinkers tend to believe that everyone sees the world as they do, and they ignore the possibility that other perspectives exist. As another example, we can see this tendency in preoperational children's gift giving; they'll typically give gifts that *they* would enjoy, such as a stuffed animal, ignoring the fact that they are giving these to an adult. To them, others view the world as they do.

THE CONCRETE OPERATIONAL STAGE (7 TO 11 YEARS)

The concrete operational stage, which is characterized by the ability to think logically when using concrete materials, marks another advance in children's thinking (Flavell, Miller, & Miller, 2002). For instance, when facing the conservation-of-number task, learners in this stage simply say, "You just made the row longer" or "You just spread the coins apart" (so, the number must remain the same).

Concrete operational learners also overcome some of the egocentrism of preoperational thinkers. They are able to understand the perspectives of storybook characters and better understand the views of others, which makes them better able to work effectively in groups.

Classification and Seriation. Classification, the process of grouping objects on the basis of common characteristics, and seriation, the ability to order objects according to increasing or decreasing length, weight, or volume, are two logical operations that develop during this stage, and both are essential for understanding number concepts (Piaget, 1977). For example, before age 5, children can form simple groups, such as separating black and white circles into two sets based on color. When a black square is added, however, they typically include it with the black circles, instead of forming subclasses of black circles and black squares. By age 7 they can form subclasses, but they still have problems with more complex classification systems.

When children are able to order objects according to some dimension, such as length (seriation), they can master transitivity, the ability to infer a relationship between two objects based on their relationship with a third. For example, suppose we have three sticks, you're shown sticks 1 and 2, and you see that 1 is longer than 2.

Now, stick 1 is removed, you're shown 2 and 3, and you see that 2 is longer than 3. You demonstrate transitivity when you conclude that 1 is longer than 3, reasoning that since 1 is longer than 2, and 2 is longer than 3, 1 must be longer than 3.

Though concrete operational thinkers have made dramatic progress, their thinking is still limited. For instance, they interpret sayings such as "Make hay while the sun shines" literally, such as concluding, "You should gather your crop before it gets dark."

Let's see how this compares to formal thinkers.

THE FORMAL OPERATIONAL STAGE (AGE 11 TO ADULT)

Although concrete operational learners are capable of logical thought, their thinking is tied to the real and tangible. Formal thinkers, in contrast, can think *abstractly, systematically,* and *hypothetically.* For example, formal thinkers would suggest that "Make hay while the sun shines" means something abstract, such as "Seize an opportunity when it exists." Their ability to think in the abstract allows the study of topics such as algebra in math, or allegory in literature, to be meaningful. Formal thinkers also reason systematically and recognize the need to control variables in forming conclusions. For example, consider the following problem:

> You're making sandwiches for a picnic. You have rye and whole wheat bread, turkey, ham, and beef for meat, and Swiss and cheddar cheese. How many different kinds of sandwiches can you make?

Formal thinkers attack the problem systematically such as rye, turkey, and Swiss; rye, turkey, and cheddar; rye, ham, and Swiss; and so on. A concrete thinker attacks the problem haphazardly, forming ad hoc solutions such as rye, turkey, and Swiss; whole wheat, beef, and cheddar; and so on.

Formal operational learners can also think hypothetically. For instance, considering what our country might be like today if the British had won the Revolutionary War requires hypothetical thinking for American history students, as does considering the influence of dominant and recessive genes for biology students.

When students can't think abstractly, systematically, or hypothetically, they revert to memorizing what they can, or, in frustration, give up completely.

Ed Psych and You

Look at the figure below. The blocks on the balance are solid cubes that aren't compressible. Which of the following statements is true of the relationships between block A and block B?

1. A is bigger than B.
2. The mass of A is greater than the mass of B.
3. A is more dense than B.
4. A is made out of a different material than B.

What stage of development is required to respond correctly to each question?

Block A   Block B

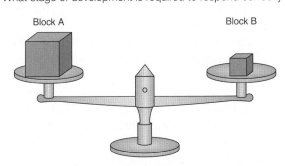

PIAGET'S STAGES AND RESEARCH ON STUDENT THINKING

Let's see how you did. Statement 1 is true, and, because we *can see* that A is bigger (greater volume), it is a preoperational task. A first grader, for example, would be likely to respond successfully.

Responding correctly to statement 2 requires logical thought. The beam is balanced; therefore, the masses of the two objects are the same, so the statement is false. It requires logical thought with concrete materials, so it is a concrete operational task.

Statement 3 is also false. A is larger than B, but the masses are the same, so the density of A is less than B, not greater. Finally, statement 4 is true; if the blocks are solids and have different densities, they must be made of different materials. Statements 3 and 4 require abstract thinking, so they are formal operational tasks.

Don't feel badly if you struggled with one or more of these problems. Here's why. Even as adults, *virtually all of us are formal operational thinkers only in areas where we have considerable experience* (Berk, 2013; Miller, 2011). Research indicates that the thinking of nearly half of all college students isn't formal operational with respect to topics outside their majors (Wigfield, Eccles, & Pintrich, 1996). Many individuals, including adults, never reach the stage of formal operations in a number of content areas.

This creates a dilemma, particularly for those of you who are planning to teach in middle, junior high, or high schools, because understanding many topics—and particularly those in high schools—requires formal operational thinking. It was clear that Karen's students' thinking was not formal operational with respect to the concept *density*. Further, while *centering* is viewed as characteristic of young children's thinking, we see it in older students and even adults.

Neo-Piagetian Views of Cognitive Development

Piaget did his work many years ago, and more recent research has built on and refined his theory. For instance, neo-Piagetian theories of development retain Piaget's basic insights into children's construction of knowledge but focus more on the ways people process information to explain movement from one stage to the next than on Piaget's global stages (Siegler, 2000, 2006).

To illustrate this perspective, look at the following list for 15 seconds, cover it up, and see how many items you can remember.

apple	bear	cat	grape
hammer	pear	orange	cow
chair	sofa	chisel	lamp
saw	table	elephant	pliers

Most adults organize the list into categories such as *furniture, fruit, tools,* and *animals,* and use the categories to remember specific items (Bruning, Schraw, & Norby, 2011; Radvansky & Ashcraft, 2014). Young children tend to use less efficient strategies such as repeating the items verbatim. Their ability to gradually begin using more efficient strategies marks an advance in development.

Neo-Piagetian theory also emphasizes the important role that *working memory,* the part of our memory system that is capable of holding only small amounts of information for short periods of time while we process and attempt to make sense of it, plays in development (Jack, Simcock, & Hayne, 2012; Morra & Camba, 2009). As children develop, their working memory capacity increases, which allows them to think about more items of information simultaneously as they solve problems (Case, 1992, 1998; Marchand, 2012). These theorists also suggest that advancing *executive functioning,* such as the ability to maintain attention and suppress intuitive conclusions in favor of more logical processing, marks an advance in development. For instance, some researchers suggest that this increase in executive functioning helps explain why concrete operational thinkers succeed on the conservation-of-number task that was illustrated in Figure 2.4, whereas younger children do not (Houdé et al., 2011).

Neo-Piagetian theory suggests that teachers should consciously focus on helping children acquire learning strategies and develop their executive functioning, which will facilitate both immediate learning and long-term development (Davidse, de Jong, Bus, Huijbregts, & Swaab, 2011).

Educational Psychology and Teaching: Applying Piaget's Theory with Your Students

Now, let's see what Piaget's theory suggests for our work with our students. The following guidelines can help us in our efforts to apply this understanding.

1. Provide concrete experiences that represent abstract ideas.
2. Help students link the concrete representations to the abstract idea.

3. Use social interaction to help students advance and refine their understanding.
4. Design learning experiences as developmental bridges to more advanced stages of development.

Let's examine these guidelines now.

Provide Concrete Experiences That Represent Abstract Ideas. As we saw earlier, most students, including those in middle and high schools—and even those in colleges and universities—are not formal operational in their thinking with respect to many of the topics they study. This means that they will benefit from concrete experiences that help them make the transition to formal operational thinking. To illustrate this process, let's sit in on another conversation between Karen and Ken the Tuesday following their Friday discussion.

"What's that for?" Ken asks, seeing Karen walking into the teachers' lounge with a plastic cup filled with cotton balls.

"I just had the greatest class," Karen replies. "You remember how frustrated I was on Friday when the kids didn't understand basic concepts like *mass* and *density*. . . . I thought about it over the weekend, and decided to try something different, even if it seemed sort of elementary.

"See," she goes on, compressing the cotton in the cup. "Now the cotton is more dense. And now it's less dense," she points out, releasing the cotton.

"Then, I made some different-sized blocks out of the same type of wood. Some of the kids first thought the density of the big block was greater. But then we weighed the blocks, measured their volumes, and computed their densities, and the kids saw they were the same. They gradually began to get it.

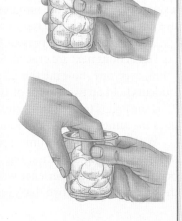

"This morning," she continues, "I had them put equal volumes of water and vegetable oil on our balances, and when the balance tipped down on the water side, they saw that the mass of the water was greater, so water is more dense than oil. I had asked them to predict which was more dense before we did the activity, and most of them said oil. We talked about that, and they concluded the reason they predicted oil is the fact that it's thicker.

"Now, here's the good part. . . . Ethan, he hates science, remembered that oil floats on water, so it made sense to him that oil is less dense. He actually got excited about what we were doing and came up with the idea that less dense materials float on more dense materials. . . . You could almost see the wheels turning. We even got into population density and compared a door screen with the wires close together to one with the wires farther apart, and how that related to what we were studying. The kids were really into it. A day like that now and then keeps you going."

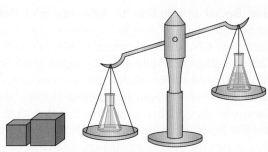

This helps us answer the second question we asked at the beginning of the chapter: "What, specifically, can Karen do in response to her students' struggles?" She addressed their difficulties by providing the specific, concrete experiences—the cotton balls in the cup, the blocks, and the balance with the water and oil—they needed to understand the concept.

The many examples that we include in discussions of the topics we present in this book are consistent with this idea and are our efforts to provide you with the concrete experiences you need to understand abstract ideas in educational psychology.

Link Concrete Representations to Abstract Ideas. Karen didn't simply provide the concrete examples; she also linked the examples to the concept of *density,* which is somewhat abstract. For instance, in seeing that the side of the balance with the water on it went down, and the side with the oil on it went up, her students had to link the example—the balance with the vials of oil and water on it—to the idea that the volumes of the two vials were the same, but the one with water in it had more mass (that side of the balance went down), so the water had to be more dense.

Teachers sometimes fail to help students make this connection. For instance, suppose a first-grade teacher is working with her students on the concept of *place value* to meet the following standard:

> Understand place value
> CCSS.Math.Content.1.NBT.B.2 Understand that the two digits of a two-digit number represent amounts of tens and ones. (Common Core State Standards Initiative, 2014h)

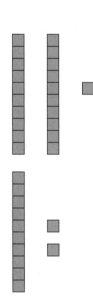

For this lesson, she wants them to understand that the number 21 represents two 10's and a single one, whereas the number 12 represents one 10 and two ones. She has the students use interlocking cubes to represent the 21.

And, she has them represent the 12 as you see on left.

Her actions next are crucial. She writes the numbers 21 and 12 on the board and directs, "Now, everyone show me this 2," as she points to the 2 in 21 and watches to be sure that the students hold up two groups of 10 interlocking cubes. She then directs, "Now, show me this 2" as she points to the 2 in 12 and watches to be sure they hold up two individual cubes. She does the same with the 1 in 21 and the 1 in 12.

Without making this link explicit, young children sometimes see the experience as two separate learning activities, one with the cubes and the other with the numbers on the board. Neither the experience with the cubes nor the numbers on the board is sufficient. It's the link between the two that's essential.

Use Social Interaction to Advance and Refine Understanding. Concrete representations alone and even links between the concrete examples and the abstract ideas are unlikely to advance development as fully as possible. Discussion is necessary. For instance, Karen's students, in spite of being eighth graders, initially *centered* on the "thickness" of the cooking oil and concluded that it's more dense than water. Many adults initially do the same. However, as Karen commented to Ken, "We talked about that, and they concluded the reason they predicted oil is the fact that it's thicker." The discussion gave her students insights into their own thinking that they probably wouldn't have gotten without it. Further, during the discussion Ethan realized that oil floats on water, concluded that less dense materials float on more dense materials, and shared his insights with the class. Without the discussion, the rest of the class wouldn't have benefited from his thinking.

Similarly, the first-grade teacher had her students describe their understanding in words, by directing, "Describe this number," as she pointed first to the 2 and then to the 1 in 21, and then guided the students into saying, "This is two groups of 10, and this is one all by itself."

Classroom **Connections**

Promoting Cognitive Development in Classrooms Using Piaget's Theory

1. Concrete experiences are essential to cognitive development. Provide concrete examples, particularly when abstract concepts are first introduced.

   ■ **Elementary:** A first-grade teacher begins her unit on animals by taking her students to the zoo, and she uses craft sticks with beans glued on them to represent groups of 10 in math.

   ■ **Middle School:** A geography teacher draws lines on a beach ball to represent latitude and longitude. He initially uses the ball so his students aren't distracted by the detail on a globe.

   ■ **High School:** An American government teacher involves his students in a simulated trial to provide a concrete example of the American court system.

2. Social interaction contributes to cognitive development. Use interaction to assess students' development and expose them to more advanced thinking.

   ■ **Elementary:** After completing a demonstration on light refraction, a fifth-grade science teacher asks students to describe their understanding of what they see. He encourages the students to ask questions of each other.

   ■ **Middle School:** An English teacher has her students discuss different perspectives about a character's motives in a novel they've read.

   ■ **High School:** A geometry teacher asks students to explain their reasoning as they demonstrate proofs at the chalkboard. She requires the students to clarify their explanations when their classmates are confused.

3. Development is advanced when learning tasks stretch the developmental capabilities of learners. Provide your students with developmentally appropriate practice in reasoning that not only matches their current level of understanding, but also encourages them to advance developmentally.

   ■ **Elementary:** A kindergarten teacher gives children in pairs a variety of geometric shapes, asks the students to group the shapes, and then has the pairs explain their different grouping patterns while he represents them on a flannel board.

   ■ **Middle School:** An algebra teacher has her students factor this polynomial expression: $m^2 + 2m + 1$. She then asks, "If no 2 appeared in the middle term, would the polynomial still be factorable?"

   ■ **High School:** A history class concludes that people often emigrate for economic reasons. Their teacher asks, "Consider an upper-class family in Mexico. Would they be likely to immigrate to the United States?" The class uses this and other hypothetical cases to examine the generalizations they've formed.

Design Learning Experiences as Developmental Bridges to More Advanced Stages of Development. As Karen presents her examples, links them to the concept of *density,* and discusses the relationships between the two, her students are becoming equipped to explain additional events, such as population density, why people float more easily in the ocean than in fresh-water lakes, why hot-air balloons rise, what allows massive oil tankers to float, and many others. Their thinking is more sophisticated because of the experiences she provided, and their development has advanced.

The same is true for the experiences with place value. As the first graders' understanding develops, they are more nearly ready to understand what numbers such as 55, 84, 95, and eventually, numbers such as 367 and beyond mean. These ideas apply to all of the topics we teach in schools. Further, as students are provided with experiences, they gradually become more aware of their own thinking, which also represents an advance in development and applies neo-Piagetian views of the developmental process.

Vygotsky's Sociocultural Theory of Cognitive Development

Piaget viewed developing children as busy and self-motivated individuals who—on their own—explore, form, and test ideas with their experiences. Lev Vygotsky (1896–1934), a Russian psychologist, provided an alternative view, a **sociocultural theory of development**, which emphasizes the role of social interaction, language, and culture on the child's

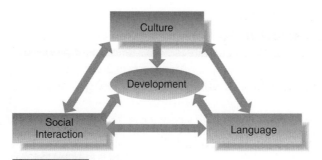

Figure 2.5

Learning and development in a cultural context

developing mind (Vygotsky, 1978, 1986, 1987, 1997). These relationships are outlined in Figure 2.5 and discussed in the sections that follow.

> **Overview of Vygotsky's Theory**
>
> Vygotsky's theory suggests that cognitive development occurs when learners, with the support of more knowledgeable others—usually parents, teachers, or other adults—acquire the knowledge and skills unique to a particular culture through the use of social interaction and language. Adults and other more knowledgeable individuals gauge learners' readiness for new tasks and provide the support needed to acquire more developmentally advanced knowledge and skills through language-rich social interactions.

Learning and Development in a Cultural Context

To begin our study of Vygotsky's theory, let's look at two short case studies. As you read them, consider how culture influences the process.

> Suzanne is reading *The Little Engine That Could* to her daughter, Perri, who sits on her lap. "I think I can, I think I can," she reads enthusiastically from the story.
>
> "Why do you think the little engine kept saying, 'I think I can, I think I can'?" Suzanne asks as they talk about the events in the story.
>
> "We need to try . . . and try . . . and try," Perri finally says hesitantly and with some prompting.
>
> Sometime later, Perri is in school, working on a project with two of her classmates.
>
> "I don't get this," her friend Dana complains. "It's too hard."
>
> "No, we can do this if we keep trying," Perri counters. "We need to work a little harder."
>
> ———————
>
> Limok and his father look out and see a fresh blanket of snow on the ground.
>
> "Ahh, beautiful," his father observes. "Iblik, the best kind of snow for hunting, especially when it's sunny."
>
> "What is iblik?" Limok wonders.
>
> "It is the soft, new snow; . . . no crystals," his father responds, picking up a handful and demonstrating how it slides easily through his fingers. "The seals like it. They come out and sun themselves. Then, we only need the spear. Our hunting will be good today."
>
> Sometime later, as Limok and his friend Osool hike across the ice, Limok sees a fresh blanket of snow covering the landscape.
>
> "Let's go back and get our spears," Limok says eagerly. "The seals will be out and easy to find today."

SOCIAL INTERACTION AND DEVELOPMENT

Vygotsky (1978, 1986) believed that social interaction is central to and directly promotes development. To see how, let's look again at Perri's and Limok's experiences. First, as she and her mother talked, Perri learned about perseverance, and Limok learned about hunting as he interacted with his father. Vygotsky would say that their thinking developed as a direct result of this interaction.

Second, the interactions were between the children and a *more knowledgeable other*, and as a result, the children developed understanding that they wouldn't have been able to acquire on their own. This understanding exists in the form of **cognitive tools**, the concepts and symbols (numbers and language) together with the real tools that allow people to think, solve problems, and function in a culture. For example, the Yu'pik people, who live in the Bering Sea just west of Alaska, have 99 different ways to describe ice. There are concepts describing wavy ice, shoreline broken ice, small cakes of ice, and thin ice overlapped like shingles (Block, 2007). These culturally embedded ideas, along with physical tools such as harpoons and nets, help them function in their immediate environments, just as concepts, such as freedom of speech and managing money, together with real tools, such as computers and the Internet, help us function in ours.

Vygotsky suggested that children need not reinvent the knowledge of a culture on their own; rather, this knowledge has accumulated over thousands of years and should be appropriated (internalized) through social interaction (Leontiev, 1981). **Internalization** is the process through which learners incorporate external, society-based ideas into internal cognitive structures. "Every function in the child's cultural development appears twice: first, on the social level, and later on the individual level. . . . All the higher functions originate as actual relationships between individuals" (Vygotsky, 1978, p. 57). Vygotsky (1978) believed that the developmental process first occurs at a social level and is later internalized by individuals, and he believed that it applies to all forms of development.

Perri and Limok both internalized cultural knowledge; Perri learned about perseverance, which is valued in our culture, and Limok learned about the conditions for good hunting. Later, they applied their understanding in a new context. Perri, for example, encouraged Dana, who wanted to quit, to keep trying, and Limok recognized the conditions for good hunting as he and Osool were hiking across the ice. Incorporating understanding into a new context marks an advance in development.

Finally, Perri and Limok were active participants in the interactions. The concept of *activity* is essential in sociocultural theory (Roth & Lee, 2007), and Vygotsky believed that children learn through active involvement with more knowledgeable people.

Ed Psych and You

Have you ever said to yourself, "I know what I'm trying to say; I just don't know how to say it"? Most of us have. Why do you suppose this is so common?

LANGUAGE AND DEVELOPMENT

Social interaction requires the use of language, and sociocultural theory suggests that language plays three important roles in development. First, it gives learners access to knowledge others already possess, and second, as you saw in the previous section, it's a *cognitive tool* that people use to help make sense of their experiences. For example, when Limok learned *iblik*, he didn't just learn the word and how to pronounce it; he also learned that it is soft, fresh, crystal-free snow and something that increases the likelihood of a successful hunt. This is related to the question we asked in *Ed Psych and You*. The ability to put our understanding into words marks an advance in our understanding and in development.

Third, language is a means for regulating and reflecting on our own thinking (Winsler & Naglieri, 2003). Let's look at this process in more detail.

PRIVATE SPEECH AND SELF-REGULATION

We all talk to ourselves; we grumble when we're frustrated, and we talk ourselves through uncertain situations. "Oh, no, a flat tire. Now what? I haven't changed a tire in years. I'd better look up how to do it in the owner's guide."

Children also talk to themselves. During free play, for example, we will often hear them muttering to no one in particular, and if we listen closely, we notice that they talk as they attempt to complete various tasks. Vygotsky believed this free-floating speech is the precursor of internal, private speech, self-talk that guides thinking and action. Private speech provides an *executive function*, one example of which is the ability to maintain attention, which we saw earlier in the chapter, and another example of which is the ability to monitor our thoughts and steer them in productive directions, which become increasingly important as we learn complex ideas and solve sophisticated problems. For example, it forms the foundation for cognitive skills such as remembering ("If I repeat the number, I'll be able to remember it") and problem solving ("Let's see, what kind of answer is the problem asking for?") (Winsler, Fernyhough, & Montero, 2009). Private speech provides children with a tool they can use to examine their thinking, help with problem solving and other higher order functions, and control emotions and actions, all of which mark the beginnings of *self-regulation*.

As development advances, private speech becomes silent and internalized but remains important for cognitive functioning. Children who use private speech achieve more than their peers, enjoy learning more, and learn complex tasks more effectively than those who don't (Lidstone, Meins, & Fernyhough, 2010). The absence of private speech, which helps monitor learning during reading, math, and complex thinking in other areas, may also be a factor in the problems encountered by students with learning disabilities (Friend, 2011).

Zone of Proximal Development

As we saw in the examples with Perri and Limok, children benefit from interacting with more knowledgeable others. Learners, however, benefit most from interaction when working in their zones of proximal development, a range of tasks that an individual cannot yet do alone but can accomplish when assisted by others (Berger, 2012; Gredler, 2012). Vygotsky (1978) described it as "the distance between the actual developmental level as determined by independent problem solving and the level of potential development as determined through problem solving under adult guidance or in collaboration with more capable peers" (p. 106).

Learners have a zone of proximal development for each task they're expected to master, and they must be in the zone to benefit from assistance. We will illustrate this process in the section "Educational Psychology and Teaching: Applying Vygotsky's Theory with Your Students," later in our discussion.

Scaffolding: Interactive Instructional Support

More knowledgeable others, most commonly parents and teachers, play essential roles in helping learners progress through the zone of proximal development for each task they are attempting. For example, as small children learn to walk, their parents often walk behind them, holding onto their hands as they take their tentative steps. As children gain

Table 2.3	Types of instructional scaffolding
Type of Scaffolding	**Example**
Modeling	An art teacher demonstrates drawing with two-point perspective before asking students to try a new drawing on their own.
Think-alouds	A physics teacher verbalizes her thinking as she solves momentum problems at the board.
Questioning	After modeling and thinking aloud, the same physics teacher "walks" students through several problems, asking them questions at critical junctures.
Adapted instructional aids	An elementary physical education teacher lowers the basket while teaching shooting techniques and then raises it as students' skills improve.
Prompts and cues	Preschoolers are taught that "the bunny goes around the hole and then jumps into it" as they learn to tie their shoelaces.

confidence, parents hold only one hand, and later, let the children walk on their own. This support illustrates the concept of **scaffolding**, which is assistance that helps children complete tasks they cannot accomplish independently (Pentimonti & Justice, 2010; Torrez-Guzman, 2011).

As with toddlers' development with respect to walking, learners' academic development is advanced by their teachers' support (Rogoff, 2003; Gredler, 2012). Without this support, development is impaired. It is important to note, however, that effective scaffolding provides only enough support to allow learners to progress on their own. Doing tasks for them can actually delay development.

Scaffolding can take a number of forms. Table 2.3 includes the forms most commonly found in classrooms. Each is designed to ensure successful task completion and ultimately cognitive growth.

Diversity: Culture and Development

Piaget and Vygotsky provide very different perspectives on the role of culture in development (Bjorklund, 2012; P. Miller, 2011). Piaget believed that children in different cultures develop in basically the same way. In that respect, he considered his stages of development to be universal and context- and culture-free.

In contrast, Vygotsky believed that culture provides the context in which development occurs; we develop by internalizing the cognitive tools embedded within specific cultures. Research supports this view (Cole & Packer, 2011; Morra, Gobbo, Marini, & Sheese, 2008; Rogoff, 2003).

The role of culture was illustrated most concretely in the example with Limok and his father. As they interacted, they used the term *iblik*, a concept unique to their culture that provided a cognitive tool they used for both thinking and communication. The same is true for all learners. Perri's development, for instance, was influenced by Suzanne's work ethic, a factor prominent in our culture. Different cultures emphasize different values and ideas, and so how children develop is influenced by the culture in which they are immersed.

These factors have implications for our teaching, because, as the diversity of our students continues to increase, they will bring many different cultures with them to our classrooms. And some may not bring with them the cognitive tools they need to thrive in our culture, which means that we must provide those tools.

As we saw earlier in our discussion, language is one of the most important tools of any culture, so we will need to provide the concrete experiences students who aren't native English speakers need to function effectively in our classrooms. Further, the more we have all our students—and particularly those who aren't native English speakers—practice using language to describe their increasing understanding, the more fully their development will be. We elaborate on this idea in the next section. Let's turn to it now.

Educational Psychology and Teaching: Applying Vygotsky's Theory with Your Students

Vygotsky's theory emphasizes the role of culture, social interaction, and language in development. As with Piaget's work, it has important implications for our teaching. The following guidelines can help us apply his ideas in our classrooms.

1. Embed learning activities in culturally authentic contexts.
2. Involve students in social interactions, and encourage them to use language to describe their developing understanding.
3. Create learning activities that are in learners' zones of proximal development.
4. Provide instructional scaffolding to assist learning and development.

Now, let's examine these guidelines in more detail.

Embed Learning Activities in Culturally Authentic Contexts. To begin, let's look at the efforts of Jeff Malone, a seventh-grade math teacher, as he works with his students to help them solve problems involving fractions, decimals, and percents with the goal of meeting the following standard.

> CCSS.Math.Content.7.NS.A.3 Solve real-world and mathematical problems involving the four operations with rational numbers. (Common Core State Standards Initiative, 2014w).

> Jeff begins his math class by passing out two newspaper ads for the same computer tablet. Techworld advertises "The lowest prices in town"; Complete Computers says, "Take an additional 15% off our already low prices."
> Jeff then asks, "So, where would you buy your tablet?"

Technology is an integral part of our culture, so Jeff built his lesson around the cost of computer tablets, items about which most students are familiar and are interested in. Using a familiar topic in this way also can increase students' interest and motivation (Brophy, 2010; Schunk, Meece, & Pintrich, 2014).

Embedding learning activities in culturally authentic contexts doesn't have to be difficult; it merely requires a bit of creativity in linking the learning activity to some aspect of your students' culture. For instance, a teacher with several Hispanic students in his class compared the Mexican War of Independence from 1810 through 1821 to our own American revolutionary war with Great Britain, and helped his students identify similarities between the two. This simple effort had a double benefit; it made the American revolutionary war more meaningful to his students with Hispanic backgrounds, and it enriched the experience for all his students, some of whom had no idea that a Mexican war of independence even existed or confused it with Cinco de Mayo, a widely held celebration of Mexican heritage and pride, but not Mexican independence.

Involve Students in Social Interactions, and Encourage Them to Use Language to Describe Their Developing Understanding. As we saw earlier in our discussion of Vygotsky's work, he believed that social interaction and the use of language are essential for promoting development. To see how Jeff capitalizes on these factors, let's rejoin his lesson.

After showing his students the two advertisements, and asking, "So, where would you buy your tablet?" Jeff, as expected, finds that his students disagree.

He then asks, "How can we find out?"

After some additional discussion, the students decide they need to find the price with the 15% discount.

Jeff reviews decimals and percentages and then puts students into groups of three and gives them two problems.

A store manager has 45 video games in his inventory. Twenty-five are out of date, so he puts them on sale. What percentage of the video games is on sale?

Joseph raised gerbils to sell to the pet store. He had 12 gerbils and sold 9 to the pet store. What percentage did he sell?

As he moves around the room, he watches the progress of one group—Sandra, Javier, and Stewart. Sandra zips through the problems. Javier knows that a fraction is needed in each case, but he struggles to compute the decimal; and Stewart doesn't know how to begin.

"Let's talk about how we compute percentages in problems like this," Jeff says, kneeling in front of the group. "Sandra, explain how you did the first problem."

Sandra begins, "Okay, the problem asks what percentage of the video games are on sale. First, I thought, how can I make a fraction? . . . Then I made a decimal out of it and then a percent. . . . So here's what I did first," and she then demonstrates how she solved the problem.

"Okay, now let's try this one," Jeff says, pointing to the second problem. "The first thing," he continues, "I need to find out is what fraction he sold. Why do I need to find a fraction? . . . Javier?"

". . . So we can make a decimal and then a percent."

"Good," Jeff smiles. "What fraction did he sell? . . . Stewart?"

". . . 9 . . . 12ths."

"Excellent. Now, Javier, how might we make a decimal out of the fraction?"

". . . Divide the 12 into the 9," Javier responds hesitantly.

"Good," and he watches Javier get .75. Stewart also begins hesitantly, beginning to grasp the idea.

After the groups have finished the review problems, Jeff calls the class back together and has some of the other students explain their solutions. When they struggle to put their explanations into words, Jeff asks questions that guide both their thinking and their descriptions.

He then returns to his original computer tablets problem and asks them to apply their knowledge of percentages to it.

Jeff capitalized on the second guideline in three ways. First, he had his students discuss where they would buy their tablets, and after they disagreed, he didn't simply tell them to find the price of the tablet at Complete Computers with the 15% discount. Rather, with his guidance they made the decision for themselves. This both capitalized on social interaction and also increased the students' motivation because it was their decision rather than his.

Second, Jeff had his students work in groups to solve his review problems, and third, he encouraged his students' use of language as they worked. As an example, let's look again at some of the dialogue when he worked with Sandra, Javier, and Stewart.

> Jeff: Let's talk about how we compute percentages in problems like this. . . . Sandra, explain how you did the first problem.
>
> Sandra: Okay, the problem asks what percentage of the video games are on sale. First, I thought, how can I make a fraction? . . . Then I made a decimal out of it and then a percent. . . . So here's what I did first (and she then demonstrates how she solved the problem).

And let's look at a bit more dialogue later in the discussion.

> Jeff: Okay, now let's try this one. . . . The first thing I need to find out is what fraction he sold. Why do I need to find a fraction? . . . Javier?"
>
> Javier: . . . So we can make a decimal and then a percent.
>
> Jeff: Good. What fraction did he sell? . . . Stewart?
>
> Stewart: . . . 9 . . . 12ths.
>
> Jeff: Excellent. Now, Javier, how might we make a decimal out of the fraction?
>
> Javier: . . . Divide the 12 into the 9.

In both brief sets of dialogue, we see that Jeff had all three students in the group verbalize what they were doing. Vygotsky believed that the use of language, such as we see illustrated here, is essential for development, and it has important implications for our teaching. The more language our students use to describe their developing understanding, the deeper that understanding becomes. Initially, they will likely struggle to put their understanding into words, so we will need to help them. With practice, however, they will gradually become more able to articulate their understanding, and the result will be increased learning and advances in development.

Finally, after he called the groups back together, Jeff had some of the students explain their solutions, which gave them additional practice in using language and presented the rest of the class with modeling that illustrated the students' thinking.

Create Learning Activities That Are in Learners' Zones of Proximal Development. As we saw earlier, when a task is within students' zones of proximal development, they can complete it with support from someone more knowledgeable—most often a teacher—but they cannot complete the task on their own. To illustrate this idea, let's look again at Jeff's work with Sandra, Javier, and Stewart, each of whom was at a different developmental level. Sandra could solve the problem without assistance, so Jeff asked her to explain her solution, which is a more advanced task. The task was within Javier's zone of proximal development, because he was able to solve the problems with Jeff's help. But Stewart's zone was below the task, so Jeff had to adapt his instruction to find the zone for him. Stewart didn't initially know how to attack the problem, but with assistance he found the fraction of the gerbils that had been sold to the pet store. By asking Stewart to identify the fraction, Jeff adapted his instruction to find the zone for this task.

Jeff's instruction seems simple enough, but it is, in fact, very sophisticated. By observing and listening to his students, Jeff assessed their current understanding and then adapted the learning activity so that it was within each student's zone of proximal development.

Provide Instructional Scaffolding to Assist Learning and Development. As we saw earlier, scaffolding is instructional support that we provide for students that helps them accomplish tasks that are in their zones of proximal development. To illustrate this process, let's look again at the dialogue from Jeff's work with Sandra, Javier, and Stewart. They were working on the second review problem, which we see again here.

> Joseph raised gerbils to sell to the pet store. He had 12 gerbils and sold 9 to the pet store. What percentage did he sell?

Jeff: The first thing . . . I need to find out is what fraction he sold. Why do I need to find a fraction? . . . Javier?

Javier: . . . So we can make a decimal and then a percent.

Jeff: Good. . . .What fraction did he sell? . . . Stewart?

Stewart: . . . 9 . . . 12ths.

Jeff: Excellent. Now, Javier, how might we make a decimal out of the fraction?"

Javier: . . . Divide the 12 into the 9.

Jeff: Good [as he watches Javier get .75. Stewart also begins hesitantly, and then begins to grasp the idea.]

Jeff's questions provided the scaffolding Javier and Stewart needed to make progress with the problem. And he provided only enough support to ensure that they made progress on their own. Effective scaffolding adjusts instructional requirements to learners' capabilities and levels of performance (Puntambekar & Hübscher, 2005). The relationship between the students' zones of proximal development and the scaffolding Jeff provided is illustrated in Figure 2.6.

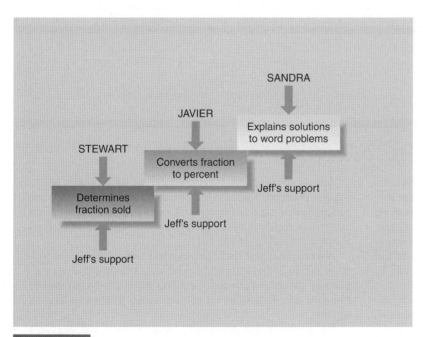

Figure 2.6

Scaffolding tasks in three zones of proximal development

Classroom **Connections**

Promoting Cognitive Development in Classrooms Using Vygotsky's Theory

1. Cognitive development occurs within the context of meaningful, culturally embedded tasks. Use authentic tasks as organizing themes for your instruction.

   - **Elementary:** A second-grade teacher teaches bar graphing by having students graph the different transportation modes that students in the class use to get to school.

   - **Middle School:** A science teacher structures a unit on weather by having her students observe the temperature, barometric pressure, and relative humidity; record and graph the data; and compare the actual weather to that forecasted in the newspaper.

   - **High School:** Before a national election, an American government teacher has his students poll their parents and students around the school. Students then have a class election, compare these results with their findings at the local and national levels, and discuss differences.

2. Scaffolding is instructional support that assists learners as they progress through their zones of proximal development. Provide enough scaffolding to ensure student success as they progress through each zone.

   - **Elementary:** When her students are first learning to print, a kindergarten teacher initially gives them dotted outlines of letters and paper with half lines for gauging letter size. As students become more skilled, she removes these aids.

   - **Middle School:** A science teacher helps her students learn to prepare lab reports by doing an experiment with the whole class and writing the report as a class activity. Students then use it as a model for writing their own reports.

   - **High School:** An art teacher begins a unit on perspective by sharing his own work and displaying works from other students. As students work on their own projects, he provides individual feedback and asks the students to discuss how perspective contributes to each drawing. Later they can use perspective effectively on their own.

3. Vygotsky believed social interaction to be a major vehicle for cognitive development. Structure classroom tasks to encourage student interaction.

   - **Elementary:** After fifth-grade students complete a writing assignment, their teacher has them share their products with each other. To assist them in the process, she provides them with focusing questions that students use to discuss their work.

   - **Middle School:** An English teacher uses cooperative learning groups to discuss the novel the class is studying. The teacher asks each group to respond to a list of prepared questions. After students discuss the questions in groups, they share their perspectives with the whole class.

   - **High School:** Students in a high school biology class work in groups to prepare for exams. Before each test, the teacher provides an outline of the content covered, and each group is responsible for creating one question on each major topic.

Analyzing Theories

Piaget's and Vygotsky's Views of Cognitive Development

Similarities and differences exist in Piaget's and Vygotsky's descriptions of cognitive development. For example, both held the now widely accepted idea that learners, instead of passively receiving knowledge from others, actively construct it for themselves. Piaget, however, believed that learners construct knowledge essentially on their own, whereas Vygotsky believed that knowledge is first constructed in a social environment and then internalized by individuals.

Also, Piaget believed that social interaction and language are primarily mechanisms for disrupting equilibrium, which is then reestablished when people individually reconstruct their understanding and advance their thinking. Vygotsky, in contrast, believed that social interaction and language directly cause development (Rogoff, 2003).

Also, as we saw earlier in our discussion of culture, Piaget viewed cognitive development as occurring largely outside the boundaries of a particular culture, whereas Vygotsky believed that development provides the cognitive tools that individuals use to function within a particular culture (Bjorklund, 2012; P. Miller, 2011).

Perhaps most important, both suggest that individuals are cognitively active in the process of constructing knowledge, which suggests we should limit our use of lecturing and explaining as teaching strategies and instead should actively involve students in learning activities.

The similarities and differences between Piaget's and Vygotsky's theories, including contributions and criticisms of each, are outlined in Table 2.4.

Table 2.4	**Analyzing theories: Comparing Piaget's and Vygotsky's theories of development**	
	Piaget	**Vygotsky**
Key question	How does development occur in all cultures?	How does development occur in a particular culture?
Description of cognitive development	Advances in thinking that result from experiences that disrupt cognitive equilibrium in individuals Development is primarily an individual process.	Advances in thinking that result from social interactions with more knowledgeable others in a cultural context Development is primarily a social process.
Catalysts for cognitive development	Maturation combined with experiences in the physical and social world that disrupt cognitive equilibrium	Language-rich interactions with more knowledgeable others in a social environment
Important concepts	Equilibrium Assimilation Accommodation Schemes Stages of development	Zone of proximal development Scaffolding Internalization Cognitive tools Private speech
Role of social interaction and language	Mechanisms to disrupt equilibrium which is reestablished by the individual	Direct causes of development, which first occurs in a social environment, then is internalized by individuals
Role of peers and adults in development	Promote development by providing experiences and interactions that disrupt equilibrium	Promote development by serving as more knowledgeable others who use language and social interaction to directly cause development
Contributions	• Was first to take a comprehensive look at cognitive development • Made educators aware that children's thinking is qualitatively different from adults' thinking • Helped educators understand that learning is an active process during which learners construct their own knowledge • Has had an enormous influence on school curriculum with his emphasis on the importance of experience in development	• Made educators realize that culture has a powerful influence on cognitive development • Recognized the role that adults and more knowledgeable peers play in cognitive development • Helped educators understand that learning and development are substantively social processes • Provided the theoretical foundation for many of today's approaches to classroom teaching and learning
Criticisms	• Underestimated the abilities of young children and overestimated the abilities of older students • Failed to recognize that students' thinking depends more on their background knowledge and experience than Piaget suggested • Piaget's stages don't adequately describe development for a number of tasks • Piaget's theory doesn't adequately consider the role of culture in development	• Was vague about the specific mechanisms of cognitive growth • Failed to account for the impact of individual experiences and their influence on cognitive development

Sources: Berk, 2013; Feldman, 2014; Piaget, 1952, 1959, 1965, 1970, 1977, 1980; Piaget & Inhelder, 1956; Vygotsky, 1978, 1986.

Developmentally Appropriate **Practice**

Promoting Cognitive Development with Learners at Different Ages

As you saw in the sections describing Piaget's and Vygotsky's theories, developmental differences have important implications for the way we teach. We examine these implications here.

Working with Students in Early Childhood Programs and Elementary Schools

Preoperational and concrete operational thinkers are capable of learning a great many concepts, but they need concrete examples that connect abstract ideas to the real world. Those of you who teach early childhood and elementary students should use concrete experiences like squares of candy bars to illustrate fractions, real crabs to demonstrate exoskeletons in animals, and experiences in their neighborhoods to illustrate the concept of *community*.

Elementary students need continual scaffolding to help them progress through their zones of proximal development for each new skill. Provide enough assistance to ensure success, and then reduce scaffolding as development advances.

Working with Students in Middle Schools

Cognitive development varies considerably among students at this age. Some will grasp abstract ideas quickly, while others will struggle. Assess frequently to ensure that your instruction is within each student's zone of proximal development. Don't assume that lack of questions means that all students understand an idea.

Though middle school students are chronologically on the border of formal operations, their thinking remains largely concrete operational. As a result, they still need the concrete experiences that make abstract concepts meaningful, such as Karen Johnson provided for her eighth graders when they struggled with the concept *density*.

Middle school students continue to need a great deal of scaffolding when working with topics that are becoming increasingly abstract, such as in prealgebra and algebra. The more practice they get with putting their ideas into words, the more effective their learning and development.

Working with Students in High Schools

Though high school students are chronologically at the stage of formal operations, the ability to think in the abstract depends on their prior knowledge and experiences. When new concepts are introduced, high school students still need concrete examples. Lecture as a teaching method, though widely used, is less effective than instruction that promotes interaction and discussion.

The social dimension of learning assumes a powerful role for high school students; how they look and what other people think of them is very important. They like to socialize, so periodically using small-group work can be effective. Small-group work can easily become a simple gab session, however, so it must be carefully monitored.

This discussion helps answer the third question we asked at the beginning of the chapter: "How will an understanding of the way students think increase your expertise as a teacher?" Because you know, for example, that students' thinking depends on their experiences, you will provide as many rich experiences as possible for your students, regardless of the grade level or content area you teach. Also, for those of you planning to be middle or high school teachers, because you realize that the thinking of most students at these levels continues to be concrete, you will initially provide them with the concrete experiences necessary to help them make the transition to abstract thinking. And you will be a more effective teacher as a result.

Language Development

A miracle occurs in children in their early years. Born with limited ability to communicate, 6-year-olds know between 8,000 and 14,000 words, and by the sixth grade, their vocabulary has expanded to 80,000 (MacWhinney, 2011; Marinellie & Kneile, 2012). Perhaps more importantly, they can use the vocabulary to read text with meaning and to describe what they've read both verbally and in writing.

Understanding how language develops is important for three reasons. First, it's the foundation for reading and writing, both essential tools for learning. Second, language is a catalyst for all forms of cognitive development; it's the vehicle students use to think and talk about the cognitive changes they're experiencing (Al-Namlah, Meins, & Fernyhough, 2012). And, third, language provides a tool for social and personal development, as we'll see in Chapter 3.

Theories of Language Development

Theories of language development differ, and these differences reflect varying emphases experts place on the roles heredity and environment play in the process.

Nativist theory, for example, emphasizes heredity and suggests that all humans are genetically wired to learn language. Noam Chomsky (1972, 2006), the father of nativist theory, proposed that an innate, genetically controlled **language acquisition device (LAD)** predisposes children to learn the rules governing language. When children are exposed to language, the LAD analyzes patterns for the rules of grammar—such as the subject after a verb when asking a question—that govern a language. Some research suggests that young infants are indeed neurologically wired or predisposed to attend to human speech (Gervain & Mehler, 2010; Koenig & Woodward, 2010; MacWhinney, 2010, 2011).

Other theories more strongly emphasize the influence of the environment. Behaviorism, for instance, suggests that children learn language through practice and reinforcement (Skinner, 1953, 1957). For example, a 2-year-old picks up a ball and says, "Baa." Mom smiles broadly and says, "Yes, ball! Good job!" Mom's "Good job!" reinforces the child's efforts, and over time, language is shaped. (We examine behaviorism in detail in Chapter 6.)

Social cognitive theory emphasizes the role of modeling, feedback, and children's imitation of adult speech (Bandura, 1986, 2001; Balog, 2010). For example,

> "Give Daddy some cookie."
> "Cookie, Dad."
> "Good. Jacinta gives Daddy some cookie."

The father modeled an expression, Jacinta attempted to imitate it, and he expanded and refined it when he said, "Good. Jacinta gives Daddy some cookie."

Vygotsky's sociocultural theory provides another perspective. It suggests that children learn language by practicing it in their day-to-day interactions with others, and adults adjust their speech to operate within children's zones of proximal development (Karniol, 2010). For instance, infant-directed speech, once called *motherese,* uses simple words, short sentences, and voice inflections to provide linguistic scaffolding for young children. As their children's language skills advance, parents use bigger words and more complex sentences, which adjust the process to each child's changing zone of proximal development (Lieven & Stoll, 2010; Sterponi, 2010).

Early Language Development

Language development begins in the cradle when adults say "Ooh" and "Aah" and "Such a smart baby!" to encourage the infant's gurgling and cooing (Arnon & Ramscar, 2012). The first words, usually spoken between ages 1 and 2, are holophrases, one- and two-word utterances that carry as much meaning for the child as complete sentences. For example, "Mama car" means "That's Momma's car."

Children also gradually learn to use intonation and emphasis to convey meaning (Mac-Whinney, 2011). For example, "Cookie" means "That's a cookie," but "Cookie!" says "I want a cookie." Differences in intonation signal the beginning of using language to communicate.

Two patterns emerge and continue with the child through later stages. **Overgeneralization** occurs when a child uses a word to refer to a broader class of objects than is appropriate, such as using the word *car* to also refer to buses and trucks. **Undergeneralization**, which is harder to detect, occurs when a child uses a word too narrowly, such as using "kitty" for her own cat but not for cats in general (Feldman, 2014; Gelman & Kalish, 2006). Both are normal aspects of language development. In most instances they're corrected through routine interactions, such as a parent saying, "No, that's a truck. See, it has more wheels and a big box on it," and "Oh, look. There's another kitty."

Young children bring to school a healthy and confident grasp of language and how it can be used to communicate with others. The importance of this foundation for learning in general, and particularly for reading and writing, can't be overstated (Hammer, Farkas, & Maczuga, 2010; Tompkins, 2014).

Language Development in the School Years

Cognitive and language development go hand in hand, and two aspects of language development are crucial for cognitive development: *vocabulary* and the *development of syntax and grammar*. We look at them next.

Ed Psych and You

Look at these sentences:

They were too close to the door to close it.
The wind was too strong to wind up the sail.
The bandage was wound around the wound.

What is significant about these sentences, and what do they suggest about language development?

DEVELOPING VOCABULARY

Before you read this chapter, you may not have understood terms such as *centration*, *object permanence*, and *zone of proximal development*, but hopefully you do now. The ideas represented by these terms are part of the knowledge base that helps you understand cognitive development, and the same is true for any area of study. In addition to subject-specific vocabulary, we also want our students to understand abstract concepts, such as *justice*, *truth*, and *beauty*, which broaden our views of the world and enrich our lives.

Elementary students enter school knowing approximately 10,000 words, but by the time they leave, they have mastered more than eight times that many (Marinellie & Kneile, 2012; MacWhinney, 2011)! They accomplish this prodigious feat in two ways. One is experience with explicit instruction that focuses on key concepts. This is a strategy widely used by teachers and one that Karen used to help her students understand concepts, such as *mass, weight, volume,* and *density*. Explicit instruction is valuable for learning terms that are unlikely to be acquired incidentally, and it's particularly important for abstract, complex, and technical terms with precise definitions, such as the concepts Karen taught (Manolitsis, Georgiou, & Parrila,

2011; Reutzel & Cooter, 2012). (We use explicit instruction in this text with our "Important Concepts," which identify, define, and illustrate the important concepts in each chapter.)

Encountering words in context is a second way new terms are used, and this process relates to **semantics**, a branch of linguistics that examines the meanings of words (Mayor & Plunkett, 2010). This process was illustrated in *Ed Psych and You* at the beginning of this section. In the sentence, "They were too close to the door to close it," the word *close* has two different meanings, and the meanings are determined by the context of the sentence. The same applies to the other two sentences. These examples illustrate the complexity of language development and help us understand why it's so challenging for young students.

GRAMMAR AND SYNTAX

Vocabulary makes up the building blocks of language, but just as a house is more than a collection of bricks, language development is more than learning isolated words. It also involves an understanding of **syntax**, the rules we use to create meaningful sentences (Haskill & Corts, 2010). For example, "I do love you." and "Do I love you?" contain identical words, but the meanings are very different because of syntax. Grammar, a subcategory of syntax that includes punctuation and capitalization, also aids communication.

Learning syntax and grammar proceeds slowly and with practice (Tomasello, 2006, 2011). During the school years children gradually learn more complex language constructions, and this development parallels other aspects of cognitive development. For instance, "Jackie paid the bill" and "She had asked him out" becomes "Jackie paid the bill because she had asked him out." The ability to use more complex sentences reflects the child's developing understanding of cause-and-effect relationships.

Using Language to Learn

Language is the foundation for both learning and communication, and children typically develop the four language skills—*listening, speaking, reading,* and *writing*—sequentially and in that order (MacWhinney, 2011; Otto, 2014). Regardless of the order, however, they have one important feature in common: *They all depend on prior knowledge and experience* (Owens, 2012). When children have visited zoos, for example, listening to or reading information about lions, elephants, and giraffes is much more meaningful, as is speaking and writing about them. The same is true for all topics. Now, let's look at these language processes in more detail.

Listening. Listening is the first language skill that develops in children, and as all teachers know, students—and especially young ones—are not very good at it. They tend to think that good listening means sitting quietly, and they don't realize that it should be a cognitively active process where they think and question themselves about what they're hearing (McDevitt, Spivey, Sheehan, Lennon, & Story, 1990).

Speaking. Speaking is a naturally occurring process in most students that complements listening and provides a vehicle for organizing thoughts and sharing them with others. As with all language skills, effective speaking depends on background knowledge, but it also requires correct pronunciation and grammar, which is challenging for all students and particularly non-native English speakers (Echevarria & Graves, 2015; Peregoy & Boyle, 2013).

As with any skill, our ability to speak clearly improves with practice (Otto, 2014). In many classrooms, however, teachers do most of the talking, so students don't have many opportunities to practice speaking.

Reading. In about second or third grade, the emphasis shifts from *learning to read* to *reading to learn* (Reutzel & Cooter, 2012; Tompkins, 2014). As with listening, many students have a tendency to read passively, never realizing that they are understanding little of what they've read. They need help in learning to ask themselves questions, such as, "What am I trying to learn here?" and "What parts of this information are most important?"

Writing. As all of us who have written papers can attest, writing is a cognitively demanding process, which helps us understand why it typically develops more slowly than listening, speaking, and reading (Berk, 2013).

Writing promotes language development in three ways. First, because it involves the organization or reorganization of ideas, it requires us to be cognitively active and to think deeply about a topic; it's virtually impossible to write passively. Second, because writing encourages us to think about our audience, it helps develop perspective taking, the ability to consider the thoughts and feelings of the reader, an important social skill. And third, we can't write about what we don't understand, so it requires us to learn new vocabulary and ideas (Cooper & Kiger, 2009).

Now, before we examine strategies for helping our students develop these important skills, let's consider what impact technology is having on cognitive and language development.

Technology, Learning, and Development

Is Technology Interfering with Cognitive and Language Development?

Throughout this chapter we've emphasized the importance of experience in cognitive development. As we've moved into the 21st century, technology is providing an increasing amount of this experience, and some experts wonder if it is interfering with healthy cognitive development. For example, in *The Dumbest Generation*, Mark Bauerlein (2008) questions whether our dependence on computers is making us less able to function in the real world. Nicholas Carr (2010) in *The Shallows* goes further, suggesting that, as a result of the Internet, we are more distractible and less able to concentrate on important ideas. Both authors suggest that technology is literally rewiring our brains. "With the exception of alphabets and number systems, the Net may well be the single most powerful mind-altering technology that has ever come into general use" (Carr, 2010, p. 116).

Let's examine these concerns more closely. In *The Shallows*, Carr argues that the amount and accessibility of information on the Internet encourage people to examine ideas superficially, and this shallow processing is having negative effects on our cognitive development. He cautions, "[W]hen we start using the Web as a substitute for personal memory, bypassing inner processes of consolidation, we risk emptying our minds of their riches" (Carr, 2010, p. 192). Could easy access to computers actually have an adverse effect on our students' thinking and cognitive development?

Some research suggests that the answer to the question is yes, and it raises some thorny questions. For example, three studies found that the development of computer skills was the only significant educational benefit that resulted from students being supplied with home computers. Achievement in math, language arts, and writing actually declined in some instances, especially for low-income students. Instead of using the computers to access information and provide study aids, students were instead using them to play video games and socialize (Malamud & Pop-Eleches, 2010; Stross, 2010; Vigdor & Ladd, 2010). International research confirms these findings (Belo, Ferreira, & Telang, 2010). In addition, research suggests that most adolescents view cell phones and other technologies not as a source of new information, but as a vehicle to initiate and maintain social relationships (Warschauer, 2011).

Part of the problem with children learning from the Internet is the huge amount of information on it and students' inability to filter through and learn from it (Afflerbach & Cho, 2010; Manning, Lawless, Goldman, & Braasch, 2011). Students are overwhelmed by the sheer magnitude of information, they aren't familiar with ways to distinguish between good and bad sites, and they have problems integrating information from different sites into coherent understanding. Schools need to do a better job of preparing students for productive use of the Internet.

Not all experts share this pessimistic view of technology's effects on learning and development. Steven Pinker (2007, 2010), a Harvard psychologist, believes that the Internet, when used wisely, can be a valuable resource. Clive Thompson (2013), in his book, *Smarter*

Than You Think, contends that the Internet augments our memories instead of replacing them, and, he argues, it opens up avenues for us to communicate with and understand other people. In addition, some research suggests that viewing children's educational programming is associated with gains in early literacy and math skills as well as academic success in the elementary grades (Ennemoser & Schneider, 2007; Linebarger & Piotrowski, 2010). However, other research suggests that the more time children spend watching prime-time shows and cartoons, the less time they spend reading and interacting with others and the poorer their academic skills (Courage & Howe, 2010; Sisson, Broyles, Newton, Baker, & Chernausek, 2011). In addition, research has also found a link between extensive television viewing and aggression as well as gender stereotyping (Collins, 2011; Coyne, Robinson, & Nelsen, 2010; Hofferth, 2010; Kahlenberg & Hein, 2010).

Technology supporters also point to the *Flynn effect*, named after the researcher who discovered it, which concludes that average intelligence test scores have been rising steadily since intelligence testing first began in the early 1900s (Flynn, 1999). Experts believe that exposure to stimulating environments, including technologies like television and the Internet, are contributing factors in this upward trend (Nettelbeck & Wilson, 2010).

And much-maligned video games, which often have action and violence as their main focus, are also causing researchers to reconsider their stance. Some research suggests that video games can actually have a positive effect on vision, attention, spatial reasoning, and decision making (Denworth, 2013). And other research has found that video games can improve older players' short-term memory and long-term focus, and these brain-changing results were confirmed when researchers found increased activity in the prefrontal cortex, the part of the brain that controls attention (Anguera et al., 2013). These results are impressive because the results extended beyond the immediate video games to other cognitive tasks as well. However, experts are still cautious about the violence that permeates most video games (Denworth, 2013; Gentile, 2011).

Similar debates exist with respect to language development. For example, the nearly ubiquitous practice of texting by young people has raised questions about its impact on people's ability to use standard language accurately and effectively. Some research suggests that the use of "techspeak," shortcuts, such as homophones, omissions, nonessential letters, and initials, to quickly text messages hinders people's ability to switch between techspeak and the normal rules of grammar (Cingel & Sundar, 2012). Others go farther, and even the popular media have raised the question, "Is texting killing the English language?" (McWhorter, 2013). Other researchers disagree, and some argue that texting is actually improving language development (Patterson, 2011).

So, is technology interfering with or even warping cognitive and language development? You, as you read this, are in the best position to answer this question for yourself. You likely use some form of technology every day, and perhaps you're spending several hours a day online. Almost certainly, you're frequently sending texts. What effects, if any, do you believe these practices are having on your own cognitive and language development? Only you can answer this question.

In a broader sense, and as with many questions about teaching and learning, questions about the impact of technology on development can't be answered with a simple yes or no. For example, the Internet is, without question, a phenomenal source of information. As we often joke, "You can find anything on Google." On the other hand, used improperly, such as spending inordinate amounts of time playing video games or corresponding on Facebook, instead of studying, technology is indeed likely to detract from learning and development.

One clear message exists. Merely exposing our students to technology won't produce learning, and it may even detract from it. As with all learning activities and tools, clear learning objectives and careful planning are essential if students are to derive maximum benefit from technology. And we need to work closely with parents to help them understand that technology must be used appropriately to contribute to learning and development.

Educational Psychology and Teaching: Helping Your Students Develop Language Abilities

We can promote language development in our students in several ways, and each of the suggestions below requires students to be active participants in the learning process.

Developing Vocabulary. We can help our students learn vocabulary by emphasizing new terms during instruction, providing examples in context to illustrate the concepts represented by the terms, and encouraging our students to use the new vocabulary in discussions and other classroom activities (M. Collins, 2010; Manolitsis et al., 2011; Reutzel & Cooter, 2012). For example, if students encounter the term *tarmac* in a story, we can show a picture of an airport, point out the location of the tarmac, and ask students to use the term in a sentence. Well written textbooks assist in the process by putting important concepts in bold print, providing definitions, and listing key concepts at the end of chapters.

Developing Grammar and Syntax: Writing. Having students do as much writing as possible is the most effective way to help them develop grammar and syntax, and this applies to all content areas. Just because we're science teachers, for instance, doesn't imply that our students don't need to write. And when they write in their science, history, or any other class, correct grammar and syntax should be required. Good writing is a skill, and the more our students practice, the better writers they will become (Tompkins, 2014). We—Paul and Don, your authors—have been writing extensively for more years than we care to remember, and we want to believe that our writing continually improves. As you study this textbook, we hope you feel all our hard work has paid off in understandable content.

We can also help our students develop their writing abilities, and the grammar and syntax integral to them, by preparing model paragraphs, short essays, and responses to questions, which provide positive examples of the ideas we are teaching. Because most classrooms now have document cameras, we can also easily display and analyze examples of student work (covering their names so they remain anonymous), which can also be effective for helping students develop their writing. Writing assignments that are short and integrated into regular lessons provide an effective way to simultaneously teach content and develop students' writing skills.

Although writing will be the primary vehicle through which students will develop their understanding of grammar and syntax, we can also promote their development with modeling and having our students practice these in their speech. For instance, "Tanya and her" is a grammatically incorrect, but common, response to the question, "Who went downtown?" When our students use incorrect grammar, we can model the correct response with a statement such as, "Oh, you mean Tanya and she went downtown." Correction without criticism is particularly important for students who aren't native English speakers.

Developing Reading and Listening Skills. Developing listening and reading skills means that students understand the ideas they are talking and reading about, and their background knowledge will strongly influence this understanding. If they lack background knowledge, we can help them by supplementing our lessons with high-quality examples, demonstrations, pictures, video clips, and other representations that illustrate key ideas (Collins, 2010; Manolitsis et al., 2011). For example, simply showing students pictures of different Native American dwellings and them hunting buffalo and gathering other kinds of food makes listening to or reading about their culture more meaningful. Similarly, simply pushing a ball off a table to demonstrate the transfer from potential to kinetic energy makes reading a science book easier and more understandable.

In essence, this practice amounts to providing experiences students need to promote their cognitive development—and which we so strongly emphasized in that discussion.

Further, Vygotsky's emphasis on language helps us understand that cognitive and language development have a hand-in-glove relationship with each other.

We can also emphasize the importance of active listening, with frequent reminders, such as "Now, listen carefully, because we want to understand this idea." Also, encouraging students to ask questions and reminding them, when reading, to periodically stop and ask themselves if they understand what they've just read can help them develop their reading and listening skills.

Developing Speaking Abilities. To learn to speak well, students need practice, just as is the case with their writing or any other skill (Tomasello, 2011). When we ask questions, we should direct them to the whole class, give all students time to think about and organize a response, and then call on an individual to respond. When they struggle, we can then help them put their thoughts into words.

We can also supplement whole-class instruction with small-group work to provide students with additional opportunities to practice their language skills. Small-group work, however, requires careful planning and monitoring to be sure that students stay on task and don't use group work as an opportunity to socialize. For example, think-pair-share is a strategy where students think about an answer to a question or problem and share it with a partner before responding to the teacher. Done properly it can be an effective way to combine the benefits of teacher-led discussions with opportunities for developing students' oral language skills.

Classroom **Connections**

Promoting Language Development in Classrooms

1. Language development depends on opportunities to hear and use language. Provide students with activities during which they can practice speaking, listening, and writing in your classroom.

   - **Elementary:** A fourth-grade teacher says to a student who has solved a problem involving the addition of fractions with unlike denominators, "Okay, explain to us exactly what you did. Be sure to include each of the terms we've been learning in your description."

   - **Middle School:** An eighth-grade history teacher, in a study of the American Revolution, says to his class, "Now, go ahead and take a few moments to put into words the parallels we've discussed between the American, French, and Russian revolutions."

   - **High School:** A biology teacher, in a discussion of genetics, says, "Describe in your own words what we mean by the term *hybrid*. How does it relate to the terms *genotype* and *phenotype* we've been discussing?"

2. Language development requires that students practice in emotionally safe and supportive environments. Create an emotional climate in your classroom that makes students feel safe as they practice language.

   - **Elementary:** When a third grader struggles to explain how he solved a problem, his teacher says, "That's okay. We all struggle to express ourselves. The more you practice, the better you'll get at it."

   - **Middle School:** In response to snickers as a student struggles to describe the parallels in the American, French, and Russian revolutions, the teacher states sternly, "We listen politely when a classmate is trying to explain his or her thoughts. We're here to support each other."

   - **High School:** In response to a student who says, "I kinda know what a 'hybrid' is, but I can't quite say it," the biology teacher says, "That's okay. We all struggle. Give it a try, and say as much as you can, and we'll take it from there."

3. Understanding and supportive teachers are an essential component of healthy language development. Provide scaffolding when students struggle with language.

   - **Elementary:** When a fifth grader says, "I tried to find for these numbers and . . ." as he struggles to explain how he found a lowest common denominator, his teacher offers, "You attempted to find the lowest common denominator?"

   - **Middle School:** As the student hesitates in his attempts to describe differences in the American, Russian, and French revolutions, the history teacher says, "First describe one thing the three revolutions had in common."

   - **High School:** In response to the student's struggles, the biology teacher says, "Go ahead and tell us what a hybrid looks like and how it's different from its parents."

Developmentally Appropriate **Practice**

Promoting Language Development with Learners at Different Ages

Working with Students in Early Childhood Programs and Elementary Schools

Language is a foundation for understanding and communication regardless of learners' ages. Developmental differences exist, however, as we discuss here.

If you're an elementary teacher, language development will be one of your most important goals. Active participation in both whole-group and small-group activities, together with writing about the topics they're learning, provide elementary students with the practice that is essential for their language development.

Sensitivity to individual differences is important when working with young children. For example, boys' language skills develop less rapidly than girls', and some cultural minorities may not be comfortable interacting with adults as conversation partners (Berk, 2013).

Questioning is one of the most useful tools that you have for promoting language development. It not only provides students with access to advanced vocabulary and modeled correct sentence constructions, but it also provides them with opportunities to practice their own developing language skills. When students struggle, you can provide prompts and model responses to questions. Elaborating on responses also provides an opportunity to model correct grammar and syntax as well as clarify content.

Young students' working memories are still developing, which limits their ability to understand complex directions (Jack, Simcock, & Hayne, 2012). Simplifying directions is important for these students.

Working with Students in Middle Schools

Social interaction becomes increasingly important for middle school students, which presents both opportunities and challenges for their teachers. When well organized, group work can provide opportunities to expose students to different perspectives and to develop their communication skills. Creating groups that are developmentally and culturally diverse provides students with opportunities to learn from each other.

Middle schoolers' listening skills are still developing, so writing definitions and other important ideas on the board or document camera is important.

Middle school students' skills with complex sentence structures and their understanding of figurative speech and metaphorical language are also developing. Jokes based on double meanings, such as "Hey, did you take a bath today? . . . Why, are you missing one?" provide opportunities to talk about language and its central role in communication (Berk, 2013).

Working with Students in High Schools

High school students want to appear grown up and are sometimes hesitant to participate in whole-class activities, so explaining why you call on everyone as equally as possible to encourage participation is important.

Because high school students often want to hide the fact that they don't understand an idea, they are often reluctant to ask questions. So, the fact that no questions are asked doesn't necessarily mean that students understand what you're teaching. Questioning, particularly as a form of informal assessment, is important with these students. Their ability to answer gives you an indication of their developing understanding.

Providing high school students with practice in writing is important, regardless of your content area. It develops language and thinking skills, encourages deeper understanding, and prepares them for college or the world of work, where the abilities to write are essential. Despite extensive practice with texting, high school students need instruction in formal conventions of grammar, spelling, and punctuation, and practice with writing is even more important than it has been in the past (Pence Turnbull & Justice, 2012). Like all of us, high school students get better at writing by practicing, so the more practice you provide, the better writers they'll become.

2 Summary

1. Describe development, and explain how Bronfenbrenner's theory and neuroscience research contribute to our understanding of development.
   - Development describes the physical, cognitive, social, and emotional changes that occur in people as they grow from infancy to adulthood.
   - Principles of development suggest that development depends on both heredity and environment, that it is continuous and relatively orderly, and that learners develop at different rates.
   - Bronfenbrenner's theory of development describes how different aspects of the environment interact with each other and genetics to influence development.
   - Neuroscience helps us understand how the brain changes when development occurs. The concept of neuroplasticity reminds us that the brain can physically change in response to experience.
   - Understanding development helps teachers adapt their instruction to meet the developmental needs and capabilities of their students.

2. Use concepts from Piaget's theory of intellectual development to explain both classroom and everyday events.
   - Concepts from Piaget's theory help explain why people want order and certainty in their lives, and how they adapt their thinking in response to new experiences.
   - According to Piaget, people organize their experiences into schemes that help them make sense of their experiences and achieve equilibrium. New experiences are assimilated if they can be explained with existing schemes. Accommodation and a change in thinking are required if new experiences can't be explained with existing schemes.
   - Maturation and experiences with the physical and social world advance development.
   - As children develop, they progress through stages that describe general patterns of thinking, ranging from perceptual dominance in preoperational thinkers to the ability to think logically and hypothetically for formal operational thinkers.

3. Use Vygotsky's sociocultural theory to explain how language, culture, and instructional support influence development.
   - Vygotsky describes cognitive development as the interaction between social interaction, language, and culture.
   - Social interaction and language provide the mechanism and tools that help children develop understandings that they wouldn't be able to acquire on their own and advance their development.
   - Social interaction and language are embedded in a cultural context that uses the language of the culture as the mechanism for promoting development.

4. Use theories of language development to explain language patterns in children.
   - Behaviorism describes language development by suggesting that children are reinforced for demonstrating sounds and words, and social cognitive theory focuses on the imitation of language that is modeled.
   - Nativist theory suggests that children are genetically predisposed to language.
   - Sociocultural theory suggests that language is developed through scaffolded practice that occurs within children's zones of proximal development.
   - Children progress from an early foundation of one- and two-word utterances, ultimately to elaborate language that involves complex sentence structures.
   - Language development during the school years focuses on word meanings (semantics), grammar (syntactics), and using language to learn through listening, reading, and writing.
   - We can promote language development in students by providing them with the experiences and opportunities to practice language that are integral to all forms of development.

Preparing for Your Licensure Exam

Understanding Cognitive and Language Development

You will be required to take a licensure exam before you go into your own classroom. This exam will include information related to cognitive and language development, and the following exercises are similar to those that appear on licensure exams. They are designed to help you practice for the exam in your state. This book and these exercises will be a resource for you later in your program as you prepare for the exam.

In this chapter, you saw how Karen Johnson used her understanding of student development to help her students learn about density. Let's look now as Jenny Newhall, a first-grade teacher who is working with her children in a lesson on the properties of air, uses her knowledge of development to promote learning. Read the case study, and then answer the questions that follow. (The case study you see here is based on the video episode you saw in "Practice Using What You Have Learned: Applying Piaget's and Vygotsky's Theories in First Grade". To make the written case more meaningful, you may want to review the video episode again.)

Jenny is working with her students on the following standard.

> CCSS.ELA-Literacy.W.1.2 Write informative/explanatory texts in which they name a topic, supply some facts about the topic, and provide some sense of closure. (Common Core State Standards Initiative, 2014f).

She plans to provide her students with experiences related to the properties of air and then have them write about their experiences.

Jenny gathers the children around her on the rug in front of a small table to begin her science lesson. After they're settled, she turns to a fishbowl filled with water and an empty glass and asks students to observe and describe them. She then says, "I'm going to put this glass upside down in the water. What's going to happen? What do you think? . . . Michelle?"

". . . Water will go in the glass."

"No, it'll stay dry," Samantha counters.

Jenny then says, "Raise your hand if you think it will get water in it. . . . Okay, . . . raise your hand if you think it'll remain dry. . . . How many aren't sure? . . . Well, let's see if we can find out.

She has the students confirm that the glass is dry, and then has the students watch carefully as she pushes the inverted glass under the water, as shown here:

Jenny carefully pulls the glass out of the water, but the students don't agree about whether or not the glass is dry on the inside, so she wads up a paper towel, pushes it to the bottom of the glass, and asks, "Now if water goes in the glass, what is the paper towel going to look like?"

The class agrees it will be wet and soggy.

The class watches as Jenny pushes the glass into the water again, pulls it back out, and says, "Okay, Marisse, come up here and check the paper towel and tell us whether it's wet or dry."

"Dry," Marisse says, after feeling the towel.

"Why did it stay dry? . . . What do you think, Jessica?"

"'Cause it's inside and the water is outside?"

"But why didn't the water go into the glass? What kept the water out? . . . Anthony?"

"A water seal."

"A water seal," Jenny repeats, fighting back a smile. Hmm. . . . There's all that water on the outside. How come it didn't go inside? . . . How can the towel stay dry?"

A quiet voice volunteers, "Because there's air in there."

"Air. . . . Is that what kept the water out?" Jenny asks. "Well, earlier Samantha said that when she was swimming in a pool and put a glass under the water, it stayed dry, but when she tipped it, it got wet inside. Now what do you think will happen if I put the glass under the water and tip it? . . . Devon?"

"It'll get wet."

Jenny removes the paper towel and returns the glass to the fishbowl.

"What's happening?" Jenny asks as she slowly tips the inverted glass, allowing some of the bubbles to escape. ". . . Andrea?"

"There are bubbles."

"Andrea, what were those bubbles made of?"

"They're air bubbles."

Jenny continues to tip the glass, allowing more air bubbles to escape, and asks again, "So, why did the towel stay dry?"

"The air kept the water out," several students respond in unison.

Jenny then divides the class into pairs, and the students use tubs of water, glasses, and paper towels to experiment on their own. After each student has a chance to try the activities, she again calls the children together, and they review and summarize what they have found.

Questions for **Case Analysis**

In answering these questions, use information from the chapter, and link your responses to specific information in the case.

Multiple-Choice Questions

1. At what level of cognitive development were Jenny's students most likely to be?

   a. Sensorimotor

   b. Preoperational

   c. Concrete operational

   d. Formal operational

2. What, specifically, was the most important thing Jenny did to promote cognitive development in her students?

   a. She introduced the activity by having students gather around her on the rug.

   b. She provided direct, concrete experiences for her students through her learning activities.

   c. She accepted every answer that students provided, avoiding damaging criticism and feedback.

   d. She called on a large number of students, encouraging participation in her activity.

Constructed-Response Question

3. Did Jenny conduct the lesson in her students' zones of proximal development? Explain why you do or do not think so. What forms of scaffolding did Jenny provide? How effective was the scaffolding?

Important **Concepts**

accommodation
assimilation
axons
centration
chronosystem
classification
cognitive development
cognitive tools
conservation
dendrites
development
egocentrism
equilibrium

exosystem
internalization
language acquisition device (LAD)
macrosystem
maturation
mesosystem
microsystem
myelination
nativist theory
neo-Piagetian theories of development
neurons

neuroplasticity
object permanence
overgeneralization
personal, social, and emotional development
physical development
prefrontal cortex
private speech
reversibility
scaffolding
schemes
semantics
seriation

social experience
sociocultural theory of development
stages of development
synapses
synaptic pruning
syntax
transformation
transitivity
undergeneralization
zone of proximal development

3 Personal, Social, and Moral Development

Arthur Tilley/Getty Images

OUTLINE	LEARNING OUTCOMES
	After you've completed your study of this chapter, you should be able to:
Personality Development Temperament Environmental Influences on Personality Development Personality Development and Emotions Personality Development and Achievement Educational Psychology and Teaching: Supporting Your Students' Personality Development	1. Describe personality development and explain how it can influence academic success and success in life after the school years.
Development of Identity and Self-concept Erikson's Theory of Psychosocial Development ▶ Analyzing Theories: Evaluating Erikson's Work Contemporary Views of Identity Development Diversity: Ethnic Identity The Development of Self-Concept Educational Psychology and Teaching: Supporting Your Students' Identity and Self-concept Development	2. Use descriptions of psychosocial, identity, and self-concept development to explain learner behavior.
Social Development Influences on Social Development Perspective Taking: Understanding Others' Thoughts and Feelings Social Problem Solving Educational Psychology and Teaching: Applying an Understanding of Social Development with Your Students	3. Describe components of social development, and explain how social development is related to success and satisfaction in school.
Development of Morality, Social Responsibility, and Self-Control Society's Interest in Moral Development Social Domain Theory of Moral Development Piaget's Theory of Moral Development Kohlberg's Theory of Moral Development ▶ Analyzing Theories: Evaluating Kohlberg's Theory of Moral Development Gender Differences: The Morality of Caring Emotional Factors in Moral Development Educational Psychology and Teaching: Promoting Moral Development in Your Students	4. Use theories of moral development to explain differences in people's responses to ethical issues.
Obstacles to Healthy Development Obesity Alcohol and Drugs Child Abuse Peer Aggression ▶ Technology, Learning, and Development: Cyberbullying ▶ Developmentally Appropriate Practice: Personal, Social, and Moral Development with Learners at Different Ages	5. Identify obstacles to development and explain how they detract from healthy development.

Think about people we all know. Some have great personalities, but we wonder about others. We know people who are socially skilled and also individuals who appear clueless. And we likely have encountered people who are scrupulously honest and others who might press the limits of right and wrong.

When we teach, we obviously want our students to understand ideas and skills, such as the causes of the Civil War and the ability to solve word problems, but we also want them to learn to manage their emotions, interact effectively with others, and develop a sense of honesty and fair play. Keep these ideas in mind as you study this chapter. We begin with a brief discussion between two middle school teachers as they describe their concerns about a student.

> "Ahh," Amanda Kellinger, an eighth-grade English teacher, sighs as she slides into a chair in the faculty lounge.
>
> "Tough day?" her friend Bill asks.
>
> "Yes, it's Sean again," Amanda nods. "I can't seem to get through to him. He jumps on other students for no apparent reason, and when I talk to him about it, he says some of them are 'out to get him.' He has a bad attitude about school in general, and when I talked with his mother, she said he's been a handful since birth. And . . . I think it's affecting his academic work."
>
> "I know what you mean," Bill responds. "I had him for English last year. At times he would almost open up to me, but then the wall would go up again. . . . And his older brother was so different, eager and cooperative, and he seemed to get along with everyone. . . . Same home, very different kids."
>
> "He's a bright boy, too," Amanda continues, "I'd love to help him . . . if I could just figure out how."

We'll return to this conversation as the chapter unfolds, but for now, think about these questions:

1. How might we explain why Sean and his older brother are so different?
2. Is Amanda's assessment likely to be accurate, that is, will Sean's attitude affect his academic work?
3. Why doesn't Sean get along with the other students?

An understanding of personal, social, and moral development can help us answer these and other questions about both ourselves and our students. We focus on these topics in this chapter as we examine

- *Personality development*, changes in our attitudinal, emotional, and behavioral responses that occur over time.
- The development of *identity* and *self-concept,* growth in the sense of who we are and an assessment of our competence in different areas.
- *Social development*, improvements we make in our ability to interact and get along with others.
- *Moral development*, advances in our conceptions of right and wrong and prosocial traits such as honesty and respect for others.

We begin with personality development.

Personality Development

Ed Psych and You

Have your friends ever set you up with a blind date? If they have, they will likely say your date has a "great personality." What does this mean?

Personality is a comprehensive term that describes our attitudinal, emotional, and behavioral responses to experiences in our environment, and, as you saw above, **personality development** involves changes in those responses. Researchers generally describe personality as being composed of five relatively independent traits, often described as the "Big Five" (Barrick, Mount, & Li, 2013; Hahn, Gottschling, & Spinath, 2012; Mõttus, Johnson, & Deary, 2012; Woods, Lievens, Fruyt, & Wille, 2013). They include:

- *Extraversion:* The extent to which individuals are socially outgoing and inclined to engage in social interaction, as opposed to being shy and withdrawn.
- *Agreeableness:* The tendency of people to empathize and get along with others, such as being warm and compassionate compared to being distant and aggressive.
- *Openness:* The extent to which people are curious and seek new experiences, such as embracing new ideas and having a wide range of interests versus being narrow and close-minded.
- *Conscientiousness:* The tendency of individuals to follow through on their commitments and to be organized and responsible, such as reliable and thorough compared to being shortsighted, scattered, and disorganized.
- *Neuroticism:* The tendency of people to be vulnerable to negative emotions and to view the world as threatening, such as anxious, tense, and worrisome versus emotionally stable, positive, and balanced.

These characteristics help us answer the question we asked in *Ed Psych and You* about the meaning of "great personality." If your friends described your date this way, they probably were suggesting that he or she was *extraverted, agreeable, open*, and *emotionally stable*. Most of us would like to believe that we possess these desirable traits.

It appears that Sean, in our case study at the beginning of the chapter, has some issues with respect to these traits. For example, he appears to be low in *agreeableness* and *openness*, and he also appears vulnerable to negative emotions, which, if they remain unchanged, are unlikely to serve him well, either in school or in later life. So, how do we acquire these traits? Genetics and the environment both play a role. Let's look at them, beginning with the influence of genetics.

Temperament

Temperament is generally described as our relatively consistent inclinations to respond to events in the environment in particular ways (Shiner et al., 2012). For instance, if we tend to have strong emotional reactions to happenings in the daily news, whereas a friend has little reaction, our different temperaments could be the cause.

Temperament is determined in large part by our genes, and patterns appear early in life (Rutter, 2011). For instance, some infants tend to react positively to new experiences, such as the willingness to try new foods and adjust to change, whereas others are more irritable and "difficult" and react negatively to new situations. And, identical twins reared in different homes often have similar temperaments (Casalin, Luyten, Vliegen, & Meurs, 2012).

Temperament influences our overall personality development (Casalin et al., 2012; Thompson, Winer, & Goodvin, 2011; Walters, 2011). For example, children with irritable and anger-prone temperaments are often low in *openness* and *agreeableness,* which can cause negative reactions from others and result in them having a hard time making friends (Bridgett et al., 2009; van den Akker, Deković, Prinzie, & Asscher, 2010). Also, difficult temperaments are associated with behavioral problems at school and adjustment problems later in life (Christensen, Mitrou, Lawrence, Sanson, & Zubrick, 2011). It also helps answer the first question we asked at the beginning of the chapter: "How might we explain why Sean and his older brother are so different?" The most likely answer is that they differ in genetically influenced temperaments.

Our temperaments provide us with the raw materials that shape our personalities, but our environments also affect personality development. "A common metaphor for thinking about personality development has been that young children display genetically influenced temperament traits and that life experiences 'layer' personality traits onto the early biological temperament" (Shiner et al., 2012, p. 440). We examine these influences next.

Environmental Influences on Personality Development

Suppose someone experiences a traumatic event, such as the death of a parent or sibling, a crippling disease like cancer, an economic disaster, or even a family move to a strange new city. Factors such as these can influence personality development (Eccles, 2009; Peterson et al., 2014; Rothbart, 2011). School environments can also shape students' personalities. For instance, making new friends, being bullied, and even the transition from elementary to middle school can influence our students' developing personalities (Schunk, Meece, & Pintrich, 2014; Schwerdt & West, 2011).

Parenting is foremost among environmental influences on personality development, and a great deal of research has examined different parenting styles. We examine this research next.

Ed Psych and You

How did your parents raise you? What kinds of expectations for your achievement and behavior did they have? How "strict" were they? How involved were they in your school activities?

PARENTING AND PERSONALITY DEVELOPMENT

Personality development begins in the home, and parents and other immediate caregivers strongly influence this aspect of development. Research indicates that certain **parenting styles**, general patterns of interacting with and disciplining children, promote more healthy development than others (Baumrind, 2005; Baumrind, Larzelere, & Owens, 2010; Gunnoe, 2013). Parents' expectations, their warmth and responsiveness, and the way they interact with their children are central to these differences (Schaffer, Clark, & Jeglic, 2009). Using these factors as a framework, researchers have linked parenting styles with the following general patterns of personality development associated with them (Chan, 2010; Cipriano & Stifter, 2010; Kakihara, Tilton-Weaver, Kerr, & Stattin, 2010; Thompson & Newton, 2010):

- *Authoritative parents* set high expectations and are warm and responsive. They are firm, caring, and consistent. They explain reasons for rules and frequently interact with their children, who tend to be agreeable, open, conscientious, and successful in school.
- *Authoritarian parents* have high expectations but tend to be cold and unresponsive. They expect conformity, they don't explain reasons for rules, and they don't encourage verbal give-and-take. Their children tend to be withdrawn, sometimes defiant, and often lack social skills.
- *Permissive parents* are warm but hold few expectations for their children, who tend to be immature, compulsive, and unmotivated. Used to getting their own way, the children are sometimes disagreeable and have trouble relating to their peers.

- *Uninvolved parents* have few expectations for their children and are cold and unresponsive. They have little interest in their children, who tend to acquire negative personality traits, lack self-control and long-term goals, and can be disobedient and easily frustrated.

These parenting styles help answer the questions we asked in *Ed Psych and You* in this section. If they held high expectations, established boundaries for your acceptable behavior, and were involved in your school activities, they fit the description of authoritative parents. Authoritative parenting tends to promote positive personality traits, such as *agreeableness, openness,* and *conscientiousness.* Adolescents whose parents are authoritative also tend to be better adjusted, less aggressive, and less likely to be swayed by peer pressure to use alcohol and other drugs. And they connect to others who are well-rounded (Cipriano & Stifter, 2010; Luyckx, Tildesley, Soenens, & Andrews, 2011; Thompson & Newton, 2010). At the other extreme, students who characterize their parents as uninvolved are more likely to party, use drugs, and reject adult values (Fite et al., 2010; Huesmann, Dubow, & Boxer, 2011).

On the other hand, we're certainly not suggesting that if your parents were authoritarian, permissive, or uninvolved, you are doomed to a life of incomplete personality development, because these parenting styles describe general patterns, and exceptions will exist.

Parents influence personality development in three important ways. First, effective parents provide a safe and nurturant environment that promotes personal security (Cipriano & Stifter, 2010). Second, they talk with their children, explain why rules are important, and emphasize the effects of actions on others, which also promotes social development (Thompson & Newton, 2010). And third, they model effective personality traits that provide their children with concrete examples they can emulate.

DIVERSITY: CULTURAL DIFFERENCES IN PARENTING STYLES

The original research on parenting styles was done primarily with European American, middle-class families. With an authoritative parenting style viewed as desirable, families in the United States and Western Europe tend to encourage independence, competition, and freedom of expression (Chen & Eisenberg, 2012; Spicer et al., 2012). However, many families with Asian, African, Middle Eastern, Native American, and Hispanic backgrounds believe in a more collectivist orientation, valuing obedience, deference to authority figures (especially parents), and the importance of the family (Leavell, Tamis-LeMonda, Ruble, Zosuls, & Cabrera, 2012; Spicer et al., 2012). In these cultures, parents combine high demands for obedience with close, supportive parent–child relationships. In addition, many of these cultures treat female children more protectively, tend to be more demanding, and are less likely to grant autonomy to their female children (Dixon, Graber, & Brooks-Gunn, 2008; Domenech, Rodriguez, Donovick, & Crowley, 2009).

A considerable amount of research has focused on Asian American families because of a general pattern of high academic achievement in their children. This research suggests that these families teach children that obedience is good and devotion to the family is more important than individual wants and desires (Calzada, Huang, Anicama, Fernandez, & Brotman, 2012; J. Chen, Chen, & Zheng, 2012).

A widely publicized, and somewhat controversial, book, *Battle Hymn of the Tiger Mother,* written by Amy Chua (2011), a Yale Law School professor, outlines some of the parenting characteristics described above. In her book she describes "Chinese mother" as loosely including parents who practice traditional, strict child rearing. She points out that the majority of Chinese immigrant mothers believe that their children can be good students, that achievement is a result of successful parenting, and that parents aren't doing their jobs if their children aren't academically successful. She goes on to say that "Western" parenting puts more of a premium on children's self-esteem instead of hard work and obedience.

She does acknowledge, however, that Western parents vary in their child-rearing practices and that not all ethnically Chinese parents are overly strict.

Since the publication of *Battle Hymn of the Tiger Mother*, additional research—although not all triggered by the book—has examined Asian American parenting styles. This research doesn't suggest strict and harsh parenting as a general pattern by Asian American parents. For example, a study directly asking, "Does tiger parenting exist?" found that contrary to the common perception, tiger parenting is not the most typical profile in Chinese American families, and where it does exist, it doesn't lead to optimal adjustment among Chinese American adolescents (Kim, Wang, Orozco-Lapray, Shen, & Murtuza, 2013). And in a study of Korean parents, researchers found a pattern of both authoritative and authoritarian—but not harsh—parenting (Choi, Kim, Kim, & Park, 2013).

Similar patterns have been found in other cultures. For instance, in a study of Pakistani parenting practices, researchers found that authoritative parenting was positively associated with emotional regulation in adolescents, whereas permissive parenting had the opposite effect (Jabeen, Anis-ul-Haque, & Riaz, 2013).

On the other hand, a study examining parenting in a neighborhood having a high concentration of Chinese American families found higher levels of authoritarian parenting and higher levels of behavior problems with their children (Lee et al., 2013).

What patterns can we find in this body of research? First, it suggests that the stereotype of Asian American parents being strict, demanding, harsh, and cold is not valid. The patterns suggest high and unyielding expectations for academic achievement, but they also suggest high levels of parental warmth and emotional support. These parenting patterns seem to produce higher achievement along with greater emotional maturity (Spera, 2005).

These results have implications for parents from all cultural backgrounds. Having high expectations for children is positive, but children also need the involvement, warmth, and emotional support from parents that it takes to meet those expectations. The results make perfect sense. A long history of research suggests that children will rise to meet expectations, but they need the support necessary to do so. Meeting these high expectations will result in the increased self-esteem commonly valued in Western cultures.

Personality Development and Emotions

Ed Psych and You

Pause for a moment and think about how you're feeling right now. Are you happy or sad? Confident or anxious? Why do you feel the way you do, and can you change this if you try?

The questions we asked in *Ed Psych and You* involve **emotions**, feelings that are often short-lived, intense, and specific (Schunk et al., 2014). For instance, we've all been anxious in anticipating a test, and the anxiety might even be quite intense. The feeling is specific to the test, however, and it likely disappears after we're finished, so the anxiety is short-lived. This is the case with most emotions.

But some emotional reactions can be more global and enduring. As we saw earlier, *neuroticism*, the tendency to experience negative emotions, is one of the "Big Five" personality traits, so emotions are integral to overall personality development.

Emotions exist in a range from those that are positive, such as happiness, excitement, hope, pride, and contentment, to a number that are negative, such as boredom, anger, guilt, stress, and depression.

A great deal of research has been conducted on emotions and their influence on physical and psychological health as well as their effects on learner motivation and achievement. With respect to general health, much of the research has focused on the adverse impact of negative emotions. For instance, well-established links have been found between anxiety, stress, and anger, and the development of cardiovascular disease (Mostofsky, Maclure, Tofler, Muller, & Mittleman, 2013; Roest, Martens, de Jonge, & Denollet, 2010). And a pattern of negative emotions appears to generally detract from health. "[T]he chronic experience of negative emotions can influence the development of disease via cumulative effects. . ." (DeSteno, Gross, & Kubzansky, 2013, p. 476). Further, negative emotions can produce adverse health outcomes indirectly by influencing decisions and choices (DeSteno et al., 2013). For instance, "anxiety eaters" may gain unhealthy amounts of weight, and serious depression can leave people without the energy to interact with other people or exercise.

Good news exists, however. Researchers have also identified links between positive emotions and overall health and well-being. "People who experience warmer, more upbeat emotions live longer and healthier lives" (Kok et al., 2013, p. 1123). "Moreover, it appears that positive affect may influence health not only by buffering effects of stress, but also by inducing positive biological function and marshaling additional healthy beneficial psychosocial resources" (DeSteno et al., 2013, p. 477).

Even though we think of emotions as "feelings," they also have cognitive, physiological, and behavioral components as well (Pekrun, Goetz, Frenzel, Barchfeld, & Perry, 2011). For instance, suppose we're confronted by an immediate threat, such as a car running a red light as we're about to enter an intersection. Fear is the emotion we experience, but we also perceive danger (a form of cognition), our muscles tense and our heart rates accelerate (physiological reactions), and we likely slam on our breaks to avoid a collision—a behavioral response. The cognitive component of emotions is particularly significant because it suggests that with awareness—a form of cognition—we have a certain degree of control over our emotions, and with practice we can move toward the positive end of the emotional continuum (Kok et al., 2013). This leads us to the idea of *emotional self-regulation.*

Ed Psych and You

Have you ever had a person make a rude remark to you, and you thought, "I'd love to tell him [or her] where to go!" But you don't. Why not?

EMOTIONAL SELF-REGULATION

The answer to the question "Why not?" in *Ed Psych and You* illustrates the concept of **emotional self-regulation** (sometimes called *emotional regulation* or simply *emotion regulation*), the processes people use to influence the emotions they have, when they have them, and how they express these emotions (Dan-Glauser & Gross, 2013). Emotional self-regulation helps us cope with our changing environments and accomplish goals. It's an important component of emotional health and overall personality development. It includes factors such as the following (Davis, Levine, Lench, & Quas, 2010; Eisenberg, Spinrad, & Eggum, 2010; Thompson et al., 2011):

- Controlling impulses to behave in socially unacceptable ways, such as controlling the impulse to tell the other person where to go in our example in *Ed Psych and You*.

- Managing negative emotions, such as being able to forget about the rude remark after initially feeling angry about it.
- Behaving in socially acceptable ways, such as deciding to talk calmly to the person about the remark, or simply leaving the scene of the incident.

Developing emotional self-regulation has two components (Buckley & Saarni, 2009). First, we learn to control how, when, and where to express our feelings. Second, we learn to reinterpret potentially negative events in a positive light, such as concluding that we simply need to study more effectively instead of being devastated by a low test score. Mastering these two components marks a significant step forward in understanding and harnessing our emotions (Aikins & Litwack, 2011). With experience, and particularly through social interactions, both slowly develop over time.

Emotional self-regulation is closely related to emotional intelligence, the ability to perceive, understand, and manage emotions in ourselves and others, and to use emotional knowledge to enhance cognition (thought) (Humphrey, 2013; Reissland, 2012). The definition of emotional self-regulation includes the term *influence* in reference to emotions, and emotional intelligence includes the term *manage* with a similar reference, so we can see the connection between the two.

The concept of emotional intelligence was popularized by Daniel Goleman (2006), who asserts that it may be more important to success in life than traditional measures of ability, such as IQ. Although the concept has been criticized as lacking validity and predictive ability (Harms & Credé, 2010), it appears widely in the research literature of education and the business world, both in our country and internationally (e.g., Gondal & Husain, 2013; Zakieh, Fatemeh, & Mahmood, 2013; Arghode, 2013; Bharti, 2013).

DIVERSITY: DIFFERENCES IN EMOTIONAL SELF-REGULATION

As we would expect, children differ considerably in their emotional self-regulation. And, as is intuitively sensible, older children are better at emotional control than their younger counterparts (Loman & Gunnar, 2010).

Gender differences also exist (Rothbart, 2011; Wentzel, Battle, Russell, & Looney, 2010). In general, girls are better at both reading and controlling their emotions. Boys are more likely to display anger and aggression, whereas girls tend to report feeling sad, fearful, or guilty. In classrooms, girls are more compliant and less likely to act out (Emmer & Evertson, 2013; Evertson & Emmer, 2013). Explanations for these gender differences include maturational differences in the brain, that is, the part of the brain responsible for controlling emotions develops more quickly in girls (Rothbart, 2011), hormonal influences (Davila, 2008), and differences in the ways boys and girls are socialized (Kennedy Root & Denham, 2010; Weisgram, Bigler, & Liben, 2010). These differences are reflected in the fact that boys are diagnosed as having emotional or behavioral problems much more often than girls (Hallahan, Kauffman, & Pullen, 2012; Hardman, Drew, & Egan, 2014).

Cultural differences also exist. Western cultures, such as ours, which tend to emphasize individualism, are more likely to teach and reinforce individuals' expressions of emotions (Morelli & Rothbaum, 2007; Miller, 2013). Collectivist cultures, such as those found in many Asian countries, are more likely to reward conformity, encourage individuals to think of the common good, and suppress individual emotions for the good of the group.

Poverty is an additional factor, and it influences emotional development in several ways. For example, the physical and psychological challenges that children experience growing up in poverty can inhibit healthy brain development (Hackman & Farah, 2012). Also, students worried about where their next meal will come from are more prone to depression, anxiety, and behavior problems (Crossnoe & Cooper, 2010; Kagan, 2010). And the challenges that many families in poverty face, such as paying bills and putting food on the table, can create home environments where the security needed for healthy emotional development is missing.

For all children, some emotional stress can be healthy because it provides experience that can contribute to healthy emotional development (Pulvermüller & Fadiga, 2010). However, emotional challenges that are too great can have a negative impact on emotional self-regulation and overall personality development (Braaten, 2011; Sawyer et al., 2010).

Personality Development and Achievement

So what does personality development have to do with academic achievement in schools and later workplace achievement and success after the school years? A considerable amount of research has examined this question, and we discuss this research in this section.

PERSONALITY AND SCHOOL ACHIEVEMENT

First, with respect to schools and learning, a strong link exists between academic achievement and *openness* and *conscientiousness,* particularly in adolescents. This is likely the result of conscientious students being able to set learning goals, regulate their behavior, and persist until goals are met. Similarly, students open to experiences may achieve higher because they respect and appreciate knowledge and discovery (Caprara, Vecchione, Alessandri, Gerbino, & Barbaranelli, 2011; Zuffianò et al., 2013). Additional research has identified links between academic achievement and *extraversion, openness,* and *conscientiousness* in younger students (Neuenschwander, Cimeli, Röthlisberger, & Roebers, 2013). These results make sense. We would intuitively predict, for example, that conscientious students who are open to new ideas would learn more and be higher achievers.

Emotions are also linked to achievement. For example, positive emotions, such as enjoyment, hope, and pride, are associated with both motivation and learning (Pekrun et al., 2011), likely because students experiencing positive emotions are able to focus on learning tasks (Durlak, Weissberg, Dymnicki, Taylor, & Schellinger, 2011; Helmsen, Koglin, & Petermann, 2012).

Negative emotions are a bit more complex. For instance, boredom, a sense of hopelessness, and shame—particularly if shame results from students believing that they lack ability—have negative effects on motivation and learning (Linnenbrink, 2007; Pekrun et al., 2011). On the other hand, some research suggests that slightly increased levels of anxiety and feelings of guilt—particularly if the guilt results from students' believing that they didn't try hard enough—can increase persistence on challenging tasks (Tulis & Fulmer, 2013).

Emotions and particularly emotional self-regulation are also linked to social success and social satisfaction. For example, students who are able to regulate their emotions are happier and better able to make and keep friends than those who exhibit less self-control (Durlak et al., 2011; Helmsen et al., 2012; Kross & Grossman, 2012).

This research also helps us answer the second and third questions we asked at the beginning of the chapter: "Is Amanda's assessment likely to be accurate, that is, will Sean's attitude affect his academic work?" and "Why doesn't Sean get along with the other students?" Yes, Sean's attitude is indeed likely to be affecting his academic work, and his personality characteristics are making it difficult for him to get along with his peers.

PERSONALITY AND WORKPLACE ACHIEVEMENT

Personality and workplace achievement have also been thoroughly researched. The relationship between high conscientiousness, low neuroticism, and high job performance is one of the best-known findings (Hurtz & Donovan, 2000). These traits are also linked to work motivation and satisfaction (Woods et al., 2013). As we might expect, workers high in *extraversion* have higher levels of job satisfaction when employed in positions that require a great deal of social interaction, such as sales (Saksvik & Hetland, 2011).

The foundation for these relationships begins early in children's lives and is strongly influenced by schooling. "[T]here appears to be an early interaction of personality and work . . . The pathways of working life and the role of work in identity seem to be set in 'skeleton form' in early years of childhood" (Woods et al., 2013, p. S9). Researchers also believe that schooling is a primary influence on the development of positive personality traits, such as *agreeableness, openness,* and *conscientiousness,* and an important source of socialization for the world of work. For instance, to succeed in school, students must take on duties and responsibilities and commit to role expectations and social norms. They must also be able to delay gratification and to be task and goal directed and organized, all of which contribute to the development of positive personality traits and success in the workplace (Bleidorn, 2012). Further, some research suggests that personality, and particularly *conscientiousness,* has a stronger influence on success in both school and work performance than does cognitive ability (Zyphur, Chaturvedi, & Arvey, 2008).

So, what can we, as teachers, do to develop these positive personality traits? We address this question next.

Educational Psychology and Teaching: Supporting Your Students' Personality Development

Two aspects of our study to this point are important. First, our students don't come to us with personalities that are fixed and unalterable; as we saw above, schooling can have a positive impact on personality development. Second, our jobs involve much more than teaching reading, math, history, and other forms of content. They also include helping our students develop the positive personality traits associated with school achievement and satisfaction with school, as well as success in later life.

The following guidelines can help us meet these goals.

- Learn about our students as people.
- Model positive personality traits.
- Use concrete examples to teach positive personality traits.
- Discuss positive personality traits and their relationships with success and achievement.
- Use an authoritative classroom management style.

As we discuss these guidelines, we will be focusing on the cognitive component of personality development, because it is largely through awareness and understanding that students can positively alter their personalities. We turn to them now.

Learn About Our Students as People. Our students are obviously unique, and, in order to best promote their development, we need to know about their unique personality characteristics. We can make formal efforts to learn about our students with simple activities such as having them to fill out a short questionnaire that asks about their favorite foods, hobbies, sports, and other aspects of their lives. Doing so doesn't take a great deal of effort, and merely asking the questions communicates that we're interested in them as human beings and promotes a positive relationship with them. "There is a growing consensus that the nature and quality of children's relationships with their teachers play a critical and central role in . . . teaching them what they need to know to become knowledgeable and productive citizens" (Wentzel, 2010, p. 75).

Also, as we interact with our students, we will learn a great deal about who is extraverted, agreeable, shy, and other personality traits, and we can adapt our instruction accordingly, again without a great deal of extra effort. For instance, we can adjust our questioning in learning activities for students low in extraversion, so they are assured of being able to answer, and, over time, they can at least partially overcome their shyness. Let's look at an example.

Suppose you're an elementary teacher working with your students in math, and you've presented the following problem:

> Jeremy has been working on his tablet computer for 20 minutes, and Cindy has been working on hers for 35 minutes. How much longer has Cindy worked than has Jeremy?

You can then call on a student who is reluctant to speak up in class with the directive: "Tell us something about this problem." The student can then offer a wide variety of answers, such as:

> The students are working on tablet computers.
> It's about a boy and a girl.
> The boy worked on his tablet for 20 minutes.
> The girl worked on hers longer than the boy.
> The problem asks us to find out how much longer that girl worked.

When students get used to this process (i.e., instead of asking for a specific response, which is typical in classroom activities, *you really are* simply asking them to tell you something about the problem), they often become much more willing to respond. Our ability to adapt our work with our students in this way is called **goodness of fit** (Rothbart, 2011; Rudasill, Gallagher, & White, 2010).

We can also combine whole-group learning activities with small-group work to help develop traits such as *openness* and *agreeableness.* As we introduce the group work, we can emphasize positive behaviors, such as listening politely while group mates are talking and providing supportive comments, and then monitor groups to ensure that students are demonstrating these behaviors.

Using strategies such as these to develop positive personality traits will obviously take time, and they won't work with every student, but over the course of a school year, they can make a difference. This is what we're trying to accomplish.

Model Positive Personality Traits. Arguably, modeling positive personality characteristics is the most effective action we can take in promoting these same characteristics in our students. Modeling openness, agreeableness, conscientiousness, and emotional stability takes no extra effort, and over time it can increase the likelihood of students developing these same characteristics. Since most people who go into teaching possess positive personality characteristics, modeling them will quickly become second nature. And we have nothing to lose in doing so. They will make a difference with at least some students, and even if they didn't, we are still happier people as a result of our modeling.

Use Concrete Examples to Teach Positive Personality Traits. We have emphasized *awareness* in this discussion because students often don't realize that they possess undesirable personality traits. For instance, how many people would describe themselves as disagreeable? Very few. We all like to think of ourselves as open, agreeable, conscientious, and emotionally stable.

We can't simply tell students that they are, for example, disagreeable. But we can illustrate and discuss desirable and undesirable personality characteristics, and this is what we mean by "Use concrete examples to teach positive personality traits." Let's look at an illustration.

> Ramon Jiménez, a middle school teacher, is making a formal effort to help his students develop positive personality traits. He displays a description of each of the traits on his document camera and then says, "These traits can influence our success in school and life outside of school. Let's look at a couple examples."
>
> Collin brings all his materials to school every day, and he always carefully does his homework. When he is involved in group work, he listens patiently

when a group mate is talking and he will often make comments, such as "That's a good thought," and even when he disagrees, he'll say, "I don't quite agree with that, but it's an interesting point." Collin also eagerly dives into the study of new topics.

Collin is learning a lot and he is well liked by the other students.

Jonathan often gets into trouble with his teachers because he forgets to bring his book, notebook, or pencil to class, and he will periodically blow off his homework with comments like, "When will I ever need to understand this stuff?" When he works in groups, he'll sometimes make fun of his group mates and make comments such as, "That was a dumb idea."

Jonathan's grades aren't very good, and his classmates will sometimes say they don't want to be in the same group with him.

"What are some differences you notice between Collin and Jonathan?" Ramon asks after giving students a minute to read the vignettes.

The students make several comments, and in the process, Ronise concludes, "It's his own fault," in response to someone pointing out that Jonathan isn't learning very much and not getting along with the other students.

"Yes," Ramon nods, "if we aren't conscientious and don't take responsibility for ourselves and control our own actions and emotions, whose fault is it if we don't learn?"

"Our own," several students respond.

"Yes," Ramon emphasizes. "We're all responsible for ourselves."

With Ramon's guidance, the students also conclude that Collin is open and agreeable, which—in addition to his conscientiousness—helps explain why he is doing well in school and is well liked by his classmates.

Formally teaching personality traits such as *conscientiousness, agreeableness,* and *openness,* the way Ramon did, capitalizes on the cognitive component of personality development. In fact, seeing behaviors and consequences concretely illustrated is more effective than hearing them described by teachers. It becomes harder, for example, for students to be disagreeable when they understand that disagreeableness leads to negative outcomes, and they know that other students are aware of both the trait and its consequences.

Discuss Positive Personality Traits and Their Relationships with Success and Achievement. We've emphasized the cognitive component of personality development, and the term *cognitive* refers to thinking. This means that with awareness and thought, students can work to develop positive personality traits. Concrete examples, such as those Ramon used, provide a reference point for discussions of personality traits and their impact on success, and discussions centered on the examples are the mechanisms we can use in our attempts to increase students' awareness and understanding. For instance, disagreeable people aren't "stuck" with being disagreeable forever. Realizing that agreeableness can lead to improved social relationships, they can try to develop this desirable trait. Further, if students understand that openness and conscientiousness are associated with academic success, they're also more likely to attempt to develop these characteristics.

Again, we have nothing to lose in making our students aware of desirable personality traits and attempting to help them understand how these traits link to academic and social success.

Use an Authoritative Classroom Management Style. Earlier in our discussion, we saw that an authoritative parenting style is generally more effective than those that are authoritarian, permissive, or uninvolved. The same tends to be true for classroom management. The interaction styles of effective teachers are similar to those of effective parents,

Classroom **Connections**

Promoting Personality Development in Classrooms

1. The development of positive personality traits is important for both success in school and success in life after the school years. Systematically promote these characteristics in students.

   ■ **Elementary:** In an effort to promote agreeableness and conscientiousness, a kindergarten teacher emphasizes and models being kind to classmates, sharing materials, and always doing assigned work. Knowing that young children bask in praise, she openly praises students when she sees them display these traits.

   ■ **Middle School:** Over the school year, a seventh-grade teacher discusses each of the "Big Five" personality traits with her students, and, knowing that peers and social acceptance are becoming increasingly important to them, emphasizes that personality traits, such as agreeableness and emotional stability, are important for making and keeping friends. She conducts periodic classroom meetings to discuss what can be done to make their classroom a positive learning environment.

   ■ **High School:** An 11th-grade teacher presents information about personality traits and how they're related to success when her students go to college or enter the workplace. She particularly emphasizes the relationships between high conscientiousness, emotional self-regulation, and success in the world of work. She uses classroom incidents as opportunities to discuss the relationships between personality traits and success in life after school.

2. Emotions and particularly emotional self-regulation are related to both school and social success. Promote emotional self-regulation in your students.

   ■ **Elementary:** When one of her students displays inappropriate emotions, such as an emotional outburst, a first-grade teacher stops her learning activity and discusses the incident and what the child might have done differently. She then models an appropriate emotional response, and she openly praises students when she sees them demonstrate appropriate behaviors.

   ■ **Middle School:** An eighth-grade teacher describes the characteristics of emotional self-regulation, and to reinforce the process, periodically has her students role-play inappropriate and appropriate emotional responses to illustrate emotional self-regulation. She emphasizes the relationship between emotional self-regulation and social success.

   ■ **High School:** A 10th-grade teacher uses written case studies (similar to the case study with Ramon Jiménez) to illustrate the relationships between emotions and both physical and psychological health. He also illustrates the characteristics of emotional self-regulation with the same strategy. He revisits the discussions throughout the school year to emphasize the relationships between emotions and overall well-being.

and the description of authoritative parenting strongly parallels recommended classroom management practices for teachers (Emmer & Evertson, 2013; Evertson & Emmer, 2013). This suggests that we should set boundaries for our students, provide reasons for our rules, enforce the rules consistently, and explain how rules help protect the rights and feelings of others. Over time, these practices contribute to positive personality traits, such as openness, agreeableness, and conscientiousness. (You will likely take a classroom management course as part of your teacher preparation program, and Chapter 12 of this text focuses on classroom management. In either case, you will be able to study the topic in much more detail than in this short section.)

Development of Identity and Self-Concept

As we navigate through life, we construct beliefs about who we are and our capabilities for dealing with life's challenges. These beliefs influence how happy and productive we become. They also apply in schools; students' **identities**, their self-constructed definitions of who they are, what their existence means, and what they want in life, combine with their **self-concepts**, cognitive assessments of their physical, social, and academic competence, to influence the way they respond to school and life in general. We consider these aspects of development in this section, beginning with a discussion of Erik Erikson's theory of psychosocial development and how it relates to the concept of identity.

Ed Psych and You

Do you generally trust people? Do you feel capable and competent? Are you in a relationship with someone "special," and do you believe the relationship will help you develop as a person?

Erikson's Theory of Psychosocial Development

Questions such as the ones we asked in *Ed Psych and You* are central to the work of Erik Erikson (1902–1994), a developmental psychologist and psychoanalyst who addressed issues such as trust, competence, and intimacy in his work with clients. He also personally wrestled with them in what he called a "crisis of identity" in his own life (Cross, 2001). Based on these experiences, he developed a theory of "psychosocial" development. The term *psychosocial* derives from the integration of identity (the psychological component of the term) and his belief that people have an innate desire to connect with others, making social factors primary motivators for human behavior (Erikson, 1968, 1980).

Erikson believed that all people have the same basic needs, which center on human relations. He also believed that personal development occurs in response to those needs, and healthy development depends on the quality of support provided by the social environment, particularly parents and other caregivers. Like other developmental psychologists, such as Piaget, he believed that development proceeds in stages, each characterized by a **crisis**, a psychosocial challenge that presents opportunities for development. Although never permanently resolved, the positive resolution of a crisis at one stage contributes to healthy identity formation and increases the likelihood of a positive resolution at the next.

Analyzing **Theories**

Evaluating Erikson's Work

Erikson's work was popular and influential in the 1960s and 1970s, but since then, developmental theorists have taken issue with it on three major points. First, they contend that his theory doesn't adequately address the role of culture in development. For instance, some cultures discourage autonomy, initiative, and self-assertiveness in children, instead emphasizing a collective sense of belonging and concern for others (Chen & Eisenberg, 2012). Research suggests that culture is indeed an important influence in all forms of development (Cole & Cagigas, 2010; Cole & Packer, 2011).

Second, critics point out that Erikson based his theory primarily on his work with males, and research suggests that females may take different paths to identity development (DiDonato & Berenbaum, 2013; Gilligan, 1977, 1982, 1998).

Third, Erikson based his theory on his personal notes and experiences dealing with clients, and his theory is difficult to validate empirically. Also, his work is grounded in the time in which he lived and practiced, and it may not accurately explain developmental changes influenced by our current society, which is quite different.

Erikson's work is intuitively sensible, however, and he was the first to recognize the role that identity formation plays in becoming a productive, happy adult. In addition, it helped focus attention on our need for relatedness, the innate need to feel loved, connected to, and respected by other people (Deci & Ryan, 2008; Moller, Deci, & Elliott, 2010; Pavey, Greitemeyer, & Sparks, 2010). It also helps us understand problems we encounter in classrooms. For example, we might explain Sean's contention (in our case study at the beginning of the chapter) that the other students are "out to get him" by saying that he hasn't positively resolved the trust–distrust crisis. This has left him less able to develop a sense of autonomy, initiative, or industry, which helps us understand why it's affecting his academic work. We've all met people we admire because of their positive outlook, openness, and commitment to making the world better. We've also encountered those who believe that others are trying to take advantage of them or are somehow inherently evil. We see good minds sliding into lethargy because of a lack of initiative or even substance abuse. We become frustrated by people's apathy and lack of a zest for living. Erikson's work helps us understand these issues. His theory, including its contributions and criticisms, is outlined in Table 3.2.

Table 3.1	Erikson's eight life-span stages
Trust vs. Mistrust (Birth to 1 year)	Trust develops when infants receive consistently loving care. Mistrust results from unpredictable or harsh care.
Autonomy vs. Shame (1–3 years)	Autonomy develops when children use their newly formed mental and psychomotor skills to explore their worlds. Parents support autonomy by encouraging exploration and accepting the inevitable mistakes.
Initiative vs. Guilt (3–6 years)	Initiative, a sense of ambition and responsibility, develops from encouragement of children's efforts to explore and take on new challenges. Overcontrol or criticism can result in guilt.
Industry vs. Inferiority (6–12 years)	School and home provide opportunities for students to develop a sense of competence through success on challenging tasks. A pattern of failure can lead to feelings of inferiority.
Identity vs. Confusion (12–18 years)	Adolescents experiment with various roles in an atmosphere of freedom with clearly established limits. Confusion results when the home environment fails to provide either the necessary structure or when it is overly controlling, failing to provide opportunities for individual exploration with different identity roles.
Intimacy vs. Isolation (Young adulthood)	Intimacy occurs when individuals establish close ties with others. Emotional isolation may result from earlier disappointments or a lack of developing identity.
Generativity vs. Stagnation (Adulthood)	Generativity occurs when adults give to the next generation through child rearing, productive work, and contributions to society or other people. Apathy or self-absorption can result from an inability to think about or contribute to the welfare of others.
Integrity vs. Despair (Old age)	Integrity occurs when people believe they've lived as well as possible and accept the inevitability of death. Remorse over things done or left undone leads to despair.

Erikson's stages help us answer the questions we asked in *Ed Psych and You*. For instance, if you generally trust people, he would say that you have positively resolved the *trust versus mistrust* crisis, and if you feel capable and competent, you've successfully resolved the *industry versus inferiority* crisis. Similarly, if you are in a meaningful and rewarding relationship with a significant other, he would say you've positively resolved the *intimacy versus isolation* crisis.

Failure to resolve a crisis at one or more stages doesn't doom people to dysfunctional lives, and we all have personal "flaws." For example, we know people who seem to lack initiative, but function well in roles where initiative isn't a major requirement. Similarly, we know self-described "loners" who have satisfying careers and who seem perfectly happy with their lives. Erikson's stages are summarized in Table 3.1.

Contemporary Views of Identity Development

Erikson believed that questions about identity begin in adolescence and attempts to answer them involve temporary periods of distress during which teenagers explore alternatives before committing to values and goals that will guide them throughout life. We've all heard—or perhaps have even used—the term *identity crisis*, which is his description of these periods of distress. He believed they were both inevitable and desirable as young people evolve into healthy adults.

Contemporary perspectives view identity development not so much as a crisis, but rather a gradual process of experimenting with different potential life directions and ultimately deciding on a course of action (Marcia, 1980, 1987, 2010). Let's look at an illustration.

Table 3.2	Analyzing theories: Erikson's theory of psychosocial development
Major question	How does psychosocial development occur throughout the life span?
Key concepts	Crisis (psychosocial challenge) Stages of development • Trust v. mistrust • Autonomy v. shame • Initiative v. guilt • Industry v. inferiority • Identity v. confusion • Intimacy v. isolation • Generativity v. stagnation • Integrity v. despair
Description of psychosocial development	Psychosocial development occurs when individuals accomplish positive resolutions of crises (psychosocial challenges) at a particular stage of development, which increases the likelihood of a positive resolution at the next stage.
Catalyst for development	• Meeting (or not meeting) life's challenges, which differ at various stages of our lives • Quality of support provided by the social environment, particularly parents and other caregivers
Contributions	• Reminds us that development is a process that continues throughout our life spans • Places the individual at the center of identity development and describes development as an active process • Helps explain a considerable amount of behavior we observe in others
Criticisms	• His theory fails to adequately account for the influence of culture (e.g., some cultures discourage rather than encourage autonomy and initiative). • Erikson based his theory primarily on his work with men, and for women the psychosocial challenge of intimacy often occurs before a focus on personal identity. • His theory is based on his notes and experiences rather than systematic research. • His theory may not reflect current societal conditions.

Sources: Berk, 2013; Erikson, 1963, 1968, 1972, 1980; Feldman, 2014.

Four high school seniors are talking about what they plan to do after they graduate.

"I'm not sure what I want to do," Sandy comments. "I've thought about veterinary medicine, and also about teaching. I've been working at the vet clinic, and I like it, but I'm not sure about doing it forever. Some of my parents' friends are teachers, so I hear what they say about it. I don't know."

"I'm off to the university in the fall," Nathan replies. "I'm going to be a lawyer. At least that's what my parents think. It's not a bad job, and lawyers make good money."

"How can you just do that?" Nancy wonders. "You said you don't want to be a lawyer. . . . I'm going to think about it for a while. . . . I'm only 17, and I'm not willing to decide yet."

"I'm going into nursing," Taylor comments. "I've been working part-time at the hospital, and it feels good to work with people and help them. I've talked with the counselors, and I think I can do the chemistry and other science courses."

To study the development of identity, researchers interviewed adolescents and found that young people's decisions can be classified into one of four states, which vary in their

Table 3.3	States in identity development
State	**Description**
Identity diffusion	A state of identity development that occurs when individuals fail to make clear choices. The state is characterized by haphazard experimentation with different career options. Individuals may not be developmentally ready to make decisions.
Identity foreclosure	A state of identity development that occurs when individuals prematurely adopt the positions of others, such as parents.
Identity moratorium	A state of identity development that occurs when individuals pause and remain in a "holding pattern." Long-range commitment is delayed.
Identity achievement	A state of identity development that occurs after individuals make decisions about goals and commitments.

ability to produce healthy outcomes (Marcia, 1980, 1987, 1999, 2010). The states are outlined in Table 3.3.

As we see in Table 3.3, *identity diffusion*, common in younger adolescents and illustrated by Sandy's consideration of both veterinary medicine and teaching, reflects haphazard consideration of different career choices. If it persists over time, it can result in apathy and confusion (Berzonsky, 2011; Berzonsky, Cieciuch, Duriez, & Soenens, 2011). *Identity foreclosure*, illustrated by Nathan's comment, occurs when adolescents prematurely adopt the goals and values of others—usually their parents—without thoroughly examining the implications for their futures.

Identity moratorium, as illustrated by Nancy's comment, involves exploration without reaching a firm commitment or conclusion. This is a positive exploratory state that involves thinking and weighing options that may eventually lead to *identity achievement*, which is also positive. Taylor's commitment to nursing illustrates this state. As we might expect, many adolescents experience both identity diffusion and identity moratorium before arriving at identity achievement.

Our example involved a discussion among high school students, and as we saw there, only Taylor had reached the state of identity achievement. This is consistent with research indicating, in contrast with Erikson's theory, that identity achievement in our modern society more commonly occurs after—instead of during—high school (Berzonsky, 2011; Duriez, Luyckx, Soenens, & Berzonsky, 2012; Kroger, Martinussen, & Marcia, 2010). This delay is especially true for college students, who have more time to consider what they want to do with their lives and often change their majors a number of times during their college careers (Klimstra, Hale, Raaijmakers, Branje, & Meeus, 2010).

SEXUAL IDENTITY

Sexual identity, people's definitions of who they are with respect to gender orientation, is another important element of identity formation. Sexual identity influences student choices ranging from clothes and friends to the occupations they consider and ultimately pursue (Martin & Ruble, 2010). **Sexual orientation**, the gender to which an individual is romantically and sexually attracted, is an important dimension of sexual identity.

For most students, sexual orientation is not a major issue, but for an estimated 3% to 10% of the student population it is confusing and stressful (Macionis, 2013). Attempts to pinpoint the causes of homosexuality are controversial, with some believing that it is genetic and others attributing it to learning and choice (Gollnick & Chinn, 2013). Most researchers point to genetic causes, however. "The evidence to date indicates that genetic and prenatal biological influences are largely responsible for homosexuality" (Berk, 2013, p. 215). Further evidence exists in studies of twins. If one member of identical twins is homosexual, for example, the other is much more likely to also be homosexual than is the case with fraternal twins (Bailey, 1993).

Research also suggests that homosexuals go through a three-phase sequence in their attempts to understand who they are (Berk, 2013). The first is feeling different, a slowly developing awareness that they aren't like other children, which is followed by a feeling of confusion, often occurring in adolescence. In this phase, homosexuals attempt to understand their developing sexuality, looking for both social support and role models. Finally, in the third phase, the majority of gay and lesbian teenagers accept their homosexuality and share it with those who are close to them.

Diversity: Ethnic Identity

"**Ethnic identity** [emphasis added] refers to an individual's sense of belonging to an ethnic group, which is defined by one's cultural heritage, and includes attributes such as values, traditions, and language" (Brittian, Umaña-Taylor, & Derlan, 2013, p. 178). Researchers suggest that ethnic identity is particularly important for members of cultural minorities living in a heterogeneous society, because the identity may provide members with a sense of belonging and acceptance in societies where the majority group sometimes holds negative stereotypes about them. This sense of belonging helps diffuse the negative effects of social devaluation that members of minorities sometimes feel (Brittian et al., 2013).

The family is key in this process (Umaña-Taylor, Alfaro, Bámaca, & Guimond, 2009). It is through the family that minority adolescents investigate their ethnicity and come to understand what it means to be a member of their ethnic group, and it can be particularly important in societies such as the United States where members of ethnic minorities often believe that majority groups have access to privileges that minority groups don't have. In these contexts, positive ethnic identity can protect individuals' sense of self-worth (Brittian et al., 2013).

Let's examine this idea in more detail.

ETHNICITY AND SELF-ESTEEM

Self-esteem, or **self-worth**, as it is sometimes called, is an emotional reaction to, or an evaluation of, the self (Schunk et al., 2014), and it raises a number of personal questions. Will others like us? Are we perceived as smart? Do people think we're attractive? Culture plays a role in helping answer these questions, and it is particularly important for members of cultural minorities.

Collective self-esteem refers to individuals' perceptions of the relative worth of the groups to which they belong. When these groups are valued by society and perceived as having positive status, personal identities and self-esteem are enhanced (Jaspal & Cinnirella, 2012). The opposite is also true.

Even very young children know they are members of an ethnic minority, and research dating back nearly 80 years indicates that children who are members of cultural minorities such as African Americans (Clark & Clark, 1939), Mexican Americans (Weiland & Coughlin, 1979), and Chinese Americans (Aboud & Skerry, 1984) evaluate their ethnic reference groups as less worthy than the White majority. As children who are in ethnic minority groups develop, they become increasingly aware of problems with inequality and discrimination (Brittian et al., 2013; Coker et al., 2009). These problems are especially acute for recent immigrants, who also face language barriers (Glick & Bates, 2010; Hernandez, Denton, & Macartney, 2010).

Many cultural minorities experience hardships linked to poverty, crime, and drug use, and schools that are unresponsive to their needs can retard the development of self-esteem (Jaspal & Cinnirella, 2012; Olmedo, 2009). Unique challenges often exist for students who are members of ethnic minorities, and sensitive teachers are crucial in helping these students form positive, healthy identities.

ETHNIC PRIDE AND IDENTITY FORMATION

Students with positive ethnic identities are better adjusted, achieve higher in school, and have more positive beliefs about their ability to cope with their environments (Ghavami, Fingerhut, Peplau, Grant, & Wittig, 2011; Marks, Patton, & Coll, 2011). In addition they are less likely to use drugs or engage in risky behaviors (Brook, Zhang, Finch, & Brook, 2010). We discuss ways you can contribute to positive ethnic identity formation in the section "Educational Psychology and Teaching: Supporting Your Students' Identity and Self-Concept Development" later in our discussion.

Ed Psych and You

How smart are you? What subjects, such as math or history, are you best at? Are you athletic? How popular are you?

The Development of Self-Concept

Your responses to our questions in *Ed Psych and You* reflect different dimensions of your **self-concept**, which, as we saw at the beginning of this section, is a cognitive appraisal of our academic, physical, and social competences (Schunk et al., 2014). If you believe you're good at math, for instance, you have a positive academic self-concept in math. Or, if you believe you're a good athlete, you have a positive physical self-concept, and if you think you're good at getting along with people, you have a positive social self-concept. Self-concepts are formed largely on the basis of experiences and feedback, and forming healthy self-concepts is important for personal and social development (Kail, 2012).

SELF-CONCEPT AND SELF-ESTEEM

The terms *self-concept* and *self-esteem* are often used interchangeably, but they are actually quite different. Self-concept is cognitive, whereas, as we saw earlier in our discussion, self-esteem (self-worth) is an emotional reaction to the self (Matsumoto & Juang, 2012; Schunk et al., 2014). People who have high self-esteem believe that they are inherently worthy people and feel good about themselves. It's important, because low self-esteem during adolescence predicts poor health, criminal behavior, and limited economic prospects as adults (Baumeister, Campbell, Krueger, & Vohs, 2003; Trzesniewski et al., 2006).

Young children tend to have both high self-esteem and positive self-concepts—sometimes unrealistically so—probably because of few social comparisons and the support they receive from parents. This optimism is functional because it encourages young children to take chances and try new activities (Verschueren, Doumen, & Buyse, 2012). Self-esteem tends to drop during the transition from elementary to middle school, probably because of physical changes brought on by puberty and the less personal nature of middle schools. It then rises again during the high school years—to a greater extent for boys than girls (Matsumoto & Juang, 2012; Harter, 2006; Seaton, Marsh, & Craven, 2010).

Self-concepts become more realistic as interactions with others give students more accurate measures of their performance compared to their peers (Schunk et al., 2014; Seaton et al., 2010). As students move into adolescence, self-concept interacts with a developing sense of identity. Each influences the other, and both influence self-esteem (Chen, Hwang, Yeh, & Lin, 2012).

SELF-CONCEPT AND ACHIEVEMENT

A strong and robust relationship exists between academic self-concept and achievement, and this relationship makes sense intuitively. For example, students who believe they're good at math have this belief because they have a history of doing well in math, and the same is true for other academic areas.

Little relationship exists between physical self-concept and achievement (S. Chen et al., 2012), and this also makes sense. We've all known highly skilled athletes, for example, who are modest achievers.

The relationship between social self-concept and achievement is more complex. For instance, believing that we're socially skilled doesn't necessarily relate to achievement, but a link between social competence and academic achievement has been found beginning with children in early elementary school (Walker & Henderson, 2012). We examine these ideas in more detail when we discuss social development later in the chapter.

Educational Psychology and Teaching: Supporting Your Students' Identity and Self-Concept Development

As teachers we can strongly influence our students' developing identity and academic self-concepts. The following guidelines can help in our efforts to promote healthy development in these areas.

1. Support autonomy and initiative in your students.
2. Maintain high expectations and provide students with evidence of increasing competence.
3. Create a safe and caring learning community in your classroom.
4. Communicate that students' ethnic backgrounds are valued and contribute to learning.

Let's see how John Adler, an eighth-grade English teacher, attempts to implement these guidelines with his students.

"Here are your papers," John announces on Friday as he hands back a set of quizzes from the day before. "You did a good job and I'm proud of you. Your writing is really improving. . . . I know I expect a lot, but you've always risen to the task.

"Put your scores in your logs, and add your improvement points."

"Who improved the most, Mr. Adler?" Jeremy asks.

"That's not important," John replies. "Remember, we're all in this together. You take responsibility for your learning, I help you as much as I can, and we all try to improve . . . That's why I put your scores on the last page of the quizzes. They're your business, and no one else's.

"Now, I'd like to have a classroom meeting," he continues, changing the direction of the discussion. "One of you came to me after school yesterday, concerned about the way some of you are treating each other outside of class. . . . She didn't name names; she simply expressed a concern, and I really like it when someone acts on their own and takes the initiative to make our classroom better.

"I concur with her concern. . . . For instance, I saw one of you get tripped when you walked down the aisle, and another had water splashed on him at the water fountain. . . . I'm also seeing more litter on the floor.

"I'm disappointed with these behaviors. We're here to help one another. . . . So, I want to hear some ideas. What can we do to make our classroom better?"

The students offer comments, with suggestions ranging from kicking perpetrators out of class to talking to them to adding more rules. The students agree that John has been attempting to enforce the rules fairly, but because he expects everyone to be responsible, perhaps he has been too lenient in some cases.

At the meeting's end, the students agree to be more responsible, and John agrees to renew his efforts to consistently enforce classroom rules.

Now, let's look at John's attempts to apply the guidelines.

Support Autonomy and Initiative in Your Students. As teachers, we can support psychosocial development in a variety of ways. For example, if you're planning to teach in preschool or early elementary grades, you can encourage children to complete tasks for themselves and reward them for taking initiative. And even though John is a middle school teacher, he realizes that no crisis is ever permanently resolved, so he publicly reinforced one of his student's autonomy and initiative with his comment, "I really like it when someone acts on their own and takes the initiative to make our classroom better." Although the comment targeted one student, its positive tone communicated to all that personal initiative was valued in John's classroom.

Maintain High Expectations and Provide Students with Evidence of Increasing Competence. As we saw earlier, students develop self-concepts on the basis of feedback they receive about their competence. Efforts to improve self-concept (and self-esteem) directly through activities that focus explicitly on these constructs, such as having minority students study multicultural learning materials, sending children to summer camps, and implementing support groups, are misguided and largely unsuccessful (O'Mara, Marsh, Craven, & Debus, 2006; Schunk et al., 2014). The only legitimate way to improve students' self-concepts is by providing them with evidence that their competence is increasing. Let's look again at the case study with John and his students.

John:	Here are your papers. You did a good job and I'm proud of you. Your writing is really improving. . . . I know I expect a lot, but you've always risen to the task. Put your scores in your logs, and add your improvement points.
Jeremy:	Who improved the most, Mr. Adler?
John:	That's not important. . . . Remember, we're all in this together. You take responsibility for your learning, I help you as much as I can, and we all try to improve. That's why I put your scores on the last page of the quizzes. They're your business, and no one else's.

Personal improvement is the key to perceptions of increasing competence, and it also helps students achieve a positive resolution of the industry–inferiority crisis. This is the reason John emphasized improvement versus actual scores, and it's also why he put students' scores in the last page of their quizzes in a symbolic gesture of deemphasizing competition.

This makes sense. In competitive classrooms, only the very highest achievers consistently receive top scores on assessments, which makes achieving a sense of competence—and with it, improved self-concepts—virtually impossible for many, if not most students.

Create a Safe and Caring Learning Community in Your Classroom. To understand how John attempted to make his classroom a safe and caring learning community, let's look again at some of John's comments:

"Now, I'd like to have a classroom meeting. . . . One of you came to me after school yesterday, concerned about the way some of you are treating each other outside of class. . . .

> I concur with her concern. . . . For instance, I saw one of you get tripped when you walked down the aisle, and another had water splashed on him at the water fountain. . . . I'm also seeing more litter on the floor.
>
> "I'm disappointed at these behaviors. We're here to help one another. . . . So, I want to hear some ideas. What can we do to make our classroom better?"

Creating a safe learning environment for all his students was John's goal in conducting the classroom meeting. A classroom structure that sets predictable limits for acceptable behavior, combined with the empathy that helps students negotiate the uncertainties of this period in their lives, is important. "[S]tudents . . . say that they want teachers to articulate and enforce clear standards of behavior. They view this not just as part of the teacher's job but as evidence that the teacher cares about them" (Brophy, 2010, p. 24). John teaches middle school students, but a safe and caring learning community is essential for students at all levels. This is particularly true for students who have exceptionalities and students who are gay or lesbian, who are often mistreated and experience discrimination at the hands of other students (Patrick, Bell, Huang, Lazarakis, & Edwards, 2013). Homosexual students are at greater risk for problems ranging from depression and substance abuse to suicide (McGuire, Anderson, Toomey, & Russell, 2010; Needham & Austin, 2010). Peer harassment is a major contributor to these problems, and you play an essential role in setting the tone for your classroom, ensuring that it is a safe place for all students.

Communicate That Students' Ethnic Backgrounds Are Valued and Contribute to Learning. To begin this section, let's look at an example based on an actual incident between a teacher and one of his students.

> Because Valdo Ayala, one of his Hispanic students, appears withdrawn and emotionally negative in class, David Haughy, an American history teacher, calls Valdo into his classroom early in the school year.
>
> "Where are you from, Valdo?" David asks.
>
> ". . . Puerto Rico."
>
> "Oh, wow!" David exclaims enthusiastically. "My wife and I were in San Juan during the summer, and we loved it. . . . We went down into old San Juan, ate in some of the local restaurants, and listened to some great music. . . . San Juan was great, and we're already talking about going back." (Excerpt based on a conversation Paul, one of your authors, had with a teacher and graduate student in one of his classes.)

As David described it in the conversation, this simple expression of enthusiasm about being in San Juan resulted in a complete turnaround in Valdo's attitude. We're all emotional beings, and David's affirmation communicated to Valdo that he was welcome and valued in David's classroom.

Let's look at another teacher's efforts.

> Maria Robles squeezes her mother's hand as they enter her new school. Her mother can tell she is nervous as she anxiously eyes the bigger boys and girls walking down the hallway.
>
> As they enter a kindergarten classroom, Carmen Avilla, her teacher, comes to greet them. "Hola. ¿Cómo te llamas, niña?" (Hello. What is your name, little one?)
>
> Maria, hiding behind her mother, is still uneasy but feels some relief.

"Dile tu nombre" (Tell her your name), her mother prompts, squeezing her hand and smiling.

". . . Maria," she offers hesitantly.

Her mother adds quickly, "Maria Robles. Yo soy su madre." (I am her mother.)

Carmen looks on her list, finds Maria's name, and checks it off. Then she invites them, in Spanish, to come into the room and meet the other boys and girls. Music is playing in the background. Maria recognizes some of her friends who are playing with toys in a corner of the room.

"Maria, ven aquí y juega con nosotros." (Maria, come here and play with us.)

Maria hesitates for a moment, looks up at her mother, and then runs over to join her friends.

You may not be able to greet a student in Spanish, but you can make them feel welcome in your classroom with simple gestures, such as those Carmen used. The way we react to students, as Carmen did with Maria, has a powerful impact on their developing identities and sense of cultural self-worth (Ahrens, DuBois, Lozano, & Richardson, 2010).

We can go farther by recognizing the achievements of ethnic minorities. For instance, providing a short biography of Julian Castro, a politician of Mexican descent, who was elected mayor of San Antonio, Texas, in 2009, reelected in 2011, and appointed to lead the Department of Housing and Urban Development in our nation's capital in 2014, communicates that the achievements of cultural minorities are recognized and respected. As another example, if you have students with Middle Eastern backgrounds in your class, you could emphasize the contributions of Omar Khayyám, a Persian philosopher and mathematician, who in the 11th and 12th centuries laid down the principles of algebra.

Examples for members of all minorities can be found, and emphasizing them communicates that you value and respect the backgrounds of all students in your classes. Doing so can make an important contribution to their sense of identity and increase their motivation to learn.

Classroom **Connections**

Promoting Psychosocial and Self-Concept Development

1. Erikson believed that social connections to others play a major role in promoting psychosocial development. Use social connection as an umbrella under which you interact with your students.

  - **Elementary:** A kindergarten student, while watering plants, knocks one over on the floor. Her teacher says evenly, "Sweep up the dirt, and wipe up the water with some paper towels." When the student is finished, the teacher hugs her and comments, "Everyone makes mistakes. The important thing is what we do about them."

  - **Middle School:** A math teacher designs her instruction so that all students are successful enough to develop a sense of industry. She spends extra time with students after school, and she lets students redo some of their assignments if they make an honest effort the first time. She frequently comments, "Math is for everyone—if you try!"

  - **High School:** A biology teacher pays little attention to the attire and slang of his students as long as offensive language isn't used, the rights of others are recognized, and learning occurs.

2. Success on challenging tasks is important for developing a sense of industry in students. Help students understand that effort leads to success and competence.

  - **Elementary:** A second-grade teacher carefully teaches a topic and provides precise directions before making seatwork assignments. She conducts "monitored practice" with the first few items to be sure all students get started correctly. When students encounter difficulties, she meets with them separately to provide extra support.

  - **Middle School:** A sixth-grade teacher develops a grading system based partially on improvement so that students can succeed by improving their performance. He regularly meets with them to help them monitor their learning progress.

  - **High School:** An art teacher uses portfolios and individual conferences to help her students set goals and see their growth over the year. During conferences, she emphasizes improvement and the link between effort and accomplishments.

3. Self-concepts develop from students meeting challenging experiences. Make students feel wanted and valued in your class. Provide learning experiences that promote success.

  ■ **Elementary:** A fourth-grade teacher starts the school year by having students bring in pictures of themselves and places them on a bulletin board together with personal information that students volunteer. They list interests and favorite activities and describe what they want to be when they grow up.

  ■ **Middle School:** A homeroom teacher for entering middle schoolers tries to make his classroom a place where students feel safe and secure. He begins the school year with classroom meetings where students get to know one another and form homeroom rules. As the year progresses, he uses these meetings to discuss issues and problems important to students.

  ■ **High School:** A ninth-grade English teacher begins each school year by announcing that everyone is important and that she expects everyone to learn. She structures her classrooms around success and minimizes competition. She also stays in her room after school and invites students who are having problems to come by for help.

Social Development

Social development describes the advances we make in our ability to interact and get along with others. A strong link exists between social development, school success, and success in later life. Children who have well-developed social skills achieve at higher levels, have higher self-esteem and fewer behavioral problems, attend school more regularly, and are more satisfied with their school experiences (Bornstein, Hahn, & Haynes, 2010; Vaughn et al., 2009; Zins, Bloodworth, Weissberg, Wang, & Walberg, 2004).

Social cognition, the ability to use cues to understand social interactions, is at the heart of social development (Hughes, Ensor, & Marks, 2010; Parke & Clarke-Stewart, 2011). **Social referencing**, people's ability to use vocal and nonverbal cues to evaluate ambiguous events and regulate their behaviors accordingly, is an aspect of social cognition (Pelaez, Virues-Ortega, Field, Amir-Kiaei, & Schnerch, 2013). For example, suppose we're in a social gathering with people we don't know well. Someone tells a story that has an unexpected ending, and we don't know whether to laugh or extend sympathy. So, we wait to see how others react in an effort to behave appropriately.

Even very young children have this ability, and some research suggests that toddlers acquire fear/avoidance behaviors from parents with anxiety disorders or depression through social referencing (Aktar, Majdandžić, Vente, & Bögels, 2014; Pelaez et al., 2013).

Influences on Social Development

As with all forms of development, social development depends on experience, and opportunities to interact with others and observe the consequences of our own and others' interactions are essential for healthy social development. This helps us understand why mothers of young children form "play groups" that provide these experiences for toddlers.

Parents, siblings, and peers are the groups that most strongly influence children's early social development. Initially, because of their proximity in the home, parents and siblings play the most important role, and later, as children mature and go to school, peers play a larger role. Let's look at the influence of these different groups.

PARENTS AND SIBLINGS

Social development begins in the home. Through their interactions with parents and siblings, young children learn how to use social interaction to get what they want (Bornstein & Lansford, 2010), and later they use these interactions to begin to understand others (Beisert et al., 2012; Cipriano & Stifter, 2010). As we saw in our discussion of parenting styles earlier in the chapter, parental influences are very powerful; parents who talk to their children about other people's thoughts, feelings, and motives promote young children's social cognition (Gehlbach, Brinkworth, & Harris, 2011; Sanders, 2010). And children learn social skills by observing their parents interact with others (Beisert et al., 2012).

Siblings assist in the process of social development. When we're young, we're in constant contact with our families and frequently interact with our brothers and sisters. Competition, negotiation, and compromise are a part of family life, and these experiences also help us acquire social skills (Caspi, 2012).

PEERS' INFLUENCE ON SOCIAL DEVELOPMENT

Ed Psych and You

Think back to the friends you had in middle and high school. How did your friends influence you then, and how do your friends influence who you are today?

As children grow older, peers—friends and classmates—play an increasingly prominent role in social development. Their influence exists in three areas (Hartup, 2009; Howe, 2010; Parke & Clarke-Stewart, 2011):

- Attitudes and values
- Opportunities to practice social skills
- Emotional support

Attitudes and Values. Peers communicate attitudes and values in areas ranging from the importance of schoolwork to definitions of right and wrong (Crossnoe, 2011; Parke & Clarke-Stewart, 2011). Our choice of friends predicts grades, involvement in school, and even behavior problems (Matjasko, Needham, Grunden, & Farb, 2010). If peer groups are academically oriented, they promote effort and achievement, but if they reject school values, students are more likely to cut classes, skip school, cheat, and even use drugs. The academic climate in classes in the same school can differ dramatically depending on the dominant peer groups in a particular classroom (Rubin et al., 2010).

Opportunities to Practice Social Skills. The extent to which we are able to make friends and establish meaningful relationships in life depends on social skills. Peers, and especially close friends, provide opportunities to practice these skills (Meadows, 2010; Coplan & Arbeau, 2009).

A snowballing effect exists. Students who have well-developed social skills are accepted by others, which gives them even more opportunities to practice and refine their social skills, whereas those lacking these skills are often rejected by peers, leading to fewer opportunities to practice and develop (Cillessen, Schwartz, & Mayeux, 2011; Mayeux, Houser, & Dyches, 2011; Rubin, Coplan, Chen, Bowker, & McDonald, 2011). Rejected students are often impulsive and aggressive, and over time they tend to withdraw. As a result, their learning and development often suffer (Bellmore, 2011; Swearer, Espelage, Vaillancourt, & Hymel, 2010).

Emotional Support. Peers, and especially friends, provide both emotional support and a sense of identity, and they also help adolescents understand that they aren't the only ones going through the sometimes confusing changes that occur during this period (Wentzel, 2009; Troutman & Fletcher, 2010; Jordan, 2006).

Students tend to select friends and seek emotional support from those who are similar in gender, ethnicity, socioeconomic status, academic orientation, and long-term goals (Peters,

Cillessen, Riksen-Walraven, & Haselager, 2010; Witvliet, van Lier, Cuijpers, & Koot, 2010). This makes sense, since we all tend to gravitate toward others who are like us. For example, when Paul's kids were in high school, they described themselves as "band nerds," since they tended to hang out with other students in the band. And Don's daughter, a volleyball player, tended to associate with other athletes.

These influences address the questions we asked in *Ed Psych and You* in this section. As you think about what you've just read, you will realize that your friends' attitudes and values are likely to be similar to yours, you practiced social skills in interacting with them, and they provided you with emotional support.

We turn now to perspective taking and social problem solving, two important dimensions of social development.

Perspective Taking: Understanding Others' Thoughts and Feelings

Perspective taking, the ability to understand other people's thoughts, feelings, and actions, is at the heart of social development (Hughes et al., 2010; Parke & Clarke-Stewart, 2011). Initially, children believe that everyone thinks and feels like they do, but over time they acquire a **theory of mind**, "[T]he ability to attribute mental states such as intentions and emotions to oneself or other persons" (Leipold, Vetter, Dittrich, Lehmann-Waffenschmidt, & Kliegel, 2013, p. 236). Or, put more simply, it is the understanding that others have distinctive perceptions, feelings, desires, and beliefs apart from our own (Parke & Clarke-Stewart, 2011). This is the beginning of perspective taking.

To see what perspective taking looks like in a classroom, let's look at four fifth graders working on a project. Notice how Mindy, one of the students in the group, uses this ability to negotiate a compromise when conflict occurs.

> Octavio, Mindy, Sarah, and Bill are studying American westward expansion in social studies. They'd been working as a group for 3 days and are preparing a report to be delivered to the class. There is some disagreement about who should present which topics.
>
> "So what should we do?" Mindy asks, looking at the others. "Octavio, Sarah, and Bill all want to report on the Pony Express."
>
> "I thought of it first," Octavio argues.
>
> "But everyone knows I like horses," Sarah counters.
>
> "Why don't we compromise?" Mindy suggests. "Octavio, didn't you say that you were kind of interested in railroads because your grandfather worked on them? Couldn't you talk to him and get some information for the report? And Sarah, I know you like horses. Couldn't you report on horses and the Plains Indians? . . . And Bill, what about you?"
>
> "I don't care . . . whatever," Bill replies, folding his arms and peering belligerently at the group.

As with all aspects of development, perspective taking develops slowly over time (Thompson et al., 2011; Burack et al., 2006). Before age 8, children typically don't understand events from others' perspectives, and it is often missing even in older children, as illustrated by Octavio's assertion, "I thought of it first," or Bill's angry response. As they mature and acquire social experiences, however, it improves.

People skilled in perspective taking can handle difficult social situations, are able to display empathy and compassion, and are better liked by their peers. Those less skilled tend to interpret others' intentions as hostile, which can lead to conflict, and they don't feel guilty or remorseful when they hurt other people's feelings (Spinrad & Eisenberg, 2009; Thompson & Newton, 2010).

This section addresses the third question we asked at the beginning of the chapter: "Why doesn't Sean get along with the other students?" His belief that the other kids are "out to get him" suggests underdeveloped perspective taking. He may also lack social problem-solving skills, the topic of our next section.

Social Problem Solving

Social problem solving is the ability to resolve conflicts in ways that are beneficial to all involved. As we would expect, social problem solving is linked to emotional intelligence (Erzözkan, 2013), and students who are good at it have more friends, fight less, and work more efficiently in groups than those who are less skilled (Honig, 2009; Patrick, Anderman, & Ryan, 2002). Mindy displayed this ability when she suggested a compromise acceptable to everyone.

Social problem solving typically occurs in four sequential steps (Eisenberg, Fabes, & Spinrad, 2006).

1. Observe and interpret social cues. ("Bill seems upset, probably because he isn't getting his first choice.")
2. Identify social goals. ("If we are going to finish this project, everyone must contribute.")
3. Generate strategies. ("Can we find different topics that will satisfy everyone?")
4. Implement and evaluate the strategies. ("This will work if everyone agrees to shift their topic slightly.")

Like perspective taking, social problem solving develops gradually and with practice (Parke & Clarke-Stewart, 2011; Jones, Brown, & Aber, 2011; Johnson & Johnson, 2006). Young children, for example, are not adept at reading social cues, and they tend to create simplistic solutions that satisfy themselves but not others. Older children realize that persuasion and compromise can benefit everyone, and they're better at adapting when initial efforts aren't successful.

Educational Psychology and Teaching: Applying an Understanding of Social Development with Your Students

In our discussion of personality development, we suggested that you do the following to promote it in your students:

- Model positive personality traits.
- Use concrete examples to teach positive personality traits.
- Discuss positive personality traits and their relationships with success and achievement.
- Use an authoritative classroom management style.

Parallel suggestions exist for social development. As with all forms of development, it has a cognitive component, and it's on this factor—students' awareness and understanding—that we want to capitalize as we attempt to help our students develop socially. In other words, we should model, explicitly teach and discuss social skills, and use a classroom management style that promotes social development.

Let's see how Teresa Manteras, a first-year teacher, attempts to promote social development in her students.

"How are you doing, Teresa?" Carla Ambergi, a veteran colleague, asks as Teresa enters the teachers' lounge.

"A little discouraged," Teresa sighs. "I learned about all those great cooperative learning activities in my university classes, but when I try them with my kids, all they do is snip at each other and argue about who is doing what. Maybe I should just lecture."

"They're not used to working in groups," Carla smiles, "and they haven't learned how to cooperate. They need practice."

"Yes, I know, . . . but I don't even know where to start."

"Would you like me to come in during my planning period? Maybe I can help."

"That would be great!" Teresa replies with a sense of relief.

Carla comes in the next day, and then she and Teresa sit down together after school. "First, I think you do an excellent job of modeling social skills," Carla comments. "You consider where the kids are coming from, you treat disagreements as an opportunity to solve problems, and you are supportive. . . . But, your modeling goes right over their heads. They don't notice what you're doing. So, I suggest that you be more specific; tell the kids what you're modeling and give them some examples. Then, add a few rules that will help guide their interactions with each other. It will take some time, but it will make a difference."

"Good points," Teresa nods. "I hadn't quite thought about it that way before."

Carla then helps Teresa develop several rules that address behavior in groups:

1. Listen politely until other people are finished before speaking.
2. Treat other people's ideas with courtesy and respect.
3. Paraphrase other people's ideas in your own words before disagreeing.
4. Encourage everyone to participate.

Teresa starts the next day. Before breaking students into groups, she tells them that they are going to work on their social skills, and she models several examples, such as making eye contact, checking perceptions, and listening attentively. Then, she presents and explains the new rules, has volunteers role-play an example for each, and guides a discussion of the examples.

Students then begin their group work. Teresa monitors the groups, intervenes when they have difficulties, and reconvenes the class when she sees a similar problem in several groups. The students are far from perfect, but they are improving.

Now let's look at Teresa's attempts to apply the guidelines.

Model Social Skills. As with promoting all forms of development, modeling social skills is arguably the most effective action we can take in promoting these same skills in our students. For example, Teresa modeled making eye contact, checking perceptions, and listening attentively with her students, and we can also model more advanced social skills, such as perspective taking and social problem solving. As with all positive traits, attitudes, and behaviors, this modeling takes little extra time and effort. It is more a matter of becoming aware of the value of modeling these behaviors, and promoting your awareness is our goal in writing this section.

Explicitly Teach Social Skills. Earlier in the chapter we saw how Ramon Jiménez used vignettes to illustrate desirable and undesirable personality traits. Teresa used a similar approach in her attempts to teach social skills, but instead of using vignettes to illustrate the skills, she first modeled them and then had her students provide examples through role play. She used role play because it provided opportunities to concretely illustrate the skills.

Then Teresa had her students practice their social skills during group work, and she gave them feedback. Students won't become socially skilled after one or two activities, but with time, practice, and explicit instruction, these skills can be developed and refined.

Discuss Social Skills and Their Relationships with School Success. Interestingly, students are often unaware of how they "come across," and they can't develop their social skills if they don't realize—in the first place—that their skills can be improved. So, our goal is to help students understand social skills and their impact on success and satisfaction in school. In attempting to reach this goal we're capitalizing on the cognitive component of social development. Specific examples, such as those provided by the students during role play, provide concrete reference points for discussions, and the discussions are the mechanisms that can lead to students' awareness and understanding. For example, when a discussion helps students realize that a lack of social skills can lead to peer rejection, which then leads to fewer opportunities to practice social skills and fewer friends, the likelihood of them attempting to improve their skills increases.

Use Classroom Management to Promote Social Development. Finally, Teresa created a set of rules designed to support students as they worked together. She presented only four rules, first because they supplemented her general classroom rules, and because a small number makes them easier to remember. Her combination of the rules, her students' role playing, discussions, and her own modeling all contributed to her students' awareness and understanding of social skills and their importance. In time, and with effort and practice, these efforts can make a difference in students' social development.

Classroom **Connections**

Advancing Social Development in Classrooms

1. Perspective taking, the ability to understand the thoughts and feelings of others, is an important part of social development. Provide opportunities for students to consider the perspectives of others.

   ▪ **Elementary:** A fourth-grade teacher has her students analyze different characters' motives and feelings when they discuss a story they've read. She asks, "How does the character feel? Why does the character feel that way? How would you feel if you were that person?"

   ▪ **Middle School:** A middle school science teacher stays after school to provide opportunities for students to talk about both class work and issues with parents and friends. When social conflicts are brought up, she listens patiently but encourages students to think about the motives and feelings of the other people involved.

   ▪ **High School:** A history teacher encourages his students to consider point of view when they read reports of historical events. For example, when his students study the Civil War, he reminds them that both sides thought they were morally right and asks questions such as, "How did the different sides in the war interpret the Emancipation Proclamation?"

2. Social problem solving is the ability to resolve conflicts in ways that are beneficial to all involved. Provide opportunities for students to engage in social problem solving as they work with others.

   ▪ **Elementary:** A third-grade teacher periodically has groups of four students check each other's math homework. When conflicts arise, he encourages students to work out the problems themselves and intervenes only if they cannot resolve the problems.

   ▪ **Middle School:** An eighth-grade English teacher sometimes purposefully leaves decisions about individual assignments up to the groups in cooperative learning activities. When disagreements occur, she offers only enough assistance to get the group back on track. If the problem is widespread, she calls a whole-class meeting to discuss the problem.

   ▪ **High School:** When art students argue about space and access to materials and supplies, their teacher calls a class meeting and requires them to discuss the problem and suggest solutions acceptable to everyone.

Development of Morality, Social Responsibility, and Self-Control

Moral development involves advances in people's conceptions of right and wrong, as well as the development of prosocial traits such as honesty and respect for others. As we'll see in this section, moral development advances when children encounter moral issues, try to make sense of them, and in the process construct an individual sense of right and wrong (Fung & Smith, 2010; Gibbs, 2010).

Moral issues are common in schools. Let's look at a simple example.

> Amanda Kellinger (our teacher in the case study at the beginning of the chapter) says to her students as they're working on a seatwork assignment, "I need to run to the main office for a moment. Work quietly until I get back. I'll only be gone a few minutes."
>
> Amanda leaves, and amidst a shuffling of papers Gary whispers, "Psst, what math problems are we supposed to do?"
>
> "Shh! No talking," Talitha says, pointing to the rules on the bulletin board.
>
> "But he needs to know so he can do his work," Krystal replies. "It's the evens on page 79."
>
> "Who cares?" Jacob growls. "She's not here. She won't catch us."

What influences our students' interpretation of classroom rules? For example, how might we explain the differences between Talitha's, Krystal's, and Jacob's reactions to the rule about no talking? More importantly, as students move through life, how do they think about and act upon their moral beliefs? These are all moral issues.

Society's Interest in Moral Development

Moral development has always been a priority in our society, and interest in it has increased in recent years, partially due to disturbing trends in our country. For example, nearly half of all students in our nation's schools report having been bullied (Josephson Institute Center for Youth Ethics, 2010). Also, cheating is common in our schools, and many students don't see a connection between cheating and morality (Honz, Kiewra, & Yang, 2010).

Outside of schools, political corruption and scandals that led to the economic downturn in the latter part of the last decade have sent shock waves through the financial community and American society in general. The American public is increasingly looking to education for solutions to problems such as these (Bushaw & Lopez, 2010).

Moral issues are also embedded in the curriculum. History is more than a chronology of events; it's the study of people's responses to moral issues, such as human suffering, justice, and whether decisions to go to war are justified. Teachers commonly have students study novels such as *To Kill a Mockingbird, The Scarlet Letter,* and *A Tale of Two Cities,* not only because they are good literature but also because they examine moral issues.

Moral development is an integral part of development in general, and students' beliefs about right and wrong influence their behavior. For instance, research suggests that the extent to which adolescents believe the world is fair and just influences their attitudes toward the victims of bullying (Fox, Elder, Gater, & Johnson, 2010), and incidents of cheating and vandalism decrease if students believe they are morally wrong (Murdock, Miller, & Kohlhardt, 2004). Also, the moral atmosphere of a school—for example, democratic and prosocial versus authoritarian—can influence not only moral development, but also student motivation and the value students place on their learning experiences (Christenson & Havsy, 2004; Haidt & Kesebir, 2010). Understanding moral development helps us better guide our students in this vital area.

Social Domain Theory of Moral Development

Ed Psych and You

Think about these questions:

Is it okay to pass a parked school bus with its stop sign out if no children are leaving the bus?

Is it okay to drive faster than the speed limit if everyone else is driving about the same speed?

Is it okay to respond in class if your instructor hasn't called on you?

Is it okay to get a tattoo or pierce your nose or eyebrow?

To understand moral development, we first need to make distinctions between *moral, conventional,* and *personal* domains (Killen & Smetana, 2010; Parke & Clarke-Stewart, 2011; Turiel, 2008a, 2008b), and these distinctions are the essence of social domain theories of moral development (Nucci, 2008).

Moral domains deal with basic principles of right, wrong, and justice. For example, even young children recognize that intentionally hurting someone is wrong (Thompson, 2012). The conventional domain, in contrast, addresses societal norms and ways of behaving in specific situations. For instance, it's likely that your instructors allow students to respond in class without being called on, and it's okay to yell at an athletic event but not in a classroom. Social conventions also vary according to culture and setting. For example, young people addressing adults by their first names is acceptable in some cultures but not in others.

Finally, the personal domain refers to decisions that are not socially regulated and do not harm or violate others' rights. For instance, parents and other adults may think that tattoos and body piercing look awful, but they aren't morally wrong, and they aren't usually addressed by social conventions such as dress codes.

Children as young as 2 or 3 begin to make distinctions between moral, conventional, and personal domains (Hamlin & Wynn, 2011; Nucci, 2009; Thompson, 2012). They understand, for example, that it's wrong to hit and hurt someone regardless of where you are and whether or not rules prohibiting it exist. Some researchers even suggest that we are born with a rudimentary sense of justice that can be observed in the first months of life (Bloom, 2010).

As children interact with others and observe the consequences of their actions, they gradually develop a more sophisticated understanding of differences among the domains (Nucci, 2009; Turiel, 2008a, 2008b; Parke & Clarke-Stewart, 2011). For example, when children push a classmate down on the playground, they see the impact of their actions on others, and they are often reprimanded by adults. They also begin to realize that conventions are arbitrary and situation specific, which can result in their questioning both school regulations and rules at home.

The lines between the moral, conventional, and personal domains are often blurred and depend on individuals' interpretations. Some preservice teachers, for example, view giving all students the opportunity to participate in class as a moral issue, whereas others are more likely to classify it in the conventional domain (Schellenberg & Eggen, 2008). Further, some researchers view reasoning about social conventions and society's rules as advances in moral development (Kohlberg, 1981, 1984).

Piaget's Theory of Moral Development

Although cognitive development usually comes to mind when we think about Piaget, he also examined moral development. He studied the two forms of development in much the same way—by observing children, presenting them with problems, and asking questions to probe their thinking (Piaget, 1965).

Piaget found that children's responses to moral problems can be divided into two broad stages. In the first, called **external morality**, children view rules as fixed, permanent, and enforced by authority figures. When Talitha said, "Shh! No talking," and pointed to the rules, she was thinking at this stage. It didn't matter that Gary was only asking about the assignment; rules are rules. In responding "Who cares? She's not here. She won't catch us," Jacob demonstrated a similar level of thinking; he was focusing on the fact that no authority figure was there to enforce the rule. External morality typically lasts to about age 10. Piaget believed that parents and teachers who stress unquestioned adherence to adult authority retard moral development and unintentionally encourage students to remain at this level.

When students advance to **autonomous morality**, Piaget's second stage, they develop rational ideas of fairness and see justice as a reciprocal process of treating others as they would want to be treated (Gibbs, 2010). Children at this stage begin to rely on themselves instead of others to regulate moral behavior. Krystal's comment, "But he needs to know so he can do his work," demonstrates this kind of thinking; she viewed Gary's whispering as an honest request for assistance rather than an infraction of rules.

Kohlberg's Theory of Moral Development

Lawrence Kohlberg, a Harvard educator and psychologist, built on and extended Piaget's work. To do this he used **moral dilemmas**, ambiguous, conflicting situations that require a person to make a moral decision, as the basis for his research. Let's look at an example.

> Steve, a high school senior, works at a night job to help support his mother, a single parent of three. Steve is conscientious and works hard in his classes, but he doesn't have enough time to study.
>
> Because of his night work and lack of interest in history, he is barely passing. If he fails the final exam, he will fail the course and won't graduate. He isn't scheduled to work the night before the exam, so he has extra time to study. But early in the evening his boss calls, desperate to have Steve come in and replace another employee who called in sick at the last moment. His boss pressures him, so Steve goes to work at 8:00 p.m. and comes home exhausted at 2:00 a.m. He tries to study but falls asleep on the couch with his book in his lap. His mother wakes him for school at 6:30 a.m.
>
> Steve goes to history, looks at the test, and goes blank. Everything seems like a jumble. Clarice, one of the best students in the class, happens to have her answer sheet positioned so that he can clearly see every answer by barely moving his eyes.
>
> Is he justified in cheating?

This is a moral issue because it deals with matters of right and wrong, and it's a dilemma because any decision Steve makes has positive and negative consequences. If he cheats, he will pass the test, but cheating is wrong. On the other hand, if he doesn't cheat, he will likely fail the course and not graduate.

Kohlberg (1963, 1969, 1981, 1984) used children's responses to moral dilemmas as the basis for his research, which he later developed into his theory. Like Piaget, he concluded that moral reasoning exists in stages, and development occurs when people's reasoning advances to a higher stage. On the basis of research conducted in Great Britain, Malaysia, Mexico, Taiwan, and Turkey, Kohlberg concluded that the development of moral reasoning is similar across cultures.

Kohlberg originally described moral reasoning as occurring at three levels, consisting of two stages each. They're outlined in Table 3.4 and discussed in the sections that follow. As you read the descriptions, remember that the specific response to a moral dilemma isn't the primary issue; the level of moral development is determined by the reasons a person gives for making the decision.

Table 3.4	Kohlberg's stages of moral reasoning
Level 1 Preconventional Ethics (*Typical of preschool and elementary students.*)	The ethics of egocentrism. Typical of children up to about age 10. Called preconventional because children typically don't fully understand rules set down by others.
Stage 1: Punishment–Obedience	Consequences of acts determine whether they're good or bad. Individuals make moral decisions without considering the needs or feelings of others.
Stage 2: Market Exchange	The ethics of "What's in it for me?" Obeying rules and exchanging favors are judged in terms of the benefit to the individual.
Level II Conventional Ethics (*Seen in older elementary and middle school students and many high school students.*)	The ethics of others. Typical of 10- to 20-year-olds. The name comes from conformity to the rules and conventions of society.
Stage 3: Interpersonal Harmony	Ethical decisions are based on concern for or the opinions of others. What pleases, helps, or is approved of by others characterizes this stage.
Stage 4: Law and Order	The ethics of laws, rules, and societal order. Rules and laws are inflexible and are obeyed for their own sake.
Level III Postconventional Ethics (*Rarely seen before college, and the universal principles stage is seldom seen even in adults.*)	The ethics of principle. Rarely reached before age 20 and only by a small portion of the population. The focus is on the principles underlying society's rules.
Stage 5: Social Contract	Rules and laws represent agreements among people about behavior that benefits society. Rules can be changed when they no longer meet society's needs.
Stage 6: Universal Principles	Rarely encountered in life. Ethics are determined by abstract and general principles that transcend societal rules.

LEVEL I: PRECONVENTIONAL ETHICS

Preconventional morality is an egocentric orientation that focuses on the consequences of actions for the self. In the **punishment–obedience** stage, people make moral decisions based on their chances of getting caught and being punished. If a person is caught and punished, an act is morally wrong; if not, the act is right. A person believing that Steve is justified in cheating because he is unlikely to get caught is reasoning at this stage. At Stage 2, **market exchange**, people reason that an act is morally justified if it results in reciprocity, such as "You do something for me, and I'll do something for you."

LEVEL II: CONVENTIONAL ETHICS

When development advances to the **conventional level of morality**, reasoning no longer depends on the consequences for the individual but instead is linked to acceptance of society's conceptions of right and wrong and the creation of an orderly world. In Stage 3, **interpersonal harmony**, people make decisions based on loyalty, living up to the expectations of others, and social conventions. For example, a teenager on a date who believes she should meet a curfew because she doesn't want to worry her parents is reasoning at this stage. A person reasoning at Stage 3 might offer two different perspectives on Steve's dilemma. One could argue that he needs to work to help his family and therefore is justified in cheating. A contrasting view, but still at this stage, would suggest that he should not cheat because people would think badly of him if they found out.

At Stage 4, **law and order**, people follow laws and rules for their own sake. They don't make moral decisions to please other people or follow social norms as in Stage 3; rather, they believe that laws and rules exist to guide behavior and create an orderly world, and they should be followed uniformly. A person reasoning at Stage 4 would argue that Steve should not cheat because "It's against the rules to cheat," or "What kind of world would we live in if people thought cheating was okay?"

Stages 3 and 4 relate to the question, "Is it okay to drive faster than the speed limit if everyone else is driving about the same speed?" that we asked earlier in *Ed Psych and You*. People reasoning at Stage 3 might conclude that speeding is okay, since everyone else is doing it. On the other hand, they could conclude that it isn't okay, because it isn't safe, and it's wrong to put people in danger. People reasoning at Stage 4 would conclude that the speed limit is the law, and breaking the law is wrong.

LEVEL III: POSTCONVENTIONAL ETHICS

Postconventional morality, also called *principled morality*, views moral issues in terms of abstract principles of right and wrong. People reasoning at Level III have transcended both the individual and societal levels. They don't follow rules for their own sake, as a person reasoning at Stage 4 would suggest; rather, they follow rules because the rules are principled agreements. Only a small portion of the population attains this level, and most don't reach it until their middle to late 20s.

In Stage 5, **social contract**, people make moral decisions based on socially agreed-upon principles. A person reasoning at Stage 5 would say that Steve's cheating is wrong because teachers and learners agree in principle that grades should reflect achievement, and cheating violates this agreement.

At the sixth and final stage, **universal principles**, the individual's moral reasoning is based on abstract, general principles that transcend society's laws. People at this stage define right and wrong in terms of internalized universal standards. "The Golden Rule" is a commonly cited example. Because very few people operate at this stage, and questions have been raised about the existence of "universal" principles, Kohlberg deemphasized this stage in his later writings (Kohlberg, 1984).

Analyzing Theories

Evaluating Kohlberg's Theory of Moral Development

As with all theories, Kohlberg's work has made contributions to our understanding of people. For instance, research generally supports his theory's suggestion that moral development depends on cognitive development and is a gradual, constructive process. For instance, reasoning at Stages 1 and 2 decreases in early adolescence, reasoning at Stage 3 tends to decline in late adolescence, and reasoning at Stage 4 tends to predominate by early adulthood (Nucci, 2009; Turiel, 2006). This makes sense with respect to cognitive development; young children are typically preoperational thinkers, adolescents tend to be concrete operational, and at least some adults are formal operational thinkers.

Also, people generally move through the stages in the order and rate predicted by his theory (Gibbs, 2010; Thornberg, 2010), and links exist between moral reasoning and moral behavior. For instance, reasoning at the higher stages is associated with altruistic behaviors, such as defending victims of injustice, the rights of minorities, and free speech (Nucci, 2009; Spinrad & Eisenberg, 2009). On the other hand, adolescents reasoning at the lower stages are likely to be less honest and to engage in more antisocial behavior, such as delinquency and drug use. And learners reasoning at higher stages tend to experience more academic and social success (Brugman, 2010; Nucci, 2009; Spinrad & Eisenberg, 2009).

A number of criticisms have also been directed at Kohlberg's work. For example, research suggests that few people move beyond Stage 4

(Gibbs, 2010), so if postconventional reasoning is required for people to be morally mature, few measure up.

Moral reasoning also depends on context to a greater extent than Kohlberg acknowledged (Haidt & Kesebir, 2010; Spinrad & Eisenberg, 2009; van IJzendoorn, Bakermans-Kranenburg, Pannebakker, & Out, 2010). For instance, in *Ed Psych and You* we asked if it was okay to pass a school bus with its sign out, and, as we addressed earlier, is it okay to exceed speed limits. Most people don't think passing a school bus is acceptable, because it could potentially injure a child, but, even though technically against the law, most people believe exceeding speed limits is okay.

Thinking about moral dilemmas is also influenced by domain-specific knowledge (Nucci, 2006, 2009; Turiel, 2006). Moral development depends on cognitive development, and knowledge about a topic provides additional information to use in moral decision making (Gibbs, 2010; Thornberg, 2010). For example, a medical doctor asked to deliberate about an educational dilemma or a teacher asked to resolve a medical issue would be hampered by their lack of professional knowledge.

Finally, because moral development, as with all forms of development, depends on experience, diversity is a factor (Nucci, 2009; Rubin, Cheah, & Menzer, 2010). We examine this issue in our discussion of gender differences in morality. Table 3.5 outlines Kohlberg's theory, including its contributions and criticisms.

Table 3.5	Analyzing theories: Evaluating Kohlberg's theory of moral development
Key question	How do changes in moral reasoning occur?
Basic description of moral development	Moral development is a gradual, continuous cognitive process that occurs as a result of experience with moral issues and interactions with others.
Catalysts for change	• Encounters with moral dilemmas in everyday life • Social interactions with others
Key concepts	• Moral dilemma • Preconventional morality • Conventional morality • Postconventional morality • Punishment–obedience stage • Market exchange stage • Interpersonal harmony stage • Law and order stage • Social contract stage • Universal principles stage
Contributions	• Kohlberg's theory recognizes that moral development is a gradual, constructive process that depends on cognitive development. • People tend to move through the stages of moral reasoning in the order and rate predicted by his theory. • Evidence identifies links between moral reasoning and moral behavior. • Kohlberg's stages generally correspond to children's thinking about right and wrong. • Kohlberg's theory is consistent with Piaget's views of moral development.
Criticisms	• Many people never reach the postconventional level of moral reasoning, which raises questions about moral maturity. • Moral reasoning depends more on context than Kohlberg acknowledged. • Performance at a certain stage depends more on domain-specific knowledge than Kohlberg suggested. • The links between moral reasoning and moral behavior are relatively weak; people often reason at one stage but behave at another. • Kohlberg's theory doesn't adequately take cultural differences into account.

Sources: Berk, 2013; Feldman, 2014; Kohlberg, 1963, 1969, 1981, 1984; Piaget, 1965; Spinrad & Eisenberg, 2009.

Gender Differences: The Morality of Caring

Some critics of Kohlberg's work also argue that it fails to adequately consider ways in which gender influences morality. Early research examining Kohlberg's theory identified differences in the ways men and women responded to moral dilemmas (Gilligan, 1982, 1998; Gilligan & Attanucci, 1988). Men were more likely to base their judgments on abstract concepts, such as justice, rules, and individual rights; women were more likely to base their moral decisions on interpersonal connections and attention to human needs. According to Kohlberg, these differences suggested a lower stage of development in women responding to moral dilemmas.

Carol Gilligan (1977, 1982), also a Harvard psychologist and Kohlberg's colleague, argued that the findings, instead, indicate an "ethic of care" in women that is not inferior; rather, Kohlberg's descriptions don't adequately represent the complexity of female thinking. Gilligan suggests that a morality of caring proceeds through three stages. In the first, children are concerned primarily with their own needs; in the second, they show concern for others who are unable to care for themselves, such as infants and the elderly; and in the third, they recognize the interdependent nature of personal relationships and extend compassion to all of humanity. To encourage this development, Gilligan recommends an engaging curriculum with opportunities for students to think and talk about moral issues involving caring.

Nell Noddings (1992, 2002, 2008) has also emphasized the importance of caring in schools, especially for teachers. Noddings argues that students should be taught the importance of caring through a curriculum that emphasizes caring for self, family and friends, and others throughout the world. Research corroborates this position; a just and compassionate school climate is more likely to promote students' moral development (Crystal, Killen, & Ruck, 2010).

Gilligan makes an important point about gender differences, but additional research is mixed; some studies have found gender differences, whereas others have not (Berk, 2013; Leman & Björnberg, 2010). Like cross-cultural studies, Gilligan's research reminds us of the complexity of the issues involved in moral development.

Emotional Factors in Moral Development

Piaget's, Kohlberg's, and Gilligan's works focus primarily on the cognitive domain, that is, thinking and reasoning about moral issues. However, emotions, such as feelings of sorrow, guilt, and empathy, are also linked to moral development (Davison, 2011; Gallese, Gernsbacher, Heyes, Hickok, & Lacoboni, 2011; Rothbart, 2011; Thompson & Newton, 2010). Let's see how.

> "Are you okay?" her mother asks as Melissa walks in the house after school appearing dejected.
>
> "I feel really bad, Mom," Melissa answers softly. "We were working in a group, and Jessica said something sort of odd, and I said, 'That's dumb.' Where did that come from? . . . She didn't say anything for the rest of our group time. She doesn't get really good grades, and I know saying something about her being dumb really hurt her feelings. I didn't intend to do it. It just sort of came out."
>
> "I know you didn't intend to hurt her feelings, Sweetheart. Did you tell her you were sorry?"
>
> "No, when I realized it, I just sat there like a lump. I know how I'd feel if someone said I was dumb."
>
> "Tell you what," her mom suggests. "Tomorrow, you go directly to her, tell her you're sorry you hurt her feelings, and that it won't happen again."
>
> "Thanks, Mom. I'll do it as soon as I see her. . . . I feel a lot better."

In this episode Melissa felt both shame, the painful emotion aroused when people recognize that they have failed to act in ways they believe are good, and guilt, the uncomfortable feelings people get when they know they've caused someone else's distress.

To advance moral development, researchers suggest, we should teach children to feel guilt, rather than shame, when they misbehave. Shame leads to the feeling that "I am a bad person," which can be devastating, particularly for young children. Guilt, on the other hand, leads to the feeling that I have done a bad thing, which can be remedied by improving behavior (Bafunno & Camodeca, 2013). Melissa's mother wisely focused on Melissa's guilt, and by suggesting that she apologize to Jessica, offered a remedy. Although unpleasant, experiencing guilt indicates that moral development is advancing and future behavior is likely to improve.

When Melissa said, "I know how I'd feel if someone said I was dumb," she was also describing feelings of empathy, the ability to experience the same emotion someone else is feeling. Empathy promotes moral and prosocial behavior, even in the absence of wrongdoing (Spinrad & Eisenberg, 2009; Thompson & Newton, 2010).

Ultimately, as parents and teachers, we want our young people to grow up kind, caring, and compassionate. In fact, for many people these values are more important than academic achievement (Grant, 2014).

Some interesting research has examined the development of these values. For instance, when we work with young people to promote academic achievement, we're encouraged to praise behaviors, such as effort, rather than personal characteristics (e.g., "Keep up the good work" is considered more effective than, "You're good at this") (Cimpian, Arce, Markman, & Dweck, 2007; Zentall & Morris, 2012).

With respect to moral development, however, the opposite appears to be the case. For instance, in a study of young children, researchers found that statements such as "Please be a helper" and "Don't be a cheater" were more effective than, "Please help" and "Don't cheat." In the moral domain, research suggests, praising personal characteristics is more effective than praising behavior (Bryan, Adams, & Monin, 2013).

The combination of cognitive and emotional aspects of moral development can lead to improvements in both moral reasoning and moral behavior. As with all forms of development, making improvements is our goal. We turn now to what we, as teachers, can do to guide our students' moral development.

Educational Psychology and Teaching: Promoting Moral Development in Your Students

We have many opportunities to promote moral development in our students. We do so primarily with our modeling, the kind of classroom environments we create, and the way we guide students' interactions with each other. The following guidelines can provide a framework for us as we attempt to promote this essential form of development:

1. Model ethical thinking, behavior, and emotions in interactions with students.
2. Use moral dilemmas as concrete reference points for examining moral issues.
3. Use discussions to help students understand and respect the perspectives of others.
4. Use classroom management as a vehicle for promoting moral development.

Let's see how Rod Leist, a fifth-grade teacher, uses these guidelines as he works with his students:

Rod begins language arts by saying, "Let's look in the story we've been reading and talk about Chris, the boy who found the wallet. He was broke, so would it be wrong for him to keep it, . . . and the money in it? . . . Jolene?"

"Yes, it would be wrong because the wallet didn't belong to him."

"Ray?"

"Why not keep it? He didn't steal it; and . . . "

"That's terrible," Helena interrupts. "How would you like it if you lost your wallet?"

"Helena," Rod admonishes. "Remember, we agreed that we would let everyone finish their point before we speak.

"Sorry for interrupting. . . . Please finish your point, Ray," Rod adds.

" . . . It wasn't his fault that the person lost it. . . . And he was broke."

"Okay, Helena, go ahead," Rod says.

"Just . . . how would you feel if you lost something and somebody else kept it? . . . That's why I think he should give it back."

"That's an interesting point, Helena. When we think about these issues, it's good for us to try to put ourselves in someone else's shoes. . . . Of course, we would feel bad if we lost something and it wasn't returned. Go ahead, . . . Juan?"

"I agree. It was a lot of money, and Chris's parents would probably make him give it back anyway."

"And what if the person who lost the money really needs it?" Kristina adds.

After continuing the discussion for several more minutes, Rod says, "These are all good points. . . . Now, I want each of you to write a short paragraph that describes what you would do if you found the wallet and explain why you feel it would be right or wrong to keep it. Then, we'll discuss your reasons some more tomorrow."

Now, let's look at Rod's attempts to apply the guidelines.

Model Ethical Thinking, Behavior, and Emotions in Interactions with Students.

"Almost all approaches to moral education recognize the importance of modeling. If we would teach the young to be moral persons, we must demonstrate moral behavior for them" (Noddings, 2008, p. 168). Rod's actions were consistent with this quote. His simple and brief apology for interrupting the discussion communicated that he also obeyed their classroom rules. Also, he reinforced Helena for being empathic and modeled his own empathy by saying, "That's an interesting point, Helena. When we think about these issues, it's good for us to try to put ourselves in someone else's shoes." Efforts to be fair, responsible, and democratic in dealings with students speak volumes about teachers' values and views of morality, and research suggests that a warm, supportive classroom atmosphere supports their efforts (Crystal et al., 2010; Noddings, 2008).

Use Moral Dilemmas as Concrete Reference Points for Examining Moral Issues.

As research consistently indicates, most people's thinking is concrete operational, which means that they need concrete examples if they are to develop a meaningful understanding of the topics they study. This is certainly true when dealing with abstract issues, such as morality, and it's particularly true of students in elementary schools, such as Rod's fifth graders.

Rod recognized this factor and used the lost wallet as a concrete reference point for discussion. It was a moral dilemma because Chris—the boy in the example who found the wallet—was broke and needed the money, but, on the other hand, the wallet and money didn't belong to him.

Moral issues come up in classes more often than we realize. For instance, in elementary classrooms discussions about whether it's okay to retaliate if someone on the playground pushes you down, or someone butts in front of you in the lunch line, can lead to meaningful discussions about issues of right and wrong. With older students, a friend, for example, asks if we think a new hairstyle looks good, and we think it is most unflattering. Do we respond truthfully, and likely hurt her feelings, or do we say it looks good, which is technically a lie? Alcohol use is another common example. Many teenagers use alcohol, and we know that drinking and driving is dangerous. However, if no one drives anywhere, is it immoral to drink before the legal age limit? Many other examples exist, and discussing them when they come up can, in time, lead to moral growth.

Use Discussions to Help Students Understand and Respect the Perspectives of Others.

Moral dilemmas provide concrete reference points, but discussions are the mechanisms that lead to higher levels of moral reasoning. To see an illustration, let's look again at some of the dialogue in Rod's lesson.

Rod: Let's look in the story we've been reading and talk about Chris, the boy who found the wallet. He was broke, so would it be wrong for him to keep it, . . . and the money in it? . . . Jolene?

Jolene: Yes, it would be wrong because the wallet didn't belong to him.

Rod: Ray?

Ray: Why not keep it? He didn't steal it; and . . .

Helena: That's terrible. How would you like it if you lost your wallet?

Rod: Helena. . . . Remember, we agreed that we would let everyone finish their point before we speak. . . . Sorry for interrupting. . . . Please finish your point, Ray.

Ray: It wasn't his fault that the person lost it. . . . And he was broke.

Rod: Okay, Helena, go ahead.

Helena: Just . . . how would you feel if you lost something and somebody else kept it? . . . That's why I think he should give it back.

Rod: That's an interesting point, Helena. When we think about these issues, it's good for us to try to put ourselves in someone else's shoes. . . . Of course, we would feel bad if we lost something and it wasn't returned. . . . Go ahead, . . . Juan?

Juan: I agree. It was a lot of money, and Chris's parents would probably make him give it back anyway.

Kristina: And what if the person who lost the money really needs it?

In this discussion, the students each offered slightly different perspectives with respect to the issue. Discussing these differences can lead to advances in moral reasoning. And students generally enjoy the opportunity to express their opinions, particularly when they are not in danger of being judged right or wrong. So discussions such as these are often motivating.

Rod then followed up on the discussion by having the students write a paragraph in which they were asked to justify their moral positions with respect to the issue. Research supports this approach. Discussions that encourage students to examine their own reasoning combined with exposure to more advanced thinking promotes moral development (Carlo, Mestre, Samper, Tur, & Armenta, 2011; Crystal et al., 2010).

Use Classroom Management as a Vehicle for Promoting Moral Development. As we've seen throughout the chapter, classroom management can be used to promote much more than an orderly classroom, and Rod's management system is an illustration. For example, he stopped Helena's interruption and reminded the class that they agreed to let people finish a point before speaking. In doing so, he was teaching fairness and tolerance for differing opinions. Understanding these values is an important part of self-regulation, which can only be developed if students understand rules and why they're important, and agree to follow them. This kind of learning environment, an environment in which students follow rules because the rules make sense, promotes *autonomous morality* (Fung & Smith, 2010; Rothbart, 2011).

As we've examined classroom applications designed to promote each of the forms of development in this chapter, themes have emerged. For instance, a cognitive component exists for each of the forms of development, and it's on this component that we try to capitalize. In other words, we want our students to *understand* and *think about* the various aspects of personality, identity, social skills, and morality and how development in each of these areas can contribute to both success and satisfaction in school and quality of life after the school years.

Classroom **Connections**

Supporting Moral Development in Classrooms

1. Moral development is enhanced by opportunities to think about moral dilemmas and hear the positions of others. Openly discuss ethical issues when they arise.

   ■ **Elementary:** The day before a new student with an exceptionality joins the class, a second-grade teacher has students discuss how they would feel if they were new, how new students should be treated, and how they should treat one another in general.

   ■ **Middle School:** A seventh-grade teacher has a classroom rule that students may not laugh, snicker, or make remarks of any kind when a classmate is trying to answer a question. She has the students discuss reasons for the rule, emphasizing how people feel when others laugh at their efforts.

   ■ **High School:** A teacher's students view cheating as a game, seeing what they can get away with. The teacher addresses the issue by saying, "Because you feel this way about cheating, I'm going to decide who gets what grade without a test. I'll grade you on how smart I think you are." This provocative statement precipitates a lively classroom discussion on fairness and cheating.

2. Moral development advances when students are exposed to moral behavior and moral reasoning at higher levels. Model moral and ethical behavior for students.

   ■ **Elementary:** One election November, fifth-grade students jokingly ask if the teacher votes. The teacher uses this as an opportunity to discuss the importance of voting and each person's responsibilities in our democracy.

   ■ **Middle School:** A science teacher makes a commitment to have students' tests and quizzes scored by the following day. One day, when asked if he has the tests ready, he replies, "Of course. . . . At the beginning of the year, I said I'd have them back the next day, and we can't go back on our agreements."

   ■ **High School:** A group of students finishes a field trip sooner than expected. "If we just hang around a little longer, we don't have to go back to school," one student suggests. "Yes, but that would be a lie, wouldn't it?" their teacher counters. "We said we'd be back as soon as we finished, and we need to keep our word."

In each case, modeling and explicitly teaching the skills using concrete examples are essential. Then, discussions of the examples combined with a classroom management style that promotes fairness and self-regulation are the mechanisms we use to promote each of the forms of development. We won't succeed with all students, but for the ones with whom we do, we will have made an immeasurable contribution to their total education.

Obstacles to Healthy Development

Healthy development is essential for our quality of life, but our modern world includes challenges that can detract from this development. Some of these challenges include:

- Obesity
- Alcohol and drugs
- Child abuse
- Peer aggression

We examine them in this section.

Obesity

We've all heard a great deal about the obesity "epidemic" in our country, and it has emerged as a major health issue facing our youth. More than one of six children in our country aged 6 to 19 is overweight or obese, triple the proportion in 1980 (Ogden & Carroll,

2010). Further, the risk of becoming obese begins earlier in life than previously thought. For instance, a major study of over 7,000 children found that the risk of overweight kindergarteners being obese in the eighth grade was four to five times that of their thinner classmates (Cunningham, Kramer, & Narayan, 2014). These statistics are even more pronounced for students who are members of cultural minorities or who come from low SES (socioeconomic status) backgrounds (Moreno, Johnson-Shelton, & Boles, 2013), as well as gay, lesbian, and bisexual youth (Austin, Nelson, Birkett, Calzo, & Everett, 2013). In addition to immediate health risks, such as high cholesterol and blood pressure, overweight youth often become heavy adults with additional health issues, such as heart disease and diabetes. In recognition of these health risks, combined with the fact that obesity-related health conditions cost our nation more than $150 billion and result in an estimated 300,000 premature deaths each year, the American Medical Association has labeled obesity a disease and not just a risk factor for other disorders (Brody, 2013).

Overweight youth also face social problems, such as peer rejection and negative perceptions. For example, some research indicates that overweight people are unconsciously perceived as less intelligent than their normal-weight peers (Vedantam, 2010).

Several factors contribute to the obesity problem, with lack of exercise being one of the most important. "A substantial number of children fail to engage in any physical activity outside of school" (Chin & Ludwig, 2013, p. 1229). Unhealthy diets, exacerbated by television advertising, and even schools also contribute to the problem (Goldfield, 2012). For instance, elementary school recess has largely been eliminated, daily physical education classes are offered in only 2 percent of our nation's high schools, and barely 50% of students take any physical education classes at all (U.S. Department of Health & Human Services, 2010). In addition, the typical adolescent spends more than 5 hours a day watching television, playing video games, and communicating on the Internet (Rideout, Foehr, & Roberts, 2010). Also, school districts, which are constantly cash strapped, often sign contracts with corporations to place soft-drink machines in school hallways (Molnar, Boninger, Wilkinson, Fogarty, & Geary, 2010).

What can we do? Information and our own modeling are our best weapons. For example, some research suggests that students have a limited understanding of what constitutes healthy eating, so teaching them about healthy eating habits can make a difference (Leatherdale, 2013; Powers, Bindler, Goetz, & Daratha, 2010). Modeling these habits, exercising, and making an effort to control our own weight (which is good for our health as well) can be even more important.

THE NEED FOR RECESS IN ELEMENTARY SCHOOLS

As we just saw, many elementary schools have cut back or eliminated recess time, and lack of recess has been linked to childhood problems ranging from obesity to anxiety and hyperactivity (Ridgers, Carter, Stratton, & McKenzie, 2011). The benefits of physical activity are undisputed (Parrish, Okely, Stanley, & Ridgers, 2013). "There is a consensus among developed countries that children and youth should accumulate a minimum of 60 minutes of moderate-to-vigorous physical activity (MVPA) every day" (Parrish et al., 2013, p. 288). As we just saw above, many children get little exercise outside of school, which makes recess even more important (Chin & Ludwig, 2013).

Free play during recess also provides students with opportunities to interact with others that can contribute to cognitive, social, and emotional development (Mathieson & Banerjee, 2010).

Given these benefits, why are so many schools cutting back on recess? *Time* is the answer. Many schools are pressured to improve scores on high-stakes tests, so they allocate extra time to the areas—such as reading and math—that are covered on the tests. These decisions, however, are having adverse effects on children's development (Berk, 2013).

Alcohol and Drugs

Think about the following statistics gathered from national surveys (Centers for Disease Control & Prevention, 2010a, 2010c; Johnston, O'Malley, Bachman, & Schulenberg, 2012):

- More than 4 of 10 high school students reported using alcohol, and nearly 25% of high school seniors reported binge drinking in the two weeks prior to the survey.
- Nearly half of adolescents reported using marijuana, and one in 15 high school seniors admitted to being daily, or almost daily, users.
- Twenty percent of high school students have taken a prescription drug, such as Oxycontin, Ritalin, or Xanax, without a doctor's prescription.
- Nearly 1 of 5 high school students report current use of cigarettes.

The dangers of drug use are well known. For example, research has identified a link between long-term marijuana use and lowered IQ (Khamsi, 2013; Rogeberg, 2013). In addition to cognitive factors, teenagers who abuse alcohol and drugs place themselves at risk for problems such as damage to their health, car accidents, and even suicide (Grilly & Salamone, 2012; Levinthal, 2013). Alcohol and drug users are less likely to exercise, and they're less likely to develop healthy mechanisms for coping with life's problems.

School connectedness, the belief by students that adults and peers in the school care about both their learning and them as individuals, is an important protective factor against drug and alcohol abuse. Young people who feel connected to their school are less likely to smoke, use alcohol and drugs, or initiate sex. They also achieve higher, have better attendance, and are less likely to drop out of school (Centers for Disease Control and Prevention, 2010b).

We can help students develop connections to their school by getting to know our students as individuals, calling them by name, and creating classroom environments that are physically and emotionally safe. We can also use teaching strategies that involve students in learning activities, instead of expecting them to primarily listen passively to lectures.

Child Abuse

> Denise, one of your students, historically has been a bright, outgoing, and high-achieving girl, but she has changed quite abruptly. She is withdrawn, and she looks down and doesn't respond when you call on her. And, although she is normally well groomed, she has been coming to school looking a bit disheveled. Then you see a welt on her face, and your concern turns to alarm. You go to your assistant principal and report what you've observed.

Denise's changes in behavior, academic performance, and appearance, and particularly the welt on her face, suggest the possibility of child abuse, and you did precisely what you should have in reporting it.

Teachers in all 50 states are required by law to report suspected child abuse. In addition, you and your school are protected from civil or criminal liability if the report is made honestly and includes behavioral data, such as observations of the symptoms we described (Schimmel, Stellman, & Fischer, 2011).

Statistics indicate that in 2011 child protective services agencies received 3.4 million reports of child abuse, and further investigation found more than 681,000 had been victims of abuse or mistreatment (Child Welfare Information Gateway, 2013). Because abuse and neglect are often hidden or not reported, reliable figures are hard to obtain. More than

78% of abuse victims suffered from neglect, about one fifth experienced physical abuse, and 9% were either sexually or psychologically abused. When sexual abuse occurs, it most commonly involves a family member, relative, or friend. Although child abuse can occur at any level of society, it tends to be associated with poverty and is often linked to parental substance abuse (Children's Defense Fund, 2012).

Abuse is obviously an obstacle to development, and you're in a unique position to identify it because you work with children for much of the day, 5 days a week. The probability that you will have abused or neglected children in your classes is low, although it is somewhat higher if you teach in a high poverty area. You need to be aware of the possibility, however, because you could literally save a life.

Peer Aggression

How students treat each other affects not only themselves, but also the people around them. Children who are aggressive not only have difficulties relating to their peers, but also can become maladjusted adults. In addition, aggression in schools creates an atmosphere of fear and distrust (Mayer & Furlong, 2010).

Aggression exists in several forms. Instrumental aggression, the most common, is an action aimed at gaining an object or privilege, such as cutting in line, or a young child grabbing another's toy. Hurting the other child isn't the goal, but it may result. On the other hand, physical and relational aggression are actions intended to hurt others, such as pushing another child down on the playground as in physical aggression, or spreading a rumor about someone, which involves relational aggression. Boys are more likely to be physical aggressors, whereas girls more commonly use relational aggression (Ostrov & Godleski, 2010). Aggression can be proactive, where students deliberately initiate aggressive acts, or reactive, behaving aggressively in response to frustration or a perceived aggressive act (Mayeux et al., 2011).

Highly aggressive students tend to be rejected by peers and do poorly in school. By adolescence, they often seek out peer groups that lead them to delinquency, and at an extreme, criminal behavior as adults (Chung, Mulvey, & Steinberg, 2011; Simons & Burt, 2011). Aggressive students often grow up to be aggressive adults who have trouble getting along with others in both the workplace and the world at large (Marsee & Frick, 2010).

Although genetics can play a role, the home environment is a primary cause of aggression (Campbell, Spieker, Vandergrift, Belsky, & Burchinal, 2010; Rhee & Waldman, 2011). Parents of aggressive children are often authoritarian, punitive, and inconsistent, and they commonly use physical punishers, such as slapping, hitting, and spanking for unacceptable behavior. So aggressive behavior is both modeled and reinforced. These home environments can result in hostile attributional bias, a tendency to interpret others' behaviors as hostile or aggressive (Hubbard, Morrow, Romano, & McAuliffe, 2010). Sean, in this chapter's opening case study, appears to have this problem; he thinks other students are "out to get him." Aggression is also linked to deficits in perspective taking, empathy, moral development, and emotional self-regulation (Eisenberg, Eggum, & Edwards, 2010).

SCHOOL VIOLENCE

School violence is an extreme form of aggression that involves serious bodily injury or death. A number of horrific incidents of violence have occurred over the last two decades, ranging from the Columbine massacre in 1999, in which 12 students were killed, the terrible event in 2012 at Sandy Hook Elementary School in Newtown, Connecticut, in which 20 children and 6 adults were fatally shot, the death of a student at Arapahoe High School in a Denver suburb in 2013, to the epidemic of violence in January of 2014, in which 11 school shootings occurred in 19 days (Ohlheiser, 2014). Because of these widely publicized cases, many people understandably believe that school violence is increasing. And as a result of the Sandy Hook shooting, school security is receiving a great deal of attention. "Perhaps never before has our nation been more focused on school security" (Nance, 2013, p. 3). Additional research suggests that school violence, including violence against teachers, is a serious problem (Espelage et al., 2013).

The publicity surrounding school violence combined with the threat of violence has left many students feeling less safe in school. Obviously, learning and development suffer whenever students don't feel safe (Chung et al., 2011; Ihlo & Nantais, 2010).

As you read this, you may feel a bit uneasy about your safety and the safety of your students when you begin teaching. This is completely understandable. However, try to keep in mind that—in spite of the horrific examples with which we're all familiar—incidents of school violence actually remain rare. Also, as we noted above, security has become a high priority in schools across our country, and your school will undoubtedly have specific security measures in place. Hopefully, this will put you a bit more at ease.

BULLYING

Although incidents of serious crime and violence are rare, bullying, a form of peer aggression that involves a systematic or repetitive abuse of power between students, is much more common. For example, in a survey of more than 43,000 high school students—the largest ever conducted about the attitudes and conduct of adolescents—half admitted they had bullied someone in the past year, and nearly the same percentage said they were bullied, teased, or taunted in a way that upset them (Josephson Institute Center for Youth Ethics, 2010).

Bullying can exist as either physical or relational aggression, and its victims are typically different in some ways. They might be students who are overweight, immature, anxious, or have disabilities. And they may also be socially isolated and lack self-confidence (Russell, Ryan, Toomey, Diaz, & Sanchez, 2011). Bullying can have long-term negative effects on students, and in the extreme, victims of repeated bullying incidents begin to ask, "Why me?" and "Am I someone who deserves to be picked on?" which can lead to destructive emotions, such as depression and even suicide (Wagner, 2009; Card & Hodges, 2008). In cases of suicide, however, other factors, such as dysfunctional families, easy access to weapons or medications, and social hopelessness, usually also exist (Bonanno & Hymel, 2010).

Historically, bullying has been viewed as a maladjusted reaction from adolescents who are socially marginalized or psychologically troubled, but more recent research suggests that this isn't true. In fact, many students bully to achieve social status, and their bullying tends to escalate until high status is reached, at which time bullying is no longer necessary (Faris & Felmlee, 2011). These researchers found that, over time, students at the very bottom and at the very top of the social hierarchy become the least aggressive youth.

Because of the perceived seriousness of bullying as a school problem, 44 states have passed anti-bullying laws, and many districts have implemented zero-tolerance policies. These laws and policies have been largely ineffective for reducing incidents of bullying, however (Graham, 2010; Walker, 2009).

Peer juries and peer counselors are infrequently used, and their effectiveness is also uncertain, whereas school-wide efforts that include increasing adult supervision, talking with bullies after bullying incidents, and immediate, appropriate, and consistent consequences for bullying have been found to be more effective (Sherer & Nickerson, 2010).

These findings have important implications for you. First, when you begin teaching, you will almost certainly encounter incidents of bullying. When you do, you should intervene immediately, apply appropriate consequences for the perpetrators, and perhaps more importantly, use the incident as a teachable moment, where you discuss the idea of right and wrong, appropriate treatment of others, tolerance for differences, and abuse of power (Graham, 2010). These discussions obviously won't produce immediate results, but, over the long term, they can make a difference not only in discouraging bullying but also in the healthy development of your students.

Also, other research suggests that if you can find alternate, appropriate ways to help students achieve social status, such as excelling in sports, academics, or class or school leadership, the likelihood of their bullying might decrease (Faris & Felmlee, 2011). Many ways of achieving social status exist, and an approach to dealing with bullying that focuses on social status might be more effective than existing programs with marginal records of success (Shah, 2013).

Technology, Learning, and Development

Cyberbullying

Bullying, in general, is a serious school problem, and because of the rapidly expanding presence of the Internet in students' lives, cyberbullying, a form of bullying that occurs when students use electronic media to harass or intimidate other students, has also become a growing problem. As an example, a girl breaks up with her boyfriend, and he then spreads ugly rumors or private pictures of her on the Internet. Cyberbullying has received enormous attention in response to the suicides of Rutgers University freshman Tyler Clementi in 2010, after his roommate streamed video of his sexual encounter with another male student, and Florida 12-year-old Rebecca Ann Sedwick in 2013, after a year and a half of constant cyberbullying, made headlines across our country. Both school officials and parents have become increasingly aware of this growing problem.

Cyberbullying tends to follow the same patterns as traditional forms of bullying; students who are bullies and bullied on the playground play similar roles in cyberspace (Twyman, Saylor, Taylor, & Comeaux, 2010; Tokunaga, 2010). In fact, two-thirds of cyberbullies also exhibit aggressive behaviors in other contexts. The anonymity of the Internet is what distinguishes cyberbullying from other types, and it can make bullies even less sensitive to the hurtful nature of their bullying actions (Ang & Goh, 2010; Smith & Slonje, 2010).

Cyberbullying is hard to measure because victims often don't report the problem to adults, but experts estimate that between 20% and 40% of youths have experienced it (Twyman et al., 2010; Rivers, Chesney, & Coyne, 2011). Given the popularity of Internet use among teenagers, cyberbullying is likely to remain a persistent problem. Because of its anonymity, cyberbullying is also difficult to combat; consequences for perpetrators rarely exist.

There are several things that victims can do to discourage cyberbullying (Ang & Goh, 2010; Smith & Slonje, 2010). First, if possible, victims should obtain the email address of the bully. They should be encouraged to print out the offensive message as proof of their harassment and provide it to adults. And, if they don't know who the bully is, victims should change their screen name and only share it with good friends. Long term, you should discuss the problem in class, emphasizing the hurt it causes to others and promoting a sense of empathy, fair play, and appropriate treatment of others.

Developmentally Appropriate **Practice**

Personal, Social, and Moral Development with Learners at Different Ages

Important differences exist in the personal, emotional social, and moral development of elementary, middle, and high school students. The following paragraphs outline suggestions that will help you respond to these differences.

Working with Students in Preschool Programs and Elementary Schools

As children enter preschool, they are developing autonomy and taking the initiative to seek out experiences and challenges. "Let me help!" and "I want to do it" are signs of this initiative. Criticism or overly restrictive directions detract from a sense of independence and, in extreme cases, lead to feelings of guilt and dependency. At the same time, children need the structure that helps them learn to take responsibility for their own behavior.

As children move through the elementary years, teachers attempt to help them succeed in learning activities challenging enough to promote feelings of competence and industry. This is demanding. Activities that are so challenging that students frequently fail can leave them with a sense of inferiority, but success on trivial tasks does little to make students feel competent (Brophy, 2010).

During the elementary years, students need opportunities to practice perspective taking and social problem solving. Discussions and small-group work where students can interact with others and practice these skills are effective learning experiences.

The elementary grades also lay the foundation for students' moral growth and the development of social responsibility and self-control. Teachers who encourage students to understand the impact of their actions on others help them make the transition from preconventional morality, with its egocentric orientation, to conventional morality, at which stage students understand why rules are important for both classrooms and the world outside of school.

Working with Students in Middle Schools

Adolescence is a time of considerable physical, emotional, and intellectual changes, and adolescents are often uncertain about how to respond to new sexual feelings. They are concerned with what others think of them and are preoccupied with their looks. They want to assert their independence, yet long for the stability of structure and discipline. They want to rebel to assert their independence but need something solid to rebel against.

Most adolescents successfully negotiate this period, however, exploring different roles and maintaining positive relationships with their parents, teachers, and other adults. Students in middle and junior high schools need firm, caring teachers who empathize with them and their sometimes capricious actions while simultaneously providing the security of clear limits for acceptable behavior (Emmer & Evertson, 2013). Classroom management provides opportunities to advance moral reasoning from preconventional to conventional thinking. Effective teachers create clear classroom rules, discuss the reasons for them, and enforce them consistently.

Instruction in middle school classrooms should promote deep understanding of the topics being studied, while simultaneously providing students with opportunities to practice prosocial behaviors, such as tolerance for others' opinions, listening politely, and avoiding hurtful comments. Effective instruction in middle schools is highly interactive, and lecture is held to a minimum.

Working with Students in High Schools

High school students are continuing to wrestle with who they are and what they want to become. Peers become increasingly important to students and have an important influence on social, emotional, and moral development.

Linking content to students' lives is particularly valuable at this age. For example, examining ideas about gender and occupational trends in social studies and showing how math and science can influence their futures are important for these students.

Like younger learners, high school students need opportunities to try out new ideas and link them to their developing sense of self. Discussions, small-group work, and focused writing assignments provide valuable opportunities for students to integrate new ideas into their developing self-identities.

chapter

3 Summary

1. Describe personality development and explain how it can influence academic success and success in life after the school years.
   - Personality is composed of five relatively independent traits that include openness, conscientiousness, extraversion, agreeableness, and neuroticism, and personality development describes improvements with respect to these traits.
   - Temperament, determined largely by genetics, describes relatively consistent inclinations to respond to events in the environment in particular ways.
   - Because of their early and extensive interactions with a child, parents have the largest influence on personality development, and some parenting styles are more effective than others.
   - Cultural differences exist with respect to parenting styles, with some cultures emphasizing characteristics such as individuality, and others focusing on a more collectivist orientation.
   - Emotional growth and the developing ability to regulate emotions is part of healthy personality development.
   - Personality development is strongly linked to both success in school and success in life after the school years.

2. Use descriptions of psychosocial, identity, and self-concept development to explain learner behavior.
   - Erik Erikson integrated identity together with social factors to develop a theory of psychosocial development.
   - Psychosocial development occurs in stages, each marked by a psychosocial challenge called a crisis. Positive resolution of the crisis in each stage prepares the individual for the challenge at the next.
   - Contemporary views of identity development suggest that career identities usually occur during high school and beyond. Identity moratorium and identity achievement are healthy developmental states; identity diffusion and identity foreclosure are less healthy.
   - Self-concept, developed largely through personal experiences, describes individuals' cognitive assessments of their academic, physical, and social competence. Academic self-concept, particularly in specific content areas, is strongly correlated with achievement.
   - Attempts to improve self-concept as an outcome of increased achievement in specific areas are often successful, unlike attempts to improve students' self-concepts by direct interventions.

3. Describe components of social development, and explain how social development is related to success and satisfaction in school.

   - Social development describes the advances children make in their ability to interact and get along with others.
   - A number of factors influence our social development, including parents, siblings, and peers. Peers influence social development through their attitudes and values, through opportunities to practice social skills, and through their emotional support.
   - Perspective taking and social problem solving are important components of social development. Perspective taking allows students to consider problems and issues from others' points of view, and social problem solving includes the ability to read social cues, generate strategies, and implement and evaluate strategies for solving social problems.
   - Students with well-developed social skills are generally more successful and satisfied with school than are their less skilled peers.
   - Teachers promote social development when they model effective social skills and give students opportunities to practice social skills in the context of classroom learning activities.

4. Use theories of moral development to explain differences in people's responses to ethical issues.
   - Piaget suggested that moral development represents individuals' progress from external morality, the enforcement of rules by authority figures, to autonomous morality, the perception of morality as rational and reciprocal.
   - Kohlberg's theory of moral development is based on people's responses to moral dilemmas. He developed a classification system for describing moral reasoning that occurs in three levels.
   - At the preconventional level, people make egocentric moral decisions; at the conventional level, moral reasoning focuses on the consequences for others; and at the post-conventional level, moral reasoning is based on principle.
   - Feeling empathy and even unpleasant emotions such as shame and guilt mark advances in moral development.
   - Teachers promote moral development by emphasizing personal responsibility and the functional nature of rules designed to protect the rights of others.

5. Identify obstacles to development and explain how they detract from healthy development.
   - There are a number of obstacles to healthy development. These include obesity, alcohol and drugs, child abuse, and bullying.
   - Obesity, defined as a greater than 20% increase over healthy body weight, is influenced by a number of factors, including diet, lack of exercise, and technologies that encourage a sedentary lifestyle.

- Alcohol and drug use are quite common in teenagers and prevent adolescents from developing healthy coping mechanisms.
- Child abuse is a major problem in our society and often involves neglect. Family members are most likely to engage in child abuse.

- Bullying is a pervasive problem in our schools, and teachers can do much to discourage it. Cyberbullying, a relatively recent phenomenon, is difficult to stop and follows many of the same patterns as regular bullying.

Preparing for Your Licensure Exam

Understanding Personal, Emotional, Social, and Moral Development

Your licensure exam will include items related to students' personal, emotional, social, and moral development, and we include the following exercises to help you practice for the exam in your state. This book will be a resource for you as you prepare for the exam.

Let's look now at a teacher working with a group of middle school students and how she contributes to these important aspects of development. Read the case study, and answer the questions that follow:

Maria, a ninth-grade English teacher, was drinking tea in the teachers' room. At the same time, she was frantically trying to brainstorm new teaching strategies and note them down on a piece of paper, when her friend and teaching colleague Beth walked in.

"What is worrying you so much?" Beth asked with concern.

"Maria replied, "Do you remember that student Thabani I had told you about at the beginning of the year? His personality traits predisposed him to do well in school, as he was eager to learn and always had his homework and assignments completed on time. But due to his problems dealing with emotional self-regulation, he was having difficulty completing his scholastic evaluations. He was so anxious and nervous that he could not finish any of the class tests and examinations."

"Oh yes! The government-appointed educational psychologist seemed to have had helped him control his emotions really well. What has happened to him now?"

"He did really well for a while in controlling his anxiety," responded Maria, "but now he is causing havoc in the classroom. He has not been responding or participating in class anymore. He always stares blankly, and constantly day dreams. He also does not seem to be as well-groomed as he used to be. He has been disturbing the other students by passing notes in class to his friends. He has also suddenly started to behave in a rowdy and rough manner in all of his social interactions. He has not been performing well academically. He had earlier understood the concepts I had discussed in class, but now he has not been able to answer them correctly in the tests any more.

"I was so concerned about him that I telephoned his mother to ask if I could meet her. I had driven to their house. She had been working so much lately that she was hardly home, so she had not noticed these changes in her son. The only thing that she had noticed was the money that she had left for Thabani to buy food for the household had gone missing and as a result, there was barely any food in the house. His siblings had been complaining that he is never at home. His mother also told me about the rumors about him that have been circulating in the village. The village elders have also been concerned about him. It seems that he has started associating with a group of boys who are known to drink alcohol, take illegal drugs and steal."

"No wonder you are so concerned," remarked Beth. "Do you think all these rumors are true?"

Maria sighed, "I wish they were not true, but they are. I spoke to Thabani as well. Although he admitted to consuming alcohol, he vehemently denied taking illegal drugs. But I just don't know if he is telling the truth about this. I am at my wits end. I don't know who I should speak to about this. He has so much potential; it is such a shame that he is losing his way."

"Oh come now, cheer up! You are always so positive. Let me help you think of the steps we can follow. We can also try to get some books that can help us," comforted Beth.

Questions for Case Analysis

In answering these questions, use information from the chapter and link your responses to specific information in the case.

Multiple-Choice Questions

1. Based on research, there is a strong link between personality and academic achievement. Which of the following personality traits that Thabani displayed are linked to higher academic achievement?

    a. Agreeableness and introversion

    b. Neuroticism and openness

    c. Agreeableness and conscientiousness

    d. Openness and conscientiousness

2. What emotional self-regulation strategies do you think the government-appointed educational psychologist taught Thabani?

    a. Physical outlets for emotion

    b. Impulse control, management of negative emotions and socially acceptable behavior

    c. Management of positive emotions and impulse control

    d. Development of self-esteem

Constructed-Response Question

3. What preventative strategies could Maria and Beth apply to avoid the problem of alcohol and possibly drug abuse becoming rife among their students?

Important Concepts

autonomous morality
bullying
collective self-esteem
conventional domain
conventional level of
    morality
crisis
cyberbullying
emotional intelligence
emotional self-regulation
empathy
ethnic identity
external morality

goodness of fit
guilt
hostile attributional bias
identity
instrumental aggression
interpersonal harmony
law and order
market exchange
moral development
moral dilemma
moral domain
parenting style
personal domain

personality
personality development
perspective taking
physical aggression
postconventional morality
preconventional morality
proactive aggression
punishment–obedience
reactive aggression
relational aggression
school connectedness
self-concept
self-esteem (self-worth)

sexual identity
sexual orientation
shame
social cognition
social contract
social conventions
social development
social problem solving
social referencing
temperament
theory of mind
universal principles

chapter

4 Learner Diversity

OUTLINE	LEARNING OUTCOMES
	After you've completed your study of this chapter, you should be able to:
Culture Ethnicity Culture and Classrooms	**1.** Describe culture and ethnicity, and explain how they can influence learning.
Linguistic Diversity English Learners English Dialects Educational Psychology and Teaching: Teaching Students in Your Classes Who Are Culturally and Linguistically Diverse	**2.** Explain why so much linguistic diversity exists in our country, and describe ways that teachers can accommodate this diversity.
Gender School-Related Gender Differences Boys' and Girls' Classroom Behavior Educational Psychology and Teaching: Responding to Gender Issues with Your Students	**3.** Explain how gender can influence learning, and describe steps for eliminating gender bias in classrooms.
Socioeconomic Status Poverty Socioeconomic Factors that Influence Learning Socioeconomic Status and Students at Risk Students at Risk and Resilience SES: Some Cautions and Implications for Teachers Educational Psychology and Teaching: Promoting Resilience in Your Students ▶ Developmentally Appropriate Practice: Student Diversity at Different Ages	**4.** Define socioeconomic status, and explain how it can affect learning.

Imagine that your family is moving to France, and you will be attending school there from this point forward. Will you succeed? What barriers will you face? How might you feel? This experience is increasingly similar to the experiences of many students in our country's schools today.

Learner diversity refers to both the group and individual differences in our students, it exists in every classroom, and it can strongly impact learning. As you read the following case study involving Jay Evans, a third-grade teacher, think about the diversity in his class and how it might influence the way he works with his students.

> Jay teaches in a large, urban elementary school. He has 29 students—16 girls and 13 boys—in his class. It includes 8 African Americans, 7 students of Hispanic descent, 3 Asian Americans, and 2 recent immigrants from Russia. English is not the native language for several, and most of his students come from low-income families.

He smiles as he walks by Katia's desk. She is his "special project," and she is blossoming in response to his efforts. When she first came to school, she was hesitant to participate because she came from Mexico, where Spanish was her native language. Initially, she could understand simple English sentences but struggled with speaking and reading English from textbooks. Jay made a point of involving her in learning activities, paired her with students who could help her with English, spent time with her after school, and gave her second-grade books to read at home. Her parents support Jay's efforts, and home–school communication is very good. Her progress since the beginning of the year has been remarkable.

As he steps past Angelo, his glow turns to concern. Angelo struggles to keep up with the rest of the class, and he is quiet and easily offended by perceived slights from his classmates. Because his parents are Mexican migrant workers, the family moves frequently, and he repeated first grade. His parents are separated, and his mother has settled in this area so the children can stay in the same school.

Jay consults with Jacinta Morales, a colleague who is bilingual, about additional efforts he might make with Angelo. Together they develop a plan to help him with both his English and his academic work.

If we stood outside and watched students come out of the schools in our country today, we would see that their backgrounds vary more than at any time in our nation's history. Jay's class is quickly becoming more typical than atypical. Cultural and linguistic background, gender, and socioeconomic status are all types of diversity. They're outlined in Figure 4.1.

When we examine this diversity, however, we must remember that it describes general patterns characteristic of groups, and a great deal of variation exists within each group. For instance, both Katia and Angelo come from Mexico, and both are native Spanish speakers. However, Katia is thriving in Jay's class, whereas Angelo is struggling. Learner diversity also involves individual differences in our students.

These differences lead to two questions:

1. How might learner diversity influence learning?
2. How should we as teachers respond to this diversity?

Research helps answer these and other important questions about our students. We begin by looking at studies examining the impact of culture on learning.

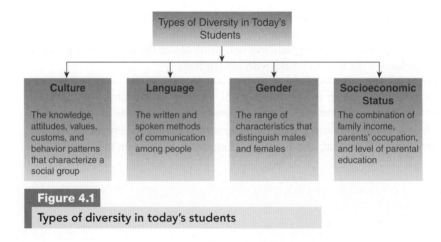

Figure 4.1

Types of diversity in today's students

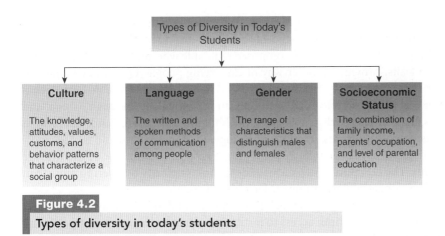

Figure 4.2

Types of diversity in today's students

Ed Psych and You

Think about the clothes you wear, the music you like, and the activities you share with your friends. Or even think about food. What and when do you eat? Do you use a knife and fork, or chopsticks, or even your fingers?

Culture

The answers to the questions in *Ed Psych and You* all depend on your **culture**, which includes the knowledge, attitudes, values, and customs that characterize a social group (Banks, 2014; Ember & Ember, 2011). Culture is one of the most powerful and important influences in our lives, and it can also influence success in school (see Figure 4.2).

The cultural diversity in our country is rapidly increasing. For example, census estimates indicate that members of cultural minorities now make up over a third of our nation's population, and projections suggest that by 2021 it will be more than half (National Center for Education Statistics, 2013). The 2000 census found, for the first time, that the Hispanic surnames Garcia and Rodriguez are among the 10 most common in our country (Roberts, 2007).

This trend is reflected in our classrooms, where more than 4 of 10 students in the P–12 population are members of cultural minorities. More recently—and significantly—2010 census data indicate that for the first time in history, less than half of 3-year-olds in our country were White (Frey, 2011). This means that White students will no longer be a majority as these children move through school.

Ethnicity

Ethnicity, a person's ancestry and the way individuals identify with the nation from which they or their ancestors came, is an important part of culture (Banks, 2014). Members of an ethnic group have a common source of origin, language (although sometimes not actively used), value system, and customs. Experts estimate that nearly 300 distinct ethnic groups live in our country (Gollnick & Chinn, 2013).

Immigration and other demographic shifts have resulted in dramatic changes in the ethnic makeup of our nation's school population. The Immigration Act of 1965, which ended quotas based on national origin, resulted in more immigrants coming to our country from a wider variety of places. For example, in the early 1900s most came from Europe, but nearly 40% of more recent immigrants come from Mexico and Central America, about 25% come from Asia, and

10% come from the Caribbean. Less than 15% now come from Europe (U.S. Bureau of Census, 2010). This helps us understand why Jay's students have such diverse backgrounds.

Race, a socially constructed category composed of people who share important biologically transmitted traits, provides another way of classifying people. Our country tends to see three major racial categories—Black, White and Asian—but considerable heterogeneity exists within each. For example, *Asian* can refer to individuals from Japan, China, and Korea, as well as many others, such as Viet Nam, the Philippines, and Thailand, all of whom have distinct customs and cultures. In addition, a single racial category could include individuals whose ancestors have been in our country for several generations, or others who are recent immigrants. The U.S. Bureau of Census adds to the complexity by offering more than 60 different options for racial descriptions (Macionis, 2013).

Historically, the concept of race was much more important than it is today. For example, a number of states used race to limit access to institutions and services, such as schools and colleges, restaurants, public restrooms and drinking fountains, swimming pools, and even seats on buses (Ehlers, 2012). In addition, prior to a Supreme Court decision in 1967, it was illegal in 16 states for mixed-race couples to marry, cohabit, or have sex. Even today, *de facto* racial segregation—labeled this way because it isn't formalized by law—still occurs in housing, and many urban schools in our country are largely segregated by race (Macionis, 2013).

Because of immigration and intermarriage—one in seven new marriages is now between people of different ethnicities—an increasing number of people are classifying themselves as multiracial or multiethnic (Saulny, 2011). So, as we think about culture, ethnicity, and race, it is important to remember that these are simply labels, they are constantly changing, and we teach people, not categories.

Culture and Classrooms

All students bring a set of values and beliefs with them when they enter our classrooms, and these values often complement and reinforce classroom practices. If they don't, however, mismatches that interfere with learning can occur. A **cultural mismatch** is a clash between a child's home culture and the culture of the school that creates conflicting expectations for students and their behavior. Most classrooms in our country reflect mainstream, middle-class values; students are expected to spend most of their time working independently, answer questions when called on, and speak Standard English (Banks, 2014; Gollnick & Chinn, 2013). If students' cultures don't emphasize values such as verbal assertiveness, competition, and working alone, cultural mismatches can occur. Being aware of these possible mismatches is the first step in dealing with them.

Let's look at an example.

Cynthia Edwards, a second-grade teacher in an elementary school in the Southwest, is reading a story. "What do you think is going to happen next? . . . Tony?" Cynthia asks in response to his eagerly waving hand.

"I think the boy is going to meet his friend."

"How do you think the boy feels about meeting his friend?" she continues.

After Tony responds, Cynthia calls on Sharon Nighthawk, one of several Native Americans in her class. When Sharon doesn't answer, Cynthia prompts her by rephrasing the question, but Sharon continues to look at her in silence.

Cynthia is slightly exasperated because Sharon seems to both understand and enjoy the story. Why won't she answer?

Thinking about the lesson later, Cynthia realizes that this has happened before, and, in fact, her Native American students rarely answer questions in class.

She can't get them to talk.

Why do students respond differently to our instruction, and how does culture influence these differences? We consider these questions in this section as we examine:

- Cultural attitudes and values
- Patterns of adult–child interactions
- Classroom organization and its match with students' home cultures

CULTURAL ATTITUDES AND VALUES

Cultural attitudes and values have a powerful influence on learning, which makes complete sense. If, for example, we grow up in a household where studying and learning are viewed as important, we will undoubtedly achieve higher than if they aren't valued. Research corroborates this view. For instance, international comparisons indicate that students in Asian countries, such as Taiwan, Hong Kong, Korea, and Japan, typically score higher on math and science achievement tests than their counterparts in the United States (Trends in International Mathematics and Science, 2013). While structural differences in education probably account for some of these differences—the school year in some of these countries is up to 50 days longer than in the United States—cultural attitudes about the importance of studying and hard work are also likely factors.

These values transfer to Asian American students, who also tend to score higher on achievement tests and have higher rates of college attendance and completion than do other groups, including European Americans (National Center for Education Statistics, 2010a; 2010b). Asian American parents usually have high expectations for their children and encourage them not only to attend college but also to earn graduate or professional degrees (Gollnick & Chinn, 2013). They often translate these aspirations into academic activities at home that augment school-assigned homework.

In contrast, members of some cultural minorities, such as African American, Native American, and Hispanic American, consistently score lower on achievement tests (National Assessment of Educational Progress, 2013a). But the reasons for these lower scores go well beyond cultural differences and include a history of segregated and subpar schools, limited English proficiency, economic hardships, and societal discrimination (Macionis, 2013; Pulliam & Van Patten, 2013).

Sometimes members of these groups form **resistance cultures**, cultures with beliefs, values, and behaviors that reject the values of mainstream culture (Factor, Williams, & Kawachi, 2013; Ogbu, 1992, 2003, 2008; Ogbu & Simons, 1998). To maintain their identity within their chosen group, members of resistance cultures reject attitudes and behaviors that lead to school success, such as doing homework, studying, and participating in class. To become a high achiever is to "become White," and students who study, want to succeed, and become actively involved in school face rejection from their peers. Low grades, classroom management and motivation problems, truancy, and high dropout rates can be the result. Students with higher levels of social resistance also tend to engage in more risky and unhealthy behaviors, such as smoking, drinking, and failure to use seat belts, than do those with lower levels of social resistance (Factor et al., 2013).

Some researchers, however, believe that the problem of resistance cultures may be overstated and misdirected (Archer-Banks & Behar-Horenstein, 2012; Stinson, 2006). Many members of minority cultures do well in school, feel connected to classrooms and their teachers, and don't experience tensions between school success and their peers. In addition, these researchers believe that the problem of limited success in school may indicate a failure on the part of schools to effectively motivate and instruct students who don't fit into mainstream school culture. For example, a review of research examining African American high school students identified a number of obstacles to school success, including low teacher expectations, school rules and regulations that were not uniformly applied, and instruction that failed to address the unique background experiences of minority students (Stinson, 2006).

The likelihood of this problem is also reduced when minority students have developed a positive ethnic identity (Cook & Ludwig, 2008). Doing well at school does not have to mean rejecting the home and neighborhood cultures.

Stereotype Threat. As minority students struggle to adapt to and compete in schools, they sometimes experience stereotype threat, anxiety felt by members of a group resulting from concern that their behavior might confirm a stereotype (Aronson, Wilson, & Akert, 2013; Guyll, Madon, Prieto, & Scherr, 2010). It adversely affects performance through heightened anxiety that reduces students' capacity for thinking and problem solving (Walton & Spencer, 2009).

Stereotype threat is most problematic for high-achieving members of cultural minorities, but it can be an issue for other groups as well. For instance, it exists when women fear that they will do less well than men on tests involving math or computer science, because they think that these are male domains, or when White males fear they will perform less well on math tests because they're competing with Asian students who they believe are better at math.

CULTURAL DIFFERENCES IN ADULT–CHILD INTERACTIONS

Cultural interaction patterns in the home also influence student behavior in school (Hoff, 2010; Leavell, Tamis-LeMonda, Ruble, Zosuls, & Cabrera, 2012). For example, Barbara Rogoff (2003) found that White children tend to respond comfortably to questions requiring specific answers, such as "What's this story about?" African American children, accustomed to questions that are more "open-ended, story-starter" types, are sometimes confused by the specific questions, because they aren't viewed as information givers in their homes.

Cultural mismatches can also occur in interpretations of time and acceptable school-related behaviors (Pang, Han, & Pang, 2011). Let's look at an example in an elementary school with a large population of Pacific Island students.

The school principal had been invited to a community awards ceremony honoring students from her school. She readily accepted, arrived a few minutes early, and was ushered to a seat of honor on the stage. After an uncomfortable (to her) wait of over an hour, the ceremony began. The children received their awards and returned to their seats, which led to an eye-opening experience.

As the children became bored, they started to fidget, which soon evolved into poking, prodding, and open chatting. The principal became uneasy, but the parents didn't seem to even notice, so she attempted to also ignore it.

Then, the children were soon out of their chairs, running around the seating area, playing tag, and yelling gleefully.

All adult faces continued looking serenely at the speaker on the stage.

At this point, the principal realized that when these children came to school late, ran around the classroom, squirmed under desks, and failed to pay attention in learning activities, it didn't mean that they or their parents didn't care about learning; that's how all the adults in their world operate. They aren't intentionally being disrespectful or defiant; they're doing what they do everywhere else [adapted from Winitzky, N. (1994). Multicultural and mainstreamed classrooms. In R. Arends (Ed.), *Learning to teach* (3rd ed). Copyright (C) 1994. Reprinted by permission of McGraw-Hill Companies].

Students from different cultures bring with them ways of acting and interacting with adults that may differ from the traditional teacher-as-authority-figure role (Hoff, 2010; Leavell et al., 2012). The principal's experience with Pacific Island culture helped her understand why her students often acted as they did.

CLASSROOM INSTRUCTION AND CULTURE

In many classrooms, individual performance is emphasized, which leads to competition reinforced by test scores and grades. Students from some cultures, such as Native American, Hispanic, and Asian, often value cooperation, view competition as unnecessary or even distasteful, and may experience difficulties in competitive classrooms (Aronson et al., 2013). A cultural mismatch then exists when they come to school and are asked to compete. Raising hands and jousting for the right to answer isn't congruent with the ways they interact at home. In addition, the typical teacher questions–student answers–teacher responds sequence found in many classrooms isn't a normal part of family life in many cultures. Children aren't routinely asked questions to which adults already know the answer, instead being expected to quietly observe adult interactions (Goodnow, 2010; Paradise & Rogoff, 2009).

This helps us understand the problem Cynthia Edwards encountered with her students who wouldn't answer questions. The Native American children sat quietly because doing so was consistent with their culture.

This discussion also helps us answer the first question we asked at the beginning of the chapter: "How might learner diversity influence learning?" When cultural mismatches exist, less learning occurs. Sensitivity to these factors is important for us all.

Multicultural Education. Multicultural education examines the influence of culture on learning and attempts to find ways to use culture to increase achievement (Banks, 2014; Gay, 2010). James Banks (2014) has created a comprehensive model of multicultural education that encompasses the entire school. Banks's model emphasizes the integration of ideas and experiences from students' cultures, prejudice reduction, and the influence of culture on the way we think about the world. Information adapted from the model is outlined in Table 4.1.

Classroom Instruction and Culture: Some Cautions. When encountering cultural mismatches, teachers sometimes conclude that parents of children who are minorities don't value schooling or support teachers' efforts (Walker, Shenker, & Hoover-Dempsey, 2010). This isn't true. Research consistently indicates that these parents care deeply about their

Table 4.1	Dimensions of multicultural education
Dimension	**Goal**
Prejudice reduction	To modify students' attitudes toward other groups of students
Content integration	To illustrate ideas using content from a variety of cultures
Equity pedagogy	To use instruction that facilitates the academic achievement of students from diverse racial, cultural, and social class groups
Understanding the knowledge-construction process	To investigate and understand how implicit cultural assumptions, frames of reference, perspectives, and biases within a discipline affect the knowledge within that discipline
An empowering school culture and social structure	To examine the total school culture (e.g., grouping, sports, and interactions with faculty and staff) to ensure that it empowers students from diverse racial, ethnic, and cultural groups

Source: Adapted from Banks (2014).

children's learning but don't realize that cultural mismatches exist (Calzada, Huang, Anicama, Fernandez, & Brotman, 2012; Chen & Eisenberg, 2012). This makes sense. Most of us grow up tacitly assuming that all homes are like ours.

Research also reminds us of the need to bridge cultural differences and adapt our instruction to the backgrounds and needs of our students (Gay, 2010). This begins when we realize that they often enter our classrooms with different beliefs, values, and behaviors.

As we said at the beginning of the chapter, we also must remember that our discussion of culture is focusing on group differences, and individuals within the groups vary, sometimes greatly.

Linguistic Diversity

When you begin your teaching career, it's likely that some, if not several, of your students will speak a native language other than English. For that matter, English may not be your first language. More than one of five students in our country's schools come from homes where English is not the native language, and this number is increasing (National Center for Education Statistics, 2011). Further, about 5% of these children come to school speaking no English at all. More than half are in the lower elementary grades, where they face the dual tasks of learning to read and write while they're learning a new language (Cushner, McClelland, & Safford, 2012). Figure 4.3 reflects this linguistic diversity.

Let's look at the characteristics of these students in more detail.

English Learners

English learners (ELs) are students whose first or home language is not English (Linquanti & Cook, 2013). (*English learners* are also commonly called *English language learners* [ELLs], and you will see both EL and ELL used in research literature.) As a result of immigration and high birth rates among immigrant families, the number of students who are ELs and those with limited English have increased significantly over the last three decades (U.S. Bureau of Census, 2010). In 2011, eight states—Alaska, California, Colorado, Hawaii, Nevada, New Mexico, Oregon, and Texas—had public school populations with more than 10% English learners, and in California this figure was nearly 3 of 10 (U.S. Department of Education, 2012). The language diversity in our country is staggering; more than 440 languages other than English are spoken in our schools, with Spanish being far and away the most common (Migration Policy Institute, 2010).

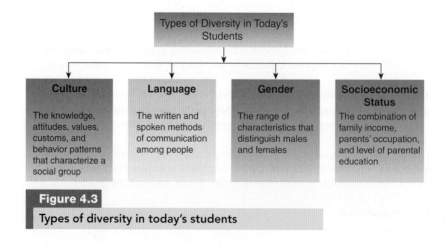

Figure 4.3

Types of diversity in today's students

Being an EL creates challenges and obstacles for students; they have to learn both English and classroom content simultaneously. As a result, they typically lag behind in achievement, they're more often referred for special education services, and they're more likely to drop out of school (Turnbull, Turnbull, Wehmeyer, & Shogren, 2013; Vaughn, Bos, & Schumm, 2014). How do schools respond to these challenges? We address this question next.

Ed Psych and You

Have you ever tried to learn a foreign language? Was it more difficult to learn to speak the language, understand it when spoken, or read it? How proficient were you after 2 or 3 years? How successful would you have been if all the instruction in your other classes was in that language?

TYPES OF EL PROGRAMS

Your answers to our questions in *Ed Psych and You* give us some insights into the challenges ELs face. Teaching English is the primary goal of all EL programs, but the way they attempt to reach the goal varies considerably. Table 4.2 outlines some different approaches.

Immersion Programs. Immersion programs place students who are ELs in general education classrooms to help them learn both English and academic content (Clark, 2009;

Table 4.2	Types of EL programs		
Type of Program	**Description**	**Advantages**	**Disadvantages**
Immersion	Places students in classrooms where only English is spoken, with few or no linguistic aids.	Increased exposure to new language and multiple opportunities to use it.	Sink or swim approach may be overwhelming and leave students confused and discouraged.
Maintenance	Students maintain first language through reading and writing activities in first language while teachers introduce English.	Students become literate in two languages.	Requires teachers trained in first language. Acquisition of English may not be as fast.
Transitional	Students learn to read in first language, and teachers give supplementary instruction in English as a second language. After mastering English, students enroll in regular classrooms and discontinue learning in first language.	Maintains first language. Transition to English is eased by gradual approach.	Requires teachers trained in first language. Literacy skills in first language not maintained and may be lost.
ESL Pullout Programs	Pullout programs in which students are provided with supplementary English instruction along with regular instruction in content classes.	Easier to administer when dealing with diverse language backgrounds because it requires only the pullout teachers to have EL expertise.	Students may not be ready to benefit from content instruction in English. Pullout programs segregate students.
Sheltered English	Teachers adapt content instruction to meet the learning needs of EL students.	Easier for students to learn content.	Requires an intermediate level of English proficiency. Also requires teachers with EL expertise.

Peregoy & Boyle, 2013). Pure-immersion programs offer no extra assistance to these students; continual exposure is believed to be sufficient to learn English.

Structured immersion, in contrast, attempts to assist students by introducing academic topics at a slower pace while simultaneously teaching English. You may have encountered a form of structured immersion in foreign language classes, where your teacher attempted to instruct as much as possible in that language.

Maintenance EL Programs. Maintenance EL programs build on students' native languages by teaching in both that language and English (Diaz-Rico, 2013; Peregoy & Boyle, 2013). Found primarily at the elementary level, these programs are designed to develop students who can speak, read, and write in two languages. They have the advantage of retaining and building on students' heritage language and culture, but they're often difficult to implement because they require groups of students with the same native language and bilingual teachers who speak that language.

Transitional EL Programs. Transitional EL programs attempt to use the native language as an instructional aid until English becomes proficient. They begin by teaching reading and writing in the first language and gradually develop learners' English skills. The transition period is often too short, however, which leaves students inadequately prepared for learning in English (Echevarria & Graves, 2015). In addition, loss of the first language and lack of emphasis on home cultures can result in communication gaps between children who no longer speak the first language and parents who don't speak English (Cushner et al., 2012; Wong & Xiao, 2010).

ESL Pullout Programs. In English as a second language (ESL) pullout programs, students receive most of their instruction in general education classrooms but are pulled out for extra help (Diaz-Rico, 2013; Peregoy & Boyle, 2013). Instruction in these programs focuses on English language development, with emphasis on pronunciation, grammar, vocabulary, and oral comprehension. In addition, ESL teachers assist with subject matter content, such as math or social studies, which is taught in general education classrooms. These programs require students whose English skills are developed to the point that they can benefit from general instruction. When this isn't the case, sheltered English classes are more effective.

Sheltered English. Sheltered English classrooms modify instruction to assist students in learning content, such as math or science. Also called *Specially Designed Academic Instruction in English*, these classes require students with intermediate levels of English proficiency as well as instructors who know both the content and EL strategies.

EVALUATING EL PROGRAMS

English learner programs, and particularly immersion, maintenance, and transitional EL programs, are controversial. For example, advocates of immersion claim that this approach teaches English more rapidly and efficiently; critics question whether this "sink or swim" approach is either effective or humane. Critics also argue that immersion ignores the first language, resulting in a loss of bilingualism, the ability to speak, read, and write in two languages.

EL children who retain their native language and become bilingual enjoy advantages. For example, bilingual children better understand the sounds words make, how languages work, and the role language plays in communication (Mertz & Yovel, 2010). Bilingual children also tend to perform better on tasks requiring advanced cognitive functions, such as intelligence tests and measures of creativity (Bialystok, 2011; Han, 2010; Leung, Maddux, Galinsky, & Chiu, 2008; Yow & Markman, 2011).

As we said above, maintenance and transitional EL programs are also controversial (Williams, 2009). Critics contend that these programs are:

- Divisive, encouraging groups of non-native English speakers to remain separate from mainstream American culture.
- Ineffective, slowing the development of English for students who are ELs.
- Inefficient, requiring expenditures for the training of bilingual teachers and materials that could be better spent on quality English programs (U.S. English, 2011).

Proponents counter that the programs build on students' first languages and provide a smooth and humane transition to English (Adesope, Lavin, Thompson, & Ungerleider, 2010). They also argue that being able to speak two languages has practical benefits in today's world.

Research on these programs is also controversial. For example, advocates of immersion cite research suggesting that students learn English faster when they're given increased opportunities to practice it in classroom activities (Hipfner-Boucher, Lam, & Xi, 2014; Nakamoto, Lindsey, & Manis, 2012). Critics counter with research suggesting that students in maintenance programs have more positive attitudes toward school and learn more math and reading. They also argue that the knowledge and skills acquired in a native language promote transfer to English (Bialystok, 2011; Mertz & Yovel, 2010; Ukrainetz, Nuspl, Wilkerson, & Beddes, 2011).

Comparing programs is difficult, because researchers study different variables (Padilla, 2006). For instance, some focus on the speed of English acquisition, whereas others examine achievement measures, such as standardized test scores or grades. And a third line of research studies the effects of different programs on general intellectual functioning and the brain's executive control and metalinguistic capabilities (Bialystok, 2011; Han, 2010; Yow & Markman, 2011).

Overall, evidence suggests that bilingualism is a desirable goal, but bilingual programs are hampered by political and economic barriers (Nieto & Bode, 2012). In addition, teachers are under increased pressure from accountability advocates to help ELs learn English as quickly as possible so they can perform well on standardized tests (Garcia & Tyler, 2010). The debate is likely to continue, as the issues are both complex and emotional.

As with students in general, significant differences exist in English learners (Echevarria & Graves, 2015). Some live in households where books and newspapers are readily accessible and parents talk and read to their children; others come from homes where both parents work and opportunities for language development are limited, making the transition to English challenging.

Developmental differences also exist. Learning to pronounce words in a second language such as English is easier for younger children than for those who are older, particularly if the second language is fundamentally different from the first (Petitto, 2009). For example, it is much easier for a native Spanish speaker to learn English than it is for someone whose first language is Chinese. On the other hand, older students have a greater knowledge of language and have mastered more learning strategies, making second language learning more efficient (Diaz-Rico, 2013, 2014). Students of all ages can learn a new language, however, if they make the effort and are provided with adequate instruction.

English Dialects

If you've traveled around our country, you've likely noticed that people, although speaking English, talk differently, and sometimes the differences are great enough that we have trouble understanding each other. These differences are the result of **dialects**, variations of Standard English—distinct in vocabulary, grammar, or pronunciation—that are associated with a particular regional or social group. Everyone speaks a dialect; we merely react to those different from our own. Dialects are such an integral part of our lives that researchers have found they even appear on Twitter (Eisenstein, O'Connor, Smith, & Xing, 2011).

Many different dialects are spoken in our country; experts have identified at least 11 that are distinct (Brice & Brice, 2009; Owens, 2014). Some are more accepted than others, however, and research suggests that teachers frequently have lower expectations for students who use nonstandard English and assess the students' work accordingly (Godley, Sweetland, Wheeler, Minnici, & Carpenter, 2006). These language patterns are often confused with mistakes during oral reading, and some believe that dialects, such as Black English, are substandard (Alim & Baugh, 2007; Snow, Griffin, & Burns, 2005). Linguists, however, believe that these variations are just as rich and semantically complex as Standard English (Pearson, Velleman, Bryant, & Charko, 2009; Labov, 1972).

Let's turn now to the implications that culture and linguistic diversity, including dialects, have for our teaching.

Educational Psychology and Teaching: Teaching Students in Your Classes Who Are Culturally and Linguistically Diverse

It's a virtual certainty that you will teach students who are members of cultural minorities, and it is highly likely that English will not be the first language for some. Effective instruction for these students doesn't differ fundamentally from effective instruction in general (Brophy, 2010; MacWhinney, 2011; Otto, 2014).

However, to promote as much learning as possible for all students, we must make some accommodations for those from varying cultural and linguistic backgrounds. The following guidelines can help us in this process.

1. Communicate that you respect all cultures and value the contributions that cultural differences make to learning.
2. Involve all students in learning activities.
3. Use concrete experiences as reference points for language development.
4. Emphasize vocabulary, and have all students practice language.
5. Help students adapt to the culture of school.

Let's see how Gary Nolan, a fourth-grade teacher in an urban elementary school, uses these guidelines as he works with his students.

> As is the case with many urban classrooms, Gary's students come from diverse backgrounds. Of his 28 students, 9 are Hispanic, 6 are African American, 4 are Asian, and 2 are from Morocco. Eight are ELs.
>
> "You're improving all the time," Gary smiles at his students who are ELs as the rest of the class files into the room on a Friday morning. He spends a half hour with them each morning to help them keep up with their classmates.
>
> "Good morning, Tu . . . Nice haircut, Shah," Gary greets students as they come in the door.
>
> "Who's up today?" he asks as the students settle down.
>
> "Me," Anna says, raising her hand.
>
> "Go ahead, Anna."
>
> Anna moves to the front of the room. "I was born in Mexico, but my father is from Guatemala, and my mother is from Columbia," she explains, pointing to each of the countries on a map at the front of the room.

Every Friday Gary has one of the students make a presentation. They bring food, costumes, art, and music that illustrate their backgrounds, and they place a pushpin with their name on it on the map.

Gary frequently comments about how lucky they are to have classmates from so many parts of the world. "Remember when Shah told us about Omar Khayyam?" Gary had asked. "He solved math problems that people in Europe didn't solve until many years later. If Shah wasn't in our class, we would never have learned that."

Gary also has a chart displaying common words and phrases, such as "Hello," "Goodbye," and "How are you?" in Spanish, Vietnamese, Arabic, and English. He has also labeled objects around the room, such as the clock, windows, and chairs, in both the students' native languages and English. And he displays a calendar that identifies holidays in different cultures. Students make special presentations on the holidays, and parents are invited.

"Okay, story time," Gary says when Anna is finished. He reads a story from a book that is liberally illustrated with pictures. After reading a portion of the story he stops and directs, "Tell us something about the story. . . . Serena?"

Serena responds, and Gary then directs, "Something else . . . Issa?"

After Issa answers, he calls on two more students, reads another portion of the story, and repeats the process. He also holds up the pictures and has students identify the object or event being illustrated. For example, one picture shows a cave in some woods that the boy and girl in the story explore.

"Everyone say 'cave,'" Gary directs, pointing at the picture, and the students say "cave" in unison. He does the same with other objects in the picture, such as a tree, rock, and stream.

After finishing, he begins, "Tell us something you remember about the story. . . . Carmela?"

". . . A boy and a girl . . . are lost," Carmela responds in her halting English.

"Yes, good. . . . The story is about a boy and a girl who got lost in a cave," Gary says slowly and clearly, pointing again to each of the objects in the picture.

"Have any of you ever been in a cave? . . . How is a cave different from a hole?"

Gary has the students briefly talk to each other and then has them share their personal experiences with digging holes and going into caves. When they struggle with a term, he provides it, has the class say it in unison, and repeats the process with another student.

"Good, everyone," Gary smiles after they've discussed the story for several more minutes. "Let's get ready for math."

Now, let's look at Gary's efforts to apply the guidelines.

Communicate Respect for all Cultures and the Contributions That Culture Makes to Learning. Gary implemented the first guideline by having students make presentations about their cultural heritage and emphasizing how lucky they are to have classmates from different parts of the world. His emphasis on the contributions of Omar Khayyam, for example, and comments like, "If Shah weren't in our class, we probably would never have learned that," communicates that students' cultures are respected and valued, which can promote both pride and motivation (Banks, 2014; Gollnick & Chinn, 2013).

Gary's actions illustrate culturally responsive teaching, approaches to instruction that attempt to understand the cultures of the students we teach, communicate positive attitudes about cultural diversity, and employ a variety of instructional approaches that build on students' cultural backgrounds (Banks, 2014; Gollnick & Chinn, 2013; Gay, 2010).

Culturally responsive teaching can make classrooms effective learning environments for all students. For instance, learning about the food, dress, art, and music from different cultures, as well as contributions of individuals from those cultures is indeed enriching for all students.

In addition to instruction that was culturally responsive, Gary communicated that he valued all his students as people by spending personal time before school with his students who were ELs and personally greeting each of his students as they came into his room. A simple greeting is a subtle gesture, but it's important when working with members of cultural minorities (Koppelman, 2014; Suarez-Orozco, Pimentel, & Martin, 2009).

Involve All Students in Learning Activities. Gary applied the second guideline by attempting to involve all his students in his learning activity. Calling on all students as equally as possible is a simple—but admittedly demanding—strategy for involving students. Doing so signaled that he expected each one to participate and learn, and when they struggled, he helped them answer.

Earlier in the chapter we said that members of cultural minorities are sometimes more comfortable when teachers ask questions that are more "open-ended, story-starter" types (Rogoff, 2003). Gary capitalized on this factor with directives such as "Tell us something about the story." Questions such as this are effective with all students, and they are particularly applicable with students who are learning English at the same time as they're studying content.

Some teachers believe that students don't *want* to answer questions. This isn't true. All students, including those who are minorities, want to be called on if they believe they will be able to answer, and you can emphasize that answering incorrectly is simply a part of learning. When learning a second language, listening and reading are easier than speaking, so they commonly develop first (Pinter, 2012). ELs' reluctance to respond may not reflect their knowledge of, or interest in, the topic you're discussing. Instead it's more likely due to the difficulty they have putting thoughts into words in a second language.

Use Concrete Experiences as Reference Points for Language Development. When we learn a new language, we typically first learn terms that represent concrete concepts, such as *dog, car,* and *mom* and *dad.* In helping our students who are English learners, the more concrete we can be the better. For instance, when using the term *force,* actually demonstrating the concept, such as pushing a book across a desk, makes the term meaningful (Diaz-Rico, 2014; Morrow, Gambrell, & Duke, 2011; Peregoy & Boyle, 2013). And, just as when we learned our own language, the knowledge we accumulate about words and how language works helps us in learning a second language (Echevarria & Graves, 2015).

Gary capitalized on this guideline by using a book filled with pictures, such as the pictures of the hole and the cave, as concrete reference points when introducing new vocabulary. He also provided concrete experiences for his students by labeling objects around the room in both English and their native languages.

Emphasize Vocabulary and Have All Students Practice Language. Language development is obviously a demanding process. For instance, it takes about 2 years in language-rich environments for students to develop basic interpersonal communication skills, a level that allows them to interact socially with their peers (Cummins, 2000). Then, they often need an additional 5 to 7 years to develop academic language proficiency, a level that allows them to handle the demanding learning tasks found in classrooms (Echevarria & Graves, 2015; Diaz-Rico, 2014). Vocabulary, and especially the technical vocabulary found in many content areas, is challenging for all students, and it's particularly challenging for ELs who are simultaneously learning English and specific content (Echevarria, Vogt, & Short, 2013). This suggests that we should encourage all our students to use as much language as possible to describe their understanding, and this process is even more important for ELs (MacWhinney, 2011; Otto, 2014).

Earlier we suggested using open-ended questions as a strategy for involving students, and these questions are also effective for promoting vocabulary development. For instance, a question/directive such as "Tell us something about the story . . . . Carmela?" allowed her to focus on language without the pressure of having to provide a specific answer (Echevarria & Graves, 2015). Context clues together with specific strategies that differentiate closely related words, such as Gary did with *cave* and *hole*, are particularly important. He also had his students practice by saying vocabulary words in unison and encouraging them to share personal experiences related to the concepts.

Finally, patience is essential in this process. If students perceive impatience in their teachers, or even worse, criticism or sarcasm, they are likely to emotionally withdraw, which makes it less likely that they will try to use language, and their opportunities to practice are reduced (Peregoy & Boyle, 2013).

Help Students Adapt to the Culture of School. Earlier in our discussion we presented the example with the school principal and students whose backgrounds were from the Pacific Islands. To maximize student achievement, and particularly the achievement of cultural and linguistic minorities, our classroom environments must be orderly and learning focused (Emmer & Evertson, 2013; Evertson & Emmer, 2013). Our students must come to class on time and stay on task. And they can't disrupt learning activities and run around the room on whims. To reach these goals, John Ogbu (2003) described a process called "accommodation without assimilation." It suggests that members of cultural minorities adapt to the school culture, including the use of language, without losing their cultural identities.

The process of accommodation without assimilation also applies to the use of dialects, and different dialects don't have to form barriers between home and school.

Bidialecticism, the ability to switch back and forth between a dialect and Standard English, allows access to both (Godley & Escher, 2011; Gollnick & Chinn, 2013). For example, a high school teacher read a series of poems by Langston Hughes and focused on how Hughes used Black English to create vivid images. The class discussed contrasts with Standard English and ways in which differences between the two dialects could be used to accomplish different goals. As time went on, the students learned to use Standard English in school but understood that using different dialects in their home cultures was perfectly acceptable.

Minority role models are especially valuable in promoting the process of accommodation without assimilation. Minority role models provide learners with evidence that they can both succeed in mainstream culture and still retain their cultural identity (Tiedt & Tiedt, 2010).

As you saw in Gary's efforts, working with students who come from diverse backgrounds is challenging. However, these students respond very positively to caring and genuine attempts to help them adapt to both school and mainstream American culture. It will take time, but for those with whom you succeed, the responses you get from them will be among the most rewarding you will have as a teacher.

Classroom Connections

Working with Students Who Are Culturally and Linguistically Diverse in Classrooms

1. Students' cultural attitudes and values can have a powerful effect on school learning. Communicate that you respect and value all cultures, and emphasize the contributions that cultural differences make to learning.

   ■ **Elementary:** A third-grade teacher designs classroom "festivals" that focus on different cultures and invites parents and other caregivers to help celebrate and contribute to enriching them. He also emphasizes values, such as courtesy and respect, which are common to all cultures.

   ■ **Middle School:** An art teacher in the Southwest decorates his room with pictures of Native American art and discusses how it contributes to art in general and how it communicates Native American values, such as a sense of harmony with nature and complex religious beliefs.

   ■ **High School:** An urban English teacher has students read works written by African American, Middle Eastern, South Asian, and Far Eastern authors. They compare both the writing approach and the different points of view that the authors represent.

2. Language development is facilitated when teachers use concrete examples to refer to abstract concepts. Begin language development and concept learning activities with experiences that provide a concrete frame of reference.

   ■ **Elementary:** A fifth-grade teacher, in a unit on fractions, has students fold pieces of paper into halves, thirds, fourths, and eighths. At each point, she has them state in words what the example represents, and she writes important terms on the board.

   ■ **Middle School:** A science teacher begins a unit on the skeletal and muscular systems by having students feel their own legs, arms, ribs, and heads. As they touch parts of their bodies, such as their Achilles tendon, she has them repeat the term *tendon* and has them state in words that tendons attach bones to muscles.

   ■ **High School:** An English teacher stops whenever an unfamiliar word occurs in a reading passage or discussion and asks for a definition and example of it. He keeps a list of these words on a bulletin board and encourages students to use them in class and in their writing.

3. Learning a second language requires that students use the language in speaking, writing, and reading. Provide students with multiple opportunities to practice language in your classroom.

   ■ **Elementary:** The fifth-grade teacher who had the students fold the papers has them describe each step they take when they add fractions with both like and unlike denominators. When they struggle to put their understanding into words, she prompts them, in some cases providing essential words and phrases for them.

   ■ **Middle School:** A social studies teacher has students prepare oral reports in groups of four. Each student must make a 2-minute presentation to the other three members of the group. After students practice their reports with each other in groups, each person presents a part of a group report to the whole class.

   ■ **High School:** A history teacher calls on a variety of students to provide part of a summary of the previous day's work. As she presents new information, she frequently stops and has other students describe what has been discussed to that point and how it relates to topics discussed earlier.

Ed Psych and You

Think about this class. What is the ratio of males to females? Is it similar to other classes you're taking? How would the ratio differ if it was an engineering or computer science class?

Gender

What Marti Banes sees on the first day of her advanced-placement chemistry class is surprising and disturbing. Of her 26 students, only 5 are girls, and they sit quietly, responding only when she asks them direct questions. Sharing her interest in science is one reason she has chosen teaching as a career, but this situation is giving her little opportunity to do so.

Lori Anderson, the school counselor at an urban middle school, looks up from the desk where she is working on her annual report to the faculty. She knows that boys traditionally outnumber girls with respect to behavioral problems, but the numbers she is seeing are troubling. In every category—referrals by teachers, absenteeism, tardies, and fights—boys outnumber girls by more than 2 to 1. In addition, the number of boys that have been referred to her for special education testing far exceeds referrals for girls.

Why did you choose your current major? Did your gender play a role in the decision? If you are like students in other areas, there's a chance it did (Hill, Corbett, & Rose, 2012). For example, research indicates that more than 8 of 10 elementary and middle school teachers are female, and the figure rises to 98% for preschool and kindergarten teachers (U.S. Department of Labor, 2013). On the other hand, Paul's two brothers are both on computer science faculties at their universities, and they report just the opposite—the vast majority of their students are male.

The fact that some of our students are boys and others are girls is so obvious that we tend to not think about it. When we're reminded, however, we notice that they often act and think differently. This is natural and positive in many ways, but problems can occur if societal or school influences limit the academic potential of either girls or boys. Gender is a form of diversity, and it can also influence learning and development (see Figure 4.4).

Boys and girls are different, and these differences manifest themselves almost from birth; male infants tend to be more active and fussier, and they don't sleep as well as female babies (Brannon, 2011; Helgeson, 2012). Girls mature faster, master verbal and motor skills at an earlier age, prefer activities with a social component, and tend to be more cooperative. Boys are more oriented toward roughhouse play and tend to be more physically aggressive and competitive (Pellegrini, 2011; Wentzel, Battle, Russell, & Looney, 2010).

Girls also tend to be more extroverted and anxious, and they are more trusting, less assertive, and have slightly lower self-esteem than boys of the same age and background. These gender differences appear early; children as young as 18 to 24 months begin to sort themselves out as male or female and gravitate toward gender-specific toys such as blocks and cars for boys and dolls for girls (Martin & Ruble, 2010; Thommessen & Todd, 2010). Both prefer to play with members of the same sex (Parke & Clarke-Stewart, 2011).

Experts believe that genetics and the environment both contribute to gender differences (Jorde, Carey, & Bamshad, 2010; Halpern et al., 2007). For example, genes control physical differences such as size and growth rate as well as differences in temperament, aggressiveness, and early verbal and exploratory behaviors. Male and female hormones also play a role (Valla & Ceci, 2011; Vuoksimaa, 2010).

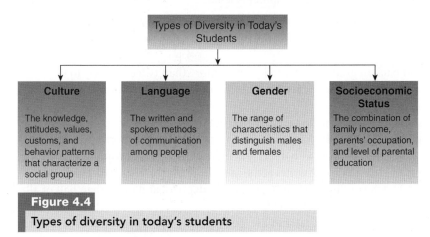

Figure 4.4

Types of diversity in today's students

Although controversial, some researchers suggest that boys' and girls' brains are wired differently (Auyeung & Baron-Cohen, 2012; Barber et al., 2012; Szaflarski et al., 2012). Components of the brain that build word centers and fine-motor skills are a year ahead in girls, which gives them an advantage in reading, using pencils, and other small-motor tasks. Centers in the brain that control emotions are also advanced for girls, making them more able to sit still for the long periods that school often requires. Some argue that school systems as a whole are more compatible with girls' genetic and physiological makeups.

Girls and boys are also treated differently by parents, peers, and teachers, and this treatment, combined with the influence of genes and hormones, creates gender-role identities, beliefs about appropriate characteristics and behaviors of males and females (Cassano & Zeman, 2010; Kennedy Root & Denham, 2010).

The school curriculum also subtly influences gender-role identity (Brannon, 2011; Helgeson, 2012). For example, male characters in stories are typically presented as strong and adventurous, but seldom warm and sensitive. Computer software programs and video games are heavily oriented toward boys, with male heroes as the main characters (Griffiths, 2010; Hamlen, 2011; Rideout, Foehr, & Roberts, 2010).

School-Related Gender Differences

Gender differences in classrooms are more significant than many people realize. Some of these differences include the following (Cvencek, Meltzoff, & Greenwald, 2011; Valla & Ceci, 2011; Weis & Cerankosky, 2010):

- In the early grades, girls score as high as, or higher than, boys on almost every standardized measure of achievement and psychological well-being. By the time they graduate from high school or college, they have fallen behind boys.
- In math, girls are initially better at basic skills such as counting, arithmetic computation, and basic concepts. During adolescence, boys perform better on math tests requiring abstract reasoning. Boys also perform better on visual-spatial tasks, a difference often attributed to the kinds of toys they play with, participation in sports, and greater exposure to computers and computer games. And boys are more confident in their abilities in math, even when achievement levels are the same.
- Girls score lower on the SAT and the ACT, both of which are important for college admission. The greatest gaps are in science and math.
- Women score lower on all sections of the Graduate Record Exam, the Medical College Admissions Test, and admissions tests for law, dental, and optometry schools.
- Women lag far behind men in college majors considered traditionally male, such as math, physics, engineering, and computer science.

On the other hand, boys have a number of issues as well. They include the following (Halpern et al., 2007; National Center for Education Statistics, 2011; Sommers, 2008; Turnbull et al., 2013):

- Boys are held back in grade more often, they're more than twice as likely to be classified as special-needs students, and they far outnumber girls in remedial English and math classes.
- Boys receive the majority of failing grades, drop out of school four times more often than girls, and are cited for disciplinary infractions as much as 10 times more often than girls.
- Boys score lower than girls on both direct and indirect measures of reading and writing, and the average 11th-grade boy writes at the same level as an average 8th-grade girl.
- Nearly 6 of 10 bachelor's degrees, 60% of master's degrees, and more than half of all doctoral degrees are earned by women.
- Boys also encounter problems later in life. For example, men are arrested for more than 60% of all property crimes and 80% of all violent crimes (Federal Bureau of Investigation, 2011).

We need to place gender achievement differences in perspective, however, because the overlap between boys' and girls' performance is much greater than any differences. In any group of boys and girls, we are likely to see students who both struggle and excel. As we would expect, on tests of general intelligence, gender differences are negligible. Boys' performance on achievement tests vary more than girls', however, with more boys at both the upper and lower ends of the spectrum (Halpern, 2006; Else-Quest, Hyde, & Linn, 2010; Valla & Ceci, 2011).

Boys' and Girls' Classroom Behavior

Given these differences, it's not surprising that boys and girls behave differently in classrooms. Girls are more engaged in classroom activities, are more diligent in completing school assignments, and are more concerned about doing well in school (Robinson & Lubienski, 2011). Boys interact with teachers more often, both because they are more assertive and because they cause more behavioral problems, and they are more likely to ask questions and make comments (Brophy, 2010; Gay, 2006; Wentzel et al., 2010).

Behavioral differences are particularly pronounced in science and math (Halpern et al., 2007; Martin & Ruble, 2010). For example, boys are more likely to lead in setting up science experiments, relegating girls to passive roles such as recording data (Brophy, 2010). These differences increase as students move through school, with a significant decrease in girls' participation in science and math activities during the middle school years. In addition, girls are more likely to attribute success in science to luck, and failure to lack of ability. In general, girls are less confident about their abilities, even when aptitude and achievement are comparable (Brophy, 2010; Schunk, Meece, & Pintrich, 2014; Wigfield, Byrnes, & Eccles, 2006).

The creation of **single-gender classes** (and schools), where boys and girls are segregated for part or all of the day, is one response to gender-related learning differences and issues. The number of single-sex classrooms in the United States has increased significantly, from less than a dozen in 2000 to 510 in 2011 (Zubrzychi, 2012). Of this number, 116 qualified as single-sex schools (NASSPE, 2013).

Advocates claim that both girls and boys benefit from single-sex schools (Sullivan, Joshi, & Leonard, 2010). Girls in these schools are more likely to assume leadership roles, take more math and science courses, and have higher self-esteem. Advocates of all-male schools claim that they promote male character development and are especially effective with boys from low-income and minority families (Patterson, 2012). Minimizing distractions from the other sex is one argument for these adaptations. One director of a single-sex school noted, "The boys don't feel like they need to put on a big show for the girls, and the girls feel like they can strive academically without having to dumb down their ability" (Standen, 2007, p. 47). Separating boys and girls also allows teachers to adjust their instruction to the specific needs and interests of each.

However, critics dispute these claims and even call for a ban on the practice (Halpern et al., 2011). These critics assert that academic achievement is no higher in single-sex classrooms, gender stereotypes are reinforced, boys become more aggressive, and girls' assertiveness is reduced.

Research raises other issues. Because boys and girls are isolated from one another, single-sex schools and classes might not prepare students for the "real world" in which males and females must work together (Standen, 2007). One critic observed, "A boy who has never been beaten by a girl on an algebra test could have some major problems having a female supervisor" (Medina, 2009, p. A24). More research is needed to determine the long-term effects of this experiment and whether these changes are effective for helping students learn and develop. At this point, the research is inconclusive (Zubrzycki, 2012).

What does the information about gender differences suggest to us as teachers? We address this question next.

Educational Psychology and Teaching: Responding to Gender Issues with Your Students

We can do a great deal to eliminate gender bias and stereotyping in our teaching. The following guidelines can assist us in our efforts:

1. Communicate openly with students about gender issues.
2. Eliminate gender bias in instructional activities.
3. Present students with nonstereotypical role models.

Let's return to Marti's work with her advanced-placement chemistry students to see how she applies these guidelines.

Marti decides to take positive steps to address the gender issue in her class. First, she initiates a discussion. "I almost didn't major in chemistry," she begins. "Some of my girlfriends scoffed, and others were nearly appalled. 'You'll be in there with a bunch of geeks,' some of them said. 'Girls don't major in chemistry,' others added. They all thought science and math were only for guys."

"It is mostly for guys," Amy shrugs. "Look at us."

"It isn't our fault," Shane responds. "Guys didn't try to keep you out of the class."

After several other students add comments, Marti continues. "I'm not blaming either you guys or the girls. . . . And there's no rule that says that girls can't be engineers or boys can't be nurses or special education teachers," she emphasizes. "In fact, there's a shortage of all of them."

As they continue, she discusses historical reasons for gender stereotypes and encourages both the boys and the girls to keep their career options open.

She has similar discussions in her other classes. During learning activities, she makes a special effort to encourage both girls and boys to participate equally, and she tells her students why she is doing so. For Career Week, she invites a female chemistry professor from a nearby university to come and talk about opportunities for women in chemistry, and she invites a male nurse from one of the local hospitals to talk about the role of science in his job and his experiences in a female-dominated profession.

Marti also talks with other science teachers and counselors about gender stereotyping, and they work on a plan to encourage both boys and girls to consider career options in nonstereotypical fields.

Let's look now at Marti's attempts to apply the guidelines in her teaching.

Communicate Openly with Your Students about Gender Issues. As with many aspects of teaching, as well as human relations in general, awareness resulting from open communication can make an important contribution toward eliminating stereotypes and perceptions. As an example, let's look again at some of the dialogue between Marti and her students.

Marti: I almost didn't major in chemistry . . . Some of my girlfriends scoffed, and others were nearly appalled. "You'll be in there with a bunch of geeks," some of them said. "Girls don't major in chemistry," others added. They all thought science and math were only for guys.

Amy: It is mostly for guys. . . . Look at us.

Shane: It isn't our fault. . . . Guys didn't try to keep you out of the class.

Marti: I'm not blaming either you guys or the girls. . . . And there's no rule that says that girls can't be engineers or boys can't be nurses or special education teachers. . . . In fact, there's a shortage of all of them."

This type of discussion opens communication and can be important for changing perceptions about gender issues. For instance, the boys heard the girls' perspectives and vice versa. And the students hearing Marti emphasize career choices, such as engineering for girls and nursing for boys, can make a difference to the students' potential career choices (Evans-Winters & Ivie, 2009).

Eliminate Gender Bias in Instructional Activities. Throughout this text, we have consistently encouraged you to call on your students as equally as possible. This strategy is important for working with students from different cultural and linguistic backgrounds, and it's equally important for boys and girls. When girls see that they're being called on as often as boys in an algebra II class, for example, or boys realize that they're being asked to participate in a unit on poetry in an English class, the practice communicates that math is as much for girls as it is for boys and that poetry is as much for boys as for girls. These actions are both concrete and symbolic and probably do more to break down stereotypes than do any other strategies.

We want to emphasize that we're focusing here on *academic* behaviors. Boys and girls are indeed different, and no one is suggesting that they should be, or behave, the same in every way. Academically, however, boys and girls should be given the same opportunities and encouragement, just as students from different cultures and socioeconomic backgrounds should be.

Present Students with Nonstereotypical Role Models. Modeling is one of the most powerful influences that exist on people's behaviors, and by inviting a female chemistry professor and a male nurse into her classes, Marti made a powerful statement about potential career choices. Seeing that men and women can succeed and be happy in nonstereotypical fields can broaden the career horizons for both girls and boys (Weisgram, Bigler, & Liben, 2010; Martin & Ruble, 2010).

Classroom **Connections**

Eliminating Gender Bias in Classrooms

1. Gender bias often results from a lack of awareness by both teachers and students. Actively attack gender bias in your teaching.

   - Elementary: A first-grade teacher consciously deemphasizes sex roles and differences in his classroom. He has boys and girls share equally in chores, and he eliminates gender-related activities, such as competitions between boys and girls and forming lines by gender.

   - Middle School: A middle school language arts teacher selects stories and clippings from newspapers and magazines that portray men and women in nontraditional roles. She matter-of-factly talks about nontraditional careers during class discussions about becoming an adult.

   - High School: At the beginning of the school year, a social studies teacher explains how gender bias hurts both sexes, and he forbids sexist comments in his classes. He calls on boys and girls equally, and emphasizes equal participation in discussions.

Ed Psych and You

Were finances ever an important concern in your family? Did your parents go to college? What kinds of jobs do they have?

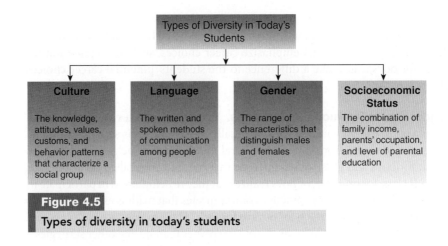

Figure 4.5
Types of diversity in today's students

Socioeconomic Status

The questions in *Ed Psych and You* relate to your **socioeconomic status (SES)**, the combination of parents' income, level of education, and the kinds of jobs they have. Socioeconomic status describes people's relative standing in society and is a powerful factor influencing student achievement (see Figure 4.5).

Researchers divide families into four classes: upper, middle, working, and lower. Table 4.3 outlines characteristics of these classes.

Socioeconomic status consistently predicts intelligence and achievement test scores, grades, truancy, and dropout and suspension rates (Macionis, 2013; Willingham, 2013). It exerts its most powerful influence at the lower income levels. For example, students from families in the highest income quartile score higher on both math and reading achievement tests, drop out of school less often, and are much more likely to graduate from high school and college than their low-SES peers (Berliner, 2005; J. Lee & Bowen, 2006).

Let's look at the issues facing lower income levels.

Table 4.3	Characteristics of different socioeconomic levels			
	Upper Class	**Middle Class**	**Working Class**	**Lower Class**
Income	$160,000+	$80,000–$160,000 (½) $40,000–80,000 (½)	$25,000–$40,000	Below $25,000
Occupation	Corporate or professional (e.g., doctor, lawyer)	White collar, skilled blue collar	Blue collar	Minimum wage unskilled labor
Education	Attended college and professional schools and expect children to do the same	Attended high school and college or professional schools.	Attended high school; may or may not encourage college	Attended high school or less; cost is a major factor in education
Housing	Own home in prestigious neighborhood	Usually own home	About half own a home	Rent

Source: Macionis, 2013 and U.S. Bureau of Census, 2013

Poverty

When Kirsten gets a spare moment, and there aren't many of these, she loves to draw fantasy creatures on her computer (when it works; when it doesn't, she uses paper and pencil). She likes to draw mermaids, fairies, and monsters—escapes from reality. But Kirsten's life is not a fairy tale. She hurries home from school with her brother, fixes them both a snack, and does her homework. Then she straightens up the small apartment, cleans up the room she shares with her brother, does the dishes left over from breakfast and last evening's meal, and cooks dinner. Quite an accomplishment for a fifth grader! She is sometimes hungry and she worries that she and her mother and brother won't have enough to eat.

Kirsten has to work like this because her single mother works 10 hours a day on two jobs—one as a waitress and the other cleaning people's houses—to make ends meet. When her mother returns home from work, she collapses on the sofa exhausted. Life is tough.

In 2012, the federal government defined the poverty level for a family of four as $23,492 (DeNavas-Walt, Proctor, & Smith, 2013). This definition is determined primarily by the cost of food, and it largely ignores other factors such as housing, transportation, and energy.

Nearly one of five students in our country live in poverty (Aud et al., 2013; Rebell & Wolff, 2012). And poverty rates are increasing; for example, the number of children living in poverty rose by 33% between 2000 and 2009 (U.S. Bureau of Census, 2010). A third of the children living in poverty have at least one parent working full time, and the low-paying jobs available to poorly educated parents can't keep up with the continually rising cost of living (Federal Interagency Forum on Child and Family Statistics, 2010). Also, the percentage of American families below the poverty level is consistently higher than in other industrialized countries (Rebell & Wolff, 2012).

Many students—such as yourself—in teacher-preparation programs nationwide come from suburban middle-class backgrounds, so they don't often think about poverty as a potential issue in their classrooms. However, many changes have occurred over the years, and more than half of the poor populations in metropolitan areas now live in suburbs. For example, in the metropolitan Cleveland, Ohio, area the suburban poverty rate, fueled by unemployment and real estate problems, increased by more than 50% between 2000 and 2010 (Tavernise, 2011). This suggests that poverty will be a factor regardless of where you teach.

Poverty is not distributed equally among racial and ethnic groups (see Figure 4.6). The actual number of White children living in poverty is greater than for any other group, but their percentage is the lowest. For example, 13% of white children live in poverty, whereas 34% of Hispanic children, 36% of Native American, and 39% of Black children experience the same plight (U.S. Department of Education, 2012). Experts estimate that 40% of American children will live in poverty at some time in their lives (Koppelman, 2014).

The federal government attempts to address some of the problems of poverty through the National School Lunch Program. Children from families at or below 130% of the poverty level are eligible for free breakfasts and lunches; those with incomes between 130% and 185% of the poverty level are eligible for reduced-price meals, for which students can be charged no more than 40 cents (U.S. Department of Agriculture, 2013). This program provided free or low-cost lunches to more than 31 million students each day in 2012. Many families that qualify don't participate, however, being either unaware that the programs are available or too proud to take advantage of them (Brimley, Verstegen, & Garfield, 2012).

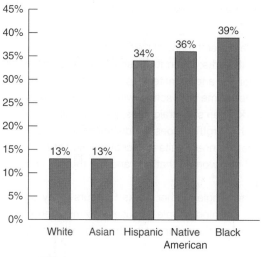

Figure 4.6

Child poverty rates by race/ethnicity
Sources: U.S. Bureau of Census, Department of
Commerce, American Community Survey (ACS),
2013; Digest of Education Statistics, 2012.

Teachers report that nearly two-thirds of their students periodically come to school hungry (Shah, 2011), and they respond in a variety of ways, such as keeping boxes of crackers, granola bars, and other snacks in their desks. They also help students sign up for free or reduced-priced meals at school.

HOMELESSNESS

Emily sleeps on a mat on the floor of a city-managed shelter, with a tattered comforter as her only cover. "I'm cold," she murmurs through her half sleep. Her mother covers her with a worn winter coat while trying to not wake her younger brother, who is sleeping nearby.

Emily, her younger brother, and her single mom have been living in one room in the shelter since her mom lost her job as a result of the downturn in the economy. She has been actively searching for a new job, but so far, no luck.

They must go to a community wash area both to clean up and go to the bathroom. The only heat in their room is a space heater that they must share with the people in the next room. It isn't uncommon for Emily and her brother to go to bed hungry, and her mom often skips meals so her children will have enough to eat. Her mother continues to hope for a job so they can get back to some semblance of a normal life again (adapted from Elliott, 2013).

This is what homelessness feels like to one of the 22,000 homeless children in New York City. Homelessness is a direct result of poverty, and the problems of poverty are particularly acute for these children. Over a million homeless students attended our schools in 2011–2012, and 40 states reported an increase in the number of homeless students, with 10 reporting an increase of 20% or more (National Center for Homeless Education, 2013).

The typical homeless family is headed by a single woman in her 20s with limited education and two children, one or both under six. Homeless children often lack adequate nutrition and medical care, and their development in speech, motor coordination, and social skills is often delayed.

The problem of homelessness has been exacerbated by the downturn in our country's economy, and many families that were barely getting by face eviction from their homes (Winerip, 2011).

Socioeconomic Factors That Influence Learning

Socioeconomic status influences learning in three important ways:

- Basic needs
- Learning experiences in the home
- Attitudes and values

Let's look at them.

BASIC NEEDS

One in five children in America experiences "food insecurity," which means that they don't always know where they will find their next meal. And members of cultural minorities and single-parent families made up a disproportionate share of this figure (Feeding America, 2013).

Food insecurity leads to both physical and psychological problems. For example, poor nutrition and inadequate prenatal care lead to higher rates of premature births and infant mortality (Ballot, Potterton, Chirwa, Hilburn, & Cooper, 2012). Premature babies have higher incidences of brain abnormalities, sensory impairments, language delays, emotional and behavioral problems, and poor motor coordination. Poor nutrition can also affect attention and memory and even lead to lower intelligence test scores (Berk, 2013).

The school nurse in high-poverty schools often serves as a substitute for the family doctor because many families don't have insurance and can't afford to seek medical care. One school nurse commented that her schools' students didn't have the "luxury" of calling a pediatrician if a child gets sick, and weekends are particularly difficult. "When our kids get sick on the weekends, they go to the emergency room, or they wait. Monday morning, they are lined up, and they have to see the nurse" (Smith, 2005, p. 49). Obviously, students will learn less when they're hungry or ill.

Economic problems can also lead to family and marital conflicts, which result in less stable and supportive homes (Repetti & Wang, 2010). Children of poverty often come to school without the sense of security that equips them to tackle school-related tasks. As a result, they often have a greater incidence of depression, anxiety, and other emotional and behavioral problems than do their more advantaged peers (Crossnoe & Cooper, 2010; Kagan, 2010).

Children of poverty also relocate frequently; in some low-income schools, mobility rates are above 100% (Dalton, 2013; Hattie, 2009). Nearly a third of the poorest students attend at least three different schools by third grade, compared to only 1 of 10 for middle-class students. These frequent moves are stressful for students and a challenge for teachers attempting to develop caring relationships with them.

LEARNING EXPERIENCES IN THE HOME

Socioeconomic status also influences the kinds of learning experiences provided in the home. High-SES parents are more likely to provide their children with educational activities, such as travel and visits to libraries, museums, and zoos (Aikens & Barbarin, 2008). They also have more computers, books, newspapers, and stimulating games in the home, and they provide more formal training, such as music and dance lessons—all of which complement classroom learning.

Higher SES parents also talk to their children more and differently than do lower SES parents (Fernald, Marchman, & Weisleder, 2012; Weisleder & Fernald, 2013). They ask more questions, explain the causes of events, provide reasons for rules, and use much more language with their children (Fernald et al., 2012). Their language is also more elaborate, their directions are clearer, and they are more likely to encourage problem solving. These differences show up in children as young as 18 months and influence future learning (Fernald et al., 2012). Called "the curriculum of the home," these interaction patterns, together with enriched background experiences, provide a strong foundation for future learning, especially in the areas of reading and writing.

Socioeconomic status also influences how children use technology. Research indicates that higher SES parents are more likely to monitor computer use, which results in significantly less time spent on entertainment programs (Wood & Hawley, 2012). Lower SES students spend more time with media such as video games and social networking and less on homework (Rideout et al., 2010). Some experts are now calling these differences the "new digital divide" (Richtel, 2012).

The summer months are also relevant. While their more affluent peers are reading books, playing educational games, and taking family trips during the summer, lower SES students spend much less time in activities that support school learning. The cumulative effects of these experiences result in *summer learning loss* for less advantaged students (Kim & Guryan, 2010; McCombs et al., 2011; Patall, Cooper, & Allen, 2010).

Higher SES parents also tend to be more involved in their children's schooling (Bolívar & Chrispeels, 2011). They attend school functions, help with projects, monitor homework, and talk to their children about school. Time spent working, often at two jobs or more, is a major obstacle to greater school involvement for low-SES parents (Murphy, 2010; Gerstel, 2011; Repetti & Wang, 2010).

ATTITUDES AND VALUES

The influence of SES is also transmitted through parental attitudes and values. For example, many high-SES parents encourage autonomy, individual responsibility, and self-control. An expanding body of research indicates that learning self-control as a child strongly influences success in later life (Moffitt et al., 2011). Low-SES parents are more likely to emphasize conformity and obedience (Patrick & Gibbs, 2011; Thompson & Newton, 2010).

Values are also communicated by example. For instance, children who see their parents reading and studying learn that reading is valuable, which increases the likelihood that they will also become readers. And as we would expect, students who read at home show higher reading achievement than those who don't (Huebner & Payne, 2010; Li, 2010).

High-SES parents also tend to have higher expectations for their children and encourage them to graduate from high school and attend college (Koppelman, 2014; Macionis, 2013). Often college graduates themselves, they understand the importance of education. They also know how to play the "schooling game," steering their sons and daughters into advanced high school courses and contacting schools for information about their children's learning progress (Englund, Egeland, & Collins, 2008; Davis & Yang, 2005). Low-SES parents, in contrast, tend to have lower aspirations for their children, allow them to "drift" into classes, and rely on the decisions of others. Students get lost in the shuffle, ending up in inappropriate or less challenging classes.

THE IMPACT ON STUDENTS

The differences in SES that we have just described, and particularly the influence of poverty, can have dramatic effects on the amount students learn. For instance, in addition to lower achievement, they are more likely to have emotional and behavioral problems in school, and they're twice as likely as their peers to be suspended and repeat a grade (Macionis &

Parrillo, 2013; McCoy-Roth, Mackintosh, & Murphy, 2012). Research also suggests that children of poverty are five times more likely to drop out of school than are their more afflu-ent peers (Chapman, Laird, Ifill, & KewalRamani, 2011). These problems are particularly pronounced for homeless children, who, as we would predict, don't attend school regularly, which exacerbates all of these problems.

The powerful negative effects of poverty on learning are further illustrated in integration-by-income programs implemented by a number of districts around the country, including Louisville, Kentucky, Omaha, Nebraska, and San Francisco (Kahlenberg, 2012). These programs integrate students from different SES levels using such means as magnet schools, vouchers, and even busing. Research suggests that low-SES students achieve higher in these environments with little or no decrements for higher SES students (Kahlenberg, 2012).

Socioeconomic Status and Students at Risk

> Laurie Ramirez looks over the papers she has been grading and shakes her head. "Fourth grade, and some of these kids don't know what zero means or how place value affects a number. Some can't add or subtract, and most don't understand mul-tiplication. How am I supposed to teach problem solving when they don't understand basic math facts?"
>
> "Reading isn't much better," she thinks. "I have a few who read at a fourth-grade level, but others are still sounding out words like *dog* and *cat*. How can I teach them comprehension skills when they are struggling with ideas this basic?"

We find failing learners in every school. For some, a combination of obstacles makes them **students at risk** of failing to complete their education with the skills necessary to succeed in today's society. Historically these students were described as *underachiev-ers*, but the term *at risk* more clearly reflects the long-term consequences of school failure.

Socioeconomic status is a primary factor in placing students at risk. As we saw ear-lier, poverty creates a number of stress factors that detract from learning (Alloway, Gather-cole, Kirkwood, & Elliott, 2009; Evans & Schamberg, 2009; Joe, Joe, & Rowley, 2009). For example, students who are eligible for free or reduced-cost lunches because of their family's income consistently score below other students on achievement tests in reading, math, and science (National Assessment of Educational Progress, 2013b).

In addition, being a member of a cultural minority or a non-native English speaker, who are also over-represented at lower income levels and often experience issues associated with poverty, increases the likelihood of placing a student at risk (Cushner et al., 2012; Diaz-Rico, 2013; Koppelman, 2014).

The combination of these factors can result in a history of low achievement, which makes new learning even more challenging because students lack the background knowl-edge and skills on which new learning depends (Aikens & Barbarin, 2008). A history of low achievement is compounded by lack of motivation, disengagement from school, and misbehavior (Brophy, 2010; Schunk et al., 2014). The problem can be exacerbated by the fact that students who need quality education the most are often provided with underqualified teachers and substandard buildings and equipment (Amrein-Beardsley, 2012).

THE DROPOUT PROBLEM

Because it has an enormous impact on subsequent employment and income, dropping out of school is one of the most pernicious outcomes of being at risk, with poverty being a major factor. As we saw earlier, students from low-income families are five times more likely to drop out than their more fortunate peers (Chapman et al., 2011). Family instability, high rates of student mobility, and higher graduation standards also contribute to the problem (Holme, Richards, Jimerson, & Cohen, 2010; Rumberger, 2011).

Students who drop out of school decrease their chances of personal success and are more likely to have problems with transiency, crime, and drug abuse (Macionis, 2013). High school dropouts often end up in dead-end minimum wage jobs. The minimum wage in our country was $7.25 an hour at the end of 2013, which amounts to $14,500 a year. We can all imagine trying to live—let alone support a family—on that amount of money. The average high school dropout earns almost 50% less than a high school graduate (Swanson, 2011). In addition, dropping out of high school closes the door to college and well-paying jobs that require advanced training and expertise with technology. In the past, factory and farm jobs offered viable alternatives for dropouts; today with outsourcing to other countries and consolidation of smaller farms, these jobs no longer exist.

As a general pattern, large urban districts have lower graduation rates, but these rates vary dramatically. For example, Chicago had a graduation rate of 70% in 2008 compared to Detroit's 33% (EPE Research Center, 2011b).

Students at Risk and Resilience

Attempts to assist students at risk now focus on developing **resilience**, a learner characteristic that, despite adversity, increases the likelihood of success in school and later life (Noltemeyer, 2013; Noltemeyer & Bush, 2013). Researchers have studied young people who have survived and even prospered despite obstacles such as poverty, poor health care, and fragmented support services, and they've found that resilient children have well-developed self-systems, including high self-esteem, optimism, and feelings that they are in control of their destinies. Resilient children set personal goals, expect to succeed, and believe they are responsible for their success. They are motivated to learn and satisfied with school (Hoff, 2012; Tucker-Drob & Harden, 2012).

How do these skills develop? Resilient children come from emotionally supportive environments, and one characteristic is striking. In virtually all cases, these children have one or more adults who have taken a special interest in them and hold them to high moral and academic standards, essentially *refusing to let the young person fail* (Gauvain & Parke, 2010; Murphy, 2010; Reis, Colbert, & Hébert, 2005). These adults are often parents, but they can also be older siblings or other adults, such as teachers, who take a young person under their wing (Flores, Cicchetti, & Rogosch, 2005; Kincheloe, 2009).

Schools also make important contributions to resilience. Let's see how.

SCHOOLS THAT PROMOTE RESILIENCE

Research has identified four school practices that promote resilience:

- *Safety and structure.* The school and classes are orderly and highly structured. Teachers work with administrators to make the school a safe and welcoming place to learn, and teachers consistently enforce rules and procedures (Bryk, Sebring, Allensworth, Luppescu, & Easton, 2010; Emmer & Evertson, 2013; Evertson & Emmer, 2013).
- *Strong personal bonds between teachers and students.* Teachers become the adults who refuse to let students fail, and students feel connected to the schools (Durlak et al., 2011; Kincheloe, 2009).
- *High and uncompromising academic standards.* Teachers emphasize mastery of content and do not accept passive attendance and mere completion of assignments (Bryk et al., 2010; Reis, McCoach, Little, Muller, & Kaniskan, 2011; Tenenbaum & Ruck, 2007).
- *Community outreach.* Schools reach out to the community and invite parents and caregivers to participate in school activities (Bryk et al., 2010; Peters et al., 2010).

These schools work closely with other community agencies to provide a web of services that support students and their families.

These schools are both demanding and supportive; in many instances, they serve as refuges, essentially homes away from home (Danner, 2011). The emphasis on school–community links reduces alienation and increases academic engagement and achievement (Murphy, 2010; Peters et al., 2010). School-sponsored activities also give teachers the chance to know students in contexts outside the classroom.

TEACHERS WHO PROMOTE RESILIENCE

Schools are no more effective than the teachers who work in them. So how do teachers promote resilience? As we would expect, easy answers don't exist, but research does provide some insights.

The student–teacher relationship is the foundation on which resilience is developed (Henderson, 2013; Jennings, Frank, Snowberg, Coccia, & Greenberg, 2013; Warshof & Rappaport, 2013), and this process is even more important with young children (Miller-Lewis, Searle, Sawyer, Baghurst, & Hedley, 2013). To become resilient, students must believe beyond any doubt that their teachers are committed to their learning and their well-being as people, regardless of their attitude or how they behave. The relationship is analogous to children who come from stable, loving families; the children never consider the possibility that their parents have anything but their best interests at heart.

So how is this relationship developed? Just as loving parents have high expectations for their children, set limits for acceptable behavior, and frequently interact with them, so do teachers who promote resilience. When students inevitably misbehave, don't care, or sometimes even resist learning, teachers don't give up on them; instead, they redouble their efforts and even display the "tough love" that students sometimes need in order to succeed in school.

Recalling some of the anxieties and demands your parents experienced when you were growing up, it's easy to understand that promoting resilience in students who come from disadvantaged backgrounds is highly stressful and challenging. Teachers who succeed have the high levels of social–emotional competence and the emotional sturdiness and sense of personal well-being being that helps them manage stress and avoid burnout (Jennings et al., 2013). Finally, and this is particularly important when working with members of cultural minorities, a sense of personal efficacy—the unrelenting belief that you can and will make a difference with these students—is essential (Sosa & Gomez, 2012).

In addition to being emotionally demanding, promoting resilience is time consuming. It requires spending extra time before or after school both helping students with academic work and being a person students can talk to about personal issues, problems, and goals. Some who work with troubled students suggest that "empathetic listening" is one of the most important personal strategies we can use in building relationships with students who come from disadvantaged backgrounds (Warshof & Rappaport, 2013).

What else do we know about teachers who promote resilience? As we indicated in our analogy with parenting above, research indicates that they interact frequently with students, learn about their families, and share their own lives. They maintain high expectations, use interactive teaching strategies, and emphasize success and mastery of content (Reis et al., 2011; Kincheloe, 2009). They motivate students through personal contacts, instructional support, and attempts to link school to students' experiences (Brophy, 2010; Patrick, Kaplan, & Ryan, 2011).

SES: Cautions and Implications for Teachers

As with culture, language, and gender, it's important to remember that the patterns we're describing represent group differences, and individuals within groups will vary widely. For example, many low-SES parents read and talk to their children, encourage their involvement in extracurricular activities, and attend school events. We (Paul and Don, your authors) both come from low-SES families, but—fortunately for us—were given all the enriching experiences we've discussed in reference to high-SES parents. Conversely, belonging to a high-SES family doesn't guarantee a child enriching experiences and caring, involved parents (Luthar & Latendresse, 2005).

We know that certain home conditions can make it difficult for students to succeed in school, but we also know that schools and teachers can do much to overcome these problems (Darling-Hammond & Bransford, 2005; Durlak, Weissberg, Dymnicki, Taylor, & Schellinger, 2011). Let's turn now to some specifics with respect to promoting resilience.

Educational Psychology and Teaching: Promoting Resilience in Your Students

We know that the student–teacher relationship is the foundation on which resilience is developed. So, what can you do that communicates to students that you're committed to them both as learners and as people? Teaching that helps—even demands—that students work hard and succeed communicates this process better than anything else. Students appreciate and respect teachers who hold high expectations and then help students reach those expectations (Jansen & Bartell, 2013). Here's what one student had to say: "She used to, like, pull me aside, and only me, and, like, make sure that I knew everything, . . . and she would do, like, . . . extra practice, like, to make sure that I got everything" (Jansen & Bartell, 2013, p. 40).

Research suggests that the same strategies proven effective for all students promote resilience in students at risk (Good & Brophy, 2008; Jennings et al., 2013). We don't need to teach in fundamentally different ways, but we do need to do it just that much better. The following guidelines can support these efforts.

1. Create and maintain a safe classroom environment with predictable routines.
2. Combine high expectations with frequent feedback about learning progress.
3. Use teaching strategies that involve all students and promote high levels of success.
4. Use high-quality examples that provide the background knowledge students need to learn new content.

Let's see how Diane Smith, a fourth-grade teacher, applies the guidelines with her students.

> Diane's students are studying adjectives in language arts, and she now wants them to be able to use comparative and superlative forms of adjectives in their writing.
>
> Students file into the room from their lunch break, go to their desks, and begin working on a set of exercises where they identify all the adjectives and the nouns they modify in a paragraph displayed on the document camera. As they work, Diane identifies students who have pencils of different lengths and those whose hair color varies.
>
> Diane reviews the passage, has students explain their choices, and provides feedback. When they finish, she directs, "Okay, very good, everyone. Look up here."
>
> "Sofia and Daniel, hold your pencils up so everyone can see. What do you notice? . . . Natia?"
>
> "The pencils are yellow."
>
> "Clarence?"
>
> "They're sharp."
>
> "Angela?"

"Sofia's is longer."

Diane then goes to the board and writes:

Sofia has a long pencil.

Sofia has a longer pencil than Daniel does.

"Now, let's look at Matt and Wesley," she continues. "What do you notice about their hair? . . . Judy?"

Again the students make observations, and after hearing several, Diane asks, "Whose is darker?"

"WESLEY!" several in the class blurt out.

"Good!" Diane again goes to the board and writes three more sentences:

Sofia has a long pencil.	Wesley has black hair.
Sofia has a longer pencil than Daniel does.	Matt has brown hair.
	Wesley has darker hair than Matt does.

"Now, how do the adjectives in the sentences compare? . . . Heather?" Diane asks, pointing to the bottom sentences on each list.

"The ones at the bottom have an 'e' 'r' on the end of them," Heather responds hesitantly.

"Yes, good. . . . And, what are we doing in each of the sentences? . . . Jason?"

"We're comparing two things."

"Good thinking, Jason. We call these kinds of adjectives *comparative adjectives*," Diane smiles.

She then repeats the process with the superlative form of adjectives by having students compare three pencils and three different hair colors, leading them to conclude that superlative adjectives have an *est* on the end of them.

"Very good, everyone. In describing nouns, if we're comparing two, we use the comparative form of the adjective, which has an 'e' 'r' on the end, and if we have three or more, we have an 'e' 's' 't' on the end of the adjective.

"Now," Diane says, pointing to a softball, tennis ball, and golf ball on her desk, "I have a little challenge for you. . . . Write two sentences each that use the comparative and superlative forms of adjectives, and tell about the sizes of these balls."

As the students work, Diane checks on their progress, and when they're finished, says, "Now let's look at your sentences. . . . Someone volunteer, and I'll write it on the board. . . . Okay, Rashad?"

"The tennis ball is bigger than the golf ball."

"Very good, Rashad. And why did you write bigger in your sentence?"

"We're comparing the size of two balls."

They continue discussing the comparative and superlative forms of adjectives, and Diane then directs, "Now, I want you to write a paragraph with at least two sentences that use the comparative form of adjectives and at least two others that use the superlative form. Underline the adjectives in each case.

"And what do we always do after we write something?"

"We read it to be sure it makes sense!" several of the students say simultaneously.

"Very good," Diane smiles. "That's how we become good writers."

As students begin working, Diane circulates among them, periodically stopping for a few seconds to comment on a student's work and to offer brief suggestions.

Now, let's look at Diane's attempts to apply the guidelines.

Create a Safe Classroom Environment with Predictable Routines. As we saw earlier in our discussion, students at risk sometimes come from backgrounds where a great deal of uncertainty exists, and school often becomes a haven of security for these students (Henderson, 2013). Creating a safe and predictable environment is important for all students, and for students at risk it's essential (Emmer & Evertson, 2013; Evertson & Emmer, 2013).

Diane created this type of environment. For example, when students came in from their break, they immediately went to work on exercises on the document camera without being told to do so. For students at risk, the routine—itself—of doing the brief set of exercises is arguably even more important than the exercises themselves.

Combine High Expectations with Feedback about Learning Progress. High expectations are important for all students, and they're particularly important for students at risk (Jansen & Bartell, 2013). This process goes beyond the content or topic being studied. High expectations further remove some uncertainty for these students by symbolizing that their teachers believe in them and believe they're capable. Students from advantaged backgrounds typically don't live with this uncertainty.

By calling on individual students and requiring that they explain their answers, Diane communicated that she expected all students to participate and learn. This is a demanding process. Many students initially have trouble putting their understanding into words, and it is even more challenging for students at risk. The urge to give up—concluding "They can't do it"—can be nearly overwhelming. Students struggle because they haven't had enough practice and support. It isn't easy, but it can be done.

Diane also provided detailed feedback for the beginning-of-class exercises and the sentences at the end of the lesson. This scaffolding promotes success, minimizes mistakes, and increases motivation (Brophy, 2010; Hattie & Gan, 2011).

Use Teaching Strategies That Involve Students and Promote Success. Because students at risk come from disadvantaged backgrounds, they often don't have a history of academic success. As a result, promoting success with them is even more important than it is with their more advantaged peers who are better equipped—academically and emotionally—to cope with occasional failure.

To see how Diane involved her students and promoted their success, let's look again at some of the dialogue from her lesson.

Diane: Okay, very good, everyone. Look up here. . . . Sofia and Daniel, hold your pencils up so everyone can see. What do you notice? . . . Natia?"
Natia: The pencils are yellow.
Diane: Clarence?
Clarence: They're sharp.
Diane: Angela?
Angela: Sofia's is longer.

Because the students could respond with literally anything they observed, they were ensured of answering successfully. For students lacking a history of success, this experience can be very powerful, both emotionally and academically (Brophy, 2010). Admittedly, this strategy won't ensure that the students will be successful in all their academic experiences, but it's an important beginning. And, with additional support, students may gradually develop the perseverance that will dramatically increase the likelihood of more long-term success.

Open-ended questions, such as "What do you notice?" or "How do these compare?," have the added advantage of being easy to ask. For instance, it took Diane only a matter of seconds to call on Natia, Clarence, and Angela, so the strategy allows you to call on several of your students in a short amount of time. Promoting involvement and success is important for all students, and for students at risk it's imperative (Lemov, 2010; Rumberger, 2011).

Use High-Quality Examples That Provide Background Knowledge. Students at risk often lack the school-related experiences that prepare them to succeed. This means that we must provide these experiences for them. Diane applied this guideline by developing her lesson around real-world examples (Renkl, 2011). Teachers who promote resilience link school topics to students' lives, and using the students' pencils and hair color to illustrate comparative and superlative adjectives was a simple application of this idea (Bryk et al., 2010; Varelas & Pappas, 2006).

Helping students succeed while still presenting engaging and challenging activities is essential when working with students at risk (Ellis, Fitzsimmons, & Small-McGinley, 2010; Peters et al., 2010). It isn't easy. Promoting resilience is not a task for the faint of heart, and it's also physically demanding. However, seeing these students meet challenges will be some of the most rewarding experiences you will ever have. As you've likely heard in other contexts, "It's the toughest job you'll ever love."

Classroom **Connections**

Effective Teaching Practices for Promoting Resilience in Classrooms

1. Positive teacher expectations influence both motivation and achievement. Communicate positive expectations to students and their parents.

   - **Elementary:** A fourth-grade teacher spends the first 2 weeks of school teaching students her classroom procedures and explaining how they promote learning. She makes short assignments, carefully monitors students to be certain the assignments are turned in, and immediately calls parents if an assignment is missing.

   - **Middle School:** A math teacher carefully explains his course procedures. He emphasizes the importance of attendance and effort and communicates that he expects all to do well. He also makes himself available before and after school for help sessions.

   - **High School:** An urban English teacher sends home an upbeat letter at the beginning of the year describing her work requirements and grading practices. She has students help translate the letter for parents whose first language is not English and asks parents to sign the letter, indicating they have read it. She also invites questions and comments from parents or other caregivers.

2. Interactive teaching strategies are essential for students at risk. Use teaching strategies that elicit high levels of student involvement and success.

   - **Elementary:** A fifth-grade teacher arranges the seating in his classroom so that students who are and are not minorities are mixed. He combines small-group and whole-class instruction, and when he uses group work, he arranges the groups so they include students who are high and low achievers, students who are and are not minorities, and boys and girls.

   - **Middle School:** An earth science teacher gives students a short quiz every day. He provides feedback the following day, and students frequently calculate their averages. The teacher closely monitors these scores and spends time before school to work with students who are falling behind.

   - **High School:** An English teacher builds her teaching around questioning and examples. She comments, "My goal is to call on each student in the class at least twice during each lesson. I also use a lot of repetition and reinforcement as we cover the examples."

Developmentally Appropriate **Practice**

Student Diversity at Different Ages

While many aspects of diversity are similar across grade levels, important developmental differences exist. The following paragraphs outline suggestions for responding to these differences.

Working with Students in Early Childhood Programs and Elementary Schools

The elementary grades pose developmental challenges for students learning a second language, as they face the dual tasks of learning to read and write while simultaneously learning English (Diaz-Rico, 2013). While some research suggests that young language learners may be more adaptable than older ones, they still need special assistance to be successful (Echevarria & Graves, 2015). Instruction that maximizes opportunities for students to practice and use language is essential for these children. The strategies Gary Nolan used in *"Educational Psychology and Teaching: Teaching Students in Your Classes Who Are Culturally and Linguistically Diverse"* (p. 162) are effective for learners at all ages but are particularly important for elementary students (MacWhinney, 2011; Otto, 2014). Writing assignments that encourage English learners to use their developing language skills are also important (Tompkins, 2014).

As you saw earlier, boys develop more slowly than girls, and girls have more developed language abilities (Calvin, Fernandes, Smith, Visscher, & Deary, 2010; Marinak & Gambrell, 2010; Valla & Ceci, 2011). Some experts suggest that developmental lags explain why boys outnumber girls in the number of special education placements (Hardman, Drew, & Egan, 2014; Heward, 2013). Simple strategies such as giving children a chance to get up and move around, providing concrete examples, and using interactive instructional strategies proven effective with English learners are also effective with slower-developing boys.

Working with Students in Middle Schools

Developmental changes, such as going through puberty, and the transition to less personal middle schools where students often have five or six teachers can be problematic for students who come from diverse backgrounds (Anderman & Mueller, 2010).

Communicating that all students' backgrounds are respected and valued is even more important in diverse middle schools than it is in elementary schools. Safe and predictable classrooms provide both structure and security for middle school students (Emmer & Evertson, 2013). Well-established routines, consistent enforcement of rules, and emphasis on treating all students with courtesy and respect are essential. Establishing personal relationships with students, emphasizing that learning is the purpose of school, and deemphasizing competition and differences among students are also important (Roorda, Koomen, Spilt, & Oort, 2011; Wang & Holcombe, 2010).

Working with Students in High Schools

High school is both the capstone of students' public school experience and an important transition period for both college and careers. Many students who come from low-SES backgrounds or are members of cultural minorities are unaware of the career and higher-education opportunities available to them, especially in rapidly developing fields like technology (Turkle, 2011). Connecting content to students' future lives is particularly important for these students. For example, science teachers can discuss career options in related fields, and social studies and English teachers can examine the impact of technology on our lives.

High school is also an important time for both girls and boys who are trying to reconcile gender-role identities with societal expectations (Weisgram et al., 2010). For example, some high school girls are fearful that being intellectually assertive is not compatible with being feminine, whereas boys are struggling with decisions about whether to go to college or join the workforce (Lane, Goh, & Driver-Linn, 2012). Open discussions with high school students can do a great deal to help them resolve these issues.

chapter

4 Summary

1. Describe culture and ethnicity, and explain how they can influence learning.
   - *Culture* refers to the attitudes, values, customs, and behavior patterns that characterize a social group. The match between a child's culture and the school powerfully influences school success.
   - *Ethnicity* refers to a person's ancestry and the way individuals identify with their ancestors' nation of origin.
   - Culture and ethnicity can influence learning through the cultural attitudes and values that students bring to schools. Some values support learning, whereas others can detract from it.
   - Culture and ethnicity can also influence learning through the interaction patterns characteristic of the cultural group. If the interaction patterns are similar to those found in school, they enhance learning. If they are dissimilar, they can detract from learning.

2. Explain why so much linguistic diversity exists in our country, and describe ways that teachers can accommodate this diversity.
   - Federal legislation, which ended quotas based on national origin, resulted in more immigrants coming to the United States from a wider variety of places. This has resulted in considerably more cultural, ethnic, and linguistic diversity in our classrooms.
   - Teachers can accommodate this diversity by first communicating that all cultures are valued and respected, involving all students in learning activities, and representing topics as concretely as possible.
   - Teachers also accommodate this diversity by providing students with opportunities to practice language and emphasizing important vocabulary.

3. Explain how gender can influence learning, and describe steps for eliminating gender bias in classrooms.
   - Gender can influence learning if either girls or boys adopt gender-stereotyped beliefs, such as believing that math and computer science are male domains, or believing that girls are inherently better at English and writing than boys.
   - Teachers can attempt to eliminate gender bias by openly discussing gender issues, expecting the same academic behaviors from both boys and girls, and inviting nonstereotypical role models to their classes to discuss gender issues.

4. Define socioeconomic status, and explain how it can affect learning.
   - Socioeconomic status describes the relative standing in society resulting from a combination of family income, parents' occupations, and the level of education parents attain.
   - SES can affect learning by influencing students' basic needs. Children of poverty often live in substandard housing and don't have access to medical care.
   - Low-SES children may also lack the school-related experiences they need to be successful, and lower SES parents may need to be encouraged and helped to be involved in their children's education.
   - SES can also influence learning through the attitudes and values of parents. Many high-SES parents encourage autonomy, individual responsibility, and self-control, whereas low-SES parents tend to value obedience and conformity. High-SES parents also tend to have higher expectations for their children than do their lower SES counterparts.

Preparing for Your Licensure Exam

Understanding Learner Diversity

Because our students are becoming more diverse, your licensure exam will contain questions related to learner diversity. To help you practice for the exam in your state, we include the following exercises.

In this chapter, we've seen how culture, language diversity, gender, and SES can influence learning, and how certain combinations of these factors can place students at risk.

Let's look now at another teacher working with students from diverse backgrounds. Read the case study, and answer the questions that follow.

Mariana has been teaching the seventh-grade geography for the past 8 years. In one of her lessons, she has decided to teach about cloud types and formation. A piece of paper has been placed on each student's desk with the following instructions:

1. Form a group of three students.
2. Go outside and look at the sky.
3. Carefully observe the clouds you see (note: not all of them are the same).
4. Write down the number of clouds your group was able to spot.
5. Write down the description of each cloud type you were able to spot.

All the students are very excited and have set about forming their groups. Michael, a new transfer student from Jamaica, quietly approaches Mariana. "Miss, I cannot do what you ask; I am sorry," he squeaks.

"Why?" Mariana asks perplexed.

"My grandmother says it is bad luck to stare at the sky. I do not want bad luck. I cannot look at the sky," answers Michael.

"Oh I see, well you don't have to look at the sky. Join a group, let them look at the sky and you can write down what they observe," suggests Mariana. On hearing this, Michael beams and runs outside to join one of the groups.

After 20 minutes, Mariana calls in all the students. After they all settle in, she asks the students, "How many clouds did you see?"

Each group responds with their respective numbers, and Mariana diligently writes them on the board. She then reflects, based on the number of clouds on the board, "There were fewer number of clouds to spot today, weren't there?"

Everyone nods in agreement. She then asked them to give her descriptions of the clouds they have seen so that she can note them down on the blackboard as well. Kelly starts to give a lengthy description, but in her enthusiasm, uses her native dialect. Mariana cannot understand this dialect, so she asks Kelly to repeat her description. She enthusiastically repeats her description using her dialect. Mariana looks around the class; the other students seem to understand Kelly, but she is unable to comprehend what Kelly was saying.

A bit embarrassed, Mariana turns to the class and utters, "I am sorry Kelly; I cannot understand your dialect. Could you repeat your description of the clouds using Standard English this time?"

All the students burst out laughing and Kelly turns beetroot red with embarrassment. Mariana immediately reprimands the class, "There is nothing wrong in speaking a dialect, but you also need to learn how to speak in Standard English as not everyone will understand your dialect." Kelly then speaks in Standard English and describes the clouds that she has seen. Mariana goes on to write down the rest of group's descriptions. After listing all the descriptions, she teaches the students the name of each cloud type. The only cloud type that is missing is the storm cloud called cumulonimbus, which she goes on to describe to the students.

After completing this, she turns to the students and asks, "Which cloud stores the most water?"

Tammy answers, "Cumulonimbus."

"Good," says Mariana. "Why is water so important for us?" she queries.

Michael enthusiastically answers, "I know that water is important as we cannot live without it. We need water to drink, and to clean ourselves, our clothes and our homes. Plants and animals need water too."

"Very good," says Mariana. "Yes, water is vital for us to survive, and without clouds we would not have water. In our next lesson, I will explain how the clouds store water, that is, I will explain to you the water cycle."

At the end of the lesson, she gives the students homework. Over the weekend, they are to go to the countryside and collect as many different types of stones as they can find and bring it to their next lesson.

All the students leave as the bell rings except for Peter. He sits crying quietly at his desk. Mariana approaches him. "What is wrong? Why are you crying?"

"It is nothing," Peter sniffles.

"Come on, tell me what is wrong. I will not tell anyone, I promise," coaxes Mariana.

Peter responds, "You promise you will not tell anyone?" Mariana nods.

"I cannot do my homework," he sobs.

"Why not?" Mariana asks with concern.

"Please do not tell anyone," squeaks Peter. Once again, Mariana nods.

"I cannot afford the train ride to the countryside, so I cannot collect the stones. You know my daddy passed away last year. My mommy told me this morning that we only have enough money for one more loaf of bread for the rest of the month, and that she does not know how she is going to pay for the rent and utilities this month. I cannot ask her for money to go the countryside."

Questions for Case Analysis

In answering these questions, use information from the chapter, and link your responses to specific information in the case.

Multiple-Choice Questions

1. From the information in the case, Michael was concerned because he could not carry out the assignment. How is his background diverse from the other learners in Mariana's class?

    a. Michael's background is diverse based on his learning style.

    b. Michael's background is diverse based on his culture.

    c. Michael's background is diverse based on his gender.

    d. Michael's background is diverse based on his learning ability.

2. How did Mariana accommodate the linguistic diversity, i.e. Kelly's dialect, in her class?

    a. By providing an opportunity to practice Standard English

    b. By being honest

    c. By reprimanding the students

    d. By providing an opportunity for Kelly to speak in her dialect Constructed-Response Question

Constructed-Response Question

3. Peter is now living with limited economic resources. Explain how his low socioeconomic level can affect his learning.

Important Concepts

academic language
    proficiency
basic interpersonal
    communication skills
bidialecticism
bilingualism
cultural mismatch
culturally responsive teaching

culture
dialect
English as a second language
    (ESL) pullout programs
English learners (ELs)
ethnicity
gender-role identity
immersion programs

learner diversity
maintenance English learner
    (EL) programs
multicultural education
race
resilience
resistance culture
sheltered English

single-gender classes
socioeconomic status (SES)
stereotype threat
structured immersion
students at risk
transitional English learner
    (EL) programs

5 Learners with Exceptionalities

OUTLINE	LEARNING OUTCOMES
	After you've completed your study of this chapter, you should be able to:
Intelligence Psychometric Descriptions of Intelligence Multitrait Views of Intelligence ▶ Analyzing Theories: Psychometric, Multiple Intelligences, and Triarchic Theories of Intelligence Intelligence: Ability Grouping Learning Styles	**1.** Describe different views of intelligence, and explain how ability grouping influences learning.
The Legal Basis for Working with Students with Exceptionalities Individuals with Disabilities Education Act (IDEA) Major Provisions of IDEA Identifying Students with Exceptionalities Diversity: Cautions in the Identification Process	**2.** Describe the major provisions of the Individuals with Disabilities Education Act (IDEA) and the amendments to it.
Exceptionalities and Learning Problems The Labeling Controversy Categories of Exceptionalities ▶ Technology, Learning, and Development: Using Assistive Technology to Support Learners with Disabilities The Neuroscience of Exceptionalities	**3.** Describe the most common learning problems that classroom teachers are likely to encounter.
Students Who Are Gifted and Talented Characteristics of Students Who Are Gifted and Talented Identifying Students Who Are Gifted and Talented Programs for Students Who Are Gifted and Talented Diversity: Pursuing Equity in Special Education	**4.** Identify characteristics of students who are gifted and talented, and explain how teachers identify and teach these students.
Teachers' Responsibilities in Inclusive Classrooms Modifying Instruction to Meet Students' Needs Collaborating with Other Professionals Promoting Social Integration and Development ▶ Developmentally Appropriate Practice: Teaching Students with Exceptionalities at Different Ages	**5.** Describe general education teachers' responsibilities in inclusive classrooms.

When you begin teaching, you almost certainly will have students in your classes with some learning or behavioral issues. Some may have trouble keeping up with their classmates academically, whereas others won't seem to be able to sit still or stay mentally focused. A few may even have visual, hearing, or speech impairments. They're like all students in many ways but sometimes need extra help to succeed. Think about these issues as you read the following case study.

Celina Curtis, a beginning first-grade teacher in a large elementary school, has survived her hectic first weeks. She is beginning to feel comfortable, but at the same time, some things are bothering her.

"It's kind of frustrating," she admits to Clarisse, a veteran who has become her friend and confidante. "I think I'm teaching, but some of the kids just don't seem to get it.

"For instance, there's Rodney. You've seen him on the playground. He's cute, but his engine is stuck on fast. I can barely get him to sit in his seat, much less work. The smallest distraction sets him off. He can usually do the work if I can get him to stick to it, but it's tough. I've talked to his mother, and he's the same way at home.

"Then there's Amelia; she's so sweet, but she simply doesn't get it. I've tried everything under the sun with her. I explain it, and the next time, it's as if it's all brand new. I feel sorry for her, because I know she gets frustrated when she can't keep up with the other kids. When I work with her one-on-one, it seems to help, but I don't have enough time to spend with her. She's falling further and further behind."

"Maybe it's not your fault. You're supposed to do your best, but you're going to burn yourself out if you keep this up," Clarisse cautions. "Check with one of the special ed teachers. Maybe these students need some extra help."

As you begin your study of this chapter, consider these questions:

1. Do Rodney and Amelia have learning issues that require some extra support in order for them to succeed, and if so, what are they?
2. What more can Celina do to help them?

Learners with exceptionalities are students who need special help and resources to reach their full potential. They include students with **disabilities**—functional limitations, such as low intelligence, or an inability to perform a certain act, such as walk or hear a teacher's voice—as well as students with **gifts and talents**—abilities at the upper end of the continuum that require additional support to reach full potential. Some have both (Foley-Nicpon, Assouline, & Colangelo, 2013). **Special education** refers to instruction designed to meet the unique needs of these students.

We begin by examining the concept of *intelligence*, because it plays an important role in understanding and helping students with exceptionalities.

Intelligence

We all know people we think are "sharp," because they're knowledgeable and perceptive, or they learn new ideas quickly and easily. These are intuitive notions of **intelligence**, which experts define more formally as the ability to acquire and use knowledge, solve problems, reason in the abstract, and adapt to new experiences (Garlick, 2010; Gläscher et al., 2010; Kanazawa, 2010).

The ability to benefit from experience is a simple way to think about intelligence. For instance, if we could hypothetically give two people exactly the same set of experiences, the more intelligent of the two will derive more benefit from the experiences.

Psychometric Descriptions of Intelligence

The field of intelligence testing began in the early 1900s in France with the work of Alfred Binet (Flanagan, Genshaft, & Harrison, 1997; Salvia, Ysseldyke, & Bolt, 2013; Siegler, 1992).

France had passed a law requiring all children to attend school, and Binet was commissioned to develop a test to identify students who needed extra educational assistance. He developed a number of questions that correlated with school success, and he found that some younger students could answer questions typically answered by older learners, whereas some older students were only able to answer questions typically answered by younger learners. This led to the concept of *mental age* (MA).

Binet's work attracted attention in the United States, and the first Stanford-Binet intelligence test was introduced in 1916 (Bartholomew, 2004). It reported test performance as a single score, an intelligence quotient (IQ), in which mental age was divided by chronological age.

$$IQ = \frac{\text{mental age (MA)}}{\text{chronological age (CA)}} \times 100$$

So, a 10-year-old who performed as well as a 15-year-old would receive an IQ score of 150 (15/10 × 100). Similarly a 10-year-old who scored as well as a 5-year-old would receive an IQ score of 50. This became known as a "psychometric" approach to studying intelligence because of its emphasis on the construction of instruments to measure it. But what exactly does this number mean, and can a single number accurately reflect a person's intelligence? We address this question next.

Ed Psych and You

Consider the following questions: On what continent is Brazil? If two buttons cost 15 cents, what would be the cost of a dozen buttons? In what way are a hammer and a saw alike? What do these questions have in common?

CAUTIONS ABOUT USING AND INTERPRETING IQ SCORES

Let's look at the questions we asked in *Ed Psych and You*. Similar items appear on the Wechsler Intelligence Scale for Children—Fourth Edition (Wechsler, 2003), the most popular intelligence test in use today (Salvia et al., 2013). These items are significant for two reasons. First, experts believe that general knowledge, such as "On what continent is Brazil?" is one indicator of intelligence.

Second, and perhaps more significant, experience obviously influences our ability to answer the questions. Intelligence test scores, while determined by psychometrically reliable instruments, may not provide an accurate picture of a student's learning potential. They reflect past exposure to the contents of a test, and they're influenced by facility with the English language and the unique experiences embedded within different cultures (Chen, Moran, & Gardner, 2009; Echevarria & Graves, 2015; Robinson, 2010; Sternberg, 2007). They also reflect past opportunities for learning and can be influenced by test-specific factors, such as fatigue, anxiety, or unfamiliarity with testing procedures (Popham, 2014).

This suggests that we should be cautious about using IQ scores alone in making decisions about our students. Other factors, such as conscientiousness, perseverance, openness to new experiences, and past performance, all influence academic success (Grigorenko et al., 2009).

INTELLIGENCE: NATURE AND NURTURE

The impact of experience on intelligence test scores also relates to what is often called the *nature–nurture* issue. The extreme **nature view of intelligence** asserts that intelligence is largely determined by genes; in essence, our intelligence is inherited from our parents and determined at birth (Horn, 2008; Toga & Thompson, 2005). The nurture view of intelligence emphasizes the influence of the environment and asserts that intelligence is malleable and can be changed by the experiences we encounter. As we've just seen, evidence supports the contention that experience strongly influences intelligence test scores, and further, research in neuroscience suggests that learning potential is not fixed, that is, with the right kinds of experiences, students can literally get "smarter" (Van Dam, 2013). This evidence is important for us as teachers, because it suggests that the experiences we provide can actually increase our students' intelligence. This is indeed very good news.

Multitrait Views of Intelligence

Because scores on different measures of intelligence, such as verbal ability and abstract reasoning, are correlated, early researchers believed that intelligence was essentially a single trait (Johnson & Bouchard, 2005; Waterhouse, 2006). For example, Charles Spearman (1927) described it as "g," or general intelligence, a basic ability that affects performance on all cognitive tasks. This is consistent with the concept of IQ, a single score that describes intelligence.

Thinking about intelligence has changed, however, and many researchers now view it as composed of more than a single trait or component. For example, one perspective contrasts fluid intelligence, the flexible, culture-free ability to adapt to new situations and acquire knowledge easily, with crystallized intelligence, intelligence that is culture specific and depends on experience and schooling (Cattell, 1963, 1987). Fluid intelligence is often related to nonverbal abilities and is influenced by brain development. Some research suggests that people high in fluid intelligence tend to be more curious and interested in learning than counterparts lower in this measure (Silvia & Sanders, 2010). Fluid intelligence tends to be somewhat stable, whereas crystallized intelligence increases throughout our lives as we acquire new knowledge and skills. Current conceptions of intelligence typically include aspects of both (Ackerman & Lohman, 2006; Phelps, McGrew, Knopik, & Ford, 2005).

Another perspective views intelligence as hierarchical and multifaceted, with general ability at the top, and more specific abilities such as language and logical reasoning, at the bottom (Ackerman & Lohman, 2006). This view suggests that some cognitive abilities, such as the inclination to search for evidence in making decisions, generalize to all situations, whereas others are content specific.

Other prominent thinkers have focused on different types of intelligence. For instance, considerable research has examined social intelligence, the ability to understand and manage people; emotional intelligence, the ability to perceive, understand, and manage emotions in ourselves and others, and to use emotional knowledge to enhance cognition (thought), and cultural intelligence, an individual's ability to adjust and effectively adapt to diverse cultural situations (Crowne, 2013). As we might expect, emotional intelligence is linked to success in romantic relationships (Malouff, Schutte, & Thorsteinsson, 2014), and, probably because the world is interconnected to a greater extent than at any point in history, cultural intelligence has received even more research emphasis, particularly in the business world (Lisak, Harush, Glikson, Nouri, & Shokef, 2013; Magnusson, Westjohn, Semenov, Randrianasolo, & Zdravkovic, 2013).

We turn now to two of the more prominent multitrait descriptions of intelligence: Gardner's theory of multiple intelligences and Sternberg's triarchic theory of intelligence.

GARDNER'S THEORY OF MULTIPLE INTELLIGENCES

Howard Gardner, a Harvard psychologist, analyzed people's performance in different domains and, dismissing the idea of "g," concluded that intelligence is composed of eight relatively independent dimensions (Gardner, 1983; Gardner & Moran, 2006). They're outlined in Table 5.1. Gardner has also considered additional dimensions, but has not yet found sufficient evidence to support them (Gardner & Moran, 2006).

Table 5.1	**Gardner's theory of multiple intelligences**
Dimension	Examples
Linguistic Intelligence Sensitivity to the meaning and order of words and the varied use of language	• Noticing differences in the meanings of words • Putting thoughts into language or writing creatively
Logical-Mathematical Intelligence The ability to reason logically, particularly in mathematics and quantitative sciences	• Making and defending conclusions based on evidence • Solving math problems and generating geometric proofs efficiently
Musical Intelligence Understanding and appreciating music	• Noticing differences in pitch, melody, and tone • Playing a musical instrument or singing
Spatial Intelligence The ability to perceive the visual world accurately	• Generating mental images of objects or creating drawings • Noticing subtle differences in similar objects
Bodily-Kinesthetic Intelligence The ability to skillfully use one's body	• Playing sports, such as basketball, soccer, or tennis skillfully • Performing dances or gymnastic routines
Interpersonal Intelligence The ability to understand other person's behaviors	• Understanding others' needs, desires, and motives • Interacting with others in socially acceptable ways
Intrapersonal Intelligence Understanding one's own thoughts, moods, and needs	• Understanding what influences one's own motivations • Using knowledge of oneself to interact effectively with others
Naturalist Intelligence The ability to recognize patterns in the physical world	• Classifying natural objects, such as animals and plants • Working successfully in naturalistic settings, such as farming, ranching, forestry, or geology

Source: Adapted from Gardner & Hatch, 1989; Checkley, 1997.

Applications of Gardner's Theory. Gardner recommends that we present content in ways that capitalize on as many different intelligences as possible and help students understand their strengths and weaknesses in each (Denig, 2003; Kornhaber, Fierros, & Veenema, 2004). For example, to develop interpersonal intelligence (similar to social intelligence described above) we might use cooperative learning; we can encourage students to put their thoughts into words to develop linguistic intelligence; and we can have students practice defending their ideas with evidence to capitalize on logical-mathematical intelligence.

Gardner warns, however, that not all topics can be adapted for each intelligence: "There is no point in assuming that every topic can be effectively approached in [multiple] ways, and it is a waste of effort and time to attempt to do this" (Gardner, 1995, p. 206).

Evaluating Gardner's Theory. Gardner's theory is popular with teachers, and it makes sense intuitively (Cuban, 2004). We all know people who don't seem particularly "sharp" analytically but who excel in getting along with others, for example. This ability serves them well, and in some instances, they're more successful in life than their "brighter" counterparts. Others are extraordinary athletes or accomplished musicians. Gardner describes these people as high in interpersonal, bodily-kinesthetic, and musical intelligence, respectively.

On the other hand, Gardner's work has a number of vocal critics. For instance, some caution that the theory and its applications have not been validated by research, nor does it [if talking about the theory only] have any support from research in cognitive neuroscience (Waterhouse, 2006). Others disagree with the assertion that abilities in specific domains, such as music, qualify as separate forms of intelligence (McMahon, Rose, & Parks, 2004). Some even argue that it isn't truly a theory (Chen, 2004).

Failure to account for the essential role that working memory plays in intelligent behavior is one of the most important criticisms (Lohman, 2001). Research and theories examining the way we process information suggest that a centralized working memory—the part of our memory system that consciously organizes and makes sense of our experiences— plays a special role in intelligence (Shelton, Elliott, Matthews, Hill, & Gouvier, 2010). For example, when we solve word problems, working memory helps keep the problems' specifics in mind as we search our memories for similar problems, select strategies, and find solutions. This cognitive juggling act occurs in all types of intelligent behavior, and Gardner's work ignores this essential role (Lohman, 2001).

STERNBERG'S TRIARCHIC THEORY OF INTELLIGENCE

Robert Sternberg (2003a, 2003b, 2004), another multitrait theorist, describes intelligence as existing in three dimensions:

- *Analytical,* which is similar to traditional definitions of intelligence and is used in thinking and problem solving (Sternberg, 2003b).
- *Creative*, or experiential, which involves the ability to deal effectively with novel situations, as well as the ability to solve familiar problems efficiently (Sternberg, 1998a, 1998b).
- *Practical*, or contextual, which is the ability to effectively accommodate the task demands of the environment. Intelligent behavior involves adapting to the environment, changing it if adaptation isn't effective, or selecting a better environment if necessary (Sternberg, 2007).

The key to intelligent behavior is to use each of these dimensions to solve problems in the real world (Grigorenko et al., 2009).

Sternberg's emphasis on the creative and practical aspects of intelligence sets his theory apart from others. He sees functioning effectively in the real world as intelligent behavior, and because of this emphasis, he believes that individuals considered intelligent in one setting or culture may be viewed as unintelligent in another (Sternberg, 2004, 2006, 2007).

Influenced by Piaget's emphasis on the role of experience in development, and consistent with the research evidence we discussed earlier in this section, which documents the influence of experience on intelligence, Sternberg believes that providing students with experiences in which they're expected to think analytically, creatively, and practically can increase intelligence. Some examples are outlined in Table 5.2.

Intelligence: Ability Grouping

Ability grouping, the process of placing students of similar abilities into groups and attempting to match instruction to the needs of each, is one of the most widely applied outcomes of intelligence testing (Chorzempa & Graham, 2006; McCoach, O'Connell, & Levitt, 2006).

Ability grouping in elementary schools typically exists in two forms. **Between-class grouping** divides students in a certain grade into levels, such as high, medium, and low.

Table 5.2   **Applying analytic, creative, and practical thinking in different content areas**

Content Area	Analytic	Creative	Practical
Math	Express the number 44 in base 2.	Write a test question that measures understanding of three different number bases.	How is base 2 used in our everyday lives?
Language Arts	Why is *Romeo and Juliet* considered a tragedy?	Write an alternative ending to *Romeo and Juliet* to make it a comedy.	Write a TV ad for the school's production of *Romeo and Juliet*.
Social Studies	In what ways were the American and the French revolutions similar and different?	What would our lives be like today if the American revolution had not succeeded?	What lessons can countries take away from the study of revolutions?
Science	If a balloon is filled with 1 liter of air at room temperature, and it is then placed in a freezer, what will happen to the balloon?	How would the balloon filled with air behave on the moon?	Describe two common examples where heating or cooling affects solids, liquids, or gases.
Art	Compare and contrast the artistic styles of Van Gogh and Picasso.	What would the Statue of Liberty look like if it were created by Picasso?	Create a poster for the student art show using the style of one of the artists we studied.

For example, an elementary school with 75 third graders might have one class of high achievers, one of average achievers, and one with low achievers. Within-class grouping divides students in a single class into groups, typically based on reading and math scores, such as a second-grade teacher having two or three different reading groups.

At the middle and high school levels, tracking, the process of placing students in different curricula on the basis of aptitude and achievement, is common, and some form of tracking exists in most schools at these levels. For example, high-ability students in high schools study a curriculum intended to prepare them for college—and in some cases even earn college credit— and lower ability students receive vocational or work-related instruction (Oakes, 2005).

Analyzing Theories

Psychometric, Multiple Intelligences, and Triarchic Theories of Intelligence

The three theoretical perspectives on intelligence provide us with different ways of thinking about what it means to be "smart" and how we determine if someone is intelligent.

Psychometric perspectives focus on intelligence as essentially a single trait and tacitly assume that the trait can be measured—commonly on a paper-and-pencil test. In contrast, both Gardner and Sternberg view intelligence as composed of more than one trait, and people may be high in some but low in others. For instance, using Gardner's conception, an individual may be high in logical-mathematical intelligence but low in bodily-kinesthetic intelligence.

Sternberg differs from the other views with his emphasis on the ability to function effectively in the real world as a measure of intelligence, as well as his focus on the role of experience and context—particularly cultural context—in thinking about intelligence.

The three perspectives raise the question, "What does it mean to be intelligent?" Each answers the question in a different way, and it's impossible to decide which of the three is more nearly correct.

Collectively, the three theoretical positions offer differing, and valuable, perspectives on a complex concept central to education. Our job is to equip students to succeed, both in school and in life after the school years. These views of intelligence remind us that children and young people can't be reduced to numbers, such as IQ, or even to a range of abilities. This understanding is liberating, and it puts us in a better position to make decisions about what is best for our students. Table 5.3 summarizes the three theoretical positions, including the contributions and criticisms of each.

Table 5.3	**Analyzing theories: Evaluating psychometric, multiple intelligences, and triarchic theories of intelligence**		
	Psychometric (Traditional) Theories of Intelligence	Gardner's Theory of Intelligence	Sternberg's Triarchic Theory of Intelligence
Major Question	How is intelligence reflected in learners' abilities to perform academic tasks, as measured by intelligence tests?	How are different dimensions of intelligence reflected in different tasks?	How is intelligent behavior reflected in the ability to think and solve problems, deal effectively with novel situations, and accommodate the daily task demands of our environments?
Key Concepts	Intelligence quotient (IQ) g—general intelligence	Linguistic intelligence Logical-mathematical intelligence Spatial intelligence Musical intelligence Body-kinesthetic intelligence Interpersonal intelligence Intrapersonal intelligence Naturalist intelligence	Analytic intelligence Creative intelligence Practical intelligence
Important Names	Charles Spearman Alfred Binet David Wechsler	Howard Gardner	Robert Sternberg
Basic View of Intelligence	• Intelligence is a trait that can be measured by performance on paper-and-pencil tests. • Performance on different subtests (e.g., verbal and quantitative) reflects different aspects of intelligence.	Intelligence is multi-faceted and composed of eight relatively independent "intelligences."	Intelligence is composed of analytic, creative, and practical abilities that people selectively employ in different contexts to achieve personal goals.
Contributions	• Pioneered efforts to define and measure intelligence • Led to the development of tests (e.g., Stanford-Binet and Wechsler Intelligence Scales) that are widely used to measure learner intelligence and diagnose learning issues	• Recognized that intelligence is multi-faceted and depends on contextual demands • Encouraged professionals to look beyond one or two scores when considering what it means to be intelligent	• Increased the focus of intelligence research on creative and practical dimensions of intelligence • Recognized that culture and context play a major role in what is considered to be intelligent behavior
Criticisms	• Relies too strongly on paper-and-pencil measures of intelligence measures • Doesn't adequately attend to cultural and contextual factors that influence intelligence	• Lacks empirical evidence supporting the existence of the various dimensions of intelligence • Agreement about the specific intelligences that Gardner has proposed is lacking	• Descriptions of how the three dimensions of intelligence interact to produce intelligent behavior are vague • Empirical evidence suggesting that the three dimensions of intelligence are distinct is lacking

Sources: Berk, 2013; Gardner, 1983, 1995; Gardner & Hatch, 1989; Gardner & Moran, 2006; Garlick, 2010; Salvia, Ysseldyke, & Bolt, 2013; Siegler & Alibali, 2005; Spearman, 1904, 1927; Sternberg, 1998a, 1998b, 2003a, 2003b, 2004, 2006, 2007, 2009; Sternberg & Grigorenko, 2001.

ABILITY GROUPING: WHAT DOES RESEARCH TELL US?

Ability grouping is controversial (Yee, 2013). Advocates argue that it allows teachers to keep instruction uniform for groups, which enables them to better meet learners' needs. Most teachers endorse it, particularly in reading and math. A study by the National Assessment of Educational Progress found that ability grouping is on the rise, with approximately 7 of 10 elementary teachers reporting that they group in both reading and math, likely the result of accountability and high-stakes testing pressures on teachers (Yee, 2013).

Critics of ability grouping counter by citing several problems. They argue that within-class grouping creates logistical problems, because different lessons and assignments are required, and improper placements can occur, which tend to become permanent (Good & Brophy, 2008). And members of cultural minorities and students with low socioeconomic status (SES) are underrepresented in high-ability classes and overrepresented in those for lower ability students (McDermott, Goldman, & Varenne, 2006; O'Conner & Fernandez, 2006). Members of low-ability groups are often stigmatized by being labeled as low achievers (Oakes, 2005). Most significantly, research indicates that homogeneously grouped low-ability students achieve less than heterogeneously grouped students of similar ability (Good & Brophy, 2008).

The negative effects of grouping are often related to the quality of instruction. As we would expect, the vast majority of teachers prefer working with high-ability students, and when assigned to low-ability groups, they sometimes lack enthusiasm and commitment and stress conformity instead of autonomy and the development of self-regulation (Chorzempa & Graham, 2006; Good & Brophy, 2008). As a result, self-esteem and motivation to learn decrease, and absenteeism increases. Tracking can also result in racial segregation of students, which has a negative influence on social development and opportunities to form friendships across cultural groups (Oakes, 2005).

ABILITY GROUPING: IMPLICATIONS FOR TEACHERS

Suggestions for dealing with the issues involved in ability grouping vary. At one extreme, critics argue that its effects are so negative that the practice should be abolished. A more moderate position suggests that grouping is appropriate in some areas, such as reading and math (Good & Brophy, 2008).

When grouping is necessary, specific measures to reduce its negative effects can be taken. Some suggestions include:

- Keeping group composition flexible, and reassigning students to other groups when their achievement warrants it.
- Attempting to keep the quality of instruction high for low-ability groups.
- Teaching low-ability students learning strategies and self-regulation.
- Avoiding stigmatizing and stereotyping low-ability students.

These suggestions are demanding, and they have implications for you as you teach. Almost certainly, you will be assigned lower ability students at some point in your career, and maybe in your first year, because teachers with seniority are often given higher ability groups. Lower ability students are indeed more difficult to teach, but making every effort to help them achieve as much as possible can be rewarding when you see the light bulb come on in a child who normally struggles.

Learning Styles

Historically, psychologists have used intelligence tests to measure mental abilities and have used concepts such as introvert and extrovert to describe different personality types. Researchers who study the interface between the two examine learning styles—students' personal approaches to thinking and problem solving (Denig, 2003). The terms *learning style, cognitive style, thinking style,* and *problem-solving style* are often used interchangeably, adding to confusion in this area.

One description of learning style distinguishes between deep and surface approaches to studying new content (Evans, Kirby, & Fabrigar, 2003). For instance, as you studied the Civil War, did you relate it to the geography, economies, and politics of the northern and southern states? If so, you were using a deep-processing approach. On the other hand, if you memorized important dates, locations, and prominent leaders, you were using a surface approach.

As you would expect, deep-processing approaches result in higher achievement if tests focus on understanding, but surface approaches can be successful if tests emphasize fact learning and memorization. Students who use deep-processing approaches tend to be more intrinsically motivated and self-regulated, whereas those who use surface approaches tend to be extrinsically motivated, for example, by attaining high grades and comparing their performance to others (Schunk, Meece, & Pintrich, 2014).

Other perspectives on learning styles contrast analytic versus holistic and visual versus verbal approaches to learning. Analytical learners tend to break learning tasks into their component parts, whereas holistic learners attack problems more globally (Norenzayan, Choi, & Peng, 2007). Visual learners prefer to see ideas, whereas verbal learners prefer hearing them (Mayer & Massa, 2003). In general, an analytic approach is more beneficial for learning and develops as students mature. You can encourage this learning style with the kinds of questions you ask and the kinds of assignments, tests, and quizzes you give. You can also present information in both visual and verbal forms to capitalize on differences in this area.

LEARNING STYLES AND LEARNING PREFERENCES

The concept of learning styles is popular in education, and many consultants use this label when they conduct in-service workshops for teachers. These workshops, however, typically focus on students' preferences for a particular learning environment, such as lighting and noise level, and consultants encourage teachers to match classroom environments to students' preferences.

Research on these practices is controversial. Advocates claim that the match results in increased achievement and improved attitudes (Farkas, 2003; Lovelace, 2005); critics counter by questioning the validity of the tests used to measure learning styles or preferences (Coffield, Moseley, Hall, & Ecclestone, 2004; Krätzig & Arbuthnott, 2006). They also cite research indicating that attempts to match learning environments to learning preferences have resulted in no increases in achievement and, in some cases, even decreases (Pashler, McDaniel, Rohrer, & Bjork, 2008).

Most credible experts in the field question the wisdom of teachers' allocating energy and resources to attempts to accommodate learning styles. "Like other reviewers who pay close attention to the research literature, I do not see much validity in the claims made by those who urge teachers to assess their students with learning style inventories . . ." (Brophy, 2010, p. 283). Brophy (2010) goes on to say that the research bases encouraging learning style assessments and the differentiated curriculum and instruction based on them is virtually nonexistent, and he also points out that a teacher working with 20 or more students doesn't have the time planning and implementing such individualized instruction would take.

Others speak more strongly. "I think learning styles represents one of the more wasteful and misleading pervasive myths of the last 20 years" (Clark, 2010, p. 10).

LEARNING STYLES: IMPLICATIONS FOR TEACHERS

While little evidence supports attempts to match instruction to students' learning styles, the concept of learning style does have implications for us as teachers. First, it reminds us that we should vary our instruction, because no instructional strategy works for all students, or even the same students all the time (Brophy, 2010). Second, we should help our students understand how they learn most effectively, something that they aren't initially good at (Krätzig & Arbuthnott, 2006). Third, our students differ in ability, motivation, background

Classroom **Connections**

Accommodating Ability Differences in Classrooms

1. Performance on intelligence tests is influenced by genetics, experience, language, and culture. Use intelligence test scores cautiously when making educational decisions, keeping in mind that they are only one indicator of ability.

   ■ **Elementary:** An urban third-grade teacher consults with a school counselor in interpreting intelligence test scores, and she remembers that language and experience influence test performance.

   ■ **Middle School:** When making placement decisions, a middle school team relies on past classroom performance and grades in addition to standardized test scores.

   ■ **High School:** An English teacher uses grades, assessments of motivation, and work samples in addition to aptitude test scores in making placement recommendations.

2. Intelligence is multifaceted and covers a wide spectrum of abilities. Use instructional strategies that maximize student background knowledge, interests, and abilities.

   ■ **Elementary:** In a unit on the Revolutionary War, a fifth-grade teacher assesses all students on basic information, but bases 25% of the unit grade on special projects, such as researching the music and art of the times.

   ■ **Middle School:** An eighth-grade English teacher has both required and optional assignments. Seventy percent of the assignments

are required for everyone; the other 30% provide students with choices.

   ■ **High School:** A biology teacher provides students with choices in terms of the special topics they study in depth. In addition, he allows students to choose how they will report on their projects, allowing research papers, classroom presentations, or poster sessions.

3. Ability grouping has both advantages and disadvantages. Use ability grouping only when essential, view group composition as flexible, and reassign students when warranted by their performance. Attempt to provide the same quality of instruction for all group levels.

   ■ **Elementary:** A fourth-grade teacher uses ability groups only for reading. She uses whole-class instruction for other language arts topics such as poetry and American folktales.

   ■ **Middle School:** A seventh-grade team meets regularly to assess group placements and to reassign students to different groups based on their academic progress.

   ■ **High School:** A history teacher videotapes lessons to compare his teaching in high-ability compared to standard-ability groups. He continually challenges both types of classes with interesting and demanding questions and assignments.

experiences, needs, and insecurities. The concept of learning style can sensitize us to these differences, help us treat our students as individuals, and help us do everything we can to maximize learning for each student.

The Legal Basis for Working with Students with Exceptionalities

In the past, students with disabilities were often placed in special classrooms or schools. Instruction in these placements was often inferior, achievement was no better than in general education classrooms, and students didn't learn the social and life skills needed in the real world (Karten, 2005; Smith, Polloway, Patton, & Dowdy, 2012). In response to the problems, a series of federal laws redefined the way teachers assist and work with these students. We exam these laws next.

Ed Psych and You

You have three students in your class that you suspect have exceptionalities. Do you have professional obligations to them that go beyond those for all your students? If so, what are they?

Individuals with Disabilities Education Act (IDEA)

In 1975 Congress passed Public Law 94-142, which made a free and appropriate public education a legal requirement for all students with disabilities in our country (Sack-Min, 2007). This law, named the *Individuals with Disabilities Education Act* (IDEA), has several provisions, which we discuss in detail later in this section.

AMENDMENTS TO IDEA

Since 1975, Congress has amended IDEA three times (Sack-Min, 2007). The first amendment, passed in 1986, held states accountable for locating young children who need special education. Amendment 1997, known as IDEA 97, attempted to clarify and extend the quality of services to students with disabilities. This amendment clarifies major provisions in the original IDEA, such as protection against discrimination in testing. It also ensures that districts protect the confidentiality of children's records and share them with parents on request.

The third amendment, IDEA 2004, includes mechanisms for reducing special education paperwork, creating discipline processes that allow districts to remove students who "inflict serious bodily injury" from classrooms, and establishing methods to reduce the number of students with diverse backgrounds who are inappropriately placed in special education. It also makes meeting the "highly qualified teacher" requirements of federal legislation more flexible by allowing veteran teachers to demonstrate their qualifications by means other than a test (Council for Exceptional Children, 2014).

Most controversial is its provision that calls for including students with disabilities in accountability systems, with critics warning that testing students with exceptionalities in the standard ways harms more than helps them (Meek, 2006).

IDEA and its amendments have affected every school in the United States and have changed the roles of teachers in both general and special education. It also relates to the questions we asked in *Ed Psych and You* in this section. The unequivocal answer to the question, "Do you have professional obligations to them [students with exceptionalities in your classroom] that go beyond those for all your students?" is yes. In the following sections we answer our second question: "If so, what are they?"

We turn now to the major provisions of IDEA.

Major Provisions of IDEA

IDEA requires that educators working with students having exceptionalities do the following:

- Provide a free and appropriate public education (FAPE).
- Educate children in the least restrictive environment (LRE).
- Protect against discrimination in testing.
- Involve parents in developing each child's educational program.
- Develop an individualized education program (IEP) of study for each student.

Let's examine them in more detail.

A Free and Appropriate Public Education (FAPE). IDEA asserts that every student can learn and is entitled to a FAPE. Provisions related to FAPE are based on the 14th Amendment to the Constitution, which guarantees equal protection of all citizens under the law. The Supreme Court in 1982 defined an appropriate education as one individually designed to provide educational benefits to a particular student (Hardman, Drew, & Egan, 2014).

Least Restrictive Environment: The Evolution Toward Inclusion. Educators attempting to provide FAPE for all students realized that segregated classes and services were not meeting the needs of students with exceptionalities. Mainstreaming, the practice of moving students with exceptionalities from segregated settings into general education classrooms, was one of the first alternatives considered. Popular in the 1970s, it began the move away from segregated services and promoted interaction between students with and without exceptionalities. However, students with exceptionalities were often placed in classrooms without adequate support (Hardman et al., 2014).

As educators struggled with these problems, they developed the concept of the **least restrictive environment (LRE)**, one that places students in as typical an educational setting as possible while still meeting the students' special needs. Broader than the concept of *mainstreaming*, the LRE can consist of a continuum of services, ranging from full-time placement in the general education classroom to placement in a separate facility. Full-time placement in the general education classroom occurs only if parents and educators decide that it best meets the child's needs.

The LRE provision ensures that you will have learners with exceptionalities in your classroom, and you will be asked to work with special educators to design and implement programs for these students. The LRE means that students with exceptionalities should participate as much as possible in all aspects of schooling, ranging from academics to extracurricular activities. The form these programs take varies with the capabilities of each student. Figure 5.1 presents a continuum of services for implementing the LRE, starting with the least confining at the top and moving to the most restrictive at the bottom. If students don't succeed at one level, educators move them to the next to provide additional help and support.

The concept of **adaptive fit** is central to the LRE. It describes the degree to which a school environment accommodates each student's needs and the degree to which a student can meet the requirements of a particular school setting (Hardman et al., 2014). As educators examined mainstreaming, LRE, and adaptive fit, they gradually developed the concept of *inclusion*.

Inclusion is a comprehensive approach that advocates a total, systematic, and coordinated web of services for students with exceptionalities (Sailor & Roger, 2005; Sapon-Shevin,

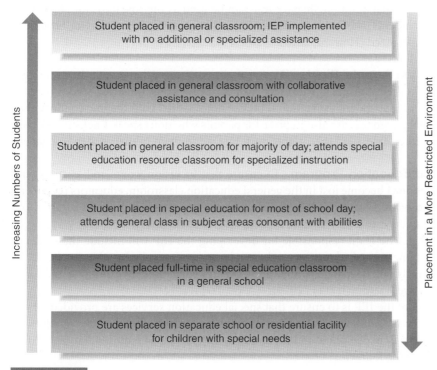

Figure 5.1

Educational service options for implementing the LRE
Sources: Hallahan, Kauffman, & Pullen, 2015; Hardman et al., 2014; Turnbull, Turnbull, Wehmeyer, & Shogren, 2013.

2007). It has three provisions: (1) students with special needs are placed on a general education school campus; (2) these students are placed in age- and grade-appropriate classrooms; and (3) general and special education services are coordinated.

The inclusion movement received a major boost from the federal government when it issued new guidelines for including students with disabilities in extracurricular sports (Pilon, 2013). Prior to that directive, guidelines were left up to individual states, creating an uneven patchwork of rules and regulations to guide coaches and athletic directors. Now the responsibility is clearly outlined and schools are required to include students with exceptionalities in sports whenever possible. For students with a hearing impairment, this might mean augmenting the sound of a starting pistol with a flashing light or allowing an interpreter on the sideline to communicate scores and assist in communicating with a doubles partner in tennis.

Inclusion is controversial, with criticisms coming from general education classroom teachers, parents, and special educators themselves (Turnbull et al., 2013). Where it works, general and special education teachers closely collaborate (Vaughn & Bos, 2015). Without close collaboration, general education teachers are overwhelmed by trying to provide the services inclusion specifies, and it isn't effective. Some parents, concerned that their children might become "lost in the shuffle," often favor special classrooms (Johnson & Duffett, 2002).

In the special education community, advocates of inclusion contend that placement in a general education classroom is the only way to eliminate the negative effects of segregation (Turnbull et al., 2013). Opponents counter that inclusion is not for everyone and that some students are better served in special classes, at least for parts of the day. Despite these controversies, inclusion is now widely accepted, and you are almost certain to encounter it in your teaching.

Fair and Nondiscriminatory Evaluation. In the past, students were often placed in special education programs based on invalid information. IDEA requires that any testing used for placement be conducted in a student's native language by qualified personnel, and no single instrument, such as an intelligence test, can be used as the sole basis for placement. More recently, students' classroom performance and general adaptive behavior have been increasingly emphasized (Heward, 2013).

Due Process and Parents' Rights. Due process guarantees that parents have the right to be involved in their children's placement in special programs, to access school records, and to obtain an independent evaluation if they're not satisfied with the one conducted by the school. Legal safeguards are also in place for parents who don't speak English; they have the right to an interpreter, and their rights must be read to them in their native language.

Individualized Education Program. To ensure that inclusion works and learners with exceptionalities don't become lost in the general education classroom, educators prepare an individualized education program (IEP), a written statement that provides a framework for delivering a FAPE to every eligible student with a disability (Rosenberg, Westling, & McLeskey, 2011). The team responsible for developing the IEP will include the students' parents; at least one special education teacher; at least one general education teacher if the student is, or likely will be, participating in the general education environment; and a district representative (Hardman et al., 2014).

The purpose of the IEP is to ensure that special education services are provided for the student on a daily and annual basis, and it is also intended to promote effective communication between the school personnel and the child's family. Idea 2004 requires that each child's IEP must include the following:

- A statement describing the child's achievement and functional performance, including a description of how the disability affects the child's progress in the general education curriculum.
- A statement of annual academic and functional goals designed to meet the special needs related to the child's disability.

- A description of how the child's progress toward meeting the goals will be measured and when reports on the child's progress will be provided.
- A statement of the special education and related services that will be provided for the child.
- An explanation of the extent, if any, to which the child will not participate with nondisabled children in the general education classroom.
- A statement of any individual accommodations, such as more time or an interpreter, that are needed to assess the academic achievement and functional performance of the child on state or district-wide assessments.

IEPs sometimes focus on adaptations in the general education classroom, and at other times they provide for outside support, such as a resource room. They are most effective when the two are coordinated, such as when a teacher working on word problems in math asks the resource teacher to focus on the same type of problems.

Identifying Students with Exceptionalities

Current approaches to identifying students who may need special help are team based, and you, as a general education teacher, will be a key member of the team. Before referring a student for a special education evaluation, you will be asked to document the problem you believe exists and the strategies you're using in attempting to solve it (Hallahan et al., 2015). You will be expected to describe the following:

- The nature of the problem and how it affects classroom performance
- Dates, places, and times problems have occurred
- Strategies you've tried
- Assessment of the strategies' effectiveness

Assessment is an essential part of the identification process. In the past, special educators relied heavily on standardized intelligence tests, but as you saw earlier, the protection-against-discrimination-in-testing provision of IDEA prevents decisions based on an intelligence test alone. Teachers are now increasingly using **curriculum-based assessments**, which measure learners' performance in specific areas of the curriculum and link assessments directly to learning objectives (Vaughn & Bos, 2015).

DISCREPANCY VERSUS RESPONSE TO INTERVENTION MODELS OF IDENTIFICATION

In the past, a **discrepancy model of identification** was used to identify students with learning problems. It looked for differences between (1) intelligence and achievement test performance, (2) intelligence test scores and classroom achievement, or (3) subtests on either intelligence or achievement tests. Inconsistency between any of the two may suggest a learning problem.

Many experts are dissatisfied with the discrepancy model, arguing that it identifies an exceptionality only after—and sometimes long after—a problem surfaces (Brown-Chidsey, 2007). Instead, they argue, educators need early screening measures, so that teachers can intervene before a major problem develops. Critics also contend that the discrepancy model does not provide specific information about the nature of the learning problem and what should be done to correct it (Sternberg & Grigorenko, 2001; Stuebing et al., 2002).

The **response to intervention model of identification** attempts to address both of these problems using a three-tiered approach (Samuels, 2009; Vaughn & Bos, 2015). In the first tier, you use instruction documented as effective for all students. The second begins when a learning problem surfaces, and you provide extra support, such as small-group activities while the rest of the students do seatwork, or help outside of school hours, in an attempt to meet the student's needs. The third tier includes intensive one-to-one help and perhaps a special needs assessment.

The model emphasizes developing skills and study strategies, such as highlighting important vocabulary, reading assignments aloud, or finding a place to study that's free of distractions. If the adaptations don't increase achievement, a learning problem that requires additional help may exist. As you adapt your instruction, you also document what is and is not working, which provides valuable information for later interventions.

ADAPTIVE BEHAVIOR

In addition to academic performance, you will also assess students' *adaptive behavior*, their ability to perform the functions of everyday school life. You observe students to assess the extent to which they perform routine school tasks, such as initiating and completing assignments, controlling their behavior, and interacting effectively with other students.

If your observations suggest that a problem exists, a number of instruments that formally assess the ability to adapt can be used (Heward, 2013). For example, the American Association on Intellectual and Developmental Disabilities Adaptive Behavior Scale—Schools contains 104 items with several questions per item (Pierangelo & Giuliani, 2006). This instrument assesses areas such as students' abilities to understand directions, express themselves, persist on tasks, and make friends.

REFERRAL FOR SPECIAL SERVICES

If you aren't able solve a student's learning problem by adapting instruction, you can then initiate a referral. When considering a referral, you should first check with an administrator or school psychologist to learn about the school's policies.

When the data suggest that a student needs additional help, a prereferral team is formed. The team usually consists of a school psychologist, a special educator, and you as the classroom teacher. The team further evaluates the problem, consults with parents, and begins the process of preparing the IEP.

Parents play an integral role in the process. They can provide valuable information about the student's educational and medical history, and notifying parents is simply the act of a professional, even if it wasn't required by law.

Diversity: Cautions in the Identification Process

The identification process that provides help to students with exceptionalities can be problematic. Evidence gathered over a number of years reveals that certain subgroups of the school-age population are referred for special education services at higher rates than others (U.S. Department of Education, 2012; Waitoller, Artiles, & Cheney, 2010). This information is important for you as a teacher because you'll play a central role in the identification process in your classroom.

Experts have quantified this disproportionate representation problem of certain culturally and linguistically diverse populations with a calculation called risk ratio (Turnbull et al., 2013). Risk ratios compare the proportion of a specific racial or ethnic group identified as needing special education services to their proportion in the general population. If the ratio is higher, the risk of being labeled as needing special services is greater; if the ratio is lower, the probability is lower. Applying this ratio to statistics gathered annually by the U.S. Department of Education reveals that African American students have a much higher probability of being labeled as having a specific learning disability, intellectual disability, or behavior disorder than the general population. Other subgroups, such as American Indian/Alaska Native, Asian/Pacific Islander, and Hispanic, display other risk ratios that differ from the general population. In addition, research on gifted and talented students reveals similar uneven identification rates, with cultural and linguistic minorities being underrepresented and White students being overrepresented (Ford, 2010).

An important question for anyone who works with students is, why do these disproportionate representation rates exist? The answer is complex and multifaceted. One interpretation targets economic and environmental factors. Cultural and linguistic minorities tend to be overrepresented in the poorer segments of our society and frequently suffer from a number of problems, such as (1) inadequate medical care, including prenatal care that is essential for healthy brain development; (2) higher than normal exposure to environmental toxins, such as lead paint and air pollution; and (3) lack of access to stimulating and enriching educational resources (Heward, 2013; Turnbull et al., 2013). These environmental risks are real and, in all likelihood, account for some of the differences that we see.

But there are other factors operating as well. State and regional differences in the interpretation of and application of different exceptionality categories exist. For example, one study of preschool placements found that Native American students identified with a disability ranged from a low risk ratio of .29 in one state to a high risk ratio of 2.25 in another state (Morrier & Gallagher, 2010). Similar differences between states in the identification of gifted and talented students have also been found (Ford, 2010). Lack of a clear consensus about the specific defining characteristics of a specific exceptionality, as well as cultural and regional differences in views of schools and classrooms, are likely at play (Aud, Fox, & KewalRamani, 2010; Ford, 2010; Waitoller et al., 2010).

Teachers are part of the puzzle, too. Many of the categories that you'll read about in the next section are what experts call "high judgment" categories (Artiles, Kozleski, Trent, Osher, & Ortiz, 2010). For example, teacher judgment is influential in determining whether a child has a learning, emotional, or behavioral disability. This makes sense, since classroom teachers work with children on a daily basis and are in the best position to observe and notice learning problems. But it also places a heavy burden of responsibility on them and creates a bit of a dilemma. From teachers' perspectives, we don't want to refer students for special services if it is unwarranted, but, on the other hand, we don't want to deprive students of access to special education services if the students really need them.

This suggests that sensitivity and caution are essential. For example, cultural and linguistic differences in students can influence classroom performance, and we know these differences also influence their behavior and test performance. We also need to be cautious about letting our own cultural backgrounds and biases influence our educational decisions. Fortunately, when you teach you'll receive assistance from special educators and other experts in your district when you wrestle with these problems. (We examine collaborative consultation and how it can help us in this process later in the chapter.)

Exceptionalities and Learning Problems

Almost 7 million students with exceptionalities are enrolled in special programs, two-thirds for relatively minor learning problems. About 13% of all students in a typical school receive special education services with issues ranging from mild learning problems to physical impairments such as being deaf or blind (National Center for Education Statistics, 2014).

Federal legislation has created categories to identify learning problems, and educators use the categories in developing special programs to meet the needs of students in each. We examine the controversies surrounding this process and the specific categories in the sections that follow.

Ed Psych and You

Do you sometimes have trouble paying attention in class or are disorganized and distracted in your studying? Do you feel as if particular areas of the curriculum are extra hard for you? Have you ever joked that you have some sort of disorder?

The Labeling Controversy

A number of categories and labels have been created to identify and accommodate learners with exceptionalities (Hardman et al., 2014). *Disorder, disability,* and *handicap* are terms commonly used to describe physical or behavioral differences. Disorder, the broadest of the three, refers to a general malfunction of mental, physical, or emotional processes. A disability is a functional limitation, such as low intelligence, or an inability to perform a certain act, such as walk or hear a teacher's voice. A handicap is a condition imposed on people's functioning that restricts their abilities, such as being unable to enter a building in a wheelchair. Some, but not all, disabilities lead to handicaps. For example, a student with a visual disability may be able to wear glasses or sit in the front of the classroom; if these measures allow the student to function effectively, the disability isn't a handicap.

The use of categories and their labels is controversial (Friend, 2014). Advocates argue that categories provide a common language for professionals and encourage specialized instruction that meets students' needs (Heward, 2013). Opponents claim that categories are arbitrary, many differences exist within them, and categorizing encourages educators to treat students as labels instead of people (National Council on Disability, 2011). Despite the controversy, labels are widely used, so you will need to be familiar with them.

Regardless of their position, special educators agree that labels shouldn't focus attention on students' weaknesses, so they endorse people-first language, which first identifies the student and then specifies the disability. For example, they use the description *students with a learning disability* instead of *learning-disabled students*. People-first language reminds us that all students are human beings who need to be treated with respect and care.

Categories of Exceptionalities

A range of categories for learners with exceptionalities exist. They include:

- Learning disabilities
- Attention-deficit/hyperactivity disorder
- Communication disorders
- Intellectual disabilities
- Emotional and behavior disorders
- Autism spectrum disorders
- Visual disabilities
- Hearing disabilities

Over 90% of students with disabilities who receive special education services in our country are identified as having *learning disabilities, communication disorders, behavior disorders, intellectual disabilities,* or *autism spectrum disorders.* Ninety-five percent of these students receive their education in inclusive programs in general education classrooms, so students with these disabilities are the ones you're most likely to encounter in your work (Hardman et al., 2014; U.S. Department of Education, 2012).

We turn to them now.

LEARNING DISABILITIES

> Tammy Fuller, a middle school social studies teacher, is surprised when she scores Adam's first quiz. He seemed to be doing so well. He is rarely absent, pays attention, and participates in class. Why is his score so low? Tammy makes a mental note to watch him more closely.
>
> In her second unit, Tammy prepares study guide questions and has students discuss their answers in groups. As she moves around the room, she notices that Adam's sheet is empty, and when she asks him about it, he mumbles something about not having time the night before. Tammy asks Adam to come in after school to complete his work.
>
> He arrives promptly and opens his book to the chapter. When Tammy checks his progress, his page is blank, and it's still empty 10 minutes later.
>
> As she sits down to talk with him, he appears embarrassed and evasive. When they start to work on the questions together, she discovers that he can't read the text.

Some students, like Adam, are average or above in intelligence but have **learning disabilities** (also called *specific learning disabilities*), difficulties with reading, writing, reasoning, listening, or math (National Joint Committee on Learning Disabilities, 1994). Problems with reading, writing, and listening are most common, but math-related difficulties also receive attention (Shaywitz & Shaywitz, 2004). The American Psychiatric Association (2013), in its latest *Diagnostic and Statistical Manual of Mental Disorders (DSM-5)*, broadened the definition of this category to include dyslexia, problems with learning to read, and dyscalculia, difficulties with math. Central nervous system dysfunction—resulting from genetics or adverse environmental conditions, such as malnutrition or alcohol or drug use during pregnancy—are believed to be the cause (Friend, 2014). Learning disabilities often exist together with—but are not caused by—other disabilities such as attention problems. Experts stress that the term *learning disability* is broad and encompasses a wide range of problems (Gregg, 2009).

The category *learning disabilities* illustrates the labeling controversy we discussed earlier. Critics contend that it's a catchall term for students who have learning problems (Sternberg & Grigorenko, 2001). Part of the criticism results from the rapid growth of the category, nonexistent in the early 1960s, but now far and away the largest percentage of exceptionalities. Estimates vary, ranging from slightly more than a third (National Center for Education Statistics, 2014) to more than 40% of all learners with exceptionalities (U.S. Department of Education, 2012).

Characteristics of students with learning disabilities are outlined in Table 5.4. Some of the characteristics are typical of general learning problems or immaturity. Unlike developmental lags, however, problems associated with learning disabilities often increase over time, resulting in lowered achievement and self-esteem and increases in classroom management problems (Heward, 2013).

Identifying and Working with Students Who Have Learning Disabilities. As with all exceptionalities, early identification is important to prevent damaging effects from accumulating. Identifying these students isn't easy, however, because students with learning disabilities who comply with rules and complete assignments on time are often passed over for referral. This is likely the reason Adam, in Tammy's class, got to middle school before his difficulties with reading were discovered.

You are almost certain to have students with learning disabilities in your classes, and they will need extra structure and support to succeed. For example, you might provide additional study aids, such as content outlines, present information both visually and verbally, and eliminate distractions during seatwork. Systematically teaching study strategies has been shown to be effective (Mastropieri & Scruggs, 2014).

Table 5.4	Characteristics of students with learning disabilities
General Patterns	
Attention deficits Disorganization and tendency toward distraction Lack of follow-through and completion of assignments Uneven performance (e.g., capable in one area, extremely weak in others) Lack of coordination and balance	
Academic Performance	
Reading	Lacks reading fluency Reverses words (e.g., *saw* for *was*) Frequently loses place
Writing	Makes jerky and poorly formed letters Has difficulty staying on line Is slow in completing work Has difficulty copying from chalkboard
Math	Has difficulty remembering math facts Has trouble with story problems Mixes columns (e.g., tens and ones) in computing

This section addresses the questions we asked in *Ed Psych and You* at the beginning of this section. Most of us periodically display characteristics similar to those in students with learning disabilities; we aren't as efficient as we could be when studying and are often disorganized and distracted. However, unlike students who actually have a disability, our problems typically aren't chronic, and we make appropriate adaptations in our study.

This has implications for our teaching. If we adapt our instruction and provide sufficient emotional and instructional support, students with learning disabilities can learn and succeed.

ATTENTION-DEFICIT/HYPERACTIVITY DISORDER

Attention-deficit/hyperactivity disorder (ADHD) is a learning problem characterized by difficulties in focusing and maintaining attention, as well as the inability to inhibit inappropriate thoughts or actions. All of us struggle to pay attention sometimes, and most of us worry and think about things when we don't need to. But students with ADHD are different; they continually struggle to control their impulses and maintain attention. In its latest *Diagnostic and Statistical Manual of Mental Disorders (DSM-5)*, the American Psychiatric Association (2013) broadened the definition of ADHD to include older students, where the symptoms are present at age 12 (versus the old cutoff of 7), and also stipulated that several symptoms must be present, and in different settings (American Psychiatric Association, 2013).

As of 2011, approximately 11% of children 4 to 17 years of age in our country have been diagnosed with ADHD, an increase of 16% since 2007, and up 53% in the last decade (Centers for Disease Control & Prevention, 2013; Schwarz & Cohen, 2013). Reporting rates vary widely. For instance, the incidence of this condition in our country is much higher than in other countries, such as Great Britain, where only 3% of the population is identified as having ADHD. The reporting rates also vary from state to state, with a low of 6% in Nevada to a high of 16% in North Carolina. Research has also identified significant racial differences; for example, African American students were 69% less likely and Hispanic students 50% less likely to be identified as having ADHD (Morgan, Staff, Hillemeier, Farkas, & Maczuga, 2013). The reasons for these country-to-country, state-to-state, and racial differences aren't clear, but lack of a clear definition of the condition might be a factor. No definitive test exists, and diagnosis is made only after lengthy interviews with parents, teachers, and the student. Regional differences in reporting rates as well as demographic factors may also be operating.

ADHD has long been associated with learning disabilities, and experts estimate an overlap of 25% to 70% in the two conditions (Hardman et al., 2014). It's relatively new as a described exceptionality and isn't listed as a distinct category in IDEA. Students with ADHD may qualify for special education under the "other health impairments" disability category, however.

Hyperactivity, inattention, difficulty in concentrating, impulsiveness, and an inordinate need for supervision are common characteristics of ADHD. It has received a great deal of media attention, and you will encounter many students who seem to fit the description. However, high activity levels and inability to focus attention are also characteristics of developmental lags, especially in young boys, so we need to be cautious about drawing conclusions on the basis of these characteristics alone.

ADHD typically appears early (at age 2 or 3) and usually persists into adolescence or beyond (Hirvikoski et al., 2011). Some experts estimate that three to four times as many boys as girls are identified (Hallahan et al., 2015). As you can imagine, teens with ADHD face considerable obstacles when involved in tasks that include distractions and require concentration and quick decision making, such as learning to drive (O'Neil, 2012). ADHD can also be a debilitating adult problem, resulting in relationship and marital problems in adulthood (Parker-Pope, 2010).

Treatments range from medication, such as the controversial drugs Ritalin and Adderall, to reinforcement programs and structured teaching environments (described later in the chapter). Experts caution against the overuse of drug treatments, instead advocating structured behavioral treatments that identify and address behavioral problems early (Clay, 2013). In addition, simple lifestyle changes, such as exercise and more sleep, also sometimes work. Diagnosis and treatment of ADHD are usually conducted in consultation with medical and psychological experts.

Rodney, in our case study at the beginning of the chapter, displays symptoms of ADHD. He's hyperactive, is easily distracted, and has difficulty focusing his attention. Clarisse gave Celina good advice in suggesting that she check with special education experts in their school. However, as we saw earlier in the chapter, Celina will be expected to document the problem, the strategies she has used to solve it, and their effectiveness before Rodney is referred. Simply moving him to a quieter part of the room might be a first step. With older students, helping them learn how to break long assignments into smaller components, keep meticulously organized assignment books, and use flash cards and other drills to develop automaticity with basic skills have been proved effective (Vaughn & Bos, 2015).

COMMUNICATION DISORDERS

Communication disorders are the second most frequently occurring exceptionality in school-age children, making up nearly 20% of the special education population (Hallahan et al., 2015). They exist in two forms. **Speech disorders** (sometimes called *expressive disorders*), which involve problems in forming and sequencing sounds, is the first. Stuttering and mispronouncing words, such as saying, "I taw it" for "I saw it," are examples. Specialists have identified three kinds of speech disorders (see Table 5.5).

Language disorders, also called *receptive disorders*, make up the second form of communication disorder, and they include problems with understanding language or, more commonly, using language to express ideas. Language disorders are often connected to

Table 5.5	Types of speech disorders	
Disorder	**Description**	**Example**
Articulation disorders	Difficulty in producing certain sounds, including substituting, distorting, and omitting	"Wabbit" for *rabbit* "Thit" for *sit* "Only" for *lonely*
Fluency disorders	Repetition of the first sound of a word (stuttering) and other problems in producing "smooth" speech	"Y, Y, Y, Yes"
Voice disorders	Problems with the larynx or air passageways in the nose or throat	High-pitched or nasal voice

other problems, such as a hearing impairment or a learning or intellectual disability (Turnbull et al., 2013).

Because they more strongly detract from learning, language disorders are more serious than speech disorders. The majority of students learn to communicate quite well by the time they start school, but a small number continue to experience problems expressing themselves verbally (Hardman et al., 2014; Heward, 2013). Seldom speaking, even during play, using few words or very short sentences, and overrelying on gestures to communicate are symptoms of language disorders.

Hearing loss, brain damage, learning or intellectual disabilities, severe emotional problems, and inadequate developmental experiences in a child's early years are the most common causes of language disorders.

The American Psychiatric Association (2013), in its latest *Diagnostic and Statistical Manual of Mental Disorders*, created a new category called *Social Communication Disorder*. This category is characterized by persistent difficulty in social uses of verbal and nonverbal communication, such as following general rules for communication and being able to greet people and exchange information. How this new category will be applied in schools is uncertain at this point.

We should keep cultural diversity in mind if we suspect that a student has a speech or language disorder. English is not the primary language for many students, and the difficulties these students encounter in learning both content and a second language should not be confused with a communication disorder. Combined with patience and understanding, English learners will respond to an enriched language environment. Students with communication disorders require the help of a speech and language specialist.

Aiding in the process of identification and modeling acceptance and respect for these students are your primary tasks in working with them. As with other exceptionalities, you play an important role in identification because you are in most direct contact with students. And ensuring that students with the disorder are accepted and respected is essential because teasing and social rejection often occur and can cause lasting emotional damage. Being patient as they try to express themselves, refraining from correcting their speech—which calls attention to the problem—and forbidding any form of demeaning comments from peers will do a great deal to help these students accommodate their disability. Cooperative and small-group activities can also provide opportunities for students to practice language in settings that are less threatening than whole-class activities.

INTELLECTUAL DISABILITIES

To begin this section, let's return to Celina's work with her students.

She watches her children as they work on a reading assignment, and most of the class works quietly. Amelia, in contrast, is out of her seat for the third time, supposedly sharpening her pencil. Celina has reminded her once to get back to work and this time goes over to see what the problem is.

"I can't do this! I don't get it!" Amelia responds in frustration when Celina asks her why she hasn't started her work.

After helping her calm down, Celina works with her for a few moments, but she can tell by Amelia's responses and her facial expressions that she truly doesn't "get" the assignment.

Some students, like Amelia, struggle with learning and become frustrated when they can't keep up with their peers. Unfortunately, this problem often isn't identified until students are several years into school. Many have mild intellectual disability. (You may also encounter the terms *cognitive impairment, educationally* or *intellectually handicapped*, and *intellectual and developmental disabilities*, which some educators prefer.) *Mental retardation*, an antiquated term, has been rejected because it's considered offensive and stigmatizing. Intellectual disabilities is the fourth largest disability category, making up about 8% of the population of students with exceptionalities (Heward, 2013). An intellectual disability is caused by either genetic factors, such as Down syndrome, or brain damage to the fetus during pregnancy (Fuchs, 2006).

The American Association on Intellectual and Developmental Disabilities (AAIDD) defines intellectual disability as a disability "Characterized by significant limitations both in intellectual functioning [emphasis added] and in adaptive behavior [emphasis added] as expressed in conceptual, social, and practical adaptive skills. This disability originates before age 18" (AAIDD, 2013, para. 1). *Intellectual functioning,* also simply called intelligence, refers to general mental capacity, such as learning, reasoning, and problem solving. *Adaptive behavior* is the collection of conceptual skills, such as the use of language, money, and time; social skills, such as interpersonal skills, social responsibility, self-esteem, gullibility, and the ability to avoid being victimized; and practical skills, such as the activities of daily living. Students with intellectual disabilities will lack general knowledge about the world, struggle with abstract ideas, and have underdeveloped motor and social skills (AAIDD, 2013).

Some of these characteristics affect learning directly; others, such as underdeveloped interpersonal skills, are less direct but still important, because they affect a student's ability to make friends and develop socially. Functioning in these areas can improve, however, when these students receive services designed to meet their needs.

Before the 1960s, definitions of intellectual disability were based primarily on below-average scores on intelligence tests, but this approach had three problems. First, tests are imprecise, so misdiagnoses sometimes occurred. Second, disproportionate numbers of minorities and non-English-speaking students were identified as mentally retarded (Hallahan et al., 2015). Third, educators found that individuals with the same intelligence test scores varied widely in their ability to cope with the real world (Heward, 2013). This is the reason *adaptive behavior* has become more important (American Psychiatric Association, 2013). When you teach, your input in this area will be essential.

Programs for students with intellectual disabilities focus on creating support systems to augment existing instruction. Schools often place these students in general education classrooms, so you are likely to work with them at some point in your career. As with other disabilities, you will be expected to adapt your instruction to meet their needs and help them develop socially.

Research indicates that these students often fail to acquire basic learning strategies, such as maintaining attention, organizing new material, and studying for tests (Heward, 2013). Amelia, in Celina's class, is an example. Celina recognized this need and attempted to provide additional support by working with her one-on-one.

EMOTIONAL AND BEHAVIOR DISORDERS

> Kyle comes in from recess sweaty and disheveled, crosses his arms, and looks at his teacher defiantly. The playground monitor has reported another scuffle, and Kyle has a history of these disturbances. He struggles with his studies but can handle them if provided with enough structure. When he becomes frustrated, he sometimes acts out, often ignoring the rights and feelings of others.
>
> Ben, who sits next to Kyle, is so quiet that his teacher almost forgets he is there. He never causes problems; in fact, he seldom participates in class. He has few friends and walks around at recess by himself, appearing to consciously avoid other children.

Although very different, Kyle and Ben both display symptoms of **emotional and behavior disorders**, serious and persistent age-inappropriate behaviors that result in social conflict and personal unhappiness. School failure is often an outcome. The terms *serious* and *persistent* are important. Many children occasionally fight with their peers, and all children periodically want to be alone. If a child shows a pattern of these behaviors, and if the behaviors interfere with normal development and school success, however, the child may have a behavior disorder.

The term *emotional and behavior disorder* is often used interchangeably with *emotional disturbance, emotional disability,* or *emotional handicap,* and you may encounter any of these in your work. Researchers prefer the term *emotional and behavior disorder* because it focuses on overt behaviors that can be targeted and changed (Turnbull et al., 2013).

Students with emotional and behavior disorders often have the following characteristics:

- Behaving impulsively and having difficulty interacting with others in socially acceptable ways
- Acting out and failing to follow school or classroom rules
- Displaying poor self-concepts
- Lacking awareness of the severity of their problems
- Deteriorating academic performance and frequently missing school (Turnbull et al., 2013)

Students with emotional and behavior disorders often have academic problems, some of which are connected with learning disabilities. The combination of these problems results in high absentee rates, low achievement, and a dropout rate of nearly 50%, the highest of any group of students with special needs (U.S. Department of Education, 2009).

Estimates of the frequency of emotional and behavior disorders vary. Some suggest that about 1% or 2% of the total school population and close to 10% of the special education population have behavior disorders, but others suggest that, because of identification problems, the percentage is much higher (Hallahan et al., 2015; Hardman et al., 2014).

Identification problems are compounded by ethnic and cultural factors. For example, American Indian/Alaska Native students are classified as having behavior disorders one and a half times more often than the general population, and African American students are over twice as likely to be labeled as having a behavior disorder (Heward, 2013).

Emotional and behavior disorders are classified as either *externalizing* or *internalizing* (Hallahan et al., 2015). Students like Kyle fall into the first category, displaying characteristics such as hyperactivity, defiance, hostility, and even cruelty. The latest *Diagnostic and Statistical Manual (DSM)* from the American Psychiatric Association (2013) has a closely related category called *Oppositional Defiant Disorder,* which is defined as an ongoing pattern of anger-guided disobedience, hostility, and defiant behavior toward authority. In its defining criteria, the *DSM* uses frequency of behaviors to differentiate this disorder from normal developmental behavioral issues in young children, such as temper tantrums and striking out when frustrated. Boys are three times more likely to be labeled as having an externalizing emotional and behavior disorder than girls, and low SES and membership in a cultural minority increase students' chances of being given this label.

Internalizing emotional and behavior disorders can be more destructive, because they don't have the high profile of students who act out, and as a result, they may go unnoticed. They're characterized by social withdrawal, few friendships, depression, and anxiety, problems more directed at the self than others. Like Ben, these children lack self-confidence and are often shy, timid, and depressed, sometimes even suicidal.

Suicide. Suicide is the third leading cause of teen death, surpassed only by car accidents and homicide (Teendriversource, 2014). Not every student with a behavior disorder is at risk for suicide, of course, but a combination of factors often connected to behavior disorders, such as depression and substance abuse, stress, and family conflict and rejection, are directly linked to the problem (Westefeld et al., 2010). Depression is a serious problem in terms of suicide because adolescents who experience this problem tend to be quiet and withdrawn and often go unnoticed by teachers. About a half million young people attempt suicide each year, and between 2,000 and 5,000 succeed, although accurate figures are hard to obtain because of the social stigma attached to suicide (Berk, 2013; Kaminski et al., 2010). The suicide rate among adolescents has tripled in the time span from the mid-1960s to the mid-1990s, due perhaps to greater stressors and less family and social support. Girls are twice as likely as boys to attempt suicide, but boys are four times more likely to succeed. Boys tend to employ more lethal means, such as shooting themselves, whereas girls choose more survivable methods, such as overdosing on drugs.

Potential suicide indicators include (American Psychological Association, 2014):

- An abrupt decline in the quality of schoolwork
- Withdrawal from friends or classroom and school activities
- Neglect of personal appearance or radical changes in personality
- Changes in eating or sleeping habits
- Depression, as evidenced by persistent boredom or lack of interest in school activities
- Comments about suicide as a solution to problems

If you observe any of these indicators in a student, contact a school counselor or psychologist immediately, because early intervention is essential.

Bipolar Disorder. Bipolar disorder is a condition characterized by alternate episodes of depressive and manic states (Heward, 2013), and the number of children treated for the disorder increased 40-fold from 20,000 in 1994 to 800,000 in 2003 (Carey, 2007). Experts believe that the incidence hasn't actually increased; rather, the numbers reflect a greater tendency to apply the diagnosis to children. The increase is also controversial, with critics claiming that the label has become a catchall term applied to any child who is either depressed, the most common symptom, or explosively aggressive. The latest *Diagnostic and Statistical Manual* from the American Psychiatric Association (2013) created a new category called *Disruptive Mood Dysregulation Disorder* that attempts to identify children up to the age of 18 who exhibit persistent irritability and frequent episodes of extreme temper tantrums. The category is intended to address concerns about the overdiagnosis and overtreatment of bipolar disorder in children. Since schools are primarily guided by the federal Individuals with Disabilities Act, it is unclear how this new psychiatric category will influence school practice (Heward, 2013).

The symptoms of bipolar disorder are similar to depression or anxiety and are often linked to other issues, especially ADHD. Treatment typically includes powerful psychiatric drugs, which generally succeed in reducing or eliminating symptoms but may have negative side effects, such as weight gain. If you encounter students with this disorder, you can expect advice and assistance from special educators and school psychologists.

Teaching Students with Emotional and Behavior Disorders. Students with emotional and behavior disorders require a classroom environment that invites participation and success while providing structure through clearly stated and consistently enforced rules.

Behavior management strategies are often used with these students (Alberto & Troutman, 2013). They include rewarding desired behaviors, such as praising a student for behaving courteously; teaching replacement behaviors, such as helping students learn to express personal feelings verbally instead of fighting; and time-out, isolating a child for brief periods of time.

Teaching self-management skills can also be effective (Heward, 2013). You will see an example when you analyze the case study at the end of the chapter.

Students with emotional and behavior disorders can be frustrating, and it's easy to forget that they have unique needs. This is where your sensitivity and acceptance are essential. Communicating to these students that their behaviors are unacceptable but they are innately worthy as human beings, and you care about them and their learning, is crucial. This acceptance and caring can do more for them than any other form of intervention.

AUTISM SPECTRUM DISORDERS

Originally thought of as a single disorder, autism spectrum disorder describes a cluster of problems characterized by communication deficits, impaired social relationships and skills, and often highly ritualized and unusual behaviors (American Psychiatric Association, 2013). A recent study found that the number of children with autism spectrum disorders may be as high as 1 in 50, up from the previous estimate of 1 in 88, making it the fastest growing serious developmental disorder (Blumberg et al., 2013). Rates are also higher for lower income and Hispanic and African American children, and early identification in these populations is essential for effective treatment (Levere, 2013).

Autism was added to the IDEA list of disabilities qualifying for special services in 1990, and since that time the term has been expanded to *autism spectrum disorders* to reflect the wide range of disabilities it encompasses. They all involve problems with social relationships, ranging from conditions in which language is severely impaired and normal social relations are virtually impossible to *Asperger's syndrome*, in which students have average to above-average intelligence and only moderately impaired language abilities and social relationships (Friend, 2014). According to the American Psychiatric Association's new *Diagnostic and Statistical Manual* (2013) Asperger's syndrome will no longer be considered a separate disorder, instead being included under the umbrella of autism spectrum disorders. The change came about because of difficulties involved in diagnosing patients with Asperger's syndrome and the finding that the diagnosis varied greatly with the person doing the diagnosis.

In addition to impaired social relationships, characteristics of autism spectrum disorder include:

- Communication and language deficits
- Unusual sensitivity to sensory stimuli such as light and sound
- Insistence on sameness and perseveration
- Ritualistic and unusual behavior patterns (Heward, 2013; Lord, 2010)

Because students with autistic spectrum disorders are different from their peers, they often face high degrees of bullying, and the problem is worse for those in regular classrooms where their unusual behaviors set them apart (Sterzing, Shattuck, Narendorf, Wagner, & Cooper, 2012). Classroom teachers play an important role with respect to this issue, both protecting these children and teaching their peers understanding and acceptance.

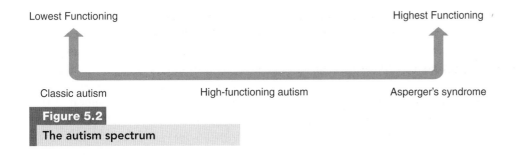

Figure 5.2

The autism spectrum

Autism spectrum disorders are thought to be caused by abnormalities in the brain (Gallese, Gernsbacher, Heyes, Hickok, & Iacoboni, 2011; Panek & Grandin, 2013). Their incidence has increased significantly in recent years, and they are four times more prevalent in boys than girls (Darden, 2007). Lack of responsiveness to social stimuli and unusual, ritualistic behaviors such as rocking or repeating words or phrases are often the first symptoms. Many children with autism spectrum disorders are in general education classes for part or all of the school day. Figure 5.2 illustrates the concept of the autism spectrum.

Two approaches to working with these students are most effective. One attempts to make the classroom environment as predictable as possible. Routines are helpful for all students; they are essential for children with an autism spectrum disorder. Also, clearly outlined rules and expectations that are consistently applied provide additional support for these students.

A second approach focuses on social skills and attempts to help these students learn to interact with their peers and adjust to the social demands of classrooms. A recent study found that a behavioral approach targeting specific social skills and behaviors was effective in improving both social and communication skills (Fein et al., 2013). Students with autism spectrum disorders are commonly unaware of the effects of their behaviors on others, so teachers' conscious efforts to teach socially acceptable behaviors can be effective.

PHYSICAL AND SENSORY CHALLENGES

Students with physical and sensory challenges also attend our schools. IDEA uses the term *orthopedic impairments*, whereas educators prefer the term *physical disabilities* to refer to a large, diverse category of students who experience health or mobility problems that affect classroom performance (Turnbull et al., 2013). In 2009, for example, more than 20% of students with exceptionalities had health problems of some sort (U.S. Department of Education, 2012). They range from mild to severe and vary greatly (Heward, 2013). Some examples include:

- Acquired immune deficiency syndrome (AIDS)
- Asthma
- Cancer
- Cerebral palsy
- Diabetes
- Epilepsy
- Seizure disorder
- Spina bifida
- Spinal cord or traumatic brain injury

You will have support from special education specialists and other health care professionals when working with any children who might have one or more of these challenges. Your caring and sensitivity will be paramount in helping these children do as well as possible.

Visual Disabilities. About one in five of us has some type of vision loss. Fortunately, most problems can be corrected with glasses, surgery, or therapy. In some situations—approximately

1 child in 3,000—the impairment cannot be corrected (Hardman et al., 2014). People with this condition have a visual handicap, an uncorrectable visual impairment that interferes with learning. Many of these students can read with the aid of a magnifying glass or large-print books, but others are entirely dependent on the spoken word or Braille.

Nearly two-thirds of serious visual disabilities exist at birth, and most children are given visual screenings when they enter elementary school. Some vision problems appear during the school years as a result of growth spurts, however, so you should remain alert to the possibility of an undetected impairment in your students. Symptoms of these problems include:

- Holding the head in an awkward position or holding a book too close or too far away
- Squinting and frequently rubbing the eyes
- Tuning out or constantly asking about procedures, particularly when information is presented on the board
- Using poor spacing in writing and having difficulty staying on the line

Students with visual disabilities differ from their peers with normal vision in areas ranging from understanding spatial concepts to general knowledge. Word meanings may not be as rich or elaborate because of the students' lack of visual experience with the world. As a result, hands-on experiences are even more important for these students than they are for other learners.

If you have students with visual disabilities in your class, you can make simple adaptations, such as seating them near writing boards and displays on screens, verbalizing while writing on the board, and ensuring that handouts are high contrast and clear (Heward, 2013). You can also supply large-print books and magnifying aids to adapt materials. Peer tutors can provide assistance in explaining and clarifying assignments and procedures.

Hearing Disabilities. Students with a hearing loss have problems perceiving sounds within the normal frequency range of human speech. Two kinds of hearing disabilities exist. A partial hearing impairment allows a student to use a hearing aid and to hear well enough to be taught through auditory channels. For students who are deaf, hearing is impaired enough so that these students use other senses, usually sight, to communicate. About 1.5% of students with exceptionalities have a hearing disability (U.S. Department of Education, 2009). Of the students with a hearing loss requiring special services, more than 60% receive instruction in general education classrooms for all or part of the school day, and the numbers have increased in recent years (Shirin, 2007).

Hearing disabilities may result from rubella (German measles) during pregnancy, heredity, complications during pregnancy or birth, meningitis, or other childhood diseases. In almost 40% of cases involving hearing loss, the cause is unknown; this makes prevention and remediation more difficult (Hardman et al., 2014; Heward, 2013).

Testing by a trained audiologist is the best method of identifying students with hearing problems, but not all schools have these programs, and problems can be overlooked if students miss the screening. When such an omission occurs, your sensitivity to possible hearing difficulties is essential. Some indicators of hearing impairment include:

- Misunderstanding or not following directions and displaying nonverbal behaviors, such as frowns or puzzled looks when directions are given
- Asking people to repeat what they've just said
- Articulating words, and especially consonants, poorly
- Turning up the volume when listening to audio recordings, radio, or television
- Showing reluctance to participate in oral activities

Lack of proficiency in speech and language are learning problems that can result from hearing disabilities. These problems affect learning that relies on reading, writing, and listening. You should remember that these language deficits have little bearing on intelligence; these students can succeed if given appropriate help.

Effective programs for students with hearing disabilities combine general education classroom instruction with additional support. Programs for students who are deaf include lipreading, sign language, and fingerspelling. Total communication is the simultaneous presentation of manual approaches, such as signing, and speech (through lipreading and residual hearing), and is increasing in popularity (Hardman et al., 2014).

You can also adapt your instruction by supplementing auditory presentations with visual information, speaking clearly and orienting yourself so students can see your face, eliminating distracting noise, and frequently checking for understanding.

Having peers without disabilities serve as tutors and work in cooperative groups with students who have hearing disabilities can also be helpful. Teaching students without disabilities the elements of American Sign Language and fingerspelling provides an added dimension to their education.

Technology, Learning, and Development

Using Assistive Technology to Support Learners with Disabilities

Julio is partially deaf, barely able to use a hearing aid to understand speech. Kerry Tanner, his seventh-grade science teacher, works closely with the special education instructor assigned to her classroom to help Julio. Seated near the front of the room to facilitate lipreading, Julio takes notes on a laptop computer during teacher presentations. Other students take turns sharing their notes with him so he can compare and fill in gaps. He especially likes to communicate with other students on the Internet, as this levels the communication playing field. When he views video clips on his computer, he uses a special device with earphones to increase the volume.

Jaleena is partially sighted, with a visual acuity of less than 20/80, even with corrective lenses. Despite this disability, she is doing well in her fourth-grade class. Tera Banks, her teacher, has placed her in the front of the room so that she can better see the chalkboard and document camera and has assigned students to work with her on her projects. Using a magnifying device, she can read most written material, but the computer is giving her special problems. The small letters and punctuation on Website addresses and other information make it difficult for her to use the computer as an information source. Tera works with the special education consultant in her district to get a monitor that magnifies the display. She knows it is working when she sees Jaleena quietly working alone at her computer on the report due next Friday.

Julio and Jaleena are benefiting from **assistive technology**, a set of adaptive tools that support students with disabilities in learning activities and daily life tasks. These tools are required by federal law under IDEA and include motorized chairs, remote control devices that turn machines on and off with the nod of the head or other muscle actions, and machines that amplify sights and sounds (Heward, 2013).

Assistive technologies are part of a larger movement in education, **universal design for learning**, which seeks to understand and adapt to the needs of diverse learners so supports are provided to all students, including those with exceptionalities (National Center on Universal Design for Learning, 2012). This movement originated in architecture with the design and construction of barrier-free physical environments such as ramps and curb cuts for wheelchair users. Educators then adapted the idea to include the redesign of flexible curriculum materials and learning technologies to accommodate the learning needs of a wide range of students, both with and without exceptionalities.

Universal design for learning has three components:

- Multiple means of representing content to give learners various ways of acquiring information and skills
- Multiple means of expression to provide learners with alternative ways to demonstrate what they know
- Multiple means of engaging students to take advantage of differing student interests and motivation

Notice that the word *multiple* appears in each component. The basic idea is to break away from the one-size-fits-all approach to instruction that basically says, "Here's the information; now learn it." Assistive technologies provide one way to implement universal design principals in the classroom.

Originally, the most widespread use of assistive technology was in the area of computer adaptations. Today, with the widespread use of mobile devices and apps, assistive technologies have spread to other types of adaptive technologies (Cook & Polgar, 2012; Lancioni, Sigafoos, & Nirbhay, 2013). For example, a new device gives the visually impaired a way to read and can be worn like the new Google Glass and travel with the user to any learning situation (Markoff, 2013). It consists of a small camera that clips onto eyeglasses and a small computer that fits into a pocket. As it reads print information, it uses a bone conduction speaker to translate printed text into speech. In addition to being portable and easy to use, this device also keeps track of frequently encountered words and phrases, and stores them in the computer for quicker and more accurate word recognition.

Other applications of assistive technologies target students with learning problems. A number of software programs exist in the areas of reading and math to help students with learning problems acquire essential facts and skills (Roblyer & Doering, 2013). Many of these programs can also be combined with modified input and output devices to make them accessible to students with physical disabilities that make it difficult to use standard technologies. Let's take a closer look at some of these adaptations.

Adaptations to Output Devices. Adaptations to output devices make it easier for students with sensory challenges to access and read information (Best, Reed, & Bigge, 2010). For example, the size of the visual display can be increased by using a special magnifying monitor, such as the one Jaleena used. For students who are blind, portable speech synthesizers can read words and translate them into sounds, such as the one that clips to glasses. In addition, special printers can convert spoken words into Braille and vice versa (Roblyer & Doering, 2013).

Adaptations to Input Devices. To use technology effectively, students must also be able to input their words and ideas. This can be difficult for those with visual or other physical disabilities that don't allow standard keyboarding. Devices that enhance the keyboard, such as making it larger and easier to see, arranging the letters alphabetically to make them easier to find, or using pictures for nonreaders, are adaptations that accommodate these disabilities. For students with limited muscular control, specially adapted mouses and joysticks, as well as a voice recognition system, can also replace standard keyboards.

Assistive technology can also help struggling writers. A number of software programs help developing writers by providing spell-check and word-prediction scaffolding (Roblyer & Doering, 2013). When a student hesitates to finish a word, the computer, based on the first few letters, then either completes it or offers a menu of suggestions. Advocates claim it frees students to concentrate on ideas and text organization.

Additional adaptations bypass the keyboard altogether. For example, speech/voice recognition software can translate speech into text on the computer screen. These systems can be invaluable for students with disabilities that affect the use of hands and fingers. Other adaptations use switches activated by a body movement, such as a head nod, to interact with the computer. Touch screens also allow students to go directly to the monitor to indicate their responses.

Students with learning disabilities encounter difficulties translating ideas into written words, and speech recognition technology eases the cognitive bottleneck in working memory by helping to produce initial drafts that are longer and have fewer errors.

And students don't even have to attend schools to benefit from new assistive technologies.

> Lexie is a third grader, who was born with a heart disorder that weakened her immune system and increased health risks for her when she attended school. Tutoring at home worked for her academically, but she missed her classmates and interacting with them. A 4-foot-tall, 18-pound camera-and-Internet-enabled robot, which Lexie named Princess, changed all that. The robot has a video camera and screen on its face, and Lexie controls it at home with a computer mouse. The robot can be moved around the room and flashes a light when Lexie needs her teacher's attention. Lexie's classmates look at the robot and say, "Hi, Lexie" when it rolls by (adapted from Brown, 2013).

About 23,000 children in our country can't attend school because of physical difficulties, and it's no fun being forced to stay at home when other kids are at school enjoying each other's company. Robot technologies such the example with Lexie and Princess can make their learning less lonely.

Assistive technologies are important because they reduce the extent to which disabilities become handicaps. As technology becomes a more integral part of classroom instruction, assistive technology will become increasingly important for students with exceptionalities.

The Neuroscience of Exceptionalities

Exceptionalities arise from a number of causes, and with the exception of physical disabilities and learned maladaptive behaviors, such as defiance and aggression, most are related to problems with the brain and neural system. The causes range from genetics to ineffective prenatal care and environmental hazards (Carlson, 2014). Our brains are adaptive and resilient, but a number of risk factors can influence the ways our brains develop and function.

Risk factors begin at conception, where gene-related issues influence brain development. For example, research indicates that ADHD runs in families and is often inherited; identical twins share it far more often than fraternal twins (Freitag, Rohde, Lempp, & Romanos, 2010). Brains of children with ADHD grow more slowly and are about 3% smaller in overall volume with a thinner cerebral cortex than the brains of unaffected age-mates (Narr et al., 2009). Similarly, genetics plays a central role in autism spectrum disorders; an identical twin of someone on the autism spectrum is around 70 times more likely to develop autism than comparable students (Baron-Cohen, 2012). Neuroscience research also reveals a number of abnormalities in these children, including excessive growth of neurons (nerve cells) and failure of synaptic pruning mechanisms—failure to eliminate neurological connections that are no longer useful, atypical movement, and abnormalities in the prefrontal cortex, the part of the brain that controls planning, inhibition of motor actions, and coordinating complex multistep actions (Fan, Decety, Yang, Liu, & Cheng, 2010; Ozonoff, 2010; Tang et al., 2014). Genetics explains why these exceptionalities occur; neuroscience helps us understand how these neural changes influence behavior.

Neuroscience research also helps us understand how challenges during pregnancy affect the developing brain. Research confirming the damage of alcohol, smoking, drugs, and malnutrition on healthy brain development has existed for many years (Berk, 2013), but new technologies allow researchers to safely study the brain activity of fetuses through the abdomens of pregnant mothers (Sheridan, Matuz, Draganova, Eswaran, & Preissl, 2010). This noninvasive technique captures the same information about the brain as an MRI (magnetic resonance imaging), but does so unobtrusively. Using these techniques, researchers have identified a number of negative consequences from these risk factors, such as decreased brain size, damage to brain structures, and abnormalities in brain functioning, including the structural and chemical activity involved in transferring messages from one part of the brain to another (Habek & Kovačević, 2011; Haycock, 2009).

These same technologies have also uncovered some intriguing findings about stimulation in the mother's uterus and prenatal brain development. One study found that fetuses can discriminate between two different spoken languages, even when they are spoken by the same person and in the same intonation (May, Byers-Heinlein, Gervain, & Werker, 2011). Other research suggests that this prenatal learning is associated with later language development and reading ability (Sheridan et al., 2010). Other research examining the effects of music on the developing fetus suggests that fetuses can hear music, that newborns prefer music similar to what they've been exposed to in the uterus, and that listening to music in the uterus might even promote cognitive development (Arya, Chansoria, Konanki, & Tiwari, 2012; Soley & Hannon, 2010). Clearly, prenatal brain development plays a powerful role in shaping each child's brain. When this development occurs in a healthy context, brain development is enhanced. The opposite is also true, with negative consequences for later school performance.

These same technologies are providing insights into the structural causes of many exceptionalities. For example, researchers have learned that blood flow to the cerebellum and prefrontal cortex is lower than normal in the brains of students with learning disabilities and ADHD, and neural activity, as measured by electrical firings, is different in the areas that control motor abilities and certain functions of working memory (Armstrong, 2010). Brain imaging research also suggests that the prefrontal cortex, responsible for regulating actions such as attention and impulse control, develops more slowly in some students with ADHD (Ahmadlou & Adeli, 2010). These results help us understand why students with ADHD encounter problems with self-regulation and monitoring their own behavior.

Neuroscience researchers have also examined the functioning of different parts of our memory systems and how they interact (Carlson, 2014). For example, students with learning disabilities have trouble holding information in working memory, the component of our memory system in which we consciously organize and combine new information with information from our long-term memories. If we can't retain information in working memory, organizing and making sense of our experiences is very difficult (Geary, 2007). Research also suggests that difficulties with reading, paying attention, and following directions may be due to an auditory processing disorder that disrupts the flow of information from the environment into the brain (Heymann, 2010; Perrachione, Tufo, & Gabrieli, 2011).

Neuroscience research is also helping us better understand the influence of educational interventions. For instance, patterns of electrical activity in parts of the brain linked to spatial and motor activity are different for deaf persons who have learned to sign compared to those who haven't developed this ability, suggesting that learning strongly influences brain development and functioning (DiSalvo, 2011; Varma, McCandliss, & Schwartz, 2008; Seung, 2012).

It's also clear that environmental conditions after birth can cause changes in brain functions. For example, we know that prolonged stimulus deprivation during the early years can result in lowered IQ and impaired cognitive function, inattention and difficulty concentrating, hyperactivity, and unruly behavior and lack of self-regulation (Berk, 2013). Neuroscience research is helping us understand how these environmental influences impact the brain's functioning and may eventually offer suggestions as to how to reverse these negative influences (Carlson, 2014).

We also know that a healthy environment can help optimize the brain's potential. In addition, stimulation, in the form of effective instruction, can play a powerful role in helping students with exceptionalities adapt to their disabilities and flourish. This is where you, the classroom teacher, are so important.

Neuroscience provides two benefits for classroom teachers. First, it helps us better understand the causes of many exceptionalities, and with this understanding comes hope for the development of better methods to maximize learning for students with exceptionalities.

This research also confirms findings from other areas of educational psychology and provides us with greater confidence in our actions. For example, earlier in the chapter we discussed the questionable recommendations of learning styles advocates, and especially those who advocate teaching to the left or right hemispheres of our brain. Neuroscience tells us that the different parts of the brain are interconnected, and targeting one hemisphere versus the other is not only misguided but also counterproductive (Alferink & Farmer-Dougan, 2010; DiSalvo, 2011).

Neuroscience also helps teachers in the process of identifying and diagnosing learners with exceptionalities. Currently, identifying many exceptionalities, such as learning disabilities, is often a high-inference process and is substantively based on teachers' observations. Often we're unsure of our diagnoses, even after consulting with special educators and testing experts. Neuroscience can help in this process, and a number of researchers are working in this area, attempting to develop screening procedures that depend on neuroscience methodologies and provide data that supplement teacher judgments. In addition, some companies are developing genetic tests and electronic screening procedures that can help parents and teachers identify, understand, and even prevent brain exceptionalities (Stewart, May, & Whitehurst, 2013; Ellison, 2010).

Students Who Are Gifted and Talented

Although we don't typically think of students who are gifted and talented as having exceptionalities, they frequently cannot reach their full potential in general education classrooms. At one time, gifted was the only term educators used, but now the enlarged category includes students who do well on IQ tests (typically 130 and above) as well as those who demonstrate talents in a range of areas, such as math, creative writing, and music (Davis, Rimm, & Siegel, 2011).

Characteristics of Students Who Are Gifted and Talented

Students who are gifted and talented have the following characteristics:

- Learn more quickly and independently than their peers
- Use advanced language, reading, and vocabulary skills
- Display more highly developed learning and metacognitive strategies
- Demonstrate higher motivation on challenging tasks and less on easy ones
- Set high personal standards of achievement (Davis et al., 2011; Grigorenko et al., 2009; Subotnik, Olszewski-Kubilius, & Worrel, 2011)

Providing rich learning experiences that help these children develop to their fullest potential is our challenge.

The history of gifted and talented education in the United States began with a longitudinal study conducted by Louis Terman and his colleagues (Terman, Baldwin, & Bronson, 1925; Terman & Oden, 1947, 1959). Using teacher recommendations and IQ scores (above 140 on the Stanford-Binet intelligence test), Terman identified 1,500 gifted individuals to be tracked over a lifetime (the study was projected to run until 2010). The researchers found that, in addition to being high academic achievers, these students were better adjusted as children and adults, had more hobbies, read more books, and were healthier than their peers. This study, combined with more current research, has done much to dispel the stereotype of gifted students as maladjusted and narrow "brains."

The current definition used by the federal government describes gifted and talented students as "Children and youth with outstanding talent who perform or show the potential for performing at remarkably high levels of accomplishment when compared with others of their age, experience, or environment" (National Society for the Gifted and Talented, 2014, para. 1). Another historically popular definition of giftedness has used three criteria: (1) above-average ability; (2) high levels of motivation and task commitment; and (3) high levels of creativity (Renzulli & Reis, 2003).

Because the federal government does not include giftedness as a recognized exceptionality in IDEA, states define it in different ways. In addition, depending on the state's definition, the percentage of students served in different states varies from 2% to 22%, with an average figure of about 12% (Friend, 2014). And as gifted education has evolved, leaders have shifted away from the concept of giftedness as a general characteristic and toward talents in specific areas (Colangelo & Davis, 2003; Davis et al., 2011).

Identifying Students Who Are Gifted and Talented

Meeting the needs of students who are gifted and talented requires early identification and instructional modifications. Failure to do so can result in gifted underachievers with social and emotional problems linked to boredom and lack of motivation (Davis et al., 2011). Conventional procedures often miss students who are gifted and talented because they rely heavily on standardized test scores and teacher nominations, and females and students from cultural minorities are typically underrepresented in these programs (Gootman & Gebeloff, 2008). When New York City moved from a comprehensive approach to identifying kindergarten students who are gifted and talented to one based solely on tests, the number of Black and Hispanic students decreased from 46% to 27% (Winerip, 2010). To address this problem, experts recommend more flexible and less culturally dependent methods, such as creativity measures, tests of spatial ability, and peer and parent nominations in addition to teacher recommendations (Davis et al., 2011).

As with all exceptionalities, you play an essential role in identifying learners who are gifted and talented because you work with these students every day and can identify strengths that tests may miss. However, research indicates that teachers often confuse conformity, neatness, and good behavior with being gifted or talented (Colangelo & Davis, 2003). You might ask yourself questions such as the following as you consider whether students in your class are gifted or talented:

- Are they curious and inquisitive?
- Do they think in the abstract and play with abstract symbol systems?
- Do they have advanced vocabularies and language skills?

Programs for Students Who Are Gifted and Talented

Programs for students who are gifted and talented are usually based on either **acceleration**, which keeps the curriculum the same but allows students to move through it more quickly, or **enrichment**, which provides alternate instruction (Dai, 2010; Davis et al., 2011). Educators disagree over which approach is better. Critics of enrichment charge that it often involves busywork and point to research suggesting that students benefit from acceleration (Feldhusen, 1998a, 1998b). Critics of acceleration counter that comparisons are unfair because the outcomes of enrichment, such as creativity and problem solving, are not easily measured. They further argue that the general education curriculum is narrow, and social development can be impaired when younger students who want accelerated content must take classes with older students. The question remains unanswered, and the debate is likely to continue.

Programs for students who are gifted and talented are typically organized in either self-contained classes or pullout programs that occupy a portion of the school day. Self-contained classes usually include both acceleration and enrichment; pullout programs focus primarily on enrichment. In both kinds of programs it is important to help these students integrate into regular classroom life, as they often feel self-conscious about being different (Mendaglio, 2010).

Diversity: Pursuing Equity in Special Education

A paradox exists in special education. The very system that was created to provide fair and humane treatment for all students has resulted in one in which culturally and linguistically diverse students are both over- and underrepresented in programs for learners with exceptionalities (Harry & Klingner, 2007). For example, African American students make up less than 15% of the school population but account for 20% of students diagnosed with exceptionalities (Blanchett, 2006). In addition, minority students, especially African American and Hispanic, have been underrepresented in gifted and talented programs (Hardman et al., 2014; Heward, 2013).

These are not recent trends. As far back as 1979, our national government recognized these disparities and asked researchers to look for possible reasons (Turnbull et al., 2013). The reasons are complex and range from problems in the students' home and neighborhood environments to factors within schools themselves (O'Conner & Fernandez, 2006). For example, poverty results in poorer prenatal care, nutrition, and health care, all of which can influence both intelligence and school performance. In addition, poverty can result in neighborhoods that are less nurturant, with limited access to early educational resources.

The children of poverty also attend poorer quality schools. For instance, classes in high-poverty schools are nearly 80% more likely to have an out-of-field teacher than those in more advantaged areas.

Critics also point to the special education placement process itself (O'Conner & Fernandez, 2006). They ask whether classrooms are culturally responsive, build on students' existing knowledge, and provide instruction sensitive to the strengths that students from diverse backgrounds possess.

The identification and placement process also depends heavily on culture and language. Tests used to identify students with exceptionalities are culturally based and depend on facility with English (Rogoff, 2003).

As a general education teacher, you can do much to address these issues. For example, making an effort to know your students as people, treating them equitably in learning activities, and emphasizing the contributions of prominent people from different cultures can do a great deal to make students feel welcome in school. The greater the extent to which they feel as though they're a part of school culture, the more motivated to learn and take responsibility they will be. Then, if learning problems occur, you can be sure that you've done everything possible before referring students for special services. And if you ultimately conclude that special services are necessary, you will be able to provide the most accurate information available for helping meet these students' needs.

Teachers' Responsibilities in Inclusive Classrooms

As we said at the beginning of the chapter, it's almost certain that you will have students with exceptionalities in your classroom, so it's important to understand how you can best help them learn as much as possible.

Ed Psych and You

Did you know any students with exceptionalities when you were in school? Do you have any of these students in your close circle of friends? How were students with exceptionalities treated in the schools you attended?

You have three responsibilities in working with these students. They're outlined in Figure 5.3 and discussed in the sections that follow. In each area, you should have assistance from special educators who have the expertise to help you.

Modifying Instruction to Meet Students' Needs

In working with the students who have exceptionalities in our classes, modifying instruction to best meet their needs will be our most important responsibility. Fortunately, instruction that is effective with students in general is also effective with students who have exceptionalities. "In general, the classroom management and instruction approaches that are effective with special students tend to be the same ones that are effective with other students" (Good & Brophy, 2008, p. 223). You will need to provide additional support, however, to help students overcome a history of failure and frustration and to convince them that renewed effort will lead to success. For instance, while the majority of the class is completing a seatwork assignment, you can work with individuals or small groups to provide additional support. Strategies effective for all students, and particularly important for students with exceptionalities, include:

- Carefully modeling solutions to problems and other assignments
- Teaching in small steps, and providing detailed feedback on homework and assessments
- Calling on students with exceptionalities as often as calling on other students
- Providing outlines, hierarchies, charts, and other forms of organization for the content you're teaching
- Increasing the amount of time available for tests and quizzes

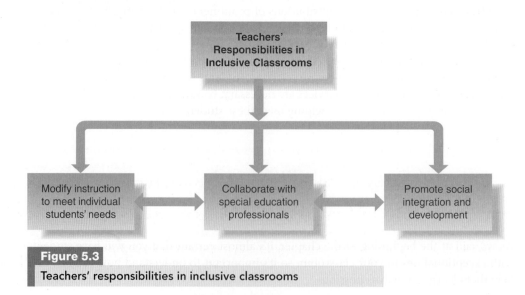

Figure 5.3
Teachers' responsibilities in inclusive classrooms

- Using available technology
- Teaching learning and study strategies

The last item deserves elaboration. Strategy training is one of the most promising approaches that has been developed for helping students with exceptionalities (Hardman et al., 2014; Heward, 2013). A strategy is a plan that students use to accomplish a learning goal. Let's look at an example.

> In working with Adam (the middle school student with a learning disability in reading that you encountered earlier in the chapter), Tammy Fuller, his teacher, helped him develop a strategy for understanding the content of a chapter in his history book. Tammy first had Adam study the chapter outline so he could see how the chapter was organized, and she had him keep the outline in front of him as he read the chapter. She then modeled reading sections of the chapter aloud, and stopped every few paragraphs and created a summary of the information he had just read. She then had him practice by doing the same. If he wasn't able to create a clear summary, she had him reread the section and again try to summarize it.

This process is admittedly demanding, but students with exceptionalities will need to make extra efforts to accommodate their learning issues, and our role is to teach them the strategies needed to help them succeed.

Because students with exceptionalities tend to approach tasks passively or use the same strategy for all types of content, we must help them actively use strategies, as Tammy did in the example above. Students also must learn to adapt their strategies to the learning task at hand (Vaughn & Bos, 2015). For instance, because Adam was attempting to comprehend the content of the chapter, Tammy taught him a different strategy than he would have used if he was simply learning to spell a list of words. Students with learning problems can use strategies but need to be taught how and provided with supervised practice until they become comfortable with the strategy (Coyne, Carnine, & Kame'enui, 2011). Your modeling and explanation, together with opportunities for practice and feedback, are essential. (The case study at the end of the chapter, involving Mike Sheppard's work with his students, illustrates a classroom application of these strategies.)

Peer tutoring, which can benefit both the tutor and the person receiving the tutoring, as well as home-based tutoring programs that involve parents, can also be effective (Vaughn & Bos, 2015).

DEVELOPING SELF-REGULATION

> Don (one of your authors) regularly tutors in a local elementary school in his city. The first-, second-, and third-grade students he works with all struggle academically and are behind in reading and math. When he works with these students and talks with their teachers, two patterns consistently emerge. First, the students are intelligent enough to succeed in school. The second is that they lack self-regulation.
>
> Paul (your other author) had a set of experiences that corroborated Don's observations. As part of a project, he was making a series of observations of first-grade classes, and he was struck by what he observed when the students were doing silent reading. Some of the students read intently for 45 minutes or more, whereas others spent little time reading, instead gazing around the room or playing with pencils or other objects. In fact, in one observation he watched a boy work for 45 minutes to make his book stand up on the desk; he spent virtually no time actually reading. As students progress through the grades, the gap between those who did and did not read conscientiously is likely to become wider and wider.

Many students with exceptionalities receive extra help in the form of tutoring but typically don't receive support that helps them develop their **self-regulation**, the ability to direct and control one's own actions and emotions. Self-regulation plays a powerful role in school success, and students who are self-regulated learn more, are happier in school, and have an easier time making friends (Berk, 2013).

Students with exceptionalities typically have poorly developed self-regulatory skills (Heward, 2013; Hallahan et al., 2015). They have problems staying on task, completing assignments, and using effective learning strategies, as Don witnessed directly and Paul observed. They also have problems controlling their impulses, such as shouting out in the middle of a teacher's explanation or interacting with peers in socially acceptable ways.

We can help these students in several ways. First, we can make them aware of their actions and how they affect learning and their ability to get along with their peers. As they become self-aware, they will gradually learn that they can influence their learning success (Turnbull et al., 2013). Second, we can teach them learning strategies, such as you saw illustrated earlier in this section with Tammy Fuller and Adam (Mastropieri & Scruggs, 2014; Vaughn & Bos, 2015). Finally, patience, support, and encouragement are essential as they gradually develop their self-regulatory abilities.

Collaborating with Other Professionals

Collaborating with other professionals is our second responsibility in helping our students with exceptionalities. **Collaboration** is the process of working with other professionals to solve common problems. Initially, educators viewed inclusion as additive; students with exceptionalities received additional services to help them function in general education classrooms (Turnbull et al., 2013). Gradually, the idea of coordination replaced addition. Today, **collaborative consultation** combines general education teachers and special educators on teams to ensure that experiences for students with exceptionalities are effectively integrated. On these teacher assistance teams, you'll work collaboratively with special educators, reading specialists, English language development teachers, school psychologists, and even school administrators to design and implement instructional programs.

Collaboration can take several forms. They include:

- Curriculum planning. One of our major tasks in the inclusion process is adjusting the curriculum to ensure that it fits the abilities and needs of students with exceptionalities. A major challenge is analyzing new instructional standards in the new Common Core so that they fit the needs of students with exceptionalities (Maxwell, 2013).
- Co-teaching. Often special educators will work alongside the classroom teacher to assist with instruction.
- Consultant teaching. Sometimes a special educator will observe, assess, and help plan instruction for students in inclusive classrooms.
- Coordination of paraprofessionals. Some students with exceptionalities are assigned paraprofessionals to help them in the classroom. Their efforts need to be planned and coordinated with the rest of the instruction that is occurring in the classroom.
- Working with parents. Parents are an integral part of every child's education and can provide valuable information and advice about their child's needs and strengths. Consulting with them helps bridge the gap between home and school (Mastropieri & Scruggs, 2014; Vaughn & Bos, 2015).

Collaboration takes more time and effort, but it is essential for effective inclusion. By working together, professionals create a safety net for students who need extra help to ensure success and guard against failure.

Collaboration typically begins when a learning problem is identified (Mastropieri & Scruggs, 2014; Vaughn & Bos, 2015). In the response to intervention model described earlier in the chapter, this occurs when the interventions you've tried fail to produce successful learning experiences for a student. Once a learning problem that requires extra services is identified, a team of professionals meets to clarify the problem; design, implement, and evaluate more intense interventions; develop IEPs; and work with parents.

Promoting Social Integration and Development

Promoting the social integration and development of students with exceptionalities is your third important responsibility. Students with exceptionalities often fall behind in their academic work, frequently misbehave, and sometimes lack social skills (Hallahan et al., 2015). As a result, other students develop negative attitudes toward them, which adversely affect their confidence and self-esteem. You'll need to make special efforts to promote the acceptance of these students in your classroom. You can do so in two ways:

- Develop classmates' understanding and acceptance of them.
- Use strategies to promote social interaction among students (Plata, Trusty, & Glasgow, 2005).

DEVELOPING CLASSMATES' UNDERSTANDING AND ACCEPTANCE

Students' negative attitudes toward their peers with exceptionalities often result from a lack of understanding, and open discussion and information about disabilities can help change these attitudes (Heward, 2013). Emphasizing that people with disabilities want to have friends, be happy, and succeed, just as we all do, can do much to change attitudes. These discussions can reduce stereotypes about learners with exceptionalities and break down the barriers between them and other students. Literature and videos that explore the struggles and triumphs of people with disabilities are also valuable sources of information.

USING STRATEGIES TO PROMOTE SOCIAL INTEGRATION AND DEVELOPMENT

Students with disabilities often lack social skills and the ability to make friends, and they may avoid other students or unknowingly alienate them (Turnbull et al., 2013). Modeling, coaching, and involving students in learning activities can all help them develop social skills. To teach a student how to initiate play, for example, you might say, "Barnell's over there on the playground. I think I'll say, 'Hi, Barnell! Want to play ball with me?' Now you try it, and I'll watch."

You can also model social problem solving. For instance, you might ask, "Mary has a toy that I want to play with. What could I do to make her want to share that toy?" Direct approaches such as these have been successful in teaching social skills such as empathy, perspective taking, negotiation, and assertiveness (Vaughn & Bos, 2015).

Calling on students with exceptionalities as frequently as possible in learning activities and expecting them to be as involved as their classmates are two of the most effective ways to promote their integration and development. Doing so communicates that all students are valued and are expected to participate and succeed.

Cooperative learning can also help students learn social skills (Mastropieri, Scruggs, & Berkeley, 2007). When students work closely in groups, emotional barriers are often broken down and students both with and without exceptionalities learn that they are more alike than they are different.

This discussion addresses the questions we asked in *Ed Psych and You* in this section. Most of us probably were aware that we had classmates with exceptionalities, but we didn't really get to know them. This was unfortunate for both them and us, because it didn't give us the chance to learn about—and possibly even become friends with—different kinds of students. As a teacher, you can do much to ensure that all students feel welcome in your classroom and have opportunities to learn about each other.

Classroom **Connections**

Teaching Students with Exceptionalities in the General Education Classroom

1. Expert teachers adapt instruction to meet the needs and capabilities of students with exceptionalities. Provide additional instructional scaffolding to ensure success on instructional tasks.

- **Elementary:** A third-grade teacher carefully monitors students during seatwork. She often gathers students with exceptionalities in a small group to provide additional assistance at the beginning of assignments.

- **Middle School:** A sixth-grade math teacher organizes his students in groups of four for seatwork assignments. Each student completes a problem and confers with a partner. When two students disagree, they confer with the other pair in their group. The teacher carefully monitors the groups to be sure that all four are participating and contributing.

- **High School:** A science teacher assesses frequently and provides detailed feedback on all assessment items. She spends time in one-on-one conferences with any students having difficulty.

2. A major obstacle to social integration and growth is other students' lack of understanding. Discuss the subject of exceptionalities in an open and positive manner.

- **Elementary:** A second-grade teacher uses role-playing and modeling to illustrate problems such as teasing and taunting others. She emphasizes treating students who look or act differently with the same respect that other students receive.

- **Middle School:** An English teacher uses literature, such as *Summer of the Swans*, by Betsy Byars (1970), as a springboard for talking about individual differences. He encourages students to reflect on their own individuality and how important this is to them.

- **High School:** An English teacher leads a discussion of students' favorite foods, activities, movies, and music, and also discusses topics and issues that concern them. She uses the discussions as a springboard for helping create a sense of community in the classroom.

3. Students with exceptionalities often pursue learning tasks passively. Use modeling and coaching to teach effective learning strategies.

- **Elementary:** A fourth-grade math teacher emphasizes questions such as the following in checking answers to word problems: Does the solution answer the problem? Does it make sense? Are the units correct? He reinforces this process throughout the school year.

- **Middle School:** A math teacher teaches problem-solving strategies by thinking aloud at the chalkboard while she's working through a problem. She breaks word problems into the following steps and places them on a poster at the front of the room: (1) *Read*: What is the question asking? (2) *Reread*: What information do I need? (3) *Stop and think*: What do I need to do—add, subtract, multiply, or divide? (4) *Compute*: Put the correct numbers in and solve. (5) *Label and check*: What answer did I get? Does it make sense?

- **High School:** An English teacher teaches and models step-by-step strategies. A unit on writing one-paragraph essays teaches students to use four steps: (1) Write a topic sentence, (2) write three sentences that support the topic sentence, (3) write a summary sentence, and (4) reread and edit the paragraph. The teacher models the strategy and provides positive and negative examples before asking the students to write their own.

4. Students who are gifted and talented need challenging learning activities to motivate them. Provide supplementary enrichment activities to challenge students who are gifted and talented.

- **Elementary:** A fifth-grade teacher allows students who are gifted and talented to substitute projects of their choice for homework assignments once they have demonstrated that they have mastered the general education curriculum.

- **Middle School:** A prealgebra teacher pretests students at the beginning of each unit. Whenever a student has mastered the concepts and skills, she receives an honor pass to work on an alternative activity in the school media center. The activities may be extensions or applications of the concepts taught in the unit, or they may involve learning about mathematical principles or math history not usually taught in the general education curriculum.

- **High School:** A social studies teacher caps off every unit with a hypothetical problem, such as "What would the United States be like today if Great Britain had won the Revolutionary War?" Students work in groups to address the question, and the teacher gives extra credit to those who want to pursue the topic further in a paper or project.

Developmentally Appropriate **Practice**

Teaching Students with Exceptionalities at Different Ages

Development plays an important role in understanding and dealing with student exceptionalities. Effective practices for students with exceptionalities are influenced by the age and developmental characteristics of students.

Working with Students in Early Childhood Programs and Elementary Schools

Early childhood and lower elementary teachers are in a unique position to help identify learning problems. Pretesting of all students at the beginning of the school year not only provides a baseline for future growth, but can also identify potential learning problems (Reutzel & Cooter, 2008; Vaughn & Bos, 2015). When pretesting data alert teachers to a potential learning problem, detailed records that identify the nature of the problem and records of intervention attempts can provide special educators with the tools they need to create effective interventions.

Sensitivity to the possibility of developmental lags is particularly important with young children. Research on learner development indicates that considerable variation exists in students' rates of development, and developmental lags are often mistaken for more serious learning problems (Lerner, 2006).

Similarly, being aware of the role of culture and language in early school success is important. Many students grow up in homes where English isn't the first language and where newspapers, magazines, and books are not readily available. Ascertaining that problems cannot be traced to cultural or language differences is important before referring a child for special services.

Working with Students in Middle Schools

The middle school years present challenges to all students, but especially to those with exceptionalities (Waber, 2010). These challenges take the form of physical and emotional changes, as well as the move from self-contained elementary classrooms to the less personal environments in middle schools.

Adaptive behaviors, such as keeping track of assignments and taking notes, present special challenges for students with exceptionalities (Vaughn & Bos, 2015). Efforts to help these students acquire learning strategies can be particularly effective.

Peers become increasingly important to middle school students. Helping students with exceptionalities learn acceptable behaviors, together with strategies for promoting interaction and cooperation, are essential. Cooperative learning and peer tutoring can be effective, but students with exceptionalities need extra support to function effectively in these settings.

Working with Students in High Schools

High school—with large schools, less personal attention, and switching classes—can be particularly challenging for students with exceptionalities (Kincheloe, 2004; Schutz, 2004). Peer acceptance continues to be a priority for all high school students.

Special efforts to help students with exceptionalities—who are sometimes painfully aware of their differences—feel welcome in their classrooms are very important for high school students. Teachers set the tone by modeling courtesy and respect and requiring students to treat each other the same way. Cooperative learning and small-group work provide opportunities for students with exceptionalities to interact socially and learn from their peers.

With respect to acquiring a deep understanding of the topics they're studying, helping learners with exceptionalities acquire effective learning strategies is even more effective with high school students than with younger learners.

5 Summary

1. Describe different views of intelligence, and explain how ability grouping influences learning.
   - Intelligence is the ability to profit from past experiences to solve future problems. It is also often defined as the ability to acquire and use knowledge, solve problems and reason in the abstract, and adapt to new situations in the environment.
   - Some theories suggest that intelligence is a single entity; others describe intelligence as existing in several dimensions.
   - Some experts believe that intelligence is largely genetically determined; others believe it is strongly influenced by experiences. Most suggest that it is determined by a combination of the two.
   - Ability grouping can influence learning through the quality of instruction with which learners are provided and through teachers' expectations for students.

2. Describe the major provisions of the Individuals with Disabilities Education Act (IDEA) and the amendments to it.
   - The major provisions of the IDEA require instruction of students with exceptionalities in the least restrictive environment (LRE), parent involvement, protection of learners against discrimination in testing, and individualized education programs (IEPs) for each student with exceptionalities.
   - Amendments to IDEA make states responsible for locating children who need special services and have strengthened requirements for nondiscriminatory assessment, due process, parental involvement in IEPs, and the confidentiality of student records.

3. Describe the most common learning problems that classroom teachers are likely to encounter.
   - The most common learning problems that classroom teachers encounter include learning disabilities, difficulties in reading, writing, reasoning, or mathematical abilities; communication disorders, which may include either speech or language disorders; intellectual disabilities, limitations in both intellectual functioning and adaptive behavior; and behavior disorders, serious and persistent age-inappropriate behaviors.
   - Teachers may also encounter autism spectrum disorders—disabilities that affect communication and social interaction—as well as visual and hearing disabilities.

4. Identify characteristics of students who are gifted and talented, and explain how teachers identify and teach these students.
   - Students who are gifted and talented learn quickly and independently, possess advanced language and metacognitive skills, and are often highly motivated and set high personal standards for achievement.
   - Methods of identifying students who are gifted and talented include intelligence testing and teacher, parent, and peer reports of unique talents and abilities.
   - The two most common methods of teaching students who are gifted and talented include acceleration, which moves students through the general education curriculum at a faster rate, and enrichment, which provides alternative instruction to encourage student exploration.

5. Describe general education teachers' responsibilities in inclusive classrooms.
   - Teachers' roles in inclusive classrooms include working with other professionals on a collaborative consultation team, adapting instruction to meet students' needs, and promoting students' social integration and growth.
   - Effective instruction for students with exceptionalities is similar to effective instruction in general. Providing additional scaffolding and helping students acquire learning strategies are also helpful.

Preparing for **Your Licensure Exam**

Understanding Learners with Exceptionalities

Because it's virtually certain that you will have students with exceptionalities in your classroom, your licensure exam will include items related to best practices for working with these students. We include the following exercises to help you practice for the exam in your state.

Let's look now at a junior high math teacher and his efforts to work with students in his class who have exceptionalities. Read the case study, and answer the questions that follow.

Antonio Marques teaches twelfth-grade zoology to the 20 students in his class in a private school in Mozambique. Since the beach is so close to the school, he has introduced marine organisms to his curriculum. He has even gone to the beach after school to collect starfishes and other marine organisms for his students. He wants to take the class to the beach to look for these, but it he realizes it would not be an ideal place for Ramiro who is wheelchair bound.

Each week, Antonio decides to focus on a particular marine organism. He begins looking at various marine organisms and teaching his students how to classify, dissect, and study each organism. As Antonio had not yet received the microscopes he had ordered a month earlier, all observations and investigations of organisms had to be done with the naked eye. Antonio does, however, attempt to download pictures of microscopic slides of the various organisms from different Web sites to complement what the students observe during the dissection. This is a challenge as the Internet service where he lives is not very reliable.

Since classifying and investigating organisms is a new experience and undertaking for the students, Antonio decides to provide extra support. He provides a laminated copy of the following table to aid the students in their weekly task. He tells the students that this is a resource that they can use throughout the year, and that they can refer to it during their tests.

Categories to classify organisms in the animal kingdom:
1. Kingdom
2. Phylum
3. Class
4. Order
5. Family
6. Genus
7. Species
What to look for and take note of during the dissection:
1. External shape of the organism
2. External size in centimeters of the organism
3. External orifices of the organism
4. Number and nature of appendages of the organism
5. Internal layers and their nature
6. Reproductive, digestive, excretory, circulatory and neurological systems of the organism
7. Miscellaneous observations of the organism

At the end of four weeks, Antonio administers a 30-minute test which focuses only on the classification of the organisms studied. Edeme, Toia, Chico, Joaquim, Afonso, and Bela has low test scores.

Perplexed, Antonio tells his students, "I have provided the guidance, support and practice needed for you to classify the different organisms in the animal kingdom. But to my utter disappointment, a number of you who were supposed to have done well in yesterday's test performed badly. Were you not able to understand what was taught in class? Was there a problem with my teaching methods?"

Edeme responds, "It is not that I did not learn. I did try to memorize the classifications, but I had difficulty holding on to this information. It was easier for me to retain information about how the organism looked, and how it interacted with the ecosystem."

Marina immediately cries out, "Oh! But the classifications are so easy to memorize. It is the ecosystem interactions and investigating the organism that I do not care to know more about. That sort of thing just does not interest me. Having to answer questions that I just have to memorize are much easier for me. I thought that was a pretty good test, Mr. Marques."

Hearing this debate, Antonio understands that he has students who have different approaches to learning. He, thus, decides to teach and evaluate in such a manner so as to cater to all the learning styles, and not be prejudiced towards a single learning style. In all his subsequent evaluations, he makes sure his tests had questions dealing with deeper understanding of the concepts as well as facts that could be memorized.

He also realizes that there are further differences in the students in his class. Antonio has not been teaching for long, he has been feeling uncertain. So he approaches the subject head at his school, Monica Rodrigues, to discuss the differences in the learners that he has been observing.

"Monica!" he exclaims, "I am so stressed. All my students are intelligent, but there are some that are very gifted, especially Candida. So I have to put in the extra effort into my teaching."

"What kind of extra effort do you mean?" asks Monica.

"Well, so far, I've introduced the students to as many marine organisms as I could possibly find on the beach. I downloaded pictures of microscope slides, and took photographs of the organisms' natural habitat and brought those to the classroom. This way the students could look at the ecosystem. I brought a number of books on the organisms we studied about each week. When the school's Internet service was not working, I also tried to give the students online access to research more about the organism of the week. I encouraged the students to use different forms and methods of taking notes, and when handing in assignments they could also use different innovative methods as long as they answered the allocated task. I also had the students sit in groups. Each member of the group was encouraged to research one aspect of the organism. At the end of each week, the students had to teach each other the allocated portion of the organism that they had investigated. All of that has still not been enough for Candida. She does soaks it all in quickly, but it still feels inadequate. Do you think we should put her in a special class for gifted learners?"

Monica comments, "There is a lot of debate around self-contained classes or pullout programs and their efficacy, so I would rather not go that route. Do you think Candida is becoming discouraged in any way?'

"No," replied Antonio confidently "she appears to be enjoying my classes, and if anything she seems to be more enthusiastic and committed to zoology than any other subject".

"How do you know that she is so committed to zoology?" queried Monica.

"I have spoken to her other teachers, and they do not seem to think Candida is surpassing the other students in the subject areas that they teach. They report that she achieves well in their subject but not exceptionally so. She must have a talent for Zoology," answers Antonio.

Monica then asks Antonio: "If she is doing well in all her subjects and is committed to Zoology, why are you feeling so stressed? You seem to be doing a good job of providing an enriched teaching environment for Candida. At the same time, you also seem to be catering to the different learning styles of the students in your class. You are using various teaching strategies and doing a good job of it."

"Well, it is a lot of extra work on my part, and it is at times stressful when I feel I will not have enough time to prepare my lesson plan," mumbles Antonio.

"But you do manage to prepare every lesson. Do you feel rewarded at all?" queries Monica.

"Yes," Antonio responds. "I was feeling insecure about my work. I am not very experienced at teaching gifted children, so I wanted to check in to see if I was doing enough. I think more than anything else I needed to expel my frustrations. Well, actually to be honest I needed some recognition for all the extra work I have been putting in. Seeing the enthusiasm in most of my students for Zoology is rewarding, but I also needed a peer to recognize and approve my work. Thank you for listening and providing incentive for me to continue as I have done so thus far.

"I wanted to also discuss with you a few problems I am facing with Laurinda. She is intelligent, but she seems to not be good at concentrating and focusing in class, and she never sits still. She was assessed by the educational psychologist last year, but I do not know the results" says Antonio.

Monica answers, "I am aware of Laurinda, but due to confidentiality reasons I cannot share her diagnosis with you. What I suggest you do is to provide her with one instruction or task to complete at a time as well help her learn organization skills. Have her sit in the front of the classroom and in a location where she is not easily distracted. Try these and then get back to me on how you are progressing with her." Antonio does as Monica suggested, and after a few months he does see some improvement in Laurinda.

Questions for **Case Analysis**

In answering these questions, use information from the chapter, and link your responses to specific information in the case.

Multiple-Choice Questions

1. What label is the most appropriate to use in the case of Ramiro who could not go to the beach for educational activities?

   a. Learning disability

   b. Handicapped

   c. Wheelchair bound

   d. Disabled

2. From the information provided in the case, what exceptionality do you think Laurinda has?

   a. Attention-deficit disorder

   b. Anxiety

   c. Attention-deficit /hyperactivity disorder

   d. Receptive disorder

Constructed-Response Question

3. What characteristics, in your opinion, did Candida have that led Antonio Marques to identify her as a gifted student?

Important **Concepts**

ability grouping
acceleration
adaptive behavior
adaptive fit
assistive technology
attention-deficit/hyperactivity
  disorder (ADHD)
autism spectrum disorder
between-class grouping
bipolar disorder
collaboration
collaborative consultation
communication disorders
crystallized intelligence
cultural intelligence

curriculum-based
  assessment
deaf
disabilities
discrepancy model of
  identification
disorder
due process
emotional and behavior
  disorders
emotional intelligence
enrichment
fluid intelligence
gifts and talents
handicap

inclusion
individualized education
  program (IEP)
intellectual disability
intellectual functioning
intelligence
language disorders
  (receptive disorders)
learners with
  exceptionalities
learning disabilities
learning styles
least restrictive environment
  (LRE)
mainstreaming

nature view of intelligence
nurture view of intelligence
partial hearing impairment
people-first language
response to intervention
  model of identification
self-regulation
social intelligence
special education
speech disorders (expressive
  disorders)
tracking
universal design for learning
visual handicap
within-class grouping

Behaviorism and Social Cognitive Theory

OUTLINE	LEARNING OUTCOMES
	After you've completed your study of this chapter, you should be able to:
Behaviorist Views of Learning	1. Use classical conditioning to explain events in and outside of classrooms.
Classical Conditioning	
Educational Psychology and Teaching: Applying Classical Conditioning with Your Students	
Operant Conditioning	
Educational Psychology and Teaching: Applying Operant Conditioning with Your Students	
▶ Technology, Learning, and Development: Capitalizing on Technology to Teach Basic Skills	2. Identify examples of operant conditioning in and outside of classrooms.
Applied Behavior Analysis	
Diversity: Capitalizing on Behaviorism in Working with Students from Diverse Backgrounds	
▶ Analyzing Theories: Evaluating Behaviorism	
Social Cognitive Theory	3. Describe the influence of modeling on people's behaviors. Include the types of models, the outcomes of modeling, the effectiveness of models, and the processes involved in learning from models.
Comparing Behaviorism and Social Cognitive Theory	
Modeling	
Vicarious Learning	
Nonoccurrence of Expected Consequences	
Self-Regulation	
Educational Psychology and Teaching: Using Social Cognitive Theory to Increase Your Students' Learning	4. Use concepts from social cognitive theory to explain people's behaviors. Include vicarious learning, the nonoccurrence of expected consequences, and self-regulation.
▶ Analyzing Theories: Evaluating Social Cognitive Theory	
▶ Developmentally Appropriate Practice: Applying Behaviorism and Social Cognitive Theory with Learners at Different Ages	

Have you ever tried harder after someone praised your efforts, or attempted some activity, such as a new dance step, after watching others do it? If the answer is yes to either of these questions, you will be able to explain why after studying this chapter. Our experiences and observations of others can strongly influence the way we act and think, and they even impact our emotions. In the following case study, you will see their effects on Tim Spencer, a 10th grader, as he struggles in one of his classes. As you read the case study, think about how Tim is influenced by his experience on a math quiz and his observations of his friend Susan.

> Tim has been doing well in Algebra II—getting mostly Bs on the weekly quizzes. On the last one, however, something inexplicably went wrong. He became confused, panicked, and failed it. He was devastated.
>
> Now, on the next quiz, he's so nervous that when he starts, the first few answers he circles have wiggly lines around them from his shaking hand. "I'm not sure I can do this," he thinks. "Maybe I should drop algebra."
>
> His hand also shakes when he takes chemistry tests, but fortunately, he isn't nervous in world history, where he is doing fine.
>
> Tim mentions his troubles to his friend Susan, who always does well on the quizzes.

"They're tough," she comments, "so I really study for them. . . . Let's get together."

Tim is skeptical but agrees, and the night before the next quiz, he goes to Susan's home to study. He sees how she selects several problems from the book and solves them completely, rather than simply reading over the sample problems and explanations. As she begins working on her third problem, he asks her why she is doing another one.

"I try to do as many different kinds as I can to be sure I don't get fooled," she explains. "So I'm more confident when I go into the quiz. . . . See, this one is different. . . . I even make a little chart. I do at least three problems of each type and then check them off as I do them, so I can see that I'm making progress. If I get them all right, I might treat myself to a dish of ice cream."

"Good idea," Tim nods. "I usually do a couple, and if I get them, I quit."

Tim adopts Susan's study habits and sets his own goal of doing three of each type of problem, selecting those with answers at the back of the book.

He does much better on the next quiz. "What a relief," he says to himself.

He's less anxious for the following week's quiz, and his efforts are paying off; he makes his highest score so far.

"Maybe I can do this after all," he says to himself.

To begin our discussion, consider these questions:

1. How can we explain Tim's nervousness on the quiz following his bad experience?
2. Why did his nervousness later decrease?
3. Why did he change his study habits and sustain his efforts?

Behaviorism and social cognitive theory help answer these questions, and in this chapter we'll see how we can apply these theories as we work with our students.

Behaviorist Views of Learning

Behaviorism is a theory that explains learning in terms of observable behaviors and how they're influenced by stimuli from the environment. It defines **learning** as a relatively enduring change in observable behavior that occurs as a result of experience (Schunk, 2012; Skinner, 1953). Notice that this definition doesn't include any references to thought processes, such as expectations, beliefs, insights, desires or goals, or permanent changes in behavior that result from maturation. Behaviorism, as the name implies, focuses on observable behavior. This narrow focus is controversial, but behaviorism continues to be widely applied in schools, especially in classroom management (Freiberg & Lamb, 2009) and in working with learners who have special needs (Daniel, Shabani, & Lam, 2013; O'Mea, 2013).

Behaviorism has two major components: *classical conditioning*, which focuses on emotional and physiological responses to stimuli from the environment, and *operant conditioning*,

Ed Psych and You

Do you get nervous at the beginning of tests, particularly if they're difficult? Do spiders or snakes make you nervous? More positively, have you ever gotten a romantic feeling from listening to a song or had an emotional reaction to being in a particular location, such as a mountain lake?

which examines changes in behaviors in response to consequences. We begin with a discussion of classical conditioning.

Classical Conditioning

Think about the questions we asked in *Ed Psych and You*. If you answered yes to any of them, we can explain your reactions using **classical conditioning**, a component of behaviorism that explains how we learn involuntary emotional or physiological responses that are similar to instinctive or reflexive responses.

Tim experienced what we commonly call *test anxiety*, and we can explain it using classical conditioning. As a result of his experience—failing the quiz—he was devastated. Tim didn't choose to feel this way; it was involuntary, that is, the feeling of devastation was out of his control. Tim associated the algebra quiz with his failure, and as a result, he was nervous when he took subsequent algebra quizzes. His nervousness was similar to the devastation he felt in response to his original failure. He *learned* to be nervous when he took later algebra quizzes; he learned an emotional response that was similar to his original instinctive response.

We usually think of learning as acquiring knowledge, such as knowing the causes of the War of 1812, or skill, such as finding 42% of 65, but emotions can also be learned, and we saw how in Tim's experience.

STIMULI AND RESPONSES IN CLASSICAL CONDITIONING

Ivan Pavlov, a Russian scientist, originally discovered classical conditioning while investigating salivation in dogs. As a part of his research, he had his assistants feed dogs meat powder so their rates of salivation could be measured. As the research progressed, however, the dogs began to salivate at the sight of the assistants, even when they weren't carrying the meat powder. This startling phenomenon caused a turn in Pavlov's work and opened the field of what is now known as classical conditioning.

Let's see how Pavlov's research applies to Tim. The original failure he experienced was an **unconditioned stimulus**, an object or event that causes an **unconditioned response**, the instinctive or reflexive (unlearned) physiological or emotional response caused by the unconditioned stimulus. The devastation Tim felt was the unconditioned response in his case.

Tim associated his algebra quiz with his failure, so quizzes became **conditioned stimuli**, formerly neutral stimuli that become associated with the unconditioned stimulus (Tim's original failure). A **neutral stimulus** is an object or event that doesn't initially affect behavior one way or the other. The algebra quizzes originally had no impact on Tim until they became associated with his failure; in other words, they were neutral.

As a result of associating algebra quizzes with failure, the quizzes produced a **conditioned response**, a learned physiological or emotional response similar to the unconditioned response.

Association is the key to learning in classical conditioning. To form the association, the unconditioned and conditioned stimuli must be *contiguous*, that is, they must occur at the same time. Without this contiguity, an association can't be formed, and learning through classical conditioning can't take place.

Both real-world and classroom examples of classical conditioning are common (Schunk, Meece, & Pintrich, 2014), and the questions we asked in *Ed Psych and You* are examples. Let's consider the last question. You're on a date that turns out to be special, and you feel the attraction and sense of romance that can occur between two people. The encounter is an unconditioned stimulus, and the romantic feeling is the unconditioned response. Now, if a particular song is playing while you're on the date, the song can become associated with

Table 6.1	Classical conditioning in our lives	
Example	Stimuli	Responses
Tim	UCS *Failure*	UCR *Devastation* (involuntary and unlearned)
	CS *Quizzes* (associated with failure)	CR *Anxiety* (involuntary but learned; similar to the original devastation)
Us	UCS *Encounter with another person*	UCR *Feeling of romance* (involuntary and unlearned)
	CS *Song* (associated with the encounter)	CR *Feeling of romance* (involuntary but learned; similar to the original romantic feeling)

Abbreviations: UCS, unconditioned stimulus; UCR, unconditioned response; CS, conditioned stimulus; CR, conditioned response.

the encounter. So, because of the association, it becomes a conditioned stimulus that produces a romantic feeling—similar to the original feeling—as a conditioned response. The mechanisms involved in Tim's case and in the romantic encounter are outlined in Table 6.1.

As other examples, we probably react warmly when we smell Thanksgiving turkey; and we may be uneasy when we enter a dentist's office and, most of us have experienced test anxiety to some degree. In each of these examples, we learned an emotional response through classical conditioning. (When you click on the link that allows you the check your understanding of the information in this section—the link is on page 220—we ask you to explain additional examples of classical conditioning.)

Even though Pavlov's original work was done at about the turn of the 20th century, the study of classical conditioning is alive and well, and it continues to be the theoretical framework for a great deal of contemporary research in areas ranging as widely as preschoolers' preferences for certain tastes (Lumeng & Cardinal, 2007), couples' therapy (Davis & Piercy, 2007), the relationships between personal power and self-esteem (Wojciszke & Struzynska-Kujalowicz, 2007), alcohol dependence (March, Abate, Spear, & Molina, 2013), and even memory (Garren, Sexauer, & Page, 2013).

GENERALIZATION AND DISCRIMINATION

You saw in our opening case study that Tim was also anxious in chemistry tests. His anxiety had *generalized* to chemistry. **Generalization** occurs when stimuli similar—but not identical—to a conditioned stimulus elicit conditioned responses by themselves (Jones, Kemenes, & Benjamin, 2001). Tim's chemistry tests were similar to his algebra quizzes, and they produced the conditioned response—anxiety—by themselves.

Generalization can also work in a positive way. Students who associate a classroom with the warmth and respect demonstrated by one teacher may generalize their reactions to other classes, club activities, and the school in general.

Discrimination, the opposite of generalization, is the process of giving different responses to related but not identical stimuli (Schunk, 2012). For example, Tim wasn't nervous in world history tests. He discriminated between world history and algebra.

EXTINCTION

After working with Susan and changing his study habits, Tim's performance began to improve on the quizzes. As a result, he was less nervous on each subsequent quiz. In time, if he continues to succeed, his nervousness will disappear, that is, the conditioned response will become extinct. **Extinction** in classical conditioning results when the conditioned stimulus occurs often enough in the absence of the unconditioned stimulus that it no longer elicits the conditioned response (Myers & Davis, 2007). As Tim took additional quizzes (conditioned stimuli) without experiencing failure (the unconditioned stimulus), his anxiety (the conditioned response) gradually disappeared.

Educational Psychology and Teaching: Applying Classical Conditioning with Your Students

A great deal of research has been conducted on emotions, their influence on our health and well-being, and their effects on learner motivation and achievement (DeSteno, Gross, & Kubzansky, 2013; Kok et al., 2013). For example, positive emotions, such as feelings of security, enjoyment, and hope, are associated with increased motivation and learning, whereas negative emotions have the opposite effect (Pekrun, Goetz, Frenzel, Barchfeld, & Perry, 2011). Classical conditioning provides us with a tool that we can use to promote positive emotions in our students. The following guidelines can help us in our efforts:

1. Consistently treat students with warmth and respect.
2. Personalize our classrooms to create an emotionally secure environment.
3. Require that students treat each other with courtesy and respect.

To see these guidelines in practice, let's look at the work of Sharon Van Horn, a second-grade teacher.

Sharon greets each of her students with the same routine each morning: As they come in the classroom, they give her a handshake, hug, high five, or any other greeting that they might prefer. During the school day, Sharon simultaneously treats her students with a warm, even manner, while requiring that they behave appropriately and are diligent in their work. She has classroom rules that forbid students from making any demeaning or hurtful comments to their classmates. They have a classroom meeting once a week, during which they discuss the importance of treating others as they would like to be treated.

Sharon takes digital pictures of her students and displays them on a large bulletin board. The students write short paragraphs about themselves, and Sharon displays them below the pictures.

Sharon also periodically displays posters and other artifacts from the heritage countries for her students who are not native English speakers. For example, colorful prints from Mexico are displayed on one wall, and vocabulary cards in both Spanish and English are hung around the room.

Alberto, who has emigrated from Mexico, comes in for extra help three mornings a week, and this morning Mariachi music is playing in the background.

"Buenos días, Alberto. How are you today?" Sharon asks before Alberto gives her a hug, which he prefers.

"Buenos días. I'm fine," Alberto responds, as he goes to his desk to take out his homework.

Now, let's look at Sharon's efforts to implement the guidelines with her students.

Treat Students with Warmth and Respect. Students are often uneasy about attending a new school or even moving to a new grade with an unfamiliar teacher. They may also be uncomfortable with a particular content area. In cases such as these their emotional reactions can have a negative effect on both their motivation and their achievement (Pekrun et al., 2011).

In an effort to help her students learn to feel comfortable in her class, Sharon behaved in a consistently warm and inviting way. Her manner acted as an unconditioned stimulus that triggered students' safe and secure feelings as unconditioned responses. Because she was consistently warm and supportive, they gradually began to associate her classroom with her emotional support, so the classroom became a conditioned stimulus that produced similar feelings of safety as conditioned responses. In time the classroom could even generalize to their school work, producing the similar positive emotions that are associated with increased motivation and achievement (Pekrun et al., 2011).

Personalize Your Classroom. Intuitively, it makes sense that we will have positive emotional reactions to pleasant personal experiences, and research corroborates this position (Ertem, 2013; Narciss et al., 2014). Sharon capitalized the emotional effects of personalization by taking pictures of her students, including descriptions the students had written, and—particularly for Alberto—playing music and displaying pictures of his native Mexico. And she made similar efforts with all her students who weren't native English speakers. Each of these efforts were attempts, through classical conditioning, to help her students feel comfortable by associating her classroom with positive personal experiences.

Require That Students Treat Each Other with Courtesy. If students are going to experience the positive emotions associated with increased motivation and learning, they must feel safe in our classrooms. Requiring that her students treat each other with courtesy and holding periodic classroom meetings to discuss the way the students treat each other capitalized on this idea. Research indicates that rules consistently applied and modeled are essential for creating positive classroom environments (Greenberg, Putman, & Walsh, 2014), and Sharon applied this research with both her manner and the enforcement of her rules.

Our goal in all our decisions is to promote learning, and students learn more in classrooms that are emotionally safe and secure. Classical conditioning is one tool we can use to promote these positive emotions.

Operant Conditioning

In the previous section, we saw that classical conditioning can explain how people learn involuntary emotional and physiological responses to classroom activities and events in our lives. However, people don't simply respond to stimuli; instead, they often "operate" on their

Classroom **Connections**

Developing a Positive Classroom Climate with Classical Conditioning

1. Classical conditioning explains how individuals learn emotional responses through the process of association. To elicit positive emotions as conditioned stimuli in your students, create a safe and welcoming classroom environment, so your classroom elicits feelings of security.

- Elementary: A first-grade teacher greets each of her students with a warm smile each morning when they come into the room. Her goal is to help her students—through classical conditioning—learn a positive emotional reaction to her classroom and their school work by associating them with her warmth and caring manner.

- Middle School: A seventh-grade teacher enforces rules that forbid students from ridiculing each other in any way. His goal is to create a safe environment, so students will associate their classroom and school work with the safety of their school environment, and, through classical conditioning, learn positive emotional reactions to school.

- High School: A geometry teacher clearly specifies what students will be held accountable for on her weekly quizzes. She also drops the students' lowest quiz score for grading purposes. Her goal is to use extinction to eliminate test anxiety in her students.

Table 6.2   A comparison of operant and classical conditioning

	Classical Conditioning		Operant Conditioning	
	Description	Example	Description	Example
Behavior	Involuntary (person does not have control of the behavior)	Tim could not control his test anxiety	Voluntary (person can control behavior)	Tim could control the way he studied
Order	Stimulus precedes behavior	The stimulus (the test) preceded and caused Tim's anxiety	Stimulus (consequence) follows behavior	Tim's improved test score (the consequence) came after (followed) Tim's changed study behavior
How learning occurs	Neutral stimulus becomes associated with an unconditioned stimulus	Tests (originally neutral stimuli) became associated with failure	Consequences of behaviors influence subsequent behaviors	Tim's improved test scores (consequences) influenced the way he studied (he continued to study diligently)
Can explain	How people learn involuntary emotional or physiological responses	How we learn to fear dogs if we're bitten by a dog How a song elicits a romantic feeling if we have had a romantic encounter while the song is playing	How voluntary behaviors are strengthened or weakened	Why a student increases his efforts to answer questions if his teacher praises him for attempting to answer Why a student sits quietly if she is admonished for speaking in class without permission

environments by initiating behaviors. This is the source of the term **operant conditioning**, which describes learning in terms of observable responses that change in frequency or duration as the result of **consequences**, events that occur following behaviors. B. F. Skinner (1953, 1954), historically the most influential figure in operant conditioning, suggested that our behaviors are controlled primarily by consequences. For example, being stopped by a highway patrol for speeding is a consequence, and it decreases the likelihood that we'll speed in the near future. A teacher's praise after a student's answer is also a consequence, and it increases the likelihood of the student trying to answer other questions. A myriad of consequences exist in classrooms, such as high test scores, attention from peers, and reprimands for inappropriate behavior. Each can influence students' subsequent behaviors.

Operant and classical conditioning are often confused. To help clarify important differences, we compare the two in Table 6.2. As you see in the table, learning occurs as a result of experience for both, but the type of behavior differs, and the behavior and stimulus occur in the opposite order for the two.

Now, let's see how different consequences in operant conditioning affect behavior. They're outlined in Figure 6.1 and discussed in the following sections.

Ed Psych and You

During a class discussion, you make a comment, and your instructor responds, "Very insightful idea. Good thinking." How are you likely to behave in later discussions? On the other hand, if you tend to be a little sloppy, your significant other or roommate may nag you to pick up after yourself. What will you probably do to get them to stop?

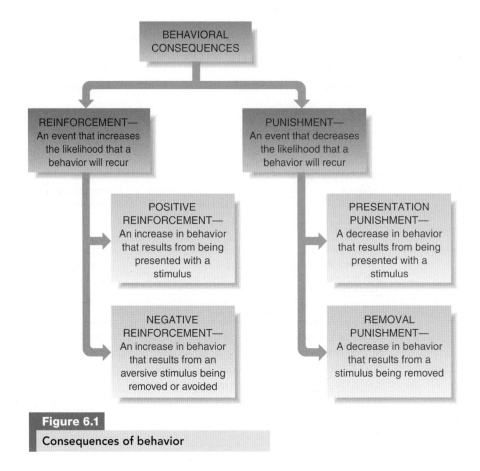

Figure 6.1

Consequences of behavior

REINFORCEMENT

Consider the first question we asked in *Ed Psych and You*. If you're praised for your comments, it's likely that you'll try to make similar comments in the future. Your instructor's comment is a **reinforcer**, a consequence that increases the likelihood of a behavior recurring, and **reinforcement** is the process of applying reinforcers to increase behavior.

Using reinforcers effectively requires good professional judgment. For instance, praising a student for no observable reason, or for answering a trivial question, is not sound practice. We should only reinforce students when they display desired behaviors, such as an insightful answer or diligent effort (Panahon & Martens, 2013), and reinforcers should be administered as soon as possible after the desired behavior is displayed; delaying a reinforcer reduces its impact (Melanko & Larkin, 2013).

We can also reinforce too much as well as too little. Reinforcing too much can result in **satiation**, the process of using a reinforcer so frequently that it loses its ability to strengthen behaviors. Just as we're "satiated" right after eating a big meal, the overuse of praise, for example, reduces its effectiveness.

On the other hand, if we don't reinforce behavior enough, **extinction**, the cessation of a behavior as a result of nonreinforcement, can occur. Let's look at an example.

Renita, a 10th grader, enjoys school and likes to respond in her classes. She is attentive and eager to answer questions.

When Mr. Frank, her world history teacher, asks a question, Renita raises her hand, but someone usually blurts out the answer before she can respond. This happens repeatedly.

Now Renita rarely raises her hand and often catches herself daydreaming in class.

For Renita, being called on reinforced both her attempts to respond and her attention. Because she wasn't called on, she wasn't reinforced, so her behaviors (raising her hand and paying attention) became extinct. So we need to be alert to be sure we provide enough, but not too much, reinforcement when we try to influence our students' behaviors, or with people in general.

With these ideas in mind, we discuss three aspects of reinforcement in the following sections:

- Primary and secondary reinforcers
- Positive reinforcement, including different types of positive reinforcers, *shaping,* and *reinforcement schedules*
- Negative reinforcement

Let's look at them.

Primary and Secondary Reinforcers. Two basic types of reinforcers exist. **Primary reinforcers** are consequences that satisfy basic biological needs, such as food, water, air, sleep, and sex. Physical affection and touching, particularly for infants, may also be primary reinforcers (Berk, 2013), and alcohol and other drugs, including caffeine, can be primary reinforcers under certain conditions (Sheppard, Gross, Pavelka, Hall, & Palmatier, 2012).

The reinforcing value of primary reinforcers can also vary. For instance, one person may prefer a certain type of food, whereas another abhors it. Or one person may be a big eater while another eats very little. So even though food is a primary reinforcer for both people, the value of food as a reinforcer differs between them.

Secondary reinforcers are consequences that become reinforcing over time through their association with other reinforcers. Money is a commonly cited example; it allows people to get food, water, sleep, and, under certain conditions, even sex.

The vast majority of reinforcers in classrooms are secondary. For instance, teacher praise, attention, tokens, high test scores, good grades, and free time are all used in classrooms, and they're all secondary reinforcers.

We should remember that secondary reinforcers are learned and they're socially dependent. For example, if praise, attention, or good grades weren't valued by others, they wouldn't serve as reinforcers. This reminds us that reinforcers we commonly consider to be effective, such as praise, may not be if they embarrass students or make them feel awkward (Bhutto, 2011).

Positive Reinforcement. **Positive reinforcement** is the process of increasing the frequency or duration of a behavior as the result of *presenting* a reinforcer. For example, your instructor *presenting* you with the comment, "Very insightful idea. Good thinking" was a positive reinforcer because it increased the likelihood that you'd contribute again.

Positive reinforcers can be classified into different categories depending on the way they increase behaviors. They include:

- *Social reinforcers,* comments, signs, or gestures, such as your instructor's praise, high test scores, a teachers' smile or positive nonverbal behavior.
- *Concrete reinforcers,* objects that can be touched or held, such as "happy faces," tokens, candy, or stars on the bulletin board.
- *Activity reinforcers,* privileges or desired actions, such as free time or the opportunity to talk to peers.

In classrooms, we typically think of positive reinforcers as something *desired* or *valued,* such as the examples above, but we should remember that *any increase in behavior* as a result of being presented with a consequence is positive reinforcement, and we sometimes unintentionally reinforce undesirable behavior in our students. For instance, if a student is acting out, we reprimand him, and his misbehavior increases, the reprimand is a positive reinforcer. Our reprimand was intended to decrease the behavior, but we inadvertently reinforced it instead; the student's behavior *increased* as a result of being *presented* with the reprimand.

We also use positive reinforcement when we take advantage of the **Premack principle** (named after David Premack, who originally described it in 1965), which states that a more-desired activity can serve as a positive reinforcer for a less-desired activity. For example, you're using the Premack principle if you wait to watch a favorite movie until after you clean up your room; the movie serves as a reinforcer for cleaning up.

You can also use the Premack principle in your work with students. If you're a geography teacher, for example, and you know your students like map work, you might say, "As soon as you've finished your summaries, you can start working on your maps." The map work serves as a positive reinforcer for completing the summaries.

Our students also—probably unintentionally—reinforce us when we teach. Their attentive looks, nods, and raised hands are positive reinforcers, and they increase the likelihood that we'll call on them, or keep doing what we're doing. High student test scores and compliments from students or their parents are also positive reinforcers for all of us.

Positive reinforcers are often used for **shaping**, the process of reinforcing successive approximations of a behavior. For example, you might have a student who is so shy and reluctant to interact with his peers that he rarely speaks. To "shape" his behavior you might first reinforce the student for any interaction with others, such as a simple smile or sharing a pencil; later, you reinforce him for greeting other students as they enter the classroom; and finally you reinforce him only for more prolonged interactions. By reinforcing successive approximations of the desired behavior, you have shaped his behavior.

The process of using positive reinforcers isn't as simple as merely presenting a reinforcer and having the behavior increase, because *the timing and spacing of reinforcers have different effects on the rate of increase and the durability of behavior*. These effects are illustrated in **reinforcement schedules**, patterns in the frequency and predictability of reinforcers (Tanno, Silberberg, & Sakagami, 2012).

For example, suppose you initially praise a student for every attempt to answer a question, but later praise answers only some of the time. Your reinforcement schedule is initially **continuous**—every desired behavior is reinforced—but later you turn to an **intermittent schedule**, where some, but not all, of the desired behaviors are reinforced.

Two types of intermittent schedules exist, and they influence behavior differently. **Ratio schedules** depend on the number of individual behaviors, and **interval schedules** depend on time. Both can be either fixed or variable. In fixed schedules, the individual receives reinforcers predictably; in variable schedules the reinforcers are unpredictable. For instance, when playing slot machines, you insert a coin, pull the handle, and other coins periodically drop into the tray. Receiving coins (reinforcers) depends on the number of times you pull the handle—not on how long you play—and you can't predict when you'll receive coins, so it is a *variable-ratio schedule*.

Many examples of variable-ratio schedules exist in classrooms. Teacher praise and comments on papers are two. The praise and comments depend on students' behaviors—not on time, and students usually cannot predict when they will receive either.

Fixed-ratio schedules are uncommon in classrooms, except for some forms of drill-and-practice computer software. For instance, a student signs on to the program, receives a personalized greeting, and solves three problems. The program then replies, "Congratulations, Antonio, you have just correctly solved three problems." If the program then gives a similar response for every three problems answered correctly, it is using a fixed-ratio schedule.

Now, suppose you're in a class that meets Mondays, Wednesdays, and Fridays, you have a quiz each Friday, and your instructor returns the quiz on Monday. You study on Sunday, Tuesday, and particularly on Thursday evenings, but you aren't reinforced for studying until the following Monday, when you receive your score. Reinforcement for your studying occurs at a predictable interval—every Monday—so it is a *fixed-interval schedule*. On the other hand, if some of your instructors give "pop" quizzes, they are using a *variable-interval schedule*, because you can't predict when you will be reinforced.

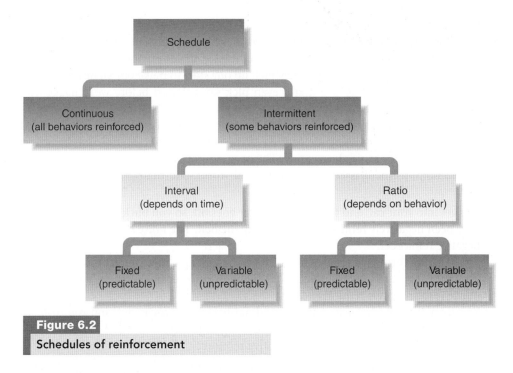

Figure 6.2

Schedules of reinforcement

Reinforcement schedules affect behavior differently, and each has advantages and disadvantages. For instance, a continuous schedule yields the fastest rates of initial learning, so it is effective when students are acquiring new skills such as solving equations in algebra (Lee, Sturmey, & Fields, 2007). However, when teachers eliminate these reinforcers, the frequency of continuously reinforced behaviors decreases more quickly than behaviors reinforced using intermittent schedules (Costa & Boakes, 2007).

Intermittent schedules of reinforcement create more enduring behaviors but also have disadvantages (Lee et al., 2007). With fixed schedules, behavior increases rapidly just before the reinforcer is given and then decreases rapidly and remains low until just before the next reinforcer is given. Giving Friday quizzes is an example; students often study carefully just before the quiz and then don't study again until just before the next quiz.

The relationships among the different types of reinforcement schedules are illustrated in Figure 6.2, and additional classroom examples are outlined in Table 6.3.

Table 6.3	Reinforcement schedules and examples
Schedule	Example
Continuous	A teacher "walks students through" the steps for solving simultaneous equations. Students are liberally praised at each step as they first learn the solution.
Fixed-ratio	The algebra teacher announces, "As soon as you've done two problems in a row correctly, you may start on your homework assignment so that you'll be able to finish by the end of class."
Variable-ratio	Students volunteer to answer questions by raising their hands and are called on at random.
Fixed-interval	Students are given a quiz every Friday.
Variable-interval	Students are given unannounced quizzes.

Negative Reinforcement. Now, think about the second question we asked in *Ed Psych and You* at the beginning of this section: "On the other hand, if you tend to be a little sloppy, your significant other or roommate may nag you to pick up after yourself. What will you probably do to get them to stop?" We likely pick up our stuff to make our significant other or roommate stop nagging us. We might even pick up our stuff before we're nagged to avoid it in the first place. This is an example of negative reinforcement, the process of increasing behavior by removing or avoiding an aversive stimulus (Bernier, Simpson, & Rose, 2012; Skinner, 1953). Being nagged is aversive, so our *picking-up-our-stuff* behavior increases to eliminate or avoid the nagging. The nagging stopping is the negative reinforcer.

Negative reinforcement is common in the real world, and many examples exist. For instance:

- You get into your car, and the seatbelt buzzer goes off, so you buckle the belt. You have been negatively reinforced for buckling the belt. The noise stopping is the negative reinforcer.
- You're sitting through a terrible movie. It's so bad, in fact, that you get up and leave. You are being negatively reinforced for leaving the movie, and escaping the bad movie is the negative reinforcer.
- You are melting in the heat of an extraordinarily hot day. You're out, and you rush home to get into air conditioning. You are being negatively reinforced for rushing home, and escaping the heat is the negative reinforcer.

Negative reinforcement is often offered as an explanation for the problems people have with quitting smoking or stopping alcohol or drug abuse (Melanko & Larkin, 2013; Thompson et al., 2012). For example, lighting up helps alleviate the aversive experience of craving the cigarette, and similar relief occurs when the addicted individual takes a drink or uses a drug.

Negative reinforcement is also common in classrooms. For example, you say to your students, "If you're all sitting quietly when the bell rings, we'll go to lunch. If not, we'll miss 5 minutes of our lunch period." In this case avoiding the aversive stimulus—missing some lunch time—acts as a negative reinforcer for the desired behavior—sitting quietly.

As with positive reinforcement, we sometimes negatively reinforce our students unintentionally.

> Kathy Long is discussing the skeletal system with her science students.
> "Why do you suppose the rib cage is shaped the way it is? . . . Jim?" she asks.
> He sits silently for several seconds and finally says, "I don't know."
> "Can someone help Jim out?" Kathy continues.
> "It protects our heart and other internal organs," Athenia volunteers.
> "Good, Athenia," Kathy smiles.

Later, Kathy calls on Jim again. He hesitates briefly and says, "I don't know."

In this example, Kathy—unintentionally—negatively reinforced Jim for failing to respond. When she called on Athenia after Jim said, "I don't know," she removed the potentially anxiety-provoking question. We have evidence that he was being negatively reinforced, because he said, "I don't know" more quickly after being called on the second time. If students struggle to answer our questions, being called on can be aversive, so they're likely to try and "get off the hook" as Jim did, or avoid being called on at all by looking down and not making eye contact with us.

This example has important implications for our teaching. We want to reinforce students *for* answering, as Kathy did with Athenia, instead of *for not* answering, as she did with Jim. Instead of turning the question to another student, prompting Jim to help him provide an acceptable answer would have been more effective, and she could then have positively reinforced him for the answer.

PUNISHMENT

Positive and negative reinforcers are consequences that increase behavior. Other consequences, called punishers, *weaken* behaviors—decrease the likelihood of the behaviors' recurring. The process of using punishers to decrease behavior is called punishment, and two kinds exist. As you saw in Figure 6.1, presentation punishment occurs when a learner's behavior decreases as a result of being presented with a punisher. For example, when a teacher puts her fingers to her lips, signaling "Shh," and students stop whispering, the students are presented with the teacher's signal, and their behavior—whispering—decreases.

Removal punishment occurs when a behavior decreases as a result of removing a stimulus, or the inability to get positive reinforcement. For example, if students are noisy and their teacher keeps them in the room for 5 minutes of their lunch period, he is using removal punishment. Under normal conditions, they go to lunch at the scheduled time, and he takes away some of that free time.

Using Punishment Effectively. Some critics (e.g., Kohn, 1996) suggest that punishment should never be used because of students' negative emotional reactions to being punished, which, the critics argue, can then generalize to academic work, the classroom, and school in general. And because punishment only decreases undesirable behaviors but doesn't affect or teach desirable ones, systems based on reinforcement are superior to those using punishment (Alberto & Troutman, 2013). However, some students can become disruptive when all punishers are removed, and experts suggest that consequences for misbehavior are a necessary part of an effective classroom management system, so using punishment is sometimes necessary (Greenberg et al., 2014). The most practical approach is to use punishment sparingly and judiciously, combined with appropriate reinforcement for good behavior, with positive reinforcement being more effective than negative reinforcement (Bernier et al., 2012).

Some punishers generally viewed as effective include:

- *Desists.* Desists are verbal or nonverbal communications that teachers use to stop a behavior (Kounin, 1970). A simple form of presentation punishment, such as a teacher putting her fingers to her lips, signaling "Shh," as you saw earlier, is a desist. When administered immediately, briefly, and unemotionally, they can be effective for reducing or eliminating a variety of inappropriate behaviors (Emmer & Evertson, 2013; Evertson & Emmer, 2013).

- *Response cost.* Response cost involves the removal of reinforcers already given (Zhou, Goff, & Iwata, 2000). For example, some teachers design systems where students receive tokens or other reinforcers for desirable behavior, which they can then use to purchase items from a school store or redeem for free time and other privileges. Taking them away because of inappropriate behavior is a form of response cost. Further, some research indicates that people in general are *loss averse,* meaning that they react more strongly to loss, or the prospect of loss, such as the tokens, than they do to the possibility of gaining a reward (Kahneman, 2011). This research suggests that response cost should be effective as a form of punishment.

- *Nonexclusion time-out.* Nonexclusion time-out involves seating a student near the teacher or on the edge of the classroom, with the goal of preventing the student from receiving reinforcers from other students (Ryan, Sanders, Katsiyannis, & Yell, 2007). Nonexclusion time-out is a variation of the traditional "seclusion" time-out, which involves completely removing students from the class and physically isolating them in an area away from classmates. Commonly used by parents to eliminate undesirable behaviors in their young children (Alberto & Troutman, 2013), traditional time-out is controversial. Questions about violating students' rights when it's used have been raised, and lawsuits have even been filed in some cases (Ryan, Peterson, & Rozalski, 2007). As a result, nonexclusion time-out is viewed as more appropriate.

- *Detention.* Similar to time-out, and typically used with older students, detention involves taking away some of the students' free time (typically a half hour or more) by keeping students in school either before or after school hours. Although somewhat controversial (Johnson, 2004), it is generally viewed as effective (Gootman, 1998). It is most effective when students are required to sit quietly and do nothing, because the possibility of positive reinforcement is eliminated (imagine sitting doing absolutely nothing for a half hour). When a parent "grounds" a teenager for inappropriate behavior, the parent is using a form of detention.

    Logistical problems exist with detention because some students simply can't stay after school, transportation doesn't exist for getting them home, or they have other responsibilities, such as after-school jobs or taking care of younger siblings. If logistical problems can be solved, detention can be an effective form of punishment.

Ineffective Forms of Punishment. Although judicious use of punishment can be effective, some forms are unacceptable, counterproductive, and should not be used. They include:

- *Corporal punishment.* Corporal punishment is a form of physical punishment, such as "swats" on the buttocks, designed to inflict pain for the purpose of disciplining a wrongdoer (Rollins, 2012). Although legal in 20 states, evidence suggests that it is detrimental to a productive learning environment (Murphy, Vagins, & Parker, 2010). It can also result in individuals' later demonstrating similar behaviors (e.g., hitting other students) as undesirable side effects (Bandura, 1986), becoming even more defiant after receiving the punishers (Nilsson & Archer, 1989), or learning more sophisticated ways to avoid getting caught. And as we would intuitively expect, research indicates that corporal punishment detracts from student motivation and learning (Ahmad, Said, & Khan, 2013).
- *Embarrassment and humiliation.* Embarrassment and humiliation can lead to some of the same negative side effects as corporal punishment. It can also dampen students' interest in school and lower their expectations for success (Ellis, Fitzsimmons, & Small-McGinley, 2010).
- *Extra class work.* Using class work as a form of punishment can teach students that the topic or subject is aversive and may, through classical conditioning, cause negative emotional reactions to it (Baldwin & Baldwin, 2001). Learners may generalize their aversion to other assignments, other teachers, and the school as well.
- *Out-of-school suspension.* Out-of-school suspension can negatively reinforce misbehaving students because they likely misbehave, at least in part, because school is aversive for them. Being suspended removes the aversive environment. Further, in most cases suspended students are academic underachievers, so being suspended exacerbates their learning problems, detracts from their emotional attachment to school, and increases the likelihood that they will drop out before they graduate (Gregory, Skiba, & Noguera, 2010).

As with using reinforcers, the use of punishers requires sound judgment. For example, if you use desists with your students, but they're reinforced by the attention you're giving them, the desists are ineffective, and you should try a different strategy, such as nonexclusion time-out. On the other hand, if participating in class is aversive, time-out—instead of being an effective punisher—may be a negative reinforcer. In either case, we need to change the strategy.

THE INFLUENCE OF ANTECEDENTS ON BEHAVIOR

So far, we have discussed the influence of consequences—reinforcers and punishers—on behavior. But we can also influence behavior through antecedents, stimuli that precede and induce behaviors. The two most common types of antecedents are (1) environmental conditions, and (2) prompts and cues. Let's look at them.

Ed Psych and You

You walk into a dark room. What is the first thing you do? Why do you do that?

Environmental Conditions. Think about our first question in *Ed Psych and You*. The answer, most likely, is "turn on the light." The darkness is an environmental antecedent that causes us to flip the light switch. The light coming on reinforces us for flipping the switch, so we continue to do so, which answers our second question. On the other hand, a traffic light turning red is an antecedent that causes us to stop, because running the light increases the likelihood of being punished by getting a ticket or being hit by another car.

Some teachers dim the lights when students come into the classroom or when the noise level becomes too great, using it as an environmental antecedent to remind them that they are inside and need to use inside voices and behaviors. We can use classroom environments as antecedents for desirable behaviors, which we can then reinforce.

Prompts and Cues. Prompts and cues are specific actions and questions you can use to elicit desired behaviors in students, particularly in learning activities. For example:

> Alicia Wendt wants her students to understand the concept *adverb*. She writes this sentence on the board:
>
> *John quickly jerked his head when he heard his name called.*
>
>   She then asks, "What is the adverb in the sentence? . . . Jacob?"
>   " . . . "
>   "How did John jerk his head?"
>   " . . . Quickly."
>   "Okay, good. . . . So, what is the adverb in the sentence?"
>   " . . . Quickly."
>   "Yes, . . . good thinking, Jacob."

When Jacob didn't respond to Alicia's question, "What is the adverb in the sentence?" she prompted him by asking, "How did John jerk his head?" Jacob responded, "Quickly," which Alicia positively reinforced by saying, "Okay, good." She prompted him again when she asked, "So, what is the adverb in the sentence?" and after Jacob responded, she again reinforced him by saying, "Yes, good thinking, Jacob."

A variety of cues exists. For instance, when you move to the front of the class or walk among students as they do seatwork, you are cuing them to turn their attention toward you or to remain on task. In each case, you can then reinforce the desired behaviors.

Educational Psychology and Teaching: Applying Operant Conditioning with Your Students

Although cognitive learning theory is the framework most commonly used to guide instruction (we examine cognitive learning theory in detail in Chapters 7-9), behaviorism can also be used as a tool to develop basic skills, and it is widely used in classroom management (Freiberg & Lamb, 2009). The following guidelines can help you use behaviorism as a tool in your work with your students.

1. Use antecedents to elicit desired behaviors, which can then be reinforced.
2. Reinforce students for genuine accomplishments and good behavior.

3. Use reinforcers and punishers appropriately to help maintain an orderly classroom.
4. Employ drill-and-practice technologies to help your students develop basic skills.

To see these guidelines in practice, let's look in on Danielle Stevens, a third-grade teacher, who is working with her students on rounding numbers as she attempts to help them reach the following Common Core Standard:

CCSS.Math.Content.3.NBT.A.1 Use place value understanding to round whole numbers to the nearest 10 or 100. (Common Core State Standards Initiative, 2014s).

Danielle introduces the topic of rounding numbers by having her students count to 100 by 10s, and then says, "Okay, keeping 10s in mind, let's think about the numbers 34 and 36. To which 10 are they the closest? . . . Juan?"

". . . 34 is closest to 30, and 36 is closest to 40," Juan responds after thinking for a couple seconds.

"Good," Danielle nods. "That's what we mean by *rounding*. Rounding helps us when we estimate answers, and we'll be using it throughout the year." After two more examples, she then says, "Now, think about 128. . . . Let's round this to the nearest 10," as she walks down the aisle, makes eye contact with Henry, and shakes her head, signaling "No," in response to his tapping Gretchen's desk with his foot.

Henry stops.

"A hundred," Andrea volunteers.

"Count from 100 to 200 by 10s," Danielle directs.

Andrea counts 100, 110, 120, and so on until she reaches 200.

"Good. So which 10 is 128 closest to?"

". . . One hundred . . . thirty," Andrea hesitantly responds.

"Very good," Danielle nods. "Yes, 128 is closer to 130 than it is to 120. . . . Good thinking."

Danielle then continues the process by having her students count to 1,000 by hundreds, and gives them additional examples, such as 462, which they round to the nearest hundred.

"Now, let's be good thinkers," she continues. "Let's round 6,457 to the nearest 10. Everyone write your answer on your chalkboard and hold it up when you're finished." (Danielle's students have small individual chalkboards at their desks, which they use to write and display answers to math problems.)

Seeing 6,460 on Michael's chalkboard, Danielle says, "Michael, explain to everyone how you arrived at your answer."

Michael explains that because they're thinking about 10s, 6,457 is closer to 6,460 than it is to 6,450.

"That's excellent thinking, Michael," Danielle smiles. "You showed a very good understanding of the problem."

Danielle continues the process with some additional examples, and she then assigns 10 problems for homework.

As she checks on the students while they work, she sees that Andrea, David, Gus, and Suzanne are still struggling with the process. To provide them with additional practice, she sends them to four of the computers at the back of her room, has them log on to a "Rounding Numbers" program, and has them practice until the end of their allocated time for math.

As the students approach the end of their math time, Danielle kneels down by Jon's desk and quietly says, "Jon, I'm very proud of you today. You were paying attention, and I didn't have to remind you even once all period. How many checks did you give yourself?"

"Four," Jon responds.

"Very good, you earned them. . . . Keep it up," Danielle says, smiling warmly. Jon has ADHD and has trouble concentrating and controlling his behavior. Danielle has him keep a "behavior" chart, and for each 10 minutes that he is attentive, he gives himself a check. Danielle had to guide him carefully as they began the process, but he's now much improved.

Now, let's look at Danielle's efforts to apply the guidelines.

Use Antecedents to Elicit Desired Behaviors. Using antecedents in interactions with students can be a useful application of operant conditioning and an effective strategy for helping students generate desired responses. To illustrate, let's look again at some of the dialogue from Danielle's work with her students.

Danielle: Now, think about 128. . . . Let's round this to the nearest 10.
Andrea: A hundred.
Danielle: Count from 100 to 200 by 10s.
Andrea: [Counts 100, 110, 120, and so on until she reaches 200.]
Danielle: Good. So which 10 is 128 closest to?
Andrea: . . . One hundred . . . thirty.
Danielle: Very good. Yes, 128 is closer to 130 than it is to 120. . . . Good thinking.

When Andrea incorrectly responded "100" to the question about rounding 128 to the nearest 10, Danielle had her count from 100 to 200 by 10s and asked, "Which 10 is 128 closest to?" Her directive and question were antecedents (cues) that helped Andrea correctly answer, "One hundred thirty."

This strategy can be applied with virtually any topic in any content area. For instance, a coach is working with his basketball team on fundamentals of the jump shot, and he displays the following photo.

> Coach: Look at the player shooting the jump shot. What is important about the shooter's fundamentals? . . . Jason?
>
> Jason: . . .
>
> Coach: Look at the shooter's wrist. What do you notice about it?
>
> Jason: It's bent. . . . And pointing to the basket.
>
> Coach: Yes, . . . good. It's important to follow through with your wrist when shooting a jump shot.

In this case, the coach's question, "What do you notice about it?" in reference to the shooter's wrist served as an antecedent that focused Jason on an important aspect of jump shooting technique and allowed him to respond correctly.

Reinforce Students for Genuine Accomplishments. It makes sense that being able to respond to questions correctly makes us all feel good, and being reinforced for doing so is even better. Research corroborates this idea, indicating that being reinforced for genuine accomplishment can increase both motivation and learning (Brophy, 2010; Cameron, Pierce, & Banko, 2005; Schunk et al., 2014).

Danielle's comment, "Very good. Yes, 128 is closer to 130 than it is to 120. . . . Good thinking," and the coach's response, "Yes, . . . good. It's important to follow through with your wrist when shooting a jump shot," were both applications of this idea.

In these examples, Danielle's and the coach's reinforcers followed prompts (antecedents). Danielle further applied the use of reinforcement for genuine accomplishment with Michael when she commented, "That's excellent thinking, Michael. You showed a very good understanding of the problem," after the students had been directed to round 6,457 to the nearest 10 and Michael explained how he arrived at 6,460.

Use Reinforcers and Punishers Appropriately to Maintain an Orderly Classroom. Research suggests that reinforcing students for good behavior is an important classroom management technique, and using punishment appropriately is sometimes necessary to create and maintain an orderly classroom (Greenberg et al., 2014). Danielle used this application of operant conditioning as she worked with her students. Let's look again at some dialogue from her work with her students.

> Danielle: [As she kneels down by Jon's desk] Jon, I'm very proud of you today. You were paying attention, and I didn't have to remind you even once all period. How many checks did you give yourself?
>
> Jon: Four.
>
> Danielle: Very good, you earned them. . . . Keep it up.

Because Jon is a student with ADHD and has trouble maintaining attention and controlling his behavior, historically he likely has been reprimanded more often for misbehavior than praised for good behavior. Demonstrating that he can control his behavior and then being reinforced for doing so can mean a great deal to a student like Jon. And it can make an important contribution to his long-term development.

Danielle also used punishment appropriately when she walked down the aisle, made eye contact with Henry, and signaled "No" with a head shake in response to him tapping Gretchen's desk with his foot. Her signal was a simple and effective presentation punisher; it stopped his behavior and didn't disrupt the flow of her lesson.

Employ Drill-and-Practice Technologies to Develop Basic Skills. Behaviorism can be used to help students acquire basic skills, and if employed judiciously, it can promote an orderly classroom environment and even increase motivation.

Technology designed to help students develop basic skills also commonly applies operant conditioning principles. We examine these applications in our "Technology, Learning, and Development" feature.

Technology, Learning, and Development

Capitalizing on Technology to Teach Basic Skills

Behaviorism, and particularly operant conditioning, has historically had a strong influence on the use of technology in classrooms. At the turn of the 21st century, experts estimated that 85% of existing educational software emphasized skill learning based on behaviorist principles, and the figure was nearly as high 10 years later (Tamim, Bernard, Borokhovski, Abrami, & Schmid, 2011).

Technology has since become more sophisticated, but drill-and-practice software based on operant conditioning continues to be an effective tool to develop students' basic skills. You saw how Danielle used it to provide her students with practice in rounding numbers in the previous section, so let's examine this application a bit further with the following example (adapted from IXL Learning, 2013).

You open the program, and the following appears:

When you click on "New Problem," a problem, such as you see here, is displayed.

You type in 675,000, as you see here.

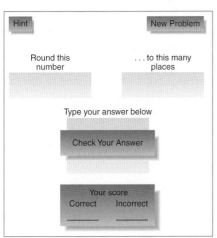
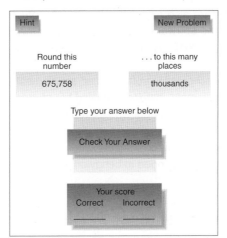
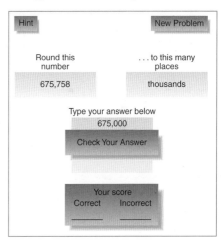

When you click on "Check Your Answer," "No, try again," pops up in a separate box. A bit uncertain about why your answer is incorrect, you click on "Hint," which tells you, "Look to the digit to the right of the rounding place. Is it 5 or greater?" Using the hint, you type in 676,000, and "Correct!" pops up. Had you answered incorrectly a second time, "Sorry, here is the answer," would have appeared, and the answer would have been displayed.

Let's see how this is an application of behaviorism. Your responses (behavior) changed from giving the incorrect answer, 675,000, to the correct answer, 676,000, as a result of (1) being told your first answer was incorrect ("No, try again"); (2) the information you received in the hint; and (3) being told that your second answer was correct ("Correct!"). "No, try again," is a punisher, and "Correct!" is a reinforcer. The likelihood of your repeating the first answer decreases, whereas the likelihood of repeating the second answer increases. You can use software applications such as these with your students in a variety of areas; the most common are drill-and-practice exercises in math and science.

Many programs provide more detailed feedback than simple hints, such as "Look at the digit to the right of the rounding place. Is it 5 or greater?," and they can also be designed to increase learner interest and motivation. Some software asks students to enter information into the program, such as their names, friends, parents, and teacher, and it then personalizes problems. For instance, consider this problem designed for elementary students in math:

There are four objects, and each one is cut in half. In all, how many pieces will there then be?

Now, compare it to the one below, personalized for a student named Josh, whose teacher is Mrs. Gonzalez.

> *Mrs. Gonzalez surprised Josh with a treat for his good behavior by giving him four small candy bars. He wanted to share them with his friend Zach, so he cut each one in half. How many pieces does Josh now have?*

The program took the information Josh had previously entered and used it in the problem. Personalizing problems in this way can increase both learning and motivation (Schunk et al., 2014).

Drill-and-practice software based on behaviorist principles is controversial, and some critics describe it as little more than "electronic flashcards" (Inan, Lowther, Ross, & Strahl, 2010). Used properly, however, evidence doesn't support this position. "Although drill-and-practice software is often disparaged . . . as 'drill and kill,' the benefits of this software function have been well-established by research" (Roblyer & Doering, 2013). As you saw in the examples with rounding, it provides students with individualized practice and increases student engagement, because the student must answer every question. Learners using the software also report that they feel more comfortable because they can set their own pace (if the software allows), and their answers and the feedback they receive are private (Inan et al., 2010). And a computer, unlike a human, can be programmed to have unlimited patience.

Drill-and-practice software can supplement your teaching, but it isn't designed to replace you. For example, instead of having her students simply memorize a set of steps for rounding numbers, Danielle's goal was for rounding to make sense to them, and she, not the software, was instrumental in helping her students reach that goal. Then she used the software to provide extra practice for students who continued to struggle. This is an appropriate application of technology grounded in behaviorism, and used this way, it can contribute to your students' learning.

Applied Behavior Analysis

Applied behavior analysis (ABA) is the process of systematically implementing the principles of operant conditioning to improve students' behavior (Alberto & Troutman, 2013). (It has historically been called *behavior modification*, but this term has a negative connotation for some people, so experts prefer the term we use here.) Widely applied in schools with students having exceptionalities who are disruptive or demonstrate other maladaptive behaviors (Matson et al., 2012; O'Mea, 2013), it has also been used successfully to help people increase their physical fitness, overcome fears and panic attacks, learn social skills, and stop smoking (Ryan, Katsiyannis, & Peterson, 2007).

Nearly half of the research on ABA has focused on its use with students having autism or other developmental delays, another 20% on students with intellectual disabilities, and the remainder on an array of learning or behavioral issues (Daniel et al., 2013). Considerable employment opportunities exist for people with advanced degrees in ABA, so if you're a psychology or special education major, you may want to look into the possibility of further work in this area.

Classroom **Connections**

Using Operant Conditioning Effectively in Classrooms

Reinforcers and Punishers

1. Reinforcers are consequences that increase behavior, and punishers are consequences that decrease behavior. Use positive reinforcement if possible, and removal punishment if necessary.

   ■ **Elementary:** After assigning seatwork, a first-grade teacher gives tickets as positive reinforcers to students who are working quietly. If a student has to be reminded to stay on task, the teacher takes one of the students' tickets as an application of response cost—a type of removal punishment. Accumulated tickets can be exchanged for opportunities to play games and work at learning centers.

   ■ **Middle School:** A seventh-grade teacher implements a system whereby all students in her class start off the week with three "behavior points." If they break a classroom rule, she applies removal punishment by removing one of their behavior points. For each day in which they break no rules, they are awarded an additional behavior point as a positive reinforcer. If they earn an additional point every day of the week, they receive additional positive reinforcement by having their names entered on a behavior honor roll in the class newsletter that goes home to parents at the end of each week.

   ■ **High School:** A math teacher increases the effectiveness of grades as positive reinforcers by awarding bonus points for quiz scores that are higher than students' personal averages.

Reinforcement Schedules

2. Reinforcement schedules influence both the acquisition of responses and their extinction. Continuous schedules increase behavior most rapidly, but intermittent schedules result in the most enduring behavior. Select a schedule that is most effective for meeting your goals.

   ■ **Elementary:** At the beginning of the school year, a first-grade teacher plans activities that all students can accomplish successfully. He uses a continuous reinforcement schedule by praising all desirable behaviors. As students' capabilities increase, he shifts to an intermittent schedule to increase the durability of the behaviors.

   ■ **Middle School:** A sixth-grade teacher employs a variable-ratio reinforcement schedule by complimenting students only when they display conscientious effort and demonstrate thorough understanding. She also applies a variable-interval schedule by periodically sending emails home to parents when students demonstrate extra effort and insight in their class work.

   ■ **High School:** A geometry teacher uses a fixed-interval schedule of reinforcement by giving frequent announced quizzes. He gives at least one quiz a week to prevent the decline in effort that can occur immediately after reinforcement when a fixed-interval schedule is used.

Shaping

3. Shaping is the process of reinforcing successive approximations of a desired behavior. Capitalize on the process to develop complex skills.

   ■ **Elementary:** A preschool teacher is attempting to help one of her students learn to share toys. Initially, she praises any social behavior that the student demonstrates. As the student gradually progresses, she requires that he actually share his toys during play to receive praise as positive reinforcers.

   ■ **Middle School:** At the beginning of the year a language arts teacher is initially generous with positive comments as she scores students' paragraphs, but as students' writing develops they have to demonstrate higher levels of expertise to earn compliments as positive reinforcers.

   ■ **High School:** An Algebra II teacher liberally praises students as they make the initial steps in solving equations. As they continue their work, they have to demonstrate higher levels of skill to receive compliments as reinforcers.

Antecedents

4. Antecedents are signals that induce desired behaviors, which can then be reinforced. Provide cues to elicit appropriate behaviors.

   ■ **Elementary:** Before students line up for lunch, a first-grade teacher reminds them to stand quietly while waiting to be dismissed. The reminder serves as an antecedent for the desired behavior, and when they stand quietly, she positively reinforces them with compliments on their good behavior.

   ■ **Middle School:** After assigning seatwork, a seventh-grade English teacher circulates around the room, reminding students to stay on task. Moving around the room serves as an antecedent for the conscientious work, for which she periodically compliments them, which is an application of a variable-interval schedule.

   ■ **High School:** When a chemistry teacher's students don't respond, or respond incorrectly, he prompts them with additional questions that help them respond acceptably. The prompts serve as antecedents, and when they respond acceptably he positively reinforces them with a smile and nod or a compliment if they demonstrate a deeper level of understanding.

STEPS IN ABA

The application of operant conditioning principles in ABA typically involves the following steps (Alberto & Troutman, 2013; Lovitt, 2012).

1. Identify target behaviors.
2. Establish a baseline for the target behaviors.
3. Choose reinforcers and punishers (if necessary).

4. Measure changes in the target behaviors.
5. Gradually reduce the frequency of reinforcers as behavior improves.

   To see how to implement these steps, let's look in on Mike Sheppard, a middle school math teacher, as he works with his students. (Mike is the same teacher you saw in our "Practicing for Your Licensure Exam" feature in Chapter 5.)

Mike has 28 students in his second-period class, including, as do most teachers, some with exceptionalities. Todd in particular has difficulty controlling his behavior, and other teachers describe him as verbally abusive, aggressive, and lacking in self-discipline. He is extremely active, and he has trouble sitting through a class period.

As the bell rings, most students are studying the screen at the front of the room as they begin a warm-up problem that Mike displays as part of his beginning-of-class routine. He quickly takes roll and then walks to Todd's desk.

"Let's take a look at your chart," he says. "You've improved a lot, haven't you?"

	2/9–2/13	2/16–2/20	2/23–2/27
Talking out	HHT HHT HHT HHT	HHT IIII HHT	HHT II
Swearing	HHT HHT	HHT II	IIII
Hitting/ touching	HHT III	HHT IIII	III
Out of seat	HHT HHT HHT III	HHT HHT HHT IIII	HHT HHT HHT III
Being friendly	II	IIII	HHT II

"Yeah, look," Todd responds, proudly displaying the chart you see here.

"That's terrific," Mike whispers as he leans over the boy's desk. "You're doing much better. We need some more work on 'out of seat,' don't we? I don't like getting after you about it, and I know you don't like it either. . . . Stop by at the end of class. I have an idea that I think will help. . . . Okay. Get to work on the problem." Mike taps Todd on the shoulder and then returns to the front of the room.

Mike goes over the warm-up exercise with the class, conducts the lesson, and gives the students five problems for homework. "Go ahead and get started now," he directs with 15 minutes left in the period.

The bell rings, and the students begin filing out of the room. Todd stops by Mike's desk, and Mike leads him to a small area in the back of the room where a partition has been set up. The area is partially enclosed but faces the class.

"Here's what we'll do," Mike directs. "When you have the urge to get out of your seat, quietly get up and move back here for a few minutes. Stay as long as you want, but be sure you pay attention to what we're doing. When you think you're ready to move back to your seat, go ahead. All I'm asking is that you move back and forth quietly and not bother the class. . . . What do you think?"

Todd nods, and Mike comments, "You're doing so well on everything else; this will help, I think. You're a good student. If you keep trying, this will work. . . . Now, here's a pass into Mrs. Miller's class."

Now, let's see how Mike implemented the steps in ABA.

Identify Target Behaviors. Identifying the specific behaviors you want to change is the first step in ABA. As we saw in Todd's chart, Mike identified five target behaviors: talking out, swearing, hitting/touching other students, being out of seat, and being friendly. Some experts might argue that Mike included too many target behaviors and might further suggest that "being friendly" isn't specific enough. As with most teaching–learning applications, these decisions are a matter of professional judgment.

Establish a Baseline. A baseline is established when the target behaviors are initially measured to provide a reference point for later comparison. For instance, during the baseline period (the week of 2/9 to 2/13), Todd talked out in class 20 times, swore 10 times, hit or touched another student 8 times, was out of his seat 18 times, and was friendly to other students twice. The teacher or an objective third party typically makes observations to determine the baseline. Mike created the behavior tally for the first week.

Choose Reinforcers and Punishers. Before attempting to change behavior, you'll need to identify the reinforcers and punishers that are likely to work for an individual student. Ideally, an ABA system is based on reinforcers instead of punishers, and this is what Mike used with Todd. If punishers are necessary, they should also be established in advance.

Mike used personal attention and praise as his primary reinforcers, and they were effective, as indicated by the positive changes in Todd's behavior. And Todd could see concrete evidence that his behavior was improving, which was, in itself, reinforcing. If the undesirable behaviors had not decreased, Mike would need to modify his system by trying some alternate reinforcers and perhaps some punishers as well.

Measure Changes in Behavior. After establishing a baseline and identifying reinforcers and punishers, you then measure the target behaviors for specified periods to see if changes occur. For example, Todd talked out 20 times the first week, 14 times the second, and only 7 times the third. Except for "out of seat," improvement occurred for each of the other behaviors during the 3-week period.

Because Mike's first intervention didn't change Todd's out-of-seat behavior, he designed an alternative, the area at the back of the room where Todd could go when the urge to get out of his seat became overwhelming. He was free to move back and forth at his own discretion, which was also reinforcing for him.

Reduce Frequency of Reinforcers. As Todd's behavior improved, Mike gradually reduced the frequency of reinforcers. Initially, you might use a continuous, or nearly continuous, schedule and then move to an intermittent one. Reducing the frequency of reinforcers helps maintain the desired behaviors and increases the likelihood of the behaviors generalizing to other classrooms and everyday activities.

FUNCTIONAL ANALYSIS

In the preceding sections we focused on measuring changes in behavior based on the use of reinforcers, and punishers when necessary. However, some experts recommend expanding the focus to identify antecedents that trigger inappropriate behaviors (Lydon, Healy, O'Reilly, & Lang, 2012; Miltenberger, 2012). For example, Mike found that Todd's abusive behavior most commonly occurred during class discussions, and he believed that the attention Todd received for the outbursts was reinforcing. Similarly, Todd was out of his desk most often during seatwork, probably because it allowed him to avoid the tasks with which he struggled. Class discussions were antecedents for abusive behavior, and seatwork was an antecedent for leaving his seat. The strategy used to identify antecedents and consequences that influence behavior is called functional analysis (Miltenberger, 2012; Schlinger & Normand, 2013), and some researchers view it as an essential component of ABA because it focuses on the antecedents of behavior and attempts to understand how environmental conditions affect behavior (Lydon et al., 2012). A functional analysis of Todd's behavior is outlined in Figure 6.3.

Functional analyses are useful for creating effective interventions, and attempts to reduce undesirable behaviors are usually coupled with reinforcing behaviors that are more appropriate or effective (Alberto & Troutman, 2013; Lydon et al., 2012). For example, Mike's positively reinforcing Todd for "being friendly" was a form of attention, so it served the

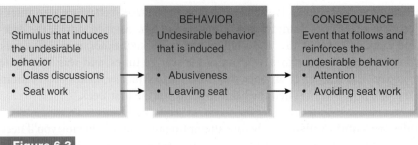

Figure 6.3

A functional analysis of Todd's behavior

same purpose that being abusive had previously served. This process of using interventions that replace problem behaviors with others serving the same purpose for the student, but which are more appropriate, is called positive behavior support.

Like all interventions, ABA won't work magic, and it is labor intensive (Alberto & Troutman, 2013; Matson et al., 2012). For example, you can't automatically assume that a student will accurately measure the target behaviors, so you have to monitor the behaviors yourself. This makes managing an already busy classroom even more complex.

Also, personal attention and praise were effective reinforcers for Todd, but if they hadn't been, Mike would have needed others. Finding a reinforcer that is simple to administer yet consistent with school procedures can be challenging. However, it can provide you with an additional tool if conventional classroom management methods, such as a basic system of rules and procedures, aren't working.

Diversity: Capitalizing on Behaviorism in Working with Learners From Diverse Backgrounds

For some students, schools can seem cold and uninviting, and this can be particularly true for members of cultural minorities (Balagna, Young, & Smith, 2013). Let's see how behaviorism can be used to help every student succeed and feel a part of the classroom.

> Julian, a fourth grader, shuffles into class and hides behind the big girl in front of him. If he is lucky, his teacher won't discover that he hasn't done his homework—12 problems! How can he ever do that many? Besides, he isn't good at math. Julian hates school. It seems strange and foreign. His teacher sometimes frowns when he speaks because his English isn't as good as the other students'. And often he has trouble understanding what the teacher is saying.
>
> Even lunch isn't much fun. If his friend Raul isn't there, he eats alone. One time when he sat with some other students, they started laughing at the way he talked and made fun of the tortillas he was eating. He can't wait to go home.

The way teachers and other students treat members of cultural minorities has a strong impact on their emotional reactions to school. School wasn't associated with positive feelings for Julian, and he didn't feel comfortable, safe, or wanted.

It doesn't have to be this way. For example, if Julian's teacher learned to be emotionally warm and supportive, such as we saw in the example with Sharon Van Horn in our section "Educational Psychology and Teaching: Applying Classical Conditioning with Your Students," he will, through classical conditioning, gradually associate school and his academic work with his teacher's support. For example, Alberto, in the example illustrating Sharon's work with her students, had an instinctive positive emotional reaction to Sharon's warmth, and over time, her classroom became associated with her manner, which then produced positive emotions as conditioned responses. These responses were similar to the instinctive positive emotions—as unconditioned responses—that were triggered by Sharon's warm and supportive manner. These experiences are particularly important for students who are members of cultural minorities, as are rules that forbid students from mistreating each other (Balagna et al., 2013).

We can also effectively apply operant conditioning principles with members of cultural minorities. For instance, when students struggle, we can use prompts as antecedents to encourage them, and then use praise when they give acceptable answers. These efforts are effective with all students, and they are even more important for members of cultural minorities because they communicate that we want these students in our classes and believe they are capable and competent (Balagna et al., 2013).

Analyzing **Theories**

Evaluating Behaviorism

As with any theory, behaviorism has both proponents and critics. Criticisms focus on the following areas:

- The ineffectiveness of behaviorism as a guide for instruction
- The inability of behaviorism to explain higher order learning functions
- The impact of reinforcers on intrinsic motivation
- Philosophical positions on learning and teaching

Let's look at them in more detail.

First, critics charge that behaviorism distorts and oversimplifies the teaching–learning process. Instruction based on behaviorism requires that content is organized so that students can respond with observable behaviors—such as the examples with rounding that we saw earlier—which allows students to be reinforced for providing correct responses. Most of what we learn doesn't exist as specific, decontextualized items of information, however. For example, we learn to write by practicing writing, not by responding to isolated grammar or punctuation exercises often found in workbooks.

Also, learners often hold misconceptions and sometimes generate "off-the-wall" ideas for which they haven't been reinforced. Because these are original ideas, behaviorism is unable to explain how students come up with them. Instead, cognitive theories that focus on learners' thought processes are required.

Also, behaviorism cannot adequately explain higher order functions, such as language development. For instance, Chomsky (1959) demonstrated that even people with small vocabularies would have to learn sentences at a rate faster than one per second throughout their lifetimes if their learning was based on specific behaviors and reinforcers. Some psychologists have even argued that Chomsky's criticism ". . . [H]ammered a nail in the lid of behaviorism's coffin" (Schlinger, 2008, p. 329).

Critics also argue that behaviorism's emphasis on rewards can have a negative impact on learner motivation. Research suggests that offering reinforcers for intrinsically motivating activities, such a solving puzzles or playing video games, can actually decrease interest in these activities (Ryan & Deci, 1996).

Some critics of behaviorism focus on larger, philosophical issues related to learning goals. Because behaviorism focuses on how the environment influences behavior, critics have historically argued, it fails to develop self-regulated learners who take responsibility for their own achievement (Anderman & Maehr, 1994; Kohn, 1993). These critics believe that, instead of promoting meaningful learning, behaviorism is essentially a means of controlling people.

Despite these criticisms, behaviorism is alive and well; a survey of research publications suggests that behaviorism, now referred to by some as *behavior analysis,* has undergone slight but steady growth over the last several decades, and "To borrow the words of Mark Twain, reports of the death of behaviorism were greatly exaggerated" (Schlinger, 2008, p. 329). Further, applied behavior analysis is a thriving area, particularly in working with students having exceptionalities, and many universities in our country offer masters and doctoral degrees in the area (O'Mea, 2013; Gambrill, 2013).

Proponents of behaviorism also counter critics by simply arguing that it works; reinforcers and punishers can and do impact the way we behave, and they also influence both motivation and achievement. For example, research indicates that sincere compliments can increase both student motivation and the way students feel about themselves (Brophy, 2010; Schunk et al., 2014), and teachers' experiences corroborate these findings. Also, a large experimental study found that monetary incentives had a statistically significant positive effect on high school students' performance on a test modeled on the National Assessment of Educational Progress (Braun, Kirsch, & Yamamoto, 2011). Supporters of behaviorism also ask how many of us would continue working if we stopped receiving paychecks, and do we lose interest in our work merely because we get paid for it (Gentile, 1996)?

Also, aspects of behaviorism provide teachers with tools they can use to create orderly classrooms. For instance, research suggests that praise for good behavior and consequences for misbehavior should be part of effective classroom management programs (Greenberg et al., 2014), and behaviorist classroom management techniques are often effective when others are not (Smith & Bondy, 2007).

Finally, as you saw in Danielle's use of technology, drill-and-practice software based on behaviorism can provide students with valuable practice in basic skills.

No learning theory is complete, and this is particularly true of behaviorism. However, if judiciously applied by knowledgeable professionals, it can be a useful tool for creating environments that optimize opportunity to learn for all students.

Table 6.4 summarizes behaviorism, including its contributions and criticisms.

Table 6.4	Analyzing theories: Behaviorism
Key question	What influences changes in observable behavior?
Definition of learning	Enduring change in observable behavior that occurs as a result of experience
Catalysts for learning	• Associations between stimuli • Reinforcement • Punishment
Key concepts	Unconditioned and conditioned stimuli Unconditioned and conditioned responses Reinforcement Punishment Generalization Discrimination Extinction Satiation Shaping
Contributions of theory	• Helps explain how the environment (in the form of associations, reinforcements, and punishments) influences a wide variety of behaviors • Is widely used as a conceptual framework for managing student behavior in classrooms • Is used as a conceptual framework for a range of drill-and-practice computer software
Criticisms of theory	• Is generally ineffective as a conceptual framework for guiding instruction • Cannot explain higher order functions, such as problem solving or language acquisition • Some evidence suggests that the use of behavioral techniques decreases intrinsic motivation in learners • Is viewed by some as mechanistic and even manipulative

Social Cognitive Theory

To begin our discussion, let's look at three examples of learning taking place and ask how they're similar.

"What are you doing?" Jason asks Kelly as he comes around the corner and sees her swinging her arms back and forth as if swinging a bat to try and hit a softball.

"I'm trying to swing at a ball like the softball players in college do, but I haven't been able to quite do it," Kelly responds. "I was watching a game on TV last night, and the way those girls swing looks so easy, but they hit it so hard. I think I can do that if I work at it."

Three-year-old Jimmy crawls up on his dad's lap with a book. "I read too, Dad," he says as his father puts down his own book to help Jimmy up.

"I really like the way Juanita has quickly put away her materials and is ready to listen," Karen Engle, a second-grade teacher, comments as the students are making the transition from one activity to another.

The other students quickly put away their materials and turn their attention to Karen.

These examples are similar in two ways. First, each involved learning by observing the behavior of others; Kelly tried to imitate the swing of big-time college softball players she observed on TV, and Jimmy saw his dad reading and wanted to imitate him. The second graders in Karen's class observed the consequence—being praised by Karen—of Juanita's putting her materials away, so they did the same.

Second, behaviorism can't explain them. It focuses on changes in behavior that have direct causes outside the learner. For instance, in our chapter-opening case study, taking algebra quizzes directly caused Tim's hand to shake. And in these vignettes, Karen's comment directly reinforced Juanita. But nothing directly happened to Kelly, Jimmy, or the other second graders in Karen's class; observing others caused them to change their behavior.

Social cognitive theory, a theory of learning that focuses on changes in behavior, thinking, and affect that result from observing others, emerged from the work of Albert Bandura (1925–) (Bandura, 1986, 1997, 2001). Because behaviorism and social cognitive theory both examine changes in behavior, let's compare the two.

Comparing Behaviorism and Social Cognitive Theory

As you begin this section, you might be asking yourself, "If behaviorists focus on observable behavior, and the term *cognitive* implies memory and thinking, why is a cognitive learning theory included in the same chapter with behaviorism?"

Here's why: Social cognitive theory has its historical roots in behaviorism, but, as the name implies, it has evolved over the years into a more cognitive perspective (Kim & Baylor, 2006; Schunk et al., 2014). Some authors continue to include aspects of social cognitive theory in books focusing on behavioral principles (e.g., Baldwin & Baldwin, 2001).

In addition, behaviorism and social cognitive theory are similar in three ways. Both:

- Focus on experience as an important cause of learning (and an important principle of cognitive theories also states that learning and development depend on learners' experiences).
- Include the concepts of reinforcement and punishment in their explanations of learning.
- Emphasize that feedback is an important aspect of the learning process.

Three important differences exist between the two, however. First, they define learning differently. Second, social cognitive theory emphasizes the role of cognitive processes—*beliefs, perceptions,* and *expectations*—in learning. And third, social cognitive theory emphasizes the concept *reciprocal causation,* which suggests that the environment, personal factors, and behavior are interdependent. Let's look at these differences.

DEFINITION OF LEARNING

Behaviorists define **learning** as a change in observable behavior, whereas social cognitive theorists view learning as a change in mental processes that creates the capacity to demonstrate different behaviors (Schunk, 2012). So, learning may or may not result in immediate behavioral change. The role of mental activity (cognition/thinking) is illustrated in our examples. Kelly, for instance, didn't try to imitate the baseball swing until the next day, so her observations had to be stored in her memory or she wouldn't have been able to reproduce the behaviors. Also, nothing directly happened to Kelly, Jimmy, or Karen's second graders—other than observing Juanita. They were reacting to mental processes instead of reinforcers and punishers that directly influenced them.

THE ROLE OF EXPECTATIONS

Instead of viewing reinforcers and punishers as directly causing behavior, as behaviorists do, social cognitive theorists believe that reinforcers and punishers create *expectations*, cognitive processes that then influence behavior. For instance, you study for an exam for several days, but you aren't reinforced until you receive your score. You sustain your efforts because you *expect* to be reinforced for studying. Karen's second graders expected to be praised for following Juanita's example, so they all imitated her. Behaviorists don't consider the role of expectations in learning, but they are central to social cognitive theory.

The fact that people respond to their expectations means they are aware of which behaviors will be reinforced or punished. This is important because, according to social cognitive theory, reinforcement changes behavior only when learners know what behaviors are being reinforced (Bandura, 1986). Tim, for instance, in our case study at the beginning of the chapter, expected his changed study habits to improve his math scores, so he maintained those habits. If he had expected some other strategy to be effective, he would have used it. He wasn't merely responding to reinforcers; he was actively assessing the effectiveness of his strategy.

RECIPROCAL CAUSATION

Behaviorism suggests a one-way relationship between the environment and behavior; the environment—unconditioned or conditioned stimuli in the case of classical conditioning, and reinforcers and punishers in the case of operant conditioning—influences behavior, but the opposite doesn't occur. Social cognitive theory's explanation is more complex, suggesting that behavior, the environment, and personal factors are interdependent, meaning each influences the other two. The term reciprocal causation describes this interdependence.

For instance, Tim's low score on his algebra quiz (an environmental factor) influenced both his expectations (a personal factor) about future success on algebra quizzes and his behavior (he changed his study habits). His behavior influenced the environment (he went to Susan's home to study) and his later expectations (he became more confident about his capability in algebra). And the environment (his initial low score) influenced both his expectations and his behavior. Figure 6.4 outlines the process of reciprocal causation, illustrated with Tim's example.

We turn now to the core concepts in social cognitive theory, beginning with modeling.

Modeling

Modeling is the central concept of social cognitive theory. We discuss modeling in detail in this section, including the following aspects associated with it:

- Outcomes, or results, of modeling
- Effectiveness of models
- Processes involved in learning from models

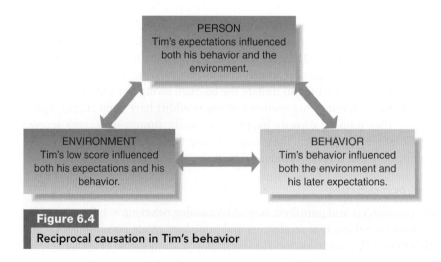

Figure 6.4

Reciprocal causation in Tim's behavior

We begin with the concept of modeling itself. Modeling is a general term that refers to *behavioral, cognitive,* and *affective* changes deriving from observing the actions of others (Schunk, 2012). Tim, for example, observed that Susan was successful in her approach to studying for exams. As a result, he imitated her behavior; direct imitation is one form of modeling, and it resulted in a behavioral change in Tim.

In other cases, cognitive changes can occur in individuals when they observe models articulate their thinking as they demonstrate skills, a process called cognitive modeling (Schunk, 2012). For example:

> "Wait," Jeanna Edwards says as she sees Nicole struggling with the microscope. "Let me show you. . . . Watch closely as I adjust it. The first thing I think about is getting the slide in place. Otherwise, I might not be able to find what I'm looking for. Then, I want to be sure I don't crack the slide while I lower the lens, so I watch from the side. Finally, I slowly raise the lens until I have the object in focus. You were trying to focus as you lowered it. It's easier and safer if you try to focus as you raise it. Go ahead and try it."

By modeling her thinking as she demonstrated how to use the microscope, Jeanna created the potential for a change in her students' thinking, that is, a change in their cognition (Braaksma, Rijlaarsdam, van den Bergh, & van Hout-Wolters, 2004).

Modeling can also result in affective or emotional changes; when we see a person who is obviously uneasy or nervous in some situation, for example, we may also feel a bit uneasy. Or when we watch a sitcom on TV and we see people laughing, we tend to spontaneously smile, or maybe even laugh out loud ourselves. The emotions we feel are the affective changes we experience as a result of seeing models display emotions.

Modeling can be *direct, symbolic,* or *synthesized.* For example, when teachers or coaches model intellectual or physical skills, they are *direct models*. Video recorded examples, as well as characters in movies, television, books, and plays, are *symbolic models*, and combining different portions of observed acts represents *synthesized modeling* (Bandura, 1986). Table 6.5 outlines these different forms of modeling.

We find a great many applications of modeling in both our personal and our professional lives. At a personal level, for example, children learn acceptable ways of behaving by observing their parents and other adults. Teenagers' hair and dress are influenced by

Table 6.5	**Different forms of modeling**	
Type of Modeling	Description	Examples
Direct modeling	An individual attempts to imitate the behavior or thinking of a live model.	Tim imitated Susan's study habits. A first grader forms letters in the same way that the teacher forms them.
Symbolic modeling	People imitate behaviors and thinking displayed by characters in books, plays, movies, television, or the Internet.	People adopt fashion patterns displayed by influential people, such as movie stars or the First Lady of the United States. Teenagers adopt slang and slogans displayed by characters in a popular movie or television show oriented toward teens.
Synthesized modeling	People combine behaviors observed in different acts.	A child uses a chair to get up and open a cupboard door after seeing her brother use a chair to get a book from a shelf and seeing her mother open the cupboard door.

characters they see on television and in movies, and even as adults, we pick up cues from others in deciding how to dress and act.

In the professional world, modeling is important as businesses try to find leaders that can serve as models for both effective business practice and ethical behavior (Whitaker & Godwin, 2013; Wurthmann, 2013). In schools, teachers demonstrate a variety of skills, such as solutions to math problems, effective writing techniques, and critical thinking (Braaksma et al., 2004). When you teach, you will also model courtesy and respect for others, tolerance for dissenting opinions, motivation to learn, and other positive attitudes and values in hopes that your students will develop these same abilities and attitudes. Coaches use modeling to demonstrate the proper techniques for skills, such as hitting a serve in volleyball or making a corner kick in soccer, and they also model important ideas such as teamwork, a sense of fair play, humility in victory, and graciousness in defeat. Modeling is one of the most important mechanisms used to change learner behavior in applied behavior analysis (Daniel et al., 2013).

Modeling can also have negative or unwanted consequences, and we see examples in a range of areas. For instance, if a business culture focuses exclusively on profits or "the bottom line," and employees see their leaders modeling unethical behavior, they're more likely to behave in the same way (Whitaker & Godwin, 2013). In schools, modeling is suggested as a contributor to homophobic aggression in students (Prati, 2012). And professional athletes and other celebrities often unintentionally model inappropriate behaviors such as violence, aggression, and drug and alcohol abuse, inadvertently sending messages that these behaviors are acceptable or even valued.

As teachers, we are models for our students, regardless of whether we choose to be or not. Our responsibility is to model the best that leaders and professionals have to offer.

OUTCOMES OF MODELING

At the beginning of this section we said that modeling refers to behavioral, cognitive, and affective changes deriving from observing the actions of others. These changes can be classified into the categories we see in Figure 6.5. Let's look at them.

Learning New Behaviors. Through imitation, people can acquire abilities they didn't have before observing a model. Solving an algebra problem after seeing the teacher demonstrate a solution, making a new recipe after seeing it done on television, or learning to

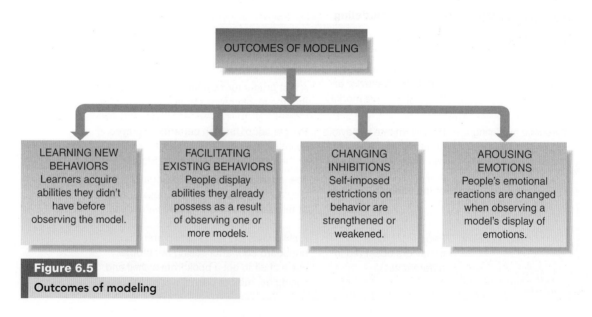

Figure 6.5

Outcomes of modeling

write a clear paragraph after seeing an exemplary one are all examples. Kelly's comment, "I'm trying to swing at a ball like the softball players in college do, but I haven't been able to quite do it," indicates that she was attempting to learn a new behavior by watching players on television.

Facilitating Existing Behaviors. You're attending a concert, and at the end of one of the numbers, someone stands and begins to applaud. You, and others, join in to create a standing ovation. You already know how to stand and applaud, so you didn't learn something new. Instead, observing the model facilitated your behavior.

This outcome is also illustrated in Tim's case. He practiced solving problems before quizzes but admitted, "I usually do a couple, and if I get them, I quit." After observing Susan, he changed the way he studied. Her approach to preparing for quizzes facilitated Tim's studying behavior.

Learning new behaviors and facilitating existing behaviors represent the "behavioral" changes we see in the definition of modeling.

Changing Inhibitions. An inhibition is a self-imposed restriction on our behavior, and observing a model and the consequences of the model's behavior can either strengthen or weaken it. Unlike actions that facilitate existing behaviors, changing inhibitions focus on socially unacceptable behaviors, such as breaking classroom rules (Schunk et al., 2014).

For example, students are less likely to break a rule if one of their peers is reprimanded; their inhibition about breaking the rule has been strengthened. Jacob Kounin (1970), a pioneer researcher in the area of classroom management, called this phenomenon the *ripple effect*. On the other hand, if a student speaks without permission and isn't reprimanded, other students are more likely to do the same. The inhibition is weakened.

Changed inhibitions represent some of the cognitive changes that can occur as a result of modeling. And, as you saw earlier, *cognitive modeling* can result in additional cognitive changes in learners.

Arousing Emotions. Finally, a person's emotional reactions can be changed by observing a model's display of emotions, and these are the affective changes we see in the definition of modeling. For example, observing the uneasiness of a diver on a high board may cause an observer to become more fearful of the board. On the other hand, modeling can also result in positive emotional outcomes; observing teachers genuinely enjoying themselves as they discuss a topic can generate similar enthusiasm in students (Brophy, 2010).

An interesting aspect exists with respect to the affective changes that can result from modeling: the emotions we see modeled aren't necessarily the emotions that are aroused. For instance, suppose we observe two people get involved in an angry and heated argument in a public setting. Anger is the emotion that is being modeled, but embarrassment or awkwardness is likely the emotion that we experience.

Ed Psych and You

We see a wide array of both direct models—people we encounter—and symbolic models, people we see in movies and home videos, on TV, and in written materials. We are likely to model the behavior, thinking, or emotions of some of them more than others. Why might this be the case?

EFFECTIVENESS OF MODELS

The question we asked in *Ed Psych and You* relates to the "effectiveness" of a model—the likelihood that we will experience the behavioral, cognitive, or affective changes that can occur as a result of modeling. A model's effectiveness depends on three factors:

- Perceived similarity
- Perceived competence
- Perceived status

Let's look at them.

Perceived Similarity. When we observe a model's behavior, we are more likely to imitate him or her if we perceive the model as similar to us. This helps us understand why presenting nontraditional career models and teaching students about the contributions of members of cultural minorities are important. Either gender can effectively demonstrate that engineering presents career opportunities, for example, but girls are more likely to believe that it is a viable career if they observe a female instead of a male engineer, just as boys are more likely to consider nursing as a potential career if they observe male rather than female nurses. Similarly, Hispanic students are more likely to believe they can accomplish challenging goals if they see the accomplishments of a successful Hispanic adult than one from another cultural group.

Perceived Competence. Perception of a model's competence, the second factor influencing a model's effectiveness, interacts with perceived similarity. People are more likely to imitate models they perceive to be competent, regardless of similarity. Tim believed Susan was competent because she was a successful student. Although Tim and Susan are similar—they are classmates—he wouldn't have imitated her study habits if she hadn't been successful.

Perceived Status. Perceived status is the third factor. Status is acquired when individuals distinguish themselves from others in their fields, and people tend to imitate models they perceive as having high status, such as professional athletes, stars in entertainment, and world leaders. At the school level, athletes, cheerleaders, and in some cases even gang members or leaders have high status.

High-status models enjoy an additional benefit. They are often tacitly credited for competence outside their own areas of expertise. This is why you see professional athletes (instead of nutritionists) endorsing breakfast cereal, and actors (instead of engineers) endorsing automobiles and motor oil.

PROCESSES INVOLVED IN LEARNING FROM MODELS

How does the process of modeling work? In other words, how do the behavioral, cognitive, or affective changes occur when we observe models? We address these questions in this section.

Four processes are involved in learning from models: *attention, retention, reproduction,* and *motivation* (Bandura, 1986). They're outlined in Figure 6.6 and described as follows:

- *Attention:* A learner's attention is drawn to the essential aspects of the modeled behavior.
- *Retention:* The modeled behaviors are transferred to memory. Storing the modeled behavior allows the learner to reproduce it later.
- *Reproduction:* Learners reproduce the behaviors that they have stored in memory.
- *Motivation:* Learners are motivated by the expectation of reinforcement for reproducing the modeled behaviors.

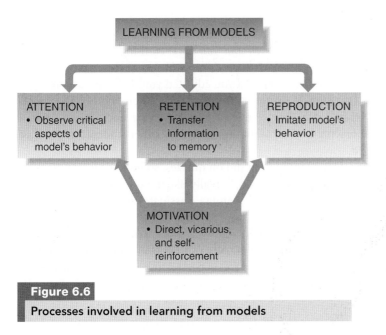

Figure 6.6

Processes involved in learning from models

Three aspects of these factors are important. First, to learn from a model, our attention must be drawn to the essential aspects of the modeled behavior (Bandura, 1986). If we don't know what we're looking for, we don't know what behaviors we should be attempting to retain and reproduce. This is common in teacher education. For instance, preservice teachers often go into schools and observe expert veterans in action; the classroom is operating like a well-oiled machine, and the observer misses the actions the expert takes to make the class work this way. Whenever we formally attempt to be models, we should call attention to the specific behaviors we're modeling.

Second, attending to the modeled behaviors and recording them in memory don't ensure that observers will be able to reproduce them. Additional scaffolding and practice with feedback are often required. (We examine this issue in more detail in the section "Educational Psychology and Teaching: Using Social Cognitive Theory to Increase Your Students' Learning," later in the chapter.)

Third, although motivation appears as a separate component in Figure 6.6, it is integral to each of the other processes. Motivated learners are more likely to attend to a model's behavior, to remember it, and to reproduce it. This is illustrated by the arrows from "motivation" pointing to each of the other processes.

Having examined modeling in detail, we turn now to other core concepts in social cognitive theory, beginning with vicarious learning.

Ed Psych and You

You're driving 75 miles an hour on the interstate, and you're passed by a sports car that appears to be going at least 80. The posted speed limit is 65. A moment later, you see the sports car that passed you pulled over by a highway patrol. You immediately slow down. Why do you slow down?

Vicarious Learning

Think about the question we asked in *Ed Psych and You* here. Nothing directly happened to you, and you didn't imitate anyone's behavior; you simply observed the consequence of the other driver's actions (he got pulled over), and you adjusted your behavior accordingly, a process called **vicarious learning** (Gholson & Craig, 2006). When you saw the sports car pulled over and you slowed down, you were *vicariously punished*, and when a student is publicly reprimanded for leaving his seat without permission, other students in the class are also vicariously punished.

On the other hand, Tim saw how well Susan did on quizzes, so he was *vicariously reinforced* by her success. And when Karen Engle said, "I really like the way Juanita has quickly put away her materials and is ready to listen," Juanita's classmates were also vicariously reinforced.

The influence of expectations helps us understand vicarious learning. Tim expected to be reinforced for imitating Susan's behavior, and the other students in Karen's class expected to be reinforced for putting their materials away. You expected to be ticketed (punished) if you continued speeding, so you slowed down.

Nonoccurrence of Expected Consequences

Earlier we saw that expectations are an integral part of social cognitive theory, and they're also important because they can influence behavior when they *are not* met. For example, suppose you have an instructor who gives you a homework assignment, you work hard on it, but he or she doesn't collect it. The nonoccurrence of the *expected* reinforcer (credit for the assignment) can act as a punisher; you are less likely to work as hard on the next assignment.

Just as the nonoccurrence of an expected reinforcer can act as a punisher, the nonoccurrence of an expected punisher can act as a reinforcer (Bandura, 1986). For example, students expect to be reprimanded (punished) for breaking rules, so if they break rules and aren't reprimanded, they are more likely to break rules in the future (Skatova & Ferguson, 2013). The nonoccurrence of the expected punisher (the reprimand) acts as a reinforcer for the misbehavior.

The nonoccurrence of expected consequences is common in our everyday world. For example, if you send an email to an acquaintance, you expect a reply, and receiving the reply is reinforcing. If the person doesn't reply, you're less likely to send her emails in the future. Sports fans buy season tickets to see their local team play, but if the team consistently loses, they're less likely to buy tickets in the future. Seeing the team win is reinforcing, and its nonoccurrence decreases fans' season-ticket-buying behavior.

Ed Psych and You

How well do you control your emotions? Are you impulsive? Do you set goals? How important is it to you to believe that you control the events that influence your life?

Self-Regulation

The answers to the questions we asked in *Ed Psych and You* are all related to the concept of **self-regulation**, the ability to direct and control one's own actions, thoughts, and emotions toward meeting goals (Schunk, 2012; Zimmerman, 2000). Social cognitive theory assumes that people desire "to control the events that affect their lives" (Bandura, 1997, p. 1). By self-regulating, they gain this control. Self-regulation is important for student learning because it makes students less dependent on teachers and allows them to take control of their own learning.

Self-regulation is a profoundly important aspect of our lives. "[D]eficits in self-regulation are found in a large number of psychological disorders including . . . addiction, eating disorders, and impulse control disorders . . . In contrast, good self-regulators—those who can aptly manage the circumstances and impulses that obstruct goal attainment—are happier, healthier, and more productive" (Legault & Inzlicht, 2013, p. 123).

Some specifics related to "happier, healthier, and more productive" involve improved social relationships, including relationships among siblings (Padilla-Walker, Harper, & Jensen, 2010) and the ability to eliminate bad habits (Quinn, Pascoe, Wood, & Neal, 2010). Self-regulation has also been identified as a primary influence on adolescents' tendency to exercise (Plotnikoff, Costigan, Karunamuni, & Lubans, 2013), and it's essential in dealing with health issues, such as how conscientiously patients undergo rehab after joint replacement surgery (Fiala, Rhodes, Blanchard, & Anderson, 2013) or deal with chronic diseases (Jang & Yoo, 2012).

Self-regulation is particularly important to you as a college or university student because of the many demands on your time, your thinking, and your emotions. Some research suggests that self-regulation is the primary factor influencing the success or failure of university students (Cohen, 2012).

Let's look at an example. You're tired from a long day at school, perhaps combined with work, and one of your friends suggests that you go out for a while. You have a homework assignment for one of your classes, but it's about the last thing you want to do. Your first thought is to simply bag it and go out with your friend, since the assignment probably won't have a major impact on your grade in the class.

You know that completing the assignment is important, however, so you set the goal of finishing at least half of it before you go to bed, and you get a cup of coffee, sit down, and before too long, you see that you've reached your goal. Rejuvenated, you redouble your efforts and finish the entire assignment.

Self-regulation is complex, and you have demonstrated several of its dimensions (which are outlined in Figure 6.7). First, you demonstrated impulse control by resisting the

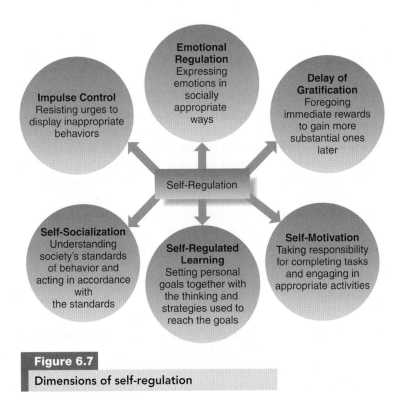

Figure 6.7

Dimensions of self-regulation

temptation to go out instead of working on your homework, and because you received little immediate reward for doing your homework, you also demonstrated **delay of gratification**, the ability to forgo an immediate pleasure or reward in order to gain a more substantial one later—the greater reward being the knowledge and skills you acquire in doing your homework and the higher grade you'll earn at the end of the class. You also displayed both self-motivation and *self-regulated learning* by accepting responsibility for doing the assignment, setting the goal, and completing it. Let's examine the concept of *self-regulated learning* in more detail.

SELF-REGULATED LEARNING

In Figure 6.7 we see that *self-regulated learning* is one of the dimensions of the general concept of self-regulation. **Self-regulated learning** is the process of setting personal goals, combined with the motivation, thought processes, strategies, and behaviors that lead to reaching the goals (Zimmerman & Schunk, 2013). It was the process Tim, in our chapter-opening case study, used to change his study strategies and improve his performance on his algebra quizzes. He knew that Susan was a successful student, so he went to her home, observed her in action, and, as a result of her modeling, adopted study strategies similar to hers. Self-regulated learning is the mechanism that allows students like Tim to capitalize on what they learn from observing models (Greene & Azevedo, 2007).

Choice is an essential element of self-regulated learning (Schunk, 2012). When learners have choices, they decide who to observe and how they will integrate the modeled behaviors into their own lives. Tim, for example, *chose* to go to Susan's house and work with her and, based on the behaviors she modeled, he *chose* his own goals. The development of self-regulated learning is difficult, if not impossible, when all aspects of a task are controlled. For example, if a teacher requires that students write 5 typewritten pages on an assigned topic, in a given format, that includes a minimum of 10 references, opportunities to develop self-regulated learning are reduced.

Self-regulated learning includes the following components:

- Goal setting
- Self-monitoring
- Self-assessment
- Strategy use (Meichenbaum, 2000; Paris & Paris, 2001)

Goal Setting. Goals provide direction for our actions and benchmarks for measuring progress. The goals and actions we select are often outcomes of behaviors we see modeled by others. For instance, Susan set the goal of working at least three of each type of algebra problem, and Tim imitated her behavior by setting a similar goal of his own. As a result of seeing other people exercise or succeed in losing weight, you might set the goal of jogging 25 miles a week, or limiting your food intake to 1,800 calories per day, for example.

Goal setting is at the heart of self-regulated learning, and it is one of the most difficult aspects of the process to implement with students. For it to work, students must be committed to challenging but realistic goals, and they are more likely to commit to goals they set for themselves than to goals set by others (Schunk et al., 2014). This is often problematic, because many students aren't motivated to set goals in the first place, and when they do, the goals are often simple and low level.

Self-Monitoring. Once they've set goals, self-regulated learners continually monitor their actions. For instance, you can keep track of the number of miles you've jogged during a week, or monitor the number of calories you consume each day. Susan said, "I even make a little chart. I do at least three problems of each type and then check them off as I do them."

Students can be taught to monitor a variety of behaviors. For example, they can keep a chart and make a check every time they catch themselves "drifting off" during an hour of study, whenever they blurt out an answer in class, or when they compliment a classmate. Self-monitoring combined with appropriate goals can improve concentration, study habits, and even social skills (Alberto & Troutman, 2013).

Self-Assessment. Self-assessment helps us determine the extent to which our goals are being met. For example, if you jog 5 miles on Sunday, 3 on Monday, 5 on Tuesday, and 5 more on Thursday, you know that you'll need to get in 7 more miles by Saturday to reach your goal of 25 miles for the week. Similarly, if you've consumed 1,200 calories but still haven't had your evening meal, you might forgo dessert.

Students can also learn to assess their own work (Stiggins & Chappuis, 2012). For example, they can determine the quality of their solutions to word problems by comparing their answers with estimates and asking themselves if the answers make sense. Tim's comparing his answers to those in the back of the book is a form of self-assessment.

Self-assessment can also contribute to motivation and personal satisfaction. For instance, when you realize that you need 7 more miles to reach your goal for the week, you will be motivated to go out for a run. The satisfaction associated with reaching goals often leads to a form of self-reward (Schunk, 2012). For instance, if you've reached your weekly calorie goals for a month straight, you may reward yourself with a nice dinner out with your friends, a new outfit, or a couple days off from dieting. Susan, for example, commented, "If I get them [the problems] all right, I might treat myself with a dish of ice cream." Reaching the goal is satisfying, and the more challenging—within reason—the goal, the more satisfying reaching it will be. In fact, the more times you reach your weekly goal, the more motivated you'll be to attain it in the future.

Self-assessment can also help solve the problem of students' not wanting to set goals or wanting to set trivial and easily attainable goals. As they see progress toward reaching their goals, their motivation will increase, and they're more likely to commit to other goals in the future.

Strategy Use. Strategy use connects actions to our goals. To be effectively self-regulated, learners must be able to match effective strategies to their goals. For example, Tim initially worked a few practice problems, and if he was able to do them, he quit. But, because of Susan's modeling, he selected a wider variety of problems. This simple change was a more effective strategy.

Even young children can use strategies. For example, if a first grader practices more on spelling words he doesn't know than on those he can already spell, he is being strategic.

Helping students become self-regulated learners is powerful but demanding. For example, students need a great deal of help in setting challenging but realistic goals, and students won't initially be good at monitoring their own progress, conducting self-assessments, and selecting appropriate strategies (Yell, Robinson, & Drasgow, 2001). Cognitive behavior modification, a procedure that promotes behavioral change and self-regulation in students through self-talk and self-instruction, is a tool that you can use to help your students develop these abilities (Meichenbaum, 2000). The procedure begins with cognitive modeling. If a student is disorganized and scattered, for example, you model both the actions and the thinking involved in setting an appropriate goal, such as bringing a pencil, notebook paper, textbook, and completed homework assignment to class each day. You also model the process of monitoring progress and assessing the extent to which your student is meeting the goal. For example, the student can use a simple checklist that includes each of the items, and you can demonstrate how the items are checked off each day.

After observing the cognitive modeling, your students practice the skill with your support and then use self-talk as a guide when performing the skills without supervision.

Cognitive behavior modification strategies are particularly effective with students having exceptionalities (Turnbull, Turnbull, Wehmeyer, & Shogren, 2013).

In spite of our best efforts, not all of our students will become self-regulated learners, but for those with whom we succeed, we will have made a life-long contribution to their success as a student and to their lives in general.

DIVERSITY: LEARNER DIFFERENCES IN SELF-REGULATION

As with all aspects of learning and development, students differ with respect to self-regulation. For example, self-regulation develops over time, and older students are better at self-regulating their learning than their younger counterparts (Berk, 2013). But even students of the same age will differ considerably in their ability to regulate their cognition, behavior, and emotions, and these differences are caused by both genetics and the environment (Rothbart, 2011). For instance, when self-regulation breaks down, as it inevitably will for all of us at times, learners who have developed a greater sense of autonomy tend to react more effectively by making adaptations in their goals and approaches to both social and cognitive problem solving (Legault & Inzlicht, 2013). This suggests that we should be doing whatever we can to help learners acquire a sense of autonomy and independence when we work with young people; it can make a significant difference in their development of self-regulation. Providing students with choices in their learning and communicating that they are personally responsible for their own behavior can help promote a sense of autonomy.

Gender differences in self-regulation also exist, particularly in the ability to resist potentially destructive impulses and substitute behaviors that are more productive (Chapple & Johnson, 2007). For example, girls are more likely to discuss a disagreement and seek a cognitive resolution than boys, who are more inclined to behave aggressively in a similar circumstance (Walker, Shapiro, Esterberg, & Trotman, 2010). Brain development tends to progress more quickly in girls than in boys, and differences in self-regulation can be found as early as kindergarten (Matthews, Ponitz, & Morrison, 2009).

Cultural differences exist as well. For instance, as a general pattern, students from East Asian cultures, such as Chinese, Japanese, and Korean, place a great deal of emphasis on self-discipline and emotional control. They also strongly emphasize the role of hard work and sustained effort in academic success, and they develop self-regulated learning processes, such as goal setting and monitoring, and strategy use at an early age (Chen & Wang, 2010; Morelli & Rothbaum, 2007).

As with all aspects of diversity, remember that we're describing general patterns here, and many exceptions exist. The patterns contribute to our professional knowledge, but ultimately we are working with individuals and we must make decisions that we believe are in those individuals' best interests, even if they don't fit a pattern.

Ed Psych and You

Are you as impulsive now as you were when you were in your middle teens? Are you more self-regulated than you were then? Has your social development advanced?

THE NEUROSCIENCE OF SELF-REGULATION

Your answers to the questions in *Ed Psych and You* may relate to changes in your brain as you develop. Research suggests that, for most of us, the answer to the first question is no, the answers to the second and third are yes, and the reasons lie, at least in part, in neuroscience (Fassler, 2012; Whelan et al., 2012). Our ability to regulate our behavior and emotions

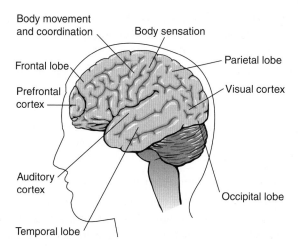

depends largely on the *prefrontal cortex*, the anterior (front) part of the frontal lobes of our brains, as you see here.

The prefrontal cortex is the region of the brain that controls impulses and emotions, monitors efforts to reach goals, manages conflicting thoughts, examines potential consequences and makes decisions about what might be wise or unwise, and suppresses socially unacceptable urges (DeYoung et al., 2010; Yang & Raine, 2009). In other words, it's the region of the brain associated with self-regulation.

The prefrontal cortex develops less rapidly than other parts of the brain, such as the *amygdala*, which is located deep within the temporal lobes and is responsible for more primitive reactions, such as impulses, fear, and aggression (Berk, 2013). This disconnect in brain development particularly manifests itself in adolescents, who tend to rely more on the amygdala and less on the prefrontal cortex in their decision making and action. This helps us understand why teenagers are more likely to act on impulse, misread social cues and others' emotions, get into fights and accidents, or engage in more serious risk-taking behaviors, such as unprotected sex or driving while intoxicated (Steinberg, 2009). The simile, "Teenagers' brains are like cars without brakes," is sometimes used. This neurological delay in development also helps us understand why every state in our country has laws restricting adolescents from activities that require mature judgment, including voting, serving on juries, and purchasing alcohol (Fassler, 2012).

The problem for teenagers is compounded by the fact that they're going through puberty and their changing hormone levels increase their sensitivity and reactions to stress. For example, their increasing testosterone levels make boys particularly vulnerable to aggressive impulses, which can be difficult to control (Walker et al., 2010). We discuss strategies for responding to these issues in our next section: "Educational Psychology and Teaching: Using Social Cognitive Theory to Increase Your Students' Learning."

Educational Psychology and Teaching: Using Social Cognitive Theory to Increase Your Students' Learning

Social cognitive theory has a wide range of classroom applications, and these applications can make a significant difference in student learning. Suggestions for applying the theory with your students include:

- Capitalize on modeling.
- Use vicarious reinforcement and punishment as learning and management tools.
- Follow through on all aspects of instruction and classroom management.
- Promote self-regulation.

Let's examine these suggestions in more detail.

Capitalize on Modeling. Modeling is one of the most powerful influences on learning and behavior that exist, and it is at the heart of social cognitive theory. We can capitalize on it in several ways. They include:

- Putting students in modeling roles and emphasizing cognitive modeling.
- Using guest role models.
- Modeling our own desirable behaviors and emotions.

Let's see how Sally Campese, an eighth-grade algebra teacher, capitalizes on modeling with her students. Sally has several students in her class who are cultural minorities.

Sally is working with her students to help them meet the standard:

CCSS.Math.Content.8.EE.C.8b. Solve systems of two linear equations in two variables algebraically, and estimate solutions by graphing the equations. Solve simple cases by inspection. (Common Core State Standards Initiative, 2014x).

"We'd better get going," Arthur says to Tameka, as they approach Sally's room. "You know how she is. She thinks algebra is sooo important."

"Yes, and I hope you did your homework. She makes such a big deal about being responsible for doing it every night," Tameka comments in return.

As Sally begins her class, she comments, "Just a reminder. I've invited a man named Javier Sanchez to speak on Friday. He is an engineer who works at a local factory, and he's going to tell you how he uses math in his job.

"Okay, look here," Sally says, turning to the day's topic. "We're having a little difficulty with simultaneous equations, so let's go over a few more problems.

"Try this one," she says, writing the following on the board:

$$4a + 6b = 24$$
$$5a - 6b = 3$$

Sally watches, and seeing that Gabriela has solved the problem successfully, says, "Gabriela, come up to the board and describe your thinking for us as you solved the problem."

Gabriela explains that she added the two equations to get $9a + 0b = 27$, and as she writes the new equation on the board, Sally then asks, "So what do we get for the value of a? . . . Chris?"

". . . Three."

"And how did you get that?"

"Zero b is zero, and I divided both sides by 9, so I have $1a$ equals 3."

"Good! . . . Now, let's find the value of b. What should we do first? . . . Mitchell?"

Now, let's look at Sally's attempts to use modeling to promote learning in her students. First, she put Gabriela in a modeling role, and by asking Gabriela to explain her thinking, she also took advantage of cognitive modeling. A classmate can at times be an even more effective model than a teacher because of perceived similarity.

Sally also utilized modeling by inviting Mr. Sanchez to her class. Because he was Hispanic, he would, also through perceived similarity, be an effective model for her students who are members of cultural minorities. Inviting someone like Mr. Sanchez even once or twice a year can do much to capitalize on the influence of minority role models.

Finally, and perhaps most important, Sally—herself—was a positive model. Evidence exists in Arthur's comment, "She thinks algebra is sooo important," which almost certainly resulted from Sally's modeling her own genuine interest in the topic. Modeling won't make all students enthusiastic learners, but it can make a difference in student motivation, as we saw in Arthur's comment (Brophy, 2010). Tameka's reply, "Yes, and I hope you did your homework. She makes such a big deal about being responsible for it every night," provides more evidence of modeling. Sally modeled elements of self-regulation that we hope to see our students develop. She is working with students early in their teen years, and teens learn what's effective and appropriate by observing their parents, teachers, and other adults. When we communicate by our words and actions that learning is not only important, but also requires hard work and self-discipline, over time our students will get the message. Sally's modeling probably did as much to promote self-regulation in her students as any formal strategy would have done.

Use Vicarious Reinforcement and Punishment as Learning and Management Tools. Vicarious learning can be an effective tool, particularly when working with younger children. Comments, such as, "Stephanie is doing a very good job of staying on task," and "I really like the way Fernando is standing so quietly in line," have a positive impact on both the behavior and the achievement of your students.

With older students, comments that suggest progress toward goals can be helpful. For instance, saying, "Good job of identifying evidence to support your conclusion, Natalie. That's one of our goals," helps keep the focus on achievement rather than personal behavior or characteristics, and reduces issues that sometimes exist when publically praising older students.

Follow Through on All Aspects of Classroom Management and Instruction. "Never establish a rule or procedure you aren't committed to enforcing" is a principle that applies in classroom management, and expectations are important cognitive processes that apply to the principle. We know that the nonoccurrence of expected punishers can act as reinforcers, so if you establish a rule, for example, students *expect* to be admonished—or punished in some other way—for breaking the rule. If they aren't, its nonoccurrence can act as a reinforcer, making it more likely that they'll break the rule in the future. If we aren't committed to consistently enforcing rules, we're better off without the rules in the first place.

Expectations are also important with respect to academic work. For instance, if we give assignments, students expect some recognition, such as credit on their final grades and feedback for what they've done, which are reinforcers. If the reinforcers aren't received, their nonoccurrence can act as punishers, making it less likely that they will exert the same amount of effort on subsequent assignments. This is why follow-through is so important, both in classroom management and in instruction.

Promote Self-Regulation. As we saw earlier, "[G]ood self-regulators—those who can aptly manage the circumstances and impulses that obstruct goal attainment—are happier, healthier, and more productive" (Legault & Inzlicht, 2013, p. 123). Developing our students' self-regulation is one of the most worthwhile goals we can strive for in our teaching.

We can promote self-regulation in a number of ways. With young students it can be as simple as establishing rules, such as listening quietly while classmates are talking and raising hands for permission to speak; instituting routines, such as turning in papers and lining up for breaks; and having discussions about how to treat others, combined with practicing appropriate social responses. Because cognition (thinking) is an important component of self-regulation, it's important to discuss reasons for each of these processes.

The cognitive component of self-regulation is even more important with older students, who are still learning how to control their actions and emotions. Several suggestions to help them in the process include (Miller, 2013):

- Discussing the importance of different aspects of self-regulation, such as impulse control and the consequences of not controlling impulses. The adolescent years are filled with temptations for instant gratification and the disregard of control. Helping students understand consequences can make a difference.
- Explaining expectations for appropriate behavior. Adolescents sometimes display inappropriate behaviors simply because they're not clear about what is expected of

them. Clear expectations also communicate that you care and help them acquire a sense of equilibrium in their lives.

- Teaching students positive self-talk and stress management techniques to help them stay cool in stressful or anxiety-provoking circumstances. This can help when they feel anxious or experience the impulse to behave aggressively.
- Encouraging physical activity or participation in sports. Physical activity has a calming effect by helping students blow off steam and release stress. And it has general health benefits and can teach the importance of setting and monitoring goals.

Developing self-regulation in students will be a challenge regardless of the age of the students you teach. For those that you reach, however, you will have made an immeasurable contribution to their learning.

Analyzing **Theories**

Evaluating Social Cognitive Theory

Like all theories, social cognitive theory has both limitations and strengths. The following are some criticisms:

- Social cognitive theory can't explain why learners attend to some modeled behaviors but not others, and it can't explain why learners can reproduce some behaviors they observe but can't reproduce others.
- It doesn't account for the acquisition of complex abilities—beyond mere mechanics—such as learning to write.
- It can't explain the role of context and social interaction in complex learning environments. For example, research indicates that student interaction in small groups facilitates learning (Schunk, 2012). The processes involved in these settings extend beyond simple modeling and imitation.

On the other hand, social cognitive theory has important strengths. For example, modeling is one of the most powerful factors influencing both our behavior and classroom learning that exist, and social cognitive theory provides us with suggestions about how to use modeling effectively in our teaching. Social cognitive theory also overcomes many of the limitations of behaviorism by helping us understand the importance of learner cognitions, and particularly expectations, on our actions (Schunk et al., 2014). It provides us with additional tools that we can use to maximize learning for all our students.

Table 6.6 outlines social cognitive theory, including its contributions and criticisms.

Classroom **Connections**

Capitalizing on Social Cognitive Theory in Classrooms

1. Cognitive modeling involves verbalizing your thinking as you demonstrate a skill. Use cognitive modeling in your instruction, and act as a role model for your students.

   - Elementary: A kindergarten teacher helps her children form letters by saying as she writes on the board, "I start with my pencil here and make a straight line down," as she begins to form a *b*.

   - Middle School: A seventh-grade teacher has a large poster at the front of his room that says, "I will always treat you with courtesy and respect, you will treat me with courtesy and respect, and you will treat each other with courtesy and respect." When a problem surfaces in his classroom he talks about it, discussing possible causes and alternate solutions. He hopes that by modeling this strategy his students will learn to problem solve interpersonal problems themselves.

   - High School: A physics teacher solving acceleration problems writes F = ma on the board and says, "First, I know I want to find the force on the object. Then, I think about what the problem tells me. Tell us one thing we know about the problem, . . . Lisa."

2. Effective modeling requires that students attend to a behavior, retain it in memory, and then reproduce it. To capitalize on these processes, provide group practice by walking students through examples before having them practice on their own.

   - Elementary: A fourth-grade class is adding fractions with unlike denominators. The teacher displays the problem 1/4 + 2/3 = ? and then asks, "What do we need to do first? . . . Karen?" She continues guiding the students with questioning as they solve the problem.

- **Middle School:** After showing students how to find exact locations using longitude and latitude, a seventh-grade geography teacher says to his students, "We want to find the city closest to 85° west and 37° north. What do these numbers tell us? . . . Josh?" He continues to guide students through the example until they locate Chicago as the closest city.

- **High School:** After demonstrating several proofs, a geometry teacher wants her students to prove that angle 1 is greater than angle 2 in the accompanying drawing.

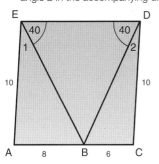

She begins by asking, "What are we given?" After students identify the givens in the problem, she asks, "What can we conclude about segments BE and BD?" and continues to guide students to a completion of the proof with her questions.

3. When learners observe a classmate being reinforced, they are vicariously reinforced. Use vicarious reinforcement to improve behavior and increase learning.

- **Elementary:** As students in a reading group move back to their desks, a first-grade teacher comments, "I like the way this group is quietly returning to their desks. Karen, Vicki, Ali, and David each get a star."

- **Middle School:** An eighth-grade English teacher displays examples of well-written paragraphs on the overhead and comments,

"Each of these has excellent paragraph structure, and each shows some imagination. Let's look at them more closely."

- **High School:** An art teacher displays several well-done pottery pieces and comments, "Look at these, everyone. These are excellent. Let's see why. . . . "

The English and art teachers accomplished three things. First, the students whose paragraphs or pottery were displayed were directly reinforced, but they weren't put on the spot, because the teachers didn't identify them. Second, the rest of the students in the classes were vicariously reinforced. Third, the teachers gave their classes feedback and provided concrete models for future imitation.

4. Self-regulated learning is the process of students taking responsibility for their own understanding. Teach students to be self-regulated learners by providing opportunities for them to set goals, use strategies, and monitor progress toward those goals.

- **Elementary:** A third-grade teacher helps his students who are having problems staying in their seats design a checklist that they can use to monitor their own behavior. The teacher initially reminds them to make a check when they are out of their seats, and later he monitors the students to see if they've given themselves checks when appropriate.

- **Middle School:** A prealgebra teacher helps her students create a rating scale to assess their progress on homework. For each assignment, they circle a 3 if they complete the assignment and believe they understand it, a 2 if they complete it but are uncertain about their understanding, and a 1 if they do not complete it. The teacher asks for feedback on these ratings and discusses common problems the students encountered.

- **High School:** An English teacher helps his students set individual goals by asking each to write a study plan. He returns to the plan at the end of the unit and has each student assess his or her progress.

Table 6.6	Analyzing theories: Social cognitive theory
Key question	How does observing others influence cognition and behavior?
Definition of learning	Change in mental processes that creates the capacity to demonstrate a change in behavior
Catalysts for learning	• Observations of others' behaviors • Observations of the consequences of others' behaviors • Expectations
Key concepts	Modeling Reciprocal causation Vicarious learning • Vicarious reinforcement • Vicarious punishment Nonoccurrence of expected consequences Self-regulation
Contributions of theory	• Explains how observations of others' behaviors (modeling and the consequences of modeled behavior) influences our behavior, and modeling is one of the most powerful influences on people's behavior • Is able to explain changes in behavior that behaviorism cannot explain • Provides an effective framework for working with students in general and teaching practice in particular
Criticisms of theory	• Cannot explain why people attend to and reproduce some modeled behaviors, but not others • Has difficulty explaining the acquisition of complex cognitive abilities • Doesn't account for the role of context and social interaction in learning

Developmentally Appropriate **Practice**

Applying Behaviorism and Social Cognitive Theory with Learners at Different Ages

Although many applications of behaviorism and social cognitive theory apply at all grade levels, some important developmental differences exist. The following paragraphs outline some of these differences.

Working with Students in Early Childhood Programs and Elementary Schools

The emotional environment we create for our students is important at all levels but is crucial when we work with young children. This explains why preschool, kindergarten, and first-grade teachers make a special effort to connect with students by, for example, giving hugs or "high fives" when children come into their classrooms.

Young children bask openly in positive reinforcement, and it is virtually impossible to satiate them with praise. On the other hand, they respond to punishment quite differently. Because their moral reasoning tends to be external, they conclude that they must be "bad" if they're punished, so punishment should be used sparingly and judiciously (Berk, 2013). Physical punishment and humiliation should never be used in classrooms, and they are particularly destructive with young children.

When using modeling, attention is important. Because young children's attention wanders, modeling can be problematic; children often don't attend to the modeled behavior and may not focus on important aspects of the modeled behavior. This means that modeling must be very explicit and concrete.

Working with Students in Middle Schools

A warm and supportive classroom environment continues to be important with middle school students, and because they are going through many physical, intellectual, and emotional changes, consistent enforcement of rules and procedures is essential to help them maintain their sense of equilibrium. Middle school students become increasingly sensitive to inconsistent treatment by their teachers, and fairness is very important to them.

Middle school students evaluate the praise they receive and may even react negatively to praise they view as insincere or unwarranted.

Because of improved language skills, cognitive modeling becomes a valuable instructional tool. They are capable of developing self-regulation but are unlikely to do so without extensive guidance and support.

Working with Students in High Schools

Classroom climate remains important with high school students, but the focus turns more to treating students with respect and communicating that you're genuinely committed to their learning. These students continue to be sensitive to perceptions of fairness and teachers' favoring some students over others (Emmer & Evertson, 2013).

Praise that communicates that their understanding is increasing is very effective and can increase these students' intrinsic motivation (Deci & Ryan, 2002).

High school students are increasingly self-regulated, and they're capable of setting and monitoring goals and using sophisticated learning strategies. However, they—and particularly lower achievers—are unlikely to use strategies effectively without extensive monitoring and support (Pressley & Hilden, 2006). Modeling effective strategy use becomes particularly important, and cognitive modeling can be a very effective tool for promoting self-regulation.

chapter

6 Summary

1. Use classical conditioning to explain events in and outside of classrooms.
   - Classical conditioning occurs when a formerly neutral stimulus, such as a teacher's room, becomes associated with a naturally occurring (unconditioned) stimulus, such as the teacher's warm and inviting manner, to produce a response similar to an instinctive or reflexive response, such as feelings of safety.
   - Generalization occurs when a stimulus similar to a conditioned stimulus triggers the conditioned response, and discrimination occurs when a stimulus fails to trigger the conditioned response.
   - Extinction occurs when the conditioned stimulus occurs often enough in the absence of the unconditioned stimulus that the conditioned response disappears.

2. Identify examples of operant conditioning in and outside of classrooms.
   - Operant conditioning focuses on voluntary responses that are influenced by consequences. Consequences that increase behavior are reinforcers. Teacher praise, high test scores, and good grades are common reinforcers.
   - Schedules of reinforcement influence both the rate of initial learning and the persistence of the behavior.
   - Shaping is the process of reinforcing successive approximations of a behavior.
   - Antecedents precede and induce behaviors that can then be reinforced. They exist in the form of environmental stimuli, prompts and cues, and past experiences.
   - Consequences that decrease behavior are punishers. Teacher reprimands and removing students' free time are common punishers.

3. Describe the influence of modeling on people's behaviors. Include the types of models, the outcomes of modeling, the effectiveness of models, and the processes involved in learning from models.
   - Modeling is the core concept of social cognitive theory. Modeling can be direct (from live models), symbolic (from books, movies, and television), or synthesized (combining the acts of different models).
   - Cognitive modeling occurs when models describe their thinking as they demonstrate skills.
   - The outcomes of modeling include learning new behaviors, facilitating existing behaviors, changing inhibitions, and arousing emotions.
   - The effectiveness of models describes the likelihood of an observer imitating a model's behavior, and it depends on the perceived similarity, perceived status, and perceived competence of the model.
   - When modeling occurs, observers first attend to the model, retain the modeled behaviors in memory, and reproduce the modeled behavior. Motivation supports each of the other modeling processes.

4. Use concepts from social cognitive theory to explain people's behaviors. Include vicarious learning, the nonoccurrence of expected consequences, and self-regulation.
   - Vicarious learning occurs when people observe the consequences of others' behaviors and adjust their own behavior accordingly, such as students increasing their attempts to answer teachers' questions after seeing a classmate attempt to answer, or students stopping talking after seeing a classmate reprimanded for talking without permission.
   - The nonoccurrence of expected reinforcers can act as punishers, and the nonoccurrence of expected punishers can act as reinforcers. As an example, students expect to be reprimanded if they break a rule, and if they aren't, the nonoccurrence of the expected reprimand can become a reinforcer for talking without permission, thereby increasing the likelihood of speaking without permission.
   - Social cognitive theory assumes that people want to control events that affect their lives, and they exercise this control by directing and controlling their actions, thoughts, and emotions toward meeting goals, a process called *self-regulation*. People who are self-regulated are more successful in both school and life after the school years than are their less well-regulated peers.
   - Self-regulation includes factors such as impulse control, delay of gratification, self-motivation, and self-regulated learning.
   - Self-regulated learning, one aspect of self-regulation, includes setting goals, monitoring and assessing goal attainment, and strategy use.

Preparing for Your Licensure Exam

Understanding Behaviorism and Social Cognitive Theory

You will be required to take a licensure exam before you go into your own classroom. This exam will include information related to behaviorism and social cognitive theory, and it will include both multiple-choice and constructed-response questions. We include the following exercises to help you practice for the exam in your state. This book and these exercises will be a resource for you as you prepare for the exam.

You've seen how you can use behaviorism and social cognitive theory to explain and influence student learning. Let's look now at a lesson to see how effectively the teacher applied these theories in his work with his students.

Warren Rose's fifth graders are working on a unit on decimals and percentages. He begins class on Thursday by saying, "Let's look at this problem."

Hearing some mumbles, he notes wryly, "I realize that percentages and decimals aren't your favorite topic, and I'm not wild about them either, but we have to learn them, so we might as well get started."

> You are at the mall, shopping for a jacket. You see one that looks great, originally priced at $84, marked 25% off. You recently got a check for $65 from the fast-food restaurant where you work. Can you afford the jacket?

"Now, . . . when I see a problem like this, I think, 'What does the jacket cost now?' I have to figure out the price, and to do that I will take 25% of the $84. . . . That means I first convert the 25% to a decimal. I know when I see 25% that the decimal is understood to be just to the right of the 5, so I move it two places to the left. Then I can multiply 0.25 times 84."

Warren demonstrates the process as he talks, working the problem to completion. He has his students work several additional examples at their desks and discusses their solutions. He then continues, "Okay, for homework, do the odd problems on page 113."

"Do we have to do all eight of them?" Robbie asks.

Several other students chime in, arguing that eight word problems are too many. "Wait, people, please," Warren holds up his hands. "All right. You only have to do 1, 3, 5, 7, and 9."

"Yeah!" the class shouts, and they then go to work on the problems.

Questions for Case Analysis

In answering these questions, use information from the chapter, and link your responses to specific information in the case.

Multiple-Choice Questions

1. Which of the following best illustrates a case of negative reinforcement in Warren's interaction with his students?

   a. Warren commenting, "I realize that percentages and decimals aren't your favorite topic, and I'm not wild about them either, but we have to learn them, so we might as well get started."

   b. Warren saying, "Now, . . . when I see a problem like this, I think, 'What does the jacket cost now?' I have to figure out the price . . ."

   c. The students working several examples at their desks and discussing the solutions.

   d. The students complaining and Warren decreasing the length of the homework assignment in response to their complaints.

2. Which of the following best illustrates a case of punishment in Warren's interaction with his students?

   a. Warren reducing the length of the homework assignment in response to the students' complaints.

   b. Warren originally assigning eight problems for homework.

   c. Warren commenting, "I'm not wild about them either," as he talked about decimals and percentages.

   d. Warren having his students solve several problems at their desks and discussing their solutions.

Constructed-Response Question

3. Assess Warren's application of modeling in his work with his students. Include both effective and ineffective applications if they exist.

Important **Concepts**

antecedents
applied behavior analysis (ABA)
behaviorism
classical conditioning
cognitive behavior modification
cognitive modeling
conditioned response
conditioned stimuli
consequences
continuous reinforcement schedule
corporal punishment
delay of gratification

desist
discrimination
extinction (classical conditioning)
extinction (operant conditioning)
functional analysis
generalization
inhibition
intermittent reinforcement schedule
interval schedule of reinforcement
learning (behaviorism)
learning (cognitive)

modeling
negative reinforcement
neutral stimulus
nonexclusion time-out
operant conditioning
positive behavior support
positive reinforcement
Premack principle
presentation punishment
primary reinforcers
punishers
punishment
ratio schedule of reinforcement
reciprocal causation

reinforcement
reinforcement schedules
reinforcer
removal punishment
response cost
satiation
secondary reinforcers
self-regulated learning
self-regulation
shaping
social cognitive theory
unconditioned response
unconditioned stimulus
vicarious learning

chapter

7 Cognitive Views of Learning

Monkey Business Images/iStock/Getty Images

*C*ognitive is in the title of this chapter, and the terms *cognitive* and *cognition* imply "thinking." Because cognitive learning theory has become the predominant framework for examining learning and teaching, we begin our discussion of learning, both in classrooms and in our daily lives, with it.

In the following case study, Mike Davis, a ninth-grade English teacher, has been working with his students on *To Kill a Mockingbird,* a classic of modern American literature. The novel is renowned for dealing with serious issues such as prejudice, racial inequality, legal integrity, and the loss of innocence. It is a staple of the curriculum in our country's schools. We join Mike's class now.

The class discussed these and other issues on Monday and Tuesday of the current week, and Mike now wants to use it as a vehicle to help his students understand figurative language and help them meet the Common Core standard,

CCSS.ELA-Literacy.RL.9-10.4 Determine the meaning of words and phrases as they are used in the text, including figurative and connotative meanings . . . (Common Core State Standards Initiative, 2014i).

On Wednesday Mike describes and provides examples of figurative language, with particular focus on the concepts *personification, metaphor,* and *simile*. For homework he asked his students to find in the novel at least two examples of each of the three forms of figurative language, and after his beginning-of-class review, he now has the students working in groups to share and evaluate their examples.

Let's look now at the thinking of three students—Miguel, Patty, and Steve—as they work in their group.

"Here's one of mine," Steve volunteers. "On page 100 it says, 'The day after Jem's twelfth birthday his money was burning up his pocket, so we headed for town in the early afternoon.' This is an example of a metaphor."

"Why?" Patty wonders.

"Because it's impossible for money to burn in your pocket when you want to spend it so badly," Steve replies.

"But," Miguel interjects, "a metaphor has to make a comparison, and nothing is being compared in the sentence. . . . I think a better example is on page 48 where it says, 'Summer was our best season . . . it was a thousand colors in a parched landscape.' Summer is being compared to a thousand colors, but it's a figurative comparison, not a real or literal comparison, so it's a metaphor."

"What do you mean?" Steve shrugs.

"Well, figurative language deals with words that exaggerate or change actual meanings of words. They're not saying that summer actually is, . . . literally is . . . a thousand colors . . . so, it's figurative. . . . Here's another one. On page 276 it says, 'Saying that blaming Jem for Mr. Ewell's death would be something like shooting a mockingbird.' . . . That's a simile. It makes a comparison, but it doesn't literally say that blaming Jem for Mr. Ewell's death is like shooting a mockingbird. And it uses the word 'like' in the statement. That's how similes are different from metaphors."

"So, what's Steve's example?" Patty asks.

"I think it's personification," Miguel answers. "When it says 'his money was burning up his pocket,' they are sort of attaching human character to money, and that's what personification does."

"Wait . . . This is a little too much. . . . You're talking about *literal* and *figurative* and *metaphor* and *simile* and *personification*. Mr. Davis went a little too fast for me when he was explaining it, so I got sort of mixed up," Patty responds.

"How do you know all this?" Steve asks, pointing at Miguel.

"My English teacher last year loved this stuff, and she was always making up metaphor and simile examples. We did it all year, and she even used examples in history and science and everything."

"Wait. . . . Let me write some of this down, so I'll remember it better," Steve responds.

We'll return to the lesson as the chapter unfolds, but for now, consider these questions related to the students' thinking.

1. Why was Miguel able to make connections in the different examples that Patty and Steve were initially unable to make?

2. Why did Patty say, "This is a little too much," and why did Mike seem to go "a little too fast" for her when he was explaining figurative language, so ". . . I got sort of mixed up."

3. What effect will Steve's decision to "write some of this stuff down" have on his learning?

Cognitive learning theory helps answer these and other questions, and in this chapter we'll see how Mike applies this theory in his teaching.

Cognitive Perspectives on Learning

Behaviorism explains learning in terms of observable changes in behavior that result from experience, such as your students attempting to answer questions after you've praised them for previous attempts to answer. Social cognitive theory focuses on the effects of observing others, such as the tendency in all of us to imitate other people's behaviors.

However, think about times when you've gotten ideas, essentially "out of the blue." You haven't been reinforced for the ideas, and they haven't been modeled for you, so neither behaviorism nor social cognitive theory can explain how you came up with them. Different explanations are required. Similarly, neither theory can explain why Miguel was able to identify relationships, such as connections between literal and figurative language, and *personification*, *simile*, and *metaphor*, that neither Steve nor Patty were able to make.

Research examining the development of complex skills, the inability of behaviorism to adequately explain how individuals learn language (Chomsky, 2006), and the development of computers all led to different explanations for learning. The result was a revolution in thinking, which resulted in a shift toward **cognitive learning theories**, theories that explain learning in terms of changes in the mental structures and processes involved in acquiring, organizing, and using knowledge (Sawyer, 2006; Schunk, 2012). These theories help us explain tasks from as simple as remembering a phone number to ones as complex as solving problems or understanding complex literary relationships in a novel such as *To Kill a Mockingbird*. This "cognitive revolution" occurred between the mid-1950s and early 1970s, and its influence on education has steadily increased since that time (Berliner, 2006).

Principles of Cognitive Learning Theory

Principles, or laws, are statements about an area of study that are generally accepted as true. For example, a prominent science principle (one of Newton's laws of motion) states, "A moving object will keep moving in a straight line unless a force acts on it." This principle helps us understand events in our world, such as why we wear seatbelts while driving.

Principles of cognitive learning theory serve the same function; they help us understand the way people of all ages think, learn, and develop. These principles, outlined in Figure 7.1, provide the framework for cognitive learning theories, and the arrows in the figure remind us that the principles are interdependent.

Ed Psych and You

Do you own a tablet computer, such as Apple's iPad or Google's Android? If you do, are you skilled with its functions, such as using its wireless mobile browser, email, social media devices, taking still pictures and video, doing photo and video viewing and editing, and working with other applications? If you're skilled with these functions, why are you? If not, why not?

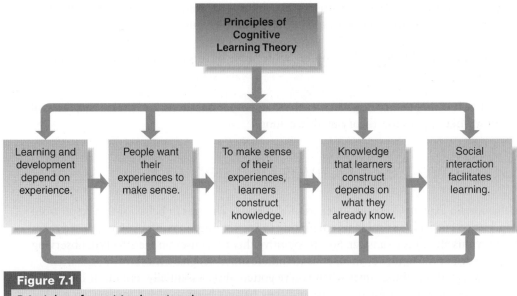

Figure 7.1

Principles of cognitive learning theory

LEARNING AND DEVELOPMENT DEPEND ON LEARNERS' EXPERIENCES

Our experiences, both in and out of classrooms, provide the raw material for learning and development, and this principle helps answer our first question at the beginning of this section: "Why was Miguel able to make connections in the different examples that Patty and Steve were initially unable to make?" The simple answer is that he had more experiences with figurative language than did either Patty or Steve. In response to Steve's question: "How do you know all this?" he said,

> "My English teacher last year loved this stuff, and she was always making up metaphor and simile examples. We did it all year, and she even used examples in history and science and everything."

His exposure to figurative language the year before provided him with a framework that Steve and Patty lacked.

Now, at a personal level think about the questions we asked in *Ed Psych and You*. If you own a tablet (surveys indicate that as of 2012 nearly a third of all Internet users did [Moscaritolo, 2012] and the percentage is almost certainly higher today), and you're skilled with its functions, it's because you've been living and working with them. If you aren't skilled, you lack these experiences, and your skills aren't as fully developed; it's as simple as that.

The same is true for all learning and development. To learn how to write effective essays, we need to practice writing; to learn to solve problems, we need experiences with problem solving. In a similar way, athletes acquire experience as they practice and compete in their sports, and your teaching experiences will help you develop expertise in your field.

PEOPLE WANT THEIR EXPERIENCES TO MAKE SENSE

Think about the number of times we've all said or heard statements such as "That makes sense" or its opposite, "I don't get it; it just *doesn't* make any sense." They are so common in our everyday lives that we don't even react when we hear them. Why is this the case?

The need to make sense of our experiences may be the most basic cognitive principle. "Human beings want and need to make sense of things that happen—or don't happen—in the short run as well as over the long haul" (Marinoff, 2003, p. 3). NBC newscaster Brian Williams comments, "Our job is to make sense of it all," in referring to the day's news. All societies and cultures, ranging from the ancient Egyptians, Greeks, and Romans to Native

Americans and our own, have constructed systems of beliefs about life, what it means, why we're here, and what happens when we die. These belief systems are mechanisms these societies have used to make sense of experiences they couldn't make sense of in any other way.

The same is true in classrooms. Cognitive learning theorists describe students as (cognitively) active beings who continually strive to make sense of their learning experiences (Bransford, Brown, & Cocking, 2000). Information that makes sense is easier to learn and also easier to remember than isolated facts, and this helps us understand why students often recall so little of what we've taught. Too much of what students study isn't meaningful to them, so they memorize enough to pass tests and then promptly forget the information. (We examine the concept of *meaningfulness* in depth later in the chapter.)

Helping our students make sense of what we teach is one of our most important goals. This book is designed to help you reach that goal.

TO MAKE SENSE OF THEIR EXPERIENCES LEARNERS CONSTRUCT KNOWLEDGE

Experts now believe that knowledge is "constructed by learners as they attempt to make sense of their experiences" (Hattie & Gan, 2011, p. 256). For instance, at the beginning of their group discussion Steve said,

> "On page 100 it says: 'The day after Jem's twelfth birthday his money was burning up his pocket, so we headed for town in the early afternoon.' This is an example of a metaphor."

Where did he get this idea (which was actually a misconception)? Since it was a misunderstanding, he didn't get it from either the book or his teacher. Simply, he *constructed* it because concluding that the statement was a metaphor made sense to him.

Making sense of our experiences is a fundamental cognitive need, and it helps us understand why people construct knowledge rather than duplicate it as a recording device might do. It also helps us understand why we get ideas essentially "out of the blue" and why we develop misconceptions as Steve did with respect to his understanding of the concept *metaphor*. In our attempts to make sense of our experiences, we fill in gaps and construct ideas that are sometimes inaccurate (Beil, 2011). And even if the ideas are accurate and make sense to us, they may not make sense to others. The fact that people, in general, and students, in particular, construct knowledge has important implications for our teaching. If the way we present information doesn't make sense to them, they will (mentally) reorganize it so that it does, or they will memorize as much of the information as they can and then quickly forget it.

KNOWLEDGE THAT LEARNERS CONSTRUCT DEPENDS ON WHAT THEY ALREADY KNOW

When we construct knowledge in our attempts to make sense of our world, we rely on what we already know, and the power of this idea is succinctly captured in a statement made by Bill Gates, multibillionaire founder of Microsoft, "The more you learn, the more you have a framework that knowledge fits into" (Sakr, 2013). Because of his prior knowledge, Miguel was able to construct relationships between literal and figurative ideas, and *personification, simile*, and *metaphor,* that Steve and Patty were initially unable to construct.

Prior knowledge can, however, be a double-edged sword, sometimes leading to misconceptions. For instance, consider this problem:

$$\frac{1}{3} + \frac{1}{4}$$

Which answer, 2/7 or 7/12, makes more sense? Initially, for some students it's 2/7. They have experience with adding numbers, so simply adding the numerators and then adding the denominators is very sensible. (And knowing that if we want to multiply the fractions, we do indeed multiply the numerators and multiply the denominators to get an answer of 1/12, makes the misconception even more understandable.) And some children, knowing that 5 is a larger number than 3, for example, even believe that a fraction with a larger denominator, such as 1/5, is greater than one with a smaller denominator, like 1/3. Similarly, because we've all had experiences such as feeling warmer when we move closer to a burning fireplace, or moving our hand closer to a hot stove burner, some people believe that our summers are warmer than our winters because we're closer to the sun in the summer.

When we teach, our job is to help our students acquire the background experiences they need to construct valid knowledge. We discuss ways to do this later in the chapter.

SOCIAL INTERACTION FACILITATES LEARNING

We've all heard the expression, "Two heads are better than one," and we've worked with someone on a task, with neither of us understanding it completely. However, as we talk and struggle we are gradually able to complete the task together, whereas alone we wouldn't have been successful. These simple examples illustrate the powerful role that social interaction plays in learning.

Social interaction has three important learning benefits for us all:

- Providing information
- Building on others' ideas
- Putting thoughts into words

To illustrate these benefits let's look at the following interchange between two students.

> Liam: (Holding a beetle between his fingers and pointing at a spider.) Look at the bugs.
> Jayden: Yech . . . Put that thing down. Besides (gesturing to the spider), that's not a bug. It's a spider.
> Liam: What do you mean? A bug is a bug.
> Jayden: Nope. Bugs . . . actually, insects . . . have six legs. See (touching the legs of the beetle). This one has eight. . . . Look (pointing to the spider).
> Liam: So . . . bugs . . . insects . . . have six legs, and spiders have eight . . . I didn't know that. . . . That means that a grasshopper is an insect, and it's different than a spider.

Providing information is the most important contribution of social interaction because it allows us to access the knowledge and expertise of others (Thaler & Sunstein, 2008). As they talked, for example, Jayden provided Liam with information about spiders and insects, and the new information caused Liam to change his incorrect views about "bugs."

This sharing also allowed Liam to build on Jayden's ideas and put his thoughts into words. By simply saying "So, . . . bugs . . . insects . . . have six legs, and spiders have eight," and "That means that a grasshopper is an insect, and it's different than a spider," Liam built on Jayden's ideas. And, instead of using the vague term "bug," he used the more precise term "insect" and linked it to having six legs. Seemingly minor differences such as these can have long-term learning benefits (Applebee, Langer, Nystrand, & Gamoran, 2003), and promoting productive interactions is an essential aspect of all effective instruction (Eggen & Kauchak, 2013; Good & Brophy, 2008).

A Model of Human Memory

Our memories are so much a part of our daily lives that we rarely think about it. We rack our brains to remember isolated facts, such as the capital of Columbia (Bogotá), and we also use our memories to solve problems, identify relationships, and make decisions. And,

Ed Psych and You

Have you ever felt that you know some fact, such as a person's name, but can't think of it right then, only to have the fact pop into your mind sometime later? Have you made a comment, such as, "I'm suffering from memory overload," or "It's on the tip of my tongue; I just can't dredge it up." Most of us have, but why do our minds work like this?

almost certainly, we've all encountered the memory problems we asked about in *Ed Psych and You*. In this section of the chapter, we'll see why our minds work the way they do.

Although cognitive learning theorists don't totally agree on the structure of human memory, most use a model similar to what you see in Figure 7.2, which was initially proposed by Atkinson and Shiffrin (1968) and has become a central component of **information processing theory**. Since it was originally proposed, this theory has been analyzed and criticized, has generated a great deal of research, and has undergone considerable refinement (Proctor & Vu, 2006; Schacter, Gilbert, & Wegner, 2011). (We examine criticisms of the theory later in the chapter.)

A **model**, as we use it in this context, is a representation that we use to help visualize what we can't observe directly. It's used in the same way the model of the atom is used in science courses you've taken. Just as we can't directly observe the nucleus or electrons in an atom, we can't look inside our heads to see working memory or attention, for example. So we create a model to help us visualize and understand them.

The human memory model is composed of three major components:

- *Memory stores*—Sensory memory, working memory, and long-term memory. These are repositories that hold information, in some cases very briefly and in others almost permanently.
- *Cognitive processes*—Attention, perception, rehearsal, encoding, and retrieval. These mental processes move information from one memory store to another.
- *Metacognition*—The cognitive mechanism we have for monitoring and regulating both the storage of information and how the information is moved from one store to another.

Although this model is only a representation, it provides us with valuable information about how our minds work when we learn and remember information. For instance, in the model we see that working memory is smaller than either sensory memory or long-term

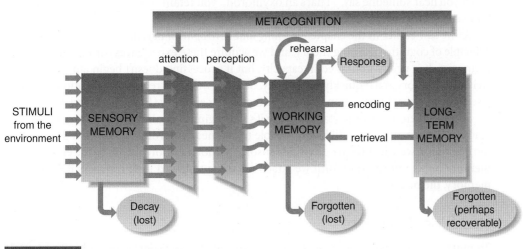

Figure 7.2

A model of human memory

memory. This reminds us that its capacity is smaller than the other two stores. Also, in Figure 7.2 you see fewer arrows to the right of attention than to its left. This tells us that we don't attend to all the stimuli we encounter; attention is a screen, and we don't notice many of the stimuli we encounter until someone or something reminds us of them.

As you see in Figure 7.2, the memory stores, cognitive processes, and metacognition are interconnected, but we examine each separately for the sake of clarity, beginning in the next section with the memory stores.

Memory Stores

The **memory stores**—sensory memory, working memory, and long-term memory—are repositories that hold information as we organize it in ways that make sense to us and store it for further use. We examine them in this section.

Ed Psych and You

Hold your finger in front of you and rapidly wiggle it. What do you notice? Also, press hard on your arm with your finger, and then release it. What do you feel?

Sensory Memory

Think about the questions we asked in *Ed Psych and You*. Did you see a faint "shadow" that trails behind your finger as it moved? Did the sensation of pressure remain for an instant after you stopped pressing on your arm? These phenomena are related to your **sensory memory** (also called the *sensory register*), the information store that briefly holds incoming stimuli from the environment in a raw, unprocessed form until they can be meaningfully organized (Bradley & Pearson, 2012; Neisser, 1967; Vlassova & Pearson, 2013). The shadow is the image of your finger that has been briefly stored in your visual sensory memory, and your tactile sensory memory stored the pressure of your finger for an instant. Likewise, when you hear someone say, "That's an oxymoron," you retain "Ox see moron" in your auditory sensory memory, even if it has no meaning for you.

As we saw earlier in the chapter, *learning and development depend on experience* is a basic principle of cognitive learning theory, and we acquire these experiences through our sensory memories. It is nearly unlimited in capacity, but if processing doesn't begin almost immediately, the memory trace quickly fades away. Sensory memory retains information for about 1 second for visual information and 2 to 4 seconds for auditory (Pashler & Carrier, 1996).

Sensory memory is important because it's the beginning point for further processing. In reading, for instance, it would be impossible to get meaning from a sentence if the words at the beginning were lost from our visual sensory memories before we got to the end. Sensory memory holds information until we attach meaning to it and then transfers it to working memory, the next store.

Working Memory

To make sense of their experiences learners construct knowledge is also a basic principle of cognitive learning theory, and this is where **working memory** comes into play. Working memory is the conscious component of our memory system, and it's often called a "workbench," because it's where our thinking occurs, and it's where we try to make sense of our experiences by linking them to what we already know (Paas, Renkl, & Sweller, 2004). We aren't aware of the contents of either sensory memory or long-term memory until they're pulled into working memory for processing.

A MODEL OF WORKING MEMORY

Figure 7.2 represents working memory as a single unit, and this is how it was initially described (Atkinson & Shiffrin, 1968). However, additional research suggests that working memory has three components—a *central executive*, a *phonological loop*, and a *visual-spatial sketchpad*—that work together to process information (Baddeley, 1986, 2001). They're outlined in Figure 7.3.

To see how these components work together, find the area of the figure you see here.

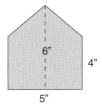

To solve the problem you probably subtracted the 4 from the 6 to determine that the height of the triangular portion of the figure was 2 inches. You recalled that the formula for the area of a triangle is ½(b)(h) and for a rectangle it's (l)(w), and you calculated the areas to be (½)(5)(2) = 5 sq. in. for the triangular portion and (5)(4) = 20 sq. in. for the rectangular part, making the total area of the figure 25 square inches.

Now, let's see how the components of your working memory executed the task. The **central executive**, a supervisory system, controls and directs the flow of information to and from the other components. For instance, your decision to break the figure into a triangle and rectangle, find the area of each, and add the two was a function of your central executive.

The **phonological loop**, a short-term storage component for words and sounds, temporarily held the formulas and the dimensions of the figure while you made the calculations. Information can be kept in the phonological loop indefinitely through **maintenance rehearsal**, the process of repeating information over and over, either out loud or silently, without altering its form. (*Maintenance rehearsal* is defined this way because it is used to "maintain" information in working memory.) For example, you look up a phone number, repeat it to yourself until you dial it, and then forget it. The ability to keep information in the phonological loop through maintenance rehearsal is represented by the "loop" with the term *rehearsal* in it above working memory in Figure 7.2.

The **visual-spatial sketchpad**, a short-term storage system for visual and spatial information, allowed you to visualize the figure and see that it could be broken into a rectangle and triangle. The visual-spatial sketchpad and the phonological loop are independent, so each can

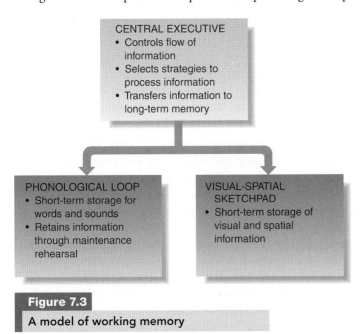

Figure 7.3

A model of working memory

perform mental work without taxing the resources of the other (Baddeley, 1986, 2001). They serve the functions that historically have been attributed to **short-term memory**.

The phonological loop can hold about as much information as we can say to ourselves in 1½ to 2 seconds, and the duration of the visual-spatial sketchpad is also limited (Baddeley, 1986, 2001). These limitations have important implications for your work with different types of students. For instance, researchers have found that learners with attention-deficit/hyperactivity disorder (ADHD) rehearse verbal and spatial information as effectively as other children, but their central executive is impaired (Karatekin, 2004), whereas learners with reading disabilities have impaired functioning of the phonological loop (Kibby, Marks, & Morgan, 2004). Students with ADHD have trouble controlling their attention and selecting effective learning strategies, and students with reading difficulties have trouble processing verbal information.

LIMITATIONS OF WORKING MEMORY

We asked about "memory overload" in *Ed Psych and You* earlier, and most of us have experienced it at one time or another. This feeling is directly related to working memory, and it's because working memory capacity is severely limited (Sweller, van Merrienboer, & Paas, 1998). Early research suggested that adult working memories can hold about seven items of information at a time and can hold the items for only about 10 to 20 seconds (Miller, 1956). (Children's working memories are even more limited.) Selecting and organizing information also uses working memory space, so we "are probably only able to deal with two or three items of information simultaneously when required to process rather than merely hold information" (Sweller et al., 1998, p. 252). As you saw in Figure 7.2, working memory is smaller than either sensory memory or long-term memory, and it's represented this way to remind us that its capacity is limited.

Working memory's limited capacity is arguably its most important feature, because working memory is where we make sense of our experiences and construct our knowledge (Clark & Mayer, 2003). Think about that. *The most important process in learning—the construction of meaningful knowledge—takes place in the component of our memory system that is the most limited!* Little wonder that students are frequently confused, miss important information, and construct misconceptions.

We see the effects of this limitation illustrated in classrooms. For instance:

- Students write better essays using computers or word processors if their keyboarding skills are well developed. If not, handwritten essays are superior (Roblyer & Doering, 2013).
- Students' writing often improves more rapidly if they are initially allowed to ignore grammar, punctuation, and spelling (McCutchen, 2000).
- In spite of research about its ineffectiveness and staff-development efforts to promote more effective forms of instruction, lecturing persists as the most common teaching strategy (Brophy, 2006b; Cuban, 1993; Lemov, 2010).

We can explain these—and many other—examples using the concept of **cognitive load**, which is the amount of mental activity imposed on working memory. Cognitive load depends on two factors. The first is the number of elements we must attend to (Paas et al., 2004), such as remembering a sequence of digits like 7 9 5 3 versus one like 3 9 2 4 6 7 8. The second sequence imposes a heavier cognitive load than the first simply because there are more numbers in it. The complexity of the elements is the second factor (Paas et al., 2004). For example, attempting to create a well-organized essay, while at the same time thinking about where to place their fingers on a keyboard, or use correct grammar, punctuation, and spelling, is a complex task that imposes a heavy cognitive load on young writers.

The idea of cognitive load also helps us understand why so many teachers lecture instead of promoting more student involvement in their lessons. Using sophisticated teaching strategies, such as guiding students with questioning, is both complex and demanding. We must remember our learning goals, decide what question to ask and who to call on, and how to prompt students when they're unable to answer, while simultaneously monitoring the rest of the class to see if students are drifting off. This process imposes a very heavy cognitive load on teachers, so they often reduce the load by simply lecturing.

Cognitive load also helps us answer the second question we asked at the beginning of the chapter: "Why did Patty say, 'This is a little too much,' and why did Mike seem to go 'a little too fast' for her when he was explaining figurative language, so '. . . I got sort of mixed up'" Mike's explanations imposed too heavy a cognitive load on Patty's working memory, and some of the information was lost before she could make sense of it.

Students must, however, learn to use correct grammar, spelling, and punctuation in their writing, and teachers who interact with their students are much more effective than those who simply lecture (Brophy, 2006b; Lemov, 2010; Lukowiak & Hunzicker, 2013; Regmi, 2012). So what can we—both as learners and as teachers—do about the limitations of working memory? We address this question next.

Ed Psych and You

If you have an electric garage door opener, have you ever wondered whether or not you've put the garage door down and gone back to check? Or do you ever wonder if you've shut off your coffee pot or failed to complete some other routine task? If so, why might this have happened?

ACCOMMODATING THE LIMITATIONS OF WORKING MEMORY: REDUCING COGNITIVE LOAD

Cognitive load is a significant factor in our lives, and anything we can do to reduce it is valuable. Three strategies are effective.

- Developing automaticity
- Using distributed processing
- Chunking

Developing Automaticity. Automaticity is the ability to perform mental operations with little awareness or conscious effort (Feldon, 2007), and it's enormously important for both learning and in our everyday living. For instance, once keyboarding and grammar skills become automatic (i.e., we can type and use correct grammar, punctuation, and spelling, essentially "without thinking about it"), we can then devote all of our limited working memory space to composing quality written work. Similarly, if our learning objectives are clear, we use good examples when we teach, and we work to develop our teaching skills, calling on our students will become nearly automatic, and we'll be able to devote our working memory space to interacting effectively with our students.

The importance of automaticity for reducing cognitive load is hard to overstate, and research indicates that **experts**, people who are highly skilled or knowledgeable in a domain, such as math, athletics, or teaching, have many of their skills developed to automaticity. And, we all develop simple routines that reduce cognitive load. For instance, without thinking about it, Paul (one of your authors) immediately puts his keys and wallet in a cabinet drawer the moment he walks into his house. The result is one less thing he has to think about.

Automaticity is a double-edged sword, however, and it helps answer our question in *Ed Psych and You*. If you answered yes to either of our questions, it was because you put the garage door down or completed the other routine task "automatically." You did it without thinking about it. And because driving is nearly an automatic process, many people tacitly believe that they can drive and simultaneously talk on their cell phones, or text while driving, both of which are dangerous (Cismaru, 2014).

Using Distributed Processing. Earlier we saw that the phonological loop and the visual-spatial sketchpad operate independently in working memory, so each can perform mental work without taxing the resources of the other. Doing so "distributes" the processing load across the two components; the visual processor supplements the verbal processor and vice versa. This suggests that we should combine our verbal explanations with visual representations whenever possible. "The integration of words and pictures is made easier by lessons that present the verbal and visual information together rather than separated" (Clark & Mayer, 2003, p. 38).

Unfortunately, teachers often use words, alone, to present information, which fails to capitalize on working memory's distributed processing capability. If, instead, we supplement our verbal presentations with figures, diagrams, and pictures, we reduce the cognitive load for our students. So, for instance, if we're teaching about factors leading to the Civil War in American history, a geographic map of the North and the South could be used to supplement our discussion. In math, diagrams are helpful in problem solving; pictures of cells with their components are used in biology; videos illustrating the correct technique for shooting a jump shot are used in coaching; and replicas of great art pieces are obviously used in art classes. Each capitalizes on the capacity of working memory to distribute cognitive load.

Chunking. Chunking is the process of mentally combining separate items into larger, more meaningful units (Miller, 1956). For example, 9 0 4 7 5 0 5 8 0 7 is a phone number, but it isn't written as phone numbers typically appear. Now, as normally written, 904-750-5807, it has been "chunked" into three larger units, which reduces cognitive load by making it both easier to read and remember. Phone numbers are virtually always chunked, and, without the area code, they're 7 digits, approximately the capacity of adult working memory.

Chunking is common in our daily lives. For instance, American Express credit cards are 15 digits long chunked into 3 units; Visa cards are 16 digits chunked into 4 units. Drivers' license numbers, memberships in organizations, such as the American Automobile Association, and the long license numbers on purchased computer software are all presented as chunks instead of a continuous string of numbers or numbers and letters.

Long-Term Memory

Knowledge that learners construct depends on what they already know is another principle of cognitive learning theory, and this is where long-term memory, our permanent information store, comes into play. What we know is stored in long-term memory, and being able to access this knowledge plays a powerful role in subsequent learning. Long-term memory's capacity is vast and durable, and some experts suggest that information in it remains for a lifetime (Schacter, 2001; Sweller, 2003).

Long-term memory contains three kinds of knowledge: *declarative, procedural*, and *conditional*. They're outlined in Figure 7.4, and described in the following sections.

DECLARATIVE KNOWLEDGE IN LONG-TERM MEMORY

Declarative knowledge is knowledge of facts, concepts, procedures, and rules, often described as knowing "what," and within this category, some researchers (e.g., Tulving, 2002) distinguish between semantic memory, which is memory for concepts, principles, and the relationships among them, and episodic memory, which is memory for our personal experiences. For example, the definitions of *figurative language, simile*, and *metaphor* that Miguel had stored in his long-term memory are all forms of declarative knowledge, and they were stored in his semantic memory. By comparison, when he recalled:

"My English teacher last year loved this stuff, and she was always making up metaphor and simile examples. We did it all year, and she even used examples in history and science and everything,"

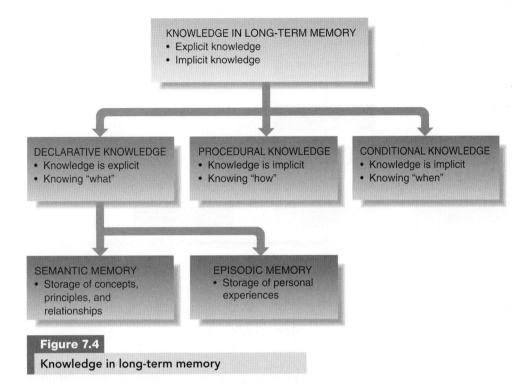

Figure 7.4

Knowledge in long-term memory

this information was stored in his episodic memory.

The lines between episodic and semantic memory are often blurred, but one difference is significant. When people have strong emotional reactions to an event, episodic memories are enduring. For example, those of us who are older remember exactly where we were and what we were doing when we received word of the infamous terrorist attacks of 9/11. You likely recall the events surrounding your first date or kiss. They're stored in your episodic memory and highlighted by emotions (Steinmetz & Kensinger, 2013). We can capitalize on episodic memory when we teach by personalizing content or teaching it, when possible, in a way that has an emotional impact on our students.

As we see in Figure 7.4 declarative knowledge is *explicit,* meaning that we are aware of what we know, and it can be determined by a person's statements. For instance, when he said, "Summer was a thousand colors in a parched landscape," we know that Miguel understood the concept *metaphor,* and he was also aware of his understanding.

Declarative Knowledge as Schemas. Acquiring declarative knowledge involves integrating new information with existing knowledge, and you saw this process illustrated with Miguel's thinking in his discussion with Steve.

Our declarative knowledge is organized in the form of schemas (also called schemata), cognitive structures that represent the way information is organized in long-term memory (Schunk, 2012; Willingham, 2007). For instance, Figure 7.5 represents Miguel's schema for figurative language. He constructed this schema, and it represents relationships among the different concepts that make sense to him. Schemas are idiosyncratic to the person who constructs them. If, for instance, when you look at Miguel's schema, it doesn't appear meaningful to you, it's because you didn't construct it. However, it is meaningful to Miguel.

The same thing occurs in classrooms when our students construct schemas that make sense to them, but not to us.

Developing Meaningful Schemas. Now, let's look at Miguel's schema again. We see that eight items of information are in it, but they're all interconnected. This interconnectedness illustrates the concept of meaningfulness, the extent to which experiences or items of

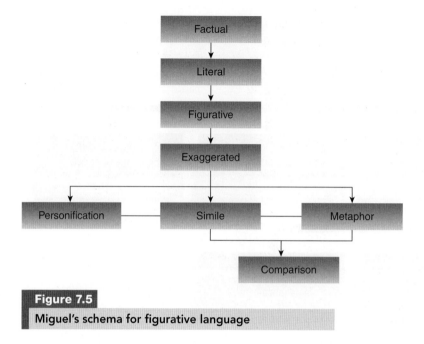

Figure 7.5

Miguel's schema for figurative language

information are linked and related to each other. Because, for Miguel, the information is interconnected, his schema is very *meaningful* for him. In contrast, Steve's schema is simple and lacks meaning. He concluded that the statement,

> "The day after Jem's twelfth birthday his money was burning up his pocket, so we headed for town in the early afternoon,"

was a metaphor, and he defended his conclusion by saying,

> "Because, it's impossible for money to burn in your pocket when you want to spend it so badly."

His schema didn't connect the idea of a comparison to the concept of *metaphor*, so his understanding—his schema—was superficial and inaccurate.

Meaningfulness is crucial in learning, for three reasons. First, our schemas represent our understanding of the topics we study, and the more meaningful—interconnected—they are, the more thoroughly we understand the topic. Second, research indicates that the number of chunks working memory can hold is limited, but the size and complexity of the chunks are not (Sweller et al., 1998). Because the individual items in Miguel's schema are all connected, it behaves like a single chunk, so it uses only one working memory slot and reduces cognitive load (Bransford et al., 2000). In contrast, because Steve's schema isn't as meaningful to him, it imposes a heavier cognitive load on his working memory than does Miguel's for him.

Third, the more meaningful (interconnected) a schema is, the more places exist to which we can connect new information. This helps us better understand Bill Gates' statement that we quoted earlier in the chapter: "The more you learn, the more you have a framework that knowledge fits into" (Sakr, 2013). Now that we've connected the statement to this discussion, the statement is more meaningful to us.

Meaningful Schemas: Implications for Learners and Teachers. *Learning and development depend on experience* is a principle of learning, which makes providing quality experiences for students one of our most important roles as teachers. Unfortunately, students' experiences often exist in isolated pieces of information, famously labeled "inert knowledge" by the renowned English philosopher Alfred North Whitehead, who described the existence of inert knowledge as the central problem of all education (Whitehead, 1929).

This problem continues today (Eggen & Kauchak, 2013; Lemov, 2010; Schunk, 2012). For instance, from our study of American history, we know about events leading up to the American Revolution, such as the French and Indian War and the Boston Tea Party. In many cases we only learned specific, isolated facts about each, such as the French and Indian War occurring between 1754 and 1763, colonists dumping tea into Boston harbor in 1773, and a number of events in the Revolutionary War itself. They are all interconnected, however. For instance, the French and Indian War was very costly for the British, so in order to raise revenue, they imposed onerous taxes on goods, such as tea, on the colonists. The colonists resented the taxes, which led to the Boston Tea Party, and, combined with other events, the Revolutionary War itself. This suggests that as learners, we should always be looking for relationships in the topics we study. It also suggests that although we need to know the definitions of concepts, simply memorizing definitions and other individual items of information is an ineffective study strategy.

Similarly, as teachers, we should make an effort to help our students identify—and hold them accountable for understanding—the connections among the ideas we teach, rather than teaching information in isolated pieces and asking factual questions on our quizzes. A question, such as, "How did the French and Indian War contribute to the Boston Tea Party?," is a much better way to promote meaningful learning than having students memorize specific facts and dates about each event.

Isolated information also imposes a heavy load on students' working memories, which helps explain why they seem to retain so little of what they're taught. Connecting ideas—making the information more meaningful—both reduces the load and makes the information more interesting and easier to remember.

Schemas in Our Daily Lives. We all have a great many schemas that represent our understanding of our personal, social, and academic worlds. For instance, Paul's wife has several close female friends that she meets socially once a month. Before she goes, she'll make comments, such as, "Sharon will probably be late" and "I'll be home early, since Libby has trouble with her eyes after dark." These comments illustrate the way her knowledge of her friends is represented in her memory. They're organized in a schema and influence how we think about the world.

In addition to organizing information, schemas also guide our actions. For example, when you first enter a college class, you may ask yourself questions, such as:

- What are the instructor's expectations?
- How should I prepare for quizzes and other assessments?
- How will I interact with my peers?

Answers to these questions come from **scripts**, schemas for events, developed over years of experience (Nuthall, 2000). You have a script that guides your actions as you prepare for, attend, and participate in your classes. In this regard, scripts also contain *procedural knowledge*, which we consider next.

PROCEDURAL KNOWLEDGE IN LONG-TERM MEMORY

Procedural knowledge is knowledge of how to perform tasks, such as solving problems, composing essays, performing pieces of music, executing physical skills (such as a back flip in gymnastics), and teaching. Procedural knowledge depends, in part, on declarative knowledge. For instance, look at this problem:

$$\frac{1}{4} + \frac{2}{3}$$

Knowing that we must find a common denominator before we can add the fractions is a form of declarative knowledge. Actually finding the common denominator and then adding the fractions requires procedural knowledge.

The same is true for all forms of procedural knowledge. To compose an essay or other form of writing, for instance, we must know grammar, punctuation, and spelling rules, all forms of declarative knowledge, but actually composing the essay represents procedural knowledge.

Our goal in developing procedural knowledge is to reach automaticity, which requires a great deal of time and effort (Colvin, 2010; Taraban et al., 2007). This suggests that we need to provide students with ample opportunities to practice. To become a good writer, we must practice; to play a musical instrument well, we must practice; to execute an effective corner kick in soccer, we must practice. The same is true for acquiring all forms of procedural knowledge.

When we help our students develop their procedural knowledge, the learning context is important (Star, 2004). For example, students should practice their grammar, spelling, and punctuation in the context of their writing, rather than on isolated sentences. And math students should develop their skills in the context of word problems that require a variety of operations (Bransford et al., 2000). Similarly, we must learn to drive a car in different contexts to ensure that our procedural knowledge transfers to different driving conditions, and athletes must perform their skills in the context of competition.

In contrast to declarative knowledge, procedural knowledge is *implicit,* meaning that we often cannot recall or explain it. For instance, when we become skilled, we aren't able to explain what we're doing as we type. We may not even be able to describe where the keys are located on the keyboard.

CONDITIONAL KNOWLEDGE IN LONG-TERM MEMORY

Conditional knowledge is knowledge of where and when to use declarative and procedural knowledge (Radvansky & Ashcraft, 2014). For example, consider again the problem:

$$\frac{1}{4} + \frac{2}{3} =$$

and also this problem:

$$\frac{2}{7} + \frac{4}{7} =$$

Recognizing that we must find a common denominator in the first problem but that we don't need one in the second represents conditional knowledge. Similarly, recognizing that we place an apostrophe before the *s* in the sentence "Both of the boy's shoes got muddy when he ran outside in the rain," but after the s in the sentence "The boys' shoes got muddy because they all ran outside in the rain," requires conditional knowledge.

As with procedural knowledge, conditional knowledge is *implicit,* and context is important for its development. When students write in a variety of content areas, or solve a variety of word problems, they acquire the practice that will help them identify different conditions and the actions they should take based on those conditions.

The characteristics of the memory stores are summarized in Table 7.1.

Developmental Differences in the Memory Stores

Because it doesn't address developmental differences, the model of human memory tacitly implies that people of all ages process information in essentially the same way, and to a certain extent this is true. For example, small children and adults both briefly store stimuli from the environment in their sensory memories, make sense of it in their working memories, and store it in their long-term memories.

Table 7.1	Characteristics of the memory stores			
	Capacity	Duration	Form of Information	Awareness
Sensory memory	Virtually unlimited	Very short	Raw, unprocessed	Unaware
Working memory	Severely limited	Relatively short unless rehearsed	In the process of being organized	Aware (the conscious part of our memory system)
Long-term memory	Virtually unlimited	Durable (some researchers believe permanent)	Schemas organized in ways that make sense to individuals	Unaware

Important developmental differences exist, however. For instance, older children retain sensory memory traces longer than their younger counterparts (Nelson, Thomas, & De Haan, 2006). This means that if you're planning to teach young children, such as first graders, your students will be less likely to understand detailed directions than would older students.

In addition, both the capacity and the efficiency of working memory increase as children develop (Berk, 2013). For example, more of older children's procedural knowledge becomes automatic, so they can process information more quickly and can handle complex tasks more efficiently than their younger counterparts (Feldman, 2014; Luna, Garver, Urban, Lazar, & Sweeney, 2004). Also, because they've simply had more experiences, older children bring a broader and deeper store of prior knowledge to learning activities, which increases their ability to make new learning meaningful. Experience can also result in differences in learners who are the same age, and this was illustrated in Mike's class. Because he had experiences with figurative language that Steve and Patty lacked, Miguel's understanding was more fully developed than theirs, so the information Mike presented was more meaningful to him.

The Cognitive Neuroscience of Memory

Cognitive neuroscientists consider memory as the retention, reactivation, and reconstruction—when necessary—of internal representations (Oudiette, Antony, Creery, & Paller, 2013). For instance, Miguel's internal (mental) representation of the concept *metaphor* included its characteristics such as a comparison—but not a literal comparison—and how it related to other concepts, such as *simile.* He had retained this representation and reactivated it during his discussion with Steve and Patty.

The process of retaining, reactivating, and reconstructing these internal representations is neural, that is, it depends on neurons. Neurons are nerve cells composed of cell bodies together with *dendrites*—short, branchlike structures that extend from the cell body and receive messages from other neurons—and *axons*—longer branches that also extend from the cell body and transmit messages. Messages are transmitted across *synapses,* tiny spaces between neurons that allow signals to be sent from axons to dendrites. The learning capability of our brains depends on the strength and permanence of these neural connections (Feldman, 2014).

As with all other aspects of learning and development, forging neural connections depends on our experiences (DiSalvo, 2011; Seung, 2012). For instance, a classic study of taxi drivers in London found that navigating its labyrinth-like streets resulted in increased growth of the visual-spatial part of their brains, and the longer they drove these streets, the greater the increase (Maguire et al., 2000). Another study found differences in the brain functions of Chinese and English speakers during problem-solving activities in math (Tang et al., 2006). Chinese speakers' brains showed increased activity in the motor or movement area as they thought about math problems, whereas the English speakers showed increases in the language areas of the brain. The researchers concluded that the differences were linked to Chinese speakers' use of the abacus, a calculating tool historically used by Chinese students that requires physical movement and spatial positioning. These findings confirm other research that shows that mental exercise causes different parts of the brain to enlarge and develop (Seung, 2012; Kurzweil, 2012). Our job as teachers is to provide quality learning experiences that encourage this growth.

Additional research demonstrates the benefits of physical exercise, and particularly continuous aerobic exercise such as running, cycling, and swimming, on the cognitive neuroscience of our brains. Further, these benefits exist throughout our entire life spans. Exercise increases neural activity—connections between neurons—and improved oxygen and nutrient delivery are some of its benefits (Erickson et al., 2011; Ruscheweyh et al., 2009). For schools, this research suggests that activities such as recess and P.E. have more benefits for students than simply helping them blow off steam or even control their weight. It can literally improve academic performance, and its benefits are particularly pronounced for the executive functioning of working memory (Chaddock, Hillman, Buck, & Cohen, 2011; Chaddock et al., 2010). And hope exists for us all as we get older; research indicates a positive link between exercise and general cognitive function in older individuals (Dik, Deeg, Visser, & Jonker, 2003).

Researchers have also found links between neural activity and students' learning orientations (Delazer et al., 2005). For instance, students who memorized problem solutions had more neural activity in parts of the brain involved in retrieval of verbal information, whereas students who implemented cognitive strategies had more activity in visual and spatial parts of the brain.

This research has two implications for us as teachers (Dubinsky, Roehrig, & Varma, 2013). First, our job is to provide students with a rich and varied menu of experiences, quality learning activities that increase the number of neural connections in our students' brains, which ultimately lead to the formation of permanent links, such as the brain growth in the London taxi drivers.

Second, neural connections forged by our teaching determine important learning outcomes such as retention and transfer—the ability to apply learning acquired in one context to a new context. For example, as certain synapses are used over and over, "neural commitments" are formed that streamline and speed the transmission of neural messages that ultimately result in automaticity, such as being able to state that $7 \times 8 = 56$ without thinking about it (Kuhl, 2004). Practice over time facilitates this streamlining.

As with many aspects of teaching and learning, this streamlining is another double-edged sword. For instance, it helps us understand why bad habits, such as making the same error while keyboarding, are so hard to break. As some neural connections are streamlined, others atrophy from lack of use. Experts suggest that this is one reason learning to pronounce a second language is often difficult for adult learners; the neural pathways for the first language dominate and overpower new ones (Kuhl, 2004).

Overly tuned neural pathways can also impede transfer. This suggests that we should present new content in a variety of contexts, so that new information will be connected in a number of alternate pathways. For instance, presenting a range of word problems that require different operations and wording problems differently when the same operation is required help create these different neural pathways. The same processes apply in all content areas.

The way our brains function also helps us understand why meaningful learning is more effective than learning isolated facts. When our students study relationships among different ideas, they form neural connections that both promote more effective encoding and transfer to new contexts (Mayer, 2008).

Research on brain functioning reinforces much of what we already know about teaching and learning. For instance, it reinforces the importance of a rich and varied set of experiences

Classroom **Connections**

Capitalizing on the Characteristics of the Memory Stores to Promote Learning in Your Students

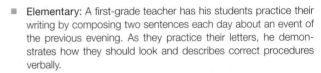

Sensory Memory

1. Sensory memory briefly holds incoming stimuli from the environment until the information can be processed. To keep students from losing important information, allow them to attend to one message before presenting a second one.

   ■ **Elementary:** A second-grade teacher asks one question at a time and gets an answer before asking a second question.

   ■ **Middle School:** A prealgebra teacher displays two similar problems on the document camera and waits until students have copied them before she starts discussing them.

   ■ **High School:** A geography teacher places a map on the document camera and says, "I'll give you a minute to examine the geography of the countries on this map in the front of the room. Then we'll discuss what you're noticing."

Working Memory

2. Working memory is where learners consciously process information, and its capacity is limited. To avoid overloading learners' working memories, develop lessons with questioning and avoid extended periods of lecturing.

   ■ **Elementary:** A third-grade teacher writes directions for seatwork on the board. He asks different students to repeat and explain the directions before they begin.

   ■ **Middle School:** A teacher in a woodworking class begins by saying, "The density of wood from the same kind of tree varies, depending on the amount of rainfall." He waits a moment, holds up two pieces of wood, and says, "What do you notice about the rings on these pieces?"

   ■ **High School:** An Algebra II teacher "walks" students through the solutions to problems by having a different student describe each step in the solution.

3. Automaticity is the ability to perform tasks with little conscious effort. To develop automaticity in your students, provide frequent practice

and present information in both verbal and visual forms.

   ■ **Elementary:** A first-grade teacher has his students practice their writing by composing two sentences each day about an event of the previous evening. As they practice their letters, he demonstrates how they should look and describes correct procedures verbally.

   ■ **Middle School:** To capitalize on the distributed processing capability of working memory, an eighth-grade history teacher prepares a flowchart of the events leading to the Revolutionary War. As she questions students, she refers to the chart for each point and shows students how to use the chart to organize their notes.

   ■ **High School:** A physics teacher demonstrates the relationship between force and acceleration by pulling a cart along a desktop with a constant force so students can see that the cart accelerates. He then asks them to describe what they see.

Long-Term Memory

4. Information is organized into schemas in learners' long-term memories. To help your students make these schemas as meaningful as possible, encourage them to look for relationships among the ideas they study.

   ■ **Elementary:** During story time, a second-grade teacher uses "how," "when," and "why" questions to encourage students to explain how the events in a story are related and contribute to the conclusion.

   ■ **Middle School:** In developing the rules for solving equations by substitution, an algebra teacher asks, "How does this process compare to solving equations by addition?"

   ■ **High School:** To help his students understand cause-and-effect relationships, a world history teacher asks questions such as "Why was shipping so important in ancient Greece?," "Why was Troy's location so important?," and "How do these questions relate to the location of today's big cities?"

for learners; it reinforces the need for meaningful learning; and it reinforces the importance of applying content to real-world contexts. It validates the applications we suggest in this chapter.

Cognitive Processes

How does information move from sensory memory to working memory and from working memory to long-term memory? How can we help our students store the information we want them to learn most efficiently? To answer these questions, let's look at Figure 7.6, which is similar to the model you first saw in Figure 7.2 (on page 269), but this time with

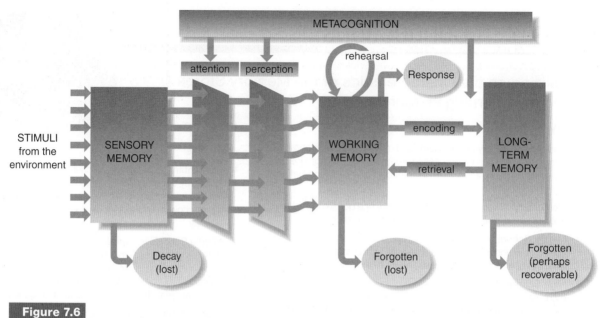

Figure 7.6

Cognitive processes in the model of human memory

cognitive processes—*attention, perception, encoding,* and *retrieval*—highlighted. As you compare Figure 7.6 to Figure 7.2, focus on these processes, and as you study the following sections, remember that they are responsible for moving information from one information store to another.

Ed Psych and You

Think about a quarter (the coin). What is on one face of the coin? What is on the opposite face for your state?

Attention

We know that learning and development for all of us depends on experience. These experiences exist in the form of stimuli that are gathered through everything we see, hear, touch, taste, or smell, and they're represented in Figure 7.6 as arrows to the left of the model. However, we remain unaware of many, if not most, stimuli until we pay *attention* to them. **Attention** is the process of selectively focusing on one stimulus in the environment while ignoring others (Radvansky & Ashcraft, 2014). For instance, think about our questions in *Ed Psych and You.* We frequently handle quarters, but most of us don't know what's on either side, and we may not know that each state has developed its own unique face. We don't *pay attention* to this information.

It is impossible to attend to all the stimuli we encounter, so we use attention as a screen that allows us to focus on the important ones and ignore the rest. Without this focus and screening, our lives would be chaotic, inundated by an endless stream of overwhelming stimuli (Davidson, 2012). This screening function is represented by fewer arrows to the right than to the left of attention in Figure 7.6.

Attention has two important characteristics. First, although individual differences exist, everyone's attention is limited, both in capacity and duration (Jiang, Swallow, & Rosenbaum, 2013; Zhou, Hofer, & Eisenberg, 2007). People miss parts of conversations, even when they're directly involved, and students often miss parts of teachers' explanations.

Second, we're easily distracted; our attention often wanders from one stimulus to another (Jiang et al., 2013; Zhou et al., 2007). This helps explain why students seem to learn less from our lessons than they should. A myriad of distractions exist in classrooms—other students (especially those of the opposite sex for adolescents), noises both inside and outside the room, and people in the hallway, among many others. Any of these can distract students' attention and cause them to miss parts of our lessons. (We discuss ways to attract and maintain students' attention in our section "Educational Psychology and Teaching: Applying Information Processing and the Model of Human Memory with Your Students" later in the chapter.)

Technology, Learning, and Development

The Influence of Technology on Attention

The impact of technology on learning and development has become the subject of considerable research, with much of it focusing on attention. For instance, studies suggest that drivers are over 20 times more likely to be involved in an accident if texting while driving, and using cell phones as we drive is comparable to driving while drunk (Virginia Tech Transportation Institute, 2009). People talking on their cell phones or texting aren't paying adequate attention to their driving. Some experts call this problem "attention blindness," a condition that exists when we concentrate intensely on one task, causing us to miss other aspects of our environment (Davidson, 2012).

Maggie Jackson (2009), in her book *Distracted: The Erosion of Attention and the Coming Dark Age,* contends we have developed a form of attention-deficit disorder, which limits our ability to remain focused. Immersed in an important writing project, we hear the familiar "ping" telling us we have a new email, and we can't resist checking. We then spend time reading emails, responding, and maybe even making a little sojourn to the Internet. Suddenly we've spent an hour away from our project. Some researchers argue that this constant stimulation appeals to a primitive impulse, provoking excitement—a dopamine squirt—that can be addictive. In its absence, people feel bored (Small & Vorgan, 2008).

Stress can also be a factor. Research indicates that people continually interrupted by emails experience increased stress, and stress hormones reduce our brain's efficiency (Mark, Gudith, & Klocke, 2008).

Multitasking. Multitasking, the process of engaging in two or more activities at the same time, is a technologically related factor influencing attention. Although it's certainly not a new phenomenon, media saturation and the wide variety of technologies available to people have made it increasingly prominent, particularly among young technology users (Wang & Tchernev, 2012). Some evidence suggests that teenagers often use as many as six different kinds of media simultaneously during out-of-school time, and as a result they pay "continuous partial attention" to everything but have a difficult time attending carefully to any one thing (Rosen, 2012).

Multitasking is a paradox. Even as it continues to increase in popularity, an expanding body of evidence indicates that it detracts from learning and performance (Junco & Cotten, 2012). "In stark contrast to the escalating popularity of media multitasking, growing research evidence consistently confirms its adverse impacts on task performance and learning" (Wang & Tchernev, 2012, pp. 493–494). Further, in spite of what multitaskers believe, multitasking doesn't save time. In fact, it takes longer to multitask than it does to do the individual tasks one after the other (Rosen, 2012).

Why is multitasking so popular? Researchers believe three factors are important. First, the sheer pervasiveness of technology and ease of use is a factor. For instance, with today's smartphones, we can simultaneously talk to a friend, look up information related to the conversation, and watch TV, all without getting up from a chair. And the experience is satisfying. We enjoy the conversation and we learn something new in the process. This is a safe and positive experience and it's related to the second factor: meeting emotional needs. For instance, if students study for a test while watching TV, their multitasking might lead them to feel satisfied, not because their studying is effective, but rather because the addition of TV made the studying entertaining. And the emotional satisfaction associated with multitasking leads to the misperception that it is efficient and productive. For instance, talking on a cell phone while driving seems like an efficient way to stay socially connected and even take care of some business, so people tend to dismiss the dangers associated with it (Wang & Tchernev, 2012).

Third, because of technology, we are socially connected to a greater degree than we ever have been in the history of civilization, and for many people, this social connection can result in a fear of missing out on something important (Rosen, 2012).

So, what should we, as both learners and teachers, do? We can't simply remove technology and other distractions; they're too intricately woven into students' lives, particularly in middle and high school. And some forms of multitasking are actually positive, such as learning something new while in an informal conversation with a friend. Rather, we must try to teach our students metacognitive skills—and acquire these skills ourselves—so we all learn to appropriately switch our attention from one task to another and from one technology to another (Davidson, 2012; Rosen, 2012). (We discuss *metacognition* in detail later in the chapter.) Some suggestions for promoting these metacognitive skills include the following:

- Put your computer speakers on mute and shut your cell phone off, or put it on vibrate, while you're studying. Require students to turn off cell phones, MP3 players, and other electronic gadgets as they enter your classroom, and explain why you are doing so. Encourage parents to eliminate distractions when their children study and do homework (Jackson, 2009).
- Create a to-do work or study list, prioritize the items on it, begin with the first item, complete it, and move on through the list. Cross items off as you finish them, so you experience the satisfaction of completing each task. Avoid the temptation of jumping back and forth. If you have tasks that you can't complete in one work session, do as much as you can before turning to another activity.
- Set time aside during the day—perhaps near the end of your workday—to respond to emails, text messages, and phone calls and avoid allowing them to interrupt your work or study.
- Avoid multitasking. Research consistently indicates that it detracts from learning (Song, Nam, Lim, & Kim, 2013). Further, some researchers suggest that technically it doesn't really exist. Rather what we commonly call multitasking is merely switching—quickly—back and forth between tasks (Wang & Tchernev, 2012).
- Provide a clear rationale for each strategy and explain to your students how these actions increase learning.

Technology has revolutionized the way we live. In adapting to this way of life, we want to be sure that it works for us instead of the other way around.

Perception

Look at the picture in the margin. Do you see a young, glamorous woman or an old, wrinkled one? This classic example illustrates the nature of **perception**, the process people use to find meaning in stimuli (Feldman, 2014). For those of you who "saw" an old woman, for instance, this is the meaning you attached to the picture, and the same is true for those of you who "saw" a young woman. Technically, we were asking, "Do you 'perceive' a young or an old woman?" All perception involves signals in the nervous system that result from the stimulation of our sense organs. For example, vision results from light striking the retinas of our eyes, smell involves odor molecules, and pressure waves influence hearing (Feldman, 2014).

In our everyday world, the term *perception* is commonly used to describe the way we interpret objects and events (Way, Reddy, & Rhodes, 2007), and it's influenced by our experiences, motivations, and expectations (Cole, Balcetis, & Zhang, 2013; Huan, Yeo, & Ang, 2006). To illustrate this idea, let's look at the following conversation between two people interviewing for teaching positions at the same school.

> "How was your interview?" Emma asked her friend, Kelly.
>
> "Terrible," Kelly responded. "He grilled me, asking me specifically how I would teach a certain topic and what I would do in the case of two students disrupting my class. He treated me like I didn't know anything. Madison, a friend of mine who teaches there, told me about him. . . . How was yours?"
>
> "Gosh, I thought mine was good," Emma responded. "He asked me the same questions, but I thought he was just trying to find out how we would think about teaching if he hired us. I had an interview at another school, and the principal there asked almost the same questions."

Kelly's and Emma's perceptions—the way they interpreted their interviews—were very different, Kelly viewing hers as being "grilled," but Emma feeling as if the interviewer only wanted to examine her thinking. Kelly's interpretation was influenced by her friend, Madison, who created negative expectations for her. And Emma had a similar experience at another school, which further influenced her perception.

Perceptions are personally constructed, so they differ among people. The arrows to the right of "perception" in Figure 7.6 are curved to remind us that our students' perceptions will vary. Because the knowledge learners construct depends on what they already know, learners' perceptions will also depend on their prior knowledge. This helps us understand why Steve's interpretations of the passages in *To Kill a Mockingbird* were less sophisticated than Miguel's. Miguel had experiences Steve lacked.

Accurate perceptions in learning activities are essential, because students' perceptions of what they see and hear enter working memory. If these perceptions are inaccurate, the information ultimately stored in long-term memory will also be inaccurate.

The primary way to determine if our students accurately perceive the information we're presenting is to ask them. For instance, if we're teaching geography and are discussing the economies of different countries, we can check students' perceptions by asking a question, such as "What do we mean by the term *economy*?" Students also commonly misperceive questions on homework and tests, which is why discussing frequently missed items and providing feedback is so important.

Encoding and Encoding Strategies

After students attend to and perceive information, and organize it in working memory so that it makes sense to them, they next **encode** the information, which means they represent it in long-term memory (Radvansky & Ashcraft, 2014; Bruning, Schraw, & Norby, 2011). Let's see how this process is illustrated in Miguel's thinking in Mike's lesson based on the following interchange between Miguel and Steve:

> Steve: Here's one of mine. . . . On page 100 it says, "The day after Jem's twelfth birthday his money was burning up his pocket, so we headed for town in the early afternoon." This is an example of a metaphor.

> Miguel: But, . . . a metaphor has to make a comparison, and nothing is being compared in the sentence. . . . I think a better example is on page 48 where it says, "I had never thought about it, but summer was a thousand colors in a parched landscape." Summer is being compared to a thousand colors, but it's a figurative comparison, not a real or literal comparison, so it's a metaphor.
>
> Steve: What do you mean?
>
> Miguel: Well, figurative language deals with words that exaggerate or change actual meanings of words. They're not saying that summer actually is, . . . literally is . . . a thousand colors in a parched landscape . . . so, it's figurative.

Miguel had the definitions of *figurative language*, *simile*, and *metaphor* stored in his long-term memory. Then, he heard Steve suggest that the example on page 100 was a metaphor, and he briefly stored it in his working memory while he retrieved the definitions from his long-term memory (pulled them back into his working memory). He conceptually organized all the information in his working memory and constructed his conclusion that the statement, "Summer was our best season . . . it was a thousand colors in a parched landscape," was a better example of a metaphor than the one Steve offered, and he then transferred the newly constructed information back into his long-term memory (i.e., he *encoded* it).

Earlier in the chapter we defined **meaningfulness** as the extent to which items of information are interconnected, and we also said that we want the schemas we store in long-term memory to be as meaningful as possible. This means that we want to encode information meaningfully (i.e., as we construct our schemas in working memory, we identify relationships and connections in the information, so these connections exist when we represent the information in our long-term memories).

A number of strategies that promote meaningful encoding exist, and we examine four of the most important in this section:

- Schema activation
- Organization
- Elaboration
- Imagery

These strategies are outlined in Figure 7.7 and discussed in the sections that follow.

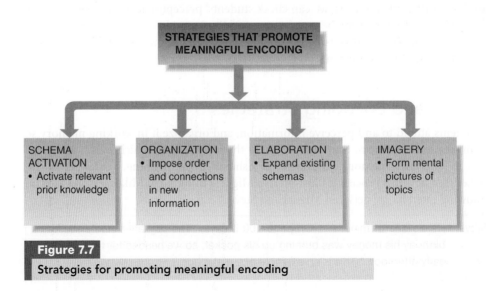

Figure 7.7

Strategies for promoting meaningful encoding

SCHEMA ACTIVATION

Think back to some of your most effective teachers. In most cases they probably began their classes with a review, and a long history of research supports the effectiveness of well-structured reviews in promoting learning (Rutter, Maughan, Mortimore, Ouston, & Smith, 1979; Good & Brophy, 2008).

Reviews capitalize on **schema activation**, which is an encoding strategy that involves activating relevant prior knowledge so that new information can be connected to it (Mayer & Wittrock, 2006). Schema activation was illustrated in Miguel's comment,

> "I think a better example is on page 48 where it says, 'Summer was our best season . . . it was a thousand colors in a parched landscape.' Summer is being compared to a thousand colors, but it's a figurative comparison, not a real or literal comparison, so it's a metaphor."

He had a schema for *figurative language*, and more specifically for *metaphor*, and both were activated by the discussion. He then related the new information—Steve's example—to his schema and used this understanding to explain why Steve's suggestion was not a good example of a metaphor.

The most effective way of activating students' prior knowledge is to ask them what they already know about a topic or to ask them to provide some personal experiences related to it. Any teaching strategy that helps students form conceptual bridges between what they already know and what they are to learn is a form of schema activation.

ORGANIZATION

Organization is an encoding strategy that clusters related items of content into categories that illustrate relationships. Because well-organized content contains connections among its elements, cognitive load is decreased, and encoding (and subsequent retrieval) is more effective. Research in reading, memory, and classroom instruction confirms the value of organization in promoting learning (Mayer, 2008). Research also indicates that experts in different fields learn more efficiently than novices because their knowledge in long-term memory is better organized, allowing them to access it and connect it to new information (Radvansky & Ashcraft, 2014; Bruning et al., 2011).

We can help our students organize information in several ways:

- *Charts and matrices:* Useful for organizing large amounts of information into categories. For instance, Table 7.1 is our attempt to organize information about the memory stores so it is meaningful to you.
- *Hierarchies:* Effective when new information can be subsumed under existing ideas. For instance, in Figure 7.4 we used a hierarchy to represent the different types of knowledge stored on long-term memory.
- *Models:* Helpful for representing relationships that cannot be observed directly. The models of human memory in Figure 7.2 and 7.6 in this chapter are examples.
- *Outlines:* Useful for representing the organizational structure in a body of written material. The detailed table of contents for this book is an example.

Other ways to organize content include graphs, tables, flowcharts, and maps. As a student, you can also use these organizers as aids as you attempt to make the information you're studying meaningful.

A word of caution: We know that people construct knowledge in ways that make sense to them, so if the organizational structure we offer doesn't make sense to our students, they will cope in one of three ways: (1) They will (mentally) reorganize and encode the information in a way that does, whether it's correct or not; (2) they'll memorize as much of it as they can, and promptly forget it later; or (3) they will ignore it altogether. To ensure that this doesn't happen, we can use questioning and discussion, both to help our students make new information meaningful and to help us determine if their developing understanding is valid.

ELABORATION

You're at a noisy party, and when you miss some of a conversation, you fill in details, trying to make sense of an incomplete message. You do the same when you read a text or listen to a lecture. You expand on (and sometimes distort) information to make it fit your expectations and current understanding. In each case, you are elaborating on either the message or what you already know.

Elaboration is an encoding strategy that involves "expanding upon new information by adding to it or linking it to what one knows. Elaborations assist encoding and retrieval because they link to-be-remembered information with other knowledge" (Schunk, 2012, p. 188). For example, a student who remembers the location of the Atlantic ocean on the globe because it starts with an "a" and is in between the Americas and Africa, which also begin with "a", or a student who remembers $6 \times 9 = 54$ because the sum of the digits in the product of a number times 9 always equals $9(5 + 4 = 9)$, is using elaboration as an encoding strategy.

Two elaboration strategies are especially effective in encoding new information: (1) the use of examples and analogies, and (2) mnemonics.

Examples and Analogies. Using examples and other representations that illustrate topics being taught is one of the most effective ways of promoting elaboration. For instance, Mike taught his students the concept of metaphor (and other forms of figurative language) and defined it as *a comparison between two ideas that is not literally true*. This statement is quite abstract, and, in itself, not very meaningful. However, when elaborated with the example, "Summer was our best season . . . it was a thousand colors in a parched landscape," the statement is much more meaningful. The same is true for all topics.

Constructing, finding, and analyzing examples is arguably the most powerful elaboration strategy that exists because it also capitalizes on schema activation (Cassady, 1999). When learners create or identify a new example of an idea, they activate their prior knowledge and then elaborate on that knowledge by connecting the example to it. Using examples also helps accommodate students' lack of experience. For example, most of Mike's students had little prior knowledge about figurative language, and they didn't know how it was used in *To Kill a Mockingbird*. By finding examples in the novel, his students elaborated on their knowledge.

Our extensive use of examples throughout this book demonstrates our belief in this strategy, and we encourage you to focus on the examples when you study. You can do the same with the concepts you teach.

When examples aren't available, using **analogies**, descriptions of relationships that are similar in some but not all respects, can be an effective elaboration strategy (Radvansky & Ashcraft, 2014). As an example, consider the following analogy from science:

> Our circulatory system is like a pumping system that carries the blood around our bodies. The veins and arteries are the pipes, and the heart is the pump.

The veins and arteries are similar—but not identical—to pipes, and the heart is a type of pump. The analogy is an effective form of elaboration because it links new information to a pumping station, an idea learners already understand.

Mnemonics. **Mnemonics** are memory strategies that create associations that don't exist naturally in the content (Schunk, 2012). Mnemonics are used to help remember vocabulary, names, rules, lists, and other kinds of factual knowledge. Mnemonics link knowledge to be learned to familiar information, and they have been proven effective in a variety of content areas and with a wide range of learners (Brehmer & Li, 2007; Bruning et al., 2011).

Table 7.2	Types and examples of mnemonic devices	
Mnemonic	**Description**	**Example**
Method of loci	Learner combines imagery with specific locations in a familiar environment, such as the chair, sofa, lamp, and end table in a living room.	Student wanting to remember the first seven elements in order visualizes hydrogen at the chair, helium at the sofa, lithium at the lamp, and so on.
Peg-word method	Learner memorizes a series of "pegs"—such as a simple rhyme like "one is bun" and "two is shoe"—on which to-be-remembered information is hung.	A learner wanting to remember to get pickles and carrots at the grocery visualizes a pickle in a bun and carrot stuck in a shoe.
Link method	Learner visually links items to be remembered.	A learner visualizes *homework* stuck in a *notebook*, which is bound to her *textbook, pencil* and *pen* with a rubber band to remember to take the (italicized) items to class.
Key-word method	Learner uses imagery and rhyming words to remember unfamiliar words.	A learner remembers that *trigo* (which rhymes with *tree*) is the Spanish word for *wheat* by visualizing a sheaf of wheat sticking out of a tree.
First-letter method	Learner creates a word from the first letter of items to be remembered.	A student creates the word *Wajmma* to remember the first six presidents in order: Washington, Adams, Jefferson, Madison, Monroe, and Adams.

For example, mnemonics have been used to increase cognitive performance of aging adults (Willis et al., 2006), and one study was so successful that it was picked up and discussed in the popular press (Begley, 2010).

Mnemonics can take several forms. We can use acronyms, such as HOMES to remember the names of the Great Lakes (Huron, Ontario, Michigan, Erie, and Superior), and phrases, such as "Every good boy does fine" to remember the names of the notes in the treble clef (E, G, B, D, and F). When learners think of the mnemonic, they link it to the information it represents, which aids the recall of information. Some additional mnemonics are outlined and illustrated in Table 7.2.

Ed Psych and You

Look at the two excerpts below.

1. Traveling by rail from the Midwest to California is a pleasant experience. As you sit in the dining car, you might meet interesting people, it's relaxing, and you hear the sound of the train rolling over the rails.
2. At the next table a woman stuck her nose in a novel; a college kid pecked at a laptop. Overlaying all this, a soundtrack: choo-k-chook, choo-k-chook, choo-k-chook, the metronomic rhythm of an Amtrak train rolling down the line to California (Isaacson, 2009).

IMAGERY

How are the two excerpts in *Ed Psych and You* different? The first is rather bland, whereas in the second we can virtually "see" in our mind's eye the woman reading her novel and the student at his computer, and we can almost hear the clicking of rails. It capitalizes on **imagery**, the process of forming mental pictures of an idea (Schunk, 2012; Schwartz & Heiser, 2006), and it's a common strategy novelists and other writers use to make their stories vivid and interesting. Imagery is also widely used by coaches to help their athletes develop skills ranging from corner kicks in soccer to jump shots in basketball and even performance in Olympic events (Clarey, 2014; Glover & Dixon, 2013; Guillot, Moschberger, & Collet, 2013).

Imagery is an effective encoding strategy, and its value is supported by **dual-coding theory**, which suggests that long-term memory contains two distinct memory systems: one for verbal information and one for images (Paivio, 1991; Sadoski & Paivio, 2001). According to dual-coding theory, ideas that can be represented both visually and verbally, such as *ball, house,* or *dog,* are easier to remember than abstract ideas that are more difficult to visualize, such as *honesty, truth,* and *ability* (Paivio, 1986).

As we study human memory, for example, the fact that we can both visualize the models in Figures 7.2 and 7.6 and read about the information in them helps us capitalize on the dual-coding capability of long-term memory. Information in the model becomes more meaningfully encoded than if we had only described it verbally (Clark & Paivio, 1991).

Dual-coding theory again reminds us of the importance of supplementing verbal information with visual representations and vice versa (Igo, Kiewra, & Bruning, 2004). Using both capitalizes on both the distributed processing capabilities of working memory and the dual-coding capability of long-term memory.

As we teach, we can take advantage of imagery in many ways (Schwartz & Heiser, 2006). For instance, we can use pictures and diagrams, we can ask students to form mental pictures of processes or events, and we can ask students to draw their own diagrams about ideas they are learning.

Imagery can be particularly helpful in problem solving (Bruning et al., 2011; Schunk, 2012). It would have been harder for you to solve the area-of-the-pentagon problem that we presented in our discussion of working memory, for example, if you hadn't used the drawing. Seeing the sketch makes the problem much more meaningful than simply being asked to find the area of a pentagon that is 5 inches at the base, 4 inches at the side, and 6 inches at the peak. In this regard, imagery is actually a form of elaboration because the drawing elaborates the original problem.

All of these encoding strategies are closely related and each is grounded in schema activation, because we retrieve background knowledge to capitalize on the strategy in each case.

IS REHEARSAL AN ENCODING STRATEGY?

Maintenance rehearsal, as we described it earlier in the chapter, is the process of repeating information over and over to retain it in working memory until it is used or forgotten. If rehearsed enough, however, information can be transferred into long-term memory through "brute force," and we've all used rehearsal to remember factual information, such as $8 \times 9 = 72$, Abraham Lincoln was our country's president during the Civil War, or a *verb* is a part of speech that shows action or a state of being. Using flash cards to remember math facts or definitions is a common form of rehearsal, and knowing some factual information, such as math facts, is important.

Rehearsal is an inefficient mechanism for getting information into long-term memory, however, because it often results in **rote learning**, learning that involves storing information in isolated pieces, most commonly through memorization (Lin, 2007; Mayer, 2002).

Elaborative rehearsal, the process of relating to-be-remembered factual information to other information, helps overcome the weaknesses of rote learning (Bruning et al., 2011). For instance, when we connect the location of the Atlantic Ocean—a form of factual information—to Africa and the Americas, we're using elaborative rehearsal. And we're using it again when we remember that the sum of the digits in the product of any number times 9 is always equal to 9 (e.g., $6 \times 9 = 54 [5 + 4 = 9]$; $8 \times 9 = 72 [7 + 2 = 9]$). Research confirms the superiority of elaborative rehearsal compared to simple "brute force" rehearsal for long-term retention (Schunk, 2012). This makes sense, because more connections are formed in long-term memory, increasing the likelihood that information can be later retrieved.

So is simple rehearsal an encoding strategy? When encoding is defined as "placing information into long-term memory" (Bruning et al., 2011, p. 65), the answer is "yes," and this is the way we describe it in this book. Some researchers have historically disagreed, arguing that encoding requires connecting the new information to other information (Craik & Watkins, 1974; Watkins & Watkins, 1974). Whether simple—nonelaborative—rehearsal is technically a form of encoding is not particularly important. Much more important is the idea that we should always attempt to connect any information we learn to other information. If we do, it will be meaningfully encoded, and this is the essence of effective learning.

Ed Psych and You

You and a friend are studying this book. You click on the link at the end of each of the major sections of the text to access questions that check your understanding of the section, you answer the questions, and you then click on the feedback to see how well you've answered.

Your friend also clicks on the links, reads each question, and then clicks on the feedback. Which of you is likely to learn more?

COGNITIVE ACTIVITY: THE ESSENCE OF ENCODING

The answer to our question in *Ed Psych and You* is that you will learn more, because you are more cognitively active than your friend. **Cognitive activity** is the process of focusing our thinking on the learning task in which we're involved and the factors related to the task. For instance, writing an answer encourages you to search your long-term memory for connections and construct a response. It requires you to think carefully about an answer, and focused thinking is the essence of cognitive activity. No matter how hard we try, when we simply read the question and the feedback, we aren't likely to focus as clearly and think as deeply about our answer. It is less cognitively active, resulting in fewer connections to information in long-term memory and less meaningful learning. Similarly, asking students to provide or recognize additional examples of an idea places them in more cognitively active roles than simply providing them with an example (Bransford et al., 2000).

Regardless of the encoding strategy we use, putting ourselves in cognitively active roles—thinking carefully about the information we're studying—is essential.

Forgetting

Forgetting is the loss of, or inability to retrieve, information from memory, and it is both a real part of our everyday lives and an important factor in classroom learning.

To understand forgetting, look again at the model first presented in Figure 7.2. There we see that information lost from both sensory memory and working memory is unrecoverable. It is literally forgotten. However, information in long-term memory has been encoded. Why can't we find it?

FORGETTING AS INTERFERENCE

The concept of **interference**, the loss of information because something learned either before or after detracts from understanding, is one way to explain forgetting (Howe, 2004). For example, students first learn the rule for forming singular possessives by adding an apostrophe *s* to the singular noun. If their understanding of this rule for forming singular possessives later interferes with learning the rules for forming plural possessives and contractions, or if the rules for forming plural possessives confuse their prior understanding, interference has occurred.

Teaching closely related ideas together—such as adjectives and adverbs, longitude and latitude, and adding fractions with similar and different denominators—can help reduce interference. In doing so, we help students recognize similarities and differences and identify areas that are easily confused.

We can also reduce interference by using reviews to capitalize on schema activation, comparing the new topic to the closely related information that our students have already studied. This helps students identify easily confused similarities and promotes elaboration.

FORGETTING AS RETRIEVAL FAILURE

Retrieval failure is a second explanation for forgetting. **Retrieval** is the process of pulling information from long-term memory back into working memory, and it's represented in Figures 7.2 and 7.6 by the arrow pointing from long-term memory back to working memory. We've all had the experience of realizing that we know a name or a fact, but we simply can't dredge it up.

This is an example of retrieval failure, and many researchers believe that "forgetting" is actually our inability to retrieve information from long-term memory (Williams & Zacks, 2001).

Ed Psych and You

Quickly state the months of the year. Now, do the same, but this time list them alphabetically. Why were you so much slower the second time?

The Role of Context in Retrieval. Retrieval also depends on context and the way we originally encoded information, and this helps answer the question we asked in *Ed Psych and You* (Williams & Zacks, 2001). The context in which we encode the months of the year is chronological, since that's the way we usually encounter them, and remembering them this way becomes automatic. Attempting to state them alphabetically presents a different context and different retrieval challenge. We can do it, but we must laboriously go through the process. Similarly, you know a person at school, but you can't remember his name when you see him at a party; his name was encoded in the school context, and you're trying to retrieve it in the context of the party.

Meaningfulness is the key to retrieval. The more interconnected our knowledge is in long-term memory, the easier it is to retrieve. Mike attempted to make information about figurative language meaningful by having his students identify examples in the context of the novel *To Kill a Mockingbird*. In doing so, he capitalized on schema activation and elaboration as encoding strategies. Using these strategies made the information more meaningful, and as a result made retrieval easier.

Practice to the point of automaticity, such as we've done with the months of the year, also facilitates retrieval (Chaffen & Imreh, 2002). When math facts are automatic, students easily retrieve them for use in problem solving, leaving more working memory space to focus on solutions.

Developmental Differences in Cognitive Processes

As with memory stores, developmental differences exist in our cognitive processes (Feldman 2014; Nelson et al., 2006). One of the most important involves attention, because the development of attention is essential for all of us in dealing with the demands of everyday life (Atkinson & Braddock, 2012). Over time, children gradually learn to focus their attention and screen out irrelevant stimuli (Davidson, 2012). Older children are less easily distracted, and attention becomes more purposeful. Developmental differences can appear by age two, with those better able to focus their attention later developing superior language skills (Beuker, Rommelse, Donders, & Buitelaar, 2013). Significantly, students with learning disabilities, such as ADHD, lag developmentally behind their peers in this important dimension of learning (Bental & Tirosh, 2007).

Developmental differences also exist in perception; because older students have more background experiences than their younger counterparts, their perceptions are more likely to be accurate. Differences also exist in encoding. For instance, students typically don't use rehearsal until about the second or third grade (Jarrold & Citroën, 2013), and as they further develop, they begin to use more advanced encoding strategies, such as imagery, organization, and elaboration (Pressley & Hilden, 2006). If you're planning to teach young children, you can promote their development by modeling cognitive processes, encouraging their use with your students, and liberally praising students when they demonstrate these abilities.

Diversity: The Impact of Diversity on Cognition

Our students' diversity has a powerful effect on their cognitive processes, with their prior knowledge and experiences being two of the most important factors. For instance, because Miguel's English teacher the year before emphasized figurative language, he had background knowledge that made his perceptions more accurate and his encoding more efficient. Steve and Patty lacked these experiences, so identifying examples of figurative language in *To Kill a Mockingbird* was harder for them.

Differences in background knowledge and experience are particularly important when students come from a variety of socioeconomic and cultural backgrounds. For example, Paul (one of your authors) grew up in a rural, relatively low socioeconomic environment and attended a very small high school. As a result, access to a rich menu of educational experiences, such as advanced math and science courses, foreign languages, and technology, was limited. When he went on to college, he competed with students from larger schools and had to work extra hard to overcome these deficiencies. Don (your other author), who taught in a low socioeconomic status neighborhood outside of Chicago, found that many of his urban students, because of parental work pressures, family issues, and other factors, never had the chance to capitalize on the educational opportunities available in the city. Although his students lived less than an hour away from world-class museums, a planetarium, and an aquarium, for example, many didn't even know they existed. More advantaged students frequently visited these sites, and their performance in class reflected the educational benefits of these experiences.

In spite of these differences, however, we can do a great deal to accommodate the diversity in our students' background knowledge. The following are some suggestions (Huan et al., 2006):

- Assess students' prior knowledge and perceptions by asking them what they already know about a topic. For example, because he has several recent-immigrant children in his class, a third-grade teacher begins a unit on communities by saying, "Tell us about the communities where you lived before coming to this country." He then uses the information as a framework for the study of their community.
- Supplement students' prior experiences with rich examples that promote elaboration and aid meaningful encoding. For instance, a middle school science teacher introduces refraction by having students put coins in opaque dishes and backing up until they can't see the coins. Partners pour water into the dishes until the coins become visible, and the teacher then shows a model illustrating how the light rays are bent when they enter and leave the water.
- Use students' experiences to augment the background knowledge of their classmates. For instance, a teacher whose class is studying modern Europe says, "Celeena, you lived in Europe. Tell us about the thinking of people in countries that were part of the former Eastern Bloc."

In each case, the teacher then uses students' existing background knowledge as a launching point for the lesson. Some evidence suggests that sharing information in this way leads to collaborative encoding, encoding information in a group setting that wouldn't be possible alone (Harris, Barnier, & Sutton, 2013). This ability is particularly valuable when working with students from diverse backgrounds, because they bring a rich array of prior experiences to learning activities. The ability to adapt lessons in this way is an important component of teaching expertise.

Classroom Connections

Helping Your Students Capitalize on Cognitive Processes to Increase Their Learning

Attention

1. Attention is the beginning point for learning. Begin and conduct lessons to attract and maintain attention.

   ■ **Elementary:** To be sure that all students are attending to the lesson, a third-grade teacher calls on all his students whether they have their hands up or not.

   ■ **Middle School:** A science teacher introducing the concept *pressure* has students stand by their desks, first on both feet and then on one foot. They then discuss the force and pressure on the floor in each case.

   ■ **High School:** To be sure that her students attend to important points, a world history teacher uses emphasis, "Everyone, listen carefully now, because we're going to look at three important reasons that World War I broke out in Europe."

Perception

2. Perception is the process of attaching meaning to the information we attend to, so accurate perceptions are essential for understanding. Check frequently to be certain that students perceive your examples and other representations accurately.

   ■ **Elementary:** In a lesson on living things, a kindergarten teacher holds up a large potted plant, asks, "What do you notice about the plant?," and calls on several children for their observations.

   ■ **Middle School:** A geography teacher downloads colored pictures of different landforms from the Internet and asks students to describe each.

   ■ **High School:** Students are reading an essay and encounter the line, "The revolution often bordered on anarchy; the citizens were out of control." Their teacher stops and asks, "What does the author mean by 'anarchy'?"

Meaningful Encoding

3. Meaningful encoding is the process of connecting new information to information already in long-term memory. To aid encoding, carefully organize the information you present to students and promote cognitive activity with interactive teaching strategies.

   ■ **Elementary:** A fourth-grade teacher illustrates that heat causes expansion by placing a balloon-covered soft drink bottle in a pot of hot water and by presenting a drawing that shows the spacing and motion of the air molecules before and after the bottle is heated. She then guides the students with questioning to understand the relationship between heat, molecular activity, and expansion.

   ■ **Middle School:** A math teacher presents a flowchart with a series of questions students should ask themselves as they solve word problems (e.g., What do I know? What am I trying to find out?). As the class works on problems, he asks them to describe their thinking and tell where they are on the flowchart.

   ■ **High School:** A history teacher presents a matrix comparing different immigrant groups, their reasons for relocating to the United States, the difficulties they encountered, and their rates of assimilation. The students then search for patterns in the information in the chart.

4. Learners elaborate their understanding when they make new connections between the items of information they're studying. Encourage students to relate items of information to each other and form mental images as often as possible.

   ■ **Elementary:** A fourth-grade teacher, after a demonstration at the front of the room, says, "Let's see what we've found out about chemical and physical changes. Give two new examples of each that show the differences between the two."

   ■ **Middle School:** A geography teacher encourages her students to visualize parallel lines on the globe as they think about latitude, and vertical lines coming together at the North and South Poles as they think about longitude. She then asks her students to compare them.

   ■ **High School:** An English teacher asks students to imagine the appearance of the characters in a novel by pretending they are casting them for a movie version. He then asks them to suggest a current actor or actress to play each role.

Retrieval

5. Retrieval occurs when learners pull information from long-term memory back into working memory, and interference can inhibit this process. To prevent interference and aid retrieval, teach closely related ideas together.

   ■ **Elementary:** To teach area and perimeter, a fifth-grade teacher has her students lay squares side by side to illustrate area, and she has them measure the distance around the pieces to illustrate perimeter.

   ■ **Middle School:** An English teacher displays a passage on the document camera that includes gerunds and participles. He then asks the students to compare the way the words are used in the passage to demonstrate that gerunds are nouns and participles are adjectives.

   ■ **High School:** A biology teacher begins a unit on arteries and veins by saying, "We've all heard of hardening of the arteries, but we haven't heard of 'hardening of the veins.' Why not?"

Ed Psych and You

Have you ever said to yourself, "I'm beat today. I'd better drink a cup of coffee before I go to class," or, "I better sit near the front of the class so I won't fall asleep." What do these comments suggest about your approach to learning?

Metacognition: Knowledge and Regulation of Cognition

Think about the questions we asked in *Ed Psych and You*. If you answered yes to either, or have had similar thoughts about your learning, you were being *metacognitive*. **Metacognition**, commonly described as "knowing about knowing," is knowledge and regulation of our cognition (Bruning et al., 2011; Pressley & Hilden, 2006). **Meta-attention**, knowledge and regulation of our attention, is one type of metacognition. For example, you knew that your drowsiness might affect your ability to attend—*knowledge of your attention*—and you regulated your attention by drinking coffee or sitting near the front of the class.

Metamemory, knowledge and regulation of memory strategies, is another form of metacognition, and Steve demonstrated metamemory when he said,

> "Wait. . . . Let me write some of this down, so I'll remember it better."

His statement also helps us answer the third question we asked at the beginning of the chapter (What impact will Steve's decision to "write some of this stuff down" have on his learning?). Realizing that he needed to write down some information and then doing so will improve his encoding and increase his learning, and the more metacognitive he becomes, the greater impact it will have.

Metacognition explains a variety of actions in our everyday lives. Paul, for instance, knows that he is likely to misplace his keys (knowledge of cognition), so he always immediately puts them in a desk drawer when he comes in from the garage (regulation of cognition). Don, a self-described absent-minded professor, realizes that he sometimes forgets important dates like his wedding anniversary and kids' birthdays, so he's put them on his computer with a reminder. Virtually everyone prepares lists when grocery shopping. In all cases we have knowledge about the limitations of our memories, and we regulate our cognitive processes with our lists and other strategies.

Research on Metacognition

A great deal of research on metacognition and teaching practices designed to improve students' metacognitive abilities has been conducted since about the mid-1970s (e.g., see Fuchs & Fuchs, 2007; Pressley & Harris, 2006; Pressley & Hilden, 2006; Waters & Kunnmann, 2010). And metacognition has found its way into areas other than learning and teaching. For instance, it has been emphasized as a tool for dealing with emotional issues, such as stress, negative thinking, and worry in both adults and children (Kertz & Woodruff-Borden, 2013; McEvoy, Moulds, & Mahoney, 2013).

This research has produced four important findings. First, metacognition plays an essential role in classroom learning. "Accurate metacognition drives effective study behavior and can improve cognition without significant increases in work or effort, while inaccurate or biased metacognition may lead learners to adopt suboptimal study behaviors and lead to inferior levels of learning" (Tullis, Finley, & Benjamin, 2013, p. 440). Note that the quote includes the phrase "without significant increases in work or effort." When we attempt to teach our students to be metacognitive, we're not asking them to work harder; we're suggesting that they work "smarter."

Second, as we would expect, metacognition depends on task difficulty (Kalyuga, 2010). When tasks are difficult, the cognitive load on working memory may be too great to allow effective metacognitive monitoring. This suggests that we need to help students break difficult tasks down into manageable parts so they can employ metacognitive strategies.

Third, as we would also predict, neither students—including college students—nor adults are particularly good at metacognitive monitoring, but metacognition can be improved significantly by directly teaching and modeling metacognitive skills (Bruning et al., 2011).

Finally, metacognition is relatively independent of general academic ability (Anderson & Nashon, 2007; Pressley & Harris, 2006). In fact, "evidence suggests that metacognitive awareness can compensate for low ability and insufficient knowledge" (Bruning et el., 2011; p. 82). For instance, realizing that attention to a task is essential doesn't depend on ability, and with this realization students are more likely to create personal learning environments free of distractions, which can be as simple as moving to the front of the class or turning off a cell phone and TV while studying at home.

All this suggests that teaching all students to be metacognitive is important, and it might be even more important with low-ability learners than with their higher ability peers.

The metacognitive components of the memory model are illustrated in Figure 7.8.

Developmental Differences in Metacognition

As we would expect, young learners' metacognitive abilities are limited. For instance, young children are often unaware of the need to pay attention in learning activities, whereas their older counterparts are more likely to realize that attention is important and can better direct it to learning tasks (Von der Linden & Roebers, 2006). With teacher support, however, even young children quickly become more strategic about their learning. For example, students as early as the third grade can be taught metacognitive learning strategies. They do, however, tend to sometimes be overconfident and overestimate their cognitive abilities, particularly when tasks are challenging (Metcalfe & Finn, 2013).

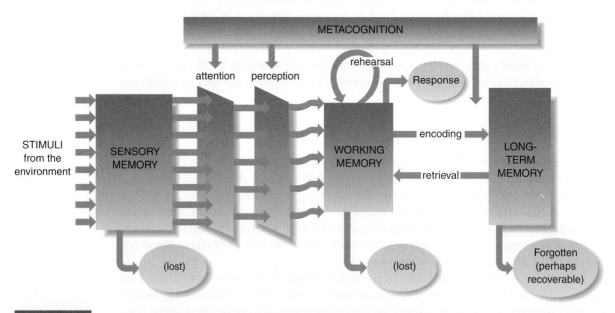

Figure 7.8

Metacognition in the model of human memory

More sophisticated metacognition, such as using advanced encoding strategies like organization, elaboration, and imagery, often begin to appear in early adolescence, advance with age, and then level off in adulthood (Weil et al., 2013).

In spite of these developmental differences, older learners and even some college students are not as metacognitive about their learning as they should be (Peverly, Brobst, & Graham, 2003), so, if you're planning to teach in middle or high schools, your students will still need a great deal of guidance and support to develop their metacognitive abilities.

Finally, as with much of learning and development, the development of metacognition has an important social component (Brinck, & Liljenfors, 2013). When parents, other adults, and siblings talk to and play with infants, for example, they help the young children begin the process of adapting to their surroundings and thinking about the way the world works.

Diversity: Metacognitive Differences in Gender, Culture, and Learners with Exceptionalities

As with most aspects of learning and development, differences exist in our students with respect to metacognition. For instance, some evidence indicates that girls tend to be more metacognitive than boys in their approaches to learning (Weil et al., 2013).

Language is also a factor. For instance, the cognitive load on second language learners' working memories is often high because they are dealing with both language and the topic they're studying. As a result, metacognitive monitoring is often pushed off the working memory workbench, taking a backseat to the immediate task at hand (Wright, 2012).

Students' cultural beliefs are another factor that influences their metacognition. Asian students, for example, tend to believe that learning is a demanding process that requires a great deal of effort and perseverance (Chen & Trommsdorff, 2012; Li, 2005). As a result of these beliefs, Asian parents and teachers often emphasize memorization and rote learning to a greater extent than do teachers from mainstream Western cultures, such as the United States (Dahlin & Watkins, 2000). In our country, as we've emphasized throughout this chapter, meaningful learning, and the metacognitive strategies needed to promote it, receive more emphasis.

Learners with exceptionalities represent another aspect of diversity with respect to metacognition. For instance, students with learning disabilities and behavioral disorders are often "cognitively inert," that is, they don't acquire metacognitive strategies through the normal course of development in the same way as their peers. However, with effort and practice they can be taught to be metacognitive, and promoting the development of these abilities represents one of the most promising educational trends in working with students having exceptionalities (Hardman, Drew, & Egan, 2014).

| Classroom **Connections**

Promoting Metacognition in Your Students

1. Metacognition is knowledge of and control over the way we study and learn, and learners who are metacognitive learn more and retain information longer. To capitalize on metacognition, integrate metacognitive strategies into your instruction and model your own metacognition.

   ■ **Elementary:** During a lesson, a fourth-grade teacher holds up a card with the sentence, "If you're paying attention, raise your hand." He acknowledges those who are and encourages them to share their strategies for maintaining attention during class.

   ■ **Middle School:** A social studies teacher emphasizes metamemory by saying, "Suppose you're reading, and the book states that there are three important differences between capitalism and socialism. What should you do?"

   ■ **High School:** An economics teacher models metacognitive strategies by making statements like, "Whenever I read something new, I always ask myself, 'How does this relate to what I've been studying?' For example, how is the liberal economic agenda different from the conservative agenda?"

In summarizing this section, we want to emphasize that these are only general patterns. For instance, Asian students wouldn't enjoy the academic success they do if they focused exclusively on memorization, and teachers in mainstream Western cultures realize that some content must simply be memorized to the point of automaticity. As with all aspects of learning and teaching, we need to be cautious about overgeneralizing and stereotyping.

Analyzing Theories

Evaluating Information Processing and the Model of Human Memory

Information processing and the model of human memory make an important contribution to our understanding of the way we learn and remember. However, critics suggest that the model, as initially presented in Figure 7.2, is an inappropriate oversimplification of the complex processes involved. For example, the model presents attention as one filter between sensory memory and working memory, but some evidence indicates that the central executive in working memory influences both our attention and how we perceive that information. So, attending to incoming stimuli and attaching meaning to them are not as simple as the one-way flow of information suggested by the model (Demetriou, Christou, Spanoudis, & Platsidou, 2002; Kiyonaga & Egner, 2013; Shipstead & Engle, 2013). "Put simply, we argue that WM and attention should no longer be considered as separate systems or concepts, but as competing and influencing one another because they rely on the same limited resource" (Kiyonaga & Egner, 2013, p. 228).

Further, some researchers question whether working memory and long-term memory are as distinct as the model suggests, and some argue that they simply represent different **activation states**, that is, differences in the extent to which individuals are attending to and actively processing information in a single memory. According to this view, when people are attending to and processing information, it's in an *active* state, which is information we typically describe as being in working memory. As attention shifts, other information becomes active, and the previously activated information becomes inactive. Most of the information in our memories is inactive, information we typically describe as being in long-term memory (Radvansky & Ashcraft, 2014; Baddeley, 2001).

The memory model has also been criticized for failing to adequately consider the social context in which learning occurs, as well as cultural and personal factors that influence learning, such as students' emotions (Nasir, Rosebery, Warren, & Lee, 2006). Critics also argue that it doesn't adequately account for the extent to which learners construct their own knowledge, a basic principle of cognitive learning theory (Kafai, 2006).

Finally, the model of human memory, as typically described, is assumed to be an information processing system that is logical, sequential, and governed by metacognition. It also assumes that information is *consciously processed*, that is, we attend to the information, attach meaning to it through perception, consciously organize and make sense of it in working memory, and then encode the information in long-term memory. An expanding body of evidence indicates, however, that we make many decisions and conclusions essentially without thinking about

them (Kahneman, 2011; Thaler & Sunstein, 2008; Vedantam, 2010). Others go even further and argue that much of what we do happens below our level of awareness (Aronson, Wilson, & Akert, 2013).

Examples, both in our everyday lives and in classrooms, corroborate this view. Retailers, for example, pay big bucks to supermarkets to have their products placed at eye level, because marketing research indicates that we—subconsciously—are more likely to buy products placed this way. Dairy products are usually placed in the back so we have to weave our way through the store to get a carton of milk, and the more time we spend in the supermarket, the greater the likelihood that we'll spend extra money (SupermarketPage.com, 2010; Underhill, 2009).

Subconscious processing also exists in classrooms. For instance, a long history of research indicates that teachers assess physically attractive students as more intelligent and more socially skilled than those who are less attractive, and they have different expectations for attractive students, which can result in differences in achievement for the two groups (Ritts, Patterson, & Tubbs, 1992). In addition, these subconscious evaluations also influence teachers' perceptions of different ethnic and cultural groups. For example, a study examining preservice and practicing teachers' assessments of students' ability found that both groups rated unattractive black males lower in perceived ability and social skills than any other group (Parks & Kennedy, 2007). Teachers are obviously not consciously making these assessments, and information processing and the model of human memory cannot account for these research results.

Despite these criticisms, virtually all cognitive descriptions of learning accept the basic structure of human memory, including a limited-capacity working memory, a long-term memory that stores information in organized form, cognitive processes that move the information from one store to another, and the regulatory mechanisms of metacognition (Bransford et al., 2000). These components help explain learning events that other theories are unable to explain.

Perhaps most important for our development as teachers, information processing and the model of human memory arguably offer more guidance for instruction than does any other theory of learning. It provides, through metacognition, a mechanism for dealing with processing that occurs below the level of consciousness. (We offer suggestions for both in the next section of the chapter.)

Table 7.3 summarizes information processing and the model of human memory, including criticisms of it and the contributions it makes to our understanding of learning and teaching.

Table 7.3	Analyzing theories: Information processing and the model of human memory
Key question	How do people gather, organize, and store information in memory?
Information stores Sensory memory (SM) Working memory (WM) Long-term memory (LTM)	Repositories that hold information: • Vary from large capacity but short duration (SM) to small capacity and relatively short duration (WM) to large capacity and long duration (LTM) • Vary in function from initial input (SM) to the conscious organizer information (WM) to the permanent information store (LTM)
Cognitive processes Attention Perception Rehearsal Encoding Retrieval	Processes that move information from one information store to another by: • Initially focusing on a stimulus (attention) • Finding meaning in the stimulus (perception) • Repeating information to keep it in WM or move it to LTM (rehearsal) • Representing organized information in LTM (encoding) • Pulling information from LTM back to WM for further processing (retrieval)
Metacognition	Executive mechanism that: • Controls cognitive processes • Regulates the flow and storage of information through the memory system
Catalysts for effective processing	• Reducing cognitive load—decreasing the amount of mental activity imposed on working memory • Developing automaticity—overlearning cognitive operations to where they can be performed without thinking about them • Using encoding strategies—finding relationships in separate items of information which make information meaningful and reduce cognitive load
Key concepts	• Sensory memory • Working memory • Long-term memory • Cognitive load • Automaticity • Chunking • Attention • Perception • Rehearsal • Encoding • Retrieval • Meta-attention • Metamemory
Criticisms of information processing theory	• Doesn't adequately explain important influences on learning, such as social context, culture, and emotion • Oversimplifies the processes involved in gathering, organizing, and storing information by implying a one-way transfer of information through the memory stores • Doesn't adequately explain the constructive processes in knowledge acquisition • Considers all information processing as a conscious, deliberate process, but some evidence indicates that a considerable amount of processing is below the conscious level
Contributions of information processing theory	• Explains how we gather information through our senses, organize it, and store it in memory • Most descriptions of learning accept this basic structure of our memory system, including a limited-capacity WM and a LTM that stores organized information, cognitive processes that move information from one store to another, and the regulatory mechanisms of metacognition • Provides important implications for designing and implementing instruction

Educational Psychology and Teaching: Applying Information Processing and the Model of Human Memory with Your Students

Applying an understanding of information processing and the model of human memory in our teaching can increase learning for all students. Guidelines for applying this information in teaching are outlined below and discussed in the sections that follow:

- Conduct reviews to activate schemas and check perceptions
- Begin learning activities with attention-getting experiences
- Develop learners' background knowledge with high-quality representations of content
- Interact with students to promote cognitive activity and reduce cognitive load
- Capitalize on meaningful encoding strategies
- Model and encourage metacognition

The guidelines overlap and interact with each other. We will see how as we discuss each.

CONDUCT REVIEWS TO ACTIVATE SCHEMAS AND CHECK PERCEPTIONS

To begin this section let's return to Mike's Thursday lesson before he had his students work in their groups.

> He begins, "What were we talking about yesterday? . . . Alexandria?"
>
> ". . . Figurative language . . . and figures of speech," Alexandria responds hesitantly.
>
> "And what do we mean by figurative language? . . . Greg?"
>
> "It's like . . . language where . . . the real meaning of the words is not quite true."
>
> "Give us an example. . . . Gabrielle."
>
> ". . . Well, like the example you used yesterday, 'Laughter is the music of the soul.' We're not saying that laughter really is music or anything like that. . . . So, it's figurative."
>
> "What is 'Laughter is the music of the soul' an example of? . . . Jason?"
>
> ". . . It's a metaphor."
>
> Mike continues by reviewing *simile* and *personification* and then assigns his students to their groups.

Three aspects of Mike's review are important and relate to the model of human memory. First, by simply asking his students what they talked about yesterday and then calling on Greg with, "What do we mean by figurative language?" he began the process of activating prior knowledge and checking perceptions. As Greg responded, he retrieved his understanding of figurative language from his long-term memory—and helped his classmates also retrieve the meaning from theirs, which made the information available for further processing. Greg's explanation also revealed his perception of figurative language, and if it had been inaccurate, Mike could have provided additional examples and explanation to help clarify the concept.

Second, notice that the students were somewhat hesitant in their responses. This is typical in classrooms; students often struggle to put their developing understanding into words. So asking them to put their thoughts into words is crucial; the more they work on articulating their thoughts, the deeper their understanding becomes.

Third, notice that Mike called on a different student for each question. This is important for two reasons. First, it communicated that he expected all his students—regardless of gender, ability, cultural background, or exceptionality—to be involved and answer, all of which contributes to a positive classroom climate (Wright, 2012).

Second, when students believe they'll be called on, they are more likely to pay attention (Good & Brophy, 2008). This leads us to the second suggestion.

BEGIN LEARNING ACTIVITIES WITH ATTENTION-GETTING EXPERIENCES

We know that our students' attention is limited and they are easily distracted. And because attention is where information processing begins, attracting students' attention is essential for learning at any level (Jiang et al., 2013). So when we prepare our **learning activities**, the new learning experiences that follow our reviews and help students reach standards and learning goals, we should consciously plan to begin our lessons in ways that attract students' attention. If we pull a live crab out of a cooler to begin a lesson on crustaceans, for example, even our most disinterested students are likely to pay attention, at least for a while. Some additional strategies for attracting attention are outlined in Table 7.4.

DEVELOP LEARNERS' BACKGROUND KNOWLEDGE WITH HIGH-QUALITY REPRESENTATIONS OF CONTENT

As we saw earlier in the chapter, the development of meaningful schemas is a primary goal of learning, and these schemas represent the way knowledge is organized in working memory and stored in long-term memory.

This means that our students must have the background knowledge required to form meaningful schemas, and in many cases they don't have it. So, simply, we must provide it

Table 7.4	Strategies for attracting attention
Type	**Example**
Discrepant events	• A world history teacher who normally dresses conservatively comes to class in a sheet, makeshift sandals, and a crown to begin a discussion of ancient Greece. • A science teacher blows between two sheets of paper, but instead of the papers flying apart, they come together.
Pictures	• An English teacher shows a picture of a bearded Ernest Hemingway as she introduces 20th-century American novels. • An art teacher displays Pablo Picasso's *Les Demoiselles d'Avignon* as an introduction to *Cubism,* the avant-garde art movement.
Problems	• A math teacher says, "We want to go to the concert on Saturday night, but we're broke. The tickets are $80 and we need another $25 for something to eat. We make $7.50 an hour in our part-time jobs. How many hours will we have to work to be able to pay for the concert? • An economics teacher says, "Sally is having a drink with her friend Kristen, who encourages her to have a Coke, but she responds, 'I would love one, but I think I'd better stick with water today. So I'll pass.' . . . What is the opportunity cost of drinking the water?"
Thought-provoking questions	• A history teacher begins a discussion of World War II with the question, "Suppose Germany had won the war. How would the world be different now?" • A fourth-grade teacher says, "When we add two fractions, we get a larger fraction, but when we multiply fractions, we get a smaller number. How can this be?"
Emphasis	• A physical education teacher says, "Pay careful attention to the way the person rolls in the video," as she prepares to show a video clip demonstrating a move in gymnastics. • A music teacher says, "Listen carefully now to the blend of the two instruments," just before she plays a musical excerpt.

for them. To illustrate this idea, let's look back on Mike's teaching. To meet the standard, he wanted his students to understand figurative language and to be able to identify the concepts *personification, simile,* and *metaphor* in the context of the novel *To Kill a Mockingbird.* Mike realized, however, that his students didn't have the background knowledge they needed, so on Wednesday (the day before) he defined the concepts and provided some examples. Let's flash back to his Wednesday lesson.

"We've been discussing *To Kill a Mockingbird* for a few days now," Mike begins, ". . . so today I want to kick it up a notch to help us see how Harper Lee, the author, uses figurative language to make the novel more interesting and attractive to read.

He then displays the following on his document camera.

Figurative language is the use of words designed to imply a meaning different than the literal meaning, and it often involves an exaggeration or comparison.

He then displays

The Rock (the actor) is an ox.

on the document camera, and asks, "What do you notice about this statement?"

The students make observations, and with Mike's guidance they conclude that it doesn't imply that the Rock literally is an ox, but rather, through exaggeration and comparison to an ox, implies that he's strong and powerful.

"A statement that makes a comparison in this way is called a *metaphor,*" Mike continues. "When we see it, we can almost visualize how strong and powerful he is."

He then displays some additional metaphors, defines the concept *simile,* provides examples of similes, and does the same for *personification.*

He then assigns the students the task of identifying two examples each of the concepts *simile, metaphor,* and *personification* in *To Kill a Mockingbird,* and to avoid overloading their cognitive resources, he gives them some page numbers in the novel to focus on.

By defining figurative language and providing examples the way he did, Mike helped his students develop their background knowledge and prepare them for the more demanding task of identifying additional examples of figurative language in the novel. Table 7.5 provides some additional ways that teachers help their students develop the background knowledge needed to construct meaningful schemas. We include them to help you begin the process of thinking about how you can help your students learn abstract ideas in a meaningful way.

INTERACT WITH STUDENTS TO PROMOTE COGNITIVE ACTIVITY AND REDUCE COGNITIVE LOAD

Because of its limited capacity, working memory has long been called an information processing bottleneck, and it's easy to impose too heavy a cognitive load on our students when we teach (Marois & Ivanoff, 2005). The biggest culprit is going too fast and providing too much information with lectures and explanations and spending too little time asking questions and interacting with our students. "This traditional approach has its place, but we rely on it all too often" (Goldsmith, 2013, p. 49). Lectures also place students in cognitively passive roles, and teachers who predominantly lecture are perceived by students as less effective than those who interact with their students (Latif & Miles, 2013).

This means that *we should be making interaction with our students, and the students with each other, a high priority in our teaching.* Doing so promotes learners' cognitive activity, and it also reduces cognitive load, because we can only move through a learning activity as rapidly as our students can correctly respond to our questions. If students are able to answer, they're processing the information, and their working memories are not overloaded. In

Table 7.5	Developing students' background knowledge
Content Area and Goal	**Example/Representation**
American history: For students to understand factors leading to the Civil War	A chart comparing the Northern and Southern states before the war. The chart includes information about the people, the land and climate, and the economies of the North and the South. The chart is combined with a geographic map of the United States before the war.
Health: For students to be able to identify healthy and unhealthy foods	A matrix showing a number of popular foods, such as soft drinks, potato chips, vegetables, fruits, and meats in the left column and the amount of fat, protein, fiber, sugar, and salt in the other columns.
Science: For students to understand the concepts *work* and *force*	A demonstration where the teacher has students push down on their desks and blow on their hands to demonstrate that *force* is a push combined with having them pull up on their chairs to demonstrate that *force* is also a pull. A demonstration where the teacher has her students slide a book across a desk to demonstration that *work* is a combination of force and movement.
Physical education: For students to understand the mechanics of an effective serve in tennis	Video clips of several tennis players demonstrating different service motions.
Math: For students to understand how to solve simultaneous equations	Sets of simultaneous equations together with step-by-step solutions showing how the equations have been solved.
Language arts: For students to understand *folk tales*	Folk tales about different teachers in the school constructed to include the essential characteristics of folk tales.

addition to promoting cognitive activity, student motivation is higher when they're interacting in lessons (Schunk, Meese, & Pintrich, 2014).

The way Mike interacted with his students illustrates the importance of effective interaction. Three aspects of his interaction are important:

- He conducted his review and learning activity primarily through questioning.
- He called on all his students individually and by name.
- He used open-ended questions as a tool for promoting student involvement.

Open-ended questions are questions for which a variety of answers are acceptable. For instance, Mike displayed the statement "The Rock is an ox," and then asked, "What do you notice about this statement?" Answers ranging from "It's about a movie actor" to "It is a metaphor" are all acceptable. Open-ended questions are particularly effective with students who are reluctant to respond and students who are not native English speakers (Goldsmith, 2013; Wright, 2012). The fact that a variety of answers are acceptable is what makes open-ended questioning a valuable tool, because they pose a nonthreatening invitation to participate. And because questions such as "What do you notice?" or "How are these alike or different?" are easy to ask, they reduce the cognitive load on us when we teach.

Interacting with our students illustrates the way these guidelines overlap and reinforce each other. When students are involved and cognitively active, they are also more attentive. So interacting with students is also a way of maintaining their attention during learning activities.

Small-group work is another strategy Mike used to encourage his students to become cognitively active, reduce their cognitive load, and maintain their attention. This doesn't imply that group work is automatically effective, however. We are sometimes lulled into concluding that if our students are talking or physically active, they are also cognitively active, but this isn't necessarily the case (Mayer, 2004). They may be talking to each other during group work and hands-on activities but may not be "thinking about" what they're doing. Group work is popular in schools, but if these activities aren't carefully structured to cognitively engage students and monitored carefully, they may be no more effective than a dry lecture. Group work and hands-on activities aren't necessarily "minds-on" activities (Brophy, 2006a; Mayer, 2004).

CAPITALIZE ON MEANINGFUL ENCODING STRATEGIES

Schema activation, organization, elaboration, and imagery are all effective strategies for promoting meaningful encoding. We capitalize on schema activation when we begin lessons with reviews, and we promote the other encoding strategies in the way we conduct our lessons. For instance, in Table 7.5 we saw that a social studies teacher used a matrix and map as a way to represent conditions in the Northern and Southern states before the Civil War. Representing her content in this way helped her capitalize on both organization and imagery as encoding strategies.

Let's analyze her efforts further. Her matrix and map appear in Figure 7.9. As students analyze the information in the matrix, for example, they can see how the land and climate differ in the two regions, and the map helps them visualize these differences. As they continue their analysis, they can see how the land and climate influenced the economies of the two regions, and making these connections promotes elaboration.

Mike also capitalized on encoding strategies by having his students identify examples of figurative language in *To Kill a Mockingbird*. As they identified the examples they elaborated on the content of the novel, all of which made their understanding deeper and more meaningful.

This discussion again illustrates how the guidelines we outlined at the beginning of this section overlap and reinforce each other. For instance, the history teacher used

	People	Land and Climate	Economy
Northern states	Small towns Religious Valued education Cooperative	Timber covered Glacial remains Poor soil Short growing season Cold winters	Syrup Rum Lumber Shipbuilding Fishing Small farms
Southern states	Aristocratic Isolated Social class distinction	Fertile soil Hot weather Long growing season	Large farms Tobacco Cotton Unskilled workers Servants and slaves

Figure 7.9

Promoting encoding with organization, elaboration, and imagery

her matrix and map to help her students develop their background knowledge, but these content representations also capitalized on organization, elaboration, and imagery to promote meaningful encoding. Further, they provided a focal point for the students, which helped maintain their attention and make interacting with them easier. For instance, after displaying the matrix, the teacher asked questions such as, "How are the land and climate different in the Northern states compared to the Southern states?" These questions are easy to ask, so they reduce the teacher's cognitive load as she guides the students' developing understanding. As the lesson develops, the students then make more and more connections, which make all the information more meaningful for them.

MODEL AND ENCOURAGE METACOGNITION

As we saw earlier, directly teaching and modeling metacognition can help students develop their metacognitive skills (Bruning et al., 2011). So how do we "directly teach" metacognition?

One approach is to illustrate and discuss metacognition in the same way we would teach any other topic. For example, Norma Layton, a language arts teacher, is attempting to help her students develop their study skills, and she displays the following vignette on her document camera.

Danielle is reading a difficult chapter in her science text. She first looks at the organization of the chapter so she can identify the main topics and the subtopics that fit under each main heading. Then, she reads the section under the first main heading, stops, and asks herself, "Okay, what was this section about?" She repeats the process for each of the sections of the chapter.

"I need to study this way," she comments to Ginger, her friend. "If I don't, I don't remember anything I've read."

"Really?" Ginger replies. "I mostly just read and try to remember as much as I can."

"Now, let's look at the vignette," Norma directs her students. "What are some differences in the way Danielle approaches her study compared to the way Ginger approaches hers?"

As students discuss the vignette, they gradually arrive at the conclusion that Danielle is more aware of the way she studies and learns, and she takes steps to regulate her study.

Norma then emphasizes that this is the way that everyone should approach their study, and most important, to think about the ways that work best for them.

Approaching the development of metacognition in this way (i.e., teaching it directly), as we would teach any other topic, is often more effective than simply encouraging students to "think about what you're doing." Students hear a lot of suggestions from their teachers, and, as a result, they sometimes tune out. Using a conceptual approach, as Norma did, is often more effective (Bruning et al., 2011).

Then, combining direct instruction of metacognition with modeling, such as making statements like, "The first thing I do when I'm faced with a new task is to ask myself what I'm trying to accomplish," and "Whenever I run into a word or phrase I'm not quite sure of, I immediately 'Google' it."

As with all instruction, the combination of direct teaching and modeling of metacognition won't work magic, and it won't work with all students. With time and effort, however, it can make a difference with most.

Teacher Metacognition. In our "Analyzing Theories" feature we saw that the model of human memory treats information processing as a linear, conscious process, but an expanding body of evidence suggests that we make many of our decisions below the conscious level. Also, we're all human, and we're going to like some of our students more than others, most likely because they have better attitudes and perhaps more attractive personalities. These reactions are subconscious, as are the tendencies of teachers to treat perceived high achievers better than students they perceive as lower achievers, tendencies confirmed by a large body of evidence (Good & Brophy, 2008).

So what can we do to address these tendencies? We certainly don't want to subconsciously treat physically and socially attractive students, or higher achievers, more favorably than those less fortunate, for example.

Simply being aware of our tendencies to make subconscious decisions and taking steps to accommodate them, that is, being metacognitive about our teaching, can help prevent or overcome many of the potentially destructive aspects of subconscious processing. Two practices—systematic assessment and equitable distribution—can help.

Systematic Assessment. First, frequent and systematic assessment carries with it a learning bonus. Evidence indicates that assessment is one of the most powerful learning tools at our disposal. Simply, "The quality of learning is determined by the quality of assessment practices in the classroom" (Khan, 2012, p 576). And self-testing is an effective study strategy. "A combination of study and tests is more effective than spending the same amount of time reviewing the material in some other way, such as rereading" (Rohrer & Pashler, 2010).

Second, to overcome the possibility of subconsciously evaluating students' work based on factors other than their academic performance, assessing students' understanding thoroughly, frequently, and as objectively as possible is essential. This means giving students frequent quizzes and assignments that provide reliable, detailed information about each student's learning progress.

Equitable Distribution. Second, we know that students are sensitive to differential treatment from their teachers (Good & Brophy, 2008). We can overcome any tendencies we might have for inappropriate differential treatment of students by consciously attempting to implement a practice called equitable distribution, the process of treating all students in classrooms as equitably as possible. The concept of *equitable distribution* was conceived nearly than 40 years ago (Kerman, 1979), and it has been strongly emphasized by prominent educators since that time (Good & Brophy, 2008; Lemov, 2010). Equitable distribution means that we call on all students as equally as possible, provide them all with similar feedback, use the same body language with them, and assess them all in the same way. Mike's interaction with his students—calling on them individually and by name—is an example of equitable distribution in practice.

Applying information processing theory and the model of human memory in our teaching need not take a great deal of extra effort. For instance, after Mike first created his examples of figurative language, he stored them in his computer and can reuse them with little further preparation. The same is true for the history teacher with her matrix and map, and Norma Layton with her efforts to promote her students' metacognition. And guiding students' learning instead of lecturing to them can—with practice—become essentially automatic. As your expertise develops, you will be able to implement most of the suggestions we're making here without a great deal of effort, and in doing so will maximize learning for all your students.

Developmentally Appropriate **Practice**

The Human Memory Model with Students at Different Ages

Although the implications of cognitive learning theory and the model of human memory apply at all grade levels, important developmental differences exist. The following guidelines outline ways to respond to these differences.

Working with Students in Early Childhood Programs and Elementary Schools

Our attention is limited, and this limitation is even more pronounced in young children. Young children haven't learned to activate and maintain their attention during lessons (Berk, 2013). If you plan to teach young children, it will be doubly important to start lessons with an activity that attracts their attention, and you'll need to continually monitor attention during lessons. To maintain the attention of young children, learning activities must be short and frequently changed.

You'll also need to make directions for every task simple and precise and continually check children's perceptions of the task requirements to make sure they understand what you want them to do. Complex tasks should be broken into shorter and simpler ones, and each should be completed before moving to the next one (Trawick-Smith, 2014).

Young children's thinking tends to be concrete, so abstract ideas need to be illustrated with concrete and personalized examples. Because their language is developing, young children benefit from opportunities to practice putting their developing understanding into words.

Modeling metacognition and helping children develop an awareness of factors that influence their learning is particularly helpful with young students (Meltzer, Pollica, & Barzillai, 2007). Children who become aware of how attention influences learning acquire a learning skill that they can use throughout their lifetimes.

Working with Students in Middle Schools

Middle school students are beginning to understand how their metacognitive capabilities influence learning. To capitalize on their increased ability to monitor their own learning, effective middle school teachers help their students develop learning strategies that emphasize metacognition. For example, encouraging students to ask themselves questions, such as "How is this idea similar to and different from the previous idea?" and "What would be a real-world example of this idea?," models effective learning strategies that can significantly increase learning.

Much of middle school students' thinking still remains concrete, however, especially when the topic is new or abstract, so you'll need to continue to use concrete examples and analyze them using questioning. And because so much of learning is verbal, guiding students as they put their understanding into words not only increases learning but also promotes language development.

Working with Students in High Schools

High school students can use sophisticated learning strategies, but they are unlikely to use them unless the strategies are modeled and encouraged (Pressley & Hilden, 2006). If you're a high school teacher, modeling the use of encoding strategies, such as organization, elaboration, and imagery, is an effective way to promote their use in classrooms. Even high school students are likely to use rehearsal as a strategy when material is difficult for them, however, so practice with other strategies is important.

Teaching strategies such as questioning and small-group work that place students in cognitively active roles are important. Unfortunately, many high school teachers tend to rely on lecture in the mistaken belief that "telling" is teaching. High school students are social beings and love nothing more than to sit around and talk about who is dating whom and what's happening that weekend. Carefully structuring and monitoring group work to ensure that students who are socially active are also cognitively active is important.

High school students are capable of abstract thinking and problem solving but may need prompting to do so. They should be encouraged to examine questions in depth and consider cause-and-effect relationships.

chapter

7 Summary

1. Describe and explain the principles of cognitive learning theory.
   - *Learning and development depend on experience* is a basic principle of cognitive learning theory. Teachers apply this principle when they provide quality experiences for their students.
   - *People want their experiences to make sense.* This principle is illustrated in how commonly statements such as "That makes sense" or "That doesn't make any sense" are used both in and outside of school.
   - *To make sense of their experiences, people construct knowledge.* This helps us understand how people generate original ideas, ideas that they haven't gotten from any outside source.
   - *Knowledge that is constructed depends on what people already know.* Knowledge isn't constructed in a vacuum. Effective teachers link new knowledge to information learners already possess.
   - *Social interaction facilitates learning.* We are social beings, and social interaction contributes to learning. Effective teachers use questioning and small-group work to encourage students to actively engage with content.

2. Use the memory stores in the human memory model to explain events in classrooms and in the everyday world.
   - Sensory memory is the store that briefly holds stimuli from the environment until they can be processed.
   - Working memory is the conscious part of our information processing system, and its capacity is limited. The limitations of working memory help us understand why learners miss information in lectures and why we all periodically experience "memory overload."
   - We accommodate the limitations of working memory by developing skills to automaticity, organizing and interconnecting information so that it behaves as large chunks, and distributing processing.
   - Long-term memory is our permanent information store, and it is where knowledge is stored until it is needed for further processing.
   - Information in long-term memory makes more sense to people and is more easily retrieved when it is meaningfully organized.

3. Describe the cognitive processes in the human memory model and identify applications in everyday events.
   - Attention and perception move information from sensory memory to working memory. Attention is the pro-cess of consciously focusing on a stimulus, and perception attaches meaning to a stimulus.
   - Learners use rehearsal to retain information in the phonological loop of working memory, and intensive rehearsal can move information into long-term memory.
   - Encoding represents information in long-term memory. Learners encode information more effectively if it is represented both visually and verbally.
   - Retrieval is the process of pulling information from long-term memory back into working memory for problem solving or further processing.
   - Students' use of the cognitive processes improve as they develop, with older learners better focusing their attention and more effectively using strategies to promote meaningful encoding.

4. Define metacognition and explain how it influences learning.
   - Metacognition is individuals' knowledge of, and regulation of, their cognitive processes.
   - Metacognition influences learning by making learners aware of the way they study and learn, and providing strategies to increase learning.
   - Metacognition is developmental, with young children being less aware of their cognitive activities than their older counterparts.

5. Describe how information processing and the model of human memory can be applied to increase learning for all students.
   - Beginning lessons with reviews of previously learned content activates prior knowledge and helps students connect new information to existing understanding.
   - Beginning lessons with learning activities that attract student attention helps students focus on appropriate stimuli and ignore irrelevant information.
   - Using examples and other representations of content to be taught during learning activities helps students acquire the background knowledge they need to construct meaningful schemas.
   - Interacting with students during learning activities puts them in cognitively active roles and reduces cognitive load.
   - Together with schema activation, capitalizing on organization, elaboration, and imagery can help students meaningfully encode information.
   - Modeling and encouraging metacognition can help learners become aware of the ways they best study and learn.

Preparing for **Your Licensure Exam**

Understanding Information Processing and Human Memory

You will be required to take a licensure exam before you go into your own classroom. This exam will include information related to information processing and human memory, and it will include both multiple-choice and constructed-response questions. We include the following exercises to help you practice for the exam in your state. This book and these exercises will be a resource for you as you prepare for the exam.

In the following case, a high school English teacher wants her students to understand different characters in the novel *The Scarlet Letter* and to meet the standard

CCSS.ELA-Literacy.RL.11-12.3 Analyze the impact of the author's choices regarding how to develop and relate elements of a story or drama (e.g., where a story is set, how the action is ordered, how the characters are introduced and developed) (Common Core State Standards Initiative, 2014j).

At this point in the discussion of the novel, she is focusing on the character development aspect of the standard. Read the case study, and then answer the questions that follow.

Sue Southam has her students reading Nathaniel Hawthorne's *The Scarlet Letter*. The novel, set in Boston in the 1600s, describes a tragic and illicit love affair between the heroine (Hester Prynne) and a minister (Arthur Dimmesdale). The novel's title refers to the letter A, meaning "adulterer," which the Puritan community makes Hester wear as punishment for her adultery. The class has been discussing the book for several days and is now examining Reverend Dimmesdale's character.

Sue begins by reading a passage from the text describing Dimmesdale, has the students write down what they believe are the most important aspects of the description in their logs, and then reads a speech he gives in front of the congregation in which he confronts Hester and exhorts her to identify her secret lover and partner in sin (while all the time hoping and believing that she will not confess and name him as her lover).

Sue then divides the class into "Dimmesdales" and "Hesters," directs the "Dimmesdales" to write in their logs what they believe Dimmesdale is thinking during his speech, and tells the "Hesters" to write what they believe Hester is thinking as she listens.

After the students write in their logs, she organizes them into groups, each composed of two Hesters and two Dimmesdales, and says, "In each group, I want you to start off by having Dimmesdale tell what he is thinking during the first part of the speech. Then I'd like a Hester to respond. Then continue with Dimmesdale's next part, then Hester's reaction, and so on. . . . Go ahead and share your thoughts in your groups."

She gives the students 5 minutes to share their perspectives, calls the class back together, and then says, "Okay, let's hear it. A Dimmesdale first. What was he thinking during his speech? . . . Mike?"

"The only thing I could think of was, 'Oh God, help me. I hope she doesn't say anything. If they find out it's me, I'll be ruined.' And then here comes Hester with her powerful speech," Mike concludes, turning to Nicole, his partner in the group.

"I wrote, 'Good man, huh. So why don't you confess then? You know you're guilty. I've admitted my love, but you haven't. Why don't you just come out and say it?'" Nicole comments.

"Interesting. . . . What else? How about another Hester? . . . Sarah?"

"I just put, 'No, I'll never tell. I still love you, and I'll keep your secret forever,'" Sarah offers.

Sue pauses for a moment, looks around the room, and comments, "Notice how different the two views of Hester are. . . . Nicole paints her as very angry, whereas Sarah views her as still loving him." Sue again pauses, Karen raises her hand, and Sue nods to her.

"I think the reason Hester doesn't say anything is that people won't believe her, because he's a minister," Karen suggests. "She's getting her revenge just by being there, reminding him of his guilt."

"But if she accuses him, won't people expect him to deny it?" Brad adds.

"Maybe he knows she won't accuse him because she still loves him," Julie offers.

"Wait a minute," Jeff counters. "I don't think he's such a bad guy. I think he feels guilty about it all, but he just doesn't have the courage to admit it in front of all of those people."

The students continue their analysis of Dimmesdale's character, including a debate about whether he is a villain or a tragic figure.

"Interesting ideas," Sue says as she closes the discussion for the day. "Be sure to keep them in mind, and for tomorrow, I'd like you to read Chapter 4, in which we begin our analysis of Hester's husband."

Questions for Case Analysis

In answering these questions, use information from the chapter, and link your responses to specific information in the case.

Multiple-Choice Questions

1. Of the following, which guideline for applying information processing theory and the model of human memory did Sue most nearly apply in her work with her students?

   a. Activate students' prior knowledge and check their perceptions by beginning lessons with reviews.

   b. Attract and maintain students' attention with effective lesson beginnings and strategies that maintain interest.

   c. Put students in cognitively active roles and reduce cognitive load by interacting with them and using group work appropriately.

   d. Model metacognition and encourage metacognitive strategies in your students.

2. During the discussion, Nicole made the following statement about Hester's reaction to Dimmesdale's speech: "Good man, huh. So why don't you confess then? You know you're guilty. I've admitted my love, but you haven't. Why don't you just come out and say it?"

Sarah, on the other hand, made this statement as a reaction to the speech: "I just put, 'No, I'll never tell. I still love you, and I'll keep your secret forever.'"

Of the following, which is the best explanation for the difference between Nicole's and Sarah's statements?

   a. Nicole's experiences were different from Sarah's, and learning and development depend on experience.

   b. Nicole and Sarah each constructed their respective statements because the statements made sense to them.

   c. The information Nicole and Sarah had stored in their long-term memories was different, and they made the statements based on this difference.

   d. Nicole primarily used organization as an encoding strategy, whereas Sarah primarily used elaboration as an encoding strategy.

Constructed-Response Question

3. Assess the extent to which Sue applied information processing theory and the model of human memory model in her lesson. Include both strengths and weaknesses in your assessment.

Important **Concepts**

activation state
analogies
attention
automaticity
central executive
chunking
cognitive activity
cognitive learning theories
cognitive load
conditional knowledge
declarative knowledge
dual-coding theory
elaboration

elaborative rehearsal
encoding
episodic memory
equitable distribution
experts
forgetting
imagery
information processing
   theory
interference
learning activities
long-term memory
maintenance rehearsal

meaningfulness
memory stores (sensory
   memory, working memory,
   and long-term memory)
meta-attention
metacognition
metamemory
mnemonics
model
multitasking
open-ended questions
organization
perception

phonological loop
principles (laws)
procedural knowledge
retrieval
rote learning
schema activation
schemas
scripts
semantic memory
sensory memory
short-term memory
visual-spatial sketchpad
working memory

OUTLINE	LEARNING OUTCOMES
	After you've completed your study of this chapter, you should be able to:
Concept Learning Theories of Concept Learning Concept Learning: A Complex Cognitive Process Educational Psychology and Teaching: Applying Theories of Concept Learning with Your Students	**1.** Define concepts, and describe strategies for helping students learn concepts.
Problem Solving Well-Defined and Ill-Defined Problems The Problem-Solving Process Creativity Educational Psychology and Teaching: Helping Your Students Become Better Problem Solvers ▶ Technology, Learning, and Development: Using Technology to Promote Problem Solving	**2.** Recognize examples of ill-defined and well-defined problems, and describe strategies to teach problem solving in classrooms.
The Strategic Learner Metacognition: The Foundation of Strategic Learning Study Strategies Critical Thinking Educational Psychology and Teaching: Helping Your Students Become Strategic Learners	**3.** Identify applications of study strategies and critical thinking.
Transfer of Learning General and Specific Transfer Factors Affecting the Transfer of Learning Diversity: Learner Differences that Influence the Transfer of Complex Cognitive Processes Educational Psychology and Teaching: Applying an Understanding of Transfer with Your Students ▶ Developmentally Appropriate Practice: Developing Complex Cognitive Skills with Learners of Different Ages	**4.** Analyze factors that influence the transfer of learning.

The title of this chapter is "Complex Cognitive Processes," and *cognitive* implies "thinking," so this chapter focuses on complex forms of thinking. Definitions of *thinking* vary, but they typically include reasoning, solving problems, or reading and understanding conceptually demanding material (Willingham, 2009). We focus on these aspects of thinking in this chapter.

To begin, let's look at fourth graders as they try to solve—what is for them—a complex problem. Keep the students' thinking in mind as you read the case study.

Laura Hunter is working with her students on problem solving as she attempts to help them reach the following standard:

CCSS.Math.Content.4.MD.A.3 Apply the area and perimeter formulas for rectangles in real world and mathematical problems (Common Core State Standards Initiative, 2014t).

She gives them the problem of finding the area of the carpeted portion of their classroom, which has an irregular shape because parts of the floor are covered with linoleum (which are marked L in the drawing you see here).

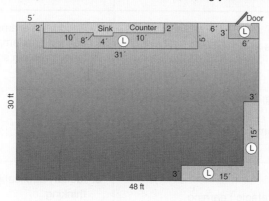

She begins the lesson on Monday by reviewing the concepts *area* and *perimeter* and then says, "When we try to solve a problem, we first need to identify what the problem actually is. . . . We're going to get new carpeting for this room, but we don't know how much to order, and your job is to figure that out."

Having identified the problem, Laura organizes her students into groups and asks them what they should do next. They decide that they first need to know the size of the room, so she has the groups measure the room and the different parts in it. She then gives each group a diagram (the one shown here) showing its dimensions and tells students that the places marked with an "L" are the parts of the floor covered with linoleum. She also displays the diagram on her document camera and says, "Okay, look at the diagram. . . . It represents our room and the carpeted area. . . . What's your next job?"

Nephi volunteers, "We didn't actually measure the area of the carpeted part; we just measured the perimeter. We need to figure out the area from our measurements."

Laura then tells the groups to work together to select a strategy for finding the carpeted area, and they go to work.

Different groups identify two strategies; one finding the area of the room and subtracting the areas covered with linoleum, and the other finding the area of an interior rectangle and then adding the extra areas of carpeting.

The students work in their groups, and after they're done, she has them report to the whole class. The different groups get the following areas for the carpeted portion: 1,173, 1,378, 1,347, 1,440, 1,169, and 1,600 square feet.

When asked if they are comfortable with the fact that the groups all got different answers, surprisingly, several say yes.

These results and the students' reactions raise the following questions:

1. Why did the groups get such varying answers to the same problem?
2. What should Laura now do to help her students improve their problem solving?
3. Because no group got the correct answer, was the time spent on the activity used wisely, or was it largely wasted?

The students' experiences and our questions help us understand why this chapter is titled "Complex Cognitive Processes." We examine these processes in the sections that follow, beginning with concept learning.

Concept Learning

Ed Psych and You

Look at the first list of 16 words below for 10 seconds. Cover up the list, and try to write down as many as you can remember in any order.

Then, do the same with the second list of 16 words. Which list is easier to remember? Why do you think so?

Here is the first list.

broom	work	salary	some
sooner	plug	jaw	fastener
jug	president	friend	evening
planet	else	salmon	destroy

Now, here is the second list:

north	blue	cucumber	quarter
celery	west	nickel	purple
red	penny	brown	east
dime	carrot	south	cauliflower

Think about the lists and our questions in *Ed Psych and You*. If you're like most people, you were able to recall more items from the second list than the first, because it was easy to classify the items into four simple categories—*directions, colors, vegetables,* and *coins.* The first list is difficult to categorize, so it is harder to remember.

Now, let's see how your experience relates to principles of cognitive learning theory. The principles are:

- Learning and development depend on experience.
- People want their experiences to make sense.
- To make sense of their experiences, people construct knowledge.
- The knowledge that people construct depends on what they already know.
- Social interaction facilitates learning.

For now, we'll focus on the first three. We all have experiences, and we want to make sense of them. So we construct knowledge. **Concepts**, mental representations of categories that allow us to identify examples and nonexamples of those categories, are some of the most basic forms of knowledge that we construct (Schunk, 2012). The categories—*directions, colors, vegetables,* and *coins*—that appear in the second list above are concepts. The idea of categorizing our experiences was pioneered by Jerome Bruner (1960, 1966, 1990), who argued that people interpret the world in terms of similarities and differences, ultimately forming concepts. Constructing concepts allows us to simplify the world, which also helps reduce the cognitive load on our working memories. Remembering the concept *coin,* for instance, imposes a lower cognitive load than remembering penny, nickel, dime, and quarter separately.

Concepts are the fundamental building blocks of our thinking, and they provide a foundation for more complex cognitive processes, such as problem solving (Schunk, 2012). Before they could find the area of the carpeted portion of their classroom, for example, Laura's students needed to understand that the concept *area* is a physical quantity describing the size of surfaces, such as those in Figure 8.1. The concept *area* allows us to think about and compare the surfaces of figures regardless of dimension or orientation.

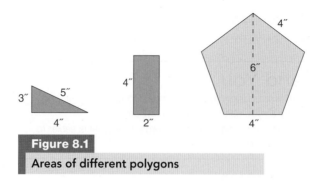

Figure 8.1

Areas of different polygons

Concepts represent a major portion of the school curriculum, and Table 8.1 includes examples in language arts, social studies, science, and math, and many others exist. For instance, students also study *rhythm* and *tempo* in music, *perspective* and *balance* in art, and *aerobic* and *isotonic exercises* in physical education. Other concepts such as *honesty, bias, love,* and *internal conflict* appear across the curriculum.

Theories of Concept Learning

Theorists offer different explanations for how people construct concepts. In this section, we examine *rule-driven* and *exemplar* theories, each explaining concept learning differently.

RULE-DRIVEN THEORY OF CONCEPT LEARNING

Rule-driven theory suggests that we construct concepts based on their attributes or **characteristics**—concepts' essential elements. For some concepts, such as *square, longitude,* or *adverb,* these elements are well-defined. For instance, *closed, equal sides,* and *equal angles* are the characteristics of the concept *square.* When we see plane figures with these characteristics, we classify them as squares based on the rule stating that squares must have these attributes. Other characteristics, such as size or color, aren't essential, so we don't consider them in making our classifications. Early researchers (e.g., Bruner, Goodnow, & Austin, 1956) investigated this rule-driven theory of concept learning and found that people differentiate concepts based on their defining characteristics. Because remembering a rule, such as saying an *adverb* must modify a verb, adjective, or other adverb, allows us to identify a huge number of adverbs based on that one simple rule, it doesn't impose a heavy load on working memory. This makes concept learning based on rules easier than those based on exemplars, which we examine next.

Table 8.1	Concepts in different content areas		
Language Arts	**Social Studies**	**Science**	**Math**
Adjective	Culture	Acid	Prime number
Verb	Longitude	Conifer	Equivalent fraction
Plot	Federalist	Element	Set
Simile	Democracy	Force	Addition
Infinitive	Immigrant	Inertia	Parabola

EXEMPLAR THEORY OF CONCEPT LEARNING

Many concepts don't have well-defined characteristics, so creating rules to help differentiate them is difficult. For instance, what are the characteristics of the concepts *Democrat* or *Republican*? They're familiar, but most people can't define them with any precision. Even common concepts, such as *car*, don't have precise characteristics. For instance, some people describe sport utility vehicles as cars, but others don't. And how about minivans, crossovers, or railroad "cars"?

A second theory of concept learning suggests that people don't construct concepts based on rules, but rather they store **exemplars**, the most highly typical examples of a concept (Radvansky & Ashcraft, 2014). For instance, prominent politicians may be exemplars for *Democrat* or *Republican;* popular autos, such as a Honda Accord, Toyota Camry, or Ford Mustang, might be stored as exemplars for the concept *car;* and a child may construct the concept *dog* by storing images of a golden retriever, cocker spaniel, collie, and German shepherd in memory as exemplars.

Exemplar theory helps explain how we construct concepts that don't have well-defined characteristics. It does have two disadvantages, however (Schunk, 2012). First, we may store a large number of exemplars for a concept in long-term memory, so when retrieved, they impose a heavy cognitive load on working memory. This makes elaborating on the concept more difficult than simply retrieving a rule, such as the rule for squares or adverbs. Second, for some concepts learners may store an incomplete set of exemplars, or even exemplars that are incorrect. For instance, if a child stored *eagle, hawk, robin,* and *cardinal,* but didn't store *penguin* or *ostrich* (birds that don't fly) for the concept *bird*, she would have an incomplete set of exemplars. On the other hand, if a child stored *dolphin* as one of his exemplars for the concept *fish,* he would be storing an incorrect exemplar.

Each theory explains different aspects of concept learning. For instance, concepts such as *square* or *odd number* are likely constructed based on their characteristics. Others, such as *car* or *dog,* are probably represented with exemplars.

Concept Learning: A Complex Cognitive Process

As you've read this section, you might have said to yourself, "Concept learning seems simple enough. Why is it described as a 'complex cognitive process'?" In fact, the thinking involved in constructing concepts is often more demanding and complex than it appears on the surface. For example, Paul taught a group of fourth graders the concept *arthropods,* animals such as insects, spiders, crabs, and lobsters, which have an *exoskeleton, three body parts,* and *jointed legs* as characteristics. After showing the students examples, such as a crab, beetle, and spider, and helping them identify the characteristics of arthropods, he showed them a clam and asked them if it was an arthropod. Surprisingly, several of the students said yes, reasoning that its hard shell was an exoskeleton. They didn't think about the fact that to be an arthropod an animal must have *all* the essential characteristics. He then asked them if their teacher was an arthropod, and again, some of them said yes, focusing on the fact that she had jointed legs.

Now, consider concepts such as *above, large, far,* and *right.* These concepts are "relational," meaning that they exist only in relation to other concepts (Schunk, 2012). For example, *above* exists only in relation to *below,* and *large* exists only in relation to *small.* In spite of the complexity of these concepts, we expect young children to learn them, as anyone who has watched *Sesame Street* knows. For example, Murray—the Muppet—sits next to a flowerpot and says, "Now, I'm *near*," then runs off in the distance and says, "Now, I'm *far.*"

These hard-to-learn concepts are important for future learning. For example, consider these problems:

$$\begin{array}{r} 76 \\ -\ 24 \\ \hline \end{array} \quad \text{and} \quad \begin{array}{r} 74 \\ -\ 26 \\ \hline \end{array}$$

If children don't understand relational ideas, they may get 52 for both answers by ignoring their location and simply subtracting the 4 from the 6 in each case.

Other forms of concept learning are also complex. For example, in math, the concept *integer* can be a negative number, a positive number, *or* zero. A polynomial can be a single number, such as 4, a number and variable, such as *4x,* or a more complex expression, such as $4x^2 + 2x + 3$. This either–or nature can be confusing for students. These examples help us understand why concept learning is indeed a complex cognitive process.

Educational Psychology and Teaching: Applying Theories of Concept Learning with Your Students

Concepts make up a substantial portion of the school curriculum, so promoting effective concept learning in our students is essential.

The following guidelines can help us in this process.

1. Promote meaningful learning by defining the concept and linking it to related concepts.
2. Provide a variety of examples and nonexamples of the concept.
3. Sequence the examples beginning with the most typical and ending with those least familiar.
4. Present the examples in a real-world context.

Now, let's see how Martina Lopez, a sixth-grade teacher, applies these guidelines as she attempts to help her students understand the concepts *fact, opinion,* and *reasoned judgment* and meet the standard:

CCSS.ELA-Literacy.RH.6-8.8 Distinguish among fact, opinion, and reasoned judgment in a text (Common Core State Standards Initiative, 2014c).

The class has been studying events leading to the Civil War, so Martina decides to use this topic as the context for studying the concepts.

She begins by saying, "The ability to distinguish among fact, opinion, and reasoned judgment is important in both school and in our lives outside of school, and it's also one that appears in the standards for this grade. . . . So that's what we're focusing on today," and she then displays the following on her document camera:

Fact: A statement that is based on observation or directly proven.
Example: Diet soda contains less sugar than regular soda.

Opinion: A statement that describes a belief that depends on a person's personal perspective, feelings, or desires.
Example: Diet soda tastes bland compared to regular soda.

Reasoned judgment: An assertion or conclusion that is supported by objective information.
Example: Diet soda is preferable to regular soda because it contains fewer calories.

After giving the students a couple minutes to study the definitions and examples, she has the students explain the differences among the three concepts. After some discussion she then displays the following:

Eli Whitney invented the cotton gin in 1793. This reduced the amount of time it took to separate the cotton seeds from the cotton fibers. As a result, raising cotton became very profitable, so the South became a one-crop economy that depended on cotton. As it turns out, the lack of variety in the Southern economy was a big mistake.

Abraham Lincoln was the best president in our country's history. He was president from 1861 until his assassination in 1865. One of Lincoln's primary accomplishments was getting the 13th amendment to the Constitution passed, because it permanently outlawed slavery.

"Look at the information you see on the document camera. . . . Think about it and identify an example of a fact. . . . Juanita?"

". . . Eli Whitney invented the cotton gin in 1793," Juanita responds.

Martina has the students identify other facts in the text, and then does the same with opinions and reasoned judgments.

After Jeremy identifies the statement "One of Lincoln's primary accomplishments was passing the 13th amendment to the Constitution" as a reasoned judgment, Martina asks, "What makes this a reasoned judgment? . . . Kristie?"

". . . It says, 'because it permanently outlawed slavery,' so that is some information that supports the conclusion about Lincoln's accomplishments."

Martina then has the students provide rationales for the other examples they identify as reasoned judgments, they summarize what they've done, and she closes the lesson.

Now, let's examine Martina's efforts to implement the guidelines.

Define the Concept and Link it to Related Concepts. Martina began her lesson by noting that the ability to distinguish among fact, opinion, and reasoned judgment is important, both in and out of school, and she then displayed definitions of the three concepts together with an example of each. Each definition contained the essential characteristics of the concepts, and by presenting the three definitions together, she linked fact, opinion, and reasoned judgment—concepts that are closely related and sometimes confused—to each other.

Provide a Variety of Examples and Nonexamples of the Concept. Regardless of a concept's complexity or the theory that explains concept learning, our students will construct their understanding of a concept based on the examples we present, combined with nonexamples that help them differentiate the concept from others that are closely related. For instance, if you want your students to understand the concept *reptile,* you would use positive examples, such as an alligator, turtle (both sea and land, so they don't conclude that all reptiles live on land), lizard, and snake. You would also include a *frog* as a nonexample, because many people believe frogs are reptiles. Similarly, if you're teaching the concept *metaphor,* you would include a variety of metaphors, combined with *similes* as nonexamples, because *metaphors* and *similes* are closely related and often confused with each other.

Martina presented the definitions of fact, opinion, and reasoned judgment together, and by doing so, examples of opinions and reasoned judgments served as nonexamples of facts, and the same applied for the other two concepts. This made her instruction efficient and made the concepts more meaningful for her students.

Martina also provided at least two examples of each. For instance, the following are examples of facts that she included:

- Eli Whitney invented the cotton gin in 1793.
- This reduced the amount of time it took to separate the cotton seeds from the cotton fibers.
- He [Lincoln] was president from 1861 until his assassination in 1865.

Opinions included:

- The lack of variety in the Southern economy was a big mistake.
- Abraham Lincoln was the best president in our country's history.

And, the following were examples of reasoned judgments:

- The South became a one-crop economy that depended on cotton.
- One of Lincoln's primary accomplishments was getting the 13th amendment to the Constitution passed.

In teaching concepts, some experts suggest that we should present a sequence of examples and guide students' constructions of the concept, and this is the approach advocated by Jerome Bruner (1960, 1966). Others suggest that presenting a definition and then illustrating it with examples is more effective, an approach preferred by David Ausubel (1963, 1977). Martina chose the strategy advocated by Ausubel, but either approach can be effective.

Sequence the Examples Beginning with the Most Typical and Ending with the Least Familiar. Martina also sequenced the examples so the most obvious fact, such as "Eli Whitney invented the cotton gin in 1793," appeared first in the passage, and more nuanced examples, such as, "One of Lincoln's primary accomplishments was getting the 13th amendment to the Constitution passed, because it permanently outlawed slavery"— which included both a reasoned judgment and a fact—were displayed at the end of the text. Sequencing examples this way capitalizes on elaboration as an encoding strategy by helping students link less-obvious examples to those that are clear and concrete.

Present Examples in a Real-World Context. Finally, by embedding the examples and nonexamples in the context of the historical passage, Martina helped her students see how fact, opinion, and reasoned judgment apply in the world outside of school. Presenting the examples this way also helped her directly focus on the standard, which emphasized that learners are to distinguish among the concepts *in a text*.

Martina grounded her lesson in the principles of cognitive learning theory and our understanding of human memory. Her examples provided the experiences the students needed to construct their knowledge of the concepts, the examples made sense to the students, and they also provided the background knowledge students needed to construct their understanding of the concepts.

Finally, she capitalized on the social nature of learning by using questioning to place her students in cognitively active roles—to *think* about what they were doing. Involving her students in this way also reduced the cognitive load on their working memories, because she couldn't move through the learning activity any faster than the students could correctly answer her questions. Her examples combined with the social interaction made the information meaningful to the students and helped them encode the concepts in their long-term memories.

Classroom Connections

Promoting Concept Learning in Schools

1. Examples provide learners with the experiences they need to construct concepts. To connect concepts to the real world, use realistic examples that include all the information learners need to understand the concept.

   - Elementary: To illustrate the concept *mammal,* a second-grade teacher brings a hamster to class and has the students feel and pet it. He also has the students think about themselves, and he shows pictures of a horse, dog, bat, dolphin, and seal. He also includes pictures of an eagle, lizard, and salmon as nonexamples.

   - Middle School: An eighth-grade English teacher provides her students with examples of verbals—gerunds, participles, and infinitives—to help them understand their function in general, as well as how they work in particular sentences.

   - High School: A tennis coach is helping his students learn how to serve. He videotapes several people, some with good serves and others less skilled. He shows students the videotapes and asks them to identify the differences in the serves.

2. To help make concepts meaningful, link new concepts to related concepts.

- ■ **Elementary:** A kindergarten teacher wants her class to understand that living things exist in many different forms. She tells her children that they themselves, as well as pets and plants in their classroom, are living things. In a discussion they identify "the ability to grow and change" and "the need for food and water" as two characteristics the examples have in common.

- ■ **Middle School:** To help his students understand the relationships between descriptive and persuasive writing, an English teacher displays paragraphs illustrating each and asks the class to identify their similarities and differences.

- ■ **High School:** A social studies teacher instructs her students to compare cultural revolutions to other revolutions, such as the Industrial Revolution, the American Revolution, and the technological revolution, pointing out similarities and differences in each case.

Ed Psych and You

What do the following have in common?

- You want to send a birthday card to a friend who has moved to New York, but you don't know her address.
- You're in a romantic relationship, but the relationship isn't very satisfying.
- You're taking classes, but also have a job, and you never seem to have enough time for anything.

Problem Solving

To begin this section, let's look at the examples in *Ed Psych and You*. They each illustrate a **problem**, which exists when people have a goal but don't have an obvious—or automatic—way to reach the goal (Schunk, 2012). For instance, the goals are accessing your friend's address, making your relationship more satisfying, and finding more time in your life. Laura's students, in the lesson at the beginning of the chapter, also faced a problem, the goal for which was finding the area of the carpeted portion of their classroom. This broad view of problem solving reminds us that problems are a part of our daily lives, and we can apply general, effective strategies to solve them.

Well-Defined and Ill-Defined Problems

Experts distinguish between **well-defined problems**, problems with clear goals, only one correct solution, and a certain method for finding it, and **ill-defined problems**, problems with ambiguous goals, more than one acceptable solution, and no generally agreed-upon strategy for reaching a solution (Radvansky & Ashcraft, 2014; Mayer & Wittrock, 2006). Our first example in *Ed Psych and You* is well-defined; your friend has only one address, and a straightforward strategy for finding it exists. Many problems in math, physics, and chemistry are well-defined.

On the other hand, your unsatisfactory relationship, and lack of time to do anything other than work and study, are ill-defined problems, because your goals aren't clear. For instance, you want your relationship to be more satisfying, but what does that mean? Perhaps you want to communicate more openly, spend more time together, or feel better emotionally when you're together. In our third example, lack of time "for anything" is also vague. Do you want more time to study? To exercise? To simply kick back and relax?

Because the goals in ill-defined problems are ambiguous, no straightforward solutions exist for them. For instance, in the case of your relationship, you might try to talk to your partner about your feelings, consider couples' counseling, or even end the relationship. With respect to your lack of time, you might try to use your time more wisely, cut back on your work hours if possible, drop a class, or even take a semester off from school.

A bit of a paradox with problem solving also exists. Our formal training with problem solving largely occurs in schools, but most of our experiences there involve well-defined problems. For instance, students in elementary schools are asked to solve problems such as the following:

> Jeremy and Melinda are saving up so they can go to iTunes to buy some of their favorite songs. They need 15 dollars. Jeremy has saved 5 dollars, and Melinda has saved 7. How much more money do they have to save to get their 15 dollars?

In high school, students solve problems such as this one:

> Kelsey and Mitch are dating but live in different cities, and they adopt the same cell phone plan. Over one billing period, Kelsey used 45 peak minutes and 50 nonpeak minutes, and her bill was $27.75. Mitch used 70 peak minutes and 30 nonpeak minutes at a charge of $36. What is the peak and the nonpeak rate in their cell phone plan?

Even though the second is more complex, both are well-defined.

On the other hand, in life we face problems related to money, careers, social relationships, and personal happiness, and they are usually ill-defined. Our lack of experience in solving problems such as these helps us understand why so many people struggle with these issues (Mienaltowski, 2011; Schraw, Dunkle, & Bendixen, 2006).

The Problem-Solving Process

Some learning theorists believe that most human learning involves problem solving (Radvansky & Ashcraft, 2014), and problem solving is one of the most thoroughly researched areas in the study of learning and teaching. A number of approaches to solving problems exist, including, among others, mathematician George Pólya's famous *How to Solve It* (1957) as well as more recent efforts of other well-known researchers (e.g., Bransford & Stein, 1993; Mayer & Wittrock, 2006; Montague, 2003). The approaches are similar and, although slightly different language may be used, they typically include the steps outlined in Figure 8.2. Experts have applied these steps to problems varying from well-defined problems in math and science to ill-defined problems with school leadership (Canter, 2004),

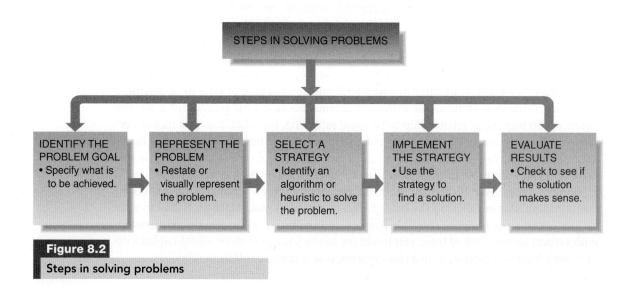

Figure 8.2

Steps in solving problems

counseling in response to classroom management issues (Dwairy, 2005), efforts to make businesses more productive (Leclerc & Moldoveanu, 2013), and even family therapy (Williamson, Hanna, Lavner, Bradbury, & Karney, 2013). We turn to these steps next.

Identify the Problem Goal. Problem solving begins when a problem solver has a goal but lacks an obvious or automatic way of reaching the goal. Understanding the problem so the goal can be identified is the first step. The *central executive*—the supervisory system in working memory that controls the flow of information to and from long-term memory— is essential in this process. For instance, appropriate information must be retrieved from long-term memory, and the meaning of the problem must be encoded. The central executive controls this process, but it sometimes goes awry. For instance, consider the following problem, which was presented to a group of second graders.

> There are 26 sheep and 10 goats on a ship. How old is the captain?

In one study, 75% of the children answered 36 (cited in Prawat, 1989)! Obviously, the students didn't understand the problem.

In some cases, identifying the problem goal is straightforward, such as it was in Laura's lesson. In other cases, particularly when working with ill-defined problems, it can be one of the most difficult aspects of problem solving (Jitendra et al., 2007), and even advanced university students have trouble with this step (Naci, 2013).

When attempting to solve ill-defined problems, identifying subgoals can be a helpful first step. Then, as we reach each subgoal, we eventually solve our problem. For instance, suppose you identify spending more time together, improving communication, and feeling better emotionally as subgoals in the problem of your dissatisfying relationship. In doing so you've better defined your problem with clear goals.

Represent the Problem. If a problem is complex, it can be helpful to represent it in ways that make it more meaningful, such as stating it in more familiar terms, relating it to problems you've previously experienced, or, if possible, representing it visually, which is probably the most effective.

Representing a problem visually capitalizes on the fact that working memory has both a visual and a verbal processor that "distribute" the processing task across the two components and reduce cognitive load on problem solvers (Clark & Mayer, 2003; Moreno & Duran, 2004). For instance, consider the following problem:

> Find the area of a pentagon with a base of 3 inches, a vertical height of 2 inches, and a total height of 4 inches.

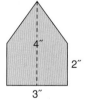

Without a diagram this might be difficult for many students, but with it, such as the one shown to the right, the problem becomes straightforward, and solving it is much easier.

Select a Strategy. After identifying and representing the problem, we need to select a strategy for solving it. If a problem is well-defined, an **algorithm**, a specific step or set of steps for finding the solution, can be used. For example, to find the area of a rectangle, we follow a simple algorithm—multiply the length times the width—and we use other simple algorithms when we solve problems such as adding fractions with unlike denominators or finding the percent decrease of a marked-down retail item. In a similar way, computer experts use complex algorithms to solve sophisticated, but well-defined, programming problems.

Many problems can't be solved with algorithms, because algorithms don't exist for ill-defined problems or for some that are well-defined. In those cases, problem solvers use heuristics, general, widely applicable problem-solving strategies (Chronicle, MacGregor, & Ormerod, 2004). The more complex and unfamiliar the task, the greater the need for heuristics (Lee & Reigeluth, 2003).

Several widely applicable heuristics exist. Trial and error is one. It's primitive and inefficient, but it gives learners practice in grappling with problems, and many people use it as a first step in trying to solve problems that are unfamiliar (Davidson & Sternberg, 2003).

Drawing analogies, a strategy used to solve unfamiliar problems by comparing them with those already solved, is a second heuristic (Mayer, 2002). It can be difficult to implement, however, because learners often can't retrieve problems from their long-term memories that are analogous to the one they want to solve, or they may make inappropriate connections between the two problems.

Means–ends analysis, a strategy that breaks the problem into subgoals and works successively on each, is another heuristic that is effective for solving ill-defined problems, and this is what you might use in attempting to solve your dissatisfying-romantic-relationship problem. Even this can be difficult, however. For instance, you identified spending more time together, improving communication, and feeling better emotionally as subgoals. What strategy, or strategies, will you use to feel better emotionally, for example? No easy answers to this question exist, but you must identify clear and workable strategies, or reaching the subgoal will be virtually impossible. This is the case for many ill-defined problems.

Teaching heuristics can improve your students' problem-solving abilities, even with early elementary students (Hohn & Frey, 2002), but ultimately, prior knowledge and practice with problem solving are essential for successfully selecting a strategy, and no heuristic can replace them (Lester, 2013).

Implement the Strategy. Having selected a strategy, problem solvers are now ready to implement it. If the problem goal is clear, the strategy for reaching it is understandable and specific, and the problem is represented effectively, implementing the strategy is straightforward.

Even then, difficulties may exist, however. To see how this occurs, we turn to an interview with four of Laura's students after the lesson. The interviewer showed the students the figures to the left, and then began questioning them.

Interviewer:	What do we mean by perimeter? . . . Show us on one of these figures. . . . Yashoda?
Yashoda:	It's the distance around the figure, like here (moving her finger around the rectangle and then the pentagon).
Interviewer:	So, what is the perimeter here (pointing to the rectangle)? . . . Erica?
Erica:	. . . 12. . . . I added 4 and 4 and 2 and 2.
Interviewer:	How about the perimeter of this (pointing to the pentagon)? . . . Hasan?
Hasan:	. . . 9. . . . I added 3 and 1 and 1 and 2 and 2.
Interviewer:	Now, what do we mean by area? . . . Show us. . . . Daniel?
Daniel:	It's like if you covered it up with paper or something (moving his hand back and forth over the rectangle). It's how much you need to cover it up.
Interviewer:	So, what is the area of the rectangle?
Daniel:	. . . 8. I multiplied 4 times 2 because the area is the length times the width.
Interviewer:	Good. So, how would you find the area of this (pointing to the pentagon)? . . . Yashoda?
Yashoda:	(After thinking for several seconds) I would multiply the 3 times the 1, which would be 3, and then I would take that times 2 (pointing at the 2 in the figure), so the area would be 6.
Interviewer:	How do the rest of you feel about that?
The others nod, agreeing that Yashoda's strategy makes sense.	

This interview helps us begin to answer the first question we asked at the beginning of the chapter: "Why did the groups get such varying answers to the same problem?" Lack of background knowledge is the obvious answer, but some subtle distinctions exist. For instance, the students had declarative knowledge about the concept *area;* Daniel's explanation of area, for example—"It's like if you covered it up with paper or something. It's how much you need to cover it up"—was valid and sensible. And when students were asked to calculate the area of the rectangle, they were quickly able to do so. However, because they hadn't encountered more complex shapes in their problem-solving efforts, they used the same strategy for finding the area of the pentagon. So, since they multiplied 4×2 to find the area of the rectangle, they multiplied $3 \times 1 \times 2$ to find the area of the pentagon.

Cognitive learning theory helps explain the students' thinking. The knowledge we construct depends on what we already know, so the students—incorrectly—applied what they knew about finding the area of the rectangle to finding the area of the pentagon. They lacked the background knowledge needed to find the area of a more complex shape. This contributed to their struggle with finding the area of the carpeted portion of their classroom.

Evaluate the Results. Evaluating results is the final step in effective problem solving, and it requires that our students think about their results (Lester, 2013; Mayer & Wittrock, 2006; Schraw et al., 2006). Often, they simply don't, as we saw in the example with the second graders adding the number of sheep and goats on a ship to get the age of the captain. We also saw this tendency in Laura's students. For instance, Laura's classroom was 48 feet long and 30 feet wide, so its area was 1,440 square feet. Yet, one group got an answer of 1,600 square feet for *the carpeted portion of the classroom*—160 square feet more than the area of the entire room. And they were perfectly satisfied with their answer! This tendency is understandably maddening for teachers. Also, students tend to accept answers they see on calculator screens whether or not the answers make sense, and this problem is becoming more prominent as students increasingly rely on technology for basic mathematical operations (Lester, 2013). (We offer suggestions for dealing with these issues in the section "Educational Psychology and Teaching: Helping Your Students Become Better Problem Solvers" later in the chapter.)

Creativity

As we said earlier in this section, most of the problems we face in life are ill-defined, and solving them often requires original thinking and solutions. This leads us to the concept of **creativity**, the ability to produce original works or solutions to problems that are productive and task appropriate (Beghetto & Kaufman, 2013). *Original* implies that the action is not learned from someone else, *productive* means that the product or solution is useful in our culture, and *task appropriate* means that the result of the creative process, such as a unique problem solution, concrete product, written document, or new idea, meets a set of task requirements. "Teachers who understand that creativity combines both originality and task appropriateness are in a better position to integrate student creativity into the everyday curriculum in ways that complement, rather than compete with, academic learning" (Beghetto & Kaufman, 2013, p. 12). As an example, Dan Stevens, a physics teacher, attempted to promote creative thought in his students when they conducted their labs. After the students completed the required portion of the lab, he told them to design and complete an extension of the experiment that wasn't described as an original part of the lab. Significantly, the students not only performed well with respect to this requirement, but they reported that designing and conducting these extensions were the most fun and interesting aspects of their lab work. (Based on a conversation Paul, one of your authors, had with a teacher taking one of his classes.)

This simple teaching example meets the criteria for creativity. Dan's students had to create original investigations (they didn't get the ideas from someone else), the investigations were productive, and they were conducted within the framework of their labs, so they were task appropriate.

The creative process exists on a continuum. At one end, for instance, it involves unique, personal interpretations, such as Dan's students extending their lab investigations, a student's insight into a different approach to solving a math problem, or a company employee designing a new marketing strategy. At the other end, it might result in a time-honored symphony, great work of art, Pulitzer Prize–winning piece of literature, or contribution to science, such as Einstein's general theory of relativity (Kaufman & Beghetto, 2009). Both ends and everything in between are important, and most of the creativity that exists in schools and in our daily lives involves individual, personal interpretations (Beghetto & Kaufman, 2013).

MEASURING CREATIVITY

Historically, creativity has usually been measured by giving students a picture or object and asking them to generate responses, such as listing as many uses for a brick as possible (e.g., doorstop, bookshelf, paperweight, weapon, building block), or suggesting ways to improve a common object such as a chair (Davis et al., 2011). These methods of measuring creativity are controversial, with critics charging that existing tests are too narrow and fail to capture its varying aspects (Tannenbaum, 2003).

Other approaches, attempting to respond to these criticisms, have used self-report measures to examine creativity. They also attempt to broaden the view of creativity to include creative products, creative thinking, creative traits, and creative behavior and accomplishments in their assessments (Silvia, Wigert, Reiter-Palmon, & Kaufman, 2012).

The nature of creativity makes it difficult to determine, in advance, whether a person is—or will be—creative, so formal measures of creativity will likely remain controversial. More probable is that we will continue to measure it informally as we've always done, that is, we will recognize examples of creativity when we see them. And more important than attempts to measure creativity are environments that encourage it. We consider these environments next.

ENVIRONMENTS THAT ENCOURAGE CREATIVITY

Discussions of creativity may lead to the impression that it should be encouraged and expressed—both in schools and in the workplace—at all times. This isn't true, however (Beghetto, 2010; Kaufman, 2009). For example, you go to a dental office for a routine teeth-cleaning procedure, or you take your car in for an oil change. Do you want your dental hygienist or mechanic to be "creative" in cleaning your teeth or changing the oil? Probably not. In cases like these we prefer that they conform to a routine procedure. On the other hand, if the mechanic, for example, discovers a problem with our car engine that could involve a costly repair, we would much appreciate a creative alternative that would be less costly.

This relates to the concept of metacognition, which is important for learning in general, and for problem solving and creativity, in particular. Creativity is important and valuable, but it must be applied judiciously (Beghetto, 2010; Kaufman, 2009).

So, what are the personal and environmental conditions that promote judicious creativity? Research provides some insights. First, at a personal level, divergent thinking, the ability to generate a variety of alternate, original solutions to questions or problems, is an important component of creativity (Davis, Rim, & Siegle, 2011). And people who think divergently have two important characteristics. First, they possess a great deal of domain-specific knowledge. It's impossible to think creatively in the absence of knowledge, and people who are creative in one domain, such as art, may not be in another, such as writing or music. Second, divergent thinkers are intrinsically motivated. They're curious and committed, and they have a passion for the task. Creativity is not an innate talent; rather it is developed through years of practice and commitment (Elder & Paul, 2007).

At a broader contextual level, creativity can suffer when people are promised rewards for creative work, when learning conditions stress competition and social comparisons, or when individuals are highly aware of being monitored and evaluated by others. Conversely, creativity generally thrives in environments that provide challenging tasks and support personal interest, involvement, and enjoyment (Hennessey & Amabile, 2010).

These conditions are important, because attempts at creativity involve risk. For instance, when a student shares a new and personally meaningful perspective on how to solve a problem, she risks being laughed at by her peers or having her idea dismissed or misunderstood by her teacher. It doesn't take many incidents for students to learn that it's not worth the effort and risk to share personal ideas; rather it's easier to conform and provide the suggestions or solutions that teachers and other students expect.

From a teaching perspective, the following are some suggestions for fostering creativity in our students:

- Creating a safe environment where students feel free to risk offering unique ideas and opinions. Communicating that creativity is valued, expressing enthusiasm in response to unusual ideas, and rewarding students for original thinking.
- Helping learners develop their domain-specific knowledge, which provides the raw materials for creativity.
- Avoiding social comparisons when assessing learning, increasing the number of assessments to reduce the pressure on any single assessment, and emphasizing the role of assessment in promoting learning (Elder & Paul, 2007; Hennessey & Amabile, 2010; VanDeWeghe, 2007).

Teachers sometimes complain that the emphasis on standards and high-stakes testing reduces opportunities to be creative or encourage creativity in students. This doesn't have to be the case. Creativity in teaching is the ability to find, or develop, original ways to explain and illustrate the topics being taught, regardless of the emphasis on standards and accountability. Dan's effort with his physics students is an example. It was original, productive, and task appropriate, so it met the criteria for creativity, but perhaps more importantly, it was simple, and he didn't have to spend any time preparing it. Fostering creativity in students depends more on the kind of learning environment you create than on whether or not they're expected to meet certain standards (Kaufman & Sternberg, 2007).

Educational Psychology and Teaching: Helping Your Students Become Better Problem Solvers

As we attempt to create better ways to teach problem solving, we realize that we have an ill-defined problem of our own. Our goal is to help our students become effective problem solvers, but often they aren't very good at it. In fact, developing students' problem-solving abilities is one of the most challenging aspects of teaching (Lester, 2013). Let's look at this challenge in a bit more depth.

CHALLENGES IN TEACHING PROBLEM SOLVING

Two aspects of teaching problem solving contribute to this challenge. They are (1) experience and background knowledge, and (2) people's thinking.

Ed Psych and You

You want to buy a new smartphone, and you're faced with the problem of finding the one that best meets your needs, yet isn't too costly. What features are you looking for? What carrier offers the best service for the least cost? What kind of problem is this?

Background Knowledge. Think about the questions we asked in *Ed Psych and You.* What do you need in order to be able to answer them? Background knowledge is the answer. The better you understand the features you're looking for, and the more you know about the options available from different carriers, the easier solving your problem will be.

Regardless of whether our problems are well-defined or ill-defined, background knowledge is essential for solving them, and lack of background knowledge is almost always an issue in teaching problem solving (Lester, 3013). We saw how lack of background knowledge impacted Laura's students as they attempted to solve their problem.

People's Thinking. A second challenge in problem solving involves our thinking. For instance, think again about your problem of selecting a new smartphone. A salesperson might encourage a more expensive one—because he or she will make more money—with more features than we need or will ever use. So, because we didn't think carefully enough about the problem, we spend money unnecessarily.

The issue of mindset is particularly important in schools, and one of the most frustrating aspects of the process is students' tendencies to accept answers whether or not they make sense. We saw this tendency illustrated in the example with the second graders, who added the number of sheep and goats to get the age of the captain, and we also saw it in Laura's students. It's an ongoing issue in attempts to help students become better problem solvers.

Students' tendencies to use superficial strategies for solving problems is an additional challenge (Gamo, Sander, & Richard, 2010). For instance, the tendency to look for key words, such as *altogether,* which suggests addition, or *how many more,* which implies subtraction, is a common strategy. Others include using the operation most recently taught or looking at cues in the chapter headings of the text. These strategies can bypass understanding completely, yet are often quite successful (Schoenfeld, 1991).

Knowing that background knowledge is a pervasive issue and that our students have a tendency to use superficial strategies for solving problems and accept answers whether or not they make sense, we turn now to strategies for improving our students problem-solving abilities.

STRATEGIES FOR DEVELOPING STUDENTS' PROBLEM SOLVING

We know from principles of cognitive learning theory that *learning and development depend on experience, we want our experiences to make sense, we construct knowledge, the knowledge we construct depends on what we already know,* and *social interaction promotes understanding.* If we use these principles as a framework, the following strategies can help improve our students' problem-solving abilities.

1. Present problems in real-world contexts, and provide practice in identifying problem goals.
2. Develop students' expertise with deliberate practice and worked examples.
3. Capitalize on social interaction to engage students and monitor their learning progress.
4. Encourage sense making in the problem-solving process.

Let's see what these suggestions look like in the classroom.

Present Problems in Real-World Contexts, and Provide Practice in Identifying Problem Goals. To help our students become better problem solvers, we need to provide two forms of practice. First, they must practice solving problems immersed in real-world contexts. An emerging field of study in educational psychology called the *learning sciences* is placing increased emphasis on learning as it exists in real-world settings. Leaders in this field argue that education in our country has, for too long, emphasized fact learning and memorized procedures, and this approach is no longer adequate for our 21st century technological world (Sawyer, 2006). This makes sense. Solving problems, such as the one Laura posed for her students, will obviously result in deeper and more useful understanding than will solving a series of abstract addition, subtraction, multiplication, and division problems.

Second, students need practice in identifying problem goals (Lester, 2013). This is a challenge, because, as we said earlier, most of the problems students encounter in schools are well-defined. Mixing the types of problems you're asking students to solve can be a useful first step (Taylor & Rohrer, 2010). For instance, when elementary students learn to add fractions, they typically first practice with problems with like denominators and then move to problems with unlike denominators. This is followed by practice with subtraction, multiplication, and division. Simply mixing these problems will encourage deeper thought and help prevent students' tendencies to use superficial strategies. So, an assignment might include problems such as the following:

$$\frac{3}{5} - \frac{2}{5} = \qquad \frac{2}{3} + \frac{3}{4} = \qquad \frac{4}{7} \div \frac{3}{4} = \qquad \frac{5}{6} \times \frac{2}{3} =$$

Then, students could be given real-world problems requiring the same operations. This strategy won't immediately make students expert problem solvers, but it's a good first step.

You can also present students with problems outside the context of math, and one of the benefits of working on problems such as these is that they're usually ill-defined and virtually always set in real-world contexts. For instance, you might have your students work on a problem such as the following:

> A new girl, named Rosalina, has recently joined our class. She is a native Spanish speaker, and she struggles with English. She is quite shy and appears to be uneasy in our class. So, we're faced with the problem of making her feel more at ease and welcome in school. What can we do to solve the problem?

This is an ill-defined real-world problem, and practicing solving problems such as this one provides students with valuable experience in social problem solving. Problem solving need not be restricted to math in the elementary schools and math, chemistry, and physics in the high schools.

Develop Students' Expertise with Deliberate Practice and Worked Examples.
Increasing learners' expertise is the general goal of all schooling. Experts are individuals who are highly knowledgeable or skilled in a specific domain, such as math, history, chess, or teaching. The term *specific domain* is important. An expert in math, for example, may be a novice in teaching or history, because a great deal of time and effort are required to develop expertise. "Experts are made, not born. This is not to say that intellectual ability and talent do not exist, or are unimportant, but that effort, deliberate practice, and feedback from experts are essential to the development of high-level expertise" (Schraw, 2006, p. 255).

The idea in the previous paragraph is important. Deliberate practice is a systematic approach to the development of a wide range of abilities including music, art, athletics, and academic skills, such as writing, problem solving, critical thinking, and others. Deliberate practice has the following components (Colvin, 2010; Ericsson, 2003):

- The practice is goal directed. We identify the skills we want to improve and practice those skills extensively.
- The practice focuses on understanding and sense making rather than rote drill.
- The practice is systematic, requiring learners to practice frequently until they have overlearned the idea.

- Learners practice in real-world settings.
- Learners receive extensive feedback.

Research also suggests that **interspersed practice**, the process of mixing the practice of different skills, is superior to **blocked practice**, practicing one skill extensively and then moving to a different one (Taylor & Rohrer, 2010). For instance, if elementary students are practicing subtraction problems that require regrouping, such as 45 − 27, their learning will be enhanced if they are also given subtraction problems that don't require regrouping, such as 74 − 43, as well as addition problems that do and do not require regrouping. This applies in all domains. For example, soccer practice is more effective if players practice dribbling for a few minutes, passing for a few more, goal scoring for an additional time, and then return to each skill instead of massing practice on a particular skill and then turning to a different one. "Students will improve as problem solvers only if they are given opportunities to solve a variety of types of problematic tasks" (Lester, 2013, p. 272).

Simply, if our students are to increase their problem-solving expertise, they need a great deal of practice in solving a variety of problems over an extended period of time.

Worked examples, problems with completed solutions, provide us with an additional tool for implementing deliberate practice. To see how, let's look at the efforts of David Chin, a fifth-grade teacher, who is working with his students on the standard:

CCSS.Math.Content.5.NF.A.1 Add and subtract fractions with unlike denominators (including mixed numbers) by replacing given fractions with equivalent fractions in such a way as to produce an equivalent sum or difference of fractions with like denominators (Common Core State Standards Initiative, 2014u).

He begins by displaying the following on his document camera.

We're at a party, and our host serves pizza. She orders several pizzas, all of which are the same size, but some are cut into six pieces and others cut into 8 pieces. You eat 2 pieces from a pizza cut into six pieces, and 1 piece from a pizza cut into 8 pieces. How much pizza did you eat?

Step 1:

$$\frac{2}{6} + \frac{1}{8} =$$

Step 2:

$$\frac{2}{6} = \frac{8}{24}$$

Step 3:

$$\frac{1}{8} = \frac{3}{24}$$

Step 4:

$$\frac{8}{24} + \frac{3}{24} = \frac{11}{24}$$

"Now, let's look at our problem," David begins. "Read the problem and then look at step 1."

He waits for a moment and then asks, "Where did we get the 2/6 and the 1/8 in step 1? . . . Lenore?"

". . . It's the amount of pizza we ate. We ate two sixths of one pizza and one eighth of another."

"Now look at steps 2 and 3. Why did we do these steps? Why were they necessary? . . . Take a few minutes to check with your partner and see if you know.

"Derek, what did you and your partner conclude," David asks after a few minutes.

". . . We need to have the same denominator," Derek responds hesitantly after peering at the steps for several seconds.

David continues guiding the students, asking them to explain each step as they go, and ends the activity by asking, "So, what did we find out? . . . Juanita?"

"We ate 11/24ths of a pizza altogether."

Research with learners ranging from lower elementary to university students indicates that worked examples can make problem solving more meaningful than traditional instruction, particularly when students are first learning a procedure (Ngu & Yeung, 2013; Shen & Tsai, 2009). And worked examples have also been shown effective when combined with other resources, such as technology (Reed, Corbett, Hoffman, Wagner, & MacClaren, 2013).

Using worked examples in this way applies cognitive learning theory. The worked examples provided David's students with the experiences they needed to help them construct their understanding of the procedure; each step made sense to them; and David used social interaction in the form of learning pairs to walk them through the process.

Students often prefer worked examples to traditional instruction (Renkl, Stark, Gruber, & Mandl, 1998; Van Gog & Kester, 2013), and David's activity helps us understand why. Students prefer learning experiences that make sense to them, and where they're successful, to trial and error or those where they memorize a set of steps with little understanding.

Capitalize on Social Interaction to Engage Students and Monitor Their Learning Progress. At the beginning of the chapter we saw how Laura's students struggled with their problem, as indicated by their widely varying answers. Now, let's return to her class the next day—Tuesday—to see how she modifies her instruction.

She begins by saying, "Let's look at our diagram again," as she displays the following diagram on the document camera.

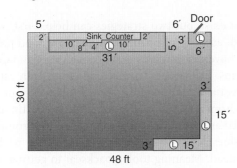

The class agrees to try the first strategy: Find the area of the room, and subtract the parts with the linoleum (marked "L"). So, using the diagram Laura first has them calculate the area of the room.

She watches to see that they get 1,440 square feet and then asks, "What do we do next?"

The students agree that they must subtract the parts marked "L," and they suggest starting at the top of the diagram.

"How will we find the area of this part? . . . Fred?" Laura asks.

". . . Multiply 31 times 5."

"Why? . . . Tu?"

". . . That part is a rectangle, and it's 31 feet long and 5 feet wide, . . . so we multiply them," Tu responds.

The students calculate the area, and she checks to be sure they all get 155 square feet. She then has them repeat the process with the portion by the door, where they get 18 square feet, and the portion at the lower right, where they get 81 square feet.

"Now what? . . . Nephi?" Laura asks.

"We need to add the 155, 18, and 81, and then subtract them from 1,440."

Laura has Nephi explain her thinking, the students add the 155, 18, and 81 to get a total of 254 square feet, which they subtract from 1,440 to get an area of 1,186 square feet for the carpeted portion of the classroom.

The interaction with her students is the most significant aspect of this learning activity. Monday's lesson made Laura realize that her students needed more scaffolding, and she provided it as she worked with them on Tuesday. But she didn't simply explain what they should do to find the area of the carpeted portion of their classroom. Rather, she guided them with her questioning. This interaction is essential for two reasons. First, it puts students in cognitively active roles and applies the cognitive learning principle: *Social interaction facilitates learning.* Second, the interaction allowed Laura to informally assess her students' learning progress. If, for example, her students had not been able to explain where they got the 155, 18, and 81, she could intervene and provide more scaffolding.

Laura's Monday lesson reminds us, however, that interaction—as with many other aspects of teaching, such as group work—isn't automatically effective. Her students were interacting in groups in her Monday lesson, but much of the interaction was unproductive. She provided much more structure and guidance in her Tuesday lesson while simultaneously maintaining the interaction. Research indicates that effective instruction involves both types of interaction—student to student and teacher to student (Kirschner, Sweller, & Clark, 2006). This discussion also helps answer our second question from the beginning of the chapter: "What should Laura now do to help her students improve their problem solving?" She needed to provide more guidance, which she did in her Tuesday lesson.

Encourage Sense Making in the Problem-Solving Process. Earlier we saw that students have a tendency to accept answers whether or not they make sense, and this tendency is an ongoing source of teacher frustration. And students' increasing dependency on technology, such as calculators, can exacerbate the problem. Whatever answer appears on the calculator screen must be right.

A simple solution to this problem doesn't exist, but two strategies can help. First, we can model and emphasize sense making in all aspects of learning and teaching, and particularly in problem solving. Second, we can have our students practice making estimates of answers before they actually solve problems. Deliberate practice combined with estimating is an effective form of practice, and requiring estimates is a powerful tool for promoting sense making. Estimates far removed from reasonable answers, such as an estimate of more than 1,440 square feet for the carpeted area of Laura's classroom—the classroom's total area—would indicate that the student doesn't have a conceptual grasp of the problem and is simply performing mechanics instead. Meaning took a backseat to getting an answer, any answer.

This section leads us to our third question at the beginning of the chapter: "Was the time spent on the activity [Monday's lesson] used wisely, or was it largely wasted?" A clear answer doesn't exist. For example, the students spent valuable class time floundering, so Laura had to spend a full additional lesson guiding them to a solution for the problem. On the other hand, the first principle of cognitive learning theory says, *learning and development depend on experience,* and her students acquired considerable experience with attempting to design and implement problem-solving strategies. In addition, they gained valuable experience learning to work together on a common problem, a skill they'll use throughout life. Research on a highly effective math program from Singapore, one of the countries that consistently scores high on international math tests, suggests that examining problems from different perspectives, as Laura had her students do, is one aspect of successful math instruction (Hu, 2010).

Deliberate practice with solving problems includes fits and starts, and we're not always successful. Whether the experiences Laura's students acquired in her Monday lesson were valuable enough to warrant the time spent on them is a matter of professional judgment.

PROBLEM-BASED LEARNING

Laura's lessons also illustrate **problem-based learning**, a teaching strategy that uses problems as the focus for developing content, skills, and self-regulation (Hmelo-Silver, 2004; Serafino & Cicchelli, 2005). Problem-based learning is widely used in a variety of areas ranging from medical education and public health (Wardley, Applegate, & Van Rhee, 2013; de Jong, Verstegen, & Tan, 2013) to computer programming (Tiantong & Teemuangsai, 2013) and to business (Smart, Hicks, & Melton, 2013), among others.

Problem-based learning activities have the following characteristics (Gijbels, Dochy, Van den Bossche, & Segers, 2005; Krajcik & Blumenfeld, 2006):

- Lessons begin with a problem, and solving it is the lesson's focus.
- Students are responsible for designing strategies and finding solutions to the problem. Groups need to be small enough (typically three or four) so that all students are involved in the process.
- The teacher guides students' efforts with questioning and other forms of scaffolding.

As we saw in Laura's lessons, the third characteristic is essential. Because her students floundered on Monday, she provided considerably more scaffolding the next day. Some would argue that she should have intervened sooner and more specifically, whereas others would suggest that the experience students gained through their struggles was a worthwhile goal in itself.

Some evidence indicates that content learned in problem-based lessons is retained longer and transfers better than content learned with instruction that is more direct (Mayer & Wittrock, 2006; Sungur & Tekkaya, 2006). Additional evidence indicates that learners are more motivated in problem-based lessons than in traditional teacher-centered activities (Luft, Brown, & Sutherin, 2007). However, most of the research has been conducted with older or advanced students, and additional evidence indicates that insufficient guidance from teachers in problem-based learning lessons is ineffective (Kirschner et al., 2006). Further, some research indicates that students, including many university students, sometimes use the most superficial strategies possible to solve problems, particularly if they aren't carefully monitored by their instructors (Loyens, Gijbels, Coertjens, & Côté, 2013). This research suggests that problem-based learning, as with all other teaching strategies, requires the measured guidance of expert teachers to be effective.

Technology, Learning, and Development

Using Technology to Promote Problem Solving

A number of factors make developing problem-solving abilities in our students a challenge. Students' lack of background knowledge, problems that are too abstract for students' developmental levels, and students' lack of motivation are common obstacles to effective instruction. Technology can be a valuable resource to address these issues.

Many forms of technology solutions exist, and those we describe here are merely examples designed to give you an idea of the kinds of resources available to you when you begin to teach.

Manipulatives are among the most prominent. Physical manipulatives, such as blocks, Cuisenaire rods, and coins are mainstays of elementary school classrooms because they provide concrete representations of abstract ideas, such as place value and regrouping. The logistics involved in using them can be prohibitive, however, so teachers are sometimes reluctant to use them (Moyer-Packenham & Suh, 2012). **Virtual manipulatives**, replicas of physical manipulatives that are accessed using technology and manipulated with a keyboard or mouse, address this problem (Roblyer & Doering, 2013). An expanding body of research indicates that virtual manipulatives generally result in as much learning as their physical counterparts (Hwang & Hu, 2013; Moyer-Packenham & Suh, 2012), and some researchers suggest that they may even be better. "Compared with their physical counterparts, computer representations may be more manageable, flexible, extensible, and 'clean' (i.e., free of potentially distracting features)" (Sarama & Clements, 2009, p. 147).

Virtual manipulatives are used most often with elementary students, but evidence suggests they can increase motivation in older learners (Lee & Chen, 2010), and virtual experimentation can also be effective with older students in science courses, such as physics (Zacharia & Olympiou, 2011). Virtual manipulatives are also available as mobile apps on smartphones and tablet computers, which means that they can be used essentially anywhere (ABCya.com, 2013).

Simulations are also valuable resources for teaching problem solving, and many exist. For instance, the *Geometer's Sketchpad* (which is, not surprisingly, advertised by its manufacturer as the world's leading software for teaching mathematics [Keycurriculum, 2013]) provides visual representations of abstract math concepts and principles. For instance, using this software, elementary students can use the simulations to manipulate fractions, number lines, and geometric patterns, and then observe the outcomes. Middle and high school students can use the software to explore ratio and proportion, graphical representations of physical events, such as a dropped ball, and linear and trigonometric functions. The software also allows students to gather and manipulate data used in problem solving, and it is quite engaging, which can contribute to students' involvement and motivation (Roblyer & Doering, 2013). Sketchpad and other simulations are also compatible with **interactive whiteboards**, large interactive displays that connect to computers. A projector is used to display information from the computer's desktop onto the board's surface, while the teacher or a student controls the information on the computer.

Historically, the best-known problem-solving technology was created more than 20 years ago by the Cognition and Technology Group at Vanderbilt (1992). Called *The Adventures of Jasper Woodbury,* the series consists of 12 videodisc-based adventures that focus on problem finding and problem solving. Each of the "adventures" is designed to present engaging and real-world problems. The following is an abbreviated version of one of the problems called "Journey to Cedar Creek":

> Jasper has just purchased a new boat and is planning to drive it home. The boat travels 8 mph and consumes 5 gallons of gas per hour. The tank holds 12 gallons of gas. The boat is at mile marker 156, and Jasper's dock is at marker 132. There are two gas stations on the way home. One is at mile marker 140.3 and the other is at mile marker 133. They charge $1.10[9] and $1.25 per gallon, respectively. They don't take credit cards. Jasper started the day with $20. He bought 5 gallons of gas at $1.25 per gallon (not including a discount of 4 cents per gallon for paying cash) and paid $8.25 for repairs to his boat. It's 2:35. Sundown is at 7:52. Can Jasper make it home before sunset without running out of fuel?

The problems in the series are purposely made complex and left ill-defined to give students practice in solving ill-defined problems, and they include extraneous material, so students learn to separate relevant from irrelevant information. Because the problems are complex, students also practice identifying subgoals, such as finding out how much money Jasper has left for the trip home. Students work on these problems in teams over several class periods (ranging from a few days to more than a week). They share their ideas, receive feedback to refine their thinking, and present their solutions to the class.

Unfortunately, as we've pointed out earlier, students get little practice in solving ill-defined problems, and the Jasper series is designed to address this shortcoming. Attempting to use technology, such as the Jasper Series, to teach problem solving is not a panacea, however. Students, used to straightforward and well-defined problems, often struggle and become frustrated in attempting to solve problems such as those in the Jasper series. So, to be successful, when you use technology such as this, you'll need to carefully monitor students' efforts and make decisions about when and how to intervene. If you intervene too soon, you rob your students of the practice they need in working with ill-defined problems; if you don't intervene soon enough, you risk students turning off and tuning out. And unfortunately you're on your own. No one can tell you when to step in. Using this technology successfully is very demanding, which likely explains why it isn't found in more classrooms around our country.

We want to close this section with an important reminder. Without question, we live in a technological world, and technology is changing our lives, in both classrooms and the world outside. However, technology, no matter how sophisticated, will not automatically increase learning, and its effectiveness will always depend on the professional ability of the teacher using it. Used with professional skill, it has the potential to be a major contributor to learning; used improperly, it can be largely a waste of valuable learning time.

Classroom **Connections**

Developing Learners' Problem-Solving Abilities

1. The learning sciences suggest that real-world applications are important, and principles of cognitive learning theory suggest that social interaction facilitates learning. Embed problems in real-world contexts and use high levels of interaction to improve your students' problem-solving abilities.

   - **Elementary:** A fourth-grade teacher breaks her students into pairs and gives each pair a chocolate bar composed of 12 square pieces. She gives them problems involving 1/4 and 1/3 and has students break off certain numbers of pieces to represent the numbers as fractions of the whole bar. She has them explain their thinking in each case.

   - **Middle School:** A middle school teacher has a "problem of the week." Each student is required to bring in one real-world problem each week that relates to the topics they are studying. The teacher selects from among them, and the class solves them.

   - **High School:** A physics teacher gives students problems such as "If you're shooting a free throw and launch it at a 45-degree angle, what velocity will you need to put on the ball in order for it to go through the hoop?" After students attempt the problem, she uses questioning to guide them to a solution.

2. Learners require extensive practice and instructional support to develop their problem-solving abilities. As students practice solving problems, provide students with scaffolding and encourage them to put their understanding into words.

   - **Elementary:** A second-grade teacher begins a lesson on graphing by telling students that she's planning for a party and asking them how they might determine their classmates' favorite jelly bean flavor. She guides them as they identify the problem and how they might represent and solve it.

   - **Middle School:** A prealgebra teacher uses categories such as "We Know" and "We Need to Know" as scaffolds for analyzing word problems. His students then use the scaffolds to solve at least two word problems each day.

   - **High School:** In a unit on statistics and probability, a teacher requires her students to make estimates before solving problems. They then compare the solutions to their estimates.

The Strategic Learner

How did you answer the questions in *Ed Psych and You*, and what do your answers tell you about what kind of learner you are? If you're like most students, "take notes" is probably the answer to the first; lecture is the most common teaching method in universities, and virtually all university students take notes (Bui, Myerson, & Hale, 2013). And "highlight," underline, or something similar is the likely answer to the second. If you take notes and highlight or underline, you're using **strategies**, cognitive operations that exceed the normal activities required to carry out a task (Pressley & Harris, 2006). Note taking is a strategy because it goes beyond merely listening to your instructor, and highlighting is also a strategy, because it goes beyond simply reading, the normal activity involved in trying to understand a written passage. A number of general learning strategies exists, such as note taking, highlighting, summarizing, self-questioning, and concept mapping (Alexander, 2006). Each can enhance learning.

Metacognition: The Foundation of Strategic Learning

Think again about the questions we asked in *Ed Psych and You*. You most likely take notes because you believe that doing so will help you better understand and remember the information your instructor is presenting. In doing so, you're being *metacognitive*. **Metacognition** is knowledge and regulation of our cognition. You know you'll remember more of your instructor's presentation if you take notes (knowledge of cognition), and you regulate your cognition by actually taking the notes. Metacognition is the mechanism we use to match a strategy to a goal, and students who are metacognitive perform better than their peers who are less so (Tullis, Finley, & Benjamin, 2013; Veenman & Spaans, 2005).

When taking notes, for example, metacognitive learners ask questions such as:

- Am I writing down important ideas or trivial details?
- Am I taking enough notes, or am I taking too many?
- When I study, am I simply reading my notes, or do I ask myself questions and search for examples to elaborate on them?

Without this kind of metacognitive monitoring, strategies are largely ineffective.

Effective strategy users also have extensive background knowledge (Coiro & Dobler, 2007; Wetzels, Kester, van Merriënboer, & Broers, 2011). Without this knowledge base, strategy use is difficult (Sternberg, 2009). Background knowledge allows students to make better decisions about what is important to study and helps them efficiently allocate their mental resources to the task (Verkoeijen, Rikers, & Schmidt, 2005).

Just as expert problem solvers draw on a wealth of experiences with problems, effective strategy users have a variety of strategies at their disposal (Alexander, 2006). For instance, they take notes, skim, use outlines, take advantage of bold and italicized print, capitalize on examples, and create concept maps. Without this repertoire, it is difficult to match strategies to different tasks.

Becoming a strategic learner takes time and effort, and even after strategy instruction, many students use them only when prompted to do so by their teachers (Pressley & Harris,

2006). Also, most students, including those in college, tend to use primitive strategies, such as rehearsal, regardless of the difficulty of the material (Peverly, Brobst, & Graham, 2003).

Study Strategies

Study strategies are specific techniques students use to increase their understanding of written materials and teacher presentations. Some of the most widely used include:

- Note taking
- Using text signals
- Summarizing
- Elaborative questioning
- Concept mapping

We examine them in the sections that follow.

NOTE TAKING

Note taking is probably the most common study strategy, it's the most widely researched, and it works—effective note taking increases achievement (Bui et al., 2013; Peverly et al., 2013). But despite its popularity, many students, including those in college, are not good note takers (Chen, 2013; Peverly et al., 2007). Effective notes include both the main ideas presented in lectures or texts and supporting details (Peverly et al., 2007), but students often fail at one or both (Chen, 2013).

Our understanding of cognitive learning theory and human memory help us explain the positive effects of note taking. First, taking notes helps maintain attention and encourages students to cognitively engage with the topic (think about the topic), and second, the notes provide a form of external storage that reduces the cognitive load on working memory (Igo, Bruning, & McCrudden, 2005). Because working memory capacity is limited, we often lose information before it's encoded, or we may reconstruct our understanding in a way that makes sense to us but isn't valid. Notes provide a source of information against which we can check our understanding (Igo et al., 2005).

We can help our students improve their note taking with **guided notes**, teacher-prepared handouts that "guide" students with cues combined with space available for writing key ideas and relationships. Using guided notes increases achievement in students ranging from those with learning disabilities (Boyle, 2013; Hamilton, Seibert, Gardner, & Talbert-Johnson, 2000) to college students (Austin, Lee, & Carr, 2004). Figure 8.3 illustrates a guided-notes form used for different climate regions of the United States by a geography teacher.

Guided notes also model the organization and key points of a topic. As students acquire experience, they gradually develop organizational skills that they can apply on their own.

USING TEXT SIGNALS

Text signals are elements in written materials that communicate the organization of the content and key ideas. Common text signals include:

- *Headings*. For example, in this chapter, *note taking, using text signals*, and *summarizing* are subheadings under the heading *study strategies*, so this organization signals that each is a study strategy.
- *Numbered and bulleted lists*. For instance, the bulleted list you're reading now identifies different text signals.
- *Underlined, bold, or italicized text*. Each of the important concepts in this text, for example, is emphasized in bold print.

Strategic learners use these signals to develop a framework for the topic they're studying (Vacca, Vacca, & Mraz, 2014). You can encourage the use of this strategy with your students

---

1. Give an example of how each of the following influences climate:

Latitude _____

Wind direction _____

Ocean currents _____

Land forms _____

2. Describe each climate, and identify at least one state that has this climate. Then identify one type of plant that lives in this climate and two different animals that are typically found in the climate.

The Mediterranean Climate _____

_____ State _____

Plant _____ Animals _____

The Marine West Coast Climate _____

_____ State _____

Plant _____ Animals _____

The Humid Subtropical Climate _____

_____ State _____

Plant _____ Animals _____

The Humid Continental Climate _____

_____ State _____

Figure 8.3

A guide for note taking in U.S. geography

---

by discussing the organization of a topic and reminding them of other text signals that can help make the information they're studying meaningful.

SUMMARIZING

Summarizing is the process of preparing a concise description of verbal or written passages. It's effective for **comprehension monitoring**—checking to see if we understand what we've read or heard. If we can prepare an accurate summary of a topic, it indicates that we understand it. As we would expect, learning to summarize takes time, effort, and training (Alexander, 2003, 2006). Training usually involves walking students through a passage and helping them construct general descriptions, generate statements that relate ideas to each other, and identify important information (Pressley & Harris, 2006).

For instance, we might summarize the problem-solving section of this chapter as follows:

> To solve problems, we must identify the problem goal, represent the problem, select and implement a strategy to solve it, and check to see if the solution makes sense. We can help our students become better problem solvers by providing students with a great deal of deliberate practice and focusing on sense making in the problem-solving process.

Research suggests that summarizing increases both students' understanding of the topics they study and their metacognitive skills (Leopold & Leutner, 2012; Thiede & Anderson, 2003). Having your students generate key terms that capture the essence of a text passage is a modified form of summarizing that can also increase comprehension (Thiede, Anderson, & Therriault, 2003).

ELABORATIVE QUESTIONING

Elaborative questioning is the process of drawing inferences, identifying examples, and forming relationships. Often described as *elaborative interrogation,* it is an effective strategy for increasing comprehension of written information in both traditional and online text (Dornisch & Sperling, 2006, 2008; Chen, Teng, Lee, & Kinshuk, 2011). It is an effective comprehension-monitoring strategy because it encourages students to create connections in the material they're studying. Three elaborative questions are especially effective:

- What is another example of this idea?
- How is this topic similar to or different from the one in the previous section?
- How does this idea relate to other ideas I've been studying?

For example, as you were studying the section on problem solving, the following questions might have been helpful:

What is another example of a well-defined problem in this class?

What is an example of an ill-defined problem?

What makes the first well-defined and the second ill-defined?

How are problem-solving and learning strategies similar? How are they different?

Questions such as these create links between new information and knowledge in long-term memory, making the new information more meaningful and increasing the likelihood that it will be retained and remembered.

CONCEPT MAPPING

A **concept map** is a visual representation of the relationships among concepts that includes the concepts themselves, sometimes enclosed in circles or boxes, together with relationships among concepts indicated by lines linking them to each other. Words on the line, referred to as *linking words* or *linking phrases,* specify the relationship between the concepts (Novak & Cañas, 2006). A concept map is somewhat analogous to the way a road map represents locations of highways and towns or a circuit diagram represents the workings of an electrical appliance. Figure 8.4 is a concept map for the complex cognitive processes that we've discussed to this point in the chapter.

Concept mapping is an effective study strategy because it encourages students to be cognitively active (think) as they study topics and employs dual-coding theory—the process of encoding information in both visual and verbal form (Hagemans, van der Meij, & de Jong, 2013; Rye, Landenberger, & Warner, 2013). It also capitalizes on effective encoding strategies (Nesbit & Adesope, 2006). A concept map visually represents relationships among concepts, so it uses *imagery,* and preparing the map itself requires *organization.* As learners' understanding increases, maps can be modified and expanded, which is a form of *elaboration.* Research indicates that the strategy makes initial learning more effective and conceptual change more durable (Hakkarainen & Ahtee, 2007).

Conceptual hierarchies are concept maps that visually illustrate superordinate, subordinate, and coordinate relationships among concepts. Because each subordinate concept is a subset of the one above it, the relationships among the concepts are clear in a conceptual hierarchy, so linking words or phrases aren't needed. Many concepts, such as our number system, the animal and plant kingdoms, parts of speech, and figurative language, can be organized hierarchically.

A conceptual hierarchy for the concept *closed-plane figures* is illustrated in Figure 8.5. *Closed-plane figures* is superordinate to all the other figures in the hierarchy; *four-sided figures, three-sided figures,* and *curved figures* are subordinate to *closed-plane figures* (they are all subsets); and *four-sided figures, three-sided figures,* and *curved figures* are coordinate to each other. Similar relationships exist among the other concepts in the hierarchy.

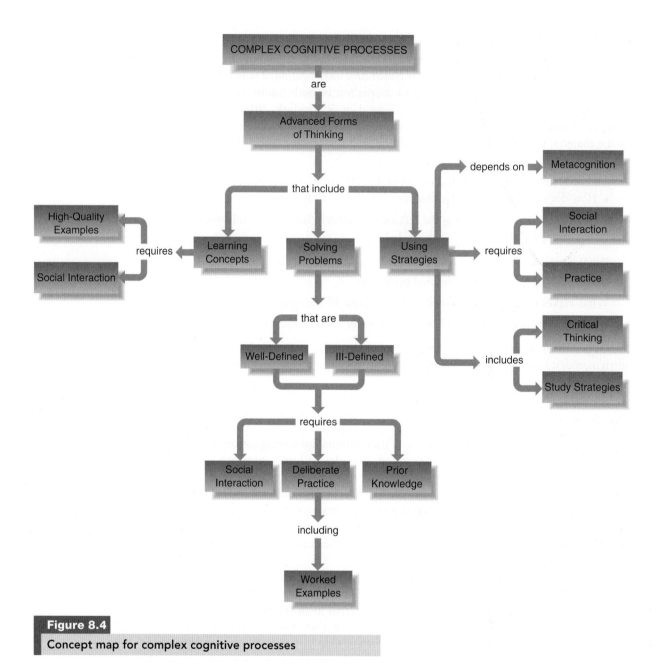

Figure 8.4

Concept map for complex cognitive processes

Concept mapping can be used to measure conceptual change in learners, and it's also an effective assessment tool (Dougherty, Custer, & Dixon, 2012; Hilbert & Renkl, 2008). For example, the student who created the conceptual hierarchy in Figure 8.5 didn't include figures with more than four sides or curved shapes other than circles. If you use a concept map as a form of assessment, and you see that your students' understanding is incomplete, you can then provide additional examples, such as pentagons and ellipses in the case of closed-plane figures.

The type of concept map students use should be the one that best illustrates relationships among the concepts. Hierarchies often work best in math and science; in other areas, such as reading or social studies, a traditional concept map may be more effective.

Most students can learn study strategies, and strategy instruction is especially valuable for younger students and low achievers, because they have a smaller repertoire of strategies and are less likely to use them spontaneously (Bruning, Schraw, & Norby, 2011). However,

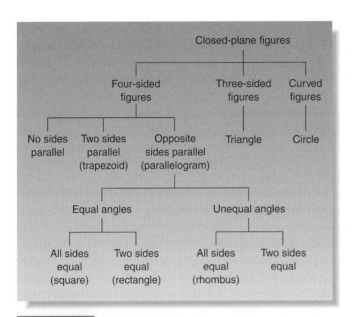

Figure 8.5

Conceptual hierarchy for the concept
closed-plane figures

the effectiveness of any strategy depends on learners' motivation, their ability to activate relevant prior knowledge, and their metacognition. If one or more of these factors is missing, no strategy is effective.

Ed Psych and You

How do you study? Do you study one topic thoroughly and then move on to the next? Do you have a designated place in your home where you usually do your studying? Do you study in large chunks of time, or shorter ones? In your estimation, how effective are your study strategies?

RESEARCH ON STUDY STRATEGIES

Think about the questions we ask in *Ed Psych and You*. Conventional wisdom suggests that we should study a topic until we thoroughly understand it and then move on to a second topic. It also suggests that we should have a designated place to study that is free of distractions. However, some of this conventional wisdom is misguided. For example, in a classic study conducted nearly four decades ago, researchers found that simply varying the environment in which students studied resulted in more recall of information than studying the same information in a single environment (Smith, Glenberg, & Borg, 1978). This suggests that studying at home some of the time, in the library at other times, and even in a coffee shop is more effective than always studying in your home. Research also indicates that studying different but related topics in one sitting is more effective than focusing intensely on a single topic (Kornell, Castel, Eich, & Bjork, 2010; Taylor & Rohrer, 2010). For example, your study of the human memory model is likely to be more effective if you also study cognitive learning principles and the relationships between the two in a single study session, rather than studying the human memory model in one session and cognitive learning principles in another. "Forcing the brain to make multiple associations with the same material may, in effect, give the information more neural scaffolding" (Carey, 2010, para. 11).

Also, as we've known for decades, spacing study is vastly superior to intense periods of cramming. So, an hour of study tonight, another hour tomorrow, and a third hour over the weekend will result in more learning than cramming three hours in one session. Cognitive scientists even suggest that seeming to forget a fact or idea and then struggling to remember it later can actually benefit learning. You don't literally forget it, and the relearning results in deeper and more thorough understanding (Kornell et al., 2010). This research gives us all something to think about as we study.

Critical Thinking

The ability to "think critically" is becoming increasingly important in today's world because of the explosion of information available with only a few key strokes, combined with questionable advertising claims, propaganda, and the conscious distortions we must constantly sift through (Buffington, 2007; Kassin, Fein, & Markus, 2011; Wade, 2009). **Critical thinking** has been defined in various ways, and complex descriptions are often offered, but most definitions include an individual's ability and inclination to make and assess conclusions based on evidence (van Gelder, 2005; Willingham, 2009). For example, an advertisement says, "Doctors recommend . . . more often," touting a health product. A person thinking critically is wary because the advertisement provides no evidence for its claims. Similarly, a critical thinker listens to another person's argument with guarded skepticism because people are known to have unconscious biases.

We like this definition of critical thinking because it's simple and straightforward, and perhaps even more importantly, it can be integrated into your regular curriculum without a great deal of extra effort on your part. Providing evidence is also an integral part of the Common Core State Standards, which are being implemented in most of the states in our country. A number of examples exist, but here is one at the elementary level: **"CCSS. ELA-Literacy.W.5.1b Provide logically ordered reasons that are supported by facts and details" (Common Core State Standards Initiative, 2014m).** And here is another example at the high school level: **"CCSS.ELA-Literacy.W.9-10.1 Write arguments to support claims in an analysis of substantive topics or texts, using valid reasoning and relevant and sufficient evidence" (Common Core State Standards Initiative, 2014n).** Critical thinking isn't an "add on" in our schools' curriculum of the future; it is instead an integral aspect of the entire learning–teaching process.

Ed Psych and You

Which do you fear more: terrorism or gunshot deaths? Sharks or dogs? Flying or driving? How do you think your feelings compare to people in general?

THE CHALLENGE OF CRITICAL THINKING

People's fears are interesting, and they relate to the questions we asked in *Ed Psych and You*. In a majority of cases, it is the first of each pair (i.e., terrorism, sharks, and flying). Now, let's look at some statistics. In 2011, 17 Americans *worldwide* were killed in terrorist attacks (Infowars.com, 2013), whereas in the same year more than 8,500 were gun-murder victims in our country (Federal Bureau of Investigation, 2013). In 2012, 80 people worldwide were bitten by sharks (Ichthyology, 2013), but over 4.5 million were bitten by dogs in this country alone (American Humane Association, 2013). In 2012 no one died in an airline crash in our country (Planecrashinfo.com, 2013), whereas slightly more than 34,000 died in auto accidents (U.S. Department of Transportation, 2013).

How can we explain these fears, when reason is supposed to be the highest achievement of the human mind, and the facts so strongly counter them? Making and assessing conclusions based on evidence, in general, and avoiding irrational emotional reactions, in particular, are more difficult than they appear, and most people are not good at this (Buskist & Irons, 2009; Lawrence, Serdikoff, Zinn, & Baker, 2009; Willingham, 2009). For example, when asked to justify an opinion, "more than half the population flounder. . . . The problem is that they do not have a general grasp of the notion of evidence and what would properly count as providing evidence in support of their view" (van Gelder, 2005, p. 42).

Some experts suggest that humans are not naturally disposed to think critically. "Humans don't think very often because our brains are designed not for thought, but for the avoidance of thought" (Willingham, 2009, p. 4). In essence, our brains are on autopilot and thinking critically about ideas is not a high priority. Why is this the case? First, thinking has three properties: It is *slow,* it requires *effort,* and the results are *uncertain.* Second, thinking occurs in working memory, which we know is limited in capacity. We function more efficiently when we perform tasks automatically, essentially without conscious thought (Willingham, 2009).

Belief preservation, the tendency to make evidence subservient to belief, rather than the other way around, and **confirmation bias**, the tendency to focus only on evidence that supports our beliefs, pose additional challenges to critical thinking (Buskist & Irons, 2009; Douglas, 2000). When we strongly believe an idea, or desire it to be true, we tend to seek evidence that supports the belief and avoid or ignore evidence that disputes it, or we retain beliefs in the face of overwhelming contrary evidence if we can find some minimal support for the belief. Young children's belief in Santa Claus is an example. Virtually no evidence supports Santa's existence, but young children cling to the belief, sometimes for years, and give it up only reluctantly. And confirmation bias is far from limited to children and Santa Claus. For example, it is an issue in many fields, such as forensics, health, and even "pure" research (Hernandez & Preston, 2013; Kassin, Dror, & Kukucka, 2013).

Cognitive learning theory and Piaget's work help us understand these tendencies. We want our experiences to make sense, so we construct knowledge that makes sense to us. When experiences do make sense, even if they're illusory or distorted, we are at equilibrium, so we have no need to pursue a matter further. And this tendency often applies as much to high achievers as it does to lower achievers (Macpherson & Stanovich, 2007).

In addition, people sometimes have a personal investment in existing beliefs. They feel that changing their beliefs reflects negatively on their intelligence or their resolve, so the change threatens their sense of self-worth (Linnenbrink & Pintrich, 2003). Also, beliefs are sometimes integral to their culture or religion (Southerland & Sinatra, 2003).

On a more positive note, research indicates that with practice and feedback critical thinking can be developed, and experts recommend that it be integrated into the regular curriculum (Burke, Williams, & Skinner, 2007; Niu, Behar-Horenstein, & Garvan, 2013). We offer suggestions for doing so in the next section.

Educational Psychology and Teaching: Helping Your Students Become Strategic Learners

Cognitive learning theory offers suggestions for helping our students become better strategy users. The following guidelines can help you in your efforts (Pressley & Harris, 2006):

1. Explicitly teach and have students practice study strategies.
2. Model critical thinking and use questioning to promote critical thinking in your students.
3. Use assessment with feedback as learning tools.

We discuss the guidelines in the following sections.

Explicitly Teach Study Strategies. Regardless of what we are attempting to learn—physical skills, such as dribbling a basketball, art or music performance, critical thinking, or academic skills, such as concept learning, problem solving, or academic writing—explicit instruction combined with modeling and the regulation of our thinking (metacognition) are essential to maximize the amount learned (Peverly et al., 2013; Pressley & Harris, 2006). This applies to study strategies as well. To see how to do this in a classroom, let's look in on Donna Evans, a middle school social studies teacher, who is attempting to help her students learn to summarize and meet the following standard:

CCSS.ELA-Literacy.RI.7.2 Determine two or more central ideas in a text and analyze their development over the course of the text; provide an objective summary of the text (Common Core State Standards Initiative, 2014h).

Donna begins her geography class by directing her students to a section of the text that describes the low-, middle-, and high-latitude climates, and says, "One way to become more effective readers is to summarize the information we read in a few short statements. This makes the information easier to remember, and it will help us understand how one climate region compares with another. You can do the same thing in all of your classes. . . . Now read the section on page 237 and see if you can identify the features of a low-latitude climate."

After the class reads the section, Donna continues, "As I was reading, here's how I thought about it." She then displays the following information on the document camera and describes her thinking as she writes it.

Low latitudes can be hot and wet or hot and dry. Close to the equator, the humid tropical climate is hot and wet all year. Farther away, it has wet summers and dry winters. In the dry tropical climate, high-pressure zones cause deserts, like the Sahara.

She then says, "Now, let's all give it a try with the section on the middle-latitude climates. Go ahead and read the section, and try to summarize it the way I did. . . . Write your summaries, and we'll share what you've written."

After they finish, Donna asks a student to volunteer a summary.

Kari volunteers, displays her summary on the document camera, and Donna and other students add information and comments to what Kari has written. Donna then has two other students display their summaries, and then the class practices again with the section on the high-latitude climates.

Throughout the school year, Donna continues to have her students practice summarizing at least twice a week.

Now let's look at Donna's efforts. She explicitly taught the process of summarizing by describing it and explaining why it's useful. For instance, she said, "One way to become more effective readers is to summarize the information we read in a few short statements. This makes the information easier to remember, and it will help us understand how one climate region compares with another. . . ."

She also modeled both the skill and her thinking when she commented, "As I was reading, here's how I thought about it." Research indicates that students' metacognitive awareness can be increased with explicit instruction such as this (Alexander, Johnson, & Leibham, 2005).

Donna then had her students practice reading a passage and preparing a summary, and she provided them with feedback. She displayed a student's example on the document camera, so everyone would be responding to the same information. And she continued the process throughout the school year. This process provides the deliberate practice that students need to develop their ability as strategic learners.

Model and Promote Critical Thinking. With some awareness and thought, critical thinking can become an integral part of your instruction, and more importantly, it requires little additional effort (Macpherson & Stanovich, 2007). Two suggestions can be helpful. First, model thinking dispositions, such as the use of evidence in making conclusions, a sense of curiosity, a desire to be informed, and a willingness to respect opinions different from your own. Statements such as "The first thing I ask myself when I read an opinion piece in the newspaper is, 'what evidence does the writer provide?'" can, over time, make a significant difference in our students' inclination to look for evidence when they hear opinions or conclusions. Your own modeling is probably the most powerful contribution you can make to your students' inclination to think critically.

Second, continually asking questions such as "How do you know?" and "Why do you say that?" throughout your lessons can be helpful. These questions require students to provide evidence for their conclusions, and, in many cases, they follow naturally from other questions. As an example, suppose you're teaching your students about *verbals,* verb forms that behave as other parts of speech in sentences, and you display the following for your students:

> Swimming and running are great forms of exercise. And, if we like to run, it's simple. All we have to do is jump into our running gear, and off we go.

You then ask your students to identify a participle, and one of your students identifies "running" in the third sentence. You can simply ask, "How do we know it's a participle?" This question follows automatically from your first, and requires a statement from the student such as "It is a verb form, and it modifies the noun *gear,* so it behaves as an adjective. And verb forms that behave as adjectives are participles." Your students will unlikely be able to make statements as complete as the one you see here, so you will have to guide them with your questioning, which also promotes learning. As they practice putting their evidence into words, they are simultaneously developing their critical thinking abilities and deepening their understanding.

Use Assessment and Feedback as Learning Tools. Research suggests that we, as teachers, have a powerful learning tool at our immediate disposal: assessment. Assessment not only measures knowledge but also changes it, and, if the assessments measure more than fact learning, the change is in the direction of deeper understanding and more meaningful learning (Stiggins & Chappuis, 2012). "Testing has such a bad connotation; people think of standardized testing or teaching to the test. Maybe we should call it something else, but this is one of the most powerful learning tools that we have" (Carey, 2010, p. 5). This suggests that we should frequently and thoroughly assess student learning, and these assessments should do more than measure recall of factual information.

Assessment is relevant to study skills and critical thinking, because students tend to study and learn based on the way they're assessed (Miller, Linn, & Gronlund, 2013). If, for example, our assessments require that our students know factual information, they will tend to memorize and use rehearsal as a study strategy. On the other hand, if our assessments require students to identify relationships and evidence to support conclusions, they will use deeper study strategies, such as concept mapping and elaborative questioning. In other words, our assessments can become learning tools that encourage our students to develop their critical thinking and use effective study strategies.

In all cases, assessments should be accompanied by feedback. "There is a preponderance of evidence that feedback is a powerful influence in the development of learning outcomes. . . .

Classroom **Connections**

Promoting Strategic Learning in Classrooms

Study Strategies

1. Students use study strategies to increase their understanding of written materials and teacher presentations. Teach study strategies across the curriculum and throughout the school year to make them most effective.

   - **Elementary:** A second-grade teacher models elaborative questioning and encourages her children to ask themselves what each lesson was about and what they learned from it.

   - **Middle School:** A sixth-grade teacher introduces note taking as a study skill. He then provides note-taking practice in his social studies class by using skeletal outlines to organize his presentations and by having his students use them as a guide for their note taking.

   - **High School:** A biology teacher closes each lesson by having her students provide summaries of the most important parts of the lesson. She adds material to summaries that are incomplete.

Critical Thinking

2. Helping students learn to make and assess conclusions based on evidence promotes critical thinking. Integrate critical thinking into the regular curriculum.

   - **Elementary:** A fourth-grade teacher makes it a point to ask questions such as (1) What do you observe? (2) How are these alike or different? (3) Why is A different from B? (4) What would happen if . . . ? (5) How do you know?

   - **Middle School:** A seventh-grade geography teacher develops her topics with examples, charts, graphs, and tables. She develops lessons around students' observations, comparisons, and conclusions related to the information they see, and she requires students to provide evidence for their conclusions.

   - **High School:** An English teacher helps his students analyze literature by asking questions such as "How do you know that?" and "What in the story supports your idea?"

The average effects of feedback are among the highest we know in education" (Hattie & Gan, 2011, p. 249). Common forms of feedback include discussing frequently missed items on quizzes and tests, providing written comments or model answers for students' written work, and comments, checklists, or rating scales for student presentations. Because student interest is high when discussing quiz items, for example, feedback often results in more learning than the original instruction (Hattie & Gan, 2011).

Transfer of Learning

Ed Psych and You

You're studying for a quiz in one of your classes with a friend, and after a considerable amount of discussion, you comment, "Talking it over this way sure helps. I get it better than when I study by myself."

What idea from your study of Ed Psych does your comment best illustrate?

How did you answer the question in *Ed Psych and You*? If you concluded that your comment illustrates an application of the cognitive learning principle *social interaction facilitates learning*, you have demonstrated **transfer**, the ability to take understanding acquired in one context and apply it to a different one (Mayer & Wittrock, 2006). "A primary goal of education is transfer of knowledge from the learning context to future novel situations" (Kaminski, Sloutsky, & Heckler, 2013, p. 14). Recognizing or providing a new example of a concept, solving a unique problem, or applying a learning strategy to a new situation are all examples of transfer.

Recalling information doesn't involve transfer. If, for example, your instructor had previously discussed the example in *Ed Psych and You*, you merely remembered the information.

Transfer can be either positive or negative. Positive transfer occurs when learning in one context facilitates learning in another, whereas negative transfer occurs when learning in one situation hinders performance in another (Mayer & Wittrock, 2006). For instance, positive transfer occurs if students know that a mammal nurses its young and breathes through lungs and if they then conclude that a whale is a mammal because it does the same. On the other hand, if they believe that a fish is an animal that lives in the sea and conclude that a whale is a fish, negative transfer has occurred.

General and Specific Transfer

At one time, educators advocated taking courses such as Latin or mathematics to "discipline" the mind. If they had accomplished this goal, general transfer, the ability to apply knowledge or skills learned in one context to a variety of different contexts, would have occurred (Phye, 2005). For example, if playing chess would help a person learn math because both require logic, general transfer would occur. Specific transfer is the ability to apply information in a context similar to the one in which it was originally learned. For example, when students know that the Greek prefix *photos* means "light" and it helps them better understand the concept *photosynthesis,* specific transfer has occurred.

Research over many years has consistently confirmed that general transfer is rare (Barnett & Ceci, 2002; Thorndike, 1924). Studying Latin, for example, results in specific transfer to the Latin roots of English words; it does little to improve thinking in general.

Factors Affecting the Transfer of Learning

Several factors affect students' ability to transfer. They include:

- *Meaningfulness.* The more thoroughly and meaningfully information is encoded, the greater the likelihood that it will transfer to new contexts. This also applies to skills. Procedural knowledge overlearned to the point of automaticity is more likely to transfer than are skills less thoroughly learned.
- *Similarity*. Transfer is more likely when the new context is similar to the context in which the information is learned.
- *Conceptual knowledge.* Conceptual knowledge—concepts, principles, and theories— is more likely to transfer than are isolated facts.
- *Real-world applications.* Knowledge and skills are more likely to transfer when they are learned and applied to real-world contexts.

Let's look at these factors in more detail.

Meaningfulness. Successful transfer requires a high level of original understanding, and students often fail to transfer because the topic wasn't meaningful to them—they didn't fully understand it—in the first place (Bereiter & Scardamalia, 2006). The more practice and feedback learners have with the topics they study, the greater the likelihood that transfer will occur (Moreno & Mayer, 2005).

Similarity. The more closely two learning situations are related, the more likely transfer is to occur (Kaminski et al., 2013). For instance, when first graders are given this problem to solve first,

> Angi has two pieces of candy. Kim gives her three more pieces of candy. How many pieces does Angi have now?

they do well on this one:

> Bruce had three pencils. His friend Orlando gave him two more. How many pencils does Bruce have now?

However, when they're given the first problem followed by this problem,

> Sophie has three cookies. Flavio has four cookies. How many do they have together?

they perform less well. The first two are more closely related than the first and third, and transfer is more likely to occur between them.

Similarly, if children understand that a dog, horse, mouse, and deer are mammals, they're more likely to conclude that a cow is a mammal than to conclude that a seal is one, because a cow is more similar to the other examples than is a seal. These results further demonstrate that transfer is specific.

Conceptual Knowledge. Facts, such as $6 \times 9 = 54$, Abraham Lincoln was our president during the Civil War, and Leo Tolstoy wrote *War and Peace*, are important parts of learning, but alone, they contribute little to transfer. In contrast, conceptual knowledge—such as understanding the characteristics of *longitude and latitude,* or the principle *moving objects continue moving in a straight line unless a force acts on them*—is more likely to transfer (Bransford & Schwartz, 1999). For example, when we understand longitude and latitude, we can identify any location on the globe, and understanding that moving objects continue to move unless a force acts on them helps us understand why we should maintain a safe driving distance between ourselves and the car in front of us. This suggests that we should emphasize concepts and principles in our instruction more strongly than isolated facts.

Real-World Applications. Content that is applied to our everyday lives is more likely to transfer than ideas that are abstract and distant (Barnett & Ceci, 2002). For instance, the principle *moving objects continue to move in a straight line unless a force acts on them* transfers to an understanding of why we have seatbelts in our cars and why cars traveling too fast sometimes "miss" curves.

Similarly, students' grammar skills are more likely to transfer when they are developed in the context of written passages than in isolated sentences, and math skills are more likely to transfer if they are practiced in the context of realistic word problems. The same applies in all content areas.

Diversity: Learner Differences that Influence Transfer of Complex Cognitive Processes

The basic cognitive processes involved in concept learning, problem solving, and strategic learning are essentially the same for all students. However, their cultural knowledge, approaches to problem solving, and attitudes and beliefs will vary, and each can influence transfer. For example, the Yu'pik people living in the Bering Sea just west of Alaska have 99 different concepts for ice (Block, 2007). This is knowledge important to their culture as they travel and hunt, but it's alien to most of us. So when they think about weather and travel, the connections they make and the ideas they transfer differ from ours.

Cultural differences also exist in the way people approach concept learning. For example, adults in Western cultures tend to classify items taxonomically, such as putting animals in one group, food items in another, and tools in a third. However, adults in some other cultures classify items into functional categories, such as putting a shovel and potato together, because a shovel is used to dig up a potato (Luria, 1976).

Attitudes and beliefs are also influenced by cultural differences. For instance, learning-related attitudes are offered as an explanation for the impressive problem-solving achievements of Japanese students, who consistently score high on international comparisons. "Attitudes toward achievement emphasize that success comes from hard work (not from innate ability). . . . Teachers examined a few problems in depth rather than covering many problems superficially; children's errors were used as learning tools for the group" (Rogoff, 2003, pp. 264–265). Students exposed to this type of instruction learn different perspectives about math than they would using a more fact-based, memory-oriented approach.

In view of their impressive academic achievements, the fact that early childhood education in Japan focuses on social development instead of academics may be surprising (Abe & Izzard, 1999). Some experts believe that this emphasis helps children feel part of a group and responsible to it, which results in greater attention to the topics being taught and fewer classroom management problems (Rogoff, 2003).

Culture also influences strategic learning. For example, students use more effective comprehension-monitoring strategies when exposed to written materials consistent with their cultural experiences (Pritchard, 1990). Once again, we see how important background knowledge is to thinking.

Interestingly, fewer cultural differences are found when tasks are embedded in real-world contexts. For example, when people such as vendors, carpenters, or dieters use math for practical purposes, they rarely get answers that don't make sense. "However, calculations in the context of schooling regularly produce some absurd errors, with results that are impossible if the meaning of the problem is being considered" (Rogoff, 2003, p. 262). This was illustrated in Laura's lesson in our case study at the beginning of the chapter. Even though finding the carpeted area of the classroom was a real-world task for her students, some were willing to accept widely varying answers to the problem, even answers that didn't make sense. This demonstrates the need to promote metacognition and provide a great deal of scaffolding for all learners, regardless of their cultural backgrounds.

Experiences and cultural and religious beliefs can also influence critical thinking. Learners whose early school experiences involve a great deal of memory-level tasks are more likely to use primitive study strategies, such as rehearsal, and they are less equipped to be critical thinkers than are their peers who have opportunities to practice higher order thinking. Memory-level tasks are common in urban schools, and urban schools typically have large numbers of minorities. This results in fewer opportunities to think about and practice complex mental processes for members of cultural minorities (Kozol, 2005). Also, members of cultures who have been taught to respect elders and learners with strong authoritarian religious beliefs may be less disposed to critical thinking (Kuhn & Park, 2005).

These differences all point to the need to be aware of the differences students bring to our classrooms. Despite these differences, the need to embed learning experiences in real-world contexts, promote high levels of interaction, and provide the scaffolding that helps learners make sense of those experiences is essential for all students, regardless of their cultural backgrounds.

Educational Psychology and Teaching: Applying an Understanding of Transfer with Your Students

Principles of cognitive learning theory provide a framework for promoting transfer in our students. To promote transfer, our goal is to make the topics we teach as meaningful for students as possible. The following guidelines are intended to help us reach this goal.

1. Provide students with a variety of high-quality examples and other experiences.
2. Apply content to real-world contexts whenever possible.
3. Use high levels of interaction to promote learning and to provide different perspectives on the topics students are learning.

Now, let's analyze the extent to which the teachers you've studied in this chapter—Martina Lopez in her lesson on the concepts *fact, opinion,* and *reasoned judgment*, Laura Hunter in her problem-solving lesson, and Donna Evans in her attempts to help her students develop their study skills—applied these guidelines in their instruction.

Provide Students with a Variety of High-Quality Examples and Other Experiences.

To begin, let's look again at the passages Martina used to illustrate the concepts *fact, opinion,* and *reasoned judgment* with her students.

> Eli Whitney invented the cotton gin in 1793. This reduced the amount of time it took to separate the cotton seeds from the cotton fibers. As a result, raising cotton became very profitable, so the South became a one-crop economy that depended on cotton. As it turns out, the lack of variety in the Southern economy was a big mistake.

> Abraham Lincoln was the best president in our country's history. He was president from 1861 until his assassination in 1865. One of Lincoln's primary accomplishments was getting the 13th amendment to the Constitution passed, because it permanently outlawed slavery.

The students could see, for example, that "Eli Whitney invented the cotton gin in 1793 is a fact," whereas "Abraham Lincoln was the best president in our country's history" is an opinion, and the same was true for the examples of reasoned judgment. These examples provided the experiences her students needed to construct their knowledge of the concepts. Martina's use of examples in this way applied the cognitive learning principles "Learning and development depend on experience," "People want their experiences to make sense," and "To make sense of their experiences, learners construct knowledge."

The passage also provided an adequate variety of examples, which research indicates is valuable for constructing knowledge and promoting transfer (Renkl, 2011; Schwartz, Bransford, & Sears, 2005). For instance, "He [Lincoln] was president from 1861 until his assassination in 1865" is another example of a fact, and "As it turns out, the lack of variety in the Southern economy was a big mistake" is a second example of an opinion. Each example adds information that increases the likelihood of experiencing examples that are meaningful to students and capitalizes on elaboration as an encoding strategy.

Problem solving is similar. To become good problem solvers students need to solve a wide variety of problems, and worked examples are particularly valuable in this process. "Proponents of teaching and learning by examples propose that after the explicit introduction of one or more domain principles (e.g., mathematical theorem . . .), learners should be presented with several examples" (Renkl, 2011, p. 273). Laura could apply this guideline by having her students find the area of a school parking lot, another area of the classroom, the area of an irregularly shaped desk, or a variety of others that are part of her school's environment.

The same applies with strategic learning. As you saw earlier, Donna had her students practice creating summaries throughout the year. She also needs to model these strategies and have students practice with other study strategies in the same way she did with summarizing.

Apply Content to Real-World Contexts. Martina's vignette also applied this guideline. Her examples of fact, opinion, and reasoned judgment were embedded in the context of paragraphs, which is more "real world" than a series of sentences would have been. Similarly, Laura having her students find the area of a school parking lot or other parts of the school environment is more real world and much more meaningful than solving written problems on a worksheet would be, and Donna having her students practice their study skills in a variety of content areas would meet the same goal.

Use High Levels of Interaction. Learning is largely a social process (Aronson, Wilson, & Akert, 2013), and *social interaction facilitates learning* is a cognitive learning principle. This makes sense. We've all had the experience of coming to understand an idea as a result of discussing it with someone else that we initially struggled to comprehend on our own. Each of the teachers applied this principle by conducting her lessons with high levels of interaction with her students. And the use of examples, connecting them to the real world, and promoting interaction are synergistic. "To fully exploit the potential of example-based instruction, it is necessary to elicit explanations from the learners" (Renkl, 2011, p. 273). The combination of the three is greater than the sum of their individual parts.

Promoting transfer is the ultimate goal of schooling. It takes time, but with effort it can be accomplished. Our job as teachers is to make this effort.

Classroom **Connections**

Promoting Transfer of Learning in Schools

1. Transfer occurs when knowledge learned in one context is applied in a different context. To promote transfer, apply the content you teach in a variety of different contexts.

   ■ **Elementary:** A fourth-grade teacher selects samples of student writing to teach grammar and punctuation rules. She displays samples on the document camera and uses the samples as the basis for her instruction.

   ■ **Middle School:** A science teacher begins a discussion of light refraction by asking students why they can see better with their glasses on than they can without them. He then illustrates refraction by putting a pencil in a glass of water, so the pencil appears differently above and below the water line, and asks the students to look at objects through magnifying lenses.

   ■ **High School:** A geometry teacher uses examples from architecture to illustrate how geometry applies to structural design. She also uses photographs from magazines and slides to illustrate how math concepts relate to the real world.

2. Involve students in activities that allow them to construct knowledge and understand the topics you are teaching. Use high-quality examples and representations to promote transfer by applying content to diverse settings.

   ■ **Elementary:** A fifth-grade teacher illustrates the concept *volume* by putting 1-cm cubes in a box 4 cm long, 3 cm wide, and 2 cm high. He instructs the students to count the cubes until the box is filled with 24 cubes. Then he relates the activity to the formula for finding volume.

   ■ **Middle School:** A history teacher writes short vignettes to illustrate hard-to-understand concepts, such as *mercantilism*. She guides students' analyses of the vignettes, helping them identify the essential characteristics of the concepts.

   ■ **High School:** An English teacher prepares a matrix illustrating the characters, setting, and themes for several of Shakespeare's plays. Students use the information to summarize and draw conclusions about Shakespeare's works.

Developmentally Appropriate **Practice**

Developing Complex Cognitive Skills with Learners of Different Ages

Although learners of all ages can develop higher level cognitive skills, important developmental differences exist. The following paragraphs outline these and offer suggestions on how to adapt your instruction to the developmental needs of your students.

Working with Students in Early Childhood Programs and Elementary Schools

The concepts that we teach young children are generally concrete and best explained by rule-driven theories of concept learning. This explains why we see concepts such as *triangle, circle, pets,* and *farm animals* taught to kindergarten children. Young learners often overgeneralize, classifying spiders as insects, for example, or they undergeneralize, such as limiting adverbs to words that end in *ly*. Because of this tendency, providing a variety of high-quality examples and discussing them thoroughly are important with young learners.

Their tendencies to center on prominent information also impact their problem solving. For example, young children tend to use superficial strategies in solving word problems, such as looking for key words like *altogether,* which suggests addition, *or how many more,* which suggests subtraction. These strategies can bypass understanding completely but are often quite successful (Schoenfeld, 1991, 2006). To accommodate these developmental patterns, ask young students to put their thinking into words, explaining how they solved a problem. They need a great deal of scaffolding, so patience and effort are required.

Young children also tend to be "strategically inert," either not using learning strategies at all or employing primitive strategies such as rehearsal. Although their lack of prior knowledge is often a factor, with effort and patience, they can learn to use strategies quite effectively (Kato & Manning, 2007).

Working with Students in Middle Schools

Middle school students' maturation makes them capable of constructing abstract concepts, such as *culture* and *justice,* which are often learned through prototypes and exemplars. However, many older students lack the experiences needed to make abstract concepts meaningful, so they are best represented as concretely as possible. For example, a seventh-grade teacher used vignettes, such as the following, to illustrate the concept *anaphylactic shock* (a body's overreaction to a minor stimulus) for her students:

> Chet is walking through some tall grass on property he has just purchased. He hears a buzzing sound and suddenly feels a sharp sting on his leg. Within minutes Chet feels his throat swelling up, and it becomes very difficult for him to breathe. Beginning to panic, he calls 911 on his cell phone.

> Twelve-year-old Amiel recently moved from Alaska to Florida. It's her first day of school, and while sitting with her classmate Janine at lunch, Amiel unwraps her tuna sandwich as Janine munches on her peanut butter and jelly sandwich. Amiel smells something she has never smelled before and asks Janine what she is eating. Before Janine can answer, Amiel falls off her chair and is curled up on the floor gasping for breath. The students at Amiel's table yell for help. One of the lunchroom workers calls 911. (S. Schellenberg, personal communication, April 13, 2014)

Concrete representations of topics such as these are much more meaningful for middle school students than simply describing them.

Middle school students also tend to lack the metacognition needed to monitor their problem solving. For example, 13-year-olds were given the following problem:

> An army bus holds 36 soldiers. If 1,128 soldiers are being bused to their training site, how many buses are needed?

Fewer than one fourth of the 13-year-olds answered it correctly; most of the other students either dropped the remainder or reported 31 1/3 buses, ignoring the fact that a third of a bus is meaningless (O'Brien, 1999). With middle school students, teachers need to emphasize evaluating the results of problem solving to ensure that the results make sense (Schoenfeld, 2006).

Middle school students can use sophisticated learning strategies but rarely do so unless their teachers model and encourage the strategies (Pressley & Harris, 2006). Efforts such as those Donna Evans made can be very effective (see "Educational Psychology and Teaching: Helping Your Students Become Strategic Learners" on page 343).

Working with Students in High Schools

Although Piaget described high school–aged students as formal operational, many are not, especially when the content is new to them. This suggests that using analogies, role plays, simulations, and vignettes, such as the ones illustrating anaphylactic shock, continues to be important for making abstract concepts meaningful to these students.

With respect to problem solving, authentic activities and real-world applications are particularly important for older students who want to see the utility of their learning activities.

Many older students use strategies, such as highlighting, passively instead of making decisions about what is most important to highlight (Pressley & Harris, 2006). Often, they fail to monitor their comprehension as well as they should, which leads them to overestimate how well they understand the topics they study (Schneider & Lockl, 2002). This is why it's important for you to encourage study strategies across the curriculum and to emphasize metacognition when working with high school students.

chapter

8 Summary

1. Define *concepts,* and describe strategies for helping students learn concepts.
   - A *concept* is a mental construct or representation of a category that allows us to identify examples and nonexamples of the category.
   - Rule-driven theories of concept learning explain how people learn well-defined concepts such as perimeter, adjective, and latitude.
   - Exemplar theories explain how learners construct concepts on the basis of the most highly typical examples of a class or category.
   - Theories of concept learning can be applied in classrooms by embedding examples and nonexamples of concepts in real-world contexts, sequencing the examples from most typical to least familiar, and linking the concept to related concepts.

2. Recognize examples of ill-defined and well-defined problems, and describe strategies to teach problem solving in classrooms.
   - A problem exists when a person has a goal but lacks an obvious way of achieving the goal.
   - A well-defined problem, such as finding the solution for $3x + 4 = 13$, has only one correct solution and a certain method for finding it.
   - An ill-defined problem, such as students' failing to accept personal responsibility for their own learning, has an ambiguous goal, more than one acceptable solution, and no generally agreed-upon strategy for reaching a solution.
   - Identifying the problem goal, representing the problem, selecting a strategy, implementing the strategy, and evaluating the results are stages in the problem-solving process.

- Deliberate practice involves purposeful and systematic practice combined with detailed feedback.
- Worked examples can be an effective part of deliberate practice, particularly for novice problem solvers.

3. Identify applications of study strategies and critical thinking.
   - Strategies are cognitive operations that exceed the normal activities required to carry out a task. Taking notes is a strategy, for example, because it is a cognitive operation used to help learners remember more of what they hear or read.
   - Learners who use strategies effectively are metacognitive about their approaches to learning. They also possess a repertoire of strategies and prior knowledge about the topics they're studying. Ineffective strategy users are less metacognitive, and they lack prior knowledge and possess fewer strategies.
   - Critical thinking is the process of making and assessing conclusions based on evidence. Teachers promote critical thinking when they ask students to justify their thinking and provide evidence for their conclusions.

4. Analyze factors that influence the transfer of learning.
   - Transfer occurs when learners can apply previously learned information in a new context. Specific transfer involves an application in a situation closely related to the original; general transfer occurs when two learning situations are quite different.
   - Teachers promote transfer when they provide students with a variety of high-quality examples embedded in a real-world context. These examples provide the experiences learners need to construct their knowledge and apply it in new settings.
   - Transfer tends to be specific, but metacognitive and self-regulatory skills may transfer across domains.

Preparing for **Your Licensure Exam**

Understanding Complex Cognitive Processes

You will be required to take a licensure exam before you go into your own classroom. This exam will include information related to concept learning, problem solving, learning strategies, and transfer, and it will include both multiple-choice and constructed-response questions. We include the following exercises to help you practice for the exam in your state. This book and these exercises will be a resource for you as you prepare for the exam.

In the following case study, Sue Brush, is working with her second graders in a lesson on graphing to meet the standard **CCSS.Math.Content.2.MD.D.10 Draw a picture graph and a bar graph (with single-unit scale) to represent a data set with up to four categories. Solve simple put-together, take-apart, and compare problems using information presented in a bar graph** (Common Core State Standards Initiative, 2014g).

Read the case study, and answer the questions that follow.

Sue introduces the lesson by saying that she is planning a party for the class but has a problem because she wants to share jelly beans with the class but doesn't know the class's favorite flavor of jelly bean.

Students offer suggestions for solving the problem, and they finally settle on having students taste a variety of jelly beans and indicate their favorite.

Having anticipated the idea of tasting the jelly beans, Sue has prepared plastic bags, each with seven different-flavored jelly beans. She gives each student a bag, and after students taste each one, she says, "Okay, I need your help. . . . How can we organize our information so that we can look at it as a whole group?"

Students offer several suggestions, and Sue then says, "Here's what we're going to do. Stacey mentioned earlier that we could graph the information, and we have an empty graph up in the front of the room." She moves to the front of the room and displays the outline of a graph:

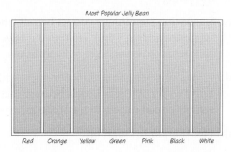

Most Popular Jelly Bean

She then asks students to come to the front of the room and paste colored pieces that represent their favorite jelly beans on the graph, and the results are what we see here.

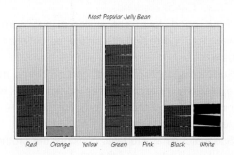

Most Popular Jelly Bean

"Now, look up here," she smiles. "We collected and organized the information, so now we need to analyze it. I want you to tell me what we know by looking at the graph. . . . Candice?"

"People like green," Candice answers.

"How many people like green?"

". . . Nine."

"Nine people like green. . . . And how did you find that out? Come up here and show us how you read the graph."

Candice goes up to the graph and moves her hand up from the bottom, counting the nine green squares as she goes.

Sue continues asking students to interpret the graph, and then changes the direction of the lesson by saying, "Okay, here we go. . . . How many more people liked green than red? . . . Look up at the graph, and set up the problem on your paper."

She watches as students look at the graph and set up the problem, and when they're finished, she says, "I'm looking for a volunteer to share an answer with us. . . . Dominique?"

"Nine plus 5 is 14," Dominique answers.

"Dominique says 9 plus 5 is 14. Let's test it out," Sue responds, asking Dominique to go up to the graph and show the class how she arrived at her answer.

As Dominique walks to the front of the room, Sue says, "We want to know the difference. . . . How many more people liked green than red, and you say 14 people, . . . 14 more people liked green. Does that work?"

Dominique looks at the graph for a moment and then says, "I mean 9 take away 5."

"She got up here and she changed her mind," Sue says with a smile to the rest of the class. "Tell them."

"Nine take away 5 is 4," Dominique says.

"Nine take away 5 is 4," Sue continues, "so how many more people liked green than red? . . . Carlos?"

"Four," Carlos responds.

"Four, good, four," she smiles at him warmly. "The key was, you had to find the difference between the two numbers."

Sue has students offer additional problems, they solve and explain them, and she then continues, "I have one more question, and then we'll switch gears. How many people took part in this voting?"

Sue watches as students consider the problem for a few minutes, and then says, "Matt? . . . How many people?"

"Twenty-four."

"Matt said 24. Did anyone get a different answer? So we'll compare. . . . Robert?"

"Twenty-two."

"How did you solve the problem?" she asks Robert.

"Nine plus 5 plus 3 plus 3 plus 1 plus 1 equals 22," he answers, adding up all the squares on the graph.

"Where'd you get all those numbers?"

"There," he says, pointing to the graph. "I went from the highest to the lowest, added them, and the answer was 22."

Sue then breaks the children into groups and has them work at centers where they gather and summarize information in bar graphs. They tally and graph the number of students who have birthdays each month, interview classmates about their favorite soft drinks, and call pizza delivery places to compare the cost of comparable pizzas.

As time for lunch nears, Sue calls the groups back together, and after they're settled, says, "Raise your hand if you can tell me what you learned this morning in math."

"How to bar graph," Jenny responds.

"So, a graph is a way of organizing information, so we can look at it and talk about it. Later we'll look at some additional ways of organizing information," and she ends the lesson.

Questions for Case Analysis

In answering these questions, use information from the chapter, and link your responses to specific information in the case.

Multiple-Choice Questions

1. Of the following, which strategy for developing students' problem solving did Sue *most prominently* illustrate in her lesson?

   a. Present problems in real-world contexts, and provide practice in identifying problem goals.

   b. Develop students' expertise with deliberate practice and worked examples.

   c. Capitalize on social interaction to engage students and monitor their learning progress.

   d. Encourage sense making in the problem-solving process.

2. Of the following, which aspect of Sue's lesson was most effective for promoting transfer?

   a. Sue initially using the jelly bean activity to illustrate bar graphs, because the activity provided students with a real-world experience

   b. Sue asking the students how many people took part in the voting

   c. Sue having Dominique correct herself when she initially suggested adding 9 and 5 to find out how many more children liked green than red jelly beans

   d. Combining her group work at centers with her learning activity using the jelly beans, because each center activity added variety to the students' experiences

Constructed-Response Question

3. To what extent did Sue promote critical thinking in her lesson? What could she have done to give her students more practice with critical thinking? Offer specific suggestions in your response.

Important **Concepts**

algorithm
belief preservation
blocked practice
characteristics
comprehension monitoring
concept map
concepts
conceptual hierarchies
confirmation bias

creativity
critical thinking
deliberate practice
divergent thinking
drawing analogies
elaborative questioning
exemplars
experts
general transfer

guided notes
heuristics
ill-defined problem
interactive whiteboards
interspersed practice
means–ends analysis
metacognition
problem
problem-based learning

specific transfer
strategies
study strategies
summarizing
text signals
transfer
virtual manipulatives
well-defined problem
worked examples

9 Knowledge Construction in Social Contexts

OUTLINE	LEARNING OUTCOMES
	After you've completed your study of this chapter, you should be able to:
The Social World Social Influences in Our Lives The Neuroscience of Social Connection ▶ Technology, Learning, and Development: Technology and Social Connection	1. Describe how social factors influence both our daily living and the way we learn.
Knowledge Construction The Transition from Cognitive to Social Constructivism Knowledge Construction and the Learning Sciences Diversity: Its Influence on Knowledge Construction	2. Describe the processes involved in knowledge construction and analyze examples that illustrate these processes.
Misconceptions: When Learners Construct Invalid Knowledge Misconceptions in Teaching and Learning The Origin of Misconceptions Misconceptions' Resistance to Change	3. Explain misconceptions, how they occur, and how they can be eliminated.
Educational Psychology and Teaching: Guiding Your Students' Knowledge Constructions Teachers' Roles in Knowledge Construction Suggestions for Classroom Practice ▶ Technology, Learning, and Development: Capitalizing on Technology to Provide Meaningful Experiences ▶ Analyzing Theories: Evaluating Constructivism ▶ Developmentally Appropriate Practice: Principles of Learning with Students at Different Ages	4. Describe suggestions for classroom practice, and explain how they are grounded in the learning sciences and the processes involved in knowledge construction.

We know that people don't behave like recording devices, such as cell phone cameras, that store information in the form in which it's presented. Instead, we construct our knowledge as we attempt to make sense of our experiences, and it commonly occurs in a social environment. This process is illustrated in the following case study, and as you read it, keep the idea of knowledge construction in social environments in mind.

> The students in this case are third graders, and their teacher, Alicia Evans, is working with them on *Common Core State Standard* **CCSS.ELA-Literacy.L.3.1f "Ensure subject-verb and pronoun-antecedent agreement" (Common Core State Standards Initiative, 2014f).**
>
> After completing her routines for the beginning of language arts, Alicia explains and demonstrates the rules with some examples on the board. She then displays the following short paragraph on her document camera.
>
> Bill takes his lunch to the cafeteria when it's time to eat. His friend Leroy and his other friend Antonio (takes, take) (his, theirs) to the cafeteria, too. Each of the boys has (his, their) own lunch box with pictures of cars

on (it, them). Bill doesn't like apples, so he will give his to anyone else if (he, they) (wants, want) it.

"Now," she directs, "Read the paragraph carefully, . . . think about it, and then decide which one of the words in the parentheses in each case is correct. Remember, our reasons and thinking are as important as the actual answers."

After giving the students a couple minutes to study the paragraph, she begins, "How about the first one?," pointing to the first set of parentheses (takes, take) in the paragraph.

The students conclude that "take" is correct in the sentence because "Leroy and Antonio" is a plural subject, so it requires the plural verb "take." They also conclude that "theirs" is correct in the sentence because "theirs" agrees with its antecedent (Leroy and Antonio).

"Now, how about this one?" she asks, pointing to the next set of parentheses (his, their) in the third sentence—Each of the boys has (his, their) own lunch box with pictures of cars on (it, them). "What do you think, and why do you think so . . . Brittany?"

". . . I think it should be 'their' because it says *boys* and boys is more than one. 'His' is only one, so that doesn't fit."

After pausing a few seconds to give the students a chance to think about Brittany's answer, Alicia recognizes Carlos's raised hand. "I think it should be 'his,' . . . because it says *each,* and each is 'one' (singular), so it should be 'his' because 'his' is also 'one.'"

After some additional discussion, the class agrees that it should be "his," and Alicia then asks, "What about this one?" pointing to the parentheses (it, them) at the end of the sentence.

"I know," Brittany says, raising her hand. "'It' is correct."

"Tell us why," Alicia, pleased, directs.

"They're talking about one lunch box, and 'it' is one, so it can't be 'them.'"

Alicia asks the rest of the class if Brittany's thinking makes sense, they agree it does, and they then analyze the examples in the last sentence.

Finally, as a seatwork assignment, Alicia directs the students to write a paragraph of their own that includes at least two examples illustrating subject-verb agreement, and two more examples illustrating pronoun-antecedent agreement.

We'll return to the lesson later in the chapter, but for now, think about these questions.

1. Where did Brittany initially get the idea that the pronoun should be "their" instead of "his" for the first example in the sentence "Each of the boys has (his, their) own lunch box with pictures of cars on (it, them)"?
2. Why did she change her mind, and conclude that the pronoun should be "it" instead of "them" in the second example in the sentence?
3. What implications does this episode have for our teaching?

We answer these and other questions in this chapter.

The Social World

This is a book about learning and what we as teachers can do to promote it. To fully understand learning in classrooms, however, we must first recognize the powerful influence that social environments have on our lives. Let's look at these influences in a bit more depth.

Ed Psych and You

You notice that your two best friends have gained a considerable amount of weight. Will this influence you in any way? Are you more likely to be careful about what you eat, so the same thing doesn't happen to you?

"Yes," is the answer to the first question, but, unfortunately, the answer to the second question is "no." We'll see why below.

Social Influences in Our Lives

We are social animals, and most of us enjoy both the company of—and interacting with—others (Brooks, 2011). In fact, we spend an enormous amount of time in social interaction. Research conducted more than 20 years ago indicates that some of us spend up to 80% of our time awake in the company of others and can average 6 hours or more a day in conversations, mostly with people we know well (Emler, 1994). Because of population increases and urbanization, the figure is probably higher today.

As we'll see throughout the chapter, social factors are also powerful in schools. For example, research indicates that social factors in neighborhoods can influence students' school attendance (Gottfried, 2014). Further, researchers have found that being absent from school not only has a negative impact on the students who are absent, but being absent also has a negative impact on the students' classmates, probably, according to the researchers' interpretation, because the absences have a negative impact on the classroom climate (Gottfried, 2011).

Now, let's see why the answer to the first question in *Ed Psych and You* above is "yes," but "no" is the answer to the second. Researchers believe that "we are biologically hardwired to mimic others" (Christakis & Fowler, 2009, p. 37). When we see our friends eat large meals, we're inclined to do so ourselves, so we're also likely to gain weight (Thaler & Sunstein, 2008). When students see their classmates misbehaving, they are more likely to misbehave, all of which detracts from the learning climate.

Positive social influences exist as well. Programs such as *Weight Watchers* and *Alcoholics Anonymous* are based on the influence of social support. For example, researchers have found that people with support groups lost 33% more weight than people did alone, and they were more likely to keep the weight off (Wing & Jeffrey, 1999). If you and your friends are smokers, and your friends quit, you're more likely to quit than if your friends continue smoking.

Social influences also extend to our emotions. "[I]n mimicking their [our friends] outward displays, we come to adopt their inward states. If your friend feels happy, she smiles, you smile, and in the act of smiling you also come to feel happy" (Christakis & Fowler, 2009, p. 37). If your friends make a concerted effort to lose weight, and, as a result, feel good about it, you're likely to do and feel the same way.

The Neuroscience of Social Connection

Think about the enormous complexities of social living. Among many others, they include learning by observing others; recognizing changes in the status of friends and foes; anticipating and coordinating group efforts; using language to communicate, teach, and learn; navigating personal relationships, social hierarchies, and changes in culture; and subjugating self-interests for the interests of a social group in exchange for the possibility of long-term benefits. This social complexity, social neuroscience researchers argue, contributes to the rapid increase in neural connectivity in the *neocortex*, the technical term for what we colloquially call "grey matter." The neocortex is the top layer of the brain that is responsible for higher levels of functioning, such as sensory perception, spatial reasoning, conscious thought, and in humans, language (Cacioppo & Ortigue, 2011). In other words, we evolved as social animals because it increased our chances for survival (Christakis & Fowler, 2009; Gazzaniga, 2008).

Evidence supporting the biological need for social connection is broad and deep. For instance, new mothers are urged to hold their newborn infants "skin-to-skin," and babies deprived of social connection develop a variety of problems, such as impaired intellectual development, hyperactivity, inattention, and unruly behavior (Kreppner et al., 2007). Research conducted more than 30 years ago found that older people who lacked social ties had shorter life spans than those with more extensive contacts, even when factors such as smoking, obesity, and physical activity were taken into account (Berkman & Syme, 1979). Additional research suggests that social connection is as beneficial to long-term health as avoiding cigarettes (The *PLoS Medicine* Editors, 2010). Researchers have also found that people who are self-absorbed, as measured by the number of self-references in their speech (I, me, my) were more likely to have heart disease than their more social peers (Scherwitz et al., 1983).

Social issues even extend to our justice system. For instance, medical ethicists suggest that the solitary confinement of prisoners increases the likelihood of mental illness or exacerbates mental conditions that already exist, and some suggest that solitary confinement constitutes "cruel and unusual punishment," which is prohibited by the Eighth Amendment to our country's constitution (Metzner & Fellner, 2010).

Having seen how important social influences are in our lives, we turn now to a closer examination of social influences in learning.

Technology, Learning, and Development

Technology and Social Connection

If you had grown up in the 1800s, your social connections would likely have been limited largely to your family if you lived in a rural area, and to your family and neighbors if you lived in a city. As the use of automobiles and air travel increased in the 20th century, our social connections widened, but driving long distances and particularly flying were still relatively rare events. Now, however, with the invention of the Internet and the widespread use of social media, social connection is literally global. As a simple example, Paul (one of your authors) has a cousin who lives in Australia and a friend in New Zealand, and he regularly corresponds with both via email and Skype. Closer to home, surveys indicate that a typical American teen may send and receive 50 text messages per day, and nearly 1 of 3 send and receive more than 100 (Pew Charitable Trust, 2010)!

With respect to social media, at the end of 2012 Facebook reported more than 1 billion—yes, billion—active monthly users, and many now use the site on their cell phones. Users also uploaded more than 2 billion photos during the year. And Twitter reports 500 million users, some of which are, of course, also on Facebook (Tam, 2013).

How is the dramatic increase in social connection impacting our lives? Research is beginning to provide some answers, and, as with most influences, the results are mixed. For instance, using cell phones—and particularly texting—while driving have become matters of national concern. One survey indicated that more than 90% of respondents sent text messages while driving and also exceeded speed limits and wandered from lane to lane in the process. Additional research indicates that texting while driving is as dangerous as driving with a blood alcohol level above the legal limit (EpiMonitor, 2011). Interestingly, these young drivers agreed that texting while driving is dangerous and should be illegal, but believing this way didn't seem to change their behavior (Harrison, 2011).

Some research also suggests that texting may have an impact on social development. For instance, one of the tasks of adolescence is to separate from parents and become an independent person, but if technology makes staying in touch very, very easy, the process of separating becomes more difficult. "Now you have adolescents who are texting their mothers 15 times a day, asking things like, 'Should I get the red shoes or the blue shoes?'" (Hafner, 2009, para. 8).

Facebook use is also being examined. Research suggests that its extensive use may hinder academic adjustment and be an indicator of lowered self-esteem in undergraduate college students (Kalpidou, Costin, & Morris, 2011); the more Facebook friends people collect, the greater their degree of narcissism (Schwartz, 2010); and increased Facebook use can result in jealousy, particularly in romantic relationships (Muise, Christofides, & Desmarais, 2009). Research suggests that people are now beginning to experience "Internet addiction disorder" or "problematic Internet use" (PIU) (Moreno, Jelenchick, & Christakis, 2013). People with this disorder are unable to function "normally" without the Internet and particularly social media. For them, life is complex and stressful when cut off from their virtual life (Summers, 2011).

Based on this research, we might be led to conclude that the effects of technology on our social connection are generally negative. And, as with excess in most domains, they can be. On the other hand, as we said at the beginning of the chapter, we are social animals with a need to be connected to others, and texting can help meet this need. And Facebook, used properly, can also be a wonderful tool for staying connected to long-time friends. For instance, Don's (your other author) college-age daughter uses Facebook to stay in touch with high school friends who live in other states. This allows them to "not miss a beat" when they get together.

At a broader level, we've all heard about the impact of social media on organized protests around the world, and, in 2013, outrage that went viral on Twitter as a result of a privileged Mexican girl having her influential father close a restaurant in Mexico City because she wasn't given the table she wanted, quickly resulting in an apology from both the girl and her father. "[T]he times are changing, in part because social media are capable of focusing a huge amount of attention, instantly, on such bad behavior" (Stevenson, 2013, para. 17). Technology has given people the power to force social change that wouldn't have been possible even as recently as 10 or 15 years ago.

As with virtually all innovations and trends, the influence of technology on social connection is neither all good nor all bad; it's a matter of how we use it, and the responsibility for using it wisely is ours. Obviously texting while driving or being addicted to Facebook is undesirable. On the other hand, staying connected to family and close friends can be wonderful, and using social media to make the world a better place is obviously positive. The key is controlling the technology, not allowing it to control us.

Knowledge Construction

That learners construct their own knowledge based on their existing understanding is the core idea of constructivism, and it's consistent with principles of cognitive learning theory that state (1) learning and development depend on learners' experiences, (2) people want their experiences to make sense, and (3) to make sense of their experiences, learners construct knowledge. "[C]onstructivism considers knowledge as constructed by learners as they attempt to make sense of their experiences" (Hattie & Gan, 2011, p. 256). This core idea was illustrated in Brittany's thinking in Alicia's lesson (in our chapter opening case study), and it answers the first question we asked at the beginning of the chapter: "Where did Brittany initially get the idea that the pronoun should be 'their' instead of 'his' for the first example in the sentence 'Each of the boys has (his, their) own lunch box with pictures of cars on (it, them)'?" She *constructed* the idea on her own because, as a result of seeing "the boys" in the sentence, "their" made more sense to her than did "his."

The Transition from Cognitive to Social Constructivism

Historically, theorists haven't completely agreed on the process of knowledge construction. Initially, based on Piaget's work, theorists and researchers focused on what is commonly called *cognitive constructivism* (Brainerd, 2003). Let's look at it.

COGNITIVE CONSTRUCTIVISM

Cognitive constructivism is a view of knowledge construction that describes it as an individual, internal process (Brainerd, 2003; Greeno, Collins, & Resnick, 1996). It emphasizes individuals' efforts to make sense of their experiences as they interact with the environment and test and modify their existing understanding. Social interaction influences the process, but primarily as a catalyst for individual cognitive conflict. When one child suggests an idea that causes disequilibrium in another, for instance, the second child resolves the disequilibrium by individually reconstructing his or her understanding (Brainerd, 2003). For example, in our chapter opening case study Brittany saw the sentence:

> "Each of the boys has (his, their) own lunch box with pictures of cars on (it, them),"

and she concluded that "their" was the correct pronoun in the first part of the sentence. Carlos replied, "I think it should be 'his,' . . . because it says *each,* and each is 'one' (singular), so it should be 'his' because 'his' is also 'one.'" Then, later in the discussion Brittany correctly concluded that "it" was the correct pronoun at the end of the sentence.

Cognitive constructivists would interpret this exchange by saying that Brittany's equilibrium was disrupted as a result of Carlos's comment together with the discussion that followed, and—individually—she resolved the problem by reconstructing her thinking to accommodate the new evidence Carlos and other classmates offered.

A literal interpretation of this position emphasizes experience-based and discovery-oriented learning activities. This view suggests, for example, that children learn math most effectively if they discover math ideas while manipulating concrete objects, such as blocks and sticks, rather than having them presented by a teacher or other expert.

One interpretation of this perspective suggests that we should avoid directly teaching or imposing our thinking on our students, but many others question it (Clark, Kirschner, & Sweller, 2012). As a result, cognitive constructivism as a framework for guiding instruction has largely receded in favor of the current views of learning that focus more strongly on social processes in knowledge construction.

SOCIAL CONSTRUCTIVISM

Ed Psych and You

You and a friend are working on a problem, but neither of you understands it completely, and neither is able to solve it alone. As you continue to struggle and discuss the problem, however, gradually you arrive at a solution. Why do you suppose you were able to solve the problem together when neither could solve it alone?

As researchers have come to better understand the complexities of learning, they now realize that in the real world, the world outside of classrooms, learning is largely social in nature. Research has "revealed that outside of formal schooling, almost all learning occurs in a complex social environment, and learning is hard to understand if one thinks of it as a mental process occurring within the head of an isolated learner" (Sawyer, 2006, p. 9).

Our example in *Ed Psych and You* illustrates this process. We've all had the experience of talking to another person about an idea or problem, with neither understanding it completely, but as the discussion continues, understanding increases for both of us. This illustrates the basic premise of social constructivism, which suggests that learners first construct knowledge in a social context and then individually internalize it. Lev Vygotsky, a Russian psychologist, often viewed as the inspiration for social constructivism, observed, "Every function in the child's cultural development appears twice: first, on the social level, and later, on the individual level. . . . All the higher functions originate as actual relations between human individuals" (Vygotsky, 1978, p. 57).

To illustrate social constructivism in action, think again about the exchange between Brittany and Carlos and the discussion that followed in Alicia's lesson. In contrast with cognitive constructivists, who interpret this episode as Brittany individually resolving the problem by changing her thinking, social constructivists suggest that the change in Brittany's thinking was a direct outcome of the discussion itself. The dialogue—directly—helped Brittany more clearly understand the grammar rule, and, following the discussion, she then individually internalized it, a process called appropriating understanding (Leont'ev, 1981; Li et al., 2007).

This exchange between the students, in addition to illustrating the social nature of learning, also helps us understand why merely explaining topics to students often doesn't work very well. If our explanations don't make sense to them, they will (mentally) restructure what we've said so it *does*—or they will memorize as much of it as they can and then quickly forget it. Explanations are also ineffective if our students don't listen carefully while we're explaining—a common problem—or they remain cognitively passive (i.e., don't think carefully enough about the explanation to encode the information in their memories). This may also have been a factor in Brittany's thinking.

Social constructivism has become the primary framework for designing and delivering instruction in our schools (Martin, 2006). It doesn't imply that learners should discover everything on their own, nor does it suggest that teachers shouldn't offer their thinking to students, "as Piagetian theory often seemed to imply" (Resnick & Klopfer, 1989, p. 4). Rather, it suggests that teachers consider all the traditional questions related to instruction: how to plan, conduct learning activities, motivate students, and assess learning. The focus, however, is on facilitating students' constructions of knowledge using social interaction as a catalyst, instead of simply explaining ideas while they listen passively (Fleming & Alexander, 2001). From a social constructivist perspective, creating learning environments in which learners are cognitively active in the process of constructing and internalizing valid ideas is an essential role for us as teachers.

We turn now to some of the processes involved in creating these learning environments as we examine:

- Sociocultural learning theory
- The classroom as a community of learners
- Cognitive apprenticeships

Sociocultural Learning Theory. Sociocultural theory, while still emphasizing the social dimensions of learning, places greater emphasis on the larger cultural contexts in which learning occurs (Mason, 2007). Patterns of interaction in homes illustrate this emphasis. In some cultures, for instance, children are not viewed as legitimate partners in conversation, and as a result, they may be reluctant to raise their hands in attempts to volunteer answers to our questions. And they may even be hesitant to respond when we call on them directly (Au, 1992; Tharp & Gallimore, 1991). Differences also exist in the cultural experiences, attitudes, and values that students bring to school, all of which influence learning (Rogoff, 2003). As teachers, we need to be sensitive to these differences and help our students understand and adapt to the culture of our classrooms.

The Classroom as a Community of Learners. A sociocultural view of learning shifts the emphasis from the individual to the group and from acquiring knowledge, per se, to belonging, participating, and communicating within a community of learners (Mason, 2007).

A **community of learners** is a learning environment in which the teacher and students all work together to help everyone learn (Brown & Campione, 1994; Palincsar, 1998). This perspective reminds us that our management, rules and procedures, and the way we interact with students create microcultures in our classrooms, making them cooperative and inviting or competitive and even frightening.

In a learning community:

- All students participate in learning activities. Alicia developed her lesson by interacting with the students; she didn't simply explain the rules to them and then have them practice with some exercises.
- Teachers and students work together to help one another learn; promoting learning isn't the teacher's responsibility alone. Brittany, for example, changed her thinking as a result of Carlos's comment. She learned from him.
- Student–student interaction is an important part of the learning process. Again, it was Brittany's interaction with Carlos, not with Alicia, that resulted in her increased understanding.
- Teachers and students respect differences in interests, thinking, and progress. Carlos, for example, didn't offer his thinking until Alicia recognized his raised hand, and, even though they were only third graders, the students in Alicia's class listened patiently as their classmates offered their thinking, even if the thinking differed from their own.
- The thinking involved in learning activities is as important as the answers themselves. Alicia even said to her students, "Remember, our reasons and thinking are as important as the actual answers."

Each of these characteristics is grounded in the idea that knowledge is first socially constructed before it is appropriated and internalized by individuals.

In attempting to create a community of learners, we are trying to develop a classroom culture in which students feel as if "we're all in this together." We do our best to support our students' efforts to understand the topics we're teaching, and students help each other whenever they can. Scores and grades reflect the extent to which they've mastered the content instead of how well they compete with each other.

Cognitive Apprenticeship. Historically, apprenticeships have helped novices—as they worked with experts—acquire skills they couldn't learn on their own (Black, 2007). Apprenticeships are common in trades such as plumbing, weaving, or cooking, but they are also used in areas such as learning to play musical instruments or creating pieces of art. **Cognitive apprenticeships** are also social learning processes that occur when less-skilled learners work alongside experts in developing cognitive skills, such as reading comprehension, writing, or problem solving (Collins, 2006). Cognitive apprenticeships focus on developing thinking and commonly include the following components:

- *Modeling*: Teachers, or other, more knowledgeable students, demonstrate skills, such as solutions to problems, and simultaneously model their thinking by describing it out loud.
- *Scaffolding*: As students perform tasks, teachers ask questions and provide support, decreasing the amount of scaffolding as students' proficiency increases.
- *Verbalization*: Students are encouraged to express their developing understanding in words, which allows teachers to assess students' developing thinking.
- *Increasing complexity*: As students' proficiency increases, teachers present them with more challenging problems or other tasks.

We saw cognitive apprenticeship in Alicia's lesson. Carlos modeled his thinking with his comment,

> "I think it should be 'his,' . . . because it says *each,* and each is 'one' (singular), so it should be 'his' because 'his' is also 'one,'"

and this modeling, together with the discussion that followed his comment, scaffolded Brittany's thinking. Then, she verbalized her thinking when she said,

> "I know . . . . 'It' is correct . . . . They're talking about one lunch box, and 'it' is one, so it can't be 'them,'"

as she explained the second example in the sentence. Verbalizing understanding helps students put their sometimes fuzzy thoughts into words and helps clarify their thinking (Kastens & Liben, 2007). By participating in a cognitive apprenticeship, Brittany's understanding increased.

Despite a large and consistent body of evidence indicating that social interaction increases learning (Brophy, 2006), it is quite rare; teachers spend most of their instructional time lecturing and explaining or having students do seatwork (Pianta, Belsky, Houts, & Morrison, 2007). Scaffolding and verbalization, two essential components of cognitive apprenticeships, are not possible if we simply explain the topics we teach. A rule of thumb for all of us is: *If we explain an idea, our students may or may not "get" it; if they explain it to us, we know they have it.*

Knowledge Construction and the Learning Sciences

Ed Psych and You

1. For which of the following problems will the answer be greater:

$$392 \div 14 = \text{or } 360 \div 12 =$$

2. Now, consider these problems:

   Jennifer makes a trip to see a college friend in a town 392 miles from her hometown. Her car uses 14 gallons of gas to make the trip. Christina is going home for spring break from college, 360 miles from her hometown. Her car uses 12 gallons of gas on the trip. Whose car, Jennifer's or Christina's, is more fuel efficient?

Which set of problems is more meaningful to you? Why do you think so?

Let's look now at the problems in *Ed Psych and You.* In both sets we simply divide 392 by 14 and 360 by 12 to answer the questions, but you likely found the second set more meaningful, as most people do, because they focus on common, real-world problems. We all spend a lot of money on gas, so we want to know how fuel efficient our cars are.

Studying learning in real-world contexts, such as examining how people learn to solve problems like the ones in our second set above, is the focus of an emerging field of study called the *learning sciences.* We examine it next.

THE LEARNING SCIENCES

The **learning sciences** is a field of study that focuses on "learning as it exists in real-world settings and how learning may be facilitated both with and without technology" (ISLS, 2004, para. 1).

Leaders in the learning sciences suggest that the schools in our country have traditionally been designed to help students acquire facts, such as "Lincoln was president during our Civil War," and procedures, such as the procedure for solving the first two problems in *Ed Psych and You* above. These leaders assert that historically, "The goal of schooling is to get these facts and procedures into the student's head. People are considered to be educated when they possess a large collection of these facts and procedures" (Sawyer, 2006, p. 1). Then, the way to determine whether schooling has been successful is to see how many of these facts and procedures students can identify or produce on a standardized test (Sawyer, 2006). This approach to schooling prepared students for our country's industrialized economy of the early 20th century, but as we've moved into a technological and knowledge-based society in the later 20th century (and particularly now in the 21st century), researchers and educational leaders find this approach to be inadequate. Knowing that learning is largely a social process, and that learners construct rather than receive knowledge, learning scientists came to several additional conclusions about learning and teaching. We outline them in Figure 9.1 and discuss them in the sections that follow.

Useful Learning Requires Deep Conceptual Understanding. The two sets of problems in *Ed Psych and You* provide a simple example of the assertion in the heading here; the second two problems require deeper conceptual understanding than simply following the memorized procedure for solving the problems in the first set. This emphasis applies in all content areas. For instance, as students we all learned about Marco Polo's visit to the Far East, the names of Portuguese explorers such as Prince Henry the Navigator and Vasco Da Gama, and Columbus's trip to the New World in 1492. We usually learned this information as a set of isolated facts and dates, consistent with the historical emphasis on teaching and learning that we described above. They are conceptually connected, however. Because of Marco Polo's travels and the influential book he wrote afterward, many merchants and traders, including the Portuguese explorers, wanted to get to the Far East. The passage around the tip of Africa and through the Indian Ocean was dangerous, however, so Columbus seized on the idea of getting to the Far East by traveling west (not realizing, of course, that he would run into the Americas instead). Understanding the connections between Marco Polo's travels, the Portuguese navigators, and Columbus's voyage to the New World at this deeper conceptual level makes all the information much more meaningful. All schooling should focus on this understanding instead of facts and memorized procedures (Bransford, Brown, & Cocking, 2000; Sawyer, 2006).

Deep Conceptual Understanding Requires Personal Reflection. "Students learn better when they express their developing knowledge—either through conversation or by creating papers, reports, or other artifacts—and then are provided the opportunities to reflectively analyze their state of knowledge" (Sawyer, 2006, pp. 2–3). This suggests that students must "do something" with their developing knowledge and skills—solve real-world

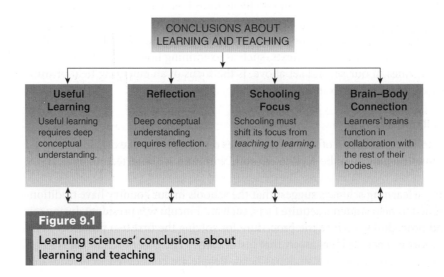

Figure 9.1

Learning sciences' conclusions about learning and teaching

problems, apply the information to their daily lives, or connect it to other information. For example, Alicia had her students write a paragraph of their own in which examples of the rules for subject-verb and pronoun-antecedent agreement were illustrated. This is a challenging task for third graders, but with practice and Alicia's support, they will succeed, and when they do, they will develop the deep conceptual understanding, and the ability to apply their understanding in the real world (their own writing), that is the goal of the learning sciences.

Schooling Must Shift Its Focus from Teaching to Learning. The statement in our heading here may appear paradoxical (i.e., haven't schools always focused on learning?). On the surface, yes, but, as we see in the example with Columbus's voyage, when probed a bit deeper, not quite.

As another example, let's look again at Alicia's work with her third graders. She could have simply presented the rules for subject-verb and pronoun-antecedent agreement, then given her students some sentences, such as

> "Neither Mary nor Laura has turned in (her, their) report."

and had them select the correct choice. And, doing so would have essentially met the standard. Instead she chose to present her examples in the context of a paragraph, which is much more "real world" than isolated sentences. For example, in our everyday lives we read information in newspapers and magazines and on the Internet. This information is always in the form of paragraphs; it never appears in isolated sentences.

She also asked her students to describe their thinking, and the discussion that followed helped Brittany resolve a misunderstanding. The difference between the way Alicia taught the rules and the way they have historically been taught is subtle but important. Her use of a real-world example and her focus on discussion and her students' thinking are essential for the development of deep conceptual understanding. "The notion is that the teacher needs to construct environments and activities that optimize making the learning of the student visible to the teacher (and preferably also to the student)" (Hattie & Gan, 2011, p. 257). Alicia created this type of environment, and her approach was consistent with a *learning sciences* emphasis.

Learners' Brains Function in Collaboration with the Rest of Their Bodies. Our brains are obviously part of our bodies, and almost as obviously, we don't think well if we're overtired or undernourished. Less obvious, however, is the concept of **embodied cognition**, the idea that cognition (our thinking) depends on characteristics of our physical bodies, and our bodies significantly influence the way we process information (Pfeifer & Bongard, 2012; Wilson & Foglia, 2011).

Many examples exist. For instance, researchers have found that people perceive hills as steeper and distances walked as longer if they're carrying a heavy backpack than if they're merely walking unencumbered (Proffitt, 2006), and learners remember more details of a story when they physically act it out (Scott, Harris, & Rothe, 2001). Also, people are able to detect the emotion expressed on another person's face more quickly if they mimic the facial expression being evaluated (Balcetis & Dunning, 2007), and participants asked to fill out a form for donations to the victims of the earthquake in Haiti in 2010, while firmly grasping a pen, were significantly more charitable than participants who merely held the pen in their fingertips (Hung & Labroo, 2011). In the last example, the researchers hypothesized that firmly grasping the pen helped participants get over their physical aversion to viewing the devastation in Haiti and made them more likely to be charitable (Hung & Labroo, 2011).

This all suggests that, when appropriate, encouraging students to use their bodies when thinking about tasks may enhance their thinking. For instance, simply forming the shape of a parallelogram with our fingers or moving our hands over a map can sometimes help us think about problems and visualize distances and situations more effectively than we would without using these gestures (Alibali, Spencer, Knox, & Kita, 2011).

SITUATED COGNITION

As we've seen above, the learning sciences focus on the study of learning as it occurs in real-world settings. Situated cognition (or situated learning) goes further to suggest that learning depends on, and cannot be separated from, the context in which it occurs (Brown, Collins, & Duguid, 1989; Robbins & Aydede, 2009). So, for instance, not only is it important to apply knowledge and understanding to real-world situations, as the learning sciences suggest, but, in fact, situated cognition researchers suggest that literally a different kind of learning occurs in real-world contexts.

For instance, when Alicia's third graders reflect on their understanding of rules for subject-verb and pronoun-antecedent agreement by writing paragraphs in which the rules are illustrated, they don't merely apply their understanding to their writing (a real-world task), they actually engage in a different, and more meaningful, kind of learning than would occur if they merely responded to exercises such as

Identify the correct pronoun in the following sentence:

"Neither Mary nor Laura has turned in (her, their) report."

As another example, proponents of situated cognition would argue that a different kind of learning occurs with you solve the second set of problems in *Ed Psych and You* than occurs when you solve the first set (Rogoff, 2003; Kirsch, 2009). Similarly, when you apply your understanding of learning theories to case studies and examples from classrooms, you acquire a different understanding than you would if you studied them in the abstract.

Situated cognition, when taken to the extreme, suggests that transfer, the ability to apply understanding acquired in one context to a different context, is difficult, if not impossible. It would suggest, for example, that people who learn to drive in rural areas would be unable to drive in big cities with their heavy traffic, because their driving expertise is situated (located) in the rural setting. Transfer does exist, however, or we would be faced with learning everything anew (Mayer & Wittrock, 2006). For example, the ability to drive in a myriad of contexts occurs, and with practice people become comfortable driving in rural areas, large cities, and even other countries.

Similarly, we can promote transfer in school by consciously varying the contexts in which learning occurs (Vosniadou, 2007). Math students, for example, should practice solving a variety of real-world problems, and language arts students should practice writing in each of their content areas (Mayer & Wittrock, 2006). Situated cognition reminds us that context is crucial, and we can accommodate it by asking our students to apply their developing knowledge in a number of different contexts. All this is consistent with the learning sciences.

Diversity: Its Influence on Knowledge Construction

Our students' diversity can have important influences on the way they construct knowledge and respond to our instruction, and the beliefs they bring to school are one of the most powerful influences on the knowledge they construct. For example, because of their different beliefs, Muslim and Jewish students are likely to construct very different understandings about issues in the Middle East, such as the Arab–Israeli conflict and the American interventions in Iraq and Afghanistan. Also, students whose religious beliefs conflict with scientists' description of the earth being four and a half billion years old, or the idea that humans evolved from more primitive species, will construct ideas that reject the tenets of evolution (Southerland & Sinatra, 2003).

Diversity, and particularly students' cultures, also influences the way they use feedback to modify their knowledge constructions. "[S]tudents from collectivist cultures (e.g., Confucian-based Asia, South Pacific nations) preferred indirect and implicit feedback, more group-focused feedback and no self-level feedback. Students from individualistic/Socratic cultures (e.g., the USA) preferred more . . . individual focused self-related feedback" (Hattie & Gan, 2011, p. 262).

So, knowing that our students will bring different beliefs to our learning activities, and desire different forms of feedback, what should we do? We know that beliefs are unlikely to change unless compelling evidence indicates that the belief is invalid, but completely compelling evidence sometimes doesn't exist, as we see with differing political views or even issues such as global warming.

The most effective approach is to clearly communicate to our students that they are accountable for understanding an idea, theory, or interpretation, whether or not they agree with or believe it (Southerland & Sinatra, 2003). For instance, the theory of evolution being controversial for some students doesn't mean that they shouldn't be required to understand its principles. Whether or not they choose to accept the principles is up to them.

With respect to feedback we can provide both indirect—feedback given to the whole class—and direct feedback whenever appropriate. If we create a classroom climate in which we're all in this together, our students who prefer indirect and implicit feedback will realize that we're on their side and will accept our direct feedback in the spirit we intend—to produce as much learning as possible.

Classrooms as learning communities are important when dealing with all forms of diversity. All students should be given the opportunity to share their beliefs, and diversity in thinking should be respected. Recognizing that classmates have beliefs different from their own and have different preferences with respect to interaction and feedback, and learning to acknowledge and respect those differences, is a worthwhile learning experience in itself.

Ed Psych and You

Are you right brained or left brained? If you think you're right brained, do you believe you're more intuitive and subjective than logical, analytical, and objective (which are considered to be left-brain orientations)? How does your left-brain or right-brain orientation influence the way you operate in the world?

Misconceptions: When Learners Construct Invalid Knowledge

Think about the questions in *Ed Psych and You*. The idea that we tend to be right brained or left brained is a sensible idea that grew out of research conducted in the 1970s and has been popularized since that time. It is, however, a myth, or misconception (Boehm, 2012; Dietrich & Kanso, 2010; Jarrett, 2012). "This popular myth, which conjures up an image of one side of our brains crackling with activity while the other lies dormant, has its roots in outdated findings from the 1970s . . . " (Boehm, 2012, para. 1).

Misconceptions are ideas we construct that make sense to us but are inconsistent with evidence or commonly accepted explanations. They are most common in science. Some, among a great many others, include: We are closer to the Sun in the summer (our summer is actually caused by the tilt of the earth); we "feed" plants in much the same way as we feed animals (plants manufacture their own food); our Moon's phases are caused by the Earth casting a shadow on the Moon (the Moon's phases are caused by the Moon's location with respect to the Earth and the Sun); and the force pushing forward on an object moving at constant speed, such as a car traveling along a highway at 70 mph, is greater than the force pushing backward (the forces are equal).

And, although misconceptions are most common in science, they exist in other content areas as well. For instance, when faced with the following math problems:

$$\begin{array}{r} 15 \\ -\ 3 \\ \hline \end{array} \qquad \begin{array}{r} 13 \\ -\ 5 \\ \hline \end{array}$$

young children sometimes get an answer of 12 for both by simply subtracting the smaller number from the larger, without considering the numbers' position. And knowing that $1 \times 1 = 1$, some students conclude that $.1 \times .1 = .1$. Language arts students commonly believe that an adverb is a word that ends in *ly* and adjectives always precede the nouns they modify. And in social studies many people believe that communism and socialism represent the same ideology. Each is a misconception, as was Brittany's conclusion,

> "I think it should be 'their' [in the sentence 'Each of the boys has (his, their) own lunch box with pictures of cars on (it, them),'] because it says *boys* and boys is more than one. 'His' is only one, so that doesn't fit."

Misconceptions in Teaching and Learning

A number of misconceptions also exist in teaching and learning. For instance, many teachers believe that the most effective way to help students understand a topic is to simply explain it to them (Cuban, 1993; Andrew, 2007), even though research indicates that explanations alone often don't work very well, and interacting with students is much more effective (Kunter et al., 2013). And many people, and even some educational leaders, believe that knowledge of content, such as math, English, or history, is all that is necessary to be an effective teacher (Mayer, 2002). This is another misconception. Knowledge of content is essential, of course, but teaching expertise requires much more, such as how to represent content in ways that are understandable to students, how to organize and manage classrooms, and understanding how students learn and develop (Kunter et al., 2013; Sadler, Sonnert, Coyle, Cook-Smith, & Miller, 2013).

Misconceptions about learner development also exist. For example, because middle and high school students' chronological ages suggest that they are formal operational in their thinking, some teachers believe they can be taught in the abstract—using words alone to help students understand the ideas they're teaching. This is a common misconception about Piaget's (1970, 1977) developmental theory. If they lack experience related to a topic, learners of all ages need concrete experiences to help them understand the topic.

Now, let's see how misconceptions originate.

The Origin of Misconceptions

The following principles of cognitive learning help us understand the origin of misconceptions:

- Learning and development depend on experience
- People want their experiences to make sense
- To make sense of their experiences, people construct knowledge

Simply, misconceptions are constructed; we form misconceptions because they make sense to us when we construct them; and they're usually consistent with our own prior personal knowledge and experiences (diSessa, 2006; Vosniadou, 2007). For instance, when we move our hand closer to a hot stove burner, or move closer to a fire in a fireplace, it feels warmer, so it makes sense to think that we are closer to the Sun in the summer. And most of the adverbs we encounter do indeed end in *ly*, so concluding that adverbs are words that end in *ly* also makes sense. Seeing "boys" in the sentence "Each of the boys has (his, their) own lunch box with pictures of cars on (it, them)" made sense and led Brittany to conclude that "their" was more accurate than "his."

Language, appearances, and "intuitive appeal" can also contribute to misconceptions. For instance, with respect to language, we refer to lead and mercury as "heavy" metals, which can lead to misconceptions about relationships between the concepts *weight, mass,* and *density*. And we describe the Sun and Moon as "rising" and "setting." Further, they both *appear* to rise and set as they move across the sky, which can lead children to believe that they revolve around the Earth.

As an example of "intuitive appeal," think again about our example in *Ed Psych and You*. The idea of right-brain–left-brain dominance is indeed intuitively appealing, and some clever people have capitalized on it. "[T]he seductive idea of the right brain and its untapped creative potential also has a long history of being targeted by self-help gurus peddling pseudo-psychology" (Jarrett, 2012, para. 2). Makers of self-improvement video games and smartphone apps perpetuate the misconception. "Did you know that the different sides of the brain control different human traits? Scientific studies have shown that the right brain and the left brain have different effects on the way we think and act" (Mirpuri, 2014, para. 1). A statement such as this, although lacking any valid research evidence, can be quite compelling.

Learning styles, students' personal approaches to thinking and problem solving (Denig, 2003), is another misconception with intuitive appeal, and schools have spent a great deal of staff development money helping teachers attempt to capitalize on their students' "learning styles." However, believing that students' learning styles influence how much they learn is also a misconception. Jere Brophy (2010), a prominent educational researcher, comments, "I do not see much validity in the claims made by those who urge teachers to assess their students with learning style inventories and follow with differentiated curriculum and instruction" (p. 283). Others speak more strongly. "I think learning styles represents one of the more wasteful and misleading pervasive myths of the last 20 years" (Clark, 2010, p. 10).

Misconceptions' Resistance to Change

As teachers we typically try to correct students' misconceptions by providing information that contradicts the misconception (Alparsian, Tekkaya, & Geban, 2004; Yip, 2004). This often doesn't work, however, because the misconception they've constructed makes sense to them, perhaps more sense than our explanation.

Why are misconceptions so resistant to change? The answer lies in Piaget's concept of equilibrium. If a misconception makes sense to us, we're at cognitive equilibrium (Sinatra & Pintrich, 2003). Changing thinking requires us to reconstruct our understanding, which is disequilibrating. Assimilating an experience into an existing understanding is simpler and less cognitively demanding.

Knowing that students bring misconceptions to learning experiences and realizing that these misconceptions are resistant to change, what can we do in response? We attempt to answer this question in the next section.

Classroom **Connections**

Promoting Conceptual Change in Your Students

1. Students construct their own knowledge, and this knowledge is sometimes invalid. Use experiences and questions to challenge students' existing understanding.

   ■ **Elementary:** A first-grade teacher's students are struggling with the following standards for understanding place value, tending to see 12 and 21 as the same numbers:

   CCSS.Math.Content.1.NBT.B.2b The numbers from 11 to 19 are composed of a ten and one, two, three, four, five, six, seven, eight, or nine ones.

   CCSS.Math.Content.1.NBT.B.2c The numbers 10, 20, 30, 40, 50, 60, 70, 80, 90 refer to one, two, three, four, five, six, seven, eight, or nine tens (and 0 ones). (Common Core State Standards Initiative, 2014o)

   He has them use blocks to demonstrate that 12 is one 10 and two ones, whereas 21 is two 10s and a single one.

   ■ **Middle School:** When one of her eighth graders explains that transparent objects are objects that we can see through and opaque objects are those we can't see through, ignoring the role of light rays, a physical science teacher asks, "If we can see through a transparent object, why can't we see through it at night?"

   ■ **High School:** When one of his students describes all Native Americans as nomadic hunter-gatherers, a history teacher shows pictures of pueblos and other permanent living structures and asks, "If they are nomadic, why would they build dwellings like these?"

2. Conceptual change requires that students are able to apply their revised thinking to new situations. Provide students with tasks that require them to apply reconstructed knowledge to new situations.

   ■ **Elementary:** The first-grade teacher in suggestion 1 writes a series of numbers on the board and has his students demonstrate the numbers with their blocks.

   ■ **Middle School:** The eighth-grade teacher in suggestion 1 asks her students to explain why they can't see a person they hear walking down the hall outside their classroom. She guides them to conclude that the light rays that are reflected from the person won't pass through the opaque wall of the classroom.

   ■ **High School:** The social studies teacher in suggestion 1 has the students describe the cultural and economic characteristics of different Native American groups, such as plains Indians and those who lived in the Southwest and Northeast.

Educational Psychology and Teaching: Guiding Your Students' Knowledge Constructions

So, what—specifically—does our understanding of the social influences on learning, knowledge construction (including the tendency to form misconceptions), and the learning sciences suggest that we should be doing when we work with our students? We now try to answer this question.

Teachers' Roles in Knowledge Construction

Our teaching roles—such as specifying learning objectives, preparing learning activities, and designing assessments—are the same when instruction is grounded in an understanding of social influences on learning, knowledge construction, and the learning sciences as they are in "traditional" classrooms. The primary difference is a shift in emphasis away from simply presenting information and "telling" students and toward providing experiences, promoting interaction, and applying content to the real world that the learning sciences suggest (Donovan & Bransford, 2005; Sawyer, 2006).

Suggestions for Classroom Practice

In applying these ideas to our teaching, our goals are to help our students construct a valid understanding of the topics we're teaching and apply their understanding to the real world. These goals have several suggestions for classroom practice. They include the following:

- Provide students with experiences that promote deep understanding
- Connect content to the real world
- Make interaction an integral part of instruction
- Teach for conceptual change
- Promote learning with assessment

Let's look at these suggestions in more detail.

PROVIDE STUDENTS WITH EXPERIENCES THAT PROMOTE DEEP UNDERSTANDING

Learning and development depend on experience, and prior experiences contribute to the knowledge students bring to our classrooms. So, what do we do when students lack experiences and come to our classrooms with insufficient or even inaccurate prior knowledge? The answer is simple (but admittedly, often not easy): *We provide the necessary experiences.*

Most commonly, these experiences exist in the form of **high-quality examples**, examples that—ideally—include all the information our students need to understand the topic. Alicia provided this experience with her paragraph that illustrated the rules for subject-verb and pronoun-antecedent agreement, and Table 9.1 provides some illustrations of teachers' use of examples in different content areas.

Table 9.1	Teachers' use of examples in different content areas	
Content Area	**Learning Objective**	**Example and Topic**
Language arts: Parts of speech	For students to understand comparative and superlative adjectives	Students' pencils of different lengths to show that one is "longer" and another is "longest" Students' hair color to show that one is "darker" and another is "darkest"
Social studies: Longitude and latitude	For students to understand longitude and latitude	A beach ball with lines of longitude and lines of latitude drawn on it (as you see here)
Math: Decimals and percents	For students to understand decimals and percents by calculating cost per ounce to determine which product is the best buy	12-ounce soft drink and its cost 16-ounce soft drink and its cost 6-pack of soft drinks and its cost
Science: Properties of matter	For students to understand the concept *density*	Cotton balls pressed into a drink cup Wooden cubes of different sizes to show that the ratio of weight to volume remains the same Equal volumes of water and vegetable oil on a balance

High-Quality Examples: The Theoretical Framework. To understand the theoretical framework for using high-quality examples, think about our experiences in the world outside of classrooms. For instance, in the natural world, as small children learn about dogs, they see, pet, and play with friendly pooches, and they gradually construct the concept *dog*. The dogs they see, pet, and play with are examples, and the wider the variety they encounter, the more fully their concept of *dog* is developed. The same is true for the myriad of other concepts we all acquire from our natural experiences. As a further illustration, watch *Sesame Street* with a child sometime. Elmo, for instance, jumps above a group of flowers, and says, "I'm above the flowers." Then, he pops up below the flowers, and says, "Now, I'm below the flowers." Elmo is simply providing examples of the concepts *above* and *below*. Everything children's educational programming teaches is through the clever and attractive use of examples.

When we use examples with our students, we use the same processes that children use in the natural world (Renkl, 2011). We, however, create specific examples to help our students reach specified learning objectives and standards. Literally, our examples provide the experiences our students use to construct their knowledge. High-quality examples are important for all topics at all grade levels, and they are especially important when learners first encounter a new idea, or for limited-English-proficiency learners who may lack the school-related experiences of their peers (Echevarria & Graves, 2015). As you plan for your instruction, and having identified the learning objective or standard you want your students to meet, the first question you should ask yourself is, "What can I show my students?" or "What can I have them do that will help them meet the objective?" This will provide them with the experience they need to construct their knowledge.

Technology, Learning, and Development

Capitalizing on Technology to Provide Meaningful Experiences

Providing the experiences our students need to construct their knowledge is demanding, and one of the most important reasons is the fact that it's difficult to find or create representations—examples—for many of the topics we teach. And the lack of examples is precisely the reason the topics are hard for students to learn (Renkl, 2011). In these cases technology can often be a valuable tool (Roblyer & Doering, 2013). We might simply drop heavy and light objects, for example, to demonstrate that all objects fall at the same rate, regardless of weight, but it's virtually impossible to illustrate the actual acceleration of a falling object.

Here, technology can be used to simulate the acceleration of the object (Roblyer & Doering, 2013). For example, Figure 9.2 simulates the position of a falling ball at uniform time intervals. We see that the distance between the images becomes greater and greater, indicating that the ball is falling faster and faster. This simulation provides an example of acceleration that is impossible to represent without the use of technology.

An expanding variety of technology simulations exist that we can use to illustrate ideas that are difficult to represent directly. For instance, if you're a biology teacher, you might use software to simulate a frog dissection rather than using an actual frog. Although the simulation doesn't allow students the hands-on experience of working with a real frog, it's less expensive because it can be used over and over; it's more flexible because the frog can be "reassembled"; and it avoids sacrificing a frog for science (Roblyer & Doering, 2013).

Simulations that can be used to illustrate topics exist in all the content areas. In language arts, for instance, simulations exist that illustrate letters and their matching sounds,

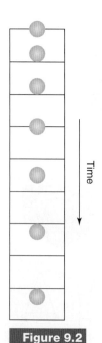

Time

Figure 9.2

Simulation of a falling object

words and their meanings, and vocabulary development. In math, software, such as The Geometer's Sketchpad (Key Curriculum, 2013), provides visual representations of abstract math concepts; in social studies, software allows students to take virtual field trips, visits to Internet sites that allow them to experience locations that they are unlikely to see in real life, such as the ancient Egyptian pyramids; and in art, Internet and CD collections allow access to a variety of different art forms. These are merely examples; simulations exist in content areas ranging from the samples seen here to special education, foreign language, music, and physical education (Roblyer & Doering, 2013). When you begin teaching and have your own classroom, you will be able to explore the resources available to you for your content area. And as the quality of software continually improves, representations are becoming more sophisticated, and the simulations are more interactive, further increasing learner motivation and understanding.

Your classroom computer can also be an efficient tool for storing the examples you create. For instance, as Alicia planned her lesson, all she did was pull her example (the paragraph) out of her computer and display it on her document camera. Her lesson required no preparation beyond simply accessing the file. This efficiency is essential in teaching. Teachers' workloads are enormous, so anything you can do to reduce the workload—without sacrificing learning—is important and valuable. Simply being able to efficiently store and retrieve your examples is an important part of this process.

Technology will never replace you and your teaching expertise. It can, however, be a valuable tool for helping you provide your students with the experiences they need to construct valid knowledge and develop the deep conceptual understanding called for by the learning sciences.

CONNECT CONTENT TO THE REAL WORLD

To replicate as closely as possible students' natural experiences, we want to connect the topics we teach to the real world whenever possible. This suggestion is supported by social constructivist learning theory and particularly situated cognition (Brown et al., 1989; Lave, 1997). And as you saw earlier in the chapter, connecting content to the real world is the essential goal of the learning sciences.

Alicia made an effort to connect her topic to the real world when she presented her rules in the context of a paragraph instead of isolated sentences, and she reinforced the connection by having her students write their own paragraphs in which the rules were illustrated. Making this connection to the real world will also lead to a much deeper conceptual understanding than would be gained from simply responding to sentences.

As illustrations in other content areas, when geography students, for instance, connect longitude and latitude to the location of a favorite hangout, science students relate the concept *inertia* to seatbelts in their cars, art students create a portrait of a family member, or math students solve making-change problems for items purchased at the school store, their learning is more meaningful than it would be if they studied the topics in the abstract, and their experiences are consistent with the learning sciences (van Merriënboer, Kirschner, & Kester, 2003). The same is true for each of the teachers in Table 9.1.

MAKE INTERACTION AN INTEGRAL PART OF INSTRUCTION

Although essential, high-quality examples won't—by themselves—necessarily produce learning (Moreno & Duran, 2004). Our students sometimes misinterpret the examples or focus on aspects of them that aren't important for reaching our learning objectives. For example, when Brittany saw the sentence

"Each of the boys has (his, their) own lunch box with pictures of cars on (it, them),"

she focused on the word *boys* in it and concluded that the correct pronoun was "their" instead of "his" in the first set of parentheses. For her, this conclusion made sense. However, after Carlos offered an alternative explanation, she changed her thinking and correctly chose "it" instead of "them" in the second set of parentheses; she reconstructed her understanding based on the social interaction. This process illustrates the social nature of knowledge construction and helps us see why interacting with our students is so important. Research indicates that instruction, as illustrated by the way Alicia taught the rules, is more effective than it would have been if Alicia had simply attempted to explain the rule to Brittany after she demonstrated her original misconception (Hattie & Gan, 2011; Renkl, 2011).

Making interaction an integral part of our instruction serves three important learning purposes. First, it puts students in cognitively active roles; they think about what they're studying. As we saw in Alicia's lesson, she explained the rules, but Brittany remained cognitively passive—as do many students during teacher explanations—so she constructed her misconception in spite of Alicia's explanation. This reminds us again that simply explaining often isn't as effective as we would like it to be. (We aren't suggesting that you shouldn't explain topics to students. Rather, we're saying *don't conclude that your students understand an idea because you've explained it to them.*) Interacting with them is essential.

Second, interaction makes students' thinking visible, which allows us to informally assess their learning progress. (We discuss assessment in more detail in the next section.) For instance, if Alicia had not made interaction an integral part of her instruction, she wouldn't have known that Brittany had constructed a misconception about the rule. And if Brittany had a misconception, it's likely that some of her classmates did as well. The interaction revealed Brittany's misconception and helped eliminate it.

Third, interaction makes feedback—both peer and teacher feedback—more effective (Hattie & Gan, 2011). For instance, because the students were interacting, Carlos was able to offer his thinking: "I think it should be 'his,' . . . because it says *each,* and each is 'one' (singular), so it should be 'his' because 'his' is also 'one.'" Brittany changed her thinking as a result of Carlos's feedback.

A positive and supportive classroom climate is essential to make interaction and feedback as effective as possible. Most effective is "high trust and a climate where being wrong is seen as a positive part of learning—and thence feedback can be sought when a student does not attain a goal" (Hattie & Gan, 2011, p. 266).

Using Cooperative Learning to Complement Whole-Group Instruction. Whole-class instruction, such as we saw in Alicia's lesson, is effective and widely used in classrooms. But if we have 30 or more students in our classes, the sheer numbers often make it difficult to involve all of them. Less confident or less assertive students may get few chances to participate, so they drift off.

Cooperative learning, instructional methods in which students are organized into groups—typically ranging from 2 to 5—to reach both academic and social development goals, offers an alternative that can be effectively used to complement our whole-group instruction. Considerable research has examined cooperative learning methods, and it suggests that "under certain, well specified conditions, they are known to substantially improve student achievement in most subjects and grade levels" (Slavin, 2011, p. 344). Slavin (2011) goes on to point out, however, that the highly structured forms of cooperative learning that have been thoroughly researched are used less often than more informal forms, such as simply putting students into groups.

Cooperative learning is popular and widely used in schools for involving students in activities ranging from having kindergarten students identify materials that will sink or float to solving word problems in math to critiquing products peers have written at a range of grade levels. For instance, Alicia gave her students the task of writing a paragraph that included at least two examples illustrating subject-verb agreement and two more illustrating pronoun-antecedent agreement. After completing the task, she could have had students work in pairs, read each other's paragraphs, and provide feedback. In addition to the interaction in the pairs, the cooperative learning activity adds variety to instruction, and periodic change is more effective than teaching the same way all or most of the time (Good & Brophy, 2008).

Cooperative learning has the added benefit of helping develop social skills and social relationships among students from different backgrounds and ability levels. When a girl who is a recent immigrant from Vietnam, an African American, and a White boy work together in a group, for example, they learn that—in many ways—they're more alike than they are different. They all want to be liked and respected, to learn, and to get along with each other. When groups are mixed by ethnicity, gender, and ability, boundaries between peer groups tend to blur, attitudes toward different ability and ethnic groups improve, and interethnic friendships develop (Aronson, Wilson, & Akert 2013; Johnson & Johnson, 2013). Some experts suggest that these outcomes are the greatest benefits of cooperative learning (Jadallah et al., 2011; Johnson & Johnson, 2013). Further, cooperative learning activities can help integrate students with exceptionalities into the regular classroom (Hardman, Drew, & Egan, 2014).

Using Open-Ended Discussions to Support Interaction. Alicia's students were involved in a form of discussion when they made conclusions about subject-verb and pronoun-antecedent agreement, but the discussion focused on specific right-or-wrong answers. For instance, in the sentence

"Each of the boys has (his, their) own lunch box with pictures of cars on (it, them),"

"his" and "it" are correct, and "their" and "them" are incorrect.

In contrast, open-ended discussions involve topics that aren't cut and dried. Examples might include analysis of a novel's characters and plot in English, issues in American government, and controversial topics, such as stem-cell research, cloning, or even evolution in science.

Properly conducted, many of the benefits of cooperative learning apply to open-ended discussions. Students learn abilities, such as courtesy, tolerance for differing opinions, and respect for evidence, again outcomes that may be more important than the actual topic being discussed.

Discussions are used more commonly with older students, and, to be successful, students' background knowledge is essential if the discussions are to be meaningful. It's impossible to conduct a successful discussion if students lack background knowledge with respect to the topic.

Emphasis on social interaction is the common thread in both cooperative learning and open-ended discussion, and they both capitalize on the fact that learning is—substantively—a social process.

Developing Interactive Teaching Abilities. Learning to make interaction an integral part of our instruction is one of the most challenging aspects of our development as teachers—for two reasons. First, most of the instruction we experience involves lecture or "teaching as telling," and, as we said earlier in the chapter, many teachers continue to believe that the best way to help students learn is to lecture to them (Alparsian et al., 2004; Yip, 2004). Rarely do we take classes, and particularly classes at the university level, where our instructors make interaction an integral part of their instruction. So, we don't have many instructional models to emulate.

Second, until we develop high levels of expertise—expertise developed to the point where promoting interaction is essentially automatic—interacting with students is demanding. It's hard work, much harder than simply telling our students what we want them to know. This likely explains why so few teachers ever become truly expert with it.

We strongly encourage you to persevere—literally practice—questioning and other interaction skills until you can interact with your students using a minimum of effort. When your expertise is developed to this point, you will find that your students will be more attentive and motivated, they will learn more, and your teaching will be more satisfying. Most people can learn to deliver acceptable lectures, but developing the skills needed to interact effectively with students requires a true professional.

TEACH FOR CONCEPTUAL CHANGE

We know that, in efforts to make sense of their experiences, our students will sometimes construct misconceptions. Teaching for conceptual change, which involves attempting to fundamentally alter students' thinking about a topic, attempts to address this tendency. Teaching for conceptual change capitalizes on Piaget's concepts of disequilibrium, accommodation, and assimilation (Alparsian et al., 2004). Three conditions are required for students to change their thinking:

- The existing conception must become dissatisfying; it must cause disequilibrium.
- An alternative conception must be understandable. Students must be able to accommodate or change their thinking so the alternative conception makes sense.
- The new conception must be useful in the real world; it must reestablish equilibrium, and students must be able to assimilate new experiences into it.

As an example, consider again the problems with subtraction:

$$\begin{array}{cc} 15 & 13 \\ -\ 3 & -\ 5 \end{array}$$

We can use concrete examples to demonstrate that the answers are indeed different. For instance, we can give children blocks representing the number 15, such as you see here, and simply remove 3 of them:

Then, we can give the children blocks representing 13, such as the following, and remove 5 of them.

In doing so, the children will see that 12 blocks remain in the first case, but only 8 are left in the second. The original conception is no longer satisfying, the alternate conception will become understandable, and the new conception is useful in the real world; students will be able to use the subtraction operation successfully.

Alicia Evans in our case study at the beginning of the chapter also taught for conceptual change. Let's look again at a portion of her lesson.

She had displayed the following on her document camera.

Bill takes his lunch to the cafeteria when it's time to eat. His friend Leroy and his other friend Antonio (takes, take) (his, theirs) to the cafeteria, too. Each of the boys has (his, their) own lunch box with pictures of cars on (it, them). Bill doesn't like apples, so he will give his to anyone else if (he, they) (wants, want) it.

Now let's look at some of the dialogue.

Alicia: Now, how about this one? [Pointing to the set of parentheses (his, their) in the sentence "Each of the boys has (his, their) own lunch box with pictures of cars on (it, them)."]. What do you think, and why do you think so . . . Brittany?

Brittany: I think it should be "their" because it says *boys* and boys is more than one. "His" is only one, so that doesn't fit.

Carlos: I think it should be "his," . . . because it says *each,* and each is "one" (singular), so it should be "his" because "his" is also "one."

Alicia: What about this one? [After some additional discussion and pointing to the parentheses (it, them) at the end of the sentence.]

Brittany: I know. "It" is correct.

Alicia: Tell us why.

Brittany: They're talking about one lunch box, and "it" is one, so it can't be "them."

Because of Carlos's comment and the discussion that followed, Brittany's original conclusion became dissatisfying, and an alternative conception was understandable to her—as indicated by her correctly selecting "it" rather than "them" at the end of the sentence.

Even with these conditions in place, conceptual change is challenging, as anyone who has attempted to convince someone to change their thinking will attest. Considerable cognitive inertia exists, requiring us to take an active role in guiding the conceptual change process in our students (Vosniadou, 2007).

Experiences, such as the example with subtraction above, and questions that reveal misconceptions and require students to apply their revised thinking to new situations, are the most effective tools we have for promoting conceptual change (Yip, 2004).

PROMOTE LEARNING WITH ASSESSMENT

If our students behaved like video recorders, teaching and learning would be simple. We could merely explain a topic accurately, and our students would record the information in that form. Straightforward, uncomplicated. This isn't how the learning and teaching world works, however; we know they don't. Instead, they construct their knowledge and store it in their long-term memories in a form that makes sense to them, and because they do, individuals' understanding of the topics they study will vary. For example, Brittany's misconception made sense to her, and she would likely have retained it if Alicia had not called on her, which revealed the misconception, and allowed Carlos to share his thinking.

However, when we teach we have classes of 20, or perhaps many more, so it's impossible to know how all of our students are thinking. Alicia knew that Brittany had a misconception about the rule, and from Brittany's response she could infer that some of the other students had misconceptions as well. She also knew that Carlos understood the rule, and others probably also understood it, but that's essentially all she knew about her students' thinking at that point. Even when we make interaction an integral part of our instruction, we can't involve all students all the time, so we need a mechanism to determine the extent to which our students are learning and their knowledge constructions are valid. This leads us to the role of **assessment**, the process of gathering information and making decisions about students' learning progress. We tend to think of assessment as giving tests and assigning grades, but it is much more than that. It is an essential part of the entire teaching–learning process. "Testing has such a bad connotation; people think of standardized testing or teaching to the test. Maybe we need to call it something else, but this is one of the most powerful learning tools we have" (Carey, 2010, para. 28).

We use two kinds of assessments to gauge learning progress. **Informal assessment,** gathering incidental information during learning activities, allows us to assess learning while it is occurring. For instance, Alicia was involved in informal assessment when she listened to Brittany's and Carlos's comments during her lesson. It's important because it helps us make decisions during learning activities. For example, if, based on their answers to your questions, your students seem to understand a topic, you move on. If they don't, you can provide additional examples or continue the discussion until they are ready to move forward (Hattie & Timperley, 2007; Shute, 2008). Informal assessment helps you make these decisions.

Informal assessment is important but incomplete and potentially misleading. For instance, if Alicia had first called on Carlos and she saw that he demonstrated an understanding of the rule, and particularly if she called on another student who also understood the rule, she might tacitly conclude that all her students understood it. In fact, her informal assessments would provide little information about the rest of her students' understanding.

Formal assessment, the process of systematically gathering information about learning from all students, addresses this problem. Alicia, realizing that it was impossible for her to informally assess all her students' understanding, gave her students the seatwork assignment in which her students were to write a paragraph of their own that included at least two examples illustrating subject-verb agreement and two more examples illustrating pronoun-antecedent agreement.

This was obviously a challenging assignment for third graders, and if she found that a number of her students weren't quite ready for the challenge, she could give them another paragraph similar to the one she used in her learning activity and have the students select the choices they believed to be correct. This exercise would also be a formal assessment, and it, combined with feedback, would provide a developmental bridge to the writing assignment she chose.

She can then store her paragraphs in her computer, and the next time she teaches the topic she's ready to go without any additional preparation.

Analyzing Theories

Evaluating Constructivism

Principles of cognitive learning theory suggest that people construct knowledge in attempts to make sense of their experiences. Constructivism makes an important contribution to our understanding of learning because it reminds us that people don't behave like recording devices, and it helps us understand why prior knowledge, social interaction, and making students' thinking visible are so important in the learning process (Carver, 2006). Because we know that students want their experiences to make sense and that they construct their own knowledge, we better understand why they don't grasp an idea that's been discussed several times, why they seem to ignore a point that's been emphasized, and why they retain misconceptions.

Misconceptions about constructivism, itself, also exist, and one of the most pervasive is confusing constructivism as a theory of learning with constructivism as an approach to teaching. "[M]any educators confuse 'constructivism,' which is a theory of how one learns and sees the world, with a prescription for how to teach" (Clark, Kirschner, & Sweller, 2012, p. 8). "The notion of constructivism postulates that learners actively construct their reality or knowledge based on their prior experiences, mental structures, and beliefs. This firmly places constructivism as a theory of learning and *not* a theory of teaching" (Hattie & Gan, 2011, p. 256).

When it is misinterpreted, *constructivism* may suggest that teachers shouldn't guide student learning, but rather students should discover it for themselves. This is a widely held and incorrect assumption (Clark et al., 2012).

It also implies that teaching methods such as small-group discussions, cooperative learning, pure discovery, and hands-on activities are "constructivist," whereas other methods, such as whole-class discussions, are not. This is also a misconception. Large-group instruction, effectively done, can promote knowledge construction, and cooperative learning, improperly done, may not.

Hands-on activities are particularly problematic. It's easy to assume that if students are working in groups and behaviorally active as they work with concrete materials, they are also cognitively active (Mayer, 2004). This may or may not be the case. "Simply put, cognitive activity can happen with or without behavioral activity, and behavioral activity does not in any way guarantee cognitive activity" (Clark et al., 2012, p. 8).

Constructivism, as a description of learning, is also incomplete. It doesn't, for example, take into account the way our human memory systems work, the important role of practice in developing skills, and the influence of emotions on motivation and learning. These topics are better explained with other theories. The idea that learners construct their own knowledge instead of passively recording it, as a recording device would do, marks an important advance in our understanding of learning, however, and it has important implications for our teaching.

Table 9.2 summarizes constructivism and outlines its contributions and criticisms.

Table 9.2	Analyzing theories: Evaluating constructivism
Basic question	What are the processes involved in people's attempts to make sense of their experiences?
Catalysts for learning	• Experiences with the physical and social world • Background knowledge • Social interaction and language
Key concepts	• Communities of learners • Cognitive apprenticeship • Appropriating understanding • Situated cognition • Misconceptions
Primary theorist	• Vygotsky • Piaget (historically)
Suggestions for teaching	• Provide students with the experiences they need to construct valid knowledge • Connect content to real-world applications • Make interaction an integral part of instruction • Use assessment as a tool to increase learning
Contributions	• Explains how learners develop original ideas and form misconceptions • Helps us understand why prior (background) knowledge is crucial for learning • Demonstrates the essential role that social interaction plays in promoting learning • Helps us understand why assessment is an essential part of the teaching–learning process
Criticisms	• Is sometimes misinterpreted as a theory of teaching instead of a theory of learning • Fails to consider the influence of our memory systems and particularly the limitations of working memory • Doesn't account for the role of practice in developing skills • Doesn't explain how emotional responses are developed or how emotions influence learning • Doesn't account for the role of praise and other reinforcers in learning

Classroom **Connections**

Helping Students Construct Valid Knowledge

1. Students construct their own knowledge, and the knowledge they construct depends on what they already know. To accommodate differences in prior knowledge, provide a variety of examples and other representations of the content you want students to understand.

- ▪ **Elementary:** A third-grade teacher in a unit on chemical and physical change has students melt ice, crumple paper, dissolve sugar, and break toothpicks to illustrate physical change. She then has them burn paper, pour vinegar into baking soda, and chew soda crackers to illustrate chemical change.

- ▪ **Middle School:** An English teacher presents the following excerpts to illustrate internal conflict:

   Kelly didn't know what to do. She was looking forward to the class trip, but if she went, she wouldn't be able to take the scholarship-qualifying test.

   Calvin was caught in a dilemma. He saw Jason take Olonzo's calculator but knew that if he told Mrs. Stevens what he saw, Jason would realize that it was he who reported the theft.

- ▪ **High School:** While teaching about the Great Depression, a social studies teacher has students read excerpts from *The Grapes of Wrath*, shows a video of people standing in bread lines, shares statistics on the rash of suicides after the stock market crash, and discusses how a current recession is similar to and different from the Great Depression.

2. Knowledge construction is most effective when learners have real-world experiences. Develop learning activities around realistic problems.

- **Elementary:** In a lesson relating geography and the way we live, a third-grade teacher has students describe the way they dress for their favorite forms of recreation. She also asks students who have moved from other parts of the country to do the same for their previous locations. She then guides them as they construct an understanding of the effect of geography on lifestyle.

- **Middle School:** In a unit on percent increase and decrease, a math teacher has students look for examples of marked-down clothes while shopping. He also brings in newspaper ads. The class discusses the examples and calculates the amount saved in each case.

- **High School:** To help her students understand the importance of persuasive writing, an English teacher brings in three examples of "Letters to the Editor" on the same topic. Students discuss the letters, determine which is most effective, and with the teacher's guidance, identify the characteristics of effective persuasive writing.

3. Social constructivist views of learning emphasize the role of social interaction in the process of knowledge construction. Make social interaction an integral part of your instruction, and avoid relying too heavily on explanations to promote learning.

- **Elementary:** A fourth-grade teacher wants his students to understand the concept of scale on a map. He places them in groups and has them create a map of their desktops. Then he has them draw a map of their room, and finally, they go outside and draw a map of their playground. When finished, he guides a class discussion to help them understand how the maps are similar and different.

- **Middle School:** A sixth-grade science teacher has his students take 8 identical wooden cubes and make one stack of 5 and another stack of 3. He has them discuss the mass, volume, and densities of the two stacks. Then, with questioning, he guides them to conclude that the mass and volume of the stack of 5 are greater than the mass and volume of the stack of 3 but that the densities of the two stacks are equal.

- **High School:** An algebra teacher "walks" students through the solutions to problems by calling on individuals to provide specific information about each step and explain why the step is necessary. When students encounter difficulties, the teacher asks additional questions to help them understand the step.

Developmentally Appropriate **Practice**

Guiding Knowledge Construction with Students at Different Ages

Although students at all ages construct knowledge, a number of developmental differences exist. The following sections outline suggestions for responding to these differences.

Working with Students in Early Childhood Programs and Elementary Schools

Young children want their experiences to make sense, and in order to make sense of their experiences they construct knowledge, as do learners of all ages. However, they lack many of the experiences that older students have acquired, so providing *concrete learning experiences* is crucial in working with early childhood and elementary students.

Young children tend to center on the most perceptually obvious aspects of objects and events, such as Brittany centering on the word *boys* in the sentence "Each of the boys has (his, their) own lunch box with pictures of cars on (it, them)," and as a result, they commonly form misconceptions or incomplete understanding. They also tend to be quite literal in their thinking, which can also lead to the construction of misconceptions. For instance, they tend to equate size with age, believing someone who is bigger is older, and in social studies they may think that lines of latitude and longitude actually exist on the earth.

As a result, explanations presented in the abstract are often nearly useless with elementary students. When working with young children, concrete, high-quality examples are even more important than with older learners. In addition, interactive instruction allows teachers both to investigate the ideas students currently hold and to assist them as they construct new ones.

Using language to describe their world and communicate with each other not only develops language skills but also promotes meaningful learning. Language is crucial for later learning, and the more opportunities young children have to practice and use language, the better.

Young children also need to learn to accept responsibility for their learning and how to interact positively with their peers. This suggests learning tasks in which young students can interact with their peers in challenging activities. These experiences provide the foundation for later learning.

Working with Students in Middle Schools

Middle school students overcome much of the tendency to interpret events literally, but often, in the process of knowledge construction, they fail to recognize relationships among objects and events. For instance, instead of recognizing that rectangles and squares are subsets of parallelograms, they often classify the figures into different categories.

Middle school students are also developing interaction skills, such as perspective taking and social problem solving. This allows you to use cooperative learning and other small-group strategies to integrate social interaction into your instruction. Cognitive apprenticeships, in which students work with other students in small groups, can provide opportunities for students to think and talk about new ideas. Encouraging students to verbalize their developing understanding during learning activities is important for promoting learning. Experts caution, however, that you should carefully structure and monitor small-group activities to ensure that they're cognitively active and remain on task (Ding, Li, Piccolo, & Kulm, 2007).

Working with Students in High Schools

High school students' experiences provide them with a rich store of prior knowledge that increases the validity of their knowledge constructions. However, they continue to construct a variety of misconceptions, particularly when working with symbols and abstract ideas. For instance, in simplifying the expression $2 + 5 \times 3 - 6$, they often get 15 ($2 + 5 = 7$; $7 \times 3 = 21$; $21 - 6 = 15$) instead of the correct answer: 11 ($5 \times 3 = 15$; $15 + 2 = 17$; $17 - 6 = 11$).

As students move to more advanced classes in high school, such as physics, chemistry, and calculus, making interaction an integral part of instruction is even more important. It is in these classes that teachers tend to act more like college instructors, where lecture is the most common instructional strategy. High school teachers sometimes even resist the idea of interaction, believing that lectures are efficient and that students will be subject to lectures in college, so they might as well "get used to it." This is neither valid nor wise. The most effective way to prepare students for advanced studies is to help them acquire the background knowledge needed to understand more abstract and sophisticated topics. And using high-quality examples, connecting content to the real world, making interaction an integral part of instruction, and using assessment as a learning tool is as important with high school students as it is with students at other developmental levels for helping them acquire this background knowledge.

High school students can also participate in and benefit from classroom discussions, which provide opportunities to refine their thinking based on the ideas of others (Hadjioannou, 2007). As with all forms of instruction, high school teachers need to structure and monitor discussions closely to ensure that they are aligned with learning goals.

9 Summary

1. Describe how social factors influence both our daily living and the way we learn.
   - Humans are primarily social beings who spend a great deal of time interacting with other people.
   - Other people influence our behaviors, the way we think, our emotions, and even the way we learn.
   - Evidence from neuroscience suggests that we have a biological need for social connection, and we evolved as social animals because it increased our chances for survival.
   - Technology, and particularly social media, such as Facebook and Twitter, has dramatically increased our social connection, with both positive and negative consequences.

2. Describe the processes involved in knowledge construction and analyze examples that illustrate these processes.
   - Learning and development depend on experience, people want their experiences to make sense, and they construct knowledge in attempts to make sense of their experiences.
   - Cognitive constructivism focuses on individual construction of knowledge. Cognitive constructivists believe that when an experience disrupts an individual's equilibrium, she reconstructs understanding to reestablish equilibrium.
   - Social constructivism emphasizes that individuals first construct knowledge in a social environment and then appropriate it. Knowledge grows directly out of the social interaction. Social constructivism has become the primary framework for guiding instruction in our nation's schools.
   - Emphasis on sociocultural theory, communities of learners, cognitive apprenticeships, and situated cognition are all applications of social constructivism to instruction.

3. Explain misconceptions, how they occur, and how they can be eliminated.
   - Misconceptions are beliefs that are inconsistent with evidence or commonly accepted explanations.

- Prior experiences, appearances, misuse of language, and "intuitive appeal" can all contribute to misconceptions.
- Changing misconceptions is difficult because the change disrupts individuals' equilibrium, the misconceptions are often consistent with everyday experiences, and individuals don't recognize inconsistencies between new information and their existing beliefs.
- For conceptual change to occur, existing conceptions must become dissatisfying, an alternative conception must be understandable, and the alternative must be useful in the real world.

4. Describe suggestions for classroom practice, and explain how they are grounded in the learning sciences and the processes involved in knowledge construction.
   - Suggestions for classroom practice include providing high-quality experiences, connecting content to the real world, making interaction an integral part of instruction, and using assessment to promote learning.
   - High-quality experiences include examples and other representations learners use to construct knowledge that makes sense to them.
   - Connecting content to the real world applies the primary emphasis of the learning sciences, which focuses on learning as it exists in real-world settings.
   - Making interaction an integral part of instruction capitalizes on the premise that learning is primarily a social process.
   - Using assessment to promote learning recognizes that learners' knowledge constructions will vary and these constructions will sometimes be invalid. Assessment can then be used to help learners reconstruct their knowledge and increase their understanding.

Preparing for **Your Licensure Exam**

Understanding the Process of Knowledge Construction

You will be required to take a licensure exam before you go into your own classroom. This exam will include information related to the processes involved in knowledge construction, and it will include both multiple-choice and constructed-response questions. We include the following exercises to help you practice for the exam in your state. This book and these exercises will be a resource for you as you prepare for the exam.

At the beginning of the chapter, you saw how Alicia Evans designed and conducted a lesson to help her students construct knowledge about the rules for subject-verb and pronoun-antecedent agreement.

In the following case, Scott Sowell, a middle school science teacher, wants his students to understand how to design experiments and control variables to meet the standard **"SC.8.N.1.2 Design and conduct a study using repeated trials and replication" (Sunshine State Standards, 2012)**. To do so, he wants his students to design and conduct a study to examine factors that influence the frequency of a simple pendulum. Read the case study, and answer the questions that follow.

To help his students meet the standard, Scott carefully explains the process for controlling variables, and explains and demonstrates how they would control variables with an experiment using plants, explaining that plant growth is essential for maintaining the world's food supply. He then decides to give them additional experience with controlling variables with simple pendulums in small groups.

Scott begins by demonstrating a simple pendulum with paper clips attached to a piece of string. He explains that frequency means the number of swings in a certain time period and asks students what factors they think will influence the frequency. After some discussion they suggest length, weight, and angle of release as possible hypotheses. (In reality, only the length of the pendulum determines its frequency.)

"Okay, your job as a group is to design your own experiments," Scott continues. "Think of a way to test how each affects the frequency. Use the equipment at your desk to design and carry out the experiment."

One group of four (Marina, Paige, Wensley, and Jonathan) ties a string to a ring stand and measures its length, as shown here:

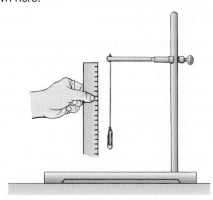

They measure the length of the string to be 49 centimeters, select 15 seconds as the amount of time to let the

pendulum swing, and add one paper clip as weight. Maria counts 21 swings.

A few minutes later, Scott again walks by the group, examines their results, and says, "So you've done one test so far. . . . What are you going to do next? . . . I'm going to come back after your next test and look at it," and he moves to another group.

The group conducts their second test by shortening the string and adding a second paper clip (which violates the principle of altering only one variable at a time).

"Mr. Sowell, we found out that the shorter it is and the heavier it is, the faster it goes," Marina reports to Scott when he returns to the group.

Scott then asks which of the two variables—length or weight—was responsible for the change in the frequency, and Wensley and Jonathan say simultaneously, "They both changed."

"Think about that. You need to come up with a conclusion about length, about weight, and about angle—how each of them influences the frequency of your pendulum," Scott reminds them as he moves from group to group.

As the group investigates the three variables—length, weight, and height (angle of release)—they continue to change two of these at the same time, confounding their results. And as Scott moves from group to group, he finds that most of the groups are doing the same thing. As a result the groups, in general, conclude that each of the three variables—length, weight, and height (angle of release)—influences a pendulum's frequency.

In response to this misconception, Scott reassembles the class and conducts a whole-class demonstration. "Let's take a look at something here," Scott says, placing a ring stand on his demonstration table. He attaches a paper clip to the pendulum, puts it in motion, and asks a student to count the swings. He adds a second paper clip and again has the students count. They find that the number of swings is the same with one, two, three, and four paper clips, which demonstrates that weight doesn't affect the frequency. He has a student state this conclusion, and he writes it on the board. Then he does a second demonstration with different angles of release to show that angle also has no effect on the frequency and again asks a student to make a conclusion so he can write it on the board.

After the demonstrations, he says, "Now I want someone to make a conclusion about what we learned about designing experiments and how we use our variables when we design experiments. . . . Who wants to talk about that? . . . Wensley? Tell me what we learned about how to set up an experiment. What did we learn from this?"

"Each time you do a different part of the experiment, only change one of the variables," Wensley explains.

"Why is that?"

"You're only checking one thing at a time. If you do two, you can't tell which one caused the change," Wensley continues.

"Right, you couldn't tell which one was causing it, could you? . . . It might go faster, but you would wonder, is it the weight or is it the length?"

Seeing that it is near the end of the class period, Scott asks if there are any questions, and hearing none, he has Marina summarize what they learned about designing experiments, hears the bell ring, and dismisses the students.

Questions for Case Analysis

In answering these questions, use information from the chapter, and link your responses to specific information in the case.

Multiple-Choice Questions

1. Scott's students changed more than one variable at a time—such as changing both the length and the weight—when they designed their experiments. Of the following, which statement *best explains* why they changed more than one variable, even though Scott had explained the process for controlling variables?

   a. The students were cognitively passive during the group work.

   b. The students constructed the idea of changing more than one variable at a time, because doing so made sense to them.

   c. The students failed to reflect on the processes involved, so they used an inappropriate technique.

   d. Scott grounded his learning activity in cognitive constructivism rather than social constructivism, so the learning activity was ineffective.

2. Scott explained the process of controlling variables and did a demonstration with plants to illustrate the process.

However, the groups in his class failed to control variables when they did their activities with the pendulum. Of the following, which statement is the *best explanation* for the students' continued inability to control variables?

   a. Scott failed to provide a high-quality example that illustrated how to control variables.

   b. Scott didn't connect his topic with plants to the real world, so he didn't adequately apply the suggestions of the learning sciences to his lesson with simple pendulums.

   c. Scott failed to adequately make social interaction an integral part of his instruction.

   d. As Scott explained the process of controlling variables, the students remained cognitively passive, so the information wasn't meaningful to them.

Constructed-Response Question

3. Scott's students had some misconceptions about controlling variables. They failed to keep length constant, for example, as they changed the weight. How effectively did Scott teach for conceptual change in responding to this misconception? Use information from the case study to support your explanation.

Important **Concepts**

appropriating understanding
assessment
cognitive apprenticeships
cognitive constructivism
community of learners

embodied cognition
formal assessment
high-quality examples
informal assessment
learning sciences

learning styles
misconceptions
situated cognition
social constructivism
sociocultural theory

transfer
virtual field trips

10 Motivation and Learning

OUTLINE	LEARNING OUTCOMES
	After you've completed your study of this chapter, you should be able to:
What Is Motivation? Extrinsic and Intrinsic Motivation Motivation to Learn Theoretical Views of Motivation	**1.** Define motivation, and describe different theoretical explanations for learner motivation.
The Influence of Needs on Motivation to Learn Maslow's Hierarchy of Needs The Need for Self-Determination ▶ Technology, Learning, and Development: The Motivating Influence of Technology The Need to Preserve Self-Worth Educational Psychology and Teaching: Using the Influence of Needs to Increase Your Students' Motivation to Learn	**2.** Describe learners' needs and how they influence motivation to learn.
The Influence of Beliefs on Motivation to Learn Beliefs about Outcomes: Expectations Beliefs about Intelligence: Mindset Beliefs about Capability: Self-Efficacy Beliefs about Value: Attainment Value, Utility Value, and Cost Beliefs about Causes of Performance: Attributions Educational Psychology and Teaching: Using the Influence of Beliefs to Increase Your Students' Motivation to Learn	**3.** Explain how learners' beliefs can influence their motivation to learn.
The Influence of Goals on Motivation to Learn Mastery and Performance Goals Social Goals Work-Avoidance Goals Diversity: Learner Differences in Goal Orientation Educational Psychology and Teaching: Using the Influence of Goals to Increase Your Students' Motivation to Learn	**4.** Describe how learners' goals can influence their motivation to learn.
The Influence of Interest and Emotion on Motivation to Learn Personal and Situational Interest Emotion and Motivation ▶ Analyzing Theories: Summarizing and Evaluating Theories of Motivation Educational Psychology and Teaching: Using the Influence of Interest and Emotion to Increase Your Students' Motivation to Learn ▶ Developmentally Appropriate Practice: Motivation to Learn with Students at Different Ages	**5.** Explain how interest and emotion influence learner motivation.

If you're like most students, you like some of your classes more than others. Why? And why do you enjoy certain activities, such as talking to friends, listening to music, reading, or sports? The answers to these questions involve motivation, arguably the greatest influence on learning that exists for all of us. Understanding student motivation is an essential part of your professional knowledge, and it can make the difference between a successful year of teaching and one that you'd rather forget. In this chapter we examine how you can use this knowledge to increase your students' learning and make your life as a teacher more enjoyable.

As you read the following case study involving a world history class, think about the students' motivation and how Kathy Brewster, their teacher, influences it.

Kathy is working with her students on the historical period spanning the 11th through the 16th centuries, which encompasses part of the Middle Ages, the Renaissance, and the Crusades. She wants her students to meet the following standard:

CCSS.ELA-Literacy.RH.11-12.9 Integrate information from diverse sources, both primary and secondary, into a coherent understanding of an idea or event, noting discrepancies among sources (Common Core State Standards Initiative, 2014e).

"We'd better get moving," Susan urges Jim as they approach the door of Kathy's classroom. "The bell's going to ring, and you know how Brewster is about this class. She thinks it's sooo important."

"Did you finish your homework?" Jim asks and then stops himself. "What am I talking about? You always do your homework."

"Actually, I've always liked history and knowing about the past, . . . and I'm pretty good at it. My dad helps me. He says he wants to keep up with the world," Susan laughs.

"In some classes, I just do enough to get a decent grade, but not in here," Jim responds. "I used to hate history, but I sometimes even read ahead a little, because Brewster makes you think. She's so gung ho, and it's kind of interesting the way she's always telling us about the way we are because of something that happened a zillion years ago—I never thought about this stuff in that way before."

"Gee, Mrs. Brewster, that assignment was impossible," Mason grumbles as he enters her classroom.

"That's good for you," Kathy smiles. "I know it was a tough assignment, but you need to be challenged. It's hard for me too when I'm studying and trying to put together new ideas, but if I hang in, I always feel like I can get it."

"Aw, c'mon, Mrs. Brewster. You know everything."

"I wish. I study every night to keep up with you people, and the harder I study, the better I get. . . . If I struggle, I just redouble my efforts. . . . And it really feels good when I finally get it."

"But you make us work so hard," Mason continues.

"Yes, I know you're working hard, and it's paying off. Hard work is the key to everything. Look at how much your writing has improved as a result of your effort. You did an excellent job on your last paper of comparing and contrasting the information about the Crusades using the excerpts from the two authors we studied. That directly addresses the standard we're working on, your thinking is much improved, and so is your writing."

"Yeah, yeah, I know," Mason replies on his way to his desk, "being good thinkers and writers will help us in everything we do in life," echoing a message the students often hear from Kathy.

"Just a reminder," Kathy says after the students are settled at their desks, "group presentations on the Renaissance are on Thursday and Friday. You decide what groups will present on each day. Remember, we're all doing our best; we're not competing with each other. . . . Also, for those who chose to write the paper on the Middle Ages, we agreed that they're due on Friday."

We'll return to Kathy's lesson later in the chapter, but for now let's consider three questions:

1. How is Susan's general orientation toward school different from Jim's?
2. How does Jim's motivation in Kathy's class differ from his other classes?
3. How has Kathy influenced both Jim's and Mason's motivation?

Theories of motivation help us answer these and other questions as we examine the relationship between motivation and learning in this chapter.

What Is Motivation?

"**Motivation** is the process whereby goal-directed activity is instigated and sustained" (Schunk, Meece, & Pintrich, 2014, p. 5). Other authors, such as Jere Brophy (2010), provide more elaborate definitions, but they also focus on initiating and continuing behaviors in an effort to reach goals. If we work hard to solve a math problem or attempt to perfect a serve in tennis, for example, we say we are motivated in each case. Solving the problem and perfecting the serve are the goals, and motivation helped us initiate and sustain our efforts to reach each one.

As we said in our introduction, motivation is arguably the most important factor influencing learning and achievement because motivated students:

- Have more positive attitudes toward school and describe it as more satisfying.
- Persist longer on difficult tasks and cause fewer management problems.
- Process information in depth and excel in classroom learning experiences (Perry, Turner, & Meyer, 2006).

Simply, motivated students learn more than their less motivated peers, and this is the reason our chapter is titled *Motivation and Learning*.

Ed Psych and You

Think about your classes. Do you study primarily to get good grades, or is understanding the course content more important to you? Do you believe understanding the content is important, even if you're not terribly interested in it?

Extrinsic and Intrinsic Motivation

Motivation is often classified into two broad categories. **Extrinsic motivation** is motivation to engage in an activity as a means to an end, whereas **intrinsic motivation** is motivation to be involved in an activity for its own sake (Schunk et al., 2014). If you answered the questions in *Ed Psych and You* by saying that you study primarily to get good grades, you are extrinsically motivated, whereas if you said understanding the course content is more important, you're intrinsically motivated. This difference helps answer our first question (How is Susan's general orientation toward school different from Jim's?). Jim's comment, "In some classes, I just do enough to get a decent grade," reflects extrinsic motivation, whereas Susan's comment, "I've always liked history and knowing about the past," suggests intrinsic motivation. As you would expect, intrinsic motivation is preferable because of its focus on learning and understanding (Brophy, 2010), and it has implications for you. Research on college and university students suggests that "the single most influential learning and study skill promoting positive academic performance was level of intrinsic motivation" (Griffin, MacKewn, Moser, & VanVuren, 2013, p. 53).

However, motivation is also contextual and can change over time (Wigfield, Guthrie, Tonks, & Perencevich, 2004). For example, we saw that Jim is extrinsically motivated in his other classes, but his comment, "I sometimes even read ahead a little," and "it's kind of interesting . . ." suggests that he is intrinsically motivated in Kathy's class. This helps answer our second question (How does Jim's motivation in Kathy's class differ from his other classes?).

We can also begin to answer the third question (How has Kathy influenced both Jim's and Mason's motivation?) by looking at intrinsic motivation in more detail. Learners are intrinsically motivated by experiences that:

- *Present a challenge.* Meeting challenges is emotionally satisfying, and challenge exists when goals are moderately difficult and success isn't guaranteed (Ryan & Deci, 2000; Stipek, 2002).
- *Promote autonomy.* Learners are more motivated when they feel that they have influence over and can control their own learning (Ryan & Deci, 2000).
- *Evoke curiosity.* Novel, surprising, or discrepant experiences arouse our curiosity and increase intrinsic motivation (Brophy, 2010).
- *Involve creativity and fantasy* (Lepper & Hodell, 1989). All we have to do is watch a small child mesmerized by a Disney movie, *Sesame Street,* or other children's programming, or notice the success of the *Harry Potter* stories to see that people are motivated by fantasy.

Some researchers suggest that aesthetic experiences associated with beauty that evoke emotional reactions, such as a beautiful sunrise or sunset, may be intrinsically motivating as well (Ryan & Deci, 2000).

Jim's comments suggest that Kathy capitalized on two of these factors. "Brewster really makes you think" suggests he was reacting to the challenge in her class, and "It's kind of interesting the way she's always telling us about the way we are because of something that happened a zillion years ago" suggests her teaching aroused his curiosity.

People tend to think of extrinsic and intrinsic motivation as two ends of a single continuum, meaning the higher the extrinsic motivation, the lower the intrinsic motivation and vice versa, but they are actually on separate continua (Schunk et al., 2014). For example, we asked if you study to understand the content or primarily to get good grades. You may want good grades but also want to understand the content, as many students do. This suggests that you're high in both intrinsic and extrinsic motivation. People may be high in both, low in both, or high in one and low in the other.

The relationships between extrinsic and intrinsic motivation are outlined in Figure 10.1.

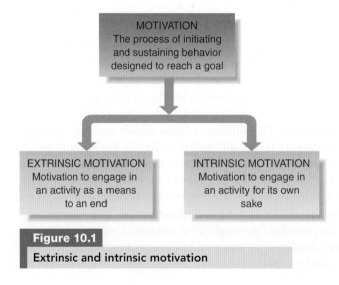

Figure 10.1

Extrinsic and intrinsic motivation

FLOW

Have you ever been so immersed in an activity that you've even lost track of time and space? This experience is described as **flow**, an intense form of intrinsic motivation in which an individual is in a state of complete absorption, focus, and concentration in a challenging activity (Csikszentmihalyi, 1990, 1996, 1999). It's the experience musicians feel when they're "in the groove," or athletes experience "in the zone." And because intrinsic motivation is linked to high performance, the concept of flow has even sparked interest in the business world as leaders attempt to increase productivity in their employees (Cranston & Keller, 2013; Moneta, 2012).

We—your authors—experience it periodically as we work on this book. We literally do lose track of time, and when we're most immersed in study and writing, we don't even want to stop to eat. It's not easily captured, but little like it exists when you have the good fortune to experience it.

As would be expected, experiencing flow is quite rare, and it has important prerequisites. They include:

- *Autonomy*: We are much more likely to experience intense intrinsic motivation in activities we choose for ourselves than in those imposed on us by others (Cranston & Keller, 2013; Ryan & Deci, 2000).
- *Expertise*: The effortless performance that is associated with flow occurs because skills and techniques are so well practiced that they've become automatic (Csikszentmihalyi, 1999).
- *Optimal challenge*: We all quickly become bored when our skill level exceeds task demands, but challenge that is too great can cause anxiety.
- *Concentration*: As we saw above, when experiencing flow, we are so immersed in the activity that we lose a sense of time and space.

Some research has linked *flow* to personality and has found that optimistic and conscientious people are more likely to experience it, whereas people who have a "glass half empty" outlook on life are less likely (Ullén et al., 2012). A bit of a paradox also exists. To experience flow, we need to be in control of the activity but not consciously try to control our behavior or the activity itself (Schunk et al., 2014).

Flow is not the same as "going with the flow," which suggests that the activity is simply spontaneous and feels good. Flow requires expertise, concentration, and effort, not simply feeling good (Csikszentmihalyi, 1999). We offer some suggestions that can help contribute to *flow* in classrooms in the section "Educational Psychology and Teaching: Using the Influence of Needs to Increase Your Students' Motivation to Learn" later in the chapter.

Motivation to Learn

It would be great if our students were intrinsically motivated to the point where our learning activities elicited flow, and we are sometimes led to believe that if our instruction is stimulating enough they will be. This is a worthwhile ideal, but it isn't realistic for all, or even most, learning activities. The following are some reasons why (Brophy, 2010):

- School attendance is compulsory, and content reflects what society believes students should learn, not necessarily what students would choose for themselves.
- Teachers work with large numbers of students and can't always meet individual needs.
- Students' performances are evaluated and reported to parents and other caregivers, so students focus on meeting external demands instead of on personal benefits they might derive from the experiences.

Jere Brophy (2010) offers an alternative. "I believe that it is realistic for you to seek to develop and sustain your students' **motivation to learn**: their tendencies to find academic activities meaningful and worthwhile and to try to get the intended learning benefits from them" (Brophy, 2010, p. 11).

Motivation to learn is related to the second question we asked in *Ed Psych and You* earlier: "Do you believe understanding the content is important, even if you're not terribly interested in it?" If you answered yes, your *motivation to learn* is high. Motivation to learn will be our focus in this chapter, and if students' intrinsic motivation also increases in the process, so much the better.

Theoretical Views of Motivation

As with learning, different theoretical orientations help us understand students' motivation to learn (Brophy, 2010; Schunk et al., 2014). We outline them in Figure 10.2 and discuss them in the sections that follow.

BEHAVIORIST VIEWS OF MOTIVATION

Behaviorism views learning as a change in observable behavior that occurs as a result of experience, and it treats motivation the same way. An increase in the amount of time spent studying, for example, is viewed as evidence of motivation, so reinforcers, such as praise, comments on homework, and good grades, are motivators (Schunk et al., 2014).

Critics argue that using rewards to motivate students sends the wrong message about learning, and some research suggests that rewards actually decrease interest when tasks are already intrinsically motivating (Ryan & Deci, 1996).

Critics also suggest that behaviorism cannot adequately explain motivation (Perry et al., 2006). For instance, if we believe we can't complete a difficult task, we're unlikely to work hard on it despite being reinforced for completing related tasks in the past. Our motivation is influenced by our beliefs, a cognitive factor not considered by behaviorists.

In spite of these criticisms, rewards are commonly used as motivators in classrooms. For example, teachers in elementary schools use praise, candy, and entertainment, such as computer games, as rewards, and middle and secondary teachers use high test scores, comments on written work, free time, and quiet compliments in attempts to motivate students.

Also, research suggests that judicious use of rewards can be effective. For instance, praise for genuine achievement and rewards that recognize increasing competence can increase intrinsic motivation (Cameron, Pierce, & Banko, 2005). We revisit this issue later in the chapter.

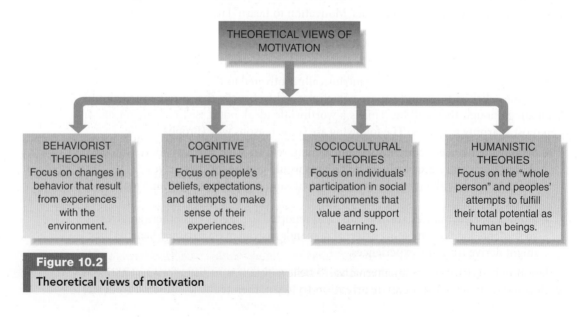

Figure 10.2

Theoretical views of motivation

COGNITIVE THEORIES OF MOTIVATION

> "C'mon, let's go," Melanie urges her friend Yelena as they're finishing a series of homework problems.
>
> "Just a sec," Yelena mutters. "I'm not quite getting this one."
>
> "Let's work on it tonight. Everybody's leaving," Melanie urges.
>
> "Go ahead, I'll catch up to you in a minute. I know that I can figure this out. . . . I just don't get it right now."

How might we explain Yelena's persistence? Behaviorism doesn't provide much help. Although getting the right answer would be reinforcing, it doesn't account for her attempt to understand why the problem made sense but still came out wrong. Also, behaviorism doesn't consider cognitive factors in motivation, so it can't explain her saying, "I know that I can figure this out," which indicates that she believes she can resolve the discrepancy and expects to do so.

People's desire to make sense of their experiences is at the heart of both cognitive learning theory and cognitive motivation theory: "Children are seen as naturally motivated to learn when their experience is inconsistent with their current understanding" (Greeno, Collins, & Resnick, 1996, p. 25). For example, why do young children so eagerly explore their environments? Why did Yelena want to stay until she solved the problem? Cognitive theorists suggest that both are motivated by the need to understand and make sense of their experiences.

Cognitive motivation theory helps explain a variety of behaviors, such as why people

- Try to solve puzzles, such as Sudoku, and other problems with no practical application.
- Are curious when something occurs unexpectedly.
- Persevere on challenging activities and then quit after they've mastered the tasks.
- Want feedback about their performance.

These tendencies all involve an innate desire to make sense of our experiences.

Social cognitive theories elaborate on these views by emphasizing learners' expectations and the influence of observing others on our motivation (Schunk & Pajares, 2004). They help explain Jim's comment in our case study at the beginning of the chapter, "She's so gung ho, and it's kind of interesting the way she's always telling us about the way we are because of something that happened a zillion years ago." His motivation in Kathy's class increased as a result of observing her model her enthusiasm and her interest in the topic she was teaching.

SOCIOCULTURAL VIEWS OF MOTIVATION

Sociocultural theories emphasize the important role of social interaction in motivation, and they focus on individuals' participation in classroom communities where all students participate in learning activities and where the teacher and students work together to help everyone learn (Hickey & Zuiker, 2005). These theories suggest that students will be more motivated in classrooms that are cooperative and supportive than in competitive environments, and they help us understand why people are more motivated to engage in an activity if others in their social group are participating in it.

Some experts suggest that a motivational zone of proximal development exists (Brophy, 2010). It describes the match between a learning activity and learners' prior knowledge and experiences that is close enough to stimulate interest and perceived value in the activity but not so familiar that learners are satiated by it. For example, multiplying 243×694 would not be a motivating task for us, nor would calculating the effects of the moon's perigee and apogee on the earth's tides. The first is so familiar that it's trivial, and the second is too complex and difficult for most of us to understand or appreciate. Neither falls within our motivational zone of proximal development.

From a sociocultural perspective, our task is to design learning experiences that are familiar enough so our students see their potential value, but not so familiar that they are no longer challenging.

HUMANISTIC VIEWS OF MOTIVATION

In the mid-20th century when the "cognitive revolution" in learning was in full swing, a parallel movement called *humanistic psychology* also began. It focused on the "whole person" and viewed motivation as people's attempts to fulfill their total potential as human beings and become "self-actualized" (Schunk et al., 2014). According to this view, understanding motivation requires an understanding of people's thoughts, feelings, and actions. Understanding behaviors or even thinking—alone—is not sufficient to understand our students; we need to focus on the total picture, including who they are as human beings (Schunk & Zimmerman, 2006). This perspective remains popular both in schools and in the workplace.

Carl Rogers, a psychologist who founded "person-centered" therapy, and Abraham Maslow, famous for his hierarchy of needs (we discuss his hierarchy in the next section of the chapter), were the two most prominent leaders in the humanistic movement, and both emphasized people's attempts to become self-actualized (Maslow, 1968, 1970; Rogers, 1963).

Rogers believed this actualizing tendency is oriented toward competence and autonomy, but experiences in our environment can foster or hinder growth (Rogers & Freiberg, 1994). He also believed that the concept of **unconditional positive regard**, treating students as if they are innately worthy, regardless of their behavior, is essential if students are going to reach their maximum potential (Rogers & Freiberg, 1994).

Unconditional positive regard isn't as simple as it appears. Parents usually feel it for their small children, but as they get older, their regard often becomes "conditional" and depends on factors such as high grades or choosing the right partner or career (Kohn, 2005a). Outside the home, regard is almost always conditional, and in schools, high achievers are regarded more positively than their lower achieving peers, as are students who are well behaved and who excel in extracurricular activities such as music or sports.

According to Rogers (1963), conditional regard hinders personal growth, and more recent work corroborates his views. "Students who felt unconditionally accepted by their teachers were more likely to be interested in learning and to enjoy challenging academic tasks, instead of just doing schoolwork because they had to" (Kohn, 2005b, p. 21).

The theoretical views you've seen here provide the conceptual framework for examining motivation in more detail. Using this framework, we examine the topics below in the sections that follow. Each is a variable that influences motivation, and they include:

- *Needs,* such as the need to feel safe, respected by others, and smart.
- *Beliefs* about ourselves and our capacity to learn.
- *Goals,* outcomes we hope to attain.
- *Interests,* our affinity or attraction to certain topics or activities.
- *Emotions,* such as joy, pride, fear, boredom, or anxiety.

Each of these influences motivation to learn, and each is grounded in the theoretical views we've discussed in this section. We begin by examining needs.

Ed Psych and You

Think about the number of times you've said something like, "I need to get organized," "I need to lose weight," or simply, "I need to pick up some milk at the store." What role do statements like these play in your own motivation?

The Influence of Needs on Motivation to Learn

As you see illustrated in *Ed Psych and You*, the notion of *needs* is so pervasive in our lives, and we use the term so often, that we don't think about it. In motivation theory a **need** is an internal force or drive to attain or to avoid a certain state or object (Schunk et al., 2014), and it makes sense that responding to these needs influences our motivation. For instance, when we say, "I need to get organized," the need pushes us to the desired state—being organized.

Food, water, and sex are considered to be the most basic needs in all species, because they're necessary for survival. Getting them is the force, and survival is the desired state. However, human needs are more complex, and we react to a number of needs in our daily lives.

In this section we examine the influence of three sets of needs on motivation to learn:

- Maslow's hierarchy of needs
- The need for self-determination
- The need to preserve self-worth

Maslow's Hierarchy of Needs

Earlier we said that humanistic views of motivation emphasize the *whole person*—physical, social, emotional, intellectual, and aesthetic. Maslow's (1968, 1987) hierarchy of needs is grounded in this holistic view of human motivation. As we look at Maslow's hierarchy, outlined in Figure 10.3, we see the needs of the whole person reflected in it. For instance, we see the *physical* person in survival and safety needs, the *social* person in belonging needs, the *emotional* person in self-esteem needs, and the intellectual and aesthetic person in the need for self-actualization.

Maslow (1968, 1970) described human needs as existing in two major groups: *deficiency needs* and *growth needs*. Let's look at them more closely.

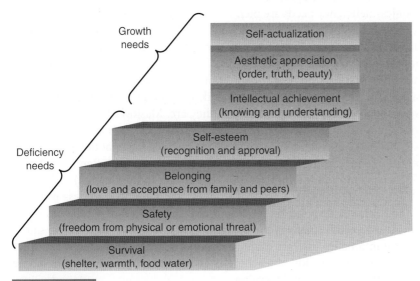

Figure 10.3

Maslow's hierarchy of needs
Source: Adapted figure from "Maslow's Hierarchy of Needs" from MOTIVATION AND PERSONALITY, 3rd Edition by Abraham H. Maslow, Edited by Robert D. Frager and James Fadiman. Copyright © 1978 by Abraham H. Maslow, Robert D. Frager, and James Fadiman. Printed and electronically reproduced by permission of Pearson Education, Inc., Upper Saddle River, New Jersey.

DEFICIENCY NEEDS

Deficiency needs are needs that energize people to meet them if they're unfulfilled. *Survival, safety, belonging,* and *self-esteem* are the deficiency needs in the hierarchy, and, according to Maslow, people won't move to a higher need unless the one below it is met. So, for example, if people's safety needs are not being met, they won't move to the need for belonging or any need above it. Representing the deficiency needs as a series of steps in Figure 10.3 is intended to remind us of this idea.

GROWTH NEEDS

After all their deficiency needs are met, people can then move to growth needs, needs in intellectual achievement and aesthetic appreciation that increase as people have experiences with them. Ultimately, growth can lead to self-actualization, reaching our full potential and becoming all that we are capable of being. In contrast with deficiency needs, the needs for intellectual achievement and aesthetic appreciation are never "satisfied." For instance, as we develop a greater understanding of a certain area, such as literature, our interest in it increases rather than decreases. Using Maslow's work, we could explain this by saying that we are responding to our need for intellectual achievement. Similarly, we would explain some people's continuing desire to experience fine art or music by saying they're responding to their need for aesthetic appreciation. Engaging in these activities also gives them pleasure and can lead to *peak experiences,* a concept that originated with Maslow.

EVALUATING MASLOW'S WORK

Maslow's work has been criticized because little research evidence exists to support his description of needs and because his work is unable to consistently predict people's behavior (Schunk et al., 2014). For instance, we've all known of people who have serious illnesses or disabling conditions, suggesting that their survival and safety needs are not being met, yet who accomplish significant intellectual or aesthetic achievements. Maslow's work would predict that this could not happen, because he suggested that people will not move to growth needs unless deficiency needs are met.

On the other hand, Maslow's work is intuitively sensible and appealing and it helps explain a number of aspects of our lives. For instance, after we first meet someone, we're likely to say, "He seemed really nice" (hopefully not, "Wow, what a jerk."), rather than "He sure seemed smart." We first react to how friendly, outgoing, and "human" people are, not how bright or successful they seem to be. The same likely applies to your instructors; you first notice how personable, supportive, and helpful they are. Maslow's hierarchy suggests that personal, social, and emotional needs precede intellectual ones, our day-to-day experiences corroborate this suggestion, and research supports the idea that emotions are important in both motivation and learning (Hunter, 2012; Mega, Ronconi, & De Beni, 2013). (We examine the influence of emotions on motivation in detail later in the chapter.)

Perhaps most important, it makes sense that students are going to learn less if they're hungry or tired, and schools respond by providing free or reduced-cost breakfasts and lunches for them. And research supports the contention that students need to feel safe—both physically and emotionally—to learn as much as possible (Perry et al., 2006). Maslow's work reminds us that the human side of teaching is essential, and ignoring it will have a negative impact on both motivation and learning.

The Need for Self-Determination

Self-determination is the need to act on and control one's environment, and having choices and making decisions are intrinsically motivating (Ryan & Deci, 2000). According to self-determination theory, people have three innate psychological needs: needs for *competence, autonomy,* and *relatedness* (Levesque, Stanek, Zuehlke, & Ryan, 2004; Ryan & Deci, 2000). We examine how they influence our motivation next.

THE NEED FOR COMPETENCE

As you interact with people, think about the number of times they attempt to demonstrate how much they know about a topic or how good they are at some skill. We all want to be "smart." Self-determination theory explains these efforts by saying that we are attempting to meet our need for competence, the ability to function effectively in the environment. The need for competence was originally described by Robert White (1959) in a paper that has become a classic. He suggested that people acquire proficiency and skill "because it satisfies an intrinsic need to deal with the environment" (p. 318).

Our need for competence can be explained at several levels. At a most basic level, for instance, if an organism can't function effectively in its environment, it isn't likely to survive (Schunk et al., 2014). Competent people succeed and grow in their careers, whereas those less competent languish and stagnate, and competent students are successful learners who find school satisfying and rewarding (Morgan & Fuchs, 2007).

Evidence that their knowledge and skills are increasing is the most important factor influencing students' perceptions of competence, and this helps explain why praise for genuine accomplishment, high teacher expectations, challenging activities, and activities that evoke curiosity are intrinsically motivating. The praise, meeting expectations and challenges, and understanding novel or puzzling experiences provide evidence that our competence is increasing. In contrast, completing trivial tasks, solving predictable problems, and receiving grades that haven't been earned provide little evidence about developing competence, so they often detract from motivation.

THE NEED FOR AUTONOMY

Do you prefer to study at home, in the library, or perhaps in a coffee shop? Would you rebel if someone dictated to you how and where you had to study? These questions relate to autonomy, independence and the ability to alter the environment when necessary. It is the second innate need described by self-determination theory, and lack of autonomy causes stress and reduces intrinsic motivation. For instance, it has historically been believed that the stress of assembly line work results from workers' having little control over their environments (Lundberg, Granqvist, Hansson, Magnusson, & Wallin, 1989). And extreme stress can become toxic and destructive. "So, the stress that kills . . . is characterized by a lack of a sense of control over one's fate" (Velasquez-Manoff, 2013; para. 7). We want to feel that we are in control of our lives, and when we don't, motivation decreases.

Autonomy and competence are strongly related. As learners' competence increases, so do their perceptions of autonomy (Bruning, Schraw, & Norby, 2011). So if we can help students feel competent, we also help them feel autonomous, and we increase both motivation and learning. (We offer some suggestions for increasing our students' perceptions of autonomy later in this section.)

THE NEED FOR RELATEDNESS

Relatedness, the feeling of being connected to others in one's social environment and feeling worthy of love and respect, is the third innate need described by self-determination theory. Relatedness and Maslow's concept of *belonging* are often treated synonymously (Juvonen, 2006), and the need for relatedness is also similar to the need for *affiliation* as described by early motivational researchers (e.g., Exline, 1962; Terhune, 1968).

The need for relatedness can sometimes have unintended consequences when students develop an unhealthy need for approval, the desire to be accepted and judged positively by others (Urdan & Maehr, 1995). Children in elementary schools generally seek the approval of their teachers, but older students with a strong need for approval often have low self-esteem and engage in activities primarily to get praise from any number of sources (Davis, 2003). If the need becomes excessive, they often fear rejection and easily submit to peer pressure. These efforts can be counterproductive, however, because students with excessive needs for approval tend to be unpopular with their peers (Rudolph, Caldwell, & Conley, 2005).

We can help meet students' needs for relatedness and approval by communicating unconditional positive regard and a genuine commitment to their learning. Students are more engaged—behaviorally, cognitively, and emotionally—in classroom activities when they believe their teachers understand, like, and empathize with them. They also report more interest in their class work, behave in more socially responsible ways, and are more likely to seek help when they need it (Cornelius-White, 2007; Marchand & Skinner, 2007).

Self-determination theory explains a number of school-related phenomena. As students' perceptions of self-determination increase, they are more likely to be intrinsically motivated and finish school (Eisenman, 2007), their literacy skills improve (Crow, 2007), and they can even develop a more healthy, active lifestyle (Bryan & Solmon, 2007).

DIVERSITY: LEARNER DIFFERENCES IN THE NEED FOR SELF-DETERMINATION

Self-determination theory describes general patterns in people's needs for self-determination that are true for most people and students. For instance, virtually everyone we've ever met, regardless of culture, gender, or socioeconomic status, has needs for competence, autonomy, and relatedness.

How these factors influence motivation to learn can vary among groups and individuals, however (Rogoff, 2003). For instance, with respect to competence, *demonstrating* that we're knowledgeable and skilled in areas such as school or the workplace tends to be more important in our culture than in East Asian cultures, where self-improvement is more strongly valued (Li, 2005; Sedikides & Gregg, 2008).

Gender differences with respect to competence also exist. For instance, boys' perceptions of their competence tend to be higher than girls' in spite of the fact that girls get higher grades (Eccles, Wigfield, & Schiefele, 1998), and girls are more easily discouraged by failure than are boys (Dweck, 2000).

With respect to autonomy, research indicates that some Native American groups give young children more autonomy in decision making than do parents in mainstream Western culture (Deyhle & LeCompte, 1999), whereas African American parents give their students less autonomy, possibly to protect them in potentially dangerous environments (Smetana & Gettman, 2006). Also, while being allowed to make choices increases learner autonomy, Asian students may prefer letting people they trust, such as parents or teachers, make choices for them (Vansteenkiste, Zhou, Lens, & Soenens, 2005).

Differences in learners' need for relatedness also exist. Some Asian students, for example, meet this need by excelling in school and gaining the approval of their parents and teachers (Li, 2005), whereas members of other minorities meet the need for relatedness by not achieving in school. "Indeed, many students from minority groups experience peer pressure discouraging them from adopting attitudes and behaviors associated with achieving good grades" (Rubinson, 2004, p. 58).

Technology, Learning, and Development

The Motivating Influence of Technology

Paul, one of your authors, was recently at an airport seating area at 5:00 a.m. waiting for an early morning flight. He was struck by the fact that, in spite of the very early hour, 23 of 26 people who were also there were studying either their smartphones or tablets. This behavior illustrates a pattern so common that we almost don't notice it; wherever we go, we see people hunched over their phones, tablets, and laptops; drivers seem to constantly be talking on their cell phones, in some cases in violation of state or city laws; and at the end of 2012, Facebook reported more than 1 billion active monthly users, with many now accessing the site on their smartphones (Tam, 2013). Further, estimates suggest that many suffer from "Facebook addiction syndrome" (Rosen, Whaling, Rab, Carrier, & Cheever, 2013). If use and involvement are indicators of motivation, the motivating influence of these devices is inescapable.

The question is "why"? What is it about technology, or at least these forms of technology, that is so motivating? Self-determination theory may provide some answers, and meeting our need for relatedness is one possible factor. Some researchers suggest that connecting with others through technology is rewarding; it makes us feel as if we're not alone in the world. And we like to talk about ourselves, share information that makes us look good or compare favorably to others, and give advice (Berger, 2013). Additional research suggests that these factors keep taking people back to social media, such as Facebook (Al-Debei, Al-Lozi, & Papazafeiropoulou, 2013).

On the other hand, as with many factors in our lives, this connection can be a double-edged sword. When people spend a lot of time on social networking sites, the anonymous intimacy can give them the feeling that their social media "friends" are truly friends even though they may not be (Morgan, 2013). Some evidence even suggests that Facebook has contributed to an increase in divorce (Fottrell, 2012). Neither of these factors, however, changes the fact that people are motivated to spend time on social media.

Meeting the need for competence is a second factor that might help explain technology's effect on our motivation. The ability to manipulate the devices to carry out tasks that once were laborsome, such as finding obscure locations in an unfamiliar city instead of struggling with a map, quickly and conveniently accessing information about virtually any topic from the convenience of an easy chair or a coffee shop, or downloading and using a new app, contributes to people's feelings of competence (Jacobs, 2012). Additional research suggests that the ease of use and perceived usefulness of these devices is a significant factor in people's motivation to use them (Chang, Liang, Yan, & Tseng, 2013). We like to use technology because it makes our lives easier, and becoming skilled with it makes us feel competent.

Certain forms of educational technology found in schools can contribute to feelings of competence as well. For instance, drill-and-practice software allows learners to proceed at their own rate, provides corrective feedback, and reinforces learning progress, all of which can contribute to perceptions of competence.

Autonomy may also be an important factor. People using their smartphones and tablets have complete autonomy—they can choose when, where, and how long they use their devices, and *they* choose the topics of discussion or inquiry. This raises an issue with respect to harnessing technology for classroom use because complete autonomy in classrooms is impossible. For instance, learners usually don't get to choose the topics they study, time is scheduled and restricted, and students are required to be in assigned seats in classrooms. This is very different from the autonomy they have when using their smartphones, tablets, and other devices, and it helps explain why technology use in classrooms isn't as motivating as many people believe it to be (Jacobs, 2012).

The advances in technology present challenges for teachers. For instance, we know that students are motivated to play with their devices, even during learning activities. In the not-too-distant past, teachers had to deal with students passing notes; today it's texting. And some experts suggest that the issue with respect to technology, such as smartphones, is not *if they should be used in classrooms*, but how to best use them. Although critics cite the opportunities for cheating, unauthorized socializing, and the social isolation issues involved, the fact is students are using smartphones every day, and they are using them to learn (Jacobs, 2012; Yang, 2013).

This raises an additional issue. In spite of appearing ubiquitous, not all students have access to smartphones, so attempting to use them for classroom activities, such as gathering information from the Internet, poses a problem for teachers (Henderson, 2011). What can be done for the students who don't have them?

Easy answers to these questions don't exist. However, we know that students are motivated to use technology, particularly when they have autonomy, so if we look for, and take notes on, any and all ideas for exploiting technology in our classrooms, we will be able to take advantage of these opportunities when they present themselves.

The Need to Preserve Self-Worth

> "I'm a genius; I'm a genius," Andrew, an eighth grader, enthusiastically shouts to his mom as he bounces into the house after school. "I got a 97 on my history test, and I didn't study a lick. I'm a genius; I'm a genius."

We can explain Andrew's behavior using the concept of **self-worth** (or self-esteem, as it is more commonly called), which is an emotional reaction to or an evaluation of the self (Schunk et al., 2014). Self-worth theorists suggest that people have an innate need to protect their sense of self-worth and accept themselves as they are. As you saw earlier—according to self-determination theory—we all have a basic need for competence, which is often reflected in our efforts to "look smart." We appear to have higher ability—look smarter— if we're able to accomplish tasks without having to work hard (Covington, 1992). So, by emphasizing that he got his high score without studying, Andrew was implying that he had high ability, which enhanced his feelings of self-worth.

Some interesting developmental patterns in learners' perceptions of effort and ability exist. For instance, when asked, most kindergarteners say they're smart. Young children assume that people who try hard are smart, and people who are smart try hard (Stipek, 2002). However, as students move through school, they begin to equate effort with low ability, and simultaneously their need to *appear* smart increases. For instance, we've all heard statements such as, "He isn't all that sharp, but he really works hard."

Because of their need to be perceived as having high ability, older students may hide the fact that they've studied hard for a test, for example, so if they do well, they can, at least in the eyes of their peers, attribute their success to being smart. Others engage in "self-handicapping" strategies to protect their self-worth, such as procrastinating ("I could have done a lot better, but I didn't start studying until after midnight"), making excuses ("This test was so tricky"), anxiety ("I understand the stuff, but I get nervous in tests"), or making a point of not trying. If they didn't try, failure isn't evidence of low ability (Covington, 1998; Wolters, 2003). Self-handicapping behaviors have been found in a range of academic areas including even physical education (Standage, Treasure, Hooper, & Kuczka, 2007). They are most common in low achievers, who often choose to not seek help when it's needed (Marchand & Skinner, 2007).

We examine ways that you can respond to these tendencies in the section "Educational Psychology and Teaching: Using the Influence of Needs to Increase Your Students' Motivation to Learn," which is next.

Educational Psychology and Teaching: Using the Influence of Needs to Increase Your Students' Motivation to Learn

Understanding learners' needs has important implications for us as we attempt to increase our students' motivation to learn. The following suggestions can help you in your efforts to apply this understanding with your students.

- Treat students as *people* first.
- Involve students in decision making.

- Praise students for effort and evidence of accomplishment.
- Avoid social comparisons among students.

Let's look at them.

Treat Students as People First. "Treat students as people first" means that we're first committed to our students as human beings who are worthy of the respect that all people deserve, regardless of their behavior. Treating students as human beings helps meet their needs for belonging and relatedness (Cornelius-White, 2007), and it also applies the concept of unconditional positive regard. To see an example, let's look at a conversation Kathy has with Mason, one of her students, after school.

As she is working in her room after school, Mason pokes his head into the room.

"Come in," she smiles. "How's our developing writer?"

"I just came by to say I hope you're not upset with me, complaining so much about all the work."

"Not at all. . . . I haven't given it a second thought."

"You already know how much you've done for me. . . . You believed in me when the rest of the world wrote me off. . . . My drug conviction is off my record now, and I'm okay. I couldn't have made it without you. You made me work, and you put in all kinds of extra time with me. You wouldn't let me give up on myself. I was headed for trouble, and now . . . I'm headed for college."

"We all need a nudge now and then," Kathy smiles. "That's what I'm here for. I appreciate your kind words, but I didn't do it; you did. . . . Now, scoot. I'm working on a rough assignment for you tomorrow."

"Mrs. Brewster, you're relentless," Mason waves as he heads out the door.

Students know when their teachers are committed to them as people. Asking a student to stop by after class because she doesn't seem to be herself is an example, as was separating Mason's drug conviction from his innate worth as a person. And research suggests that this commitment may be particularly important for boys; "boys need to *feel* their teachers—their warmth, their mastery, their inspiration—before opening up to invest themselves in learning" (Reichert, 2010, p. 27). In working with her students Kathy demonstrated the unconditional positive regard that is important to us all, but rare in the everyday world.

Treating students "as people first" in no way implies that we lower our learning or behavioral expectations for them. Kathy also demonstrated her commitment to her students by maintaining high standards, helping her students meet them, and emphasizing the value of what they were learning. She also expected her students to treat her and each other with the same respect she demonstrated with them.

Involve Students in Decision Making. Involving our students in decision making can help meet students' need for autonomy and can also contribute to a positive classroom climate. Allowing students to make choices is one of the most effective strategies, and it can involve small actions, such as asking elementary students which snacks they should have for a classroom party or having the students decide the order of the group presentations, as Kathy did in our case study at the beginning of the chapter. Or it can involve more substantive choices, such as Kathy allowing her students to decide whether they wanted to make a group presentation on the Renaissance or write a paper on the Middle Ages.

Some additional suggestions for promoting feelings of autonomy by involving our students in decision making include:

- Soliciting student input in creating classroom rules and procedures.
- Encouraging students to set and monitor their own learning goals.

- Emphasizing the influence of effort and strategy use, and deemphasizing the influence of ability, on achievement.
- Asking for and accepting a variety of opinions during class discussions.
- Conducting classroom meetings to discuss issues, such as student behavior and treatment of others. Even young children are capable of providing this type of input.

Praise Students for Effort and Evidence of Accomplishment. To begin this section, let's look again at Kathy's reply to Mason in the case study at the beginning of the chapter, after he complained about how hard she makes them work. She commented,

> "Yes, I know you're working hard, and it's paying off. Hard work is the key to everything. Look at how much your writing has improved as a result of your effort. You did an excellent job on your last paper of comparing and contrasting the information about the Crusades using the excerpts from the two authors we studied. That directly addresses the standard we're working on, your thinking is much improved, and so is your writing."

Now, let's look at the comment in a bit more detail. To begin, in saying, "Yes, I know you're working hard, and it's paying off," Kathy praised Mason for his effort, and in commenting, "Look how much your writing has improved as a result of your effort," she praised him for his accomplishments while simultaneously linking effort to ability.

Two aspects of Kathy's praise are significant. First, praise for genuine accomplishment can increase motivation in students of all ages because the praise provides students with evidence that their competence is increasing (Cameron et al., 2005). Developing perceptions of our own competence is one of the most powerful motivating factors that exist, and, in fact, if we could make all our students feel competent, motivation and learning issues would largely disappear.

Second, notice that Kathy said, "Look at how much your writing has improved," but did not say, "Look at how good a writer you are." This is a subtle but important difference. A significant body of research indicates that praise worded in "person" terms, such as, "You are a smart girl," can decrease subsequent motivation, particularly if learners later experience failure, whereas praise worded in "process" terms, such as, "you tried hard" or "you found a good way to do it," increases subsequent motivation (Cimpian, Arce, Markman, & Dweck, 2007; Zentall & Morris, 2012). Interestingly, this pattern also applies to mothers as they interact with their own children (Pomerantz & Kempner, 2013).

Self-worth theory helps us understand these findings. If children are told they're "smart," for example, and they later fail, the failure suggests that they might not be so smart after all, which can detract from their sense of self-worth, and subsequently, their motivation. On the other hand, if they're praised for working hard, and they later fail, the failure suggests that work, not intelligence, is involved and they should redouble their efforts or change their strategies. In either case, motivation increases.

Avoid Social Comparisons among Students. Social comparisons are destructive in classrooms because they emphasize competition rather than mastery of content. Actions such as writing distributions of scores on the board divide classes into winners and losers, and for students who are consistently at the bottom end of the distribution, it can strongly detract from motivation (Corpus, Ogle, & Love-Geiger, 2006). Very few people want to play games in which they lose all the time. To preserve their sense of self-worth, students may conclude that what they're studying isn't important and give up completely.

In contrast, comments such as Kathy saying, "Remember, we're all doing our best; we're not competing with each other" remind students that effort and increasing competence are more important than "winning." Consistently emphasized over time, it can make a difference in both motivation and learning.

As with all suggestions, the ones we offer here won't work all the time or with all students. And in the real world, you won't turn every student into a motivated learner. You can make a difference with many, however, and for them, you will have made an immeasurable contribution to their lives.

Classroom **Connections**

Capitalizing on Students' Needs to Increase Motivation in Classrooms

Maslow's Hierarchy of Needs

1. Maslow described people's needs in a hierarchy with deficiency needs—survival, safety, belonging, and self-esteem—preceding the growth needs. Address students' deficiency and growth needs both in instruction and in the way you interact with students.

   - **Elementary:** A fourth-grade teacher calls on all students to involve everyone and promote a sense of belonging in his classroom. He makes them feel safe by helping them respond correctly when they are unable to answer.

   - **Middle School:** To help meet learners' belonging needs, a seventh-grade teacher asks two of the more popular girls in her class to introduce a new girl to other students and to take her under their wings until she gets acquainted.

   - **High School:** To address learners' growth needs, an American government teacher brings in a newspaper columnist's political opinion piece, comments that it was interesting to her, and asks students for their opinions on the issue.

Learners' Needs for Self-Determination

2. Self-determination theory suggests that people have innate needs for competence, autonomy, and relatedness. Design challenging learning tasks that, when completed, can provide evidence for increasing competence, and emphasize these accomplishments when students succeed.

   - **Elementary:** A fifth-grade teacher drops an ice cube into a cup of water and a second cube into a cup of alcohol and asks them why it floats in one and sinks in the other. He guides students' efforts until they solve the problem and then praises them for their thinking.

   - **Middle School:** A math teacher has students bring in a challenging "problem of the week." He helps them solve each problem and comments on how much their problem solving is improving.

   - **High School:** A biology teacher guides a discussion of our skeletal system until students understand the function of the skull, rib cage, and other bones, and then comments on how much the students have improved in their analyses of our body systems.

3. Learners' perceptions of autonomy increase when teachers ask them for input into classroom procedures, involve them in learning activities, and give them feedback on assessments. Create a classroom environment that helps meet learners' needs for autonomy.

   - **Elementary:** A fourth-grade teacher holds periodic class meetings in which she encourages students to offer suggestions for improving the classroom environment.

   - **Middle School:** A prealgebra teacher returns all tests and quizzes the following day and discusses frequently missed problems in detail. He comments frequently on students' continually improving skills.

   - **High School:** In a simulation, a world history teacher asks students to identify specific archeological evidence for sites that represent different civilizations. She comments that the students' ability to link evidence to conclusions has improved significantly.

4. Learners' needs for relatedness are met when teachers communicate a commitment to students both as people and as learners.

   - **Elementary:** A first-grade teacher greets her students each morning at the door with a hug, "high five," or handshake. She tells them what a good day they're going to have.

   - **Middle School:** A seventh-grade teacher calls a parent to express concern about a student whose behavior and attitude seems to have changed.

   - **High School:** A geometry teacher in an urban school conducts help sessions after school on Mondays through Thursdays. When they come in for extra help, she also encourages students to talk about their personal lives and their hopes for the future.

Learners' Needs to Preserve Self-Worth

5. Self-worth theory suggests that people link self-worth to high ability. Emphasize that ability can be increased with effort.

   - **Elementary:** When her second graders succeed with word problems during their seatwork, a teacher comments, "You're really understanding what we're doing. The harder we work, the smarter we get."

   - **Middle School:** A life-science teacher comments, "You're really seeing the connections between animals' body structures and their ability to adapt. This is not an easy idea to grasp, and you should feel good about figuring this out."

   - **High School:** As students' understanding of balancing equations increases, a chemistry teacher comments, "Balancing equations is important in chemistry and I know it isn't easy, but you people are really improving with this stuff."

The Influence of Beliefs on Motivation to Learn

To begin this section, look at the following statements and think about what they tell us about each person's motivation.

1. "If I study hard for the next test, I'm going to do well."
2. "Learning a foreign language doesn't come naturally for me, but with some more work, I'm going to be good at it by the end of the year."
3. "I'm not that crazy about algebra, but I need to get good at it. I want to major in engineering in college, and I know I'll need it."

Each of these statements describes a **belief**, an idea we accept as true without necessarily having definitive evidence to support it. As with needs, people's beliefs about their abilities have a strong influence on their motivation to learn, and in this section we examine how the following sets of beliefs influence motivation.

- Beliefs about outcomes: Expectations
- Beliefs about intelligence: Mindset
- Beliefs about capability: Self-efficacy
- Beliefs about value: Attainment value, utility value, and cost
- Beliefs about causes of performance: Attributions

Ed Psych and You

Do you like to play games? Do you like playing all games or only certain ones? Why do you enjoy playing some and not others? Is succeeding in some games more important to you than succeeding in others?

Beliefs about Outcomes: Expectations

Look again at the statement, "If I study hard for the next test, I'm going to do well." It describes an **expectation**, a belief about a future outcome—in this case a high score on the next test (Schunk & Zimmerman, 2006). The influence of expectations on motivation is often described using **expectancy x value theory**, which states that people are motivated to engage in a task to the extent that they expect to succeed on the task *times* the value they place on the success (Wigfield & Eccles, 1992, 2000). (We examine the influence of task value on motivation later in this section.) The "x" implies multiplication, and it is important because anything times zero is zero. So, if learners don't expect to succeed on a task, their motivation will be low regardless of how much they value success on it (Tollefson, 2000). Similarly, if people don't value success on a task, their motivation will also be low, even if success is assured. This relates to the questions in *Ed Psych and You*. For most people, the games they most enjoy are those in which they generally succeed, winning more often than not. Their expectations for success are quite high, or they quit playing. It's a unique person who continues to play a game he or she rarely wins.

Students with high expectations for success persist longer on tasks, choose more challenging activities, and achieve more than those whose expectations are lower (Eccles et al., 1998; Wigfield, 1994).

Past experience is the primary factor influencing expectations. Students who usually succeed expect to do so in the future, and the opposite is true for those who are unsuccessful. This helps us understand why promoting motivation to learn is such a challenge when working with low achievers. Because they have a history of failure, their motivation to learn is low as a result of low expectations for success. This, combined with their need to preserve their sense of self-worth, creates a problem that is doubly difficult for all of us who teach.

The only way we can increase motivation to learn in students whose expectations for success are low is to design learning experiences that ensure some degree of success. This is, of course, an enormous challenge, but in time, and with effort, it can be done.

Beliefs about Intelligence: Mindset

Our beliefs about intelligence also affect our motivation. To see how, let's look at the words of an eighth grader, Sarah, as she talks about her ability in math: "My brother, I, and my mom aren't good at math at all, we inherited the 'not good at math gene' from my mom and I am good at English, but I am not good at math" (Ryan, Ryan, Arbuthnot, & Samuels, 2007, p. 5).

Sarah is describing a **fixed mindset**, a belief that intelligence, or ability, is relatively fixed, stable, and unchanging over time and for different task conditions (Dweck, 2008a, 2008b). (A *fixed mindset* is also described as an *entity view of intelligence or ability*). According to Sarah, "some have it and some don't," and there is little she can do about it.

Compare this view with our second statement at the beginning of this section: "Learning a foreign language doesn't come naturally for me, but with some more work, I'm going to be good at it by the end of the year." This statement reflects a **growth mindset** (also called an *incremental view of intelligence*), the belief that intelligence, or ability, can be increased with effort. People with a growth mindset roughly equate ability with learning (Schunk et al., 2014).

The concept of *mindset* was originated by Carol Dweck, whose book *Mindset: The New Psychology of Success* (2008b) has received a great deal of attention both in academic circles and in the popular media. Dweck's research suggests that mindset is a powerful motivational factor that begins to appear in childhood and impacts aspects of our lives ranging from academic success to work, sports, parenting, and even personal relationships and self-regulation. Additional work has corroborated her findings. For instance, one study found that mothers with a growth mindset were more supportive and positive with their children than those with a fixed mindset (Moorman & Pomerantz, 2010). Additional research has found that people in the workforce with a stress-is-enhancing mindset perform better than those with a stress-is-debilitating mindset (Crum, Salovey, & Achor, 2013). And additional research suggests that mindset is even more important for productivity than are skills, because needed skills can be learned, whereas mindset impacts people's entire approach to their work (Kennedy, Carroll, & Francoeur, 2013).

Mindset has important implications for parents and the way they praise their children. Dweck's (2008a, 2008b) research suggests that children who continually hear how smart they are shy away from challenges, become sensitive to failure, and learn to believe that effort is an indicator of low ability. As a result their performance declines. Instead, she asserts, parents should praise their children for qualities they can control, such as concentration, effort, and the strategies they use.

In schools, mindset helps us understand why learners sometimes engage in self-handicapping behaviors to protect their self-worth. Failure suggests a lack of ability, so if students have a fixed mindset, they protect their self-worth by avoiding situations that may reflect negatively on their ability, and motivation and learning decrease. On the other hand, if learners believe that ability can be increased with effort—a growth mindset—challenge and failure merely suggest that more effort or better strategies are needed. As a result, their motivation and learning increase, and their success provides evidence that their ability is increasing (Schunk & Zimmerman, 2006).

Beliefs about Capability: Self-Efficacy

To begin this section let's look again at the conversation between Melanie and Yelena, which introduced the discussion of cognitive theories of motivation.

> "C'mon, let's go," Melanie urges her friend Yelena as they're finishing a series of homework problems in math.
>
> "Just a sec," Yelena mutters. "I'm not quite getting this one."
>
> "Let's work on it tonight. Everybody's leaving," Melanie urges.
>
> "Go ahead, I'll catch up to you in a minute. I know that I can figure this out. . . . I just don't get it right now."

Yelena's statement suggests that she believes she is capable of solving this problem if she perseveres. It illustrates the concept of **self-efficacy**, our belief that we are capable of accomplishing a specific task (Bandura, 1997, 2004). *Self-efficacy, self-concept,* and *expectation for success* are closely related, but they aren't synonymous (Schunk, 2012). For example, if Yelena believes she is generally competent in math, we would say that she has a positive self-concept in math. Self-efficacy is more specific. She believes she can solve this problem and those similar to it, but it doesn't mean that she believes she will succeed in all forms of math or in other domains, such as writing essays. Also, believing that she can solve problems such as this one isn't identical to her expectations for success. For example, even though she believes she can solve problems like this one, she won't expect to succeed on her next math quiz if she doesn't study and do her homework.

The concept of self-efficacy has wide-ranging applications, and it is particularly important in the areas of health and well-being. For instance, research indicates that patients who believe they will recover fully—high self-efficacy—after total joint replacement are much more conscientious about their rehab than patients with lower self-efficacy, and, as a result, do indeed recover more completely and quickly (Fiala, Rhodes, Blanchard, & Anderson, 2013). Additional research suggests that self-efficacy, which leads to self-regulation, is the primary factor influencing whether or not young people will exercise on a regular basis (Dewar, Lubans, Morgan, & Plotnikoff, 2013; Nehl et al., 2012).

Self-efficacy depends on four factors (see Figure 10.4). Past performance on similar tasks is the most important. If you have a history of success giving oral reports in your classes, for example, your self-efficacy in this area will be high. Modeling, such as seeing

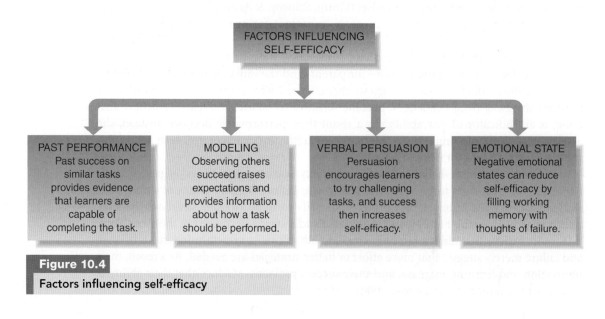

Figure 10.4

Factors influencing self-efficacy

others deliver excellent reports, can also increase your self-efficacy by raising expectations and providing information about the way a skill should be performed (Bandura, 1997; Kitsantas, Zimmerman, & Cleary, 2000).

Although limited in effectiveness, verbal persuasion, such as a teacher's comment, "I know you will give a fine report," can also increase self-efficacy by encouraging students to attempt challenging tasks, which increases efficacy if they succeed.

Finally, students' emotional state as well as physiological factors, such as fatigue or hunger, can also influence self-efficacy. If they're anxious, for example, their working memories might be filled with thoughts of failure, so they're less likely to succeed, and self-efficacy then decreases (Linnenbrink-Garcia & Pekrun, 2011). Or, if they're too tired to study, their self-efficacy is likely to be temporarily reduced.

Self-efficacy strongly influences motivation to learn, and it is commonly described as a component of social cognitive theory. "Self-efficacy is a central motivational variable in social cognitive theory and can affect choice of activities, effort, and persistence" (Schunk et al., 2014, p. 145). For instance, compared to low-efficacy students, high-efficacy learners accept more challenging tasks, exert more effort, persist longer, use more effective strategies, and generally perform better (Bandura, 1997; Schunk & Ertmer, 2000).

Beliefs about Value: Attainment Value, Utility Value, and Cost

Value refers to the benefits, rewards, or advantages that individuals believe can result from participating in an activity, and it is the second component of expectancy x value theory.

Three types of values influence motivation (Wigfield & Eccles, 2000, 2002):

- Attainment value
- Utility value
- Cost

Attainment Value. To understand attainment value, let's think about the last question we asked in *Ed Psych and You* earlier: "Is succeeding in some games more important to you than succeeding in others?" The answer is almost certainly "yes," and success is more important to you if you believe you're good at the game. This relates to attainment value, the importance an individual attaches to doing well on a task (Wigfield & Eccles, 2000, 2002). For example, it's important to Don (one of your authors) that he swims his laps in a certain amount of time because he believes that he's a good swimmer, and winning in tennis is important to Paul (your other author) because he—perhaps naively—believes he plays tennis well. Succeeding validates their beliefs about their ability (Anderman & Wolters, 2006). On the other hand, winning at chess isn't important to either one, since neither believes that he's a good chess player.

Utility Value. Now, think about your study of educational psychology and this book. We hope you view it as interesting for its own sake, but perhaps more importantly, we want you to believe that understanding its content will make you a better teacher. If you do, it has high utility value, the belief that a topic, activity, or course of study will be useful for meeting future goals, including career goals (Wigfield & Eccles, 1992). Believing that studying educational psychology will make you a better professional increases its utility value and increases your motivation to study educational psychology.

Cost. Have you ever dropped a class because your workload was too heavy? Many of us have, and we can explain why using the concept of cost, the consideration of what a person must give up to engage in an activity (Wigfield & Eccles, 2002). In the case of an impossible workload, the cost is too high, so you're not motivated to continue in the class.

Beliefs about outcomes (expectations), intelligence or ability (mindset), capability (self-efficacy), and value help us understand why our students are likely to engage in and persevere on tasks. Their beliefs about their performances and why they perform the way they do can also influence their motivation. This leads us to a discussion of attributions.

Beliefs about Causes of Performance: Attributions

When you succeed on a task, why are you successful? If you don't succeed, why not? The explanations we offer for our successes and failures influence our motivation, and to see how, let's look at four students' reactions to the results of a test.

> "How'd you do, Bob?" Anne asks.
>
> "Terrible," Bob answers sheepishly. "I just can't do this stuff. I'm no good at essay tests. . . . I'll never get it."
>
> "I didn't do so good either," Anne replies, "but I knew I wouldn't. I just didn't study hard enough. I won't let that happen again."
>
> "Unbelievable!" Armondo adds. "I didn't know what the heck was going on, and I got a B. I really lucked out. I don't think she read mine."
>
> "I think the test was too tough," Ashley shakes her head. "I looked at it and just went blank. All I could think was, 'I've never seen this stuff before. Where did it come from?' I thought I was going to throw up."

The students are offering **attributions**, explanations, or beliefs related to the causes of their performance. Bob, for example, believed that his poor performance resulted from lack of ability, whereas Anne believed that lack of effort caused hers. Armondo believed he was lucky, and Ashley thought the test was too hard. **Attribution theory** attempts to systematically describe learners' beliefs about the causes of their successes and failures and how these beliefs influence motivation to learn. It is a cognitive theory of motivation; that is, it is based on the assumption that people want to understand—make sense of—their environments (White, 1959; Weiner, 1992). Understanding why they perform the way they do helps them meet this goal, and it helps explain why they seek information about their performance (Savolainen, 2013).

Students most commonly form attributions for academic performance, but also in other areas, such as why they're being harassed or bullied (Visconti, Sechler, & Kochenderfer-Ladd, 2013). Adults also form attributions for the degree to which they're successful in their work, personal relationships, and even their health and well-being (Schunk et al., 2014). Historically, research on attributions for academic achievement focused on four major causes for success or failure—*ability, effort, task difficulty,* and *luck*—but more recent research has expanded the list (Schunk et al., 2014). Some examples of attributions in different domains are listed in Table 10.1. In spite of the variety of attributions we see in the table, attribution theory categorizes them along three causal dimensions (Weiner, 1992, 2000).

- *Stability*: Whether the attribution—perceived cause—is likely or not likely to change in the near future. For instance, in the physical skills domain in Table 10.1, natural ability would be considered stable, because it isn't going to change.
- *Locus*: Whether the attribution is within or outside the learner. As an example, in the academic achievement domain, ability and effort would be considered *internal*—within the learner—whereas task difficulty and quality of instruction would be considered *external*—outside the learner.

Table 10.1	**Attributions in different domains**		
Academic Achievement	**Physical Skills**	**Interpersonal Relationships**	**Health and Well-Being**
Ability	Natural ability	Personality	Heredity
Effort	Amount of practice	Physical attractiveness	Exercise
Task difficulty	Quality of coaching	Social status	Luck
Luck	General health	Money	Working conditions
Interest	Diet	Personal hygiene	Personal habits
Quality of instruction	Body structure	Availability	Attitude
Fairness of teachers	Emotional makeup	Character of others	
Fatigue			
Help from others			

Adapted from Weiner (2000).

- *Control*: Whether or not the learner can influence or change the factor. In the respective domains, the individual can control effort (academic achievement), amount of practice (physical skills), personal hygiene (interpersonal relationships), and personal habits (health and well-being). On the other hand, in these same domains the individual cannot, for the most part, control the fairness of teachers, quality of coaching, social status, or heredity.

In general, people tend to attribute successes to internal causes, such as high ability or effort in the case of academic achievement, and their failures to external causes, such as quality of coaching in the case of physical skills, or character of others in the case of interpersonal relationships (Rhodewalt & Vohs, 2005). This makes sense. In the academic domain, for example, attributing success to internal causes, such as ability, and failures to external causes, such as poor teaching, allows learners to maintain their sense of self-worth.

THE INFLUENCE OF ATTRIBUTIONS ON EMOTIONS, COGNITION, AND MOTIVATION

Attributions influence learners in three ways (Weiner, 2000, 2001):

- *Emotions*: Emotional reactions to success and failure
- *Cognition*: Expectations for future success
- *Motivation*: Future effort

To see how these influences work, let's look at Anne's and Bob's attributions again. Anne attributed her poor score to lack of effort. She was responsible for her effort, so guilt was her most prominent emotional reaction. Her comment, "I won't let that happen again," suggests that she will increase her effort. As a result, she will expect to succeed, and improved achievement is likely.

Bob attributed his failure to lack of ability. He has a *fixed mindset*, as indicated by his comment, "I'm no good at essay tests. . . . I'll never get it." So, instead of guilt, his emotional reaction is embarrassment and shame, since he views himself as having low ability. His comment, "I'll never get it," suggests that he doesn't expect future success, so both his effort and his achievement are likely to decrease.

Motivation tends to increase when students attribute failure to lack of effort, as Anne did, or ineffective strategies, because effort and strategy use can be controlled, whereas it tends to decrease when they attribute failure to causes they can't control, such as luck or ability if they believe ability is fixed (Weinstock, 2007).

LEARNED HELPLESSNESS

If attributing failure to lack of ability becomes a pattern, **learned helplessness**, the debilitating belief that one is incapable of accomplishing tasks and has little control of the environment, can result. Bob's comment, "I just can't do this stuff. . . . I'll never get it," indicates that he is a potential candidate for learned helplessness. Concluding "I'll never get it" can result in overwhelming feelings of shame and self-doubt and giving up without trying.

Learned helplessness has both an affective and a cognitive component. Affectively, students in this state often have low self-esteem and suffer from anxiety and depression (Graham & Weiner, 1996). Cognitively, they expect to fail, so they exert little effort and use ineffective strategies, which result in less success and an even greater expectation for failure (Dweck, 2000). Fortunately, efforts to intervene through attribution training have been successful.

ATTRIBUTION TRAINING

Learners can improve the effectiveness of their attributions with training, and teachers are central to the process (Robertson, 2000). In a pioneering study, Dweck (1975) provided students who demonstrated learned helplessness with both successful and unsuccessful experiences. When the students were unsuccessful, the experimenter specifically stated that the failure was caused by lack of effort or ineffective strategies. Comparable students were given similar experiences but no training. After the training, learners responded more positively to failure by persisting longer and adapting their strategies more effectively. More recent research has corroborated Dweck's findings (Schunk et al., 2014).

Educational Psychology and Teaching: Using the Influence of Beliefs to Increase Your Students' Motivation to Learn

Earlier in the chapter we saw that capitalizing on students' needs can increase their motivation to learn, and the same applies to their beliefs. The following suggestions can help you apply an understanding of students' beliefs to increase their motivation to learn.

- Model a growth mindset, internal attributions for successes, and control attributions for failures.
- Promote expectation for success and self-efficacy with modeling and effective teaching.
- Emphasize the utility value of what you're teaching.

Model a Growth Mindset, Internal Attributions for Successes, and Control Attributions for Failures. To begin this section, let's look again at the brief conversation between Kathy and Mason in the case study at the beginning of the chapter.

> Mason: Gee, Mrs. Brewster, that assignment was impossible.
> Kathy: That's good for you. I know it was a tough assignment, but you need to be challenged. It's hard for me too when I'm studying and trying to put together new ideas, but if I hang in, I always feel like I can get it.
> Mason: Aw c'mon, Mrs. Brewster. You know everything.
> Kathy: I wish. I study every night to keep up with you people, and the harder I study, the better I get. . . If I struggle, I just redouble my efforts, and it really feels good when I finally get it.

In saying, "the harder I study, the better I get," Kathy modeled a growth mindset. Then, in saying, "It's hard for me too when I'm struggling and trying to put together new ideas, but if I hang in, I always feel like I can get it," she modeled an internal attribution for success by suggesting that it was the result of her personal effort and not some factor outside of herself. Finally, in saying, "If I struggle, I just redouble my efforts," she suggested that even when she struggled she was in control, that is, she modeled a control attribution for failure, and she even modeled an emotional reaction to finally succeeding by saying "and it really feels good when I finally get it."

This modeling, combined with encouraging our students to believe the same way, is the most effective strategy we have for promoting a positive mindset and healthy attributions. Also, encouraging students to attribute failure to ineffective strategies is particularly effective for students who believe they are already trying hard. And as students see their competence increase, their motivation to learn will also increase.

Promote Self-Efficacy and Expectations for Success with Modeling and Effective Teaching. Let's look once again at Kathy's comments in her conversation with Mason. She said,

> "It's hard for me too when I'm struggling and trying to put together new ideas, but if I hang in, I always feel like I can get it."

In making this statement she modeled not only an internal attribution for her success, but also the belief that she was capable of accomplishing a specific task (self-efficacy) and would succeed (expectation for success). As we saw earlier in our discussion, modeling is one of the factors that influence self-efficacy.

Success on similar tasks is the other important factor influencing both self-efficacy and expectations for future success, because students high in both choose more challenging tasks, persist longer on them, and generally learn more than their peers lower in either.

Promoting self-efficacy and expectations for success is obviously a challenge, particularly for students with a history of underachievement. The situation is not hopeless, however. The following suggestions, all components of effective teaching, can make a difference.

- Establish clear goals and create learning activities, assignments, and assessments that directly address the goals. When students know exactly what they're supposed to learn, they know how to study and the likelihood of their success increases, and with it, their self-efficacy.
- Provide students with practice in developing their abilities. For instance, Kathy's comment to Harvey, "Look at how much your writing has improved as a result of your effort," suggests that she has her students do a considerable amount of writing in her class. No substitute exists for practice in developing skills and abilities, and some experts believe that deliberate practice is even more important than natural ability (Colvin, 2010; Schraw, 2006).
- Thoroughly discuss assignments and assessments after they're given, and provide students with the information they need to improve their abilities.
- Make statements such as, "If you study hard, I know you can do well on the quiz," "Yes, this assignment will be a challenge, but I know you can do it," or even, "I know we struggled a little on the last quiz, but if we work a little harder, we'll improve on the next one." Statements such as these have a much more positive effect on motivation than saying something such as, "I'm not sure what you were thinking about on the last quiz," "You'd better get going or you'll be back in this class next year," or "I'm not sure what your problem is." Our use of language can have an important impact on our students' motivation to learn.

Because of its influence on motivation, increasing our students' self-efficacy is one of our most important goals, and modeling and effective instruction are our most effective tools. When we model effective study strategies, involve students in learning activities, thoroughly assess understanding, and provide detailed feedback, we promote the success that contributes to self-efficacy. Ultimately, we "help them to appreciate that they are developing their abilities by accepting challenges and applying consistent effort" (Brophy, 2010, p. 53).

Emphasize the Utility Value of What You're Teaching. Earlier in our discussion we saw that *utility value* is the belief that a topic, activity, or course of study will be useful for meeting future goals. Kathy's emphasis on utility value was indicated by Susan's, Jim's, and Mason's comments in the case study at the beginning of the chapter. For instance, Susan said,

> "We'd better get moving. The bell's going to ring, and you know how Brewster is about this class. She thinks it's sooo important."

Believing that what we teach is important and valuable won't automatically cause our students to believe the same way. However, even subtly communicating that what we're teaching isn't important will surely detract from their motivation. So we have nothing to lose by demonstrating that we believe what we're teaching is important and valuable, and it takes virtually no additional time or energy to communicate this belief to our students.

We saw how this belief influenced Jim as he commented,

> "I used to hate history, but sometimes I even read ahead a little, because Brewster makes you think. She's so gung ho, and it's kind of interesting the way she's always telling us about the way we are because of something that happened a zillion years ago—I never thought about this stuff in that way before."

And Mason's comment is an even more concrete example of Kathy's emphasis on utility value.

> "Yeah, yeah, I know, being good thinkers and writers will help us in everything we do in life," echoing a message the students often hear from Kathy.

"Why do we have to learn this?" is a question students commonly ask, or at least wonder about if they're afraid to ask. Communicating the utility value of what we're teaching can help address this issue.

As with applying an understanding of needs in an effort to increase our students' motivation to learn, the suggestions for capitalizing on beliefs are synergistic—the effect of their combination and interaction is greater than the sum of the individual elements. For instance, if our students believe that we're committed to them both as people and as learners, the likelihood of them taking us seriously when we model a growth mindset increases. Similarly, if we involve our students in decision making, they are more likely to believe that we respect them as people, and the likelihood of them believing us when we emphasize the utility value of what we're teaching also increases. The same is true for all the suggestions we offer.

Classroom **Connections**

Using Students' Beliefs to Increase their Motivation to Learn

Beliefs About Future Outcomes and Capability: Expectations and Self-Efficacy

1. Expectations are beliefs about future outcomes, and self-efficacy describes beliefs about our capability to accomplish specific tasks. Develop expectations for success and self-efficacy by providing enough scaffolding to ensure that students make progress on challenging tasks.

- **Elementary:** A fourth-grade teacher presents students with a word problem, has them try it, and then provides enough guidance so they are successful in solving it.
- **Middle School:** A seventh-grade English teacher has his students write paragraphs, and he then displays some of them on the document camera and makes suggestions for improvement.
- **High School:** An art teacher has students keep a portfolio of their work. She periodically asks them to review their products to see evidence of progress.

Beliefs About Intelligence: Mindset

2. Learners with a growth mindset believe that ability can increase with effort. Emphasize a growth mindset with your students.

- **Elementary:** After her students have solved a series of word problems, a second-grade teacher comments, "See how our work is paying off. When we work hard, we get better and better."
- **Middle School:** A seventh-grade geography history teacher says, "Your efforts to understand how geography influences countries' economies and politics are really helping. I tell your other teachers how much you're improving in my class."
- **High School:** A chemistry teacher emphasizes that he studies every night. "The harder I work, the more capable I become," he smiles. "And you can do the same thing."

Beliefs About Value: Utility Value

3. Utility value is the belief that a topic or activity will be useful for meeting future goals. Emphasize the utility value of the topics students study.

- **Elementary:** A fifth-grade teacher emphasizes the importance of understanding our bodies so we can make good decisions about keeping our bodies healthy.
- **Middle School:** A seventh-grade math teacher working on percentage problems brings in newspaper advertisements for marked-down products. The class determines the actual reduction in cost, and the teacher then emphasizes the value of percentages in understanding how much people save in promotions.
- **High School:** An English teacher displays examples of well-written (and not so well-written) attempts to make and defend an argument. She uses the examples to emphasize the value of being able to express oneself clearly.

Beliefs About Causes of Performance: Attributions

4. Attributions describe beliefs about causes of performance. Model and encourage students to attribute success to increasing competence and failure to lack of effort or ineffective strategies.

- **Elementary:** As his students initially work on word problems, a second-grade teacher carefully monitors student effort during seatwork. When he sees assignments that indicate effort, he makes comments to individual students, such as "Your work is improving all the time."
- **Middle School:** A sixth-grade English teacher comments, "I wasn't good at grammar for a long time. But I kept trying, and I found that I could do it. You can become good too, but you have to work at it."
- **High School:** A chemistry teacher comments, "The way we're attacking balancing equations is working much better, isn't it? You tried to memorize the steps before, and now you're understanding what you're doing."

The Influence of Goals on Motivation to Learn

To begin this section, let's examine the thinking of several of Kathy's students as they prepare their group presentations on the Renaissance.

Susan: This should be interesting. I don't know much about the Renaissance, and it began a whole new emphasis on learning all over the world. Mrs. Brewster has given us a lot of responsibility, so we need to come through. We need to make a presentation she'll like.

Damien: I'll get my Dad to help us. He's really up on history. Our presentation will be the best one of the bunch, and the class will be impressed.

Sylvia: Yikes! Everyone in my group is so smart. What can I do? They'll think I'm the dumbest one. I'm going to just stay quiet when we're working together.

> **Charlotte:** This should be fun. We can get together to work on this at one of our houses. If we can get the project out of the way quickly, I might have time to get to know Damien better.
>
> **Antonio:** I don't know anything about this. I'd better do some studying so my group will think I'm pulling my weight.
>
> **Patrick:** I like group activities. They're usually easy. Somebody is always gung ho and does most of the work.

Each of the students' thinking reflects a **goal**, an outcome an individual hopes to attain (Anderman & Wolters, 2006). Susan's, for example, was to understand the Renaissance and please Mrs. Brewster, Charlotte wanted to socialize, and Patrick simply wanted to do as little work as possible. These different goal orientations influence both their motivation and learning, as we'll see in the next section.

Ed Psych and You

When you take tests or quizzes in your classes, do you want to know how you do compared to others in the course? Why do you think this is the case?

Mastery and Performance Goals

Much of the research examining goals has focused on differences between **mastery goals** (also called *learning goals*)—goals that focus on accomplishing tasks, improving, and increasing understanding—and **performance goals**—goals that focus on ability and how learners compare to others (Midgley, 2001). For instance, Susan's desire to understand the Renaissance is a mastery goal. Students with a mastery orientation persist in the face of challenge and difficulty, attribute success to effort, use effective strategies (such as self-questioning), and maintain their interest and effort even after formal instruction is finished (Wolters, 2003).

In comparison, our questions in *Ed Psych and You* relate to performance goals, and if you answered yes to the first one, you're typical. Because ability becomes increasingly important to students as they get older, they want to know how they perform compared to others, which helps explain why most people answer yes to the first question. Teachers contribute to this orientation if they post distributions of scores on tests or use course management systems that display class averages. Although some performance orientation in students is inevitable, performance goals are less effective than mastery goals. Let's see why.

Performance goals exist in two forms (Elliot & Thrash, 2001). **Performance-approach goals** emphasize looking competent and receiving favorable judgments from others. Damien's wanting to make the best presentation and impress the class is an example. Students with performance-approach goals tend to be confident and have high self-efficacy, but they may exert only minimal effort or use superficial strategies, such as memorization, to reach them. When goals become challenging, they may engage in self-handicapping behaviors, such as not trying when they're not sure they can meet the goals, or they may even cheat (Brophy, 2010; Midgley, Kaplan, & Middleton, 2001).

Sylvia's thinking, "They'll think I'm the dumbest one. I'm going to just stay quiet when we're working together," reflects a **performance-avoidance goal**, an attempt to avoid looking incompetent and being judged unfavorably, and this is the most detrimental for motivation and achievement (Ryan et al., 2007). Students who attempt to avoid looking incompetent tend to have low self-efficacy, lack self-confidence, and experience anxiety about tests and other assessments (Midgley et al., 2001). They often try to avoid tasks that will help them master new skills. For example, Sylvia only wanted to avoid looking "dumb" to the other students; learning was essentially irrelevant to her.

Students with a fixed mindset tend to adopt performance goals, whereas those with a growth mindset are more apt to adopt mastery goals (Dweck, 1999, 2006). This relationship makes sense. For example, wanting to make the best presentation in the class—a performance goal—could be interpreted as an indicator of high ability, which is important for individuals who view intelligence, or ability, as fixed. This can be a problem, however, because we all periodically fail, and failure, for them, is an indicator of low ability. In contrast, individuals with growth mindsets are more likely to seek challenge and persevere, because failure merely indicates that more work is required, and, as competence increases, so does intelligence.

Social Goals

Let's look at the students' thinking again. Charlotte, for example, thought, "If we can get the project out of the way quickly, I might have time to get to know Damien better," and Antonio decided, "I don't know anything about this. I'd better do some studying so my group will think I'm pulling my weight." Both are **social goals**, goals to achieve particular social outcomes or interactions (Wentzel, 2002). More specifically, Antonio had a *social-responsibility* goal. Other social goals include:

- Forming friendships.
- Gaining teacher or peer approval.
- Meeting social obligations.
- Assisting and supporting others.
- Underachieving to make others feel better (Davis, 2003; Wentzel, 2000).

Social goals can both increase and decrease motivation to learn (Horst, Finney, & Barron, 2007). For instance, Charlotte's wanting to "get the project out of the way quickly" detracted from her motivation. As we would expect, low achievers report this orientation more often than do high achievers (Wentzel, 1999). On the other hand, social-responsibility goals, such as Antonio's, are associated with both high motivation and achievement (Wentzel, 1996).

Motivation to learn is highest when mastery and social-responsibility goals are combined (Wentzel, 2000). This is illustrated in Susan's thinking, "This should be interesting. I don't know much about the Renaissance" (a mastery goal) and, "Mrs. Brewster has given us a lot of responsibility, so we need to come through. We need to make a presentation she'll like" (a social-responsibility goal).

Work-Avoidance Goals

Patrick's comment, "I like group activities. They're usually easy. Somebody is always gung ho and does most of the work," indicates a work-avoidance goal. Students with this goal orientation feel successful when tasks are easy or can be completed with little effort (Dowson & McInerney, 2001). They also tend to use ineffective learning strategies, make minimal contributions to group activities, ask for help even when they don't need it, and complain about challenging activities. Not surprisingly, students like Patrick are a source of frustration for teachers.

Table 10.2 summarizes the different types of goals and their influence on motivation and achievement.

Table 10.2 Goals, motivation, and achievement

Type of Goal	Example	Influence on Motivation and Achievement
Mastery goals	Understand the influence of the Renaissance on American history.	Leads to sustained effort, high self-efficacy, willingness to accept challenges, and high achievement.
Performance-approach goals	Produce one of the best presentations on the Renaissance in the class.	Can lead to sustained effort and high self-efficacy for confident learners. Can increase achievement. Can detract from willingness to accept challenging tasks, which decreases achievement.
Performance-avoidance goals	Avoid the appearance of low ability in front of peers and teachers.	Detracts from motivation and achievement, particularly for learners lacking confidence.
Social goals	Be perceived as reliable and responsible.	Can increase motivation and achievement. *Social-responsibility goals* enhance motivation and achievement, particularly when combined with mastery goals.
	Make friends and socialize.	Can detract from motivation and achievement if social goals compete for time with mastery goals.
Work-avoidance goals	Complete assignments with as little effort as possible.	Detracts from effort and self-efficacy. Strongly detracts from achievement.

Diversity: Learner Differences in Goal Orientation

As with many aspects of learning and motivation, learner differences with respect to goal orientation sometimes exist. For instance, research indicates that both Asian American and African American students tend to focus on mastery goals, whereas European American students focus more on performance goals, and Asian American students are also more likely to have growth mindsets (Qian & Pan, 2002).

This goal orientation and mindset influences learners' attributions. For instance, Asian American students are also more likely to attribute their successes to effort and their failures to lack of effort than are Caucasian students (Lillard, 1997; Steinberg, 1996). This makes sense. We would expect learners with growth mindsets to attribute both success and failure to effort—or lack of—and we would also expect them to have a mastery goal orientation.

Gender differences also exist with respect to goal orientations. As a general pattern, research suggests that girls are more likely to have a mastery goal orientation than are boys (Dekker et al., 2013; Nie & Liem, 2013; Yeung, Lau, & Nie, 2011). And as would be expected, girls tend to have a strong social goal orientation (Dekker et al., 2013). On the other hand, particularly for high achievers, boys tend to adopt a performance-approach orientation more often than do girls, who, perhaps because they are less confident than boys, more often adopt a performance-avoidance orientation (Dekker et al., 2013). This was illustrated by Sylvia's comment earlier, "Yikes! Everyone in my group is so smart. What can I do? They'll think I'm the dumbest one. I'm going to just stay quiet when we're working together." Interestingly, however, in classes considered to be male domains, such as math and physics, boys sometimes adopt performance-avoidance goals, likely to preserve the perception of high ability in these areas (Koul, Roy, & Lerdpornkulrat, 2012).

One of the most significant findings relates to changes in goal orientation as students approach adolescence. As they move into high school, boys' mastery approach decreases, and they become much more likely than girls to adopt a work-avoidance orientation. These age and gender differences in goal orientations may be a possible explanation for boys' lower academic achievement compared to girls', and they indicate a need for early intervention to help prevent boys' academic slide (Dekker et al., 2013).

As you apply this information with your students, it's important to remember that individuals within groups vary significantly. For instance, many European American students and many boys set mastery goals, whereas some Asian American students and many girls set performance goals, and particularly performance-approach goals. As teachers, we want to avoid thinking that can result in stereotyping any group.

The suggestions we offer in the next section for applying our understanding of goal orientations with our students apply to all—cultural minorities and nonminorities, boys, girls, learners with exceptionalities, and learners from all socioeconomic backgrounds. We turn to these suggestions next.

Educational Psychology and Teaching: Using the Influence of Goals to Increase Your Students' Motivation to Learn

We obviously can't adapt our instruction to each student's goal orientation, and, as students progress through school, their performance orientation tends to increase while their mastery orientation decreases (Elliot & McGregor, 2000). Further, to suggest to students that grades aren't important and they should forget about grades is unrealistic. Parents focus on grades, grade-point averages are part of the reality of applying for colleges, and you're concerned about your grade in this class. However, you can take steps to avoid an unhealthy emphasis on performance goals. The following suggestions can help.

- Focus on a mastery and social-responsibility orientation by emphasizing that learning is the goal of schooling, and creating an emotionally supportive classroom climate.
- Create assessments that measure deep understanding of content, and avoid focusing exclusively on factual information.
- Encourage students to set and monitor moderately challenging, measurable, near-term goals.

Let's look at these suggestions in more detail.

Focus on a Mastery and Social-Responsibility Orientation. The emphases and values we communicate to our students can make a major contribution to their goal orientations. For instance, if we focus on and emphasize deep understanding of the topics we teach, our students may eventually realize that grades will take care of themselves if they understand the content. This is the ideal we strive for. Students will compete, and we can't eliminate it completely, but we can contribute to a mastery orientation with statements like Kathy's comment, "Remember, we're all doing our best; we're not competing with each other," and by avoiding any comments such as, "Only four people got A's on the last test," or "Karen and Liam got the highest grades on this quiz," which promote competition among students and a performance orientation.

We can make additional symbolic gestures by writing students' scores on the last page of their tests and telling them that they are not to share their scores with each other. You won't be able to enforce the "don't share" policy, but it symbolizes a focus on learning instead of performance. We can also combine small-group work, which responds to students' social goals, with whole-class instruction, which is often preferred by students with performance-approach goals (Bong, 2001). And we can help create a social-responsibility orientation by creating a learning community that emphasizes a we're-all-in-this-together learning climate.

Create Effective Assessments. How do you feel after you've solved a challenging problem, generated a new idea, or found a relationship in information that you hadn't thought of before? For virtually all of us, it's a good feeling. We aren't thinking about anyone else or how we compare to them. It simply feels good to figure something out after we've worked hard at it. In fact, research in neuroscience indicates that the pleasure centers in our brains are activated when we accomplish something challenging, particularly as a result of hard work (Zink, Pagnoni, Martin-Skurski, Chappelow, & Berns, 2004).

This relates to the process of assessment. The most effective mechanism we have for contributing to a mastery goal orientation in our students is to provide them with evidence that their understanding is increasing, and assessment is the most powerful tool we have for providing them with this evidence (Rohrer & Pashler, 2010). Some suggestions for using assessment effectively include (Schunk et al., 2014; Stipek, 2002):

- Provide clear expectations for students, and ensure that assessments are consistent with the expectations.
- Assess at levels beyond knowledge and recall.
- Assess frequently, and emphasize the assessments' learning benefits. Avoid comments that make assessments appear punitive or controlling.
- Discuss frequently missed items, and emphasize the reasons for answers as much as the answers themselves.
- Drop one or two of students' lowest test or quiz scores for purposes of grading.

Clear expectations and assessments that are aligned with them increase the likelihood that students will be successful, and succeeding on assessments that measure more than knowledge and recall is one of the most effective tools we have for making students feel competent. And the more competent students feel, the less concerned they are about their performance compared to others.

Clear expectations also contribute to students' feelings of autonomy. If they know what is expected of them, they can either choose to study or not study, and they will understand the consequences of not studying. Either way, they're in control, which is the essence of autonomy.

Assessing frequently removes the pressure students often feel, because doing poorly on one assessment doesn't mean they're doomed to failure. Discussing frequently missed items provides students with information they can use to increase their understanding, which further contributes to perceptions of both competence and autonomy (El, Tillema, & van Koppen, 2012). And dropping one or two quizzes for purposes of grading communicates that learning is the primary purpose of assessment (Stiggins & Chappuis, 2012). Each of these factors contributes to a mastery orientation.

Encourage Students to Set and Monitor Goals. Goal setting has been widely used to increase motivation and performance in a variety of areas. For example, the weight loss program, Weight Watchers, is based on setting and monitoring goals, and research indicates that it can be effective (MacMillan, 2012). Goal setting and monitoring has also been used in the business world (Crossley, Cooper, & Wernsing, 2013), areas of health behavior in addition to weight loss (Mann, de Ridder, & Fujita, 2013), and athletics (Guan, Xiang, McBride, & Keating, 2013). For example, suppose you set the goal of jogging 20 miles a week. You jog 4 miles each on Sunday and Monday, rest Tuesday, do 5 on Wednesday, rest again Thursday, and do 4 more on Friday. You don't feel like going for a run on Saturday, but you do anyway because you need to get 3 more miles to reach your goal. If you're committed to the goal, your motivation will be high, and you go for a run even if you don't want to.

Goal setting and monitoring can also be used to increase learners' motivation in academic settings (Schunk et al., 2014). Effective goals have three characteristics:

- Specific (versus broad and general).
- Immediate or close at hand (versus distant).
- Moderately challenging.

For instance, "to answer and understand all of the self check questions at the end of each major section of the chapter" is an effective goal, because it is specific and immediate, whereas, "to learn more in this class" is not, because it is general and distant.

The appropriate degree of challenge is a matter of personal judgment. For example, 20 miles a week would not be challenging enough for a serious runner, whereas it might be too challenging for someone just beginning an exercise regimen.

Speaking from personal experience, setting and monitoring goals can be highly motivating if, and this is a big *if*, we're committed to the goal (Schunk et al., 2014). For example, Paul and Don, your authors, have both used goals to increase their level of exercise and lose weight. This can be problematic in classrooms, however, because students tend to be reluctant to set goals in the first place, set goals that are too easy to attain, or lack commitment to the goals.

However, if you are able to induce your students to set and monitor learning goals, you will have implemented one of the most powerful motivators that exist. Some examples of effective goals might include:

- To answer and understand each problem in all their math homework assignments.
- To Google each new vocabulary term they encounter and write down the definition.
- To solve a minimum of five practice problems or practice exercises before each quiz.
- To write a brief summary at the end of each class period that outlines the important ideas discussed in class.

As students monitor progress toward their goals, their level of commitment is likely to increase, because their perceptions of competence and sense of self-efficacy will have increased. And you can support their efforts in your instruction. For instance, you can help your students create personal charts that they can use to check the number of homework problems they're able to solve. You can also ask students to share new vocabulary they've learned, and you can give them a few minutes at the end of each class period to write and discuss their summaries. You can also enlist the support of parents in encouraging their sons and daughters to set and monitor goals. The combination of your encouragement and parental support can play a powerful role in influencing both the kinds of goals learners set and their commitment to the goals.

In spite of your best efforts, not all of your students will set goals, or if they do, will remain committed to them. Those who do, however, will make your efforts well worth it.

Classroom **Connections**

Capitalizing on Goals to Increase Student Motivation

1. Goals are outcomes learners hope to achieve. Emphasize mastery goals in your work with your students.

   - **Elementary:** As a fifth-grade teacher begins a writing project, he comments, "Our goal is to improve our writing. When it improves, the grade you get will take care of itself."

   - **Middle School:** An eighth-grade history teacher puts her students' test scores on the last page of their tests and says, "Our scores are our own business. We're here to learn, not compete with each other."

   - **High School:** In response to students asking how many A's were on the last test, a biology teacher says, "We don't care about that. Instead, ask yourself if your understanding is increasing."

2. A combination of mastery goals and social-responsibility goals can lead to the highest levels of motivation to learn. Emphasize social responsibility with your students.

   - **Elementary:** A third-grade teacher instructs her students to work in pairs to solve a series of math problems. "Work hard," she emphasizes, "so you can help out your partner if he or she needs it."

   - **Middle School:** An eighth-grade English teacher is discussing *To Kill a Mockingbird* with her students. "In order for us to get the most out of the book, we're all responsible for making a contribution to the class discussions," she emphasizes.

   - **High School:** An American history teacher asks her students to work in groups of four to prepare a project comparing the American, French, and Russian revolutions. "Remember, the quality of your project depends on all of you doing your parts to contribute to the final product," she emphasizes.

The Influence of Interest and Emotion on Motivation to Learn

"Because it's interesting" is an intuitively sensible answer to why learners would be motivated to engage in an activity, and as teachers we commonly attempt to capitalize on student interest in our instruction (Anderman & Wolters, 2006; Brophy, 2010). Let's look at it in more detail.

Ed Psych and You

Have you ever wondered why there are so many "cop" shows on TV? Or why outright sex or barely concealed sexual overtones are such a big part of movies and television?

Personal and Situational Interest

Let's go back to the conversation in the case study at the beginning of the chapter between Susan and Jim as they entered Kathy's classroom. Susan commented, "I've always liked history and knowing about the past, . . . and I'm pretty good at it," to which Jim replied, "In some classes I just do enough to get a decent grade, but not in here. . . . It's kind of interesting the way she's always telling us about the way we are because of something that happened a zillion years ago."

Susan's and Jim's comments suggest that they're both interested in Kathy's class, but the nature of their interest differs. Susan expressed **personal interest**, "a person's ongoing affinity, attraction, or liking for a domain, subject area, topic, or activity" (Anderman & Wolters, 2006, p. 374), whereas Jim demonstrated **situational interest**, a person's current enjoyment, pleasure, or satisfaction generated by the immediate context (Schraw & Lehman, 2001). Intrinsic interest—in addition to attainment value, utility value, and cost—is one of the factors increasing value according to expectancy x value theory (Wigfield & Eccles, 1992, 2000).

Personal interest is relatively stable, and it depends heavily on prior knowledge (Renninger, 2000). This stability and knowledge are illustrated in Susan's comment, "I've always liked history, . . . and I'm pretty good at it." Situational interest, in contrast, depends on the current situation and can change quickly.

Some topics, such as death, danger, power, money, romance, and sex, seem to be universal in their ability to create situational interest (Hidi, 2001), and this helps answer the questions we asked in *Ed Psych and You*. For younger students, scary stories, humor, and animals also seem to generate situational interest.

When we teach, we tend to focus on situational interest more than personal interest, because we have more control over the former (Schraw, Flowerday, & Lehman, 2001), and some research suggests that it is essential for student persistence on challenging tasks (Tullis & Fulmer, 2013). However, as a person's expertise develops, situational interest can lead to personal interest, so our goal in creating personal interest can be reached by helping our students develop as much expertise as possible with respect to the topics we teach.

We examine strategies for increasing student interest in more detail in the section "Educational Psychology and Teaching: Using the Influence of Interest and Emotion to Increase Your Students' Motivation to Learn" later in this discussion.

Emotion and Motivation

Our emotions, in addition to our interests, also affect our motivation to learn. To see how, consider how you would react to the following experiences:

- You've just solved a challenging problem.
- Your instructor brings a newspaper clipping to class that graphically describes atrocities occurring in the Middle East.
- You study carefully for a test in one of your classes, and you still don't do well.

In the first example, you probably felt a sense of accomplishment and pride; the second may have caused feelings of outrage, and the third likely left you feeling discouraged and frustrated. Each is an **emotion**, a feeling that is often short-lived, intense, and specific (Schunk et al., 2014).

Our definition describes emotions as "feelings," but they have cognitive, physiological, and behavioral components as well (Pekrun, Goetz, Frenzel, Barchfeld, & Perry, 2011). For instance, suppose we're confronted by an immediate threat, such as a large, snarling, barking dog. Fear is the emotion we experience, but we also perceive danger (a form of cognition), our muscles tense and our heart rates accelerate (physiological reactions), and we likely run—a behavioral response.

Over the past several years, interest in the influence of emotions in academic settings has grown (Linnenbrink-Garcia & Pekrun, 2011). Academic emotions can vary widely, such as experiencing the enjoyment and sense of accomplishment resulting from succeeding on a challenging task, to the boredom we've all experienced in dry lectures, to the anger and frustration that can result from dealing with seemingly intractable difficulties.

Positive emotions, such as enjoyment, hope, and pride, have generally positive effects on success and achievement, but they don't create these effects directly; the increases in achievement result from increased self-regulation and higher levels of motivation (Pekrun et al., 2011), which is why we're discussing emotions in a chapter on motivation instead of in a chapter on learning.

The motivational benefits of positive emotions include the following (Goetz et al., 2012; Linnenbrink, 2007; Linnenbrink-Garcia & Pekrun, 2011; Pekrun et al., 2011):

- *Mindset*: Learners experiencing positive emotions are more likely to adopt a growth mindset.
- *Goal orientation*: Positive emotions are associated with a mastery goal orientation.
- *Self-regulation*: Learners with positive emotions are more likely to self-regulate by preparing more strategically for tests, being more metacognitive during their study, and exerting more effort and persistence on homework.
- *Information processing*: Emotions are encoded together with information, and positive emotions facilitate positive memories.
- *Evaluation of learning*: Positive emotions have a positive effect on students' evaluation of learning and performance.

Negative emotions, on the other hand, are a bit more complex. Boredom, a sense of hopelessness, and shame—particularly if shame is associated with beliefs about lack of ability—are particularly destructive for factors, such as persistence and self-regulation, that increase motivation and achievement (Linnenbrink, 2007; Pekrun et al., 2011). On the other hand, some research suggests that slightly increased levels of anxiety and feelings of guilt—particularly if the guilt results from students' believing that they didn't try hard enough—can increase persistence on challenging tasks (Tullis & Fulmer, 2013). To illustrate these ideas, let's look again at part of the conversation among the students in our discussion of attribution theory earlier in the chapter.

> Anne: How'd you do, Bob?
> Bob: Terrible. . . . I just can't do this stuff. I'm no good at essay tests. . . . I'll never get it.
> Anne: I didn't do so good either . . . but I knew I wouldn't. I just didn't study hard enough. I won't let that happen again.

Both Anne and Bob experienced negative emotions, but the impact on their motivation is likely to be very different. Bob expressed a sense of hopelessness, which is linked to decreased motivation and achievement, whereas Anne felt guilty about her lack of effort, which is associated with increased motivation and achievement.

As we would expect, classroom climate and perceptions of teachers' support have an important influence on students' emotions. For example, high-quality instruction, teacher enthusiasm, and achievement-contingent feedback, such as praise for achievement and support after failure, are positively linked to enjoyment, whereas perceptions of teacher punishment and ineffective instruction are linked to boredom (Jang & Liu, 2012).

MOTIVATION AND ANXIETY

Now, let's look at the conversation among the students that introduced our discussion of attributions once more. In it Ashley commented,

> "I looked at the test, and just went blank. All I could think of was, 'I've never seen this stuff before. Where did it come from?' I thought I was going to throw up."

Ashley experienced **anxiety**, a general uneasiness and feeling of tension relating to a situation with an uncertain outcome. We've all experienced it at one time or another, and it's one of the most studied emotions in motivation and learning.

The relationship between anxiety, motivation, and achievement is curvilinear; some is good, but too much can be damaging (Cassady & Johnson, 2002; Tullis & Fulmer, 2013). For example, some anxiety makes us study harder and develop competence, and relatively high anxiety improves performance on tasks where our expertise is well developed, such as in the case of highly trained athletes (Covington & Omelich, 1987). Too much, however, can decrease motivation and achievement, and classrooms where the evaluation threat is high are particularly anxiety producing (Hancock, 2001). Our understanding of human memory helps explain its debilitating effects (Cassady & Johnson, 2002). First, anxious students have difficulty concentrating, and because they worry about—and even expect—failure, they often misperceive the information they see and hear. In addition, test-anxious students often use superficial strategies, such as memorizing definitions, instead of strategies that are more productive, such as self-questioning (Ryan et al., 2007). In essence, highly test-anxious students often don't learn the content very well in the first place, which increases their anxiety when they're required to perform on tests. Finally, during assessments, they often waste working memory space on thoughts similar to Ashley's, "I've never seen this stuff before. Where did it come from?," leaving less cognitive energy and space available for focusing on the task.

Some interesting and highly applicable research also addresses the issue of anxiety. Researchers found that simply writing about test-related worries for 10 minutes immediately before taking an exam improved test scores in a classroom setting, and particularly when high-stakes tests were involved (Ramirez & Beilock, 2011). These researchers concluded that writing about their worries unloaded the thoughts that were occupying students' working memories, thereby making more working memory space available to devote to the assessment task.

It's important to remember that our descriptions of learner anxiety represent general patterns, and individuals will vary. For instance, some high achievers continue to experience anxiety in spite of a long history of success. In all cases, we teach individuals and not groups, and we want to treat our students in the same way.

THE NEUROSCIENCE OF EMOTION

Neuroscience is now beginning to provide us with the tools to help us better understand how emotions affect motivation. Emotions are thought to be related to activities in our brains that influence our attention, motivation, and assessment of the significance of stimuli we encounter. In humans and other complex vertebrates, the amygdalae, almond-shaped sets of neurons located deep in the middle of the brain's temporal lobe (see Figure 10.5), perform primary roles in the formation and storage of memories associated with emotional events (Amunts et al., 2005). The functions of the amygdalae help us understand the research results we discussed earlier in this section, such as why positive emotions are associated with increased motivation and achievement. For instance, when we experience the enjoyment of succeeding on a challenging task, the amygdalae create a memory associating the challenge and the success, which primes us for taking on additional challenges (Phelps & Sharot, 2008).

Emotions are also linked to neurotransmitters—chemicals that transmit signals from a neuron (nerve cell in the brain) to a target neuron across a synapse (a tiny space between neurons that allows messages to be transmitted from one to another). Three neurotransmitters associated with emotions are involved. The first is dopamine, an organic chemical strongly associated with the reward system of the brain. Dopamine is released when people have rewarding experiences, such as food, sex, and stimuli that become associated with them through classical conditioning (Arias-Carrión, Stamelou, Murillo-Rodríguez, Menéndez-González, & Pöppel, 2010).

Noradrenaline, another organic compound, is the second neurotransmitter, and it is released in response to stress by increasing heart rate, releasing glucose from energy stores, and increasing blood flow to muscles and oxygen to the brain (Lövheim, 2012). Serotonin, the third neurotransmitter, and another organic compound, is generally considered to be a contributor to feelings of well-being and happiness (Young, 2007).

Lövheim (2012) has proposed a model linking these neurotransmitters to basic emotions, such as anger, fear, excitement, joy, and disgust.

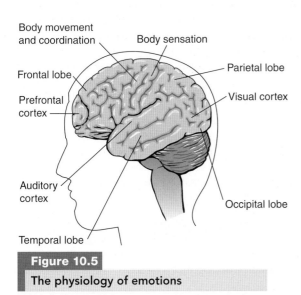

Figure 10.5

The physiology of emotions

According to his model, joy, for example, is produced by a combination of high dopamine, high serotonin, and low noradrenaline. This makes sense. Experiencing joy is rewarding (dopamine); it isn't stressful (noradrenaline); and it gives us a sense of well-being (serotonin). So, according to Lövheim's model, emotions are strongly chemically based.

Additional research sheds some light on the neuroscience of emotional control, which is generally considered to be a positive aspect of self-regulation (Legault & Inzlicht, 2013). However, researchers have found that an initial act of self-control (suppressing emotions) later decreased activity in the prefrontal cortex (see Figure 10.5), the area of the brain responsible for the use of memory, reasoning, planning, and problem solving (Friese, Binder, Luechinger, Boesiger, & Rasch, 2013). In other words, suppressing emotions may have a negative effect on later thinking and problem solving.

One of the most important findings in the neuroscience of emotion relates to the link between effort, challenge, and reward. Researchers found that the reward centers of people in their study were more strongly activated when they had to work to receive rewards than when the rewards were given without having to earn them (Zink et al., 2004). This also makes sense. We all have had the experience of accomplishing difficult tasks as a result of hard work. This experience is much more satisfying than getting something for nothing. It strongly suggests that we should be challenging our students as much as possible.

Analyzing Theories

Summarizing and Evaluating Theories of Motivation

Studying the topic of motivation is challenging. The topic is complex and includes a number of individual theories of motivation; a unified theory that might be comparable to behaviorism, social cognitive theory, or information processing doesn't exist. Further, concepts from different theories overlap. For instance, *self-worth* and *self-esteem* are often used interchangeably, and the concept of *belonging* from Maslow's hierarchy and *relatedness* from self-determination theory are essentially the same. Also, *competence* from self-determination theory and *self-efficacy* are sometimes equated (Schunk et al., 2014). Further, concepts such as *expectancy for success, self-efficacy,* and *self-concept* are so closely related that distinguishing among them is a challenge, particularly for readers who don't have a great deal of background knowledge in the field of motivation.

Inconsistencies also exist. For example, the concept of needs has been criticized by some of the most prominent leaders and researchers in the field. "Given these problems, needs are not investigated often in current research. However, reconceptualizing needs as goals, contemporary cognitive theories represent an improvement on traditional needs theories" (Schunk et al., 2014, p. 174). Self-determination theory, one of the most prominent and powerful theories of motivation, is based on the concept of needs, however, with the premise that we all have the needs for competence, autonomy, and relatedness; Maslow's hierarchy of needs remains prominent in the field; and "Covington (1992) proposed that the need for self-worth is a basic need of all individuals" (Schunk et al., 2014, p. 224). So, needs remain prominent in theories of motivation.

Despite their complexity, overlap, and inconsistency, theories of motivation help explain a great deal about our behavior, and some examples are outlined in Table 10.3. And the theories have many implications for both the way we live our daily lives and the way we teach. For example, we commonly see many cases of people attempting to demonstrate how smart they are or how good they are at some activity. And everyone appreciates receiving a quick reply to an email or being asked how we feel or how we're doing after we've been ill, and we're all annoyed when someone says they'll call us back, but they don't. The concepts of competence and relatedness from self-determination theory help us understand why.

As another simple example, it makes sense that we will be motivated to engage in an activity if we've been successful in similar activities in the past, and we all want to understand why we succeed or fail on different tasks. The concept of self-efficacy and attribution theory help us understand these tendencies. And setting and monitoring goals can be very motivating if we are committed to reaching the goals. It also makes sense that we will persist longer and more diligently in activities that we enjoy and give up more quickly when we're bored. Many other examples exist.

We, Paul and Don, your authors, have spent major portions of our careers studying motivation. The topic is a challenge, but it is always stimulating, and seeing motivation theory illustrated both in everyday living and in classrooms is enormously rewarding.

Table 10.3 outlines variables involved in motivation, the basic premise involved in each, examples that can be explained using the variables, and the theoretical framework that supports the variables.

Table 10.3 Variables that influence motivation

Variable Influencing Motivation	Basic Premise	Examples the Variables Can Explain	Theoretical Framework
Needs			
Needs for • Survival • Safety • Belonging • Self-esteem • Intellectual achievement • Aesthetic appreciation • Self-actualization	People are motivated to satisfy deficiency needs and have continuing experiences with growth needs	• Why we first react to how "nice" people are rather than how "smart" they are (need for belonging) • Why some people have an insatiable thirst for learning (continuing experiences with intellectual achievement)	Maslow's hierarchy of needs
Needs for • Competence • Autonomy • Relatedness	People are motivated to meet needs for competence, autonomy, and relatedness	• Why praise for genuine accomplishment increases motivation but accomplishment of trivial tasks does not (perceptions of competence) • Why leaders in large corporations experience less stress than those who work for them (higher levels of autonomy) • Why we first react to people at a human level (need for relatedness)	Self-determination theory
Need to • Preserve self-worth	People are motivated to preserve their sense of self-worth and perceptions of high ability	• Why students value being able to succeed without studying (evidence of high ability) • Why students sometimes engage in self-handicapping behaviors (preserve perceptions of high ability in case of failure)	Self-worth theory
Beliefs about			
• Future outcomes (expectations)	Motivation to engage in an activity increases when people expect to succeed in the activity	• Why we persist longer and choose more challenging tasks if we expect to succeed on them	Expectancy x value theory
• Intelligence/ability (mindset)	Motivation tends to increase if people believe that intelligence can be increased with effort	• Why people who believe "some got it and some don't" attempt to communicate perceptions of high ability by avoiding challenging tasks (preserve perceptions of high intelligence) • Why people who believe "the harder we work, the smarter we get" choose challenging tasks and persevere (failure simply indicating more effort or better strategies needed)	Self-worth theory Attribution theory
• Capability (self-efficacy)	Motivation increases if people believe they're capable of accomplishing specific tasks	• Why a person who has been scoring consistently in the high 80s believes that he will have a good day on the golf course (past success being the source of beliefs about capability) • Why a teacher's students work harder when she models effort and perseverance for them (modeling influencing self-efficacy)	Self-efficacy theory (social cognitive theory)

Continued

• Attainment value • Utility value • Cost	Motivation increases if an activity is important to them, will have some future benefit, and they don't have to give up too much to engage in the activity	• Why a person who plays tennis is motivated to win if she believes she is a good player but less so if she believes she isn't a good player (high attainment value) • Why a student takes an extra course in math if she wants to major in engineering in college (high utility value) • Why a student drops a course if he has to care for an ailing parent (too high a cost)	Expectancy x value theory
• Causes of performance	People are motivated to understand the causes of their performance	• Why students get upset when they don't get feedback on tests, quizzes, and other assignments (the desire to understand reasons for performance) • Why doing poorly because of too little effort is motivating (internal and controllable attribution)	Attribution theory
Goals			
• Mastery goals • Performance goals • Social goals • Work-avoidance goals	Specific, moderately challenging, and near-term goals that focus on understanding and improvement increase motivation to learn	• Why a person who has resolved to consume no more than 1,500 calories a day avoids eating a cookie because it is a measurable, short-term goal (near-term and specific goal) • Why a person who resolves to lose weight fails to do so (distant and general goal)	Goal theory
Interest (particularly situational interest)			
• Sex and violence • Power and money • Involvement • Personalization	People are motivated to participate in activities they find interesting	• Why there are so many "cop" shows in TV, and why "sex sells" (intrinsically interesting) • Why being able to apply understanding to a personal, real-world application is satisfying (increases intrinsic interest) • Why people enjoy conversations when they're directly involved but drift off when they are not (increases intrinsic interest)	Expectancy x value theory
Emotions			
• Enjoyment • Hope • Pride • Anger • Boredom	Positive emotions contribute to motivation and learning and negative emotions generally detract from motivation and learning	• Why we persist longer in activities we enjoy • Why we set mastery goals and regulate our learning when we take pride in our learning progress • Why we pay attention and process information less effectively when we're bored	Information processing theory Social cognitive theory

Educational Psychology and Teaching: Using the Influence of Interest and Emotion to Increase Your Students' Motivation to Learn

An understanding of learners' interests and emotions has important implications for the way we work with our students. As we saw earlier in this section, situational interest is essential if students are going to persist in their efforts (Tullis & Fulmer, 2013). We also saw that some topics, such as death, danger, power, money, romance, and sex, seem to be universally interesting (Hidi, 2001). It is difficult to build much of our instruction around these topics, but we can increase situational interest in several other ways (Brophy, 2010; Schraw & Lehman, 2001):

- Personalize content by linking topics to students' lives.
- Focus on real-world applications.
- Promote high levels of student involvement.
- Model our own interest in the topics we teach.

Personalizing content and connecting topics to the real world can also capitalize on students' emotions by increasing their enjoyment. And involving students essentially eliminates the chances of boredom, one of the most destructive emotions for learner motivation (Pekrun et al., 2011). It's harder for students to be bored when they're actively involved in lessons and know they're likely to be called on, even if they don't have high personal interest in the topics.

To see what these suggestions look like in a classroom, let's return to Kathy's work with her students in a later learning activity.

"We've been discussing the Crusades for several days now. . . . How did we start?" she asks.

"We imagined that Lincoln High School was taken over by people who believed that extracurricular activities should be eliminated," Carnisha volunteers.

"Good. . . . Then what?"

"We decided we'd talk to them. . . . We'd be on a 'crusade' to change their minds and save our school."

"Very good. . . . Now, what were the actual Crusades all about? . . . Selena?"

"Well, the Christians wanted to get the Holy Land back from the Muslims, but according to the first book we studied [Armstrong, 2001], they were a bunch of bad wars conducted in the name of religion . . . that has contributed to the problems between Christians, Jews, and Muslims that we still see in the Middle East today."

"Excellent analysis. . . . Think about that. The Crusades nearly 1,000 years ago have had an influence on us here today," she continues energetically. "Now, how about a different perspective? . . . What did our other author [Asbridge, 2012] have to say? . . . Becky?"

"His book almost read more like an adventure novel. He focused more on the role of leaders like Richard the Lionheart and Saladin."

"And who were they? . . . Miguel?"

"Richard the Lionheart was king of England, and Saladin was the great Muslim leader who fought against the Crusaders."

"What else did our author, Asbridge, offer? . . . Anyone?"

After pausing several seconds, Josh volunteers, "He talked about how the religious aspects of the Crusades were also tied up in secular politics, like hanging on to power and that kind of thing."

"And he also talked a lot about the way they fought high-risk wars in medieval times, where one battle could turn the tide of a war," Ashley adds.

"Can you think of any other historical examples of battles that have turned the tides of wars?"

The students discuss some possibilities, such as the battle of Gettysburg in our Civil War, and Zach even offers the Battle of the Bulge in World War II as a possibility.

"Outstanding, everyone," Kathy smiles, and she then continues, "Now, for today's assignment, you were asked to write an analysis comparing our two sources. We did this to address our standard that says,

> *Integrate information from diverse sources, both primary and secondary, into a coherent understanding of an idea or event, noting discrepancies among sources,*
>
> as she reads the standard that is written on the board.
>
> "So let's see how we did. Go ahead. . . . Nikki?"
>
> Kathy asks three students to present their positions and then closes the discussion by saying, "See how interesting this is? Here we see ourselves influenced by people who lived hundreds of years ago. . . . This is what history is all about."
>
> "Brewster loves this stuff," David whispers to Kelly.
>
> "Now, we heard from Nikki, Steve, and Mike," Kathy continues, "but the rest of you haven't had your analyses critiqued. So, exchange your work with your partner, and give each other some feedback based on our discussion of Nikki's, Steve's, and Mike's papers."

Now, let's see how Kathy applied the guidelines.

Personalize Content by Linking Topics to Students' Lives. A large and expanding body of research confirms that personalizing topics can significantly increase student motivation (Ertem, 2013; Narciss et al., 2014). Kathy capitalized on this factor by using the students' "crusade" to prevent having extracurricular activities eliminated from the school as a metaphor for the real Crusades. It isn't as hard as it might initially appear. For instance, simply putting students' names in examples, applications, and even quizzes and tests is a simple and positive first step. Being aware of the need to do so, you'll think of additional ways to personalize your topics when you plan.

Connect Topics to the Real World. When students see how the topics they study link to the real world, their motivation is also likely to increase. The class's "crusade" to prevent extracurricular activities from being eliminated also capitalized on this guideline. Word problems in math can easily be applied to the real world, writing can focus on real-world topics, and with some thought and effort, most topics can be connected to the way we live today.

Promote High Levels of Student Involvement. Kathy involved her students in two ways. First, during their discussion she directly called on them by name and asked for their points of view. When students expect to be called on, they become more attentive and interested, and boredom decreases (Lemov, 2010). She further involved her students by having them work in pairs to critique each other's analyses. Combining whole-group instruction with small-group work adds variety to learning activities and also helps reduce the likelihood of boredom.

Model Our Own Interest in the Topics We Teach. Finally, Kathy modeled her own interest in the topic by saying, "Think about that. The Crusades nearly 1,000 years ago have had an influence on us here today" and "See how interesting this is? Here we see ourselves influenced by people who lived hundreds of years ago. . . . This is what history is all about."

David's comment, "Brewster loves this stuff," is a testimony to the influence teachers' modeling of their own interest can have on students.

We can also take steps to reduce anxiety in our students by making expectations clear, assessing frequently and thoroughly, and providing specific and detailed feedback on the assessments (Rohrer & Pashler, 2010). And, particularly if you teach older students, you might simply offer them the opportunity to write about their worries for a few minutes before they take a test. As we saw earlier, this process can help reduce the debilitating effects of anxiety (Ramirez & Beilock, 2011).

The suggestions we've outlined in this chapter won't increase motivation to learn in all situations or for all students, but they can increase motivation and learning for many. This is the essence of professionalism. We do our best to maximize motivation and learning for as many of our students as possible.

Classroom **Connections**

Using Students' Interests and Emotions to Promote Motivation in Classrooms

1. Promote interest in your learning activities by using personalized, concrete examples and promoting high levels of student involvement.

   ■ **Elementary:** A fourth-grade teacher puts his students' names into word problems. He is careful to be sure that all students' names are used by jotting down the names he uses and keeping track over time.

   ■ **Middle School:** A geography teacher begins the study of longitude and latitude by asking the students how they would tell a friend the exact location of one of their favorite hangouts.

   ■ **High School:** A physics teacher creates problems using the velocity and momentum of soccer balls after they've been kicked, and she asks students to determine the acceleration and speed players must run to intercept the kicks.

2. To reduce anxiety, emphasize understanding the content of tests instead of grades, provide opportunities for practice, and give students ample time to finish assessments.

   ■ **Elementary:** A second-grade teacher monitors his students as they work on a quiz. When he sees their attention wander, he reminds them of the work they have done on the topic and to concentrate on their work.

   ■ **Middle School:** An eighth-grade algebra teacher gives her students extensive practice with the types of problems they'll be expected to solve on their tests.

   ■ **High School:** An AP American history teacher knows that her students are nervous about passing the end-of-year exam. She frequently reminds them, "If you thoroughly understand the content, you'll be fine on the test. So, as you study, try to connect the ideas, and don't just memorize information."

Developmentally Appropriate **Practice**

Motivation to Learn in Students at Different Ages

Many applications of motivation theory apply to learners at all grade levels, such as using high-quality and personalized examples, involving students, and creating safe and orderly learning environments. Developmental differences exist, however. The following paragraphs outline suggestions for responding to these differences.

Working with Students in Early Childhood Programs and Elementary Schools

In contrast with older students, young children bask openly in praise, and they rarely evaluate whether the praise is justified. They also tend to have growth mindsets and set mastery goals. Because of these factors emphasizing that all students can learn, avoiding social comparisons, praising students for their effort, and reminding them that hard work "makes us smart" can increase motivation to learn.

Working with Students in Middle Schools

As learners grow older, their mastery orientation tends to decrease, while their performance orientation increases. Modeling a growth mindset and emphasizing the relationship between effort and increased competence and ability are important. Middle school students increasingly meet their needs for belonging and relatedness with peer experiences, so social goals tend to increase in importance. Combining whole-group with small-group activities can help students meet these needs and goals.

Middle school students' need for autonomy also increases, so involving them in activities that increase their sense of autonomy, such as asking them to provide input into classroom rules, can be effective.

Working with Students in High Schools

High school students are beginning to think about their futures, so emphasizing the utility value of the topics they study and the skills they develop can increase their motivation to learn.

Because of the many experiences that high school students can access, such as video games and the Internet, generating interest in school topics can be a challenge. However, using concrete and personalized examples and promoting high levels of interaction remain effective.

Evidence that their competence is increasing is important to high school students, so sincere praise and other indicators of genuine accomplishment can increase motivation to learn.

chapter

10 Summary

1. Define motivation, and describe different theoretical explanations for learner motivation.
   - Motivation is a process by which goal-directed activity is instigated and sustained.
   - Extrinsic motivation is motivation to engage in an activity as a means to an end; intrinsic motivation is motivation to be involved in an activity for its own sake.
   - Behaviorism describes motivation and learning in the same way; an increase in behavior is evidence of both learning and motivation.
   - Cognitive theories of motivation focus on learners' beliefs, expectations, and the desire to make sense of their experiences.
   - Sociocultural views of motivation focus on individuals' participating in learning communities.
   - Humanistic views of motivation are grounded in the premise that people are motivated to fulfill their total potential as human beings.

2. Describe learners' needs and how they influence motivation to learn.
   - A need is an internal force or drive to attain or avoid certain states or objects.
   - According to Maslow, all people have needs for survival, safety, belonging, and self-esteem. Once these needs are met, people are motivated to fulfill their potential as human beings.
   - According to self-determination theory, all people have needs for competence, autonomy, and relatedness. Helping students meet these needs increases motivation.
   - Self-worth theory suggests that all people have the need to protect their sense of self-worth, which depends on maintaining the perception that they have high ability.

3. Explain how learners' beliefs can influence their motivation to learn.
   - A belief is an idea we accept as true without necessarily having definitive evidence to support it.
   - Learners' motivation increases when they expect to succeed.
   - Learners with a growth mindset—those who believe that ability can be improved with effort—tend to have higher motivation to learn than learners with a fixed mindset—those who believe that ability is fixed.

- Students who believe they are capable of accomplishing specific tasks have high self-efficacy and are more motivated to learn than students whose self-efficacy is lower.
- Believing that increased understanding will help them meet future goals increases students' motivation to learn.
- Students who believe that effort and ability are the causes of their success, or that lack of effort is the cause of failure, are likely to be more motivated to learn.

4. Describe how learners' goals can influence their motivation to learn.
   - A goal is an outcome an individual hopes to attain.
   - Learners whose goals focus on mastery of tasks, improvement, and increased understanding have higher motivation to learn than do learners whose goals focus on social comparisons.
   - Social goals can decrease motivation to learn if they focus exclusively on social factors. Social-responsibility goals, however, and particularly social-responsibility goals combined with mastery goals, can lead to sustained motivation and achievement.

5. Explain how interest and emotion influence learner motivation.
   - As would be expected, learners are more motivated to study topics in which they're interested.
   - Students who have high personal interest in a topic or course of study generally have extensive background knowledge related to the topic, and their interest is usually quite stable.
   - Situational interest depends on the immediate context and can change quickly.
   - Personalized topics, real-world applications, involvement, and seeing interest modeled all contribute to situational interest.
   - Positive emotions, such as enjoyment, hope, and pride, generally increase both motivation to learn and achievement, whereas negative emotions, such as anger, frustration, and particularly boredom, generally decrease motivation to learn.

Learners with positive emotions are more likely to adopt mastery goals, self-regulate their learning, and have a growth mindset than are students with negative emotions.

Preparing for Your Licensure Exam

Understanding the Relationship Between Motivation and Learning

You will be required to take a licensure exam before you go into your own classroom. This exam will include information related to learner motivation, and it will include both multiple-choice and constructed-response questions. We include the following exercises to help you practice for the exam in your state. This book and these exercises will be a resource for you as you prepare for these tests.

You saw in this chapter how Kathy Brewster applied an understanding of the relationship between motivation and learning in her teaching. We look in now at another world history teacher who is also teaching about the Crusades. Read the case study, and then answer the questions that follow.

Michael Marcus watches as his students take their seats, and then announces, "Listen, everyone, I have your tests here from last Friday. Liora, Ivan, Lynn, and Segundo, super job on the test. They were the only A's in the class."

After handing back the tests, Michael comments, "There were 7 D's or F's on this test. It wasn't that hard. . . . We have another one in 2 weeks. Let's give these sharp ones with the A's a run for their money. . . . Maybe this will motivate you.

"Now let's get going. We have a lot to cover today. . . . As you'll recall from yesterday, the Crusades were an attempt by the Christian powers of Western Europe to wrestle control of what is now the Middle East away from the Muslims. Pope Urban II proclaimed the first crusade in 1095 with the goal of restoring Christian access to the holy places around Jerusalem, and the Crusades went on for another 200 years, but finally ended in failure, because, as we know today, the Middle East remains largely Muslim with respect to religion."

Michael continues presenting information about the Crusades until he sees that 20 minutes are left in the period.

"I know that has been a lot to write down," he continues, "and I realize that learning dates and places isn't the most pleasant stuff, but you might as well get used to it, because that's what you'll have to do when you go to college. Plus, they'll be on the next test.

"Now, in the time we have left in the period, I want you to write a summary of the Crusades that outlines the major people and events and tells why they were important. You should be able to finish by the end of the period, but if you don't, turn your papers in at the beginning of class tomorrow. You may use your notes. Go ahead and get started."

As he monitors students, he sees that Jeremy has written only a few words on his paper. "Are you having trouble getting started?" Michael asks quietly.

"Yeah, . . . I don't quite know how to get started," Jeremy mumbles.

"I know written assignments are hard for you. . . . Let me help you," Michael nods.

He takes a blank piece of paper and starts writing as Jeremy watches. He writes several sentences on the paper and then says, "See how easy that was? That's the kind of thing I want you to do. Go ahead—that's a start. Keep that so you can see what I'm looking for. Go back to your desk, and give it another try."

Questions for Case Analysis

In answering these questions, use information from the chapter, and link your responses to specific information in the case.

Multiple-Choice Questions

1. In an attempt to motivate his students, Michael listed the names of the students who earned A's on the test, and encouraged the rest of the students to ". . . give these sharp ones with the A's a run for their money." Of the following, which choice describes the best assessment of the effectiveness of Michael's strategy for motivating his students?

a. It was an effective strategy, because it encouraged his students to increase their effort.

b. It was an effective strategy, because it provided students with feedback about their performance.

c. It was an effective strategy, because it encouraged the students who did well to attribute their success to high ability and those who did poorly to lack of effort.

d. It was an ineffective strategy, because it encouraged social comparisons, which detract from motivation.

2. Michael spent most of the class period lecturing to his students about the Crusades, and lectures have consistently been identified as ineffective teaching strategies. With respect to motivation, which of the following best explains why his lecture might have a negative impact on his students' motivation to learn?

   a. Lectures are inconsistent with self-determination theory, because lectures cannot provide students with information that helps increase their perceptions of competence.

   b. Lectures are commonly boring, and boredom is a negative emotion shown to detract from motivation to learn.

   c. Lectures are inconsistent with expectancy x value theory because they cannot provide students with information that students believe has utility value.

   d. Lectures detract from motivation to learn because it isn't possible for students to establish mastery goals when their teachers lecture.

Constructed-Response Question

3. Assess the extent to which Michael promoted situational interest in his topic (the Crusades). Provide evidence from the case study and the chapter in making your assessment.

Important **Concepts**

anxiety
attainment value
attribution theory
attributions
autonomy
belief
competence
cost
deficiency needs
emotion
expectancy x value theory

expectation
extrinsic motivation
fixed mindset
flow
goal
growth mindset
growth needs
intrinsic motivation
learned helplessness
mastery goals
motivation

motivation to learn
motivational zone of
    proximal development
need
need for approval
performance goals
performance-approach goals
performance-avoidance goal
personal interest
relatedness
self-actualization

self-determination
self-efficacy
self-worth
situational interest
social goals
unconditional positive
    regard
utility value
value

11
A Classroom Model for Promoting Student Motivation

OUTLINE	LEARNING OUTCOMES
	After you've completed your study of this chapter, you should be able to:
Creating a Mastery-Focused Classroom A Model for Promoting Student Motivation The Teacher–Student Relationship	**1.** Describe the differences between a mastery-focused and a performance-focused classroom.
The Teacher: Personal Qualities that Increase Motivation to Learn Personal Teaching Efficacy: Beliefs about Teaching and Learning Modeling and Enthusiasm: Communicating Genuine Interest Caring: Meeting Needs for Belonging and Relatedness Teacher Expectations: Promoting Competence and Healthy Attributions Educational Psychology and Teaching: Demonstrating Personal Qualities that Increase Your Students' Motivation to Learn	**2.** Describe the personal qualities of teachers who increase students' motivation to learn.
Learning Climate: Creating a Motivating Classroom Environment Order and Safety: Classrooms as Secure Places to Learn Success: Developing Self-Efficacy Challenge: Increasing Perceptions of Competence Task Comprehension: Increasing Feelings of Autonomy and Value Educational Psychology and Teaching: Applying an Understanding of Climate Variables in Your Classroom	**3.** Identify the learning climate variables that increase students' motivation to learn.
Instructional Variables: Developing Interest in Learning Activities Introductory Focus: Attracting Students' Attention Personalization: Links to Students' Lives Involvement: Increasing Situational Interest Feedback: Information about Learning Progress Educational Psychology and Teaching: Applying the Instructional Variables to Increase Your Students' Motivation to Learn ▶ Developmentally Appropriate Practice: Applying the Model for Promoting Student Motivation with Learners of Different Ages	**4.** Explain how different instructional variables increase students' motivation to learn.

As we all know from experience, some students are more motivated to learn than are others. This doesn't suggest that we're helpless with respect to student motivation, however; when we work with our students, both as individuals and in groups, we can do a great deal to influence their motivation to learn. In this chapter we focus on specific strategies we can use to increase our students' motivation.

Let's begin by looking in on DeVonne Lampkin, a fifth-grade teacher, as she works with her students. As you read the case study, think about her students' motivation and how DeVonne influences it.

DeVonne is working with her students on the following science standard:

4. Structure, Function, and Information Processing. 4-LS1-1. Construct an argument that plants and animals have internal and external structures that function to support survival, growth, behavior, and reproduction (National Science Teachers Association, 2013a, p. 25.).

She decides to compare the structures of arthropods to our own body structures to address this standard, and she uses examples and nonexamples of arthropods to help her students think critically and address the standard's "construct an argument" component.

She begins her day's lesson by reaching into a cooler and taking out a live lobster.

The students "ooh" and "aah" at the wriggling animal, and DeVonne asks Stephanie to carry it around the room so her classmates can observe and touch it.

As Stephanie circulates around the room, DeVonne says, "Look carefully, because I'm going to ask you to tell us what you see."

When everyone has had a chance to observe the lobster, DeVonne asks, "Okay, what did you notice?"

"Hard," Tu observes.

"Pink and green," Saleina comments.

"Wet," Kevin adds.

As students make additional observations, DeVonne lists them on the board and prompts students to conclude that the lobster has a hard outer covering (exoskeleton), three body parts, and segmented legs. She identifies them as essential characteristics of the body structure of arthropods.

Reaching into her bag again, DeVonne pulls out a jar with a cockroach in it. Amid more squeals, she walks around the class holding it with tweezers and has the students decide whether it's an arthropod.

After some discussion to resolve uncertainty about whether the cockroach has an exoskeleton, the class concludes that it does.

DeVonne next takes a clam out of her cooler, and asks, "Is this an arthropod?"

Some students conclude that it is, reasoning that it has a hard shell.

"But," A.J. comments, "it doesn't have any legs," and, following additional discussion, the class decides that it isn't an arthropod.

"Now," DeVonne asks, "Do you think Mrs. Sapp [the school principal] is an arthropod? . . . Tell us why or why not."

Amid more giggles, some students conclude that she is, because she has segmented legs. Others disagree because she doesn't look like a lobster or a roach. After some discussion, Tu observes, "She doesn't have an exoskeleton," and the class finally agrees that she is not an arthropod.

DeVonne then instructs the students to form pairs, passes out shrimp for examination, calms the excited students, and asks them to observe the shrimp carefully and decide whether they're arthropods.

During the whole-group discussion that follows, she discovers that some of the students are still uncertain about the idea of an exoskeleton, so she has them peel the shrimp and feel the head and outer covering. After seeing the peeled covering, they conclude that the shrimp does indeed have an exoskeleton.

We'll revisit DeVonne's lesson later in the chapter, and as you study this material, keep the following questions in mind:

1. How did DeVonne's personal qualities contribute to her students' motivation to learn?
2. How did the classroom environment DeVonne created influence her students' motivation?
3. What impact did DeVonne's instruction have on her students' motivation?

Classroom applications of both motivation and learning theories help answer these and other questions about student motivation. We examine these applications in this chapter.

Creating a Mastery-Focused Classroom

We begin answering our questions by considering two types of classrooms. A **mastery-focused classroom** emphasizes effort, continuous improvement, and understanding, whereas a **performance-focused classroom** stresses high grades, public displays of ability, and performance compared to others (Anderman & Wolters, 2006).

DeVonne attempted to create a mastery-focused classroom in four ways: (1) She used her personal qualities to develop a positive teacher–student relationship, which provided the emotional foundation that supported all her other efforts; (2) she created high levels of interest by using concrete examples, such as the real lobster, cockroach, and shrimp, to teach the concept *arthropod*, and she promoted high levels of involvement throughout the learning activity; (3) instead of performance, she emphasized increasing understanding and learning; and (4) she promoted cooperation instead of competition as students studied the topic. Differences in mastery-focused compared to performance-focused classrooms are summarized in Table 11.1 (Anderman & Wolters, 2006; Pintrich, 2000).

A Model for Promoting Student Motivation

Within this mastery-oriented framework, in this chapter we present a model for promoting student motivation, which synthesizes learning and motivation theory and research. It is outlined in Figure 11.1 and has three essential components:

1. *The teacher*: Demonstrates personal qualities that increase student motivation to learn.

Table 11.1	Mastery-focused and performance-focused classrooms	
	Mastery Focused	Performance Focused
Success defined as . . .	Mastery, improvement	High grades, doing better than others
Value placed on . . .	Effort, improvement	High grades, demonstration of high ability
Reasons for satisfaction . . .	Meeting challenges, hard work	Doing better than others, success with minimum effort
Teacher oriented toward . . .	Student learning	Student performance
View of errors . . .	A normal part of learning	A basis for concern and anxiety
Reasons for effort . . .	Increased understanding	High grades, doing better than others
Ability viewed as . . .	Incremental, alterable	An entity, fixed
Reasons for assessment . . .	Measure progress toward preset criteria, provide feedback	Determine grades, compare students to one another

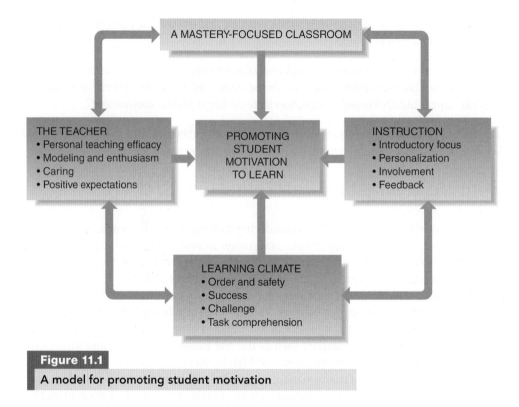

Figure 11.1

A model for promoting student motivation

   2. *Learning climate*: Creates a motivating environment for learning.
   3. *Instruction*: Develops interest in learning activities.

Four variables exist within each component, and the variables and components in the model operate in synergy; that is, the effect of their combination and interaction is greater than the sum of the individual variables; a single variable cannot be effectively applied if the others are missing. The arrows connecting each of the components in the model are intended to remind us of this interdependence.

The Teacher–Student Relationship

A positive teacher–student relationship is at the core of a motivating classroom environment, and the synergy in the model's variables depends to a major extent on this relationship. For instance, positive and supportive teachers tend to create emotionally safe and low-conflict learning environments, which are particularly important for students who struggle in school and lack self-regulation (Liew, Chen, & Hughes, 2010). Further, a positive teacher–student relationship contributes to students' intrinsic motivation. As we would expect, these factors contribute to learners' academic achievement.

   This research also suggests that a positive student–teacher relationship not only supports learner motivation in the present learning environment, but also provides a foundation for future motivation and academic achievement. Further, this social and emotional support from teachers appears to be particularly important for children who are academically at-risk and/or who come from predominantly low-income and ethnic minority backgrounds (Liew et al., 2010). This benefit is supported by theory. "Consistent with attachment and self-determination theories, our findings suggest that academically at-risk learners' perceptions of teachers as supportive have a beneficial effect on their academic effort in the classroom and confidence in their academic abilities" (Hughes, Wu, Kwok, Villarreal, & Johnson, 2012, p. 362).

Teachers able to create a positive teacher–student relationship and a positive classroom environment realize that teaching—instead of being a *personal* endeavor—is an *interpersonal* endeavor, and they consciously set "relational goals," goals to create close and caring relationships with students. Further, teachers with this goal orientation also tend to use mastery rather than performance approaches in their instruction; that is, they focus on increasing understanding, emphasize that grades take care of themselves if students understand content, avoid social comparisons among students, and use assessment primarily as a tool for increasing learning (Butler, 2012).

Creating positive teacher–student relationships in no way implies that we lower either achievement or behavioral standards for our students. Classrooms are for conscientious work and rigorous learning, not horseplay and off-task behaviors. Nor does a positive teacher–student relationship suggest that we are our students' "buddies." Rather, we are adults who are committed to our students both as people and as learners, and we're there to guide and support their learning and development.

As we turn to the variables in the model for promoting student motivation, remember that the teacher–student relationship is the emotional architecture that provides a framework and foundation for each variable and the interdependence that exists among them.

Now, let's look at the characteristics of teachers who promote student motivation to learn.

The Teacher: Personal Qualities that Increase Motivation to Learn

Other than their parents and home environment, you—their teacher—are the most important influence on your students' learning and motivation. You establish the teacher–student relationships in your classroom, create a positive emotional climate, implement effective instruction, and establish a mastery-oriented learning environment as the umbrella for all your learning experiences. None of the other components of the model are effective if the teacher qualities highlighted in Figure 11.2 are lacking.

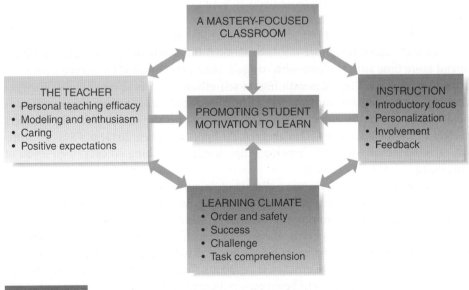

Figure 11.2

Teacher qualities in the model for promoting student motivation

Ed Psych and You

Think about some of your best teachers. What were they like? What kind of learning environment did they create? What did they do that made their classes interesting and worthwhile?

Personal Teaching Efficacy: Beliefs about Teaching and Learning

Self-efficacy describes individuals' beliefs about their capability of accomplishing specific tasks. **Personal teaching efficacy**—teachers' believing that they're capable of getting all students to learn, regardless of prior knowledge, ability, or personal backgrounds—is an extension of the concept of self-efficacy (Woolfolk Hoy, Davis, & Pape, 2006).

Significant differences exist between teachers high in personal teaching efficacy compared to their low-efficacy peers. For instance, high-efficacy teachers take personal responsibility for student learning. They are demanding but fair, they maximize time available for instruction, they praise students for their increasing competence, and they persevere with low achievers. In contrast, low-efficacy teachers are more likely to blame low achievement on students' lack of intelligence, poor home environments, or other causes outside the classroom. They have lower expectations, spend less time on learning activities, give up on low achievers, and are more critical when students fail. They are also more controlling and value student autonomy less than do high-efficacy teachers (Ware & Kitsantas, 2007).

Differences also exist with respect to the goal orientations of the two groups. For instance, high-efficacy teachers tend to have a mastery goal orientation, and they maintain it even if their schools emphasize performance goals, such as focusing on high-stakes testing results. Low-efficacy teachers, in contrast, tend to adopt the performance-oriented goals promoted by their schools (Yoon & Sungok, 2013).

These factors influence students' goal orientations, and ultimately their learning. For instance, students tend to adopt goals consistent with the goal orientations of their schools and teachers; that is, students are more likely to adopt mastery goals if they perceive their schools and teachers as having this orientation (Wolters, 2004).

These results make sense. For instance, if we believe we can influence learning for all students, we will indeed maximize our instructional time, demand more of our students, and spend more time with students who struggle. And these intuitively sensible results are confirmed by research. "Teachers with higher self-efficacy beliefs showed higher instructional quality, as indicated by the three dimensions of cognitive activation, classroom management, and individual learning support, whether instruction was rated by the teachers themselves or by their students" (Holzberger, Philipp, & Kunter, 2013, p. 782). To summarize, "in classrooms where teachers have high levels of teaching efficacy, high levels of learning occur" (Tanel, 2013, p. 7).

Efficacy can also affect the learning climate of an entire school. Students benefit from **collective efficacy**, beliefs that the faculty as a whole can have a positive effect on student learning, and it is particularly important for students who come from diverse backgrounds (Hoy, Tarter, & Hoy, 2006). In schools where collective efficacy is high, low-socioeconomic status (SES) students have achievement gains almost as high as those of high-SES students from schools with low collective efficacy (Lee, 2000). Teachers in high-collective-efficacy schools reduce the achievement gap between advantaged and disadvantaged students.

As with self-efficacy, personal teaching efficacy depends on background, experience, and the culture of the school in which we work. Our professional knowledge is important;

teachers with extensive professional knowledge tend to be higher in personal teaching efficacy than their colleagues who are less knowledgeable (Tanel, 2013). And if we experience the rewards of seeing our students learning, our efficacy will be higher, as it also will be if we work with high-efficacy colleagues (Holzberger et al., 2013).

Maintaining high personal teaching efficacy can be a challenge. You may work with students who don't seem to care, virtually refuse to do homework, and, in spite of your best efforts to involve them, won't pay attention in class. Understandably, this will be discouraging. However, if you maintain the belief that you can and do make a difference with students, you will. Even if you don't succeed with every student, you will have done your job.

Modeling and Enthusiasm: Communicating Genuine Interest

Social cognitive theory explains why teacher modeling is one of the most powerful influences on student interest. Increasing student motivation is virtually impossible if teachers model distaste or disinterest with statements such as "I know this stuff is boring, but we have to learn it" or "This isn't my favorite topic, either." In contrast, if we model the belief that what we're teaching is important for students to learn, the likelihood that they will adopt that same belief increases. It won't work for every student or for every learning activity, but we have nothing to lose in doing so.

Video 11.1 Teachers can demonstrate enthusiasm in a variety of ways. This teacher's excitement and energy communicate his enthusiasm.

Expert teachers model several aspects of the learning–teaching process that influence student motivation, all of which are supported by theory and research (Brophy, 2010; Schunk, Meece, & Pintrich, 2014). They include:

- *A growth mindset*, the belief that our intelligence or ability can be increased with hard work.
- *A mastery and social-responsibility goal orientation*, a focus on learning and improvement and meeting our commitments to others.
- *Internal attributions*, the belief that we control both our successes and our failures.
- *A link between hard work and self-worth*, the view that our self-worth is determined by our work ethic and not the appearance of high ability.

Expert teachers also model enthusiasm, and teacher enthusiasm is linked to both motivation and learning. "Enthusiastic teachers provided better learning support and classroom management, which in turn had positive effects on students' motivation" (Kunter et al., 2013, p. 815).

We can demonstrate enthusiasm in a variety of ways, such as using humor, describing our own personal experiences, and demonstrating excitement and energy. However, given that we won't always have a relevant personal experience to describe, and we won't always feel humorous or energetic, the way we can most consistently demonstrate enthusiasm is to communicate our own genuine interest in the topics we're teaching. We all have different personalities, and some of us are naturally more energetic and outgoing than others. However, we can all make statements such as the following that increase student motivation: "Geography is interesting because it strongly influences our lives. For example, most of our major cities, such as New York, Chicago, and San Francisco, became important because of their geography," or "Think about the needles on a cactus compared to the leaves on an oak tree; they're actually related and they're adaptations to their environments. Now, that's interesting." Regardless of our personalities, statements such as these increase the likelihood that our students will also be interested in the topic and believe that the content is valuable and worth learning (Brophy, 2010). And it takes no extra preparation or energy on our part. Better yet, with a bit of awareness and practice, it will become essentially automatic.

Caring: Meeting Needs for Belonging and Relatedness

> A first-grade teacher greets each of her children every morning with a hug, handshake, or "high five."
>
> A fifth-grade teacher immediately calls parents if one of his students fails to turn in a homework assignment or misses more than 2 days of school in a row.
>
> An algebra teacher learns the name of each student in all five of her classes by the end of the first week of school, and she stays in her room during her lunch hour to help students who are struggling.

Each of these teachers is demonstrating caring, which refers to a teacher's empathy and investment in the protection and development of young people (Noddings, 2001; Roeser, Peck, & Nasir, 2006).

The importance of "caring" as a personal characteristic is grounded in both philosophy and theory. "The ethics of care," which originated as part of a philosophical movement that became prominent in the second half of the 20th century, emphasizes that all people are vulnerable and interdependent, and these characteristics should be considered in dealing with others (Gilligan, 2008; Noddings, 2001; Tong, 2009). From a theoretical perspective, caring people help meet others' needs for belonging, which is preceded only by safety and survival in Maslow's (1970) hierarchy of needs. And caring helps meet people's needs for relatedness, one of the three innate needs described by self-determination theory (Deci & Ryan, 2008; Ryan & Deci, 2000).

Caring is important in schools. All parents want teachers who care about their children, and caring is one of the characteristics principals first look for when they attempt to recruit new teachers (Engel, 2013). And evidence suggests that caring teachers strongly impact students' motivation and learning. "Students who perceived that teachers cared about them reported positive motivational outcomes such as more prosocial and social-responsibility goals, academic effort, and greater internal control beliefs" (Perry, Turner, & Meyer, 2006, p. 341). Students want teachers to care for them both as learners and as people.

Caring is particularly important for boys (Reichert & Hawley, 2010) and newcomer immigrant youth (Suarez-Orozco, Pimentel, & Martin, 2009). This might be surprising, because on the surface boys want to appear tough, resilient, and unemotional. Research suggests that exactly the opposite is true; all students, and especially boys, need to feel wanted and cared about.

The concept of caring is sometimes misinterpreted as "touchy-feely" and even flaky education that emphasizes emotions, feelings, and self-esteem above academic learning. This is a misconception, and in fact quite the opposite is the case; requiring appropriate behavior from students and holding students to high academic standards is at the core of a caring classroom environment. "Ironically, reactions that are often intended to protect students' self-esteem—such as accepting low quality work—convey a lack of interest, patience, or *caring* [emphasis added]" (Stipek, 2002, p. 157).

Research corroborates this view. When junior high students were asked, "How do you know when a teacher cares about you?" they responded that paying attention to them as human beings was important, but more striking was their belief that teachers who care are committed to their learning and hold them to high standards (Wilson & Corbett, 2001).

Respect is also an important aspect of caring; we model it for our students, we expect students to respect us, and we require them to respect each other. Further, respect and appropriate standards of behavior are interrelated. "Treat everyone with respect" is a rule that should be universally enforced. An occasional minor incident of rudeness can be overlooked, but chronic disrespect, either for us or other students, should not be tolerated; it has no place in a caring classroom environment.

Teacher Expectations: Promoting Competence and Healthy Attributions

Communicating positive expectations is the final teacher quality in our model for promoting student motivation (Figure 11.2), and research and theory both support its importance. For example, high teacher expectations are consistently linked to increased achievement in a long history of classroom research (Brophy, 2006; Sorhagen, 2013). In fact, teacher *expectations* can have a profound impact on students' achievement, and this influence can remain in effect years later. "High school students whose first-grade teachers underestimated their abilities performed significantly worse on standardized tests. . . . Conversely, when early abilities were overestimated, high school students performed better than expected" (Sorhagen, 2013, p. 472). Think about this; teachers' expectations are so important that expectations in first grade continue to have an effect on students' achievement as much as 10 years later!

From a theoretical perspective, when students' achievement increases, their perceptions of their competence also increase, and competence is one of people's three innate psychological needs according to self-determination theory. Meeting high expectations also contributes to learners' sense of self-efficacy (which is sometimes equated with competence [Schunk et al., 2014]), and as perceptions of competence and self-efficacy increase, so do students' motivation to learn.

Teachers' expectations influence the way they interact with students, and they often treat students they perceive to be high achievers differently from those they perceive to be low achievers (Weinstein, 2002). This differential treatment typically occurs in four ways (Good & Brophy, 2008):

- *Emotional support*: Teachers interact more with perceived high achievers, their interactions and nonverbal behaviors are more positive, and they seat these students closer to the front of the class.
- *Effort*: Teachers are more enthusiastic when working with high achievers, their instruction is more thorough, and they require more complete and accurate student answers.
- *Questioning*: Teachers call on perceived high achievers more often, they allow these students more time to answer, and they provide high achievers with more prompts and cues when they're unable to answer.
- *Feedback and assessment*: Teachers praise perceived high achievers more, criticize them less, and offer perceived high achievers more complete feedback on assessments.

At an extreme, teachers' expectations for students can become **self-fulfilling prophecies**, phenomena that occur when people's performance results from and confirms beliefs about their capabilities (Weinstein, 2002). Let's see how this works. Communicating positive expectations suggests to students that they will be successful. As we saw earlier, when they are successful, their perceptions of their competence and self-efficacy increase, their motivation increases, and with it, their achievement is greater.

The reverse also occurs, and it is most significant when teachers underestimate their students' capabilities. For instance, "underestimated students have a lower expectancy of success, have a lower self-concept, and report more test anxiety than overestimated students" (Zhou & Urhahne, 2013, p. 283). Communicating low expectations can result in students exerting less effort, so they perform less well, which confirms perceptions about their capabilities. These experiences also influence their attributions. For instance, students who believe their teachers have low expectations for them tend to attribute success to external factors, such as luck, and attribute failure to internal attributions, such as lack of ability (Zhou & Urhahne, 2013). Either can have a negative impact on motivation.

Research conducted over the past several decades consistently indicates that children of all ages are aware of teachers' expectations. For instance, in a study conducted more than 20 years ago, researchers concluded, "After ten seconds of seeing and/or hearing a teacher, even very young students could detect whether the teacher talked about or to an excellent or a weak student" (Babad, Bernieri, & Rosenthal, 1991, p. 230). More recently, researchers concluded, "Although teachers in general seem to be fair and objective . . . differential teacher treatments, even sometimes implicit or unintentional, will be sensitively perceived by students and impact their self-concept" (Zhou & Urhahne, 2013, p. 276).

Unfortunately, our expectations for our students are often out of our conscious control. For instance, without thinking about it, we can fall into a pattern of calling on our higher achievers more often than our lower achievers, and we're a bit surprised when higher achievers are unable to answer, so we prompt them more. On the other hand, if we call on a lower achiever, and he isn't able to answer, we're not surprised, so we don't try as hard to prompt him, instead turning the question to another student, with a "Can someone help out?"

As we saw earlier, students are aware of this differential treatment, and it has a negative impact on their perceptions of competence, self-efficacy, and attributions, which then have a negative influence on motivation and ultimately achievement.

Our goal in writing this section is first to remind us of the powerful influence expectations have on student learning and motivation and second to make us aware of the fact that our expectations are often below the conscious level. With awareness, we are more likely to maintain appropriately high expectations for all students, such as calling on our lower achievers as often as our high achievers.

This discussion helps answer the first question we asked in *Ed Psych and You* at the beginning of the section, "Think about some of your best teachers. What were they like?" Most likely they cared about you both as a person and as a student, they communicated their beliefs in your ability to succeed and learn, they were enthusiastic, and they had high expectations for all your work. These are the qualities we all want to display in our work with our students.

Educational Psychology and Teaching: Demonstrating Personal Qualities that Increase Your Students' Motivation to Learn

Personal qualities that promote motivation to learn can be applied in a number of ways. The following guidelines can help you in your efforts to demonstrate these qualities with your students.

1. Strive to maintain high personal teaching efficacy.
2. Maintain appropriately high expectations for all students.
3. Model responsibility, effort, and interest in the topics you're teaching.
4. Demonstrate caring and commitment to your students' learning.

To see these guidelines in action, let's look again at DeVonne's work with her students.

"Wow, you're here early," Karla Utley, another teacher in the school, says to DeVonne early one morning.

"I've got kids coming in," DeVonne replies. "I did a writing lesson yesterday, and we evaluated some of their paragraphs as a whole class." (DeVonne's writing lesson is the case study at the end of this chapter.) "Several of the kids, like Tu and Saleina, did really well . . . but some are behind. So, Justin, Picey, and Rosa are coming in before school this morning, and we're going to get some more practice. They aren't my highest achievers, but I know I can get more out of them than I am right now. They're good kids; they're just a little behind."

A half hour before school, DeVonne is working at her desk as the three students come in the door. She smiles and says, "We're going to practice a little more on our writing. I know that you can all be good writers, and it's the same thing for me. I've practiced and practiced, and now my effort is paying off. . . . And the more we improve, the more fun writing becomes. I enjoy it more now than I ever have. You can do the same thing. . . . Let's look at your paragraphs again."

She displays Justin's paragraph on the document camera and asks, "What did we suggest that you might do to improve this?" (The lesson in which Justin's paragraph was initially evaluated is the case study at the end of the chapter in the section "Preparing for Your Licensure Exam." You will see his paragraph again there.)

> There was a boy named Josh. He lives in a house with the roof falling in and the windows were broke. He had holes in the wall and the ceiling leaked when it rained. But then again it always rained and thunder over his house. Noone ever goes to his gate because he was so weird. They say he is a vampire.

"He needs to stay on either the boy or the house," Rosa offers.

"Good," DeVonne nods. "Staying focused on your topic sentence is important."

Together, the group examines each student's original paragraph and makes specific suggestions for improvement.

DeVonne then says, "Okay, now each of you rewrite your paragraphs based on our suggestions. When you're finished, we'll look at them again."

The students rewrite their paragraphs, and they again discuss the products.

"Much improvement," DeVonne says after they've finished. "If we keep at it, we're going to get there. . . . I'll see you again tomorrow at 7:30."

Now, let's see how DeVonne's work with her students applies the guidelines.

Strive to Maintain High Personal Teaching Efficacy. As we said earlier, teachers with high personal teaching efficacy believe that they are capable of promoting learning in their students regardless of conditions, either in their homes or in the schools they attend. DeVonne's comment to Karla, "I know I can get more out of them than I am right now. They're good kids; they're just a little behind," reflects this belief. And her efforts were consistent with her stated belief, which applied the first guideline.

Maintain Appropriately High Expectations for All Students. In having Justin, Picey, and Rosa come to school a half hour early to get some extra practice with their writing, and saying to them, "I know that you can all be good writers," she communicated positive expectation for her students.

In some rare cases, students may essentially refuse to come in for extra help. In situations such as these, you've still done your best, and this is all you can do. You can sleep at night knowing that you've made all the efforts that can be expected of a professional.

Model Responsibility, Effort, and Interest in the Topics You're Teaching. As she worked with Justin, Picey, and Rosa, DeVonne said to them, "It's the same thing for me. I've practiced and practiced, and now my effort is paying off. . . . And the more we improve, the more fun writing becomes. I enjoy it more now than I ever have." This comment modeled responsibility, effort, and interest in writing. It won't work all the time or with every student, but it will make a difference with many, and moreover, it takes little extra effort to model these characteristics, and we have nothing to lose in doing so.

Demonstrate Caring and Commitment to Your Students' Learning. Finally, and perhaps most significantly, DeVonne demonstrated caring and commitment by arriving at school an hour early to devote extra time to helping students who needed additional support. She kept the study session upbeat and displayed the respect for the students that is essential for promoting motivation to learn.

We can also demonstrate that we care about our students in other ways. Some examples include (Aaron, Auger, & Pepperell, 2013; Brophy, 2010):

- Learning students' names quickly, and calling on them by their first names.
- Getting to know students as individuals by commenting on, and asking about, personal items, such as a family member, friend, or activity.
- Making eye contact, smiling, demonstrating relaxed body language, and leaning toward them when talking.
- Using the terms "we" and "our" rather than "you" and "your" in reference to class activities and assignments.
- Spending time with students.

The last item deserves special emphasis. We all have exactly 24 hours in our days, and the way we allocate our time is the truest measure of our priorities. Choosing to spend some of our time with an individual student, or a small group, as DeVonne did, communicates caring better than any other single factor. Helping students who have problems with an assignment, or calling a parent after school hours, communicates that you care about students as learners. Spending your personal time to ask a question about a baby brother or compliment a new hairstyle communicates caring about students as people.

These personal qualities won't turn all your students into motivated learners, but you have nothing to lose by demonstrating these qualities, and they take little extra effort. And in doing so, for the students you do impact, you will have made an invaluable contribution to their lives.

Classroom Connections

Demonstrating Personal Characteristics in the Model for Promoting Student Motivation

Caring

1. Caring teachers promote a sense of belonging and relatedness in their classrooms and commit to the development of students both as people and as learners. Demonstrate caring by respecting students and giving them your personal time.

- **Elementary:** A first-grade teacher greets each of her students every day as he or she comes into the classroom and makes it a point to talk to each student about something personal several times a week.

- **Middle School:** A geography teacher calls parents as soon as he sees a student having academic or personal problems. He solicits parents' help and offers his assistance in solving problems.

- **High School:** An algebra II teacher conducts help sessions after school three afternoons a week. Students are invited to attend to get help with homework or to discuss any other concerns about the class or school.

Modeling and Enthusiasm

2. Teachers demonstrate enthusiasm by modeling their own interest in the content of their classes. Communicate interest in the topics you're teaching.

   - **Elementary:** During individual reading time, a fourth-grade teacher comments on a book she's interested in, and she reads while the students are reading.

   - **Middle School:** A life science teacher brings science-related clippings from the local newspaper to class and asks students to do the same. He discusses the clippings and pins them on a bulletin board for students to read.

   - **High School:** A world history teacher frequently describes connections between classroom topics and their impact on today's world.

Positive Expectations

3. Teacher expectations strongly influence motivation and learning. Maintain appropriately high expectations for all students.

   - **Elementary:** A second-grade teacher makes a conscious attempt to call on all her students as equally as possible.

   - **Middle School:** When his students complain about word problems, a prealgebra teacher reminds them of how important problem solving is for their lives. Each day, he guides a detailed discussion of at least two challenging word problems.

   - **High School:** When her American history students turn in sloppily written essays, the teacher displays a well-written example on the document camera, discusses it, and requires her students to revise their original products.

Learning Climate: Creating a Motivating Classroom Environment

As students spend time in school, they can sense whether the classroom is a safe and positive place to learn. In a **positive learning climate**, the teacher and students work together as a community of learners to help everyone achieve. Our goal in creating a positive learning climate is to promote students' feelings of safety and security, together with a sense of success, challenge, and understanding (see Figure 11.3).

Let's see how we can create this type of learning environment.

Order and Safety: Classrooms as Secure Places to Learn

Order and safety are two important climate variables that create a predictable learning environment and promote feelings of physical and emotional security. The importance of safe and orderly classrooms for learner motivation is well established by a long history of

Video 11.2 A positive learning climate is essential for motivation and achievement. This teacher attempts to establish a positive learning climate by emphasizing that he and his students are "in this together" and that it's okay to be wrong.

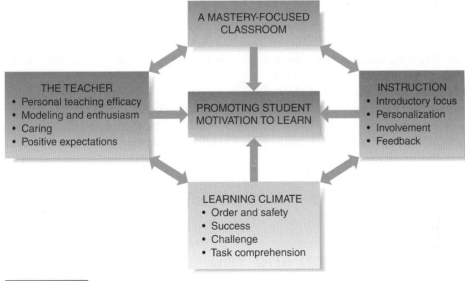

Figure 11.3

Learning climate variables in the model for promoting student motivation

research (Schunk et al., 2014), and additional work suggests that a safe environment is particularly important for students who are members of cultural minorities (Cooper, 2013). Further, your ability to create this type of environment is a high priority for principals; it's one of the first characteristics they look for as they recruit prospective teachers (Engel, 2013).

The importance of order and safety for promoting motivation can be explained from three different theoretical perspectives:

- *Piaget's concept of equilibrium.* The need for equilibrium, when students feel that their surroundings are safe and predictable and events in their environment make sense to them, is the foundation of Piaget's theory of cognitive development, and a safe, orderly, and predictable classroom helps students meet this need (Piaget, 1977).
- *Maslow's work and self-determination theory.* According to Maslow's (1970) hierarchy, safety is a deficiency need preceded only by survival, and learners feel more autonomous and in control—an innate need according to self-determination theory—in a safe environment (Brophy, 2010; Deci & Ryan, 2008; Ryan & Deci, 2000).
- *Information processing and human memory.* A safe environment allows learners to focus their limited working memory space on learning tasks. In environments that aren't safe, students waste some of this crucial learning space to think about ways to avoid criticism, ridicule, or threat (Schunk et al., 2014).

We set the tone for this essential variable by creating positive student–teacher relationships, communicating positive expectations, establishing routines that create an orderly environment, modeling and requiring mutual respect, and consistently enforcing rules and standards for appropriate behavior (Jones, Jones, & Vermete, 2013).

Success: Developing Self-Efficacy

Students' beliefs in their capabilities of accomplishing specific tasks—their self-efficacy—are among the most powerful motivators that exist. Success is the most significant factor that contributes to these beliefs, so, once we've established a safe and orderly learning environment, helping our students succeed on their learning tasks becomes our most important goal. To feel a sense of self-efficacy, they must believe that their own learning is progressing. Merely scoring higher than classmates on a test might temporarily increase these beliefs, but this kind of success can be fleeting, and students aren't always able to score higher than classmates regardless of how hard they try. They can make personal learning progress, however, and this is the most enduring form of success and the form that most contributes to self-efficacy, and ultimately to self-worth.

Attempting to inoculate our students against periodic failure is an integral part of this process. We all fail now and then, and we should try to help students understand that some failure experiences are inevitable and perhaps even valuable. Mistakes and failure are normal parts of learning, and students who understand this and persevere are those who succeed over the long term (Zhou & Urhahne, 2013).

Challenge: Increasing Perceptions of Competence

Ed Psych and You

Think about how you feel when you solve a difficult problem, make a computer application work, or figure out a puzzling event. Why do you feel this way?

According to self-determination theory, developing a sense of competence is an innate need in all of us, and seeing our competence increase is intrinsically motivating (Deci & Ryan, 2008; Ryan & Deci, 2000). Further, "all students, even the seemingly unmotivated, care about being seen as competent and able in the eyes of others" (De Castella, Byrne, & Covington, 2013, p. 861).

This helps answer the question we asked in *Ed Psych and You*. Solving difficult problems or figuring out a computer application or puzzling event increases our perception of competence. "Attainment of challenging goals conveys to learners that they are becoming more competent, which raises self-efficacy and perceived control over outcomes. In turn, learners are apt to set new, challenging goals, which serve to maintain intrinsic motivation" (Schunk et al., 2014, p. 268). Further, research in neuroscience indicates that successfully responding to challenges can provide a dopamine-reward rush in the pleasure sensors of our brains (Carey, 2010; Zink, Pagnoni, Martin-Skurski, Chappelow, & Berns, 2004). It's personally rewarding to attempt and succeed on challenging tasks.

Video 11.3 Challenging tasks can increase motivation because meeting challenges increases perceptions of competence. This student comments that he tries harder in challenging classes.

This suggests that success, alone, is not sufficient for promoting student motivation. Students can successfully memorize lists of facts and rules or solve routine problems, but this success does little to increase their perceptions of competence, and it is not emotionally satisfying. They need to experience success in activities they perceive as challenging. In addition, students' beliefs about both attainment value and utility value are increased when they succeed on challenging tasks (Lam & Law, 2007).

We can capitalize on the motivating characteristics of challenge by presenting students with challenging tasks such as identifying relationships in the topics they study and the implications of these relationships for new learning (Brophy, 2010). For example, DeVonne didn't immediately tell her students that arthropods had an exoskeleton, three body parts, and segmented legs. Instead, with her guidance they identified these characteristics for themselves. Then, she had them observe and decide if a cockroach, clam, and even Mrs. Sapp (the school principal) were arthropods. Her approach was challenging for students, because some of them initially concluded that both the clam and Mrs. Sapp were indeed arthropods.

We can readily see how this approach was richer and more motivating for students than memorizing a set of characteristics for these animals. And when tasks are challenging, students might initially complain, but when they finally do succeed, their sense of accomplishment will be just that much greater.

Task Comprehension: Increasing Feelings of Autonomy and Value

Understanding what they are expected to learn and why it's important also influence motivation. To see how, let's return to DeVonne's work with her students the day after her lesson on arthropods.

> "Now, let's review for a few minutes," she begins. "What were the characteristics of arthropods that we identified yesterday?"
>
> "Exoskeleton," Saleina volunteers.
>
> "Three body parts," Tu adds.
>
> "Jointed legs," Kevin offers.
>
> "Good. . . . And what are some examples of arthropods?"
>
> The students offer crabs, lobsters, roaches, beetles, spiders, and others as examples, and DeVonne then asks, "Why is it important to study these animals?"
>
> After hesitating for a moment, Stephanie says, "We eat them, like shrimp and stuff."

"Good," DeVonne smiles. "Indeed, they're an important food source. In fact, did you know that insects are as nutritious as meat, and they're eaten both cooked and raw in many cultures?"

Amid, "Eeww," "Yuk," "Gross," and other reactions from students, DeVonne adds, "More than 80% of all animal species are arthropods, and there are more than a million different species. . . . Think about that. More than 8 out of 10 animals on this earth are arthropods. . . . And they're essential for pollinating our plants. Without them, we wouldn't have enough food. We really do need to understand our most abundant, and one of our most important, neighbors."

This discussion reflects DeVonne's attempts to capitalize on **task comprehension**, learners' awareness of what they are supposed to be learning and an understanding of why the task is important and worthwhile.

As with success, a challenging task won't increase motivation to learn if students don't believe that it is meaningful and worth understanding (Vavilis & Vavilis, 2004). For example, DeVonne could have simply said, "Be sure you know the characteristics of arthropods and some examples of them, because they will be on our next test," and statements such as this are common in classrooms. Instead, she suggested that the reason they were studying arthropods is because they have a major impact on our daily lives.

The importance of task comprehension can be explained with the value component of expectancy x value theory, which says that people are motivated to engage in a task to the extent that they expect to succeed on that task times the value they place on the success. Task comprehension contributes to the value learners place on their successes. This makes sense. If we understand why we study a topic, we will certainly value it more than we would if we simply studied it for no apparent reason. And evidence suggests that understanding why we study a topic contributes to our feelings of autonomy, an innate psychological need according to self-determination theory (Deci & Ryan, 2008; Ryan & Deci, 2000).

A number of ways to increase task comprehension exist. For instance, DeVonne emphasized the contributions of arthropods to our food supply, and in doing so helped her students understand the world around them. In other cases, we study a topic because it is a prerequisite for more advanced work, such as taking algebra because we need it for trigonometry and calculus. We study other topics because they help make a contribution to our work and careers. We, Paul and Don—your authors—want to believe that this is an important reason you study educational psychology; we hope you believe that it will help you become a better teacher. And we study some topics simply because they're intrinsically interesting. Any and all of these reasons are worthwhile, and it's important that we communicate the reasons to our students. This is the essence of task comprehension.

As with teacher qualities, climate variables are synergistic. For instance, if students feel safe enough to share their thinking without fear of criticism or ridicule, the motivating effects of challenge will be increased. Similarly, if students know why they're studying a topic, experiencing success as they work will be more enjoyable than if they don't understand why they're studying it.

Educational Psychology and Teaching: Applying an Understanding of Climate Variables in Your Classroom

As with all aspects of learning and teaching, creating a classroom climate that promotes students' motivation to learn isn't easy, particularly with learners who have a history of low achievement. Our goal with all students should be to help them feel physically and emotionally safe in our classrooms, to succeed on tasks they perceive as challenging, and to understand why they're studying the topics we select.

Let's see how we might promote this type of positive learning climate.

Creating a Safe and Orderly Environment. Creating a safe and orderly learning environment is a classroom management issue, and it's understandably one of teachers' primary concerns (Emmer & Evertson, 2013; Evertson & Emmer, 2013). If you haven't already done so, you will likely take an entire course in your teacher preparation program devoted to this very important topic. Or at the very least one or more of your other courses will have significant components that focus on classroom management. (In fact, courses in educational psychology, such as the one you're now taking, often include classroom management as one of their topics, and Chapter 12 of this text is devoted to it.) As you study this topic, remember that a strong relationship exists between student motivation and a safe and orderly classroom.

Promoting Student Success. As teachers, promoting student success can be an enormous challenge, certainly one of our most demanding tasks. If it were easy, we wouldn't see mainstream media lament school dropout rates, teachers complaining about students who don't seem to care about learning—or their own futures—and a myriad of other motivation-related issues.

We can, however, take steps that increase the likelihood of our students experiencing success. Two of the most important include (1) using open-ended questions and (2) using high-quality examples. Let's look at them.

Open-ended questions are questions for which a variety of answers are acceptable. To illustrate, let's look again at some dialogue from DeVonne's lesson as she has Stephanie carry the lobster around the room.

> DeVonne: Look carefully, because I'm going to ask you to tell us what you see. . . . Okay, what did you notice?
>
> Tu: Hard.
>
> Saleina: Pink and green.
>
> Kevin: Wet.

Notice that DeVonne asked a simple, straightforward question: "What do you notice?" and Tu, Saleina, and Kevin each responded with a different answer. This question, or others that are similar, such as "What do you observe?" or "What do you see?," can be very effective for helping students—and particularly those who are often unable to answer questions requiring a single answer—experience success, because virtually anything they say in response is acceptable.

Using open-ended questions often takes a little "getting used to." Students are so often asked questions requiring one specific answer that they may initially be reluctant to try and respond. In our own teaching we've even had students say, "I'm not sure what you're looking for," to which we reply, "I'm looking for whatever you notice."

Our experience suggests that open-ended questions work. As one example, Paul was recently teaching a lesson with a group of fifth graders, and within a matter of minutes, students who were initially reluctant to respond were raising their hands attempting to volunteer answers. Using open-ended questions isn't an immediate panacea for success, but using them can be an effective strategy for helping students who are rarely successful experience the pleasure of being able to answer and participate.

High-quality examples are examples for which all the information students need to understand a topic is observable in them. DeVonne's lobster was a high-quality example. For instance, she wanted her students to understand that arthropods have an *exoskeleton,* *three body parts,* and *segmented legs.* Her students could see these characteristics in the lobster. When students *can see* the characteristics in an example, they essentially can't miss, so again, they experience success.

Combining open-ended questions with high-quality examples also makes it easier to prompt students when they are initially unable to answer. To illustrate, let's look again at some dialogue.

> DeVonne: [holding up the lobster] What do you notice about the lobster's legs? . . . Damien?
>
> Damien: They're long.
>
> DeVonne: [wiggling the legs] Are they all in one part or more than one part?
>
> Damien: More than one.
>
> DeVonne: Yes, good. When we see legs like this, we say they're segmented.

Damien was able to answer successfully, to which DeVonne responded, "Yes, good." This is admittedly a small success, but if he has enough experiences like this one, in time his motivation is likely to increase.

In other content areas, such as math or language arts, where students must develop problem-solving or grammar and punctuation skills, providing scaffolded practice before expecting students to work independently can also contribute to their success.

Here's what we mean by scaffolded practice. You're teaching percent increase and percent decrease, and you've presented your students with the following problem:

> You see a sharp looking shirt at one of the stores in the mall that was originally priced at $70, and it's now marked down to $50. What is the percent decrease in the price?

You then have the students all work the problem while you monitor their efforts. When they've finished, you discuss the solution, give them another problem, and continue until you believe most of the students understand the process. Then, you give your students a homework assignment, and while the majority of the students work on the assignment, you provide extra support in a small group for those who need it. Instructional scaffolding such as this is one of the most effective strategies we have for maximizing our students' success.

The importance of promoting success also illustrates the synergy among the variables in the model for promoting student motivation. For instance, open-ended questions and scaffolded practice are only effective if the classroom environment is safe and orderly. Students won't answer if they're afraid of being laughed at or ridiculed. And if students are involved in horseplay instead of doing their homework, it will be impossible for you to provide extra help for the students who need it. Similarly, students will make more of an effort to answer if they believe that you're truly committed to their learning and care about them as people. The variables in the model are interdependent and build upon one another.

Capitalizing on Challenge. As we found earlier, success—alone—won't necessarily increase students' motivation; they need to believe that they're succeeding on tasks that are meaningful and worthwhile.

Before we continue, we want to remind you of what *challenge* is not. All teachers want to believe that they're challenging their students, but many are often uncertain about how to do so. So, in misguided efforts, they simply increase students' workload, such as, instead of assigning 10 problems for homework, they assign 15, or, instead of assigning 20 pages to be read, they assign 40. This often has precisely the opposite of the intended effect. Instead of increasing motivation, students often interpret these efforts as meaningless busy work, or even worse, a form of punishment.

Instead of simply piling on more work, we should be requiring our students to examine the topics they're studying in more depth, to link ideas to each other, and to find different ways to solve problems. In essence, challenge requires students to "think."

And doing so need not be difficult; it's more a matter of "getting used to." For instance, DeVonne's asking her students if the clam, and even Mrs. Sapp—the school principal—were arthropods was a simple form of challenge. Also notice that some of her students thought they were; they centered on the hard shell of the clam and Mrs. Sapp's jointed legs in concluding that both were arthropods. This form of challenge provided additional benefits: students developed a deeper understanding of arthropods, and they learned that concepts must include all the essential characteristics rather than only one, such as the clam's hard shell.

Questions that ask students to explain or offer conjectures are excellent for challenging students. For instance, again suppose you're teaching percent increase and percent decrease and you pose this problem:

> An item marked down from $40 to $30 is a 25% decrease, but an item whose value increases from $30 to $40 is a 33% increase. How can that be?

Students often struggle with problems such as this, but when they eventually meet the challenge, their perceptions of their competence will markedly increase, as will their motivation.

Similarly, a question such as "We know the clam shell has two parts. What if it had three parts instead? Would it then be an arthropod?" asks students for a conjecture about arthropods and their characteristics. And again, in addition to challenging students, it promotes deeper understanding of the topic.

Challenging students has an additional benefit: Teaching is a more fun when we challenge students and listen to their thinking. And we may be surprised by the results. Students who are traditionally low achievers sometimes come up with ideas we didn't believe they were capable of. The result is a win-win. The students win because their understanding and motivation increase; we win because it's more fun, and our personal teaching efficacy also gets a boost.

Ensuring Task Comprehension. A common student question is, "Why do we have to learn this?" Task comprehension helps answer it. The single most effective way to ensure that students understand why they're studying a topic is to apply it to their daily lives. For instance, after asking her students why it's important to study arthropods, DeVonne pointed out facts, such as arthropods being an important food source and their role in pollinating plants.

Similarly, valid reasons exist for studying virtually all the topics we teach, and we merely need to communicate these reasons to our students. As teachers, we know why it's important to learn something; we need to also help our students reach this same understanding. They won't all be convinced, but as we've repeatedly said in our discussion of motivation, we have nothing to lose by doing so, and the effort it takes is minimal.

Classroom **Connections**

Promoting a Positive Learning Climate in Classrooms

Order and Safety

1. Order and safety create a predictable learning environment and support learner autonomy and security. Create a safe and secure learning environment.

   ■ Elementary: A first-grade teacher establishes and practices daily routines until they're predictable and automatic for students.

   ■ Middle School: An eighth-grade American history teacher leads a discussion focusing on the kind of environment the students want to work in. They conclude that all "digs" and discourteous remarks should be forbidden. The teacher consistently enforces the agreement.

   ■ High School: An English teacher reminds her students that all relevant comments about a topic are welcome, and she models acceptance of every idea. She requires students to listen courteously when a classmate is talking.

Success and Challenge

2. Succeeding on challenging tasks promotes self-efficacy and helps students develop a sense of competence. Structure instruction so that students succeed on challenging tasks.

- **Elementary:** A fourth-grade teacher comments, "Our understanding of fractions is getting better and better. So, now I have a problem that is going to make us all think. It will be a little tough, but I know that we'll be able to do it." After students attempt the solution, he guides a discussion of the problem and different ways to solve it.

- **Middle School:** A sixth-grade English teacher has the class practice two or three homework exercises as a whole group each day and discusses them before students begin to work independently.

- **High School:** As she returns their homework, a physics teacher gives her students worked solutions to the most frequently missed problems. She has students put solutions in their portfolios to study for the weekly quizzes.

Task Comprehension

3. Task comprehension reflects students' awareness of what they are supposed to be learning and an understanding of why the task is important and worthwhile. Promote task comprehension by describing rationales for your learning activities and assignments.

- **Elementary:** As he gives students their daily math homework, a third-grade teacher says, "We know that understanding how math applies to our lives is really important, so that's why we practice word problems every day."

- **Middle School:** A seventh-grade English teacher carefully describes her assignments and due dates and writes them on the board. Each time, she explains why the assignment is important and how it links to other things they've learned.

- **High School:** A biology teacher displays the following on the document camera:
  We don't just study flatworms because we're interested in flatworms. As we look at how they've adapted to their environments, we'll gain additional insights into ourselves.
  He then says, "We'll return to this idea again and again to remind ourselves why we study each organism."

Instructional Variables: Developing Interest in Learning Activities

Teacher qualities and climate variables form a general framework for motivation. Within this context, we can do much to ensure that students' learning experiences enhance their motivation to learn. From an instructional perspective, a motivated student is someone who is actively engaged in learning activities (Brophy, 2010). To promote both learning and motivation, we need to initially capture—and then maintain—students' attention and engagement throughout a learning activity. Different ways of doing this are outlined in Figure 11.4.

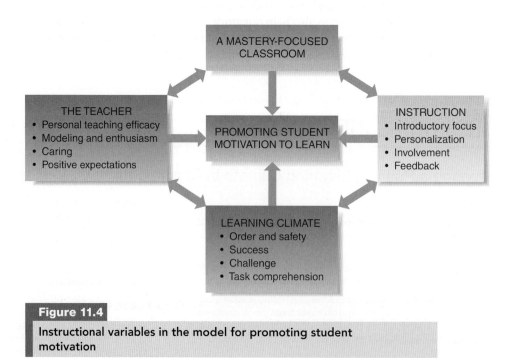

Figure 11.4

Instructional variables in the model for promoting student motivation

Introductory Focus: Attracting Students' Attention

Our understanding of learning reminds us that all information processing begins with attention, and simply, students can't learn if they aren't paying attention. **Introductory focus** is a lesson beginning that attracts student attention and provides a conceptual framework for the learning activity (Kauchak & Eggen, 2012; Lemov, 2010). It also attempts to capitalize on the effects of curiosity and novelty, which are characteristics of intrinsically motivating activities (Brophy, 2010). For example, DeVonne began her lesson on arthropods by bringing a live lobster to class. The squeals and "oohs" and "aahs" suggested that she had indeed attracted their attention. Let's look at another example of introductory focus.

> As an introduction to studying cities and their locations, Marissa Allen, a social studies teacher, hands out a map of a fictitious island. On it are physical features such as lakes, rivers, and mountains. Information about altitude, rainfall, and average seasonal temperature is also included.
>
> Marissa begins, "The name of this activity is *Survival*. Our class has just been sent to this island to settle it. We have information about its climate and physical features. Where should we make our first settlement?"

We can attract our students' attention with unique problems, such as Marissa's survival task, by asking paradoxical questions ("If Rome was such a powerful and advanced civilization, why did it collapse?"); by using demonstrations with seemingly contradictory results (e.g., dropping two balls of different weights and seeing that they hit the floor at the same time); or with eye-catching examples, such as DeVonne's lobster (Hidi & Renninger, 2006).

Unfortunately teachers tend to use effective lesson introductions infrequently (Brophy, 2010), but it need not be as difficult as it might initially appear. All that is required is an effort to connect the content of each lesson to students' prior knowledge and interests. We offer several additional examples for providing introductory focus in the section "Educational Psychology and Teaching: Applying the Instructional Variables to Increase Your Students' Motivation to Learn" later in the chapter.

Once our students are paying attention, and we've provided a conceptual framework for the lesson, it has to maintain their attention and provide information about learning progress. *Personalization, involvement,* and *feedback* can help meet these goals.

Personalization: Links to Students' Lives

> Sue Crompton, a second-grade math teacher, introduces the topic of graphing by measuring her students' heights. She continues by giving them a length of construction paper and has them place their strip of paper on the spot on a graph that corresponds to their height. After discussing the results, she does a similar activity with hair color to reinforce the idea of graphing.
>
> Chris Emery, a science teacher, begins a unit on genetics by saying, "Reanne, what color are your eyes?"
>
> "Blue," Reanne responds.
>
> "And how about yours, Eddie?"
>
> "Green."
>
> "Interesting," Chris smiles. "When we're done with this unit on genetics, we'll be able to figure out why Reanne's eyes are blue and Eddie's are green, and a whole bunch of other things related to the way we look."

Sue and Chris both attempted to increase their students' interest through **personalization**, the process of using intellectually and/or emotionally relevant examples to illustrate a topic. DeVonne also capitalized on personalization when she helped her students understand why they were studying arthropods and how these animals affect their lives, and by asking them if Mrs. Sapp, their school principal, was an arthropod.

The value of personalization as a motivational strategy can be explained with both practical experience and with theory, and research confirms its importance (Ertem, 2013; Narciss et al., 2014). First, it's intuitively sensible (we all like to learn things that relate to us) and widely applicable. Experienced teachers describe it as one of the most important ways they have of promoting their students' interest in learning activities (Schraw & Lehman, 2001; Wortham, 2004).

Second, from a theoretical perspective, we can explain the value of personalization with both information processing theory and self-determination theory. With respect to information processing, personalized content is meaningful because it encourages students to connect new information to structures already in long-term memory (Moreno & Mayer, 2000). In the end, all learning is personal, and students' ability to link new information to what they already know is essential. With respect to self-determination theory, students feel an increased sense of autonomy when they study topics to which they can personally relate (Iyengar & Lepper, 1999).

As with introductory focus, we offer additional examples for personalizing content in the section "Educational Psychology and Teaching: Applying the Instructional Variables to Increase Your Students' Motivation to Learn" later in the chapter.

DIVERSITY: PERSONALIZING CONTENT TO INCREASE MOTIVATION TO LEARN IN STUDENTS HAVING DIVERSE BACKGROUNDS

> Jack Seltzer, a high school biology teacher in the Navajo Nation reservation, uses his students' background experiences to illustrate hard-to-understand science concepts. He uses Churro sheep, a local breed that Navajos use for food and wool, to illustrate genetic principles. When they study plants, he focuses on local varieties of squash and corn that have been grown by students' ancestors for centuries. Geologic formations in nearby Monument Valley are used to illustrate igneous, sedimentary, and metamorphic rocks (Baker, 2006).

We know that belonging (from Maslow's theory) and relatedness (from self-determination theory) are needs that strongly influence students' motivation to learn (Baumeister & DeWall, 2005), and students who don't develop a sense of belonging or identify with their schools have higher dropout rates (Juvonen, 2006, 2007). This problem is particularly acute among members of cultural minorities and students who are disadvantaged (Wentzel & Wigfield, 2007). Further, minority students' disengagement is often exacerbated by the school curriculum, much of which is oriented toward mainstream, middle-class, nonminority students (Anderson & Summerfield, 2004).

Gender differences in interest also exist (Buck, Kostin, & Morgan, 2002). For instance, males tend to be more interested in topics such as war, politics, hard science, and business, whereas females are more interested in human relationships, arts, literature, marginalized groups, and social reform. Some researchers even link these gender-based interests to performance differences on standardized exams, such as advanced placement tests in high school (Halpern, 2006).

Now, let's look back to Jack Seltzer and his work with his Navajo students. He attempted to create a sense of belonging and interest in his class by capitalizing on the motivating effects of personalization. This variable is important for all students, but it can be particularly effective with members of cultural minorities, who commonly say they don't belong or don't feel welcome in school (Rubinson, 2004). When these students are presented with examples and experiences that directly relate to their lives, as Jack did, their interest and sense of belonging can significantly increase.

Involvement: Increasing Situational Interest

Ed Psych and You

Think about your experiences at lunch with friends or at a party. How do you feel when you're engaged in conversations compared to when you're on the fringes?

The question in *Ed Psych and You* addresses the idea of **involvement**, the extent to which people are directly participating in an activity. For instance, when we're talking and actively listening (involved), we pay more attention to the conversation, and our interest in it is higher than when we're on its fringes. The same applies in classrooms. Involvement increases situational interest, and it encourages students to become cognitively active. And we know from our study of human memory that cognitive activity is essential for meaningful learning (Blumenfeld, Kempler, & Krajcik, 2006).

Expectancy x value theory helps us understand the importance of involvement. As suggested by this theory, intrinsic interest is one of the factors that increases task value in learning activities, and involvement increases intrinsic interest. This makes sense. When we're involved in a conversation, such as we suggested in *Ed Psych and You*, we almost can't help being interested in the topic of discussion.

Questioning is our most generally applicable tool for increasing involvement; students' attention is high when they're thinking about and answering questions, but it drops during teacher monologues. In our discussion of strategies for promoting student success earlier in the chapter, we talked about *open-ended questioning,* and in addition to promoting success, these questions can also be effective for involving students (Brophy, 2006). Questions such as "What do you see?" are easy to ask, and once students get used to them, they're easy to answer, so we can call on several different students very quickly.

In addition to questioning in general, and open-ended questioning in particular, *hands-on activities* and *group work* can also be effective for promoting involvement. For example, when students work with manipulatives in math, concrete materials in science, maps and globes in geography, or computers in language arts, their level of interest often increases significantly. In DeVonne's lesson, for instance, her students' involvement was highest when they actually worked with the shrimp. Periodically using hands-on activities adds variety to learning activities, and variety also increases learner interest (Perry et al., 2006).

Group work, in which students work together toward common learning goals, can also increase involvement (Slavin, 2011; Wentzel & Watkins, 2011). Group work provides opportunities for students to interact and compare their ideas with others, both of which increase interest.

As with virtually all aspects of teaching and learning, hands-on activities or group work won't automatically increase motivation and learning—for two reasons. With respect to hands-on activities, we often tacitly assume that students who are behaviorally active—that is, they are working with the materials—are also cognitively active and are actually thinking about the learning task. This often isn't the case. A hands-on activity may be interesting to students, and even fun, but it doesn't automatically result in meaningful learning.

With respect to group work, students are often inclined to merely socialize instead of focusing on the learning task they've been given; the group work does nothing more than help students meet social goals.

Three strategies can help deal with these potential problems. First, we need to give our students very specific directions and requirements for each activity; they're less likely to go off task if they know exactly what they're supposed to be doing. Second, the students should be required to produce a product, such as written responses to a series of questions. When they're required to produce a product, they are also less likely to go off task, and the process of producing the product also promotes involvement (and learning). And third, we must carefully monitor the activities. Students are more likely to remain on task and avoid socializing if we're walking around the room, asking questions, and making comments. Our goal is to ensure that students are learning from the activities, not merely enjoying the experience (Brophy, 2010; Mayer, 2004).

Feedback: Information about Learning Progress

We all want to know how we're doing when we learn something new, and information about our current understanding helps us make sense of our efforts and experiences. Feedback contributes to motivation by providing this information (El, Tillema, & van Koppen, 2012). Its value can be explained in several ways, which include the following (Hattie & Timperley, 2007):

- *Self-determination theory*. Feedback indicating that competence is increasing contributes to self-determination.
- *Attribution theory*. Feedback helps us understand why we perform the way we do, which attribution theory considers an important need.
- *Knowledge construction*. Feedback gives us information about the validity of our knowledge constructions, which allows us to change our thinking and reconstruct our understanding if necessary.
- *Self-regulated learning*. Feedback gives us information about progress toward goals, and when they're met, our self-efficacy increases. If they're not met, we can then increase our effort or change strategies.

The type of feedback is important (Hattie & Timperley, 2007; Hattie & Gann, 2011). When it provides information about learning progress, motivation increases, but if it has a performance orientation, such as emphasizing high grades, competition, and social comparisons, it can detract from motivation to learn (Brophy, 2010; Schunk et al., 2014). Performance-oriented feedback has a particularly detrimental effect on lower ability students and detracts from intrinsic motivation for both low and high achievers.

Educational Psychology and Teaching: Applying the Instructional Variables to Increase Your Students' Motivation to Learn

In this section we've focused on the instructional variables in the model for promoting student motivation, but throughout the chapter, we've emphasized that the variables in each component are interdependent and exist in synergy. The instructional variables, without teachers' personal qualities and the climate variables, won't—alone—increase students' motivation to learn.

With that thought in mind, the following guidelines can help us apply the instructional variables in the model for promoting student motivation in our teaching.

- Begin lessons with an example, question, or activity designed to attract students' attention.
- Create links between topics and students' personal lives.

- Maintain high levels of student involvement in learning activities.
- Use assessment and feedback to increase interest and self-efficacy.

To see how a teacher attempts to apply the guidelines with his students, let's look at a lesson taught by David Crawford, a world history teacher.

David is working with his students to develop their skills with examining evidence, eventually leading to their abilities to identify textual evidence to meet the following standard.

CCSS.ELA-Literacy.RH.9-10.1 Cite specific textual evidence to support analysis of primary and secondary sources, attending to such features as the date and origin of the information (Common Core State Standards Initiative, 2014d).

As the bell rings, his students are in their seats and have their notebooks on their desks. David moves to the front of the room and begins, "I'm going to show you some objects on the table here, and as you look at them, think about this question: What do the items have to do with technology?"

David reaches into a box, pulls out two animal skulls, a piece of woven fabric, and a stone spear point that is ground to a fine edge, and puts them on the table at the front of the room. Then, he puts another stone spear point that is also sharp but chipped, two small animal bones, and a fragment from an animal skin on the table next to the first group.

As students look at the objects, they offer a few ideas, and then David begins directing the lesson with the question, "What are some common forms of technology in our world today? Go ahead. . . . Brenda?"

The students offer examples such as computers, smartphones, tablets, and iPods, and then David continues, "Good examples. . . . Now, we tend to think of technology as something recent, but it's existed throughout history, and we can tell a great deal about a civilization by looking at its artifacts."

He defines the term *artifact* and then says, "Today we're going to examine some artifacts to see what they might tell us about the technologies people used who left them behind. This will give us the thinking tools to understand the civilizations we study as we look at the history of the world."

"We'll call this Civilization A, and this one Civilization B," he says, pointing to the sets of materials.

"What do you notice about the artifacts?" David directs. "Go ahead and start . . . Kelly?"

As he calls on them, a number of students make observations, and then with David's guidance they conclude that the skulls are from a cow and a sheep and the bones are leg and rib bones from an antelope or deer.

"Now," David smiles, "We're archeological teams, and we found these sites. . . . I want you to work with your partners and write down as many conclusions as you can about the people who used these from each group, and any comparisons between the two, such as which one you believe was more advanced. In each case, provide evidence for your conclusions."

At the end of their allotted time, David says, "Okay, what did you come up with?"

"We think those are newer," Lori says, pointing at the chipped spear points. "The points are sharp, and they're sort of like art."

"Rod?" David acknowledges, seeing his raised hand.

"I sort of disagree," Rodney responds, referring to the points with fine edges. "These look like they're ground, and grinding would be more advanced technology than chipping."

The class continues discussing the artifacts, and from the cow and sheep skulls and the cloth, the students conclude that Civilization A had domesticated animals and the ability to weave. They decide that the antelope bones and skin indicate that Civilization B probably consisted of hunter-gatherers.

After completing the discussion, David says, "Okay, for tonight, I want you to read about the Old, Middle, and New Stone Ages on pages 35 to 44 of your books and decide what ages these artifacts probably belonged to. . . . You did a great job today. You made some excellent conclusions and supported them in each case."

Now, let's look at David's attempts to apply the guidelines.

Attracting Students' Attention: Introductory Focus.

When we teach, we can begin lessons in a variety of ways. David began his with a conscious effort to attract his students' attention by displaying artifacts and asking his students, "What do the items have to do with technology?" The combination of the two was a good form of introductory focus because we don't typically think of skulls, bones, and spear points as forms of technology.

Creating motivating lesson beginnings need not take a great deal of extra work and preparation; it's more a matter of a little extra thought about ways to start lessons. Once doing so becomes a habit, the process will become nearly automatic.

Some additional examples for providing introductory focus are outlined in Table 11.2.

Linking Topics to Students' Lives: Personalization.

David attempted to personalize his learning activity by beginning the lesson with examples of today's technology and by placing his students in the role of archeologists. As with introductory focus, personalizing content merely requires a bit of thought; it need not require a great deal of extra planning and effort.

Expectancy x value theory helps us understand the motivating influence of personalizing topics. Students value success on topics that affect them personally, or to which they can personally relate, more than remote and disconnected topics.

Table 11.3 outlines additional examples of teachers' attempts to personalize the topics they teach.

Involving Students: Creating Interest.

To begin this section, let's think again about the way David conducted his lesson. Three aspects are significant.

- He began by saying, "I'm going to display some objects on the table here, and as you look at them, think about this question: What do the items have to do with technology?"
- He asked, "What are some common forms of technology in our world today?"
- As he directed the students to the items on the table he asked, "What do you notice about the artifacts?"

Each question was open-ended, which allowed him to call on several different students easily and quickly. Using questions such as these is the most widely applicable strategy we have for involving students. As you attempt to use open-ended questioning in your

Table 11.2	**Tools and techniques for providing introductory focus**
Tool/Technique	**Example**
Problems and questions	• A literature teacher shows a picture of Ernest Hemingway and says, "Here we see 'Papa' in all his splendor. He seemed to have everything—fame, adventure, romance. Yet he took his own life. Why would this happen?" • A science teacher asks the students to explain why two pieces of paper come together at the bottom (rather than move apart) when students blow between them. • An educational psychology instructor introducing social cognitive theory displays the following vignette: *You're driving 75 mph on the interstate—with a posted speed limit of 65—when another car blazes past you. A minute later, you see the car stopped by the highway patrol. You immediately slow down. How would behaviorism explain your slowing down?*
Inductive sequences	• An English teacher displays the following: *I had a ton of homework last night! I was upset because I had a date with the most gorgeous girl in the world! I guess it was okay, because she had on the ugliest outfit ever!* The students find a pattern in the examples and develop the concept hyperbole. • An educational psychology instructor begins a discussion of development with these questions: Are you bothered when something doesn't make sense? Do you want the world to be predictable? Are you more comfortable in classes when the instructor specifies the requirements, schedules the classes, and outlines the grading practices? Does your life in general follow patterns more than random experiences? The class looks at the pattern and arrives at the concept of *equilibrium*.
Concrete examples	• An elementary teacher begins a unit on amphibians by bringing in a live frog. • A geography teacher draws lines on a beach ball to demonstrate that longitude lines intersect at the poles and latitude lines are parallel to each other. • An educational psychology instructor introduces the concept *negative reinforcement* by describing his inclination to take a pain killer to reduce his discomfort after a demanding workout.
Objectives and rationales	• A math teacher begins, "Today we want to learn about unit pricing. This will help us decide which product is a better buy. It will help us all save money and be better consumers." • A world history teacher says, "Today we're going to look at the concept of *mercantilism*. It will help us understand why, throughout history, Europe came to the New World and went into South Asia and Africa." • An educational psychology instructor says, "We know that learners construct, rather than record, understanding. Today we want to see what that principle suggests about the way we should teach most effectively."

teaching, remember that any question you ask that has a variety of acceptable answers can be effective for involving students. For instance, a teacher in a lesson on Shakespeare's *Julius Caesar* might ask questions such as:

"What has happened so far in the play?"
"What are some of the major events?"
"How are Brutus and Marc Antony similar? How are they different?"
"How does the setting for Act I compare with that for Act II?"

As another example, a teacher in a lesson on amphibians and reptiles might ask questions such as:

"How is a frog similar to a lizard?"
"How are the frog and a toad similar to or different from each other?"

Table 11.3	Teachers' efforts to personalize examples
Topic	**Example**
Creating bar graphs	A second-grade teacher uses her students' favorite flavor of jelly beans to create a large bar graph at the front of her classroom.
The concept *population density*	A teacher uses masking tape to create two identical areas on the classroom floor. She then has three students stand in one area and five students stand in the other to demonstrate that the population density of the second is greater. The class then looks up the population density of their city and other cities in their state.
Comparative and superlative adjectives	A language arts teacher has students hold up different length pencils and writes on the board: *Devon has a long pencil.* *Andrea has a longer pencil.* *Steve has the longest pencil.* She then has students identify the characteristics of comparative and superlative adjectives.
Finding equivalent fractions	A math teacher arranges the 24 desks in his classroom into 4 rows of 6 desks each with two rows close together and the other two rows close together. He then guides the students to conclude that two rows are 12/24ths of the desks. He next guides students to conclude that the two rows together are also 1/2 of the desks, so 12/24ths is equivalent to 1/2.
The Crusades	A World History teacher uses the class's "crusade" to prevent extracurricular activities from being eliminated at the school as an analogy for the actual Crusades in history.
Shakespeare	A literature teacher introduces the study of *Hamlet* by saying, "Suppose you've been away from home for several years. When you return, you learn that your father has died and your mother has married your uncle—your father's brother. Then, you begin to find clues suggesting that your uncle might be responsible for your father's death" (Brophy, 2010).

Open-ended questions also provide us with insights into our students' thinking and allow us to build on their prior knowledge (Powell & Caseau, 2004). For instance, if we ask them to make observations, and the observations have little or nothing to do with the characteristics we want to identify, we know our students lack relevant background knowledge, and we can then try to provide it.

In addition to his use of open-ended questions, David had his students work with partners to make conclusions about the civilizations. This simple form of group work also promotes involvement. The discussion that followed also promoted involvement—perhaps even at a higher level—because the students had a personal investment in their conclusions. So they were keenly interested in their classmates' reactions to their ideas.

Some additional strategies for promoting involvement are outlined in Table 11.4, and each promotes cognitive engagement. Improvement drills add an element of game-like novelty to otherwise routine activities, and personal improvement increases self-efficacy. Having students use chalkboards in individual workspaces is similar to having them solve problems on paper at their desks, but the chalkboards allow sharing and discussion, and students often will use them to attempt problems they wouldn't try on paper.

Assessing Students and Providing Feedback: Providing Information about Learning Progress. Feedback is the final variable in the model for promoting student motivation. We combine the discussion of feedback with assessment, because assessment is one of the most powerful influences on learning and motivation (Carey, 2010; Rohrer & Pashler, 2010).

Table 11.4	Strategies for promoting involvement	
Technique	**Example**
Improvement drills	Students are given a list of 10 multiplication facts on a sheet. Students are scored on speed and accuracy, and points are given for individual improvement.
Games	The class is divided equally according to ability, and the two groups respond in a game format to teacher questions.
Individual work spaces	Students are given their own chalkboards on which they solve math problems and identify examples of concepts. They hold the chalkboards up when they've solved the problem or when they think an example illustrates a concept. They also write or draw their own examples on the chalkboards.
Student group work	Student pairs observe a science demonstration and write down as many observations of it as they can.

To examine this influence, let's return to David's work with his students.

> The next day, David begins by saying, "One of our goals for yesterday and throughout the year is to be able to examine evidence and conclusions. . . . You did a good job on this, but we need a little more practice. . . . I'm going to display the conclusions and evidence that some of you offered. . . . Now, remember the spirit we're doing this in. It's strictly for the sake of learning and improvement. It's not intended to criticize any of you. . . . I've covered up your names, so everyone can remain anonymous. . . . Let's take a look at what two groups wrote," as he displays the following on the document camera:
>
> Conclusion: The people had cloth.
>
> Evidence: There is cloth from Civilization A.
>
> Conclusion: The people in Civilization A were more likely to survive.
>
> Evidence: They had cows and sheep, so they didn't have to find wild animals. The cloth piece suggests that they wove cloth, so they didn't have to depend upon animal skins.
>
> "What comments can you make about the two sets of conclusions?"
>
> "The first one isn't really a conclusion," Shantae offers. "You can see the cloth, so it really doesn't say anything."
>
> "Good observation, Shantae. . . . Yes, a conclusion is a statement based on a fact; it isn't the fact itself."
>
> The class then discusses the second example and agrees that the conclusion is based on evidence.
>
> "This is the kind of thing we're looking for," David comments. "I know that you're all capable of this kind of thinking, so let's see it in your next writing sample."
>
> He then brings out several cans of soup and asks students to make conclusions about the civilization that might have produced such an artifact and to give evidence that supports each conclusion.
>
> The class, beginning to understand the process, makes a number of comments, and David writes the students' conclusions and supporting evidence on the board.

Assessment with detailed feedback is essential for learning, and collecting and reading the students' papers was a form of assessment. Because they had limited experience with forming conclusions based on evidence, without the assessment and accompanying feedback, David's students were unlikely to understand the difference between good and poor conclusions. The same is true for all forms of learning beyond simple memory tasks.

Detailed feedback on traditional assessments, such as tests and quizzes, is equally important. Frequently missed test and quiz items should be discussed in sufficient detail so students know why they missed the item. This may seem time consuming, but it's time well spent. If questions persist, students should be offered the opportunity to come in and discuss their tests and quizzes one-on-one.

Feedback is important for motivation because it helps students improve the quality of their work. As they see their quality increasing, their perceptions of competence, self-determination, and intrinsic motivation also increase. None of this is possible without ongoing assessment and feedback.

Classroom **Connections**

Using Instructional Variables to Promote Motivation to Learn

Introductory Focus

1. Introductory focus attracts students' attention and provides a conceptual umbrella for the lesson. Plan lesson introductions to capitalize on this variable.

   - **Elementary:** A fifth-grade teacher introduces a lesson on measuring by bringing in a cake recipe and ingredients that have to be modified if everyone in the class is going to get a piece of cake. He says, "We want to make enough cake so we can all get a piece. This is what we're going to figure out today."

   - **Middle School:** A physical science teacher begins her lessons with a simple demonstration, such as whirling a cup of water suspended on the end of a string around her head. "Why doesn't the water fly out of the cup? . . . Let's try to figure this out," she says in beginning the lesson.

   - **High School:** An English teacher introduces *A Raisin in the Sun* (Hansberry, 1959) by saying, "Think about a Muslim family in Detroit. How do you think they felt after the events of 9/11? Keep those questions in mind as we read *A Raisin in the Sun*."

Personalization

2. Personalization uses intellectually or emotionally relevant examples to illustrate a topic. Personalize content to create links between content and students' lives.

   - **Elementary:** A fourth-grade teacher begins a lesson comparing animals with exoskeletons and those with endoskeletons by having students squeeze their legs to demonstrate that their bones are inside. He then passes out a number of crayfish and has the students compare the crayfish to themselves.

   - **Middle School:** A seventh-grade teacher begins a lesson on percentages by bringing in an ad for computer games and products from a local newspaper. The ad says "10% to 25% off marked prices." The class works problems to see how much they might save on popular computer games.

   - **High School:** As her class studies the Vietnam War, a history teacher asks students to interview someone who served in the military at the time. The class uses the results of the interviews to remind themselves of the "human" dimension of the war.

Involvement

3. Involvement describes the extent to which students are actively participating in a lesson. Promote high levels of involvement in all learning activities.

   - **Elementary:** Each day a second-grade teacher passes out a sheet with 20 math facts on it. The students quickly write the answers and then score the sheets. Students who improve their scores from the previous day or get all 20 facts correct receive a bonus point on their math averages.

   - **Middle School:** A seventh-grade prealgebra teacher assigns students to work in pairs to complete seatwork assignments. He requires them to work each problem individually, then check with each other, and ask for help if they can't agree on the solution.

   - **High School:** An English teacher randomly calls on all students as equally as possible, whether or not they raise their hands. At the beginning of the year, he explains that his intent is to encourage participation, and that students will soon get over any uneasiness about being "put on the spot." He prompts students who are unable to answer until they give an acceptable response.

Feedback

4. Feedback provides students with information about their learning progress. Provide prompt and informative feedback about learning progress.

   - **Elementary:** A fourth-grade teacher discusses the most frequently missed items on each of her homework assignments and quizzes, providing detailed information about each of the items.

   - **Middle School:** A seventh-grade teacher writes on a student paper, "You have some very good ideas. Now you need to rework your essay so that it is grammatically correct. Look at the notes I've made on your paper."

   - **High School:** A world history teacher displays an "ideal answer" on the document camera for each of the items on his homework assignments and essay items on his tests. Students compare their answers to the ideal and take notes with suggestions for improving their responses.

Developmentally Appropriate **Practice**

Applying the Model for Promoting Student Motivation with Learners at Different Ages

The components of the model for promoting student motivation apply to learners at all grade levels. For example, caring teachers, a safe and orderly environment, success, and high levels of student involvement are essential for all students. Developmental differences exist, however. We outline these differences in this section.

Working with Students in Early Childhood Programs and Elementary Schools

Elementary students enter school wide-eyed and optimistic, with only vague ideas about what they will do or learn. However, school is often the first time they are separated from their homes and parents, and anxiety about the unfamiliar may result. Taking extra time to make classrooms inviting places to learn is important with these children.

Interest can be a powerful motivating factor for elementary students (Hidi, Renninger, & Krapp, 2004). Topics such as animals, cartoon characters, sports, dinosaurs, and fantasy are interesting for most children. Incorporating these topics into reading, writing, and math assignments can be effective.

Elementary students' ability to set goals and use learning strategies are largely undeveloped, but the beginnings of self-regulation can be established with conscious efforts to model and teach metacognition (Paris, Morrison, & Miller, 2006).

Working with Students in Middle Schools

Middle school students have become savvy about rules and procedures and the schooling "game." However, the transition to middle school can be challenging for adolescents, and both motivation and learning often suffer (Wigfield, Byrnes, & Eccles, 2006). Classes are usually larger and less personal, and students leave the security of one teacher for a schedule that sends them to different classrooms and teachers. Caring teachers who take the time to form personal relationships with their students are essential at this age.

Peers become increasingly important during the middle school years, and cooperative learning and group work become effective vehicles for increasing involvement and motivation. However, the growing influence of peers can result in off-task behaviors during group work, so structuring it carefully, monitoring students during activities, and holding students accountable for a product are important.

Variables such as challenge and task comprehension become more important than they were with elementary students. Middle school students also begin to assess the relevance and value of what they're studying, so personalization also becomes an increasingly important variable.

Working with Students in High Schools

Although more mature, many high school students still have not reached a high level of self-regulation. Modeling self-regulation and conscious efforts to teach more sophisticated and effective learning strategies can help these students meet their needs for self-determination (Pressley & Hilden, 2006).

High school students are also self-aware and are thinking about their futures after high school, so they frequently assess the value of the topics they study. In addition, high school students' needs for competence and autonomy are prominent. As a result, climate variables, such as challenge and task comprehension, and instructional variables, such as personalization and feedback, become increasingly important.

chapter

11 Summary

1. Describe the differences between a mastery-focused and a performance-focused classroom.
   - Mastery-focused classrooms emphasize effort and increased understanding. Performance-focused classrooms emphasize demonstrating high ability and comparisons among students.
   - Mastery-focused environments increase student motivation to learn, whereas performance-focused environments can detract from motivation to learn for all but the highest achievers.

2. Describe the personal qualities of teachers who increase students' motivation to learn.
   - Teachers who are high in personal teaching efficacy believe that they can help students learn, regardless of students' prior knowledge or other factors.
   - Modeling courtesy and respect is essential for motivation, and communicating genuine interest in the topics they teach demonstrates teacher enthusiasm.
   - Teachers demonstrate that they care about their students by spending personal time with them and demonstrating respect for each individual. Holding students to high standards is one of the most effective ways to simultaneously show respect and communicate that teachers expect all students to succeed.

3. Identify the learning climate variables that increase students' motivation to learn.
   - Motivating environments are safe, secure, and orderly places that focus on learning.
   - Success on tasks that students perceive as challenging increases motivation to learn. Meeting challenges provides evidence that competence is increasing and leads to feelings of autonomy.
   - In motivating environments, students understand what they're expected to learn. Understanding what they're learning and why increases perceptions of autonomy and contributes to task value.

4. Explain how different instructional variables increase students' motivation to learn.
   - Teachers can increase motivation to learn by beginning lessons with examples, activities, or questions that attract students' attention and provide frameworks for information that follows.
   - Students maintain their attention and interest when teachers make content personally relevant to them and keep them involved in learning activities.
   - Teachers increase student motivation to learn by providing feedback about learning progress. When feedback indicates that competence is increasing, self-efficacy and self-determination both improve, and intrinsic motivation increases.

Preparing for **Your Licensure Exam**

Understanding Student Motivation

You will be required to take a licensure exam before you go into your own classroom. This exam will include information related to students' motivation, and it will include both multiple-choice and constructed-response questions. We include the following exercises to help you practice for the exam in your state. This book and these exercises will be a resource for you prepare for the exam.

We saw at the beginning of the chapter how DeVonne Lampkin taught the concept *arthropod*. Now read about a language arts lesson on the construction of paragraphs that DeVonne taught later that same day. After reading the case study, answer the questions that follow.

DeVonne is working with her fifth graders on their writing skills. She plans to have them practice writing paragraphs and conduct self-assessments using criteria in a 3-point rubric.

She begins, "Today, we're going to practice some more on composing good paragraphs. . . . Now, we know the characteristics of a good paragraph, but let's review for a moment. . . . What do we look for in a well-composed paragraph?"

"Topic sentence," several students say immediately.

"Okay, what else?"

"Sentences that go with the topic," others add.

"Yes, 'go with the topic' means that the sentences support your topic sentence. You need to have at least four supporting sentences."

DeVonne reminds students that they also need to use correct grammar and spelling, and then displays the following paragraphs:

Computers come in all shapes and sizes. One of the first computers, named UNIVAC, filled a room. Today, some large computers are as big as refrigerators. Others are as small as books. A few are even tiny enough to fit in a person's pocket.

Ann's family bought a new color television. It had a 54-inch screen. There were controls for color and brightness. Ann likes police stories. There were also controls for sound and tone.

After some discussion, the class concludes that the first example meets the criteria for an acceptable paragraph, but the second one does not, because the topic sentence doesn't have four supporting sentences and the information "Ann likes police stories" doesn't pertain to the topic.

She then says, "Now, you're going to write a paragraph on any topic that you choose, and then the class is going to grade your paper." DeVonne smiles as she hears several calls of "Woo-hoo" from the students.

The students go to work, and when they've finished, DeVonne says, "Okay, now we're going to grade the paragraphs." She reviews the criteria from the 3-point rubric, and then says, "Okay, who wants to go first?"

"Me!" several of the students shout.

"I should have known that," DeVonne smiles. "Okay, Tu, come on up."

Tu displays his paragraph on the document camera and reads it aloud:

The class discusses his paragraph, agrees that it deserves a 3, and then several students call out, "I want to go next! I want to go next!"

DeVonne asks Justin to display his paragraph:

There was a boy named Josh. He lives in a house with the roof falling in and the windows were broke. He had holes in the wall and the ceiling leaked when it rained. But then again it always rained and thunder over his house. Noone ever goes to his gate because he was so weird. They say he is a vampire.

She asks students to raise their hands to vote on the score for this paragraph. The students give it a mix of 2s and 1s.

"Samantha, why did you give it a 2?" DeVonne asks, beginning the discussion.

"He didn't stay on his topic. . . . He needs to stay on either the boy or the house," Samantha notes.

"Haajar? . . . You gave him a 1. . . . Go ahead."

"There was a boy named Josh, and then he started talking about the house. And then the weather and then the boy again," Haajar responds.

A few more students offered comments, and the class agrees that Justin's paragraph deserves a 1.5. DeVonne then asks for another volunteer.

"Me, me! I want to do mine!" several students exclaim with their hands raised. DeVonne calls on Saleina to display her paragraph, the students agree that it deserves a 3, and DeVonne then says, "I am so impressed with you guys. . . . Your work is excellent."

"Okay, let's do one more," DeVonne continues. "Joshua."

"No! No!" the students protest, wanting to continue the activity and have theirs read.

"Okay, one more after Joshua," DeVonne relents with a smile. The class assesses Joshua's paragraph and one more, and just before the end of the lesson, several students ask, "Are we going to get to do ours tomorrow?"

DeVonne smiles and assures them that they will get to look at the rest of the paragraphs the next day.

Questions for Case Analysis

In answering these questions, use information from the chapter, and link your responses to specific information in the case.

Multiple-Choice Questions

1. The students were very eager to display their paragraphs. Of the following, which variable in the model for promoting student motivation likely best explains why the students were so eager to display their paragraphs?

   a. Teacher modeling and enthusiasm

   b. Personalization

   c. Introductory focus

   d. Task comprehension

2. After each student displayed his or her paragraph, the class discussed the paragraph and then gave it a score of 3, 2, or 1. The variable in the model for promoting student motivation that is best illustrated by this process is:

   a. positive expectations.

   b. order and safety.

   c. task comprehension.

   d. feedback.

Constructed-Response Question

3. In spite of the fact that they were having their paragraphs publicly evaluated, DeVonne's students were very enthusiastic about displaying their work. Offer an explanation for their enthusiasm, including as many of the variables in the model for promoting student motivation as apply.

Important **Concepts**

caring
collective efficacy
high-quality examples
introductory focus

involvement
mastery-focused classroom
open-ended questions
order and safety

performance-focused
    classroom
personal teaching efficacy
personalization

positive learning
    climate
self-fulfilling prophecy
task comprehension

Classroom Management: Developing Self-Regulated Learners

Robert Daly/Getty Images

OUTLINE	LEARNING OUTCOMES
	After you've completed your study of this chapter, you should be able to:
Goals of Classroom Management Developing Learner Self-Regulation Creating a Community of Caring and Trust Maximizing Time for Teaching and Learning	**1.** Describe the goals of classroom management, and identify applications of the goals.
Planning for Classroom Management Planning for Instruction Planning for Classroom Management in Elementary Schools Planning for Classroom Management in Middle and Secondary Schools Planning for the First Days of School Educational Psychology and Teaching: Creating and Teaching Your Classroom Rules	**2.** Identify characteristics of elementary, middle, and secondary school students and how they influence planning for classroom management.
Communicating with Parents Benefits of Communication Strategies for Involving Parents	**3.** Describe effective communication strategies for involving parents.
Intervening When Misbehavior Occurs Emotional Factors in Interventions Cognitive Interventions Behavioral Interventions An Intervention Continuum Educational Psychology and Teaching: Responding Effectively to Misbehavior in Your Students	**4.** Use cognitive and behavioral learning theories to explain effective interventions.
Serious Management Problems: Defiance and Aggression Responding to Defiant Students Responding to Fighting Responding to Bullying Diversity: Classroom Management with Students from Diverse Backgrounds ▶ Developmentally Appropriate Practice: Classroom management with learners at different ages	**5.** Describe your legal and professional responsibilities in cases of aggressive acts and steps you can take to respond to defiance and aggression.

Classroom management includes all the actions teachers take to create an environment that supports academic learning, self-regulation, and social and emotional development. As the definition suggests, it's much more than simply creating an orderly classroom. Effectively done, it also promotes learning, motivation, and a sense of safety and security in students (Emmer & Evertson, 2013; Evertson & Emmer, 2013), and this is true across cultures, content areas, and grade levels (Adeyemo, 2013; Hochweber, Hosenfeld, & Klieme, 2013; Morris et al., 2013). Keep these ideas in mind as you read the following case study and see how Judy Harris, a middle school teacher, handles the classroom management incidents illustrated in it.

Judy's seventh-grade geography class is involved in a cultural unit on the Middle East.

As the students enter the room, they see a large map, together with the following directions displayed on the document camera.

Identify the longitude and latitude of Damascus and Cairo.

Judy's students begin each class by completing a review exercise while she takes roll and returns papers. They also pass their homework forward, each putting his or her paper on top of the stack.

Judy waits for the students to finish, and then begins, "About what latitude is Damascus, . . . Bernice?" as she walks down one of the rows.

". . . About 34 degrees north, I think," Bernice replies.

Judy's 30 students are in a room designed for 24, so the aisles are narrow, and as Judy walks past him, Darren reaches across the aisle and pokes Kendra with his pencil.

Darren watches Judy from the corner of his eye.

"Stop it, Darren," Kendra mutters loudly.

Judy turns, comes back up the aisle, stands near Darren, and continues, "Good, Bernice. It is close to 34 degrees.

"So, would it be warmer or colder than here in the summer? . . . Darren?" she asks, looking directly at him.

". . . Warmer, I think," Darren responds after Judy repeats the question for him, because he didn't initially hear it.

"Okay. Good. And why might that be the case? . . . Jim?"

As she waits for Jim to answer, Judy moves over to Rachel, who has been whispering to Deborah and playing with her cell phone, and kneels down so they are at eye level. She points to the rules displayed on a poster, and says quietly but firmly, "We agreed that it was important to listen when other people are talking, and you know that we all have to honor our agreements. . . . We can't learn when people aren't paying attention, and I'm uncomfortable when my class isn't learning."

"Damascus is south of us and also in a desert," Jim responds.

"Good, Jim. Now let's look at Cairo," Judy directs as she stands up and watches to ensure that Rachel is looking at the map.

Now, as you read this chapter, keep the following questions in mind:

1. What, specifically, did Judy do to create an environment that was orderly and simultaneously promoted student learning and development?
2. How can you establish and maintain a similar environment in your own classroom?

We answer these questions in this chapter.

Ed Psych and You

As you anticipate your first teaching position, what is your greatest concern? Why do you feel that way?

Goals of Classroom Management

If you're typical, *classroom management* is the answer to the first question we asked in *Ed Psych and You*. It was for both of us (Paul and Don, your authors) as we started our first jobs in the P–12 world, and most beginning teachers perceive it as their most serious challenge (Kaufman & Moss, 2010). It's also a major cause of teacher burnout and job dissatisfaction for veteran teachers (Evertson & Weinstein, 2006).

Administrators also understand the challenges involved in classroom management, and the ability to create and maintain orderly classrooms is one of the characteristics they most look for in teachers, a capability they rank above knowledge of content and teaching skills (Engel, 2013). And as has historically been the case, public opinion polls continue to identify it as one of schools' most challenging problems, with only inadequate funding ranked higher (Bushaw & Lopez, 2013).

The complexities of classrooms help us understand why creating orderly learning environments is so challenging (Doyle, 2006), and it helps answer the second question (*why* classroom management is likely your greatest concern) we asked in *Ed Psych and You*. For example, Judy had to deal with Darren's and Rachel's misbehavior while simultaneously maintaining the flow of her lesson. And to prevent the incident between Darren and Kendra from escalating, she needed to immediately react to Darren while simultaneously deciding if she should intervene in the case of Rachel's whispering and off-task behavior. Also, had she reprimanded Kendra instead of Darren—the perpetrator of the incident—it would have suggested that she didn't know what was going on in her class.

To accommodate this complexity and to create a classroom that facilitates "academic learning, self-regulation, and social and emotional development," the major goals of classroom management include:

- Developing learner self-regulation.
- Creating a community of caring and trust.
- Maximizing time for teaching and learning.

We discuss them next.

Developing Learner Self-Regulation

Teachers frequently lament students' lack of effort and willingness to take responsibility for their own learning.

> "My kids are so irresponsible," Kathy Hughes grumbles to her friend and colleague, Mercedes Blount, in a conversation at lunch. "They don't bring their books, they forget their notebooks in their lockers, they come without pencils. . . . I can't get them to come to class prepared, let alone get them to read their assignments."
>
> "I know," Mercedes responds, smiling wryly. "Some of them are totally spacey, and others just don't seem to give a rip."

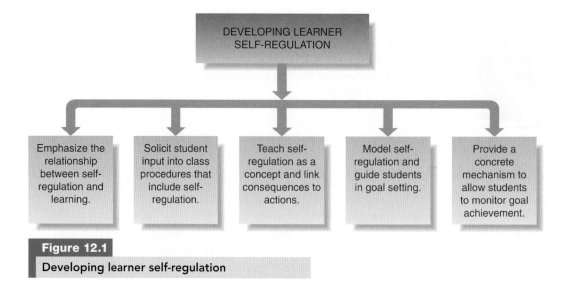

Figure 12.1

Developing learner self-regulation

The solution to this problem, while not simple or easy, is the development of student **self-regulation**, which is the ability to direct and control our actions and emotions (Berk, 2013). Self-regulation is multifaceted and includes:

- *Self-motivation*—taking responsibility for completing tasks and engaging in appropriate activities
- *Delay of gratification*—forgoing immediate rewards to gain more substantial ones later
- *Impulse control*—resisting urges to display inappropriate behaviors
- *Emotional regulation*—expressing emotions in socially appropriate ways
- *Self-socialization*—understanding society's standards of behavior and acting in accordance with those standards
- *Self-regulated learning*—setting personal learning goals together with the thinking and strategies used to reach these goals

Developing self-regulation takes time and effort, and students need a great deal of support to develop it (Bohn, Roehrig, & Pressley, 2004). Suggestions for providing your students with the assistance they need to develop self-regulation are outlined in Figure 12.1 and illustrated in the case study that follows.

Let's see how Sam Cook, a middle school math teacher, attempts to apply the suggestions in Figure 12.1 with his students.

Sam begins the first day of school by welcoming his students, having them introduce themselves, and then saying, "To learn as much as possible, we need to work together and support each other. For instance, I need to bring the examples and materials that will help you understand our topics. . . . That's my part. . . . So, what is your part?"

With some guidance from Sam, the students conclude that they should bring their books and other materials to class each day. They also realize that they need to be in their seats when the bell rings, listen until their classmates finish talking, support their classmates' efforts, and attempt to understand their homework instead of merely doing it.

"Now, who is responsible for all this?" Sam asks.

"We are," several students respond.

"Yes. . . . I'm responsible for my part, and you're responsible for your parts.

"Now, let's see what happens when people aren't responsible," Sam says, displaying the following on the document camera:

Josh brings all his materials to school every day, and he carefully does his homework. He has a list that he checks off to be sure that he has each of the items and that he understands his homework. If he's uncertain about any part, he asks the next day. He participates in class discussions and is supportive when his classmates talk.

Josh is learning a lot, and he says his classes are interesting. His teachers respect his effort.

Andy gets in trouble with his teachers because he often forgets to bring his book, notebook, or pencil to class. He sometimes forgets his homework, so he doesn't get credit for the assignment, and he isn't learning very much. Andy also snaps at his classmates in discussions, and sometimes hurts their feelings. Now some of the other students don't want to talk to him.

Andy's teacher called his mom to discuss his behavior and lack of responsibility, and now Andy can't watch TV for a week.

"What are some differences you notice between Josh and Andy?" Sam asks after giving students a minute to read the vignettes.

The students make several comments, and in the process, Ronise concludes, "It's his own fault," in response to someone pointing out that Andy isn't learning very much and not getting along with the other students.

"Yes," Sam nods, "if we don't take responsibility for ourselves and control our own actions and emotions, whose fault is it if we don't learn?"

"Our own," several students respond.

"Yes," Sam emphasizes. "We're all responsible for ourselves."

With Sam's guidance, the students set goals that will help them take responsibility and control themselves, and the next day, he distributes a monitoring sheet (see Figure 12.2), which he has prepared based on the discussion. He has them put the sheet in the front of their notebooks and check off the items the first thing each morning. As the sheets accumulate, the students have a "self-regulation portfolio" that gives them a record of their progress.

Sam then asks the students how they will determine whether they understand their homework, and they agree that they will either explain it in class or to their parents. Finally, they decide that each week the students who get 18 or more checks for the self-regulation goals and 8 or more for the learning goals will have free time on Fridays. Those with fewer than 15 checks on the self-regulation goals will spend "quiet time" alone during that period, and those with fewer than 8 checks for the learning goals will work with Sam on areas that need improvement.

Now, let's see how Sam attempted to apply the suggestions in Figure 12.1. First, he emphasized from the beginning of the year that they were in school to learn and that self-regulation was necessary if they were to learn as much as possible. Second, he asked for students' input into class procedures, which increases the likelihood that students will follow them. Further, being asked to provide input promotes students' feelings of autonomy, a basic psychological need for all of us according to self-determination theory (Ryan & Deci, 2000; Deci & Ryan, 2008).

Third, Sam treated self-regulation as a concept, and he illustrated it with an example (Josh) and nonexample (Andy). Students often aren't self-regulated simply because they don't realize that they're behaving irresponsibly or are failing to control their impulses and emotions. Also, they sometimes don't recognize the relationship between their actions and the consequences of those actions. By illustrating the consequences of being—or not being—self-regulated, Sam helped promote this awareness and understanding (Charles & Senter, 2012).

Week of _____ Name _____					
Self-Regulation Goals	Monday	Tuesday	Wednesday	Thursday	Friday
Bring sharpened pencil					
Bring notebook					
Bring textbook					
In seat when bell rings					
Listen while a classmate is speaking					
Extend courtesy and respect					
Learning Goals	Monday	Tuesday	Wednesday	Thursday	Friday
Finish homework					
Understand homework					

Figure 12.2

Monitoring sheet

Fourth, in saying, "To learn as much as possible, we need to work together and support each other. For instance, I need to bring the examples and materials that will help you understand our topics. . . . That's my part," he personally modeled responsibility, and he also guided his students as they set goals. And finally, he prepared a concrete mechanism (the monitoring sheet) to help his students track their progress toward their goals. We want our students to gradually accept responsibility for following these procedures and also learn to make decisions that will increase their own learning. Doing so marks progress on the path to self-regulation.

Sam's students initially met goals to receive rewards (free time) and avoid punishers (quiet time alone during the free period). As self-regulation develops, his students hopefully will begin setting their own goals because they see that setting and monitoring goals increase learning.

Regardless of how hard you try, some of your students will periodically misbehave and fail to accept responsibility, as you saw with Darren and Rachel in Judy's class. However, for students who do become self-regulated, you will have made a lifelong contribution to their learning and overall well-being.

Creating a Community of Caring and Trust

As you saw in the definition of classroom management, it should support academic and social–emotional learning. We can promote both by creating a **community of caring and trust**, a classroom environment in which learners feel physically and emotionally safe and their needs for belonging and relatedness are met (Watson & Battistich, 2006). "This requires a school and classroom climate in which students can afford to be emotionally vulnerable, and in which that vulnerability extends to the student's willingness to risk engagement in acts of kindness and concern for others" (Nucci, 2006, p. 716). In addition, we want our students to feel emotionally connected to us and their classmates and worthy of love and respect (O'Connor, Dearing, & Collins, 2011).

Teachers are at the core of communities of caring and trust (Jones, Jones, & Vermete, 2013). We communicate caring by spending time with our students; by demonstrating that we're committed to them both as learners and as people; and by modeling prosocial behaviors, such as courtesy, respect, and fairness, and expecting the same in return. And systematically teaching self-regulation, as you saw with Sam and his students, creates an environment in which caring and a sense of community can develop (Watson & Ecken, 2003).

Maximizing Time for Teaching and Learning

When students' self-regulation develops and a community of caring and trust is created, disruptions and misbehavior decrease, so we have more time to devote to teaching and learning, the third goal of classroom management.

But "time" isn't as simple as it appears on the surface, and different types exist. They include:

- Allocated time—the amount of time a teacher or school designates for a content area or topic, such as elementary schools' allocating an hour a day to math or middle and secondary schools' having 55-minute periods.
- Instructional time—the amount of time left for teaching after routine management and administrative tasks are completed.
- Engaged time—the amount of time students are paying attention and involved in learning activities.
- Academic learning time—the amount of time students are successful while engaged in learning activities.

When reformers suggest lengthening the school day or year, they're suggesting an increase in allocated time. Its value, however, depends on how efficiently it's used. For instance, the benefits of increased allocated time are reduced if instructional time is lost because we have to deal with misbehavior; engaged time is lost if students aren't paying attention; or academic learning time is decreased because students are confused and unsuccessful.

The ideal we strive for is to maximize instructional, engaged, and academic learning time so that as much of our allocated time as possible is devoted to teaching and learning. Although all teachers must spend some time on routine activities, such as taking roll and collecting homework, we try to come as close as possible to this ideal. For example, Judy gave her students a review exercise to complete while she took roll and handed back papers. The exercise activated students' prior knowledge, focused their attention on the day's topic, and eliminated noninstructional time when disruptions are most common. She also maintained the flow of her lesson—so she didn't lose instructional time—while simultaneously dealing with both Darren's and Rachel's misbehavior.

Her actions begin to answer the first question we asked at the beginning of the chapter: "What, specifically, did Judy do to create an environment that was orderly and simultaneously promoted student learning and development?" She maximized the time available for learning.

The different types of time help us understand why classroom management is so essential for motivation and learning. A long history of research suggests that students learn more in orderly classrooms (Good & Brophy, 2008; Hochweber et al., 2013), and this research is consistent for different age groups (Morris et al., 2013), content areas (Adeyemo, 2013), and cultural groups (Adeyemo, 2013; Balagna, Young, & Smith, 2013). In classrooms where students are engaged and successful, achievement is high, learners feel a sense of competence and self-efficacy, and interest in the topics increases (Good & Brophy, 2008).

Planning for Classroom Management

Some of the earliest research examining classroom management was conducted by Jacob Kounin (1970), who found that the key to orderly classrooms is a teacher's ability to prevent management problems before they occur, rather than focusing on **discipline**, responses to misbehavior after they happen. His findings have been consistently corroborated over the years (Brophy, 2006; Hochweber et al., 2013).

Our goal should be to prevent as many management problems as possible, leaving fewer incidents of misbehavior to deal with later. This requires planning, and beginning teachers tend to underestimate the amount of time and energy it takes. Because they don't plan carefully enough to prevent problems, they often find themselves responding to misbehavior, which increases their uncertainty about classroom management (Reupert & Woodcock, 2010). We discuss planning for classroom management in the sections that follow. However, because classroom management and effective instruction are so interdependent, we first briefly consider planning for instruction.

Ed Psych and You

As you reflect on your experiences as a student, in which classes are you most likely to pay attention to your instructor? In which are you most likely to drift off, perhaps text a friend, or even chat with the person next to you?

Planning for Instruction

Think about the questions we ask here in *Ed Psych and You* and also about Judy's work with her students. Typically, we're most likely to drift off, text, or talk to a neighbor if our instructor stands at the front of the class droning on in a lecture. "Dry lessons with limited opportunities for students to participate are boring and erode students' motivation; this is when management problems begin" (Evertson & Emmer, 2013, p. 102). This was certainly true when we—Paul and Don—were students, and you've likely had similar experiences. In Judy's case, it would have been virtually impossible for her to maintain an orderly and learning-focused classroom if her instruction had been ineffective. "Walk the halls of any school, and you'll find that it's not the strictest teacher with the most rules, but the personable teacher with the most interesting and challenging lesson plan that has the best behaved students" (Kraft, 2010, p. 45).

This suggests that as we plan for classroom management, we must simultaneously plan for effective instruction (Good & Brophy, 2008; Greenberg, Putman, & Walsh, 2014). The close link between management and instruction has been consistently corroborated by research, and it is true whether we plan to teach in elementary, middle, or high schools (Gay, 2006).

Expert teachers plan for several factors (Greenberg et al., 2014). They include:

- Being very clear about our learning goals, preparing examples or representations of the topics we're planning to teach, and having these and other learning materials ready so instruction can begin immediately. For instance, Judy's map was displayed when her students walked into the classroom, and Sam had his vignettes prepared and waiting when he began his instruction.
- Planning to involve students to maximize the likelihood that they will maintain their attention. For instance, as soon as they finished their warm-up activity, Judy immediately began involving her students with her questions.

- Starting classes and activities on time. For instance, Judy had a warm-up activity waiting for the students when they walked in the room. Having a task waiting for students helps eliminate "dead time" when disruptions are most likely to occur.
- Creating well-established routines. Judy had established the routine of students completing a warm-up activity every day when they came into the room, so they began the activity without being told to do so. Routines help establish equilibrium for students, and they reduce the cognitive load on both teachers' and students' working memories.
- Making transitions quickly and smoothly. This includes seating members of groups near each other, so they merely have to turn slightly in their seats to move from whole-group to small-group activities and back again. If students have to get up from their chairs to move back and forth from group work, time is wasted, and disruptions are more likely. Also, clear and precise directions for seatwork decrease the likelihood of disruptions, because students know what they're expected to do in the small-group activity.

Having planned carefully for instruction, we turn now to the specific planning challenges for classroom management at different grade levels. We begin with elementary classrooms.

Planning for Classroom Management in Elementary Schools

Regardless of whether you're preparing to teach in elementary, middle, or high schools, a clear system of **rules**, standards for acceptable behavior, and **procedures**, guidelines for accomplishing recurring tasks, such as turning in papers and making transitions from one activity to another, will be the core of your classroom management system (Emmer & Evertson, 2013; Evertson & Emmer, 2013; Greenberg et al., 2014). However, if you're preparing to teach in an elementary school, preparing rules and procedures will be different than if you're working with older students. To understand why, let's look at one intern's experience with first graders.

> Jim Cramer, an elementary education major, is beginning his internship in a first-grade classroom. It's a disaster. Students get up from their seats and wander around the room. They begin playing with materials at their desks while he is trying to explain a topic. They argue about their roles in cooperative learning activities. Reminders to pay attention have no effect. They're not destructive or intentionally misbehaving; they're little kids. His directing teacher has a rather laissez faire approach to classroom management, and the lack of focus in her classroom doesn't seem to bother her.

The characteristics of young children help us understand why Jim's first experience didn't go well.

CHARACTERISTICS OF ELEMENTARY STUDENTS

As we know, young children's thinking tends to focus on the concrete and tangible, and their attention spans are limited (Jiang, Swallow, & Rosenbaum, 2013; Piaget, 1970; Zhou, Hofer, & Eisenberg, 2007). Socially and emotionally, they are eager to please their teachers and are vulnerable to criticism and harsh treatment (Carter & Doyle, 2006).

Developing a sense of personal autonomy as they move from their family to the school setting is one of the most important tasks young children face. An orderly and predictable school environment is important, because it mirrors the stability they—

hopefully—experience in the home. For children who don't have this structure and stability, an orderly classroom can be a stabilizing force that helps build a sense of trust and security (Watson & Ecken, 2003).

Young children need enough freedom to develop initiative but sufficient structure to maintain their sense of equilibrium. As they progress through the elementary grades, they continue to need acceptance and the recognition that helps them develop a sense of industry and self-assurance. This is a challenge. "It is difficult to meet the misbehaving child's needs for autonomy, belonging, and competence, and also maintain a safe and productive classroom" (Watson & Ecken, 2003, p. 3).

Our rules and procedures help us meet this challenge. We turn to them next.

RULES AND PROCEDURES IN ELEMENTARY CLASSROOMS: THE THEORETICAL FRAMEWORK

As with most aspects of learning and teaching, creating and implementing rules and procedures in elementary classrooms are grounded in cognitive learning theory. "People want their experiences to make sense" is arguably the most basic principle of cognitive learning theory, which means that first, and most important, if they are to be effective, our rules and procedures must make sense to our students. This means that they must be understandable and provide the behavioral support needed to help students reach learning goals. For instance, one elementary teacher had the following rules:

- We raise our hands before speaking.
- We listen when someone else is talking.
- We leave our seats only when given permission by the teacher.
- We stand politely in line at all times.
- We keep our hands to ourselves.

These rules make sense. For instance, waiting to speak, listening while a classmate is talking, and remaining in seats until given permission help maximize time for learning and contribute to self-regulation, both goals of classroom management. Standing politely and keeping hands to themselves contribute to social and emotional development, an important goal of classroom management. The opposite is also true. For instance, blurting out answers or comments indicates a lack of self-regulation, and failing to listen while a classmate is talking demonstrates a form of insensitivity to classmates that detracts from the social–emotional learning important in elementary classrooms.

Research provides further evidence for the importance of rules in promoting social and emotional development. For example, researchers have found that implementing a rule preventing the exclusion of classmates promoted social acceptance to a greater extent than did individual efforts to help the excluded children (Harriet & Bradley, 2003).

The rules above are merely examples, and you will make your own decisions about your rules when you begin teaching. Most important, your rules must make sense to your students to promote the academic learning, self-regulation, and social and emotional development so important in elementary classrooms.

Second, we must keep the number of rules and procedures small enough to keep the cognitive load on our students' working memories manageable. Too many can overload students' working memories—particularly for elementary students—so they often break rules, or fail to follow procedures, because they simply forget.

Third, we know that automaticity—the ability to perform an action essentially without thinking about it—is important for reducing cognitive load. This means that procedures, such as turning in papers and lining up for lunch, must be practiced to the point that students perform them without thinking about it. For instance, because Judy's students completed a warm-up activity every day when they began class, they immediately began the activity without Judy having to remind them to do so.

Judy teaches in a middle school. Let's look at an elementary teacher's efforts.

Martha Oakes, a first-grade teacher, is helping her students understand the procedure for putting away worksheets.

"I put each of their names, and my own, on cubby holes on the wall of my room. Then, while they were watching, I did a short worksheet myself and walked over and put it in my storage spot, while saying out loud, 'I'm finished with my worksheet. . . . What do I do now? . . . I need to put it in my cubby hole. If I don't put it there, my teacher can't check it, so it's very important. . . . Now, I start on the next assignment.'

"Then I gave my students the same worksheet, directing them to take it to their cubbies, quietly and individually, as soon as they were finished. After everyone was done, we spent a few minutes discussing the reasons for taking the finished work to the cubbies immediately, not touching or talking to anyone as they move to the cubbies and back to their desks, and starting right back to work. Then I gave them another worksheet, asked them what they were going to do and why, and had them do it. We then spent a few more minutes talking about what might happen if we didn't put papers where they belong.

"We have a class meeting nearly every day just before we leave for the day. We discuss classroom life and offer suggestions for improvement. Some people might be skeptical about whether or not first graders can handle meetings like this, but they can. This is also one way I help them keep our rules and procedures fresh in their minds."

We can see how Martha's approach is grounded in cognitive learning theory. First, she modeled the process for taking worksheets to the cubbies, used cognitive modeling in verbalizing what she was doing, and had the students practice doing the same. Being specific and concrete was essential for Martha's students because they're first graders, and these actions provided the concrete examples they needed to construct their understanding of the process and promote self-regulation. With enough practice, the procedure will become automatic, which will reduce the cognitive load on both Martha and the children.

We offer specific suggestions for creating your own rules and procedures in the section "Educational Psychology and Teaching: Creating and Teaching Your Classroom Rules" later in the chapter.

ARRANGING THE PHYSICAL ENVIRONMENT IN ELEMENTARY CLASSROOMS

Because it is the space in which a variety of activities takes place, the physical environment in elementary classrooms plays an important role in classroom management (Evertson & Emmer, 2013; Weinstein & Romano, 2015). "You will facilitate these activities if you arrange your room to permit orderly movement, keep distractions to a minimum, and make efficient use of available space" (Evertson & Emmer, 2013, p. 13). Tables, chairs, cubbies, carpeted areas, plants, easels, building blocks, and shelves should physically accommodate whole-group, small-group, and individual study and should be flexible and adaptable to various instructional formats.

Although everyone's classroom will look different, several guidelines can help you as you think about your room arrangement (Evertson & Emmer, 2013):

- Be sure that all students can see the writing board, document camera or overhead projector, and other displays. If students have to move or crane their necks to see, disruptions are more likely.
- Design your room so you can see all your students. Monitoring their reactions to instruction is important for both learning and classroom management.
- Make sure that students can easily access commonly used materials without disrupting their classmates.
- Keep high-traffic areas free from obstructions, and provide ample space for student movement.

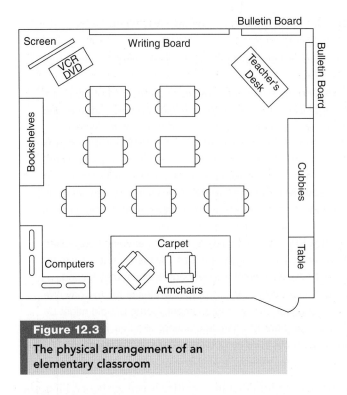

Figure 12.3

The physical arrangement of an elementary classroom

Figure 12.3 illustrates the physical arrangement of one elementary classroom. Note how it is designed to maximize these guidelines. This is merely an example, of course, and you may choose to arrange your classroom differently.

Planning for Classroom Management in Middle and Secondary Schools

Middle and secondary classes are populated by adolescents, and their developmental characteristics are different from those of elementary students. So, if you're preparing to be a middle or secondary teacher, you'll need to consider these characteristics as you plan. Let's take a look.

CHARACTERISTICS OF MIDDLE AND SECONDARY STUDENTS

As students move through school, several developmental trends become significant:

- The influence of peers increases.
- Needs for belonging and social acceptance increase.
- Search for a sense of identity begins.
- Desire for autonomy and independence increases.

Learning and motivation theories help us understand the implications of these developmental changes for classroom management. For example, social cognitive theory helps us understand how peers influence student behavior. Peers become important models, and students tend to imitate peers who are accomplished in academics, athletics, or even delinquency (Kidron & Fleischman, 2006). Vicarious reinforcement and punishment can be effective if peers believe that the reinforcers and punishers are fairly administered, that is, they make sense to the students. Judy's interventions with Darren and Rachel are examples. Their classmates could see that they were breaking rules the class had agreed upon and that Judy was enforcing the rules fairly.

Second, Maslow's work and self-determination theory remind us that belonging and relatedness are important to all students, and the need to be accepted by peers increases as students move into adolescence. This helps us understand why they tend to be conforming in their speech, dress, and behavior even if seemingly bizarre by adult standards. Peer rejection can lead to academic, personal, and social problems, which can then result in disruptive behavior (Wentzel, 2003). We promote feelings of belonging and relatedness in our students by communicating a genuine commitment to them, both as people and as learners, calling on all students as equally as possible, and enforcing rules forbidding students from mistreating each other (Kraft, 2010).

Third, adolescents are beginning their search for identity, and their needs for autonomy and independence increase. This can result in rebellious and seemingly capricious behavior, which can be frustrating. However, while attempting to exercise their newfound independence, adolescents need the stability and equilibrium that result from the firm hand of a caring teacher who sets clear limits for acceptable behavior.

RULES AND PROCEDURES IN MIDDLE AND SECONDARY CLASSROOMS: THE THEORETICAL FRAMEWORK

Much of the theoretical framework for rules and procedures in middle and secondary schools is the same as in elementary schools, but some differences exist. For instance, the need for rules and procedures to make sense to students is even more important as students mature, and perceptions of fairness, inequitable treatment, and teachers having "favorites" or "pets" increase. Because students are increasingly sensitive to these issues, understanding why rules exist and consistent enforcement of them become increasingly important.

Self-determination theory also identifies autonomy as a basic psychological need for all of us, and soliciting students' input into the formation of rules and procedures helps meet this need.

The following are rules from one seventh-grade class:

- Be in your seat and quiet when the bell rings.
- Follow directions the first time they're given.
- Bring covered textbooks, notebook, pen, pencils, and planner to class every day.
- Raise your hand for permission to speak or leave your seat.
- Keep hands, feet, and objects to yourself.
- Leave class only when dismissed by the teacher.

As with the examples of rules for elementary classrooms, these rules make sense, accommodate the developmental characteristics of middle school students, and help meet the goals of classroom management. For instance, middle school students tend to be "social," so the first rule accommodates this characteristic. And as students gradually learn to control their tendencies to socialize, follow directions, and take the responsibility for bringing necessary materials to class, their self-regulation develops. Similarly, keeping hands, feet, and objects to themselves also contributes to self-regulation and the social–emotional learning goals central to effective classroom management.

As in elementary classrooms, the specific rules you create will depend on your professional judgment. For example, the third rule might appear to be too specific to you, but this teacher noted that the specifics were necessary to ensure that her students actually brought the materials to class (J. Holmquist, personal communication, January 14, 2014).

As students move into high school, their behavior tends to stabilize, they communicate more effectively at an adult level, and they respond generally well to clear rationales.

The following are rules taken from a tenth-grade class:

- Do all grooming outside of class.
- Be in your seat before the bell rings.
- Stay in your seat at all times.
- Bring all materials daily. This includes your book, notebook, pen/pencil, and paper.
- Give your full attention to others in discussions, and wait your turn to speak.
- Leave when I dismiss you, not when the bell rings.

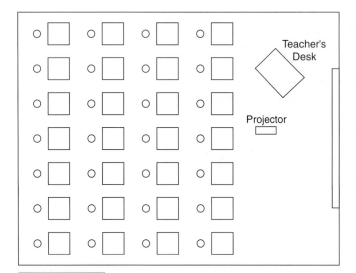

Figure 12.4

Classroom arrangement in traditional rows

Again, the rules are designed to accommodate the characteristics of older, more mature students. For example, older students sometimes obsess about their looks and decide, for example, to brush their hair in the middle of a class discussion, which explains, "Do all grooming outside of class." Rules requiring students to be in their seats when the bell rings, and stay in their seats, contribute to self-regulation. And listening attentively to their classmates contributes to the social and emotional learning that is so important.

ARRANGING THE PHYSICAL ENVIRONMENT IN MIDDLE AND SECONDARY CLASSROOMS

The physical environment in middle and secondary classrooms tends to be the more nearly traditional arrangement of desks in rows or in a semicircle facing the front of the room. Figures 12.4 and 12.5 illustrate these arrangements.

If you use a combination of whole-group and small-group instruction, you may want to arrange the room as you see in Figure 12.6, which helps simplify making transitions back and forth. Students are seated with their group mates so they don't have to move to get into their groups. Then, when the learning activity moves from small to whole group, students merely have to turn their heads to see you, the board, and the document camera or overhead.

No single room arrangement works for all situations. You will need to experiment and use the arrangement that works best for you. Specific guidelines for effective room arrangements in secondary schools include (Emmer & Evertson, 2013):

- Being sure the room arrangement is consistent with instructional goals.
- Keeping high-traffic areas free of congestion.
- Ensuring that you can easily see all your students and that all students can see instructional presentations and displays.
- Keeping frequently used materials and supplies readily accessible.

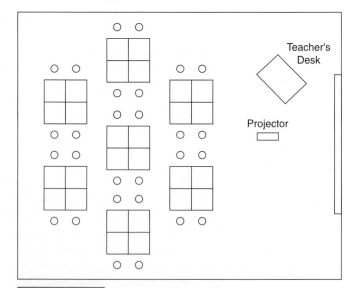

Figure 12.6

Sample seating arrangement for group work

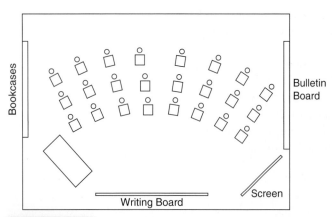

Figure 12.5

Classroom arrangement in a semicircle

PERSONALIZING YOUR CLASSROOM

Many classrooms, and particularly those in middle and secondary schools, are quite impersonal, and they reveal little about the people who spend time in them (Emmer & Evertson, 2013).

Our classrooms are more inviting if we post personal items, such as individual or class pictures, artwork, poetry, and other products prepared by students, on bulletin boards or posters. A section of a bulletin board can display names of students who improved from one test to another or some other form of recognition so all students have an equal chance of being honored.

We can also personalize our classrooms by involving students in decisions about its arrangement. If they know that the goal is promoting learning, and if self-regulation is stressed, their input provides a sense of ownership that increases their security, sense of belonging, and perceptions of autonomy.

Planning for the First Days of School

Research consistently indicates that the patterns of behavior for the entire year are established in the first few days of school (Gettinger & Kohler, 2006; Jones & Jones, 2013). In elementary schools, "the beginning of school is an important time for classroom management because your students will learn attitudes, behavior, and work habits that will affect the rest of the year" (Evertson & Emmer, 2013, p. 69). In middle and secondary schools, "the first few weeks of school are especially important for classroom management because during this time your students will learn behaviors and procedures needed throughout the year" (Emmer & Evertson, 2013, p. 64).

Let's look at the differences between two middle school teachers in how they begin their school year.

> Donnell Alexander is waiting at the door for her eighth graders with prepared handouts as students come in the room. As she distributes them, she says, "Take your seats quickly, please. You'll find your name on a desk. The bell is going to ring in less than a minute, and everyone needs to be at his or her desk and quiet when it does. Please read the handout while you're waiting."
>
> She is standing at the front of the room, surveying the class as the bell rings. When it stops, she begins, "Good morning, everyone."
>
> Vicki Williams, who also teaches eighth graders across the hall from Donnell, is organizing her handouts as the students come in the room. Some take their seats while others mill around, talking in small groups. As the bell rings, she looks up and says over the hum of the students, "Everyone take your seats, please. We'll begin in a couple minutes," and she turns back to organizing her materials.

In these first few minutes, Donnell's students learned that they were expected to be in their seats and ready to start at the beginning of class, whereas Vicki's learned just the opposite. Students quickly understand these differences, and unless Vicki changes this pattern, she will soon have problems, perhaps not dramatic, but chronic and low grade, like nagging sniffles that won't go away. Problems such as these cause more teacher stress and fatigue than any other (Friedman, 2006). Specific suggestions for the first few days include the following:

- *Establish expectations.* Hand out a description of the class requirements and your grading system the first day. Emphasize that all the decisions you make are intended to promote learning.
- *Plan structured instruction.* Begin your instruction with an eye-catching and motivating learning activity, and avoid group work for the first few days.

- *Teach rules and procedures.* Begin teaching your rules and procedures the first day of class, and discuss and practice the rules with extra frequency the first few days.
- *Begin communication with parents.* Write a letter to parents, which includes a description of your class requirements and rules and procedures, display it for your students, email it to parents, and request that they reply back to you. (If parents don't have access to email, give students a hard copy and have them return the letter with parents' signatures the following day.)

Establishing expectations and communicating with parents immediately demonstrates that you're in charge of your classroom and that you have your act together. Combined with effective instruction, nothing does more to prevent classroom management problems.

Educational Psychology and Teaching: Creating and Teaching Your Classroom Rules

As we've seen in the preceding sections, clear and specific rules and procedures help promote academic learning, self-regulation, and social and emotional development. Combined with effective instruction, they are the cornerstone of an effective classroom management system. The following guidelines can help in your efforts to create and teach rules effectively:

1. Create a small number of positively stated rules.
2. Solicit student input in the rule-setting process.
3. Emphasize rationales for rules.
4. Use concrete examples to illustrate rules and procedures.

(We focus on rules in this section, but the guidelines apply equally well to procedures.)

Let's do a flashback to the beginning of the school year to see how Judy Harris created and taught her rules:

> Judy begins by having students introduce themselves, including any personal information they would like to share, and she does the same.
>
> When they're finished, she says, "Our goal for this class is to learn about the geography of our world and how it impacts the way we live. In order to learn as much as possible, we need some rules that will guide the way we operate. So, think about some rules that make sense and are fair to all of us. . . . Go ahead, Jonique."
>
> ". . . We should listen," Jonique offers after pausing for several seconds.
>
> The class agrees that the rule makes sense, Judy writes it on the board, and then asks, "Why is this rule so important?"
>
> ". . . It's rude if we don't listen to each other or if we interrupt when someone is talking," Enita offers.
>
> "Of course," Judy smiles. "What's the very most important reason?"
>
> "To learn," Antonio responds, remembering what Judy said at the beginning of the discussion.
>
> "Absolutely, that's what school is all about. We learn less if we don't listen. . . . And we're all responsible for our own behavior, so this will also help us meet that goal. . . . And listening attentively is a part of treating everyone with courtesy and respect."
>
> The students agree that they all want to be treated courteously, Judy writes it on the board, and she continues to lead the discussion until the rules you see below appear on the list.

In each case she emphasizes why the rule is important, how it will increase learning, and why it will increase their ability to take responsibility for their own behavior.

Particularly during the first few weeks of school, and then throughout the year, when an incident occurs, such as one student interrupting another, Judy stops what they are doing, reminds the class of the rule, and again asks the students why it's important. The students gradually adapt to the rules and become acclimated to the classroom environment.

Let's look now at Judy's attempts to apply the guidelines.

Create a Small Number of Positively Stated Rules. The first guideline is illustrated in the rules themselves: She created only five and she stated them positively. A small number decreases the cognitive load on students' working memories and increases the likelihood that students will remember the rules. As we said earlier, students commonly break rules—particularly in elementary schools—because they simply forget.

Stating rules positively is grounded in cognitive learning theory: the rules establish expectations for students, which they can encode in their long-term memories as schemas. Negatively stated rules merely identify what students are "not to do" and don't contribute to schema construction. Also, stating rules positively helps promote a classroom environment that supports self-regulation and the social and emotional development we are trying to nurture.

Solicit Student Input. Judy applied the second guideline—solicit student input in the rule-setting process—when she said, "In order to learn as much as possible, we need some rules that will guide the way we operate. So, think about some rules that make sense and are fair to all of us. . . . Go ahead, Jonique." Being asked for input creates social contracts that can increase moral development, students' feelings of autonomy, and motivation to learn (Brophy, 2010; Deci & Ryan, 2008; Ryan & Deci, 2000). This guideline is more important at the middle and secondary level than in elementary schools, and some teachers choose to create effective rules and procedures without student input (Carter & Doyle, 2006). We endorse the process, particularly at the middle and secondary levels, because it reinforces the message that students are responsible for their actions.

Emphasize Rationales for Rules. As we said earlier, the need to make sense of our experiences is arguably the most basic principle of cognitive learning theory, and providing rationales for rules helps students make sense of them. If, for example, we emphasize that *learning* in all its forms is the reason we're in school, and students understand that blurting out answers and comments detracts from learning, they are more likely to regulate their behavior and refrain from speaking without permission because the rule makes sense to them. And if the rule makes sense, they're more likely to obey it.

Let's look again at some of the dialogue to see how Judy applied this guideline.

> Judy: Why is this rule [to listen] so important?
>
> Enita: It's rude if we don't listen to each other or if we interrupt when someone is talking.
>
> Judy: Of course. . . . What's the very most important reason?
>
> Antonio: To learn.

As we can see from this brief dialogue, providing rationales is easy to do; we merely discuss why the rule is important. It doesn't take much time, and the benefits can be greater than we might expect.

Whether or not you solicit student input into the rule-making process, providing reasons (rationales) for rules is essential. Without reasons, students might view rules as arbitrary, or even punitive, which increases the likelihood that they will disobey the rules.

Use Concrete Examples to Illustrate Rules and Procedures. Judy applied the final guideline by using classroom incidents that occurred during the normal course of learning activities to illustrate rules. As an example, let's review a brief excerpt from the case study at the beginning of the chapter.

> As she waits for Jim to answer, Judy moves over to Rachel, who has been whispering to Deborah and playing with her cell phone, and kneels down so they are at eye level. She points to the rules displayed on a poster, and says quietly but firmly, "We agreed that it was important to listen when other people are talking, and you know that we all have to honor our agreements. . . . We can't learn when people aren't paying attention."

Here, Judy used Rachel's off-task behavior as an opportunity to reinforce the rule "Listen attentively when someone else is talking." Using examples in this way can be very effective because they're immediate, concrete, and personal. In time, students will construct understanding of the rule and disruptions will gradually decrease.

Also, you saw earlier how Martha Oakes had her first graders practice the procedure for putting worksheets in their cubbies. Concrete examples such as these help students construct their understanding of the procedures, just as they construct understanding of any concept.

Classroom Connections

Planning and Teaching Rules and Procedures in Classrooms

Planning Rules and Procedures

1. Effective classroom management begins with planning. Carefully plan your rules and procedures before you meet your first class.

   - Elementary: A third-grade teacher prepares a handout for his students and their parents and gives it to his students the first day of school. The students take the handout home, have their parents sign it, and return it the next day.

   - Middle School: A prealgebra teacher prepares a short written list of rules before she starts class on the first day. She plans to ask her students to suggest additional rules that will increase everyone's opportunity to learn.

   - High School: An English teacher prepares a description of his procedures for the way writing drafts will be handled and how his class will use peer comments to improve essays. He displays and discusses the procedure the first day of class.

Teaching Rules and Procedures

2. The developmental characteristics of students influence teachers' management strategies. Consider the developmental level of your students when teaching rules and procedures.

- **Elementary:** At the beginning of the school year, a first-grade teacher takes a few minutes each day to have her students practice procedures such as turning in materials and lining up for lunch. She continues having them practice until students follow the procedures without being reminded.

- **Middle School:** A sixth-grade teacher has a rule that says, "Treat everyone with respect." She offers specific examples and asks students to discuss whether or not the examples illustrate treating everyone with respect.

- **High School:** A chemistry teacher takes a full class period to teach safe lab procedures. She models correct procedures, explains the reasons for them, and carefully monitors students as they work in the lab.

Communicating with Parents

Students' home environments have a powerful influence on both learning and classroom management, so involving parents in their children's life at school is essential (Adamski, Fraser, & Peiro, 2013; O'Connor et al., 2011). And classrooms with large numbers of students from diverse backgrounds present unique communication challenges (Walker & Hoover-Dempsey, 2006). Lower parent participation in school activities is often associated with families who are members of cultural minorities, are lower in socioeconomic status, or have a child enrolled in either special education or programs for students who are English learners (ELs) (Hong & Ho, 2005). You will need to make special efforts to initiate and maintain home–school communication with these parents (Zaragoza, 2005).

Benefits of Communication

Students benefit from home–school cooperation in several ways, such as more positive attitudes and higher long-term achievement, better attendance, greater self-regulation, and increased enrollment in postsecondary education (Hong & Ho, 2005; Sheldon, 2007).

These outcomes result from a variety of influences. For instance, some research indicates that when parents are involved, their children are more motivated in school, partially to please their parents. And because of students' increased motivation, their achievement also increases (Cheung & Pomerantz, 2012). Other research suggests that parents' participation in school activities, higher expectations for their children, and teachers' increased understanding of learners' home environments contribute to students' higher achievement (Adamski et al., 2013). Some research suggests that parental involvement can even increase students' cognitive ability (Phillipson & Phillipson, 2012).

Parent–teacher collaboration also has benefits for us as teachers. For example, teachers who encourage parental involvement report more positive feelings about teaching and their school and rate parents higher in helpfulness and follow-through (Weinstein & Romano, 2015).

Strategies for Involving Parents

All schools have formal communication channels, such as open houses—usually occurring within the first 2 weeks of the year—when teachers introduce themselves and describe their policies; interim progress reports, which tell parents about their youngsters' achievements at the midpoint of each grading period; parent–teacher conferences; and, of course, report cards. These processes are school-wide and valuable, but you can go well beyond them. Let's see how Jacinta Escobar attempts to increase communication with her students' parents.

Every year, as soon as she's able to access the email addresses of her students' parents, Jacinta creates an email list and prepares a letter stating that she expects to have a productive and exciting year, outlines her expectations and classroom procedures, and solicits parents' support. She shares and discusses it with her students the first day of class, and explains why having their parents involved is so important. She also asks for their suggestions for rules and procedures to include in the letter. She then takes the letter home, revises it, and emails a copy of the letter to parents, and requests that parents reply to the email as a form of contract indicating their support. She follows up on those that aren't returned with additional emails and even phone calls in some cases.

Her letter appears in Figure 12.7.

Every other week throughout the year, Jacinta sends assignments and graded homework home to be signed by parents—to indicate that the parents have looked at the artifacts. She also encourages parents to contact her if they have any questions about the packets.

During the evening, Jacinta periodically calls parents to let them know about their children's progress. If students miss more than one assignment, she calls immediately and expresses her concern. She also makes a point of emailing parents to report positive news, such as a student exceeding requirements, overcoming an obstacle, or showing kindness to a classmate.

Jacinta attempted to promote communication with parents in three ways. The first was her letter. (Her letter is simply an example. You will tailor your letter to best meet your students' needs.) It began the communication process, expressed positive expectations, specified class rules (described as "guidelines"), and outlined procedures for homework, absences, and extra credit.

The letter also asked for the parents' reply, which makes it a contract soliciting their support. Replies aren't guarantees, but they symbolize a commitment and increase the likelihood that parents and students will attempt to honor it. Also, because students have input into the content of the letter, they feel greater ownership of the process.

Notice also that the letter is free from grammar, punctuation, and spelling errors. Teachers sometimes send communications home with errors in them. Don't. First impressions are important and lasting. Your first letter creates a perception of your competence, and errors detract from your credibility.

In her second attempt to enhance communication, Jacinta sent packets of students' work home every other week and asked parents to sign and return them. In addition to creating a link between home and school, these packets give parents an ongoing record of their child's progress.

Third, she periodically called and emailed parents, which effectively maintains communication and enlists their cooperation (Anderson & Minke, 2007). Allocating some of your personal time to call or email parents communicates caring better than any other way. Also, talking to a parent allows you to be specific in describing a student's needs and gives you a chance to again solicit support. If a student is missing assignments, for example, you can find out why and can encourage parents to more closely monitor their child's study habits.

When we talk to parents, we need to establish a positive, cooperative tone that lays the foundation for joint efforts. Consider the following:

"Hello, Mrs. Hansen? This is Jacinta Escobar, Jared's geography teacher."

"Oh, uh, is something wrong?"

"Not really. I just wanted to call to share with you some information about Jared. He's a bright, energetic boy, and I enjoy seeing him in class every day. But he's missing some homework assignments."

August 24, 2015

Dear Parents,

I am looking forward to a productive and exciting year, and I am writing this letter to encourage your involvement and support. You always have been and always will be the most important people in your youngster's education. We cannot do the job without you.

For us to work together most effectively, some guidelines are necessary. With the students' help, we prepared the ones listed here. Please read this information carefully, and reply to this email with a simple statement saying, "I have read and support these guidelines."

If you have any questions, please feel free to call me at Southside Middle School (441-5935) or personally (221-8403) in the evenings.

Sincerely,

Jacinta Escobar

AS A PARENT, I WILL TRY MY BEST TO DO THE FOLLOWING:

1. I will ask my youngsters about school every day (evening meal is a good time). I will ask them about what they're studying and try to learn about it.
2. I will provide a quiet time and place each evening for homework, and I will set an example by also working, studying, or reading while my youngsters are working.
3. I will ask to see my youngsters' homework after they've finished it, and I will have them explain some of the information to see if they understand it.

STUDENT GUIDELINES FOR SUCCESS:

Self-regulation guidelines:

1. I will be in class and seated when the bell rings.
2. I will follow directions the first time they are given.
3. I will bring a covered textbook, notebook, paper, and two sharpened pencils to class each day.
4. I will raise my hand for permission to speak or leave my seat.
5. I will keep my hands, feet, and objects to myself.

Homework guidelines:

1. Our class motto is "I will always try and I will never give up."
2. I will complete all assignments. I understand that I will not receive credit for homework turned in late.
3. If I am absent, I am responsible for coming in before school to get makeup work as soon as I return to school.
4. I know that I have one day for each day I'm absent to make up missed work.
5. I understand that extra credit work is not given. If I do the required work, extra credit isn't necessary.

Student Signature _____

Figure 12.7

Letter to parents

"I didn't know he had geography homework. He never brings any home."

"That might be part of the problem. He just might forget that he has any to do. . . . I have a suggestion. I have the students write their homework assignments in their folders each day. Please ask Jared to share his folder with you in the evening, and make sure that his homework is done. Then, please initial it so I know you and he talked. I think that will help. How does that sound?"

"Sure. I'll try that."

"Good. We don't want him to fall behind. If he has problems with the homework, have him come to my room before or after school, and I'll help him. Is there anything else I can do? . . . If not, I look forward to meeting you soon."

This conversation was positive, created a partnership between home and school, and offered a specific plan of action.

Decisions about when to call parents about a management issue depend on your professional judgment. The question, "To what extent does the issue influence learning?" is a good guideline. For instance, you should probably handle an incident where a student slips and uses a cuss word in class. On the other hand, if the student's language or behaviors are detracting from other students' learning, you should probably contact the parents.

Finally, emphasizing accomplishments should be uppermost in all types of communication with parents. When you call about a problem, first try to describe accomplishments and progress if possible. You can also initiate communication for the sole purpose of reporting good news, as Jacinta did in her emails. All parents want to feel proud of their children, and sharing accomplishments can further improve the home–school partnership.

As it continues to expand, technology will provide an ever more important channel for improving home–school communication. For example, you can create an electronic template and involve your students in inserting information into it, which can then be used as a class newsletter. As it becomes a routine you can maintain communication with parents efficiently and with a minimum of time and effort.

Classroom Connections

Communicating Effectively with Parents

1. Communication with parents is an essential part of effective classroom management. Establish communication links during the first few days of school, and maintain them throughout the year.

- **Elementary:** A kindergarten teacher calls each of her students' parents during the first week of school, tells them how happy she is to have their children in her class, learns as much as she can about them, and encourages them to contact her at any time.

- **Middle School:** Each week, a sixth-grade social studies teacher sends home a "class communicator," describing the topics his students will be studying and giving suggestions parents can follow in helping their children. Students write notes to their parents on the communicator, describing their personal efforts and progress.

- **High School:** A geometry teacher sends a letter home at the beginning of the school year, describing his homework and assessment policies. He calls parents when more than one homework assignment is missing.

2. Effective communication with parents is positive, clear, and concise. Communicate in nontechnical language, and make specific suggestions to parents for working with their children.

- **Elementary:** A third-grade teacher asks all her parents to sign a contract agreeing that they will (a) designate an hour each evening when the television is turned off and children do homework; (b) ask their children to show them their homework assignments each day; and (c) look at, ask their children about, and sign the packet of papers that is sent home every other week.

- **Middle School:** A sixth-grade teacher discusses a letter to parents with his students. He has them explain what each part of the letter says and then asks the students to read and explain the letter to their parents.

- **High School:** A ninth-grade basic math teacher makes a special effort at the beginning of the school year to explain to parents of students with exceptionalities how she'll modify her class to meet their children's needs. She strongly encourages parents to monitor homework and assist if they can.

3. Take extra steps to communicate with the parents of children who are members of minorities.

- **Elementary:** A second-grade teacher in an urban school enlists the aid of teachers who are bilingual. When he sends messages home, he asks them for help in translating notes for parents.

- **Middle School:** At the beginning of each grading period, a sixth-grade teacher sends a letter home, in each student's native language, describing the topics that will be covered, the tests and the approximate times they will be given, and any special projects that are required.

- **High School:** A biology teacher, who has many students with parents who speak little English, holds student-led conferences in which the students report on their progress. As she participates in each conference she has students serve as translators.

Intervening When Misbehavior Occurs

Our focus to this point has been on efforts to *prevent* as many management problems as possible. We have emphasized the interdependence of management and instruction, the importance of planning, and the central role rules and procedures play in creating a classroom environment that promotes both academic and social–emotional learning. Despite our best efforts, however, some students will periodically misbehave or fail to pay attention. For example, Judy, in our opening case study, had carefully planned her rules and procedures, she was well organized, and she promoted high levels of student involvement in her learning activity, but she still had to intervene with Darren and Rachel. This is common in classrooms.

In the following sections, we discuss interventions from emotional and humanistic, cognitive, and behaviorist perspectives. Each contributes to our understanding and provides guidance as we make decisions about how to intervene most effectively.

Ed Psych and You

Have you ever been criticized or chewed out in front of other people or been in an argument in public? How did it make you feel? How did you feel afterward?

Emotional Factors in Interventions

From our study of humanistic views of motivation, and particularly Maslow's work, we understand that safety—including emotional safety—is an important need for all of us. This need relates to the questions we ask in *Ed Psych and You*. We all want to avoid being humiliated in front of our peers, and the same applies in classrooms. The emotional tone of our interventions influences both the likelihood of students complying with them and their attitudes toward us and the class afterward. Loud public reprimands, criticism, and sarcasm reduce students' sense of safety and are particularly destructive in elementary schools, where children are vulnerable and strongly seek the approval of their teachers. In middle and secondary schools, they create resentment, detract from classroom climate, and lead to students finding creative ways to be disruptive without getting caught (Emmer & Evertson, 2013; Evertson & Emmer, 2013).

Similarly, arguing with students about the interpretation of a rule or compliance with it also detracts from the emotional climate of classrooms. You never "win" an argument with students. You can exert your authority, but doing so is not sustainable throughout a school year, resentment is often a side effect, and the encounter may expand into major conflict (Pellegrino, 2010).

Consider the following incident that occurred after a teacher directed a chronically misbehaving student to move:

> Student: I wasn't doing anything.
> Teacher: You were whispering, and the rule says listen when someone else is talking.
> Student: It doesn't say no whispering.
> Teacher: You know what the rule means. We've been over it again and again.
> Student: Well, it's not fair. You don't make other students move when they whisper.
> Teacher: You weren't listening when someone else was talking, so move.

The student knew what the rule meant and was simply playing a game with the teacher, who allowed herself to be drawn into an argument. In contrast, consider the following.

> Teacher: Please move up here (pointing to an empty desk in the first row).
> Student: I wasn't doing anything.
> Teacher: One of our rules says that we listen when someone else is talking. If you would like to discuss this, come in and see me after school. Please move now (turning back to the lesson as soon as the student moves).

This teacher maintained an even demeanor and didn't allow herself to be pulled into an argument or even a brief discussion. She handled the event quickly and efficiently, offered to discuss it with the student later, and immediately turned back to the lesson.

Students' inclination to argue with teachers strongly depends on the emotional climate of the classroom. If rules and procedures make sense to students, and if they're enforced consistently and fairly, students are less likely to argue. When students break rules, simply reminding them of the rule and why it's important, and requiring compliance, as Judy did with Rachel, are as far as minor incidents should go. (We examine serious management issues, such as defiance and aggression, later in the chapter.)

Cognitive Interventions

The term *cognitive* implies thinking, and as we've said repeatedly in this chapter, the desire for our experiences to make sense is arguably the most basic principle of cognitive learning theory. We also said earlier that rules and procedures should make sense to students, and we want our interventions to make sense to them as well. If they do, the likelihood of serious management problems is sharply reduced. Also, rules, procedures, and interventions that make sense contribute to students' self-regulation. When students understand the impact of their behavior on others and on learning, they are more likely to begin regulating their own actions and emotions. Keep these ideas in mind as we examine the following interventions.

DEMONSTRATE WITHITNESS

Withitness, a teacher's awareness of what is going on in all parts of the classroom at all times, and communicating this awareness to students, is an essential component of successful interventions (Emmer & Evertson, 2013; Evertson & Emmer, 2013; Kounin, 1970). Withitness is often described as "having eyes in the back of your head." Let's compare two teachers.

> Ron Ziers is explaining the process for finding percentages to his seventh graders. While Ron illustrates the procedure, Steve, in the second desk from the front of the

room, is periodically poking Katilya, who sits across from him. She retaliates by kicking him in the leg. Bill, sitting behind Katilya, pokes her in the arm with his pencil. Ron doesn't respond to the students' actions. After a second poke, Katilya swings her arm back and catches Bill on the shoulder. "Katilya!" Ron says sternly. "We keep our hands to ourselves! . . . Now, where were we?"

Karl Wickes has the same group of students in life science. He puts a drawing displaying a flowering plant on the document camera. As the class discusses the information, he notices Barry whispering something to Julie, and he sees Steve poke Katilya, who kicks him and loudly whispers, "Stop it." As Karl asks, "What is the part of the plant that produces fruit?" he moves to Steve's desk, leans over, and says quietly but firmly, "We keep our hands to ourselves in here." He then moves to the front of the room, watches Steve out of the corner of his eye, and says, "Barry, what other plant part do you see in the diagram?"

We can see why demonstrating withitness is a cognitive intervention. In Ron's class, being reprimanded when she was completely innocent didn't make sense to Katilya, whereas seeing Karl immediately respond to Steve's misbehavior did. This is why withitness is so important.

Karl demonstrated withitness in three ways:

- He identified the misbehavior immediately, and quickly responded by moving near Steve. Ron did nothing until the problem had spread to other students.
- He correctly identified Steve as the cause of the incident. In contrast, Ron reprimanded Katilya, leaving students with a sense that he didn't know what was going on.
- He responded to the more serious infraction first. Steve's poking was more disruptive than Barry's whispering, so Karl first responded to Steve and then called on Barry, which drew him back into the activity and made further intervention unnecessary.

Withitness goes further (Hogan, Rabinowitz, & Craven, 2003). It also involves watching for evidence of inattention or confusion and responding with questions, such as "Some of you look puzzled. Do you want me to rephrase the question?" And it includes approaching or calling on inattentive students to bring them back into lessons.

Lack of withitness is often a problem for beginning teachers because the complexities of teaching add to the heavy cognitive load on their working memories, making the process of continually monitoring student behavior difficult (Wubbels, Brekelmans, den Brok, & van Tartwijk, 2006). You can best address this issue by creating well-established routines and carefully planning your instruction, which reduce your cognitive load during teaching and contribute to your own self-confidence (Greenberg et al., 2014). As you acquire experience, you will learn to be sensitive to students and make adjustments to ensure that they are as involved and successful as possible.

MAINTAIN CONSISTENCY AND FOLLOW-THROUGH

"Be consistent" is recommended so often that it has nearly become a cliché, but it is essential nevertheless. If one student is reprimanded for breaking a rule and another is not, for example, students are unable to make sense of the inconsistency. They are likely to conclude that the teacher doesn't know what's going on or has "pets," either of which detracts from classroom climate.

Although consistency is important, achieving complete consistency in the real world is virtually impossible, and we should adapt our interventions to both the student and context. For example, most classrooms have a rule about speaking only when recognized by the teacher. So, as you're monitoring seatwork, suppose one student asks another a question about the assignment and then immediately goes back to work. Failing to remind the student that talking is not allowed during seatwork is technically inconsistent, but an intervention in this case is both unnecessary and counterproductive. On the other hand, a student who repeatedly turns around and whispers becomes a disruption, and intervention is necessary. Students understand the difference, and the "inconsistency" is appropriate and effective.

Following through means doing what we've said we'll do. Without follow-through, our management systems break down because students learn that we aren't fully committed to ensuring that our classroom environments are orderly. This is confusing and leaves them with a sense of uncertainty.

In fact, failing to follow through can—by decreasing students' inhibitions about misbehaving—actually increase misbehavior (Skatova & Ferguson, 2013). The concept of expectations within social cognitive theory helps us understand why. When students break a rule, they expect to be reprimanded. If the reprimand doesn't occur, it serves as a reinforcer, making it more likely that students will continue to display the misbehavior.

Once again, the first few days of the school year are important. If you follow through consistently during this period, enforcing rules and reinforcing procedures will be much easier during the rest of the year.

KEEP VERBAL AND NONVERBAL BEHAVIORS CONGRUENT

For interventions to make sense to your students, your verbal and nonverbal behaviors must be congruent (Doyle, 2006). Compare the following interventions:

> Karen Wilson's eighth graders are working on their homework as she circulates among them. She is helping Jasmine when Jeff and Mike begin whispering loudly behind her.
>
> "Jeff. Mike. Stop talking, and get started on your homework," she says, glancing over her shoulder.
>
> The two slow their whispering, and Karen turns back to Jasmine. Soon, the boys are whispering as loudly as ever.
>
> "I thought I told you to stop talking," Karen says over her shoulder again, this time with irritation in her voice.
>
> The boys glance at her and quickly resume whispering.
>
> Isabel Rodriguez is in a similar situation with her prealgebra students. As she is helping Vicki, Ken and Lance begin horseplay at the back of the room.
>
> Isabel excuses herself, turns, and walks directly to the boys. Looking Lance in the eye, she says evenly and firmly, "Lance, we have plenty to do before lunch, and noise during seatwork detracts from learning. Begin your work now." Then, looking directly at Ken, she continues, "Ken, you, too. Quickly now. We have only so much time, and we don't want to waste it." She waits briefly until they are working quietly and then returns to Vicki.

The teachers had similar intents, but the impact of their actions was very different. When Karen glanced over her shoulder as she was telling the boys to stop whispering, and then failed to follow through, her communication was confusing; her words said one thing, but her body language said another. When messages are inconsistent, people attribute more credibility to tone of voice and body language than to spoken words (Aronson, Wilson, & Akert, 2013).

In contrast, Isabel's communication was clear and consistent. She responded immediately, faced her students directly, explained how their behavior detracted from learning, and made sure her students were on task before she went back to Vicki. Her verbal and nonverbal behaviors were consistent, so her message made sense. Characteristics of effective nonverbal communication are outlined in Table 12.1.

Table 12.1	Characteristics of effective nonverbal communication
Nonverbal Behavior	**Example**
Proximity	A teacher moves close to an inattentive student.
Eye contact	A teacher looks an off-task student directly in the eye when issuing a directive.
Body orientation	A teacher directs himself squarely to the learner, rather than over the shoulder or sideways.
Facial expression	A teacher frowns slightly at a disruption, brightens her face at a humorous incident, and smiles approvingly at a student's effort to help a classmate.
Gestures	A teacher puts her palm out (Stop!) to a student who interjects as another student is talking.
Vocal variation	A teacher varies the tone, pitch, and loudness of his voice for emphasis and displays energy and enthusiasm.

USE I-MESSAGES

Successful cognitive interventions should both focus on the inappropriate behavior and help students understand the effects of their actions on others. To illustrate, let's look again at Judy's encounter with Rachel in the case study at the beginning of the chapter. Judy pointed to the rule and then said:

> "We agreed that it was important to listen when other people are talking, and you know that we all have to honor our agreements. . . . We can't learn when people aren't paying attention, and I'm uncomfortable when my class isn't learning."

In this encounter, Judy sent an **I-message**, a nonaccusatory communication that addresses a behavior and describes the effects on the sender and the feelings it generates in the sender (Gordon, 1981). "A rationale for using an I-message is that students often act without much awareness of the effects their behavior has on others, and they will change when they realize that they are causing someone a problem" (Emmer & Evertson, 2013, p. 174).

Judy's I-message reminded Rachel that her behavior was unacceptable while simultaneously communicating that she was still valued as a person. Judy also described the behavior's effect on the sender—herself—and the feelings it generated: "We can't learn when people aren't paying attention, and I'm uncomfortable when my class isn't learning." The intent of an I-message is to promote understanding, as it always is in cognitive interventions. Judy wanted Rachel to understand the effects of her actions on others, and if successful, her message contributes to Rachel's self-regulation.

Judy was also assertive in her directive to Rachel, and research indicates that teacher assertiveness, combined with perseverance and consistency, is part of expert classroom management (Jones et al., 2013). **Assertive discipline**, an approach to classroom management that promotes a clear and firm response style, suggests that teachers are often ineffective because their responses to students are either passive or hostile (Canter, 1996). For example, a passive response to Rachel might be, "Please. How many times do I have to remind you of our rule about paying attention?" A hostile response would be, "Your whispering is driving me up the wall," which implies a weakness in students' characters and detracts from the classroom's emotional climate. In comparison, an assertive response style signals that you know what you're doing and you're in charge of your class.

APPLY LOGICAL CONSEQUENCES

Logical consequences are outcomes that are conceptually related to misbehavior; they help learners make sense of an intervention by creating a link between their actions and the consequences that follow. For example:

> Allen, a rambunctious sixth grader, is running down the hall toward the lunchroom. As he rounds the corner, he bumps Alyssia, causing her to drop her books.
>
> "Oops," he replies, continuing his race to the lunchroom.
>
> "Hold it, Allen," Doug Ramsay, who is monitoring the hall, says. "Go back and help her pick up her books and apologize."
>
> Allen walks back to Alyssia, helps her pick up her books, mumbles an apology, and then returns. As he approaches, Doug again stops him.
>
> "Now, why did I make you do that?" Doug asks.
>
> "Cuz we're not supposed to run."
>
> "Sure," Doug says evenly, "but more important, if people run in the halls, they might crash into someone, and somebody might get hurt. . . . Remember that you're responsible for your actions. Think about not wanting to hurt yourself or anybody else, and the next time you'll walk whether a teacher is here or not. . . . Now, go on to lunch."

Doug applied a logical consequence in this incident, and we can see why it's important. Having to pick up Alyssia's books after bumping her and causing her to drop them made sense to Allen, and this is our goal in applying logical consequences. They help students understand the effects of their actions on others and promote the development of self-regulation (Watson & Battistich, 2006).

Behavioral Interventions

Although interventions that make sense and lead to learner understanding and self-regulation are the ideals we strive for, in the real world, some students seem either unable or unwilling to direct and control their actions and emotions. In these cases, behaviorism with its applications of reinforcement and appropriate punishment may be necessary (Fabiano, Pelham, & Gnagy, 2007; Ryan, Katsiyannis, & Peterson, 2007). Further, in the real world actions have consequences, and learning that consequences exist for misbehavior is part of students' total education (Greenberg et al., 2014). Experts recommend using behavioral interventions as short-term solutions to specific problems, with development of self-regulation remaining the long-term goal (Emmer & Evertson, 2013; Evertson & Emmer, 2013).

Let's see how Cindy Daines, a first-grade teacher, uses a behavioral intervention with her students:

> Cindy has a problem with her students' making smooth and orderly transitions from one activity to another.
>
> In an attempt to improve the situation, she makes "tickets" from construction paper, gets local businesses to donate small items to be used as prizes, and displays the items in a fishbowl on her desk. She then explains, "We're going to play a little game to see how quiet we can be when we change lessons. . . . Whenever we change, I'm going to give you 1 minute, and then I'm going to ring this bell," and she rings the bell to demonstrate. "Students who have their books out and are waiting quietly when I ring the bell will get one of these tickets. On Friday afternoon, you can turn them in for prizes you see in this fishbowl. The more tickets you have, the better the prize will be."

During the next few days, Cindy moves around the room, handing out tickets and making comments such as "I really like the way Merry is ready to work," "Ted already has his books out and is quiet," and "Thank you for moving to math so quickly."

She realizes her strategy is starting to work when she hears "Shh" and "Be quiet!" from the students, so she is gradually able to space out the rewards as the students become more responsible.

Cindy used concepts from both behaviorism and social cognitive theory in her system. Her tickets and prizes were positive reinforcers for making quick and quiet transitions, and her comments, such as "I really like the way Merry is ready to work" and "Ted already has his books out and is quiet," were vicarious reinforcers for the other children.

When using behavioral interventions we need to remember that reinforcement is more effective for changing behavior than punishment (Landrum & Kaufman, 2006). However, punishment may be necessary in some cases, and desists, detention, and nonexclusionary time-out—the process of seating a student near the teacher or on the edge of the classroom, with the goal of preventing the student from receiving reinforcers—can be effective punishers. The following are guidelines for using punishment in management interventions:

- Use punishment as infrequently as possible.
- Apply punishers immediately and directly to the behavior.
- Apply punishers only severe enough to eliminate the misbehavior.
- Apply punishers dispassionately, and avoid displays of anger.
- Explain and model alternative desirable behaviors.

Now, let's briefly examine corporal punishment, which should never be used, and removing students from classrooms, which should be used only as a last resort.

CORPORAL PUNISHMENT

Corporal punishment is a form of physical punishment that involves the deliberate infliction of pain in response to misbehavior. It's common in our culture, with more than 90% of parents reporting that they spank their toddlers (Simons, Simons, & Su, 2013). It is highly controversial, however, and professional organizations, such as the American Academy of Pediatrics, have come out strongly opposed to hitting children for any reason (American Academy of Pediatrics, 2011).

Corporal punishment in schools is permitted in 81 countries around the world, including the United States (Lenta, 2012). Although its use is declining in our country, it remains legal in 19 states (Rollins, 2012). However, virtually all educational leaders and professional organizations are strongly opposed to corporal punishment in schools (Rollins, 2012; Simons et al., 2013), and some argue that the practice is immoral and should be totally banned (Lenta, 2012).

Arguments against corporal punishment can also be made on theoretical grounds. For instance, corporal punishment, through modeling, suggests that hitting people is an acceptable response to unacceptable behavior. This doesn't make any sense when we're trying to develop self-regulation in students, aspects of which are impulse control (resisting urges to display inappropriate behaviors), emotional regulation, and expressing emotions in socially appropriate ways. We certainly don't teach these characteristics by hitting students.

We endorse all of these arguments and suggest to you that corporal punishment is never an acceptable behavioral intervention under any circumstance. There are better ways to manage behavior and teach self-control.

REMOVING STUDENTS FROM CLASSROOMS

Unfortunately, in the real world of classrooms a few students will be incorrigible and disruptive enough that they must be removed. This practice isn't as simple as it appears on the surface, however, because students who can't or won't accept responsibility for their behavior often blame their teachers for the exclusion (being removed from the classroom). This has implications for us if we feel we must ultimately have a student taken out of our classroom. We should, before deciding to have students removed, first remind them that their behaviors are unacceptable, and if the reminder doesn't work, punish them using acceptable forms of punishment, such as nonexclusionary time-out. If neither works, and the student is removed, we should have a follow-up conversation with the student, explaining why the removal was necessary. In the process, we should highlight the impact of the misbehavior on classmates and how it detracts from learning and the emotional atmosphere in our classroom (Lewis, Romi, & Roache, 2012).

Ideally, we should try to avoid removing students from classrooms if possible. Research indicates that frequent use of exclusionary discipline strategies (removing students from classrooms) is associated with higher frequencies of discipline problems and less positive classroom climates and teacher–student relationships (Mitchell & Bradshaw, 2013). Except in extreme circumstances, removing students from our classrooms should be an intervention of last resort.

DESIGNING AND MAINTAINING A BEHAVIORAL MANAGEMENT SYSTEM

Clear rules and expectations followed by consistently applied consequences (reinforcers and punishers) are the foundation of a behavioral management system. Designing a management system based on behaviorism involves the following steps:

- Prepare a list of specific rules that clearly define acceptable behavior.
- Specify reinforcers for obeying each rule and punishers for breaking the rules, such as the consequences in Table 12.2.
- Display the rules, and explain the consequences.
- Consistently apply consequences.

A behavioral system doesn't preclude providing rationales or creating the rules with learner input. However, in contrast with a cognitive approach, which emphasizes understanding and self-regulation, the primary focus is on clearly specifying behavioral guidelines and applying consequences.

Table 12.2   Sample consequences for breaking or following rules

Consequences for Breaking Rules	
First infraction	Name on list
Second infraction	Check by name
Third infraction	Second check by name
Fourth infraction	Half-hour detention
Fifth infraction	Call to parents
Consequences for Following Rules	
A check is removed for each day that no infractions occur. If only a name remains, and no infractions occur, the name is removed.	
All students without names on the list are given 45 minutes of free time Friday afternoon to do as they choose. The only restrictions are that they must stay in the classroom, and they must not disrupt the students who didn't earn the free time.	

In designing a comprehensive management system, you probably will combine elements of both cognitive and behavioral approaches. Behavioral systems have the advantage of being immediately applicable; they're effective for initiating desired behaviors, particularly with young students; and they're useful for reducing chronic misbehavior. They also help students understand that actions have consequences, and we're all accountable for our behaviors (Greenberg et al., 2014). Cognitive systems take longer to produce results but are more likely to develop learner self-regulation.

POSITIVE BEHAVIOR SUPPORT

When you begin teaching, you will almost certainly have students in your classes who have exceptionalities, such as specific learning disabilities or behavior disorders. You will be expected to create a classroom environment that meets the needs of all of your students, including those with exceptionalities. Let's look at an example.

> You have a student named Tanya who has been diagnosed with a mild form of autism. She displays behaviors typical of the disorder, such as underdeveloped social skills, highly ritualistic behavior, and a strong emotional attachment to a particular adult. For example, she is sometimes abusive to other students when you do group work, so you remove her from the group. And she frequently becomes upset and will even periodically shout and run out of the room when you have your students begin their homework for the next day.
>
> With the help of your school's special education specialist, you analyze Tanya's behavior and conclude that her abuse and running out of the room serve two purposes: (1) they allow her to escape social situations in which she is uncomfortable, and (2) they get your attention.
>
> Based on the analysis, you both work with Tanya to help her learn to make appropriate comments and ask questions during group work, and you design a system so she earns points that she can trade for treats of her choosing when she behaves appropriately. You also spend extra time helping her with her seatwork, and you create a private area in the back of the room where she can go whenever she feels she needs a break from academic tasks.

Your interventions are examples of **positive behavior support**, interventions that replace problem behaviors with alternative, appropriate actions that serve the same purpose for the student (Carter & Van Norman, 2010). For example, Tanya was negatively reinforced for behaving abusively (she was allowed to escape the uncomfortable situation), and when she was taught some specific interaction skills, the negative reinforcer was replaced with a positive reinforcer (the points). Similarly, the attention she received when she shouted and ran out of the room was replaced with your attention when you worked with her one-on-one.

Positive behavior support is widely used and is commonly implemented on a school-wide basis (Scott, Gagnon, & Nelson, 2008). Research indicates that it is generally effective for dealing with problems that traditional classroom management systems can't solve (Scott, Alter, Rosenberg, & Borgmeier, 2010). You are likely to be involved in positive behavior support when you begin teaching, and you will be provided with extra support from special educators as well as staff development experiences that will help you implement it in your classroom.

An Intervention Continuum

Despite your best efforts to plan for both classroom management and instruction, students will misbehave, so you will periodically have to intervene, as Judy did in the case study at the beginning of the chapter. Let's look at some options that you can implement in your work with students.

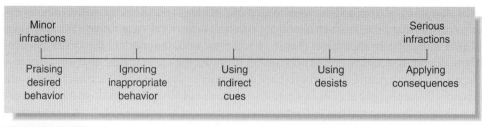

Figure 12.8

An intervention continuum

Disruptions vary from isolated incidents, such as a student briefly whispering to a neighbor, to chronic infractions, such as a student repeatedly poking a classmate, or even fighting. Because the severity of infractions varies, your interventions should also vary, and they will include both cognitive and behavioral elements.

To maximize instructional time, intervening should be as unobtrusive as possible. A continuum of interventions is outlined in Figure 12.8 and discussed in the following sections.

Praising Desired Behavior. Because promoting positive behaviors is an important goal, praising students for displaying them is a sensible first intervention, and experts suggest that praise for desirable behavior should be a part of all effective classroom management systems (Greenberg et al., 2014). Praise occurs less often in classrooms than we might expect, so efforts to "catch 'em being good" are worthwhile, especially as a method of prevention. Elementary teachers praise openly and freely, and middle and secondary teachers often make private comments, such as "I'm extremely pleased with your work this week. . . . Keep it up," or write private notes to students praising them for their work and behavior. Some research suggests that praising middle school students in notes significantly reduces discipline referrals (Nelson, Young, Young, & Cox, 2010).

Reinforcing behaviors that are incompatible with misbehavior is an extension of this idea (Alberto & Troutman, 2013). For instance, participating in a learning activity is incompatible with daydreaming, so calling on a student and reinforcing any attempt to respond are more effective than reprimanding a student for not paying attention.

Ignoring Inappropriate Behavior. Behaviors that aren't reinforced become extinct. The attention students receive when they're admonished for minor misbehaviors is often reinforcing, so ignoring the behavior can eliminate the reinforcers you might inadvertently provide (Landrum & Kaufman, 2006). This is effective, for example, when two students briefly whisper but soon stop. A combination of praising desired behaviors, reinforcing incompatible behaviors, and ignoring misbehavior are all effective ways to deal with minor disruptions.

Using Indirect Cues. You can also use indirect cues—such as proximity, methods of redirecting attention, and vicarious reinforcers—when misbehaviors can't be ignored but can be stopped or diverted without addressing them directly (Jones & Jones, 2013). For example, Judy moved near Darren and called on him after she heard Kendra mutter. Her proximity stopped his misbehavior, and calling on him directed his attention back to the lesson.

Vicarious reinforcement can also be effective. If you plan to be an elementary teacher, you can use students as models and vicariously reinforce the rest of the students with statements such as "I really like the way Row 1 is working quietly" or "Elisa has already started the assignment." If you plan to teach in middle or secondary schools, you can also use vicarious reinforcers, but you need to be sensitive to possible student reactions to the process, because older students are sometimes uncomfortable being singled out in front of their peers.

Using Desists. A **desist** is a verbal or nonverbal communication a teacher uses to stop a behavior (Dhaem, 2012; Kounin, 1970). "Glenys, we leave our seats only when given permission," "Glenys!" and a finger to the lips, or a stern facial expression are all desists. They are the most common teacher reactions to misbehavior.

Clarity and tone are important when using desists. For example, "Randy, what is the rule about touching other students?" or "Randy, how do you think that makes Willy feel?" are more effective than "Randy, stop that," because they link the behavior to a rule or to the behavior's effects. Students react to these subtle differences and prefer rule and consequence reminders to teacher commands (Brophy, 2006).

The tone of desists should be firm but not angry. Kounin (1970) found that kindergarten students managed with rough desists actually became more disruptive, and older students are uncomfortable in classes where harsh desists are used. In contrast, firm, even reprimands, the suggestion of alternative behaviors, and questioning that maintains student involvement in learning activities can reduce off-task time in most classrooms.

Clear communication, including congruence between verbal and nonverbal behavior, an awareness of what is happening in the classroom (withitness), and effective instruction, are essential in using desists. However, even when these elements exist, simple desists may not be enough.

Applying Consequences. If you've tried all other options on the intervention continuum, and they simply aren't working, you'll then need to apply consequences. Logical consequences are most desirable and should be tried first, but classrooms are complex and busy, so it isn't always possible to solve problems with them. In these cases behavioral consequences—simply intended to change a behavior quickly and efficiently—can be effective (Greenberg et al., 2014; Murphy, 2007). Let's look at an example.

> Jason is an intelligent and active fifth grader. He loves to talk and seems to know just how far he can go before Mrs. Aguilar becomes exasperated with him. He understands the rules and the reasons for them, but his interest in talking seems to take precedence. Ignoring him isn't working. A call to his parents helped for a while, but soon he's back to his usual behavior—never quite enough to require a drastic response, but always a thorn in Mrs. Aguilar's side.
>
> Finally, she decides to give him only one warning. At a second disruption, he's placed in time-out from regular instructional activities. She meets with him and explains the rules. The next day, he begins to misbehave almost immediately.
>
> "Jason," she warns, "you can't work while you're talking, and you're keeping others from finishing their work. Please get busy."
>
> He stops, but a few minutes later, he's at it again.
>
> "Jason," Mrs. Aguilar says quietly as she moves back to his desk, "Please go back to the time-out area."
>
> Now, a week later, Jason is working quietly with the rest of the class.

Behavior such as Jason's is common, particularly in elementary and middle schools, and it causes more teacher stress than do highly publicized threats of violence and bodily harm (Friedman, 2006). The behavior is disruptive, so it can't be ignored; praise for good work helps to a certain extent, but students get much of their reinforcement from friends; desists work briefly, but the constant monitoring is tiring. Mrs. Aguilar had little choice but to apply behavioral consequences with Jason.

Consistency is the key to promoting change in students like Jason. He understood what he was doing, and he was capable of controlling himself. When he could predict the consequences of his behavior, he quit. He knew that his second infraction would result in a time-out, and when it did, he quickly changed his behavior. There was no argument, little time was used, and the class wasn't disrupted.

Educational Psychology and Teaching: Responding Effectively to Misbehavior in Your Students

Incidents of misbehavior will inevitably occur in your classroom. The following guidelines can help you intervene effectively.

1. Maintain the flow of instruction while intervening in cases of misbehavior.
2. Protect students' emotional safety when intervening.
3. Use cognitive interventions when possible; revert to behavioral interventions when necessary.
4. Move along the intervention continuum only as far as necessary.

Let's look at the guidelines in more detail.

Maintain the Flow of Instruction While Intervening. If possible, we should intervene without disrupting the flow of our instruction. To illustrate, let's look again at Judy's work with her students in the case study at the beginning of the chapter.

> Judy: About what latitude is Damascus, . . . Bernice?
> Bernice: About 34 degrees north, I think.
> Judy: Good, Bernice. It is close to 34 degrees. . . . So, would it be warmer or colder than here in the summer? . . . Darren? (seeing that Darren has poked Kendra with his pencil, and walking near him).
> Darren: . . . Warmer, I think. (after Judy repeats the question for him, because he didn't initially hear it).
> Judy: Okay. Good. And why might that be the case? . . . Jim? (moving over to Rachel and telling her to move to a different desk).

In this brief episode, Judy intervened with both Darren and Rachel without disrupting the flow of her lesson, an ability called **overlapping** (Kounin, 1970). This amounts to doing two things at once, which imposes a heavy cognitive load on teachers, so you might not be good at it immediately. However, with careful planning—both for instruction and for classroom management—and with practice, the process will gradually become much easier. Judy's work is an example. Because her expertise was highly developed, her questioning was essentially automatic, so she was able to devote most of her working memory space to monitoring her students' behavior.

Protect Students' Emotional Safety. As we said earlier, interventions should take students' emotional reactions into account. We're all human, we can't help becoming angry with students at times, and it's even appropriate to acknowledge that we're angry. However, harsh, critical, and sarcastic interventions do little to eliminate problem behaviors, and they detract from classroom climate. If you feel angry, give yourself a few seconds to calm down before you do something you might be sorry for later. Judy maintained an even demeanor in her interventions, which helped her students feel emotionally safe, and she intervened with virtually no interruption in the flow of her lesson.

Use Cognitive Interventions When Possible. In all cases, we should do our best to ensure that our interventions make sense to students. If they do, all but the most incorrigible of students are likely to comply because they understand why we're intervening.

Judy's interventions were primarily cognitive. For example, she was "withit" in recognizing that Darren was the perpetrator of the incident with Kendra; she was consistent and followed through to be sure Rachel complied; she kept her verbal and nonverbal behavior consistent, such as looking directly at Darren when she called on him and making eye contact with Rachel when talking to her; and she responded to Rachel with an I-message. Further, she knelt down to eye level when talking to Rachel. This move tacitly communicates to students that a problem exists, and they and their teacher are working on it together (Dhaem, 2012).

Move Along the Intervention Continuum Only as Far as Necessary. When we intervene, we should only go as far as necessary. For instance, if a simple desist stops a misbehavior, this is as far as we should go. Elaborating on the intervention gives the incident more significance than it deserves. Judy only had to go as far as using indirect cues with both Darren and Rachel. She simply moved over near Darren and called on him, she referred Rachel to the class rule and ensured that she complied, and neither action disrupted the flow of her lesson.

Careful planning for classroom management combined with efforts to promote self-regulation can prevent many management problems from occurring in the first place, and applying the guidelines we've discussed here can quickly eliminate most others. Unfortunately, however, serious problems can sometimes occur. We discuss them in the next section of the chapter.

Classroom **Connections**

Intervening Successfully in Classrooms

1. Cognitive interventions target learners' need to make sense of their experiences. Use logical consequences to help students develop responsibility. Hold discussions regarding fairness or equity after class and in private.

   ■ **Elementary:** During daily classroom chores, two first graders begin a tug-of-war over a cleaning rag and knock over a potted plant. Their teacher talks to them, they agree to clean up the mess, and they write a note to their parents explaining that they will be working in the classroom before school the next week to pay for a new pot.

   ■ **Middle School:** A social studies teacher makes her interventions learning experiences by identifying rules that were broken and explaining why the rules exist. In cases of uncertainty, she talks privately to students.

   ■ **High School:** After having been asked to stop whispering for the second time in 10 minutes, a ninth grader protests that he was asking about the assigned seatwork. His teacher reminds him of the incidents, points out that his behavior is disruptive, and reprimands him without further discussion. His teacher talks to him after class, explaining why rules exist, and reminding him that he is expected to accept responsibility for his behavior.

2. Positive reinforcement can be used to increase appropriate behavior. Use positive reinforcers to initiate and teach desirable behaviors.

   ■ **Elementary:** A first-grade teacher, knowing that the time after lunch is difficult for many students, gives students 1 minute after a timer rings to settle down and get out their materials. When the class meets the requirement, they earn points toward free time.

   ■ **Middle School:** To encourage students to clean up quickly after labs, a science teacher offers 5 minutes of free time to talk in their seats if the lab is cleaned up in time. Students who don't clean up in time are required to finish in silence.

   ■ **High School:** A ninth-grade basic math teacher is encountering problems getting his students to work quietly in small groups. He discusses the problem with the class and then closely monitors the groups, circulating and offering praise and reinforcement when they are working smoothly.

3. Linking consequences to behaviors helps students see the connection between their actions and their effects on others. To help students see the logical connection between behaviors and consequences, follow through consistently in cases of disruptive behavior, and explain your actions.

   ■ **Elementary:** A second-grade teacher finds that transitions to and from lunch and bathroom breaks are sometimes disruptive. She talks with the class about the problem, initiates a "no-talking" rule during these transitions, and carefully enforces the rule.

   ■ **Middle School:** A teacher separates two seventh graders who disrupt lessons with their talking, telling them the new seat assignments are theirs until further notice. The next day, they sit in their old seats as the bell is about to ring. "Do you know why I moved you two yesterday?" the teacher says immediately. After a momentary pause, both students nod. "Then move quickly now, and be certain you're in your new seats tomorrow. You can come and talk with me when you believe you're ready to accept responsibility for your talking."

   ■ **High School:** An eleventh-grade history teacher reminds students about being seated when the bell rings. As it rings the next day, two girls remain standing and talking. The teacher turns to them and says, "I'm sorry, but you must not have understood me yesterday. To be counted on time, you need to be in your seats when the bell rings. Please go to the office and get a late-admit pass."

Ed Psych and You

We've all heard about highly publicized incidents of school shootings and other stories about teachers being assaulted by students. Do you worry about these possibilities as you anticipate your first teaching job?

Serious Management Problems: Defiance and Aggression

If you answered yes to our question in *Ed Psych and You*, you're like many other beginning teachers. Many, perhaps most, think—and worry—about incidents of school violence and even the possibility of being assaulted by a student. However, incidents of defiance and aggression toward teachers are rare in schools, with research indicating that the assault rate is slightly over 3 per 1,000 teachers (Moriarty, 2009). However, these incidents can happen, and you need to be aware of the possibility and be prepared to deal with an incident in the unlikely event that it occurs.

Responding to Defiant Students

> Tyrone, one of your students, has difficulty maintaining attention and staying on task. He frequently makes loud and inappropriate comments in class and disrupts learning activities. You warn him, reminding him that being disruptive is unacceptable, and blurting out another comment will result in a time-out.
>
> Within a minute, Tyrone blurts out again.
>
> "Please go to the time-out area," you say evenly.
>
> "I'm not going, and you can't make me," he says defiantly. He crosses his arms and remains seated at his desk.

What do we do when a student like Tyrone says, "I'm not going, and you can't make me?" Experts offer two suggestions (Moriarty, 2009; Smith & Bondy, 2007). First, remain calm to avoid a power struggle. Teachers' natural tendencies are to become angry and display a show of force to demonstrate to students that they "can't get away with it." Remaining calm gives us time to control our tempers, and the student's mood when facing a calm teacher is likely to change from anger and bravado to fear and contrition (Good & Brophy, 2008).

Second, if possible, give the rest of the class a brief assignment, and then tell the student calmly but assertively to please step outside the classroom so you can talk. Communicate an assertive, but not threatening, tone.

Defiance is often the result of negative student–teacher relationships, and they occur most commonly with students who display externalizing behavior problems, such as aggression, temper tantrums, or impulsiveness and hyperactivity (Henricsson & Rydell, 2004). When a problem occurs with such students, it's important to let them say everything that's on their minds in private conferences, such as outside the classroom, before responding. Finally, arrange to meet with the student before or after school, focus on the defiance as a problem, and attempt to generate solutions that are acceptable to both of you.

If the student refuses to leave your classroom, or becomes physically threatening, immediately send someone to the front office for help. Many schools now have security personnel who can be summoned through the communication system from the classroom. In this case, immediately contact security. Defiance at this level likely requires help from a mental health professional.

Responding to Fighting

> As you work with a small group of your fourth graders, a fight suddenly breaks out between Trey and Neil, who are supposed to be working on a group project together. You hear sounds of shouting and see Trey flailing at Neil, who is attempting to fend off Trey's blows. Trey is often verbally aggressive and sometimes threatens other students.
>
> What do you do?

Incidents of student aggression toward each other are much more common than threats to teachers. Information from the Centers for Disease Control and Prevention (2012) indicates that in 2011 about 12% of all middle and high school students were involved in a physical fight on school property. Incidents between younger children, such as your fourth graders, are lower, and the figures in both cases may also be lower, because statistics indicate that violent crime in schools—in spite of some unspeakable and widely publicized incidents of school violence—has been declining steadily since the early 1990s (Neuman, 2012).

In a situation such as the one between Trey and Neil, you are required by law to intervene. If you don't, you and the school can be sued for **negligence**, the failure to exercise sufficient care in protecting students from injury (Schimmel, Stellman, Conlon, & Fischer, 2015). However, the law doesn't require you to physically break up the fight; immediately reporting it to administrators is acceptable.

An effective response to fighting involves three steps: (1) stop the incident (if possible), (2) protect the victim, and (3) get help. For instance, in the case of the classroom scuffle, a loud noise, such as shouting, clapping, or slamming a chair against the floor, will often surprise the students enough so they'll stop (Evertson & Emmer, 2013). At that point, you can begin to talk to them, check to see if the victim is all right, and then take the students to the main office, where you can get help. If your interventions don't stop the fight, you should immediately send an uninvolved student for help. Don't attempt to separate the students unless you're sure you can do so without danger to yourself or them. You are responsible first for the safety of the other students and yourself, second for the involved students, and finally for property (Good & Brophy, 2008).

Responding to Bullying

> Matt, one of your seventh graders, is shy and a bit small for his age. As he comes into your class this morning, he appears disheveled and depressed. Concerned, you take him aside and ask if anything is wrong. With some prodding he tells you that he repeatedly gets shoved around on the school grounds before school, and two boys have been taunting him and calling him gay. "I hate school," he comments.
>
> How do you respond?

Bullying, a form of peer aggression that involves a systematic or repetitive abuse of power between students, is a serious management problem in our schools. Students learn less when they're afraid of being bullied, and their social and emotional growth is decreased. In a survey of more than 43,000 high school students, half admitted that they had bullied someone in the past year, and nearly the same percent said they had been bullied, teased, or taunted (Josephson Institute Center for Youth Ethics, 2010).

Dramatically increased attention has been directed at bullying in recent years, partially because of more frequent incidents of **cyberbullying**, a form of bullying that occurs when students use electronic media to harass or intimidate other students. Attention has also increased because of some widely publicized cases of students committing suicide after being bullied, particularly after being cyberbullied (Low & Espelage, 2013). For example, in a Florida case in 2013, authorities even pressed charges against two adolescent girls because of allegations that they harassed 12-year-old Rebecca Sedwick to the point that she jumped to her death from the top of an abandoned concrete plant (Almasy, Segal, & Couwels, 2013).

Our society in general and school officials in particular are now recognizing that bullying is a serious problem. "The courts are very clear that all facets of the school community must police and report any bullying behavior that is observed. . . . It is no longer OK . . . to call bullying 'horse play'" (Padgett & Notar, 2013, p. 88). Bullying obviously detracts from students' feelings of safety, and it can carry serious problems for both perpetrators and victims. Some research even indicates that adults vividly remember incidents of being bullied many years after they've completed their schooling (Cooper & Nickerson, 2013).

Forty-four states have passed anti-bullying laws, and many districts have implemented zero-tolerance policies. However, these laws and policies have been largely ineffective in reducing incidents of bullying (Graham, 2010; Walker, 2009). Further, seeing that zero-tolerance policies are leading to increased arrest records, low academic achievement, and high dropout rates that particularly affect minority students, many school districts around the country are moving away from these policies, particularly for minor offenses (Alvarez, 2013).

Teachers are central to schools' efforts to eliminate bullying, so you will play an important role in the process (Peron, 2013). Because you will be on the "front line" with students, you will be in a better position than other school authorities to observe incidents of bullying, and you must be prepared to deal with this serious problem. Three levels of intervention exist.

At the first level, you should intervene immediately and apply appropriate consequences for the perpetrators. Trey, for example, must understand that his aggressive actions won't be tolerated. Because immediately stopping the practice is imperative, behavioral interventions will probably be needed, particularly in the near term (Kuppens, Laurent, Heyvaert, & Onghena, 2013). Most important, bullies must learn that their actions are unacceptable.

At the second level, open and frank discussions about bullying that include information about the maladaptive personal and social characteristics of bullies can reduce their social status among other students. For instance, research indicates that, as general patterns, bullies tend to have the following characteristics.

- They often lack empathy and don't understand the negative impact their behaviors are having on others (Craig & Pepler, 2007).
- Academically, bullies tend to perform poorly and don't adjust well to school (Dake, Price, & Telljohann, 2003).
- Bullies are more likely than other students to have problems with substance abuse, criminal activity, delinquency, and school misconduct (Merrell, Gueldner, Ross, & Isava, 2008).

Your goal in these discussions is to make bullying a socially unacceptable practice. We're all human, we all have feelings, and it will be harder for students to behave as bullies when they realize that other students may see them as unintelligent delinquents who don't care about anyone else. These discussions can also address topics such as ideas about right and wrong, appropriate treatment of others, tolerance for differences, and abuse of power. They can also focus on aspects of self-regulation, such as impulse control, emotional regulation, and self-socialization (Graham, 2010).

We can also talk to bullies in private, ask them if they want to be seen in this way by their peers, and discuss more socially acceptable ways to express themselves. Because bullies tend to also come from homes with poor parental role models who fail to set limits on their children's behavior and who tend to use physical discipline to control their children (Merrell et al., 2008; Veenstra et al., 2005), you may be an adult they can turn to for guidance and emotional support (Kuppens et al., 2013).

Openly discussing the maladaptive characteristics of bullies may seem a bit extreme, but it's heartbreaking, for example, to see a student small for his age being pushed around every day by bigger boys who think the abuse is funny or even cool, or to see a girl socially ostracized for some capricious reason. Bullying is a serious problem and we must do what it takes to stop it. As you can see, bullying is an issue about which we feel strongly. We've witnessed it firsthand, and the destruction is palpable. It must be stopped, and you will be on the first line of intervention.

At the third level, and long term, the most effective responses to bullying are school-wide and include all members of the school community—administrators, teachers, students, support staff, custodians, parent–teacher organizations, bus drivers, cafeteria personnel, and parents. These programs are time and energy intensive and demanding but they are effective (Padgett & Notar, 2013). If students know, for example, that their bus driver will report an incident of bullying on the ride home from school, and consequences exist, they are less likely to bully. The same is true for incidents in the cafeteria, on the school grounds, and activities outside of school.

Both intermediate and long-term interventions will take time, and they won't reach every student. But they can make a difference, and for the students you—and your school—reach, the results can be increased self-regulation, healthier social development for individuals, and a safer and more positive school environment for all students.

Diversity: Classroom Management with Students from Diverse Backgrounds

Working with learners from diverse backgrounds presents a unique set of challenges. A long history of research suggests that discrepancies exist in disciplinary referrals and punishment for students who are members of cultural minorities (Balagna et al., 2013; Gay, 2006; Murphy, Vagins, & Parker, 2010). For example, African American boys are referred for behavior problems at a much higher rate than their peers, and they also receive harsher punishments. Also, European American students are often disciplined for observable infractions, such as smoking, leaving school without permission, or profanity, whereas African American students are more often disciplined for infractions that require a teacher's interpretation, such as disrespect, defiance, or class disruptions (Skiba et al., 2011).

Additional evidence suggests that communication breakdowns between teachers and students who are English language learners sometimes result in students being punished for what teachers thought they heard and not for what children actually said (Kirylo, Thirumurthy, & Spezzini, 2010). Some researchers believe that this miscommunication occurs because most teachers are middle class, female, and White, whereas students who are ELs are cultural minorities and are often from families with lower socioeconomic status.

Culturally responsive classroom management, which combines cultural knowledge with teachers' awareness of possible personal biases, can help overcome some of these problems. A culturally responsive classroom management model designed to address this problem has five elements:

- Become personally aware of possible cultural biases.
- Learn about students' cultural heritage.
- Learn about student's neighborhoods and home environments.
- Create caring and inclusive learning environments.
- Develop culturally responsive classroom management strategies (Milner & Tenore, 2010).

As we become aware of our own possible fears and biases and come to understand our students' interaction patterns, we will realize that student responses that appear threatening or disrespectful often are not intended that way. Increased awareness and knowledge, combined with culturally responsive classroom management strategies, can contribute a great deal toward overcoming racial discrepancies in classroom management issues (Balagna et al., 2013; McCurdy, Kunsch, & Reibstein, 2007). These strategies, to a large extent, include those we've discussed in this chapter, such as promoting student responsibility and self-regulation, creating communities of caring and trust, and establishing clear expectations for behavior. Combined with conducting highly interactive lessons and providing students with specific and nonjudgmental feedback about their behavior and learning progress, these strategies are effective with all students, and they're particularly important for students from diverse backgrounds. As with all strategies, they won't solve every problem, but they will contribute to your students' academic and social–emotional learning.

Developmentally Appropriate **Practice**

Classroom Management with Learners at Different Ages

Although many aspects of classroom management, such as creating a caring classroom community, developing learner responsibility, and planning carefully, apply across the K–12 continuum, developmental differences exist. The following paragraphs outline suggestions for responding to these differences.

Working with Children in Early Childhood Programs and Elementary Schools

Earlier in the chapter we discussed the importance of teaching rules and procedures to elementary students. Young children are often unaware of rules and procedures and may not understand how they contribute to learning. Because their cognitive development is likely to be preoperational, special efforts to explain the importance of rules and their connection to personal responsibility and learning can be helpful.

Young children are trusting and vulnerable, so criticism and harsh reprimands and desists are particularly harmful (Carter & Doyle, 2006). They respond well to praise, but ignoring inappropriate behavior and using indirect cues are less likely to be effective with them than with older students. Behavioral interventions, such as time-outs for chronic interruptions, can be effective if they are not overdone. Developing personal responsibility for behavior should be an important long-term goal.

Working with Students in Middle Schools

As students develop, they become more cognitively, personally, and socially aware. As a result, consistency and logical consequences become increasingly important and effective. Middle school students continue to need a caring teacher; clear boundaries for acceptable behavior and consistently enforced boundaries are indicators of caring for these students. Timely and judicious praise continues to be important, but ignoring inappropriate behavior and using indirect cues can also be effective for minor rule infractions.

The increasing importance of peers presents both challenges and opportunities in middle schools. Whispering, note passing, and general attempts to socialize become problems, and clear, consistently applied rules are essential. Middle school students appreciate being involved in rule setting, and periodic class meetings are effective in enlisting student commitment to and cooperation with classroom rules and procedures.

Working with Students in High Schools

High school students react well to being treated as adults. Developing personal responsibility is important, and private conferences that appeal to their sense of responsibility can be effective. Peers continue to exert a powerful influence on behavior, so avoiding embarrassing students in front of their peers is important. Often, a simple request to turn around or get busy is all the intervention needed.

High school students are also becoming increasingly skilled at reading social and nonverbal cues, so congruence between verbal and nonverbal channels is important. Honest interventions that directly address the problem and leave students' dignity intact, but still communicate commitment and resolve, are very effective.

A positive teacher–student relationship remains the foundation of an effective management system, and high school students react well to personal comments, such as a compliment about a new outfit or hairstyle, or questions, such as asking about an ill parent's progress or how a new brother or sister is doing.

chapter

12 Summary

1. Describe the goals of classroom management, and identify applications of the goals.
   - Promoting student self-regulation, the ability to control one's actions and emotions, is a primary goal of classroom management.
   - When students learn to behave in acceptable ways and control their impulses, communities of caring and trust, classroom environments where students feel safe to share their thinking without fear of humiliation or ridicule, are developed.
   - In classrooms where learners are self-regulated and communities of caring and trust are created, time available for learning is maximized.

2. Identify characteristics of elementary, middle, and secondary school students and how they influence planning for classroom management.
   - Young children's thinking is perceptual and concrete; they are eager to please their teachers and are vulnerable to criticism and harsh treatment.
   - Effective teachers in elementary schools teach rules and procedures and provide concrete opportunities to practice them, which creates orderly and predictable environments that build trust and develop autonomy.
   - Middle school students are increasingly influenced by peers, and needs for social acceptance and independence increase.
   - Effective teachers in middle schools treat students with unconditional positive regard and provide the firm hand of a caring teacher who sets clear limits for acceptable behavior.
   - As students move into high school, they communicate more effectively at an adult level, and they respond well to clear rationales for rules and procedures that make sense to them.

3. Describe effective communication strategies for involving parents.
   - Effective communication with parents begins with early communication and maintains links throughout the school year.
   - Home–school cooperation increases students' achievement, increases willingness to do homework, improves attitudes and behaviors, and increases attendance and graduation rates.

4. Use cognitive and behavioral learning theories to explain effective interventions.
   - Cognitive learning theory is grounded in the premise that people want their experiences to make sense.
   - Demonstrating withitness—being consistent, keeping verbal and nonverbal messages congruent, using I-messages, and applying logical consequences—is a cognitive intervention.
   - Praising desired behavior, ignoring inappropriate behavior, using desists, and applying consequences all capitalize on behavioral concepts, such as reinforcement, extinction, and punishment, to maintain an orderly classroom.

5. Describe your legal and professional responsibilities in cases of aggressive acts and steps you can take to respond to defiance and aggression.
   - Teachers are required by law to intervene in cases of violence or aggression.
   - Stopping the incident, protecting the victim, and seeking assistance are the first steps involved in responding to fighting.
   - Responding immediately and applying appropriate consequences are the most effective responses to incidents of bullying.

Preparing for Your Licensure Exam

Understanding Classroom Management

You will be required to take a licensure exam before you go into your own classroom. This exam will include information related to classroom management, and it will include both multiple-choice and constructed-response questions. We include the following exercises to help you practice for the exam in your state. This book and these exercises will be a resource for you as you prepare for the exam.

In the opening case study, you saw how Judy Harris maintained an orderly and learning-focused classroom. In the following case study, Janelle Powers, another seventh-grade geography teacher, also has her students working on a lesson about the Middle East. Analyze Janelle's approach to classroom management, and answer the questions that follow.

In homeroom this morning, Shiana comes through the classroom doorway just as the tardy bell rings.

"Please quickly take your seat, Shiana," Janelle directs. "We need to get started. . . . All right. Listen up, everyone," she continues. "Ali?"

"Here."

"Gaelen?"

"Here."

"Chu?"

"Here."

When Janelle finishes taking the roll, she walks around the room, handing back a set of papers.

"You did quite well on the assignment," she comments. "Let's keep up the good work. . . . Howard and Manny, please stop talking while I'm returning papers. Can't you sit quietly for 1 minute?"

The boys, who were whispering, turn back to the front of the room.

"Now," Janelle continues, returning to the front of the room, "we've been studying the Middle East, so let's review for a moment. . . . Look at the map, and identify the longitude and latitude of Cairo. Take a minute, and jot these down right now. I'll be collecting these in a few minutes."

The students begin as Janelle goes to her file cabinet to get out some materials to display on the document camera.

"Stop it, Damon," she hears Leila blurt out behind her.

"Leila," Janelle responds sternly, "we don't talk out like that in class."

"He's poking me, Mrs. Powers."

"Are you poking her, Damon?"

". . ."

"Well?"

"Not really."

"You did, too," Leila complains.

"Both of you stop it," Janelle warns. "Another outburst like that, Leila, and your name goes on the board."

As the students are finishing their work, Janelle looks up from the materials on her desk to check an example on the overhead. She hears Howard and Manny talking and laughing at the back of the room.

"Are you boys finished?"

"Yes," Manny answers.

"Well, be quiet then until everyone is done," Janelle directs and goes back to rearranging her materials.

"Quiet, everyone," she again directs, looking up in response to a hum of voices around the room. "Is everyone finished? . . . Good. Pass your papers forward. . . . Remember, put your paper on the top of the stack. . . . Roberto, wait until the papers come from behind you before you pass yours forward."

Janelle collects the papers, puts them on her desk, and then begins, "We've talked about the geography of the Middle East, and now we want to look at the climate a bit more. It varies somewhat. For example, Syria is extremely hot in the summer but is actually quite cool in the winter. In fact, it snows in some parts."

Janelle then continues presenting information about the Middle East for the remainder of the period, stopping twice to remind Manny and Howard to stop talking and pay attention.

Questions for **Case Analysis**

In answering these questions, use information from the chapter, and link your responses to specific information in the case.

Multiple-Choice Questions

1. Think about the way Janelle began her class—by first taking roll and then handing back a set of papers. With respect to classroom management, which of the following is the best assessment of Janelle's class beginning?

    a. It was effective because she began taking roll just as the tardy bell finished ringing.

    b. It was effective, because she immediately began handing the papers back as soon as she had finished taking roll.

    c. It was ineffective, because she told Shiana to quickly take her seat as the bell was ringing.

    d. It was ineffective, because the time spent taking roll and handing back papers allowed off-task behavior, such as Manny and Howard's talking.

2. Look at the encounter between Damon and Leila that began with Leila saying, "Stop it, Damon," and ending with Janelle saying, "Another outburst like that, Leila, and your name goes on the board." Of the following, which is the best assessment of Janelle's handling of this incident?

    a. It was effective because she intervened immediately to stop the disruption.

    b. It was ineffective because Janelle's reprimand of Leila indicated a lack of withitness.

    c. It was effective because Janelle responded assertively instead of aggressively or passively in responding to Leila.

    d. It was ineffective because Janelle didn't use an I-message in responding to Leila.

Constructed-Response Question

3. With respect to classroom management and the synergy between classroom management and instruction, assess Janelle's overall effectiveness. Provide evidence from the case study to support your assessment.

Important **Concepts**

academic learning time	corporal punishment	engaged time	overlapping
allocated time	culturally responsive	I-message	positive behavior support
assertive discipline	classroom management	instructional time	procedures
bullying	cyberbullying	logical consequences	rules
classroom management	desist	negligence	self-regulation
community of caring and	discipline	non-exclusionary timeout	withitness
trust			

Learning and Effective Teaching

OUTLINE	LEARNING OUTCOMES

Imagine you're sitting in the back of a classroom observing a teacher working with students. How would you know if the teacher is "good" or "effective"? What would you look for? What would you expect to see? Keep these questions in mind as we follow the work of Scott Sowell, a middle school science teacher, through this chapter.

As Scott is working on a Saturday afternoon to plan his next week, he looks at his textbook and the standards from the National Science Teachers Association, one of his most important professional organizations. He decides that he will work with his students on the following standard:

MS.Forces and Interactions. MS-PS2-2. Plan an investigation to provide evidence that the change in an object's motion depends on the sum of the forces on the object and the mass of the object (National Science Teachers Association, 2013, p. 61).

As he plans, he also thinks about his past experience with the topic and decides that he will incorporate the standard into lessons on Bernoulli's principle, the law that helps explain how different forces enable airplanes to fly. "The kids like it," he remembers, "because it's both interesting and has a lot of real-world applications."

He identifies three objectives for his Monday lesson. His first is for students to know that a force is a push or a pull, and his second is for them to identify examples of the concept *force*. He thinks about simple demonstrations to illustrate *force,* such as pulling a student's chair across the floor, pushing on the chalkboard, and having the students lift their books off their desks.

Then, he thinks, "My third objective is for them to determine what will happen to an object when different forces act on it" (the sum of the forces on an object). "So," he smiles to himself, "I'll demonstrate it with a little tug of war with one of the kids. I'll let him pull me to show that because his force is greater, we'll move that way. It'll help them understand the part of the standard that says, 'change in an object's motion depends on the sum of the forces on the object.' And the demonstration will provide the evidence called for in the standard."

Finally, he decides to teach Bernoulli's principle on Tuesday and Wednesday, review on Thursday, and give a quiz on Friday.

We have made "Learning and Effective Teaching" the title of this chapter simply because **effective teaching** is instruction that promotes as much learning as possible in all students. Our purpose in writing this chapter is to help you understand what effective teachers do to maximize their students' learning, how their actions relate to cognitive learning theory, and how you can become an effective teacher when you begin your career. We'll use Scott's work with his students as the framework for our discussion.

Effective teaching can be summarized in three phases, which are outlined in Figure 13.1. As you see in the figure, the phases are interdependent and cyclical. The process begins with planning, and we turn to it next.

Ed Psych and You

You have a personal project that you want to complete, such as redecorating the living room in your apartment or house. What is the first thing you think about? What else do you consider?

Planning for Instruction

Think about the questions we ask in *Ed Psych and You* here. After identifying the project, such as redecorating the living room in your apartment, you'll then probably ask yourself a series of questions, the first being the project's purpose, or objective. Maybe you want it to be more comfortable; perhaps you want it to be warmer and more inviting for guests; you might simply want to use the space more efficiently; or maybe your objective is to incorporate all three. Then, you'll ask yourself how you'll achieve your objective, such as repainting the room, rearranging the furniture, or adding some artwork. When

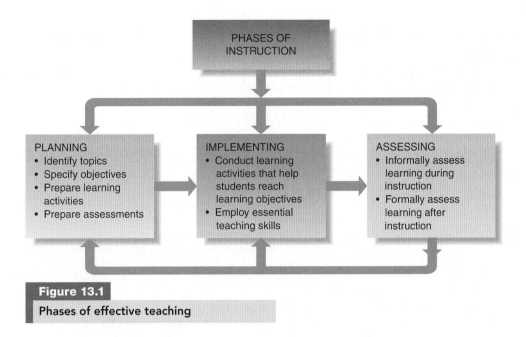

Figure 13.1

Phases of effective teaching

you're finished, you'll consider some way of determining whether or not you did indeed achieve your purpose.

As we plan for teaching, we go through a similar process. We ask ourselves a series of questions, and we make decisions that answer them, just as you did with your redecorating project (Anderson & Krathwohl, 2001; Lemov, 2010). We make four decisions when we plan for teaching. They include:

- Identifying topics
- Specifying learning objectives
- Preparing and organizing learning activities
- Planning for assessment

The planning decisions Scott made, the question each decision answers, and examples that illustrate each are outlined in Table 13.1. We examine these planning decisions in more detail next.

Identifying Topics

"What is important to learn?" is the first question we ask ourselves when we begin planning (Lemov, 2010). In answering the question, we rely on textbooks, curriculum guides, and particularly standards, such as the one Scott used. Students' interests in the topic and the availability of real-world applications will also influence our decisions. Scott, for example, identified *force* and relationships among forces as his Monday topic and Bernoulli's principle for his Tuesday and Wednesday topic. He decided that *force* is important because it's a basic science concept, and Bernoulli's principle is important because it can help us understand real-world events, such as how airplanes are able to fly.

More content appears in textbooks than can be learned in depth. So, instead of teaching a topic simply because it's the next one that appears in our books, we need to make decisions about whether a topic is important enough to teach. Standards, together with our knowledge of content and our understanding of our students' backgrounds and interests, help us make decisions in this process (Bereiter & Scardamalia, 2006).

Table 13.1 Planning for instruction

Planning Decision	Question the Decision Answers	Examples from Scott's Lesson
Identify topic(s)	What is important for students to learn?	Scott decided that his students should understand: • the concept *force* • relationships among forces • Bernoulli's principle
Specify learning objectives	What, specifically, do I want students to know or be able to do with respect to the topic?	Scott wanted his students to: • know that a force is a push or a pull • identify examples of forces • understand that objects move in the direction of the greatest force on them (change in an object's motion depends on the sum of the forces on the object) • explain examples of Bernoulli's principle (examples showing that as the speed of air over a surface increases, the force the air exerts on the surface decreases)
Prepare and organize learning activities	What will I do to help students reach the learning objectives?	Scott decided he would: • show a series of examples, such as pushing on the chalkboard, to illustrate the concept *force* • conduct a "tug of war" to demonstrate that objects move in the direction of the greater force • conduct a series of demonstrations of Bernoulli's principle (illustrated on pp. 551–553)
Planning for assessment	How will I determine the extent to which students have reached the learning objective(s)?	Scott decided he would: • have students sketch and describe the relationship between speed of air over a surface and the force the air exerts on the surface (illustrated on p. 584)

Specifying Learning Objectives

After identifying a topic, we specify **learning objectives**, what we want students to know or be able to do with respect to the topic. Clear learning objectives are essential because they guide the rest of our planning decisions. For example, **learning activities** are all the actions we take to help our students reach our learning objectives, and it's impossible to design effective learning activities if we're not clear about what we're trying to accomplish (our objectives) in the first place, and the same is true for designing assessments. Unsuccessful lessons are often the result of teachers not being clear about their objectives.

OBJECTIVES IN THE COGNITIVE DOMAIN

Scott had three objectives for his Monday lesson. He wanted his students to (1) know that a *force* is a push or a pull, (2) identify examples of forces, and (3) determine that objects will move in the direction of the greatest force on them (change in an object's motion depends on the sum of the forces on the object). For his Tuesday and Wednesday lesson he wanted his students to *explain examples of Bernoulli's principle (examples showing that as the speed of air over a surface increases, the force the air exerts on the surface decreases).*

These are learning objectives in the **cognitive domain**, the area of learning that focuses on students' thinking and the processes involved in acquiring, applying, and analyzing knowledge. Objectives can also be written for the **affective domain**, which centers on people's attitudes, values, and emotion, and the **psychomotor domain**, the learning domain that concentrates on physical skills. Because the majority of formal instruction in our nation's schools focuses on the cognitive domain, and because a cognitive component is often involved in attitudes, emotions, and physical skills, we will limit our discussion here to this area of learning.

TAXONOMIES FOR COGNITIVE OBJECTIVES

Let's think about Scott's objectives again. Each involves thinking, so they are all in the cognitive domain, but the specific cognitive (thought) processes required of learners are quite different. To respond to these differences, experts developed a system to classify objectives, questions, and assessment items. The result was the famous "Bloom's Taxonomy," which has been a cornerstone of education for more than a half century (Bloom, Englehart, Furst, Hill, & Krathwohl, 1956). The categories in the system include:

- *Knowledge:* Knowledge of facts, definitions, and other forms of memorized information, such knowing that *force* is a push or a pull (Scott's first objective).
- *Comprehension:* Understanding information, such as the ability to state a problem in one's own words or identify an original example of a concept, such as identifying examples of force (Scott's second objective).
- *Application:* Using what one knows to solve an original problem, such as determining what will happen when different forces act on an object (Scott's third objective).
- *Analysis:* The ability to break information into component parts and provide evidence to support conclusions, such as explaining how one knows that one force is greater than another.
- *Synthesis:* Combining information to create an original process or product, such as constructing a unique process for finding a solution to a problem.
- *Evaluation:* Making judgments about the validity or quality of work based on a set of criteria, such as determining which of two approaches to solving a problem is more efficient.

To reflect our increased understanding of teaching and learning since the middle of the 20th century, when the original taxonomy was published, it has been revised and now more nearly reflects the influence of cognitive learning theory on teaching and learning (Anderson & Krathwohl, 2001). This newer taxonomy describes objectives in terms of students' cognitive processes and uses the term *knowledge* to reflect what students should know or acquire (Anderson & Krathwohl, 2001). For example, in Scott's first objective: "Know that force is a push or a pull," *force* is the knowledge, and *know* is the cognitive process.

The result is a matrix with 24 cells that represent the intersection of four types of knowledge with six cognitive processes (Anderson & Krathwohl, 2001). This taxonomy appears in Figure 13.2.

To understand this classification matrix, let's look at Scott's four objectives again:

- Know that force is a push or a pull
- Identify examples of the concept *force*
- Determine that objects will move in the direction of the greatest force on them (change in an object's motion depends on the sum of the forces on the object)
- Explain examples of Bernoulli's principle (examples showing that as the speed of air over a surface increases, the force the air exerts on the surface decreases)

The first objective focuses on the concept *force* and involves memory, so it would be classified into the cell where *conceptual knowledge* intersects with *remember.* Because being able to identify examples of the concept *force* requires understanding, the second objective would be classified into the cell where *conceptual knowledge* intersects with *understand.* The third objective, "determine that objects will move in the direction of the greatest force on them," belongs in the cell where *procedural knowledge* intersects with *apply,* because making this determination requires the application of procedural knowledge. His fourth objective, "explain examples of Bernoulli's principle (examples showing that as the speed of air over a surface increases, the force the air exerts on the surface decreases)," requires learners to analyze the influence

The Knowledge Dimension	The Cognitive Process Dimension					
	1. Remember	2. Understand	3. Apply	4. Analyze	5. Evaluate	6. Create
A. Factual knowledge						
B. Conceptual knowledge						
C. Procedural knowledge						
D. Metacognitive knowledge						

Figure 13.2

A taxonomy for learning, teaching, and assessing
Source: "A Taxonomy for Learning, Teaching, and Assessing" from *A Taxonomy for Learning, Teaching, and Assessing: A Revision of Bloom's Taxonomy of Educational Objectives, Abridged Edition*, 1st Edition by Anderson *ET AL.* Copyright © 2001 by Anderson/Krathwohl/Cruikshank/Mayer/Pintrich/Raths/Wittrock. Printed and Electronically reproduced by permission of Pearson Education, Inc., Upper Saddle River, New Jersey.

of air flowing over a surface, so it would be classified into the cell where *procedural knowledge* intersects with *analyze*.

The taxonomy helps us understand the complexities of learning, and it also reminds us that we want our students to do more than remember factual knowledge. Unfortunately, schooling often focuses more on this most basic type of learning than it does on the other 23 cells combined. These other forms of knowledge and more advanced cognitive processes are even more important now in the 21st century, as student thinking, decision making, and problem solving are increasingly emphasized.

Preparing and Organizing Learning Activities

Once Scott had specified his learning objectives, he then prepared and organized his learning activities—all the actions he took to help his students reach his objectives. This process involved four steps:

1. Identify the components of the topic—the concepts, principles, and relationships among them—that students should understand.
2. Sequence the components.
3. Prepare examples that students can use to construct their knowledge of each component.
4. Order the examples with the most concrete and obvious presented first.

Scott used a task analysis to accomplish these steps. Let's look at this planning tool.

TASK ANALYSIS: A PLANNING TOOL

Task analysis is the process of breaking content into component parts and sequencing the parts. Although different forms of task analysis exist, a subject matter analysis, such as Scott used, is most common in classrooms (Alberto & Troutman, 2013).

Table 13.2	A task analysis for teaching *force* and Bernoulli's principle	

Task-Analysis Step	Example
1. Identify components of the topic.	Scott identified the concept *force*, the influence of two different forces on an object, and *Bernoulli's principle* as different components of the topic.
2. Sequence the components.	Scott planned to teach (1) the concept of *force*; (2) the effect of different forces on an object; and (3) *Bernoulli's principle,* in that order.
3. Prepare examples of each.	Scott prepared examples of each, such as pulling a student in a chair, pushing on the chalkboard, and having a "tug of war" with a student.
4. Order the examples.	Scott first planned to push on the chalkboard, because it was the simplest and most concrete, then demonstrate other examples, and later have his "tug of war" with a student.

When we complete a task analysis, we first identify the specific concepts and principles included in the general topic, then sequence them in a way that will be most understandable to students, and finally identify examples to illustrate each.

Scott knew that his students needed to understand the concept *force* and the effect of different forces on an object in order to understand Bernoulli's principle. So, he first planned to teach *force* and the relationships among forces on Monday and Bernoulli's principle on Tuesday and Wednesday. Scott's task analysis is outlined in Table 13.2.

Planning for Assessment

Because formal assessments, such as quizzes and tests, are typically given after students complete a learning activity, we might assume that thinking about assessment also occurs then. This isn't true; thinking about assessment is an essential part of planning (Stiggins & Chappuis, 2012). As we saw in Table 13.1, effective assessments answer the question, "How can I determine if my students have reached the learning objectives?" (We examine Scott's assessment in detail later in the chapter.)

Assessment decisions are important during planning because they help us align our instruction. Let's examine this important idea further.

Instructional Alignment

Instructional alignment is the match between learning objectives, learning activities, and assessments, and it is essential for promoting learning (Martone & Sireci, 2009; Polikoff, 2012; Wonder-McDowell, Reutzel, & Smith, 2011). If instruction isn't aligned, it's hard to know what is being learned. "Students may be learning valuable information, but one cannot tell unless there is alignment between what they are learning and the assessment of that learning . . . and learning goals" (Bransford, Brown, & Cocking, 2000, pp. 151–152). Instructional alignment is also important because if instruction isn't aligned with assessments, and poor test results come back, "We can't tell if (a) students were taught what they needed to know, but they didn't learn it, or (b) students weren't taught what they needed to know" (Hess & McShane, 2013, p. 63).

Maintaining alignment isn't as easy as it appears. For instance, if our objective is for students to be able to write effectively, yet our learning activities focus on isolated grammar skills, our instruction is not aligned. It is similarly out of alignment if the objective is for students to apply math concepts to the real world, but learning activities have students practicing computation problems.

Scott's instruction was aligned. His objectives were for students to understand the concept *force*, the effect of different forces on an object, and Bernoulli's principle; his learning activity focused on those objectives, and his assessment measured the extent to which students understood these ideas.

Planning in a Standards-Based Environment

To begin this section, look at the following short statements:

> **MS.Forces and Interactions. MS-PS2-2. Plan an investigation to provide evidence that the change in an object's motion depends on the sum of the forces on the object and the mass of the object** (National Science Teachers Association, 2013, p. 61).

> **CCSS.Math.Content.1.OA.B.3 Apply properties of operations as strategies to add and subtract.** *Examples: If 8 + 3 = 11 is known, then 3 + 8 = 11 is also known. (Commutative property of addition.) To add 2 + 6 + 4, the second two numbers can be added to make a ten, so 2 + 6 + 4 = 2 + 10 = 12. (Associative property of addition.)* (Common Core State Standards Initiative, 2014p).

> **CCSS.ELA-Literacy.RH.9-10.8 Assess the extent to which the reasoning and evidence in a text support the author's claims** (Common Core State Standards Initiative, 2014d).

These statements are **standards**, descriptions of what students should know or be able to do at the end of a prescribed period of study. The first is the standard Scott was working on with his students, and the second and third are standards established by the **Common Core State Standards Initiative (CCSSI)**, launched in 2009 as a state-led effort to establish a single set of clear educational standards for all states in essential content areas (Common Core State Standards Initiative, 2014b). All states and the District of Columbia have established standards, and 45 states have adopted the Common Core standards, so standards will be a part of your teaching life when you begin your career. This means you must be able to plan instruction to help your students meet standards.

Standards are essentially statements of objectives, but because they vary in specificity, we often need to first interpret the meaning of the standard and then construct our own specific learning objectives based on our interpretation. For instance, let's look again at the standard that Scott used as a basis for planning his lesson:

> **MS.Forces and Interactions. MS-PS2-2. Plan an investigation to provide evidence that the change in an object's motion depends on the sum of the forces on the object and the mass of the object** (National Science Teachers Association, 2013, p. 61).

Based on his interpretation of the standard, he specified the following objectives, the first three for Monday, and the fourth for Tuesday and Wednesday.

1. Students will know that a force is a push or a pull.
2. Students will identify examples of forces.
3. Students will determine that objects will move in the direction of the greatest force on them (change in an object's motion depends on the sum of the forces on the object).
4. Students will explain examples of Bernoulli's principle (examples showing that as the speed of air over a surface increases, the force the air exerts on the surface decreases).

Now, let's look at Scott's thinking as he interpreted the standard and created his objectives.

Before students can "provide evidence that the change in an object's motion depends on the sum of the forces on the object," they first need to understand the concept *force* and be able to identify examples of forces. This led to his first two objectives. Then, he constructed his third and fourth objectives to illustrate "that the change in an object's motion depends on the sum of the forces on the object." Scott's learning activity was the "investigation" that provided the evidence called for in the standard. (Scott's lesson on Bernoulli's principle is presented later in the chapter in the section "Implementing Instruction.")

He then prepared his learning activities and assessments based on his objectives. Scott's lesson plan appears in Figure 13.3. This lesson plan is merely an example. Formats for lesson plans vary, and the format you will be taught in your methods courses may be different than the example you see here. (The actual lesson based on this lesson plan appears in the first "Practicing what you have learned" exercise at the end of the chapter. Merely click on the link to see the lesson.)

Topic:

Force and Bernoulli's principle

Standard:

MS. Forces and Interactions. MS-PS2-2. Plan an investigation to provide evidence that the change in an object's motion depends on the sum of the forces on the object and the mass of the object.

Learning Objectives:

Students will:

1. know that a *force* is a push or a pull.
2. identify examples of forces.
3. determine that objects will move in the direction of the greatest force on them.
4. explain examples showing that as the speed of air over a surface increases, the force the air exerts on the surface decreases.

Learning Activities:

1. Show examples of forces to review the concept *force*.
2. Tug objects back and forth to review the principle: "Objects move in the direction of the greater force."
3. Have students blow over a piece of paper, ask for observations, and use questioning to lead them to observe that the paper rises.
4. Have students blow between two pieces of paper and observe that the papers come together.
5. Have students blow through the neck of a funnel with a Ping-Pong ball in its mouth and observe that the ball stays in the mouth of the funnel.
6. Sketch the examples on the board and have them identify where the force was greater in each case. Guide them to conclude that the force under the paper, on the outside of the two papers, and in front of the ball was greater than the force on top of the paper, between the papers, and behind the ball.
7. Have students identify where the speed of the air was greater in each case.
8. Guide students to conclude that where the speed of the air was greater, the force was less (the force is greater on the opposite side). Label this relationship "Bernoulli's principle."

Assessment:

1. Have students sketch the flow of air over the surface for each of the examples and prepare a written description of the relationship between the speed and force.
2. Ask students to use Bernoulli's principle to explain how airplanes are able to fly.

Figure 13.3

Scott's lesson plan in middle school science

Now, let's look again at the second standard above, which is in first-grade math.

> CCSS.Math.Content.1.OA.B.3 Apply properties of operations as strategies to add and subtract. *Examples: If 8 + 3 = 11 is known, then 3 + 8 = 11 is also known. (Commutative property of addition.) To add 2 + 6 + 4, the second two numbers can be added to make a ten, so 2 + 6 + 4 = 2 + 10 = 12. (Associative property of addition.)* (Common Core State Standards Initiative, 2014p).

In this case, the standard is specific and concrete, so interpreting it is quite easy, and the two objectives below follow logically from it:

1. For students to understand that addition is commutative.
2. For students to understand that addition is associative.

A lesson plan based on this standard appears in Figure 13.4.

Finally, let's look at the third standard above, which is a literacy standard in History/ Social Studies, for Grade 9–10.

Topic:

Commutative and associative property of addition

Standard:

CCSS.Math.Content.1.OA.B.3 Apply properties of operations as strategies to add and subtract. *Examples: If 8 + 3 = 11 is known, then 3 + 8 = 11 is also known. (Commutative property of addition.) To add 2 + 6 + 4, the second two numbers can be added to make a ten, so 2 + 6 + 4 = 2 + 10 = 12. (Associative property of addition.)*

Learning Objectives:

1. For students to understand that addition is commutative.
2. For students to understand that addition is associative.

Learning Activity:

Commutative Property:

1. Give each student 12 plastic circular discs.
2. Have them count out 8 discs and put them in a group. Then, have them count out 3 more discs and put them in a separate group.
3. Ask them how many discs they have altogether.
4. Ask them to explain in words what they did, and guide them to say, "We first counted 8 discs and then we counted 3 more discs, and we got 11 discs altogether."
5. Write 8 + 3 = 11 on the board.
6. Now have them count 3 discs and put them in a group, then count 8 discs and put them in a group, and count how many they have altogether. Again, have them explain in words what they did, guiding them to say, "We first counted 3 discs and then we counted 8 discs, and we got 11 discs altogether."
7. Write 3 + 8 = 11 directly below where you've written 8 + 3 = 11.
8. Ask them what they notice about the two problems, and guide them to conclude that they both equal 11. Then, guide them to conclude that the order of the numbers doesn't matter when we add, and write 8 + 3 = 3 + 8. Tell them that this works for all numbers when we add and tell them this is called the commutative property of numbers.
9. Do some additional examples similar to this one.

Figure 13.4

Lesson plan for Common Core State Standard in first-grade math

Associative Property:

10. Have the students count 2 discs and put them in a group; count 6 discs and put them in a second group; count 4 discs and put them in a third group.

11. Ask them how many discs they have altogether, ask them to explain in words what they did, and guide them to conclude that they added 2 plus 6 plus 4, and they got 12 altogether.

12. Write 2 + 6 + 4 = 12 on the board.

13. Have them count 2 discs and put them in a group, count 6 discs and put them in a group, and ask them how many they have altogether. Write 2 + 6 = 8 on the board.

14. Then, have them count 4 more discs and ask them how many they have altogether. Write 8 + 4 = 12 directly below 2 + 6 + 4 = 12.

15. Ask them to explain what they did and guide them to say that they first grouped the 2 and the 6 to get 8 and then grouped the 8 and the 4 to get 12.

16. Repeat the process by first grouping the 6 and the 4 to get 10 and then adding the 10 and the 2.

17. Tell them this works for all numbers and tell them this is called the associative property of numbers.

18. Do some additional examples.

Assessment:

1. Give them a worksheet with the following problems on it:

   5 + 2 =

   7 + 1 =

   Tell them to demonstrate the commutative property on their worksheets.

2. On the same worksheet give them the following problems:

   5 + 2 + 4 =

   3 + 1 + 6 =

   Tell them to demonstrate the associative property on their worksheets.

3. Have students who demonstrate the properties correctly come to the front of the room and explain what they did in each case.

Figure 13.4

(Continued)

CCSS.ELA-Literacy.RH.9-10.8 **Assess the extent to which the reasoning and evidence in a text support the author's claims** (Common Core State Standards Initiative, 2014d).

Objectives based on this standard might appear as follows:

1. For students to determine the extent to which authors provide evidence to support the claims presented in their writing.
2. For students to determine the extent to which authors' reasoning supports the claims presented in their writing.

A lesson plan based on this standard appears in Figure 13.5.

When first faced with the task of interpreting standards and creating objectives based on them, you might feel a bit overwhelmed or intimidated. However, as you acquire experience interpreting standards and creating learning activities designed to help your students reach them, the task won't seem as daunting. We hope this section helps you get started with this process.

Topic:

Evidence and reasoning

Standard:

CCSS.ELA-Literacy.RH.9-10.8 Assess the extent to which the reasoning and evidence in a text support the author's claims.

Learning Objectives:

1. For students to determine the extent to which authors provide evidence to support the claims presented in their writing.
2. For students to determine the extent to which authors' reasoning supports the claims presented in their writing.

Learning Activity:

1. Define the concept *evidence* as facts or observations related to a claim or conclusion.
2. Provide examples of evidence supporting a claim or conclusion and provide additional examples where evidence refutes a claim or conclusion.
3. Ask students if they're familiar with the controversy over the name of the Washington Redskins professional football team. If not, explain that some people claim that the name "Redskin" is inherently racist, whereas others claim it is not.
4. Display two columns, one by Rick Reilly, a sports writer for ESPN.com (Reilly, 2013), and the other by Kathleen Parker, a *Washington Post* columnist (Parker, 2013), both of which discuss the controversy related to the name "Washington Redskins" and offer assertions as to whether or not the name "Redskin" should be changed.
5. Have students read the two columns and then work in pairs to assess the extent to which the two authors support their claims related to the need to change the name.
6. Have the groups report to the whole class.
7. As the groups report, write items they consider to be evidence supporting each author's claim on the board.
8. Discuss the items as a whole group.

Assessment:

1. Give students a column related to the issue of immigration and immigration reform in our country (Bandow, 2013).
2. Have them write a paragraph that assesses the extent to which the author supports his claims with evidence and sound reasoning.

Figure 13.5

Lesson plan for Common Core State Standard in literacy for social studies

Classroom Connections

Planning Effectively in Classrooms

1. Knowledge can vary from factual to metacognitive, and cognitive processes range from remembering to creating. Consider the level of your instruction, and prepare objectives that require students to do more than remember factual knowledge.

   - Elementary: A fourth-grade teacher wants her students to understand the different functions of the human skeleton, such as why the skull is solid, the ribs are curved, and the femur is the largest bone in the body. "This is better than simply having them label the different bones," she thinks.

   - Middle School: A seventh-grade geography teacher wants his students to understand how climate is influenced by the interaction of a number of variables. To reach his objective, he gives students a map of a fictitious island, together with longitude, latitude, topography, and wind direction, and has students make and defend conclusions about the climate of the island.

   - High School: A biology teacher wants her students to understand the relationships between an organism's body structure and its adaptation to its environment. She has her students identify the characteristics of parasitic and nonparasitic worms and the differences between them. Students then link the differences to the organisms' abilities to adapt to their environments.

2. Instructional alignment ensures that learning activities are congruent with learning objectives, and assessments are consistent with both. Prepare assessments during planning, and keep the need for alignment in mind as you plan.

   ■ **Elementary:** The fourth-grade teacher in her unit on the skeletal system prepares the following as an assessment: "Suppose humans walked on all fours, as chimpanzees and gorillas do. Describe how our skeletons would be different from our skeletons now."

   ■ **Middle School:** To assess his students' developing knowledge, the geography teacher gives them another map of a fictitious island with different mountain ranges, wind directions, ocean currents, and latitude and longitude. He then asks them to identify and explain where the largest city on the island would most likely be.

   ■ **High School:** The biology teacher describes two organisms, one with radial symmetry and the other with bilateral symmetry. She asks her students to identify the one that is most advanced with respect to evolution and to explain their choices.

Ed Psych and You

You've thought about and made the necessary decisions about redecorating your living room. In other words, you've identified your objectives and planned the redecorating process. Now what do you do?

Implementing Instruction

Now consider the question we ask in *Ed Psych and You* above. The answer is simply *implement your plans*. For example, you actually will do the painting, rearranging the furniture, or adding some artwork to your room.

Again, teaching is similar. **Implementing instruction** is the process of putting the decisions made during planning into action. Planning is largely a series of sequential thought processes combined with gathering necessary materials, whereas implementation focuses on action. A great deal of thinking is involved during implementation as well, but if you've planned carefully, the load on your working memory during implementation will be significantly reduced.

Effectively implementing instruction involves a number of sophisticated teaching skills. To illustrate them, let's return to Scott's work with his students. Scott had taught the concept of *force* and the net effect of forces on an object (objects move in the direction of the greater force) on Monday. We join him as he begins class Tuesday with a review.

"Let's go over what we did yesterday," he begins just as the bell stops ringing. "What is a force? . . . Shantae?"

" . . . A push or a pull," she responds, after thinking for a second.

"Good, Shantae," Scott smiles and then reviews the concept of force by pushing on the board, blowing on an object sitting on his desk, and asking students to explain why they are forces.

He continues by holding a stapler and having Damien try to pull it away from him to review the idea that objects move in the direction of the greater force.

Reminding students to "keep these ideas in mind" and raising his voice to emphasize his points, he gives each two pieces of paper, picks up a similar piece, and blows over it, as you see here.

He directs students to do the same, and then asks, "What did you notice when we blew over the top? . . . David?"

"The paper moved."

"How did the paper move? . . . Let's do it again."

David again blows over the surface of the paper, and Scott repeats, "What did the paper do?"

". . . It came up."

"Yes," Scott waves energetically. "When you blow over it, it comes up."

He then has students pick up both pieces of paper and demonstrates how to blow between them, as shown here.

"What did you notice here? . . . Sharon?" Scott asks after they've done the same.

". . . The papers came together."

"Okay, good. Remember that, and we'll talk about it in a minute," Scott smiles. "Now, let's look at one more example. . . . I have a funnel and a Ping-Pong ball. . . . I'm going to shoot Tristan in the head when I blow," he jokes, pointing to one of the students.

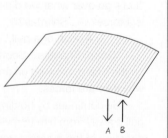

He blows through the funnel's stem, and to the students' surprise, the ball stays in the funnel.

Scott has students repeat the demonstration and make observations, and he then draws sketches of the three examples on the board and says, "Let's look at these."

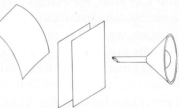

Referring to the first sketch, Scott asks, "Was I blowing on the top or the bottom? . . . Rachel?"

"The top."

"And what happened there? . . . Heather?"

"The paper rose up."

Referring to the second sketch, he asks, "What did we do here? . . . Shantae?"

"We blew in between them."

"And what happened there? . . . Ricky?"

"They came together."

Scott does a similar analysis with the ball and funnel and then says, "Let's think about the forces here. . . . What forces are acting on the paper? . . . Colin?"

"Gravity."

"And which direction is gravity pulling?"

"Down."

Scott draws an arrow pointing downward, indicating the force of gravity, and labels it "A."

"What other force is acting on the paper? . . . William?" he continues.

"Air," William says, pointing up.

"How do you know it's pushing up?"

"The paper moved up."

"Exactly. You know there's a force pushing up, because objects move in the direction of the greater force, and the paper moved up." Scott then draws an arrow pointing up and labels it "B."

Scott guides the students through a similar analysis of the second and third examples, leading them to conclude that the forces pushing the two papers together were greater than the forces pushing them apart, and the force pushing the ball into the funnel was greater than the force pushing the ball out.

"Now let's look again at the forces and where we blew," Scott continues, as he moves back to the first sketch. "Study the drawings carefully, and see what kind of relationship exists between the two."

After several seconds, Heather concludes, "It seems like wherever you blew, the force was stronger on the opposite side."

Seeing that the bell is going to ring in a minute, Scott continues, "Yes, excellent, Heather. . . . A person named Bernoulli discovered that every time you increase the speed of the air over a surface, the force goes down. . . . So, when I speed up the air over the top of the paper (holding up the single sheet of paper), the force goes down and this force takes over (motioning underneath the paper to illustrate a force pushing up)."

He summarizes the other two examples in the same way, finishing just as the bell ending the period begins to ring.

As Scott implemented his plans, he demonstrated a number of **essential teaching skills**, basic abilities that all teachers, including those in their first year, should possess to maximize student learning. They are equally important for working with learners having exceptionalities, members of cultural minorities, and those in urban, suburban, and rural environments. In short, essential teaching skills apply to all students and all teaching situations.

Essential teaching skills are analogous to what is commonly referred to as *basic skills,* the skills in reading, writing, math, and technology that all people need to function effectively in today's world. You will be expected to understand and demonstrate these skills regardless of the content area or grade level that you're planning to teach.

Derived from a long line of research (Brophy, 2006; Good & Brophy, 2008), these skills are outlined in Table 13.3 and discussed in the sections that follow.

Teacher Beliefs and Behaviors

Admittedly, beliefs are not skills, but the effectiveness of your teaching will substantively depend on your beliefs about learning, teaching, and students. For instance, if you believe that you are capable of getting all students to learn (high personal teaching efficacy), you will expect more from your students (high expectations), demonstrate your own interest in the topics you're teaching (modeling and enthusiasm), and commit yourself to your students, both as learners and as people (caring). These beliefs are fundamental for effective teaching. Each is linked to student motivation and increased achievement (Brophy, 2010; Bruning, Schraw, & Norby, 2011).

Scott's interactions with his students suggest that he held these beliefs. He was energetic and enthusiastic, he demonstrated the respect for students that indicates caring, and his questioning suggested that he expected all students to participate and learn. These are the beliefs and behaviors we hope to see in all teachers.

Organization

To teach effectively, we must first be well organized. This means that we (1) prepare the materials we need in advance, (2) start our instruction on time, (3) quickly and smoothly make transitions from one activity to another, and (4) develop well-established classroom routines. These different aspects of organization increase achievement by maximizing instructional time and helping prevent classroom management problems (Good & Brophy, 2008).

Table 13.3 Essential teaching skills, components, and cognitive learning theory applications

Essential Teaching Skill	Essential Teaching Skill Components	Application of Cognitive Learning Theory
Teacher beliefs and behaviors	• Personal teaching efficacy • High and positive expectations • Modeling and enthusiasm • Caring	Models desired behaviors, increases self-efficacy, and helps students meet their need for relatedness.
Organization	• Starting instruction on time • Having materials ready • Creating well-established routines	Reduces the cognitive load on teachers' and students' working memories and helps establish and maintain students' equilibrium.
Review	• Beginning-of-lesson review • Interim reviews	Activates prior knowledge retrieved from long-term memory, to which new knowledge is attached.
Focus	• Capture attention • Maintain attention	Attracts learners' attention and provides a conceptual umbrella for the lesson.
Questioning	• Questioning frequency • Equitable distribution • Prompting • Wait-time	Encourages learners to become cognitively active. Provides scaffolding.
Feedback	• Immediate • Specific • Corrective information • Positive emotional tone	Provides students with information they use to determine whether the knowledge they've constructed is valid.
Closure	• End-of-lesson summary	Contributes to schema construction and meaningful encoding.
Communication	• Precise terms • Connected discourse • Transition signals • Emphasis	Makes information understandable and meaningful. Maintains learner attention.

Scott was well organized. He began his lesson as soon as the bell finished ringing, he had the sheets of paper, balls, and funnels ready to hand out, and he made the transition from his review to the learning activity quickly and smoothly. This organization was the result of clear thinking and decision making during his planning.

Review

Implementing instruction is a systematic process, and it begins with a **review**, a summary that helps students link what they've already learned to the new information we're planning to teach. It can occur at any point in a lesson, although it is most common at the beginning and end.

The knowledge learners construct depends on what they already know is an important cognitive learning principle, and beginning reviews help students activate the prior knowledge needed to construct their new understanding.

Scott's beginning review on Tuesday was one of the most effective aspects of his lesson. He didn't just ask his students to recall the definition of *force* and the influence of different forces on an object; he illustrated the ideas with examples. Because he had shown examples on Monday, it may seem redundant to use additional examples, but doing so is often necessary. Using concrete examples during the review increases its effectiveness by providing additional links between new information and information already in long-term memory. And Scott's review was essential because his students had to understand force and the influence of different forces on an object in order to understand Bernoulli's principle.

Focus

We know from our understanding of human memory that all learning begins with attention, so we need a mechanism to capture and maintain students' attention throughout the lesson. **Focus** provides this mechanism, and some authors use the label "hook" to describe this function (Lemov, 2010).

Scott provided focus for his students by beginning his lesson with his demonstrations. They attracted his students' attention and provided context for the rest of the lesson. His demonstrations and sketches on the board helped maintain student attention throughout his learning activity. Concrete objects, pictures, models, materials displayed on the document camera, or even information written on the board can all act as focus during a lesson.

Questioning

We've conducted a review and used a form of focus to attract our students' attention. Our next challenge is to involve them in the lesson and encourage their cognitive activity, that is, encourage them to *think* carefully about what they're studying. Doing so is supported by a long history of research. "Teachers who elicit greater achievement gains spend a great deal of time actively instructing their students. Their classrooms feature more time spent in interactive lessons featuring teacher–student discourse and less time spent in independent seatwork" (Brophy, 2006, p. 764). Further, teachers who are the most effective spend a minimum amount of time in lecture–presentations (Brophy, 2006; Lemov, 2010).

Questioning is the most widely applicable and effective tool we have for promoting this involvement (Diaz, Whitacre, Esquierdo, & Ruiz-Escalante, 2013; Lemov, 2010). And questioning provides teachers with "the unique opportunity to facilitate higher cognitive levels in their students by the questions they ask during instruction" (Smart & Marshall, 2013, p. 265). Further, some researchers suggest that "teacher questioning is one of the indices of the quality of teaching. It plays an essential role in promoting students' knowledge construction and cognitive development through classroom interaction" (Wang & Wang, 2013, p. 1387). Questioning is one of the most important abilities that we all need to develop if we are to become expert teachers.

Skilled questioning is sophisticated, but in our work with teachers we've seen that with practice and experience they've become expert at it, and you can, too (Eggen & Kauchak, 2012; Kauchak & Eggen, 2012). To avoid overloading your working memory, you need to practice questioning strategies until they're essentially automatic, which leaves working memory space available to monitor students' thinking and assess learning progress (Feldon, 2007). Once you master this ability, you'll find that using questioning to guide your students' increasing understanding will be one of your most rewarding professional experiences.

The components of effective questioning are outlined in Figure 13.6 and discussed in the sections that follow. The connections in the figure remind us that the features are interdependent.

Questioning Frequency. Questioning frequency refers to the number of questions we ask during a learning activity. Scott developed his entire lesson with questioning, and, as with many aspects of teaching, questioning frequency isn't as simple as it appears on the surface. To maximize learning, questions must remain focused on the learning objectives,

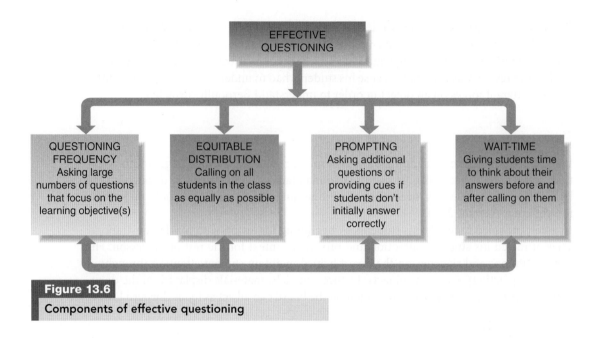

Figure 13.6

Components of effective questioning

and this is another reason careful planning is so important. If we're clear about our objectives, guiding our students' learning with questioning will be much easier.

Equitable Distribution. Equitable distribution is the process of calling on all the students in a class as equally as possible (Eggen & Kauchak, 2012; Kauchak & Eggen, 2012; Kerman, 1979), and it is intended to accommodate teachers' tendencies to call on high-achieving or more outgoing students more often than their peers (Good & Brophy, 2008). To emphasize that we should call on students whether or not they have their hands raised, some experts use the term *cold call* when describing equitable distribution (Lemov, 2010).

To illustrate this idea, let's return to Scott's lesson:

Scott:	(Referring to the sketch of the single piece of paper.) Was I blowing on the top or the bottom? . . . Rachel?
Rachel:	The top.
Scott:	And what happened there? . . . Heather?
Heather:	The paper rose up.
Scott:	(Referring to the sketch of the two pieces of paper.) What did we do here? . . . Shantae?
Shantae:	We blew in between them.
Scott:	And what happened there? . . . Ricky?
Ricky:	They came together.

In this short episode, Scott called on four different students, and he first asked the question and then identified who he wanted to respond. Equitable distribution makes everyone responsible for generating an answer and creates the expectation that all learners are capable of responding and should be paying attention. "Students benefit from opportunities to practice oral communication skills, and distributing response opportunities helps keep them attentive and accountable" (Good & Brophy, 2008, p. 322).

Equitable distribution is a simple but demanding idea because it requires careful monitoring of students and a great deal of energy. This is another reason why we should practice questioning to the point of automaticity to reduce the cognitive load it imposes on us as we work with our students (Feldon, 2007).

Prompting. In attempting to equitably distribute your questions, you might wonder, "What do I do when the student I call on doesn't answer or answers incorrectly?" Ideally, prompting—an additional question or statement used to elicit an appropriate response after a student fails to answer correctly—is the answer. Its value to both learning and motivation is well documented (Brophy, 2006).

To illustrate, let's look again at Scott's work with his students.

> Scott: What did you notice when we blew over the top? . . . David?
> David: The paper moved.
> Scott: How did the paper move? . . . Let's do it again. (David again blew over the surface of the paper.)
> Scott: What did the paper do?
> David: It came up.

David didn't initially give the answer necessary to help him understand the relationship between force and the movement of the paper, so having him recall the previous demonstration was a form of prompting.

As another example, Ken Duran, in a language arts lesson on adjectives, displays the following on his document camera:

The girl was very athletic.

Let's look at some brief dialogue:

> Ken: Identify an adjective in the sentence . . . Chandra?
> Chandra: . . .
> Ken: What do we know about the girl?
> Chandra: She was athletic.

Ken's prompt, which elicited an acceptable response, kept Chandra involved in the activity and helped her be successful. She hadn't arrived at the answer Ken wanted, but the question kept her active and in her zone of proximal development, which helped her make learning progress.

We need to be strategic when we prompt. For instance, if a question calls for factual knowledge, such as "What is 7 times 8?" or "Who was our president during the Civil War?," and a student doesn't answer, prompting isn't useful; students either know the fact or they don't. It's effective, however, when studying conceptual, procedural, and metacognitive knowledge, and when using cognitive processes beyond remembering (Anderson & Krathwohl, 2001).

Wait-Time. For questions to be effective, we need to give our students time to think. If we wait a second and survey the room after asking a question, we alert all students that they may be called on. Then, after identifying a student, we wait a couple more seconds to give the student some "think" time. This period of silence, both before and after calling on a student, is called wait-time, and in most classrooms, it is too short, often less than 1 second (Rowe, 1974, 1986; Kastens & Liben, 2007).

Significantly, increased learning is linked to longer wait-times (Kastens & Liben, 2007; Rowe, 1974, 1986). "Longer wait times consistently resulted in longer student responses, an increase in the number of students volunteering to respond, and an increase in the number of follow-up questions posed by students" (Tofade, Elsner, & Haines, 2013, p. 7). In addition, the number of times students responded "I don't know" decreased, and test scores increased (Tofade et al., 2013). Further, some research suggests that increasing wait-times is even more effective when working with students having disabilities (Johnson & Parker, 2013; Lamella & Tincani, 2012).

As with prompting, we should use wait-time strategically. For example, if students are practicing basic skills, such as multiplication facts, quick answers are desirable, and wait-times should be short (Good & Brophy, 2008). Also, if a student appears uneasy, you may choose to intervene earlier. However, if you expect students to think—using cognitive processes such as apply, analyze, or evaluate—wait-times should be longer, sometimes exceeding the 3- to 5-second rule of thumb.

Cognitive Levels of Questions. The kinds of questions we ask also influence learning, and the merits of low- and high-level questions have been widely researched. The results are mixed, however. Depending on the teaching situation, both low-level questions, such as remembering factual information, and high-level questions that require students to apply knowledge to new situations can increase achievement (Good & Brophy, 2008).

The appropriate level for a question depends on your learning objectives, and you should think about asking logical sequences of questions instead of questions in isolation. You saw this illustrated in Scott's lesson. After completing the demonstrations, Scott first asked students to describe how the papers and the ball acted, which he followed with questions asking them to identify the relationship between the speed of the air and the forces it exerted on the objects.

As you teach, you should focus on your learning objectives and not on the level of questions you ask. If your thinking about your objectives is clear, the levels of your questions will take care of themselves.

Feedback

When we teach, our students need information that will help them determine whether the knowledge they're constructing is accurate and valid. **Feedback** provides this information, and its value for promoting learning is well documented (Hattie & Timperley, 2007; Hattie & Gan, 2011). In fact, a meta-analysis of more than 800 studies identified feedback as one of the most powerful influences on learning (Hattie, 2009). It also contributes to motivation because it provides learners with information about their increasing competence, which is a basic psychological need according to self-determination theory (Brophy, 2010; Deci & Ryan, 2008).

Effective feedback has four characteristics:

- It is immediate or given soon after a learner response.
- It is specific.
- It provides corrective information for the learner.
- It has a positive emotional tone (Hattie & Gan, 2011).

To illustrate these characteristics, let's compare three kinds of feedback after the following sentences have been displayed on the document camera.

Our team's running game was in high gear last night.

Running is one of the best forms of exercise that exists.

Mr. Dole:	What does the word *running* illustrate in the first sentence displayed on the document camera, . . . Jo?
Jo:	A verb.
Mr. Dole:	Not quite. Help her out, . . . Steve?
Ms. West:	What does the word *running* illustrate in the first sentence displayed on the document camera, . . . Jason?
Jason:	A verb.
Ms. West:	No, it's a participle. How is *running* used in the second sentence, . . . Albert?

> Ms. Baker: What does the word *running* illustrate in the first sentence displayed on the document camera, . . . Donna?
> Donna: A verb.
> Ms. Baker: Not quite. . . . How is the word *running* used in the sentence?
> Donna: It tells us about the game.
> Ms. Baker: Good. So, it behaves as an adjective. Verb forms that behave as adjectives are called participles. Now, let's look at the second sentence.

Each teacher gave immediate feedback, but neither Mr. Dole nor Ms. West gave the students any corrective information. Ms. Baker, in contrast, provided Donna with specific information that helped her understand the concept, which is the most important feature of effective feedback (Hattie & Timperley, 2007).

Although these examples don't illustrate the emotional tone of the teachers' responses, it is important. Harsh, critical, or sarcastic feedback detracts from students' feelings of safety and relatedness, which decreases both motivation and learning (Schunk, Meece, & Pintrich, 2014).

Praise. Praise is the most common form of positive feedback, and a study examining college students' reactions to praise is revealing. The researchers found that the desire for praise, and the boost to self-esteem that comes with it, trumped other desires and needs, including alcohol, money, or even sex (Bushman, Moeller, & Crocker, 2010).

Other research examining the use of praise in K–12 classrooms has found the following patterns:

- Praise is used less often than most teachers believe—less than five times per class.
- Praise for good behavior is quite rare; it occurs once every 2 or more hours in the elementary grades and even less as students get older.
- Praise tends to depend as much on the type of student (e.g., high achieving, well behaved, and attentive) as on the quality of the student's response.
- Teachers praise students based on the answers they expect to receive as much as on those they actually hear (Good & Brophy, 2008).

Using praise effectively is complex. For instance, young children tend to accept it at face value even when overdone, whereas older students assess the validity of the praise and what they believe it communicates about their ability. Young children bask in praise given openly in front of a class, whereas adolescents often react better if it's given quietly and individually. However, with students of all ages, *process praise,* praise for hard work and perseverance, such as "You're trying hard," is more effective than *person praise,* praise for personal qualities, such as "You're a good student," because person praise can detract from students' motivation when they fail (Droe, 2013). This is particularly true for students who have a low sense of academic self-worth (Brummelman et al., 2013). Further, over-praising students for correct answers to easy questions can create the perception in students that their teachers believe they have low ability (Kaspar & Stelz, 2013). This research suggests that—for all students—we should praise them for their effort or for what they are accomplishing, instead of who they are, and we should praise in a simple, natural, and genuine manner.

Written Feedback. Much of the feedback we provide occurs during lessons, but students also need information about the quality of their written work. Because writing detailed comments is enormously time-consuming, providing each student with individual, written feedback is very difficult.

One solution to this problem is to provide model responses to written assignments. For instance, to help students evaluate their answers to essay items, you can write ideal answers, display them, and encourage students to compare their answers with the model. Combined with discussion and time available for individual help, the model provides informative feedback that is manageable in terms of time and effort.

Closure

Closure is a summary that occurs at the end of lessons. It pulls different aspects of the topic together, helps students construct meaningful schemas, and signals the end of a lesson. When students are involved in higher level learning, a summary statement combined with having them identify additional examples of a concept, or apply a principle or rule to a new situation, is an effective form of closure. When teaching problem solving, summarizing the thinking involved in solving the problem is also effective.

Communication

In all aspects of our lessons—reviews, focus, questioning, the feedback we provide, and the way we bring lessons to closure—clear and concise communication is important. Clear communication increases student achievement, and students are more satisfied with instruction when their teachers communicate clearly (Good & Brophy, 2008; Weiss & Pasley, 2004). In a sense, clear communication is an umbrella under which the other essential teaching skills fall.

Effective communication has four characteristics:

- Precise language
- Connected discourse
- Transition signals
- Emphasis

Precise language omits vague terms—such as *perhaps, and so on, maybe, might,* and *usually*—from explanations and responses to students' questions. For example, if you ask, "What do high-efficacy teachers do that promotes learning?" and your instructor responds, "Usually, they use their time somewhat better and so on," you're left with a sense of uncertainty about the idea. In contrast, if the instructor says, "They believe they can increase learning, and one way they do this is by using their time efficiently," you're given a clear picture, which makes the idea more understandable.

Connected discourse refers to instruction that is thematic and leads to a point. If the point of the lesson isn't clear, if it's sequenced inappropriately, or if incidental information is interjected without indicating how it relates to the topic, the discourse becomes disconnected or scrambled. This means that we should keep our lessons on track and minimize time spent on matters unrelated to the topic (Burbules & Bruce, 2001; Leinhardt, 2001).

Transition signals are verbal statements indicating that one idea is ending and another is beginning. For example, an American government teacher might signal a transition by saying, "We've been talking about the Senate, which is one house of Congress, and now we'll turn to the House of Representatives." Because not all students are cognitively at the same place, a transition signal alerts them that the lesson is making a conceptual shift—moving to a new topic—and allows them to prepare for it.

Emphasis consists of verbal and vocal cues that alert students to important information in a lesson. For example, Scott used a form of vocal emphasis—raising his voice—when he said, "Keep these ideas in mind," as he moved from his review to the lesson itself. Whenever you say something such as, "Now remember, everyone, this is very important" or "Listen carefully now," you're using verbal emphasis.

Repeating a point is another common form of emphasis. Asking students, "What did we say these problems have in common?" stresses an important feature in the problems and helps students link new information to knowledge stored in their long-term memories.

Redundancy is particularly important when reviewing abstract concepts, principles, and rules (Brophy & Good, 1986; Shuell, 1996).

Knowledge of content is essential for clear communication. If we clearly understand the topics we teach, we'll use clearer language, our lessons will be more thematic, and we will remain focused on our learning objectives to a greater extent than we would if we're uncertain or unclear about the content (Brophy, 2006; Staples, 2007). This suggests that, as we plan, we should carefully study any topics about which we're uncertain.

Classroom **Connections**

Demonstrating Essential Teaching Skills in Classrooms

Teacher Beliefs and Behaviors

1. Personal teaching efficacy, high expectations, modeling and enthusiasm, and caring are teacher beliefs and behaviors associated with increased student achievement. Try to demonstrate these beliefs during lessons to increase student motivation and achievement.

   ■ **Elementary:** A third-grade teacher communicates her personal efficacy and caring by calling a student's parents and soliciting their help as soon as the student fails to turn in an assignment or receives an unsatisfactory grade on a quiz or test.

   ■ **Middle School:** A seventh-grade teacher commits himself to being a role model by displaying the statement "I will always behave in the way I expect you to behave in this class" on the bulletin board. He uses the statement as a guiding principle in his class.

   ■ **High School:** A geometry teacher, knowing that her students initially have problems with proofs, conducts help sessions twice a week after school. "I would much rather help them than lower my expectations," she comments.

Organization and Communication

2. Effective organization helps teachers begin classes on time, have materials prepared, and maintain well-established routines. Carefully plan and organize materials and communicate clearly to maximize instructional time.

   ■ **Elementary:** A first-grade teacher has several boxes filled with frequently used science materials, such as soft drink bottles, balloons, matches, baking soda, vinegar, funnels, and a hot plate. The day before a science demonstration, he spends a few minutes selecting his materials from the boxes and sets them on a shelf near his desk so that he'll have everything ready at the beginning of the lesson.

   ■ **Middle School:** An eighth-grade American history teacher asks a member of her team to visit her class to provide feedback about her instruction. She also asks her colleague to check if she clearly emphasizes the important points in the lesson, sequences the presentation logically, and communicates changes in topics.

   ■ **High School:** A biology teacher begins each class with an outline of the day's topics and activities on the board. As she makes transitions from one activity to the other, she calls students' attention to the outline so students can understand where they've been and where they're going.

Focus and Feedback

3. Lesson focus helps maintain student attention, and feedback provides students with information about their learning progress. Use problems, demonstrations, and displays to provide focus during lessons. Provide feedback throughout all learning experiences.

   ■ **Elementary:** A fourth-grade teacher beginning a study of different groups of animals brings a live lobster, a spider, and a grasshopper to class and builds a lesson on arthropods around these animals. After making a list of arthropods' characteristics on the board, she asks students if a clam is an arthropod. When some say it is, she provides feedback by referring them to the list and asking them to identify each characteristic in the clam. After a short discussion, they conclude that the clam isn't an arthropod.

   ■ **Middle School:** A science teacher dealing with the concept of kindling temperature soaks a cloth in a water–alcohol mix, ignites it, and asks, "Why isn't the cloth burning?" He provides feedback during the class discussion by asking guiding questions to help students develop their understanding.

   ■ **High School:** A physical education teacher shows students a videotape of a professional tennis player executing a nearly perfect backhand. She then videotapes the students as they practice backhands, and they attempt to modify their swings to more nearly imitate the pros.

Questioning and Review

3. Reviews help activate and consolidate students' prior knowledge, and questioning puts them in cognitively active roles. Begin and end each class with a short review, and guide the review with questioning.

   ■ **Elementary:** A fifth-grade teacher whose class is studying different types of boundaries says, "We've looked at three kinds of boundaries between the states so far today. What are these three, and where do they occur?"

   ■ **Middle School:** An English teacher begins, "We studied pronoun–antecedent agreement yesterday. Give me an example that illustrates this idea, and explain why your example is correct."

   ■ **High School:** An art teacher says, "Today we've found that many artists use color to create different moods. Let's summarize some of the features that we've learned about. Go ahead, offer one, someone."

Models of Instruction

As we saw in the previous section, demonstrating essential teaching skills increases our students' learning regardless of the content area or grade level in which we teach. By comparison, **models of instruction** are prescriptive approaches to teaching designed to help students acquire a deep understanding of specific forms of knowledge. Each is grounded in cognitive learning theory and supported by research. Each also includes sequential steps designed to help students reach specified learning objectives.

Essential teaching skills support each model. For instance, just as students use reading in all their content areas, organization, questioning, and the other essential teaching skills are important regardless of the model being used.

Research suggests that no single model is most effective for all students or for helping students reach all learning objectives (Knight, 2002; Kroesbergen & van Luit, 2002; Marzano, 2003). In this section we examine four of the more widely used:

- Direct instruction
- Lecture–discussion
- Guided discovery
- Cooperative learning

Direct Instruction

Direct instruction is a teaching model designed to help students acquire well-defined knowledge and skills needed for later learning. Examples of these skills include young students' using basic operations to solve math problems, students' using grammar and punctuation in writing, and chemistry students' balancing equations.

Direct instruction has been thoroughly researched. When used by expert teachers, it's a highly effective model (Clark, Kirschner, & Sweller, 2012; Matlen & Klahr, 2013), and it's particularly effective in working with low achievers and students with exceptionalities (Flores & Kaylor, 2007; Turnbull, Turnbull, Wehmeyer, & Shogren, 2013).

Direct instruction ranges from a highly structured, nearly scripted, and somewhat behaviorist approach (Carnine, Silbert, Kame'enui, Tarver, Jongjohann, 2006) to one that is more flexible and cognitive (Eggen & Kauchak, 2012; Kauchak & Eggen, 2012). We discuss the latter here, which typically occurs in four phases:

- Introduction and review
- Developing understanding
- Guided practice
- Independent practice

Table 13.4 outlines the phases in direct instruction and the cognitive learning component that provides the framework for each phase.

Now let's look at the use of direct instruction in two different content areas.

Sam Barnett, a second-grade teacher, is working with his students on addition and subtraction of whole numbers to meet the following standard:

CCSS.Math.Content.2.OA.A.1 Use addition and subtraction within 100 to solve one- and two-step word problems involving situations of adding to, taking from, putting together, taking apart, and comparing, with unknowns in all positions, e.g., by using drawings and equations with a symbol for the unknown number to represent the problem (Common Core State Standards Initiative, 2014r).

He begins by displaying the following problem on the document camera:

Table 13.4	The phases in cognitive-based direct instruction
Phase	Cognitive Learning Component
Introduction and Review: Teachers begin with a form of introductory focus and review previous work.	• Attract attention. • Access prior knowledge from long-term memory.
Developing Understanding: Teachers describe and model the skill or explain and present examples of the concept. Teachers emphasize understanding.	• Acquire declarative knowledge about the skill or concept. • Encode declarative knowledge into long-term memory.
Guided Practice: Students practice the skill or identify additional examples of the concept, and the teacher provides scaffolding.	• Move through the associative stage of developing procedural knowledge.
Independent Practice: Students practice on their own.	• Develop automaticity with the skill or concept.

Jana and Patti are saving special soda cans to get a free CD. They can get the CD if they save 35 cans. Jana had 15 cans and Patti had 12. How many did they have together? [Jana and Patti are two students in Sam's class.]

He continues by reviewing the addition of single digit numbers, such as 8 + 7, and has his students represent the numbers as 1 group of 10 interlocking cubes and 5 single cubes at their desks. He also writes

$$
\begin{array}{r}
7 \\
+\ 8 \\
\hline
15
\end{array}
$$

on the board and displays images of the cubes on the screen at the front of his room.

He then refers the class back to the word problem he displayed, discusses the information in it, and then writes the following on the board:

$$
\begin{array}{r}
15 \\
+\ 12 \\
\hline
\end{array}
$$

Then he demonstrates how to add the numbers both using the interlocking cubes and numbers on the board and describes his thinking in the process.

He repeats the process with a second example and then gives the students a problem of their own to solve and demonstrate with their cubes as he watches their progress. They discuss the solution and describe their thinking during the discussion. He repeats the process with two more examples, and then assigns 5 problems to do as seatwork. He carefully monitors their efforts as they work on the problems.

Now, let's look at another example.

Vanesa Rodriguez, an eighth-grade English teacher, is working with her students on the following standard:

CCSS.ELA-Literacy.L.8.1a Explain the function of verbals (gerunds, participles, infinitives) in general and their function in particular sentences (Common Core State Standards Initiative, 2014g).

She is focusing on gerunds and participles in today's lesson, and she begins by writing the words *jumping, running, talking,* and *sleeping* on the board and asking students what part of speech they represent, to which they respond, "Verbs." She continues by reviewing other parts of speech, such as nouns, pronouns, adjectives, and adverbs.

She then says that the context can determine the way verb forms are used, and she displays the following on her document camera:

Running is a very good form of exercise, and athletes, such as running backs in football, have to be in very good physical shape. I'm going to go running this afternoon.

She notes that *running* is used in three different ways in the two sentences and explains that it is first used as a noun [Running is the subject in "Running is a very good form of exercise"]. Then "running" [in "running backs"] is used as an adjective, and in the second sentence it's used as a verb. She explains that verb forms used as nouns are called gerunds, and verb forms used as adjectives are called participles. She then has the students explain how they will know if a verb form is actually a verb or if it is a different part of speech, and she asks them to explain how this relates to context.

Vanesa then displays the following on her document camera:

I'm not going to be jumping up to do any work anytime soon. In the first place, I don't want to feel like a jumping bean in my own house, and in the second, I don't think that jumping is all that good for you.

She gives the students a few minutes to identify the way *jumping* is used in the two sentences, and then asks students to discuss what they've found. They conclude that it is used as a verb in the first sentence, as a participle in the first clause of the second sentence, and as a gerund in the second clause of the second sentence.

She gives the students an additional example and has them discuss it as they discussed the first, and finally she has them write a paragraph in which they must embed at least two examples of verb forms used as verbs, two examples where they're used as gerunds, and two examples used as participles.

Now, let's look at Sam's and Vanesa's use of direct instruction.

Introduction and Review. Sam began his lesson with the problem involving Jana and Patti, which provided focus for the lesson. He then reviewed addition of single digit numbers. Vanesa began hers by writing examples of verb forms on the board and reviewing other parts of speech.

Both lessons were grounded in cognitive learning theory. We know that learning begins with attention, and Sam used his problem—and personalized it by embedding two of his students' names in it—to attract their attention, and Vanesa did the same with her words on the board and asking her students what part of speech they represented. They both then activated their students' background knowledge with their reviews. These actions both make sense intuitively and are supported by research (Brophy, 2006; Kirschner, Sweller, & Clark, 2006). However, many classroom lessons begin with little or no attempt to attract attention or activate relevant prior knowledge (Brophy, 2010).

Developing Understanding. After a review, the next phase in direct instruction is designed to provide students with new information that they will connect to their existing understanding. Once this connection is made and organized in working memory, students will encode their new knowledge (i.e., they will represent it in long-term memory, ready to be retrieved and connected to the next set of new information presented by their teachers).

Sam completed this phase when he modeled the process—including cognitive modeling as he described his thinking—for adding two-digit numbers. Vanesa used her example displayed on the document camera for the same purpose. She also used cognitive modeling by explaining that *running* was used as a noun in the first part of her example, as an adjective in the second, and as a verb in the third.

Sam and Vanesa both emphasized understanding in this phase. When solving problems like the one Sam presented, students often follow procedures mechanically or use superficial strategies, such as adding when they see the words "how many altogether" or subtracting when they see "how many more" in a math problem (Jitendra et al., 2007; Mayer, 2008). Instead, Sam had his students demonstrate the problem with their interlocking cubes and explain what they had done.

Vanesa emphasized understanding both with her simple—but clever—example combined with her explanation and having her students verbalize their understanding. Her example provided the context that allowed her students to see that *running* was first used as a noun, then an adjective, and finally a verb.

Having students verbalize their understanding, as both Sam and Vanesa did, is important for learning. As we know from our study of Vygotsky's work, language is an essential part of learning and development, and the more opportunities students have to put their understanding into words, the deeper that understanding becomes.

Not spending the time needed to develop adequate levels of understanding is arguably the most common mistake teachers make when using direct instruction. Students won't develop deep understanding if we emphasize memorization, don't ask enough questions, or move too quickly to practice (Rittle-Johnson & Alibali, 1999). Or we may involve learners in hands-on activities but fail to establish the connection between the materials, such as the cubes, and the abstractions they represent (the numbers in the problem) (Ball, 1992). For instance, asking students to explain and demonstrate the difference between 2 in 12 and 2 in 21 is crucial for developing understanding of place value, and teachers often fail to help their students make this connection.

Guided Practice. Once students have developed an understanding of the procedure, they begin practicing as we monitor their progress. Initially, we use questioning to provide enough scaffolding support to ensure success, but not so much that challenge is reduced. As students practice, they gradually develop automaticity and become confident with the new content (Péladeau, Forget, & Gagné, 2003). Sam had his students work a problem, and they discussed it afterward so he could be sure that they understood the process. He continued with guided practice until he believed that most students were ready to work on their own.

During her guided practice Vanesa provided another example in which the verb form *jumping* was used first as a verb, second as a participle, and third as a gerund. She did this on purpose. In her first example *running* was first used as a gerund, then a participle, and finally as a verb. Vanesa purposely changed the sequence, so her students would need to use the context of the sentence to make their conclusions, rather than use the same order in which the verb form was used. This simple, but thoughtful, move on her part is a mark of teaching expertise.

Independent Practice. In this final phase of direct instruction, we reduce scaffolding and shift responsibility to the students. Our goal is for them to be able to perform the skill automatically, so working memory space can be devoted to future higher level applications (Feldon, 2007).

Monitoring students' progress continues to be important. Expert teachers circulate around the room to ensure that students are on task and working successfully; their less-effective counterparts are more likely to work at their desks or merely check to see that students are on task (Brophy, 2006; Safer & Fleischman, 2005).

Homework. Homework is a common form of independent practice, and, perhaps surprisingly, it is somewhat controversial. Some authors argue that it is ineffective and even destructive (Kohn, 2006a, 2006b). Others note that American students are assigned more homework than students in other developed countries, yet score lower in comparisons of international achievement (Baines, 2007).

Research, however, consistently indicates that homework, properly designed and implemented, increases achievement (Carr, 2013; Dettmers, Trautwein, Lüdtke, Kunter, & Baumert, 2010), and, because learners must take responsibility for completing it, it also develops self-regulation (Marzano & Pickering, 2007; Xu & Wu, 2013). *Properly designed and implemented* is essential. Simply assigning homework doesn't increase achievement, and more isn't necessarily better. Increasing the amount of homework in the name of academic rigor is ineffective at best and, at worst, can decrease both motivation and achievement (Carr, 2013; Vatterott, 2014).

The amount of cognitive effort—thinking—students apply in completing homework is the primary factor influencing its effectiveness, and cognitive motivation theory helps us understand how to increase effort (Trautwein, Lüdtke, & Schnyder, 2006). Three factors are involved. The first is perceived value. If students believe that homework will increase their understanding, they're likely to make a conscientious effort to complete it (Carr, 2013; Trautwein & Lüdtke, 2007). Homework perceived as unnecessary, or as busywork, particularly for older students, detracts from motivation and does little to promote learning. Assigning more exercises than necessary for maximizing learning can be counterproductive, and older students are unlikely to complete homework assignments for which they receive no credit (Marzano & Pickering, 2007).

Second, students must be generally successful on homework assignments, so their perceptions of competence and self-efficacy are increased (Carr, 2013). Third, students are much more likely to do homework if their parents expect it and monitor the extent to which it is done.

The characteristics of effective homework are summarized in Table 13.5, together with developmental differences between elementary and middle/secondary students (Brophy, 2006; Carr, 2013; Dettmers et al., 2010; Marzano & Pickering, 2007).

Lecture–Discussion

Lecture–discussion is an instructional model designed to help students acquire **organized bodies of knowledge**, topics that connect facts, concepts, and generalizations, and make the relationships among them explicit (Eggen & Kauchak, 2012; Rosenshine, 1987). For example, students acquire organized bodies of knowledge when they examine the relationships among plot, character, and symbolism in a novel such as *To Kill a Mockingbird* in

Table 13.5	Characteristics of effective homework at different developmental levels
Level	Characteristic
All Levels	• Aligned with learning objectives and learning activities • Clear directions • High success rates • Feedback provided • Parental involvement
Elementary	• A quiet place, free from distractions, to do homework • Part of the regular class routine
Middle and Secondary	• Clear reasons for the importance of the homework • Credit, such as points toward an overall grade

literature; study landforms, climate, and economy in different countries in geography; or compare parasitic and nonparasitic worms and how differences between them are reflected in their body structures in biology.

Because lecture–discussions are modifications of traditional lectures, and because lecturing is so common in classrooms, we briefly examine lectures before turning to a discussion of lecture–discussions.

LECTURES

The prevalence of lecturing in our nation's schools is paradoxical. Although the most criticized of all teaching methods, it is the most commonly used (Cuban, 1993; Friesen, 2011). Some reasons for the popularity of lectures include:

- They're efficient. Planning time is limited to organizing content.
- They're flexible. They can be applied to most content areas and topics.
- They're simple. Cognitive load is low, so teachers' working memory space can be devoted to organizing and presenting content.
- They're relatively easy to implement; teaching skills, such as questioning, prompting, and providing feedback, are largely unnecessary. Even novice teachers can learn to deliver acceptable lectures.

Lectures also have some strengths. For instance, they can help students acquire information not readily accessible in other ways, and they can be effective if the goal is to provide students with information that would be time-consuming to find on their own (Ausubel, 1968; Friesen, 2011). They can also help students integrate information from a variety of sources, and they can expose students to different points of view. If we're trying to accomplish one or more of these goals, lecturing can be effective.

Despite their popularity and strengths, lectures have important disadvantages:

- They put learners in cognitively passive roles. This is inconsistent with cognitive views of learning and is arguably their primary disadvantage.
- They often fail to attract and maintain students' attention. We've all sat through mind-numbing lectures with a goal of simply getting the time to pass as quickly as possible.
- They don't allow teachers to determine if students are interpreting information accurately.
- Although lowering the cognitive load for teachers, they often impose a heavy cognitive load on learners, so information is frequently lost from working memory before it can be encoded into long-term memory.

Lectures are especially problematic for young students because of their short attention spans and limited vocabularies, and they're also ineffective if higher order thinking is a goal. In a historical analysis of seven studies comparing lecturing to discussion, discussion was superior in all seven on measures of retention and higher order thinking. In addition, discussion was superior in seven of nine studies on measures of student attitude and motivation (McKeachie & Kulik, 1975). Because of a long history critical of lectures, considerable emphasis—including emphasis at the college and university level—is being placed on teaching methods that put students in more cognitively active roles (Baeten, Struyven, & Dochy, 2013; Smart, Witt, & Scott, 2012).

OVERCOMING THE WEAKNESSES OF LECTURES: LECTURE–DISCUSSIONS

Lecture–discussions help overcome the weaknesses of lectures by interspersing systematic teacher questioning between short presentations of information.

Lecture–discussions exist in four phases:

- Introduction and review
- Presenting information

Table 13.6	Phases of lecture–discussion and cognitive learning components
Phase	**Cognitive Learning Component**
Introduction and Review: The teacher begins with a form of introductory focus and reviews previous work.	• Attract attention. • Access prior knowledge from long-term memory.
Presenting Information: The teacher presents information. The teacher keeps presentations short to prevent overloading learners' working memories.	• Acquire declarative knowledge about the topic.
Comprehension Monitoring: The teacher asks a series of questions to check learners' understanding.	• Check students' perceptions. • Put students in cognitively active roles. • Begin schema construction.
Integration: The teacher asks additional questions to help learners integrate new and prior knowledge.	• Construct integrated schemas that organize information and reduce cognitive load.

- Comprehension monitoring
- Integration

Table 13.6 outlines these phases in lecture–discussion together with the cognitive learning theory components that support each phase.

Now, let's look at a lesson in which Diane Anderson, a 10th-grade American history teacher, is working with her students on events leading up to the American Revolutionary War. Look for the phases of lecture–discussion as you read the case study.

Diane's students have been reading about American history prior to the Revolutionary War in their textbooks, and she wants them to meet the following standard.

CCSS.ELA-Literacy.RH.9-10.3 Analyze in detail a series of events described in a text; determine whether earlier events caused later ones or simply preceded them (Common Core State Standards Initiative, 2014d).

She begins by reviewing a timeline that starts with Jamestown in 1607 and leads up to the middle 1700s. She then asks the students how events, such as the French and Indian War and the Boston Tea Party, relate to the Revolutionary War, noting that answering that question is the goal for the day.

She then describes French efforts to settle in North America, notes that at least 35 of our present 50 states were originally mapped by the French, and points out that they founded some of our major cities, such as St. Louis, Detroit, and New Orleans.

She then has the students summarize what she's said, uses a map at the front of the room to identify the geography of the French and British settlements, and then presents information about the French relationships with Native Americans and French policies of giving land to settlers if they would serve in the military.

She then notes that the British wanted to expand across the Appalachian Mountains, has the students discuss the conflict that was inevitable, and explain why it was costly for the British and what the British did to raise revenue. She has them link these events to the colonists' rebellion, and finally, she has the students link the entire discussion to the standard.

Now, let's look at another example.

Dan Roundfield, a seventh-grade life-science teacher, is working with his students on the classification of living things, and he wants them to meet the following standard:

CCSS.ELA-Literacy.RST.6-8.4 Determine the meaning of symbols, key terms, and other domain-specific words and phrases as they are used in a specific scientific or technical context relevant to grades 6–8 texts and topics (Common Core State Standards Initiative, 2014k).

He begins by displaying a rock, paper clip, potted plant, clamshell, lobster, and a picture of the class (which he had taken the first day of the school year) on a desk at the front of the room. He then asks the students how the rock and paper clip are different from the other items, and prompts them to say "living things."

He then notes that scientists wanted a system to organize and classify these living things, and says that developing an understanding of this classification system is their objective for the next couple days.

He then takes the rock and paper clip off the desk, points to the rest of the items, and notes that most macroscopic creatures are either plants or animals, so they belong to either the plant kingdom or animal kingdom, as he points to the plant and then to the other items. He points out that the distinction is primarily based on sources of nutrition and the capability of locomotion, with plants producing their own food through photosynthesis, but unable to move on their own. Animals, in contrast, are able to move on their own, but must eat other organisms to obtain food.

He then stops and asks the students to describe the following terms: classification, kingdom, locomotion, and photosynthesis. When they struggle with a term, such as locomotion, he writes the following on the board:

Because plants can't move on their own, we say they aren't capable of locomotion.

He does the same with the other terms, reminding the students that they should use the context in which words are used to help them understand the meaning of technical terms.

He then continues by noting that the next level of classification is the phylum; holds up the lobster noting its external skeleton, three body parts, and jointed limbs; and says it belongs to the phylum Arthropoda, commonly called arthropods. He then holds up the clam and notes that it belongs to the phylum Mollusca (mollusks) and explains that mollusks are usually enclosed in hard shells and have soft, unsegmented bodies. He notes that classification into a phylum depends largely on body structure and organization.

He stops providing information again and shows them pictures of insects, spiders, oysters, and snails, and asks them to what kingdom and phylum they belong. He also asks the students if they (the students) are either arthropods or mollusks, and after they conclude they aren't, he asks them why not.

Dan then continues the process by introducing the phylum Chordata (chordates) and asking them to identify a number of examples that would fit this phylum, such as themselves and other animals with backbones, such as fish, birds, reptiles, and other mammals. He then asks them to try and identify examples that don't fit any of the three phyla, and with some prompting, the students identify different types of worms as examples.

Now, let's look at Diane's and Dan's applications of the lecture–discussion model.

Introduction and Review. As with direct instruction, lecture–discussion is grounded in cognitive learning theory, and, as we've emphasized repeatedly, all learning begins with attention. Diane attempted to attract her students' attention by asking them how events such as the French and Indian war and the Boston Tea Party relate to the Revolutionary War. Then, to activate her students' background knowledge she had them review a historical timeline.

Dan attempted to attract his students' attention by referring them to the items he had displayed on the desk at the front of the room and asking them how the rock and paper clip were different from the other items. He then reviewed the concept of classification.

Presenting Information. Diane began this phase by presenting information about Jamestown, Quebec, French settlements in the present-day United States, and cities in our country that were originally founded by the French.

Dan presented information about the animal and plant kingdoms and the characteristics of each, such as plants lacking locomotion, but making their own food, and animals being able to move on their own, but needing to acquire food from others.

The *presenting information* phase capitalizes on the advantages of lectures, that is, it provides students with information they would have trouble acquiring on their own and integrates information from a variety of sources.

Note also that both Diane and Dan kept this phase very short. We know that attention spans, for all people, are short, and we're easily distracted, so, to maximize the likelihood of maintaining their students' attention, both Diane and Dan quickly turned to *comprehension monitoring,* the next phase.

Comprehension Monitoring. After her brief presentation, Diane used questioning to involve her students in the comprehension-monitoring phase. To check their perceptions, she had them summarize the information she presented, and she also referred them to a map so they could see how the geography of the area related to the English and French settlements.

Dan's efforts in this phase were more complex and demanding. To meet his standard he wanted his students to understand technical terms, such as *classification, kingdom, locomotion,* and *photosynthesis.* Understandably, they struggled with some of the terms, and so he elaborated by writing statements on the board that would help them use context (and meet the standard) to help determine the meaning of each term. (He would also spend a great deal more time helping them understand photosynthesis, but for today's lesson he merely wanted them to understand that it's the process by which plants make their own food.)

The comprehension-monitoring phase is designed to cognitively engage students, check their perceptions, make sure they understand new information presented, and begin the process of schema construction, ultimately leading to encoding.

Integration. After interacting with the students to check their perceptions and understanding of the topics to this point in their lessons, both teachers then presented additional information designed to be integrated with the students' existing knowledge of the topics. Diane, for example, presented information about the French policy of giving land to settlers if they served in the military, the French relationship with Native Americans, British desires to move west across the Appalachian Mountains, and the inevitable conflict it caused with the French. All this led to war, which was costly, leading to onerous tax demands on the British colonists, and ultimately to the colonists revolting.

After ensuring that his students understood key concepts and how they could use context to help them with their understanding, Dan presented information about phyla, provided examples of arthropods, mollusks, and chordates, and asked his students for examples of each.

The process of integration exists in a series of cycles with each cycle adding more related information to the preceding cycle. As the information is integrated, learners' schemas become more complex and interconnected, with the goal of well-organized understanding ultimately being encoded in students' long-term memories.

The quality of lecture–discussion lessons depends on how effectively we guide the discussions that help students understand and integrate the information we present. Because students construct their own knowledge, the schemas they construct won't necessarily mirror the way we organize the body of knowledge. Our discussions allow us to assess the validity of students' schema constructions and help them reconstruct their understanding when necessary. This is a primary reason lecture–discussion is more effective than traditional lecture.

Guided Discovery

Guided discovery is an instructional model that involves teachers' scaffolding students' constructions of concepts and the relationships among them (Eggen & Kauchak, 2012; Mayer, 2008). When using the model, we identify our learning objectives, arrange information so that patterns can be found, and guide students to the objectives.

When using "discovery" models, teachers sometimes believe that students should be left essentially on their own to "discover" the ideas being taught (Kirschner et al., 2006). Doing so allows misconceptions to form, wastes time, and often leaves students frustrated (Clark et al., 2012; Mayer, 2004). Teachers correctly believe that learners construct their own knowledge, but sometimes assume "that the best way to promote such construction is to have students try to discover new knowledge or solve new problems without explicit guidance from the teacher. Unfortunately, this assumption is both widespread and incorrect" (Clark et al., 2012, p. 8).

In contrast, "guided" discovery—and other forms of learner-centered instruction, such as inquiry and problem-based learning—is highly scaffolded, and teachers play an essential role in guiding students' learning progress (Clark et al., 2012; Hmelo-Silver, Duncan, & Chinn, 2007).

When done well, guided discovery is highly effective. "Guided discovery may take more or less time than expository instruction, depending on the task, but tends to result in better long-term retention and transfer than expository instruction" (Mayer, 2002, p. 68).

When using guided discovery, you will spend less time explaining and more time asking questions, so students have more opportunities to share their thinking and put their developing understanding into words. Also, because of the high levels of student involvement, guided discovery tends to increase students' intrinsic interest in the topic being studied (Lutz, Guthrie, & Davis, 2006).

Guided discovery occurs in five phases:

- Introduction and review
- The open-ended phase
- The convergent phase
- Closure
- Application

Table 13.7 outlines these phases and the cognitive learning components that provide the theoretical framework for them.

Let's look at an example. On pages 543–544 you saw how Vanesa Rodriguez, an eighth-grade English teacher, used direct instruction to help her students understand verbals. Steve Kapner, another eighth-grade teacher in the same school, is working with his students on the same topic and standard, but he decides to use guided discovery instead of direct instruction.

Steve begins, as Vanesa did, by reviewing parts of speech and having his students provide examples of each. He then displays the following on his document camera:

I'm running three miles on Mondays, Wednesdays, and Fridays now. I'm walking four miles a day on Tuesdays and Thursdays. And I'm relaxing on Saturdays and Sundays.

Table 13.7	The phases of guided discovery and cognitive learning components
Phase	Cognitive Learning Component
Introduction and Review: The teacher begins with a form of introductory focus and reviews previous work.	• Attract attention. • Activate prior knowledge.
The Open-Ended Phase: The teacher provides examples and asks for observations and comparisons.	• Provide experiences from which learners will construct knowledge. • Promote social interaction.
The Convergent Phase: The teacher guides students as they search for patterns in the examples.	• Begin schema production. • Promote social interaction.
Closure: With the teacher's guidance, students state a definition of the concept or a description of the relationship among concepts.	• Complete schema production.
Application: The teacher has students use the concept or principle to explain another (ideally) real-world example.	• Promote transfer.

Running is the best form of exercise that exists, I think. But walking is also good, and it's easier on my knees. Relaxing a couple days a week also helps my body recover.

My running times have gone down since I've lost some weight. I have some new walking gear, so I look decent out on the road. Both make my relaxing environment just that much more pleasant.

"Now, look at the three short paragraphs, and tell me what you notice," Steve begins.

He calls on several individual students to make observations, which range from "Each paragraph has three sentences in it" to "Each paragraph is about exercise" to "The words *running, walking,* and *relaxing* are in all three," among a number of others.

After the students have made their observations, Steve directs them to the first paragraph and has them identify the subject and verb in each sentence, to which they respond "I" for the subject in each case, and *running, walking,* and *relaxing* as the verbs.

He does the same with the second paragraph, and the students conclude that *running, walking,* and *relaxing* are the subjects of the sentences here.

Noting that the words are used differently in the first two paragraphs, he asks the students to decide how they're used in the third, and after some discussion they conclude that *running, walking,* and *relaxing* are used as adjectives in the third paragraph.

He tells the students that the words are *gerunds* in the second paragraph and *participles* in the third, and he then helps the students verbalize a definition of each, which he writes on the board.

He then has them write a paragraph in which they must embed at least two examples of verb forms used as verbs, two examples of verb forms used as gerunds, and two examples used as participles.

Now, let's look at Steve's use of guided discovery to help students reach his standard.

Introduction and Review. Steve began by reviewing parts of speech. His review activated his students' prior knowledge, and he used examples to attract his students' attention, such as having his students offer examples of each part of speech. Presenting examples, or having students provide examples of concepts that have been taught in earlier lessons, is an effective way to introduce lessons.

The Open-Ended Phase. Steve began the open-ended phase by displaying his three paragraphs and saying, "Now, look at the three short paragraphs, and tell me what you notice."

The open-ended phase has several benefits for both the teacher and the students. First, open-ended questions are easy to ask, so we can call on a wide variety of students—practice equitable distribution—very quickly. Second, questions in this phase are easy to answer—students literally describe what they're observing—so we can involve students who typically don't try to answer or are often unable to answer correctly. Third, when students understand that we really do want them to tell us what they observe—as opposed to typical questions requiring a specific answer—their efforts to respond increase, sometimes dramatically, student involvement is easier to achieve, and motivation often increases. And, finally, students respond according to what they perceive in the examples, so the questions give us some insight into their thinking.

The Convergent Phase. The convergent phase continues to capitalize on social interaction to promote the process of schema construction. In this phase, however, teachers' questions begin to guide students toward a specific understanding of the topic being taught. Steve began the move to the convergent phase when he had his students identify the subject and verb in the first paragraph and conclude that *running, walking,* and *relaxing* were the verbs in each case. He continued by moving to the second paragraph and guiding the students to conclude that *running, walking,* and *relaxing* were the subjects of the sentences in it, and he did the same with the third paragraph, guiding the students to conclude that the verb forms were used as adjectives in this case.

As we can see, Steve didn't simply "tell" his students what they were supposed to understand, as might occur in a more teacher-centered approach to instruction, but instead strongly guided his students' developing understanding. As we saw earlier in our discussion, this guidance is supported by research.

Closure. Closure completes the process of schema construction. Steve brought his lesson to closure when he had his students verbalize a definition of *gerunds* and *participles.*

When we move lessons to closure, our questioning provides scaffolding for our students as they attempt to put their understanding into words.

Closure is particularly important when using guided discovery because the direction of the lesson may be less obvious than it is with either direct instruction or lecture–discussion. Putting the definition of a concept into words, as was the case in Steve's lesson, helps eliminate uncertainty that may remain in students' thinking.

Application. Steve had his students apply their understanding by writing a paragraph in which verb forms were used as verbs, gerunds, and participles.

Notice also that Steve's and Vanesa's lessons (even though Steve used guided discovery and Vanessa used direct instruction) were similar in several ways. For instance, their reviews were similar, as were the ways in which they had their students apply their understanding. They both used examples to illustrate *gerunds* and *participles,* and they embedded their examples in the context of short paragraphs. And they both strongly guided their students' developing understanding.

The primary difference between the two was in the amount of interaction between the teacher and students. As we said at the beginning of our discussion of guided discovery, when using the model you will spend less time explaining and more time asking questions, so student involvement is higher than with direct instruction. We saw this illustrated in Steve's lesson compared to Vanesa's.

Because of this involvement and because students have more opportunities to put their developing understanding into words, guided discovery tends to increase students' intrinsic interest in the topic being studied, which can also lead to deeper understanding (Smart et al., 2012; Baeten et al., 2013).

Cooperative Learning

Cooperative learning is a set of instructional strategies in which students work in mixed-ability groups to reach specific cognitive and social development objectives. Cooperative learning strongly emphasizes social interaction, and research suggests that groups of learners co-construct more powerful understanding than individuals do alone (Hadjioannou, 2007; Li et al., 2007). This co-constructed knowledge can then be internalized and used by individuals.

Although a single view doesn't exist, most researchers agree that cooperative learning consists of students working together in groups small enough (typically two to five) so that everyone can participate in a clearly assigned task (Brown & Ciuffetelli, 2009; Cohen, 1994; Sharan, 2010; Slavin, 2011). Cooperative learning also shares four other features:

- Learning objectives direct the groups' activities.
- Learning activities require social interaction.
- Teachers hold students individually accountable for their understanding.
- Learners depend on one another to reach objectives.

The last characteristic, called *positive interdependence* (Johnson & Johnson, 2006) or *reciprocal interdependence* (Cohen, 1994), is important because it emphasizes the role of peer cooperation in learning. Accountability is also essential because it keeps students focused on the objectives and reminds them that learning is the purpose of the activity (Antil et al., 1998; Sharan, 2010; Slavin, 2011).

Unlike direct instruction, lecture–discussion, and guided discovery, cooperative learning activities don't follow a specific set of steps, which is why we describe them as "strategies" instead of "models." However, successful implementation of cooperative learning activities requires as much thought and planning as does using any model.

INTRODUCING COOPERATIVE LEARNING

Your students won't automatically be good at cooperative learning, and some—particularly those in middle schools—may view cooperative activities more as opportunities to socialize than to meet your learning objectives (Wentzel, 2009). The following suggestions can help you get the process started with your students.

- Seat group members together, so they can move back and forth from group work to whole-class activities with little disruption.
- Have materials ready for easy distribution to each group.
- Introduce students to cooperative learning with short, simple tasks, and make objectives and directions clear.
- Specify the amount of time available to accomplish the task (and keep it relatively short).
- Monitor groups while they work.
- Require that students produce a product, such as written answers to specific questions, as an outcome of the activity.

Table 13.8	Cooperative learning strategies	
Strategy	Description	Example
Think–Pair–Share	Individuals in a pair answer a teacher question and then share it with their partner. The teacher calls on pairs to respond to the original question.	A world history teacher says, "Identify two factors or events that the Russian Revolution, which began in 1917, had in common with the French Revolution that began in 1789. . . . Turn to your partner, see what both of you think, and we'll discuss your answers in a minute."
Reciprocal Questioning	Pairs work together to ask and answer questions about a lesson or text.	A teacher provides question stems, such as "Summarize . . ." or "Why was . . . important?," and students use the stems to create specific questions about the topic.
Scripted Cooperation	Pairs work together to elaborate on each other's thinking.	Math: First member of a pair offers a problem solution. The second member then checks the answer, asks clarifying questions, and the process is repeated. Reading: Pairs read a passage, and the first member offers a summary. The second edits and adds to it, and the process continues.
Jigsaw II	Individuals become expert on subsections of a topic and teach it to others in their group.	One student studies the geography of a region, another the economy, a third the climate. Each attends "expert" meetings, and the "experts" then teach the content to others in their group.
Student Teams Achievement Divisions (STAD)	Social interaction helps students learn facts, concepts, and skills.	The independent practice phase of direct instruction is replaced with team study, during which team members check and compare their answers. Team study is followed by quizzes, and individual improvement points lead to team awards.

These suggestions are designed to minimize the likelihood of disruptions and maximize the likelihood of students remaining on task, particularly when you first introduce them to cooperative learning activities.

COOPERATIVE LEARNING STRATEGIES

Social constructivism provides the framework for all cooperative learning strategies, and those most widely used are outlined in Table 13.8. Other forms of cooperative learning exist, and although they differ in format, all incorporate the suggestions described earlier. As with all forms of instruction, no single cooperative learning strategy can reach all learning objectives, and cooperative learning should not be overused.

EVALUATING COOPERATIVE LEARNING

As an instructional strategy, cooperative learning is very popular worldwide, and a great deal of research examining cooperative learning strategies has been conducted in countries ranging as widely as Saudi Arabia (Alghamdi & Gillies, 2013), Iran (Marashi & Dibah, 2013), Taiwan (Pan & Wu, 2013), and Canada (Gagné & Parks, 2013). It has also been used at all levels of instruction, including doctoral programs (Roseth, Akcaoglu, & Zellner, 2013). Further, research conducted nearly 20 years ago found that even then it was one of the most widely used approaches to instruction in our country's schools, with more than 90% of elementary teachers using some form of cooperative learning in their classrooms (Antil, Jenkins, Wayne, & Vadasy, 1998). This figure may be a bit misleading, however, because some teachers describe any form of student group work as cooperative learning, and as we saw earlier in our discussion, cooperative learning involves much more than simply having students work in groups (Cohen, 1994).

Research examining cooperative learning is somewhat mixed. For instance, some studies suggest that it can increase student achievement and that it can also improve problem-solving abilities and interpersonal skills (Gao, Losh, Shen, Turner, & Yuan, 2007; Roseth et al., 2007). It can also increase motivation. When implemented effectively, it involves all students, which can be difficult in whole-class activities where less confident learners have fewer chances to participate. If students aren't involved, they're more likely to drift off (Brophy, 2010). Cooperative learning advocates go further and suggest that research results are generally positive (Tsay & Brady, 2010) or even "overwhelmingly positive" (Brown & Ciuffetelli, 2009).

On the other hand, simply putting students into groups doesn't ensure either increased achievement or motivation. For instance, when students are organized into mixed-ability groups, those with higher ability often feel they are being exploited by slackers and, in fact, frequently prefer to work alone instead of in groups (Cohen, 1994; Sharan, 2010; Su, 2007). Also, average-ability students often do not take advantage of learning in mixed-ability groups because high-ability students tend to dominate the group interaction (Saleh, Lazonder, & de Jong, 2007). In addition, the methods used to assess the effectiveness of cooperative learning can be problematic (Tsay & Brady, 2010), so the suggestion that research uniformly supports the effectiveness of cooperative learning needs to be viewed with caution.

These results have two implications for us if we want to use cooperative learning. First, careful planning is essential. For instance, when we tell students that we expect them to collaborate, such as ensuring that they solicit comments from everyone in the groups, interaction improves (Saleh et al., 2007). Second, group grading (grading in which all students in groups receive the same grade) should be avoided because it fails to accurately evaluate learning at the individual level. Further, students are fully aware that not all group members make equal contributions to tasks, so group grading often causes resentment in students who make greater contributions. Because of these factors, individual accountability is essential (Su, 2007).

A final reminder about cooperative learning strategies: Remember, they are strategies, and only strategies, which means that you use them to help you reach different learning objectives, such as learning to work together, developing communication skills, or understanding content objectives; they are never goals or objectives in themselves. If you believe you can best reach learning objectives with a cooperative learning strategy, using it is appropriate. However, putting students into groups for its own sake is never an appropriate objective.

Also, like all strategies and models, cooperative learning has both strengths and weaknesses, and overusing any one is not effective. Used judiciously and thoughtfully, however, cooperative learning can be effective for adding variety to your instruction, increasing student interest, and improving the social skills so important for students' overall education. We examine this idea in more detail in the next section.

DIVERSITY: USING COOPERATIVE LEARNING TO CAPITALIZE ON YOUR STUDENTS' DIVERSITY

Although important for constructing knowledge, effective social interaction doesn't always occur easily, especially in classrooms with diverse student populations. People tend to be wary of those different from themselves, and this tendency also occurs in schools. Members of specific ethnic groups tend to spend most of their time together, so they don't learn that all of us are much more alike than we are different (Juvonen, 2006; Okagaki, 2006).

We can't mandate tolerance, trust, and friendship among our students. Classroom activities that encourage mixed-group cooperation are needed, and evidence suggests that they can be effective. For example, students working in cooperative groups often improve their social skills; they develop friendships and positive attitudes toward others who differ in achievement, ethnicity, and gender; and they increase their acceptance of students with exceptionalities (Juvonen, 2006; Okagaki, 2006).

Let's see how Olivia Costa, a middle school math teacher, attempts to reach these goals in her classroom.

As Olivia watches her students work, she is both pleased and uneasy. They've improved a great deal in their math, but there is little mixing among her minority and nonminority students. She worries about six children from Central and South America who are struggling with English and three students with exceptionalities who leave her class every day for extra help.

To promote a more cohesive atmosphere, Olivia spends time over the weekend organizing students into groups of four, with equal numbers of high- and low-ability students in each group. She also mixes students by ethnicity and gender, and she makes sure that no group has more than one student for whom English is a second language or more than one student with an exceptionality.

On Monday she explains how they are to work together. To introduce the process, she sits with one group and models cooperation and support for the others. After she finishes a lesson on problem solving, she sends the groups to different parts of the room to practice the skills she's been teaching. All students in each group solve a problem and then share their answers with group-mates. If they cannot solve the problem or resolve differences about the correct answer, Olivia intervenes. She carefully monitors the groups to be sure that each student first attempts the problems before conferring with others.

Monitoring the groups is demanding, but her first session is fairly successful. "Phew," she thinks to herself at the end of the day. "This isn't any easier, but it does seem to be better."

Now, let's look at Olivia's efforts in a bit more detail. First, because her objective was to promote interpersonal relationships, she organized the groups so that high- and low-ability students, boys and girls, members of minorities and nonminorities, and students with and without exceptionalities were equally represented. Letting students form their own groups is one of the most common mistakes teachers make when attempting to reach this goal (Wentzel & Watkins, 2011).

Second, knowing that effective interaction must be planned and taught, she modeled desired behaviors, such as being supportive, listening, asking questions, and staying on task. We can also directly teach interaction strategies or use role-plays and video recordings of effective groups to help students learn cooperation skills (Blatchford, Baines, Rubie-Davies, Bassett, & Chowne, 2006; Vaughn & Bos, 2015). These skills are especially important for students who are members of cultural minorities, because they sometimes hesitate to seek and give help.

Third, she carefully monitored students while they worked. Initial training alone won't ensure cooperation. Groups need constant monitoring and support, particularly with young children and when cooperative learning is first introduced (Vaughn & Bos, 2015). If problems persist, you may need to reconvene the class for additional training.

The benefits of student cooperation stem primarily from three factors:

- Students with different backgrounds work together.
- Group members have equal status.
- Students learn about each other as individuals (Slavin, 2011).

As students work together, they frequently find that they have more in common than they would expect. They all want to succeed and to get along with their peers and to be accepted and respected. Having students work together to achieve common goals can be one of the most effective tools you have for helping students meet these needs.

Flipped Instruction

Flipped instruction (commonly called the "flipped classroom") is an approach to teaching that has students study new content online by watching video lectures, usually on home computers, but also on other devices, such as smartphones. Then, they discuss the new content and do problems, exercises, and other activities that apply the content in class where teachers can offer more personalized guidance and interaction with students instead of lecturing. This is the source of the term *flipped*. Instead of listening to a teacher presentation in class and doing homework outside of class, they watch the lecture outside of class and do the "home-work" during class time.

As an example, consider Diane Anderson's lesson on the events leading up to the Revolutionary War. If she wanted to "flip" her instruction, she would create a video lecture in which she would provide all the information she presented in class and then make the video available to students through a delivery system such as YouTube. The students' assignment would be to view the video and be prepared to discuss the information in it the next day. Class time would then be spent in a detailed discussion of topics, such as the relative advantages of the French and the English during the French and Indian War, the links between that war and the Revolutionary War, why part of Canada is French speaking, and a number of others.

Similarly, if Scott wanted to flip his instruction, he would create a video lecture during which he would provide examples of Bernoulli's principle using the demonstrations he used in class. Class time would then be spent analyzing applications of Bernoulli's principle, such as explaining how it helps airplanes fly, why a shower curtain moves in and wraps around our legs when we're taking a shower, how atomizers on perfume bottles work, and many others.

Although precursors to the flipped classroom go back to about the turn of the 21st century, major impetus for the idea was created by the *Khan Academy*, a nonprofit educational website created in 2006 by Salman Khan, an MIT and Harvard Business School graduate. The website features hundreds of short video lectures stored on YouTube that teach subjects ranging from math and science to economics and art history and more (Sparks, 2011). Since its inception, the Khan Academy videos have been viewed by literally millions of people.

Flipped instruction has garnered a great deal of interest, and some educators are even describing it as revolutionary. For instance, in 2011 a school in Michigan completely converted its entire instructional delivery system to flipped instruction (Rosenberg, 2013). And an increasing number of articles focusing on flipped instruction in classrooms ranging from elementary schools to colleges and universities have been appearing in a variety of professional journals (e.g., Corcoran, 2013; Enfield, 2013; Roehl, Reddy, & Shannon, 2013; Sams & Bergmann, 2013). The results reported in these articles are uniformly positive (Pierce, 2013). However, most of the results are anecdotal, and at the time of this edition's publication, systematic research examining the efficacy of flipped instruction is largely lacking.

ISSUES INVOLVED WITH FLIPPED INSTRUCTION

As with any educational innovation, some issues exist with respect to flipped instruction. For instance, what if students don't have available technology, so they're unable to view the videos? Also, what if students choose not to view the video lectures?

In addition, considerable logistics are required. For example, if you decide to use flipped instruction in your classroom—and no school policies in our country prevent you from doing so—you will have to prepare the video lectures, and the presentation and technical quality of the videos must be good enough so they are meaningful to students. Also, you must then prepare the exercises and applications that you will use in class. Flipped instruction requires considerable work and effort by teachers.

On the other hand, flipped instruction makes sense from a learning perspective; unlike a classroom lecture, students can rewind the video and watch the lecture as many times as necessary to understand the content. Second, flipped instruction is consistent with essential teaching skills, models of instruction, and traditional modes of presentation. For instance, essential teaching skills, such as teacher enthusiasm, focus, review, clear communication, and closure, are as important in a video lecture as they are in one delivered live to students in class. Also, the video lectures essentially apply the *developing understanding* phase of direct instruction and the *presenting information* phase of lecture–discussions. If PowerPoint presentations are used in a traditional lecture, they can also be used in a video lecture. And video lectures can even incorporate aspects of guided discovery. For instance, Scott could present his demonstrations in a video and then go back and identify the patterns in them, just as he did in class. The difference, of course, is that he would be presenting all the information without any interaction with students. And, finally, students can work in groups, if appropriate, when they work on applications in class of the content delivered in the video lectures.

With respect to students not watching the videos, if they aren't inclined to watch videos at home, they're probably even less inclined to do traditional homework (Khan, 2012). Also, most schools now have facilities that allow students without access to technology at home to watch videos after school.

And, finally, with respect to logistics, once the video lectures and application materials have been prepared, and you're satisfied with their quality, they can be used over and over.

Whether or not flipped instruction is the revolutionary innovation that proponents say it is remains to be seen. The concept appears to have potential, however, and it is, and will be, applicable for you when you begin teaching.

Differentiating Instruction

Our students are more diverse than ever before in our nation's history. Because of this diversity, they all respond to our instruction a bit differently. **Differentiating instruction**, the process of adapting instruction to meet the needs of students who vary in background knowledge, skills, needs, and motivations, is a response to this diversity.

Two factors related to differentiated instruction are important. First, it is not individualized instruction (Tomlinson & McTighe, 2006). In essence, tutoring is the only true form of individualization, and it's impossible for you to tutor every one of your students.

Second, much of what you do when you plan carefull and effectively implement your instruction will include forms of differentiation. For example, differentiation experts suggest the following (Dixon, Yssel, McConnell, & Hardin, 2014; Parsons, Dodman, & Burrowbridge, 2013):

- Plan thoroughly, and carefully teach the essential knowledge and skills needed for further learning. This is part of all forms of effective instruction.
- Use assessment as a tool to extend rather than simply measure learning. (We discuss assessment as a learning tool in the next section of the chapter.) Emphasize critical thinking by requiring students to provide evidence for their conclusions. This goal is often neglected in instruction with students who are lower achievers or members of cultural minorities.
- Actively engage all learners. Equitable distribution and cooperative learning are two effective ways to reach this goal.
- Vary your instruction. For example, using direct instruction in one lesson, guided discovery in another, and cooperative learning in a third, or in combination with the other models, helps meet students' varying needs and interests.

In addition to the preceding suggestions, some specific differentiation strategies can be effective (Kauchak & Eggen, 2012). They include:

- Small-group support
- Mastery learning
- Personalizing content

Small-Group Support. Providing extra instructional support for small groups of students is one of the most applicable and practical forms of differentiation. For instance, when Sam's students began independent practice in his lesson on adding whole numbers, he called Cathy, Josh, and Jeremy to the back of the room, where he provided additional assistance to help them better grasp the ideas. Because he was working with only three students, his instruction in the small group was nearly one-on-one.

Effectively implementing the *developing understanding* and *guided practice* phases of direct instruction are crucial if small-group support is to work. The rest of the class must be working quietly and successfully. If you have to get up to help other students or deal with off-task behavior, your small-group support will be much less effective.

Mastery Learning. Mastery learning is a system of instruction that allows students to progress at their own rate through a unit of study (Tanner & Tanner, 2007). Objectives specify the learning outcomes for the unit, and frequent formative quizzes provide feedback about learning progress. When students master a learning objective, they continue; when they don't, they are provided with alternative learning activities.

Mastery learning can be effective, particularly for low achievers (Verdinelli & Gentile, 2003), but it is logistically demanding (Good & Brophy, 2008).

Personalizing Content. Much of what is written about differentiating instruction focuses on cognitive objectives. However, responding to differences in students' needs and motivations are also important.

Personalizing content is another way to differentiate instruction. For example, Sam implemented a simple form of personalization by putting two of his students' names in his original problem. Doing so took no additional effort, and it can significantly increase student interest and motivation (Schraw & Lehman, 2001).

Personalizing content primarily requires awareness and some imagination. If you're aware of the need to link content to students' lives, and you make attempts to do so, you will find that the process gets easier and easier. Improved interest and motivation will often result.

Other ways of differentiating instruction exist, such as varying learning objectives, learning materials, and assessments, but they are demanding and difficult to implement (O'Meara, 2011). Most beginning teachers begin with the strategies we've outlined here and, as they gain experience and confidence, experiment with different ways to adapt their instruction to meet individual student needs and interests.

Technology, Learning, and Development

Using PowerPoint Effectively

Earlier in the chapter we saw how Diane Anderson used the lecture–discussion model to help her students understand events leading up to the American Revolution.

Let's look now at Jack Wilson, another American history teacher, and how he teaches similar information.

> Jack introduces the topic and then comments, "We need to know why the colonists in our country originally fought the war," he says. ". . . There were several causes, and we're going to look at them today."
>
> He then brings PowerPoint up on his computer and displays the following information:
>
> > • The French and Indian War (1754–1763)
> >   The war was costly for the British, who looked to the colonies to help pay some of the costs.
>
> "This is where it all started," he comments, pointing to the display on the screen. "The French and Indian War was incredibly costly for the British, so they needed to figure out a way to make additional money to pay for the debt that resulted from the war."

As Jack watches, his students quickly write down the information they see, and he then displays the following slides, making brief comments after each one, and allowing students time to copy the information on them.

• The British impose new taxes (1764)

The British felt they were spending a great deal of money to protect the colonists, so they imposed new taxes to cover the costs of stationing British troops in North America.

• Boston Massacre (1770)

In response to taunts by colonists, British soldiers killed five colonists. The event turned colonists' opinions against the British.

• Boston Tea Party (1773)

In response to an act granting a monopoly on tea trade, colonists dumped tons of tea into Boston harbor, one of the most famous events leading up to the Revolutionary War.

After he has displayed his PowerPoint slides, made comments, and allowed the students time to copy the information, he summarizes the lesson by saying, "Keep these events in mind as we begin our discussion of the Revolutionary War. . . . We'll start our discussion of the war itself tomorrow."

Look familiar? We've all sat through PowerPoint presentations where an instructor or presenter displayed bullet points, often read them to us, and gave us time to copy the information.

Jack fell into this pattern. Instead of involving his students in a discussion of the historical events leading up to the American Revolution and how they contributed to it, he reduced the causes to a series of bullet points, and his students simply copied the information, a cognitively passive process. This isn't an effective use of PowerPoint.

Teachers are using significantly more technology in their work with students, with PowerPoint presentations being one of the most popular, particularly in middle and secondary schools and at the college level (Hill, Arford, Lubitow, & Smollin, 2012; Isseks, 2011; Lawson, 2013). However, some experts, school administrators, and even teachers themselves have begun to question the effectiveness of PowerPoint presentations, suggesting that they are inconsistent with efforts to involve students in learning activities and teach higher order thinking (Adams, 2006). Others go further and suggest that the technologies, such as this, are an impediment to using student-centered forms of instruction, such as guided discovery and problem-based learning (Hill et al., 2012; Langenegger, 2011). PowerPoint's most ardent critics are even more harsh, particularly about using this technology at the college level. "Every day, on every campus, in every town across the United States, due specifically to PowerPoint, there are lackluster students not paying attention and often sleeping in class. In these classes, the professors are reading PowerPoint slides word-for-word" (Lawson, 2013, p. 2). Although this quote is a bit overstated, most of us have had experiences similar to this one.

PowerPoint itself is not the issue. "The root problem of PowerPoint presentations is not the *power* or the *point,* but the *presentation.* . . . The presenter does everything—gathers information, eliminates extraneous points, and selects the direction and duration of the presentation" (Isseks, 2011, pp. 74–75.)

From a learning perspective, PowerPoint presentations can be problematic because they tend to put learners in even more cognitively passive roles than do standard lectures. Students can ask questions, but usually only to clarify information on a slide.

The allure of PowerPoint is understandable. Information can be easily copied onto PowerPoint slides, and the slides organize the lecture, which dramatically reduces the cognitive load on teachers. Further, in an era of high-stakes testing, PowerPoint presentations are effective for "covering" content and creating the illusion that doing so equals teaching (Isseks, 2011).

Criticisms of PowerPoint presentations have also come from outside education. For example, they are common in the business world, and members of the military complain that the near universal use of the presentation format oversimplifies military objectives and the complexity of military missions (Bumiller, 2010).

Using PowerPoint Effectively

None of the criticisms we've outlined above suggest that you shouldn't use PowerPoint in your teaching. The issue is *how* you use it. Combined with information you can get from the Internet, it can be a powerful learning tool. Two suggestions can be helpful.

First, reduce the number of bullet points, and include pictures, videos, diagrams, and maps that stimulate student interest and thought. For example, Jim Norton, an earth science teacher, simply Googled the Rocky and Appalachian mountains and downloaded detailed, colored pictures onto PowerPoint slides, which he used to illustrate the characteristics of young and mature mountains. He did the same with other landforms, such as young and old rivers, and used them to provide detailed, concrete examples of each of the concepts.

Second, make your presentations interactive. Jim, for instance, displayed the slides of the Rockies and Appalachians, had his students make observations to identify differences between them, and then suggested possible reasons for the differences. Instead of passively looking at a series of bullet points and attempting to remember the information displayed with them, his students were involved in a form of inquiry. Other suggestions include inserting questions in the slides that encourage students to think about the content and link ideas (Valdez, 2013).

Used effectively, PowerPoint has the potential to enhance learning experiences, as you saw in the example with Jim Norton and his students. Jim was also able to store everything on a thumb drive, making it easy for him to retrieve, revise, and improve the presentation for the next time he teaches the topic.

As with many aspects of teaching and learning, the issue isn't whether to use or not use a strategy or tool; it's *how* to use it. How effectively you use any strategy depends on your professional knowledge and judgment.

Classroom **Connections**

Using Models of Instruction Effectively in Classrooms

Direct Instruction

1. Direct instruction includes an introduction and review, a phase for developing understanding, and guided and independent practice. Emphasize understanding, and provide sufficient practice to develop automaticity.

   ■ **Elementary:** A fourth-grade teacher, in a lesson on possessives, first explains the difference between singular and plural possessives and then asks students to punctuate the following sentences.

   The students books were lost when he forgot them on the bus.
   The students books were lost when they left them on the playground.
   Who can describe the boys adventure when he went to the zoo?
   Who can describe the boys adventure when they swam in the river?

   He then has students write paragraphs that incorporate both singular and plural possessives.

   ■ **Middle School:** In a unit on percentages and decimals, a math teacher comments that the star quarterback for the state university completed 14 of 21 passes in last Saturday's game. "What does that mean? Is that good or bad? Was it better than the 12 of 17 passes completed by the opposing quarterback?" she asks. She then explains how to calculate the percentages with the class and then has the students practice finding percentages in other real-world problems.

   ■ **High School:** A ninth-grade geography teacher helps his students locate the longitude and latitude of their city by "walking them through" the process, using a map and a series of specific questions. He then has them practice finding the longitude and latitude of other cities, as well as finding the major city nearest sets of longitude and latitude locations.

Lecture–Discussion

2. Lecture–discussions include an introduction and review, a phase where information is presented, and questions that check comprehension and help students integrate ideas. Keep presentations short, and use high levels of interaction to maintain students' attention and promote schema production.

- **Elementary:** A first-grade teacher wants her students to know similarities and differences between farm animals and pets. To do this, she constructs a large chart with pictures of both. As they discuss the two groups of animals, she continually asks students to identify similarities and differences between the two groups.

- **Middle School:** An American history teacher discussing immigration in the 19th and early 20th centuries compares immigrant groups of the past with today's Cuban population in Miami, Florida, and Mexican immigrants in San Antonio, Texas. He asks students to summarize similarities and differences between the two groups with respect to the difficulties they encounter and the rates of assimilation into the American way of life.

- **High School:** A biology teacher is presenting information related to transport of liquids in and out of cells, identifying and illustrating several of the concepts in the process. After about 3 minutes, she stops presenting information and asks, "Suppose a cell is in a hypotonic solution in one case and a hypertonic solution in another. What's the difference between the two? What would happen to the cell in each case?"

Guided Discovery

3. When teachers use guided discovery, they present students with examples and guide students' knowledge construction. Provide examples that include all the information students need to understand the topic, and guide student interaction.

- **Elementary:** A fifth-grade teacher begins a unit on reptiles by bringing a snake and turtle to class. He includes colored pictures of lizards, alligators, and sea turtles. He has students describe the animals and pictures and then guides them to an understanding of the essential characteristics of reptiles.

- **Middle School:** A seventh-grade English teacher embeds examples of singular and plural possessive nouns in the context of a paragraph. She then guides the discussion as students develop explanations for why particular sentences are punctuated the way they are, for example, "The girls' and boys' accomplishments in the middle school were noteworthy, as were the children's efforts in the elementary school."

- **High School:** A world history teacher presents students with vignettes, such as this one:

> You're part of an archeological team, and at one site you've found some spear points. In spite of their ages, the points are still quite sharp, having been chipped precisely from hard stone. You also see several cattle and sheep skulls and some threads that appear to be the remains of coarsely woven fabric.

He then guides the students to conclude that the artifacts best represent a New Stone Age society.

Cooperative Learning

4. Cooperative learning requires that students work together to reach learning objectives. Provide clear directions for groups, and carefully monitor students as they work.

- **Elementary:** A second-grade teacher begins the school year by having groups work together on short word problems in math. When students fail to cooperate, she stops the groups and immediately discusses the issues with the class.

- **Middle School:** A life-science teacher has students create and answer questions about the characteristics, organelles, and environments of one-celled animals. He periodically offers suggestions to the pairs to help them ask more meaningful questions.

- **High School:** A geometry teacher has pairs use scripted cooperation to solve proofs. When they struggle, she offers hints to help them continue to make progress.

4. Because of its emphasis on group interdependence, cooperative learning can promote healthy interactions between students from different backgrounds. Use cooperative learning groups to capitalize on the richness that learner diversity brings to classrooms, and design tasks that require group cooperation.

- **Elementary:** A second-grade teacher waits until the third week of the school year to form cooperative learning groups. During that time, she observes her students and gathers information about their interests, talents, and friendships. She then uses the information in making decisions about group membership.

- **Middle School:** A sixth-grade math teacher uses cooperative learning groups to practice word problems. He organizes the class into pairs, forming, whenever possible, pairs that are composed of a minority and nonminority student, a student with and a student without an exceptionality, and a boy and a girl.

- **High School:** An English teacher has students work in groups of four to provide feedback on one another's writing. The teacher organizes all groups so that they're composed of equal numbers of boys and girls, minorities and nonminorities, and students who do and do not have exceptionalities.

Ed Psych and You

Think about your redecorating project again. You repainted the room, rearranged the furniture, and added some pieces of art. As you gaze at the finished product, what do you think about now?

Assessment and Learning: Using Assessment as a Learning Tool

Think about our question in *Ed Psych and You* here. The most likely answer is, *Have I accomplished my purpose?* For instance, you'll ask yourself if the room really is more comfortable and inviting, or if you really are using the space more efficiently. In other words, you'll assess the extent to which you've achieved your objective.

Again, the process you're going through is analogous to teaching. Having conducted a learning activity—or series of activities—you'll want to assess the extent to which your students have reached your learning objectives. Assessment is the third step in the planning–implementing–assessing cycle.

Let's see how Scott assessed his students' understanding of Bernoulli's principle. The following is an item on his Friday quiz and students' responses to it.

> Look at the drawing that represents the two pieces of paper that we used in the lesson. Explain what made the papers move together. Make a sketch that shows how the air flowed as you blew between the papers. Label the forces in your sketch as we did during the lesson.

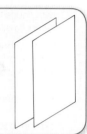

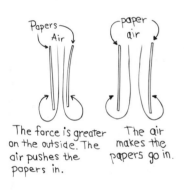

To the left are two students' sketches of the flow of air between the papers.

The students' responses illustrate an essential characteristic of effective assessments: *Assessments must provide information about students' thinking* (Chappuis, Stiggins, Chappuis, & Arter, 2012; Herman & Linn, 2014). For instance, the sketches show that students correctly concluded that the force (pressure) on the outside of the papers pushing in was greater than the force (pressure) between the papers pushing out. This doesn't provide a great deal of evidence about their understanding, however, because the lesson emphasized this conclusion.

The students' explanations of their sketches of the airflow are more revealing. They concluded that the moving air curled around the bottoms of the papers and pushed the papers together, which indicates a misconception. (The papers moved together because increasing the speed of the air over a surface [in this case over the surface of the papers] decreases the pressure the air exerts on the surface [the papers], and the still air on the outside of the papers pushes them together, as illustrated in the sketch to the left. This is an application of Bernoulli's principle.)

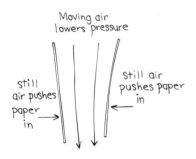

If Scott's assessment hadn't asked for both an explanation and a drawing, he might not have learned that his students left the lesson with misconceptions. Assessments such as these provide opportunities to directly address student misconceptions, which we can then attempt to correct to increase our students' understanding (which is why "Using Assessment as a Learning Tool" is the subtitle of this section). A detailed discussion of these responses together with additional examples (such as demonstrating that air exerts pressure in all directions and that all objects, including air particles, move in a straight line unless a force acts on them) would greatly expand the students' understanding of basic principles in science. In fact, teaching these principles after the assessment likely produces more learning than trying to teach them beforehand, because the students' responses to the assessment provide both motivation and context for learning. Ideally, all assessments provide similar opportunities to extend learning.

The same is true for much of classroom learning. We tend to think of assessment as giving tests and assigning grades, but it is much more than that: it's an essential part of the entire teaching–learning process. "Testing has such a bad connotation; people think of standardized testing or teaching to the test. Maybe we need to call it something else, but this is one of the most powerful learning tools we have" (Carey, 2010, para. 28).

Developmentally Appropriate **Practice**

Effective Instruction with Learners at Different Ages

Essential teaching skills are important at all developmental levels, and the models of instruction discussed in this section can be used at all levels as well. But when using the models, some adaptations are necessary to accommodate developmental differences in students. The following paragraphs outline suggestions for responding to these developmental differences.

Working with Students in Early Childhood Programs and Elementary Schools

Because it is effective for teaching basic skills, direct instruction is probably the most widely used instructional model in the lower elementary grades. When using direct instruction with young children, the developing understanding and guided practice phases are crucial because they lay a foundation for independent practice. Monitoring learner progress during guided practice and spending extra time with lower achievers while the majority of the students are practicing independently is an effective adaptation with young children.

Lecture–discussions should be used sparingly with young children because of their short attention spans and lack of prior knowledge. Verbal explanations must be kept short and combined with frequent episodes of comprehension monitoring for young children. Models other than lecture–discussion are often more effective with young students.

Guided discovery can be particularly effective with young children if the goal is for them to understand topics that you can illustrate with concrete examples, such as crustaceans, fractions, or parts of speech. When using guided discovery with young children, you should verbally link examples to the concept being taught and emphasize new terms.

Young children need a great deal of scaffolding and practice to work effectively in groups. Clearly describing procedures for turning in materials and participating in the activities is also crucial.

Working with Students in Middle Schools

In middle schools, direct instruction is an effective model for learning procedural skills that require practice, such as in prealgebra, algebra, and language arts. As with younger students, the developing understanding and guided practice phases are essential for the success of the activity.

Guided discovery is one of the most effective models with middle school students, but establishing rules about treating each other with courtesy and respect during the activities is important with these students. If you use high-quality examples, middle school students are capable of learning more abstract concepts such as symmetric and asymmetric body structures in life science or culture in social students. Guided discovery continues to be an effective model for teaching concepts that can be represented with concrete examples.

Cooperative learning can be effectively used to complement direct instruction, as Olivia Costa did with her eighth graders. Cooperative learning can also help middle school students develop social and communication skills, perspective taking, and collaboration.

Lecture–discussion can be effective for teaching organized bodies of knowledge in science, literature, and social studies.

Working with Students in High Schools

High school students typically pose fewer management challenges than younger students, but their greater willingness to sit passively can be a problem. Using lecture–discussions as an alternative to pure lectures is desirable.

Each of the other models can also be effective as instructional alternatives, depending on your goals. High school students are often familiar with the other models, as they've encountered them in earlier grades. Frequent monitoring is still needed to keep lessons on track and aligned with learning objectives.

chapter

13 Summary

1. Describe the steps in planning for instruction, including planning in a standards-based environment.
   - When planning for instruction, teachers first identify topics that are important for students to learn, specify learning objectives, prepare and organize learning activities, and design assessments.
   - When using standards to plan for instruction, teachers first need to interpret the standard and then design learning activities to help students meet the standard and assessments to determine whether the standard has been met.

2. Describe essential teaching skills, and explain why they're important.
   - Essential teaching skills are the abilities and attitudes that all effective teachers possess. These attitudes include high personal teaching efficacy—the belief that they are responsible for student learning and can increase it. These attitudes also include caring, modeling, enthusiasm, and high expectations for student achievement and behavior.
   - Essential teaching skills include the ability to organize efficiently, communicate clearly, attract and maintain student attention, provide informative feedback, and deliver succinct reviews.
   - Effective questioning is an important essential teaching skill and should include high frequency and equitable distribution, prompts when students can't answer, and sufficient wait-time for students to think about their answers.

3. Explain the relationships between models of instruction and essential teaching skills, and describe how the components of different models contribute to learning.
   - Essential teaching skills support and are incorporated in all models of instruction.
   - Direct instruction is an instructional model designed to teach knowledge and essential skills that students need for later learning. Teachers conduct direct instruction in four phases: (a) introduction and review, to attract students' attention and activate prior knowledge; (b) developing understanding, to acquire declarative knowledge about the skill; (c) guided practice, to begin the devel-

opment of procedural knowledge; and (d) independent practice, to further develop the skill to automaticity.
   - Lecture–discussion is an instructional model designed to help students acquire organized bodies of knowledge. It consists of (a) an introduction and review, to attract attention and activate prior knowledge; (b) presenting information, to provide knowledge; (c) comprehension monitoring, to check students' perceptions; and (d) integration, to promote schema production.
   - Guided discovery is an instructional model that helps students learn concepts and the relationships among them. It consists of (a) an introduction and review, to attract students' attention and activate prior knowledge; (b) an open-ended phase in which students make observations of examples; (c) a convergent phase in which teachers help students identify patterns and begin schema production; (d) closure, when students, assisted by teachers, complete schema production and clarify the learning objective; and (e) application, which helps promote transfer.
   - Cooperative learning is a set of instructional models that uses group interaction to reach specified learning objectives. Teachers hold learners individually accountable for understanding, and learners must depend on each other to reach the objectives.
   - Differentiating instruction is the process of adapting instruction to meet the needs of students who vary in background knowledge, skills, needs, and motivations.

4. Identify the essential characteristics of effective assessments.
   - Productive learning environments are assessment centered. This means that assessment is an integral part of the learning–teaching process and that assessments are aligned with objectives and learning activities.
   - Effective assessments provide teachers with information about students' thinking, which both teachers and students can use as feedback about learning progress.
   - Effective assessments provide opportunities for increasing students' understanding through detailed feedback and discussion. Discussion following assessments often increases understanding as much as or more than the learning activity itself.

Preparing for **Your Licensure Exam**

Understanding Effective Teaching

You will be required to take a licensure exam before you go into your own classroom. This exam will include information related to effective teaching, and it will include both multiple-choice and constructed-response questions. We include the following exercises to help you practice for the exam in your state. This book and these exercises will be a resource for you as you prepare for the exam.

In the chapter, you saw how Scott planned his lesson, demonstrated essential teaching skills, and assessed his students' learning. Let's look now at a teacher working with a class of ninth-grade geography students. As you read the case study, consider the extent to which the teacher applied the information you've studied in this chapter in her lesson. Read the case study, and answer the questions that follow.

Francisca has been teaching mathematics for three years. She has taught the seventh-grade students for the last two years, and has found that geometry is what most students struggle with. Hence, she has created a game of sorts with different 2D geometric shapes to aid her students' understanding. Francisca has realized that by making concepts fun for students to learn, understanding is enhanced. Furthermore, she has also discovered that students understand new concepts better when these are linked to concepts they already know.

In the first three lessons she first introduces geometry to her students by teaching them the various 2D geometric shapes with their names and properties. She has developed a chart that contains the names of the 2D geometric shapes. The students are required to pair up, choose a shape, and then write on the chart where they found that shape in the real world. They are told they have three days to complete the assignment.

2D Geometric shapes	Examples in daily lives
Circle	Wheel
Equilateral Triangle	Jewelry
Isosceles Triangle	Doritos chip
Scalene Triangle	Sail
Right Triangle	Sandwich
Obtuse Triangle	Bicycle
Acute Triangle	Steps
Square	Rubric cube
Rectangle	A bird's eye view of the top of a car
Rhombus	Brazilian flag
Parallelogram	On a guitar
Trapezoid	Pyramids
Trapezium	A handbag

2D Geometric shapes	Examples in daily lives
Kite	Kite
Pentagon	Soccer ball
Hexagon	Bee hive
Octagon	Stop sign

In the fourth geometry lesson, she asks her students for feedback on the assigned task.

Mark answers, "Some of the shapes were so obvious to spot like the kite; we have all seen a kite. But others were difficult to spot like the parallelogram; if it was my own shape that I had to look for, I would have been unable to complete the assignment."

Francisca smiles and replies, "Is it that these shapes are hidden from us? Or is it that you were not aware of these shapes before now and hence found it more difficult to spot?"

She patiently waits for a response. After a while Jeff answers, "They are there for us to see, but the funny names, definitions and properties of the shapes and trying to apply that to the shapes we see around us sometimes made the assignment difficult."

Francisca agrees with Jeff, and then provides feedback on the real world examples provided by the students. She commends the creativity and the effort students have taken to complete the task. She also congratulates all students on their work. Together with the students, she developss strategies to help them remember the 2D geometric shapes, their names and properties. The students develop mnemonics, rap songs, and poems to help them remember.

Thereafter, Francisca groups the students into different pairs from the initial assignment. She tasks the new groups with finding similarities for the uses of the objects found in the real world. Without thinking, John immediately responded, "Duh! We use them in our real world. This is stupid; we have already done the assignment". The whole class bursts out laughing. "Yes," replies Francisca patiently, "but there are similarities in how these objects are used. For example, shapes like stop sign and the top of the car are used in different ways for transportation". With this, the class calms down and sets about completing the task. Francisca gives the groups five minutes to complete the assignment. After five minutes, she asks for responses from the class and writes them on the blackboard.

She then asks the class to reflect, "If we did not have these shapes, what would life be like?" After a while Grace answers, "It would be boring. The world would be a difficult place to live in, we could not make ourselves more beautiful without jewelry, and we would not have places to live in like our houses, and there would be no pyramids like the ones in ancient Egypt. Without these shapes, our world, our society would be chaotic."

"Very good Grace, you were able to use the chart as well as the work that we just did to come up with that answer," exclaimed Francisca.

John once more blurted out "Yeah, we would be living on a flat world".

Francisca replied smiling "Yes, but even a flat world would have shape, it could be a square or a rectangle or even a circle. It could be any shape you desire; just think of the possibilities!"

Francisca then provides pieces of paper to each student and asks each student to draw a 3D design using as many 2D geometric shapes as they can. She gives them 10 minutes to complete the task. She then asks them to name the shapes that they had used in their designs. These are to be listed on the piece of paper below their designs. She observes the class closely to see who has been constantly referring to the chart. She notes their names down in her lesson preparation notes. She asks for the students' designs to be handed in to her. She will use these two formats, i.e. the 3D design as well as her observations, as a form of her students' assessment.

As the last 10 minutes of the lesson nears, Francisca asks the students to be quiet. She likes to have the students find a quiet place in their minds, and she even puts on some soothing music for a few minutes. During the last few minutes, Francisca guides the students in making a summary statement of what they have learned regarding the 2D geometric shapes and their uses in the real world. She thanks all the students for their hard work and participation.

Questions for Case Analysis

In answering these questions, use information from the chapter, and link your responses to specific information in the case.

Multiple-Choice Questions

1. Look at the information in the case study beginning with, "She observes the class closely to see who is constantly referring to the chart. She notes their names down in her lesson preparation notes. She asks for the students' designs to be handed in to her. She will use these two formats, i.e. the 3D design as well as her observations, as a form of her students' assessment."

   Why do you think Francisca chose to use this assessment towards the end of the lesson?

   a. To review

   b. To provide closure

   c. She needed to fill in time in her lesson

   d. To gather information on students' understanding

2. Francisca used many models of instruction discussed in the chapter. Which instruction model did she not use in her lesson?

   a. Direct instruction, because the progress of her lesson was directed with her questioning.

   b. Lecture–discussion, because the information on the chart was discussed by the students.

   c. Guided discovery, because patterns in the information presented on the chart was searched for by the students.

   d. Differentiating instruction, because she catered for students of varying skills, needs, motivation and knowledge with specific strategies.

Constructed-Response Question

3. In a table format and using examples from the case, state what essential teaching skills Francisca employed. Include the application of cognitive learning theory relative to each essential teaching skill you mention.

Important **Concepts**

affective domain
closure
cognitive domain
Common Core State
    Standards Initiative
    (CCSSI)
connected discourse
cooperative learning
differentiating instruction

direct instruction
effective teaching
emphasis
equitable distribution
essential teaching skills
feedback
flipped instruction
focus
guided discovery

implementing instruction
instructional alignment
learning activities
learning objective
lecture–discussion
mastery learning
models of instruction
organized bodies of
    knowledge

precise language
prompting
psychomotor domain
questioning frequency
review
standards
task analysis
transition signals
wait-time

Blend Images/Ariel Skelley/Getty Images

OUTLINE	LEARNING OUTCOMES
	After you have completed your study of this chapter, you should be able to:
Classroom Assessment Assessment *for* Student Learning Validity: Making Accurate Assessment Decisions Reliability: Consistency in Assessment	1. Describe assessment *for* learning and explain how validity and reliability are related to it.
Informal Assessment Informal Assessment During Learning Activities Reliability of Informal Assessments	2. Describe informal assessment, and explain why it is an important part of assessment *for* learning.
Formal Assessment Paper-and-Pencil Items Performance Assessments Portfolio Assessment: Helping Students Develop Self-Regulation Evaluating Formal Assessment Formats	3. Identify differences between formal and informal assessment, and analyze formal assessment items.
Effective Assessment Practices Planning for Assessment Preparing Students for Assessments Administering Assessments Analyzing Results Providing Students with Feedback Increasing the Efficiency of Your Assessment Practices	4. Explain how effective assessment practices increase student learning.
Designing a Total Assessment System Formative and Summative Assessment Designing a Grading System Assigning Grades: Increasing Learning and Motivation ▶ Technology, Learning, and Development: Using Technology to Improve Your Assessment System Diversity: Effective Assessment Practices with Students from Diverse Backgrounds	5. Describe the components and decisions involved in designing a total assessment system.

You've taught a lesson, and you believe it went well. The students were involved and seemed interested. But you're missing some essential information. What did they learn, and did they learn what you intended? Being able to answer these questions is an essential part of the learning–teaching process.

As you read the following case study, consider how DeVonne Lampkin, a fifth-grade teacher, attempts to answer the questions, and more importantly, how she uses the information she gathers to increase her students' learning. (The actual lesson on which this case study is based is the framework for the first "Practicing What You Have Learned" exercise at the end of the chapter. To see the lesson, simply click on the link.)

DeVonne is beginning a unit on fractions as she is working with her students to reach the following standard:

CCSS.Math.Content.5.NF.A.1. Add and subtract fractions with unlike denominators (including mixed numbers) by replacing given fractions with equivalent fractions in such a way as to produce an equivalent sum or difference of fractions with like denominators. *For example, 2/3 + 5/4 = 8/12 + 15/12 = 23/12. (In general, a/b + c/d = (ad + bc)/bd.)* (Common Core State Standards Initiative, 2014c).

She knows that fractions were introduced in the fourth grade, but she isn't sure how much her students remember, so she gives them a pretest. When she scores it, here's what she finds:

Draw a figure that will illustrate each of the fractions.

3/4   3/8   1/3

You need 3 pieces of ribbon for a project. The pieces should measure 2 5/16, 4 2/16, and 1 3/16 inches. How much ribbon do you need in all?

$7 \frac{10}{16}$

The students seem to understand the basic idea of a fraction, and how to add fractions with like denominators. But the following responses suggest they struggle with adding fractions when the denominators are different:

Latoya made a punch recipe for a party.

Punch Recipe
3/4 gallon ginger ale   1/2 gallon grapefruit juice
1 2/3 gallon orange juice   2/3 gallon pineapple juice

a. Will the punch she made fit into one 3-gallon punch bowl? Explain why or why not.

No because when added correctly it is more.

b. How much punch, if any, is left over?

None

On Saturday, Justin rode his bicycle 12 ½ miles.

On Sunday, he rode 8 3/5 miles.

a. How many miles did he ride altogether?

21

b. How many more miles did Justin ride on Saturday than on Sunday?

4 miles more.

Based on these results, DeVonne plans to focus on *equivalent fractions* in her first lesson, because her students need to understand this concept to be able to add fractions with unlike denominators.

She begins the lesson by passing out chocolate bars divided into 12 equal pieces, and with her guidance, the students show how 3/12 is the same as 1/4, 6/12 is equal to 1/2, and 8/12 equals 2/3. In each case she has them explain their answers.

DeVonne then goes to the board and demonstrates how to create equivalent fractions using numbers. At the end of the lesson, she gives a homework assignment that includes the following problems:

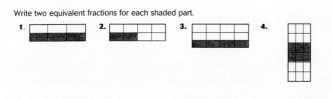

When she scores the homework, she sees that some students are still having difficulties.

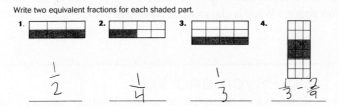

So, she designs another activity for the next day to further illustrate equivalent fractions. She begins the activity by having students construct a model fraction city with equivalent-length streets divided into different parts:

When the students are finished making their strips, she has them move cars along the different streets to illustrate equivalent fractions such as 1/2 = 3/6 and 1/3 = 3/9. Then, she illustrates adding fractions with like denominators, using the cars and strips

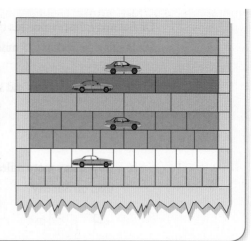

as concrete examples. Next she uses the same cars and strips to illustrate adding fractions with unlike denominators.

Finally, DeVonne goes to the board and demonstrates how to perform the same operations using numbers, and gives her students a homework assignment on adding fractions with unlike denominators.

At the end of the week, she gives a cumulative test on fractions. Her students' answers suggest that they seem to understand equivalent fractions and how to add fractions with unlike denominators.

To begin your study of this chapter, consider these questions:

1. What is classroom assessment and how does it contribute to learning?
2. What was the primary purpose of DeVonne's assessments?
3. How did DeVonne's assessments provide her with different kinds of information about her students' learning?

Research on classroom assessment helps us answer these questions and suggests ways to make our assessments more effective. In this chapter we examine how you can apply this research with your students.

Classroom Assessment

Classroom assessment includes all the processes involved in making decisions about our students' learning progress (Brookhart & Nitko, 2015). Our observations of students' written work, their answers to questions in class, and their performance on teacher-made and standardized tests are different forms of classroom assessment. It also includes performance assessments, such as watching first graders print or observing art students create a piece of pottery. Assessment also involves decisions about assigning grades or reteaching a topic, such as DeVonne's deciding to begin her unit with a lesson on equivalent fractions, to teach a second lesson on the topic, and to give her unit test at the end of the week. This answers our first question above, "What is classroom assessment?"

Ed Psych and You

Think about the classes you're now in. In which do you study the hardest, and in which do you learn the most? Why do you think so?

Assessment *for* Student Learning

Think about the questions we asked in *Ed Psych and You*. If you're typical, it's classes in which you're frequently and thoroughly assessed. Students sometimes protest that they would learn as much or more if they weren't assessed, but this assertion isn't supported by research. In fact, quite the opposite is true (Carey, 2010; Pennebaker, Gosling, & Ferrell,

2013; Rohrer & Pashler, 2010). "Testing has such a bad connotation; people think of standardized testing or teaching to the test. Maybe we need to call it something else, but this is one of the most powerful learning tools we have" (Carey, 2010, para. 28).

This captures the essence of **assessment *for* learning**, the idea that assessment is a continual, ongoing process designed to support and increase student learning (Stiggins & Chappuis, 2012). Instead of assessment occurring at the end of a unit or course of study to determine the amount students learned—assessment *of* learning—assessment *for* learning becomes an integral part of the teaching–learning process.

Assessment *for* learning also helps us answer our second question at the beginning of the chapter: "What was the primary purpose of DeVonne's assessments?" Assessments are used in assigning grades, of course, but *promoting learning* is their primary purpose. Effective assessments serve four functions, each of which contribute to learning:

- Measuring current understanding
- Increasing motivation to learn
- Developing self-regulation
- Measuring achievement

We examine them next.

DIAGNOSTIC ASSESSMENT: MEASURING CURRENT UNDERSTANDING

"Begin where learners are" is a basic tenet of teaching. This means that we should identify what our students already know and use this information as a starting point. Then, we help them understand content they don't yet know and acquire skills they don't yet have.

To illustrate this idea, let's look again at DeVonne's work with her students. Before she began her unit on fractions, she gave a pretest to determine their current level of understanding. She found that they understood the concept *fraction* and could add fractions with like denominators, but they had misconceptions about adding fractions when the denominators were different. As a result, her first learning objective was for her students to understand the concept *equivalent fraction*, and the second was for them to be able to add fractions with unlike denominators. (This process helped her reach her standard.)

DeVonne's pretest was a form of **diagnostic assessment**, an assessment designed to provide teachers with information about students' prior knowledge and misconceptions before beginning a learning activity. Diagnostic assessment helps us identify our students' zones of proximal development, so we can provide the scaffolding that helps them progress through their zones.

DeVonne's homework assignment was also a form of diagnostic assessment. For example, in scoring her students' papers, she saw responses such as the following to her first four items:

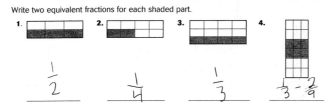

Their responses suggested that they retained misconceptions about the concept *equivalent fraction*, because they wrote only one fraction for the first three problems and answered the fourth problem incorrectly. As a result, she designed a second learning activity to teach *equivalent fractions*.

INCREASING MOTIVATION TO LEARN

Part of the reason you learn more in classes where you're frequently and thoroughly assessed is that you're more likely to study diligently when you know you're going to be held accountable for understanding the content. In other words, your motivation is increased. Initially, you're probably extrinsically motivated—you study to get a good grade—but as your understanding increases, your intrinsic motivation often increases as well (Stiggins & Chappuis, 2012).

Assessments that increase motivation to learn have the following characteristics (Schunk, Meece, & Pintrich, 2014):

- They are aligned with learning objectives.
- They focus on content mastery and improvement.
- They avoid social comparisons.
- They measure higher level learning.
- They include detailed feedback.

Assessments aligned with learning objectives provide students with the information they need to focus their efforts, which increases the likelihood of success. When students are successful and attribute their success to effort, motivation to learn increases. Focusing on improvement and content mastery and eliminating social comparisons communicates that learning—not competition or doing better than others—is the goal. Measuring higher level outcomes provides challenge, and if challenges are met, perceptions of competence and autonomy increase. "Attainment of challenging goals conveys to learners that they are becoming more competent, which raises self-efficacy and perceived control over outcomes. In turn, learners are apt to set new, challenging goals, where serves to maintain intrinsic motivation" (Schunk et al., 2014, p. 268).

Finally, feedback on all assessments—including homework—is essential. We all want and need information about our learning progress. Effective assessments combined with feedback tell us if our study efforts are paying off and what we still need to work on. The opposite is also true. Your worst classes are likely those in which assessments are infrequent or murky, leaving you wondering about how you're doing and whether you're on the right path to mastering course content.

DEVELOPING SELF-REGULATED LEARNING

Self-regulated learning occurs when we set personal learning goals and monitor progress toward those goals. High-quality assessments contribute to this process by providing us with information that helps focus our efforts. For example, if assessments require that we do more than memorize factual information, we quickly adapt our study habits and focus on deeper understanding. Many experts believe that assessment has more influence on the way students study and learn than any other aspect of the teaching–learning process (Carey, 2010; Pennebaker et al., 2013).

We can contribute to self-regulated learning by making our expectations clear, emphasizing that assessments are designed to increase learning, aligning assessments with learning objectives and learning activities, and providing detailed feedback on all assessments (Schunk et al., 2014; Stiggins & Chappuis, 2012).

MEASURING ACHIEVEMENT

In addition to increasing motivation and promoting self-regulated learning, assessment also provides students and their parents, teachers, and school leaders with information about how much students have learned (Popham, 2014). This has historically been the primary role of assessment, but as we've seen in this section, assessment *for* learning expands this role to also include increasing student motivation and helping them become more efficient learners. The relationships among these processes are outlined in Figure 14.1.

Validity: Making Accurate Assessment Decisions

Validity is the degree to which an assessment actually measures what it is supposed to measure (Miller, Linn, & Gronlund, 2013). Our classroom assessments are valid if they target important content and are aligned with our learning objectives. For example, if one of our objectives is for students to understand the causes of the Revolutionary War, but a quiz focuses on names, dates, and places, it's not valid. Based on the quiz results, we might

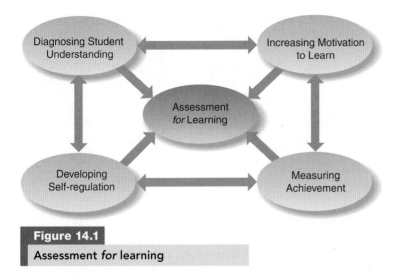

Figure 14.1

Assessment *for* learning

conclude that students have met the objective, when in fact we would have gathered little information about their understanding of the war's causes.

Assessment decisions are also invalid if they're based on personality, appearance, or other factors unrelated to our learning objectives, such as giving lower scores on essay items because of messy handwriting (Miller et al., 2013). These actions are usually unconscious; without realizing it, we sometimes base our assessments on appearance rather than sub-stance, and decreased validity is the result.

Creating valid assessments is challenging but not impossible. If we continually look for ways to improve our tests, quizzes, and other assessments; analyze trends and patterns in student responses; and conscientiously revise our assessments, validity will improve.

Reliability: Consistency in Assessment

In addition to being valid, we also want our assessments to be reliable. **Reliability**, an intui-tively sensible concept, describes the extent to which assessments are consistent and free from errors of measurement (Miller et al., 2013). For instance, if your bathroom scale is reliable, and your weight doesn't change, the readings shouldn't vary from one day to the next. Hypothetically, if we could repeatedly give a student the same reliable test, and if no additional learning or forgetting occurred, the scores would all be the same. Unreliable assessments cannot be valid, even if they are aligned with teachers' learning objectives, because they provide inconsistent information.

Ambiguous wording on test and quiz items, directions that aren't clear, and inconsistent scoring, which is common on essay items, are three factors that detract from reliability. The issue of unreliable scoring on essay items is significant enough that the essay portion of the the SAT—added to the test in 2005—was made optional as the test was being revised in 2014 (Balf, 2014). As another example, different instructors with similar backgrounds, ostensibly using the same criteria, have awarded grades ranging from excellent to failure on the same essay (Waugh & Gronlund, 2013). If scoring is inconsistent, lack of reliability makes test results invalid.

Different strategies to increase reliability include the following:

- Use a sufficient number of items or tasks on assessments to ensure that you've accurately assessed the idea or skill. For instance, a quiz of 15 items is likely to be more reliable than a quiz that has only 5 items.
- Clearly explain requirements for responding to assessment items so students know what you're asking.
- Identify criteria for scoring students' essay items in advance. Score all students' responses to a particular item before moving to a second one.

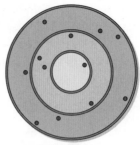

TARGET 1
(reliable and valid shooting)

TARGET 2
(unreliable and invalid shooting)

TARGET 3
(reliable but invalid shooting)

Figure 14.2

The relationships between validity and reliability

- To prevent being influenced by your expectations of students, score assessments anonymously, particularly if you're scoring essay items or solutions to problems where partial credit is given. Have students put their names on the last page of the quiz, for example, so you won't know whose quiz you're scoring until you're finished.

Visualizing a target is one way to think about the relationship between validity and reliability (Miller et al., 2013). A valid and reliable shooter consistently clusters shots in the target's bull's-eye. A reliable but invalid shooter clusters shots, but the cluster is not in the bull's-eye. And a shooter that scatters shots randomly over the target is analogous to an assessment instrument that is neither valid nor reliable. These relationships are illustrated in Figure 14.2.

Ed Psych and You

Your car is about ready to collapse, so—because the company is reputed to build high-quality cars—you buy a pre-owned Brand X with 75,000 miles on it. Within 2 months, it begins to give you trouble. First, you have the air conditioning fixed, a few months later the brakes have to be replaced, and there's a funny noise in the transmission. "I'll never own another Brand X," you conclude. How is your experience related to the process of assessment?

Informal Assessment

When we see or hear the term *assessment,* we typically think of tests and quizzes. But learning is a continual, dynamic process, and we need to continually gather assessment information as learning proceeds. For example, consider the following:

- You see some of your students drifting off during a lesson, so you stop and ask a series of questions to review what you've covered so far.
- You're circulating around the room as your students work on a seatwork assignment in math, and you see that several students have made the same error on three similar problems.

Your observations, combined with the related decisions you make based on these observations, are all part of **informal assessment**, the process of gathering incidental information about learning progress and making decisions based on that information. In our examples, you didn't plan to gather the information in advance, and you didn't get the same information from each of your students. Several of your students making an error, for instance, doesn't mean that *all* students in the class have made the same error.

Your experience with your pre-owned car in *Ed Psych and You* below is also an example of informal assessment. Your experiences with your air conditioning, brakes, and differential are all items of incidental information that you gathered during the normal course of operating your car. You made the decision to never own another Brand X based on that information.

Informal assessment is an essential part of the total assessment process because it helps us make the many decisions required every day in teaching (Miller et al., 2013; Waugh & Gronlund, 2013). Let's look at this process in more detail.

Informal Assessment During Learning Activities

To understand how informal assessments contribute to learning, let's return to DeVonne's work with her students. The class has added fractions with unlike denominators using their cars, and she now wants them to be able to add fractions having unlike denominators without the support of the concrete examples.

"Let's review what we've done," she begins. "Look at your cars again, and move one of your cars to First Street and Fourth Avenue and your other car to First Street and Eighth Avenue. . . . How far have your two cars moved altogether? . . . Write the problem on your paper using fractions."

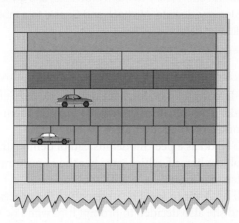

She sees that Jeremy has written the following on his paper:

$$\frac{1}{4} + \frac{1}{8} = \frac{2}{8}$$

She also sees that Juanita, Michael, and Cassie have written 1/4 + 1/8 = 2/12 on their papers.

$$\frac{1}{4} + \frac{1}{8} = \frac{2}{12}$$

$$\frac{1}{4} + \frac{1}{8} = \frac{2}{12}$$

$$\frac{1}{4} + \frac{1}{8} = \frac{2}{12}$$

"I'll work with them when I assign seatwork," she thinks to herself.

She waits for the students to finish and then, seeing that Nikki has a clear solution, says, "Nikki, please come up and show us how you solved the problem."

Nikki goes to the board and writes:

$$\frac{2}{2} \times \frac{1}{4} = \frac{2}{8}$$

"Explain why Nikki could write 2/2 times 1/4 to get 2/8. . . . Amir."

". . ."

"What does 2/2 equal?"

". . . One," Amir responds.

"Good, . . . and whenever we multiply something by one, we don't change the value. . . . So, now what can Nikki do? . . . Thelicia?"

". . . Add the 2/8 and 1/8 to get 3/8."

"Good, Thelicia," DeVonne smiles. "Now, let's try this one," and she gives the students another problem, again watches as they attempt to solve it, and discusses it as they discussed the first one. After two more problems, she gives a seatwork assignment and then calls Jeremy, Juanita, Michael, and Cassie to a table at the back of the room to provide additional help.

In this brief episode, DeVonne used informal assessment in three ways:

- She observed that Jeremy, Juanita, Michael, and Cassie didn't understand how to add fractions with unlike denominators and decided to give them extra help while the rest of the class worked on their additional problems.
- She decided to use Nikki as a peer model instead of demonstrating the correct solution to the problem herself, which gave her the opportunity to hear Nikki articulate her understanding.
- She decided to call on Amir to see if he understood the process—instead of having Nikki explain—and she also decided to prompt him when he was unable to answer instead of turning the question to another student.

DeVonne's observations and her decisions were all part of informal assessment; each was designed to promote learning and based on incidental information she gathered during the learning activity.

Other ways to gather informal data about students include:

- Observing students as they work on assignments or interact with other students in small groups.
- Watching for body language that suggests puzzlement, frustration, or just "tuning out."
- Looking for patterns of on-task and off-task behavior both in individual students and the class as a whole.
- Observing students as they enter and leave your classroom and as they interact with peers at lunch and recess.

Each of these provides valuable information about students' learning and development.

Students' personal, written products can also be valuable sources of informal assessment information. Some examples include:

- *Response journals.* Have students respond to a specific event in a work of literature or a controversial topic in social studies.
- *Personal diaries.* Ask students to share their current thinking about topics.
- *Learning logs.* Have students evaluate their own learning progress by responding to specific questions (Stiggins & Chappuis, 2012).

Classroom **Connections**

Capitalizing on Informal Assessment in Classrooms

Informal assessment is the process of gathering information during learning activities and other school events and making instructional decisions on the basis of that information. Make your informal assessments as systematic as possible and seek additional information to bolster your decisions.

■ **Elementary:** A first-grade teacher notices that one of her students appears listless and sometimes falls asleep during learning activities. She watches the student for several days, and then contacts the school counselor.

■ **Middle School:** A sixth-grade math teacher sees that one of her students has incorrectly solved a word problem involving decimals. He tells the student to recheck his answer, and then

checks several other students' answers to see if the whole class appears to have the same problem.

■ **High School:** An American history teacher wants his students to understand the relationships among Marco Polo's visit to the Far East, the Portuguese explorers, and Columbus's trip to the New World. A few students respond to open-ended questions about the topic, but most sit silently. Adapting, he changes the direction of the lesson and provides a short presentation on the main ideas, followed by a discussion in which he asks students to use the facts involved in each individual case to examine the relationships among the ideas.

These products provide us with additional sources of information. They also give us insights into our students' thinking and encourage them to become more reflective and self-regulated about their own learning.

Reliability of Informal Assessments

Informal assessments are essential in the day-to-day functioning of classrooms, but they're often unreliable and can provide an incomplete picture of learning. For example, concluding that all students understand an idea on the basis of responses from only a few (who usually have their hands up) is a common mistake. Further, students who are physically attractive or have engaging personalities are often awarded higher grades than their less fortunate peers, so important decisions, such as assigning grades, should not be made on the basis of informal assessments alone (Miller et al., 2013; Waugh & Gronlund, 2013).

Similarly, seeing a student push another down on the playground and concluding that the student is a bully could also be both unreliable and invalid. Making this judgment on the basis of one playground incident is unwise, and additional information is needed to make a valid decision about what to do next.

Your experience with your pre-owned car in *Ed Psych and You* at the beginning of this section is another example of reliability issues involved with informal assessments. For instance, your experiences don't necessarily imply that Brand X cars, in general, will have problems with air conditioning, brakes, and transmission. Because your car turned out to be a lemon doesn't mean that all Brand X cars are lemons.

To supplement the sometimes unreliable information provided by informal assessments, we need additional information. This leads us to a discussion of formal assessment, our next topic.

Formal Assessment

DeVonne used informal assessments as an integral part of her instruction, but this is only one aspect of the assessment process. For instance, she also used:

• A diagnostic pretest, which gave her information about her students' understanding of fractions and how to add them.

- Homework assignments that measured their understanding of *equivalent fractions* and adding fractions with unlike denominators.
- A unit test that covered all aspects of adding fractions.

Each was a **formal assessment**, which is the process of systematically gathering the same kind of information from every student and making decisions based on that information. This discussion addresses the third question we asked at the beginning of the chapter: "How did DeVonne's assessments provide her with different kinds of information about her students' learning?" In addition to informal assessments, she also used formal assessments to provide a comprehensive picture of their learning progress. For instance, when DeVonne gave her students the following items for homework, every student responded to the same problems. Formal assessments overcome the reliability issues that often accompany informal assessment, so the combination of the two increases the likelihood of gathering accurate information and making good instructional decisions.

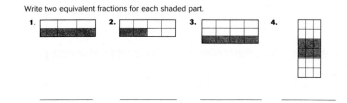

Formal assessments commonly occur in three forms:

- Paper-and-pencil items, such as multiple-choice and essay.
- Performance assessments, such as observing students making a presentation.
- Portfolios, collections of students' work that measure progress over time.

Let's look at them.

Ed Psych and You

When you prepare for a test, how do you study? What factors influence how you study? What kind of information makes your task more efficient?

Paper-and-Pencil Items

We've all studied for tests and know that different formats require different preparation. For instance, if we're expecting a multiple-choice test, we'll study differently than if we're preparing for essay items. In this section, we examine different types of paper-and-pencil test items and how they'll influence your students' learning.

Paper-and-pencil items typically exist in two formats: (1) *selected-response formats*, such as multiple-choice, true–false, and matching, because they require learners to *select* the correct answer from a list of alternatives, or (2) *supply formats*, such as completion or essay, because they require learners to supply their own answers. Items can also be classified as objective, such as multiple-choice, where scorers don't have to make decisions about the quality of an answer, or subjective, such as essay, where scorer judgment is a factor (Miller et al., 2013).

Regardless of the format, two factors are essential for making the items valid and reliable. First, to be valid, the items must be aligned with learning standards and your specific learning objectives. The best way to ensure alignment is to write items during planning so both objectives and items can be compared while they're fresh in your mind. Second, students' responses to the items should be analyzed, and items should be revised when necessary to make them more effective.

Let's look now at the most common paper-and-pencil formats.

MULTIPLE-CHOICE ITEMS

Multiple-choice is an assessment format that consists of a stem and a series of answer choices called distractors. The **stem** is the beginning part of the item. It presents the item as a problem to be solved, a question to be answered, or an incomplete statement. Multiple-choice items also include options—typically four or five. One option is the correct or best choice, and the rest are **distractors**, designed to identify students who don't understand the content the item is measuring (Miller et al., 2013). The stem should pose one question or problem to be considered, and distractors should address students' likely misconceptions. You can then discuss these distractors when providing your students with informative feedback about their test performance (Stiggins & Chappuis, 2012).

People often think that multiple-choice items can only measure factual information that students memorize, but this is a misconception. Multiple-choice items, when well designed, are a valid and highly effective format for assessing a range of thinking levels. The fact that most standardized tests use this format is evidence of its effectiveness. Guidelines to help us prepare effective multiple-choice items include the following (Waugh & Gronlund, 2013):

1. Present one clear problem or question in the stem. A clear, unambiguous stem tells students what you're looking for and how to answer the question.
2. Make all distractors plausible to students, especially those with an incomplete understanding of the content. If students can eliminate distractors based on superficial knowledge or wording in the distractor, we won't get an accurate picture of what they know.
3. Vary the position of the correct choice, and avoid overusing choice *c*. After you've completed the test or quiz, take a few minutes to ensure that the correct responses are randomly assigned.
4. Avoid using similar wording in the stem and the correct choice. For example, in the following item, forms of the term *circulate* appear in both the stem and the correct answer—choice b.

   Which of the following is a function of the circulatory system?

   a. To support the vital organs of the body
   b. To circulate the blood throughout the body
   c. To transfer nerve impulses from the brain to the muscles
   d. To provide for the movement of the body's large muscles

5. Avoid using more technical wording in the correct choice than in the distractors. For example, in the following item, the correct choice—c—is written in more technical terms than the distractors.

   Of the following, which is the definition of *population density*?
   a. The number of people who live in your city or town
   b. The number of people who voted in the last presidential election
   c. The number of people per square mile in a country
   d. The number of people in cities compared to small towns

   We might fall into this trap if we take the correct choice directly from the text and then make up the distractors. Our informal language appears in the distractors, whereas text language appears in the correct answer.

6. Keep the correct choice and the distractors similar in length. If one choice is significantly longer or shorter than others, it should be a distractor. For example, in the following item, the correct choice—d—is significantly longer than the incorrect choices. (We give a similar clue if the correct choice is shorter than the distractors.)

   Of the following, which is the most significant cause of World War II?
   a. American aid to Great Britain
   b. Italy's conquering of Ethiopia
   c. Japan's war on China
   d. The devastation of the German economy as a result of the Treaty of Versailles

7. Avoid using absolute terms in incorrect choices. Absolute terms, such as *all, always, none,* and *never,* are usually associated with incorrect answers. If used, they should be in the correct answer, such as "All algae contain chlorophyll." For example, in the following item, distractors *a* and *c* are stated in absolute terms, so test-wise students only have to choose between the correct choice—b—and distractor d.

   Which of the following is the best description of an insect?
   a. It always has one pair of antennae on its head.
   b. It has three body parts.
   c. None lives in water.
   d. It has eight legs.

8. Keep the stem and distractors grammatically consistent. Again, our goal here should be to find out what students really know, not their ability to use grammatical cues to eliminate incorrect answers.

9. Avoid including two distractors with the same meaning. For example, in the following item, choices *a* and *c* are automatically eliminated, because both are gerunds, and only one answer can be correct. Also, the item uses "All of the above" as a choice; it can't be correct if *a* and *c* are eliminated. That makes the correct choice—b—the only possible choice. A student could answer correctly and have no idea what a participle is.

   Which of the following illustrates a verb form used as a participle?
   a. Running is good exercise.
   b. I saw a jumping frog contest on TV yesterday.
   c. Thinking is hard for many of us.
   d. All of the above.

10. Emphasize negative wording if it is used. In the following item, for example, the stem is stated in negative terms without this fact being emphasized; the word *not* should be underlined, set in bold print, or italicized. Also, choice *a* is grammatically inconsistent with the stem. One solution to this problem is to end the stem with "a(n)," so grammatical consistency is preserved. (Also *c* is the correct choice, which can be a problem if it's overused.)

    The one of the following that is not a reptile is a:
    a. alligator.
    b. lizard.
    c. frog.
    d. turtle.

11. Avoid using "all of the above" as a choice, and use "none of the above" with care. It's difficult to write valid and reliable items using these alternatives, and gaps in student knowledge are harder to interpret.

    Items may be written so that only one choice is correct, or they may be in a best-answer form, in which two or more choices are partially correct but one is clearly better than the others. The best-answer form is more demanding, promotes higher level thinking, and

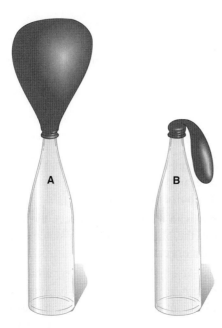

Look at the drawings above. They represent two identical soft drink bottles covered with identical balloons sitting side-by-side on a table. Bottle A was then heated. Which of the following is the most accurate statement?

  a. The density of the air in Bottle A is greater than the density of the air in Bottle B.
 *b. The density of the air in Bottle A is less than the density of the air in Bottle B.
  c. The density of the air in Bottle A is equal to the density of the air in Bottle B.
  d. We don't have enough information to compare the density of the air in Bottle A to the density of the air in Bottle B.

Figure 14.3

Interpretive exercise using the multiple-choice format

measures more complex understanding. Many of the multiple-choice questions that assess your understanding of the material in this text use the best-answer form.

Assessing Higher Level Learning. Multiple-choice can be an effective format for assessing higher order thinking, and *interpretive exercises* are useful for meeting this goal. These exercises present information covered in class in a different context, and the distractors represent different "interpretations" of it (Waugh & Gronlund, 2013). The material that students are asked to interpret may be a graph, chart, table, map, picture, or written vignette.

Figure 14.3 contains an example in science. In this case, the goal is for students to apply information about heat, expansion, mass, volume, and density to a unique situation. This type of exercise helps develop critical thinking and promotes transfer, and because it is challenging, can also increase learner motivation. Most of the higher order multiple-choice items that you will respond to as you take this class are interpretive exercises.

MATCHING ITEMS

The multiple-choice format is inefficient if all of the items require the same set of answer choices, as in the following (asterisk indicates correct answer):

  1. The statement "Understanding is like a light bulb coming on in your head" is an example of the concept:
     *a.   simile.
      b.   metaphor.

     c. hyperbole.

     d. personification.

  2. The statement, "That's the most brilliant comment ever made" is an example of the concept:

     a. simile.

     b. metaphor.

 *c. hyperbole.

     d. personification.

These assessments can be made more efficient by using a **matching format**, which requires learners to classify a series of examples using the same alternatives. The following is an example based on the multiple-choice items above.

Match the following statements with the figures of speech by writing the letter of the appropriate figure of speech in the blank next to each statement. You may use each figure of speech once, more than once, or not at all.

_____ 1. Understanding is like a light bulb coming on in your head.	a. alliteration b. hyperbole
_____ 2. That's the most brilliant comment ever made.	c. metaphor d. personification
_____ 3. His oratory was a bellow from the bowels of his soul.	e. simile
_____ 4. Appropriate attitudes are always advantageous.	
_____ 5. Her eyes were limpid pools of longing.	
_____ 6. He stood as straight as a rod.	
_____ 7. I'll never get this stuff, no matter what I do.	
_____ 8. The colors of his shirt described the complex world in which he lived.	

This example illustrates four characteristics of effective matching items. First, the content is homogeneous; all the statements are figures of speech, and only figures of speech appear as alternatives. Other topics for which the matching format is effective include people and their achievements, historical events and dates, terms and definitions, and authors and their works (Miller et al., 2013).

    Second, the item includes more statements than possible alternatives (to prevent getting the right answer by process of elimination). And, third, students may use the alternatives more than once or not at all, as specified in the directions.

    Finally, the entire item includes only 8 statements. As a rule of thumb, if a matching item involves more than 10 statements, you should create two separate items to prevent confusion.

TRUE–FALSE ITEMS

True–false is an assessment format that includes statements that learners judge as being correct or incorrect. Because true–false items usually measure lower level outcomes, and because students have a 50–50 chance of guessing the correct answer, this format should be used sparingly (Miller et al., 2013). We don't recommend that you use the format, and we include no true–false items in the test bank that accompanies this text.

    If you choose to use the format, however, the following guidelines can improve the effectiveness of these items:

- Write more false than true items. Teachers tend to do the reverse, and students tend to mark items they're unsure of as "true."
- Make each item one clear statement.
- Avoid clues that allow students to answer correctly without fully understanding the content. Examples of clues include the term *most*, which usually indicates a true statement, or *never*, typically suggesting a false statement.

COMPLETION ITEMS

Completion is an assessment format that includes a question or an incomplete statement that requires the learner to supply the answer. For example:

1. What is an opinion? _____
2. _____ is the capital of Canada.

Items that consist of questions, such as the first example, are sometimes called short-answer items. This format is popular with teachers, probably because the questions seem easy to construct. This is misleading, however, because completion items have two important disadvantages. First, it is difficult to phrase a question so that only one possible answer is correct. A number of defensible responses could be given to item 1, for example. Overuse of completion items can put students in the position of trying to guess the answer the teacher wants instead of giving the one they think is correct.

Second, unless the item requires solving a problem, completion items usually measure recall of factual information, as in item 2. Because of these weaknesses, experts recommend that you use completion formats sparingly (Waugh & Gronlund, 2013). Table 14.1 presents guidelines for preparing completion items.

ESSAY ITEMS: MEASURING COMPLEX OUTCOMES

Essay is an assessment format that requires students to make extended written responses to questions or problems. Essay items make three valuable contributions to our assessment efforts. First, they can assess dimensions of learning, such as creative and critical thinking, that can't be measured with other formats. Second, the ability to organize thinking, make and defend arguments, and describe ideas in writing is an important goal across the curriculum, and the essay format is an effective way to measure progress toward these goals (Stiggins & Chappuis, 2012). Third, essay items can improve the way students study. If they know an essay format will be used, for example, they are more likely to look for relationships in what they study and to organize information in a meaningful way.

Essay items also have disadvantages, however. Because essay tests require extensive writing time, it isn't possible to assess learning across as broad a spectrum, so breadth of coverage can be a problem. In addition, scoring is time consuming and sometimes unreliable. Making the essay portion of the revised SAT optional is largely the result of reliability issues (Balf, 2014). Scores on essay items are also influenced by writing skill, including grammar, spelling, and handwriting (Brookhart & Nitko, 2015).

Table 14.1	**Guidelines for preparing completion items**
Guideline	**Rationale**
1. Use only one blank, and relate it to the main point of the statement.	Several blanks are confusing, and one answer may depend on another.
2. Use complete sentences followed by a question mark or period.	Complete sentences allow students to more nearly grasp the full meaning of the statement.
3. Keep blanks the same length. Use "a(an)" at the end of the statement, or eliminate indefinite articles.	A long blank for a long word or a particular indefinite article commonly provides clues to the answer.
4. For numerical answers, indicate the degree of precision and the units desired.	Degree of precision and units clarify the task for students and prevent them from spending more time than necessary on an item.

1. Elicit higher order thinking by using such terms as *explain* and *compare*. Have students defend their responses with facts.
2. Write a model answer for each item. You can use this both for scoring and for providing feedback.
3. Require all students to answer all items. Allowing students to select particular items prevents comparisons and detracts from reliability.
4. Prepare criteria for scoring in advance.
5. Score all students' answers to a single item before moving to the next item.
6. Score all responses to a single item in one sitting if possible. This increases reliability.
7. Score answers without knowing the identity of the student. This helps reduce the influence of past performance and expectations.
8. Develop a model answer complete with points, and compare a few students' responses to it, to see if any adjustments are needed in the scoring criteria.

Figure 14.4

Guidelines for preparing and scoring essay items
Sources: Miller, Linn, & Gronlund, 2013; Stiggins & Chappuis, 2012; Waugh & Gronlund, 2013.

Essay items appear easy to write, but they can be ambiguous, leaving students uncertain about how to respond. As a result, students' ability to interpret the question is often the outcome measured. Figure 14.4 presents guidelines for preparing and scoring essay items (Stiggins & Chappuis, 2012). In addition to these suggestions, rubrics can help improve the reliability of scoring essays. We examine them next.

Using Rubrics. A rubric is a scoring scale that explicitly describes criteria for grading (Brookhart, 2013; Stiggins & Chappuis, 2012). Originally created to increase reliability and validity when scoring essays, rubrics are also used when assessing performances, such as a student presentation, or products other than essays, such as a lab report in science.

Rubrics provide guidance for our planning by providing targets to focus on during instruction; we can also share them with our students during learning activities to help them understand what we're looking for, and they're essential for accurate assessments. The following steps are useful when constructing rubrics:

- Establish criteria based on elements that must exist in students' work.
- Decide on the number of levels of achievement for each criterion.
- Develop clear descriptors for each level.
- Determine a rating scale for the entire rubric.

Figure 14.5 contains a rubric for assessing effective paragraphs. In it, we see that the teacher has identified a topic sentence, supporting sentences, and summarizing sentence as essential components of an effective paragraph. These elements appear in a column along the left side of the matrix. Then the rubric describes levels of achievement for each element. Clear descriptors guide students as they write and also provide reference points for you when you score student products. As a final planning step, you make decisions about grading criteria. For example, you might decide that 9 points would be an A, 7–8 points a B, and 5–6 points would be a C. So, a student would be required to be at a level of achievement of 3 on all three criteria to earn an A, for example, and would have to be at level 2 on two of the three elements and at level 3 on the third to earn a B.

	Levels of Achievement		
Criteria	**1**	**2**	**3**
Topic Sentence	Not present; reader has no idea what paragraph is about	Present but does not give the reader a clear idea what the paragraph is about	Provides a clearly stated overview of the paragraph
Supporting Sentences	Rambling and unrelated to topic sentence	Provides additional information but not all focused on topic sentence	Provides supporting detail relating to the topic sentence
Summarizing Sentence	Nonexistent or unrelated to preceding sentences	Relates to topic sentence but doesn't summarize information in paragraph	Accurately summarizes information in paragraph and is related to topic sentence
Overall Score (9 Possible)			

Figure 14.5

Sample rubric for paragraph structure

Rubrics are essential for increasing reliability when assessing students' work (Brookhart, 2013). If you were using this rubric to score students' paragraphs, for example, the descriptions of the dimensions and levels of achievement in Figure 14.5 help maintain consistency in evaluating each student's work. Without the rubric as a guide, the likelihood of inconsistent scoring and unreliable assessments is much higher.

COMMERCIALLY PREPARED TEST ITEMS

Because you will be very busy when you teach, you are likely to use test items included in the ancillary materials for your textbooks. Although using these items saves time, you should use them with care, for three reasons (Brookhart & Nitko, 2015; Popham, 2014):

1. *Compatibility of learning objectives*: The learning objectives of the curriculum developers may not be the same as yours. If items don't reflect the objectives in your lesson or unit, they are invalid.
2. *Uneven quality*: Textbook authors often don't prepare the test items included with ancillary materials; the items are prepared by a graduate student or some other person the company hires who is not intimately familiar with the content of the textbook. As a result many commercially prepared tests are poor quality.
3. *Emphasis on lower level items*: Commercially prepared items typically measure at a knowledge/recall level. This is particularly true in content areas other than math and quantitative sciences, such as chemistry and physics.

The time and energy you save in using commercially prepared items are important advantages, however. If you decide to use commercially prepared items, the following guidelines can help you capitalize on these benefits:

- Select items that are consistent with your learning objectives and put them in a computer file.
- Use feedback from students and analysis of test results to revise ineffective items.
- Create additional items that help you accurately assess your students' understanding.

If you use commercially prepared items, continually assess them to ensure that they meet your own learning objectives and are of high quality.

Performance Assessments

Some critics argue that traditional paper-and-pencil assessments, most commonly in the form of multiple-choice tests, lack validity and fail to assess higher level outcomes (Brookhart & Nitko, 2015; Corcoran, Dershimer, & Tichenor, 2004). In response to these criticisms, the use of **performance assessments**, direct examinations of student performance on tasks relevant to life outside of school, have been emphasized, especially in the language arts (Frey & Schmitt, 2005; Popham, 2014). The term *performance assessment* originated in content areas such as science and the performing arts, where students were required to demonstrate an ability in a real-world situation, such as a laboratory demonstration or recital.

Let's look at two examples.

A high school auto mechanics teacher wants his students to be able to troubleshoot and diagnose what is wrong with a car engine that won't start. He provides an overview of common starting problems along with actual examples of auto engine malfunctioning. Students discuss the problems in each example; with the assistance of the teacher, they arrive at steps and criteria for troubleshooting unresponsive engines and then use these to guide their work on other engines.

A health teacher reads in a professional journal that the biggest problem people have in applying first aid is not the mechanics per se, but knowing what to do and when. In an attempt to address this problem, the teacher periodically plans "catastrophe" days. Students entering the classroom encounter a catastrophe victim with an unspecified injury. In each case, they must first diagnose the problem and then apply first aid. The teacher observes them as they work and uses the information she gathers in discussions and assessments.

Designing performance assessments involves three steps, each designed to make them more valid and reliable (Marion & Pellegrino, 2006; Miller et al., 2013).

1. Specify the type of performance you are trying to assess.
2. Structure the evaluation setting, balancing realism with safety and other issues.
3. Design evaluation procedures with clearly identified criteria.

SPECIFYING THE PERFORMANCE COMPONENTS

Specifying the components you're attempting to measure is the first step in designing any assessment. A clear description of the performance helps students understand what is required and assists you in designing appropriate instruction. An example of component specification in the area of persuasive writing is outlined in Figure 14.6.

Persuasive essay
1. Specifies purpose of the essay
2. Provides evidence supporting the purpose
3. Identifies audience
4. Specifies likely counterarguments
5. Presents evidence dispelling counterarguments

Figure 14.6

Performance outcomes in persuasive writing

Table 14.2	Processes and products as components of performance	
Content Area	**Product**	**Process**
Math	Correct answer	Problem-solving steps leading to the correct solution
Music	Performance of a work on an instrument	Correct fingering and breathing that produce the performance
English Composition	Essay, term paper, or composition	Preparation of drafts and thought processes that produce the product
Word Processing	Letter or copy of final draft	Proper stroking and techniques for presenting the paper
Science	Explanation for the outcomes of a demonstration	Thought processes involved in preparing the explanation

In some cases the performance components will be processes—what students actually do—and in others they will be the final products. The initial focus is typically on processes, with the emphasis shifting to products after procedures are mastered (Waugh & Gronlund, 2013). Examples of how processes and products are interrelated components of performance assessments are shown in Table 14.2.

STRUCTURING THE EVALUATION SETTING

Performance assessments are valuable because they emphasize real-world tasks. However, time, expense, and/or safety often prevent assessing performance in the real world, so intermediate steps are necessary. For example, developing safe drivers is the goal of driver education. However, putting beginning drivers in heavy traffic is dangerous. So, teachers might begin by having students respond to written case studies, progress to using a simulator, then to driving on roads with little traffic, and finally to driving in a variety of conditions. As students' driving skills develop, they progress to higher degrees of realism.

Simulations provide opportunities to measure performance in cases where high realism is not feasible, and a driving simulator is an example. As another example, a geography teacher wanting to measure students' understanding of the impact of climate and geography on the location of cities might display the information shown in Figure 14.7. This simulation asks students to identify the best location for a city on the island and the criteria they would use in determining the location. Their criteria provide insights into their thinking.

DESIGNING EVALUATION PROCEDURES

Designing evaluation procedures is the final step in creating effective performance assessments. Scoring rubrics, similar to those used with essay items, increase both reliability and validity (Stiggins & Chappuis, 2012).

Strategies to assess learner performance include (1) systematic observation, (2) checklists, and (3) rating scales. Let's look at them.

Systematic Observation. Teachers routinely observe students in classroom settings, but these informal observations usually are not systematic, and records are rarely kept. Systematic observation, the process of specifying criteria for acceptable performance in an activity and taking notes based on the criteria, addresses these problems. For example,

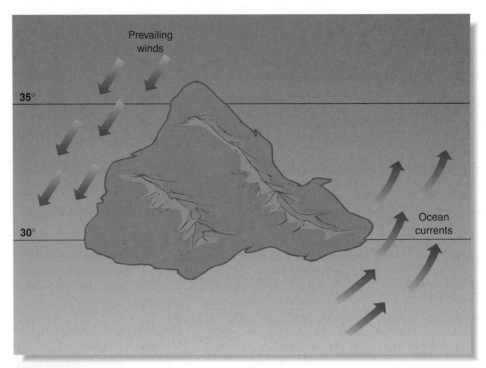

Figure 14.7

Simulation in geography

if you're a science teacher assessing your students' ability to use the scientific method, you might establish the following:

1. States problem or question
2. States hypotheses
3. Specifies independent, dependent, and controlled variables
4. Gathers and displays data
5. Evaluates hypotheses based on data

Your notes then refer directly to the criteria, making them consistent for all groups. You can also use these notes to give learners feedback and provide information for use in future planning.

Checklists. Checklists, written descriptions of dimensions that must be present in an acceptable performance, extend systematic observation by specifying important aspects of performance, which you can then share with your students. During the assessment, you check off the desired dimensions rather than describing them in notes, as in systematic observation. For instance, in the preceding example you would check off each of the five criteria for effective use of the scientific method as they appeared in students' reports.

Checklists are useful when you can clearly determine if a student has met a criterion, such as "States hypotheses." In other cases, however, such as "Evaluates hypotheses based on data," the results aren't cut-and-dried; some evaluations will be more thorough and precise than others. Rating scales address this problem.

Rating Scales. Rating scales are written descriptions of the dimensions of an acceptable performance along with scales of values on which each dimension is rated. They can be constructed in numerical, graphic, or descriptive formats and are similar to the scoring rubrics we discussed earlier. An example of a rating scale similar to one you might encounter when you begin teaching is illustrated in Figure 14.8.

Effectiveness

	1	3	5
Lesson scope	No learning objective is apparent. The focus and scope of the lesson are uncertain.	Learning objective is unclear. The lesson covers too much or too little content.	A clear learning objective is apparent. The scope of the lesson is effective for reaching the objective.
Organization	Materials are not prepared and ready prior to the lesson. Routines are not apparent. Instructional time is wasted.	Some materials are prepared in advance, and some routines are apparent. Instructional time used reasonably well.	Instructional time is maximized with materials prepared in advance and well-established routines apparent.
Quality of examples/ nonexamples	Examples/nonexamples are not used.	Examples/nonexamples are used but are inadequate to accurately represent the topic.	A variety of high-quality examples in context are used to represent the topic.
Review	No review of previous work is conducted.	A brief and superficial review of previous work is present.	A thorough review of ideas necessary to understand the present topic is conducted.
Questioning frequency	Teacher lectured. Few questions were asked.	Some questions were asked. Much of the content was delivered through lecture.	The lesson was developed with questioning throughout.
Equitable distribution of questions	Questions were not directed to specific students.	Some questions were directed to individual students. Volunteers were called on most frequently.	All students in the class were called on as equally as possible, and questions were directed to students by name.
Wait-time and prompting	Little wait-time was given. Unanswered questions were directed to other students.	Intermittent assistance was provided as well as adequate wait-time in some cases.	Students were consistently given wait-time and were prompted when they were unable to answer correctly.
Closure	Lesson lacked closure.	The teacher offered a summary and closure of the lesson.	The teacher guided students as they stated the main ideas of the lesson.
Instructional alignment	Learning objectives, learning activities, and assessment are out of alignment.	Objectives, learning activities, and assessment are partially aligned.	Learning objectives, the learning activity, and assessment are clearly aligned.

Figure 14.8

Rating scale for teaching effectiveness

Source: Adapted from *An Examination of the Relationships Between Elementary Teachers' Understanding of Education Psychology and Their Pedagogical Practice,* paper presented at the annual meeting of the American Education Research Association, Chicago, April 2007.

Portfolio Assessment: Helping Students Develop Self-Regulation

Portfolio assessment is the process of selecting collections of student work that both you and your students evaluate using preset criteria (Popham, 2014; Stiggins & Chappuis, 2012). The portfolio is the actual collection of works, and it might include essays written over the school year, projects, samples of poetry, lab reports, video recorded performances, and

Table 14.3	Portfolio samples in different content areas
Content Area	Example
Elementary Math	Homework, quizzes, tests, and projects completed over time.
Writing	Drafts of narrative, descriptive, and persuasive essays in various stages of development. Samples of poetry.
Art	Projects over the course of the year collected to show growth in an area perspective or in a medium painting.
Science	Lab reports, projects, classroom notes, quizzes, and tests compiled to provide an overview of learning progress.

quizzes and tests. The use of portfolios is common in a wide variety of areas including measuring school readiness for preschool children or assessing art students' developing skills in drawing. As the use of technology advances, electronic portfolios are becoming increasingly popular. Table 14.3 contains examples of portfolio assessments in different content areas.

Helping students develop self-regulation is an important reason for using portfolios. With respect to assessment, self-regulation means that students take responsibility for their own learning and they use assessments to gather information about their learning progress (Hofer, 2010; Schneider, 2010). For example, a student writes an essay, and his teacher provides written feedback stating that he didn't provide as much evidence as he needed to fully support his conclusions. He includes the essay in his portfolio of written products, and in his next essay, he makes an extra effort to carefully document all of his conclusions. He rereads his work and concludes that his second essay is an improvement compared to the first. In her feedback, his teacher corroborates his evaluation. This example illustrates learning progress as a result of his self-regulation.

When students become directly involved in the assessment process, as we see in this example, they become more metacognitive about their approaches to studying and more reflective about what works for them. Portfolios also help develop a sense of ownership and autonomy, both of which increase learner motivation (Schunk et al., 2014).

The following guidelines can make portfolios more effective learning tools:

- Integrate portfolios into your instruction, and refer to them as you teach.
- Provide examples of portfolios when introducing them to students.
- Involve students in the selection and evaluation of their work.
- Require students to provide an overview of each portfolio, a rationale for the inclusion of individual works, criteria they use to evaluate individual pieces, and a summary of progress.
- Provide students with frequent and detailed feedback about their decisions.

Portfolio assessment is demanding. Also, in the real world, not all students will take the responsibility to try to improve, such as we saw in the example with the student developing his writing, and their seeming lack of willingness to make the effort will be frustrating. For those who do, however, you will have made an invaluable contribution to their development—both in school and in life after the school years.

Evaluating Formal Assessment Formats

Each type of formal assessment format—paper-and-pencil items, performance assessments, and portfolios—has both strengths and weaknesses. For instance, critics of paper-and-pencil items argue that they focus on low-level knowledge and skills, fail to measure learners' ability to apply understanding in the real world, and measure only outcomes, so these assessments provide little insight into students' thinking (Solley, 2007). Advocates counter that they are a time- and energy-efficient way of gathering large amounts of information about learning progress. Further, the charge that paper-and-pencil items only measure low-level outcomes doesn't have to be true. Most aptitude and achievement tests, such as the SAT, ACT, Graduate Record Exam, and many others, primarily use the multiple-choice format. If this format only measured low-level outcomes, it wouldn't be so widely used. And earlier in our discussion, we saw how *interpretive exercises* using the multiple-choice format can be used to measure higher level learning and thinking.

Further, education is in an era of accountability, and multiple-choice, often combined with a writing component, is by far the most common format used on high-stakes tests administered by states around our country. Faced with the demands of standards-based accountability, you will feel pressure to prepare your students for these tests, and providing them with practice together with feedback is an effective way to help them develop confidence and expertise with these types of items.

As alternatives to paper-and-pencil assessments, advocates of performance and portfolio assessment contend that these formats tap higher level thinking and problem-solving skills, emphasize real-world applications, and focus on the processes learners use to produce their products (DiMartino & Castaneda, 2007).

Issues exist with these alternatives, however. First, they are time and labor intensive. Examining individual students' portfolios, for example, is very time consuming and demanding. Second, reliability is an issue, and obtaining acceptable levels of reliability has historically been a problem (Barnes, Torrens, & George, 2007; Tillema & Smith, 2007).

At the classroom level, allowing students to determine portfolio content creates additional problems. For example, when students choose different items to place in their portfolios, cross-student comparisons are difficult, which decreases reliability. To address this issue, experts recommend supplementing portfolios with traditional measures to obtain the best of both processes (Stiggins & Chappuis, 2012).

As with all aspects of learning and teaching, assessment is complex, and your knowledge, skill, and professional judgment will be crucial in designing assessments that will maximize learning for all your students.

Classroom **Connections**

Creating Valid and Reliable Classroom Assessments

1. Validity describes the extent to which an assessment measures what it is supposed to measure. Increase validity through careful planning before assessment.

- **Elementary:** A third-grade teacher compares items on her quizzes, tests, and graded homework to the standards in the curriculum guide and the objectives in her unit plan to be sure that all the important objectives are covered.

- **Middle School:** A social studies teacher writes a draft of one test item at the end of each day to be certain the emphasis on his tests is consistent with his instruction. When he puts the test together, he checks to be sure that all content areas and difficulty levels are covered.

- **High School:** After composing a test, a biology teacher rereads the items to eliminate wording that might be confusing or too advanced for her students.

2. Performance assessments directly examine students' ability to perform tasks similar to those they will be expected to perform in life outside of school. Increase the validity of your assessments by using performance assessment when appropriate.

- **Elementary:** A first-grade teacher uses a rating scale to assess his students' oral reading ability. While he listens to each student read, he uses additional notes to help him remember each student's strengths and weaknesses. He uses these at parent–teacher conferences to provide caregivers with an accurate picture of each student's reading progress.

- **Middle School:** A math teacher working on decimals and percentages brings in store ads from three local supermarkets and asks students to compare prices on five household items. Students must determine which store provided the best bargains and the percentage difference between the stores on each item.

- **High School:** A teacher in business technology has students write letters in response to job notices in the newspaper. The class then critiques the letters in terms of format, grammar, punctuation, and clarity, using a rubric the class had developed previously.

3. Portfolio assessments involve students in the assessment process. Use portfolios to develop learner self-regulation.

- **Elementary:** A fourth-grade teacher uses portfolios as an organizing theme for his language arts curriculum. Students collect pieces

of work during the year and evaluate and share them with other members of their writing teams.

- **Middle School:** A math teacher asks each student to compile a portfolio of work and present it at parent–teacher conferences. Before the conference, the teacher meets with students and helps them identify their strengths and weaknesses.

- **High School:** An auto mechanics teacher makes each student responsible for keeping track of the competencies and skills each has mastered. Each student is given a folder and must document the completion of different shop assignments.

Effective Assessment Practices

Increasing student learning and development is always our goal when making professional decisions. Gathering valid and reliable information that can be used to help us make these decisions—as DeVonne Lampkin did in our case study at the beginning of the chapter—is the primary purpose of assessment.

In this section we offer suggestions for making the assessment process as efficient and effective as possible as we discuss:

- Planning for assessment
- Preparing students for assessments
- Administering assessments
- Analyzing results
- Providing students with feedback

Planning for Assessment

As with all aspects of teaching, effective assessments require careful planning. To ensure that our assessments are aligned with our learning objectives, we should think about assessments as we plan for instruction. Teachers commonly wait to prepare assessments until after they have completed a chapter or unit of instruction, and as a result, they might give little emphasis to a topic in class but have several items on a quiz related to it, or emphasize a topic in class but give it minimal coverage on a quiz. Also, teachers often emphasize application in learning activities but write test items that merely require recall of factual information. Doing so reduces the validity of the assessments and frustrates students.

Ed Psych and You

Have you ever been studying for a test with a friend, and one of you asked, "Do you think we need to know . . .?" How did you feel about being in this situation?

TABLES OF SPECIFICATIONS: INCREASING VALIDITY THROUGH PLANNING

A **table of specifications** is a matrix that helps us organize our learning objectives by content area and cognitive level and helps us link our instruction and assessment to objectives and standards. Preparing a table of specifications is one way to ensure that learning objectives and assessments are aligned. For example, a geography teacher based her instruction in a unit on the Middle East on the following list of objectives:

Understands location of cities

1. Identifies locations of major cities
2. Explains historical factors in settlements

Understands climate

1. Identifies major climate regions
2. Explains factors that influence existing climates

Understands influence of physical features

1. Describes topography
2. Relates physical features to climate
3. Explains impact of physical features on location of cities
4. Analyzes impact of physical features on economy

Understands factors influencing economy

1. Describes economies of countries in the region
2. Identifies major characteristics of each economy
3. Explains how economies relate to climate and physical features

Table 14.4 contains a table of specifications for a content-level matrix based on these objectives. The teacher had a mix of items, with greater emphasis on physical features than other topics. This emphasis reflects the teacher's objectives, which stressed the influence of physical features on the location of cities, the climate, and the economy of the region. It also reflects the time and effort spent on each area. A table of specifications such as this increases validity by ensuring a match between objectives, instruction, and assessment.

Establishing criteria for performance assessments serves a function similar to a table of specifications. The criteria identify the performance, determine emphasis, and help ensure congruence between learning objectives and assessments.

This information addresses the questions we asked in *Ed Psych and You* at the beginning of this section. We've all experienced the frustration of trying to prepare for a test but not knowing how to study because we didn't know what would be on it. Effective assessment should not be a guessing game between a teacher and students. Students should know what is expected of

Table 14.4	Sample table of specifications			
	Outcomes			
Content	Knowledge	Comprehension	Higher Order Thinking and Problem Solving	Total Items in Each Content Area
Cities	4	2	2	8
Climate	4	2	2	8
Economy	2	2	—	4
Physical features	4	9	7	20
Total items	14	15	11	—

them, so they know how to study and prepare. We eliminate any guesswork by being clear about our objectives and ensuring that assessments are aligned with them. Using the objectives listed above, for instance, tells geography students that they need to know the locations of major cities, understand the causes of the climates in the Middle East, and how understand the economies of the countries relate to the climates and physical features of each. Now they know how to study.

Preparing Students for Assessments

Preparing students for assessments is important for validity because we want our assessments to accurately reflect what students actually know and can do. To illustrate this idea, let's look again at DeVonne's work with her students the day before she gives her unit test.

"Get out your chalkboards," she directs, referring to individual chalkboards each student has to show his or her work on math problems.

"We're having a test tomorrow on finding equivalent fractions and adding fractions, and the test will go in your math portfolios. . . . I have some problems on the test that are going to make you think. . . . But you've all been working hard, and we've been practicing, and you're getting good at this, so you'll be able to do it. You're my team, and I know you'll come through," she smiles.

"To be sure we're okay, I have a few problems that are just like ones on the test, so let's see how we do. Write these on your chalkboards."

$$\frac{1}{3} + \frac{1}{4} = ? \qquad \frac{2}{7} + \frac{4}{7} = ?$$

DeVonne watches as they work on the problems and hold up their chalkboards when they finish. Seeing that three students miss the first problem, she reviews it with the class, and then displays the following three:

$$\frac{2}{3} + \frac{1}{6} = ? \qquad \frac{4}{9} + \frac{1}{6} = ? \qquad \frac{2}{9} + \frac{4}{9} = ?$$

Two students miss the second one, so again she reviews it carefully.

"Now, let's try one more," she continues, displaying the following problem on the document camera:

You are at a pizza party with 5 other people, and you order 2 pizzas. The 2 pizzas are the same size, but one is cut into 4 pieces and the other is cut into 8 pieces. You eat 1 piece from each pizza. How much pizza did you eat in all?

Again, she watches the students work and reviews the solution with them when they finish, asking questions such as "What information in the problem is important?," "What do we see in the problem that's irrelevant?," and "What should we do first in solving it?" in the process.

After discussing two more word problems, she tells students, "The problems on the test tomorrow are like the ones we practiced here today," asks if they have any additional questions, and finishes her review by saying, "All right, when we take a test, what do we always do?"

"We read the directions carefully!" they shout in unison.

"Okay, good," DeVonne smiles. "Now, remember, what will you do if you get stuck on a problem?"

"Go on to the next one so we don't run out of time."

"And what will we be sure not to do?"

"We won't forget to go back to the one we skipped."

Now let's look at the way DeVonne prepared her students for her test in a bit more detail. She:

- Specified what would be on the test.
- Gave students a chance to practice similar items under test-like conditions.
- Established positive expectations and encouraged students to link effort and success.
- Encouraged her students to use specific test-preparation strategies.

Specifying what will be on a test and identifying the test format provides structure for students, leads to higher achievement for all students, and is particularly important for those who are struggling with the content.

Specifying test content often isn't enough, however, particularly with young learners, so giving students practice exercises and presenting them in a format that parallels their appearance on the test is important (Geno, 2014). In learning math skills, for instance, DeVonne's students first practiced adding fractions with like denominators, then learned to find equivalent fractions, and finally added fractions with unlike denominators, each in separate lessons. On the test, however, the problems were mixed, so DeVonne gave students a chance to practice integrating these skills before they took the actual test.

Because we live in an era of high-stakes testing, and these tests usually use a multiple-choice format, you should give your students practice in responding to multiple-choice items. This means that at least some of the test items you prepare for your students should be in this format.

DeVonne also communicated that she expected students to do well on the test, and the motivational benefits of establishing positive expectations have been confirmed by a long history of research (Schunk et al., 2014). She also emphasized effort and the influence of hard work on success by saying, "But you've all been working hard, and we've been practicing, and you're getting good at this, so you'll be able to do it." Encouraging students to establish a growth mindset and believe that ability can be improved through effort benefits both immediate performance and long-term motivation.

Finally, DeVonne encouraged her students to employ specific test-taking strategies. Let's look at this idea in more detail.

TEACHING TEST-TAKING STRATEGIES

We can help our students improve their test-taking skills by teaching them strategies, such as the following:

- Read directions carefully.
- Identify important information in questions.
- Use time efficiently and pace themselves.

DeVonne encouraged the use of her strategies. To illustrate, let's look again at some of the dialogue in her lesson.

DeVonne: All right, when we take a test, what do we always do?

Students: We read the directions carefully!

DeVonne: Okay, good . . . Now, remember, what will you do if you get stuck on a problem?

Students: Go on to the next one so we don't run out of time.

DeVonne: And what will we be sure not to do?

Students: We won't forget to go back to the one we skipped.

With older students, explaining how questions will be scored and describing the nuances of different testing formats is also helpful. Strategy instruction improves performance and especially benefits young, low-ability students and students who are minorities or who have limited test-taking experience (Geno, 2014).

Ed Psych and You

Have you ever felt that you were prepared for a big test and "blanked" when you turned it over? Have you ever felt like you knew the test content but did not do well on it because of being nervous? What can you do about it?

REDUCING TEST ANXIETY

Think about the first two questions we asked in *Ed Psych and You* here. If you answered yes—and most of us have had this experience—you experienced classic **test anxiety**, an unpleasant emotional reaction to testing situations that can lower performance. Usually, it is momentary and minor, but for a portion of the school population (estimates run as high as 10%), it can be a serious problem (Cassady, 2010; Lang & Lang, 2010; Schunk et al., 2014).

Test anxiety is triggered by testing situations that (1) involve pressure to succeed, (2) are perceived as difficult, (3) impose time limits, and (4) contain unfamiliar items or formats (Schunk et al., 2014). Unannounced quizzes and tests are particularly powerful triggers for test anxiety.

Research suggests that test anxiety consists of both an emotional and a cognitive component (Cassady, 2010; Englert & Bertrams, 2013). Its emotional component can lead to physiological symptoms, such as increased pulse rate, dry mouth, upset stomach, and headache, as well as feelings of dread and helplessness and sometimes "going blank." Its cognitive—or worry—component involves preoccupation with test difficulty, thoughts of failure, and other concerns, such as parents being upset by a low score. Thoughts, such as "I've never seen this stuff before," "Oh my gosh," and "I'm going to flunk," occupy working memory, which leaves less of its limited capacity to focus on the test itself.

As teachers we can also do much to reduce test anxiety in our students, and the most successful efforts focus on the worry component (Schunk et al., 2014). Suggestions include:

- Discussing test content and procedures before testing, and giving clear directions for responding to test items.
- Giving more, rather than fewer, quizzes and tests to lower the significance of any one assessment.
- Minimizing the competitive aspects of tests by focusing on criterion measures (e.g., 90 and above is an A, 80 is a B, etc.) and avoiding social comparisons, such as public displays of test scores. (We discuss criterion referencing in the next section.)
- Teaching test-taking skills, and giving students ample time to take tests.
- Using a variety of assessments to provide opportunities for students to demonstrate their understanding and skills in different ways.

Now, let's look again at the third question we asked in *Ed Psych and You*: "What can you do about it [being nervous when beginning a test]?" The first thing is to realize that a certain amount of anxiety is normal, and if you're well prepared, it can even increase test performance (Cassady, 2010). Then, the most effective way to deal with test anxiety is to study and prepare to the point that your understanding is so thorough that you succeed in spite of feeling nervous. From your—a student's—perspective, this is the single, best strategy for coping with text anxiety.

We offer this advice from personal experience. We—Paul and Don, your authors—were both terribly test anxious as students, so we would study to the point where we could say to ourselves, "There isn't anything they can ask me that I don't know." Students, including those in college, often fail to study as thoroughly as necessary, and they tend to believe they understand a topic better than they do (Bembenutty, 2009). As a result their anxiety spikes when they're faced with a test, particularly if the test measures understanding beyond recall of factual information.

As a final—and somewhat interesting—note, some research suggests that if you feel anxious as you anticipate an important test, simply taking a few minutes before the exam to write down your fears can reduce your anxiety and boost your performance (Ramirez & Beilock, 2011). We can't guarantee that it will work for you, but you have nothing to lose in doing so.

Administering Assessments

When we administer assessments, we want to ensure that results accurately reflect what students know and can do. Let's return to DeVonne's classroom to see how she does this.

> At 10:00 Thursday morning, DeVonne shuts a classroom window because of noise from delivery trucks outside. She considers rearranging the desks in the room but decides to wait until after the test.
>
> "Okay, everyone, let's get ready for our math test," she directs, as students put their books under their desks.
>
> She waits a moment, sees that everyone's desk is clear, and says, "When you're finished, turn the test over, and I'll come and get it. Now look up at the board. After you're done, work on the assignment listed there until everyone is finished. Then we'll start reading." As she hands out the tests, she says, "If you get too warm, raise your hand, and I'll turn on the air conditioner. I shut the window because of the noise outside."
>
> "Work carefully," she says after everyone has a copy. "You've all been working hard, and I know you will do well. You have as much time as you need."
>
> As students begin working, DeVonne stands at the side of the room, watching them.
>
> After several minutes, she notices Anthony doodling at the top of his paper and glancing around the room. She goes over and says, "It looks like you're doing fine on these problems," pointing to some near the top of the paper. "Now concentrate a little harder. I'll bet you can do most of the others." She smiles reassuringly and again moves to the side of the room.
>
> DeVonne goes over to Hajar in response to her raised hand. "The lead on my pencil broke, Mrs. Lampkin," she whispers.
>
> "Take this one," DeVonne responds, handing her another. "Come and get yours after the test."
>
> As students finish, DeVonne picks up their papers, and they begin the assignment on the board.

Now let's see how DeVonne's actions helped maximize her students' performance. First, she arranged her classroom to be comfortable and free from distractions. Distractions can depress test performance, particularly in young or struggling students (Vaughn, Bos, & Schumm, 2014).

Second, she gave specific directions for taking the test, turning in the papers, and spending time afterward. These directions helped maintain order and prevented distractions for late-finishing students.

Finally, she carefully monitored students as they worked on the test. This not only allowed her to encourage those who were distracted but also discouraged cheating. In the real world some students will cheat if given the opportunity. However, an emphasis on learning versus performance and efforts to create a supportive learning environment decrease the likelihood of cheating (O'Connor, 2011; Pulfrey, Buchs, & Butera, 2011). In addition, external factors, such as leaving the room, influence cheating more than whether students are inclined to do so.

In DeVonne's case, monitoring was more a form of support than of being a watchdog. For example, when she saw that Anthony was distracted, she quickly intervened, encouraged him, and urged him to increase his concentration. This encouragement is particularly important for students who are underachieving or test anxious.

Analyzing Results

The overall difficulty of the test and the difficulty of individual items are important factors to consider when analyzing our assessment results. Difficulty levels are especially important in this era of accountability and criterion-referenced assessment. We need to know how many students mastered essential content and if we can go on to the next topic. The difficulty level for the whole test can be obtained by averaging total scores for the entire class. If you teach multiple sections of the same class, which frequently occurs at the middle and high school levels, comparing average scores across classes provides us with insights into both our instruction and students' mastery of content. Some questions we might ask include:

- Did one class perform better than others and why?
- Did I teach topics differently to different sections, and what effect did that have on student performance?
- For each individual class or section, does the level of performance suggest mastery of the content, or do I need to reteach a topic or topics before moving on to the next unit?

To answer the last question, we might have to examine individual items. Experts compute difficulty levels for individual items with the following simple formula (Miller et al., 2013):

$$D = \frac{\text{Number of students answering correctly}}{\text{Number of students taking the assessment}}$$

Teachers typically use this formula informally, eyeballing the data and looking for patterns in students' responses. Most students getting an individual item or cluster of items covering the same topic correct suggests content mastery. How high the difficulty level should be is a matter of professional judgment and depends on a number of factors, such as:

- How important the concept or skill is to understanding the big picture
- Whether the knowledge or skill is a prerequisite to additional content that follows
- How much time you spent on the topic and how important other topics are in the curriculum

This last point is important. We never have enough time in the school year to teach all the topics that exist in our textbooks or curriculum guides, so we must make decisions about what content to prioritize. Analyzing assessment results provides us with information that can help us make these decisions.

We can also gather valuable information about our assessments by further analyzing individual items. In addition to questions about student mastery of content, we also want to know if individual items are functioning effectively. For example, look at these results for the following multiple-choice item. (The numbers in parentheses indicate the number of students who selected each option.)

The Vietnam War primarily occurred during which time period?
- a. 1930–1940 (0)
- b. 1940–1950 (3)
- c. 1950–1960 (4)
- d. 1960–1970 (18)
- e. 1970–1980 (4)

This suggests that most of the class (60%) got the item right and understood the relative time frame for the Vietnam War. Compare those with these results:

Which of the following is a reptile?
 a. Frog (7)
 b. Shrimp (5)
 c. Trout (6)
 d. Turtle (8)

These results paint a very different picture of content mastery and also suggest that students have misconceptions about the topic. Eight students answered correctly, but 18 did not. Armed with this data, you can then provide the students with detailed feedback, or even reteach the topic if necessary.

In analyzing our assessments, we also need to think about ways to improve them for the future. DeVonne did this when she made notes on her copy of the test before filing it. Her notes reminded her that the wording on one of her problems was confusing, so she would need to revise it before using it again. This, plus other information taken from the test, will assist her in future planning for both instruction and assessment.

Providing Students with Feedback

"Do you have our tests finished, Mrs. Lampkin?" students ask Friday morning.

"Of course!" she smiles, returning their papers.

"Overall, you did well, and I'm proud of you. I knew all that hard work would pay off. . . . There are a few items I want to go over, though. We had a little trouble with number 13, and you all made nearly the same mistake, so let's take a look at it."

She waits a moment while students read the problem and then asks, "Now, what are we given in the problem?. . . Saleina?"

"Mr. El had two dozen candy bars."

"Okay. Good. And how many is that? . . . Kevin?"

"Umm . . . two dozen is 24."

"Fine. And what else do we know? . . . Hanna?"

DeVonne continues the discussion of the problem and then goes over two others that were frequently missed. In the process, she makes notes at the top of her copy, identifying the problems that were difficult. She writes "Ambiguous" by one and underlines some of the wording in it. By another, she writes, "Teach them how to draw diagrams of the problem." She then puts her copy of the test in a folder, lays it on her desk to be filed, and turns back to the class.

To promote as much learning as possible, providing students with informative feedback for all forms of assessment is essential. In fact, in using assessment *for* learning, feedback is arguably the most important part of the process (Hattie & Gann, 2011). Feedback helps students learn from their mistakes, and knowledge of results increases student motivation. Also, because student attention is high during discussions of missed items, many teachers believe that students learn more in these sessions than they do in original instruction. Informative feedback is particularly important for items written for application, analysis, and evaluation of conceptual and procedural knowledge. These items are challenging, and students typically struggle with them because they don't have a great deal of experience in responding to items written at these levels. Discussing these items both increases students' understanding of the content and helps them learn how to respond to higher level items. This is the essence of assessment *for* learning, and the instructional time spent on it is time well spent (Stiggins & Chappuis, 2012).

When providing feedback for essay items, creating model responses and then discussing the model responses can be a valuable learning tool. As you display the model response you can identify its important features, and students can compare their responses to it. Providing detailed written feedback to individual students is an enormously demanding task, and the use of model answers can save you a great deal of time.

Finally, multiple-choice items written above the recall of factual information are often interpretive exercises that may involve a certain degree of ambiguity, so some students might misinterpret the items. Discussion and feedback will help you identify wording in any items that can be misinterpreted. You can then revise the items to make them clearer and reuse them. This leads us to suggestions for making your assessment process more efficient.

Increasing the Efficiency of Your Assessment Practices

Assessment is one of the most important components of the teaching–learning process, but creating quality assessments is demanding. Two suggestions can help you make the assessment process as efficient as possible. Let's look at them.

Create an Item File of Paper-and-Pencil Items. Creating an item file of paper-and-pencil items is one of the most important actions you can take for improving both the quality and the efficiency of your assessment practices. Use the best items from tests that are included as part of your textbook's ancillary materials and supplement these items with those you construct yourself. Store the information in your computer and create future tests and quizzes from the file.

As your item file expands, assessing your students will become more and more efficient. You merely select items from the file that best help you determine if your students are meeting your learning objectives and create your tests and quizzes from them.

You will be very busy when you teach, and it's virtually impossible to continually create new assessment items at levels above recall of factual information from scratch. You simply won't have the time. So, once you've created clear, unambiguous items that measure higher levels of learning, you should use the items over and over.

Collect Assessments and Store Them for Students. After giving a quiz or test, returning it, and providing students with detailed feedback, collect the tests and store them in a file for your students.

This suggestion may seem counterintuitive, and might even be controversial, but, again, it's impossible to continually create high-quality test items that measure more than knowledge and recall. So you need to reuse your items. By collecting quizzes and tests, and storing them for students, you're able to reuse your items, which increases your efficiency.

This suggestion in no way detracts from providing students with feedback. You will thoroughly discuss quizzes and tests when you return them to students, and after collecting the assessments, you can invite students to come in and review a quiz or test anytime after it's given. You only need to get it from the student's file and discuss it in as much detail as is necessary.

These suggestions will help you increase the quality of your assessments, because you will revise ambiguous or poorly worded items. It will also dramatically increase the efficiency of the assessment process because you won't be spending the time it takes to continually create new assessment items. This process takes time and effort, but once you have created a file of high-quality items, your assessments truly will be designed *for* learning.

Classroom **Connections**

Conducting Effective Classroom Assessment Practices

1. Preparing assessments during planning for instruction helps ensure that assessments are aligned with learning objectives. Creating assessments during planning saves time and also increases validity.

- **Elementary:** A fourth-grade teacher, as part of an extended unit on reading comprehension, is planning lessons focusing on cause-and-effect relationships. As he plans, he identifies passages that he will use for practice and as the basis for assessing his students' abilities in this area.

- **Middle School:** A middle school social studies teacher is planning a unit focusing on the relationships between technological events, such as the Industrial Revolution, and changes in societies. As she plans, she writes a series of short essay questions that she will use to assess her students' understanding of the relationships.

- **High School:** A geometry teacher is planning a unit on the construction of segments and angles, angle bisectors, and parallel and perpendicular lines. As he plans, he creates problems that he will use to assess his students' understanding of these processes.

2. Providing students with specific test-preparation procedures both increases achievement and decreases test anxiety. Allow students to practice on items similar to those that will appear on the assessment, and express positive expectations about their performance.

- **Elementary:** The fourth-grade teacher gives his students reading passages and has them identify cause-and-effect relationships in the passages.

- **Middle School:** The middle school social studies teacher presents examples of responses to essay questions similar to those she plans to use for her assessment. With her guidance, students identify both well-written and poorly written responses and explain differences between the two.

- **High School:** The geometry teacher has his students practice creating constructions similar to those that will appear on the end-of-unit test.

3. Feedback and discussion of assessment items increases students' understanding of the topics they are studying. Provide detailed feedback on frequently missed items.

- **Elementary:** The fourth-grade teacher returns students' papers and discusses each of the items in detail.

- **Middle School:** The social studies teacher creates ideal responses to the essay items and helps her students identify the components that made those responses ideal.

- **High School:** The geometry teacher demonstrates how each of the constructions of the items on the test could be created. He guides a discussion of alternate ways the constructions could be accomplished.

Designing a Total Assessment System

Creating high-quality assessment items and effective test administration procedures increases the likelihood that your assessments will be valid and reliable. But individual tests, quizzes, and assignments still need to be coordinated in a comprehensive assessment system. Designing a total assessment system raises a number of important questions, such as:

- How many tests and quizzes should I give?
- Should I give grades to all assignments and quizzes, or use some primarily for feedback?
- How will I count homework?
- How will I use performance assessments?
- How will I assess and report affective dimensions, such as cooperation and effort?

The answers to these questions will be your responsibility, a prospect that may seem daunting, because you have little experience to fall back on. However, knowing that the decisions are yours removes some of this uncertainty. We discuss these issues in this section.

Formative and Summative Assessment

Although we often think that the purpose of giving tests and quizzes is to assign grades, their most important function is to provide information about learning progress and promote additional learning (Stiggins & Chappuis, 2012). Assessment *for* learning includes diagnosing students' existing understanding, assessing their learning progress, and providing feedback. We can use assessments to increase learning but not include the results in decisions about grading, a process called **formative assessment** (Popham, 2011).

Virtually all forms of informal assessment are formative. For example, when you use students' responses to questions to provide feedback in a learning activity, the primary purpose is to promote learning and clear up misconceptions, rather than grading students. Pretests, work samples, and writing assignments that can be rewritten are other common forms of formative assessment. Providing students with feedback, which is essential for increasing motivation and helping students learn to monitor their own progress, is its primary purpose. In this respect, formative assessment is a form of instructional scaffolding that assists students during learning.

Summative assessment is the process of assessing after instruction and using the results for grading decisions. In classrooms, most assessments are used for summative purposes; however, used properly, both formative and summative assessments can be useful for making instructional decisions and increasing student motivation.

Designing a Grading System

An effective grading system provides feedback to students, helps them develop self-regulation, and can increase motivation. It also aids communication between teachers and parents. The following guidelines can help you design an effective grading system in your own classroom:

- Create a system that is clear, understandable, and consistent with school and district policies.
- Design your system to support learning and instruction by gathering frequent and systematic information from each student.
- Base grades on observable data.
- Assign grades consistently regardless of gender, class, race, or socioeconomic status.

You should be able to confidently defend your system to a parent or administrator if necessary (Miller et al., 2013).

Ed Psych and You

After taking a test, do you want to know how you did compared to the other students in your class? Or do you simply want to know what your grade is? How do these two kinds of information differ?

NORM-REFERENCED AND CRITERION-REFERENCED GRADING SYSTEMS

Assigning value to students' work is an integral part of assessment. Norm-referenced and criterion-referenced systems are two ways to assign grades to student performance. When **norm-referenced grading** is used, assessment decisions are based on an individual's performance compared to the performance of peers. The following is an example of a norm-referenced system:

A Top 15% of students

B Next 20% of students

C Next 30% of students

D Next 20% of students

F Last 15% of students

When using **criterion-referenced grading**, you make assessment decisions according to a predetermined standard, such as 90–100 for an A, 80–89 for a B, and so on. The specific standards vary among school districts, schools, and teachers. These standards are often established by the school or district, but in some cases the decision will be yours completely.

Criterion-referenced systems have two important advantages over norm-referenced ones (Stiggins & Chappuis, 2012). First, because they reflect the extent to which learning objectives are met, they more accurately describe content mastery, an important consideration in this era of accountability. Second, they deemphasize competition. Competitive grading systems can discourage students from helping each other, threaten peer relationships, and decrease motivation to learn, especially for those who find it difficult to compete. Although norm referencing is important in standardized testing, it is rarely used in classroom assessment systems.

This discussion addresses the questions we asked in *Ed Psych and You* in this section. If you're like most students, you will want to know the criteria for earning grades at the beginning of the semester. In addition, although we don't want to openly compete with our classmates, most of us want to know how we've done on a quiz or test compared to others in the class.

We encourage you to minimize these comparisons in your work with your students. Statements such as "Our goal here is to learn as much as possible, not compete with our classmates, so don't think about how you did compared to others" won't eliminate this tendency on the part of students, but it can make a difference in students' tendencies to compete with each other.

COMBINING PAPER-AND-PENCIL AND PERFORMANCE ASSESSMENTS

For those of you who will teach in upper elementary, middle, and high schools, paper-and-pencil assessments will be the cornerstones of your grading system. Some teachers add tests and quizzes together and count them as a certain percentage of the overall grade; others weigh them differently in assigning grades.

If you're using performance assessments or portfolios as part of your assessment system, you should include them in determining grades. To do otherwise communicates that they are less important than the paper-and-pencil measures you're using. If you rate student performance on the basis of well-defined criteria, scoring will have acceptable reliability, and performance assessments and/or portfolios can then be an integral part of your total assessment system.

HOMEWORK

Properly designed homework contributes to learning, but to be most effective, students must get credit for doing it, and you need to include it in your grading system. Students, and particularly older students, exert little effort on homework for which they receive no credit (Lee & Shute, 2010; Cooper, Robinson, & Patall, 2006; Marzano, 2007). Beyond this point, however, research provides little guidance as to how you should manage homework. Accountability, feedback, and your own workload will all influence this decision. Table 14.5 outlines some homework-assessment options.

As we see in Table 14.5, each option has advantages and disadvantages. The best strategy is one that results in learners making the most consistent and conscientious effort on their homework without costing you an inordinate amount of time and effort.

Assigning Grades: Increasing Learning and Motivation

Having made decisions about paper-and-pencil and performance assessments, portfolios, and homework, you are now ready to design your total grading system. At this point, you need to make two decisions: (1) what to include and (2) the weight to assign each component.

In addition to paper-and-pencil assessments, performance measures, and homework, some teachers include affective factors, such as effort, class participation, and attitude. Assessment experts discourage this practice, although it is common in classrooms (Miller et al., 2013). Gathering systematic information about affective variables is difficult, and assessing them is

Table 14.5	Homework-assessment options	
Option	**Advantages**	**Disadvantages**
Grade it yourself	Promotes learning. Allows diagnosis of students. Increases student effort.	Is very demanding for the teacher.
Grade samples	Reduces teacher work, compared with first option.	Doesn't give the teacher a total picture of student performance.
Collect at random intervals	Reduces teacher workload.	Reduces student effort unless homework is frequently collected.
Change papers, students grade	Provides feedback with minimal teacher effort.	Consumes class time. Doesn't give students feedback on their own work.
Students score own papers	Also provides feedback with minimum teacher effort. Lets students see their own mistakes.	Is inaccurate for purposes of evaluation. Lets students not do the work and copy in class as it's being discussed.
Students get credit for completing assignment	Gives students feedback on their work when it's discussed in class.	Reduces effort of unmotivated students.
No graded homework, frequent short quizzes	Is effective with older and motivated students.	Reduces effort of unmotivated students.

highly subjective. In addition, a high grade based on effort suggests to both students and parents that important content was learned when it may not have been. Factors such as effort, cooperation, and class attendance should be reflected in a separate section of the report card.

Let's look at two teachers' systems for assigning grades:

Kim Sook (middle school science)		Lea DeLong (high school algebra)	
Tests and quizzes	50%	Tests	45%
Homework	20%	Quizzes	45%
Performance assessment	20%	Homework	10%
Projects	10%		

We see that these two grading systems are quite different. Kim, an eighth-grade physical science teacher, emphasizes both homework and **alternative assessments**, which include projects and performance assessments. Traditional tests and quizzes count only 50% in his system. Lea emphasizes tests and quizzes more heavily; they count 90% in her system. The rationale in each case is simple. Kim, an experienced middle school teacher, believes that homework is important to student learning and has found that unless it is assigned and graded, students won't do it. He also includes projects as an important part of his system, believing they involve his students in the study of science. He uses performance assessments to chart students' progress as they work on experiments and other lab activities. Lea, a secondary algebra II teacher, believes that students understand the need to do their homework in order to succeed on tests and quizzes, so she deemphasizes this component in her grading system. Instead, she gives a weekly quiz and three tests during a 9-week grading period.

Standards-based grading, a practice that has become more prominent with the emphasis on standards and accountability, targets specific standards and the extent to which students have met them (Deddeh, Main, & Fulkerson, 2010). By focusing on mastery of content, standards-based grading eliminates factors such as effort or credit for homework. Teachers who implement this system claim that it simplifies communication with both students and parents because it specifically identifies content and skills that students have learned and provides students with clear messages about important ideas that still need additional work and effort.

To promote learning, students need to understand your assessment system. Even young students can understand the relationship between effort and grades if they are assessed frequently and if their homework is scored and returned promptly. Conversely, even high school students can have problems understanding a grading system if it is too complex.

Parents also need to understand your assessment system if they are to be involved in their children's learning (Stiggins & Chappuis, 2012). Parent–teacher conferences and graded examples of their child's work together with report cards are valuable sources of information parents use to gauge their children's learning progress. An understandable assessment system is essential in this process.

POINTS OR PERCENTAGES?

In assigning scores to assessments, you have two options. In a percentage system, you convert each score to a percentage and then average the percentages as the marking period progresses. In a point-based system, students accumulate raw points, and you convert them to a percentage only at the end of the marking period.

A percentage-based system has one important weakness. If a student misses 1 item on a 10-item quiz, for example, the student's score is a 90%. If you give another short quiz, and the student gets 3 of 5 items correct, the student's score on the second quiz is 60%, and the average of the two quizzes is 75%. This process gives the two quizzes equal weight, even though the first had twice as many items. The student got 12 of 15 items correct, which is 80%, so a point system more accurately reflects the student's performance.

If averaging percentages is flawed, why is it so common? Simplicity is the primary reason. It is both simpler for teachers to manage and easier to communicate to students and parents. Many teachers, and particularly those in elementary and middle schools, have attempted point systems and later returned to percentages because of pressure from students.

As with most aspects of teaching, the design of a grading system is a matter of your professional judgment. A percentage system is fair if assignments are similar in length, tests are also similar in length, and tests receive more weight than quizzes and assignments. On the other hand, a point system can work if students keep a running total of their points and you tell them the number required for an A, a B, and so on at frequent points in the marking period.

Technology, Learning, and Development

Using Technology to Improve Your Assessment System

Because of its ability to store large amounts of data and process it quickly, technology is proving to be especially valuable in classroom assessment. Technology, and particularly computers, can serve three important and time-saving assessment functions (Roblyer & Doering, 2013):

- Planning and constructing tests
- Analyzing test data, especially data gathered from objective tests
- Maintaining student records

Let's look at them.

Planning and Constructing Tests

Planning and constructing tests can be both labor- and time-intensive. We advocate collecting assessments after you've given them and revising and storing the individual items to be reused in the future. Doing so increases the quality of future assessments and also saves you time and energy.

A number of commercial software programs can assist in this process. These programs have the following capabilities:

- Develop a test file for a variety of formats that can be stored in the system. Within a file, items can be organized by topic, chapter, objective, or difficulty.
- Revise items to eliminate misleading wording and ineffective distractors.
- Select items from the file to generate the complete assessment and create multiple versions of a test to deal with absent students or to minimize cheating.
- Produce student-ready copies and an answer key.

You can also store model answers to essay items on your computer, which can be repeatedly used. So, once you've written a model answer, you need only revise it to make it clearer; you don't need to re-create the answer every time you use the item.

Analyzing Test Data

Once administered, tests need to be scored and analyzed. If you're a middle or high school teacher with 5 sections of 30 students and you've given a 40-item test, for example, you face an daunting logistical task: scoring $5 \times 30 \times 40 = 6{,}000$ individual items!

Most schools now have technology that can machine-score or scan your tests if they're in multiple-choice, true–false, or matching formats, and a number of software programs exist that can machine-score tests. These programs can:

- Score objective tests and provide descriptive statistics such as mean, median, mode, range, and standard deviation.
- Identify the numbtter of students who selected each response, the percentage of students who didn't respond to an item, and the correlation of each item with the total test.
- Sort student responses by score, grade/age, or gender.

Your school will most likely also have a technology expert who can help you with each of these tasks.

Maintaining Student Records

To maximize learning, you need to assess frequently and thoroughly, and you need to be able to easily store and access the information you gather about each student. In addition, your students need to know where they stand in the course to make the best use of their time and resources. Computers provide an efficient way of storing, analyzing, and reporting student assessments.

Let's see how one teacher uses them.

> I use an electronic gradebook in my teaching, and the program allows me to set it up either by total points or percentages. It also allows me to decide the amount of weight I want to assign to tests, quizzes, homework, and anything else, such as projects, for students' final averages.
>
> The program is very user friendly, and it's an enormous time saver (Nicole Yudin, personal communication, April 18, 2014).

Your school will have access to one or more electronic gradebook programs, and you will be provided with technical support in setting up and using this software. And as it continues to improve, technology will become an even more useful tool to make your teaching more efficient.

Diversity: Effective Assessment Practices with Students from Diverse Backgrounds

Learner diversity influences teaching and learning in a number of ways, and the process of assessment is one of the most important.

The current reform movement, with its emphasis on standards and the achievement of all students, has heightened awareness of the problem of educating students from diverse backgrounds. The problem is particularly acute in urban settings, where diversity is the most pronounced (Macionis & Parrillo, 2013).

Student diversity influences classroom assessment in three important ways. First, learners from diverse backgrounds may lack experience with general testing procedures, different test formats, and test-taking strategies. Second, because most assessments are strongly language based, language may be an obstacle (Forte, 2010; Kieffer, Lesaux, Rivera, & Francis, 2009). Third, learners may not fully understand that assessments promote learning and instead view them as punitive. The following recommendations respond to these issues (Popham, 2014):

- Attempt to create a learning-focused classroom, in which you emphasize that assessments are used to promote learning, provide feedback, and measure learning progress.
- Increase the number and frequency of assessments, and provide detailed and corrective feedback for all items. Encourage students to ask questions about test items, and when they answer incorrectly, ask them to explain their answers. Emphasize that mistakes are part of learning, and continually present students with evidence of their learning progress.
- Deemphasize grades, and keep all assessment results private. Establish a rule that students may not share their scores and grades with each other. (This is impossible to enforce, but as a symbolic gesture it attempts to protect students who want to succeed but face peer pressure not to.)
- Drop one or two quizzes a marking period for purposes of grading. This practice reduces test anxiety and communicates to students that you are "on their side" and want them to succeed. It also contributes to a positive classroom climate.
- Make provisions for non-native English speakers by allowing extra time and providing extra help with language aspects of your assessments.

Of these suggestions, feedback with discussions of frequently missed items is the most beneficial. Although important in all environments, it is essential for effective assessment with learners from diverse backgrounds. In many cases, students' explanations for their answers can reveal learning problems, which you can then address. In addition, feedback can help you identify content bias in your questions (Popham, 2014). For example, some students may have limited experiences with electrical appliances such as an iron or vacuum cleaner, summertime activities such as camping and hiking, or musical instruments such as a banjo. If assessment items require knowledge or experiences with these ideas, you are measuring both the intended topic and students' general knowledge, which detracts from validity. The only way to identify these potential sources of bias is to discuss assessment items afterward. Then you can revise and more carefully word your assessments to help eliminate bias.

The possibility of content bias is even more likely if you have non-native English speakers in your classes. Suggestions for supporting these students include the following (Forte, 2010; Kieffer et al., 2010):

- Provide extra time to take tests.
- Allow a translation glossary or dictionary to be used during the test.
- Read directions aloud. (It is even better if you can read the students the directions in their native languages.)
- Allow them to take the test at a different time, and read it to them, clarifying misunderstandings where possible.

Learners with exceptionalities pose special grading challenges; research indicates that large numbers of these students receive below-average grades in their general education classes (Heward, 2013). The effects of low grades can be devastating to students who already experience frustration in attempting to keep up with their peers. In addition, federal legislation in the form of the Individuals with Disabilities Education Act (IDEA) mandates that schools make appropriate accommodations for students with physical, mental, social, or emotional disabilities. This requirement applies to both instruction and assessment practices.

To address this problem, teachers often adapt their grading systems by grading on improvement, assigning separate grades for process and for products, and basing a grade on meeting the objectives of an individualized education program (IEP). The dilemma for teachers is how to increase motivation to learn while providing an accurate indicator of learning progress (Vaughn & Bos, 2015; Vaughn et al., 2014).

The primary function of assessment in general, and with diverse learners in particular, is to provide evidence of increasing competence. Evidence of learning progress can then be an important source of motivation to learn. The accommodations you make in your own classroom to help learners perform at the highest levels on your assessments will exert a powerful influence on how your students view themselves as well as your classroom.

Classroom **Connections**

Designing Effective Classroom Assessment Systems

1. Formative assessment is used primarily to provide feedback to students; summative assessments are used for grading. Use both to promote learning in your assessment system.

 ■ **Elementary:** A second-grade teacher discusses math problems that several students missed on their homework and then asks them to rework the problems. If students are still having problems with the content, she re-teaches it before she gives them a graded assessment.

 ■ **Middle School:** A sixth-grade science teacher has created and e-filed an item pool. He uses some of the items to create a "practice test," which the class discusses immediately after they've taken it. He then uses additional items on a summative assessment.

 ■ **High School:** A 10th-grade English teacher provides extensive individual comments on students' papers. In addition, he identifies problem areas common to the whole class and uses anonymous selections from students' papers to discuss and provide feedback to the whole class.

2. Frequent and thorough assessments, combined with feedback, promote learning. Design your assessment system so that gathering systematic information from each student is a regular part of your class routines.

 ■ **Elementary:** A second-grade teacher has his students solve two problems each morning that focus on the previous day's math topic. The class discusses the solutions before he moves to the topic for the day.

 ■ **Middle School:** A geography teacher gives a weekly quiz and three tests during each 9-week grading period with the majority of the items written above the recall of factual information level. She provides detailed feedback on each of the items and then col-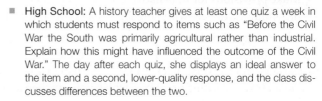lects the quizzes and tests, so she can reuse the items.

 ■ **High School:** A history teacher gives at least one quiz a week in which students must respond to items such as "Before the Civil War the South was primarily agricultural rather than industrial. Explain how this might have influenced the outcome of the Civil War." The day after each quiz, she displays an ideal answer to the item and a second, lower-quality response, and the class discusses differences between the two.

3. Effective grading systems are understandable to both students and their parents. Create a grading system that is understandable and consistent with school policies.

 ■ **Elementary:** A fourth-grade teacher's school uses a 70–79, 80–89, and 90–100 grading system for a C, B, and A, respectively. She explains the system in a letter to her students' parents, and routinely sends home packets of student papers that indicate the students' learning progress.

 ■ **Middle School:** A math teacher displays his grading system on a wall chart. He explains the system and what it requires of students. He emphasizes that it is designed to promote learning and returns to the chart periodically to remind students of their learning progress.

 ■ **High School:** A history teacher in a school with high percentages of minority students takes extra time and effort during parent–teacher conferences to explain how she arrives at grades for her students. She saves students' work samples and shares them with parents during conferences.

Developmentally Appropriate **Practice**

Assessment of Learning with Students at Different Ages

Although many aspects of assessment, such as aligning assessments with learning objectives, ensuring that they are valid and reliable, and using them to promote learning, apply at all developmental levels, important differences exist. The following paragraphs outline suggestions for responding to these differences.

Working with Students in Early Childhood Programs and Elementary Schools

Young children are just learning to play the school game, and assessment is often one of its more puzzling aspects (Berk, 2013; Trawick-Smith, 2014). They come from environments where play and informal social interaction are integral parts of their daily lives, and sit-down formal assessments are often strange and confusing to them.

This suggests that informal assessments such as systematic observation, checklists, and rating scales should be used to provide valuable sources of information about achievement. In addition, performance assessments that gauge young students' abilities to perform tasks such as counting and classifying are also useful. When formal assessments are used, structure and support in the form of detailed directions and ample opportunities to practice with immediate feedback are necessary.

In addition to gathering accurate information about progress in learning and development, one of our major assessment goals at the P–K level should be to begin the process of helping students understand how effort and assessment influence learning. Motivation to learn is starting to crystallize at this early age, and positive experiences with assessment tasks can lay a firm foundation for future classroom learning (Schunk et al., 2014).

Lower elementary grades strongly emphasize reading and math, and performance assessments are widely used. For example, first graders are asked to identify sounds of vowels and consonant digraphs in printed words, decode words, and print letters. In math, they are asked to write numbers, order whole numbers up to 100 or more, and represent numbers on a number line. Each task suggests a performance assessment.

Informal assessment and assessment of affective outcomes, such as "Gets along well with others," are also more prominent in elementary report cards than with older students. Because of these emphases, being aware of the possibility that our casual observations may be unreliable or invalid is important. Attempting to gather the same information from all students and increasing the frequency of assessments are essential when assessing young children's knowledge and skills.

Working with Students in Middle Schools

The cognitive demands on middle school students increase significantly, and teachers use paper-and-pencil assessments to a much greater degree than elementary teachers. For example, in social studies, eighth graders are expected to understand ideas such as the ways in which architecture, language, and beliefs have been transmitted from one culture to another; in science they are expected to understand the difference between weight and mass, and the relationships between the temperature and the motion of particles; in math they are expected to solve systems of linear equations; and in language arts they are expected to understand literary devices, such as meter and figurative language.

These are all abstract ideas, and instructional alignment is the key to effective assessment of these topics. If topics are taught in the abstract, they won't be meaningful to students, and students will memorize what they can in order to perform acceptably on the assessments. Instruction that includes high-quality examples and a great deal of discussion is necessary to make the topics meaningful. Then, assessments that also employ examples, such as the interpretive exercise in Figure 14.3, are effective for promoting learning.

Working with Students in High Schools

Standards for high school students typically require a great deal of abstract thinking. For instance, in language arts they are expected to understand how strategies such as hyperbole, rhetorical questioning, and glittering generalities are used as persuasive techniques; in science they are required to understand atomic theory, and in social studies they are asked to understand why ancient civilizations such as those in Mesopotamia, Egypt, and the Indus Valley evolved and were successful. As with middle school students, unless these topics are meaningfully taught, students will try memorizing enough information to survive assessments, and then information will be promptly forgotten. To make the information meaningful, teachers need to use a variety of ways to represent topics, such as vignettes, timelines, and artifacts in history, and well-designed models and simulations in science. If the topics are meaningfully taught, and assessments are aligned with the instruction, assessment *for* learning can be accomplished.

chapter

14 Summary

1. Describe assessment *for* learning and explain how validity and reliability are related to it.
   - Assessment for learning makes assessment an integral part of the teaching–learning process, designed to support and increase learning.
   - Valid assessments increase the effectiveness of the assessment process by ensuring that assessments are consistent with learning objectives.
   - Reliable assessments provide consistent measurement results. Assessments that are unreliable cannot be valid.

2. Describe informal assessment, and explain why it is an important part of assessment *for* learning.
   - Informal assessment is the process of gathering information and making decisions during lessons and other classroom activities.
   - Informal assessment is essential for the many instructional decisions that teachers make each day, such as how quickly to move a learning activity, who to call on, what questions to ask, and how long students should be given to respond. Without informal assessment, making these decisions would be impossible.

3. Identify differences between formal and informal assessment, and analyze formal assessment items.
   - Informal assessment is the process of gathering information and making decisions during learning activities and other classroom activities. Formal assessment is the process of systematically gathering the same kind of information from each student.
   - Paper-and-pencil items, performance assessments, and portfolios can all be used as formal assessments.

   - Formal assessments can be analyzed and improved using specific criteria that exist for each assessment format.

4. Explain how effective assessment practices increase student learning.
   - Teachers use effective assessment practices when they design assessments that are congruent with learning objectives and instruction, communicate what will be covered on assessments, allow students to practice on items similar to those that will appear on tests, teach test-taking skills, and express positive expectations for student performance.
   - Effective assessment practices also include attempts to reduce test anxiety, such as increasing testing frequency, using criterion referencing, providing clear information about tests, and giving students ample time.
   - Effective assessment practices increase learning by making expectations clear, providing students with opportunities to practice, and providing detailed feedback.

5. Describe the components and decisions involved in designing a total assessment system.
   - A total assessment system includes creating effective assessment items, preparing students, administering assessments, analyzing results, and assigning grades.
   - Decisions involved in designing a total assessment system include the number of tests and quizzes; the uses of alternative assessments; the level of assessment items, such as knowledge, application, or analysis; the role of homework in assigning grades; and the assessment and reporting of affective dimensions, such as cooperation and effort.

Preparing for **Your Licensure Exam**

Understanding Effective Assessment Practices

Your licensure exam will include information related to classroom assessment. We include the following exercises to help you practice for the exam in your state. This book and these exercises will be a resource for you as you prepare for the exam.

At the beginning of the chapter, you saw how DeVonne Lampkin used assessment to help increase her students' achievement.

Let's look now at Ron Hawkins, an urban middle school English teacher, who is involved in assessing his students' understanding of pronoun cases. Read the case study, and answer the questions that follow.

"Today we're going to begin studying pronoun cases," Ron announces as he starts the lesson. "Everybody turn to page 484 in your text. . . . This is important in our writing because we want to be able to write and use Standard English correctly, and this is one of the places where people get mixed up. So, when we're finished, you'll all be able to use pronouns correctly in your writing."

He then writes the following on the board:

Pronouns use the nominative case when they're subjects and predicate nominatives. Pronouns use the objective case when they're direct objects, indirect objects, or objects of prepositions.

"Let's review," Ron continues, briefly discussing direct and indirect objects, predicate nominatives, and objects of prepositions.

"Now let's look at some additional examples," he continues, as he displays the following sentences on the document camera:

1. Did you get the card from Esteban and (I, me)?
2. Will Meg and (she, her) run the concession stand?
3. They treat (whoever, whomever) they hire very well.
4. I looked for someone (who, whom) could give me directions to the theater.

"Okay, look at the first one. Which is correct? . . . Omar?"

"*Me.*"

"Good, Omar. How about the second one? . . . Lonnie?"

"*Her.*"

"Not quite, Lonnie. . . . Suppose I turn the sentence around and say, 'Meg and her will run the concession stand.' That doesn't sound right, does it? 'Meg and she' is a compound subject, and when we have a subject, we use the nominative case. . . . Okay?"

Lonnie nods and Ron continues, "Look at the third one. . . . Chloe?"

"I'm not sure . . . *whoever*, I guess."

"This one is a little tricky," Ron nods. "When we use whoever and whomever, whoever is the nominative case and whomever is the objective case. In this sentence, whomever is a direct object, so it is the correct form."

After he finishes, Ron gives students another list of sentences to practice on for homework in which they are to select the correct form of the pronoun.

On Tuesday, Ron reviews these exercises and discusses several additional examples that use *who, whom, whoever,* and *whomever.* He then discusses the rules for pronoun–antecedent agreement (pronouns must agree with their antecedents in gender and number). He again has students analyze examples as he did with pronoun cases.

He continues with pronouns and their antecedents on Wednesday and begins a discussion of indefinite pronouns as antecedents for personal pronouns—*anybody, either, each, one, someone*—and has students analyze examples as before.

Near the end of class on Thursday, Ron announces, "Tomorrow, we're going to have a test on this material: pronoun cases, pronouns and their antecedents, and indefinite pronouns. You have your notes, so study hard. . . . Are there any questions? . . . Good. I expect you all to do well. I'll see you tomorrow."

On Friday morning as students file into class and the bell rings, Ron picks up a stack of tests from his desk. The test consists of 30 sentences, 10 of which deal with case, 10 with antecedents, and 10 with indefinite pronouns. The final part of the test directs students to write a paragraph. The following are sample items from the test:

Part I. For each of the items below, mark A on your answer sheet if the pronoun case is correct in the sentence, and mark B if it is incorrect. If it is incorrect, supply the correct pronoun.

1. Be careful who you tell.
2. Will Renee and I be in the outfield?
3. My brother and me like waterskiing.

Part II. Write the pronoun that correctly completes the sentence.

1. Arlene told us about _____ visit to the dentist to have braces put on.
2. The Wilsons planted a garden in _____ backyard.
3. Cal read the recipe and put _____ in the file.
4. Each of the girls on the team wore _____ school sweater to the game.
5. None of the brass has lost _____ shine yet.
6. Few of the boys on the team have taken _____ physicals yet.

Part III. Write a short paragraph that contains at least two examples of pronouns in the nominative case and two examples of pronouns in the objective case. (Circle and label these.) Include also at least two examples of pronouns that agree with their antecedents. Remember!! The paragraph must make sense. It cannot be just a series of sentences.

Ron watches as his students work, and seeing that 15 minutes remain in the period and that some students are only starting on their paragraphs, he announces, "You only have 15 minutes left. Watch your time and work quickly. You need to be finished by the end of the period."

He continues monitoring students, again reminding them to work quickly when 10 minutes are left and again when 5 minutes are left.

Luis, Simao, Moy, and Rudy are hastily finishing the last few words of their tests as the bell rings. Luis finally turns in his paper as Ron's fourth-period students are filing into the room.

"Here," Ron says. "This pass will get you into Mrs. Washington's class if you're late. . . . How did you do?"

"Okay, I think," Luis says over his shoulder as he scurries out of the room, "except for the last part. It was hard. I couldn't get started."

"I'll look at it," Ron says. "Scoot now."

On Monday, Ron returns the tests, saying, "Here are your papers. You did fine on the sentences, but your paragraphs need a lot of work. Why did you have so much trouble with them, when we had so much practice?"

"It was hard, Mr. Hawkins."

"Not enough time."

"I hate to write."

Ron listens patiently and then says, "Be sure you write your scores in your notebooks. . . . Okay, does everyone have them written down?. . . Are there any questions?"

"Number 3," Enrique requests.

"Okay, let's look at 3. It says, 'My brother and me like waterskiing.' There, the pronoun is part of the subject, so it should be *I* and not *me*.

"Any others?"

A sprinkling of questions comes from around the room, and Ron responds, "We don't have time to go over all of them. I'll discuss three more."

He responds to the three students who seem to be most urgent in waving their hands. He then collects the tests and begins a discussion of adjective and adverb clauses.

Questions for Case Analysis

In answering these questions, use information from the chapter, and link your responses to specific information in the case.

Multiple-Choice Questions

1. During his lessons preparing for the test on Friday, Ron gave his students sample sentences similar to the ones that would appear on the test and provided them with feedback. Doing this best described:

   a. alternative assessment

   b. formative assessment

   c. performance assessment

   d. standards-based assessment

2. As Ron gave his students the sample exercise, he watched his students' nonverbal cues for confidence or confusion. This would be an example of:

   a. systematic observation

   b. performance assessment

   c. informal assessment

   d. standards-based assessment

Constructed-Response Question

3. In the section on effective assessment practices, suggestions for preparing students for assessments, administering them, and analyzing results were offered. How effectively did Ron perform each task? Describe specifically what he might have done to be more effective in these areas.

Important **Concepts**

alternative assessment
assessment for learning
checklists
classroom assessment
completion
criterion-referenced grading
diagnostic assessment

distractors
essay
formal assessment
formative assessment
informal assessment
matching
multiple-choice

norm-referenced grading
performance assessment
portfolio assessment
rating scales
reliability
rubric
standards-based grading

stem
summative assessment
systematic observation
table of specifications
test anxiety
true–false items
validity

OUTLINE	LEARNING OUTCOMES
	After you've completed your study of this chapter, you should be able to:
Standardized Testing and Accountability No Child Left Behind and Race to the Top The Common Core State Standards Initiative High-Stakes Tests Additional Developments in Standardized Testing Teacher Evaluation and the Accountability Movement	**1.** Describe the relationships between standards-based education, accountability, and standardized testing.
Standardized Tests Functions of Standardized Tests Norm- Versus Criterion-Referenced Standardized Tests Types of Standardized Tests Evaluating Standardized Tests: Validity Revisited	**2.** Describe the functions of standardized tests in the total assessment process.
Understanding and Interpreting Standardized Test Scores Descriptive Statistics Interpreting Standardized Test Results	**3.** Interpret standardized test results using statistics and standard scores.
Diversity and Standardized Testing Student Diversity and Assessment Bias Standardized Testing and English Learners Accommodating Students with Disabilities	**4.** Explain how learner diversity can influence the validity of standardized tests.
Educational Psychology and Teaching: Your Role in Standardized Testing	**5.** Describe the different roles you'll have in the process of standardized testing.

We've all had experiences with standardized tests and standardized testing. For instance, you likely took the SAT or ACT as part of your college applications, and we all took other standardized tests, such as the Stanford Achievement Test, when we were in school.

To introduce you to this topic, read the following case study and consider how standardized testing influences the work of Mike Chavez, a fourth-grade teacher.

> "Hello, Mrs. Palmer. I'm glad you could come in," Mike says, offering his hand in greeting.
>
> "Thank you," Doris Palmer responds. "I'm a little confused by a report that was sent home with David after he took the Stanford Achievement Test."
>
> "Well, let's take a look," Mike replies as he offers Mrs. Palmer a seat next to his desk.

"Here's what we received," Mrs. Palmer offers, and she shows David the following:

NATIONAL	PR	NATIONAL GRADE PERCENTILE BANDS						
		1	10	30	50	70	90	99
Total Reading	70				▬▬			
Total Math	64			‖‖‖‖				
Language	66			‖‖‖‖				
Spelling	80					‖‖‖‖		
Science	55			‖‖‖‖				
Social Science	85						▬▬	
Listening	40			▬▬				
Complete Battery	64			‖‖‖‖				

Source: "National Grade Percentile Bands" adapted from *Stanford Achievement Test Series, Tenth Edition* (Stanford 10). Copyright (C) 2003 by NCS Pearson, Inc. Reproduced with permission. All rights reserved.

"I'm not sure what this information means," she continues. "For instance, it says 'Total Reading' and then this number 70. And, then there's this information in the box."

"I understand completely," Mike smiles in response. "Let me try to clarify the information. . . . First, the PR stands for percentile rank. That means he scored as well as or better than 70% of the students who took this test around the country. . . . You already know he's in our top reading group, and these results suggest that he's properly placed."

"And what about these 'percentile bands' that we see here?" she continues, pointing to the information on the paper.

"A percentile band shows a range in which a student's true score is likely to fall. Because a possibility of some measurement error always exists in a test, the test manufacturers use the percentile band to accommodate this possibility."

"Is all this testing really necessary?" Mrs. Palmer queries. "Every time we turn around, David seems to be taking another test."

"That's a good question, and a lot of people question the amount of testing that goes in schools. . . . They do give us some valuable information, however. For example, they give us an objective, outside measure to help us understand how David and our other students are doing compared to others around the country. And we, the teachers, receive some additional and more detailed information about our students' performance, so the tests help us provide extra instructional support if it should be necessary. . . . Here, let me share some of this information about David with you."

We will examine this and other information related to standardized testing as the chapter unfolds. As you study these topics, keep the following questions in mind:

1. How have standards and accountability changed the role of standardized testing?
2. What is the purpose of standardized testing?
3. How can you use standardized tests to increase your students' learning?

We begin by addressing our first question above.

Ed Psych and You

How good were the schools you attended through your elementary, middle, and high school years? How do you know?

Standardized Testing and Accountability

A great deal has been written over the last several years about American's lack of knowledge. For example, a report from the National Assessment of Educational Progress found that only 12% of American 12th graders scored well enough to be considered "proficient" in American history (National Center for Education Statistics, 2010). In addition, when asked to name the three branches of government, only 38% of our country's citizens could name all three (Annenberg Foundation, 2011). And when *Newsweek* magazine gave 1,000 Americans the U.S. Citizenship test, nearly 40% failed (Romano, 2011).

The results are no better in science; a survey of American adults found that only slightly more than half knew how long it takes the Earth to revolve once around the Sun, and fewer than 6 of 10 realized that early humans and dinosaurs didn't live at the same time (ScienceDaily, 2009). Experts suggest that this lack of knowledge imperils our country's future, because it makes us less able to make informed political, economic, and environmental decisions (Romano, 2011).

Similar concerns are being raised at the school level. Evidence indicates that students are sometimes promoted from one grade to the next without mastering essential content and are graduating from high school without the skills needed to function effectively in life after school (West, 2012; Winters, 2012).

In response to these concerns, educators have established academic **standards**, statements that describe what students should know or be able to do at the end of a prescribed period of study. They've been developed by every state in the nation, and currently a movement exists to implement national standards (Common Core State Standards Initiative, 2014; Gewertz, 2011).

Standards-based education focuses teaching and learning on these standards, and **accountability** is the process of requiring students to demonstrate that they have met specified standards and making teachers responsible for students' performance.

No Child Left Behind and Race to the Top

The current standards-based reform movement began in 2001, with the passage of the **No Child Left Behind (NCLB)** act, a far-reaching federal government attempt to identify and serve all students in every segment of our society. The impetus behind this legislation was a growing realization that many children in our poorest schools were indeed being left behind, as indicated by major achievement gaps between poor and more well-off students and between students who are members of cultural minorities and their White counterparts. Leaders concluded that requiring states to create standards and measure students' achievement of them was the most effective way to address these disparities.

This complex and comprehensive reform effort was controversial from its beginning. Advocates have argued that NCLB has focused our nation's attention on the importance of education and especially on the basic skills essential for success both in school and later life. Also, by requiring states to report the academic progress of specific subgroups, such as members of cultural minorities, it has highlighted the problem of unequal achievement (Miller, 2012).

Critics have focused primarily on the way the legislation was implemented (Alexander, 2012). For example, NCLB requires each state to design its own standards together with the assessments that measure students' attainment of the standards. This has resulted in accountability systems that vary widely from state to state and are sometimes inaccurate and misleading. For instance, faced with the possibility of federal sanctions for not meeting their benchmarks, some states have "gamed the system" by lowering standards and creating lax accountability systems that reward mediocre, or even poor, performance (Ravitch, 2010).

The future of NCLB is unclear, especially with a Congress that is strongly divided along partisan lines. In response to legislative inaction, the Obama administration granted waivers to 34 states plus the District of Columbia (McNeil, 2013a). These waivers depended on the state developing realistic and rigorous alternatives to the NCLB–mandated standards and tests.

The waivers didn't suggest that the country was backing away from accountability, however. For example, the Obama administration poured more than four billion dollars into a program called **Race to the Top** (U.S. Department of Education, 2009). This competitive grant program encouraged individual states and districts to design comprehensive accountability programs that included common learning standards for students, data systems to track student performance, feedback to teachers, and even teacher merit pay plans based on students' standardized test performance.

The Common Core State Standards Initiative

The No Child Left Behind act was instrumental in promoting both standards and standards-based accountability. But as we saw above, it left the design of standards and the corresponding accountability tests to individual states, which resulted in standards that varied greatly in both content and rigor (Darling-Hammond & Wentworth, 2010).

The **Common Core State Standards Initiative (CCSSI)**, sponsored by the National Governors Association and the Council of Chief State School Officers—and not linked to NCLB—attempted to address these problems by creating a common set of rigorous standards for all states. Its goals are to ensure that our country's students are college and career ready, and "to provide a consistent, clear understanding of what students are expected to learn so teachers and parents know what they need to do to help them" (CCSSI, 2014, p. 1). Initial analysis of the new standards suggests that most target higher level learning outcomes (Darling-Hammond & Adamson, 2013).

By 2012, 45 states, the District of Columbia, four territories, and the Department of Defense Education Activities had adopted the Common Core and are in the process of developing standardized tests to measure achievement of the standards (McNeil, 2012, 2013b).

As we see here, standardized testing is an integral part of all efforts to improve the quality of our nation's schools and increase student learning. We turn now to a more detailed discussion of standardized testing and accountability.

High-Stakes Tests

Standardized testing intended to determine what students know and can do is central to the current accountability movement originally spawned by NCLB. Standardized testing is the mechanism used to determine if students have met standards, and its influence on schools and classrooms is enormous. The fact that students in other industrialized countries score higher than American students on these tests has alarmed leaders in our country, and current reform movements are largely due to concerns about low scores on standardized tests.

High-stakes tests are standardized tests used to make important decisions that affect students, teachers, and schools (Miller, Linn, & Gronlund, 2013). High-stakes tests usually occur at the state level and are used to measure the extent to which students have met standards. They're typically given at designated grade levels, such as 5th, 8th, and 10th, and the results are used to make decisions about student promotion and even high school graduation. When students can't move to the next grade level or graduate from high school because they fail a test, for example, the "stakes" are very high, thus the term *high-stakes tests*.

Standardized testing, in general, and high-stakes testing, in particular, are controversial (Popham, 2014). Advocates claim that the processes help clarify the goals of school systems, send clear messages to students about what they should be learning, and provide the public with hard evidence about school effectiveness (Hirsch, 2006; Phelps, 2005). They also argue that the tests are the fairest and most effective means of providing a quality education for all students.

Critics counter that teachers spend too much class time having students practice for the tests, the curriculum is narrowed to what is being tested, and the tests don't provide a true measure of what students have learned (Nichols & Berliner, 2008; Ravitch, 2010). Critics also contend that cutoff scores are arbitrary, and the instruments are too crude to be used in making crucial decisions about students, teachers, and schools. In addition, the tests have had a disproportionately negative impact on members of minority cultures and particularly those with limited proficiency in English (Viadero, 2009).

Other issues exist. For instance, in a given year, millions of students take state-mandated tests at an annual cost of billions of dollars, and many educators and parents—as you saw illustrated in Mrs. Palmer's question to Mike—feel that standardized testing is overemphasized (Bushaw & Lopez, 2013).

Finally, cheating is also a problem. For example, one report indicated that teachers in 18 schools in Washington, DC, cheated on students high-stakes tests in 2012 (Brown, 2013), and in 2013, the former superintendent of schools in Atlanta was indicted for racketeering related to a cheating scandal in the district's schools (Winerip, 2013). These are only two examples, and many others exist. Some argue that the pressures involved in high-stakes testing make cheating inevitable (Stanford, 2013).

This discussion answers the first question that we asked at the beginning of the chapter: "How have standards and accountability changed the role of standardized testing?" The weight placed on standardized test results and the influence these results have on students, teachers, and schools are two of the most important changes. As we saw earlier, students' performance on standardized tests are being used to make decisions ranging from grade promotion to graduation from high school.

These uses of standardized tests are significantly different from the way Mike Chavez used the Stanford Achievement Test; he used the results as a basis for making decisions designed to increase his students' learning.

This information addresses the questions we asked in *Ed Psych and You* at the beginning of this section. In this era of standards and accountability, the "quality" of a school is being operationally defined as how well students score on standardized tests, and particularly high-stakes tests. If the students generally score well, it's a good school; if they don't, it isn't. Further, a number of states around our country give schools grades ranging from A to F on the basis of standardized test performance, and state leaders defend the practice, arguing that it "does a good job of driving student improvement" (Smiley, 2014, para. 8). These processes help us begin to understand the expanded role of standardized testing in our nation's schools.

Additional Developments in Standardized Testing

The vast majority of standardized test items use a multiple-choice format, and many of these items are written at a knowledge/recall level. More items that effectively and efficiently assess higher level learning outcomes are needed (Darling-Hammond & Wentworth, 2010).

Professional groups have been working with states to develop tools such as **performance assessments**, direct examinations of student performance on tasks relevant to life outside of school. These items ask test takers to solve real-world problems that involve multiple steps and often require lengthy written responses (Darling-Hammond & Adamson, 2010, 2013). Examples of performance assessment items in different content areas can be found in Table 15.1.

As we might expect, technical problems exist. For example, performance items take longer to administer and are more expensive because scoring the open-ended responses requires highly trained evaluators. Advocates, however, argue that the additional cost is warranted because these tests provide a more accurate picture of student learning (Darling-Hammond & Adamson, 2013).

Benchmark assessments, short tests administered periodically throughout the school year, are additional developments in assessment. These assessments are typically found in math and reading, and, because they are computerized, they can provide immediate feedback that allows teachers to adjust their instruction to student learning needs. They address the complaint that current standardized tests are given infrequently and the results are typically not available to teachers until the school year is over (Herman, Osmundson, & Dietel, 2010; Sparks, 2013).

Computerized adaptive testing programs that adapt to students' ability levels by presenting items that are ideally suited for individual students are additional technology-related innovations in standardized testing. They are intended to address the fact that individual items are often very easy for some students but difficult for others (Davis, 2012; Sparks, 2013). When these programs are used, for instance, students who perform well on items of intermediate difficulty will be presented with more difficult items, whereas those who perform poorly are presented with easier items. Adaptive testing saves time, a major concern with many testing programs, and also prevents students from becoming frustrated

Table 15.1	Performance assessments in different content areas
Content Area	Performance Assessments
Science	Students plan an extended experimental investigation, conduct the research, analyze the results, and write a scientific report.
Technology	In a collaborative project, students create an interactive technology system to monitor the financial dealings of a rock band promoter. Students must research other systems and create one that is user friendly and suitable for the target audience.
Math	Students are asked to plot data on a graph and develop a quadratic equation that matches the graph.
English and Language Arts	Students compare and contrast two works of literature in terms of setting, plot, characters, and the social, cultural, and historical context in which they occur.

Sources: Darling-Hammond & Adamson, 2010, 2013; Herman & Linn, 2013; Pecheone & Kahl, 2011; Picus, Adamson, & Owen, 2010; Schenker, 2013.

or bored with a test. Several states are currently using computerized testing programs, and their use is likely to increase in the future.

Teacher Evaluation and the Accountability Movement

The accountability movement has also changed the way you'll be evaluated when you begin teaching. You may have encountered aspects of this process in your program already, and if you haven't, you probably will. For instance, 47 states either use national tests, such as Praxis, or state tests to ensure that teacher candidates possess essential knowledge and skills before they're licensed (Hightower, 2012).

Standardized test results may even impact the amount of money you earn when you begin teaching. For example, a number of states are considering, or have enacted, legislation tying teacher salaries to their students' scores on high-stakes tests, which could mean that your salary may be linked to your students' test performance through a process called *value-added modeling.*

Value-added modeling is a method of teacher evaluation that measures a teacher's contribution to student learning in a given year by comparing the current test scores of their students to the scores of those same students in previous school years and to the scores of other students in the same grade. When using value-added models, researchers use statistical methods to accommodate extraneous factors, such as student background, ability, and socioeconomic status, in an attempt to determine how much a teacher contributes to students' learning. This contribution is then considered the "value" the teacher added. For example, if a second grader scores at the 50th percentile on a reading test at the beginning of the year and at the 60th percentile at the end of the year, researchers conclude that the gain is a result of the teacher's expertise, and "value" had been added. This approach seeks to isolate the contribution that each teacher provides (the value added) during the year, which can then be compared to the performance of other teachers (Bausell, 2013; Darling-Hammond, Amrein-Beardsley, Haertel, & Rothstein, 2012).

This process isn't as simple as it appears on the surface, however, and value-added models are highly controversial (Martineau, 2010; Sawchuk, 2010). Critics question the assumption that tests can accurately measure what teachers are accomplishing in their classes, arguing that invalid tests necessarily produce invalid value-added measures (Papay, 2011). In addition, test results may not capture important learning outcomes that may show up later, and sometimes much later. We've all had teachers, for example, who presented intriguing ideas and asked thought-provoking questions that only made sense to us after a considerable period of time. And, we've also had teachers whose inspiration had a long-term impact on our motivation and even career choice. Value-added models can't capture these long-term outcomes, critics assert.

The move to publish the results of teacher evaluations based on students' test scores and make these evaluations open to the public—with listings of names of individual teachers in newspaper articles—have added to the controversy (Sawchuk, 2012). (How would you like to have your evaluations made public during your first year of teaching?)

Critics caution that data gathered over several years are often necessary to make valid conclusions about a teacher's performance, and publishing these data indiscriminately could damage individual teachers as well as schools (Darling-Hammond, 2012).

In spite of these controversies, it's likely that you'll be faced with value-added models when you begin teaching. In other words, the way your students perform on standardized tests will be part of your teaching evaluations. You can take steps to adapt to these trends, however. For example, becoming familiar with testing formats and providing your students with practice using them can increase students' scores. Also, knowing what content is being measured on the tests and doing everything you can to ensure that your students have mastered this content will contribute to higher test scores. (This suggestion is different from "teaching to the test," which focuses on specific test items, and provides practice with those items.)

Standardized testing will be a part of reality when you begin teaching. So you need to be as informed as possible about the strengths and limitations of these tests. We examine standardized tests in more detail in the next section.

Ed Psych and You

What standardized tests did you take as you progressed through grades K–12? How well did you do on these tests? How did these tests influence your academic career?

Standardized Tests

Standardized tests are assessment instruments given to large samples of students—nationwide in many cases—under uniform conditions and scored and reported according to uniform procedures. These uniform testing conditions and reporting procedures are the source of the term *standardized*. As we said earlier, we're all familiar with them. We took achievement tests as we moved through elementary school, and the SAT or ACT is a rite of passage from high school to college. And with increased emphasis on accountability, standardized testing has become an even more important part of teachers' and students' lives.

And the impact goes beyond accountability and high-stakes testing. For example, the New York City school system decided to use a standardized test to determine admission to gifted programs for kindergarteners. Parents, eager to have their children in the program, spent $1,000 to prepare their children for the test (Winerip, 2010). Books, test-prep materials, and $145-an-hour tutoring sessions became hot-selling items—all to pass a standardized test for entrance into a special kindergarten program!

Standardized tests are designed to answer questions that teacher-made assessments alone can't, such as:

- How do the students in my class compare with others across the country?
- How well is our curriculum preparing students for college or future training?
- How does a particular student compare to those of similar ability?
- Are students learning essential knowledge and skills that will prepare them for life as well as subsequent learning? (Miller et al., 2013; Brookhart & Nitko, 2015).

To answer these questions, individuals' test scores are compared to the scores of a **norming group**, a representative sample whose scores are compiled for the purpose of national comparisons. The norming group includes students from different geographical regions, private and public schools, boys and girls, and different cultural and ethnic groups (Miller et al., 2013). **National norms** are scores on standardized tests earned by representative groups from around the nation. Individuals' scores are then compared to the national norms.

Now, let's look at important ways that standardized tests are used.

Functions of Standardized Tests

Standardized tests serve three primary functions:

- Assessment and diagnosis of learning
- Selection and placement
- Program evaluation and accountability

ASSESSMENT AND DIAGNOSIS OF LEARNING

From a teacher's perspective, the most important function of standardized testing is to provide an external, objective picture of your students' progress. In Mike's class, for example, David consistently receives A's in reading, but this doesn't tell his parents, Mike and other teachers, or school administrators how he compares to other children at his grade level across the nation. Were his A's due to high achievement or generous grading? Standardized tests help answer this question, and, together with schoolwork, they provide a more complete and accurate picture of student progress.

Standardized tests also help diagnose student strengths and weaknesses (Popham, 2014). For example, after seeing that David scored relatively low in listening, Mike might arrange to schedule a standardized diagnostic test. These tests are usually administered individually, with the goal of obtaining more detailed information about a student's achievement or even determining whether or not a student has an exceptionality or a special learning need.

SELECTION AND PLACEMENT

Selecting and placing students in specialized or limited enrollment programs is another function of standardized tests. For instance, students entering a high school may come from "feeder" middle schools, private schools, and schools outside the district, many with different academic programs. Scores from the math section of a standardized test, for example, can help the math faculty place students in classes that will best match their backgrounds and capabilities. Similarly, teachers often use standardized test results, along with their own assessments, to place students in reading and math groups that best meet student needs.

Standardized test results are also used to make decisions about admission to college or placement in advanced programs, such as programs for the gifted. As you already know, the scores students make on the SAT or ACT are important in determining whether they're accepted by the college of their choice.

PROGRAM EVALUATION AND ACCOUNTABILITY

Providing information about the quality of instructional programs is a third function of standardized tests. For example, if an elementary school moves from a reading program based on writing and children's literature to one that emphasizes phonics and basic skills, the faculty can use standardized test results to assess the effectiveness of this change. And as you saw earlier in the chapter, high-stakes tests are increasingly being used to hold schools, teachers, and students accountable for learning.

Norm- Versus Criterion-Referenced Standardized Tests

Norm-referenced grading—sometimes called "grading on the curve"—compares a student's performance to that of others in a class, while whereas criterion-referenced systems assign grades based on predetermined standards, such as 90+ = A, 80–90 = B, and so on. Similarly, **norm-referenced standardized tests** compare (reference) a student's performance to the performance of others, whereas **criterion-referenced**

standardized tests, sometimes called standards-referenced, content-referenced, or domain-referenced tests, compare performance against a set standard. They may even be called objectives-based tests when the standards are in the form of learning objectives (Miller et al., 2013).

Norm- and criterion-referenced tests differ in the way scores are reported. Norm-referenced scores describe a student's performance compared to peers, so they don't tell us what our students actually know. In Mike's class, for instance, David's percentile rank in reading was 70, which only tells his teacher and parents that he scored as well as, or better than, 70% of the students who took the test; it doesn't give Mike any information about David's specific reading skills. In contrast, criterion-referenced scores compare students' performance to a standard, so they provide information about mastery of specific learning objectives, such as the ability to add two-digit numbers or identify the main idea in a paragraph.

With the current focus on standards and accountability, increased emphasis is being placed on criterion-referenced tests, especially at the state and district levels. Nationally, norm-referenced tests, such as the Stanford Achievement Test that David took, are still popular, because they allow location-to-location comparisons, and the general nature of test content allows them to be used in a wide variety of situations. Both are useful and depend on our assessment goals.

Types of Standardized Tests

Five kinds of standardized tests are commonly used in education.

- Achievement tests
- Diagnostic tests
- Intelligence tests
- Aptitude tests
- Readiness tests

Let's look at them.

ACHIEVEMENT TESTS

Achievement tests, the most widely used type of standardized test, are designed to assess how much students have learned in specific content areas, most commonly reading, language arts, and math, but also in areas such as science, social studies, computer literacy, and critical thinking (Thorndike & Thorndike, 2010). These areas are then usually broken down into descriptions of more specific skills. For example, David's test results included Total Reading, Total Math, Science, Listening, and others. Popular achievement tests include the Iowa Test of Basic Skills, the California Achievement Test, the Stanford Achievement Test, the Comprehensive Test of Basic Skills, and the Metropolitan Achievement Test, as well as statewide assessments developed by different states (Brookhart & Nitko, 2015; Stiggins & Chappuis, 2012). You can simply Google any of these tests if you want to find out more information about them.

Standardized achievement tests typically include batteries of subtests administered over several days. They reflect a curriculum common to most schools, which means that they will assess some, but not all, of the goals of an individual school. This is both a strength and a weakness. Because they are designed for a range of schools, they can be used in a variety of locations, but this "one size fits all" approach may not accurately measure achievement for your specific school or classroom.

The **National Assessment of Educational Progress (NAEP)** is a battery of achievement tests administered periodically to carefully selected samples of students (National Center for Education Statistics, 2014). Called the "Nation's Report Card," the NAEP is designed to provide a comprehensive picture of achievement in students across the country. It does this by strategically sampling students in terms of gender, SES, and race/ethnicity to ensure that the results accurately reflect students' achievement in our nation's schools. No results are provided for individual students, classrooms, or schools, but test scores are provided for specific groups of students such as low-SES females as well as for states and some urban areas.

NAEP tests are given in the 4th, 8th, and 12th grades in math, reading, science, and writing and less frequently in art, civics, economics, geography, and U.S. history. A pilot of a new technology and engineering test is being field tested and will be NAEP's first entirely computer-based test (Sparks, 2012). It will be oriented toward critical thinking and problem solving, with only 20% consisting of concrete facts and information. For example, students might be asked to collaborate with a simulated boss via video conference to improve the life cycle of a household toaster. Future NAEP tests will continue to expand on computer administrations and increased emphasis on performance assessments focusing on application and problem solving.

Because of increased interest in the global economy and how our students are doing compared to students in other countries, NAEP has coordinated its testing efforts in the **Trends in International Mathematics and Science Study (TIMSS)**. Using comparable standardized test score data from other industrialized countries, recent TIMSS data revealed that students in our country lag behind many other countries in the areas of science and mathematics (TIMSS, 2014). For example, American fourth graders scored ninth out of 57 countries in math, and in eighth-grade science, our students ranked 13th, trailing countries such as Singapore and Chinese Taipei. These standardized-based international comparisons have resulted in increased scrutiny of our own educational system, as well as questions about how to import the best educational practices from other countries (Carnoy & Rothstein, 2013; Cavanagh, 2012).

DIAGNOSTIC TESTS

Achievement tests measure students' progress in a range of curriculum areas; **diagnostic tests** are designed to provide a detailed description of a learner's strengths and weaknesses in specific skill areas (Thorndike & Thorndike, 2010). Their use is most common in the primary grades, where instruction is designed to match the developmental levels of children.

Diagnostic tests are usually administered individually, and, compared to achievement tests, they include a larger number of items, use more subtests, and provide scores in more specific areas. A diagnostic test in reading, for example, might measure letter recognition, word analysis skills, sight vocabulary, vocabulary in context, and reading comprehension. The *Detroit Test of Learning Aptitude*, the *Durrell Analysis of Reading Difficulty*, and the *Stanford Diagnostic Reading Test* are popular diagnostic tests.

INTELLIGENCE TESTS

Intelligence tests, also called school ability tests or cognitive ability tests, are standardized tests designed to measure an individual's capacity to acquire and use knowledge, solve problems, and accomplish new tasks. In recent years there has been a trend away from using *intelligence tests* as a label, because the term is often misinterpreted to suggest innate intelligence and because considerable disagreement about what intelligence actually is exists. The two most widely used intelligence tests in the United States are the Stanford-Binet and the Wechsler Scales (Salvia, Ysseldyke, & Bolt, 2013). Let's look at them more closely.

The Stanford-Binet. The Stanford-Binet, currently called the *Stanford-Binet Intelligence Scales, Fifth Edition*, or SB5 (Roid, 2003), is an individually administered test composed of several subtests. It comes in a kit that includes testing materials, such as manipulatives and pictures, together with a test manual. Earlier versions heavily emphasized verbal tasks, but the most recent edition also includes nonverbal knowledge. Some examples of the types of items on the test include:

- *Nonverbal knowledge*, such as explaining an absurdity like a person in a bathing suit sitting in snow.
- *Nonverbal working memory*, such as asking a student to reproduce a display of blocks after a short delay.
- *Verbal knowledge*, for instance, explaining the meaning of common words.
- *Verbal working memory*, for instance, having students identify key words in sentences after a brief delay (Roid, 2003).

The Stanford-Binet is a technically sound instrument that is second in popularity only to the Wechsler scales (described in the next section). It has been revised and renormed a number of times over the years, most recently in 2003, using 4,800 schoolchildren, stratified by economic status, geographic region, and community size. The U.S. Census was used to ensure proportional representation of White, African American, Hispanic, Asian, and Asian/Pacific Islander subcultures (Bain & Allin, 2005).

The Wechsler Scales. Developed by David Wechsler over a period of 40 years, the Wechsler scales are the most popular intelligence tests in use today (Salvia et al., 2013). The three Wechsler tests, aimed at preschool-primary, elementary, and adult populations, have two main parts: verbal and performance.

The Wechsler Intelligence Scale for Children—Fourth Edition is an individually administered intelligence test with 13 subtests, of which 6 are verbal and 7 are performance (Wechsler, 2003). (Table 15.2 outlines some sample subtests.) The performance sections were added in reaction to the strong verbal emphasis of earlier intelligence tests. Like the Stanford-Binet, the Wechsler scales are considered technically sound by testing experts (Salvia et al., 2013).

The Wechsler's two scales, yielding separate verbal and performance scores, provide valuable information to users. For example, a substantially higher score on the performance compared with the verbal scale could indicate a language problem related to poor reading or language-based cultural differences. Because performance subtests demand a minimum of verbal ability, these tasks are helpful in studying learners with disabilities, persons with limited educational background, or students who resist school-like tasks.

APTITUDE TESTS

Although *aptitude* and *intelligence* are often used synonymously, aptitude—the ability to acquire knowledge—is only one characteristic of intelligence. The concept of intelligence encompasses a wider range of cognitive abilities, such as the ability to solve problems and think in the abstract.

As opposed to measuring the general construct of intelligence, aptitude tests attempt to predict future performance in a specific domain, such as success in college. The concept of aptitude is intuitively sensible; for example, people will say, "I just don't have any aptitude for math," implying that their potential for learning math is limited.

Aptitude tests are standardized tests designed to predict the potential for future learning and measure general abilities developed over long periods of time. Aptitude tests are commonly used in selection and placement decisions, and they correlate highly with achievement tests (Miller et al., 2013; Popham, 2014).

The SAT and ACT, both designed to measure students' potential for success in college, are the two most common aptitude tests in use today. This potential is heavily influenced by

Table 15.2	Sample items from the Wechsler Intelligence Scale for Children

Verbal Section

Subtest	Description/Examples
Information	This subtest taps general knowledge common to American culture: 1. How many wings does a bird have? 2. How many nickels make a dime? 3. What is steam made of? 4. Who wrote "Tom Sawyer"? 5. What is *pepper*?
Arithmetic	This subtest is a test of basic mathematical knowledge and skills, including counting and addition through division: 1. Sam had three pieces of candy and Joe gave him four more. How many pieces of candy did Sam have altogether? 2. Three women divided eighteen golf balls equally among themselves. How many golf balls did each person receive? 3. If two buttons cost 15¢, what will be the cost of a dozen buttons?
Similarities	This subtest is designed to measure abstract and logical thinking through use of analogies: 1. In what way are a lion and a tiger alike? 2. In what way are a saw and a hammer alike? 3. In what way are an hour and a week alike? 4. In what way are a circle and a triangle alike?

Performance Section

Subtest	Description/Examples
Picture completion	Students are shown a picture with elements missing, which they are required to identify. This subtest measures general knowledge as well as visual comprehension.
Block design	This subtest focuses on a number of abstract figures. Designed to measure visual-motor coordination, it requires students to match patterns displayed by the examiner.

Picture Completion

Block Design

Source: Simulated Items similar to those found in the *Wechsler Intelligence Scale for Children, Third Edition* (WISC®-III). Copyright © 1990 by NCS Pearson, Inc. Reproduced with permission. All rights reserved.

experience, however, and classroom-related knowledge, particularly in language and mathematics, is essential for success on the tests.

The SAT was revised in 2005 when a writing component was added and the point scale was increased to 2,400 from the original 1,600. However, in 2014 the College Board, developers of the SAT, acknowledged that the writing component hasn't contributed to the predictive power of the test and announced an additional revision of the exam (Jaschik, 2014). Some of the changes include the following:

- The writing component will be revised and made optional.
- The point scale will return to 1,600.
- Points will no longer be deducted for incorrect answers on the multiple-choice portion of the test.
- The vocabulary portion will be revised to include terms believed to be more widely used in college and in the workplace.

These revisions are scheduled to take effect in 2016.

The SAT has come under increasing criticism in recent years, and even David Coleman, president of the College Board, criticized his own test (the SAT) and its main rival, the ACT, saying that both had become disconnected from the work of high schools in our country (Lewin, 2014). Other critics go further, arguing that high school grades are better predictors of college success. They further argue that the SAT discriminates against students who come from low-income families that can't afford the expensive test preparation many more advantaged students use to score well on the exam (Balf, 2014; FairTest, 2014). In spite of these criticisms, aptitude tests, such as the SAT and ACT, will likely remain a rite of passage for students in the foreseeable future.

READINESS TESTS

Readiness tests are standardized tests designed to assess the degree to which children are prepared for an academic or preacademic program (Miller et al., 2013; Salvia et al., 2013). They are most often used to assess children's readiness for academic work in kindergarten or first grade. In this regard, they have qualities of both aptitude and achievement tests. They are similar to aptitude tests in that they are designed to assess a student's potential for future learning. However, most readiness tests are narrower, measuring the extent to which students have mastered basic concepts in a certain domain. For example, a preschool readiness test might measure students' understanding of basic concepts such as *up* and *down*, *left* and *right*, or *big* and *small*, which form the foundation for reading and math. This is what makes them similar to achievement tests.

Readiness tests, like other standardized tests, can provide valuable information for educational decision making, but scores on them should not be used as the only criterion for assessing a child's readiness for school. Virtually every five- or six-year-old can benefit from school experiences, and observations of a child's ability to function in a school setting should also be a part of the assessment process.

Let's return to the questions we asked in *Ed Psych and You* earlier. Almost certainly, you took a number of standardized achievement tests, such as the Stanford Achievement Test David Palmer took. It's also likely that you took several state-sponsored achievement tests, designed to measure the extent you had mastered state standards. Both types of tests likely influenced the reading and math groups you were assigned to. You probably also took either the SAT or ACT when you applied for admission to college, and you may also have taken a high-stakes test in your state that influenced whether or not you were allowed to graduate from high school with a standard diploma. The fact that you're in college and taking this course suggests that you performed well on these tests, but this isn't the case for all students. As educators we need to be careful about the decisions we make on the basis of standardized test scores.

Evaluating Standardized Tests: Validity Revisited

Test validity is important to you and other teachers because you're the major consumers of standardized test results. Let's look at how validity can influence your classroom decisions, revisiting Mike Chavez, the teacher in the case study at the beginning of the chapter.

> Mike has been asked to serve on a district-wide committee to consider a new standardized achievement battery for the elementary grades. His job is to get feedback from the faculty at his school about the California Achievement Test as an alternative to the Stanford Achievement Test, the test they're now using.
>
> After providing an overview of the tests during a faculty meeting, Mike asks if people have questions.
>
> "How much problem solving does the California Achievement Test cover?" a fifth-grade teacher asks.
>
> "We're moving our language arts curriculum more in the direction of writing. Does the new test emphasize writing?" a second-grade teacher also asks.
>
> As the discussion continues, a confused colleague wonders out loud, "Which is better? That's really what we're here for. How about a simple answer?"

Mike couldn't offer a simple answer, not because he was unprepared, but instead because he was asked to make judgments about validity, which is the degree to which an assessment actually measures what it is supposed to measure (Miller et al., 2013). When we create our own tests, we ensure validity by aligning the test with our learning objectives. Standardized tests are already constructed, so you must judge only the suitability of a test for a specific purpose. (A complete review of more than 1,000 standardized tests can be found in *The Eighteenth Mental Measurements Yearbook* [Spies, Carlson, & Geisinger, 2011].) Validity, in this case, involves the appropriate use of a test, not the design of the test itself.

Experts describe three kinds of standardized test validity—*content, predictive*, and *construct*—and each provides a different perspective on the issue of appropriate use.

CONTENT VALIDITY

Content validity refers to a test's ability to accurately sample the content taught and measure learners' understanding of it. It is determined by comparing test content with curriculum objectives, and it is a primary concern when considering standardized achievement tests (Miller et al., 2013). The question Mike was asked about which test was "better" addresses content validity. The "better" test is the one with the closer match between your school's curriculum and the content of the test.

PREDICTIVE VALIDITY

Predictive validity is the measure of a test's ability to gauge future performance (Miller et al., 2013). It is central to the SAT and ACT, which are designed to measure a student's potential for doing college work, and it is also the focus of tests that gauge students' readiness for academic tasks in the early elementary grades.

Predictive validity is usually quantified by correlating two variables, such as a standardized test score and student grades. For example, a correlation of .47 exists between the SAT and freshman college grades (FairTest, 2008). High school grades are the only predictor that is better (a correlation of .54).

Why isn't the correlation between standardized tests and college performance higher? The primary reason is that the SAT and ACT are designed to predict "general readiness," but other factors such as motivation, study habits, and prior knowledge also affect performance (Popham, 2014).

CONSTRUCT VALIDITY

Construct validity is an indicator of the logical connection between a test and what it is designed to measure. The concept of construct validity is somewhat abstract, but is important in understanding the total concept of validity. It answers the question, "Do these items actually assess the ideas the test is designed to measure?" For instance, many of the items on the SAT are designed to tap the ability to do abstract thinking about words and numbers, tasks that students are likely to face in their college experience. Because of this, the test has construct validity.

Understanding and Interpreting Standardized Test Scores

One of the major advantages of standardized tests is the fact that they're given to thousands of students, which allows comparisons with students across the United States and around the world. Because the amount of information these tests provide is enormous, test publishers use statistical methods to summarize results. Teachers need to understand these results to use them effectively in making professional decisions about their students. We examine these statistics in the following sections.

Descriptive Statistics

As an introduction to the use of statistics in summarizing information, take a look at Table 15.3, which contains scores made by two classes of 31 students on a 50-item test, both ranked from the highest to lowest score. (As you examine this information, keep in mind that a standardized test would have a sample much larger than 31 students and would contain a larger number of items. We are using a class-size example here for the sake of illustration.)

As you see, a simple array of scores can be cumbersome and not very informative, even when the scores are ranked. We need more efficient ways of summarizing the information.

FREQUENCY DISTRIBUTIONS

A frequency distribution is a distribution of test scores that shows a simple count of the number of people who obtained each score. It can be represented in several ways, one of which is a graph with the possible scores on the horizontal (x) axis and the frequency, or the number of students who got each score, on the vertical (y) axis.

The frequency distributions for our two classes are shown in Figure 15.1. Although this information is still in rough form, we already begin to see differences between the two classes. For instance, there is a wider range of scores in the first class than in the second, and the scores are more nearly clustered near the middle of the second distribution. Beyond this qualitative description, however, the distributions aren't particularly helpful. We need a better way to summarize the information. Measures of central tendency do this.

MEASURES OF CENTRAL TENDENCY

Measures of central tendency—the mean, median, and mode—are quantitative descriptions of a group's performance as a whole. In a distribution of scores, the mean is the average score, the median is the middle score in the distribution, and the mode is the most frequent score.

To obtain a mean, we simply add the scores and divide by the number of scores. As it turns out, both distributions in Table 15.3 have a mean of 42 (1,302/31). The mean is one indicator of how each group performed as a whole.

Table 15.3	Scores of two classes on a 50-item test
Class #1	Class #2
50	48
49	47
49	46
48	46
47	45
47	45
46	44 ⎤
46	44 ⎥
45	44 ⎬ mode
45	44 ⎥
45	44 ⎦
44 ⎤	43
44 ⎥	43
44 ⎬ mode	43
44 ⎦	43
43—median	42—median & mean
42—mean	42
41	42
41	42
40	41
40	41
39	41
39	40
38	40
37	39
37	39
36	38
35	38
34	37
34	36
33	35

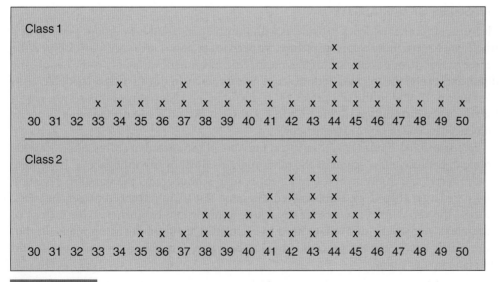

Figure 15.1

Frequency distribution for two classes on a 50-item test

Ed Psych and You

When you take your first job after college, which of the following would you prefer: A salary that matches the *average* salary of people in our country, or a salary that matches the *median* (middle) salary of people in our country? Why?

The median for the first distribution is 43, because half the scores (15) fall equal to or above 43, and the other half are equal to or below 43. Using the same process, we find that the median for the second distribution is 42.

The median is useful when extremely high or low scores skew the mean and give a false picture of the sample. For example, you commonly hear or read demographic statistics such as "The median income for families of four in this country went from . . . in 2010 to . . . in 2015." The median income is reported because a few multimillion-dollar incomes would make the mean quite high and would give an artificially rosy picture of typical families' standards of living. The median, in contrast, is not affected by these extremes and provides a more realistic picture. The median serves the same function when used with test scores.

Looking once more at the two samples, we can see that the most frequent score for each is 44, which is the mode. Small samples, such as those here, often have more than one mode, resulting in bimodal or even trimodal distributions.

Using our measures of central tendency, we see that the two groups of scores are much alike: They have the same mean, nearly the same median, and the same mode. As you saw from examining the frequency distribution, however, this doesn't give us a complete picture. We also need a measure of their variability, or *spread,* which we discuss in the next section.

Before we do, let's return to the questions we asked earlier in *Ed Psych and You.* You would be better off if your first job paid mean (average) salary in our country, which in 2011 was about $41,000. By comparison, the median salary was close to $27,000 in the United States (Social Security Administration, 2014). Here again we can see how a few wealthy billionaires at the upper end can skew the picture.

MEASURES OF VARIABILITY

Measures of central tendency provide us with information about how groups perform as a whole, but to get a more complete picture, we need to see how scores vary. **Variability** is the degree of spread, or deviation from the mean. One measure of variability is the **range**, the distance between the top and bottom score. For instance, in our first class (in Table 15.3) the range is 17, and in the second it's 13, confirming the wider range of scores we saw in the frequency distribution (in Figure 15.1). Although easy to compute, the range is overly influenced by one or more extreme scores.

The **standard deviation**, a statistical measure of the spread of scores, addresses this problem, because a few scores at the outer margins don't overly influence it. If we were to administer an achievement test to an entire high school grade, the standard deviation would be larger than if we administered the same test to an advanced placement class, because the variability of scores for the whole grade would be greater. With the use of computers, you will be unlikely to need to calculate a standard deviation manually, but we're briefly describing the procedure here to help you understand the concept. To find the standard deviation:

1. Calculate the mean.
2. Subtract the mean from each of the individual scores.

3. Square each of these values. (This eliminates negative numbers.)
4. Add the squared values.
5. Divide by the total number of scores (31 in our samples).
6. Take the square root.

In our classroom samples, the standard deviations are 4.8 and 3.1, respectively. We saw from merely observing the two distributions that the first was more spread out, and the standard deviation provides a quantitative measure of that spread.

THE NORMAL DISTRIBUTION

Standardized tests are administered to large (in the hundreds of thousands or even millions) samples of students, and the scores often approximate a normal distribution. To understand this concept, look again at our two distributions in Figure 15.1 and then focus specifically on the second one. If we drew a line over the top of the frequency distribution, it would appear as shown in Figure 15.2.

Now imagine a very large sample of scores, such as we would find from a typical standardized test. The curve would approximate the one shown in Figure 15.3. This is a **normal distribution**, a distribution of scores in which the mean, median, and mode are equal and the scores distribute themselves symmetrically in a bell-shaped curve. Many large samples of human characteristics, such as height and weight, tend to distribute themselves this way, as do the results from large samples of most standardized tests.

The sample of scores in Figure 15.2 has both a mean and median of 42, but a mode of 44, so its measures of central tendency don't quite fit the normal distribution. Also, as we see from the normal distribution in Figure 15.3, 68% of all the scores fall within 1 standard deviation from the mean, but in our sample distribution, about 71% of the scores are within 1 standard deviation above and below the mean. Our samples aren't normal distributions, which is typical of the smaller samples found in classrooms.

Interpreting Standardized Test Results

Using our two small samples, we have illustrated techniques that statisticians use to summarize standardized test scores. Again, keep in mind that data gathered from standardized tests come from hundreds of thousands of students instead of the small number in our illustrations. When standardized tests are used, comparing students from different schools, districts, states, and even countries is an important goal. To make these comparisons, and depending on the test, raw scores, percentile rank, percentile bands, stanines, grade equivalents, and standard scores are used. For example, the home report Mrs. Palmer received included percentile ranks and percentile bands. We look at these ways of describing test results in the following sections.

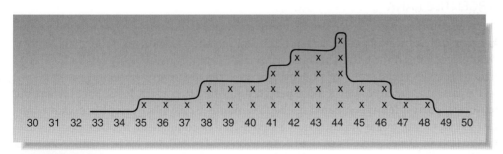

Figure 15.2

Frequency distribution for the second class

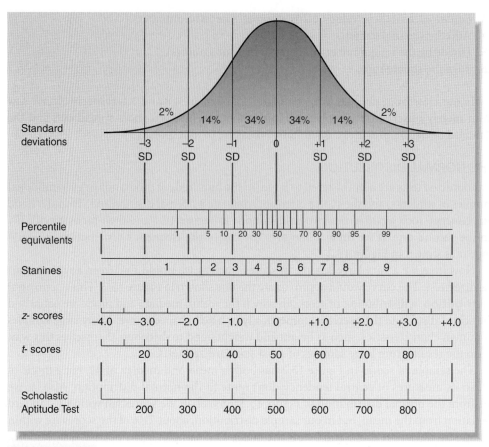

Figure 15.3

Normal distribution

RAW SCORES

All standardized tests are based on **raw scores**, simply the number of items an individual answered correctly on a standardized test or subtest. For example, the Stanford Achievement Test David took had 80 total items in math, and David answered 56 of them correctly, so his raw score for that subtest is 56. (These results were reported to Mike, as David's teacher, but they weren't sent to David's parents.)

The raw score doesn't tell us much, however, until we compare his score to others. Percentile ranks, stanines, grade equivalents, and standard scores help us do that.

PERCENTILE RANK

The **percentile rank (PR)** represents the percentage of students in the norming sample that scored at or below a particular raw score. For instance, David's raw score of 56 in Total Math placed him in the 64th percentile nationally. That means his score was as high as or higher than 64% of the scores of students who took the test across the nation.

Parents and students often confuse percentiles with percentages. Percentages reflect the number of correct items compared to the total number possible. Percentile rank, in contrast, is a description that indicates how a student did in comparison to other students taking the test. So Dave's percentage right score was 70% (56/80), but his percentile score was 64. The two measures provide us with different types of information.

Percentiles are used because they are simple and straightforward. However, they are *rankings*, and the differences between the ranks are not equal. For instance, in our first distribution of 31 students, a score of 48 would be in the 90th percentile, 46 would be in the 80th, 44 would be in the 60th, and 43 would be the 50th percentile. In this sample, the difference between scores representing the 90th and 80th percentiles is twice as great (2 points) as the difference between scores representing the 60th and 50th percentiles (1 point). With large samples, this difference is even more pronounced. Students who score at the extremes in the sample vary more from their counterparts than those who score near the middle of the distribution. For example, in Figure 15.3 we see that the range of scores from the 50th to the 60th percentile is much smaller than the range from the 90th to the 99th percentile.

Percentile bands are ranges of percentile scores on standardized tests, and they were included in the home report David's mother received. The advantage of a percentile band is that it takes into account the possibility of measurement error (McMillan, 2011). Instead of a single percentile, the band is a range of percentile scores within which an individual's test performance is likely to fall. In this respect, percentile bands function somewhat like stanines, which we discuss next.

STANINES

The stanine is another commonly used way to describe standardized test scores. A stanine, or "standard nine," describes an individual's standardized test performance using a scale ranging from 1 to 9 points. Stanine 5 is in the center of the distribution and includes all the scores within one fourth of a standard deviation on either side of the mean. Stanines 4, 3, and 2 are each a band of scores, one half a standard deviation in width, extending below stanine 5. Stanines 6, 7, and 8, also a half standard deviation in width, extend above stanine 5. Stanines 1 and 9 cover the tails of the distribution. A student's score that falls 1 standard deviation above the mean will be in stanine 7; a student's score 2 standard deviations above the mean will be in stanine 9. Figure 15.3 shows how stanines correspond to other measures we've discussed.

Stanines are widely used because they're simple, and they encourage teachers and parents to interpret scores based on a possible range, instead of fine distinctions that may be artificial (McMillan, 2011). For instance, a score in the 57th percentile may be the result of 1 or 2 extra points on a subtest compared to a score in the 52nd percentile, and the student may have guessed the answer correctly, so the difference between the two wouldn't be meaningful. Both scores fall in stanine 5, however. Because it describes performance as a range of possible scores, the stanine is probably a more realistic indicator of performance. Reducing the scores to a 9-point band sacrifices information, however, so it is important to keep the advantages and disadvantages of stanines in mind as you use these to help parents and students interpret standardized test scores.

GRADE EQUIVALENTS

The grade equivalent is a score determined by comparing an individual's score to the scores of students in a particular age group, and it is another common way test results are described. For instance, David's grade equivalent for Total Math was 5.5. That means that he scored as well on the test as the average score for those students taking the test who are in the fifth month of the fifth grade.

This does not imply that David, a fourth grader, should be in the fifth grade. Grade equivalents can be misleading because they oversimplify results and suggest comparisons that aren't necessarily valid. A grade equivalent of 5.5 tells us that David is somewhat advanced in math. It doesn't suggest that he should be promoted to fifth grade, and it doesn't necessarily suggest that he should be working with fifth graders. Because of the possibility of misinterpretation, some standardized tests no longer use grade equivalents (Miller et al., 2013; Salvia et al., 2013).

STANDARD SCORES

As you saw in our discussion of percentiles, differences in raw scores don't result in comparable differences in the percentile rank. For instance, you saw that it took only a 1-point difference—43 compared with 42—to move from the 50th to the 60th percentile, but it took a 2-point difference—48 compared with 46—to move from the 80th to the 90th percentile in our distribution in Figure 15.2. To deal with this type of discrepancy, test developers use standard scores. A **standard score** is a description of performance on a standardized test that uses the standard deviation as the basic unit (McMillan, 2011). Standardized test makers use the mean and standard deviation to report standard scores.

The **z-score**, the number of standard deviation units from the mean, is one type of standard score. A z-score of 2 is 2 standard deviations above the mean, for example, and a z-score of −1 is 1 standard deviation below the mean.

The **t-score** is a standard score that defines the mean as 50 and the standard deviation as 10. A t-score of 70 would be 2 standard deviations above the mean and would correspond to a z-score of 2.

Standard scores such as z-scores and t-scores are useful because they make comparisons convenient. Because they are based on equal units of measurement throughout the distribution, intergroup and intertest comparisons are possible.

SCALED SCORES

When you take a standardized test, somewhere on it you'll see a label, such as "Form A." Because these tests are repeatedly given to large numbers of people, the content of the test, over time, becomes "exposed," that is, test takers remember some of the questions and pass the information along to future test takers (Tan & Michel, 2011). This sharing of information reduces validity, so developers create different "forms" of the test to deal with the issue. As a result, people taking the test at different times may take different forms of the test, or people taking the test at the same time may be given different forms to address concerns about security.

Even though developers of standardized tests adhere to strict test specifications, it's virtually impossible to create different forms of tests that are exactly equal in difficulty (Tan & Michel, 2011). So, percent-correct scores or raw scores might not provide accurate comparisons of different test takers' performance. For instance, a student getting 70% correct on an easier form may actually have less knowledge or skill than a student getting 60% correct on a harder form. Similarly, if two students get the same raw score on two different forms, the one taking the harder form is demonstrating greater knowledge and skills.

In an effort to ensure that results reported from different forms represent the same level of performance, standardized testing programs report **scaled scores**. These scores are obtained by statistically adjusting and converting raw scores to a common scale in an effort to accommodate differences in difficulty among different forms of the test. For instance, a student taking an easier form of the test would need to get a slightly higher raw score to achieve the same scaled score as a student who took a harder form of the test. This effort to ensure that scores accurately represent test takers' performance is the reason standardized test results are commonly reported as scaled scores.

STANDARD ERROR OF MEASUREMENT

Although standardized tests are technically sophisticated, like all tests they contain measurement error; scores represent only an approximation of a student's "true" score. Hypothetically, if we could give a student the same test over and over, for example, and the student neither gained nor lost any knowledge, we would find that the scores would vary. If we averaged those scores, we would have an estimate of the student's "true" score. A **true score** is the hypothetical average of an individual's scores if repeated testing under ideal conditions were possible. An estimate of the true score is obtained using the **standard error of measurement**, the range of scores within which an individual's true score is likely to fall. This range is sometimes termed the *confidence interval, score band*, or *profile band*. For example, suppose Ben has a raw score of 46 and Kim has a raw score of 52 on a test with a standard error of 4. This means that Ben's true score is between 42 and 50, and Kim's is between 48 and 56. At first glance, Kim appears to have scored significantly higher than Ben, but considering the standard error, their scores may be equal, or Ben's true score may even be higher than Kim's. Understanding standard error is important when we make decisions based on standardized tests. For instance, it would be unwise to place Ben and Kim in different ability groups based solely on the results illustrated here.

In this section we described the different ways that standardized tests are reported, and this section also addressed the questions we asked in *Ed Psych and You* at the beginning of the section. Average is often defined in terms of the mean, a measure of central tendency. Average is where most students are—both in terms of intelligence and achievement. However, this single score, or series of scores, fails to capture the many ways that students are unique and different. Keep this in mind as you interpret the standardized test scores of your students.

Diversity and Standardized Testing

One of the most volatile controversies in standardized testing involves critics' claims that the tests are biased against members of cultural minorities (Freedle, 2010; Santelices & Wilson, 2010). This is particularly true for Hispanic and African American students who,

Classroom **Connections**

Using Standardized Tests Effectively in Classrooms

1. The validity of a standardized achievement test depends on the match between learning objectives and test content. Carefully analyze results to increase instructional alignment.

   ■ **Elementary:** A fourth-grade team goes over the previous year's test scores to identify areas in the curriculum that need greater attention.

   ■ **Middle School:** The math teachers in a middle school go over standardized results item by item. Seeing that a large number of students missed a particular item, the teachers plan to place more emphasis on this topic in their instruction.

   ■ **High School:** English teachers in an urban high school use a scoring rubric to analyze student scores on a statewide writing assessment. They share the rubric with their students and use it to help them improve their writing skills.

2. The value of standardized test scores to consumers depends, in large part, on the extent to which they understand the results. Communicate test results clearly to both students and their caregivers.

   ■ **Elementary:** Third-grade teachers in an urban elementary school prepare a handout that explains standardized test scores including examples and answers to frequently asked questions. They use the handout in parent–teacher conferences.

   ■ **Middle School:** A middle school team integrates standardized test scores into a comprehensive packet of assessment materials. When they meet with students and their caregivers, they use the information to identify individual student's areas of strength and those that need improvement.

   ■ **High School:** During an orientation meeting with parents, members of an English Department first give an overview of tests that students will encounter in high school and describe how scores are reported. During individual meetings with parents, teachers provide specific information about individuals' scores.

on average, consistently score lower on standardized tests than do White and Asian students (National Assessment of Educational Progress, 2014). And because scoring below established minimums on high-stakes standardized tests can result in grade retention or failure to graduate from high school, the controversy has increased (Popham, 2014). A number of cases have actually gone to the courts, and the validity of tests for cultural minorities and the extent to which students have had the opportunity to learn test content have been key issues (Schimmel, Stellman, Conlon, & Fischer, 2015). The essential question is, as standardized tests are increasingly used to make important decisions about students, will members of cultural minorities be treated fairly?

As you would expect, advocates and critics disagree, and two important issues related to standardized testing with minority students remain unresolved (Salvia et al., 2013). The first is whether the tests are valid and reliable enough to justify using results to make decisions about students' academic careers and lives. The second relates to technical problems involved in testing members of minorities and particularly students who speak English as a second language. Significantly, experts and professional organizations including the American Educational Research Association, the American Psychological Association, and the National Council on Measurement in Education are increasingly critical of making decisions about promotion or graduation on the basis of one test score (American Educational Research Association, American Psychological Association, & National Council on Measurement in Education, 1999).

Ed Psych and You

Did you ever take a standardized test where certain parts of the content were unfamiliar to you? Did you ever encounter items on a standardized test that contained vocabulary that you didn't understand? What did these mismatches between test content and you say about you, and what did these mismatches say about the test?

Student Diversity and Assessment Bias

Because of the controversies surrounding standardized testing, increased attention is being focused on the issue of assessment bias. **Assessment bias** is a form of discrimination that occurs when a test or other assessment instrument unfairly penalizes a group of students because of their gender, ethnicity, race, or socioeconomic status (SES).

Measurement experts identify three types of assessment bias that detract from validity (Miller et al., 2013):

- Bias in content
- Bias in testing procedures
- Bias in test interpretation and use

As you study these topics, remember that mean differences between groups do not necessarily indicate bias. Underlying causes, such as poverty or inadequate educational opportunities, may account for these differences (Brookhart & Nitko, 2015).

BIAS IN CONTENT

Critics contend that the content of standardized tests is geared to White, middle-class American students, and members of cultural minorities are disadvantaged by this content. For example, the following item is drawn from a standardized science test used to measure the knowledge of sixth graders:

> If you wanted to find out if a distant planet had mountains or rivers on it, which of the following tools should you use?
>
> a. binoculars
> b. microscope
> c. telescope
> d. camera (Popham, 2004, p. 48)

Performance on this item is likely to be influenced by SES and a student's exposure to high-cost items like microscopes and telescopes.

Bias can also occur in word problems (Miller et al., 2013). For example:

> Derek Jeter is batting .310 after 100 trips to the plate. In his next three times at bat, he gets a single, double, and home run. What is his batting average now?

This item requires that students know how batting averages are computed and whether doubles and home runs count more than singles. Word problems can also be biased if students have trouble reading the item because of limited skills with English.

Mismatches between test content and the cultural backgrounds of students can also result in content bias. For example, students from a remote Eskimo community were asked the following question on a standardized vocabulary test: "Which of the following would most likely take you to the hospital if you got hurt?" The "correct" answer was *ambulance*, but Eskimo students replied airplane because that is how people in their village receive emergency medical aid (Platt, 2004).

BIAS IN TESTING PROCEDURES

Because students from different cultures respond differently to testing situations, bias can also occur in testing procedures. For example, in one study researchers found that Navajo students were unaware of the consequences of poor test performance, instead treating tests as game-like events (Deyhle, 1987). Other research has found that some minority students believe tests will be biased, and as a result they don't try to do well on them (Morgan & Mehta, 2004; Ryan & Ryan, 2005).

BIAS IN TEST INTERPRETATION AND USE

Bias can also occur in the ways test results are interpreted and used. Experts are concerned about the adverse effects of testing on minority students' progress through public schools and entrance into college. Evidence suggests that test results are sometimes used in ways that discriminate against members of cultural minorities and those who do not speak English as a first language. For example, a historic study of 812 students classified as being "mentally retarded" found 300% more Mexican Americans and 50% more African Americans than would be expected from their numbers in the general population, and the study population had 40% fewer Anglo Americans than would be expected. Further, people in lower income brackets were overrepresented, whereas people in the upper brackets were underrepresented (Mercer, 1973). More recent research suggests that this problem still exists (Heward, 2013).

Standardized Testing and English Learners

Standardized testing poses special challenges for students who are English learners (ELs) and their teachers. Research indicates that students whose first language isn't English consistently score lower than other students on both standardized achievement and intelligence tests (Robinson, 2010). This isn't surprising, because most standardized tests are developed for native English speakers and depend heavily on English language skills. This presents a problem for teachers who are asked to use standardized test scores in their work with students who are ELs, because students must be able to read and understand English if a test written in English is to measure performance accurately (Echevarria & Graves, 2015).

The problem of standardized testing with limited-English speakers is not new, but its importance has increased with the current emphasis on accountability. The No Child Left Behind legislation has required that all students who are ELs and have been in this country for three consecutive years be tested in reading and language arts using a test written in English (Forte, 2010; Robinson, 2010).

Language is not the only reason for the poor performance of students who are ELs on standardized tests. These students tend to come from lower SES families, and research consistently demonstrates the adverse effects of poverty on achievement (Macionis, 2013). In addition, students who are ELs typically attend poorer schools, with fewer resources and greater numbers of unqualified or inexperienced teachers (Brimley, Verstegen, & Garfield, 2012; Kozol, 2005).

Researchers have identified additional factors influencing the performance of students who are ELs on standardized tests, all related to the linguistic complexity of the tests. In addition to the fact that the tests are administered in English, the tests contain many technical terms such as *ion*, *colonization*, and *simile* that aren't commonly used in conversation (Echevarria & Graves, 2015). This puts students who are ELs at a disadvantage, because they acquire language proficiency through everyday conversation. In addition, standardized tests are timed, placing an additional cognitive burden on EL test takers.

TESTING ACCOMMODATIONS FOR ENGLISH LEARNERS

Accommodations to address these problems focus on either the test itself or testing procedures. For example, attempts to modify the test have either attempted to translate the test into students' first language or simplify vocabulary or sentence structures, such as shortening sentences or converting from passive to active voice (Maxwell, 2013). Technical and logistical problems exist with these efforts, however. For example, testing experts question whether the modified and original forms of the test are comparable, which raises questions of validity (Maxwell, 2013), and it isn't economically feasible to translate tests into all the native languages that exist in some urban districts. Even when students speak a common language, cultural differences, such as variations in Spanish dialects spoken in Spain, Mexico, Cuba, and Puerto Rico, make it difficult to construct a test that is culturally and linguistically meaningful (Echevarria & Graves, 2015; Popham, 2014).

Attempts to increase validity through modifications of testing procedures, such as providing regular and bilingual dictionaries and allowing more time for students who are ELs, appear more promising (Abedi & Gándara, 2006). Providing more time, especially when combined with test-specific glossaries, appears to be the most feasible accommodation.

Accommodating Students with Disabilities

In the United States, the Individuals with Disabilities Education Act (IDEA) requires appropriate accommodations for students with disabilities. Many of these testing accommodations are similar to those for students who are ELs. The most common accommodations include:

- Modify the presentation format, such as reading questions out loud when reading is an issue.

- Modify the response format (e.g., allow students to dictate their answers when writing is a problem).
- Provide extra time for tests.
- Administer tests in smaller time increments to prevent fatigue or frustration.
- Administer tests individually or in separate, quieter settings free from distractions (American Educational Research Association et al., 1999; Samuels, 2013; Turnbull, Turnbull, Wehmeyer, & Shogren, 2013).

Modifying standardized assessment procedures can alter the validity of test results, however, so we need to keep this possibility in mind.

Teaching test-taking strategies is a second way to accommodate students with disabilities (Mastropieri & Scruggs, 2014). These strategies include:

- Learn to use separate bubble answer sheets.
- Sort problems by type and difficulty level, and begin with easier ones first.
- Underline key words in problems, and draw diagrams and pictures.
- Eliminate obvious wrong options, and guess where appropriate.

To be effective, these strategies need to be taught through modeling and practiced thoroughly, well before any high-stakes tests are attempted.

This section addresses the questions we asked in *Ed Psych and You* about your own experiences with standardized testing. We've all been in testing situations in which we didn't know some of the answers or didn't even understand the question. This may have resulted from our simply not understanding the topic. However, at other times it may have been the result of faulty items that failed to adequately assess our knowledge. Assessment bias exists, and it can negatively influence both our students and us. We describe ways to minimize these negative effects in the next section.

Educational Psychology and Teaching: Your Role in Standardized Testing

You will play a central role in ensuring that standardized test scores reflect what your students have actually learned. Given current demographic trends in the United States, you almost certainly will have members of cultural minorities in your classes, and some will speak a native language other than English. In addition, you will need to communicate test results to students and their caregivers and use the results to improve your instruction. The following guidelines can assist you in performing these essential functions:

1. Prepare students so that test results accurately reflect what they know and can do.
2. Make accommodations, if possible, for members of cultural minorities and students who are not native English speakers.
3. Administer tests in ways that maximize student performance.
4. Communicate results to students and their caregivers.

Let's see how these guidelines operate in classrooms.

Preparing Students. As you saw earlier in the chapter, the validity of standardized tests depends on the match between the test and the purpose for using it. With the present emphasis on district, state, and even nationally mandated tests, it will be your responsibility to ensure that students have learned the content covered on the tests.

Ensuring that students are prepared depends in large part on the effectiveness of our instruction. Students should have studied in detail the content covered on the test, and they should have opportunities to practice the skills measured on the test using a format similar to the one they'll encounter on the test (Miller et al., 2013). For example, teachers commonly assess spelling by giving quizzes in which students are asked to correctly spell lists of words. However, when spelling is assessed on standardized tests, students are given a list of four closely matched words and asked to select the one spelled correctly. To do well on these items, students need practice with this format.

Students should also be taught general test-taking strategies. These strategies are particularly important for members of cultural minorities, students whose first language isn't English, and students from low-SES backgrounds. Effective test-taking strategies for standardized tests include:

- Read and follow all directions.
- Determine how questions will be scored, such as whether penalties exist for errors in spelling or grammar in written responses, or for guessing on multiple-choice items.
- Eliminate options on multiple-choice items, and make informed guesses with remaining items (if guessing isn't penalized).
- Pace themselves so they have enough time to answer all the questions.
- Answer easier questions first, and go back to check answers if time permits.
- Check to be sure that responses on the answer sheet match the numbers in the test booklet (Brookhart & Nitko, 2015).

Accommodating Cultural Minorities and English Learners. As you saw in earlier sections, standardized tests often use technical language that is infrequently used in everyday conversation. Providing concrete examples of technical terms during instruction and emphasizing the essential characteristics of important concepts can help accommodate differences in background knowledge. This is particularly important for members of cultural minorities and non-native English speakers.

Also, providing dictionaries and allowing extra time for these students are effective accommodations if testing procedures allow it.

Administering Tests. To ensure that standardized tests yield valid results, they must be uniformly administered. Developers typically provide detailed instructions about how their tests should be administered (Brookhart & Nitko, 2015). Manuals specify the allotted time for each test and subtest—which should be written on the board for students—and provide scripts for introducing and describing the subtests. If scripts and time frames aren't followed precisely, the results can be invalid.

Interpreting Results. Once results are returned, you will be responsible for explaining them to students and their caregivers and using them to improve your instruction. To identify areas that may need improvement, you might compare the scores of one year's class with those in earlier years.

Standardized test scores should be combined with other information about students when communicating results, and you should emphasize that the scores are only approximations of student capabilities. And to the extent possible, avoid technical language in discussing results.

Testing experts are clear on the following point: No single test should be used as the basis for educational decisions about individual students (Miller et al., 2013). At the school level, you can help ensure that alternate data sources such as grades, work samples, and classroom observations are used in making decisions about individual students. At the policy level, you can become an advocate for the use of comprehensive assessment data in making these decisions.

Classroom **Connections**

Eliminating Test Bias in Classrooms

1. Test validity can be compromised when cultural factors unfairly affect test performance. Be aware of the potential effects that learner diversity can have on assessment performance.

   ■ **Elementary:** Before any of her students who are non-native English speakers are referred for special education testing, a first-grade teacher talks with a school psychologist and describes the child's background and language patterns.

   ■ **Middle School:** Before administering a statewide exam, an eighth-grade math teacher explains the purpose and format of the test and gives students practice with the content covered on the test. He reads the directions for taking the test slowly and clearly and writes the amount of time remaining on the board.

   ■ **High School:** A high school English teacher holds sessions after school to help her students with limited English proficiency prepare for a high-stakes test. She explains test purposes and formats and provides students with timed practice on similar items.

2. Testing procedures can influence student performance and ultimately test validity. Adapt testing procedures to meet the needs of all students.

   ■ **Elementary:** An urban third-grade teacher states positive expectations as her students prepare for a standardized test and carefully monitors them to be sure they stay on task during the test.

   ■ **Middle School:** Before standardized tests are given each year, a middle school language arts teacher takes time to teach test-taking strategies. She models the strategies, discusses them with her students, and provides opportunities to practice them under test-like conditions.

   ■ **High School:** An algebra teacher makes a special effort to ensure that students understand the vocabulary on the state standardized test. Before the test, he carefully reviews important concepts the class has learned during the school year.

Finally, when making decisions about students, use a variety of sources of data, such as your own quizzes, tests, homework, and informal observations, in addition to standardized test results. This is important for all students, and even more so when working with members of cultural minorities and students who are ELs. These alternate sources help provide a more comprehensive and accurate picture of your students' achievements.

Developmentally Appropriate **Practice**

Standardized Testing with Learners at Different Ages

Effective assessment with standardized tests requires that teachers take learner development into account. The following sections outline suggestions for accommodating the developmental levels of your students.

Working with Students in Early Childhood Programs and Elementary Schools

The developmental characteristics of young children can have a powerful effect on the validity of standardized tests. Their short attention spans and limited language skills influence their performance, and most won't understand that the tests are important, so they often don't make efforts to perform well. For many young children, a standardized test is just one more worksheet to be completed. They also lack experience with timed tests and multiple-choice formats, which are commonly used on standardized tests. They may not follow directions, and because they tend to be impulsive, they often select the first choice that seems plausible or may rush through the test so they can return to activities they find more enjoyable.

Because of mismatches between testing requirements and students' developmental limitations, teachers of young children should treat standardized test results skeptically, particularly when they're inconsistent with a child's classroom performance. Most importantly, teachers should avoid making long-term predictions about student potential on the basis of standardized test results, and particularly on the basis of these results alone.

Working with Students in Middle Schools

Middle school students are starting to understand the importance of standardized tests, which can have both positive and negative effects; it can increase their motivation to perform well, but it can also result in test anxiety that can decrease their performance.

While generally more test-savvy than younger children in their ability to respond to standardized tests, individual development varies a great deal. Some have acquired the study habits, self-regulatory abilities, and test-taking strategies needed to navigate through timed, standardized test formats successfully, whereas others haven't (Schunk, 2005; Zimmerman, 2005).

To accommodate these differences, middle school teachers should emphasize self-regulation and personal responsibility during tests, teach test-taking strategies, and provide ample practice with formats similar to those students will encounter on standardized tests. Emphasizing that the tests can give them valuable information about their strengths and areas that need more work, stating positive expectations about their performance, and encouraging them to do their best are also helpful with middle school students.

Working with Students in High Schools

By the time they reach high school, students have had a considerable amount of experience with standardized testing. As a result, most are familiar with test formats and procedures, but for students who have had negative experiences with standardized testing, motivation can be a problem (Ryan, Ryan, Arbuthnot, & Samuels, 2007). Motivation can be a special problem for low-performing students, and it often prevents them from performing up to their capabilities. One adolescent facing challenging problems on a test commented, "I figured I would get them wrong. . . . Yeah, because if I know I'm going to get them wrong I just kind of think why bother trying" (Ryan et al., 2007, p. 9).

Teachers of high school students should emphasize that standardized test results exist to provide students with information, and the results don't say anything about their intrinsic worth as human beings or determine whether they will be successful in life. Doing as well as possible is important, however, if the results are to provide the most useful information.

High school students also need help interpreting standardized test scores and how they can be used to make career decisions. Test results can be confusing, and both students and their parents need help understanding and translating them into useful information (Carr, 2008). Caring and understanding teachers are in the best position to help students understand test results because they are familiar with students' classroom performance and can help students make important decisions about their futures.

15 Summary

1. Describe the relationships between standards-based education, accountability, and standardized testing.
   - Standards-based education is the process of focusing instruction on predetermined goals or standards.
   - Accountability is the process of requiring students to demonstrate that they have met the standards and holding teachers responsible for students' performance. Standardized testing in the form of high-stakes tests are used to determine whether students have met the standards.
   - Advocates of accountability argue that standardized tests efficiently assess the educational achievements of students. Critics counter that misuse of standardized tests discourages innovation, narrows the curriculum, and results in teaching to the test.

2. Describe the functions of standardized tests in the total assessment process.
   - Assessing student academic progress, diagnosing strengths and weaknesses, and placing students in appropriate programs are important functions of standardized tests. Providing information for program evaluation and improvement is also an important function.
   - Achievement tests provide information about student learning; diagnostic tests provide in-depth analysis of specific student strengths and weaknesses; intelligence tests are designed to measure students' ability to acquire and use knowledge, to solve problems, and to accomplish new tasks; and aptitude tests are designed to predict potential for future learning.
   - Validity measures the appropriateness of a test for a specific purpose and includes content, predictive, and construct validity.

3. Interpret standardized test results using statistics and standard scores.
   - Standardized test scores are interpreted by using descriptive statistics to compare an individual's performance to the performance of a norming group.
   - The mean, median, and mode are measures of central tendency, and the range and standard deviation are measures of variability.
   - Percentiles, stanines, grade equivalents, and standard scores all allow a student's score to be compared with the scores of comparable students in a norming group.

4. Explain how learner diversity can influence the validity of standardized tests.
   - Learner diversity can influence the validity of standardized tests if being a member of a cultural minority or a non-native English speaker results in test bias.
   - Content bias occurs when incidental information in items discriminates against certain cultural groups.
   - Bias in testing procedures occurs when groups don't fully understand testing procedures and the implications of time limits.
   - Bias in the use of test results occurs when tests are used in isolation to make important decisions about students.

5. Describe the different roles you'll have in the process of standardized testing.
   - Ensuring that your students have learned the content covered on standardized tests will be one of your most important roles, and it will depend in large part on the effectiveness of your instruction.
   - You should also provide students with practice using formats they will encounter on standardized tests and help students acquire test-taking strategies.
   - You will also be expected to accommodate members of cultural minorities and English learners as they prepare to take standardized tests. Providing concrete examples of technical terms during instruction and emphasizing the essential characteristics of important concepts can help in this process.
   - You will also need to administer standardized tests according to guidelines specified in testing manuals and interpret standardized test scores for students and their caregivers.

Preparing for Your Licensure Exam

Understanding Standardized Testing

Your licensure exam will include information related to classroom assessment, and we include the following exercises to help you practice for the exam in your state. This book and these exercises will be a resource for you as you prepare for the exam.

At the beginning of the chapter, you saw how Mike Chavez interpreted standardized test scores for a parent. Let's look now at another situation in which using standardized tests helps answer questions about learning and teaching. Read the case study, and answer the questions that follow.

Peggy Barret looks up from the stack of algebra tests that she is grading as her colleague, Stan Witzel, walks into the teacher's lounge.

"How's it going?" Stan asks.

"Fine . . . I think. I'm scoring tests from my Algebra I class. That's the one where I'm trying to put more emphasis on problem solving. Quite a few kids are actually getting into the applications now, and they like the problem solving when they do small-group work. The trouble is, some of the others are really struggling. . . . So I'm not so sure about it all."

"I wish I had your problems. It sounds like your kids are learning, and at least some of them like it," Stan replies.

"Yeah, I know," Peggy nods. "Getting these kids to like any kind of math is an accomplishment, but still I wonder. . . . It's just that I'm not sure if they're getting all that they should. I don't know whether this class is really doing better than last year's class or even my other classes this year, for that matter. The tests I give are pretty different in the different classes. I think the kids are doing better on problem solving, but to be honest about it, I see quite a few of them struggling with mechanics. I work on the mechanics, but not as much as in other classes. I'm not sure if I'm putting the right emphasis in the class."

"Good point," Stan shrugs. "I always wonder when I make changes. By emphasizing something more, I wonder if they are they missing out on something else?"

"As important," Peggy continues, "I wonder how they'll do when they go off to college. Quite a few of them in this class will be going. . . . Got any ideas?"

"Good questions, Peggy. I wish I knew, but . . . I guess that's part of teaching."

"Yeah," she replies with her voice trailing off, "it seems as if we should be able to get some better information.

"I can see that some of the kids just don't seem to get it. I would say their background is weak; they seem to be trying. On the other hand, I checked out some of their old standardized test results, and their math scores weren't that bad. Maybe it's not background. Maybe they just don't belong in my class."

"Tell me about the kids who are struggling," Stan suggests.

"Well, Jacinta tries really hard. Quan is a whiz at computation but struggles when I ask him to think. Carlos actually seems to do fairly well with mechanics but has a hard time with word problems. For example, I tried to motivate the class the other day with several word problems involving statistics from our basketball team. Most of the class liked them and got them right. Not these three."

"Maybe you ought to talk to Yolanda," Stan suggests. "She's been in this game for a while and might know about some tests that are available that can help you answer some of your questions."

Questions for **Case Analysis**

In answering these questions, use information from the chapter, and link your responses to specific information in the case.

Multiple-Choice Questions

1. What type of standardized test would help Peggy determine "whether this class is really doing better than last year's class or even my other classes this year"?

   a. Achievement test

   b. Diagnostic test

   c. Intelligence test

   d. Aptitude test

2. What type of validity would be the primary concern with this test?

   a. Content validity

   b. Predictive validity

   c. Construct validity

   d. Ecological validity

Constructed-Response Question

3. In investigating the problems that her students were having in math, Peggy checked out their overall test scores from past standardized tests. What else might she have done?

Important **Concepts**

accountability
achievement tests
aptitude tests
assessment bias
benchmark assessments
Common Core State
 Standards Initiative
 (CCSSI)
computerized adaptive
 testing programs
construct validity
content validity
criterion-referenced
 standardized tests
diagnostic tests

frequency distribution
grade-equivalent score
high-stakes tests
intelligence tests
mean
measures of central
 tendency
median
mode
National Assessment of
 Educational Progress
 (NAEP)
national norms
No Child Left Behind
 (NCLB)

normal distribution
norm-referenced
 standardized tests
norming group
percentile bands
percentile rank (PR)
performance
 assessments
predictive validity
Race to the Top
range
raw score
readiness tests
scaled scores
standard deviation

standard error of
 measurement
standard score
standardized tests
standards
standards-based education
stanine
Trends in International
 Mathematics and Science
 Study (TIMSS)
true score
t-score
value-added modeling
variability
z-score

Using *Educational Psychology: Windows on Classrooms* (10th ed.) to Prepare for the Praxis™ *Principles of Learning and Teaching* Exam

"*The Praxis Series* tests are currently required for teacher licensure in more than 40 states and U.S. territories. These tests are also used by several professional licensing agencies and by several hundred colleges and universities" (Educational Testing Service, 2014a, p. 21). Also, teacher candidates who test in one state can submit their scores for licensure in any other *Praxis®* user state (Educational Testing Service, 2014a).

Four *Principles of Learning and Teaching* (PLT) tests, one each for teachers seeking licensure in Early Childhood, or grades K–6, 5–9, and 7–12, are among the Praxis™ exams. *Educational Psychology: Windows on Classrooms* (10th ed.) addresses virtually all of the topics covered in the PLT tests.

Each of the four *Principles of Learning and Teaching* exams consists of 70 multiple-choice (MC) and 4 constructed-response (CR) questions organized into four sections. The four sections with the approximate number of questions in each include (Educational Testing Service, 2014b, 2014c, 2014d, 2014e):

- Students as learners—21 MC and one or two CR questions
- Instructional process—21 MC and one or two CR questions

- Assessment—14 MC and zero or one CR questions
- Professional development, leadership, and community—14 MC and zero or one CR questions

The multiple-choice questions are similar to those in the test bank that accompanies *Educational Psychology: Windows on Classrooms* (10th ed.). The constructed response questions are based on "case histories" (case studies), which you will be asked to read and analyze. The case histories are very similar to the case studies that appear throughout this text. Each of the constructed-response questions are scored on a scale of 0–2. Sample questions and responses that earn scores of 2, 1, and 0 can be found at the following links: http://www.ets.org/s/praxis/pdf/0621.pdf (Early Childhood); http://www.ets.org/s/praxis/pdf/0622.pdf (Grades K–6); http://www.ets.org/s/praxis/pdf/0623.pdf (Grades 5–9); http://www.ets.org/s/praxis/pdf/0624.pdf (Grades 7–12). Sample multiple-choice questions can also be found at these links.

We have designed this text to help you succeed on the Praxis™ *Principles of Learning and Teaching* exam by including case studies at the end of each chapter, which are followed by multiple-choice and short-answer questions. The case studies and questions help you prepare for your licensure exam by providing you with items similar to those that will appear on the exam. We provide feedback for all the items.

Topics Covered on the Praxis™ Exam (Educational Testing Service, 2014b, 2014c, 2014d, 2014e)	Chapter Content in *Educational Psychology: Windows on Classrooms* (10th ed.) Aligned with Topics Covered on the Praxis™ Exam
I. Students as Learners	
Student Development and the Learning Process	
• Understands the theoretical foundations of how students learn (such as how knowledge is constructed, how skills are acquired, and the cognitive processes involved) • Knows the contributions of foundational theorists in education (such as Piaget, Vygotsky, Kohlberg, Skinner, and Bandura)	Chapter 2: Cognitive and Language Development • Principles of development (p. 57) • Bronfenbrenner's bioecological model of development (pp. 57–60) • Piaget's theory of cognitive development (pp. 65–74) • Neo-Piagetian views of cognitive development (p. 74)

- Understands concepts and terms related to a variety of learning theories (such as schema, metacognition, transfer, zone of proximal development, and classical and operant conditioning)
- Knows the distinguishing characteristics of the stages in each domain of human development (i.e., cognitive, social, and moral)
- Understands how learning theory and human development impact the instructional process (such as using learning and development theory to design instruction and solve educational problems)

- Educational psychology and teaching: Applying Piaget's theory with your students (pp. 74–77)
- Vygotsky's sociocultural theory of cognitive development (pp. 77–82)
- Educational psychology and teaching: Applying Vygotsky's theory with your students (pp. 82–85)

Chapter 3: Personal, Social, and Moral Development
- Social development (pp. 124–129)
- Development of morality, social responsibility, and self-control

Chapter 6: Behaviorism and Social Cognitive Theory (Entire chapter)

Chapter 7: Cognitive Views of Learning (Entire chapter)

Chapter 8: Complex Cognitive Processes (Entire chapter)

Chapter 9: Knowledge Construction in Social Contexts
- Knowledge construction (pp. 383–387)
- Knowledge construction and the learning sciences (pp. 387–390)
- Educational psychology and teaching: Guiding your students' knowledge constructions

Students as Diverse Learners

- Understands that a number of variables affect how individual students perform (such as culture, gender, socioeconomic status, motivation, cognitive development, prior knowledge and experience, and language)
- Recognizes areas of exceptionality and their potential impact on student learning (such as cognitive, speech/language, and behavioral)
- Understands the implications and application of legislation relating to students with exceptionalities in classroom practice
- Recognizes the traits, behaviors, and needs of intellectually gifted students
- Recognizes that the process of English language acquisition affects the educational experience of English learners (ELs)
- Knows a variety of approaches for accommodating students with exceptionalities in each phase of the educational process

Chapter 2: Cognitive and Language Development
- How experiences advance development (pp. 67–69)
- Stages of development (pp. 69–74)
- Learning and development in a cultural context (pp. 78–80)
- Diversity: Culture and development (pp. 81–82)
- Language development (pp. 89–94)

Chapter 4: Learner Diversity (Entire chapter)

Chapter 5: Learners with Exceptionalities
- The legal basis for working with students with exceptionalities (pp. 199–205)
- Exceptionalities and learning problems (pp. 205–221)
- Students who are gifted and talented (pp. 221–223)
- Teachers' responsibilities in inclusive classrooms (pp. 223–228)

Chapter 10: Motivation and Learning (Entire chapter)

Chapter 11: A Classroom Model for Promoting Student Motivation (Entire chapter)

Chapter 14: Increasing Learning Through Assessment
- Diversity: Effective assessment practices with students from diverse backgrounds

Chapter 15: Standardized Testing and Learning
- Diversity and standardized testing (pp. 661–665)

Student Motivation and Learning Environment

- Knows the major contributions of foundational behavioral theorists to education (such as Skinner, Maslow, and Erikson)

Chapter 3: Personal, Social, and Moral Development
- Erikson's theory of psychosocial development (pp. 114–116)

• Understands the implications of foundational motivation theories for instruction, learning, and classroom management (such as extrinsic and intrinsic motivation, self-determination, attribution, classic and operant conditioning, and positive and negative reinforcers)	Chapter 6: Behaviorism and Social Cognitive Theory • Classical conditioning (pp. 237–239) • Operant conditioning (pp. 240–253) Chapter 10: Motivation and Learning (Entire chapter)
• Knows principles and strategies for classroom management (such as routines and procedures, rules, and ways of promoting a positive learning environment)	Chapter 11: A Classroom Model for Promoting Student Motivation (Entire chapter) Chapter 12: Classroom Management: Developing Self-Regulated Learners (Entire chapter)

II. Instructional Process

Planning Instruction

• Understands the role of district, state, and national standards in instructional planning	Chapter 1: Educational Psychology: Understanding Learning and Teaching • Standards and accountability (pp. 40–44)
• Knows how to apply the basic concepts of predominant educational theories	Chapter 2: Cognitive and Language Development • Educational psychology and teaching: Applying Piaget's theory with your students (pp. 74–77)
• Knows how to select content to achieve lesson and unit objectives	• Educational psychology and teaching: Applying Vygotsky's theory with your students (pp. 82–86)
• Knows how to develop objectives in the cognitive, affective, and psychomotor domains	Chapter 6: Behaviorism and Social Cognitive Theory • Educational psychology and teaching: Applying classical conditioning with your students (pp. 239–240)
• Is aware of the need for and is able to identify various resources for planning enrichment and remediation activities	• Educational psychology and teaching: Applying operant conditioning with your students
	• Educational psychology and teaching: Using social cognitive theory to increase your students' learning
	Chapter 7: Cognitive Views of Learning • Educational psychology and teaching: Applying information processing and the model of human memory with your students (pp. 320–327)
	Chapter 9: Knowledge Construction in Social Contexts • Educational psychology and teaching: Guiding your students' knowledge construction (pp. 394–402)
	Chapter 13: Learning and Effective Teaching • Identifying topics (pp. 541–542) • Specifying learning objectives (pp. 542–544) • Preparing and organizing learning activities (pp. 544–545) • Planning in a standards-based environment (pp. 546–551)

Instructional Strategies

• Understands the cognitive processes associated with learning (such as critical and creative thinking, questioning, and problem solving)	Chapter 6: Behaviorism and Social Cognitive Theory • Self-regulation (pp. 268–273)
• Understands the distinguishing features of different instructional models (such as direct instruction, guided discovery, and cooperative learning)	Chapter 7: Cognitive Views of Learning • Cognitive processes (pp. 301–313) Chapter 8: Complex Cognitive Processes (Entire chapter)
• Knows a variety of instructional strategies associated with each instructional model	Chapter 12: Classroom Management: Developing Self-Regulated Learners
• Knows a variety of strategies for encouraging complex cognitive processes	• Developing learner self-regulation (pp. 497–500)

- Knows a variety of strategies for supporting student learning (such as modeling, developing self-regulation, and differentiated instruction)
- Understands the use and implications of different grouping techniques and strategies

Chapter 13: Learning and Effective Teaching

- Models of instruction (pp. 562–573)
- Cooperative learning (pp. 574–577)
- Flipped instruction (pp. 577–579)
- Differentiated instruction (pp. 579–580)

Questioning Techniques

- Knows the components of effective questioning (such as wait time, handling incorrect answers, and encouraging participation)
- Understands the uses of questioning (such as increasing motivation, reviewing previous lessons, and summarizing information)
- Knows strategies for promoting a safe and open forum for discussion

Chapter 11: A Classroom Model for Promoting Student Motivation

- The teacher–student relationship (pp. 462–463)
- Order and safety (pp. 471–472)

Chapter 12: Classroom Management: Developing Self-Regulated Learners

- Creating a community of caring and trust (pp. 500–501)

Chapter 13: Learning and Effective Teaching

- Review (pp. 554–555)
- Questioning (pp. 555–558)
- Feedback (pp. 558–560)
- Closure (p. 560)

Communication Techniques

- Understands various verbal and nonverbal communication models
- Is aware of how culture and gender can affect communication
- Knows how to use various communication tools to enrich the learning environment

Chapter 4: Learner Diversity

- Cultural differences in adult–child interactions (pp. 156–158)
- School-related gender differences (pp. 168–169)
- Boys' and girls' classroom behavior (p. 169)

Chapter 12: Classroom Management: Developing Self-Regulated Learners

- Keep verbal and nonverbal behaviors congruent (pp. 520–521)

Chapter 13: Learning and Effective Teaching

- Communication (pp. 560–561)

III. Assessment

Assessment and Evaluation Strategies

- Understands the role of formal and informal assessment in informing the instructional process
- Understands the distinctions among the different types of assessment
- Knows how to create and select an appropriate assessment format to meet instructional objectives
- Knows how to select from a variety of assessment tools to evaluate student performance
- Understands the rationale behind and the uses of students' self and peer assessment

Chapter 9: Knowledge Construction in Social Contexts

- Promote learning with assessment (pp. 401–402)

Chapter 11: A Classroom Model for Promoting Student Motivation

- Assessing students and providing feedback: Providing information about learning progress (pp. 486–488)

Chapter 13: Learning and Effective Teaching

- Planning for assessment (p. 545)
- Assessment and learning: Using assessment as a learning tool (pp. 583–584)

Chapter 14: Increasing Learning Through Assessment (Entire chapter)

Assessment Tools

- Understands the types and purposes of standardized tests
- Understands the distinction between norm-referenced and criterion-referenced scoring
- Understands terminology related to testing and scoring (such as validity, reliability, raw score, scaled score, percentile, mean, mode, median, and grade equivalent scores)
- Knows how to interpret assessment results and communicate the meaning of those results to students, parents/caregivers, and school personnel

Chapter 14: Increasing Learning Through Assessment
- Validity: Making accurate assessment decisions (pp. 596–597)
- Reliability: Consistency in assessment (pp. 597–598)
- Norm-referenced and criterion-referenced grading systems (pp. 626–627)

Chapter 15: Standardized Testing and Learning
- Functions of standardized tests (p. 647)
- Norm- versus criterion-referenced standardized tests (pp. 647–648)
- Types of standardized tests (pp. 648–652)
- Evaluating standardized tests: Validity revisited (pp. 653–654)
- Understanding and interpreting standardized test scores (pp. 654–661)
- Educational psychology and teaching: Your role in standardized testing (pp. 665–666)

IV. Professional Development, Leadership, and Community

- Is aware of a variety of professional development practices and resources (such as professional literature, professional associations, mentors, and study groups)
- Understands the implications of research, views, ideas, and debates on teaching practices
- Recognizes the role of reflective practice for professional growth
- Is aware of school support personnel who assist students, teachers, and families (such as guidance counselors, IEP team members, and special education teachers)
- Understands the role of teachers and schools as educational leaders in the greater community
- Knows basic strategies for developing collaborative relationships with colleagues, administrators, other school personnel, parents/caregivers, and the community to support the educational process
- Understands the implications of major legislation and court decisions relating to students and teachers

Chapter 1: Educational Psychology: Understanding Learning and Teaching
- The preeminence of teachers (pp. 25–26)
- Educational psychology, professional knowledge, and expert teaching (pp. 26–33)
- Professional knowledge and reflective practice (p. 35)
- The role of research in acquiring professional knowledge (pp. 35–38)

Chapter 5: Learners with Exceptionalities
- The legal basis for working with students with exceptionalities (pp. 199–205)
- Individualized education program (pp. 202–203)
- Collaborating with other professionals (pp. 226–227)

Chapter 12: Classroom Management: Developing Self-Regulated Learners
- Communicating with parents (pp. 513–516)

Glossary

Ability grouping. The process of placing students of similar abilities into groups and attempting to match instruction to the needs of these groups.

Academic language proficiency. A level of proficiency in English that allows students to handle demanding learning tasks with abstract concepts.

Academic learning time. The amount of time students are successful while engaged in learning activities.

Acceleration. Programs for students who are gifted and talented that keep the curriculum the same, but allow students to move through it more quickly.

Accommodation. The process of creating new schemes or adjusting old ones when they can no longer explain new experiences.

Accountability. The process of requiring students to demonstrate that they have met specified standards and holding teachers responsible for students' performance.

Achievement tests. Standardized tests designed to assess how much students have learned in specified content areas.

Action research. Applied research designed to answer a specific school- or classroom-related question.

Activation state. The extent to which information in memory is being actively attended to and cognitively processed.

Adaptive behavior. A person's ability to perform the functions of everyday living.

Adaptive fit. The degree to which a school environment accommodates the student's needs and the degree to which a student can meet the requirements of a particular school setting.

Affective domain. The area of learning that focuses on people's feelings, attitudes, and emotions.

Algorithm. A specific step or set of steps for finding the solution to a problem.

Allocated time. The amount of time a teacher or school designates for a content area or topic.

Analogies. Descriptions of relationships that are similar in some but not all respects.

Antecedents. Stimuli that precede and induce behaviors.

Anxiety. A general uneasiness and feeling of tension relating to a situation with an uncertain outcome.

Applied behavior analysis (ABA). The process of systematically implementing the principles of operant conditioning to change student behavior.

Appropriating understanding. The process of individually internalizing understanding after it has first been socially constructed.

Aptitude tests. Standardized tests designed to predict the potential for future learning and measure general abilities developed over long periods of time.

Assertive discipline. An approach to classroom management that promotes a clear and firm response style with students.

Assessment bias. A form of discrimination that occurs when a test or other assessment instrument unfairly penalizes a group of students because of their gender, ethnicity, race, or socioeconomic status.

Assessment. The process of gathering information and making decisions about students' learning progress.

Assimilation. The process of using existing schemes to interpret new experiences.

Assistive technology. A set of adaptive tools that support students with disabilities in learning activities and daily life tasks.

Attainment value. The importance an individual attaches to doing well on a task.

Attention-deficit/hyperactivity disorder (ADHD). A learning problem characterized by difficulties in maintaining attention.

Attention. The process of consciously focusing on a stimulus.

Attribution theory. A cognitive theory of motivation that attempts to systematically describe learners' beliefs about the causes of their successes and failures and how these beliefs influence motivation to learn.

Attributions. Explanations or beliefs related to the causes of performance.

Autism spectrum disorder. A description of a cluster of disorders characterized by impaired social relationships and skills and often associated with highly unusual behavior.

Automaticity. The ability to perform mental operations with little awareness or conscious effort.

Autonomous morality. A stage of moral development characterized by the belief that fairness and justice is the reciprocal process of treating others as they would want to be treated.

Autonomy. Independence and the ability to alter the environment when necessary.

Axons. Longer branches that extend from the cell body of neurons and transmit messages to other neurons.

Basic interpersonal communication skills. A level of proficiency in English that allows students to interact conversationally with their peers.

Behaviorism. A theory that explains learning in terms of observable behaviors and how they're influenced by stimuli from the environment.

Belief preservation. People's tendency to make evidence subservient to belief, rather than the other way around.

Belief. A cognitive idea we accept as true without necessarily having definitive evidence to support it.

Benchmark assessments. Short tests administered periodically throughout the school year that give teachers immediate feedback on how their students are meeting academic standards.

Between-class grouping. Divides students in a certain grade into levels, such as high, medium, and low.

Bidialecticism. The ability to switch back and forth between a dialect and Standard English.

Bilingualism. The ability to speak, read, and write in two languages.

Bipolar disorder. A condition characterized by alternative episodes of depressive and manic states.

Blocked practice. The process of practicing one skill extensively and then moving to a different skill.

Bullying. A form of peer aggression that involves a systematic or repetitious abuse of power between students.

Caring. A teacher's empathy and investment in the protection and development of young people.

Central executive. A supervisory component of working memory that controls the flow of information to and from the other components.

Centration (centering). The tendency to focus on the most perceptually obvious aspect of an object or event, neglecting other important aspects.

Characteristics. A concept's essential, or defining, elements.

Chronosystem. In Bronfenbrenner's theory, the time-dependent element of our developing environment.

Chunking. The process of mentally combining separate items into larger, more meaningful units.

Classical conditioning. A component of behaviorism that explains how we learn to display involuntary emotional or physiological responses that are similar to instinctive or reflexive responses.

Classification. The process of grouping objects on the basis of common characteristics.

Classroom management. All the actions teachers take to create an environment that supports academic learning, self-regulation, and social and emotional development.

Closure. A summary that occurs at the end of lessons.

Cognitive activity. The process of focusing our thinking on the learning task in which we're involved and the factors related to the task.

Cognitive apprenticeships. Social learning processes that occur when less-skilled learners work alongside experts in developing cognitive skills.

Cognitive behavior modification. A procedure that promotes behavioral change and self-regulation in students through self-talk and self-instruction.

Cognitive constructivism. A view that describes knowledge construction as an individual, internal process.

Cognitive development. Changes in our thinking that occur as a result of maturation and experience.

Cognitive domain. The area of learning that focuses on students' thinking and the processes involved in acquiring, applying, and analyzing knowledge.

Cognitive learning theories. Theories that explain learning in terms of the changes in the mental structures and processes involved in acquiring, organizing, and using knowledge.

Cognitive load. The amount of mental activity imposed on working memory.

Cognitive modeling. The process of performing a demonstration combined with verbalizing the thinking behind the actions.

Cognitive tools. The concepts and symbols (numbers and language) together with the real tools that allow people to think, solve problems, and function in a culture.

Collaboration. The process of working with other professionals to solve common problems.

Collaborative consultation. The process of general and special education teachers working together to create effective learning experiences for learners with exceptionalities.

Collective efficacy. Beliefs that the faculty as a whole in a school can have a positive effect on student learning.

Collective self-esteem. Individuals' perceptions of the relative worth of the groups to which they belong.

Common Core State Standards Initiative (CCSSI). A state-led effort to establish a single set of clear educational standards for all states in mathematics and English-language arts, together with literacy in history/social studies, science, and technical subjects, that states can share and voluntarily adopt.

Communication disorders. Exceptionalities that interfere with students' abilities to receive and understand information from others and express their own ideas.

Community of caring and trust. A classroom environment in which learners feel physically and emotionally safe and their needs for belonging and relatedness are met.

Community of learners. A learning environment in which the teacher and students work together to help everyone learn.

Competence. The ability to function effectively in the environment.

Comprehension monitoring. The process of checking to see if we understand what we have read or heard.

Computerized adaptive testing programs. Testing programs that adapt to students' ability levels by presenting items that are ideally suited for each student.

Concept map. A visual representation of the relationships among concepts that includes the concepts themselves, sometimes enclosed in circles or boxes, together with relationships among concepts indicated by lines linking the concepts.

Concepts. Mental representations of categories that allow us to identify examples and nonexamples of those categories.

Conceptual hierarchies. Types of concept maps that visually illustrate superordinate, subordinate, and coordinate relationships among concepts.

Conditional knowledge. Knowledge of where and when to use declarative and procedural knowledge.

Conditioned response. A learned physiological or emotional response that is similar to the unconditioned response.

Conditioned stimulus. A formerly neutral stimulus that becomes associated with an unconditioned stimulus.

Confirmation bias. People's tendency to focus only on evidence that supports their beliefs.

Connected discourse. Instruction that is thematic and leads to a point.

Consequences. Events (stimuli) that occur following a behavior that influence the probability of the behavior recurring.

Conservation. The idea that the "amount" of some substance stays the same regardless of its shape or the number of pieces into which it is divided.

Construct validity. An indicator of the logical connection between a test and what it is designed to measure.

Content validity. A test's ability to accurately sample the content taught and to measure the extent to which learners understand it.

Continuous reinforcement schedule. A schedule of reinforcement in which every desired behavior is reinforced.

Conventional domain. The domain of moral development that addresses societal norms and ways of behaving in specific situations.

Conventional morality. A moral orientation linked to uncritical acceptance of society's conventions about right and wrong.

Cooperative learning. A set of instructional strategies in which students work in mixed-ability groups to reach specific cognitive and social development objectives.

Corporal punishment. A form of physical punishment that involves the deliberate infliction of pain in response to misbehavior.

Correlation. A relationship, either positive or negative, between two or more variables.

Correlational research. The process of looking for relationships between variables that enables researchers to predict changes in one variable on the basis of changes in another without implying that one variable causes the other.

Cost. The consideration of what a person must give up to engage in an activity.

Creativity. The ability to produce original works or solutions to problems that are productive and task appropriate.

Crisis. In Erikson's theory, a psychosocial challenge that presents opportunities for development.

Criterion-referenced standardized tests. Standardized tests that compare performance against a set performance standard.

Critical thinking. An individual's ability and inclination to make and assess conclusions based on evidence.

Crystallized intelligence. Culture-specific mental ability, heavily dependent on experience and schooling.

Cultural intelligence. An individual's ability to adjust and effectively adapt to diverse cultural situations.

Cultural mismatch. A clash between a child's home culture and the culture of the school that creates conflicting expectations for students and their behavior.

Culturally responsive classroom management. Classroom management that combines cultural knowledge with teachers' awareness of possible personal biases.

Culturally responsive teaching. An approach to education that attempts to understand the cultures of the students we teach, communicate positive attitudes about cultural diversity, and employ a variety of instructional approaches that build on students' cultural backgrounds.

Culture. The knowledge, attitudes, values, and customs that characterize a social group.

Curriculum-based assessment. Measurement of learners' performance in specific areas of the curriculum.

Cyberbullying. A form of bullying that occurs when students use electronic media to harass or intimidate other students.

Deaf. A hearing impairment that requires the use of other senses, usually sight, to communicate.

Declarative knowledge. Knowledge of facts, concepts, procedures, and rules.

Deficiency needs. Needs that energize people to meet them if they're unfulfilled.

Delay of gratification. The ability to forgo an immediate pleasure or reward in order to gain a more substantial one later.

Deliberate practice. An approach to the development of a wide range of abilities that includes the following characteristics: (1) It is goal directed; (2) It focuses on understanding instead of rote drill; (3) It is frequent and systematic; (4) It is conducted in real-world contexts; and (5) It includes feedback about learning progress.

Dendrites. Relatively short, branchlike structures that extend from the cell body of neurons and receive messages from other neurons.

Descriptive research. Research that uses tools such as tests, surveys, and observations to describe the status or characteristics of a situation or phenomenon.

Design-based research. Research that is designed to impact classroom practice and contribute to theory by focusing on educational interventions that are conducted in real-world contexts using mixed methods and multiple interactions, and involve a partnership between researchers and practitioners.

Desist. A verbal or nonverbal communication that teachers use to stop a behavior.

Development. The changes that occur in human beings as they grow from infancy to adulthood.

Developmental differences. Changes in students' thinking, personalities, and social skills that result from maturation and experience.

Developmentally appropriate practice. Instruction that matches teacher actions to the capabilities and needs of learners at different developmental levels.

Diagnostic tests. Standardized tests designed to provide a detailed description of learners' strengths and weaknesses in specific skill areas.

Dialect. A variation of Standard English that is associated with a particular regional or social group and is distinct in vocabulary, grammar, or pronunciation.

Differentiating instruction. The process of adapting instruction to meet the needs of students who vary in background knowledge, skills, needs, and motivations.

Direct instruction. A teaching model designed to help students acquire well-defined knowledge and skills needed for later learning.

Disabilities. Functional limitations or an inability to perform a certain act.

Discipline. Teachers' responses to student misbehavior.

Discrepancy model of identification. One method of identifying students with learning problems that focuses on differences between achievement and intelligence tests or subtests.

Discrimination. The process that occurs when a person gives different responses to related but not identical stimuli.

Disorder. A general malfunction of mental, physical, or psychological processes.

Divergent thinking. The ability to generate a variety of alternate, original solutions to questions.

Drawing analogies. A heuristic used to solve unfamiliar problems by comparing them with those already solved.

Dual-coding theory. A theory suggesting that long-term memory contains two distinct memory systems, one for verbal information and the other for images.

Due process. The guarantee that parents have the right to be involved in identifying and placing their children in special programs, to access school records, and to obtain an independent evaluation if they're not satisfied with the one conducted by the school.

Educational psychology. The academic discipline that focuses on human teaching and learning.

Effective teaching. Instruction that promotes as much learning as possible in all students.

Egocentrism. The inability to see objects and events from others' perspectives.

Elaboration. An encoding strategy that increases the meaningfulness of new information by connecting it to existing knowledge.

Elaborative questioning. The process of drawing inferences, identifying examples, and forming relationships.

Elaborative rehearsal. The process of relating to-be-remembered factual information to other information.

Embodied cognition. The idea that cognition (our thinking) depends on characteristics of our physical bodies, and our bodies significantly influence the way we process information.

Emotion. A feeling that is often short-lived, intense, and specific.

Emotional and behavior disorders. Serious and persistent age-inappropriate behaviors that result in social conflict, personal unhappiness, and often school failure.

Emotional intelligence. A form of intelligence that involves the accurate perception and expression of emotion and the ability to adapt emotions and use emotional knowledge in thought processes.

Emotional self-regulation. The ability to manage our emotions so we can cope with the environment and accomplish goals.

Empathy. The ability to experience the same emotion someone else is feeling.

Emphasis. Verbal and vocal cues that alert students to important information in a lesson.

Encoding. The process of representing information in long-term memory.

Engaged time. The amount of time students are paying attention and involved in learning activities.

English as a second language (ESL) pullout programs. Programs for students who are ELs who receive most of their instruction in general education classrooms but are also pulled out for extra help.

English learners (ELs). Students whose first or home language is not English.

Enrichment. Programs for students who are gifted and talented that provide alternate instruction.

Episodic memory. Memory for personal experiences.

Equilibrium. A cognitive state in which we're able to explain new experiences by using existing understanding.

Equitable distribution. The process of calling on all the students in a class as equally as possible, whether or not they have their hands raised.

Essential teaching skills. Basic abilities that all teachers, including those in their first year of teaching, should possess to maximize student learning.

Ethnic identity. An awareness of ethnic group membership and a commitment to the attitudes, values, and behaviors of that group.

Ethnicity. A person's ancestry and the way individuals identify with the nation from which they or their ancestors came.

Exemplars. The most highly typical examples of a concept.

Exosystem. In bioecological theory, societal influences that affect both the micro- and mesosystems.

Expectancy x value theory. A theory that explains motivation by saying that learners will be motivated to engage in a task to the extent that they expect to succeed on a task times the value they place on the success.

Expectation. A belief about a future outcome. The influence of expectations on motivation is often described using expectancy x value theory.

Experimental research. A type of research that systematically manipulates variables in attempts to determine cause and effect.

Experts. People who are highly skilled or knowledgeable in a domain, such as math, athletics, or teaching.

External morality. A stage of moral development in which individuals view rules as fixed and permanent and enforced by authority figures.

Extinction (classical conditioning). The process that occurs when the conditioned stimulus occurs often enough in the absence of the unconditioned stimulus so that it no longer elicits the conditioned response.

Extinction (operant conditioning). The disappearance of a behavior as a result of nonreinforcement.

Extrinsic motivation. Motivation to engage in an activity as a means to an end.

Feedback. Information teachers provide to students that helps students determine whether or not the knowledge they're constructing is accurate and valid.

Fixed mindset (entity view of ability). The belief that abilities are relatively fixed, stable, and unchanging over time and task conditions.

Flipped instruction (commonly called the "flipped classroom"). An approach to instruction that has students study new content online by watching video lectures, usually at home, and do problems, exercises, and other activities that apply the content in class.

Flow. An intense form of intrinsic motivation in which an individual is in a state of complete absorption, focus, and concentration in a challenging activity.

Fluid intelligence. The flexible, culture-free mental ability to adapt to new situations and acquire knowledge quickly.

Focus. The essential teaching skill teachers use to capture and maintain students' attention and interest throughout the lesson.

Forgetting. The loss of, or inability to retrieve, information from long-term memory.

Formal assessment. The process of systematically gathering information about learning from all students.

Frequency distribution. A distribution of test scores that shows a count of the number of people who obtained each score.

Functional analysis. The strategy used to identify antecedents and consequences that influence behavior.

Gender-role identity. Beliefs about appropriate characteristics and behaviors of males and females.

General pedagogical knowledge. A type of professional knowledge that involves an understanding of instructional and classroom management strategies that apply to all topics and subject matter areas.

General transfer. The ability to apply knowledge or skills learned in one context to a variety of different contexts.

Generalization. The process that occurs when stimuli similar, but not identical, to a conditioned stimulus elicit the conditioned responses by themselves.

Gifts and talents. Abilities at the upper end of the continuum that require additional support to reach full potential.

Goal. An outcome an individual hopes to attain.

Goodness of fit. Matching what we do as teachers to each student's personalities.

Grade-equivalent score. A score that is determined by comparing an individual's score on a standardized test to the scores of students in a particular age group.

Growth mindset (incremental view of ability). The belief that intelligence, or ability, can be increased with effort.

Growth needs. Needs in intellectual achievement and aesthetic appreciation that increase as people have experiences with them.

Guided discovery. A model of instruction that involves teachers scaffolding students' constructions of concepts and the relationships among them.

Guided notes. Teacher-prepared handouts that "guide" students with cues and space available for writing key ideas and relationships in a written passage or presentation.

Guilt. The uncomfortable feeling people get when they know they've caused distress for someone else.

Handicap. A condition imposed on a person's functioning that restricts the individual's abilities.

Heuristics. General, widely applicable problem-solving strategies.

High-quality examples. Examples for which all the information students need to understand a topic is observable in the example.

High-stakes tests. Standardized tests used to make important decisions that affect students, teachers, schools, and school districts.

Hostile attributional bias. A tendency to view others' behaviors as hostile or aggressive.

I-message. A nonaccusatory communication that addresses a behavior and describes the effects on the sender and the feelings it generates in the sender.

Identity. Individuals' self-constructed definition of who they are, what their existence means, and what they want in life.

Ill-defined problem. A problem that has an ambiguous goal, more than one acceptable solution, and no generally agreed-upon strategy for reaching a solution.

Imagery. The process of forming mental pictures of an idea.

Immersion programs. English language programs that place students who are ELs in general education classrooms without additional assistance to help them learn both English and academic content at the same time.

Implementing instruction. The process of putting decisions made during planning into action.

Inclusion. A comprehensive approach to educating students with exceptionalities that advocates a total, systematic, and coordinated web of services.

Individualized education program (IEP). A written statement that provides a framework for delivering a free and appropriate education (FAPE) to every eligible student with a disability.

Informal assessment. The process of gathering incidental information about learning progress during learning activities.

Information processing theory. A theory that describes how information enters our memory system, is organized, and is finally stored.

Inhibition. A self-imposed restriction on one's behavior.

Instructional alignment. The match between learning objectives, learning activities, and assessments.

Instructional time. The amount of time left for teaching after routine management and administrative tasks are completed.

Instrumental aggression. An aggressive act aimed at gaining an object or privilege.

Intellectual disability. A disability characterized by significant limitations both in intellectual functioning and in adaptive behavior.

Intellectual functioning. General mental capacity, such as the ability to learn, reason, and solve problems. Also simply called intelligence.

Intelligence tests. Standardized tests designed to measure an individual's capacity to acquire and use knowledge, to solve problems, and to accomplish new tasks.

Intelligence. The ability to acquire and use knowledge, solve problems and reason in the abstract, and adapt to new situations in the environment.

Interactive whiteboard. A device that includes a display screen connected to a computer and projector that allows information displayed on the screen to be manipulated with special pens or hands, stored in the computer, and recovered later for further use.

Interference. The loss of information because something learned either before or after detracts from understanding.

Intermittent reinforcement schedule. A schedule of reinforcement in which some, but not all, of the desired behaviors are reinforced.

Internalization. The process through which learners incorporate external, society-based activities into internal cognitive processes.

Interpersonal harmony. A stage of moral reasoning in which conclusions are based on loyalty, living up to the expectations of others, and social conventions.

Interspersed practice. The process of deliberately mixing the practice of different skills.

Interval schedule of reinforcement. An intermittent reinforcement schedule in which behaviors are reinforced after a predictable (fixed) or unpredictable (variable) time interval.

Intrinsic motivation. Motivation to be involved in an activity for its own sake.

Introductory focus. A lesson beginning that attracts student attention and provides a conceptual framework for the lesson.

Involvement. The extent to which people are actively participating in an activity.

Language acquisition device (LAD). A genetically controlled set of processing skills that enables children to understand and use the rules governing language.

Language disorders (receptive disorders). Problems with understanding language or using language to express ideas.

Law and order. A stage of moral reasoning in which conclusions are based on following laws and rules for their own sake.

Learned helplessness. The debilitating belief that one is incapable of accomplishing tasks and has little control of the environment.

Learner diversity. The group and individual differences in our students.

Learners with exceptionalities. Students who need special help and resources to reach their full potential.

Learning (behaviorism). A relatively enduring change in observable behavior that occurs as a result of experience.

Learning (cognitive). A change in mental processes that creates the capacity to demonstrate different behaviors.

Learning activities. The learning experiences that follow reviews and help students reach standards and learning goals.

Learning disabilities. Difficulty in acquiring and using reading, writing, reasoning, listening, or mathematical abilities.

Learning objectives. Statements that specify what students should know or be able to do with respect to a topic.

Learning sciences. A field of study that focuses on learning as it exists in real-world settings and how learning may be facilitated both with and without technology.

Learning styles. Students' personal approaches to learning, problem solving, and processing information.

Least restrictive environment (LRE). A policy that places students in as typical an educational setting as possible while still meeting the students' special needs.

Lecture–discussion. An instructional model designed to help students acquire organized bodies of knowledge through short teacher presentations followed by interactive discussions.

Logical consequences. Outcomes that are conceptually related to misbehavior; they help learners make sense of an intervention by creating a link between their actions and the consequences.

Long-term memory. The permanent information store in our memory system.

Macrosystem. Bronfenbrenner's fourth level, which includes cultural influences on development.

Mainstreaming. The practice of moving students with exceptionalities from segregated settings into general education classrooms.

Maintenance EL programs. Programs for students who are ELs that build on students' native language by teaching in both that language and English.

Maintenance rehearsal. The process of repeating information over and over, either out loud or silently, without altering its form.

Market exchange. A stage of moral reasoning in which conclusions are based on an act of reciprocity on someone else's part.

Mastery goal. A goal that focuses on accomplishing a task, improving, and increasing understanding.

Mastery learning. A system of instruction that allows students to progress at their own rate through a unit of study.

Mastery-focused classroom. A classroom environment that emphasizes effort, continuous improvement, and understanding.

Maturation. Genetically controlled, age-related changes in individuals.

Mean. The average score in the distribution of a group of scores.

Meaningfulness. The extent to which items of information are interconnected.

Means–ends analysis. A heuristic that breaks a problem into subgoals and works successively on each.

Measures of central tendency. Quantitative descriptions of a group's performance as a whole.

Median. The middle score in the distribution of a group of scores.

Memory stores (sensory memory, working memory, and long-term memory). Repositories that hold information, both in a raw state and in organized, meaningful form.

Mesosystem. In Bronfenbrenner's model, the interactions and connections between the different elements of children's immediate settings.

Meta-attention. Knowledge and regulation of attention.

Metacognition. Knowledge and regulation of our thinking.

Metamemory. Knowledge and regulation of memory strategies.

Microsystem. In Bronfenbrenner's bioecological theory, the people and activities in a child's immediate surroundings.

Misconceptions. Ideas we construct that make sense to us but are inconsistent with evidence or commonly accepted explanations.

Mnemonics. Memory strategies that create associations that don't exist naturally in the content.

Mode. The most frequent score in the distribution of a group of scores.

Model. A representation that we use to help visualize what we can't observe directly.

Modeling. A general term that refers to behavioral, cognitive, and affective changes deriving from observing the actions of others.

Models of instruction. Prescriptive approaches to teaching designed to help students acquire a deep understanding of specific forms of knowledge.

Moral development. Advances in people's conceptions of right and wrong, and prosocial behaviors and traits such as honesty, fairness, and respect for others.

Moral dilemma. An ambiguous, conflicting situation that requires person to make a moral decision.

Moral domain. The domain of moral development that deals with basic principles of right, wrong, and justice.

Motivation to learn. Students' "tendencies to find academic activities meaningful and worthwhile and to try to get the intended learning benefits from them" (Brophy, 2010, p. 11).

Motivation. The "process whereby goal-directed activity is instigated and sustained" (Schunk, Meece, & Pintrich, 2014, p. 5).

Motivational zone of proximal development. The match between a learning activity and learners' prior knowledge and experiences that is close enough to stimulate interest and perceived value in the activity but not so familiar that learners are satiated by it.

Multicultural education. An approach to teaching that examines the influence of culture on learning and attempts to find ways that students' cultures can be used to enhance achievement.

Multitasking. The process of engaging in two or more activities at the same time.

Myelination. The process that occurs when cells grow around neurons to give them structural support, and a fatty coating of myelin, called the *myelin sheath*, develops to insulate axons and enable them to conduct electrical charges quickly and efficiently.

National Assessment of Educational Progress (NAEP). A battery of achievement tests administered periodically to carefully selected samples of students to provide a comprehensive picture of achievement in students across the country.

National norms. Scores on standardized tests earned by representative groups of students from around the nation to which an individual's score is compared.

Nativist theory. A theory of language development that suggests all humans are genetically wired to learn language.

Nature view of intelligence. The assertion that intelligence is essentially determined by genetics.

Need for approval. The desire to be accepted and judged positively by others.

Need. An internal force or drive to attain or to avoid a certain state or object.

Negative reinforcement. The process of increasing behavior by removing or avoiding an aversive stimulus.

Negligence. The failure of teachers or schools to exercise sufficient care in protecting students from injury.

Neo-Piagetian theory of development. A theory of cognitive development that accepts Piaget's stages but uses the acquisition of specific processing strategies to explain movement from one stage to the next.

Neurons. Nerve cells composed of cell bodies, dendrites, and axons, which make up the learning capability of the brain.

Neuroplasticity. The brain's ability to physically remodel itself in response to experience.

Neuroscience. The study of how the nervous system develops, how it's structured, and what it does.

Neutral stimulus. An object or event that doesn't initially influence behavior one way or the other.

No Child Left Behind (NCLB). Federal legislation requiring states to create standards in math and reading and to construct tests to measure every student's attainment of those standards.

Nonexclusion time-out. Seating a student near the teacher or on the edge of the classroom, with the goal of preventing the student from receiving reinforcers.

Norm-referenced standardized tests. Standardized tests that compare (reference) a student's performance with the performance of others.

Normal distribution. A distribution of scores in which the mean, median, and mode are equal and the scores distribute themselves symmetrically in a bell-shaped curve.

Norming group. The representative group of individuals whose standardized test scores are compiled for the purpose of national comparisons.

Nurture view of intelligence. The assertion that emphasizes the influence of the environment on intelligence.

Object permanence. The understanding that objects exist even when out of sight.

Open-ended questions. Questions for which a variety of answers are acceptable.

Operant conditioning. A behaviorist form of learning that occurs when an observable behavior changes in frequency or duration as the result of a consequence.

Order and safety. A learning climate variable that creates a predictable learning environment and supports learner autonomy together with a sense of physical and emotional security.

Organization. An encoding strategy that clusters related items of content into categories that illustrate relationships.

Organized bodies of knowledge. Topics that connect facts, concepts, and generalizations, and make the relationships among them explicit.

Overgeneralization. A language pattern that occurs when a child uses a word to refer to a broader class of objects than is appropriate.

Overlapping. The ability to intervene in cases of misbehavior without disrupting the flow of a lesson.

Parenting style. General patterns of interacting with and disciplining children.

Partial hearing impairment. An impairment that allows a student to use a hearing aid to hear well enough to be taught through auditory channels.

Pedagogical content knowledge. An understanding of how to represent topics in ways that make them understandable to learners, as well as an understanding of what makes specific topics easy or hard to learn.

People-first language. Language in which a student's disability is identified after the student is named.

Percentile bands. Ranges of percentile scores on standardized tests.

Percentile rank (PR). The percentage of students in the norming sample that scored at or below a particular raw score.

Perception. The process people use to find meaning in stimuli.

Performance assessments. Direct examinations of student performance on tasks relevant to life outside of school.

Performance goal. A goal that focuses on demonstrating ability and competence and how learners compare to others.

Performance-approach goal. A goal that emphasizes looking competent and receiving favorable judgments from others.

Performance-avoidance goal. A goal that emphasizes attempts to avoid looking incompetent and being judged unfavorably.

Performance-focused classroom. A classroom environment that emphasizes high grades, public displays of ability, and performance compared to others.

Personal domain. The domain of moral development that refers to decisions that are not socially regulated and do not harm or violate others' rights.

Personal interest. "A person's ongoing affinity, attraction, or liking for a domain, subject area,

topic, or activity" (Anderman & Wolters, 2006, p. 374).

Personal teaching efficacy. Teachers' beliefs that they can help all students learn, regardless of their prior knowledge, ability, or personal backgrounds.

Personal, social, and emotional development. Changes in our personality, the ways we interact with others, and our ability to manage our feelings.

Personality development. Age-related changes in personality and the ways that individuals react to their environment.

Personality. A comprehensive term that describes our attitudinal, emotional, and behavioral responses to experiences in our environment.

Personalization. The process of using intellectually and/or emotionally relevant examples to illustrate a topic.

Perspective taking. The ability to understand the thoughts and feelings of others.

Phonological loop. In working memory, a short-term storage component for words and sounds.

Physical aggression. An aggressive act that can cause bodily injury.

Physical development. Changes in the size, shape, and functioning of our bodies.

Positive behavior support. The process of using interventions that replace problem behaviors with behaviors serving the same purpose for the student but which are more appropriate.

Positive learning climate. A classroom climate in which the teacher and students work together as a community of learners to help everyone achieve.

Positive reinforcement. The process of increasing the frequency or duration of a behavior as the result of presenting a reinforcer.

Postconventional morality. A moral orientation that views moral issues in terms of abstract and self-developed principles of right and wrong.

Precise language. Teacher language that omits vague terms from explanations and responses to students' questions.

Preconventional morality. An egocentric orientation lacking any internalized standards for right and wrong.

Predictive validity. The measure of a test's ability to gauge future performance.

Prefrontal cortex. A portion of the cortex near the forehead that monitors and guides other parts of the brain's activities, including planning, maintaining attention, reasoning, decision making, emotional control, and the inhibition of unhealthy thoughts and behaviors.

Premack principle. The principle that a more-desired activity can serve as a positive reinforcer for a less-desired activity.

Presentation punishment. The process of decreasing a behavior that occurs when a stimulus (punisher) is presented.

Primary reinforcers. Consequences that satisfy basic biological needs.

Principles (laws). Statements about an area of study that are generally accepted as true.

Private speech. Self-talk that guides thinking and action.

Proactive aggression. A deliberate aggressive act initiated toward another.

Problem-based learning. A teaching strategy that uses problems as the focus for developing content, skills, and self-regulation.

Problem. The presence of a goal but the absence of an obvious way to achieve it.

Procedural knowledge. Knowledge of how to perform tasks, such as solving problems or composing essays.

Procedures. Guidelines for accomplishing recurring tasks.

Professional knowledge. The body of information and skills that are unique to a particular area of study.

Prompting. An additional question or statement used to elicit an appropriate student response after a student fails to answer correctly.

Psychomotor domain. The area of learning that focuses on physical skills.

Punishers. Consequences that weaken behaviors or decrease the likelihood of the behaviors' recurring.

Punishment–obedience. A stage of moral reasoning in which conclusions are based on the chances of getting caught and being punished.

Punishment. The process of using punishers to decrease behavior.

Qualitative research. A type of research that attempts to describe a complex educational phenomenon in a holistic fashion using nonnumeric data.

Quantitative research. The systematic, empirical investigation of phenomena using numerical data and often involving statistical and mathematical techniques.

Questioning frequency. Refers to the number of questions teachers ask during a learning activity.

Race to the Top. A competitive grant program encouraging individual states and districts to design comprehensive accountability programs that include merit pay plans for teachers based on student performance on standardized tests.

Race. A socially constructed category composed of people who share important biologically transmitted traits.

Range. The distance between the top and bottom score in a distribution of scores.

Ratio schedule of reinforcement. An intermittent reinforcement schedule where specific behaviors are reinforced either predictably (fixed) or unpredictably (variable).

Raw score. The number of items an individual answered correctly on a standardized test or subtest.

Reactive aggression. An aggressive act committed in response to frustration or another aggressive act.

Readiness tests. Standardized tests designed to assess the degree to which children are prepared for an academic or preacademic program.

Reciprocal causation. The interdependence of the environment, behavior, and personal factors in learning.

Reflective practice. The process of conducting a critical self-examination of one's teaching.

Reinforcement schedules. Patterns in the frequency and predictability of reinforcers that have differential effects on behavior.

Reinforcement. The process of applying reinforcers to increase behavior.

Reinforcer. A consequence that increases the likelihood of a behavior recurring.

Relatedness. The feeling of being connected to others in one's social environment and feeling worthy of love and respect.

Relational aggression. An aggressive act that can adversely affect interpersonal relationships.

Removal punishment. The process of decreasing a behavior that occurs when a stimulus is removed or when an individual cannot receive positive reinforcement.

Research. The process of systematically gathering information in an attempt to answer professional questions.

Resilience. A learner characteristic that, despite adversity, increases the likelihood of success in school and later life.

Resistance cultures. Cultures with beliefs, values, and behaviors that reject the values of mainstream culture.

Response cost. The process of removing reinforcers already given.

Response to intervention model of identification. A method of identifying a learning problem that focuses on the specific classroom instructional adaptations that teachers use and their success.

Retrieval. The process of pulling information from long-term memory into working memory.

Reversibility. The ability to mentally trace the process of moving from an existing state back to a previous state.

Review. A summary that helps students link what they've already learned to new information in the learning activity.

Rote learning. Learning that involves storing information in isolated pieces, most commonly through memorization.

Rules. Descriptions of standards for acceptable behavior.

Satiation. The process of using a reinforcer so frequently that it loses its ability to strengthen behaviors.

Scaffolding. Assistance that helps children complete tasks they cannot complete independently.

Scaled scores. Statistically adjusted and converted scores on standardized tests designed to accommodate differences in difficulty for different forms of the test.

Schema activation. An encoding strategy that involves activating relevant prior knowledge so that new knowledge can be connected to it.

Schemas. Cognitive structures that represent the way information is organized in our long-term memories.

Schemes. Mental operations that represent our constructed understanding of the world.

School connectedness. The belief by students that adults and peers in the school care about their learning as well as about them as individuals.

Scripts. Schemas for events that guide behavior in particular situations.

Secondary reinforcers. Consequences that become reinforcing over time through their association with other reinforcers.

Self-actualization. Reaching one's full potential and becoming all that one is capable of being.

Self-concept. A cognitive assessment of our physical, social, and academic competence.

Self-determination. The need to act on and control one's environment.

Self-efficacy. The belief that one is capable of accomplishing a specific task.

Self-esteem (self-worth). An emotional reaction to, or an evaluation of, the self.

Self-fulfilling prophecy. A phenomenon that occurs when a person's performance results from and confirms beliefs about his or her capabilities.

Self-regulated learning. The process of setting personal goals, combined with the motivation, thought processes, strategies, and behaviors that lead to reaching the goals.

Self-regulation. The ability to direct and control our actions and emotions.

Self-worth. An emotional reaction to or an evaluation of the self.

Semantic memory. Memory for concepts, principles, and the relationships among them.

Semantics. A branch of linguistics that examines the meaning of words.

Sensory memory. The memory store that briefly holds incoming stimuli from the environment in a raw, unorganized state until they can be processed.

Seriation. The ability to order objects according to increasing or decreasing length, weight, or volume.

Sexual identity. Students' self-constructed definition of who they are with respect to gender orientation.

Sexual orientation. The gender to which an individual is romantically and sexually attracted.

Shame. The painful emotion aroused when people recognize that they have failed to act or think in ways they believe are good.

Shaping. The process of reinforcing successive approximations of a behavior.

Sheltered English. An approach to teaching students who are ELs in academic classrooms that modifies instruction to assist students in learning content.

Short-term memory. Historically, the part of our memory system that temporarily holds information until it is processed (organized so it makes sense to the individual). Currently thought of as two systems: one that stores verbal information and one that stores images.

Single-gender classes. Classes where boys and girls are segregated for part or all of the day.

Situated cognition. A view of learning suggesting that learning depends on, and cannot be separated from, the context in which it occurs.

Situational interest. A person's current enjoyment, pleasure, or satisfaction generated by the immediate context.

Social cognition. The ability to use cues to understand social interactions.

Social cognitive theory. A theory of learning that focuses on changes in behavior, thinking, and emotions that result from observing others.

Social constructivism. A view of knowledge construction that suggests that learners first construct knowledge in a social context and then individually internalize it.

Social contract. A stage of moral reasoning in which conclusions are based on socially agreed-upon principles.

Social conventions. Societal norms and ways of behaving in specific situations.

Social development. The advances people make in their ability to interact and get along with others.

Social experience. The process of interacting with others. In Piaget's theory social experience promotes development by having learners compare their schemes to those of others.

Social goals. Goals to achieve particular social outcomes or interactions.

Social intelligence. The ability to understand and manage people.

Social problem solving. The ability to resolve conflicts in ways that are beneficial to all involved.

Social referencing. The ability to use social cues to help explain the meaning of uncertain circumstances and events.

Sociocultural theory of development. A theory of cognitive development that emphasizes the influence of social interactions and language, embedded within a cultural context, on cognitive development.

Sociocultural theory. A form of social constructivism that emphasizes the social dimensions of learning, but places greater emphasis on the larger cultural contexts in which learning occurs.

Socioeconomic status (SES). The combination of parents' income, occupation, and level of education that describes families' or individuals' relative standing in society.

Special education. Instruction designed to meet the unique needs of students with exceptionalities.

Specific transfer. The ability to apply information in a context similar to the one in which it was originally learned.

Speech disorders (expressive disorders). Problems in forming and sequencing sounds.

Stages of development. General patterns of thinking for children at different ages or with different amounts of experience.

Standard deviation. A statistical measure of the spread of scores.

Standard error of measurement. The range of scores within which an individual's true score is likely to fall.

Standard score. A description of performance on a standardized test that uses the standard deviation as the basic unit.

Standardized tests. Assessment instruments given to large samples of students under uniform conditions and scored and reported according to uniform procedures.

Standards-based education. The process of focusing curricula and instruction on predetermined goals or standards.

Standards. Statements that describe what students should know or be able to do at the end of a prescribed period of study.

Stanine. A description of an individual's standardized test performance that uses a scale ranging from 1 to 9 points.

Stereotype threat. The anxiety felt by members of a group resulting from concern that their behavior might confirm a stereotype.

Strategies. Cognitive operations intended to increase learning that exceed the normal activities required to carry out a task.

Structured immersion. A type of immersion English language program that attempts to assist students who are ELs by teaching both English and academic subjects at a slower pace.

Students at risk. Students who fail to complete their education with the skills necessary to succeed in today's society.

Study strategies. Specific techniques students use to increase their understanding of written materials and teacher presentations.

Summarizing. The process of preparing a concise description of verbal or written passages.

Synapses. The tiny spaces between neurons that allow messages to be transmitted from one neuron to another.

Synaptic pruning. The process of eliminating synapses that are unused or unnecessary.

Syntax. The set of rules that we use to put words together into meaningful sentences.

t-score. A standard score that defines the mean as 50 and the standard deviation as 10.

Task analysis. The process of breaking content into component parts and sequencing the parts.

Task comprehension. Learners' awareness of what they are supposed to be learning and an understanding of why the task is important and worthwhile.

Teacher evaluation. The process of assessing teachers' classroom performance and providing feedback they can use to increase their expertise.

Temperament. Genetically determined and relatively consistent tendencies to respond to events in the environment in particular ways.

Text signals. Elements included in written materials that communicate text organization and key ideas.

Theories. Comprehensive sets of related patterns, derived from observations, that researchers use to explain and predict events in the world.

Theory of mind. An understanding that other people have different and distinctive perceptions, feelings, desires, and beliefs.

Tracking. Placing students in different classes or curricula on the basis of achievement.

Transfer. The ability to take understanding acquired in one context and apply it to another.

Transformation. The ability to mentally record the process of moving from one state to another.

Transition signals. Verbal statements indicating that one idea is ending and another is beginning.

Transitional EL programs. English learner programs that attempt to use the native language as an instructional aid until English becomes proficient.

Transitivity. The ability to infer a relationship between two objects based on knowledge of their relationship with a third object. Concrete operational learners can think logically, but they need tangible materials to do so effectively.

Trends in International Mathematics and Science Study (TIMSS). A comparison of standardized test score data of U.S. students to students in other industrialized countries by the NAEP.

True score. The hypothetical average of an individual's scores if repeated testing under ideal conditions were possible.

Unconditional positive regard. Treating individuals as if they are innately worthy regardless of their behavior.

Unconditioned response. The instinctive or reflexive (unlearned) physiological or emotional response caused by the unconditioned stimulus.

Unconditioned stimulus. An object or event that causes an instinctive or reflex (unlearned) emotional or physiological response.

Undergeneralization. A language pattern that occurs when a child uses a word too narrowly.

Universal design for learning. Part of a larger movement in education that seeks to understand and adapt to the needs of diverse learners so supports are provided to all students, including those with exceptionalities.

Universal principles. A stage of moral reasoning in which conclusions are based on abstract and general principles that transcend or exceed society's laws.

Utility value. The belief that a topic, activity, or course of study will be useful for meeting future goals, including career goals.

Value-added modeling. A method of teacher evaluation that measures a teacher's contribution to student learning in a given year by comparing the current test scores of their students to the scores of those same students in previous school years, and to the scores of other students in the same grade.

Value-added models. Teacher evaluation procedures that assess the amount students learn, as measured by their performance on standardized tests, while in a particular teacher's classroom.

Value. The benefits, rewards, or advantages that individuals believe can result from participating in an activity.

Variability. The spread of scores, or degree of difference or deviation from the mean.

Vicarious learning. The process of observing the consequences of others' actions and adjusting our own behavior accordingly.

Virtual field trips. Visits to Internet sites that allow students to experience locations that they are unlikely to see in real life.

Virtual manipulatives. Replicas of physical manipulatives that are accessed using technology and manipulated with a keyboard or mouse.

Visual handicap. An uncorrectable visual impairment that interferes with learning.

Visual-spatial sketchpad. In working memory, a short-term storage system for visual and spatial information.

Wait-time. A period of silence, both before and after calling on a student, that gives students time to think about their answer to a question.

Well-defined problem. A problem that has a clear goal, only one correct solution, and a defined method for finding it.

Within-class grouping. Divides students in a single class into groups, typically based on reading and math scores.

Withitness. A teacher's awareness of what is going on in all parts of the classroom at all times and communicating this awareness to students.

Worked examples. Problems with completed solutions that provide students with one way of learning to solve problems.

Working memory. The conscious component of our memory system and the memory store that holds and organizes information as we try to make sense of it.

Zone of proximal development. A range of tasks that an individual cannot yet do alone but can accomplish when assisted by the guidance of others.

z-score. The number of standard deviation units from the mean.

References

Aaron J., Auger, R. W., & Pepperell, J. L. (2013). "If we're ever in trouble they're always there." A qualitative study of teacher-student caring. *The Elementary School Journal, 114,* 100–117.

ABCya.com. (2013). *Virtual manipulatives.* Retrieved from https://itunes.apple.com/us/app/virtual-manipulatives!/id471341079?mt=8#

Abe, J. A., & Izzard, C. E. (1999). Compliance, noncompliance strategies, and the correlates of compliance in 5-year-old Japanese and American children. *Social Development, 8,* 1–20.

Abedi, J., & Gándara, P. (2006). Performance of English language learners as a subgroup in large-scale assessment: Interaction of research and policy. *Educational Measurement: Issues and Practice, 25*(4), 36–46.

Aboud, F., & Skerry, S. (1984). The development of ethnic attitudes: A critical review. *Journal of Cross-Cultural Psychology, 15,* 3–34.

Ackerman, P., & Lohman, D. (2006). Individual differences in cognitive function. In P. A. Alexander & P. H. Winne (Eds.), *Handbook of educational psychology* (2nd ed., pp. 139–162). Mahwah, NJ: Erlbaum.

Adams, C. (2006). PowerPoint, habits of mind, and classroom culture. *Journal of Curriculum Studies, 38,* 389–411.

Adamski, A., Fraser, B. J., & Peiro, M. M. (2013). Parental involvement in schooling, classroom environment and student outcomes. *Learning Environments Research, 16,* 315–328.

Adesope, O., Lavin, T., Thompson, R., & Ungerleider, C. (2010). A systematic review and meta-analysis of the cognitive correlates of bilingualism. *Review of Educational Research, 80,* 207–245.

Adeyemo, S. A. (2013). The relationship between effective classroom management and students' academic achievement in physics. *Journal of Applied Sciences Research, 9,* 1032–1042.

Afflerbach, P., & Cho, B.-Y. (2010). Determining and describing reading strategies: Internet and traditional forms of reading. In H. Waters & W. Schneider (Eds.), *Metacognition, strategy use, and instruction* (pp. 201–225). New York: Guilford.

Ahmad, I., Said, H., & Khan, F. (2013). Effect of corporal punishment on students' motivation and classroom learning. *Review of European Studies, 5,* 130–134.

Ahmadlou, M., & Adeli, H. (2010). Wavelet-synchronization methodology: A new approach for EEG-based diagnosis of ADHD. *Clinical EEG Neuroscience, 41,* 1–10.

Ahrens, K., DuBois, D., Lozano, P., & Richardson, L. (2010). Naturally acquired mentoring relationships and young adult outcomes among adolescents with learning disabilities. *Learning Disabilities Research & Practice, 25,* 207–216.

Aikins, J., & Litwack, S. (2011). Prosocial skills, social competence, and popularity. In A. Cillessen, D., Schwartz, & L. Mayeux (Eds.), *Popularity in the peer system* (pp. 140–162). New York: Guilford.

Aikens, N., & Barbarin, O. (2008). Socioeconomic differences in reading trajectories: The contribution of family, neighborhood, and school contexts. *Journal of Educational Psychology, 100,* 235–251.

Aktar, E., Majdandžić, M., Vente, W., & Bögels, S. M. (2014). Parental social anxiety disorder prospectively predicts toddlers' fear/avoidance in a social referencing paradigm. *Journal of Child Psychology & Psychiatry, 55,* 77–87. doi:10.1111/jcpp.12121.

Alberto, P. A., & Troutman, A. C. (2013). *Applied behavior analysis for teachers* (9th ed.). Upper Saddle River, NJ: Merrill/Pearson.

Al-Debei, M. M., Al-Lozi, E., & Papazafeiropoulou, A. (2013). Why people keep coming back to Facebook: Explaining and predicting continuance participation from an extended theory of planned behaviour perspective. *Decision Support Systems, 55,* 43–54.

Alexander, J. M., Johnson, K. E., & Leibham, M. E. (2005). Constructing domain-specific knowledge in kindergarten: Relations among knowledge, intelligence, and strategic performance. *Learning and Individual Differences, 15,* 35–52.

Alexander, L. (2012). NCLB lessons: It is time for Washington to get out of the way. *Education Week, 31*(15), 40.

Alexander, P. (2003). The development of expertise: The journey from acclimation to proficiency. *Educational Researcher, 32*(8), 10–14.

Alexander, P. (2006). *Psychology in learning and instruction.* Upper Saddle River, NJ: Pearson.

Alferink, L., & Farmer-Dougan, V. (2010). Brain-(not)based education: Dangers of misunderstanding and misapplication of neuroscience research. *Exceptionality, 18,* 42–52.

Alghamdi, R., & Gillies, R. (2013). The impact of cooperative learning in comparison to traditional learning (small groups) on EFL learners' outcomes when learning English as a foreign language. *Asian Social Science, 9,* 19–27.

Alibali, M. W., Spencer, R. C., Knox, L., & Kita, S. (2011). Spontaneous gestures influence strategy choices in problem solving. *Psychological Science, 22,* 1138–1144.

Alim, H., & Baugh, J. (Eds.). (2007). *Talkin black talk: Language, education, and social change.* New York: Teachers College Press.

Alloway, T., Gathercole, S., Kirkwood, H., & Elliott, J. (2009). The cognitive and behavioral characteristics of children with low working memory. *Child Development, 80,* 606–621.

Almasy, S., Segal, K., & Couwels, J. (2013). Sheriff: Taunting post leads to arrests in Rebecca Sedwick bullying death. CNN Justice. Retrieved from http://www.cnn.com/2013/10/15/justice/rebecca-sedwick-bullying-death-arrests/

Al-Namlah, A., Meins, E., & Fernyhough, C. (2012). Self-regulatory private speech relates to children's recall and organization of autobiographical memories. *Early Childhood Research Quarterly.* Retrieved from http://yadda.icm.edu.pl/yadda/element/bwmeta1.element.elsevier-e92613b8-240b-3031-8fa8-37860c4f13b9

Alparsian, C., Tekkaya, C., & Geban, O. (2004). Using the conceptual change instruction to improve learning. *Journal of Biological Education, 37,* 133–137.

Alvarez, L. (2013). Seeing the toll, schools revise zero tolerance. *The New York Times.* Retrieved from http://www.nytimes.com/2013/12/03/education/seeing-the-toll-schools-revisit-zero-tolerance.html?partner=rss&emc=rss&_r=0&pagewanted=print

American Academy of Pediatrics. (2011). Where we stand: Spanking. Retrieved from http://www.healthychildren.org/English/familylife/family-dynamics/communication-discipline/Pages/Where-We-Stand-Spanking.aspx

American Association on Intellectual and Developmental Disabilities (AAIDD). (2013). *Definition of intellectual disability.* Retrieved from http://aaidd.org/intellectual-disability/definition#.Uv1HVsKYbfs

American Educational Research Association, American Psychological Association, & National Council on Measurement in Education. (1999). *Standards for educational and psychological testing* (2nd ed.). Washington, DC: Author.

American Humane Association. (2013). *Dog bite statistics.* Retrieved from http://www.americanhumane.org/animals/stop-animal-abuse/fact-sheets/dog-bites.html

American Psychiatric Association. (2013). *Diagnostic and statistical manual of mental disorders* (5th ed.). Washington, DC: Author.

American Psychological Association. (2014). *Teen suicide is preventable.* Retrieved from https://www.apa.org/research/action/suicide.aspx

Amrein-Beardsley, A. (2012). Recruiting expert teachers into high-needs schools: Leadership, money, & colleagues. *Education Policy Analysis Archives, 20*(27), 1–26.

Amunts, K., Kedo, O., Kindler, M., Pieperhoff, P., Mohlberg, H., Shah, N. J., . . . Zilles, K. (2005). Cytoarchitectonic mapping of the human amygdala, hippocampal region and entorhinal cortex: Intersubject variability and probability maps. *Anatomy and Embryology, 210,* 343–352.

Anderman, E., & Mueller, C. (2010). Middle school transitions and adolescent development. In J. Meece & J. Eccles (Eds.), *Handbook of research on schools, schooling, and human development* (pp. 198–215). Mahwah, NJ: Erlbaum.

Anderman, E. M., & Maehr, M. (1994). Motivation and schooling in the middle grades. *Review of Educational Research, 64,* 287–309.

Anderman, E. M., & Wolters, C. A. (2006). Goals, values, and affect: Influences on motivation. In P. A. Alexander & P. H. Winne (Eds.), *Handbook of educational psychology* (2nd ed., pp. 369–389). Mahwah, NJ: Erlbaum.

Anderson, D., & Nashon, S. (2007). Predators of knowledge construction: Interpreting students' metacognition in an amusement park physics program. *Science Education, 91*, 298–320.

Anderson, J. (2010). *Cognitive psychology and its implications* (7th ed.). New York: Worth.

Anderson, K., & Minke, K. (2007). Parent involvement in education: Toward an understanding of parents' decision making. *Journal of Educational Research, 199*(5), 311–323.

Anderson, L., & Krathwohl, D. (Eds.). (2001). *A taxonomy for learning, teaching, and assessing: A revision of Bloom's taxonomy of educational objectives.* New York: Addison Wesley Longman.

Anderson, P. M., & Summerfield, J. P. (2004). Why is urban education different from suburban and rural education? In S. R. Steinberg & J. L. Kincheloe (Eds.), *19 urban questions: Teaching in the city* (pp. 29–39). New York: Peter Lang.

Anderson, T., & Shattuck, J. (2012). Design-based research: A decade of progress in education research? *Educational Researcher, 41*, 16–25. doi:10.3102/0013189X11428813

Andrew, L. (2007). Comparison of teacher educators' instructional methods with the constructivist ideal. *The Teacher Educator, 42*, 157–184.

Ang, R., & Goh, D. (2010). Cyberbullying among adolescents: The role of affective and cognitive empathy, and gender. *Child Psychiatry and Human Development, 41*, 387–397.

Anguera, J. A., Boccanfuso, J., Rintoul, J. L., Al-Hashimi, O., Faraji, O., Janowich, J., . . . Gazzaley, A. (2013). Video game training enhances cognitive control in older adults. *Nature, 501*(7465), 97–101.

Annenberg Foundation. (2011). *The guardian of democracy: The civic mission of schools report.* Retrieved from http://www.civicmissionofschools.org/the-campaign/guardian-of-democracy-report

Antil, L., Jenkins, J., Wayne, S., & Vadasy, P. (1998). Cooperative learning: Prevalence, conceptualizations, and the relation between research and practice. *American Educational Research Journal, 35*(3), 419–454.

Applebee, A., Langer, J., Nystrand, M., & Gamoran, A. (2003). Discussion-based approaches to developing understanding: Classroom instruction and student performance in middle and high school English. *American Educational Research Journal, 40*(3), 685–730.

Archer-Banks, D., & Behar-Horenstein, L. (2012). Ogbu revisited: Unpacking high-achieving African American girls' high school experience. *Urban Education, 47*(1), 198–223.

Arghode, V. (2013). Emotional and social intelligence competence: Implications for instruction. *International Journal of Pedagogies and Learning, 8*, 66–77.

Arias-Carrión, O., Stamelou, M., Murillo-Rodríguez, E., Menéndez-González, M., & Pöppel, E. (2010). Dopaminergic reward system: A short integrative review. *International Archives of Medicine, 3*, 24. doi:10.1186/1755-7682-3-24. Retrieved from http://www.intarchmed.com/content/3/1/24

Armstrong, K. (2001). *Holy war: The crusades and their impact on today's world.* New York: Anchor/Random House.

Armstrong, T. (2010). *Neurodiversity: Discovering the extraordinary gifts of autism, ADHD, dyslexia, and other brain differences.* Philadelphia: Da Capo Lifelong Books.

Arnon, I., & Ramscar, M. (2012). Granularity and the acquisition of grammatical gender: How order-of-acquisition affects what gets learned. *Cognition, 122*, 292–305.

Aronson, E., Wilson, T. D., & Akert, R. D. (2013). *Social psychology* (8th ed.). Upper Saddle River, NJ: Pearson.

Artiles, A., Kozleski, E., Trent, S., Osher, D., & Ortiz, A. (2010). Justifying and explaining disproportionality, 1968–2008: A critique of underlying views of culture. *Exceptional Children, 76*(3), 279–299.

Arya, R., Chansoria, M., Konanki, R., & Tiwari, D. (2012). Maternal music exposure during pregnancy influence neo-natal behavior: An open-label randomized controlled trial. *International Journal of Pediatrics.* doi:10.1155/2012/901812

Asbridge, T. (2012). *The Crusades: The authoritative history of the war for the Holy Land.* New York: Ecco/HarperCollins.

Ashcraft, M., & Radvansky, G. (2014). *Cognition* (6th ed.). Upper Saddle River, NJ: Pearson.

Atkinson, J., & Braddick, O. (2012). Visual attention in the first years: Typical development and developmental disorders. *Developmental Medicine and Child Neurology, 54*, 589–595.

Atkinson, R., & Shiffrin, R. (1968). Human memory: A proposed system and its control processes. In K. Spence & J. Spence (Eds.), *The psychology of learning and motivation: Advances in research and theory* (Vol. 2). San Diego, CA: Academic Press.

Au, K. (1992, April). *"There's almost a lesson here": Teacher and students' purposes in constructing the theme of a story.* Paper presented at the annual meeting of the American Educational Research Association, San Francisco.

Aud, S., Fox, M., & KewalRamani, A. (2010). *Status and trends in the education of racial and ethnic minorities.* Washington, DC: U.S. Department of Education.

Aud, S., Wilkinson-Flicker, S., Kristapovich, P., Rathbun, A., Wang, X., & Zhang, J. (2013). *The Condition of Education 2013* (NCES 2013-037). U.S. Department of Education, National Center for Education Statistics. Washington, DC. Retrieved from http://nces.ed.gov/pubs2013/2013037.pdf

Austin, J. L., Lee, M., & Carr, J. P. (2004). The effects of guided notes on undergraduate students' recording of lecture content. *Journal of Instructional Psychology, 31*, 314–320.

Austin, S. B., Nelson, L. A., Birkett, M. A., Calzo, J. P., & Everett, B. (2013). Eating disorder symptoms and obesity at the intersections of gender, ethnicity, and sexual orientation in US high school students. *American Journal of Public Health, 103*, e16–e22.

Ausubel, D. P. (1963). *The psychology of meaningful verbal learning.* New York: Grune & Stratton.

Ausubel, D. P. (1968). *Educational psychology: A cognitive view.* New York: Holt, Rinehart & Winston.

Ausubel, D. P. (1977). The facilitation of meaningful verbal learning in the classroom. *Educational Psychologist, 12*, 162–178.

Auyeung, B., & Baron-Cohen, S. (2012). Fetal testosterone in mind: Human sex differences and autism. In F. de Waal & P. Ferrari (Eds.), *The primate mind: Built to connect with other minds.* Cambridge: MA: Harvard University Press.

Babad, E., Bernieri, F., & Rosenthal, R. (1991). Students as judges of teachers' verbal and nonverbal behavior. *American Educational Research Journal, 28*(1), 211–234.

Baddeley, A. D. (1986). *Working memory: Theory and practice.* London, UK: Oxford University Press.

Baddeley, A. D. (2001). Is working memory still working? *American Psychologist, 56*, 851–864.

Baeten, M., Struyven, K., & Dochy, F. (2013). Student-centred teaching methods: Can they optimise students' approaches to learning in professional higher education? *Studies in Educational Evaluation, 39*, 14–22.

Bafunno, D., & Camodeca, M. (2013) Shame and guilt development in preschoolers: The role of context, audience and individual characteristics. *European Journal of Developmental Psychology, 10*, 128–143. DOI:10.1080/17405629.2013.765796.

Bailey, S. (1993). The current status of gender equity research in American Schools. *Educational psychologist, 28*, 321–339.

Bain, S. K., & Allin, J. D. (2005). Book review: Stanford-Binet intelligence scales, fifth edition. *Journal of Psychoeducational Assessment, 23*, 87–95.

Baines, L. (2007). Learning from the world: Achieving more by doing less. *Phi Delta Kappan, 89*, 98–100.

Baker, D. (2006). For Navajo, science and tradition intertwine. *Salt Lake Tribune*, pp. D1, D5.

Baker, E. L., Barton, P. E., Darling-Hammond, L., Haertel, E., Ladd, H. F., Linn, R. L., . . . Shepard, L. A. (2010). Problems with the use of student test scores to evaluate teachers. *Economic Policy Institute.* Retrieved from http://www.epi.org/files/page/-/pdf/bp278.pdf

Balagna, R. M., Young, E. L., & Smith, T. B. (2013). School experiences of early adolescent. Latinos/as at risk for emotional and behavioral disorders. *School Psychology Quarterly, 28*, 101–121.

Balcetis, E., & Dunning, D. (2007). Cognitive dissonance and the perception of natural environments. *Psychological Science, 18*, 917–921.

Baldwin, J. D., & Baldwin, J. I. (2001). *Behavior principles in everyday life* (4th ed.). Upper Saddle River, NJ: Prentice Hall.

Balf, T. (2014). The story behind the SAT overhaul. *The New York Times*. Retrieved from http://www.nytimes.com/2014/03/09/magazine/the-story-behind-the-sat-overhaul.html?_r=0

Ball, D. (1992, Summer). Magical hopes: Manipulatives and the reform of math education. *American Educator*, pp. 28–33.

Ballot, D., Potterton, J., Chirwa, T., Hilburn, N., & Cooper, P. (2012). Developmental outcomes of very low birth weight infants in a development country. *BMC Pediatrics, 12*. Retrieved from http://www.biomedcentral.com/1471-2431/12/11

Balog, H. (2010). A comparison of maternal and child intonation: Does adult input support child production? *Infant Behavior & Development, 33*(3), 337–345.

Bandow, D. (2013). Immigration benefits the U.S., so let's legalize all work. *Forbes*. Retrieved from http://www.forbes.com/sites/dougbandow/2013/09/16/immigration-benefits-the-u-s-so-lets-legalize-all-work/.

Bandura, A. (1986). *Social foundations of thought and action: A social cognitive theory.* Upper Saddle River, NJ: Prentice Hall.

Bandura, A. (1997). *Self-efficacy: The exercise of control.* New York: Freeman.

Bandura, A. (2001). Social cognitive theory. In *Annual Review of Psychology*. Palo Alto, CA: Annual Review.

Bandura, A. (2004, May). *Toward a psychology of human agency.* Paper presented at the meeting of the American Psychological Society, Chicago.

Banks, J. (2014). *An introduction to multicultural education* (5th ed.). Boston: Allyn & Bacon.

Barber, A., Srinivasan, P., Joel, S., Caffo, B., Pekar, J., & Mostofsky, S. (2012). Motor "dexterity": Evidence that left hemisphere lateralization of motor circuit connectivity is associated with better motor performance in children. *Cerebral Cortex, 22*, 51–59.

Barnes, S. P., Torrens, A., & George, V. (2007). The use of portfolios in coordinated school health programs: Benefits and challenges to implementation. *The Journal of School Health, 77*, 171–179.

Barnett, S. M., & Ceci, S. J. (2002). When and where do we apply what we learn? A taxonomy for far transfer. *Psychological Bulletin, 128*, 612–637.

Baron-Cohen, S. (2012). Autism and the technical mind. *Scientific American, 307*(5), 72–75.

Barrick, M., R., Mount, M. K., & Li, N. (2013). The theory of purposeful work behavior: The role of personality, higher-order goals, and job characteristics. *Academy of Management Review, 38*, 132–153. http://dx.doi.org/10.5465/amr,2010.0479

Bartholomew, D. (2004). *Measuring intelligence.* New York: Cambridge University Press.

Bauerlein, M. (2008). *The dumbest generation: How the digital age stupefies young Americans and jeopardizes our future.* New York: Penguin.

Baumeister, R., Campbell, J., Krueger, I., & Vohs, K. (2003). Does high self-esteem cause better performance, interpersonal success, happiness, or healthier lifestyles? *Psychological Science in the Public Interest, 4*(1), 1–44.

Baumeister, R. F., & DeWall, C. N. (2005). The inner dimension of social exclusion: Intelligent thought and self-regulation among rejected persons. In K. D. Williams, J. P. Forgas, & W. von Hippel (Eds.), *The social outcast: Ostracism, social exclusion, rejection, and bullying* (pp. 53–73). New York: Psychology Press.

Baumrind, D. (2005). Patterns of parental authority. *New Directions in Child Adolescent Development, 108*, 61–69.

Baumrind, D., Larzelere, R., & Owens, E. (2010). Effects of preschool parents' power assertive patterns and practices on adolescent development. *Parent, 10*, 157–201.

Bausell, R. B. (2013). Putting value-added evaluation to the (scientific) test. *Education Week, 32*(17), 22, 23, 25.

Beghetto, R. A. (2010). Creativity in the classroom. In J. C. Kaufman & R. J. Sternberg (Eds.), *The Cambridge handbook of creativity* (pp. 447–466). Cambridge, UK: Cambridge University Press.

Beghetto, R., & Kaufman, J. C. (2013). Fundamentals of creativity. *Educational Leadership, 70*, 10–15.

Begley, S. (2010, June 28 and July 5). This is your brain. Aging. *Newsweek*, 64–68.

Beil, L. (2011, November 29). The certainty of memory has its day in court. *New York Times*, D1, D6.

Beisert, M., Zmyj, N., Liepelt, R., Jung, F., Prinz, W., & Daum, M. (2012). Rethinking 'rational imitation' in 14-month-old infants: A perceptual distraction approach. *Plos ONE, 7*(3) Retrieved from http://www.ncbi.nlm.nih.gov/pmc/articles/PMC3303798/

Bellmore, A. (2011). Peer rejection and unpopularity: Associations with GPAs across the transition to middle school. *Journal of Educational Psychology, 103*, 282–295.

Belo, R., Ferreira, P., & Telang, R. (2010). *The effects of broadband in schools: Evidence from Portugal.* Retrieved from http://papers.ssrn.com/sol3/papers.cfm?abstract_id=1636584

Bembenutty, H. (2009). Test anxiety and academic delay of gratification. *College Student Journal, 43*, 10–21.

Bental, B., & Tirosh, E. (2007). The relationship between attention, executive functions and reading domain abilities in attention deficit hyperactivity disorder and reading disorder: A comparative study. *The Journal of Child Psychology and Psychiatry and Allied Disciplines, 48*, 455–463.

Bereiter, C., & Scardamalia, M. (2006). Education for the knowledge age: Design-centered models of teaching and instruction. In P. A. Alexander & P. H. Winne (Eds.), *Handbook of educational psychology* (2nd ed., pp. 695–714). Mahwah, NJ: Erlbaum.

Berger, J. (2013). *Contagious: Why things catch on.* New York: Simon and Schuster.

Berger, K. (2012). *The developing person through the life span* (8th ed.). New York: Worth.

Berk, L. (2013). *Child development* (9th ed.). Boston: Allyn & Bacon.

Berk, L. (2013). *Development through the lifespan* (6th ed.). Boston: Allyn & Bacon/Pearson.

Berkman, L. F., & Syme, S. L. (1979). Social networks, host resistance, and mortality: A nine-year follow-up study of Alameda County Residents. *American Journal of Epidemiology, 109*, 186–204.

Berliner, D. (2005). Our impoverished view of educational reform. *Teachers College Record*, August 2. ID Number: 12106. Retrieved from http://www.tcrecord.org

Berliner, D. C. (2000). A personal response to those who bash education. *Journal of Teacher Education, 51*, 358–371.

Berliner, D. C. (2006). Educational psychology: Searching for essence throughout a century of influence. In P. A. Alexander & P. H. Winne (Eds.), *Handbook of educational psychology* (2nd ed., pp. 3–42). Mahwah, NJ: Erlbaum.

Bernier, S., Simpson, C. G., & Rose, C. A. (2012). Positive and negative reinforcement in increasing compliance and decreasing problematic behavior. *National Teacher Education Journal, 5*, 45–52.

Berrill, D., & Whalen, C. (2007). "Where are the children?" Personal integrity and reflective teaching portfolios. *Teaching and Teacher Education, 23*, 868–884.

Berzonsky, M. (2011). A social-cognitive perspective on identity construction. In S. Schwartz, K. Luyckx, & V. Vignoles (Eds.), *Handbook of identity theory and research* (pp. 55–76). New York: Springer.

Berzonsky, M., Cieciuch, J., Duriez, B., & Soenens, B. (2011). The how and what of identity formation: Associations between identity styles and value orientations. *Personality and Individual Differences, 50*, 195–299.

Best, S., Reed, P., & Bigge, J. (2010). Assistive technology. In S. Best, K. Heller, & J. Bigge (Eds.), *Teaching individuals with physical or multiple disabilities* (6th ed., pp. 175–220). Upper Saddle River, NJ: Merrill/Pearson.

Beuker, K. T., Rommelse, N. N., Donders, R., & Buitelaar, J. K. (2013). Development of early communication skills in the first two years of life. *Infant Behavior and Development, 36*, 71–83.

Bharti, R. (2013). A study of personality factors in relation to emotional intelligence of student-teachers. *Golden Research Thoughts, 3*, 1–7.

Bhutto, M. I. (2011). Effects of social reinforcers on students' learning outcomes at secondary school level. *International Journal of Academic Research in Business and Social Sciences, 1*, 71–86.

Bialystok, E. (2011). Coordination of executive functions in monolingual and bilingual children. *Journal of Experimental Child Psychology, 110*, 461–468.

Bjorklund, D. (2012). *Children's thinking* (5th ed.). Belmont, CA: Cengage.

Black, S. (2007). Apprenticeships: A tradition that works. *American School Board Journal, 194*(2), 38–40.

Blanchett, W. (2006). Disproportionate representation of African American students in special education: Acknowledging the role of white privilege and racism. *Educational Researcher, 35*(6), 24–28.

Blatchford, P., Baines, E., Rubie-Davies, C., Bassett, P., & Chowne, A. (2006). The effect of a new approach to group work on pupil–pupil and teacher–pupil interactions. *Journal of Educational Psychology, 98*(4), 750–765.

Bleidorn, W. (2012). Hitting the road to adulthood: Short-term personality development during a major life transition. *Personality and Social Psychology Bulletin, 38,* 12, 1594–1608. doi:10.1177/0146167212456707.

Block, M. (2007). Climate changes lives of whalers in Alaska. *All Things Considered.* National Public Radio. Retrieved from http://www.npr.org/templates/story/story.php? storyId=14428086

Bloom, B., Englehart, M., Furst, E., Hill, W., & Krathwohl, O. (1956). *Taxonomy of educational objectives: The classification of educational goals: Handbook 1. The cognitive domain.* White Plains, NY: Longman.

Bloom, P. (2010). The moral life of babies. *New York Times Magazine.* Retrieved from http://www.nytimes.com/2010/05/09/magazine/09babies-t.html?_r=0

Blumberg, S., Bramlett, M., Kogan, M., Schieve, L., Jones, J., & Lu, M. (2013). Changes in prevalence of parent-reported autism spectrum disorder in school-aged U.S. children: 2007 to 2011–2012. *National Health Statistics Reports, 65,* 1–12. Retrieved from http://www.cdc.gov/nchs/data/nhsr/nhsr065.pdf

Blumenfeld, P., Kempler, T., & Krajcik, J. (2006). Motivation and cognitive engagement in learning environments. In R. K. Sawyer (Ed.), *Cambridge handbook of the learning sciences* (pp. 475–488). Cambridge, MA: Cambridge University Press.

Boehm, K. (2012). Left brain, right brain: An outdated argument. *Yale Scientific.* Retrieved from http://www.yalescientific.org/2012/04/left-brain-right-brain-an-outdated-argument/

Bohn, C. M., Roehrig, A. D., & Pressley, M. (2004). The first days of school in the classrooms of two more effective and four less effective primary-grades teachers. *Elementary School Journal, 104*(4), 269–288.

Bolívar, J. M., & Chrispeels, J. H. (2011). Enhancing parent leadership through building social and intellectual capital. *American Educational Research Journal, 48,* 4–38.

Bonanno, R. A., & Hymel, S. (2010). Beyond hurt feelings: Investigating why some victims of bullying are at greater risk for suicidal ideation. *Merrill-Palmer Quarterly, 56,* 420–440.

Bong, M. (2001). Between- and within-domain relations of academic motivation among middle and high school students: Self-efficacy, task-value, and achievement goals. *Journal of Educational Psychology, 93,* 23–34.

Borko, H., & Putnam, R. (1996). Learning to teach. In D. Berliner & R. Calfee (Eds.), *Handbook of educational psychology* (pp. 673–708). New York: Macmillan.

Bornstein, M., & Lansford, J. (2010). Parenting. In M. Bornstein (Ed.), *Handbook of cultural developmental science* (pp. 259–277). New York: Psychology Press.

Bornstein, M., Hahn, C., & Haynes, O. (2010). Social competence, externalizing, and internalizing behavioral adjustment from early childhood through early adolescence: Developmental cascades. *Development and Psychopathology, 22*(4), 717–735. doi:10.1017/S0954579410000416

Bornstein, M., Hahn, C., & Haynes, O. (2011). Maternal personality, parenting cognitions, and parenting practices. *Developmental Psychology, 47,* 658–675.

Boyd, D., & Bee, H. (2012). *The developing child* (13th ed.). Upper Saddle River, NJ: Pearson.

Boyle, J. R. (2013). Strategic note-taking for inclusive middle school science classrooms. *Remedial and Special Education, 34,* 78–90.

Braaksma, M., Rijlaarsdam, G., van den Bergh, H., & van Hout-Wolters, B. (2004). Observational learning and its effects on the orchestration of writing processes. *Cognition & Instruction, 22*(1), 1–36.

Braaten, E. (2011). *How to find mental health care for your child.* Washington, DC: American Psychological Association.

Bradley, C., & Pearson, J. (2012). The sensory components of high-capacity iconic memory and visual working memory. *Frontiers in Psychology, 3,* 355. doi:10.3389/fpsyg.2012.00355

Brainerd, C. J. (2003). Jean Piaget, learning research, and American education. In B. Zimmerman & D. Schunk (Eds.), *Educational psychology: A century of contributions* (pp. 251–287). New York: Routledge.

Brannon, L. (2011). *Gender: Psychological perspective* (6th ed.). Boston: Pearson.

Bransford, J. D., & Schwartz, D. L. (1999). Rethinking transfer: A simple proposal with multiple implications. *Review of Research in Education* (Vol. 24, pp. 61–100). Washington, DC: American Educational Research Association.

Bransford, J. D., & Stein, B. S. (1993). *The ideal problem solver* (2nd ed.). New York: Freeman.

Bransford, J., Brown, A., & Cocking, R. (Eds.). (2000). *How people learn: Brain, mind, experience, and school.* Washington, DC: National Academy Press.

Braun, H., Kirsch, I., & Yamamoto, K. (2011). An experimental study of the effects of monetary incentives on performance on the 12th-grade NAEP reading assessment. *Teachers College Record, 113,* 2309–2344. Retrieved from http://www.tcrecord.org/Content.asp?ContentID=16008

Brehmer, Y., & Li, S-C. (2007). Memory plasticity across the life span: Uncovering children's latent potential. *Developmental Psychology, 43,* 465–478.

Brice, A., & Brice, R. (2009). *Language development: Monolingual and bilingual acquisition* (1st ed.). Upper Saddle River, NJ: Pearson.

Bridgett, D., Gartstein, M., Putnam, S., McKay, T., Iddins, R., Robertson, C., . . . Rittmueller, A. (2009). Maternal and contextual influences and the effect of temperament development during infancy on parenting in toddlerhood. *Infant Behavior and Development, 32,* 103–116.

Brimley, V., Verstegen, D., & Garfield, R. (2012). *Financing education in a climate of change* (11th ed.). Boston: Allyn & Bacon.

Brinck, I., & Liljenfors, R. (2013). The developmental origin of metacognition. *Infant and Child Development, 22,* 85–101.

Brittian, A. S., Umaña-Taylor, A. J., & Derlan, C. L. (2013). An examination of biracial college youths' family ethnic socialization, ethnic identity, and adjustment: Do self-identification labels and university context matter? *Cultural Diversity and Ethnic Minority Psychology, 19,* 177–189.

Broad Foundation. (2013). *Our education system is in deep distress.* Retrieved from http://broadeducation.org/about/crisis_stats.html

Brody, J. (2013). A label calls attention to obesity. *New York Times, July 2,* D7.

Bronfenbrenner, U. (1979). *The ecology of human development: Experiments by nature and design.* Cambridge, MA: Harvard University Press.

Bronfenbrenner, U. (2005). *Making human beings human: Bioecological perspectives on human development.* Thousand Oaks, CA: Sage.

Bronfenbrenner, U., & Morris, P. (2006). The bioecological model of human development. In R. Lerner (Ed.), *Handbook of child psychology: Vol. 1 Theoretical models of human development* (6th ed., pp. 793–828). Hoboken, NJ: Wiley.

Brook, J., Zhang, C., Finch, S., & Brook, D. (2010). Adolescent pathways to adult smoking: Ethnic identity, peer substance use, and antisocial behavior. *American Journal on Addictions, 19*(2), 178–186.

Brookhart, S. (2013). *How to create and use rubrics for formative assessment and grading.* Baltimore: American Society for Curriculum Developers.

Brookhart, S. M., & Nitko, A. J. (2015). *Educational assessment of students* (7th ed.). Upper Saddle River, NJ: Pearson.

Brooks, D. (2011). *The social animal: The hidden sources of love, character, and achievement.* New York: Random House.

Brooks, D. (2013). Beyond the brain. *The New York Times.* Retrieved from http://www.nytimes.com/2013/06/18/opinion/brooks-beyond-the-brain.html?_r=0

Brophy, J. (2006). History of research on classroom management. In C. M. Evertson & C. S. Weinstein (Eds.), *Handbook of classroom management: Research, practice, and contemporary issues* (pp. 17–43). Mahwah, NJ: Erlbaum.

Brophy, J. (2006a). Graham Nuttall and social constructivist teaching; Research-based cautions and qualifications. *Teaching and Teacher Education, 22,* 529–537.

Brophy, J. (2006b). Observational research on generic aspects of classroom teaching. In P. A. Alexander & P. H. Winne (Eds.), *Handbook of educational psychology* (2nd ed., pp. 755–780). Mahwah, NJ: Erlbaum.

Brophy, J. (2010). *Motivating students to learn* (3rd ed.). New York: Routledge.

Brophy, J., & Good, T. (1986). Teacher behavior and student achievement. In M. Wittrock (Ed.), *Handbook of research on teaching* (3rd ed., pp. 328–375). New York: Macmillan.

Brown, A., & Campione, J. (1994). Guided discovery in a community of learners. In K. McGilly (Ed.), *Classroom lessons: Integrating cognitive theory and classroom practice* (pp. 229–270). Cambridge, MA: MIT Press.

Brown, E. (2013). D.C. report: Teachers in 18 classrooms cheated on students' high-stakes tests in 2012. *The Washington Post*. Retrieved from http://www.washingtonpost.com/local/education/memo-could-revive-allegations-of-cheating-in-dc-public-schools/2013/04/12/9ddb2bb6-a35e-11e2-9c03-6952ff305f35_story.html

Brown, H., & Ciuffetelli, D. C. (Eds.). (2009). *Foundational methods: Understanding teaching and learning*. Toronto: Pearson Education.

Brown, J., Collins, A., & Duguid, P. (1989). Situated cognition and the culture of learning. *Educational Researcher, 18*, 32–42.

Brown, R. (2013, June 8). A swiveling proxy that will even wear a tutu. *New York Times*. Retrieved from http://www.nytimes.com/2013/06/08/education/for-homebound-students-a-robot-proxy-in-the-classroom.html?nl=todaysheadlines&emc=edit_th_20130608&_r=0

Brown-Chidsey, R. (2007). No more "Waiting to fail." *Educational Leadership, 65*(2), 40–46.

Brugman, D. (2010). Moral reasoning competence and the moral judgment-action discrepancy in young adolescents. In W. Koops, D. Brugman, T. Ferguson, & A. Sanders (Eds.), *The development and structure of conscience* (pp. 119–133). New York: Psychology Press.

Brummelman, E., Thomaes, S., Overbeek, G., Orobio de Castro, B., van den Hout, M. A., & Bushman, B. J. (2013, February 18). On feeding those hungry for praise: Person praise backfires in children with low self-esteem. *Journal of Experimental Psychology*: General. Advance online publication. doi:10.1037/a0031917

Bruner, J. S. (1960). *The process of education*. Cambridge, MA: Harvard University Press.

Bruner, J. S. (1966). *Toward a theory of instruction*. New York: Norton.

Bruner, J. S. (1990). *Acts of meaning*. Cambridge, MA: Harvard University Press.

Bruner, J., Goodnow, J., & Austin, G. (1956). *A study of thinking*. New York: Wiley.

Bruning, R. H., Schraw, G. J., & Norby, M. M. (2011). *Cognitive psychology and instruction* (5th ed.). Upper Saddle River, NJ: Prentice Hall.

Bryan, C. J., Adams, G. S., & Monin, B. (2013). When cheating would make you a cheater: Implicating the self prevents unethical behavior. *Journal of Experimental Psychology: General, 142*, 1001–1005. doi: 10.1037/a0030655

Bryan, C. L., & Solmon, M. A. (2007). Self-determination in physical education: Designing class

environments to promote active lifestyles. *Journal of Teaching in Physical Education, 26*, 260–278.

Bryk, A., Sebring, P., Allensworth, E., Luppescu, S., & Easton, J. (2010). *Organizing schools for improvement: Lessons from Chicago*. Chicago: University of Chicago Press.

Buck, G., Kostin, I., & Morgan, R. (2002). *Examining the relationship of content to gender-based performance difference in advanced placement exams*. (Research Report No. 2002–12). New York: College Board.

Buckley, M., & Saarni, C. (2009). Emotion regulation: Implications for positive youth development. In R. Gilman, E. Huebner, & M. Furlong (Eds.), *Handbook of positive psychology in schools* (pp. 107–118). New York: Routledge.

Buffington, M. L. (2007). Contemporary approaches to critical thinking and the world wide web. *Art Education, 60*, 18–23.

Bui, D. C., Myerson, J., & Hale, S. (2013). Note-taking with computers: Exploring alternative strategies for improved recall. *Journal of Educational Psychology, 105*, 299–309.

Bullough, R., Jr. (1989). *First-year teacher: A case study*. New York: Teachers College Press.

Bumiller, E. (2010, April 26). We have met the enemy and he is PowerPoint. *New York Times*, p. A1. Retrieved from www.nytimes.com/2010/04/27/world/27powerpoint.html

Burack, J., Flanagan, T., Peled, T., Sutton, J., Zygmuntowicz, C., & Manley, J. (2006). Social perspective-taking skills in maltreated children and adolescents. *Developmental Psychology, 42*, 207–217.

Burbules, N., & Bruce, B. (2001). Theory and research on teaching as dialogue. In V. Richardson (Ed.), *Handbook of research on teaching* (4th ed., pp. 1102–1121). Washington, DC: America Educational Research Association.

Burke, L. A., Williams, J. M., & Skinner, D. (2007). Teachers' perceptions of thinking skills in the primary curriculum. *Research in Education, 77*, 1–13.

Bushaw, W. J., & Lopez, S. J. (2010). A time for change: The 42nd annual Phi Delta Kappa/Gallup poll of the public's attitudes toward the public schools. *Phi Delta Kappan, 92*, 9–26.

Bushaw, W. J., & Lopez, S. J. (2013). The 45th annual PDK/Gallup poll of the public's attitudes toward the public schools. Retrieved from http://pdkintl.org/noindex/2013_PDKGallup.pdf

Bushaw, W. J., & Lopez, S. J. (2013). Which way do we go? The 45th annual PDK/Gallup poll of the public's attitudes toward the public schools. *Phi Delta Kappan, 95*, 9–25.

Bushman, B. J., Moeller, S. J., & Crocker. J. (2010). Sweets, sex, or self-esteem? Comparing the value of self-esteem boosts with other pleasant rewards. *Journal of Personality*. Accepted article. doi:10.1111/j.1467-6494.2010.00712.x

Buskist, W., & Irons, J. G. (2009). Simple strategies for teaching your students to think critically. In D. S. Dunn, J. S. Halonen, & R. A. Smith (Eds.), *Teaching critical thinking in psychology: A handbook of best practices* (pp. 49–57). Hoboken, NJ: Wiley-Blackwell.

Butler, R. (2012). Striving to connect: Extending an achievement goal approach to teacher motivation to include relational goals for teaching. *Journal of Educational Psychology, 104*, 726–742.

Byars, B. (1970) *Summer of the swans*. New York: Viking.

Byrnes, J. (2007). Some ways in which neuroscientific research can be relevant to education. In D. Coch, J. Fischer, & G. Dawson (Eds.), *Human behavior, learning, and the developing brain: Typical development* (pp. 30–49). New York: Guilford Press.

Cacioppo, J. T., & Ortigue, S. (2011). Social neuroscience: How a multidisciplinary field is uncovering the biology of human interactions. *The Dana Foundation*. Retrieved from http://www.dana.org/news/cerebrum/detail.aspx?id=34724

California State Board of Education. (2008). *Grade ten. History-Social Science Content Standards*. Retrieved from http://www.cde.ca.gov/be/st/ss/hstgrade10.asp

Calvin, C., Fernandes, C., Smith, P., Visscher, P., & Deary, I. (2010). Sex, intelligence, and educational achievement in a national cohort of over 175,000 11-year-old schoolchildren in England. *Intelligence, 38*, 424–432.

Calzada, E., Huang, K., Anicama, C., Fernandez, Y., & Brotman, L. (2012). Test of a cultural framework of parenting with Latino families of young children. *Cultural Diversity & Ethnic minority Psychology, 18*, 285–296.

Cameron, J., Pierce, W. D., & Banko, K. M. (2005). Achievement-based rewards and intrinsic motivation: A test of cognitive mediators. *Journal of Educational Psychology, 97*, 641–655.

Campbell, S., Spieker, S., Vandergrift, N., Belsky, J., & Burchinal, M. (2010). Predictors and sequelae of trajectories of physical aggression in school-age boys and girls. *Development and Psychopathology, 22*, 133–150.

Canter, A. (2004). A problem-solving model for improving student achievement. *Principal Leadership, 5*, 11–15.

Canter, L. (1996). First the rapport—then the rules. *Learning, 24*, 12–13.

Caprara, G. V., Vecchione, M., Alessandri, G., Gerbino, M., & Barbaranelli. C. (2011). The contribution of personality traits and self-efficacy beliefs to academic achievement: A longitudinal study. *British Journal of Educational Psychology, 81*, 78–96.

Card, N., & Hodges, E. V. (2008). Peer victimization among school children: Correlates, causes, consequences, and considerations in assessment and intervention. *School Psychology Quarterly, 23*, 451–461.

Carey, B. (2007, September 4). Bipolar illness soars as a diagnosis for the young. *New York Times*. Retrieved from http://www.nytimes.com/2007/09/04/health/04psych.html?_r=0

Carey, B. (2010). Forget what you know about good study habits. *New York Times*. Retrieved from http://www.nytimes.com/2010/09/07/health/views/07mind.html?_r=1&th=&emc=th&pagewanted=print

Carey, B. (2010). Tracing the spark of creative problem-solving. *The New York Times*. Retrieved from http://www.nytimes.com/2010/12/07/science/07brain.html?_r=1&ref=science

Carlo, G., Mestre, M., Samper, P., Tur, A., & Armenta, B. (2011). The longitudinal relations among dimensions of parenting styles, sympathy, prosocial moral reasoning, and prosocial behaviors. *International Journal of Behavioral Development, 35*, 116–124.

Carlson, N. (2011). *Foundations of behavioral neuroscience* (8th ed.). Boston: Allyn & Bacon.

Carnine, D., Silbert, J., Kame'enui, E., Tarver, S., & Jongjohann, K. (2006). *Teaching struggling and at-risk readers: A direct instruction approach.* Upper Saddle River, NJ: Merrill/Pearson.

Carnoy, M., & Rothstein, R. (2013). International tests reveal surprises at home and abroad. *Education Week, 32*(18), 20, 23.

Carr, N. (2008). Talking about test scores. *American School Board Journal, 195*(1), 38–39.

Carr, N. (2010). *The shallows: What the Internet is doing to our brains.* New York: W. W. Norton.

Carr, N. S. (2013). Increasing the effectiveness of homework for all learners in the inclusive classroom. *School Community Journal, 23*, 169–182.

Carter, D. R., & Van Norman, R. K. (2010). Class-wide positive behavior support in preschool: Improving teacher implementation through consultation. *Early Childhood Education Journal, 38*, 279–288.

Carter, K., & Doyle, W. (2006). Classroom management in early childhood and elementary classrooms. In C. M. Evertson & C. S. Weinstein (Eds.), *Handbook of classroom management: Research, practice, and contemporary issues* (pp. 373–406). Mahwah, NJ: Erlbaum.

Cartwright, K. (2012). Insights from cognitive neuroscience: The importance of executive function for early reading development and education. *Early Education & Development, 23*, 24–26.

Carver, S. (2006). Assessing for deep understanding. In R. K. Sawyer (Ed.), *Cambridge handbook of the learning sciences* (pp. 205–224). Cambridge, MA: Cambridge University Press.

Casalin, S., Luyten, P., Vliegen, N., & Meurs, P. (2012). The structure and stability of temperament from infancy to toddlerhood: A one-year prospective study. *Infant Behavior & Development, 35*, 94–108.

Case, R. (1992). *The mind's staircase: Exploring the conceptual underpinnings of children's thought and knowledge.* Hillsdale, NJ: Erlbaum.

Case, R. (1998). The development of central conceptual structures. In D. Kuhn & R. Siegler (Eds.), *Handbook of child psychology: Vol. 2. Cognition, perception, and language* (5th ed., pp. 745–800). New York: Wiley.

Casey, B. J., Jones, R. M., & Somerville, L. H. (*2011*). Braking and accelerating of the adolescent brain. *Journal of Research on Adolescence, 21*(1), 21–33.

Caspi, J. (2012). *Sibling aggression: Assessment and treatment.* New York: Springer.

Cassady, J. (1999, April). *The effects of examples as elaboration in text on memory and learning.* Paper presented at the annual meeting of the American Educational Research Association, Montreal, Canada.

Cassady, J. (2010). Test anxiety: Contemporary theories and implications for learning. In J. Cassady (Ed.), *Anxiety in the schools: The causes, consequences, and solutions for academic anxieties* (pp. 7–26). New York: Peter Lang.

Cassady, J. C., & Johnson, R. E. (2002). Cognitive anxiety and academic performance. *Contemporary Educational Psychology, 27*, 270–295.

Cassano, M., & Zeman, J. (2010). Parental socialization of sadness regulation in middle childhood: The role of expectations and gender. *Developmental Psychology 35*(5), 1214–1226.

Cattell, R. (1963). Theory of fluid and crystallized intelligence: A critical experiment. *Journal of Educational Psychology, 54*, 1–22.

Cattell, R. (1987). *Intelligence: Its structure, growth, and action.* Amsterdam: North-Holland.

Cavanagh, S. (2012). U.S. education pressured by international comparisons. *Education Week, 31*(16), 6–10.

Center for Public Education. (2012). *The United States of education: The changing demographics of the United States and their schools.* Retrieved from http://www.centerforpubliceducation.org/You-May-Also-Be-Interested-In-landing-page-level/Organizing-a-School-YMABI/The-United-States-of-education-The-changing-demographics-of-the-United-States-and-their-schools.html

Center for Public Education. (2013). How many students with disabilities are in our school(s)? Retrieved from http://www.data-first.org/data/how-many-students-with-disabilities-are-in-our-schools/

Centers for Disease Control and Prevention (CDC). (2010a). *Alcohol and drug use.* Retrieved from http://www.cdc.gov/HealthyYouth/alcoholdrug/index.htm

Centers for Disease Control and Prevention (CDC). (2010b). *Strategies for increasing protective factors among youth.* Retrieved from http://www.cdc.gov/HealthyYouth/AdolescentHealth/connectedness.htm

Centers for Disease Control and Prevention (CDC). (2010c). *Tobacco use.* Retrieved from http://www.cdc.gov/HealthyYouth/tobacco/index.htm

Centers for Disease Control and Prevention. (2012). *Understanding school violence.* Retrieved from http://www.cdc.gov/violenceprevention/pdf/schoolviolence_factsheet-a.pdf

Centers for Disease Control and Prevention. (2013). *Attention-deficit/hyperactivity disorder (ADHD).* Retrieved from http://www.cdc.gov/ncbddd/adhd/

Chaddock, I., Erickson, K. I., Prakash, R. S., Kim, J. S., Voss, M. A., VanPatter, M., . . . Kramer, A. F. (2010). A neuroimaging investigation of the association between aerobic fitness, hippocampal volume, and memory performance in preadolescent children. *Brain Research, 1358*, 172–183.

Chaddock, L., Hillman, C. H., Buck, S. M., & Cohen, N. J. (2011). Aerobic fitness and executive control of relational memory in preadolescent children. *Medicine & Science in Sports & Exercise, 43*, 344–349.

Chaffen, R., & Imreh, G. (2002). Practicing perfection: Piano performance and expert memory. *Psychological Science, 13*, 342–349.

Chan, S. (2010). Aggressive behavior in early elementary school children: Relations to authoritarian parenting, children's negative emotionality and coping strategies. *Early Child Development and Care, 180*(9), 1253–1269. doi:10.1080/030044309020981447

Chang, C-C., Liang, C., Yan, C-F., & Tseng, J-S. (2013). The impact of college students' intrinsic and extrinsic motivation on continuance intention to use English mobile learning systems. *Asia-Pacific Education Researcher, 22*, 181–192.

Chapman, C., Laird, J., Ifill, N., & KewalRamani, A. (2011*). Trends in high school dropout and completion rates in the United States: 1972–2009.* National Center for Education Statistics. Retrieved from http://nces.ed.gov/pubs2012/2012006.pdf

Chapple, C. L., & Johnson, K. A. (2007). Gender differences in impulsivity. *Youth Violence and Juvenile Justice, 5*, 221–234. doi:10.1177/1541204007301286

Chappuis, J., Stiggins, R., Chappuis, S., & Arter, J. (2012). *Classroom assessment for student learning: Doing it right — using it well* (2nd ed.). Boston: Allyn & Bacon/Pearson.

Charles, C. M., & Senter, G. W. (2012). *Elementary classroom management* (6th ed.). New York: Addison Wesley.

Checkley, K. (1997). The first seven . . . and the eighth. *Educational Leadership, 55*, 8–13.

Chen, J. (2004). Theory of multiple intelligences: Is it a scientific theory? *Teachers College Record, 106*, 17–23.

Chen, J., Chen, T., & Zheng, X. (2012). Parenting styles and practices among Chinese immigrant mothers with young children. *Early Child Development and Care, 182*, 1–21.

Chen, J., Moran, S., & Gardner, H. (2009). *Multiple intelligences around the world.* San Francisco: Jossey-Bass.

Chen, N-S., Teng, D. C-E., Lee, C-H., & Kinshuk. (2011). Augmenting paper-based reading activity with direct access to digital materials and scaffolded questioning. *Computers & Education, 57*, 1705–1715.

Chen, P-H. (2013). The effects of college students' in-class and after-class lecture note-taking on academic performance. *Asia-Pacific Education Researcher, 22*, 173–180. doi:10.1007/s40299-012-0010-8

Chen, S., Hwang, F., Yeh, Y., & Lin, S. (2012). Cognitive ability, academic achievement and academic self-concept: Extending the internal/external frame of reference model. *British Journal of Educational Psychology, 82*, 308–326.

Chen, X., & Eisenberg, N. (2012). Understanding cultural issues in child development: Introduction. *Child Development Perspectives, 6*, 1–4.

Chen, X., & Trommsdorff, G. (Eds.). (2012). *Values, religion, and culture in adolescent development.* Cambridge, UK: Cambridge University Press.

Chen, X., & Wang, I. (2010). China. In M. H. Bornstein (Ed.), *Handbook of cultural development science* (pp. 429–444). New York: Psychology Press.

Chetty, R., Friedman, J., & Rockoff, J. (2011). *The long-term impacts of teachers: Teacher value-added and student outcomes in adulthood (Executive summary).* Retrieved from http://obs.rc.fas.harvard.edu/chetty/va_exec_summ.pdf

Cheung, C. S. S., & Pomerantz, E. M. (2012). Why does parents' involvement enhance children's achievement? The role of parent-oriented motivation. *Journal of Educational Psychology, 104,* 820–832.

Child Welfare Information Gateway. (2013). *Child maltreatment 2011: Summary of key findings.* Washington, DC: U.S. Department of Health and Human Services, Children's Bureau.

Children's Defense Fund. (2012). *The state of America's children. Yearbook 2007.* Washington, DC: Author.

Chin, J. J., & Ludwig, D. (2013). Increasing children's physical activity during school recess periods. *American Journal of Public Health, 103,* 1229–1234.

Choi, Y., Kim, Y. S., Kim, S. Y., & Park, I. J. (2013). Is Asian American parenting controlling and harsh? Empirical testing of relationships between Korean American and Western parenting measures. *Asian American Journal of Psychology, 4,* 19–29.

Chomsky, N. (1959). Review of B. F. Skinner's *Verbal Behavior. Language, 35,* 26–58.

Chomsky, N. (1972). *Language and mind* (2nd ed.). Orlando, FL: Harcourt Brace.

Chomsky, N. (2006). *Language and mind* (3rd ed.). Cambridge, England: Cambridge University Press.

Chorzempa, B., & Graham, S. (2006). Primary-grade teachers' use of within-class ability grouping in reading. *Journal of Educational Psychology, 98*(3), 529–541.

Christakis, N. A., & Fowler, J. H. (2009). *Connected: The surprising power of our social networks and how they shape our lives.* New York: Little, Brown and Company.

Christensen, D., Mitrou, R., Lawrence, D., Sanson, A., & Zubrick, S. (2011, December). *Child temperament, parenting style and emotional and behavioral problems in early childhood: Findings from the Longitudinal Study of Australian Children.* Paper presented at the meeting of the LSAC-LSIC Conference, Melbourne, Australia.

Christenson, S., & Havsy, L. (2004). Family–school–peer relationships: Significance for social, emotional, and academic learning. In J. Zins, R. Weissberg, M. Wang, & H. Walberg (Eds.), *Building academic success on social and emotional learning* (pp. 59–75). New York: Teachers College Press.

Chronicle, E., MacGregor, J., & Ormerod, T. (2004). What makes an insight problem? The roles of heuristics, goal conception, and solution recoding in knowledge-lean problems. *Journal of Experimental Psychology: Learning, Memory, and Cognition, 30*(1), 14–217.

Chua, A. (2011). *Battle hymn of the tiger mother.* New York: Penguin.

Chung, H., Mulvey, E., & Steinberg, L. (2011). Understanding the school outcomes of juvenile offenders: An exploration of neighborhood influences and motivational resources. *Journal of Youth and Adolescence, 40,* 1025–1038.

Cillessen, A., Schwartz, D., & Mayeux, L. (Eds.). (2011). *Popularity in the peer system.* New York: Guilford.

Cimpian, A., Arce, H. M. C., Markman, E. M., & Dweck, C. S. (2007). Subtle linguistic cues affect children's motivation. *Psychological Science, 18,* 314–316. doi:10.1111/j.1467-9280.2007.01896.x

Cingel, D. P., & Sundar, S. S. (2012). Texting, tech-speak, and tweens: The relationship between text messaging and English grammar skills. *New Media & Society, 14,* 1304–1320.

Cipriano, E., & Stifter, C. (2010). Predicting preschool effortful control from toddler temperament and parenting behavior. *Journal of Applied Developmental Psychology, 31,* 221–230.

Cismaru, M. (2014). Using the extended parallel process model to understand texting while driving and guide communication campaigns against it. *Social Marketing Quarterly, 20,* 66–82.

Clarey, C. (2014, February 22). Olympians use imagery as mental training. *New York Times.* Retrieved from http://www.nytimes.com/2014/02/23/sports/olympics/olympians-use-imagery-as-mental-training.html?hpw&rref=sports&_r=0

Clark, J., & Paivio, A. (1991). Dual coding theory and education. *Educational Psychology Review, 3,* 149–210.

Clark, K. (2009). The case for Structured English Immersion. *Educational Leadership, 66*(7), 42–46.

Clark, K., & Clark, M. (1939). The development of consciousness of self and the emergence of racial identification in Negro preschool children. *Journal of Social Psychology, 10,* 591–599.

Clark, R. C. (2010). *Evidence-based training methods: A guide for training professionals.* Alexandria, VA: ASTD Press.

Clark, R. C., & Mayer, R. E. (2003). *e-Learning and the science of instruction: Proven guidelines for consumers and designers of multimedia learning.* San Francisco: Pfeiffer/Wiley.

Clark, R. E., Kirschner, P. A., & Sweller, J. (2012). Putting students on the path to learning: The case for fully guided instruction. *American Educator, 36,* 6–11.

Clarke, A. (2006). The nature and substance of cooperating teacher reflection. *Teaching and Teacher Education, 22,* 910–921.

Clay, R. (2013). Easing ADHD without meds. *American Psychological Association, 44*(2), 44.

Coffield, F., Moseley, D., Hall, E., & Ecclestone, K. (2004). *Learning styles and pedagogy in post-16 learning: A systematic and critical review.* London: Learning and Skills Research Centre/University of Newcastle upon Tyne.

Cognition and Technology Group at Vanderbilt. (1992). The Jasper Series as an example of anchored instruction: Theory, program description and assessment data. *Educational Psychologist, 27,* 291–315.

Cohen, E. (1994). Restructuring the classroom: Conditions for productive small groups. *Review of Educational Research, 64,* 1–35.

Cohen, M. T. (2012). The importance of self-regulation for college student learning. *College Student Journal, 46,* 892–902.

Coiro, J., & Dobler, E. (2007). Exploring the online reading comprehension strategies used by sixth-grade skilled readers to search for and locate information on the Internet. *Reading Research Quarterly, 42,* 214–257.

Coker, T., Elliott, M., Kanouse, D., Grunbaum, J., Schwebel, D., Gilliland, M., . . . Schuster, M. (2009). Perceived racial/ethnic discrimination among fifth-grade students and its association with mental health. *American Journal of Public Health, 99*(5), 878–884.

Colangelo, N., & Davis, G. (Eds.). (2003). *Handbook of gifted education* (3rd ed.). Boston: Allyn & Bacon.

Cole, M., & Cagigas, X. (2010). Cognition. In M. Bornstein (Ed.), *Handbook of cultural developmental science: An advanced textbook* (pp. 127–142). New York: Psychology Press.

Cole, M., & Packer, M. (2011). Culture in development. In M. Bornstein & M. Lamb (Eds.), *Developmental science: An advanced textbook* (6th ed., pp. 51–107). New York: Psychology Press.

Cole, M., Cole, S. R., & Lightfoot, C. (2009). *The development of children* (6th ed.). New York: W. H. Freeman.

Cole, S., Balcetis, E., & Zhang, S. (2013). Visual perception and regulatory conflict: Motivation and physiology influence distance perception. *Journal of Experimental Psychology, 142,* 18–22.

Collins, A. (2006). Cognitive apprenticeship. In R. K. Sawyer (Ed.), *Cambridge handbook of the learning sciences* (pp. 47–60). Cambridge, MA: Cambridge University Press.

Collins, M. (2010). ELL preschoolers' English vocabulary acquisition from storybook reading. *Early Childhood Research Quarterly, 25*(1), 84–97.

Collins, R. (2011). Content analysis of gender roles in media: Where are we now and where should we go? *Sex Roles, 64,* 290–198.

Colvin, G. (2010). *Talent is overrated: What really separates world-class performers from everybody else.* New York: Penguin Group.

Common Core State Standards Initiative. (2014a). *Mission statement.* Retrieved from http://www.corestandards.org/

Common Core State Standards Initiative. (2014b). About the standards. Retrieved from http://www.corestandards.org/about-the-standards/.

Common Core State Standards Initiative. (2014c). *Development Process.* Retrieved from http://www.corestandards.org/about-the-standards/development-process/

Common Core State Standards Initiative. (2014d). English Language Arts Standards, History/Social Studies, Grade 6–8. Retrieved from http://www.corestandards.org/ELA-Literacy/RH/6-8

Common Core State Standards Initiative. (2014e). Grade 5, Number & Operations—Fractions. Retrieved from http://www.corestandards.org/Math/Content/5/NF/

Common Core State Standards Initiative. (2014f). English Language Arts Standards, History/Social Studies, Grade 9-10. Retrieved from http://www.corestandards.org/ELA-Literacy/RH/9-10/.

Common Core State Standards Initiative. (2014g). English Language Arts Standards, History/Social Studies, Grade 11-12. Retrieved from http://www.corestandards.org/ELA-Literacy/RH/11-12

Common Core State Standard Initiative. (2014h). *English Language Arts Standards, Language, Grade 3.* Retrieved from http://www.corestandards.org/ELA-Literacy/L/3

Common Core State Standards Initiative. (2014i). English language arts standards, language, grade 8. Retrieved from http://www.corestandards.org/ELA-Literacy/L/8

Common Core State Standards Initiative. (2014j). English Language Arts Standards, Reading: Informational Text, Grade 7. Retrieved from http://www.corestandards.org/ELA-Literacy/RI/7

Common Core State Standards Initiative. (2014k). English Language Arts Standards, Reading: Literature, Grade 9–10. Retrieved from http://www.corestandards.org/ELA-Literacy/RL/9-10

Common Core State Standards Initiative. (2014l). English Language Arts Standards, Reading: Literature, Grade 11–12. Retrieved from http://www.corestandards.org/ELA-Literacy/RL/11-12

Common Core State Standards Initiative. (2014m). English Language Arts Standards, Science & Technical Subjects, Grade 6–8. Retrieved from http://www.corestandards.org/ELA-Literacy/RST/6-8

Common Core State Standards Initiative. (2014n). English language arts standards, writing, grade 1. Retrieved from http://www.corestandards.org/ELA-Literacy/W/1

Common Core State Standards Initiative. (2014o). English Language Arts Standards, Writing, Grade 5. Retrieved from http://www.corestandards.org/ELA-Literacy/W/5

Common Core State Standards Initiative. (2014p). English Language Arts Standards, Writing, Grade 9–10. Retrieved from http://www.corestandards.org/ELA-Literacy/W/9-10

Common Core State Standards Initiative. (2014q). Mathematics, Grade 1, Number & Operations in Base Ten. Retrieved from http://www.corestandards.org/Math/Content/1/NBT

Common Core State Standards Initiative. (2014r). Mathematics, Grade 1, Operations and Alge-braic Thinking. http://www.corestandards.org/Math/Content/1/OA/.

Common Core State Standards Initiative. (2014s). Mathematics, Grade 2, Measurement & Data. Retrieved from http://www.corestandards.org/Math/Content/2/MD

Common Core State Standards Initiative. (2014t). Mathematics, grade 2, operations & algebraic thinking. Retrieved from http://www.corestandards.org/Math/Content/2/OA

Common Core State Standards Initiative. (2014u). *Mathematics, Grade 3, Number & Operations in Base Ten.* Retrieved from http://www.corestandards.org/Math/Content/3/NBT

Common Core State Standard Initiative. (2014v). *Mathematics, Grade 4. Measurement and Data.* Retrieved from http://www.corestandards.org/Math/Content/4/MD

Common Core State Standards Initiative. (2014w). Mathematics, Grade 5, Number & Opera-tions—Fractions. Retrieved from http://www.corestandards.org/Math/Content/5/NF

Common Core State Standards Initiative. (2014x). Mathematics, Grade 6, Ratios & Proportional Relationships. Retrieved from http://www.corestandards.org/Math/Content/6/RP/.

Common Core State Standards Initiative. (2014y). Mathematics, Grade 7, The Number System. Retrieved from http://www.corestandards.org/Math/Content/7/NS

Common Core State Standards Initiative. (2014z). Mathematics, Grade 8, Expressions & Equations. Retrieved from http://www.corestandards.org/Math/Content/8/EE

Cook, A., & Polgar, J. (2012). *Essentials of assistive technology.* Waltham, MA: Elsevier.

Cook, P., & Ludwig, J. (2008). The burden of "acting White": Do Black adolescents disparage aca-demic achievement? In J. Ogbu (Ed.), *Diversity and multiculturalism: A reader* (pp. 341–361). New York: Routledge.

Cooper, H. (2006). Research questions and research designs. In P. Alexander & P. Winne (Eds.), *Handbook of educational psychology* (2nd ed., pp. 849–879). Mahwah, NJ: Erlbaum.

Cooper, H., Robinson, J. C., & Patall, E. A. (2006). Does homework improve academic achieve-ment? A synthesis of research, 1987–2003. *Review of Educational Research, 76,* 1–62.

Cooper, J. D., & Kiger, N. (2009). *Literacy: Helping students construct meaning* (7th ed.). Boston: Houghton Mifflin.

Cooper, K. S. (2013). Safe, affirming, and productive spaces: Classroom engagement among Latina high school students. *Urban Education, 48,* 490–528.

Cooper, L., & Nickerson, A. (2013). Parent retro-spective recollections of bullying and current views, concerns, and strategies to cope with children's bullying. *Journal of Child & Family Studies, 22,* 526–540.

Coplan, R., & Arbeau, K. (2009). Peer interactions and play in early childhood. In K. Rubin, W. Bukowski, & B. Laursen (Eds.), *Handbook of peer interactions, relationships, and groups* (pp. 143–161). New York: Guilford Press.

Corcoran, C. A., Dershimer, E. L., & Tichenor, M. S. (2004). A teacher's guide to alternative assessment: Taking the first steps. *The Clearing House, 77*(5), 213–216.

Corcoran, J. (2013). Flipping reading lessons at a Title I school. *School Administrator, 70,* 22–23.

Corcoran, S. P. (2010). Can teachers be evaluated by their students' test scores? Should they be? The use of value-added measures of teacher effectiveness in policy and practice. *Annenberg Institute for School Reform.* Retrieved from http://annenberginstitute.org/pdf/valueAddedReport.pdf

Cornelius-White, J. (2007). Learner-centered teacher-student relationships are effective: A meta-analysis. *Review of Educational Research, 77,* 113–143.

Corpus, J. H., Ogle, C. M., & Love-Geiger, K. E. (2006). The effects of social-comparison versus mastery praise on children's intrinsic motiva-tion. *Motivation & Emotion, 30,* 333–343.

Costa, D. S. J., & Boakes, R. A. (2007). Maintenance of responding when reinforcement becomes delayed. *Learning & Behavior, 35,* 95–105.

Council for Exceptional Children. (2014). *A primer on the IDEA 2004 regulations.* Retrieved from http://www.cec.sped.org/Policy-and-Advocacy/Current-Sped-Gifted-Issues/Individuals-with-Disabilities-Education-Act/A-Primer-on-the-IDEA-2004-RegulationsIDEA

Courage, M., & Howe, M. (2010). To watch or not to watch: Infants and toddlers in a brave new electronic world. *Developmental Review, 30,* 101–115.

Covington, M. (1992). *Making the grade: A self-worth perspective on motivation and school reform.* Cambridge, MA: Harvard University Press.

Covington, M. (1998). *The will to learn: A guide for motivating young people.* New York: Cambridge University Press.

Covington, M., & Omelich, C. (1987). "I knew it cold before the exam": A test of the anxiety blockage hypothesis. *Journal of Educational Psychology, 79,* 393–400.

Coyne, M., Carnine, D., & Kame'enui, E. (2011). *Effective teaching strategies that accommodate diverse learners* (4th ed.). Boston: Pearson.

Coyne, S., Robinson, S., & Nelsen, D. (2010). Does reality backbite: Verbal and relational aggres-sion in reality television programs. *Journal of Broadcasting and Electronic Media, 54,* 282–298.

Craig, W. M., & Pepler, D. J. (2007). Understanding bullying: From research to practice. *Canadian Psychology, 48,* 86–93.

Craik, F. I., & Watkins, M. J. (1974). The role of re-hearsal in short-term memory. *Journal of Verbal Learning and Verbal Behavior, 12,* 598–607.

Cranston, S., & Keller, S. (2013). Increasing the "meaning quotient" of work. *McKinsey Quar-terly, 1,* 48–59.

Cross, T. L. (2001). Gifted children and Erikson's theory of psychosocial development. *Gifted Child Today, 24*(1), 54–55, 61.

Crossley, C. D., Cooper, C. D., & Wernsing, T. S. (2013). Making things happen through challenging goals: Leader proactivity, trust, and business-unit performance. *Journal of Applied Psychology, 98*, 540–549.

Crossnoe, R. (2011). *Fitting in, standing out: Navigating the social challenge of high school to get an education.* Cambridge, England: Cambridge University Press.

Crossnoe, R., & Cooper, C. (2010). Economically disadvantaged children's transitions into elementary school: Linking family processes, school contexts, and educational policy. *American Educational Research Journal, 47*, 258–291.

Crow, S., R. (2007). Information literacy: What's motivation got to do with it? *Knowledge Quest, 35*, 48–52.

Crowne, K. A. (2013). An empirical analysis of three intelligences. *Canadian Journal of Behavioural Science/Revue canadienne des sciences du comportement, 45*, 105–114.

Crum, A. J., Salovey, P., & Achor, S. (2013). Rethinking stress: The role of mindsets in determining the stress response. *Journal of Personality and Social Psychology, 104*, 716–733.

Crystal, D., Killen, M., & Ruck, M. (2010). Fair treatment by authorities is related to children's and adolescents' evaluations of interracial exclusion. *Applied Developmental Science, 14*, 125–136.

Csikszentmihalyi, M. (1990). *Flow.* New York: Harper and Row.

Csikszentmihalyi, M. (1996). *Creativity: Flow and the psychology of discovery and invention.* New York: Harper Collins.

Csikszentmihalyi, M. (1999). If we are so rich, why aren't we happy? *American Psychologist, 54*, 821–827.

Cuban, L. (2004). Assessing the 20-year impact of multiple intelligences on schooling. *Teachers College Record, 106*(1), 140–146.

Cummins, J. (2000). *Language, power, and pedagogy: Bilingual children in the crossfire.* Clevedon, UK: Multilingual Matters.

Cunningham, S. A., Kramer, M. R., & Narayan, K. M. V. (2014). Incidence of childhood obesity in the United States. *New England Journal of Medicine, 370*, 403–411. doi:10.1056/NEJMoa1309753

Cushner, K., McClelland, A., & Safford, P. (2012). *Human diversity in education: An integrative approach.* Boston: McGraw-Hill.

Cvencek, D., Meltzoff, A., & Greenwald, A. (2011). Math-gender stereotypes in elementary school children. *Child Development, 82*, 766–779.

Dahlin, B., & Watkins, D. (2000). The role of repetition in the process of memorizing and understanding. A comparison of the views of Western and Chinese secondary students in Hong Kong. *British Journal of Educational Psychology, 70*, 65–84.

Dai, D. (2010). *The nature and nurture of giftedness: A new framework for understanding gifted education.* New York: Teachers College Press.

Dake, J. A., Price, J. H., & Telljohann, S. K. (2003). The nature and extent of bullying at school. *Journal of School Health, 73*, 173–180.

Dalton, J. D. (2013). Mobility and student achievement in high poverty schools. *Electronic Theses and Dissertations.* Paper 1159. Retrieved from http://dc.etsu.edu/etd/1159

Dan-Glauser, E. S., & Gross, J. J. (2013). Emotion regulation and emotion coherence: Evidence for strategy-specific effects. *Emotion, 13*, 832–842.

Daniel, B., Shabani, D. B., & Lam, W. Y. (2013). A review of comparison studies in applied behavior analysis. *Behavioral Interventions, 28*, 158–183.

Danner, F. (2011, April). *School belonging and trajectories of depressive symptoms across adolescence and young adulthood.* Paper presented at the annual meeting of the American Educational Research Association, New Orleans.

Darden, E. (2007). Autism, the law, and you. *American School Board Journal, 194*(9), 60–61.

Darling-Hammond, L. (2012). Value-added teacher evaluation: The harm behind the hype. *Education Week, 31*(24), 32.

Darling-Hammond, L., & Adamson, F. (2010). *Beyond basic skills: The role of performance assessment in achieving 21st century standards of learning.* Stanford, CA: Stanford Center for Opportunity Policy in Education.

Darling-Hammond, L., & Adamson, F. (2013). *Developing assessments of deeper learning: The cost and benefits of using tests that help students learn.* Stanford, CA: Stanford University Center for Opportunity Policy in Education.

Darling-Hammond, L., & Baratz-Snowden, J. (Eds.). (2005). *A good teacher in every classroom: Preparing the highly qualified teachers our children deserve.* San Francisco: Jossey-Bass/Wiley.

Darling-Hammond, L., & Bransford, J. (Eds.). (2005). *Preparing teachers for a changing world: What teachers should learn and be able to do.* San Francisco: Jossey-Bass.

Darling-Hammond, L., & Wentworth, L. (2010). *Benchmarking learning system: Student performance assessment in international contexts.* Stanford, CA: Stanford University Center for Opportunity Policy in Education.

Darling-Hammond, L., Amrein-Beardsley, A., Haertel, E. H., & Rothstein, J. (2011). Getting teacher evaluation right: A background paper for policy makers. *American Educational Research Association.* Retrieved from http://www.cea.org/v2/assets/includes/shared/getFile.cfm?type=pdf&loc=/professional/evaluation/articles/&getFile=Darling-Hammond-Getting-TE-Right

Darling-Hammond, L., Amrein-Beardsley, A., Haertel, E., & Rothstein, J. (2012). Evaluating teacher evaluation. *Phi Delta Kappan, 93*, 8–15.

Davidse, N., de Jong, M., Bus, A., Huijbregts, S., & Swaab, H. (2011). Cognitive and environmental predictors of early literacy skills. *Reading and Writing, 24*(4), 395–412.

Davidson, C. A. (2012). *Now you see it: How the brain science of attention will transform the way we live, work, and learn.* New York: Penguin.

Davidson, J., & Sternberg, R. (Eds.). (2003). *The psychology of problem solving.* Cambridge: Cambridge University.

Davila, J. (2008). Depressive symptoms and adolescent romance: Theory, research, and implications. *Child Development Perspectives, 2*(1), 26–31.

Davis, C., & Yang, A. (2005). *Parents and teachers working together.* Turners Falls, MA: Northeast Foundation for Children.

Davis, E., Levine, L., Lench, H., & Quas, J. (2010). Metacognitive emotion regulation: Children's awareness that changing thoughts and goals can alleviate negative emotions. *Emotion, 10*(4), 498–510.

Davis, G. (2003). Identifying creative students, teaching for creative growth. In N. Colangelo & G. Davis (Eds.), *Handbook of gifted education* (3rd ed., pp. 311–324). Boston: Allyn & Bacon.

Davis, G. A., Rimm, S. B., & Siegle, D. (2011). *Education of the gifted and talented* (6th ed.). Upper Saddle River, NJ: Merrill/Pearson.

Davis, M. (2012). Adaptive testing evolves to assess common-core skills. *Education Week.* Retrieved from http://www.edweek.org/dd/articles/2012/10/17/01adaptive.h06.html

Davis, S. D., & Piercy, F. P. (2007). What clients of couple therapy model developers and their former students say about change, part I: Model-dependent common factors across three models. *Journal of Marital and Family Therapy, 33*, 318–343.

Davison, M. (2011, April). *Are you standing in my shoes? How affective and cognitive teaching sequences influence historical empathy.* Paper presented at the annual meeting of the American Education Research Association, New Orleans.

De Castella, K., Byrne, D., & Covington, M. (2013). Unmotivated or motivated to fail? A cross-cultural study of achievement motivation, fear of failure, and student disengagement. *Journal of Educational Psychology, 105*, 861–880.

de Jong, N., Verstegen, D. M., & Tan, F. E. (2013). Comparison of classroom and online asynchronous problem-based learning for students undertaking statistics training as part of a public health masters degree. *Advances in Health Sciences Education, 18*, 245–264.

de Jong, T. (2011). Instruction based on computer simulations. In R. Mayer & P. Alexander (Eds.), *Handbook of research on learning and instruction* (pp. 446–466). New York: Routledge.

Deci, E., & Ryan, R. (2008). Facilitating optimal motivation and psychological well-being across life's domains. *Canadian Psychology, 49*, 14–23.

Deci, E., & Ryan, R. (Eds.). (2002). *Handbook of self-determination research.* Rochester, NY: University of Rochester Press.

Deddeh, H., Main, E., & Fulkerson, S. (2010). Eight steps to meaningful grading. *Phi Delta Kappan, 91*(7), 53–58.

Dekker, S., Krabbendam, L., Lee, N. C., Boschloo, A., de Groot, R., & Jolles, J. (2013). Sex differences in goal orientation in adolescents aged 10–19: The older boys adopt work-avoidant goals twice as often as girls. *Learning and Individual Differences, 26*, 196–200.

Delazer, M., Ischebeck, A., Domahs, F., Zamarian, L., Koppelstaetter, F., Siednetoph, C., . . . Felber, S. (2005). Learning by strategies and learning by drill: Evidence from an fMRI study. *NeuroImage, 25*, 838–849.

Demetriou, A., Christou, C., Spanoudis, G., & Platsidou, M. (2002). The development of mental processing: Efficiency, working memory, and thinking. *Monographs of the Society for Research in Child Development* (Serial No. 268, Vol. 67, No. 1). Boston: Blackwell.

DeNavas-Walt, C., Proctor, B., & Smith, J. (2013). *Income, poverty, & health insurance coverage in the United States: 2012.* Washington, DC: U.S. Government Printing Office.

Denig, S. J. (2003, April). *A proposed relationship between multiple intelligences and learning styles.* Paper presented at the annual meeting of the American Educational Research Association, Chicago.

Denworth, L. (2013). Brain-changing games. *Scientific American Mind, 23*(6), 28–35.

DeSteno, D., Gross, J. J., & Kubzansky, L. (2013). Affective science and health: The importance of emotion and emotion regulation. *Health Psychology, 32*, 474–486.

Dettmers, S., Trautwein, U., Lüdtke, O., Kunter, M., & Baumert, J. (2010). Homework works if homework quality is high: Using multilevel modeling to predict the development of achievement in mathematics. *Journal of Educational Psychology, 102*, 467–482.

Dewar, D. L., Lubans, D. R., Morgan, P. J., & Plotnikoff, R. C. (2013). Development and evaluation of social cognitive measures related to adolescent physical activity. *Journal of Physical Activity and Health, 10*, 544–555.

Deyhle, D. (1987). Learning failure: Tests as gatekeepers and the culturally different child. In H. Trueba (Ed.), *Success or failure?* (pp. 85–108). Cambridge, MA: Newbury House.

Deyhle, D., & LeCompte, M. (1999). Cultural differences in child development: Navajo adolescents in middle schools. In R. H. Sheets & E. R. Hollins (Eds.), *Racial and ethnic identity in school practices: Aspects of human development* (pp. 123–139). Mahwah, NJ: Erlbaum.

Dhaem, J. (2012). Responding to minor misbehavior through verbal and nonverbal responses. *Beyond Behavior, 21*, 29–34.

Diaz, Z., Whitacre, M., Esquierdo, J. J., & Ruiz-Escalante, J. A. (2013). Why did I ask that question? Bilingual/ESL pre-service teachers' insights. *International Journal of Instruction, 6*, 163–176.

Diaz-Rico, L. (2013). *Strategies for teaching English learners* (3rd ed.). Boston: Pearson.

Diaz-Rico, L. (2014). *Crosscultural, language, & academic development handbook* (5th ed.). Boston: Pearson

DiDonato, M, & Berenbaum, S. (2013) Predictors and consequences of gender typicality: The mediating role of communality.*Archives of Sexual Behavior, 42*, 429-436

Dietrich, A., & Kanso, R. (2010). A review of EEG, ERP, and neuroimaging studies of creativity and insight. *Psychological Bulletin, 136*, 822–848. doi:10.1037/a0019749

Digest of Education Statistics. (2012). *Table 429: Number and percentage of persons 16 to 24 years old who were neither enrolled in school nor working, by educational attainment, age group, family poverty status, and race/ethnicity: 2012.* Retrieved from http://nces.ed.gov/pubs2014/2014015.pdf

Dik, M. G., Deeg, D. J. H., Visser, M., & Jonker, C. (2003). Early life physical activity and cognition at old age. *Journal of Clinical and Experimental Neuropsychology, 25*, 643–653.

DiMartino, J., & Castaneda, A. (2007). Assessing applied skills. *Educational Leadership, 64*, 38–42.

Ding, M., Li, X., Piccolo, D., & Kulm, G. (2007). Teacher interventions in cooperative-learning mathematics classes. *Journal of Educational Research, 100*(3), 162–176.

DiSalvo, D. (2011). *What makes your brain happy & why you should do the opposite.* Amherst, NY: Prometheus.

diSessa, A. (2006). A history of conceptual change research: Threads and fault lines. In R. K. Sawyer (Ed.), *Cambridge handbook of the learning sciences* (pp. 265–282). Cambridge, MA: Cambridge University Press.

Dixon, F. A., Yssel, N., McConnell, J. M., & Hardin, T. (2014). Differentiated instruction, professional development, and teacher efficacy. Journal for the Education of the Gifted, 37, 111–127.

Dixon, S., Graber, J., & Brooks-Gunn, J. (2008). The roles of respect for parental authority and parenting practices in parent-child conflict among African American, Latino, and European American families. *Journal of Family Psychology, 22*, 1–20.

Dodge, K. (2011). Context matters in child and family policy. *Child Development, 82*, 433–442.

Domenech Rodriguez, M., Donovick, M., & Crowley, S. (2009). Parenting styles in a cultural context: Observations of protective parenting in first-generation Latinos. *Family Process, 48*(2), 195–210.

Donovan, M. S., & Bransford, J. D. (2005). Introduction. In M. S. Donovan & J. D. Bransford (Eds.), *How students learn: History, mathematics, and science in the classroom* (pp. 1–26). Washington, DC: National Academies Press.

Dornisch, M. M., & Sperling, R. A. (2006). Facilitating learning from technology-enhanced text: Effects of prompted elaborative interrogation. *Journal of Educational Research, 99*, 156–165.

Dornisch, M. M., & Sperling, R. A. (2008). Elaborative interrogation and adjuncts to technology-enhanced text: An examination of ecological validity. *International Journal of Instructional Media, 35*, 317–328.

Dougherty, J. L., Custer, R. L., & Dixon, R. A. (2012). Mapping concepts for learning and assessment. *Technology & Engineering Teacher, 71*, 10–14.

Douglas, N. L. (2000). Enemies of critical thinking: Lessons from social psychology research. *Reading Psychology, 21*, 129–144.

Dowson, M., & McInerney, D. (2001). Psychological parameters of students' social and work avoidance goals: A qualitative investigation. *Journal of Educational Psychology, 93*, 35–42.

Doyle, W. (2006). Ecological approaches to classroom management. In C. M. Evertson & C. S. Weinstein (Eds.), *Handbook of classroom management: Research, practice, and contemporary issues* (pp. 97–125). Mahwah, NJ: Erlbaum.

Droe, K. L. (2013). Effect of verbal praise on achievement goal orientation, motivation, and performance attribution. *Journal of Music Teacher Education, 23*, 63–78.

Dubinsky, J. M., Roehrig, G., & Varma, S. (2013). Infusing neuroscience into teacher professional development. *Educational Researcher, 42*, 317–329.

Dunn, J., Schaefer-McDaniel, N., & Ramsey, J. (2010). Neighborhood chaos and children's development: Questions and contradictions. In V. Evans & T. Wachs (Eds.), *Chaos and its influence on children's development: An ecological perspective* (pp. 173–189).

Duriez, B., Luyckx, K., Soenens, B., & Berzonsky, M. (2012). A process-content approach to adolescent identity formation: Examining longitudinal associations between identity styles and goal pursuits. *Journal of Personality, 80*, 135–161.

Durlak, J., Weissberg, R., Dymnicki, A., Taylor, R., & Schellinger, K. (2011). The impact of enhancing students' social and emotional learning: A meta-analysis of school-based universal interventions. *Child Development, 82*(1), 405–432. doi:10.1111/j.1467-8624.2010.01564.x

Dwairy, M. (2005). Using problem-solving conversation with children. *Intervention in School and Clinic, 40*, 144–150.

Dweck, C. (1975). The role of expectations and attributions in the alleviation of learned helplessness. *Journal of Personality and Social Psychology, 31*, 674–685.

Dweck, C. (1999). Self-theories and goals: Their role in motivation, personality, and development. In R. Dienstbier (Ed.), *Perspectives on motivation: Nebraska symposium on motivation 1990* (Vol. 38, pp. 199–325). Lincoln: University of Nebraska Press.

Dweck, C. (2000). *Self-theories: Their role in motivation, personality, and development.* Philadelphia, PA: Psychology Press.

Dweck, C. S. (2006). *Mindset: The new psychology of success.* New York: Random House.

Dweck, C. S. (2008a). Can personality be changed? The role of beliefs in personality and change. *Current Directions in Psychological Science, 17*, 391–394. doi:10.1111/j.1467-8721.2008.00612.x

Dweck, C. S. (2008b). *Mindset: The new psychology of success.* New York: Ballantine Books.

Eccles, J. (2009). Who am I and what am I going to do with my life? Personal and collective identities as motivators of action. *Educational Psychologist, 44,* 78–89.

Eccles, J. S., Wigfield, A., & Schiefele, U. (1998). Motivation to succeed. In W. Damon (Series Ed.) & N. Eisenberg (Vol. Ed.), *Handbook of child psychology: Vol. 3. Social, emotional, and personality development* (5th ed., pp. 1017–1095). New York: Wiley.

Echevarria, J., & Graves, A. (2015). *Sheltered content instruction: Teaching English learners with diverse abilities* (5th ed.). Boston: Pearson.

Echevarria, J., Vogt, M., & Short, D. (2013). *Making content comprehensible for English learners: The SIEP model* (4th ed.). Boston: Pearson.

Educational Testing Service. (2014a). *The Praxis series.* Retrieved from https://www.ets.org/praxis/faq_test_takers/

Educational Testing Service. (2014b). *Principles of learning and teaching: Early childhood.* Retrieved from http://www.ets.org/s/praxis/pdf/0621.pdf

Educational Testing Service. (2014c). *Principles of learning and teaching: Grades K–6.* Retrieved from http://www.ets.org/s/praxis/pdf/0622.pdf

Educational Testing Service. (2014d). *Principles of learning and teaching: Grades 5–9.* Retrieved from http://www.ets.org/s/praxis/pdf/0623.pdf

Educational Testing Service. (2014e). *Principles of learning and teaching: Grades 7–12.* Retrieved from http://www.ets.org/s/praxis/pdf/0624.pdf

Edwards, A., Esmonde, I., & Wagner, J. (2011). Learning mathematics. In R. Mayer & P. Alexander (Eds.), *Handbook of research on learning and instruction* (pp. 55–77). New York: Routledge.

Eggen, P., & Kauchak, D. (2012). *Strategies and models for teachers: Teaching content and thinking skills* (6th ed.). Boston: Pearson.

Eggen, P., & Kauchak, D. (2013, April). *Educational leaders' conceptions of effective instruction: A nine-year study.* Paper presented at the annual meeting of the American Educational Research Association, San Francisco.

Ehlers, N. (2012). *Racial imperatives: Discipline, performativity, and struggles against subjection.* Bloomington, IN: Indiana University Press.

Eisenberg, N., Eggum, N., & Edwards, A. (2010). Empathy-related responding and moral development. In W. Arsenio & E. Lemerise (Eds.), *Emotions, aggression, and morality in children: Bridging development and psychopathology* (pp. 115–135). Washington, DC: American Psychological Association.

Eisenberg, N., Fabes, R., & Spinrad, T. (2006). Prosocial development. In N. Eisenberg (Vol. Ed.), *Handbook of child psychology: Vol. 3. Social, emotional, and personality development* (6th ed., pp. 646–718). Hoboken, NJ: John Wiley & Sons.

Eisenberg, N., Spinrad, T., & Eggum, N. (2010). Emotion-related self-regulation and its relation to children's maladjustment. *Annual Review of Clinical Psychology, 6,* 495–525.

Eisenman, L. T. (2007). Self-determination interventions: Building a foundation for school completion. *Remedial and Special Education, 28,* 2–8.

Eisenstein, J., O'Connor, B., Smith, N., & Xing, E. (2011). *A latent variable model for geographical lexical variation.* Paper presented at the Linguistic Society of America, Pittsburgh.

El, R. P., Tillema, H., & van Koppen, S. W. M. (2012). Effects of formative feedback on intrinsic motivation: Examining ethnic differences. *Learning and Individual Differences, 22,* 449–454.

Elder, L., & Paul, R. (2007). Critical thinking: The nature of critical and creative thought: Part II. *Journal of Developmental Education, 30,* 36–37.

Elliot, A., & McGregor, H. (2000, April). Approach and avoidance goals and autonomous-controlled regulation: Empirical and conceptual relations. In A. Assor (Chair), *Self-determination theory and achievement goal theory: Convergences, divergences, and educational implications.* Symposium conducted at the annual meeting of the American Educational Research Association, New Orleans.

Elliot, A., & Thrash, T. (2001). Achievement goals and the hierarchical model of achievement motivation. *Educational Psychology Review, 13,* 139–156.

Elliott, A. (2013). Girl in the shadows: Dasani's homeless life. *New York Times.* Retrieved from http://www.nytimes.com/projects/2013/invisible-child/#/?chapt=1

Ellison, K. (2010, June 1). Seeking an objective test for attention disorder. *New York Times,* pp. D5–D6.

Else-Quest, N., Hyde, J., & Linn, M. (2010). Cross-national patterns of gender differences in mathematics: A meta-analysis. *Psychological Bulletin, 136*(1), 103–127.

Ember, C., & Ember, M. (2011). *Cultural anthropology* (13th ed.). Boston: Pearson.

Emler, N. (1994). Gossip, reputation, and adaptation. In R. F. Goodman & A. Ben-Ze'ev (Eds.), *Good gossip* (pp. 34–46) Lawrence: University of Kansas Press.

Emmer, E. T., & Evertson, C. M. (2013). *Classroom management for middle and high school teachers* (9th ed.). Boston: Allyn & Bacon/Pearson.

Erikson, E. (1968). *Identity: Youth and crisis.* New York: Norton.

Enfield, J. (2013). Looking at the impact of the flipped classroom model of instruction on undergraduate multimedia students at CSUN. *TechTrends: Linking Research & Practice to Improve Learning, 57,* 14–27.

Engel, M. (2013). Problematic preferences: A mixed method examination of principals' preferences for teacher characteristics in Chicago. *Educational Administration Quarterly, 49,* 52–91.

Englert, C., & Bertrams, A. (2013). The role of self-control strength in the development of state anxiety in test situations. *Psychological Reports: Disability & Trauma, 112,* 976–991.

Englund, M., Egeland, B., & Collins, W. (2008). Exceptions to high school dropout predictions in a low-income sample: Do adults make a difference? *Journal of Social Issues, 64,* 77–93.

Ennemoser, M., & Schneider, W. (2007). Relations of television viewing and reading: Findings from a 4-year longitudinal study. *Journal of Educational Psychology, 99,* 349–368.

EPE Research Center. (2011b). Most of nation's largest school systems meeting expectations. *Education Week, Diplomas Count, 30*(34), 27.

EpiMonitor. (2011). Distracted driving called "Epidemic on America's roadways." Author. Retrieved from http://epimonitor.net/Distracted_Driving.htm

Erez, M., Lisak, A., Harush, R., Glikson, E., Nouri, R., & Shokef, E. (2013). Going global: Developing management students' cultural intelligence and global identity in culturally diverse virtual teams. *Academy of Management Learning and Education, 12,* 330–355.

Erickson, K., Voss, M., Prakash, R., Basak, C., Szabo, A., Chaddock, L., . . . Kramer, A. (2011). Exercise training increases the size of hippocampus and improves memory. *Neuroscience, 108,* 3017–3022

Ericsson, K. A. (2003). The acquisition of expert performance as problem solving: Construction and modification of mediating mechanisms through deliberate practice. In J. E. Davidson & R. J. Sternberg (Eds.), *The psychology of problem solving* (pp. 31–83). Cambridge, UK: Cambridge University Press.

Erikson, E. (1980). *Identity and the life cycle* (2nd ed.). New York: Norton.

Ertem, I. S. (2013). The influence of personalization of online texts on elementary school students' reading comprehension and attitudes toward reading. *International Journal of Progressive Education, 9,* 218–228.

Erzözkan, A. (2013). Assessment of social problem solving with respect to emotional intelligence. *Online Journal of Counseling & Education, 2,* 16-32.

Espelage, D., Anderman, E. M., Brown, V. E., Jones, A., Lane, K. L., McMahon, . . . Reynolds, C. R. (2013). Understanding and preventing violence directed against teachers: Recommendations for a national research, practice, and policy agenda. *American Psychologist, 68,* 75–87.

Evans, C., Kirby, U., & Fabrigar, L. (2003). Approaches to learning, need for cognition, and strategic flexibility among university students. *The British Journal of Educational Psychology, 73,* 507–528.

Evans, G., & Schamberg, M. (2009). Childhood poverty, chronic stress, and adult working memory. *Proceedings of the National Academy of Sciences, 106,* 6545–6549.

Evans-Winters, V., & Ivie, C. (2009). Lost in the shuffle: Re-calling a critical pedagogy for urban girls. In S. Steinberg (Ed.), *Diversity and multiculturalism: A reader* (pp. 411–421). New York: Peter Lang.

Evertson, C. M., & Emmer, E. T. (2013). *Classroom management for elementary teachers* (9th ed.). Boston: Allyn & Bacon/Pearson.

Evertson, C., & Weinstein, C. S. (Eds.). (2006). *Handbook of classroom management: Research, practice, and contemporary issues.* Mahwah, NJ: Erlbaum.

Exline, R. (1962). Need affiliation and initial communication behavior in problem solving groups characterized by low interpersonal visibility. *Psychological Reports, 10,* 405–411.

Fabiano, G. A., Pelham, W. E., Jr., & Gnagy, E. M. (2007). The single and combined effects of multiple intensities of behavior modification and methylphenidate for children with attention deficit hyperactivity disorder in a classroom setting. *The School Psychology Review, 36,* 195–216.

Factor, R., Williams, D. R., & Kawachi, I. (2013). Social resistance framework for understanding high-risk behavior among nondominant minorities: Preliminary evidence. *American Journal of Public Health, 103,* 2245–2252.

FairTest. (2008). SAT I: *A faulty instrument for predicting college success.* FairTest: The National Center for Fair and Open Testing. Retrieved from http://www.fairtest.org

FairTest. (2014). FairTest questions the College Board on plans for "New" SAT. Retrieved from http://www.fairtest.org/fairtest-questions-college-board-plans-new-sat

Fan, Y., Decety, J., Yang, C., Liu, J., & Cheng, Y. (2010). Unbroken mirror neurons in autism spectrum disorders. *Journal of Child Psychology and Psychiatry, 51*(9), 981–988. doi:10.111/j.1469-7610.2010.02269.x

Faris, R., & Felmlee, D. (2011). Status struggle: Network centrality and gender segregation in same- and cross-gender aggression. *American Sociological Review, 76,* 48–73.

Farkas, R. (2003). Effects of traditional versus learning-styles instructional methods on middle school students. *Journal of Educational Research, 97*(1), 42–51.

Fassler, D. (2012). Your teen's brain: Driving without the brakes. *Scientific American.* Retrieved from http://blogs.scientificamerican.com/guest-blog/2012/03/15/your-teens-brain-driving-without-the-brakes/

Fauth, R., Roth, J., & Brooks-Gunn, J. (2007). Does the neighborhood context alter the link between youth's after-school time activities and developmental outcomes? A multilevel analysis. *Developmental Psychology, 43*(3), 760–777.

Federal Bureau of Investigation. (2011). *Crimes in the United States, 2011.* Retrieved from http://www.fbi.gov/about-us/cjis/ucr/crime-in-the-u.s/2011/crime-in-the-u.s.-2011/persons-arrested

Federal Bureau of Investigation. (2013). *US murders by weapon type 2007–2011.* Retrieved from http://www.quandl.com/FBI-FBI/WEAPONS11-US-Murders-by-Weapon-Type-2007-2011

Federal Interagency Forum on Child and Family Statistics. (2010). *America's children in brief: Key national indicators of well-being, 2010.* Retrieved from http://www.childstats.gov/pdf/ac2010/ac_10.pdf

Feeding America. (2013). *Hunger & poverty statistics.* Retrieved from http://feedingamerica.org/hunger-in-america/hunger-facts/hunger-and-poverty-statistics.aspx

Feiman-Nemser, S. (2001). From preparation to practice: Designing a continuum to strengthen and sustain teaching. *Teachers College Record, 103,* 1013–1055.

Fein, D., Barton, M., Eigsti, I., Kelly, E. Naigles, L., Schultz, R., . . . Tyson, K. (2013). Optimal outcomes in individuals with a history of autism. *Journal of Child Psychology, 54*(2), 195–205.

Feldhusen, J. (1998a). Programs and service at the elementary level. In J. VanTassel-Baska (Ed.), *Excellence in educating gifted and talented learners* (3rd ed., pp. 211–223). Denver: Love.

Feldman, R. S. (2014). *Development across the life span* (7th ed.). Boston: Pearson.

Feldon, D. F. (2007). Cognitive load and classroom teaching: The double-edged sword of automaticity. *Educational Psychologist, 42,* 123–137.

Fernald, A., Marchman, V., & Weisleder, A. (2012). SES differences in language processing skill and vocabulary are evident at 18 months. *Development Science, 16*(2), 234–248

Fiala, B., Rhodes, R. E., Blanchard, C., & Anderson, J. (2013). Using social–cognitive constructs to predict preoperative exercise before total joint replacement. *Rehabilitation Psychology, 58,* 137–147.

Fisher, C., Berliner, D., Filby, N., Marliave, R., Cohen, K., & Dishaw, M. (1980). Teaching behaviors, academic learning time, and student achievement: An overview. In C. Denham & A. Lieberman (Eds.), *Time to learn* (pp. 7–32). Washington, DC: National Institute of Education.

Fite, P., Vitulano, M., Wynn, P., Wimsatt, A., Gaertner, A., & Rathert, J. (2010). Influence of perceived neighborhood safety on proactive and reactive aggression. *Journal of Community Psychology, 38*(6), 757–768. doi:10.1002/jcop.20393

Flanagan, D., Genshaft, J., & Harrison, P. (1997). *Contemporary intellectual assessment: Theories, tests, and issues.* New York: Guilford Press.

Flavell, J., Miller, P., & Miller, S. (2002). *Cognitive development* (4th ed.). Upper Saddle River, NJ: Prentice Hall.

Fleming, V., & Alexander, J. (2001). The benefits of peer collaboration: A replication with a delayed posttest. *Contemporary Educational Psychology, 26,* 588–601.

Flores, E., Cicchetti, D., & Rogosch, F. (2005). Predictors of resilience in maltreated and nonmaltreated Latino children. *Developmental Psychology, 41*(2), 338, 351.

Flores, M. M., & Kaylor, M. (2007). The effects of a direct instruction program on the fraction performance of middle school students at-risk for failure in mathematics. *Journal of Instructional Psychology, 34,* 84–94.

Flynn, J. (1999). Searching for justice: The discovery of IQ gains over time. *American Psychologist, 54,* 5–20.

Foley-Nicpon, M., Assouline, S. G., & Colangelo, N. (2013). Twice-exceptional learners: Who needs to know what? *Gifted Child Quarterly, 57,* 169–180.

Ford, D. (2010). *Reversing underachievement among gifted Black students* (2nd ed.). Waco, TX: Prufrock.

Forte, E. (2010). Examining the assumptions underlying the NCLB federal accountability policy on school improvement. *Journal of Educational Psychology, 102,* 76–88.

Fottrell, Q. (2012). Does Facebook wreck marriages? *The Wall Street Journal.* Retrieved from http://blogs.marketwatch.com/realtimeadvice/2012/05/21/does-facebook-wreck-marriages/?mg=blogs-sm

Fox, C. L., Elder, T., Gater, J., & Johnson, E. (2010). The association between adolescents' beliefs in a just world and their attitudes to victims of bullying. *The British Journal of Educational Psychology, 80,* 183–198.

Freedle, R. (2010). On replicating ethnic test bias effects: The Santelices and Wilson study. *Harvard Education Review, 80*(30), 394–404.

Freiberg, H. J., & Lamb, S. M. (2009). Dimensions of person-centered classroom management. *Theory into Practice, 48,* 99–105.

Freitag, C., Rohde, L., Lempp, T., & Romanos, M. (2010). Phenotypic and measurement influences on heritability estimates in childhood ADHD. *European Child and Adolescent Psychiatry, 19,* 311–323.

Frey, B., & Schmitt, V. (2005, April). *Teachers' classroom assessment practices.* Paper presented at the annual meeting of the American Educational Research Association, Montreal, Canada.

Frey, W. H. (2011). A demographic tipping point among America's three-year-olds. *The Brookings Institute.* Retrieved from http://www.brookings.edu/opinions/2011/0207_population_frey.aspx

Friedman, I. A. (2006). Classroom management and teacher stress and burnout. In C. M. Evertson & C. S. Weinstein (Eds.), *Handbook of classroom management: Research, practice, and contemporary issues* (pp. 925–944). Mahwah, NJ: Erlbaum.

Friedman, T. (2013). The Shanghai secret. *New York Times.* Retrieved from http://www.nytimes.com/2013/10/23/opinion/friedman-the-shanghai-secret.html?ref=todayspaper&pagewanted=print

Friend, M. (2014). *Special education: Contemporary perspectives for school professionals* (4th ed.). Boston: Allyn & Bacon.

Friese, M., Binder, J., Luechinger, R., Boesiger, P., & Rasch, B. (2013). Suppressing emotions impairs subsequent Stroop performance and reduces prefrontal brain activation. *PLoS ONE, 8,* 1–11.

Friesen, N. (2011). The lecture as a transmedial pedagogical form: A historical analysis. *Educational Researcher, 40,* 95–102.

Fuchs, D. (2006). Cognitive profiling of children with genetic disorders and the search for a scientific basis of differentiated education. In P. Alexander & P. Winne (Eds.), *Handbook of educational psychology* (2nd ed., pp. 187–206). Mahwah, NJ: Erlbaum.

Fuchs, D., & Fuchs, L. S. (2007). Increasing strategic reading comprehension with peer-assistant learning activities. In D. S. McNamara (Ed.), *Reading comprehension strategies: Theories, interventions, and technologies* (pp. 175–197). New York: Erlbaum.

Fuhrman, S. H. (2013). Tying teacher evaluation to student achievement: Caution, yellow light ahead. *Education Week.* Retrieved from http://www.edweek.org/ew/articles/2010/04/07/28fuhrman_ep.h29.html

Fung, H., & Smith, B. (2010). Learning morality. In D. Lancy, J. Bock, & S. Gaskins (Eds.), *The anthropology of learning in childhood* (pp. 261–285). Walnut Creek, CA: AltaMira Press.

Gagné, N., & Parks, S. (2013). Cooperative learning tasks in a grade 6 intensive ESL class: Role of scaffolding. *Language Teaching Research, 17,* 188–209.

Gall, M., Gall, J., & Borg, W. (2010). *Applying educational research: How to read, do, and use research to solve problems of practice* (6th ed.). Boston: Allyn & Bacon/Pearson.

Gallese, V., Gernsbacher, M., Heyes, C., Hickok, G., & Iacoboni, M. (2011). Mirror neuron forum. *Perspectives on Psychological Science, 6,* 369–407.

Gambrill, E. (2013). Birds of a feather: Applied behavior analysis and quality of life. *Research on Social Work Practice, 23,* 121–140.

Gamo, S., Sander, E., & Richard, J. (2010). Transfer of strategy use by semantic recoding in arithmetic problem solving. *Learning and Instruction, 20,* 400–410.

Gao, H., Losh, S. C., Shen, E., Turner, J. E., & Yuan, R. (2007, April). *The effect of collaborative concept mapping on learning, problem solving, and learner attitude.* Paper presented at the annual meeting of the American Educational Research Association, Chicago.

Garcia, S., & Tyler, B-J. (2010). Meeting the needs of English language learners with learning disabilities in the general curriculum. *Theory Into Practice, 49,* 113–120.

Gardner, H. (1983). *Frames of mind: The theory of multiple intelligences.* New York: Basic Books.

Gardner, H. (1995). Reflections on multiple intelligences: Myths and messages. *Phi Delta Kappan, 77,* 200–209.

Gardner, H., & Hatch, T. (1989). Multiple intelligences go to school. *Educational Researcher, 18*(8), 4–10.

Gardner, H., & Moran, S. (2006). The science of multiple intelligences theory: A response to Lynn Waterhouse. *Educational Psychologist, 41*(4), 227–232.

Garlick, D. (2010). *Intelligence and the brain: Solving the mystery of why people differ in IQ and how a child can be a genius.* Burbank, CA: Aesop Press.

Garren, M. V., Sexauer, S. B., & Page, T. L. (2013). Effect of circadian phase on memory acquisition and recall: Operant conditioning vs. classical conditioning. *PLoS ONE, 8,* 1–8. doi:10.1371/journal.pone.0058693

Gauvain, M., & Parke, R. (2010). Socialization. In M. Bornstein (Ed.), *Handbook of cultural developmental science* (pp. 239–258). New York: Psychology Press.

Gay, G. (2006). Connections between classroom management and culturally responsive teaching. In C. Evertson, & C. Weinstein (Eds.), *Handbook of classroom management: Research,* practice, and contemporary issues (pp. 343–370). Mahwah, NJ: Erlbaum.

Gay. G. (2010). *Culturally responsive teaching: Theory, research, & practice* (2nd ed.). New York: Teachers College Press.

Gay, L. R., Mills, G. E., & Airasian, P. W. (2012). *Educational research: Competencies for analysis and applications* (10th ed.). Upper Saddle River, NJ: Pearson Education.

Gazzaniga, M. S. (2008). *Human: The science behind what makes us unique.* New York: HarperCollins.

Geary, D. (2007). An evolutionary perspective on learning disability in mathematics. *Development Neuropsychology, 32*(1), 471–519.

Gehlbach, H., Brinkworth, M., & Harris, A. (2011, April). *The promise of social perspective taking to facilitate teacher–student relationships.* Paper presented at the annual meeting of the American Educational Association, New Orleans.

Gelman, S., & Kalish, C. (2006). Conceptual development. In W. Damon & R. Lerner (Series Eds.), D. Kuhn & R. Siegler (Vol. Eds.), *Handbook of child psychology: Vol. II. Cognition, perception, and language* (pp. 687–733, 6th ed.). New York: Wiley.

Geno, J. A. (2014). Using tests to improve student achievement. *Techniques: Connecting Education and Careers, 89,* 50–53.

Gentile, D. (2011). The multiple dimensions of video game effects. *Child Development Perspectives, 5*(2), 75–81.

Gentile, J. (1996). Setbacks in the advancement of learning. *Educational Researcher, 25,* 37–39.

Gerstel, N. (2011). Rethinking families and community: The color, class, and centrality of extended kin ties. *Sociological Forum, 26,* 1–20.

Gervain, J., & Mehler, J. (2010). Speech perception and language acquisition in the first year of life. *Annual Review of Psychology, 61,* 191–218.

Gettinger, M., & Kohler, K. M. (2006). Process–outcome approaches to classroom management and effective teaching. In C. M. Evertson & C. S. Weinstein (Eds.), *Handbook of classroom management: Research, practice, and contemporary issues* (pp. 73–95). Mahwah, NJ: Erlbaum.

Gewertz, C. (2011). Progress is slow on common-standards implementation. *Education Week, 31*(4), 13.

Ghavami, N., Fingerhut, A. W., Peplau, L. A., Grant, S., & Wittig, M. A. (2011). Testing a model of minority identity achievement, identity affirmation and psychological well-being among ethnic minority and sexual minority individuals. *Cultural Diversity and Ethnic Minority Psychology, 17*(1), 79–88.

Gholson, B., & Craig, S. D. (2006). Promoting constructive activities that support vicarious learning during computer-based instruction. *Educational Psychology Review, 18,* 119–139.

Gibbs, J. C. (2010). *Moral development and reality: Beyond the theories of Kohlberg and Hoffman* (2nd ed.). Boston: Pearson Allyn & Bacon.

Gijbels, D., Dochy, F., Van den Bossche, P., & Segers, M. (2005). Effects of problem-based learning: A meta-analysis from the angle of as- sessment. *Review of Educational Research, 75*(1), 27–61.

Gilligan, C. (1977). In a different voice: Women's conceptions of the self and of morality. *Harvard Educational Review, 47,* 481–517.

Gilligan, C. (1982). *In a different voice: Psychological theory and women's development.* Cambridge, MA: Harvard University Press.

Gilligan, C. (1998). *Minding women: Reshaping the education realm.* Cambridge, MA: Harvard University Press.

Gilligan, C. (2008). Moral orientation and moral development. In A. Bailey & C. J. Cuomo (Eds.), *The feminist philosophy reader* (pp. 467–477). Boston: McGraw-Hill.

Gilligan, C., & Attanucci, J. (1988). Two moral orientations: Gender differences and similarities. *Merrill-Palmer Quarterly, 34,* 223–237.

Gimbel, P. (2008). Helping new teachers reflect. *Principal Leadership (High School Ed.), 8,* 6–8.

Ginsburg, A., Leinwand, S., & Decker, K. (2009). *Informing grades 1–6 standards development: What can be learned from high-performing Hong Kong, Korea, and Singapore?* Washington, DC: American Institutes for Research.

Gläscher, J., Rudrauf, D., Colom, R., Paul, L., Tranel, D., Damasio, H., & Adolphs, R. (2010). Distributed neural system for general intelligence revealed by lesion mapping. *Proceedings of the National Academy of Sciences of the United States of America, 107,* 4705–4709.

Glick, J., & Bates, L. (2010). Diversity in academic achievement: Children of immigrants in US schools. In E. Grigorenko & R. Takanishi (Eds.), *Immigration, diversity, and education* (pp. 112–129). New York: Routledge.

Glover, S., & Dixon, P. (2013). Context and vision effects on real and imagined actions: Support for the common representation hypothesis of motor imagery. *Journal of Experimental Psychology: Human Perception and Performance.* doi:10.1037/a0031276

Gluszek, A., & Dovidio, J. (2010). The way they speak: A social psychological perspective on the stigma of nonnative accents in communication. *Personality and Social Psychology Review, 14*(2), 214–237.

Godley, A., & Escher, A. (2011, April). *Bidialectical African-American students' views on code-switching in and out of school.* Paper presented at the annual meeting of the American Educational Research Association, New Orleans.

Godley, A., Sweetland, J., Wheeler, R., Minnici, A., & Carpenter, B. (2006). Preparing teachers for dialectally diverse classrooms. *Educational Researcher, 35*(8), 30–37.

Goetz, T., Nett, U. E., Martiny, S. E., Hall, N. C., Pekrun, R., Dettmers, S., & Trautwein, U. (2012). Students' emotions during homework: Structures, self-concept antecedents, and achievement outcomes. *Learning and Individual Differences, 22,* 225–234.

Gogtay, N., & Thompson, P. (2010). Mapping gray matter development: Implications for typical development and vulnerability to psychopathology. *Brain and Cognition, 72,* 6–15.

Goldfield, G. (2012). Making access to TV contingent on physical activity: Effects on liking and relative reinforcing value of TV and physical activity in overweight and obese children. *Journal of Behavioral Medicine, 35,* 1–7.

Goldsmith, W. (2013). Enhancing classroom conversation for all students. *Phi Delta Kappan, 94,* 48–53.

Goleman, D. (2006). *Emotional intelligence: Why it can matter more than IQ* (10th ed.). New York: Random House.

Gollnick, D., & Chinn, P. (2013). *Multicultural education in a pluralistic society* (9th ed.). Upper Saddle River, NJ: Merrill/Pearson Education.

Gondal, U. H., & Husain, T. (2013). A comparative study of intelligence quotient and emotional intelligence: Effect on employees' performance. *Asian Journal of Business Management, 5,* 153–162.

Good, T., & Brophy, J. (2008). *Looking in classrooms* (10th ed.). Boston: Allyn & Bacon.

Goodnow, J. (2010). Culture. In M. Bornstein (Ed.), *Handbook of cultural developmental science* (pp. 207–221). New York: Psychology Press.

Gootman, E., & Gebeloff, R. (2008). Gifted programs in the city are less diverse. *The New York Times.* Retrieved from http://www.nytimes.com/2008/06/19/nyregion/19gifted.html?pagewanted=all&_r=0.

Gootman, M. E. (1998). Effective in-house suspension. *Educational Leadership, 56*(1), 39–41.

Gordon, T. (1981). Crippling our children with disruption. *Journal of Education, 163,* 228–243.

Gottfried, M. A. (2011). The detrimental effects of missing school: Evidence from urban siblings. *American Journal of Education, 117,* 147–182.

Gottfried, M. A. (2014). Can neighbor attributes predict school absences? *Urban Education, 49,* 216–250.

Graham, S. (2010). What educators need to know about bullying behaviors. *Phi Delta Kappan, 92,* 66–69.

Graham, S., & Weiner, B. (1996). Theories and principles of motivation. In D. Berliner & R. Calfee (Eds.), *Handbook of educational psychology* (pp. 63–84). New York: Macmillan.

Grant, A. (2014). Raising a moral child. *The New York Times.* Retrieved from

Grant, L. W. (2006). Persistence and self-efficacy: A key to understanding teacher turnover. *The Delta Kappa Gamma Bulletin, 72*(2), 50–54.

Gredler, M. (2012). Understanding Vygotsky for the classroom: Is it too late? *Educational Psychology Review, 24,* 113–131.

Green, E. (2010). Building a better teacher. *The New York Times Magazine.* Retrieved from http://www.nytimes.com/2010/03/07/magazine/07Teachers-t.html?_r=1

Green, M., & Piel, J. (2010). *Theories of human development: A comparative approach* (2nd ed.). Boston: Allyn & Bacon.

Greenberg, J., Putman, H., & Walsh, K. (2014). *Training our future teachers: Classroom management.* National Council on Teacher Quality.

Retrieved from http://www.nctq.org/dmsView/Future_Teachers_Classroom_Management_NCTQ_Report

Greene, J. A., & Azevedo, R. (2007). A theoretical review of Winne and Hadwin's model of self-regulated learning: New perspectives and directions. *Review of Educational Research, 77,* 334–372.

Greene, M., & Kirpalani, N. (2013). Using interactive whiteboards in teaching retail mathematics. *Marketing Education Review, 23,* 49–54.

Greeno, J., Collins, A., & Resnick, L. (1996). Cognition and learning. In D. Berliner & R. Calfee (Eds.), *Handbook of educational psychology* (pp. 15–46). New York: Macmillan.

Gregg, N. (2009). *Adolescents and adults with learning disability and ADHD: Assessment and accommodation.* New York: Guilford.

Gregory, A., Skiba, R. J., & Noguera, P. A. (2010). The achievement gap and the discipline gap: Two sides of the same coin. *Educational Researcher, 39,* 59–68.

Griffin, R., MacKewn, A., Moser, E., & VanVuren, K. W. (2013). Learning skills and motivation: Correlates to superior academic performance. *Business Education & Accreditation, 5,* 53–65.

Griffiths, M. (2010). Online video gaming: What should educational psychologists know? *Educational Psychology in Practice, 26*(1), 35–40.

Grigorenko, E., Jarvin, L., Diffley, R., Goodyear, J., Shanahan, E., & Sternberg, R. (2009). Are SSATs and GPA enough? A theory-based approach to predicting academic success in secondary school. *Journal of Education Psychology, 101*(4), 964–981.

Grilly, D., & Salamone, J. (2012). *Drugs, brain, & behavior* (6th ed.). Boston: Pearson.

Guan, J., Xiang, P., McBride, R., & Keating, X. D. (2013). Achievement goals, social goals, and students' reported persistence and effort in high school athletic settings. *Journal of Sport Behavior, 36,* 149–170.

Guillot, A., Moschberger, K., & Collet, C. (2013). Coupling movement with imagery as a new perspective for motor imagery practice. *Behavioral and Brain Functions, 9,* 1–8. doi:10.1186/1744-9081-9-8

Guyll, M., Madon, S., Prieto, L., & Scherr, K. (2010). The potential roles of self-fulfilling prophecies, stigma consciousness, and stereotype threat in linking Latino ethnicity and educational outcomes. *Journal of Social Issues, 66*(1), 113–130.

Habek, D., & Kovačević, M. (2011). Adverse pregnancy outcomes and long-term morbidity after early fetal hypokinesia in maternal smoking pregnancies. *Archives of Gynecology and Obstetrics, 283,* 491–495.

Hacker, D., Bol, L., Horgan, D., & Rakow, E. (2000). Test prediction and performance in a classroom context. *Journal of Education Psychology, 92,* 160–170.

Hackman, D., & Farah, M. (2012). Socioeconomic status and the developing brain. *Trends in Cognitive Science, 16,* 91–136.

Hadjioannou, X. (2007). Bringing the background to the foreground: What do classroom environ-

ments that support authentic discussions look like? *American Educational Research Journal, 44*(2), 370–399.

Hafner, K. (2009). Texting may be taking a toll. *New York Times.* Retrieved from http://www.nytimes.com/2009/05/26/health/26teen.html?_r=0&ref=textmessaging&pagewanted=print

Hagemans, M. G., van der Meij, H., & de Jong, T. (2013). The effects of a concept map-based support tool on simulation-based inquiry learning. *Journal of Educational Psychology, 105,* 1–24.

Hahn, E., Gottschling, J., & Spinath, F. (2012). Short measurements of personality—Validity and reliability of the GSOEP Big Five Inventory (BFI-S). *Journal of Research in Personality, 46,* 355–359.

Haidt, J., & Kesebir, S. (2010). Morality. In S. Fiske & D. Gilbert (Eds.), *Handbook of social psychology* (5th ed., pp. 797–832). Hoboken, NJ: Wiley.

Hakkarainen, O., & Ahtee, M. (2007). The durability of conceptual change in learning the concept of weight in the case of a pulley in balance. *International Journal of Science and Mathematics Education, 5,* 461–482.

Hallahan, D., Kauffman, J., & Pullen, P. (2015). *Exceptional children* (13th ed.). Boston: Pearson.

Halpern, D. (2006). Assessing gender gaps in learning and academic achievement. In P. A. Alexander & P. H. Winne (Eds.), *Handbook of educational psychology* (2nd ed., pp. 635–653). Mahwah, NJ: Erlbaum.

Halpern, D., Benbow, C., Geary, D., Gur, R., Hyde, J., & Gernsbacher, M. (2007). The science of sex differences in science and mathematics. *Psychological Science in the Public Interest, 8,* 1–51.

Halpern, D., Eliot, L., Bigler, R., Fabes, R., Hanish, L., Hyde, J., . . . Martin, C. (2011). The pseudoscience of single-sex schooling. *Science, 333*(6050), 1706–1707.

Hamilton, S. L., Seibert, M. A., Gardner, III, R., & Talbert-Johnson, C. (2000). Using guided notes to improve the academic achievement of incarcerated adolescents with learning and behavior problems. *Remedial and Special Education, 21,* 133–140.

Hamlen, K. (2011). Children's choices and strategies in video games. *Computers in Human Behavior, 27*(1), 532–539.

Hamlin, J., & Wynn, K. (2011). Young infants prefer prosocial to antisocial others. *Cognitive Development, 26,* 30–39.

Hammer, C., Farkas, G., & Maczuga, S. (2010). The language and literacy development of Head Start children: A study using the Family and Child Experiences Survey Database. *Language, Speech, and Hearing Services in Schools, 41,* 70–83.

Han, W-J. (2010). Bilingualism and socioemotional well-being. *Children and Youth Services Review, 32,* 720–731.

Hancock, D. R. (2001). Effects of test anxiety and evaluative threat on students' achievement and motivation. *The Journal of Educational Research, 94,* 284–290.

Hansberry, L. (1959). *A raisin in the sun.* New York: Random House.

Hanushek, E. E., Rivkin, S. G., & Kain, J. J. (2005). Teachers, schools, and academic achievement. *Econometrica, 73,* 417–458.

Hardman, M. L., Drew, C. J., & Egan, M. W. (2014). *Human exceptionality: School community and family* (11th ed.). Stamford, CT: Cengage.

Hardman, M., Drew, C., & Egan, W. (2014). *Human exceptionality* (11th ed.). Boston: Cengage.

Harms, P. D., & Credé, M. (2010). Remaining issues in emotional intelligence research: Construct overlap, method artifacts, and lack of incremental validity. *Industrial and Organizational Psychology: Perspectives on Science and Practice, 3,* 154–158.

Harriet, A. W., & Bradley, K. D. (2003). "You can't say you can't play:" Intervening in the process of social exclusion in the kindergarten classroom. *Early Childhood Research Quarterly, 18,* 185–205.

Harris, C. B., Barnier, A. J., & Sutton, J. (2013). Shared encoding and the costs and benefits of collaborative recall. *Journal of Experimental Psychology: Learning, Memory, and Cognition, 39,* 183–195.

Harrison, M. A. (2011). College students' prevalence and perceptions of text messaging while driving. *Accident Analysis & Prevention, 43,* 1516–1520. http://dx.doi.org/10.1016/j.aap.2011.03.003

Harry, B., & Klingner, J. (2007). Discarding the deficit model. *Educational Leadership, 64*(5), 16–21.

Harter, S. (2006). The self. In N. Eisenberg (Ed.), *Handbook of child psychology: Vol. 3. Social, emotional, and personality development* (6th ed., pp. 505–570). Hoboken, NJ: Wiley.

Hartup, W. (2009). Critical issues and theoretical viewpoints. In K. Rubin, W. Bukowski, & B. Laursen (Eds.), *Handbook of peer interactions, relationships, and groups* (pp. 3–19). New York: Guilford Press.

Haskill, A., & Corts, D. (2010). Acquiring language. In E. Sandberg & B. Spritz (Eds.), *A clinician's guide to normal cognitive development in childhood* (pp. 23–41). New York: Routledge/Taylor & Francis.

Hattie, J. A. C., & Timperley, H. (2007). The power of feedback. *Review of Educational Research, 77,* 81–112. doi:10.3102/003465430298487

Hattie, J., & Gan, M. (2011). Instruction based on feedback. In R. E. Mayer & P. A. Alexander (Eds.), *Handbook of research on learning and instruction* (pp. 249–271). New York: Routledge.

Hattie, J., & Timperley, H. (2007). The power of feedback. *Review of Educational Research, 77*(1), 81–112.

Haycock, P. (2009). Fetal alcohol spectrum disorders: The epigenetic perspective. *Biology of Reproduction, 81,* 607–617.

Helgeson, V. (2012). *Psychology of gender* (4th ed.). Boston: Pearson.

Helmsen, J., Koglin, U., & Petermann, F. (2012). Emotion regulation and aggressive behavior in preschoolers: The mediating role of social information processing. *Child Psychiatry & Human Development, 43,* 87–101.

Henderson, N. (2013). Havens of resilience. *Educational Leadership, 71,* 22–27.

Henderson, R. (2011). Classroom pedagogies, digital literacies and the home-school digital divide. *International Journal of Pedagogies and Learning, 6*(2), 152–161.

Hennessey, B. A., & Amabile, T. M. (2010). Creativity. *Annual Review of Psychology, 61,* 569–598.

Henricsson, L., & Rydell, A. M. (2004). Elementary school children with behavior problems: Teacher–child relations and self-perception. A prospective study. *Merrill-Palmer Quarterly, 50,* 111–138.

Herman, J., & Linn, R. (2014). New assessments, new rigor. *Educational Leadership, 71,* 34–37.

Herman, J., & Linn, R., (2013). *On the road to assessing deeper learning: The status of Smarter Balanced and PARCC assessment consortia (CRESST Report 823).* Los Angeles, CA: University of California, National Center for Research on Evaluation, Standards, & Student Testing (CRESST).

Herman, J., Osmundson, E., & Dietel, R. (2010). Benchmark assessment for improved learning. *ACC Policy Brief.* Los Angeles, CA: University of California.

Hernandez, D., Denton, N., & Macartney, S. (2010). Children of immigrants and the future of America. In E. Grigorenko & R. Takanishi (Eds.), *Immigration, diversity, and education* (pp. 7–25). New York: Routledge.

Hernandez, I., & Preston, J. L. (2013). Disfluency disrupts the confirmation bias. *Journal of Experimental Social Psychology, 49,* 178–182.

Hess, F. M., & McShane, M. Q. (2013). Common core in the real world. *Phi Delta Kappan, 95,* 61–66.

Heward, W. L. (2013). *Exceptional children: An introduction to special education* (10th ed.). Boston: Pearson.

Heymann, L. (2010). *The sound of hope.* New York: Ballantine.

Hickey, D. T., & Zuiker, S. J. (2005). Engaged participation: A sociocultural model of motivation with implications for educational assessment. *Educational Assessment, 10,* 277–305.

Hidi, S. (2001). Interest, reading, and learning: Theoretical and practical considerations. *Educational Psychology Review, 13,* 191–209.

Hidi, S., & Renninger, K. A. (2006). The four-phase model of interest development. *Educational Psychologist, 41*(2), 111–127.

Hidi, S., Renninger, K. A., & Krapp, A. (2004). Interest, a motivational variable that combines affective and cognitive functioning. In D. Dai & R. Sternberg (Eds.), *Motivation, emotion, and cognition: Integrative perspectives on intellectual functioning and development* (pp. 89–155). Mahwah, NJ: Erlbaum.

Hightower, A. (2012). On policy, student achievement, states pressing to measure up. *Education Week, 31*(16), 43–64.

Hilbert, T. S., & Renkl, A. (2008). Concept mapping as a follow-up strategy to learning from texts: What characterizes good and poor mappers? *Instructional Science, 36,* 53–73.

Hill, A., Arford, T., Lubitow, A., & Smollin, L. M. (2012). "I'm ambivalent about it": The dilemmas of PowerPoint. *Teaching Sociology, 40,* 242–256.

Hill, C., Corbett, C., & Rose, A. (2010). *Why so few? Women in science, technology, engineering, and mathematics.* Washington, DC: AAUW.

Hipfner-Boucher, K., Lam, K., & Xi, C. (2014). The effects of bilingual education on the English language and literacy outcomes of Chinese-speaking children. *Written Language & Literacy, 17,* 116-138.

Hirsch, E. (2006). *Knowledge deficit: Closing the shocking education gap for American children.* Boston: Houghton Mifflin.

Hirvikoski, T., Waaler, E., Alfredsson, J., Pihlgren, C., Holmström, A., Johnson, A., . . . Nordström, A. (2011). Reduced ADHD symptoms in adults with ADHD after structured skills training group: Results from a randomized controlled trial. *Behavioural Research and Therapy, 49,* 175–185.

Hmelo-Silver, C. E. (2004). Problem-based learning: What and how do students learn? *Educational Psychology Review, 16,* 236–266.

Hmelo-Silver, C. E., Duncan, R. G., & Chinn, C. A. (2007). Scaffolding and achievement in problem-based and inquiry learning: A response to Kirschner, Sweller, and Clark (2006). *Educational Psychologist, 42,* 99–107.

Hochweber, J., Hosenfeld, I., & Klieme, E. (2013, August 12). Classroom composition, classroom management, and the relationship between student attributes and grades. *Journal of Educational Psychology.* Advance online publication. doi:10.1037/a0033829

Hofer, M. (2010). Adolescents' development of individual interests: A product of multiple goal regulation? *Educational Psychologist, 45,* 149–166.

Hoff, E. (2010). Context effects on young children's language use: The influence of conversational setting and partner. *First Language, 30,* 461–472.

Hoff, E. (2012). Interpreting the early language trajectories of children from low-SES and language minority homes: Implications for closing achievement gaps. *Developmental Psychology.* Retrieved from http://www.ncbi.nlm.nih.gov/pubmed/22329382

Hofferth, S. (2010). Home media and children's achievement and behavior. *Child Development, 81,* 1598–1619.

Hogan, T., Rabinowitz, M., & Craven, J. (2003). Representation in teaching: Inference from research on expert and novice teachers. *Educational Psychologist, 38,* 235–247.

Hohn, R. L., & Frey, B. (2002). Heuristic training and performance in elementary mathematical problem solving. *The Journal of Educational Research, 95,* 374–390.

Holme, J., Richards, M., Jimerson, J., & Cohen, R. (2010). Assessing the effects of high school exit examinations. *Review of Educational Research, 80,* 476–526.

Holzberger, D., Philipp, A., & Kunter, M. (2013). How teachers' self-efficacy is related to Instructional quality: A longitudinal analysis. *Journal of Educational Psychology, 105,* 774–786.

Hong, S., & Ho, H. (2005). Direct and indirect longitudinal effects of parental involvement on student achievement: Second-order latent growth modeling across ethnic groups. *Journal of Educational Psychology, 97*(1), 32–42.

Honig, A. (2009). Understanding and working with non-compliant and aggressive young children. *Early Child Development and Care, 179*(8), 1007–1023. doi:10.1080/0300443070172626217

Honz, K., Kiewra, K., & Yang, Y.-S. (2010). Cheating perceptions and prevalence across academic settings. *Mid-Western Educational Researcher, 23,* 10–17.

Horn, J. (2008). Spearman, *g*, expertise, and the nature of human cognitive capability. In P. Kyllonen, R. Roberts, & L. Stankov (Eds.), *Extending intelligence: Enhancement and new constructs* (pp. 185–230). New York: Erlbaum/Taylor & Francis.

Horst, S. J., Finney, S. J., & Barron, K. E. (2007). Moving beyond academic achievement goal measures: A study of social achievement goals. *Contemporary Educational Psychology, 32,* 667–698.

Houdé, O., Pineau, A., Leroux, G., Poirel, N., Perchey, G., Lanoë, C., . . . Mazoyer, B. (2011). Functional MRI study of Piaget's conservation-of-number task in preschool and school-age children: A neo-Piagetian approach. *Journal of Experimental Child Psychology, 110,* 332– 346. doi: 10.1016/j.jecp.2011.04.008

Howe, C. (2009). Collaborative group work in middle childhood. *Human Development, 52,* 215–239.

Howe, C. (2010). *Peer groups and children's development.* Malden, MA: Wiley-Blackwell.

Howe, M. L. (2004). The role of conceptual recoding in reducing children's retroactive interference. *Developmental Psychology, 40,* 131–139.

Hoy, W., Tarter, C. J., & Hoy, A. (2006). Academic optimism of schools: A force for student achievement. *American Educational Research Journal, 43*(3), 425–446. http://www.ed.gov/about/bdscomm/list/mathpanel/report/final-report.pdf http://www.nytimes.com/2014/04/12/opinion/sunday/raising-a-moral-child.html?ref=todayspaper

Hu, W. (2010, October 1). Making math lessons as easy as 1, pause 2, pause. . . *New York Times.* Retrieved from http://www.nytimes.com/2010/10/01/education/01math.html

Huan, V. S., Yeo, L. S., & Ang, R. P. (2006). The influence of dispositional optimism and gender on adolescents' perception of academic stress. *Adolescence, 41,* 533–546.

Hubbard, J., Morrow, M., Romano, L., & McAuliffe, M. (2010). The role of anger in children's reactive versus proactive aggression: Review of findings, issues of measurement, and implications for intervention. In W. Arsenio & E. Lemerise (Eds.), *Emotions, aggression, and morality in children: Bridging development and psychopathology* (pp. 201–217). Washington, DC: American Psychological Association. doi:10.1037/12129-01

Huebner, C., & Payne, K. (2010). Home support for emergent literacy: Follow-up of a community-based implementation of dialogic reading. *Journal of Applied Developmental Psychology, 31,* 195–201.

Huesmann, L., Dubow, E., & Boxer, P. (2011). The transmission of aggressiveness across generations: Biological, contextual, and social learning processes. In P. Shaver & M. Mikulincer (Eds.), *Human aggression and violence: Causes, manifestations, and consequences. Herzliya series on personality and social psychology* (pp. 123–142). doi:10.1037/12346-007

Hughes, C., Ensor, R., & Marks, A. (2010). Individual differences in false belief understanding are stable from 3 to 6 years of age and predict children's mental state talk with school friends. *Journal of Experimental Child Psychology, 108,* 96–112.

Hughes, J. N., Wu, J-Y., Kwok, O., Villarreal, V., & Johnson, A. Y. (2012). Indirect effects of child reports of teacher–student relationship on achievement. *Journal of Educational Psychology, 104,* 350–365.

Hull, J. (2013). Trends in teacher evaluation: How states are measuring teacher performance. *National School Boards Association Center for Public Education.* Retrieved from http://www.centerforpubliceducation.org/Main-Menu/Evaluating-performance/Trends-in-Teacher-Evaluation-At-A-Glance/Trends-in-Teacher-Evaluation-Full-Report-PDF.pdf

Humphrey, R. H. (2013). The benefits of emotional intelligence and empathy to entrepreneurship. *Entrepreneurship Research Journal, 3,* 287–294.

Hung, I. W., & Labroo, A. A. (2011). From firm muscles to firm willpower: Understanding the role of embodied cognition in self-regulation. *Journal of Consumer Research, 37,* 1046–1064.

Hunter, M. (2012). How motivation really works: Toward an emoto-motivation paradigm. *Economics, Management, and Financial Markets, 7,* 138–196.

Hurtz, G. M., & Donovan, J. J. (2000). Personality and job performance: The Big Five revisited. *Journal of Applied Psychology, 85,* 869–879. doi:10.1037/0021-9010.85.6.869

Hwang, W-Y., & Hu, S-S. (2013). Analysis of peer learning behaviors using multiple representations in virtual reality and their impacts on geometry problem solving. *Computers & Education, 62,* 308–319. doi:10.1016/j.compedu.2012.10.005

Ichthyology. (2013). *International shark attack file.* Retrieved from http://www.flmnh.ufl.edu/fish/sharks/statistics/statsw.htm

Igo, L. B., Bruning, R., & McCrudden, M. (2005). Exploring differences in students' copy-and-paste decision making and processing: A mixed-methods study. *Journal of Educational Psychology, 97*(1), 103–116.

Igo, L. B., Kiewra, K., & Bruning, R. (2004). Removing the snare from the pair: Using pictures to learn confusing word pairs. *Journal of Experimental Education, 72*(3), 165–178.

Ihlo, T., & Nantais, M. (2010). Evidence-based interventions within a multi-tier framework for positive behavioral supports. In T. Glover & S. Vaughn (Eds.), *The promise of response to intervention: Evaluating current science and practice* (pp. 239–266). New York: Guilford.

Inan, F. A., Lowther, D. L., Ross, S. M., & Strahl, D. (2010). Pattern of classroom activities during students' use of computers: Relations between instructional strategies and computer applications. *Teaching and Teacher Education, 26,* 540–546.

Infowars.com. (2013). Statistics show that you are NOT going to be killed by terrorism. Retrieved from http://www.infowars.com/statistics-show-you-are-not-going-to-be-killed-by-terrorism/

Ingersoll, R., & Smith, T. (2004). What are the effects of induction and mentoring on beginning teacher turnover? *American Educational Research Journal, 41*(3), 681–714.

Inhelder, B., & Piaget, J. (1958). *The growth of logical thinking from childhood to adolescence* (A. Parsons & S. Milgram, Trans.). New York: Basic Books.

Isaacson, A. (2009, March 5). Riding the rails. *New York Times.* Retrieved from http://travel.nytimes.com/2009/03/08/travel/08amtrak.html

ISLS. (2004). *International Society of the Learning Sciences.* Retrieved from http://www.isls.org/index.html?CFID=62939330&CFTOKEN=61074672

Isseks, M. (2011). How PowerPoint is killing education. *Educational Leadership, 68,* 74–76.

IXL Learning. (2013). *Estimation and rounding.* Retrieved from http://www.ixl.com/math/grade-3

Iyengar, S., & Lepper, M. (1999). Rethinking the role of choice: A cultural perspective on intrinsic motivation. *Journal of Personality and Social Psychology, 76,* 349–366.

Jabeen, F., Anis-ul-Haque, M., & Riaz, M. N. (2013). Parenting styles as predictors of emotion regulation among adolescents. *Pakistan Journal of Psychological Research, 28,* 85–105.

Jack, F., Simcock, G., & Hayne, H., (2012). Magic memories: Young children's verbal recall after a 6-year delay. *Child Development, 83,* 159–172.

Jackson, M. (2009). *Distracted: The erosion of attention and the coming dark age.* Amherst, NY: Prometheus Books.

Jackson, P. (1968). *Life in classrooms.* New York: Holt, Rinehart & Winston.

Jacobs, G. E. (2012). Rethinking common assumptions about adolescents' motivation to use technology in and out of school. *Journal of Adolescent & Adult Literacy, 56,* 271–274. doi:10.1002/JAAL.00139

Jadallah, M., Anderson, R., Nguyen-Jahiel, K., Miller, B., Kim, I., Kuo, L., . . . Wu, X. (2011).

Influence of a teacher's scaffolding moves during child-led small group discussion. *American Educational Research Journal, 48*(1), 194–230.

Jang, L. Y., & Liu, W. C. (2012). 2 × 2 Achievement goals and achievement emotions: A cluster analysis of students' motivation. *European Journal of Psychology of Education, 27*, 59–76. doi:10.1007/s10212-011-0066-5

Jang, Y., & Yoo, H. (2012). Self-management programs based on the social cognitive theory for Koreans with chronic disease. *Contemporary Nurse, 40*, 147–159.

Jansen, A., & Bartell, T. (2013). Caring mathematics instruction: Middle school students' and teachers' perspectives. *Middle Grades Research Journal, 8*, 33–49.

Jarrett, C. (2012). Why the left-brain right-brain myth will probably never die. *Psychology Today.* Retrieved from http://www.psychologytoday.com/blog/brain-myths/201206/why-the-left-brain-right-brain-myth-will-probably-never-die

Jarrold, C., & Citroën, R. (2013). Reevaluating key evidence for the development of rehearsal: Phonological similarity effects in children are subject to proportional scaling artifacts. *Developmental Psychology, 49*, 837–847.

Jaschik, S. (2014). A new SAT. *Inside Higher Ed.* Retrieved from http://www.insidehighered.com/news/2014/03/05/college-board-unveils-new-sat-major-overhaul-writing-exam

Jaspal, R., & Cinnirella, M. (2012). The construction of ethnic identity: Insights from identity process theory. *Ethnicities, 12* (5), 503–530.

Jennings, P. A., Frank, J. L., Snowberg, K. E., Coccia, M. A., & Greenberg, M. T. (2013). Improving classroom learning environments by cultivating awareness and resilience in education (CARE): Results of a randomized controlled trial. *School Psychology Quarterly, 28*, 374–390.

Jiang, Y. H. V., Swallow, K. M., & Rosenbaum, G. M. (2013). Guidance of spatial attention by incidental learning and endogenous cuing. *Journal of Experimental Psychology—Human Perception and Performance, 39*, 285–297.

Jitendra, A., Haria, P., Griffin, C., Leh, J., Adams, A., & Kaduvettoor, A. (2007). A comparison of single and multiple strategy instruction on third-grade students' mathematical problem solving. *Journal of Educational Psychology, 99*(1), 115–127.

Joe, S., Joe, E., & Rowley, L. (2009). Consequences of physical health and mental illness risks for academic achievement in grades K–12. *Review of Research in Education, 33*, 283–309.

Johnson, B., & Christensen, L. (2011). *Educational research: Quantitative, qualitative and mixed approaches* (4th ed.). Los Angeles: Sage.

Johnson, D. (2013). Student in-class texting behavior: Associations with instructor clarity and classroom relationships. *Communication Research Reports, 30*, 57–62.

Johnson, D. W., & Johnson, R. (2006). *Learning together and alone: Cooperation, competition, and individualization* (8th ed.). Needham Heights, MA: Allyn & Bacon.

Johnson, D., & Johnson, R. (2013). *Joining together: Group theory and group skills* (11th ed.). Boston: Pearson.

Johnson, J., & Duffett, A. (2002). *When it's your own child: A report on special education and the families who use it.* New York: The Public Agenda.

Johnson, L. (2004). Down with detention. *Education Week, 24*(14), 39–40.

Johnson, M. (2011). Developmental neuroscience, psychophysiology, and genetics. In M. Bornstein & M. Lamb (Eds.), *Developmental science: An advanced textbook* (6th ed., pp. 201–240). New York: Psychology Press.

Johnson, N., & Parker, A. T. (2013). Effects of wait time when communicating with children who have sensory and additional disabilities. *Journal of Visual Impairment & Blindness, 107*, 363–74.

Johnson, S., & Birkeland, S. (2003, April). *Pursuing a "sense of success:" New teachers explain their career decisions.* Paper presented at the annual meeting of the American Educational Research Association, New Orleans, LA.

Johnson, W., & Bouchard, T. (2005). The structure of human intelligence: It is verbal, perceptual, and image rotation (VPR), not fluid and crystallized. *Intelligence, 33*, 393–416.

Johnston, L., O'Malley, P., Bachman, J., & Schulenberg, J. (2012). *Monitoring the future: National results on adolescent drug use: Overview of key findings, 2012.* Retrieved from http://www.drugabuse.gov/related-topics/trends-statistics/monitoring-future/monitoring-future-survey-overview-findings-2012

Jones, K. A., Jones, J. L., & Vermete, P. J. (2013). Exploring the complexity of classroom management: 8 components of managing a highly productive, safe, and respectful urban environment. *American Secondary Education, 41*, 21–33.

Jones, N., Kemenes, G., & Benjamin, P. (2001). Selective expression of electrical correlates of differential appetitive classical conditioning in a feedback network. *Journal of Neurophysiology, 85*, 89–97.

Jones, S., Brown, J., & Aber, J. (2011). Two-year impacts of a universal school-based social-emotional and literacy intervention: An experiment in translational developmental research. *Child Development, 82*(2), 533–554.

Jones, V., & Jones, L. (2013). *Comprehensive classroom management: Creating communities of support and solving problems* (10th ed.). Boston: Pearson.

Jordan, J. (2006). Relational resilience in girls. In S. Goldstein & R. Brooks (Eds.), *Handbook of resilience in children* (pp. 79–90). New York: Springer-Verlag.

Jorde, L., Carey, J., & Bamshad, M. (2010). *Medical genetics* (4th ed.). Philadelphia: Mosby Elsevier.

Josephson Institute Center for Youth Ethics. (2010). *The ethics of American youth: 2010.* Retrieved from http://charactercounts.org/programs/reportcard/2010/index.html

Junco, R., & Cotten, S. (2012). No A 4 U: The relationship between multitasking and academic performance. *Computers & Education, 59*, 505–514.

Juvonen, J. (2006). Sense of belonging, social bonds, and school functioning. In P. A. Alexander & P. H. Winne (Eds.), *Handbook of educational psychology* (2nd ed., pp. 655–674). Mahwah, NJ: Erlbaum.

Juvonen, J. (2007). Reforming middle schools: Focus on continuity, social connectedness, and engagement. *Educational Psychologist, 42*, 197–208.

Kafai, Y. (2006). Constructionism. In R. K. Sawyer (Ed.), *The Cambridge handbook of the learning sciences* (pp. 35–46). New York: Cambridge University Press.

Kagan, J. (2010). Emotions and temperament. In M. Bornstein (Ed.), *Handbook of cultural developmental science* (pp. 175–194). New York: Psychology Press.

Kahlenberg, R. (2012). *The future of school integration: Socioeconomic diversity as an educational reform strategy.* New York: Century Foundation.

Kahlenberg, S., & Hein, M. (2010). Progression on Nickelodeon? Gender-role stereotypes in toy commercials. *Sex Roles, 62*, 830–847.

Kahneman, D. (2011). *Thinking fast and slow.* New York: Farrar, Straus, and Giroux.

Kail, R. (2012). *Children & their development* (6th ed.). Boston: Pearson.

Kakihara, F., Tilton-Weaver, L., Kerr, M., & Stattin, H. (2010). The relationship of parental control to youth adjustment: Do youths' feelings about their parents play a role? *Journal of Youth and Adolescence, 39*, 1442–1456.

Kaku, M. (2011). *Physics of the future: How science will shape human destiny and our daily lives by the year 2100.* New York: Doubleday.

Kalpidou, M., Costin, D., & Morris, J. (2011). The relationship between Facebook and the well-being of undergraduate college students. *Cyberpsychology, Behavior, and Social Networking, 14*, 183–189. doi:10.1089/cyber.2010.0061

Kalyuga, S. (2010). Schema acquisition and sources of cognitive load. In J. L. Plass, R. Moreno, & R. Brünken (Eds.), *Cognitive load theory* (pp. 48–64). Cambridge, England: Cambridge University Press.

Kaminski, J. A., Sloutsky, V. M., & Heckler, A. F. (2013). The cost of concreteness: The effect of nonessential information on analogical transfer. *Journal of Experimental Psychology: Applied, 19*, 14–29.

Kaminski, J., Puddy, R., Hall, D., Cashman, S., Crosby, A., & Ortega, L. (2010). The relative influence of different domains of social connectedness on self-directed violence in adolescence. *Journal of Youth and Adolescence, 39*, 460–473.

Kanazawa, S. (2010). Evolutionary psychology and intelligence research. *American Psychologist, 65*(4), 279–289.

Karatekin, C. (2004). A test of the integrity of the components of Baddeley's model of working memory in attention-deficit/hyperactivity disorder (ADHD). *The Journal of Child Psychology and Psychiatry and Allied Disciplines, 45*(5), 912–926.

Karniol, R. (2010). *Social development as preference management: How infants, children, and parents get what they want from one another.* New York: Cambridge University Press.

Karten, T. (2005). *Inclusion strategies that work: Research-based methods for the classroom.* Thousand Oaks, CA: Corwin Press.

Kaspar, K., & Stelz, H. (2013). The paradoxical effect of praise and blame: Age-related differences. *Europe's Journal of Psychology, 9,* 304–318.

Kassin, S. M., Dror, I. E., & Kukucka, J. (2013). The forensic confirmation bias: Problems, perspectives, and proposed solutions. *Journal of Applied Research in Memory and Cognition, 2,* 42–52.

Kassin, S., Fein, S., & Markus, H. R. (2011). *Social psychology* (8th ed.). Belmont, CA: Cengage.

Kastens, K., & Liben, L. (2007). Eliciting self-explanations improves children's performance on a field-based map skills task. *Cognition and Instruction, 25*(1), 45–74.

Kato, T., & Manning, M. (2007). Content knowledge—The real reading crisis. *Childhood Education, 83,* 238–239.

Kauchak, D., & Eggen, P. (2012). *Learning and teaching: Research-based methods* (6th ed.). Boston: Pearson.

Kaufman, D., & Moss, D. M. (2010). A new look at preservice teachers' conceptions of classroom management and organization: Uncovering complexity and dissonance. *The Teacher Educator, 45,* 118–136.

Kaufman, J. C. (2009). *Creativity 101.* New York: Springer.

Kaufman, J. C., & Beghetto, R. A. (2009). Beyond big and little: The four C model of creativity. *Review of General Psychology, 13,* 1–12.

Kaufman, J. C., & Sternberg, R. J. (2007). Creativity. *Change, 39,* 55–58.

Keller, B. (2013). War on the core. *New York Times.* Retrieved from http://www.nytimes.com/2013/08/19/opinion/keller-war-on-the-core.html?_r=0&pagewanted=print

Kennedy Root, A., & Denham, S. (2010). The role of gender in the socialization of emotion: Key concepts and critical issues. In A. Kennedy Root & S. Denham (Eds.), *The role of gender in the socialization of emotion: Key concepts and critical issues. New Directions for Child and Adolescent Development, 128,* 1–9. San Francisco: Jossey-Bass.

Kennedy, F., Carroll, B., & Francoeur, J. (2013). Mindset not skill set: Evaluating in new paradigms of leadership development. *Advances in Developing Human Resources, 15,* 10–26.

Kerman, S. (1979). Teacher expectations and student achievement. *Phi Delta Kappan, 60,* 70–72.

Kersey, K., & Masterson, M. (2009). Teachers connecting with families: In the best interest of children. *Young Children, 64*(5), 34–38.

Kertz, S., & Woodruff-Borden, J. (2013). The role of metacognition, intolerance of uncertainty, and negative problem orientation in children's worry. *Behavioural and Cognitive Psychotherapy, 41,* 243–248.

Keycurriculum. (2013). *The geometer's sketchpad.* Retrieved from http://www.keycurriculum.com/products/sketchpad

Khamsi, R. (2013). Going to pot. *Scientific American, 308,* 34–36.

Khan, B. (2012). Relationship between assessment and students' learning. *International Journal of Social Sciences and Education, 2,* 576–589.

Khan, S. (2012). *The one world schoolhouse: Education reimagined.* London: Hodder & Stoughton.

Kibby, M. Y., Marks, W., & Morgan, S. (2004). Specific impairment in developmental reading disabilities: A working memory approach. *Journal of Learning Disabilities, 37,* 349–363.

Kidron, Y., & Fleischman, S. (2006). Promoting adolescents' prosocial behavior. *Educational Leadership, 63*(7), 90–91.

Kieffer, J., Lesaux, N., Rivera, M., & Francis, D. (2009). Accommodations for English language learners taking large-scale assessments: A meta-analysis on effectiveness and validity. *Review of Educational Research, 79,* 1168–1201.

Killen, M., & Smetana, J. (2010). Future directions: Social development in the context of social justice. *Social Development, 19*(3), 642–657. doi:10.1111/j.1467-9507.2009.00548.x

Kim, J., & Guryan, J. (2010). The efficacy of a voluntary summer book reading intervention for low-income Latino children from language minority families. *Journal of Educational Psychology, 102,* 20–31.

Kim, S. Y., Wang, Y., Orozco-Lapray, D., Shen, Y., & Murtuza, M. (2013). Does "tiger parenting" exist? Parenting profiles of Chinese Americans and adolescent developmental outcomes. *Asian American Journal of Psychology, 4,* 7–18.

Kim, Y., & Baylor, A. L. (2006). A social-cognitive framework for pedagogical agents as learning companions. *Educational Technology Research and Development, 54,* 569–596.

Kincheloe, J. (2004). Why a book on urban education? In S. Steinberg & J. Kincheloe (Eds.), *19 urban questions: Teaching in the city* (pp. 1–27). New York: Peter Lang.

Kincheloe, J. (2009). No short cuts in urban education: Metropedagogy and diversity. In S. Steinberg (Ed.), *Diversity and multiculturalism: A reader* (pp. 379–409).

Kirsch, D. (2009). Problem solving and situated cognition. In P. Robbins & M. Aydede (Eds.), *The Cambridge handbook of situated cognition* (pp. 264–306). New York: Cambridge University Press.

Kirschner, P. A., Sweller, J., & Clark, R. E. (2006). Why minimal guidance during instruction does not work: An analysis of the failure of constructivist, discovery, problem-based, experiential, and inquiry-based teaching. *Educational Psychologist, 41,* 75–86.

Kirylo, J. D., Thirumurthy, V., & Spezzini, S. (2010). Children were punished: Not for what they said, but for what their teachers heard. *Childhood Education, 86,* 130–131.

Kitsantas, A., Zimmerman, B., & Cleary, T. (2000). The role of observation and emulation in the development of athletic self-regulation. *Journal of Educational Psychology, 92*(4), 811–817.

Kiyonaga, A., & Egner, T. (2013). Working memory as internal attention: Toward an integrative account of internal and external selection processes. *Psychonomic Bulletin and Review, 20,* 228–242.

Klimstra, T., Hale, W. Raaijmakers, Q., Branje, S., & Meeus, W. (2010). Identity formation in adolescence: Change or stability: *Journal of Youth and Adolescence, 39,* 150–162.

Knight, J. (2002). Crossing the boundaries: What constructivists can teach intensive-explicit instructors and vice versa. *Focus on Exceptional Children, 35,* 1–14, 16.

Koenig, M., & Woodward, A., (2010). Sensitivity of 24-month-olds to the prior inaccuracy of the source: Possible mechanisms. *Development Psychology, 46*(4), 815–826.

Kohlberg, L. (1963). The development of children's orientation toward moral order: Sequence in the development of human thought. *Vita Humana, 6,* 11–33.

Kohlberg, L. (1969). Stage and sequence: The cognitive-developmental approach to socialization. In D. Goslin (Ed.), *Handbook of socialization theory and research.* Chicago: Rand McNally.

Kohlberg, L. (1981). *Philosophy of moral development.* New York: Harper & Row.

Kohlberg, L. (1984). *The psychology of moral development: The nature and validity of moral stages.* San Francisco: Harper & Row.

Kohn, A. (1993). *Punished by rewards: The trouble with gold stars, incentive plans, A's, praise, and other bribes.* Boston: Houghton Mifflin.

Kohn, A. (1996). By all available means: Cameron and Pierce's defense of extrinsic motivators. *Review of Educational Research, 66,* 1–4.

Kohn, A. (2005a). *Unconditional parenting: Moving from rewards and punishments to love and reason.* New York: Atria Books.

Kohn, A. (2005b). Unconditional teaching. *Educational Leadership, 63*(1), 20–24.

Kohn, A. (2006a). *The homework myth: Why our kids get too much of a bad thing.* Cambridge, MA: Da Capo Press.

Kohn, A. (2006b). Abusing research: The study of homework and other examples. *Phi Delta Kappan, 88,* 9–22.

Kok, B. E., Coffey, K. A., Cohn, M. A., Catalino, L. I., Vacharkulksemsuk, T., Algoe, S. B., . . . Fredrickson, B. L. (2013). How positive emotions build physical health: Perceived positive social connections account for the upward spiral between positive emotions and vagal tone. *Psychological Science, 24,* 1123–1132.

Konstantopoulos, S. (2011). Teacher effects in early grades: Evidence from a randomized study. *Teachers College Record, 113,* 1541–1565.

Koppelman, K. (2014). *Understanding human differences: Multicultural education for a diverse America* (4th ed.). Boston: Pearson.

Kornell, N., Castel, A. D., Eich, T. S., & Bjork, R. A. (2010). Spacing as a friend of both memory and induction in young and older adults. *Psychology and Aging, 25*, 498–503.

Kornhaber, M., Fierros, E., & Veenema, S. (2004). *Multiple intelligences: Best ideas from research and practice.* Boston: Allyn & Bacon.

Koul, R., Roy, L., & Lerdpornkulrat, T. (2012). Motivational goal orientation, perceptions of biology and physics classroom learning environments, and gender. *Learning Environments Research, 15*, 217–229.

Kounin, J. (1970). *Discipline and group management in classrooms.* New York: Holt, Rinehart & Winston.

Kozol, J. (2005). *The shame of the nation: The restoration of apartheid schooling in America.* New York: Crown.

Kraft, M. A. (2010). From ringmaster to conductor: 10 simple techniques that can turn an unruly class into a productive one. *Phi Delta Kappan, 91*, 44–47.

Krajcik, J., & Blumenfeld, P. (2006). Project-based learning. In R. K. Sawyer (Ed.), *Cambridge handbook of the learning sciences* (pp. 317–334). Cambridge, MA: Cambridge University Press.

Krätzig, G., & Arbuthnott, K. (2006). Perceptual learning style and learning proficiency: A test of the hypothesis. *Journal of Educational Psychology, 98*(1), 238–246.

Krauss, S., Brunner, M., Kunter, M., Baumert, J., Blum, W., Neubrand, M., & Jordan, A. (2008). Pedagogical content knowledge and content knowledge of secondary mathematics teachers. *Journal of Educational Psychology, 100*, 716–725. doi:10.1037/0022-0663.100.3.716

Kreppner, J. M., Rutter, M., Beckett, C., Castle, J., Colvert, E., Groothues, C., . . . Sonuga-Barke, E. J. (2007). Normality and impairment following profound early institutional deprivation: A longitudinal follow-up into early adolescence. *Developmental Psychology, 43*, 931–946.

Kroesbergen, E. H., & van Luit, E. H. (2002). Teaching multiplication to low math performers: Guided versus structured instruction. *Instructional Science, 30*, 361–378.

Kroger, J., Martinussen, & Marcia, J. (2010). Identity status change during adolescence and young adulthood: A meta-analysis. *Journal of Adolescence, 33*, 683–698.

Kross, E., & Grossmann, I. (2012). Boosting wisdom: Distance from the self enhances wise reasoning, attitudes, and behavior. *Journal of Experimental Psychology: General, 141*, 43–48.

Kuhl, P. (2004). Early language acquisition: Cracking the speech code. *Nature Reviews Neuroscience, 5*, 831–843.

Kuhn, D. (2009). Adolescent thinking. In R. Lerner & L. Steinberg (Eds.), *Handbook of adolescent psychology, Vol. 1: Individual bases of adolescent development* (3rd ed., pp. 152–186). Hoboken, NJ: Wiley.

Kuhn, D., & Park, S. H. (2005). Epistemological understanding and the development of intellectual values. *International Journal of Educational Research, 43*, 111–124.

Kuhn, D., Pease, M., & Wirkala, C. (2009). Coordinating the effects of multiple variables: A skill fundamental to scientific thinking. *Journal of Experimental Child Psychology, 103*(3), 268–284.

Kunter, M., Klusmann, U., Baumert, J., Richter, D., Voss, T., & Hachfeld, A. (2013). Professional competence of teachers: Effects on instructional quality and student development. *Journal of Educational Psychology, 105*, 805–820.

Kuppens, S., Laurent, L., Heyvaert, W., & Onghena, P. (2013). Associations between parental psychological control and relational aggression in children and adolescents: A multilevel and sequential meta-analysis. *Developmental Psychology, 49*, 1697–1712.

Kurzweil, R. (2012). *How to create a mind.* New York: Viking.

Labov, W. (1972). *Language in the inner city: Studies in the "Black" English vernacular.* Philadelphia: University of Pennsylvania Press.

Lam, S-F., & Law, Y-K. (2007). The roles of instructional practices and motivation in writing performance. *The Journal of Experimental Education, 75*, 145–164.

Lamella, L., & Tincani, M. (2012). Brief wait time to increase response opportunity and correct responding of children with autism spectrum disorder who display challenging behavior. *Journal of Developmental & Physical Disabilities, 24*, 559–573.

Lancioni, G., Sigafoos, M., & Nirbhay, S. (2013). *Assistive technology.* New York: Springer.

Landrum, T. J., & Kaufman, J. M. (2006). Behavioral approaches to classroom management. In C. M. Evertson & C. S. Weinstein (Eds.), *Handbook of classroom management: Research, practice, and contemporary issues* (pp. 47–71). Mahwah, NJ: Erlbaum.

Lane, K., Goh, J., & Driver-Linn, E. (2012). Implicit science stereotypes mediate the relationship between gender and academic participation. *Sex Roles, 66*, 220–234.

Lang, J. W., & Lang, J. (2010). Priming competence diminishes the link between cognitive test anxiety and test performance: Implications for the interpretation of test scores. *Psychological Science, 21*, 811–819.

Langenegger, J. (2011, April). *Changes that stick: The role of sustaining forces.* Paper presented at the annual meeting of the American Educational Research Association, New Orleans.

Latif, E., & Miles, S. (2013). Students' perceptions of effective teaching. *Journal of Economics and Economic Education Research, 14*, 121–129.

Lave, J. (1997). The culture of acquisition and the culture of understanding. In D. Kirshner & J. A. Whitson (Eds.), *Situated cognition: Social, semiotic, and psychological perspectives* (pp. 17–35). Mahwah, NJ: Erlbaum.

Lawrence, N. K., Serdikoff, S. L., Zinn, T. E., & Baker, S. C. (2009). Have we demystified critical thinking? In D. S. Dunn, J. S. Halonen, & R. A. Smith (Eds.), *Teaching critical thinking in psychology: A handbook of best practices* (pp. 23–33). Hoboken, NJ: Wiley-Blackwell.

Lawson, G. W. (2013). Eliminate PowerPoint in the classroom to facilitate active learning. *Global Education Journal, 2013*, 1–8.

Leatherdale, S. T. (2013). A cross-sectional examination of school characteristics associated with overweight and obesity among grade 1 to 4 students. *BMC Public Health, 13*, 1–21.

Leavell, A., Tamis-LeMonda, C., Ruble, D., Zosuls, K., & Cabrera, N. (2012). African-American, White and Latino fathers' activities with their sons and daughters in early childhood. *Sex Roles, 66*, 53–65.

Leclerc, O., & Moldoveanu, M. (2013). Five routes to more innovative problem solving. *McKinsey Quarterly, 2*, 80–91.

Lee, C. D. (2010). Soaring above the clouds, delving the ocean's depths: Understanding the ecologies of human learning and the challenge for education science. *Educational Researcher, 39*, 643–655.

Lee, C. D., & Spratley, A. (2010). *Reading in the disciplines: The challenges of adolescent literacy.* New York: Carnegie Corporation of New York.

Lee, C., & Chen, M. (2010). Taiwanese junior high students' mathematical attitudes and perceptions toward virtual manipulatives. *British Journal of Educational Technology, 41*, 17–21.

Lee, E. H., Zhou, Q., Ly, J., Main, A., Tao, A., & Chen, S. H. (2013, September 16). Neighborhood characteristics, parenting styles, and children's behavioral problems in Chinese American immigrant families. *Cultural Diversity and Ethnic Minority Psychology.* Advance online publication. doi:10.1037/a0034390

Lee, J., & Bowen, N. (2006). Parent involvement, cultural capital, and the achievement gap among elementary school children. *American Educational Research Journal, 43*(2), 193–218.

Lee, J., & Reigeluth, C. M. (2003). Formative research on the heuristic task analysis process. *Educational Technology Research and Development, 51*, 5–24.

Lee, J., & Shute, V. (2010). Personal and social-contextual factors in K–12 academic performance: An integrative perspective on student learning. *Educational Psychologist, 45*, 185–202.

Lee, R., Sturmey, P., & Fields, L. (2007). Schedule-induced and operant mechanisms that influence response variability: A review and implications for future investigations. *The Psychological Record, 57*, 429–465.

Lee, V. (2000). Using hierarchical linear modeling to study social contexts: The case of school effects. *Educational Psychologist, 35*, 125–141.

Legault, L., & Inzlicht, M. (2013). Self-determination, self-regulation, and the brain: Autonomy improves performance by enhancing neuroaffective responsiveness to self-regulation failure. *Journal of Personality and Social Psychology, 105*, 123–138.

Leinhardt, G. (2001). Instructional explanations: A commonplace for teaching and location for contrast. In V. Richardson (Ed.), *Handbook of research on teaching* (4th ed., pp. 333–357). Washington, DC: American Educational Research Association.

Leipold, K., Vetter, N. C., Dittrich, M., Lehmann-Waffenschmidt, M., & Kliegel, M. (2013). Individual and developmental differences in the relationship between preferences and theory of mind. *Journal of Neuroscience, Psychology, and Economics, 6,* 236–251.

Leman, P., & Björnberg, M. (2010). Conversation, development, and gender: A study of changes in children's concepts of punishment. *Child Development, 81*(3), 958–971. doi:10.1111/j.1467-8624.2010.01445.x

Lemov, D. (2010). *Teach like a champion: 49 techniques that put students on the path to college.* San Francisco: Jossey-Bass

Lenta, P. (2012). Corporal punishment of children. *Social Theory & Practice, 38,* 689–716.

Leont'ev, A. (1981). The problem of activity in psychology. In J. Wertsch (Ed.), *The concept of activity in Soviet psychology* (pp. 37–71). Armonk, NY: Sharpe.

Leopold, C., & Leutner, D. (2012). Science text comprehension: Drawing, main idea selection, and summarizing as learning strategies. *Learning and Instruction, 22,* 16–26.

Lepper, M., & Hodell, M. (1989). Intrinsic motivation in the classroom. In C. Ames & R. Ames (Eds.), *Research on motivation in education* (Vol. 3, pp. 73–105). San Diego: Academic Press.

Lerner, R. (2006). Developmental science, developmental systems, and contemporary theories of human development. In W. Damon & R. Lerner (Series Eds.), R. Lerner (Vol. Ed.), *Handbook of child psychology: Vol. I. Theoretical models of human development* (6th ed., 1–17). New York: Wiley.

Lerner, R., Lewin-Bizan, S., & Warren, A. (2011). Concepts and theories of human development. In M. Bornstein & M. Lamb (Eds.), *Developmental science: An advanced textbook* (6th ed., pp. 3–50). New York: Psychology Press.

Lester, F. K. (2013). Thoughts about research on mathematical problem-solving instruction. *The Mathematics Enthusiast, 10,* 245–278.

Leung, A., Maddux, W., Galinsky, A., & Chiu, C. (2008). Multicultural experience enhances creativity: The when and how. *American Psychologist, 63,* 169–181.

Levere, J. (2013, May 21). Aiming autism ads at Hispanic and African-American parents. *New York Times,* p. B8.

Levesque, C., Stanek, L., Zuehlke, A. N., & Ryan, R. (2004). Autonomy and competence in German and American university students: A comparative study based on self-determination theory. *Journal of Educational Psychology, 96*(1), 68–84.

Levinthal, C. (2013). *Drugs, behavior, & modern society* (2nd ed.). Boston: Pearson.

Lewin, T. (2014). A new SAT aims to realign with schoolwork. *The New York Times.* Retrieved from http://www.nytimes.com/2014/03/06/education/major-changes-in-sat-announced-by-college-board.html?_r=0

Lewis, R., Romi, S., & Roache, J. (2012). Excluding students from classroom: Teacher techniques that promote student responsibility. *Teaching and Teacher Education, 28,* 870–878.

Lezotte, L. W., & Snyder, K. M. (2011). *What effective schools do: Re-envisioning the correlates.* Bloomington, IN: Solution Tree Press.

Li, G. (2010). Race, class, and schooling: Multicultural families doing the hard work of home literacy in America's inner city. *Reading & Writing Quarterly: Overcoming Learning Difficulties, 26*(2), 140–165.

Li, J. (2005). Mind or virtue: Western and Chinese beliefs about learning. *Current Directions in Psychological Science, 14,* 190–194.

Li, Y., Anderson, R., Nguyen-Jahiel, K., Dong, T., Archodidou, A., Kim, I., . . . Miller, B. (2007). Emergent leadership in children's discussion groups. *Cognition and Instruction, 25,* 75–111.

Lidstone, J., Meins, E., & Fernyhough, C. (2010). The roles of private speech and inner speech in planning during middle childhood: Evidence from a dual task paradigm. *Journal of Experimental Child Psychology, 10,* 438–451.

Lieven, E., & Stoll, S. (2010). Language. In M. Bornstein (Ed.), *Handbook of cultural developmental science* (pp. 143–160). New York: Psychology Press.

Liew, J., Chen, Q., & Hughes, J. N. (2010). Child effortful control, teacher-student relationships, and achievement in academically at-risk children: Additive and interactive effects. *Early Childhood Research Quarterly, 25,* 51–64.

Lillard, A. S. (1997). Other folks' theories of mind and behavior. *Psychological Science, 8,* 268–274.

Lin, J.-R. (2007). Responses to anomalous data obtained from repeatable experiments in the laboratory. *Journal of Research in Science Teaching, 44*(3), 506–528.

Linder Gunnoe, M. (2013). Associations between parenting style, physical discipline, and adjustment in adolescents' reports. *Psychological Reports, 112,* 933–975.

Linder, S. M. (2013). Interactive whiteboards in early childhood mathematics. *Delta-K, 50,* 46–52.

Linebarger, D., & Piotrowski, J. (2010). Structure and strategies in children's educational television: The roles of program type and learning strategies in children's learning. *Child Development, 81,* 1582–1597.

Linn, S. (2009). *Case for make believe: Saving play in a commercialized world.* New York: The New Press.

Linnenbrink, E. A. (2007). The role of affect in student learning: A multi-dimensional approach to considering the interaction of affect, motivation, and engagement. In P. A. Schutz & R. Pekrun (Eds.), *Emotion in education* (pp. 107–124). San Diego, CA: Academic. doi:10.1016/B978-012372545-5/50008-3

Linnenbrink, E. A., & Pintrich, P. R. (2003). Achievement goals and intentional conceptual change. In G. M. Sinatra & P. R. Pintrich (Eds.), *Intentional conceptual change* (pp. 347–374). Mahwah, NJ: Erlbaum.

Linnenbrink-Garcia, L., & Pekrun, R. (Eds.). (2011). Students' emotions and academic engagement: Introduction to the special issue [Special issue]. *Contemporary Educational Psychology, 36,* 1–3. doi:10.1016/j.cedpsych.2010.11.004

Linquanti, R., & Cook, H. G. (2013) Toward a "Common Definition of English Learner": A brief defining policy and technical issues and opportunities for state assessment consortia. *Council of Chief State School Officers.* Retrieved from http://files.eric.ed.gov/fulltext/ED542705.pdf

Lohman, D. (2001, April). *Fluid intelligence, inductive reasoning, and working memory: Where the theory of multiple intelligences falls short.* Paper presented at the annual meeting of the American Educational Research Association, Seattle.

Loman, M., & Gunnar, M. (2010). Early experience and the development of stress reactivity and regulation in children. *Neuroscience & Biobehavioral Reviews, 34,* 867–876.

Loughran, J., Mulhall, P., & Berry, A. (2004). In search of pedagogical content knowledge in science: Developing ways of articulating and documenting professional practice. *Journal of Research in Science Teaching, 41,* 370–391.

Lovelace, M. (2005). Meta-analysis of experimental research based on the Dunn and Dunn Model. *Journal of Educational Research, 98*(3), 176–183.

Lövheim, H. (2012). A new three-dimensional model for emotions and monoamine neurotransmitters. *Medical Hypotheses, 78,* 341–348.

Lovitt, T. C. (2012). Applied behavior analysis: A method that languished but should be restored. *Intervention in School and Clinic, 47,* 252–256.

Low, S., & Espelage, D. (2013). Differentiating cyber bullying perpetration from non-physical bullying: Commonalities across race, individual, and family predictors. *Psychology of Violence, 3,* 39–52.

Loyens, S. M., Gijbels, D., & Coertjens, L., & Côté, D. J. (2013). Students' approaches to learning in problem-based learning: Taking into account professional behavior in the tutorial groups, self-study time, and different assessment aspects. *Studies in Educational Evaluation, 39,* 23–32.

Luft, P., Brown, C. M., & Sutherin, L. J. (2007). Are you and your students bored with the benchmarks? Sinking under the standards? *Teaching Exceptional Children, 39,* 39–46.

Lukowiak, T., & Hunzicker, J. (2013). Understanding how and why college students engage in learning. *The Journal of Effective Teaching, 13,* 44–63.

Lumeng, J. C., & Cardinal, T. M. (2007). Providing information about a flavor to preschoolers: Effects on liking and memory for having tasted it. *Chemical Senses, 32,* 505–513.

Luna, B., Garver, K. E., Urban, T. A., Lazar, N. A., & Sweeney, J. A. (2004). Maturation of cognitive processes from late childhood to adulthood. *Child Development, 75,* 1357–1372.

Lundberg, U., Granqvist, M., Hansson, T., Magnusson, M., & Wallin, L. (1989). Psychological and physiological stress responses during repetitive work at an assembly line. *Work & Stress, 3,* 143–153.

Luria, A. R. (1976). *Cognitive development: Its cultural and social foundations.* Cambridge, MA: Harvard University Press.

Luthar, S., & Latendresse, S. (2005). Children of the affluent: Challenges to well-being. *Current Directions in Psychological Science, 14,* 49–53.

Lutz, S., Guthrie, J., & Davis, M. (2006). Scaffolding for engagement in elementary school reading instruction. *Journal of Educational Research, 100*(1), 3–20.

Luyckx, K., Tildesley, E. A., Soenens, B., Andrews, J. A., Hampson, S. E., Peterson, M., Duriez, B. (2011). Parenting and trajectories of children's maladaptive behaviors: A 12-year prospective community study. *Journal of Clinical Child and Adolescent Psychology, 40,* 468–478.

Lydon, S., Healy, O., O'Reilly, M., & Lang, R. (2012). Variations in functional analysis methodology: A systematic review. *Journal of Developmental & Physical Disabilities, 24,* 301–326.

Macionis, J. (2013). *Society: The basics* (12th ed.). Upper Saddle River, NJ: Prentice Hall.

Macionis, J., & Parrillo, V. (2013). *Cities and urban life* (6th ed.). Upper Saddle River, NJ: Merrill/Prentice Hall.

Macionis, J., & Parrillo, V. (2013). *Cities and urban life* (6th ed.). Upper Saddle River, NJ: Merrill/Pearson Education.

MacMillan, A. (2012). Dieters in Weight Watchers study drop up to 15 pounds in a year. Health.com. Retrieved from http://www.cnn.com/2011/09/07/health/weight-watchers-lancet

Macpherson, R., & Stanovich, K. E. (2007). Cognitive ability, thinking dispositions, and instructional set as predictors of critical thinking. *Learning and Individual Differences, 17,* 115–127.

MacWhinney, B. (2010). Computational models of child language learning: An introduction. *Journal of Child Language, 37*(3), 477–485.

MacWhinney, B. (2011). Language development. In M. Bornstein & M. Lamb (Eds.), *Developmental science: An advanced textbook* (6th ed., pp. 389–424). New York: Psychology Press.

Magnusson, P., Westjohn, S. A., Semenov, A. V., Randrianasolo, A. A., & Zdravkovic, S. (2013). The role of cultural intelligence in marketing adaptation and export performance. *Journal of International Marketing, 21,* 44–61.

Maguire, E., Gadian, D., Johnsrude, I., Good, C., Ashburner, J., Frackowiak, R., & Frith, C. (2000). Navigation-related structural change in the hippocampi of taxi drivers. *Proceedings of the National Academy of Science, USA, 97*(8), 4398–4403.

Malamud, O., & Pop-Eleches, C. (2010). *Home computer use and the development of human capital* (National Bureau of Economic Research Working Paper No. 15814).

Malouff, J. M., Schutte, N. S., & Thorsteinsson, E. B. (2014). Trait emotional intelligence and romantic relationship satisfaction: A meta-analysis. *American Journal of Family Therapy, 42,* 53–66.

Mann, T., de Ridder, D., & Fujita, K. (2013). Self-regulation of health behavior: Social psychological approaches to goal setting and goal striving. *Health Psychology, 32,* 487–498.

Manning, F., Lawless, K., Goldman, S., & Braasch, J. (2011, April). *Evaluating the usefulness of multiple sources with respect to an inquiry question: Middle school students' analysis and ranking of Internet search results.* Paper presented at the American Educational Research Association, New Orleans.

Manolitsis, G., Georgiou, G., & Parrila, R. (2011). Revisiting the home literacy model of reading development in an orthographically consistent language. *Learning & Instruction, 21*(4), 496–505.

Marashi, H., & Dibah, P. (2013). The comparative effect of using competitive and cooperative learning on the oral proficiency of Iranian introvert and extrovert EFL learners. *Journal of Language Teaching & Research, 4,* 545–556.

March, S. M., Abate, P., Spear, N. E., & Molina, J. C. (2013). The role of acetaldehyde in ethanol reinforcement assessed by Pavlovian conditioning in newborn rats. *Psychopharmacology, 226,* 491–499. doi:10.1007/s00213-012-2920-9

Marchand, G., & Skinner, E. A. (2007). Motivational dynamics of children's academic help-seeking and concealment. *Journal of Educational Psychology, 99,* 65–82.

Marchand, H. (2012). Contributions of Piagetian and post-Piagetian theories to education. *Educational Research Review, 7,* 165–176.

Marcia, J. (1980). Identity in adolescence. In J. Adelson (Ed.), *Handbook of adolescent psychology.* New York: Wiley.

Marcia, J. (1987). The identity status approach to the study of ego identity development. In T. Honess & K. Yardley (Eds.), *Self and identity: Perspectives across the life span.* London: Routledge & Kegan Paul.

Marcia, J. (1999). Representational thought in ego identity, psychotherapy, and psychosocial development. In I. E. Sigel (Ed.), *Development of mental representation: Theories and applications.* Mahwah, NJ: Lawrence Erlbaum.

Marcia, J. (2010). Life transitions and stress in the context of psychosocial development. In T. Miller (Ed.), *Handbook of stressful transitions across the lifespan* (pp. 19–34). New York: Springer Science & Business Media.

Margolis, J. (2010). Why teacher quality is a local issue (and why Race to the Top is a misguided flop). *Teachers College Record.* Retrieved from http://www.tcrecord.org/Content.asp?ContentID=16023

Marinak, B., & Gambrell, L. (2010). Reading motivation: Exploring the elementary gender gap. *Literacy Research and Instruction, 49*(2), 129–141.

Marinellie, S. & Kneile, L. (2012). Acquiring knowledge of derived nominals and derived adjectives in context. *Language, Speech, and Hearing Services in Schools, 43,* 53–65.

Marinoff, L. (2003). *The big questions: How philosophy can change your life.* New York: Bloomsbury.

Marion, S., & Pellegrino, J. (2006). A validity framework for evaluating the technical quality of alternate assessments. *Educational Measurement: Issues and Practices, 25*(4), 47–57.

Mark, G., Gudith, D., & Klocke, U. (2008). *The cost of interrupted work: More speed and stress.* Proceedings of the twenty-sixth annual SIGCHI conference on human factors in computing systems, Florence, Italy.

Markoff, J. (2013, June 4). Device from Israeli start-up gives the visually impaired a way to read. *New York Times International,* p. A7.

Markoff, J., & Gorman, J. (2013, April 21). Obama to unveil initiative to map the human brain. *New York Times,* A12.

Marks, A., Patton, F., & Coll, C. (2011). Being bicultural: A mixed-methods study of adolescents' implicitly and explicitly measured multiethnic identities. *Developmental Psychology, 47,* 270–288.

Marois, R., & Ivanoff, J. (2005). Capacity limits of information processing in the brain. *Trends in Cognitive Sciences, 9,* 296–305.

Marsee, M., & Frick, P. (2010). Callous-unemotional traits and aggression in youth. In W. Arsenio & E. Lemerise (Eds.), *Emotions, aggression, and morality in children: Bridging development and psychopathology* (pp. 137–156). Washington, DC: American Psychological Association.

Martin, C., & Ruble, D. (2010). Patterns of gender development. *Annual Review of Psychology, 61,* 353–381.

Martin, J. (2006). Social cultural perspectives in educational psychology. In P. A. Alexander & P. H. Winne (Eds.), *Handbook of educational psychology* (2nd ed., pp. 595–614). Mahwah, NJ: Erlbaum.

Martineau, J. (2010). The validity of value-added models: An allegory. *Phi Delta Kappan, 91*(7), 64–67.

Martone, A., & Sireci, S. G. (2009). Evaluating alignment between curriculum, assessment, and instruction. *Review of Educational Research, 79,* 1332–1361.

Marx, P. (2013, July 29). Mentally fit. *New Yorker,* 24–28.

Marzano, R. J. (2003). *What works in schools: Translating research into action.* Alexandria VA: Association for Supervision and Curriculum Development.

Marzano, R. J. (2007). *Classroom assessment and grading that work.* Alexandria VA: Association for Supervision and Curriculum Development.

Marzano, R. J., & Pickering, D. J. (2007). Errors and allegations about research on homework. *Phi Delta Kappan, 88,* 507–513.

Maslow, A. (1968). *Toward a psychology of being* (2nd ed.). New York: Van Nostrand.

Maslow, A. (1970). *Motivation and personality* (2nd ed.). New York: Harper & Row. (Original work published 1954.)

Mason, L. (2007). Introduction: Bridging the cognitive and sociocultural approaches in research on conceptual change: Is it feasible? *Educational Psychologist, 42*(1), 1–8.

Mastropieri, M., & Scruggs, T. (2014). *The inclusive classroom: Strategies for effective differentiated instruction* (5th ed.). Upper Saddle River, NJ: Merrill/Pearson.

Mastropieri, M., Scruggs, T., & Berkeley, S. (2007). Peers helping peers. *Educational Leadership, 64*(5), 54–58.

Mathieson, K., & Banerjee, R. (2010). Pre-school peer play: The beginnings of social competence. *Educational and Child Psychology. Special Issue: In-School Relationships and their Outcomes, 27*(1), 9–20.

Matjasko, J., Needham, B., Grunden, L., & Farb, A. (2010). Violent victimization and perpetration during adolescence: Developmental stage dependent ecological models. *Journal of Youth and Adolescence, 39*(9), 1053–1066. doi:10.1007/s10964-010-9508-7

Matlen, B. J., & Klahr, D. (2013). Sequential effects of high and low instructional guidance on children's acquisition of experimentation skills: Is it all in the timing? *Instructional Science: An International Journal of the Learning Sciences, 41*, 621–634.

Matson, J. L., Turygin, N. C., Beighley, J., Rieske, R., Tureck, K., & Matson, M. L. (2012). Applied behavior analysis in Autism Spectrum Disorders: Recent developments, strengths, and pitfalls. *Research in Autism Spectrum Disorders, 6*, 144–150.

Matsumoto, D., & Juang, L. (2012). Culture, self, and identity. In D. Matsumoto & L. Juang (Eds.), *Culture and psychology* (pp. 342–365). Independence, KY: Cengage Learning.

Matthews, J. S., Ponitz, C. C., & Morrison, F. J. (2009). Early gender differences in self-regulation and academic achievement. *Journal of Educational Psychology, 101*, 689–704.

Maxwell, L. (2013a). A look at ELL performance on Common-Core-aligned tests. *Education Week, August 23.* Retrieved from http://blogs.edweek.org/edweek/learning-the-language/2013/08/ell_performance_sinks_on_commo.html

Maxwell, L. (2013b). Consortia struggle with ELL provisions. *Education Week, 32*(27), 1, 16, 17.

May, L., Byers-Heinlein, K., Gervain, J., & Werker, J. (2011). Language and the newborn brain: Does prenatal language experience shape the neonate neural response to speech? *Frontiers in Psychology, 15.* doi:10.3389/fpsyg.2011.00222

Mayer, M., & Furlong, M. (2010). How safe are our schools? *Educational Researcher, 39*, 16–26.

Mayer, R. (2002). *The promise of educational psychology: Volume II. Teaching for meaningful learning.* Upper Saddle River, NJ: Merrill/Pearson.

Mayer, R. E. (2004). Should there be a three-strikes rule against pure discovery learning? *American Psychologist, 59*, 14–19.

Mayer, R. E. (2008). *Learning and instruction* (2nd ed.). Upper Saddle River, NJ: Pearson.

Mayer, R. E., & Wittrock, M. C. (2006). Problem solving. In P. A. Alexander & P. H. Winne (Eds.), *Handbook of educational psychology* (2nd ed., pp. 287–303). Mahwah, NJ: Erlbaum.

Mayer, R., & Massa, L. (2003). Three facts of visual and verbal learners: Cognitive ability, cognitive style, and learning preference. *Journal of Educational Psychology, 95*, 833–846.

Mayeux, L., Houser, J., & Dyches, K. (2011). Social acceptance and popularity: Two distinct forms of peer status. In A. Cillessen, D., Schwartz, & L. Mayeux (Eds.), *Popularity in the peer system* (pp. 79–102). New York: Guilford.

Mayor, J., & Plunkett, K. (2010). A neurocomputational account of taxonomic responding and fast mapping in early word learning. *Developmental Review, 117*(1), 1–31.

McCoach, D. B., O'Connell, A., & Levitt, H. (2006). Ability grouping across kindergarten using an early childhood longitudinal study. *Journal of Educational Research, 99*(6), 339–346.

McCombs, J., Sloan, R., Augustine, C., Schwartz, H., Bodilly, S., McInnis, B., Lichter, D., & Cross, A. (2011). *Making summer count: How summer programs can boost children's learning.* Santa Monica, CA: Rand Corporation.

McCoy-Roth, M., Mackintosh, B., & Murphy, P. (2012). When the bough breaks: The effects of homelessness on young children. *Child Trends, 3*(1), 1–11.

McCurdy, B. L., Kunsch, C., & Reibstein, S. (2007). Secondary prevention in the urban school: Implementing the behavior education program. *Preventing School Failure, 51*, 12–19.

McCutchen, D. (2000). Knowledge, processing, and working memory: Implications for a theory of writing. *Educational Psychologist, 35*(1), 13–23.

McDermott, R., Goldman, S., & Varenne, H. (2006). The cultural work of learning disabilities. *Educational Researcher, 35*(6), 12–17.

McDevitt, T., Spivey, N., Sheehan, E., Lennon, R., & Story, R. (1990). Children's beliefs about listening: Is it enough to be still and quiet? *Child Development, 61*, 713–721.

McEvoy, P. M., Moulds, M. L., & Mahoney, A. E. (2013). Mechanisms driving pre- and post-stressor repetitive negative thinking: Metacognitions, cognitive avoidance, and thought control. *Journal of Behavior Therapy and Experimental Psychiatry, 44*, 84–93.

McGregor, D. (2011). What can reflective practice mean for you . . . and why should you engage in it? In D. McGregor & L. Cartwright (Eds.), *Developing reflective practice: A guide for beginning teachers* (pp. 1–20). Berkshire, England: Open University Press.

McGuire, J., Anderson, C., Toomey, R., & Russell, S. (2010). School climate for transgender youth: A mixed method investigation of student experiences and school responses. *Journal of Youth and Adolescence, 39*(10), 1175–1188. doi:10.1007/s10964-010-9540-7

McKeachie, W., & Kulik, J. (1975). Effective college teaching. In F. Kerlinger (Ed.), *Review of research in education: Vol. 3* (pp. 24–39). Washington, DC: American Educational Research Association.

McKenney, S., & Reeves, T. C. (2013). Systematic review of design-based research progress: Is a little knowledge a dangerous thing? *Educational Researcher, 42*, 97–100.

McMahon, S., Rose, D., & Parks, M. (2004). Multiple intelligences and reading achievement; An examination of the Teele Inventory of Multiple Intelligences. *Journal of Experimental Education, 73*(1), 41–52.

McMillan, J. (2011). *Classroom assessment: Principles and practices for effective standards-based instruction* (5th ed.). Boston: Allyn & Bacon.

McNeil, M. (2012). Race to top districts "personalize" plans. *Education Week, 32*(26), 1, 16, 17.

McNeil, M. (2013a). California districts' waiver bid heads to review phase. *Education Week, 32*(27), 18, 21.

McNeil, M. (2013b). Race to top promises come home to roost. *Education Week, 31*(15), 1, 23.

McWhorter, J. (2013). Is texting killing the English language? *Time Ideas.* Retrieved from http://ideas.time.com/2013/04/25/is-texting-killing-the-english-language/

Meadows, S. (2010). *The child as a social person.* London, England: Routledge.

Medina, J. (2009, March 11). Boys and girls together taught separately in public school. *New York Times,* A24.

Meece, J., & Daniels, D. (2011). *Child and adolescent development for educators* (4th ed.). New York: McGraw-Hill.

Meek, C. (2006). From the inside out: A look at testing special education students. *Phi Delta Kappan, 88*(4), 293–297.

Mega, C., Ronconi, L., & De Beni, R. (2013, July 1). What makes a good student? How emotions, self-regulated learning, and motivation contribute to academic achievement. *Journal of Educational Psychology,* 1–11. Advance online publication. doi:10.1037/a0033546

Meichenbaum, D. (2000). *Cognitive behavior modification: An integrative approach.* Dordrecht, Netherlands: Kluwer Academic.

Melanko, S., & Larkin, K. T. (2013). Preference for immediate reinforcement over delayed reinforcement: Relation between delay discounting and health behavior. *Journal of Behavioral Medicine, 36*, 34–43. doi:10.1007/s10865-012-9399-z

Meltzer, L., Pollica, L., & Barzillai, M. (2007). Executive function in the classroom: Embedding strategy instruction into daily teaching practices. In L. Meltzer (Ed.), *Executive function in education: From theory to practice* (pp. 165–193). New York: Guilford Press.

Mendaglio, S. (2010). Anxiety in gifted students. In J. C. Cassady (Ed.), *Anxiety in schools: The causes, consequences, and solutions for academic anxieties* (pp. 153–173). New York: Peter Lang.

Mercer, J. (1973). *Labeling the mentally retarded.* Berkeley: University of California Press.

Merrell, K., Gueldner, B., Ross, S., & Isava, D. (2008). How effective are school bullying intervention programs? A meta-analysis of intervention research. *School Psychology Quarterly, 23*, 26–42.

Mertz, E., & Yovel, J. (2010). Metalinguistic awareness. In J. Ostman, J. Verschureren, J. Blommaert, & C. Bulcaen (Eds.), *Handbook of pragmatics* (pp. 122–144). New York: Kluwer.

MET. (2013). Ensuring fair and reliable measures of effective teaching: Culminating findings from the MET Project's three-year study. Retrieved from http://www.metproject.org/downloads/MET_Ensuring_Fair_and_Reliable_Measures_Practitioner_Brief.pdf

Metcalfe, J., & Finn, B. (2013). Metacognition and control of study choice in children. *Metacognition and Learning, 8,* 19–46. doi:10.1007/s11409-013-9094-7

Metzner, J. L., & Fellner, J. (2010). Solitary confinement and mental illness in U.S. prisons: A challenge for medical ethics. *Journal of the American Academy of Psychiatry and the Law Online.* Retrieved from http://www.jaapl.org/content/38/1/104.full.pdf

Midgley, C. (2001). A goal theory perspective on the current status of middle level schools. In T. Urdan & F. Pajares (Eds.), *Adolescence and education* (Vol. I, pp. 33–59). Greenwich, CT: Information Age Publishing.

Midgley, C., Kaplan, A., & Middleton, M. (2001). Performance-approach goals. Good for what, for whom, under what circumstances, and at what cost? *Journal of Educational Psychology, 93,* 77–86.

Mienaltowski, A. (2011). Everyday problem solving across the adult life span: Solution diversity and efficacy. *Annals of the New York Academy of Sciences, 1235,* 75–85. doi:10.1111/j.1749-6632.2011.06207.x

Migration Policy Institute. (2010). *Top languages spoken by English language learners nationally and by state.* National Center on Immigrant Integration Policy. Retrieved from http://www.migrationinformation.org/ellinfo/FactSheet_ELL3.pdf

Miller, A. (2013). How to teach a teen to have impulse control. *GlobalPost.* Retrieved from http://everydaylife.globalpost.com/teach-teen-impulse-control-11045.html

Miller, B. (2013). *Cultural anthropology* (7th ed.). Boston: Pearson.

Miller, G. (1956). The magical number seven, plus or minus two: Some limits on our capacity for processing information. *Psychological Review, 63,* 81–97.

Miller, G. (2010). Mistreating psychology in the decades of the brain. *Perspectives on Psychological Science, 5,* 716–643.

Miller, G. (2012). Equal opportunity: A landmark law for children and education. *Education Week, 31*(15), 40.

Miller, M. D., Linn, R. L., & Gronlund, N. E. (2013). *Measurement and assessment in teaching* (11th ed.). Upper Saddle River, NJ: Merrill/Pearson.

Miller, M., Linn, R., & Gronlund, N. (2009). *Measurement and assessment in teaching* (10th ed.). Upper Saddle River, NJ: Merrill/Pearson.

Miller, M., Linn, R., & Gronlund, N. (2013). *Measurement and assessment in teaching* (11th ed.). Upper Saddle River, NJ: Merrill/Pearson.

Miller, P. (2011). *Theories of developmental psychology* (5th ed.). New York: Worth.

Miller-Lewis, L. R., Searle, A., Sawyer, M. G., Baghurst, P. A., & Hedley, D. (2013). Resource factors for mental health resilience in early childhood: An analysis with multiple methodologies. *Child and Adolescent Psychiatry and Mental Health, 7,* 1–23.

Milner, H. R., & Tenore, F. B. (2010). Classroom management in diverse classrooms. *Urban Education, 45,* 560–603.

Miltenberger, R. G. (2012). *Behavior modification: Principles and procedures* (5th ed.). Belmont, CA: Cengage.

Mirpuri, D. (2014). Right brain vs left brain: Find out how the left brain and the right brain influence our personalities. About.com *Toys.* Retrieved from http://toys.about.com/od/babydvdsandmusic/qt/leftrightbrain.htm

Mitchell, M. M., & Bradshaw, C. P. (2013). Examining classroom influences on student perceptions of school climate: The role of classroom management and exclusionary discipline strategies. *Journal of School Psychology, 51,* 599–610.

Moffitt, T. E., Arseneault, L., Belsky, D., Dickson, N., Hancox, R. J., Harrington, H. , . . . Caspi, A. (2011). A gradient of childhood self-control predicts health, wealth, and public safety. *PNAS.* Retrieved from http://www.pnas.org/content/early/2011/01/20/1010076108.full.pdf+html

Mohajer, S. T. (2013). 20,000 students sue Calif. educators for not teaching English. *The Christian Science Monitor.* Retrieved from http://search.mywebsearch.com/mywebsearch/GGmain.jhtml?searchfor=non-native+english+speakers+in+california&ptb=5483FA38-861B-4C7A-AAF3-1A65937AAA3E&n=77DE8857&tpr=hpsb&ts=1384269563801&p2=%5EY6%5Exdm003%5EYY%5Eus&si=CP_KraXh5rcCFVIV7AodAV8AQQ&st=hp

Moller, A., Deci, E., & Elliott, A. (2010). Person-level relatedness and the incremental value of relating. *Personality and Social Psychology Bulletin, 36*(6), 754–767.

Molnar, A., Boninger, F., Wilkinson, G., Fogarty, J., & Geary, S. (2010*). Effectively embedded: The thirteenth annual report on schoolhouse commercializing trends: 2009–2010.* Retrieved from http://nepc.colorado.edu/publication/Schoolhouse-commercialism-2010

Molnar, M. (2014). State chambers of commerce defend Common Core. *Education Week.* Retrieved from http://www.edweek.org/ew/articles/2014/01/29/19chambers_ep.h33.html?cmp=ENL-EU-NEWS1

Moneta, G. B. (2012). Opportunity for creativity in the job as a moderator of the relation between trait intrinsic motivation and flow in work. *Motivation and Emotion, 36,* 491–503.

Montague, M. (2003). *Solve it! A practical approach to teaching mathematical problem-solving skills.* Reston, VA: Exceptional Innovations.

Moorman, E. A., & Pomerantz, E. M. (2010). Ability mindsets influence the quality of mothers' involvement in children's learning: An experimental investigation. *Developmental Psychology, 46,* 1354–1362.

Morelli, G. A., & Rothbaum, F. (2007). Situating the child in context: Attachment relationships and self-regulation in different cultures. In S. Kitayama & D. Cohen (Eds.), *Handbook of cultural psychology* (pp. 500–527). New York: Guilford.

Moreno, G., Johnson-Shelton, D., & Boles, S. (2013). Prevalence and prediction of overweight and obesity among elementary school students. *Journal of School Health, 83,* 157–163.

Moreno, M. A., Jelenchick, L. A., & Christakis, D. A. (2013). Problematic internet use among older adolescents: A conceptual framework. *Computers and Human Behavior, 29,* 1879–1887. http://dx.doi.org/10.1016/j.chb.2013.01.053

Moreno, R., & Duran, R. (2004). Do multiple representations need explanations: The role of verbal guidance and individual differences in multimedia mathematics learning. *Journal of Educational Psychology, 96,* 492–503.

Moreno, R., & Mayer, R. (2000). Engaging students in active learning: The case for personalized multimedia messages. *Journal of Educational Psychology, 92*(4), 724–733.

Moreno, R., & Mayer, R. (2005). Role of guidance, reflection, and interactivity in an agent-based multimedia game. *Journal of Educational Psychology, 97*(1), 117–128.

Morgan, M. (2013). Social media impacts real relationships. *The Deseret News.* Retrieved from http://www.deseretnews.com/article/865576858/Social-media-impacts-real-relationships.html?pg=all

Morgan, P. L., & Fuchs, D. (2007). Is there a bidirectional relationship between children's reading skills and reading motivation? *Exceptional Children, 73,* 165–183.

Morgan, P., Staff, J., Hillemeier, M., Farkas, G., & Maczuga, S. (2013). Racial and ethnic disparities in ADHD diagnosis from kindergarten to eighth grade. *Pediatrics.* Retrieved from http://pediatrics.aappublications.org/content/early/2013/06/19/peds.2012-2390

Morgan, S. L., & Mehta, J. D. (2004). Beyond the laboratory: Evaluating the survey evidence for the disidentification explanation of black–white differences in achievement. *Sociology of Education, 77*(1), 82–101.

Moriarty, A. (2009). Managing confrontations safely and effectively. *Kappa Delta Pi Record, 45,* 78–83.

Morra, S., & Camba, R. (2009). Vocabulary learning in primary school children: Working memory and long-term memory components. *Journal of Experimental Child Psychology, 104,* 156–178.

Morra, S., Gobbo, C., Marini, Z., & Sheese, R. (2008). *Cognitive development: Neo-Piagetian perspectives.* New York: Erlbaum.

Morrier, M., & Gallagher, P. (2010). *Racial disparities in preschool special education eligibility for five southern states.* Retrieved from http://sed.sagepub.com/content/early/2010/08/31/0022466910380465

Morris, P., Lloyd, C. M., Millenky, M., Leacock, N., Raver, C. C., & Bangser, M. (2013). *Using classroom management to improve preschoolers' social and emotional skills: Final impact and implementation findings from the Foundations of Learning Demonstration in Newark and Chicago.* New York: MDRC. Retrieved from http://www.eric.ed.gov.dax.lib.unf.edu/PDFS/ED540680.pdf

Morrow, L., Gambrell, L., & Duke, N. (2011). *Best practices in literacy instruction* (4th ed.). New York: Guilford Press.

Moscaritolo, A. (2012). Survey: 31 percent of U.S. Internet users own tablets. *PC Magazine.* Retrieved from http://www.pcmag.com/article2/0,2817,2405972,00.asp

Mostofsky, E., Maclure, M., Tofler, G. H., Muller, J. E., & Mittleman, M. A. (2013). *Relation of outbursts of anger and risk of acute myocardial infarction. American Journal of Cardiology, 112,* 343–348.

Mõttus, R., Johnson, W., & Deary, I. (2012). Personality traits in old age: Measurement and rank-order stability and some mean-level change. *Psychology & Aging, 27,* 243–249.

Moyer-Packenham, P., & Suh, J. (2012). Learning mathematics with technology: The influence of virtual manipulatives on different achievement groups. *Journal of Computers in Mathematics and Science Teaching, 31,* 39–59.

Muise, A., Christofides, E., & Desmarais, S. (2009). More information than you ever wanted: Does Facebook bring out the green-eyed monster of jealousy? *Cyberpsychology and Behavior, 12,* 441–444. doi:10.1089=cpb.2008.0263

Murdock, T. B., Miller, A., & Kohlhardt, J. (2004). Effects of classroom context variables in high school students' judgments of the acceptability and likelihood of cheating. *Journal of Educational Psychology, 96*(4), 765–777.

Murphy, J. (2010). *The educator's handbook for understanding and closing achievement gaps.* Thousand Oaks, CA: Corwin Press.

Murphy, J. C. (2007). Hey, Ms. A! One student teacher's success story. *Kappa Delta Pi Record, 43,* 52–55.

Murphy, L. W., Vagins, D. J., & Parker, A. (2010). *Statement before the House Education and Labor Subcommittee on Healthy Families and Communities hearing on "Corporal punishment in schools and its effect on academic success."* American Civil Liberties Union and Human Rights Watch. Retrieved from http://www.hrw.org/sites/default/files/related_material/CorpPunishStatement_041510.pdf

Murphy, P., & Benton, S. (2010). The new frontier of educational neuropsychology: Unknown opportunities and unfulfilled hopes. *Contemporary Educational Psychology, 35,* 153–155.

Myers, K. M., & Davis, M. (2007). Mechanisms of fear extinction. *Molecular Psychiatry, 12,* 120–150.

Naci, J. C. (2013). Process inquiry: Analysis of oral problem-solving skills in mathematics of engineering students. *US-China Education Review A, 3,* 73–82.

Nakamoto, J., Lindsey, K. A., & Manis, F. R. (2012). Development of reading skills from K-3 in Spanish-speaking English language learners following three programs of instruction. *Reading and Writing: An Interdisciplinary Journal, 25,* 537-567.

Nance, J. P. (2013). Students, security, and race. *Emory Law Journal, 63,* 1–57.

Narciss, S., Sosnovsky, S., Schnaubert, L., Andrès, E., Eichelmann, A., Goguadze, G., & Melis, E. (2014). Exploring feedback and student characteristics relevant for personalizing feedback strategies. *Computers and Education, 71,* 56–76.

Narr, K., Woods, R., Lin, J., Kim, J., Phillips, O., Del'Homme, M. , . . . Levitt, J. (2009). Widespread cortical thinning is a robust anatomical marker for attention-deficit/hyperactivity disorder. *Journal of the American Academy of Child and Adolescent Psychiatry, 48,* 1014–1022.

Nasir, N., Rosebery, A., Warren, B., & Lee, C. (2006). Learning as a cultural process: Achieving equity through diversity. In R. K. Sawyer (Ed.), *The Cambridge handbook of the learning sciences* (pp. 489–504). New York: Cambridge University Press.

NASSPE. (2013). National Association for Single Sex Public Education. Retrieved from http://www.singlesexschools.org/schools-schools.htm.

National Assessment of Educational Progress. (2013a). *Changes by student groups.* Washington, DC. National Center for Educational Statistics. Retrieved from http://nationsreportcard.gov/reading_math_2013/#/gains-by-group

National Assessment of Educational Progress. (2013b). *The nation's report card.* Washington, DC: National Center for Educational Statistics. Retrieved from http://nces.ed.gov/nationsreportcard/

National Assessment of Educational Progress. (2014). *The nation's report card.* Washington, DC: National Center for Educational Statistics. Retrieved from http://www.nces.ed.gov/nationsreportcard

National Center for Education Statistics. (2010a). *The nation's report card: U.S. history, 2010.* Retrieved from http://nces.ed.gov/nationsreportcard/pubs/main2010/2011468.asp

National Center for Education Statistics. (2010b). *Digest of education statistics: Table 7. Percentage of the population 3 to 34 years old enrolled in school, by age group; Selected years, 1940 through 2009.* Washington, DC: Author.

National Center for Education Statistics. (2010c). *Projections of education statistics to 2019.* Retrieved from http://nces.ed.gov/programs/projections/projections2019/tables/table_02.asp?referrer=list

National Center for Education Statistics. (2011). *The condition of education.* Retrieved from http://nces.ed.gov/programs/coe/

National Center for Education Statistics. (2012). *National assessment of educational progress* (NAEP). Retrieved from http://nces.ed.gov/nationsreportcard/about/

National Center for Education Statistics. (2013a). *A first look: 2013 mathematics and reading national assessment of educational progress at grades 4 and 8.* Retrieved from http://nces.ed.gov/nationsreportcard/pubs/main2013/2014451.aspx

National Center for Education Statistics. (2013b). *Projections of education statistics to 2021.* Retrieved from http://nces.ed.gov/programs/projections/projections2021/tables.asp

National Center for Education Statistics. (2014a). *Children and youth with disabilities.* Retrieved from http://nces.ed.gov/programs/coe/indicator_cgg.asp

National Center for Education Statistics. (2014b). *National assessment of educational progress.* Retrieved from http://nces.ed.gov/nationsreportcard/

National Center for Homeless Education. (2013). *Education for homeless children and youths program: Data collection summary.* Retrieved from http://center.serve.org/nche/downloads/data-comp-0910-1112.pdf

National Center on Universal Design for Learning. (2012). *The concept of UDL.* Retrieved from http://www.udlcenter.org/aboutudl/whatisudl/conceptofudl

National Commission on Excellence in Education. (1983). *A nation at risk: The imperative for educational reform.* Washington, DC: Government Printing Office. Retrieved from http://datacenter.spps.org/sites/2259653e-ffb3-45ba-8fd6-04a024ecf7a4/uploads/SOTW_A_Nation_at_Risk_1983.pdf

National Council on Disability. (2011). *National disabilities policy: A progress report - October 2011.* Retrieved from http://www.ncd.gov/progress_reports/Oct312011

National Joint Committee on Learning Disabilities. (1994). Learning disabilities: Issues on definition. A position paper of the National Joint Committee in Learning Disabilities. In *Collective perspectives on issues affecting learning disability: Position papers and statements.* Austin, TX: Pro-Ed.

National Science Teachers Association. (2013a). Next generation science standards. Retrieved from http://nstahosted.org/pdfs/ngss/20130509/topic-grouped/MS-PhysicalScienceStandards.pdf

National Science Teachers Association. (2013b). *Next generation science standards.* Retrieved from http://nstahosted.org/pdfs/ngss/20130509/topic-grouped/ES-LifeScienceStandards.pdf

National Society for the Gifted and Talented. (2014). *Giftedness defined.* Retrieved from http://www.nsgt.org/giftedness-defined/

Needham, B., & Austin, E. (2010). Sexual orientation, parental support, and health during the transition to young adulthood. *Journal of Youth and Adolescence, 39,* 1189–1198.

Nehl, E. J., Blanchard, C. M., Kupperman, J., Sparling, P., Rhodes, R., Torabi, M. R., & Courneya, K. S. (2012). Exploring physical activity by ethnicity and gender in college students using social cognitive theory. *Journal of Research in Health, Physical Education, Recreation, Sport & Dance, 7,* 11–17.

Neisser, U. (1967). *Cognitive psychology.* New York: Appleton-Century-Crofts.

Nelson, C., Thomas, K., & de Haan, M. (2006). Neural bases of cognitive development. In D. Kuhn,

R. Siegler (Vol. Eds.), W. Damon, & R. Lerner (Series Eds.), *Handbook of child psychology. Vol. 2: Cognition, perception, and language* (6th ed., pp. 3–57). New York: Wiley.

Nelson, J. A. P., Young, B. J., Young, E. L., & Cox, G. (2010). Using teacher-written praise notes to promote a positive environment in a middle school. *Preventing School Failure, 54,* 119–125.

Nesbit, J., & Adesope, O. (2006). Learning with concept and knowledge maps: A meta-analysis. *Review of Educational Research, 76*(3), 413–448.

Nettelbeck, T., & Wilson, C. (2010). Intelligence and IQ. In K. Wheldall (Ed.), *Developments in educational psychology* (2nd ed., pp. 30–52). New York: Routledge.

Neuenschwander, R., Cimeli, P., Röthlisberger, M., & Roebers, C. M. (2013). Personality factors in elementary school children: Contributions to academic performance over and above executive functions? *Learning and Individual Differences, 25,* 118–125.

Neuman, S. (2012). *Violence in schools: How big a problem is it?* National Public Radio. Retrieved from http://www.npr.org/2012/03/16/148758783/violence-in-schools-how-big-a-problem-is-it

New York Times Editorial Board. (2013). Moving ahead with the Common Core. *New York Times.* Retrieved from http://www.nytimes.com/2013/04/21/opinion/sunday/moving-ahead-with-common-core.html?_r=1&

Ngu, B. H., & Yeung, A. S. (2013). Algebra word problem solving approaches in a chemistry context: Equation worked examples versus text editing. *The Journal of Mathematical Behavior, 32,* 197–208.

Nichols, S., & Berliner, D. (2008). Why has high-stakes testing so easily slipped into contemporary American life? *Phi Delta Kappan, 89,* 672–676.

Nie, Y., & Liem, G. A. D. (2013). Extending antecedents of achievement goals: The double-edged sword effect of social-oriented achievement motive and gender differences. *Learning and Individual Differences, 23,* 249–255.

Nielsen, J. A., Zielinski, B. A., Ferguson, M. A., Lainhart, J. E., & Anderson, J. S. (2013). An evaluation of the left-brain vs. right-brain hypothesis with resting state functional connectivity magnetic resonance imaging. *Plos One, 8,* 1–11. Retrieved from http://www.plosone.org/article/fetchObject.action?uri=info%3Adoi%2F10.1371%2Fjournal.pone.0071275&representation=PDF

Nieto, S., & Bode, P. (2012). *Affirming diversity: The sociopolitical context of multicultural education* (6th ed.). Boston: Pearson.

Nieuwenhuis, I. L., Folia, V., Forkstam, C., Jensen, O., & Petersson, K. M. (2013). Sleep promotes the extraction of grammatical rules. *PLoS ONE, 8,* 1–10.

Nilsson, L., & Archer, T. (1989). Aversively motivated behavior: Which are the perspectives? In T. Archer & L. Nilsson (Eds.), *Aversion, avoidance and anxiety.* Hillsdale, NJ: Erlbaum.

Niu, L., Behar-Horenstein, L. S., & Garvan, C. W. (2013). Do instructional interventions influence college students' critical thinking skills? A meta-analysis. *Educational Research Review, 9,* 114–128.

Noddings, N. (1992). *The challenge to care in schools: An alternative approach to education.* New York: Teachers College Press.

Noddings, N. (2001). The caring teacher. In V. Richardson (Ed.), *Handbook of research on teaching* (4th ed., pp. 99–105). Washington, DC: American Educational Research Association.

Noddings, N. (2002). *Educating moral people: A caring alternative approach to education.* New York: Teachers College Press.

Noddings, N. (2008). Caring and moral education. In L. P. Nucci & D. Narváez (Eds.), *Handbook of moral and character education* (pp. 161–174). New York: Routledge.

Noltemeyer, A. (2013). Resilience across contexts: Introduction to the collection. *School Psychology International, 34*(5), 1–5.

Noltemeyer, A., & Bush, K. (2013). Adversity & resilience: Lessons for school psychologists. *School Psychology International, 34*(5). doi:0.1177;0143034312472762

Norenzayan, A., Choi, I., & Peng, K. (2007). Perception and cognition. In S. Kitayama & D. Cohen (Eds.), *Handbook of cultural psychology* (pp. 569–594). New York: Guilford Press.

Novak, J. D., & Cañas, A. J. (2006). The theory underlying concept maps and how to construct and use them. Retrieved from http://cmap.ihmc.us/Publications/ResearchPapers/TheoryCmaps/TheoryUnderlyingConceptMaps.htm

Nucci, L. (2006). Classroom management for moral and social development. In C. Evertson & C. Weinstein (Eds.), *Handbook of classroom management: Research, practice, and contemporary issues* (pp. 711–731). Mahwah, NJ: Erlbaum.

Nucci, L. (2009). *Nice is not enough: Facilitating moral development.* Upper Saddle River, NJ: Pearson Education.

Nucci, L. P. (2008). Social cognitive domain theory and moral education. In L. P. Nucci & D. Narváez (Eds.), *Handbook of moral and character education* (pp. 291–309). New York: Routledge.

Nuthall, G. A. (2000). The role of memory in the acquisition and retention of knowledge in science and social studies units. *Cognition and Instruction, 18*(1), 83–139.

O'Brien, T. (1999). Parrot math. *Phi Delta Kappan, 80,* 434–438.

O'Conner, C., & Fernandez, S. (2006). Race, class, and disproportionality: Reevaluating the relationship between poverty and special education placement. *Educational Researcher, 35*(6), 6–11.

O'Connor, E. E., Dearing, E., & Collins, B. A. (2011). Teacher-child relationship and behavior problem trajectories in elementary school. *American Educational Research Journal, 48,* 120–162.

O'Connor, K. (2011). *A repair kit for grading: 15 fixes for broken grades* (2nd ed.). Boston: Pearson Assessment Training Institute.

O'Mara, A., Marsh, H., Craven, R., & Debus, R. (2006). Do self-concept interventions make a difference? A synergistic blend of construct validation and meta-analysis. *Educational Psychologist, 41*(3), 181–206.

O'Mea, M. L. (2013). Implementing applied behavior analysis for effective orientation and mobility instruction of students with multiple disabilities. *Journal of Visual Impairment and Blindness, 107,* 65–70.

O'Meara, J. (2011). *Beyond differentiated instruction.* Thousand Oaks, CA: Corwin Press.

O'Neil, J. (2012, March 27). Roadblocks to a rite of passage. *New York Times,* pp. D1, D6.

Oakes, J. (2005). *Keeping track: How schools structure inequality* (2nd ed.). New Haven, CT: Yale University Press.

OECD. (2013). *OECD Skills outlook 2013: First results from the survey of adult skills.* Retrieved from http://skills.oecd.org/documents/OECD_Skills_Outlook_2013.pdf

Ogbu, J. (1992). Understanding cultural diversity and learning. *Educational Researcher, 21*(8), 5–14.

Ogbu, J. (2003). *Black American students in an affluent suburb: A study of academic disengagement.* Mahwah, NJ: Erlbaum.

Ogbu, J. U. (2008). Collective identity and the burden of "acting White" in Black history, community, and education. In J. Ogbu (Ed.), *Minority status, oppositional culture, and schooling* (pp. 29–63). New York: Routledge.

Ogbu, J., & Simons, H. (1998). Voluntary and involuntary minorities: A cultural-ecological theory of school performance with some implications for education. *Anthropology & Education Quarterly, 29*(2), 155–188.

Ogden, C., & Carroll, M. (2010). Prevalence of obesity among children and adolescents: United States trends 1963–1965 through 2007–2008. *Center for Disease Control and Prevention.* Retrieved from http://www.cdc.gov/nchs/data/hestat/obesity_child_07_08/obesity_child_07_08.htm

Ohlheiser. A. (2014). January's epidemic: 11 school shootings in 19 days. *The Wire.* Retrieved from http://www.thewire.com/national/2014/01/januarys-school-shootings/357448/.

Okagaki, L. (2006). Ethnicity, learning. In P. A. Alexander & P. H. Winne (Eds.), *Handbook of educational psychology* (2nd ed., pp. 615–634). Mahwah, NJ: Erlbaum.

Olmedo, I. (2009). Blending borders of language and culture: Schooling in La Villita. *Journal of Latinos and Education, 8*(1), 22–37.

Ostrov, J., & Godleski, S. (2010). Toward an integrated gender-linked model of aggression subtypes in early and middle childhood. *Psychological Bulletin, 117,* 233–242.

Otto, B. (2014). *Language development in early childhood* (6th ed.). Columbus. OH: Merrill.

Oudiette, D., Antony, J. W., Creery, J. C., & Paller, K. A. (2013). The role of memory reactivation during wakefulness and sleep in determining which memories endure. *Journal of Neuroscience, 33,* 6672–6678.

Owens, R. (2012). *Language development* (8th ed.). Boston: Allyn & Bacon.

Ozonoff, S. (2010). Autism spectrum disorders. In K. O. Yeates, M. D. Ris, H. G. Taylor, & B. F. Pennington (Eds.), *Pediatric neuropsychology: Research, theory, and practice* (pp. 418–446). New York: Guilford Press.

Paas, F., Renkl, A., & Sweller, J. (2004). Cognitive load theory: Instructional implications of the interaction between information structures and cognitive architecture. *Instructional Science, 32*(1), 1–8.

Padgett, S., & Notar, C. E. (2013). Anti-bullying programs for middle/high schools. *National Social Science Journal, 40*, 88–93.

Padilla, A. (2006). Second language learning: Issues in research and teaching. In P. Alexander & P. Winne (Eds.), *Handbook of educational psychology* (2nd ed., pp. 571–592). Mahwah, NJ: Erlbaum.

Padilla-Walker, L. M., Harper, J. M., & Jensen, A. C. (2010). Self-regulation as a mediator between sibling relationship quality and early adolescents' positive and negative outcomes. *Journal of Family Psychology, 24*, 419–428.

Paivio, A. (1986). *Mental representations: A dual-coding approach.* New York: Oxford University.

Paivio, A. (1991). Dual coding theory: Retrospect and current status. *Canadian Journal of Psychology, 45*, 255–287.

Palincsar, A. (1998). Social constructivist perspectives on teaching and learning. *Annual Review of Psychology, 49*, 345–375.

Pallas, A. (2010/2011). Measuring what matters. *Phi Delta Kappan, 92*, 68–71.

Palmer, L. K. (2013). The relationship between stress, fatigue, and cognitive functioning. *College Student Journal, 47*, 312–325.

Pan, C-Y., & Wu, H-Y. (2013). The cooperative learning effects on English reading comprehension and learning motivation of EFL freshmen. *English Language Teaching, 6*, 13–27.

Panahon, C. J., & Martens, B. K. (2013). A comparison of noncontingent plus contingent reinforcement to contingent reinforcement alone on students' academic performance. *Journal of Behavioral Education, 22*, 37–49. doi:10.1007/s10864-012-9157-x

Panek, R., & Grandin, T. (2013). *The autistic brain: Thinking across the spectrum.* Boston: Houghton Mifflin.

Pang, V., Han, P., & Pang, J. (2011). Asian American and Pacific Islander students: Equity and achievement gap. *Educational Researcher, 40*(8), 378–389.

Papay, J. (2011). Different tests different answers: The stability of teacher value-added estimates across outcome measures. *American Educational Research Journal, 48*(1), 163–193.

Paradise, R., & Rogoff, B. (2009). Side by side: Learning by observing and pitching in. *Ethos, 27*, 102–138.

Paris, S. G., & Paris, A. H. (2001). Classroom application of research on self-regulated learning. *Educational Psychologist, 36*, 89–101.

Paris, S. G., Morrison, F. J., & Miller, K. F. (2006). Academic pathways from preschool through elementary school. In P. A. Alexander & P. H. Winne (Eds.), *Handbook of educational psychology* (2nd ed., pp. 61–85). Mahwah, NJ: Erlbaum.

Parke, R., & Clarke-Stewart, A. (2011). *Social development.* Hoboken, NJ: Wiley.

Parker, K. (2013). Redskins name is ready for retiring. *The Washington Post.* Retrieved from http://www.washingtonpost.com/opinions/kathleen-parker-redskins-name-is-ready-for-retiring/2013/10/08/becff1e8-304a-11e3-9ccc-2252bdb14df5_story.html

Parker-Pope, T. (2010, July 20). Attention disorders can take a toll on marriage. *New York Times*, p. D5.

Parks, F. R., & Kennedy, J. H. (2007). The impact of race, physical attractiveness, and gender on education majors' and teachers' perceptions of student competence. *Journal of Black Studies, 37*, 936–943.

Parrish, A-M., Okely, A. D., Stanley, R. M., & Ridgers, M. D. (2013). The effect of school recess interventions on physical activity. *Sports Medicine, 43*, 287–299.

Parsons, S. A., Dodman, S. L., & Burrowbridge, S. C. (2013). Broadening the view of differentiated instruction. *Phi Delta Kappan, 95*, 38–42.

Pascual-Leone, A., Amedi, A., Fregni, F., & Merabet, L. B. (2005). The plastic human brain cortex. *Annual Review of Neuroscience, 28*, 377–401. doi 10.1146/annurev.neuro.27.070203.144216

Pashler, H., & Carrier, M. (1996). Structures, processes, and the flow of information. In E. Bjork & R. Bjork (Eds.), *Memory* (pp. 3–29). San Diego, CA: Academic Press.

Pashler, H., McDaniel, M., Rohrer, D., & Bjork, R. (2008). Learning styles: Concepts and evidence. *Psychological Science in the Public Interest, 9*, 105–119.

Patall, E., Cooper, H., & Allen, A. (2010). Extending the school day or school year: Systematic review of research (1985–2009). *Review of Educational Research, 80*, 401–436.

Patrick, D. L., Bell, J. F., Huang, J. Y., Lazarakis, N. C., & Edwards, T. C. (2013). Bullying and quality of life in youths perceived as gay, lesbian, or bisexual in Washington State, 2010. *American Journal of Public Health, 103*, 1255–1262.

Patrick, H., Anderman, L. H., & Ryan, A. M. (2002). Social motivation and the classroom social environment. In C. Midgley (Ed.), *Goals, goal structures, and patterns of adaptive learning* (pp. 85–108). Mahwah, NJ: Erlbaum.

Patrick, H., Kaplan, A., & Ryan, A. (2011). Positive classroom motivational environments; Convergence between mastery goal structure and classroom social climate. *Journal of Educational Psychology, 103*, 367–382.

Patrick, R., & Gibbs, J. (2010). Inductive discipline, parental expression of disappointed expectations, and moral identity in adolescence. *Journal of Youth and Adolescence, 36.* Retrieved from http://link.springer.com/article/10.1007%2Fs10964-011-9698-7

Patterson, E. (2011). Texting: An old language habit in a new media. *International Journal of the Humanities, 9*, 235–242.

Patterson, G. (2012). Separating the boys from the girls. *Phi Delta Kappan, 93*(5), 37–41.

Paufler, N. A., & Amrein-Beardsley, A. (2014). The random assignment of students into elementary classrooms: Implications for value-added analyses and interpretations. *American Educational Research Journal, 51*, 328–362.

Pavey, L., Greitemeyer, T., & Sparks, P. (2010). Highlighting relatedness promotes prosocial motives and behavior. *Personality and Social Psychology Bulletin, 37*(7) 905–917. doi:10.1177/014616721

Pearson, B., Velleman, S., Bryant, T., & Charko, T. (2009). Phonological milestones for African American English-speaking children learning mainstream American English as a second dialect. *Language, Speech, and Hearing Services in School, 40*(3), 229–244.

Pecheone, R., & Kahl, S. (2011). *Through a looking glass: Lessons learned and future direction for performance assessment.* Stanford, CA: Stanford Center for Opportunity Policy in Education.

Pekrun, R., Goetz, T., Frenzel, A. C., Barchfeld, P., & Perry, R. P. (2011). Measuring emotions in students' learning and performance: The Achievement Emotions Questionnaire (AEQ). *Contemporary Educational Psychology, 36*, 36–48. doi:10.1016/j.cedpsych.2010.10.002

Péladeau, N., Forget, J., & Gagné, F. (2003). Effect of paced and unpaced practice on skill application and retention: How much is enough? *American Educational Research Journal, 40*(3), 769–801.

Pelaez, M., Virues-Ortega, J., Field, T. M., Amir-Kiaei, Y., & Schnerch, G. (2013). Social referencing in infants of mothers with symptoms of depression. *Infant Behavior and Development, 36*, 548–556.

Pellegrini, A. (2011). "In the eye of the beholder": Sex bias in observations and ratings of children's aggression. *Educational Researcher, 40*, 281–286.

Pellegrino, A. M. (2010). Pre-service teachers and classroom authority. *American Secondary Education, 38*, 62–78.

Pence Turnbull, K. L., & Justice, L. M. (2012). *Language development from theory to practice* (2nd ed.). Upper Saddle River, NJ: Merrill/Pearson Education.

Pennebaker J. W., Gosling S. D., & Ferrell J. D. (2013). Daily online testing in large classes: Boosting college performance while reducing achievement gaps. *PLoS ONE, 8*(11), e79774. doi:10.1371/journal.pone.0079774. Retrieved from http://www.plosone.org/article/info%3Adoi%2F10.1371%2Fjournal.pone.0079774

Pentimonti, J., & Justice, L. (2010). Teachers' use of scaffolding strategies during read alouds in the preschool classroom. *Early Childhood Education, 37*, 241–248.

Peregoy, S., & Boyle, O. (2013). *Reading, writing, and learning in ESL* (6th ed.). New York: Longman.

Perrachione, T., Tufo, S., & Gabrieli, J. (2011). Human voice recognition depends on language ability. *Science, 333*(6042), 595–605.

Perron, T. (2013). Peer victimisation: Strategies to decrease bullying in schools. *British Journal of School Nursing, 8,* 25–29.

Perry, N. E., Turner, J. C., & Meyer, D. K. (2006). Classrooms as contexts for motivating learning. In P. A. Alexander & P. H. Winne (Eds.), *Handbook of educational psychology* (2nd ed., pp. 327–348). Mahwah, NJ: Erlbaum.

Peters, E., Cillessen, A., Riksen-Walraven, J., & Haselager, G. (2010). Best friends' preference and popularity: Associations with aggression and prosocial behavior. *International Journal of Behavioral Development, 34*(5), 398–405. doi:10.1177/0165025409323709

Peters, R., Bradshaw, A., Petrunka, K., Nelson, G., Herry, Y., Craig, W. , . . . Rossiter, M. (2010). The Better Beginnings, Better Futures Project: Findings from grade 3 to grade 9. *Monographs of the Society for Research in Child Development, 75*(3, Serial No. 297).

Peterson, A. M., Harper, F. W., Albrecht, T. L., Taub, J. W., Orom, H., Phipps, S., & Penner, L. A. (2014). Parent caregiver self-efficacy and child reactions to pediatric cancer treatment procedures. *Journal of Pediatric Oncology Nursing, 31,* 18–27.

Petitto, L. (2009). New discoveries from the bilingual brain and mind across the life span: Implications for education. *Brain, Mind, & Education, 3,* 185–197.

Peverly, S. P., Brobst, K. E., & Graham, M. (2003). College adults are not good at self-regulation: A study on the relationship of self-regulation, note taking, and test taking. *Journal of Educational Psychology, 95,* 335–346.

Peverly, S. T., Vekaria, P. C., Reddington, L. A., Sumowski, J. F., Johnson, K. R., & Ramsay, C. M. (2013). The relationship of handwriting speed, working memory, language comprehension and outlines to lecture note-taking and test-taking among college students. *Applied Cognitive Psychology, 27,* 115–126.

Peverly, S., Ramaswamy, V., Brown, C., Sumowski, J., Alidoost, M., & Garner, J. (2007). What predicts skill in lecture note taking? *Journal of Educational Psychology, 99*(1), 167–180.

Pew Charitable Trust. (2010). Pew Internet project: Teens and mobile phones. Retrieved from http://www.pewtrusts.org/news_room_detail.aspx?id=58543

Pfeifer, R., & Bongard, J. C. (2012). *How the body shapes the way we think: A new view of intelligence.* Boston: MIT Press.

Phelps, E. A., & Sharot, T. (2008). How (and why) emotion enhances the subjective sense of recollection. *Current Directions in Psychological Science, 17,* 147–152.

Phelps, L., McGrew, K., Knopik, S., & Ford, L. (2005). The general (g), broad, and narrow CHC stratum characteristics of the WJ III and WISC-III tests: A confirmatory cross-battery investigation. *School Psychology Quarterly, 20,* 66–88.

Phelps, R. (Ed.). (2005). *Defending standardized testing.* Mahwah, NJ: Erlbaum.

Phillipson, S., & Phillipson, S. N. (2012). Children's cognitive ability and their academic achievement: The mediation effects of parental expectations. *Asia Pacific Education Review 13,* 495–508.

Phye, G. (2005). Transfer and problem solving: A psychological integration of models, metaphors, and methods. In J. Royer (Ed.), *The cognitive revolution in educational psychology* (pp. 249–292). Greenwich, CT: Information Age Publishing.

Piaget, J. (1952). *Origins of intelligence in children.* New York: International Universities Press.

Piaget, J. (1959). *Language and thought of the child* (M. Grabain, Trans.). New York: Humanities Press.

Piaget, J. (1965). *The moral judgment of the child.* New York: Free Press. (Original work published 1932.)

Piaget, J. (1970). *The science of education and the psychology of the child.* New York: Orion Press.

Piaget, J. (1977). Problems in equilibration. In M. Appel & L. Goldberg (Eds.), *Topics in cognitive development: Vol. 1. Equilibration: Theory, research, and application* (pp. 3–13). New York: Plenum Press.

Piaget, J. (1980). *Adaptation and intelligence: Organic selection and phenocopy* (S. Eames, Trans.). Chicago: University of Chicago Press.

Piaget, J., & Inhelder, B. (1956). *The child's conception of space.* Boston: Routledge and Kegan-Paul.

Pianta, R., Belsky, J., Houts, R., & Morrison, F. (2007). Opportunities to learn in America's elementary classrooms. *Science, 315,* 1795–1796.

Picus, L., Adamson, F., & Owens M. (2010). *A new conceptual framework analyzing costs of performance assessment.* Stanford, CA: Stanford Center for Opportunity Policy in Education.

Pierangelo, R., & Giuliani, G. (2006). *Assessment in special education* (2nd ed.). Boston: Allyn & Bacon.

Pierce, R. (2013). Student performance in a flipped class module. In R. McBride & M. Searson (Eds.), *Proceedings of Society for Information Technology & Teacher Education International Conference 2013* (pp. 942–954). Chesapeake, VA: AACE. Retrieved from http://www.editlib.org/p/48235

Pilon, M. (2013, January 16). Forging path to starting line for younger disabled athletes. *New York Times,* pp. A1, A3.

Pinker, S. (2007). *Stuff of thought: Language as a window into human nature.* New York: Houghton Mifflin.

Pinker, S. (2010, June 11). Mind over mass media. *New York Times,* p. A27.

Pinter, A. (2012). Children learning second languages. *English Language Teaching Journal, 66,* 261–263.

Pintrich, P. (2000). Multiple goals, multiple pathways: The role of goal orientation in learn-ing and achievement. *Journal of Educational Psychology, 92,* 544–555.

Planecrashinfo.com. (2013). *Accident database.* Retrieved from http://www.planecrashinfo.com/database.htm

Plata, M., Trusty, J., & Glasgow, D. (2005). Adolescents with learning disabilities: Are they allowed to participate in activities? *Journal of Educational Research, 98*(3), 136–143.

Platt, R. (2004). Standardized tests: Whose standards are we talking about? *Phi Delta Kappan, 85*(5), 381–382.

Plotnikoff, R. C., Costigan, S. A., Karunamuni, N., & Lubans, D. R. (2013). Social cognitive theories used to explain physical activity behavior in adolescents: A systematic review and meta-analysis. *Preventive Medicine, 56,* 245–253. doi:10.1016/j.ypmed.2013.01.013

Polikoff, M. S. (2012). Instructional alignment under No Child Left Behind. *American Journal of Education, 118,* 341–368.

Pólya, G. (1957). *How to solve it.* Garden City, NY: Doubleday.

Pomerantz, E. M., & Kempner, S. G. (2013). Mothers' daily person and process praise: Implications for children's theory of intelligence and motivation. *Developmental Psychology.* Advance online publication. doi:10.1037/a0031840

Popham, W. J. (2004). *American's failing schools: How parents and teachers can cope with No Child Left Behind.* New York: Routledge Falmer.

Popham, W. J. (2011). Combating phony formative assessment—with a hyphen. *Education Week, 30*(21), 35.

Popham, W. J. (2014). *Classroom assessment: What teachers need to know* (7th ed.). Boston: Pearson.

Powell, R., & Caseau, D. (2004). *Classroom communication and diversity.* Mahwah, NJ: Erlbaum.

Powers, T. G., Bindler, R. C., Goetz, S., & Daratha, K. B. (2010). Obesity prevention in early adolescence: Student, parent, and teacher views. *Journal of School Health, 80,* 13–19.

Prati, G. (2012). A social cognitive learning theory of homophobic aggression among adolescents. *School Psychology Review, 41,* 413–428.

Prawat, R. (1989). Promoting access to knowledge, strategy, and disposition in students: A research synthesis. *Review of Educational Research, 59,* 1–41.

Premack, D. (1965). Reinforcement theory. In D. Levine (Ed.), *Nebraska Symposium on Motivation* (Vol. 13, pp. 3–41). Lincoln: University of Nebraska Press.

Pressley, M., & Harris, K. R. (2006). Cognitive strategies instruction: From basic research to classroom instruction. In P. A. Alexander & P. H. Winne (Eds.), *Handbook of educational psychology* (2nd ed., pp. 265–286). Mahwah, NJ: Erlbaum.

Pressley, M., & Hilden, K. (2006). Cognitive strategies. In D. Kuhn & R. Siegler (Eds.), *Handbook of child psychology* (6th ed., Vol. 2, pp. 511–556). Hoboken, NJ: John Wiley & Sons.

Pritchard, R. (1990). The effects of cultural schemata on reading processing strategies. *Reading Research Quarterly, 25,* 273–295.

Proctor, R. W., & Vu, K. P. L. (2006). The cognitive revolution at age 50: Has the promise of the information processing approach been fulfilled? *Journal of Human Computer Interaction, 23*, 253–284.

Proffitt, D. R. (2006). Embodied perception and the economy of action. *Perspectives on Psychological Science, 1*, 110–122.

Pulfrey, C., Buchs, C., & Butera, F. (2011). Why grades engender performance-avoidance goals: The mediating role of autonomous motivation. *Journal of Educational Psychology, 103*, 683–700.

Pulliam, J., & Van Patten, J. (2013). *History and social foundations of American education* (10th ed.). Columbus, OH: Merrill.

Pulvermüller, F., & Fadiga, L. (2010). Active perception: Sensorimotor circuits as a cortical basis for language. *Nature Reviews Neuroscience, 11*, 351–360.

Puntambekar, S., & Hübscher, R. (2005). Tools for scaffolding students in a complex learning environment: What have we gained and what have we missed? *Educational Psychologist, 40*(1), 1–12.

Qian, G., & Pan, J. (2002). A comparison of epistemological beliefs and learning from science text between American and Chinese high school students. In B. K Hofer & P. R. Pintrich (Eds.), *Personal epistemology: The psychology of beliefs about knowledge and knowing* (pp. 365–385). Mahwah: NJ; Erlbaum.

Quinn, J. M., Pascoe, A., Wood, W., & Neal, D. T. (2010). Can't control yourself? Monitor those bad habits. *Personality and Social Psychology Bulletin, 36*, 499–511.

Quiroga, R., Fried, I., & Koch, C. (2013). Brain cells for grandmother. *Scientific American, 308*(2), 30–5.

Radvansky, G. A., & Ashcraft, M. H. (2014). *Cognition* (6th ed.). Upper Saddle River, NJ: Pearson.

Rakison, D. (2010). Perceptual categorization and concepts. In J. Bremner & T. Wachs (Eds.), *Wiley-Blackwell handbook of infant development* (2nd ed., pp. 243–270). Oxford, UK: Wiley.

Ramirez, G., & Beilock, S. L. (2011). Writing about testing worries boosts exam performance in the classroom. *Science, 331*, 211–213. doi:10.1126/science.1199427

Ravitch, D. (2010). *The death and life of the great American school system*. New York: Basic Books.

Rebell, M., & Wolff, J. (2012). We can overcome poverty's impact on school success. *Education Week, 31*(17), 24–25.

Reed, S. K., Corbett, A., Hoffman, B., Wagner, A., & MacClaren, B. (2013). Effect of worked examples and cognitive tutor training on constructing equations. *Instructional Science: An International Journal of the Learning Sciences, 41*, 1–24.

Regmi, K. (2012). A review of teaching methods—lecturing and facilitation in higher education (HE): A summary of the published evidence. *The Journal of Effective Teaching, 12*, 61–76.

Reichert, M. C. (2010). Hopeful news on regarding the crisis in U.S. education: Exploring the human element in teaching boys. *Education Week, 30*(12), 27.

Reichert, M., & Hawley, R. (2010). Reaching boys teaching boys: Strategies that work—and why. San Francisco: John Wiley & Sons.

Reilly, R. (2013). Have the people spoken? *ESPN .com* Retrieved from http://espn.go.com/nfl/story/_/id/9689220/redskins-name-change-not-easy-sounds

Reis, S., Colbert, R., & Hébert, T. (2005). Understanding resilience in diverse, talented students in an urban high school. *Roeper Review, 27*(2), 110–120.

Reis, S., McCoach, D., Little, C., Muller, L., & Kaniskan, R. (2011). The effects of differentiated instruction and enrichment pedagogy on reading achievement in five elementary schools. *American Educational Research Journal, 48*, 462–501.

Reissland, N. (2012). *The development of emotional intelligence: A case study*. New York: Routledge/Taylor & Francis Group.

Renkl, A. (2011). Instruction based on examples. In R. E. Mayer & P. A. Alexander (Eds.), *Handbook of research on learning and instruction* (pp. 272–295). New York: Routledge.

Renkl, A., Stark, R., Gruber, H., & Mandl, H. (1998). Learning from worked-out examples: The effects of example variability and elicited self-explanations. *Contemporary Educational Psychology, 23*, 90–108.

Renninger, K. A. (2000). Individual interest and its implications for understanding intrinsic motivation. In J. M. Harackiewicz & C. Sansone (Eds.), *Intrinsic and extrinsic motivation: The search for optimal motivation and performance* (pp. 373–404). San Diego, CA:

Renzulli, J., & Reis, S. (2003). The schoolwide enrichment model: Developing creative and productive giftedness. In N. Colangelo & G. Davis (Eds.), *Handbook of gifted education* (3rd ed., pp. 184–203). Boston: Allyn & Bacon.

Repetti, R., & Wang, S.-W. (2010). Parent employment and chaos in the family. In G. Evans & T. Wachs (Eds.), *Chaos and its influence on children's development: An ecological perspective* (pp. 191–208). Washington, DC: American Psychological Association.

Resnick, L., & Klopfer, L. (1989). Toward the thinking curriculum: An overview. In L. Resnick & L. Klopfer (Eds.), *Toward the thinking curriculum: Current cognitive research* (pp. 1–18). Retrieved from http://www.ets.org/s/praxis/pdf/0624.pdf

Reupert, A., & Woodcock, S. (2010). Success and near misses: Pre-service teachers' use, confidence and success in various classroom management strategies. *Teaching and Teacher Education, 26*, 1261–1268.

Reutzel, D., & Cooter, R. (2008). *Teaching children to read: The teacher makes the difference* (5th ed.). Upper Saddle River, NJ: Merrill/Pearson.

Rhee, S., & Waldman, I. (2011). Genetic and environmental influences on aggression. In P. Shaver & M. Mikulincer (Eds.), *Human aggression and violence: Causes, manifestations, and consequences*. Washington, DC: American Psychological Association.

Rhodewalt, F., & Vohs, K. D. (2005). Defensive strategies, motivation, and the self: A self-regulatory process view. In A. J. Elliot & C. S. Dweck (Eds.), *Handbook of competence and motivation* (pp. 548–565). New York: Guilford.

Richtel, M. (2012, May 30). Wasting time is new divide in digital era. *New York Times*. Retrieved from http://www.nytimes.com/2012/05/30/us/new-digital-divide-seen-in-wasting-time-online.html?pagewanted=all&_r=0

Rideout, V., Foehr, U., & Roberts, D. (2010). *Generation M²: Media in the lives of 8- to 18-year-olds*. Menlo Park, CA: Kaiser Family Foundation. Retrieved from http://kff.org/other/event/generation-m2-media-in-the-lives-of/

Ridgers, N. D., Carter, L. M., Stratton, G., & McKenzie, T. L. (2011). Examining children's physical activity and play behaviors during school playtime over time. *Health Education Research, 26*, 586–595.

Rittle-Johnson, B., & Alibali, M. (1999). Conceptual and procedural knowledge of mathematics: Does one lead to the other? *Journal of Educational Psychology, 91*(1), 175–189.

Ritts, V., Patterson, M. L., & Tubbs, M. E. (1992). Expectations, impressions, and judgments of physically attractive students: A review. *Review of Educational Research, 62*, 413–426.

Rivers, I., Chesney, T., & Coyne, I. (2011). Cyberbullying. In C. Monks & I. Coyne (Eds.), *Bullying in different contexts* (pp. 211–230). New York: Cambridge University Press.

Rivkin, S. G., Hanushek, E. E., & Kain, J. J. (2001). *Teachers, schools, and academic achievement*. Amherst, MA: Amherst College.

Robbins, P., & Aydede, M. (2009). A short primer on situated cognition. In P. Robbins & M. Aydede (Eds.), *The Cambridge handbook of situated cognition* (pp. 3–10). New York: Cambridge University Press.

Roberts, S. (2007). *In name count, Garcias are catching up to Joneses*. Retrieved from http://www.nytimes.com/2007/22/17/us/17surnames.html?th&emc=th

Robertson, J. (2000). Is attribution training a worthwhile classroom intervention for K–12 students with learning difficulties? *Educational Psychology Review, 12*(1), 111–134.

Robinson, J. (2010). The effects of test translation on young English learners' mathematics performance. *Educational Researcher, 39*, 582–593.

Robinson, J., & Lubienski, S. (2011). The development of gender achievement gaps in mathematics and reading during elementary and middle school: Examining direct cognitive assessments and teacher ratings. *American Educational Research Journal, 48*, 268–302.

Roblyer, M. D., & Doering, A. H. (2013). *Integrating educational technology into teaching* (6th ed.). Boston: Pearson.

Roehl, A., Reddy, S. L., & Shannon, G. J. (2013). The flipped classroom: An opportunity to engage millennial students through active learning strategies. *Journal of Family & Consumer Sciences, 105*, 44–49.

Roeser, R. W., Peck, S. C., & Nasir, N. S. (2006). Self and identity processes in school motivation, learning and achievement.). In P. A. Alexander & P. H. Winne (Eds.), *Handbook of educational psychology* (2nd ed., pp. 391–424). Mahwah, NJ: Erlbaum.

Roest, A. M., Martens, E. J., de Jonge, P., & Denollet, J. (2010). Anxiety and risk of incident coronary heart disease: A meta-analysis. *Journal of the American College of Cardiology, 56*, 38–46. doi:10.1016/j.jacc.2010.03.034

Rogeberg, O. (2013). Correlations between cannabis use and IQ change in the Dunedin cohort are consistent with confounding from socioeconomic status. *Proceedings of the National Academy of Sciences of the United States of America, 110*, 4251–4254.

Rogers, C. (1963). Actualizing tendency in relation to motives and to consciousness. In M. Jones (Ed.), *Nebraska Symposium on Motivation* (Vol. 11, pp. 1–24). Lincoln: University of Nebraska Press.

Rogers, C., & Freiberg, H. J. (1994). *Freedom to learn* (3rd ed.). Upper Saddle River, NJ: Merrill/Pearson.

Rogoff, B. (2003). *The cultural context of human development*. Oxford, England: Oxford University Press.

Rohrer, D., & Pashler, H. (2010). Recent research on human learning challenges conventional instructional strategies. *Educational Researcher, 39*, 406–412.

Roid, G. (2003). *Stanford-Binet Intelligence Scales, Fifth Edition*. Itasca, IL: Riverside.

Rollins, J. A. (2012). Revisiting the issue of corporal punishment in our nation's schools. *Pediatric Nursing, 38*, 248, 269.

Romano, A. (2011, March 28). How dumb are we? *Newsweek*, 56–60.

Romboy, D., & Kinkead, L. (2005, April 14). Surviving in America. *Deseret Morning News, 155*(303), pp. 1, 11, 12.

Roorda, D., Koomen, H., Spilt, J., & Oort, F. (2011). The influence of affective teacher–student relationships on students' school engagement and achievement: A meta-analytic approach. *Review of Educational Research, 81*, 493–529.

Rosen, L. D. (2012). *iDisorder: Understanding our obsession with technology and overcoming its hold on us*. New York: Palgrave/Macmillan.

Rosen, L. D., Whaling, K., Rab, S., Carrier, L. M., & Cheever, N. A. (2013). Is Facebook creating "iDisorders"? The link between clinical symptoms of psychiatric disorders and technology use, attitudes and anxiety. *Computers in Human Behavior, 29*, 1243–1254.

Rosenberg, M., Westling, D., & McLeskey, J. (2011). *Special education for today's teachers: An introduction* (2nd ed.). Upper Saddle River, NJ: Merrill/Pearson.

Rosenberg, T. (2013). Turning education upside down. *The New York Times*. Retrieved from http://opinionator.blogs.nytimes.com/2013/10/09/turning-education-upside-down/?_r=0

Rosenshine, B. (1987). Explicit teaching. In D. Berliner & B. Rosenshine (Eds.), *Talks to teachers*. New York: Random House.

Roseth, C. J., Johnson, D. W., Johnson, R. T., Fang, F., Hilk, C. L., & Fleming, M. A. (2007, April). *Effects of cooperative learning on elementary school students' achievement: A meta-analysis*. Paper presented at the annual meeting of the American Educational Research Association, Chicago.

Roseth, C., Akcaoglu, M., & Zellner, A. (2013). Blending synchronous face-to-face and computer-supported cooperative learning in a hybrid doctoral seminar. *TechTrends: Linking Research and Practice to Improve Learning, 57*, 54–59.

Roth, W., & Lee, Y. (2007). "Vygotsky's neglected legacy:" Cultural-historical activity theory. *Review of Educational Research, 77*(2), 186–232.

Rothbart, M. K. (2011). *Becoming who we are: Temperament and personality in development*. New York: Guilford.

Rowe, M. (1974). Wait-time and rewards as instructional variables, their influence on language, logic, and fate control: Part I. Wait-time. *Journal of Research in Science Teaching, 11*, 81–94.

Rowe, M. (1986). Wait-time: Slowing down may be a way of speeding up. *Journal of Teacher Education, 37*(1), 43–50.

Rubin, K., Cheah, C., & Menzer, M. (2010). Peers. In M. Bornstein (Ed.), *Handbook of cultural developmental science* (pp. 223–237). New York: Psychology Press.

Rubin, K., Coplan, R., Chen, X., Bowker, J., & McDonald, K. (2011). Peer relationships in childhood. In M. Bornstein & M. Lamb (Eds.), *Developmental science: An advanced textbook* (6th ed., pp. 519–570). New York: Psychology Press.

Rubinson, F. (2004). Urban dropouts: Why so many and what can be done? In S. R. Steinberg & J. L. Kincheloe (Eds.), *19 urban questions: Teaching in the city* (pp. 53–67). New York: Peter Lang.

Rudasill, K., Gallagher, K., & White, J. (2010). Temperamental attention and activity, classroom emotional support, and academic achievement in third grade. *Journal of School Psychology, 48*(2), 113–134.

Rudolph, K. D., Caldwell, M. S., & Conley, C. S. (2005). Need for approval and children's well-being. *Child Development, 72*, 309–323.

Rumberger, R. (2011). *Dropping out: Why students drop out of high school*. Boston: Harvard University Press.

Ruscheweyh, R., Willemer, C., Krüger, K., Duning, T., Warnecke, T., Sommer, J., . . . Flöel, A. (2009). Physical activity and memory functions: An interventional study. *Neurobiology of Aging, 32*, 1304–1319.

Russell, S., Ryan, C., Toomey, R., Diaz, R., & Sanchez, J. (2011). Lesbian, gay, bisexual, and transgender adolescent school victimization: Implications for young adult health and adjustment. *Journal of School Health, 81*(5), 223–230.

Rutter, M. (2011). Biological and experiential influences on psychological development. In D. Keating (Ed.), *Nature and nurture in early child development* (pp. 7–44). New York: Cambridge University Press.

Rutter, M., Maughan, B., Mortimore, P., Ouston, J., & Smith, A. (1979). *Fifteen thousand hours. Secondary schools and their effects on children*. Cambridge, MA: Harvard University Press.

Ryan, J. B., Katsiyannis, A., & Peterson, R. (2007). IDEA 2004 and disciplining students with disabilities. *NASSP Bulletin, 91*, 130–140.

Ryan, J. B., Peterson, R. L., & Rozalski, M. (2007). State policies concerning the use of seclusion timeout in schools. *Education and Treatment of Children, 30*, 215–239.

Ryan, J. B., Sanders, S., Katsiyannis, A., & Yell, M. L. (2007). Using time-out effectively in the classroom. *Teaching Exceptional Children, 39*, 60–67.

Ryan, K. E., & Ryan, A. M. (2005). Psychological processes of stereotype threat and standardized math test performance. *Educational Psychologist, 40*(1), 53–63.

Ryan, K. E., Ryan, A. M., Arbuthnot, K., & Samuels, M. (2007). Students' motivation for standardized math exams. *Educational Researcher, 36*(1), 5–13.

Ryan, R., & Deci, E. (1996). When paradigms clash: Comments on Cameron and Pierce's claim that rewards do not undermine intrinsic motivation. *Review of Educational Research, 66*, 33–38.

Ryan, R., & Deci, E. (2000). Intrinsic and extrinsic motivations: Classic definitions and new directions. *Contemporary Educational Psychology, 25*, 54–67.

Rye, J., Landenberger, R., & Warner, T. A. (2013). Incorporating concept mapping in project-based learning: Lessons from watershed investigations. *Journal of Science Education and Technology, 22*, 379–392. doi:10.1007/s10956-012-9400-1

Sack-Min, J. (2007). The issues of IDEA. *American School Board Journal, 194*(3), 20–25.

Sadler, P. M., Sonnert, G., Coyle, H. P., Cook-Smith, N., & Miller, J. I. (2013). The influence of teachers' knowledge on student learning in middle school physical science classrooms. *American Educational Research Journal, 50*, 1020–1049.

Sadoski, M., & Paivio, A. (2001). *Imagery and text: A dual coding theory of reading and writing*. Mahwah, NJ: Erlbaum.

Safer, N., & Fleischman, S. (2005). How student progress monitoring improves instruction. *Educational Leadership, 62*(5), 81–83.

Sailor, W., & Roger, B. (2005). Rethinking inclusion: Schoolwide applications. *Phi Delta Kappan, 86*(7), 503–509.

Sakr, S. (2013). Charlie Rose interviews 'Bill Gates 2.0' on 60 Minutes: The man after Microsoft. *60 Minutes*. Retrieved from http://www.engadget.com/2013/05/13/bill-gates-60-minutes/?utm_medium=feed&utm_source=Feed_Classic&utm_campaign=Engadget

Saksvik, I., & Hetland, H. (2011). The role of personality in stress perception across different vocational types. *Journal of Employment Counseling, 48,* 3–16.

Saleh, M., Lazonder, A. W., & de Jong, T. (2007). Structuring collaboration in mixed-ability groups to promote verbal interaction, learning, and motivation of average-ability students. *Contemporary Educational Psychology, 32,* 314–331.

Salvia, J., Ysseldyke, J., & Bolt, S. (2013). *Assessment in special and inclusive education* (12th ed.). Boston: Cengage.

Sams, A., & Bergmann, J. (2013). Flip your students' learning. *Educational Leadership, 70,* 16–20.

Samuels, C. (2009). 'What works' guide gives RTI thumbs up on reading. *Education Week, 28*(23), 7.

Samuels, C. (2013). Test rules differ between groups of special ed. *Education Week, 32*(27), 1, 16, 17.

Sanders, W. (2010). Walking alongside children as they form compassion. *Exchange, 32*(3), 50–53.

Sanders, W. L., & Rivers, J. C. (1996). *Cumulative and residual effects of teachers on student academic achievement.* Knoxville, TN: University of Tennessee Value-Added Research and Assessment Center.

Santelices, M., & Wilson, M. (2010). Unfair treatment? The case of Freedle, the SAT, and the standardization approach to differential item functioning. *Harvard Educational Review, 80*(1), 106–133.

Sapon-Shevin, M. (2007). *Widening the circle: The power of inclusive classrooms.* Boston: Beacon Press.

Sarama, J., & Clements, D. (2009). "Concrete" computer manipulatives in mathematics education. *Child Development Perspectives, 3,* 145–150.

Satel, S., & Lilienfeld, S. (2013). *Brainwashed: The seductive appeal of mindless neuroscience.* New York: Basic Books.

Saulny, S. (2011). Black? White? Asian? More young Americans choose all of the above. *New York Times, January 29.* Retrieved from http://www.nytimes.com/2011/01/30/us/30mixed.html

Savolainen, R. (2013). Approaching the motivators for information seeking: The viewpoint of attribution theories. *Library & Information Science Research, 35,* 63–68.

Sawchuk, S. (2010). Merit-pay model pushed by Duncan shows no achievement edge. *Education Week, 29*(33), 1, 21.

Sawchuk, S. (2012). Access to teacher evaluations divides advocates. *Education Week, 31*(26), 1, 18.

Sawyer, M., Pfeiffer, S., Spence, S., Bond, L., Graetz, B., Kay, D. , . . . Sheffield, J. (2010). School-based prevention of depression: A randomized controlled study of the *beyondblue* schools research initiative. *Journal of Child Psychology and Psychiatry, 51*(2), 100–209.

Sawyer, R. K. (2006). Introduction: The new science of learning. In R. K. Sawyer (Ed.), *The Cambridge handbook of the learning sciences* (pp. 1–18). New York: Cambridge University Press.

Schachter, R. (2012). Neuroscience in schools. Improving learning capacity for young students. *District Administration, 48,* 40–45.

Schacter, D. (2001). *The seven deadly sins of memory.* Boston: Houghton Mifflin.

Schacter, D., Gilbert, D., & Wegner, D. (2011). *Psychology* (2nd ed.). New York: Worth.

Schaffer, M., Clark, S., & Jeglic, E. L. (2009). The role of empathy and parenting style in the development of antisocial behaviors. *Crime & Delinquency, 55,* 586–599.

Schellenberg, S., & Eggen, P. (2008, March). *Educational psychology students' awareness of moral issues in classroom instruction: A developmental analysis.* Paper presented at the annual meeting of the American Educational Research Association, New York.

Schenker, L. (2013). Goodbye, No. 2 pencils. *Salt Lake Tribune,* April 28, B1.

Scherwitz, I., McKelvain, R., Laman, C., Patterson, J., Dutton, L., Yusim, S. , . . . Leachman, R. (1983). Type A behavior, self-involvement, and coronary atherosclerosis. *Psychosomatic Medicine, 45,* 47–57.

Schimmel, D., Stellman, L., & Fischer, L. (2011). *Teachers and the law* (8th ed.). New York: Longman.

Schimmel, D., Stellman, L., Conlon, C., & Fischer, L. (2015). *Teachers and the law* (9th ed.). New York: Longman.

Schlinger, H. D. (2008). The long good-bye: Why B. F. Skinner's verbal behavior is alive and well on the 50th anniversary of its publication. *The Psychological Record, 58,* 329–337.

Schlinger, H. D., & Normand, M. P. (2013). On the origin and functions of the term functional analysis. *Journal of Applied Behavior Analysis, 46,* 285–288.

Schneider, W. (2010). Metacognition and memory development in childhood and adolescence. In H. Waters & W. Schneider (Eds.), *Metacognition, strategy use, and instruction* (pp. 54–81). New York: Guilford.

Schneider, W., & Lockl, K. (2002). The development of metacognitive knowledge in children and adolescents. In T. J. Perfect & B. L. Schwartz (Eds.), *Applied metacognition* (pp. 224–257). Cambridge, UK: Cambridge University Press.

Schoenfeld, A. (1991). On mathematics as sense making: An informal attack on the unfortunate divorce of formal and informal mathematics. In J. Voss, D. Perkins, & J. Segal (Eds.), *Informal reasoning and education* (pp. 311–343). Hillsdale, NJ: Erlbaum.

Schoenfeld, A. H. (2006). Mathematics teaching and learning. In P. A. Alexander & P. H. Winne (Eds.), *Handbook of educational psychology* (2nd ed., pp. 479–510). Mahwah, NJ: Erlbaum.

Schoof, R. (2013). Common core stirs furor: What's at issue. *McClatchy Washington Bureau.* Retrieved from http://www.sacbee.com/2013/06/10/5484382/common-core-stirs-furor-whats.html

Schraw, G. (2006). Knowledge structures and processes. In P. A. Alexander & P. H. Winne (Eds.), *Handbook of educational psychology* (2nd ed., pp. 245–263). Mahwah, NJ: Erlbaum.

Schraw, G., & Lehman, S. (2001). Situational interest: A review of the literature and directions for future research. *Educational Psychology Review, 13*(1), 23–52.

Schraw, G., Dunkle, M. E., & Bendixen, L. D. (2006). Cognitive processes in well-defined and ill-defined problem solving. *Applied Cognitive Psychology, 9,* 523–538. doi:10.1002/acp.2350090605

Schraw, G., Flowerday, T., & Lehman, S. (2001). Increasing situational interest in the classroom. *Educational Psychology Review, 13*(3), 211–224.

Schunk, D. (2005). Self-regulated learning: The educational legacy of Paul R. Pintrich. *Educational Psychologist, 40*(2), 85–94.

Schunk, D. (2012). *Learning theories: An educational perspective* (6th ed.). Boston: Pearson.

Schunk, D. H., & Ertmer, P. A. (2000). Self-regulation and academic learning: Self-efficacy enhancing interventions. In M. Boekaerts, P. R. Pintrich, & M. Zeidner (Eds.), *Handbook of self-regulation* (pp. 631–649). San Diego: Academic Press.

Schunk, D. H., & Pajares, F. (2004). Self-efficacy in education revisited: Empirical and applied evidence. In D. M. McInerney & S. Van Etten (Eds.), *Sociocultural influences on motivation and learning: Vol. 4. Big theories revisited* (pp. 115–138). Greenwich, CT: Information Age.

Schunk, D. H., & Zimmerman, B. J. (2006). Competence and control beliefs: Distinguishing the means and the ends. In P. A. Alexander & P. H. Winne (Eds.), *Handbook of educational psychology* (2nd ed., pp. 349–367). Mahwah, NJ: Erlbaum.

Schunk, D. H., Meece, J. L., & Pintrich, P. R. (2014). *Motivation in education: Theory, research, and applications* (4th ed.). Boston: Pearson.

Schutz, A. (2004, April). *Home is a prison in the global city: A critical review of urban school–community relationships.* Paper presented at the annual meeting of the American Educational Research Association, San Diego.

Schwartz, D., & Heiser, J. (2006). Spatial representations and imagery in learning. In R. K. Sawyer (Ed.), *The Cambridge handbook of the learning sciences* (pp. 283–298). New York: Cambridge University Press.

Schwartz, D., Bransford, J., & Sears, D. (2005). Efficiency and innovation in transfer. In J. Mestre (Ed.), *Transfer of learning from a modern multidisciplinary perspective* (pp. 1–51). Greenwich, CT: Information Age Publishing.

Schwartz, M. (2010). The usage of Facebook as it relates to narcissism, self-esteem and loneliness. *ETD Collection for Pace University.* Paper AAI3415681. Retrieved from http://digitalcommons.pace.edu/dissertations/AAI3415681

Schwarz, A., & Cohen, S. (2013, April 1). More diagnoses of hyperactivity causing concern. *New York Times,* pp. A1, A11.

Schwerdt, G., & West, M. R. (2011). The impact of alternative grade configurations on student outcomes through middle and high school. *Harvard University Program on Education Policy and Governance Working Papers Series.* Retrieved from http://www.hks.harvard.edu/pepg/PDF/Papers/PEPG11-02_Schwerdt_West.pdf

ScienceDaily. (2009). *American adults flunk basic science.* Retrieved from http://www.sciencedaily.com/releases/2009/03/090312115133.htm

Scott, C. L., Harris, R. J., & Rothe, A. R. (2001). Embodied cognition through improvisation improves memory for a dramatic monologue. *Discourse Processes, 31,* 293–305.

Scott, T. M., Alter, P. J., Rosenberg, M., & Borgmeier, C. (2010). Decision-making in secondary and tertiary interventions of school-wide systems of positive behavior support. *Education and Treatment of Children, 33,* 513–535.

Scott, T. M., Gagnon, J. C., & Nelson, C. M. (2008). School-wide systems of positive behavior support: A framework for reducing school crime and violence. *Journal of Behavior Analysis of Offender and Victim: Treatment and Prevention, 1,* 259–272.

Seaton, M., Marsh, H., & Craven, R. (2010). Big-fish-little-pond effect: Generalizability and moderation—Two sides of the same coin. *American Educational Research Journal, 47,* 390–433.

Sedikides, C., & Gregg, A. P. (2008). Self-enhancement: Food for thought. *Perspectives on Psychological Science, 3,* 102–116.

Segall, A. (2004). Revisiting pedagogical content knowledge: The pedagogy of content/the content of pedagogy. *Teaching and Teacher Education, 20,* 489–504.

Seo, K. K-J. (Ed.). (2013). *Using social media effectively in the classroom: Blogs, Wikis, Twitter, and more.* New York: Routledge.

Serafino, K., & Cicchelli, T. (2003). Cognitive theories, prior knowledge, and anchored instruction on mathematical problem solving and transfer. *Education and Urban Society, 36*(1), 79–93.

Seung, S. (2012). *Connectome.* Boston: Houghton Mifflin.

Shah, N. (2011). Childhood hunger. *Education Week, 30*(22), 5.

Shah, N. (2013). Progress, persistence seen in latest data on bullying. *Education Week, 32*(35), 14.

Sharan, Y. (2010). Cooperative learning for academic and social gains: Valued pedagogy, problematic practice. *European Journal of Education, 45,* 300–313.

Shaywitz, S. E., & Shaywitz, B. A. (2004). Reading disability and the brain. *Educational Leadership, 61*(6), 7–11.

Sheldon, S. (2007). Improving student attendance with school, family, and community partnerships. *Journal of Educational Research, 199,* 267–275.

Shelton, J. T., Elliott, E. M., Matthews, R. A., Hill, B. D., & Gouvier, W. D. (2010). The relationships of working memory, secondary memory, and general fluid intelligence: Working memory is special. *Journal of Experimental Psychology. Learning, Memory and Cognition, 36,* 813–820.

Shen, C-Y., & Tsai, H-C. (2009). Design principles of worked examples: A review of the empirical studies. *Journal of Instructional Psychology, 36,* 238–244.

Sheppard, A. B., Gross, S. C., Pavelka, S. A., Hall, M. J., & Palmatier, M. I. (2012). Caffeine increases the motivation to obtain non-drug reinforcers in rats. *Drug and Alcohol Dependence, 124,* 216–222.

Sherer, Y. C., & Nickerson, A. B. (2010). Anti-bullying practices in American schools: Perspectives of school psychologists. *Psychology in the Schools, 47,* 217–229.

Sheridan, C., Matuz, T., Draganova, R., Eswaran, H., & Preissl, H. (2010). Fetal magnetoencephalography—achievements and challenges in the study of prenatal and early postnatal brain responses: A review. *Infant and Child Development, 19,* 80–93.

Shiner, R. L., Buss, K. A., McClowry, S. G., Putnam, S. P., Saudino, K. J., & Zentner, M. (2012). What is temperament now? Assessing progress in temperament research on the twenty-fifth anniversary of Goldsmith et al. (1987). *Child Development Perspectives, 6,* 436–444.

Shipstead, Z., & Engle, R. W. (2013). Interference within the focus of attention: Working memory tasks reflect more than temporary maintenance. *Journal of Experimental Psychology: Learning, Memory, and Cognition, 39,* 277–289.

Shirin, A. (2007). *Can deaf and hard of hearing students be successful in general education classes?* Retrieved from http://www.tcrecord.org/Content.asp?ContentID=13461

Shuell, T. (1996). Teaching and learning in a classroom context. In D. Berliner & R. Calfee (Eds.), *Handbook of educational psychology* (pp. 726–764). New York: Macmillan.

Shulman, L. (1986). Those who understand: Knowledge growth in teaching. *Educational Researcher, 15,* 4–14.

Shulman, L. (1987). Knowledge and teaching: Foundations of the new reform. *Harvard Educational Review, 57,* 1–22.

Shulman, R. G. (2013). *Brain imaging: What it can (and cannot) tell us about consciousness.* New York: Oxford University Press.

Shute, V. J. (2008). Focus on formative feedback. *Review of Educational Research, 78,* 153–189.

Siegel, D. (2012). *The developing mind: How relationships and the brain interact to shape who we are* (2nd ed.). New York: Guilford.

Siegler, R. (1992). The other Alfred Binet. *Developmental Psychologist, 28,* 179–190.

Siegler, R. (2000). The rebirth of children's learning. *Child Development, 71,* 26–35.

Siegler, R. (2006). Microgenetic analyses of learning. In D. Kuhn & R. Siegler (Vol. Eds.), *Handbook of child psychology: Vol. 2. Cognition, perception, and language* (6th ed., pp. 464–510). Hoboken, NJ: Wiley.

Siegler, R. (2012). From theory to application and back: Following in the giant footsteps of David Klahr. In J. Shrager & S. Carver (Eds.), *The journey from child to scientist: Integrating cognitive development and the education sciences.* Washington, DC: American Psychological Association.

Siegler, R., & Alibali, M. (2005). *Children's thinking* (4th ed.). Upper Saddle River, NJ: Prentice Hall.

Siegler, R., & Lin, X. (2010). Self-explanations promote children's learning. In H. Waters & W. Schneider (Eds.), *Metacognition, strategy use, and instruction* (pp. 85–112). New York: Guilford Press.

Silvia, P. J., & Sanders, C. E. (2010). Why are smart people curious? Fluid intelligence, openness to experience, and interest. *Learning and Individual Differences, 20,* 242–245.

Silvia, P. J., Wigert, B. R., Reiter-Palmon, R., & Kaufman, J. C. (2012). Assessing creativity with self-report scales: A review and empirical evaluation. *Psychology of Aesthetics, Creativity, and the Arts, 6,* 19–34.

Simons, L. G., Simons, R. L., & Su, X. L. (2013). Consequences of corporal punishment among African Americans: The importance of context and outcome. *Journal of Youth and Adolescence, 42,* 1273–1285.

Simons, R., & Burt, C. (2011). Learning to be bad: Adverse social conditions, social schemas, and crime. *Criminology, 49,* 553–597.

Sinatra, G. M., & Pintrich, P. R. (2003). The role of intentions in conceptual change learning. In G. M. Sinatra & P. R. Pintrich (Eds.), *Intentional conceptual change* (pp. 1–18). Mahwah, NJ: Erlbaum.

Sisson, S., Broyles, S., Newton, R., Jr., Baker, B., & Chernausek, S. (2011). TVs in the bedrooms of children: Does it impact health and behavior? *Preventive Medicine, 52,* 104–108.

Skatova, A., & Ferguson, E. (2013). Individual differences in behavioural inhibition explain free riding in public good games when punishment is expected but not implemented. *Behavioral and Brain Functions, 9,* 1–11. Retrieved from http://www.behavioralandbrainfunctions.com/content/9/1/3

Skiba, R. J., Horner, R. H., Chung, C., Rausch, M. K., May, S. L., & Tobin, T. (2011). Race is not neutral: A national investigation of African American and Latino disproportionality in school discipline. *School Psychology Review, 40,* 85–107.

Skinner, B. F. (1953). *Science and human behavior.* New York: Macmillan.

Skinner, B. F. (1954). The science of learning and the art of teaching. *Harvard Educational Review, 24,* 86–97.

Skinner, B. F. (1957). *Verbal behavior.* Upper Saddle River, NJ: Prentice Hall.

Slavin, R. E. (2011). Instruction based on cooperative learning. In R. E. Mayer & P. A. Alexander (Eds.), *Handbook of research on learning and instruction* (pp. 344–360). New York: Routledge.

Small, G., & Vorgan, G. (2008). *iBrain: Surviving the technological alteration of the modern mind.* New York: William Morrow.

Smart, J. B., & Marshall, J. C. (2013). Interactions between classroom discourse, teacher questioning, and student cognitive engagement in middle school science. *Journal of Science Teacher Education, 24,* 249–267. doi:10.1007/s10972-012-9297-9

Smart, K. L., Hicks, N., & Melton, J. (2013). Using problem-based scenarios to teach writing. *Business Communication Quarterly, 76,* 72–81. doi:10.1177/1080569912466256

Smart, K. L., Witt, C., & Scott, J. P. (2012). Toward learner-centered teaching: An inductive approach. *Business Communication Quarterly, 75,* 392–403.

Smetana, J. G., & Gettman, D. C. (2006). Autonomy and relatedness with parents and romantic development in African American adolescents. *Developmental Psychology, 42,* 1347–1351.

Smiley, D. (2014). School grades to stay, Florida education chief says. *The Miami Herald.* Retrieved from http://www.miamiherald.com/2014/01/21/3884176/florida-education-commissioner.html

Smith, A., & Bondy, E. (2007). "No! I won't!" Understanding and responding to defiance. *Childhood Education, 83,* 151–157.

Smith, F. (2005). Intensive care. *Edutopia, 1*(9), 47–49.

Smith, P., & Slonje, R. (2010). Cyberbullying: The nature and extent of a new kind of bullying, in and out of school. In S. Jimerson, S. Swearer, & D. Espelage (Eds.), *Handbook of bullying in schools: An international perspective* (pp. 249–262). New York: Routledge/Taylor & Francis Group.

Smith, S. M., Glenberg, A., & Bjork, R. A. (1978). Environmental context and human memory. *Memory & Cognition, 6,* 342–353.

Smith, T., Polloway, E., Patton, J., & Dowdy, C. (2012). *Teaching students with special needs in inclusive settings* (6th ed.). Boston: Pearson.

Snow, C., Griffin, P., & Burns, M. S. (2005). *Knowledge to support the teaching of reading: Preparing teachers for a changing world.* San Francisco: Jossey-Bass.

Social Security Administration. (2014). *National average wage index.* Retrieved from http://www.ssa.gov/oact/cola/AWI.html

Soley, G., & Hannon, E. (2010). Infants prefer the musical meter of their own culture: A cross-cultural comparison. *Development Psychology, 46,* 286–292.

Solley, B. A. (2007). On standardized testing. *Childhood Education, 84,* 31–37.

Sommers, C. (2008). *The case against Title-Nining the sciences.* Retrieved from http://www.tcrecord.org

Song, J., & Felch, J. (2009). Judging teachers: Much of what you thought you knew is wrong. *Los Angeles Times.* Retrieved from http://latimesblogs.latimes.com/lanow/2009/10/challenging-classroom-myths.html

Song, K-S., Nam, S. C., Lim, H. K., & Kim, J. K. (2013). Analysis of youngsters' media multitasking behaviors and effect on learning. *International Journal of Multimedia & Ubiquitous Engineering, 8,* 191–198.

Sorhagen, N. S. (2013). Early teacher expectations disproportionately affect poor children's high school performance. *Journal of Educational Psychology, 105,* 465–477.

Sosa, T., & Gomez, K. (2012). Connecting teacher efficacy beliefs in promoting resilience to support of Latino students. *Urban Education, 47,* 876–909.

Southerland, S. A., & Sinatra, G. M. (2003). Learning about biological evolution: A special case of intentional conceptual change. In G. M. Sinatra & P. R. Pintrich (Eds.), *Intentional conceptual change* (pp. 317–345). Mahwah, NJ: Erlbaum.

Southern Education Foundation. (2013). *A new majority: Low income students in the south and nation.* Retrieved from http://www.southerneducation.org/getattachment/0bc70ce1-d375-4ff6-8340-f9b3452ee088/A-New-Majority-Low-Income-Students-in-the-South-an.aspx

Sparks, S. (2012). New NAEP demands application of knowledge. *Education Week, 32*(26), 18.

Sparks, S. (2013). Next stage for testing envisioned. *Education Week, 32*(24), 1, 17.

Sparks, S. D. (2011). Lectures are homework in schools following Khan Academy lead. *Education Week.* Retrieved from http://www.edweek.org/ew/articles/2011/09/28/05khan_ep.h31.html

Spearman, C. (1904). General intelligence, objectively determine and measured. *American Journal of Psychology, 15,* 201–293.

Spearman, C. (1927). *The abilities of man: Their nature and measurement.* New York: Macmillan.

Spera, C. (2005). A review of the relationship among parent practices, parenting styles, and adolescent school achievement. *Educational Psychology Review, 17,* 125–146.

Spicer, P., LaFramboise, T., Markstrom, C., Niles, M., West, M., Fehringer, K., . . . Sarche, M. (2012). Toward an applied developmental science for native children, families, and communities. *Child Development Perspectives, 6,* 49–54.

Spies, R. A., Carlson, J. F., & Geisinger, K. F. (Eds.). (2010). *The eighteenth mental measurements yearbook.* Lincoln, NE: Buros Institute of Mental Measurements.

Spinrad, T., & Eisenberg, N. (2009). Empathy, prosocial behavior, and positive development in schools. In R. Gilman, E. Huebner, & M. Furlong (Eds.), *Handbook of positive psychology in schools* (pp. 119–129). New York: Routledge.

Sprenger, M. (2010). *Brain-based teaching in the digital age.* Alexandria, VA: Association for Supervision and Curriculum Development.

Springer, K. (2010). *Educational research: A contextual approach.* Hoboken, NJ: John Wiley and Sons.

Standage, M., Treasure, D. C., Hooper, K., & Kuczka, K. (2007). Self-handicapping in school physical education: The influence of the motivational climate. *The British Journal of Educational Psychology, 77,* 81–99.

Standen, A. (2007) Gender matters: Educators battle over single-sex schools. *Edutopia, 3*(1), 46–49.

Stanford, J. (2013). High-stakes testing makes cheating inevitable. *Huff Post Politics.* Retrieved from http://www.huffingtonpost.com/jason-stanford/standardized-test-cheating_b_2993239.html

Staples, M. (2007). Supporting whole-class collaborative inquiry in a secondary mathematics classroom. *Cognition and Instruction, 25,* 161–217.

Star, J. (2004, April). *The development of flexible procedural knowledge in equation solving.* Paper presented at the annual meeting of the American Educational Research Association, San Diego.

Steinberg, L. (1996). *Beyond the classroom: Why school reform has failed and what parents need to do.* New York: Touchstone.

Steinberg, L. (2009). Should the science of adolescent brain development inform public policy? *American Psychologist, 64,* 739–750.

Steinmetz, K., & Kensinger, E. (2013). The emotion-induced memory trade-off: More than an effect of overt attention? *Memory & Cognition, 41,* 69–81.

Sternberg, R. (1998a). Applying the triarchic theory of human intelligence in the classroom. In R. Sternberg & W. Williams (Eds.), *Intelligence, instruction, and assessment* (pp. 1–16). Mahwah, NJ: Erlbaum.

Sternberg, R. (1998b). Metacognition, abilities, and developing expertise: What makes an expert student? *Instructional Science, 26*(1–2), 127–140.

Sternberg, R. (2003a). *Cognitive psychology* (3rd ed.). Belmont, CA: Wadsworth.

Sternberg, R. (2003b). *Wisdom, intelligence, and creativity synthesized.* Cambridge: Cambridge University Press.

Sternberg, R. (2004). Culture and intelligence. *American Psychologist, 59,* 325–338.

Sternberg, R. (2006). Recognizing neglected strengths. *Educational Leadership, 64*(1), 30–35.

Sternberg, R. (2007). Who are bright children? The cultural context of being and acting intelligent. *Educational Researcher, 36*(3), 148–155.

Sternberg, R. (2009). Foreword. In S. Tobias & T. Duffy (Eds.), *Constructivist instruction: Success or failure* (pp. x–xi). New York: Routledge.

Sternberg, R., & Grigorenko, E. (2001). Learning disabilities, schooling, and society. *Phi Delta Kappan, 83*(4), 335–338.

Sterponi, L. (2010). Learning communicative competence. In D. Lancy, J. Bock, & S. Gaskins (Eds.), *The anthropology of learning in childhood* (pp. 235–259). Lanham, ND: AltaMira Press/Rowman & Littlefield.

Sterzing, P., Shattuck, P., Narendorf, S., Wagner, M., & Cooper, B. (2012). Bullying involvement and autism spectrum disorders: Prevalence and correlates of bullying involvement among adolescents with an autism spectrum disorder. *JAMA Pediatrics (formerly Archives of Pediatric & Adolescent Medicine,* Retrieved from http://archpedi.jamanetwork.com/article.aspx?articleid=1355390

Stevenson, M. (2013). Andrea Benitez, Mexican official's daughter, causes restaurant to close, creating scandal. *The Huffington Post.* Retrieved from http://www.huffingtonpost.

com/2013/04/30/andrea-benitez-mexican-restaurant-closing_n_3184634.html

Stewart, K., May, H., & Whitehurst, L. (2013, January 16). U. researchers find 24 new genetic markers for autism. *Salt Lake Tribune,* pp. A1, A4.

Stinson, D. (2006). African American male adolescents, schooling, (and mathematics): Deficiency, rejection, and achievement. *Review of Educational Research, 76,* 477–506.

Stipek, D. (2002). *Motivation to learn* (4th ed.). Boston: Allyn & Bacon.

Strauss, V. (2013). Common core standards attacked by Republicans. *Washington Post.* Retrieved from http://www.washingtonpost.com/blogs/answer-sheet/wp/2013/04/19/common-core-standards-attacked-by-republicans/

Stross, R. (2010, July 21). Computers at home: Educational hope vs. teenage reality. *New York Times.* Retrieved from http://www.nytimes.com/2010/07/11/business/11digi.html

Stuebing, K., Fletcher, J., LeDoux, J., Lyon, G., Shaywitz, S., & Shaywitz, B. (2002). Validity of IQ-discrepancy classifications of reading disabilities: A meta-analysis. *American Educational Research Journal, 39*(2), 469–518.

Su, A. Y-L. (2007). The impact of individual ability, favorable team member scores, and student perception of course importance on student preference of team-based learning and grading methods. *Adolescence, 42,* 805–826.

Suarez-Orozco, C., Pimentel, A., & Martin, M. (2009). The significance of relationships: Academic engagement and achievement among newcomer immigrant youth. *Teachers College Record Volume, 111,* 712–749. Retrieved from http://www.tcrecord.org/Content.asp?ContentID=15342

Subotnik, R., Olszewski-Kubilius, P., & Worrel, R. (2011). Rethinking giftedness and gifted education: A proposed direction forward based on psychological science. *Psychological Science in the Public Interest, 12,* 3–54.

Sullivan, A., Joshi, H., & Leonard, D. (2010). Single-sex schooling and academic attainment at school and through the lifecourse. *American Educational Research Journal, 47*(1), 6–36.

Summers, A. (2011). *Facebook addiction disorder— The 6 symptoms of F.A.D.* Social Times. Retrieved from http://socialtimes.com/facebook-addiction-disorder-the-6-symptoms-of-f-a-d_b60403

Sungur, S., & Tekkaya, C. (2006). Effects of problem-based learning and traditional instruction on self-regulated learning. *Journal of Educational Research, 99*(5), 307–318.

Sunshine State Standards. (2012). *Benchmark #:SC.8.N.1.2.* Retrieved from http://www.cpalms.org/Standards/PublicPreviewBenchmark1817.aspx

SupermarketPage.com. (2010). Supermarket secrets. Retrieved from http://supermarketpage.com/secrets.php

Swanson, C. (2011). Nation turns a corner. *Education Week, 39*(34), 23–25.

Swearer, S., Espelage, D., Vaillancourt, T., & Hymel, S. (2010). What can be done about school bullying: Linking research to educational practice. *Educational Researcher, 39,* 38–47.

Sweller, J. (2003). Evolution of human cognitive architecture. *The Psychology of Learning and Motivation, 43,* 215–266.

Sweller, J., van Merrienboer, J., & Paas, F. (1998). Cognitive architecture and instructional design. *Educational Psychology Review, 10,* 251–296.

Szaflarski, J., Rajagopal, A., Altaye, M., Byars, A., Jacola, L., Schmithorst, V., . . . Holland, S. (2012). Left-handedness and language lateralization in children. *Brain Research.* Retrieved from http://www.ncbi.nlm.nih.gov/pubmed/22177775

Tam, D. (2013). Facebook by the numbers: 1.06 billion monthly active users. *CNET.* Retrieved from http://news.cnet.com/8301-1023_3-57566550-93/facebook-by-the-numbers-1.06-billion-monthly-active-users/

Tamim, R. M., Bernard, R. M., Borokhovski, E., Abrami, P. C., & Schmid, R. F. (2011). What forty years of research says about the impact of technology on learning: A second-order meta-analysis and validation study. *Review of Educational Research, 81,* 4–28.

Tan, X., & Michel, R. (2011). Why do standardized testing programs report scaled scores? *Educational Testing Service.* Retrieved from http://www.ets.org/Media/Research/pdf/RD_Connections16.pdf

Tanel, R. (2013). Prospective physics teachers' self-efficacy beliefs about teaching and conceptual understandings for the subjects of force and motion. *Journal of Baltic Science Education, 12,* 6–20.

Tang, Y., Zhang, W., Chen, K., Feng, S., Ji, Y., Shen, J., Reiman, E., & Liu, Y. (2006). Arithmetic processing in the brain shaped by culture. *Proceedings of the National Academy of Sciences USA, 103,* 10775–10780.

Tannenbaum, A. (2003). Nature and nurture of giftedness. In N. Colangelo & G. Davis (Eds.), *Handbook of gifted education* (3rd ed., pp. 45–59). Boston: Allyn & Bacon.

Tanner, D., & Tanner, L. (2007). *Curriculum development: Theory into practice* (4th ed.). Upper Saddle River, NJ: Prentice Hall.

Tanno, T., Silberberg, A., & Sakagami, T. (2012). Discrimination of variable schedules is controlled by interresponse times proximal to reinforcement. *Journal of the Experimental Analysis of Behavior, 98,* 341–354.

Taraban, R., Anderson, E. E., DeFinis, A., Brown, A. G., Weigold, A., & Sharma, M. P. (2007). First steps in understanding engineering students' growth of conceptual and procedural knowledge in an interactive learning context. *Journal of Engineering Education, 96,* 57–68.

Tavernise, S. (2011, February 5). In census, young Americans increasingly diverse. *New York Times.* Retrieved from http://www.nytimes.com/2011/02/05/us/05census.html

Taylor, K., & Rohrer, D. (2010). The effects of interleaved practice. *Applied Cognitive Psychology, 24,* 837–848.

Teendriversource. (2014). *Basic facts about teen crashes.* Retrieved from http://www.teendriversource.org/stats/teen/detail/107

Tenenbaum, H., & Ruck, M. (2007). Are teachers' expectations different for racial minority than for European American students? A meta-analysis. *Journal of Educational Psychology, 99,* 253–273.

Terhune, K. (1968). Studies of motives, cooperation, and conflict within laboratory microcosms. In G. Snyder (Ed.), *Studies in international conflict* (Vol. 4, pp. 29–58). Buffalo, NY: SUNY Buffalo Council on International Studies.

Terman, L., & Oden, M. (1947). The gifted child grows up. In L. Terman (Ed.), *Genetic studies of genius* (Vol. 4). Stanford, CA: Stanford University Press.

Terman, L., & Oden, M. (1959). The gifted group in mid-life. In L. Terman (Ed.), *Genetic studies of genius* (Vol. 5). Stanford, CA: Stanford University Press.

Terman, L., Baldwin, B., & Bronson, E. (1925). Mental and physical traits of a thousand gifted children. In L. Terman (Ed.), *Genetic studies of genius* (Vol. 1). Stanford, CA: Stanford University Press.

Texas Education Agency. (2012). *Chapter 111. Texas essential knowledge and skills for mathematics. Subchapter A. elementary.* Retrieved from http://ritter.tea.state.tx.us/rules/tac/chapter111/ch111a.pdf

Thaler, R. H., & Sunstein, C. R. (2008). *Nudge: Improving decisions about health, wealth, and happiness.* New Haven, CT: Yale University Press.

Tharp, R., & Gallimore, R. (1991). *The instructional conversation: Teaching and learning in social activity.* Washington, DC: National Center for Research on Cultural Diversity and Second Language Learning.

The *PLoS Medicine* Editors. (2010). Social relationships are key to health, and to health policy. *PLoS Med.* Retrieved from http://www.plosmedicine.org/article/info%3Adoi%2F10.1371%2Fjournal.pmed.1000334

Thiede, K. W., & Anderson, M. C. M. (2003). Summarizing can improve metacomprehension accuracy. *Contemporary Educational Psychology, 28,* 129–160.

Thiede, K. W., Anderson, M. C. M., & Therriault, D. (2003). Accuracy of metacognitive monitoring affects learning of texts. *Journal of Educational Psychology, 95,* 66–73.

Thomas, E., & Wingert, P. (2010, March 15). Why we can't get rid of failing teachers. *Newsweek,* 24–27.

Thommessen, S., & Todd, B. (2010, April). *Revisiting sex differences in play: Very early evidence of stereotypical preferences in infancy.* Paper presented at the annual meeting of the British Psychological Society, Stratford-upon-Avon, UK.

Thompson, C. (2013). *Smarter than you think: How technology is changing our minds for the better.* New York: Penguin Press.

Thompson, L. L., Claus, E. D., Mikulich-Gilbertson, S. K., Banich, M. T., Crowley, T., Krmpotich, T., . . . Tanabe, J. (2012). Negative reinforcement learning is affected in substance dependence. *Drug and Alcohol Dependence, 123*, 84–90.

Thompson, R. A. (2012). Whither the preconventional child? Toward a life-span moral development theory. *Child Development Perspectives, 6*, 423–429.

Thompson, R., & Newton, E. (2010). Emotion in early conscience. In W. Arsenio & E. Lemerise (Eds.), *Emotions, aggression, and morality in children: Bridging development and psychopathology* (pp. 13–31). Washington, DC: American Psychological Association.

Thompson, R., Winer, A., & Goodvin, R. (2011). The individual child: Temperament, emotion, self, and personality. In M. Bornstein & M. Lamb (Eds.), *Developmental science: An advanced textbook* (6th ed., pp. 427–468). New York: Psychology Press.

Thornberg, R. (2010). A study of children's conceptions of school rules by investigating their judgments of transgressions in the absence of rules. *Educational Psychology, 30*(5), 583–603. doi:10.1080/01443410.2010.492348

Thorndike, E. (1924). Mental discipline in high school studies. *Journal of Educational Psychology, 15*, 1–2, 83–98.

Thorndike, R., & Thorndike, T. (2010). *Measurement and evaluation in psychology and education.* (8th ed.). Upper Saddle River, NJ: Pearson.

Tiantong, M., & Teemuangsai, S. (2013) .The four scaffolding modules for collaborative problem-based learning through the computer network on Moodle LMS for the computer programming course. *International Education Studies, 6*, 47–55.

Tiedt, P., & Tiedt, I, (2010). *Multicultural teaching* (8th ed.). Boston: Allyn & Bacon.

Tillema, H., & Smith, K. (2007). Portfolio appraisal: In search of criteria. *Teaching and Teacher Education, 23*, 442–456.

TIMSS. (2014). *Fifth International Mathematics & Sciences Study.* Retrieved from http://nces.ed.gov/timss/

Tindell, D. R., & Bohlander, R. W. (2013). The use and abuse of cell phones and text messaging in the classroom: A survey of college students. *College Teaching, 60*, 1–9.

Tofade, T., Elsner, J., & Haines, S. T. (2013). Best practice strategies for effective use of questions as a teaching tool. *American Journal of Pharmaceutical Education, 77*, 1–9.

Toga, A., & Thompson, P. (2005). Genetics of brain structure and intelligence. *Annual Review of Neuroscience, 28*, 1–23.

Tokunaga, R. (2010). Following you home from school: A critical review and synthesis of research on cyberbullying victimization. *Computers in Human Behavior, 26*, 277–287.

Tollefson, N. (2000). Classroom applications of cognitive theories of motivation. *Educational Psychology Review, 12*, 63–83.

Tomasello, M. (2006). Acquiring linguistic constructions. In D. Kuhn & R. Siegler (Vol. Eds.), *Handbook of child psychology: Vol. 2. Cognition, perception, and language* (6th ed., pp. 255–298). Hoboken, NJ: Wiley.

Tomasello, M. (2011). Language development. In U. Goswami (Ed.), *Wiley-Blackwell handbook of childhood cognitive development* (2nd ed., pp. 239–257). Malden, MA: Wiley-Blackwell.

Tomlinson, C. A., & McTighe, J. (2006). *Integrating differentiated instruction and understanding by design: Connecting content and kids.* Alexandria, VA: Association for Supervision and Curriculum Development.

Tompkins, G. (2014). *Literacy for the 21st century: A balanced approach* (6th ed.). Upper Saddle River, NJ: Merrill/Prentice Hall.

Tong, R. (2009). *Feminist thought: A more comprehensive introduction.* Charlotte, NC: Westview Press.

Torrez-Guzman, M. (2011). Methodologies and teacher stances: How do they interact in classrooms? *International Journal of Bilingual Education and Bilingualism, 14*(2), 225–241. doi: 10.1080/13670050.2010.539675

Trautwein, U., & Lüdtke, O. (2007). Students' self-reported effort and time on homework in six school subjects: Between-student differences and within-student variation. *Journal of Educational Psychology, 99*, 432–444.

Trautwein, U., Lüdtke, O., & Schnyder, I. (2006). Predicting homework effort: Support for a domain-specific, multilevel homework model. *Journal of Educational Psychology, 98*, 438–456.

Trawick-Smith, J. (2014). *Early childhood development: A multicultural perspective* (6th ed.). Upper Saddle River, NJ: Merrill/Pearson.

Trends in International Mathematics and Science. (2013). *Highlights from TIMSS 2011.* Washington, DC: U.S. Department of Education.

Troutman, D., & Fletcher, A. (2010). Context and companionship in children's short-term versus long-term friendships. *Journal of Social and Personal Relationships, 27*(8), 1060–1074. doi:10.1177/0265407510381253

Trzesniewski, K., Donnellan, M., Moffitt, T., Robins, R., Poulton, R., & Caspi, A. (2006). Low self-esteem during adolescence predicts poor health, criminal behavior, and limited economic prospects during adulthood. *Developmental Psychology, 42*(2), 381–390.

Tsay, M., & Brady, M. (2010). A case study of cooperative learning and communication pedagogy; Does working in teams make a difference? *Journal of the Scholarship of Teaching and Learning, 10*, 78–89.

Tucker-Drob, E., & Harden, K. (2012). Intellectual interest mediates gene x socioeconomic status interaction on adolescent academic achievement. *Child Development, 83*, 743–757.

Tulis, M., & Fulmer, S. M. (2013). Students' motivational and emotional experiences and their relationship to persistence during academic challenge in mathematics and reading. *Learning and Individual Differences, 27*, 35–46.

Tullis, J. G., Finley, J. R., & Benjamin, A. S. (2013). Metacognition of the testing effect: Guiding learners to predict the benefits of retrieval. *Memory and Cognition, 41*, 429–442. doi:10.3758/s13421-012-0274-5

Tullis, M., & Fulmer, S. M. (2013). Students' motivational and emotional experiences and their relationship to persistence during academic challenge in mathematics and reading. *Learning and Individual Differences, 27*, 35–46.

Tulving, E. (2002). Episodic memory: From mind to brain. *Annual Review of Psychology, 53*, 1–25.

Turiel, E. (2006). The development of morality. In N. Eisenberg (Vol. Ed.), *Handbook of child psychology: Vol. 3. Social, emotional, and personality development* (6th ed., pp. 789–857). Hoboken, NJ: John Wiley & Sons.

Turiel, E. (2008a). The development of children's orientations toward moral, social, and personal orders: More than a sequence in development. *Human Development, 51*, 21–39.

Turiel, E. (2008b). Thought about actions in social domains: Morality, social conventions, and social interactions. *Cognitive Development, 23*(1), 136–154. doi:10.1016/j.cogdev.2007.04.001

Turkle, S. (2011). *Alone together: Why we expect more from technology and less from ourselves.* New York: Basic Books.

Turnbull, A., Turnbull, H. R., Wehmeyer, M. L., & Shogren, K. A. (2013). *Exceptional lives: Special education in today's schools* (7th ed.). Boston: Pearson.

Twyman, K., Saylor, C., Taylor, L. A., & Comeaux, D. (2010). Comparing children and adolescents engaged in cyberbullying to matched peers. *Cyberpsychology, Behavior, and Social Networking, 13*, 195–199.

U. S. Department of Transportation. (2013). *Traffic safety facts.* Retrieved from http://www-nrd.nhtsa.dot.gov/Pubs/811741.pdf

U.S. Bureau of Census. (2010). *Table 232. Children who speak a language other than English at home by region: 2008.* Washington, DC: U.S. Government Printing Office.

U.S. Census Bureau. (2013). *American Community Survey. 2013.* Retrieved from http://www.census.gov/acs/www/

U.S. Department of Agriculture. (2013). *National School Lunch Program.* Washington, DC: Author. Retrieved from http://www.fns.usda.gov/sites/default/files/NSLPFactSheet.pdf

U.S. Department of Education. (2008). *Foundations for success: The final report of the National Mathematics Advisory Council.* Retrieved from http://www.ed.gov/about/bdcomm/list/mathpanel/report/final-report.pdf

U.S. Department of Education. (2009a). *Race to Top executive summary.* Retrieved from http://www2.ed.gov/programs/racetothetop/executive-summary.pdf

U.S. Department of Education. (2009b). *Twenty-eighth annual report to Congress on the implementation of the Individuals with Disabilities Education Act.* Washington, DC: U.S. Government Printing Office.

U.S. Department of Education. (2012a). *Digest of education statistics, Table 47.* Washington, DC: Author.

U.S. Department of Education. (2012b). *Thirty-first annual report to Congress on the implementation of the Individuals with Disabilities Education Act.* Washington, DC: U.S. Government Printing Office.

U.S. Department of Health & Human Services. (2010). *Child maltreatment 2009.* Retrieved from http://archive.acf.hhs.gov/programs/cb/pubs/cm09/cm09.pdf

U.S. Department of Labor. (2013). *Occupational employment statistics.* Retrieved from http://www.bls.gov/oes/current/oes_nat.htm

U.S. English. (2011). *Official English: Why is official English necessary?* Retrieved from http://www.usenglish.org/view/10

Ukrainetz, T., Nuspl, J., Wilderson, K., & Beddes, S. (2011). The effects of syllable instruction on phonemic awareness in preschoolers. *Early Childhood Research Quarterly, 26,* 50–60.

Ullén, F., de Manzano, O., Almeida, R., Magnusson, P. K. E., Pedersen, N. L., Nakamura, J., . . . Madison, G. (2012). Proneness for psychological flow in everyday life: Associations with personality and intelligence. *Personality and individual differences, 52,* 167–172.

Umaña-Taylor, A. J., Alfaro, E. C., Bámaca, M. Y., & Guimond, A. B. (2009). The central role of familial ethnic socialization in Latino adolescents' cultural orientation. *Journal of Marriage and Family, 71,* 46–60. doi:10.1111/j.1741-3737.2008.00579.x

Underhill, P. (2009). *Why we buy: The science of shopping.* New York: Simon & Schuster Adult Publishing.

Urdan, T. C., & Maehr, M. L. (1995). Beyond a two-goal theory of motivation and achievement: A case for social goals. *Review of Educational Research, 65,* 213–243.

Vacca, R. T., Vacca, J. L., & Mraz, M. (2014). *Content area reading: Literacy and learning across the curriculum* (11th ed.). Boston: Allyn & Bacon.

Valdez, A. (2013). Multimedia learning from PowerPoint: Use of adjunct questions. *Psychology Journal, 10,* 35–44.

Valla, M., & Ceci, S. (2011). Can sex differences in science be tied to the long reach of prenatal hormones? Brain organization theory, digit ratio (2D/4D), and sex differences in preferences and cognition. *Perspectives in Psychological Science, 6,* 134–146.

Van Dam, N. (2013). Inside the learning brain. *T+D, 67,* 30–35.

van den Akker, A., Deković, M., Prinzie, P., & Asscher, J. (2010). Toddlers' temperament profiles: Stability and relations to negative and positive parenting. *Journal of Abnormal Child Psychology, 38,* 485–495.

van Gelder, T. (2005). Teaching critical thinking: Some lessons from cognitive science. *College Teaching, 53,* 41–46.

Van Gog, T., & Kester, L. (2013). A test of the testing effect: Acquiring problem-solving skills from worked examples. *Cognitive Science, 36,* 1532–1541. doi:10.1111/cogs.12002

Van Horn, R. (2008). *Bridging the chasm between research and practice: A guide to major educational research.* Lanham, MD: Rowman & Littlefield Education.

van IJzendoorn, M., Bakermans-Kranenburg, M., Pannebakker, R., & Out, D. (2010). In defence of situational morality: Genetic, dispositional and situational determinants of children's donating to charity. *Journal of Moral Education, 39*(1), 1–20. doi:10.1080/030572409328535

van Merriënboer, J., Kirschner, P., & Kester, L. (2003). Taking the load off a learner's mind: Instructional design for complex learning. *Educational Psychologist, 38*(1), 5–13.

van Ommen, C. (2013). Review of *Critical neuroscience: A handbook of the social and cultural contexts of neuroscience. Journal of Theoretical and Philosophical Psychology, 33,* 199–202.

VanDeWeghe, R. (2007). How does assessment affect creativity? *English Journal, 96,* 91–93.

Vansteenkiste, M., Zhou, M., Lens, W., & Soenens, B. (2005). Experiences of autonomy and control among Chinese learners: Vitalizing or immobilizing. *Journal of Educational Psychology, 97,* 468–483.

Varelas, M., & Pappas, C. (2006). Intertextuality in read-alouds of integrated science-literacy units in urban primary classrooms: Opportunities for the development of thought and language. *Cognition and Instruction, 24,* 211–259.

Varma, S., McCandliss, B., & Schwartz, D. (2008). Scientific and pragmatic challenges for bridging education and neuroscience. *Education Researcher, 37,* 140–152.

Vatterott, C. (2014). Student-owned homework. *Educational Leadership, 71,* 39–42.

Vaughn, B., Shin, N., Kim, M., Coppola, G., Krzysik, L., Santos, A., . . . Korth, B. (2009). Hierarchical models of social competence in preschool children: A multisite, multinational study. *Child Development, 80*(6), 1775–1796. doi:10.1111/j.1467-8624.2009.01367.x

Vaughn, S., & Bos, C. (2015). *Strategies for teaching students with learning and behavior problems* (9th ed.). Boston: Pearson.

Vaughn, S., Bos, C., & Schumm, J. (2014). *Teaching students who are exceptional, diverse, & at risk in the general education classroom* (6th ed.). Boston: Pearson.

Vavilis, B., & Vavilis, S. (2004). Why are we learning this? What is this stuff good for, anyway?: The importance of conversation in the classroom. *Phi Delta Kappan, 86*(4), 282–287.

Vedantam, S. (2010). *The hidden brain: How our unconscious minds elect presidents, control markets, wage wars, and save our lives.* New York: Spiegel & Grau.

Veenman, M. (2011). Learning to self-monitor and self-regulate. In R. Mayer & P. Alexander (Eds.), *Handbook of research on learning and instruction* (pp. 197–218). New York: Routledge.

Veenman, M. V., & Spaans, M. A. (2005). Relation between intellectual and metacognitive skills: Age and task differences. *Learning and Individual Differences, 15,* 159–176.

Veenstra, R., Lindenberg, S., Oldehinkel, A. J., De Winter, A. F., Verhulst, F. C., & Ormel, J. (2005). Bullying and victimization in elementary schools: A comparison of bullies, victims, and bully/victims, and uninvolved preadolescents. *Developmental Psychology, 41,* 672–682.

Velasquez-Manoff, M. (2013). Status and stress. *The New York Times.* Retrieved from http://opinionator.blogs.nytimes.com/2013/07/27/status-and-stress/?nl=todaysheadlines&emc=edit_th_20130728

Verdinelli, S., & Gentile, J. R. (2003). Changes in teaching philosophies among in-service teachers after experience mastery learning. *Action in Teach Education, 25,* 56–66.

Verkoeijen, P. P., Rikers, R. M., & Schmidt, H. G. (2005). The effects of prior knowledge on study-time allocation and free recall: Investigating the discrepancy reduction model. *The Journal of Psychology, 139,* 67–79.

Verschueren, K., Doumen, S., & Buyse, E. (2012). Relationships with mother, teacher, and peers: Unique and joint effects on young children's self-concept. *Attachment & Human Development, 14,* 233–248.

Viadero, D. (2009). Scholars probe diverse effects of exit exams. *Education Week, 28*(30), 1–10.

Vigdor, J., & Ladd, H. (2010). *Scaling the digital divide: Home computer technology and student achievement.* Retrieved from http://www.urban.org/uploadedpdf/1001433-digital-divide.pdf

Virginia Tech Transportation Institute. (2009). *New data from VTTI provides insight into cell phone use and driving distractions.* Retrieved from http://www.vtti.vt.edu/PDF/7-22-09-VTTI-Press_Release_Cell_phones_and_Driver_Distraction.pdf

Virginia Youth Violence Project. (2010). *Serious violent crime rate in U.S. Schools.* Retrieved from http://youthviolence.edschool.virginia.edu/violence-in-schools/national-statistics.html

Visconti, K. J., Sechler, C. M., & Kochenderfer-Ladd, B. (2013). Coping with peer victimization: The role of children's attributions. *School Psychology Quarterly, 28,* 122–140.

Vlassova, A., & Pearson, J. (2013). Look before you leap: Sensory memory improves decision making. *Psychological Science, 24,* 1635–1643. doi:10.1177/0956797612474321

Von der Linden, N., & Roebers, C. M. (2006). Developmental changes in uncertainty monitoring during an event recall task. *Metacognition and Learning, 1,* 213–228.

Vosniadou, S. (2007). The cognitive-situative divide and the problem of conceptual change. *Educational Psychologist, 42*(1), 55–66.

Vosniadou, S. (2009). Science education for young children: A conceptual-change point of view. In O. Barbarin & B. Wasik (Eds.), *Handbook of child development and early education: Research to practice* (pp. 544–557. New York: Guilford Press.

Vuoksimaa, E. (2010). *Origins of the sex differences in handedness & mental rotation ability: Genetic, environmental, & hormonal effects*. Helsinki: Helsinki University Press.

Vygotsky, L. (1978). *Mind in society: The development of higher psychological processes* (M. Cole, V. John-Steiner, S. Scribner, & E. Souberman, Eds. & Trans.). Cambridge, MA: Harvard University Press.

Vygotsky, L. (1986). *Thought and language*. Cambridge, MA: MIT Press.

Vygotsky, L. (1987). The problem and the method of investigation. In R. Rieber & A. Carton (Eds.), *Collected works of L. S. Vygotsky: Vol. 1. Problems of general psychology* (pp. 167–241). New York: Plenum Press.

Vygotsky, L. (1997). Analysis of higher mental functions. In R. Rieber & A. Carton (Eds.), *Collected works of L. S. Vygotsky: Vol. 4. The history of the development of higher mental functions* (pp. 65–82). New York: Plenum Press.

Waber, D. (2010). *Rethinking learning disabilities: Understanding children who struggle in school*. New York: Guilford.

Wade, C. (2009). Critical thinking: Needed now more than ever. In D. S. Dunn, J. S. Halonen, & R. A. Smith (Eds.), *Teaching critical thinking in psychology: A handbook of best practices* (pp. 11–21). Hoboken, NJ: Wiley-Blackwell.

Wadsworth, B. J. (2004). *Piaget's theory of cognitive and affective development* (5th ed.). Boston: Pearson Education.

Wagner, B. (2009). *Suicidal behavior in children and adolescents*. New Haven, CT: Yale University Press.

Waitoller, F., Artiles, A., & Cheney, D. (2010). The miner's canary: A review of overrepresentation research. *Journal of Special Education, 44*, 29–49.

Walker, D. (2009). Effectiveness of state anti-bullying laws questioned. *Education Week, 29*(4), 7.

Walker, E., Shapiro, D., Esterberg, M., & Trotman, H. (2010). Neurodevelopment and schizophrenia: Broadening the focus. *Current Trends in Psychological Science, 19*, 204–208.

Walker, J. M., & Hoover-Dempsey, K. V. (2006). Why research on parents' involvement is important to classroom management. In C. M. Evertson & C. S. Weinstein (Eds.), *Handbook of classroom management: Research, practice, and contemporary issues* (pp. 665–684). Mahwah, NJ: Erlbaum.

Walker, J., Shenker, S., & Hoover-Dempsey, K. (2010). Why do parents become involved in their children's education? Implications for school counselors. *Professional School Counseling, 14*, 27–41.

Walker, O. L., & Henderson, H. A. (2012). Temperament and social problem solving competence in preschool: Influences on academic skills in early elementary school. *Social Development, 21*, 761–779.

Walters, G. (2011). Childhood temperament: Dimensions or types? *Personality and Individual Differences, 50*, 1168–1173.

Walton, G., & Spencer, S. (2009). Latent ability: Grades and test scores systematically underestimate intellectual ability of negatively stereotyped students. *Psychological Science, 20*, 1132–1139.

Wang, K., & Wang, X. (2013). Promoting knowledge construction and cognitive development: A case study of teacher's questioning. *Theory and Practice in Language Studies, 3*, 1387–1392.

Wang, M.-T., & Holcombe, R. (2010). Adolescents' perceptions of school environment, engagement, and academic achievement in middle school. *American Educational Research Journal, 47*, 633–662.

Wang, Z., & Tchernev, J. M. (2012). The "myth" of media multitasking: Reciprocal dynamics of media multitasking, personal needs, and gratifications. *Journal of Communication, 62*, 493–513. doi:10.1111/j.1460-2466.2012.01641.x

Wardley, C. S., Applegate, E. B., & Van Rhee, J. A. (2013). A comparison of student knowledge acquisition by organ system and skills in parallel problem-based and lecture-based curricula. *The Journal of Physician Assistant Education, 24*, 5–14.

Ware, H., & Kitsantas, A. (2007). Teacher and collective efficacy beliefs as predictors of professional commitment. *Journal of Educational Research, 100*(5), 303–310.

Warschauer, M. (2011). *Learning in the cloud: How (and why) to transform schools with digital media*. New York: Teachers College Press.

Warshof, A., & Rappaport, N. (2013). Staying connected with troubled students. *Educational Leadership, 71*, 34–38.

Waterhouse, L. (2006). Multiple intelligences, the Mozart effect, and emotional intelligence: A critical review. *Educational Psychologist, 41*(4), 217–225.

Waters, H. S., & Kunnmann, T. W. (2010). Metacognition and strategy discover in early childhood. In H. S. Waters & W. Schneider (Eds.), *Metacognition, strategy use, and instruction* (pp. 3–22). New York: Guilford.

Watkins, M. J., & Watkins, O. C. (1974). Processing of recency items for free recall. *Journal of Experimental Psychology, 102*, 488–493.

Watson, M., & Battistich, V. (2006). Building and sustaining caring communities. In C. M. Evertson & C. S. Weinstein (Eds.), *Handbook of classroom management: Research, practice, and contemporary issues* (pp. 253–279). Mahwah, NJ: Erlbaum.

Watson, M., & Ecken, L. (2003). *Learning to trust: Transforming difficult elementary classrooms through developmental discipline*. San Francisco: Jossey-Bass.

Waugh, C., & Gronlund, N. (2013). *Assessing student achievement* (10th ed.). Needham Heights, MA: Allyn & Bacon.

Way, N., Reddy, R., & Rhodes, J. (2007). Students' perceptions of school climate during the middle school years: Associations with trajectories of psychological and behavioral adjustment. *American Journal of Community Psychology, 40*, 194–213.

Wechsler, D. (2003). *Wechsler Intelligence Scale for Children* (4th ed.) San Antonio, TX: Psychological Corporation.

Weil, L. G., Fleming, S. M., Dumontheil, I., Kilford, E. J., Weil, R. S., Rees, G., . . . & Blakemore, S-J. (2013). The development of metacognitive ability in adolescence. *Consciousness and Cognition, 22*, 264–271.

Weiland, A., & Coughlin, R. (1979). Self-identification and preferences: A comparison of White and Mexican American first and third graders. *Journal of Social Psychology, 10*, 356–365.

Weiner, B. (1992). *Human motivation: Metaphors, theories, and research*. Newbury Park, CA: Sage.

Weiner, B. (2000). Interpersonal and intrapersonal theories of motivation from an attributional perspective. *Educational Psychology Review, 12*, 1–14.

Weiner, B. (2001). Intrapersonal and interpersonal theories of motivation from an attribution perspective. In F. Salili, C. Chiu, & Y. Hong (Eds.), *Student motivation: The culture and context of learning* (pp. 17–30). New York: Kluwer Academic/Plenum.

Weinstein, C. S., & Romano, M. E. (2015). *Elementary classroom management: Lessons from research and practice* (6th ed.). New York: McGraw-Hill.

Weinstein, R. (2002). *Reaching higher: The power of expectations in schooling*. Cambridge, MA: Harvard University Press.

Weinstock, J. (2007). Don't call my kid smart. *T.H.E. Journal, 34*, 6.

Weis, R., & Cerankosky, B. (2010). Effects of video-game ownership on young boys' academic and behavioral functioning: A randomized, controlled study. *Psychological Science, 21*, 463–470.

Weisberg, D., Sexton, S., Mulhern, J., & Keeling, D. (2009). The widget effect: Our national failure to acknowledge and act on difference in teacher effectiveness (Executive summary). *New Teacher Project*. Retrieved from http://widgeteffect.org/downloads/TheWidgetEffect_execsummary.pdf

Weisgram, E., Bigler, R., & Liben, L. (2010). Gender, values, and occupational interests among children, adolescents, and adults. *Child Development, 81*(3), 778–796. doi:10.1111/j.1467-8624.2010.01433.x

Weisleder, A., & Fernald, A. (2013). Talking to children matters. *Psychological Science, 24*(11), 2143–2152.

Weiss, I., & Pasley, J. (2004). What is high-quality instruction? *Educational Leadership, 61*(5), 24–28.

Wentzel, K. (1996). Social goals and social relationships as motivators of school adjustment. In J. Juvonen & K. Wentzel (Eds.), *Social motivation: Understanding children's school adjustment* (pp. 226–247). Cambridge, England: Cambridge University Press.

Wentzel, K. (1999). Social-motivational processes and interpersonal relationships: Implications for understanding students' academic success. *Journal of Educational Psychology, 91,* 76–97.

Wentzel, K. (2000). What is it that I'm trying to achieve? Classroom goals from a content perspective. *Contemporary Educational Psychology, 25,* 105–115.

Wentzel, K. (2009). Peers and academic functioning at school. In K. Rubin, W. Bukowski, & B. Laursen (Eds.), *Handbook of peer interactions, relationships, and groups* (pp. 531–547). New York: Guilford Press.

Wentzel, K. R. (2002). The contribution of social goal setting to children's school adjustment. In A. Wigfield & J. S. Eccles (Eds.), *Development of achievement motivation* (pp. 221–246). New York: Academic Press.

Wentzel, K. R. (2003). Sociometric status and adjustment in middle school: A longitudinal study. *Journal of Early Adolescence, 23,* 5–28.

Wentzel, K. R. (2009). Peers and academic functioning at school. In K. H. Rubin, W. M. Bukowski, & B. Laursen (Eds.), *Handbook of peer interactions, relationships, and groups* (pp. 531–547). New York: Guilford.

Wentzel, K. R. (2010). Students' relationships with teachers. In J. L. Meece & J. S. Eccles (Eds.), *Handbook of research on schools, schooling, and human development* (pp. 75–91). New York: Routledge.

Wentzel, K. R., & Watkins, D. E. (2011). Instruction based on peer interactions. In R. E. Mayer & P. A. Alexander (Eds.), *Handbook of research on learning and instruction* (pp. 322–343). New York: Routledge.

Wentzel, K. R., & Wigfield, A. (2007). Motivational interventions that work: Themes and remaining issues. *Educational Psychologist, 42,* 261–271.

Wentzel, K., Battle, A., Russell, S., & Looney, L. (2010). Social supports from teachers and peers as predictors of academic and social motivation. *Contemporary Educational Psychology, 35,* 193–202.

West, M. (2012). *Is retaining students in the early grade self-defeating?* Brookings Institute. Retrieved from http://www.brookings.edu/research/papers/2012/08/16-student-retention-west

Westefeld, J., Bell, A., Bermingham, C., Button, C., Shaw, K., Skow, C., . . . Woods, T. (2010). Suicide among preadolescents: A call to action. *Journal of Loss and Trauma, 15,* 381–407.

Wetzels, S. A., Kester, L., van Merriënboer, J. J., & Broers, N. J. (2011). The influence of prior knowledge on the retrieval-directed function of note taking in prior knowledge activation. *British Journal of Educational Psychology, 81,* 274–291.

Whelan, R., Conrod, P. J., Poline, J-B., Lourdusamy, A., Banaschewski, T., Barker, G. J., . . . Garavan, H. (2012). Adolescent impulsivity phenotypes characterized by distinct brain networks. *Nature Neuroscience 15,* 920–925. doi:10.1038/nn.3092

Whitaker, B. G., & Godwin, L. N. (2013). The antecedents of moral imagination in the workplace:

A social cognitive theory perspective. *Journal of Business Ethics, 114,* 61–73.

White, R. (1959). Motivation reconsidered: The concept of competence. *Psychological Review, 66,* 297–333.

Whitehead, A. N. (1929): *The aims of education and other essays.* New York: Free Press.

Wigfield, A. (1994). Expectancy-value theory of achievement motivation: A developmental perspective. *Educational Psychology Review, 6,* 49–78.

Wigfield, A., & Eccles, J. (1992). The development of achievement task values: A theoretical analysis. *Developmental Review, 12,* 265–310.

Wigfield, A., & Eccles, J. (2000). Expectancy-value theory of achievement motivation. *Contemporary Educational Psychology, 25,* 68–81.

Wigfield, A., & Eccles, J. S. (2002). The development of competence beliefs, expectancies for success, and achievement values from childhood through adolescence. In. A. Wigfield & J. S. Eccles (Eds.), *Development of achievement motivation. A volume in the educational psychology series* (pp. 91–120). San Diego, CA: Academic Press.

Wigfield, A., Byrnes, J., & Eccles, J. (2006). Development during early and middle adolescence. In P. Alexander & P. Winne (Eds.), *Handbook of educational psychology* (2nd ed., pp. 87–114). Mahwah, NJ: Erlbaum.

Wigfield, A., Eccles, J., & Pintrich, P. (1996). Development between the ages of 11 and 25. In D. Berliner & R. Calfee (Eds.), *Handbook of educational psychology* (pp. 148–185). New York: Macmillan.

Wigfield, A., Guthrie, J., Tonks, S., & Perencevich, K. (2004). Children's motivation for reading: Domain specificity and instructional influences. *Journal of Educational Research, 97(6),* 299–310.

Williams, C., & Zacks, R. (2001). Is retrieval-induced forgetting an inhibitory process? *American Journal of Psychology, 114,* 329–354.

Williams, M. (2009). U.S. bilingual education controversy continues. Retrieved from http://www.suite101.com/content/us-bilingual-education-controversy-continues-a148086

Williamson, H. C., Hanna, M. A., Lavner, J. A., Bradbury, T. N., & Karney, B. R. (2013). Discussion topic and observed behavior in couples' problem-solving conversations: Do problem severity and topic choice matter? *Journal of Family Psychology, 27,* 330–335.

Willingham, D. (2013). Why does family wealth affect learning? *American Educator, Spring,* 33–39.

Willingham, D. T. (2007). *Cognition: The thinking animal* (3rd ed.). Upper Saddle River, NJ: Merrill/Pearson.

Willingham, D. T. (2009). *Why don't students like school? A cognitive scientist answers questions about how the mind works and what it means in your classroom.* San Francisco: Jossey-Bass.

Willis, S. L., Tennstedt, S. L, Marsiske, M., Ball, K., Elias, J., Koepke, K. M., . . . Wright, E. (2006). Long-term effects of cognitive training on everyday functional outcomes in older adults. *The*

Journal of the American Medical Association, 296. Retrieved from http://jama.ama-assn.org/cgi/content/full/296/23/2805#AUTHINFO

Wilson, B. L., & Corbett, H. (2001). *Listening to urban kids: School reform and the teachers they want.* Albany, NY: State University of New York Press.

Wilson, R. A., & Foglia, L. (2011). Embodied cognition. In E. N. Zalta (Ed.), *The Stanford Encyclopedia of Philosophy.* Retrieved from http://plato.stanford.edu/archives/fall2011/entries/embodied-cognition

Winerip, M. (2010, July 26). Equity of test is debated as children compete for gifted kindergarten. *New York Times.* Retrieved from http://www.nytimes.com/2010/07/26/education/26winerip.html?pagewanted=all&_r=0

Winerip, M. (2011, May 2). Homeless, but finding sanctuary at school. *New York Times,* A14.

Winerip, M. (2013). Ex-schools chief in Atlanta is indicted in testing scandal. *The New York Times.* Retrieved from http://www.nytimes.com/2013/03/30/us/former-school-chief-in-atlanta-indicted-in-cheating-scandal.html?hp&pagewanted=all&_r=2&

Wing, R. R., & Jeffery, R. W. (1999). Benefits of recruiting participants with friends and increasing social support for weight loss and maintenance. *Journal of Consulting and Clinical Psychology, 67,* 132–138.

Winitzky, N. (1994). Multicultural and mainstreamed classrooms. In R. Arends (Ed.), *Learning to teach* (3rd ed., pp. 132–170). New York: McGraw-Hill.

Winsler, A., & Naglieri, J. (2003). Overt and covert verbal problem-solving strategies: Developmental trends in use, awareness, and relations with task performance in children aged 5 to 17. *Child Development, 74,* 659–678.

Winsler, A., Fernyhough, C., & Montero, I. (2009). *Private speech, executive functioning, and the development of verbal self-regulation.* New York: Cambridge University Press.

Winters, M. (2012). *The benefits of Florida's test-based promotion system.* Manhattan Institute for Policy Research. Retrieved from http://www.manhattan-institute.org/html/cr_68.htm

Witvliet, M., van Lier, P., Cuijpers, P., & Koot, H. (2010). Change and stability in childhood clique membership, isolation from cliques, and associated child characteristics. *Journal of Clinical Child and Adolescent Psychology, 39(1),* 12024. doi:10.1080/15374410903401161

Wojciszke, B., & Struzynska-Kujalowicz, A. (2007). Power influences self-esteem. *Social Cognition, 25,* 472–494.

Wolfe, P. (2010). *Brain matters: Translating research into classroom practice* (2nd ed.). Alexandria, VA: Association for Supervision and Curriculum Development.

Wolters, C. (2003). Understanding procrastination from a self-regulated learning perspective. *Journal of Educational Psychology, 95,* 179–187.

Wolters, C. A. (2004). Advancing achievement goal theory: Using goal structures and goal orientations to predict students' motivation, cognition, and achievement. *Journal of Educational Psychology, 96,* 236–250.

Wonder-McDowell, C., Reutzel, D. R., & Smith, J. A. (2011). Does instructional alignment matter?: Effects on struggling second graders' reading achievement. *Elementary School Journal, 112,* 259–279.

Wong, K., & Xiao, Y. (2010). Diversity and difference: Identity issues of Chinese heritage language learners from dialect backgrounds. *Heritage Language Journal, 7,* 153–187.

Wood, L., & Hawley, A. (2012). Dividing at an early age: The hidden digital divide in Ohio elementary schools. *Learning, Media, & Technology, 37,* 20–39.

Woods, S. A., Lievens, F., Fruyt, F. D., & Wille, B. (2013). Personality across working life: The longitudinal and reciprocal influences of personality on work. *Journal of Organizational Behavior, 34,* S7–S25.

Woolfolk Hoy, A., Davis, H., & Pape, S. J. (2006). Teacher knowledge and beliefs. In P. A. Alexander & P. H. Winne (Eds.), *Handbook of educational psychology* (2nd ed., pp. 715–737). Mahwah, NJ: Erlbaum.

Wortham, S. (2004). The interdependence of social identification and learning. *American Educational Research Journal, 41*(3), 715–750.

Wright, F. (2012). Difference in metacognitive thinking as a cultural barrier to learning. *Journal of the Australia and New Zealand Student Services Association, 40,* 16–22.

Wubbels, T., Brekelmans, M., den Brok, P., & van Tartwijk, J. (2006). An interpersonal perspective on classroom management in secondary classrooms in the Netherlands. In C. M. Evertson & C. S. Weinstein (Eds.), *Handbook of classroom management: Research, practice, and contemporary issues* (pp. 1161–1191). Mahwah, NJ: Erlbaum.

Wurthmann, K. (2013). A social cognitive perspective on the relationships between ethics education, moral attentiveness, and PRESOR. *Journal of Business Ethics, 114,* 131–153.

Xu, J., & Wu, H. (2013). Self-regulation of homework behavior: Homework management at the secondary school level. *Journal of Educational Research, 106,* 1–13.

Yang, J. (2013). Mobile assisted language learning: Review of the recent applications of emerging mobile technologies. *English Language Teaching, 6,* 19–25.

Yang, Y., & Raine, A. (2009). Prefrontal structural and functional brain imaging findings in antisocial, violent, and psychopathic individuals: A meta-analysis. *Psychiatry Research, 174,* 81–88. doi:10.1016/j.pscychresns.2009.03.012

Yee, V. (2013, June 10). Grouping students by ability regains favor in classroom. *New York Times,* pp. A1, A3.

Yell, M. L., Robinson, T. R., & Drasgow, E. (2001). Cognitive behavior modification. In T. J. Zirpoli & K. J. Melloy, *Behavior management: Applications for teachers* (3rd ed., pp. 200–246). Upper Saddle River, NJ: Merrill/Pearson.

Yeung, A. S., Lau, S., & Nie, Y. (2011). Primary and secondary students' motivation in learning English: Grade and gender differences. *Contemporary Educational Psychology, 36,* 246–256.

Yip, D. Y. (2004). Questioning skills for conceptual change in science instruction. *Journal of Biological Education, 38,* 76–83.

Yoon, J. C., & Sungok, S. S. (2013). Predicting teachers' achievement goals for teaching: The role of perceived school goal structure and teachers' sense of efficacy. *Teaching and Teacher Education, 32,* 12–21.

Young, S. N. (2007). How to increase serotonin in the human brain without drugs. *Journal of Psychiatry and Neuroscience, 32,* 394–99.

Yow, W., & Markman, E. (2011). Bilingualism and children's use of paralinguistic cues to interpret emotion in speech. *Bilingualism: Language & Cognition, 14,* 562–569.

Zacharia, Z. C., & Olympiou, G. (2011). Physical versus virtual manipulative experimentation in physics learning. *Learning and Instruction, 21,* 317–331.

Zakieh, S., Fatemeh, A., & Mahmood, A. (2013). The effect of labor's emotional intelligence on their job satisfaction, job performance and commitment. *Iranian Journal of Management Studies, 6,* 29–45.

Zaragoza, N. (2005). Including families in the teaching and learning process. In J. Kincheloe (Ed.), *Classroom teaching: An introduction.* New York: Peter Lang.

Zentall, S. R., & Morris, B. J. (2012). A critical eye: Praise directed toward traits increases children's eye fixations on errors and decreases motivation. *Psychonomic Bulletin & Review, 19,* 1073–1077.

Zhou, J., & Urhahne, D. (2013). Teacher judgment, student motivation, and the mediating effect of attributions. *European Journal of Psychology of Education, 28,* 275–295.

Zhou, L., Goff, G., & Iwata, B. (2000). Effects of increased response effort on self-injury and objective manipulation as competing responses. *Journal of Applied Behavioral Analysis, 33,* 29–40.

Zhou, Q., Hofer, C., & Eisenberg, N. (2007). The developmental trajectories of attention focusing, attentional and behavioral persistence, and externalizing problems during school-age years. *Developmental Psychology, 43*(2), 369–385.

Zimmerman, B. (2005, April). *Integrating cognition, motivation and emotion: A social cognitive perspective.* Paper presented at the annual meeting of the American Educational Research Association, Montreal, Canada.

Zimmerman, B. J. (2000). Attaining self-regulation: A social cognitive perspective. In M. Boekaerts, P. R. Pintrich, & M. Zeidner (Eds.), *Handbook of self-regulation* (pp. 13–39). San Diego: Academic Press.

Zimmerman, B. J., & Schunk, D. H. (Eds.). (2013). *Self-regulated learning and academic achievement: Theory, research, and practice.* New York: Springer.

Zimmerman, F. J., Christakis, D. A., & Meltzoff, A. N. (2007). Associations between media viewing and language development in children under age 2 years. *The Journal of Pediatrics, 151,* 364–368.

Zink, C. F., Pagnoni, G., Martin-Skurski, M. E., Chappelow, J. C., & Berns, G. S. (2004). Human striatal responses to monetary reward depend on saliency. *Neuron, 42,* 509–517.

Zins, J., Bloodworth, M., Weissberg, R., & Walberg, H. (2004). The scientific base linking social and emotional learning to school success. In J. Zins, R. Weissberg, M. Wang, & H. Walberg (Eds.), *Building academic success on social and emotional learning* (pp. 3–22). New York: Teachers College Press.

Zubrzycki, J. (2012). Single-gender schools scrutinized. *Education Week, 31*(17), 1, 12–13.

Zuffianò, A., Alessandri, G., Gerbino, M., Kanacri, B. P., Di Giunta, L., Milioni, M., & Caprara, G. V. (2013). Academic achievement: The unique contribution of self-efficacy beliefs in self-regulated learning beyond intelligence, personality traits, and self-esteem. *Learning and Individual Differences, 23,* 158–162.

Zyphur, M. J., Chaturvedi, S., & Arvey, R. D. (2008). Job performance over time is a function of latent trajectories and previous performance. *Journal of Applied Psychology, 93,* 217–224. doi:10.1037/0021-9010.93.1.217

Name Index

Griffin, R., 413
Griffiths, M., 168
Grigorenko, E., 191, 194, 196, 203, 207, 221
Grilly, D., 142
Gronlund, N. E., 365, 596, 597, 599, 601, 603, 605, 607, 611, 643
Gross, A. C., 243
Gross, J. J., 107, 239
Grossmann, I., 109
Gruber, H., 351
Grunden, L., 125
Guan, J., 442
Gudith, D., 303
Gueldner, B., 532
Guillot, A., 310
Guimond, A. B., 118
Gunnar, M., 108
Gunnoe, (inits?), 104
Guryan, J., 176
Guthrie, J., 414, 571
Guyll, M., 156

H
Habek, D., 220
Hacke, D., 27
Hackman, D., 108
Hadjioannou, X., 405, 574
Hadman, M., 217
Haertel, E. H., 43, 645
Hafner, K., 383
Hagemans, M. G., 359
Hahn, C., 58, 124
Hahn, E., 103
Haidt, J., 130, 134
Haines, S. T., 557
Hakkarainen, O., 359
Hale, S., 356
Hale, W., 117
Hall, E., 198
Hall, M. J., 243
Hallahan, D., 108, 201, 203, 209, 211, 212, 226, 227
Halpern, D., 167, 168, 169
Hamilton, S. L., 357
Hamlen, J., 168
Hamlin J., 131
Hammer, C., 90
Han, P., 156
Han, W-J., 160, 161
Hancock, D. R., 446
Hanna, M. A., 343
Hannon, E., 220
Hansson, T., 421
Hanushek, E. E., 25
Harden, K., 178
Hardin T., 579
Hardman, M. L., 108, 184, 201, 202, 206, 209, 210, 212, 216, 223, 225, 317, 399
Harms, P. D., 108
Harper, J. M., 269
Harriet, A. W., 504
Harris, A., 125
Harris, C. B., 314

Harris, K. R., 316, 356, 358, 363, 364, 373
Harris, R. J., 389
Harrison, M. A., 382
Harrison, P., 190
Harry, B., 223
Harter, S., 119
Hartup, W., 125
Harush, (inits?), 192
Haselager, G., 125–126
Haskill, A., 91
Hatch, T., 193, 196
Hattie, J. A. C., 33, 175, 182, 287, 366, 383, 389, 391, 398, 402, 482, 558, 559, 623
Havsy, L., 130
Hawley, A., 176
Hawley, R., 466
Haycock, P., 220
Hayne, H., 74
Haynes, O., 58, 124
Healy, O., 257
Hébert, T., 178
Heckler, A. F., 366
Hedley, D., 179
Hein, M., 93
Heiser, J., 309, 310
Helgeson, V., 167, 168
Helmsen, J., 109
Henderson, H. A., 120
Henderson, N., 179, 182
Henderson, R., 423
Hennessey, B. A., 347
Henricsson, L., 530
Herman, J., 584, 644
Hernandez, D., 118
Hernandez, I., 363
Hess, F. M., 545
Hetland, H., 109
Heward, W. L., 45, 184, 202, 204, 205, 206, 207, 210, 211, 212, 213, 214, 215, 216, 217, 223, 225, 226, 227, 632, 663
Heyes, C., 136, 215
Heymann, L., 220
Heyvaert, W., 532
Hickey, D. T., 417
Hickok, G., 136, 215
Hicks, N., 353
Hidi, S., 444, 450, 479, 489
Hightower, A., 645
Hilbert, T. S., 360
Hilburn, N., 175
Hilden, K., 278, 313, 315, 489
Hill, A., 581
Hill, B. D., 194
Hill, C., 167
Hill, W., 543
Hillemeier, M., 209
Hillman, C. H., 300
Hipfner-Boucher, K., 161
Hirsch, E., 643
Hirvikoski, T., 209
Hmelo-Silver, C. E., 353, 571
Ho, H., 513

Hochweber, J., 495, 501, 502
Hodell, M., 414
Hodges, E. V., 144
Hofer, C., 303, 503
Hofer, M., 614
Hoff, E., 156, 178
Hofferth, S., 93
Hoffman, B., 351
Hogan, T., 519
Hohn, R. L., 344
Holcombe, R., 184
Holme, J., 178
Holmquist, J., 507
Holzberger, D., 464
Hong, S., 513
Honig, A., 127
Honz, K., 130
Hooper, K., 424
Hoover-Dempsey, K. V., 157, 513
Horgan, D., 27
Horn, J., 192
Horst, S. J., 439
Hosenfeld, I., 495
Houdé, O., 74
Houser, J., 125
Houts, R., 387
Howe, C., 68, 125, 311
Howe, M., 93
Hoy, A., 464
Hoy, W., 464
Hozberger, D., 465
Hu, S-S., 354
Hu, W., 353
Huan, V. S., 305, 313
Huang, J. Y., 122
Huang, K., 105, 158
Hubbard, J., 143
Hübscher, R., 85
Huebner, C., 176
Huesmann, L., 105
Hughes, C., 124, 126
Hughes, J. N., 462
Huijbregts, S., 74
Hull, J., 43, 44
Humphrey, R. H., 108
Hung, I. W., 389
Hunter, M., 420
Hunzicker, J., 293
Hurtz, G. M., 109
Husain, T., 108
Hwang, F., 119
Hwang, W-Y., 354
Hyde, J., 169
Hymel, S., 125, 144

I
Iacoboni, M., 136, 215
Ifill, N., 177
Igo, L. B., 310, 357
Ihlo, T., 144
Imreh, G., 312
Inan, F. A., 254
Ingersoll, R., 28
Inhelder, B., 66, 72
Inzlicht, M., 47, 269, 272, 275, 448

Irons, J. G., 363
Isaacson, A., 309
Isava, D., 532
Isseks, M., 581
Ivanoff, J., 322
Ivie, C., 171
Iwata, B., 247
Iyengar, S., 480
Izzard, C. E., 369

J
Jabeen, F., 106
Jack, F., 74
Jackson, M., 303, 304
Jackson, P., 35
Jacobs, G. E., 423
Jadallah, M., 399
Jang, L. Y., 446
Jang, Y., 269
Jansen, A., 180, 182
Jarrett, C., 393
Jarrold, C., 313
Jaschik, S., 652
Jaspal, R., 118
Jeffrey, R. W., 381
Jeglic, E. L., 104
Jelenchick, L. A., 393
Jenkins, J., 575
Jennings, P. A., 179, 180
Jensen, A. C., 269
Jensen, O., 47
Jiang, Y. H. V., 303, 321, 503
Jimerson, J., 178
Jitendra, A., 343, 565
Joe, E., 177
Joe, S., 177
Johnson, A. Y., 462
Johnson, B., 37
Johnson, D., 46, 399
Johnson, D. W., 127, 574
Johnson, E., 130
Johnson, J., 202
Johnson, K. A., 272
Johnson, K. E., 364
Johnson, L., 248
Johnson, M., 61, 62
Johnson, N., 557
Johnson, R., 127, 399, 574
Johnson, R. E., 446
Johnson, S., 28
Johnson, W., 103, 192
Johnson-Shelton, D., 141
Johnston, L., 142
Jones, J. L., 472, 501
Jones, K. A., 472, 501, 521
Jones, L., 526
Jones, N., 238
Jones, R. M., 63
Jones, S., 127
Jones, V., 526
Jongjohann, K., 562
Jonker, C., 300
Jordan, J., 125
Jorde, L., 167
Joshi, H., 169

Subject Index